Y0-ABE-709

A·N·N·U·A·L E·D·I·T·I·O·N·S

Human Resources *03/04*

Thirteenth Edition

EDITOR
Fred H. Maidment

Western Connecticut State University

Dr. Fred Maidment is associate professor of management at Western Connecticut State University in Danbury, Connecticut. He received his bachelor's degree from New York University and his master's degree from the Bernard M. Baruch College of the City University of New York. In 1983 Dr. Maidment received his doctorate from the University of South Carolina. He resides in Connecticut with his wife.

McGraw-Hill/Dushkin
530 Old Whitfield Street, Guilford, Connecticut 06437

Visit us on the Internet
http://www.dushkin.com

Credits

1. **Human Resource Management in Perspective**
   Unit photo—© 2003 by PhotoDisc, Inc.
2. **Meeting Human Resource Requirements**
   Unit photo—© 2003 by PhotoDisc, Inc.
3. **Creating a Productive Work Environment**
   Unit photo—TRW Inc. photo.
4. **Developing Effective Human Resources**
   Unit photo—TRW Inc. photo.
5. **Implementing Compensation, Beliefs, and Workplace Safety**
   Unit photo—TRW Inc. photo.
6. **Fostering Employee/Management Relationships**
   Unit photo—TRW Inc. photo.
7. **International Human Resource Management**
   Unit photo—© 2003 by PhotoDisc, Inc.

Copyright

Cataloging in Publication Data
Main entry under title: Annual Editions: Human Resources. 2003/2004.
1. Human Resources—Periodicals. I. Maidment, Fred, comp. II. Title: Human Resources.
ISBN 0–07–254861–4   658'.05   ISSN 1092–6577

Thirteenth Edition

Cover image © 2003 PhotoDisc, Inc.
Printed in the United States of America   1234567890BAHBAH543   Printed on Recycled Paper

Editors/Advisory Board

Members of the Advisory Board are instrumental in the final selection of articles for each edition of ANNUAL EDITIONS. Their review of articles for content, level, currentness, and appropriateness provides critical direction to the editor and staff. We think that you will find their careful consideration well reflected in this volume.

EDITOR

Fred H. Maidment
Western Connecticut State University

ADVISORY BOARD

Lawrence S. Audler
University of New Orleans

Donna K. Cooke
Florida Atlantic University

John L. Daly
University of South Florida

Daniel A. Emenheiser
University of North Texas

Daniel O. Lybrook
Purdue University

Faten Moussa
SUNY at Plattsburgh

Robert K. Prescott
Rollins College

Margaret A. Rechter
University of Pittsburgh

Joseph F. Salamone
SUNY at Buffalo

Stephen P. Schappe
Pennsylvania State University - Capital

Rieann Spence-Gale
Northern Virginia Community College

Richard J. Wagner
University of Wisconsin, Whitewater

Ann C. Wendt
Wright State University

Staff

EDITORIAL STAFF

Ian A. Nielsen, Publisher
Roberta Monaco, Senior Developmental Editor
Dorothy Fink, Associate Developmental Editor
Iain Martin, Associate Developmental Editor
Addie Raucci, Senior Administrative Editor
Robin Zarnetske, Permissions Editor
Marie Lazauskas, Permissions Assistant
Diane Barker, Proofreader
Lisa Holmes-Doebrick, Senior Program Coordinator

TECHNOLOGY STAFF

Richard Tietjen, Senior Publishing Technologist
Jonathan Stowe, Executive Director of eContent
Marcuss Oslander, Sponsoring Editor of eContent
Christopher Santos, Senior eContent Developer
Janice Ward, Software Support Analyst
Angela Mule, eContent Developer
Michael McConnell, eContent Developer
Ciro Parente, Editorial Assistant
Joe Offredi, Technology Developmental Editor

PRODUCTION STAFF

Brenda S. Filley, Director of Production
Charles Vitelli, Designer
Mike Campell, Production Coordinator
Laura Levine, Graphics
Tom Goddard, Graphics
Eldis Lima, Graphics
Nancy Norton, Graphics
Juliana Arbo, Typesetting Supervisor
Karen Roberts, Typesetter
Jocelyn Proto, Typesetter
Cynthia Powers, Typesetter
Cathy Kuziel, Typesetter
Larry Killian, Copier Coordinator

To the Reader

In publishing ANNUAL EDITIONS we recognize the enormous role played by the magazines, newspapers, and journals of the public press in providing current, first-rate educational information in a broad spectrum of interest areas. Many of these articles are appropriate for students, researchers, and professionals seeking accurate, current material to help bridge the gap between principles and theories and the real world. These articles, however, become more useful for study when those of lasting value are carefully collected, organized, indexed, and reproduced in a low-cost format, which provides easy and permanent access when the material is needed. That is the role played by ANNUAL EDITIONS.

The environment for human resource management is constantly changing. The events of September 11, 2001, are only just a preview of the global environment that may be developing for managers. The terrorist acts are certain to change the role of human resources in the future. At the very least, what has transpired will make the practice of human resources more difficult and more challenging. Meeting those challenges will be the task that will face human resource managers in the future and will make it a key factor in the success of any organization.

In addition to the events of September 11, the Enron scandal will also play a role in the development of human resources. These two developments have been addressed with separate sections in this edition of *Annual Editions: Human Resources 03/04*.

Management must respond to these forces in many ways, not the least of which is the effort to keep current with the various developments in the field. The 53 articles that have been chosen for *Annual Editions: Human Resources* reflect an outstanding cross section of the current articles in the field. The volume addresses the various component parts of HRM (human resource management) from compensation, training, and discipline to international implications for the worker and the employer. Articles have been chosen from leading business magazines such as *Business Week* and journals such as *Workforce* and the *Monthly Labor Review* to provide a wide sampling of the latest thinking in the field of human resources.

Annual Editions: Human Resources 03/04 contains a number of features designed to be useful for people interested in human resource management. These features include a *table of contents* with abstracts that summarize each article with bold italicized key ideas and a *topic guide* to locate articles on specific subjects. The volume is organized into seven units, each dealing with specific interrelated topics in human resources. Every unit begins with an overview that provides background information for the articles in the section. This will enable the reader to place the selection in the context of the larger issues concerning human resources. Important topics are emphasized and key points to consider that address major themes are presented.

This is the thirteenth edition of *Annual Editions: Human Resources*. It is hoped that many more will follow addressing these important issues. We believe that the collection is the most complete and useful compilation of current material available to the human resource management student. We would like to have your response to this volume, for we are interested in your opinions and recommendations. Please take a few minutes to complete and return the postage-paid *article rating form* at the back of the volume. Any book can be improved, and we need your help to continue to improve *Annual Editions: Human Resources*.

Fred Maidment

Fred Maidment
Editor

Contents

UNIT 1
Human Resource Management in Perspective

Nine unit selections examine the current environment of human resource management with special emphasis on corporate strategy, disabled workers, sexual harassment, and the war on terror following September 11, 2001.

Unit Overview   xviii

The concepts in bold italics are developed in the article. For further expansion, please refer to the Topic Guide and the Index.

UNIT 2
Meeting Human Resource Requirements

The unit's eight articles discuss the dynamics of human resource job requirements, planning, selection, recruitment, and information systems.

The concepts in bold italics are developed in the article. For further expansion, please refer to the Topic Guide and the Index.

UNIT 3
Creating a Productive Work Environment

The seven selections in this section examine how to increase productivity in the workplace by motivating employees and developing effective communication channels.

The concepts in bold italics are developed in the article. For further expansion, please refer to the Topic Guide and the Index.

UNIT 4
Developing Effective Human Resources

Five unit articles discuss how to develop resources through employee training and career and staff development.

UNIT 5
Implementing Compensation, Beliefs, and Workplace Safety

Eleven articles address employee compensation, incentive arrangements, executive pay, health and safety considerations, and benefits.

The concepts in bold italics are developed in the article. For further expansion, please refer to the Topic Guide and the Index.

The concepts in bold italics are developed in the article. For further expansion, please refer to the Topic Guide and the Index.

UNIT 6
Fostering Employee/Management Relationships

In this unit, ten selections examine the dynamics of labor relations, collective bargaining, disciplinary action, temporary and part-time employees, and workplace ethics, including details of the Enron scandal.

The concepts in bold italics are developed in the article. For further expansion, please refer to the Topic Guide and the Index.

UNIT 7
International Human Resource Management

Three articles discuss the increasing globalization of human resource management.

The concepts in bold italics are developed in the article. For further expansion, please refer to the Topic Guide and the Index.

Topic Guide

This topic guide suggests how the selections in this book relate to the subjects covered in your course. You may want to use the topics listed on these pages to search the Web more easily.

On the following pages a number of Web sites have been gathered specifically for this book. They are arranged to reflect the units of this *Annual Edition.* You can link to these sites by going to the DUSHKIN ONLINE support site at *http://www.dushkin.com/online/.*

ALL THE ARTICLES THAT RELATE TO EACH TOPIC ARE LISTED BELOW THE BOLD-FACED TERM.

Americans With Disabilities Act

6. A Statute for Liberty
9. Dealing With HR Issues Following the 9/11 Terrorist Attacks

Benefits

1. HR Outsourcing—A Money-Saving Strategy
2. What Is an Employee? The Answer Depends on the Federal Law
7. Sexual Harassment: It Doesn't Go With the Territory
9. Dealing With HR Issues Following the 9/11 Terrorist Attacks
10. Using Telecommuting to Improve the Bottom Line
11. When Good Employees Retire
19. The Extra Mile: Motivating Employees to Exceed Expectations
20. What Makes You Tick?
21. A Plan for Keeping Employees Motivated
24. How to Develop the Mind of a Strategist
26. Is Your Training a Waste of Money?
28. Career Development and Its Practice: A Historical Perspective
30. What Are Employees Worth?
32. Pay and Employee Commitment: The Missing Link
34. Executive Pay
35. The Great CEO Pay Heist
39. Health-Care Costs: HR's Crisis Has Real Solutions
40. A New Model for Controlling Health-Care Costs
46. Temporary Solution
51. Personnel Demands Attention Overseas
53. Safe Haven

Blue-collar jobs

2. What Is an Employee? The Answer Depends on the Federal Law
11. When Good Employees Retire
20. What Makes You Tick?
29. Choosing the Right Path
38. The Triangle Legacy: 90 Years After Fire, Sweatshops Persist
41. A Black Eye for Labor
42. Labor Law for Supervisors: Recent Developments in Employment Testing—Part II
43. Union Rules in Nonunion Settings: The NLRB and Workplace Investigations
49. Crisis of Confidence

Career development

1. HR Outsourcing—A Money-Saving Strategy
11. When Good Employees Retire
12. A Dearth of Good Managers
13. Matching Colors
18. Employees or Partners?
20. What Makes You Tick?
22. Enhancing Your Writing Skills
26. Is Your Training a Waste of Money?
28. Career Development and Its Practice: A Historical Perspective
29. Choosing the Right Path
32. Pay and Employee Commitment: The Missing Link
51. Personnel Demands Attention Overseas
52. Cross-Cultural Awareness

Communication

4. Managing in the New Millennium: Survivors of Organizational Downsizing
7. Sexual Harassment: It Doesn't Go With the Territory
9. Dealing With HR Issues Following the 9/11 Terrorist Attacks
10. Using Telecommuting to Improve the Bottom Line
14. Playing e-Detective
16. Teamwork Aids HRIS Decision Process
19. The Extra Mile: Motivating Employees to Exceed Expectations
20. What Makes You Tick?
22. Enhancing Your Writing Skills
23. Harmony in the Workplace: 10 Positive Strategies You Can Use
24. How to Develop the Mind of a Strategist
25. Creating a Learning Organization
26. Is Your Training a Waste of Money?
27. Brand Yourself
29. Choosing the Right Path
36. Disengage the Rage: Defusing Employee Anger
37. How Safe Is Your Job? The Threat of Workplace Violence
39. Health-Care Costs: HR's Crisis Has Real Solutions
40. A New Model for Controlling Health-Care Costs
43. Union Rules in Nonunion Settings: The NLRB and Workplace Investigations
51. Personnel Demands Attention Overseas

Corporate strategy and human resources

2. What Is an Employee? The Answer Depends on the Federal Law
3. Strategizing for HR
4. Managing in the New Millennium: Survivors of Organizational Downsizing
9. Dealing With HR Issues Following the 9/11 Terrorist Attacks
11. When Good Employees Retire
12. A Dearth of Good Managers
13. Matching Colors
34. Executive Pay
35. The Great CEO Pay Heist
42. Labor Law for Supervisors: Recent Developments in Employment Testing—Part II
47. Shades of Gray
48. Lessons From the Darkside
49. Crisis of Confidence
50. Dirty Rotten Numbers
51. Personnel Demands Attention Overseas
52. Cross-Cultural Awareness

Disciplinary action

7. Sexual Harassment: It Doesn't Go With the Territory
14. Playing e-Detective
15. Learning From Experience
36. Disengage the Rage: Defusing Employee Anger
37. How Safe Is Your Job? The Threat of Workplace Violence
38. The Triangle Legacy: 90 Years After Fire, Sweatshops Persist
43. Union Rules in Nonunion Settings: The NLRB and Workplace Investigations
44. Why Employees Commit Fraud
45. Enough Is Enough
47. Shades of Gray
48. Lessons From the Darkside
49. Crisis of Confidence
50. Dirty Rotten Numbers

Dual career couples

10. Using Telecommuting to Improve the Bottom Line

World Wide Web Sites

The following World Wide Web sites have been carefully researched and selected to support the articles found in this reader. The easiest way to access these selected sites is to go to our DUSHKIN ONLINE support site at *http://www.dushkin.com/online/*.

AE: Human Resources 03/04

The following sites were available at the time of publication. Visit our Web site—we update DUSHKIN ONLINE regularly to reflect any changes.

General Sources

Bureau of Labor Statistics
http://stats.bls.gov:80

The home page of the Bureau of Labor Statistics (BLS), an agency of the U.S. Department of Labor, offers sections that include Data, Economy at a Glance, Keyword Searches, Surveys and Programs, other statistical sites, and much more.

Economics Statistics Briefing Room
http://www.whitehouse.gov/fsbr/esbr.html

Easy access to current federal economic indicators is available at this site, which provides links to information produced by a number of federal agencies. Subjects are Output, Income, Employment, Unemployment, Earnings, Production and Business Activity, Prices and Money, Credits and Securities Markets, Transportation, and International Statistics.

Human Resource Professional's Gateway to the Internet
http://www.hrisolutions.com/index2.html

This up-to-date Web site offers links to other human relations locations, recruiting–related Web sites, human resources–related companies, as well as search tools.

In the Workplace
http://www.ilr.cornell.edu/workplace.html

The Cornell School of Industrial and Labor Relations offers this site on the Net. It consists of a useful Work Index; a list of Centers, Institutes, and Affiliated Groups; and an Electronic Archive that covers full-text documents on the glass ceiling, child labor, and much more.

Labor Force, Employment, and Unemployment
http://www.cris.com/%7Enetlink/bci/2BCllst.html

Here is helpful statistical information about the civilian labor force. The site covers job vacancies, marginal employment adjustments, employment, diffusion indexes of employees on private nonagricultural payrolls, unemployment, the labor force, and civilian labor force participation rates.

NBER Home Page
http://www.nber.org

The National Bureau of Economic Research engages in specialized research projects on every aspect of economics. The thirteen programs include asset pricing, economics of aging, labor studies, and productivity.

Voice of the Shuttle: Postindustrial Business Theory Page
http://www.qub.ac.uk/english/shuttle/commerce.html

Information on many subjects, which include Restructuring, Reengineering, Downsizing, Flattening, Outsourcing, Business and Globalism, Human Resources Management, Labor Relations, Statistics and History, is available at this site. Voice of the Shuttle also includes resources on job searches, careers, working from home ideas, and suggestions about business startups.

UNIT 1: Human Resource Management in Perspective

Employment and Labor Law
http://www.lectlaw.com/temp.html

This site offers wide-ranging Web resources and articles covering age discrimination in employment, all of the civil rights legislation, the glass ceiling commission, Americans With Disabilities statutes, the Fair Labor Standards Act, whistle-blowing support, unions today, and employment law.

Law at Work
http://www.lawatwork.com

From this site you can not only look at current labor laws, such as OSHA, but consider drug testing at work, violence in the workplace, unemployment questions, sexual harassment issues, affirmative action, and much more.

UNIT 2: Meeting Human Resource Requirements

America's Job Bank
http://www.ajb.dni.us

You can find employers or job seekers and lots of job market information at this site. Employers can register their job openings, update them, and request employment service recruitment help.

National Center for the Workplace
http://socs.berkeley.edu/~iir/ncw/execsum.html

Through interdisciplinary research, information sharing, and policy analysis and development, the NCW addresses the problems created by the convergence of broad economic, social, cultural, political, and technological changes in the workplace. It describes its grant projects here.

UNIT 3: Creating a Productive Work Environment

Commission on the Future of Worker-Management Relations
http://www.dol.gov/dol/_sec/public/media/reports/dunlop/dunlop.htm

The report of the U.S. Federal Commission on the Future of Worker-Management Relations, which covers many issues, including enhancement of workplace productivity, changes in collective bargaining practices, and intervention in workplace problems by government agencies, may be found here.

The Downsizing of America
http://www.nytimes.com/specials/downsize/glance.html

The complete 7-week series on downsizing in America is printed on the Web by the *New York Times,* in which it appeared.

Employee Incentives and Career Development
http://www.snc.edu/socsci/chair/336/group1.htm

This site states that effective employee compensation and career development is an important tool in obtaining, maintaining, and retaining a productive workforce. There are links to Pay-for-Knowledge, Incentive Systems, Career Development, Wage and Salary Compensation, and more.

www.dushkin.com/online/

Foundation for Enterprise Development
http://www.fed.org/aboutus/aboutus.htm

Access the Foundation for Enterprise Development files at this site. Their mission is to foster the development of competitive enterprises based on the premise that sharing company ownership and meaningful involvement with employees are effective ways of motivating the workforce in order to achieve business goals.

UNIT 4: Developing Effective Human Resources

Employment Interviews
http://www.snc.edu/socsci/chair/336/group3.htm

The importance of proper interview techniques to the building of a workforce is discussed here. The page has links to related sites and refers to a book by Alder and Elmhorst, *Communicating at Work: Principles and Practices for Business and the Professionals.*

Feminist Majority Foundation
http://www.feminist.org

This site houses the Feminist Career Center, an Affirmative Action page, and information of interest to women.

How to Do an Employee Appraisal
http://www.visitorinfo.com/gallery/howapp.htm

At this site learn online how to do an annual performance review appraisal and read a "horror story" of a badly done one.

Human Resource Management
http://www.ozemail.com.au/~cyberwlf/3UB/main2.html

This site leads to Employee Training facts, Human Resource Planning steps, plus Recruitment Information and a Selection Process outline.

UNIT 5: Implementing Compensation, Beliefs, and Workplace Safety

BenefitsLink: The National Employee Benefits Web Site
http://www.benefitslink.com/index.php

This link offers facts and services for employers who are sponsoring employee benefit plans and for participating workers.

Executive Pay Watch
http://www.paywatch.org/paywatch/index.htm

While keeping an eye on the issue of executive salaries, bonuses, and perks in CEO compensation packages, this labor union site offers suggestions to working families on what can be done to curb exorbitant pay schemes.

Social Security Administration
http://www.ssa.gov

Here is the official Web site of the Social Security Administration.

WorkPlace Injury and Illness Statistics
http://www.osha.gov/oshstats/work.html

The Bureau of Labor Statistics Web presents links to many issues of occupational injury and illness and offers a great deal of statistical information.

UNIT 6: Fostering Employee/Management Relationships

Fair Measures: Legal Training for Managers
http://www.fairmeasures.com/asklawyer/archive/

All the questions in this Ask the Lawyer Archive are answered by Rita Risser, an employment law attorney. They cover a range of employee/management relations and are aimed at fostering out-of-court solutions to problems.

Working Stiff Action Guide
http://www.pbs.org/weblab/workingstiff/action/

This compilation of information sources for working people includes government agencies, union and labor-related groups, legal and activist resources, workplace gripe sites, and a job stress network.

UNIT 7: International Human Resource Management

Globalization and Human Resource Management
www.cic.sfu.ca/forum/adler.html

Dr. Nancy J. Adler, a faculty member at McGill University, discusses strategic international human resource development in this thorough summary for the Internet.

Labor Relations and the National Labor Relations Board
http://www.snc.edu/socsci/chair/336/group2.htm

From this site you can explore labor relations in today's international marketplace.

We highly recommend that you review our Web site for expanded information and our other product lines. We are continually updating and adding links to our Web site in order to offer you the most usable and useful information that will support and expand the value of your Annual Editions. You can reach us at: *http://www.dushkin.com/annualeditions/.*

UNIT 1

Human Resource Management in Perspective

Unit Selections

1. **HR Outsourcing—A Money-Saving Strategy**, Stephen Norman and Rob Arbuckle
2. **What Is an Employee? The Answer Depends on the Federal Law**, Charles J. Muhl
3. **Strategizing for HR**, Kathryn Tyler
4. **Managing in the New Millennium: Survivors of Organizational Downsizing**, Patricia M. Buhler
5. **Strategic Human Resources Management in Government: Unresolved Issues**, Jonathan Tompkins
6. **A Statute for Liberty**, Peter McGeer
7. **Sexual Harassment: It Doesn't Go With the Territory**, Rachel Thompson
8. **Why 9/11 Didn't Change the Workplace**, Shari Caudron
9. **Dealing With HR Issues Following the 9/11 Terrorist Attacks**, Robert W. Lincoln Jr.

Key Points to Consider

- What social and economic trends do you feel are the most significant? Has downsizing gone too far? How will these trends impact on the labor force as it enters the twenty-first century? How does human resource management make a difference?

- What are some of the ways that firms can better utilize the skills and talents of their employees?

- What are the most important changes for the American worker during this century, and what changes do you see as likely in the next 20 years? How have changes in the family resulted in changes in human resource management?

- In the past 30 years, the government has taken a more active role in the struggle of minorities and other groups in the workforce. How has the ADA changed the workplace?

- Sexual harassment is a very important area of concern for most organizations. What do you think organizations can and should do about it?

- How do you think September 11 will affect organizations and their relations with their employees? Do you think that things will change significantly?

 **Links: www.dushkin.com/online/**
These sites are annotated in the World Wide Web pages.

Employment and Labor Law
http://www.lectlaw.com/temp.html
Law at Work
http://www.lawatwork.com

The only constant is change. Industrial society is dynamic, a great engine that has brought about many of the most significant changes in the history of the human race. Since the start of the Industrial Revolution in England, a little over 200 years ago, industrialized society has transformed Western civilization in a multitude of ways. Many great inventions of the last 200 years have significantly altered the way people live and the way they see the world.

At the time of the Declaration of Independence, the 13 colonies were an overwhelmingly agricultural society that clung to the Atlantic coast of North America. At the beginning of the twenty-first century, the United States is a continental nation with the world's largest industrial base and perhaps the smallest percentage of farmers of any major industrialized country. These changes did not happen overnight, but were both the result and the cause of the technological innovations of the Industrial Revolution. The technological marvels of today, such as television, radio, computers, airplanes, and automobiles, did not exist until after the Industrial Revolution, and a disproportionate number of them did not exist until after 1900.

Along with technological changes have come changes in the ways people earn their living. When Thomas Jefferson authored the Declaration of Independence in 1776, he envisioned a nation of small, independent farmers, but that is not what later developed. Factories, mass production, and economies of scale have been the watchwords of industrial development. Industrial development changed not only the economy, but also society. Most Americans are no longer independent farmers, but are, for the most part, wage earners, who make their living working for someone else.

Changes in the American labor force include the increase in the numbers of women and minorities working next to white males. The nature of most jobs has changed from those directly associated with production to those providing services in the white-collar economy. Many other changes are developing in the economy and society that will be reflected in the workforce. For the first time since the early days of the republic, international trade represents a significant part of the American economy, having increased greatly in the past 20 years. The economic reality is that the GM autoworker competes not only with Ford and Chrysler, but also with Toyota and Volkswagen.

The society, the economy, and the workforce have changed. Americans today live in a much different world than they did 200 years ago. It is a highly diverse, heterogeneous world, full of paradox. When people think of American industry, they tend to think of giant-sized companies like IBM and General Electric, but, in fact, most people work for small firms. The relative importance of the *Fortune* 500 companies in terms of employment in the economy has been declining both in real and percentage terms. Economic growth today is with small organizations.

Change has brought not only a different society, but a more complex one. Numerous rules and regulations must be followed that did not exist 200 years ago. The human element in any organization has been critical to its success, and foreknowing what the human resource needs of the organization are going to be 1, 5, or even 10 years into the future is a key element for continuing success.

Individual decisions have also changed. In the first part of the twentieth century, it was common for a worker to spend his or her entire life with one organization, doing one particular job. Now the worker can expect to do many different jobs, probably with a number of different organizations in different industries. Mergers, technological change, and economic fluctuations all put a premium on individual adaptability in a changing work environment for individual economic survival.

The changes in industrial society have often come at a faster rate than most people were willing to either accept or adapt to. Many old customs and prejudices have been retained from prior times. While progress has been made with regard to certain groups—no American employer today would dare to end an employment notice with the letters "NINA" (No Irish Need Apply), as was common at one time—for other groups, the progress has been slow at best. Women represent about half of American workers but they are paid only about 70 percent of what men earn, and sexual harassment still represents a problem. African Americans and other minorities have been discriminated against for centuries in American society, to the point where the federal government has been forced to step in and legislate equal opportunity, both on and off the job. People with disabilities have also sought protection as seen in "A Statute for Liberty." Finally, the clash of differing cultures seems ever more pronounced in our society. America has traditionally viewed itself as a melting pot, but it is clear that certain groups have historically "melted" more easily than others, a situation that is reflected in the workplace.

Human resource management plays an important role in industrial America. Business leaders recognize the value of their employees to the future of their organizations. Increasingly, competition in world markets is becoming based on the skills and abilities of people, not machines. Indeed, among major competitors, virtually everyone has essentially the same equipment. The difference is often what the people in the organization do with the equipment.

Of special consideration are the recent events of September 11, 2001. For the first time since the War of 1812, the United States was forcefully attacked on its home soil with a greater loss of life than at Pearl Harbor. These events will mean changes in the way the economy operates and the way organizations will treat their employees.

Society, the workplace, and the way they are viewed have all undergone major changes. Frederick W. Taylor and Elton Mayo, early writers in management, held certain views about industry at the beginning of the twentieth century, while Peter Drucker, W. Edwards Deming, and others have different ideas now, at the beginning of the twenty-first century. The American society and economy, as well as the very life of the average American worker, are different from what they were 200 or even 100 years ago, and both the workers and the organizations that employ them must respond to those changes.

HR Outsourcing—A Money-Saving Strategy

Stephen Norman and Rob Arbuckle

Workplace violence is on the rise. Employee lawsuits are multiplying. Legislatures are passing more employment-related regulations. With today's low unemployment, it's more expensive to recruit and retain good employees.

Consequently, credit unions are enlisting professionals to help tackle these problems. Some credit unions hire a human resource (HR) director or create an HR department. But an in-house department can't always provide the expertise necessary to meet the credit union's needs.

Just to handle the problems mentioned above, you'd need a trainer to train managers how to deal with workplace violence and to identify issues that could lead to violence, an attorney to monitor and explain all employment-related legal matters, a skilled recruiter to find topnotch employees, and a compensation and benefits expert to monitor competitors' wages and benefit packages. Monthly payroll costs for this bench of experts alone easily could approach $15,000 to $20,000, not including insurance benefits, resource materials, supplies, and administrative help. For many small credit unions, the benefit seems too small to justify the cost.

Executives wanting to lower overhead expenses without sacrificing the knowledge and service levels of their HR departments are outsourcing the function: contracting with HR management firms.

It's Not Consulting

Outsourcing is different from hiring consultants or temporary employees to work on projects or set up systems. Dr. Richard Noland of Advanced Management Systems, Salem, Ore., describes outsourcing: "If you buy and manage temporary employees to handle your accounting function, that is not outsourcing accounting because you still are managing the process. If you hire an accounting firm to take care of your taxes, that is outsourcing because the accounting firm is managing the process for you."

HR management is just one of many support services credit unions are outsourcing. Support services are operations that don't generate revenue but are necessary to operate a credit union, such as accounting, payroll, benefits, and administrative support.

For years, credit unions have used outside vendors to help with information systems management, enabling them to focus on providing excellent member service. Likewise, credit unions have outsourced marketing efforts to advertising agencies to develop promotional campaigns.

Some credit union leagues offer consolidated services such as telephone loan centers, enabling multiple credit unions to offer loan transaction capabilities to members 24 hours a day without incurring the cost of equipping and staffing such a center.

It's Your HR Department

But true HR outsourcing means the outsourcing firm becomes the credit union's HR department. To be effective, the firm must offer recruiting assistance, training, legal compliance monitoring, organizational development, employee relations management, policy manual and employee handbook formation, job description design, personnel file audits, and performance management systems.

Professional employer organizations (PEOs), which manage HR and personnel responsibilities, for example, create co-employment partnerships with their clients. The PEO hires the client's employees and manages and compensates them, including wages, performance bonuses, retirement packages, and insurance benefits. Then it leases the employees back to the client at a rate usually better for the employer because there's some savings on payroll taxes and other deductions. The employees benefit because the PEO can provide better insurance and other compensation at lower costs. That's because the PEO has economies of scale when it negotiates health care, life insurance, and other benefits.

It's a Cost Saver

Outsourcing firms generally charge for services in one of three ways: fee per month, fee per project, or hourly.

Fee per month. Firms that charge monthly usually have an annual contract with the credit union. Total charges for all services are divided into monthly, quarterly, or semiannual payments.

The firm agrees to provide certain services each month and to show up at the credit union site one-half day per week or some other arrangement. In many circumstances, if the firm spends more time at the credit union in a particular month—due to an emergency or other unforeseeable incident—the monthly fee stays the same. However, the credit union may have to pay for additional incidental expenses such as travel costs if the outsourcing firm is outside the client's geographic area.

Fee per project. Each project has a specific fee. For example, drafting a policy manual may cost $2,000; writing job descriptions, $5,000; and providing on-site visits, $500 per visit. Consultants use this method more than outsourcing firms do. Consultants usually don't have long-term contracts with clients, and clients have no obligation to use the consultants for additional projects.

Businesses usually use this type of arrangement to supplement work of an existing department or to provide services outside the expertise of in-house staff.

Hourly fee. This involves billing by the hour, similar to how attorneys bill for services. Typically, outsourcing firms don't charge for every service they perform by the hour. They'll perform many services on a flat-fee basis and charge an hourly fee for on-site visits, telephone calls, or to handle situations outside the standard scope of the existing contract.

Rates vary depending on the expert performing the service: A more experienced HR manager may charge $100 per hour, a less experienced one, $50 per hour.

While these dollar figures may seem high, the cost of employing one or more full-time HR professionals can be two to three times higher. One credit union in Oregon went from a monthly HR budget of $15,000 to $5,000 when it switched from an in-house department to an outsourcing firm. The credit union saved money on wages, employment taxes, benefits, office space, office supplies, administrative staff, and resource materials, including HR publications and seminars.

While the outsourcing firm has the same expenses for its employees that the credit union would have, it can leverage the employees and associated costs among several clients and pass the savings on to the credit union.

It's More Than Just Cost Savings

Saving money isn't the only advantage to outsourcing HR functions. Credit unions also gain the expertise of a full bench of HR professionals at the cost of one generalist. Managers with questions about the best way to conduct a performance review can get help from someone experienced in performance review systems, rather than relying on HR managers whose only experiences with performance reviews are ones they administer to their own employees. And credit unions have access to the latest information without incurring training expenses.

It's Proven Experience

An effective HR system takes into account the unique characteristics of the industry. So finding a firm that has worked with and developed systems for credit unions means there's no need to "reinvent the wheel." The HR firm can provide a well-developed system proven to work in credit unions.

Outsourcing firms also may act as neutral third parties to help resolve disputes. Oftentimes internal HR managers are subject to office politics or viewed as agents of management. Objectivity also is important. This means that the outsourcing firm often may recommend changes management may have resisted from someone inside the credit union.

Outsourcing firms can accomplish more than most internal departments because they may have more talent to draw from. Small- and medium-size credit unions usually can't afford more than a few people in their HR departments. Because the outsourcing firm has more employees, it can accomplish more in a shorter period of time and can absorb the impact unexpected emergencies may have on completing a project.

It's Not for Everyone

There are some disadvantages to outsourcing:

- The first challenge is there's not an HR manager on-site at all times. Some managers want answers face-to-face. It's part of the "out of sight, out of mind" mentality. Once a credit union hires an outsourcing firm, there's often a period of frustration and adjustment for managers who need some advice on how to deal with a situation. This is particularly true if managers aren't trained as supervisors and are used to offloading management responsibilities to an HR department.

- The second biggest challenge comes if employees don't establish good rapport with the outsourcing firm's professionals. If employees don't trust or get along with members of the HR firm, they won't use the firm's services, diminishing the arrangement's effectiveness.

It's Worth Considering

Your management team should answer several questions to determine whether outsourcing is a viable option:

1. How large is the credit union, and how many problems does it have? Generally, it's more difficult for an inexperienced outsourcing firm to effectively manage businesses or departments with more than 50 employees. The more employees your credit union has, the more experienced the HR firm must be.

2. Which is the best value for the dollar—to have full-time HR staff or outsource? The answer depends on how skilled your management team is at handling employee issues. The more skilled and experienced your managers, the easier it is to outsource: They're able to deal with day-to-day HR issues and rely periodically on the HR professionals for the more complicated HR matters. It also de-

Outsourcing and the Internet

During the next few years, the Internet will become a popular and viable option in outsourcing some human resource (HR) management functions. One site is E-Benefits (www.ebenefits.com). Its ad reads: "E-Benefits VirtualHR helps reduce legal exposure, track your employee records, and publish reports and documents with full security. VirtualHR automates and simplifies HR administration for free."

Three issues credit unions must address before jumping into Internet solutions for HR management are:

- Security. It's a big problem, not a little one. Privacy issues, Internet security issues, and securing your Intranet or network from Internet hackers is increasingly more difficult as prices in leading-edge technology continue to tumble.
- Accessibility. Who has access to the Internet? For example, investing in an Internet solution to benefits questions and answers doesn't make sense if your employees don't have access to the Internet.
- Exit strategy. When you outsource your HR management information to an Internet host, you're building intellectual capital in someone else's database. How do you get it back if you want to take it in-house or move it to another provider of services?

All of these issues can be resolved with good planning. While using the Internet for recruiting and finding legal information is easy, other HR activities are in their infancy.

The dollar value of professional services offered on the Internet will grow from the current $15 billion to more than $55 billion in the next two years, according to a Forrester report summarized in PC Computing. HR management services will be a big part of this growth. Credit unions at least should consider the Internet options before adding more overhead to their in-house HR departments.

pends on the efficiencies you're trying to achieve. Will outsourcing meet your criteria?

3. Is the credit union looking for someone to take over the HR operation or for a partner with the resources to handle situations that arise?
4. Can the credit union provide managers and staff with necessary services through outsourcing? Make sure the firm offers all services management requires.
5. What services does the credit union need, and what services can the outsourcing firm provide? Most outsourcing companies offer these basic services:
   - Legal compliance;
   - Employee relations advice;
   - Management training on HR issues;
   - Organization development;
   - Compensation and benefits knowledge;
   - Surveys in compensation, benefits, and employee satisfaction;
   - Job description development; and
   - Policy manual/employee handbook creation.
6. Does the outsourcing firm offer any services via the Internet, such as employee database management or legal compliance training (see "Outsourcing and the Internet," p. 35)?
7. How does the firm create rapport with credit union staff? The firm must develop relationships with your staff so they have confidence in its information and decisions.
8. Can the firm provide accurate answers within a quick timeframe? Will someone always be available who knows the credit union's personnel policies well enough to give correct information?
9. What are the track records of the firms the credit union is considering, and who is on staff? Check references.
10. How long will the contract be?

11. What are the contract's provisions? Is there a clause permitting contract termination if you're dissatisfied with the firm's performance?
12. Is this strictly a financial decision? Sometimes outsourcing will save you money; sometimes you get a chance to start over with new HR management; and sometimes you get both.

After deciding to contract with an outsourcing firm, your management team should ask for benchmarks to make sure you're receiving the service level you expect. Performance criteria can be built into the contract but should be documented.

For example, the contract may stipulate the firm will be on-site at least one day every two weeks. Another provision may require the outsourcing firm to respond to all client calls within 24 hours. Also list in the contract penalties for not meeting performance criteria.

True HR management outsourcing is relatively new to credit unions. It offers many advantages to small- and medium-size credit unions looking to reduce administrative costs and minimize headaches involved in managing employees. The key advantage to outsourcing is management gets the benefit of an entire bench of experts at the cost of one HR generalist. But it's essential to address several important questions before deciding to outsource.

Stephen Norman is an attorney working in human resources. Rob Arbuckle is vice president/chief operating officer for Washington Credit Union, Mountlake Terrace, Wash.

Editor's note: The CUNA HR Council provides a forum for HR professionals to discuss HR issues such as outsourcing. Contact CUNA HR Council executive committee member Cathleen Slone at 314-542-1345 or by e-mail at slonec@mcusstl.org.

What is an employee? The answer depends on the Federal law

In a legal context, the classification of a worker as either an employee or an independent contractor can have significant consequences

Charles J. Muhl

In the American workplace today, a full-time, 40-hour-a-week employee who stays with the same employer performing the same job over the course of an entire worklife would be viewed as a rarity, or at least as a person found in lesser proportion in the U.S. workforce than in decades past. Today's workplace includes a variety of workers in contingent arrangements—independent contractors, leased employees, temporary employees, on-call workers, and more—perceived to be a result of employers' desire to reduce labor costs and employees' desire to increase their flexibility, among other things. The Bureau of Labor Statistics recently reported that in February 2001 the contingent workforce, or those workers who do not have an implicit or explicit contract for ongoing employment and who do not expect their current job to last, totaled 5.4 million people, roughly 4 percent of the U.S. workforce.[1] According to the BLS survey, millions more were employed in alternative work arrangements:[2] 8.6 million independent contractors (representing 6.4 percent of total employment), 2.1 million on-call workers, 1.2 million temporary help agency workers, and 633,000 contract company workers. The Bureau treats these contingent workers and workers in alternative work arrangements as part of total U.S. employment, and although they are in a typical employment situation, most of the general public would probably consider them employees.

But how does Federal law treat workers in contingent and alternative work arrangements? That is, are such workers viewed as employees who are entitled to legal protections under Federal legislation? As is frequently the case with legal questions, the answer depends—in this case, on the Federal law at issue. In general, though, courts evaluate the totality of the circumstances surrounding a worker's employment, with a focus on who has the right—the employer or the employee—to control the work process.

The question "Is a worker an employee?" may seem like a simple one to answer on its surface. The dictionary definition of "employee" says succinctly that an employee is "a person who works for another in return for financial or other compensation."[3] Under that definition, independent contractors would appear to be employees. However, the legal definition of "employee" is concerned with more than the pay received by a worker for services provided. *Black's Law Dictionary* defines "employee" as "a person in the service of another under any contract of hire, express or implied, oral or written, where the employer has the power or right to control and direct the employee in the material details of how the work is to be performed."[4] In contrast, an "independent contractor" is one who, "in the exercise of an independent employment, contracts to do a piece of work according to his own methods and is subject to his employer's control only as to the end product or final result of his work."[5] This legal distinction as to how a worker must be classified has broad implications—and potentially negative consequences for mischaracterization—for both employers and workers alike.

This article examines how the legal determination is made that a worker is either an employee or an independent contractor, beginning with a discussion of why the determination is important and then discussing the tests used by courts to make the determination and the laws pursuant to which each test applies.

Employee or independent contractor?

Employers have used independent contractors and other contingent workers more frequently in recent times for a variety of reasons, including reducing the costs associated with salaries, benefits, and employment taxes and increasing the flexibility of the workforce.[6] Under U.S. law, employers are required to pay the employer's share, and withhold the worker's share, of employment taxes for employees, but not for independent contractors. Employment taxes include those collected pursuant to the

Federal Insurance Contributions Act (FICA)[7] for the U.S. Social Security system; those collected pursuant to the Federal Unemployment Tax Act (FUTA),[8] which pays unemployment benefits to displaced workers; and income tax withholding.[9]

U.S. law imposes other obligations on employers with respect to employees that are not imposed on independent contractors.[10] The Fair Labor Standards Act (FLSA)[11] requires employers to meet minimum-wage and overtime obligations toward their employees. Title VII of the Civil Rights Act of 1964[12] prohibits employers from discriminating against their employees on the basis of race, color, religion, sex, or national origin, while the Age Discrimination in Employment Act (ADEA)[13] prohibits employers from discriminating against employees on the basis of their age. The Employment Retirement Security Act (ERISA)[14] sets the parameters of qualified employee benefit plans, including the level of benefits and amount of service required for vesting of those benefits, typically in the context of retirement. The Americans with Disabilities Act (ADA)[15] prohibits employers from discriminating against qualified individuals who have disabilities. The Family and Medical Leave Act (FMLA)[16] requires employers to provide eligible employees with up to 12 weeks of unpaid leave per year when those employees are faced with certain critical life situations. The National Labor Relations Act (NLRA)[17] grants employees the right to organize and governs labor-management relations.

Clearly, then, some incentive exists for employers to classify their workers as independent contractors rather than employees, in order to reduce costs and various legal obligations. However, the failure of an employer to make the proper determination as to whether workers are employees or independent contractors can have dire consequences. Employers who are careless in their labeling of workers as independent contractors risk exposure to substantial liability in the future under Federal law if the workers are mischaracterized. The U.S. Government—in particular, the Internal Revenue Service (IRS)—can seek to recover back taxes and other contributions that should have been paid by the employer on the employee's behalf,[18] and the workers themselves can seek compensation for job benefits that the employer denied them on the basis of their supposed status as independent contractors.

One of the most striking examples of the danger of mischaracterizing workers as independent contractors rather than employees occurred in *Vizcaino* v. *Microsoft*,[19] a case in which the U.S. Court of Appeals for the Ninth Circuit held that a class of workers for the leading U.S. computer software company were employees who were entitled to participate in Microsoft's various pension and welfare plans, despite the fact that the workers had signed an agreement that labeled them as independent contractors.

Prior to 1990, Microsoft hired "freelancers" to perform various services for the company over a continuous period, in some cases extending in excess of 2 years. Upon joining Microsoft, the former freelancers executed agreements which specifically stated that they were independent contractors and not employees and that nothing contained in the agreement would be construed to create an employer-employee relationship. Despite the agreements, the workers were fully integrated into Microsoft's workforce, working under nearly identical circumstances as Microsoft's regular employees. The erstwhile freelancers worked the same core hours at the same location and shared the same supervisors as regular employees. The only distinction between the freelancers and regular employees was that the freelancers were hired for specific projects. Microsoft neither paid the employer's share, nor withheld the worker's share, of FICA taxes and did not allow the workers to participate in the company's pension plans, on the basis of the agreements the workers had signed stating that they were independent contractors.

The IRS investigated Microsoft and determined that the workers were employees, not independent contractors, and that Microsoft should have been withholding taxes for them.[20] Accepting the IRS' determination, Microsoft conferred employee status on certain of the workers, but dismissed others from employment. Those who were dismissed then filed a class-action suit seeking to have the court declare that they were eligible to participate in Microsoft's pension plans. The district court determined that the workers were employees, not independent contractors.[21] On appeal, Microsoft conceded that the workers were employees, but argued (1) that they had waived their right to participate in the company's pension plans by executing the agreements which specifically stated that they were independent contractors and not employees and (2) that nothing contained in the agreement could be construed to create an employer-employee relationship. The court of appeals rejected Microsoft's argument, finding that the company's pension plan administrator had acted arbitrarily and capriciously in denying the workers' claim that they were entitled to participate in the pension plans. The court found that the administrator should have focused on the actual circumstances surrounding the freelancers' employment and not the labeling of the workers by the agreements. In December 2000, Microsoft settled the case for $97 million.

There are circumstances in which the classification of a worker as an independent contractor is detrimental to employers and beneficial to workers. When the services being performed result in a copyrightable work, employers may wish to establish that a worker is an employee in order to obtain authorship of the copyright. The U.S. Supreme Court, in *Community for Creative Non-Violence, et al.* v. *Reid*,[22] held that an employer is the owner of a copyright if the employer had contracted for a creative "work for hire"—that is, if work prepared by an employee is within the scope of employment. If the worker is an independent contractor, the worker, and not the employer, is the owner of the copyright for the work performed. Thus, in the context of intellectual property rights, employers are protected by establishing an employer-employee relationship with a worker.

Determining a worker's status

The potential benefits to both employers and workers of the proper characterization of the working relationship raises the question, How is the legal determination made as to whether a worker is an employee or an independent contractor? Generally,

Exhibit 1.   Tests for determining whether a worker is an employee

Test	Description	Laws under which test has been applied by courts
Common-law test (used by Internal Revenue Service (IRS))	Employment relationship exists if employer has right to control work process, as determined by evaluating totality of the circumstances and specific factors	Federal Insurance Contributions Act Federal Unemployment Tax Act Income tax withholding Employment Retirement and Income Security Act National Labor Relations Act Immigration Reform and Control Act (IRS test)
Economic realities test	Employment relationship exists if individual is economically dependent on a business for continued employment	Fair Labor Standards Act Title VII Age Discrimination in Employment Act Americans with Disabilities Act Family and Medical Leave Act (likely to apply)
Hybrid test	Employment relationship is evaluated under both common-law and economic reality test factors, with a focus on who has the right to control the means and manner of a worker's performance	Title VII Age Discrimination in Employment Act Americans with Disabilities Act

the totality of the circumstances—that is, all the conditions under which a person is working—governs the characterization of that person as an employee or an independent contractor; the label a company places on the worker has no bearing on the matter. Again generally, a person is an employee if the employer has the right to control the person's work process, whereas a worker is classified as an independent contractor if the employer does not control the process, but dictates only the end result or product of the work. Note that the employer does not actually have to control the work process: the mere *ability* of the employer to take control is sufficient to create an employer-employee relationship.

The courts have developed three tests to be used in determining a worker's status: the common-law test, the economic realities test, and a hybrid test that incorporates various elements of both of those tests. Because the tests have been applied to different Federal statutes, the characterization of a worker as an employee or an independent contractor can vary, depending on which statute is being applied. As a result, the same person can be classified as an employee under one test and the relevant Federal laws to which that test is applied, but as an independent contractor under another test and its relevant Federal laws. Furthermore, different tests are applied to the same Federal law, depending on which jurisdiction a case is heard in. However, because each of the tests evaluates the totality of the circumstances behind the employment relationship, the overlap in the tests is substantial. Exhibit 1 offers a brief summary or the three tests.

Common-law test. The common-law test was developed on the basis of the traditional legal concept of agency, which, in an em-

ployment context, consists of a relationship wherein one person (the employee) acts for or represents another (the employer) by the employer's authority.[23] The common-law test involves the evaluation of 10 factors to determine whether a worker is an employee, with no one factor dispositive, but with the determination centering on who has the right to control the work process. Exhibit 2 shows the 10 factors used in the common-law test.

The IRS uses a derivation of the common-law test in assessing whether a worker is an employee, taking into account some of the common-law test's factors as part of the IRS's own 20-factor test.[24] In addition to evaluating employment tax obligations under the Federal income tax law, FICA, and FUTA, the common-law/IRS test has been applied to the National Labor Relations Act, which governs labor-management relations and collective bargaining for unionized employers, and to the Immigration Reform and Control Act. Furthermore, in *NationWide Mutual Insurance Co.* v. *Darden*,[25] the U.S. Supreme Court ruled that, for Federal laws that do not contain a clear definition of "employee," the relationship between employer and worker should be evaluated on the basis of the common-law test, focusing on who had the right to control the worker.

In a vast number of cases throughout the U.S. Federal court system, some going back several decades, the common-law test has been applied to determine whether workers are employees or contractors. For example, in *Walker* v. *Altmeyer*,[26] decided in 1943, the U.S. Court of Appeals for the Second Circuit found that an attorney who was given office space at $100 per month in return for services performed was an employee pursuant to the Social Security Act, because his landlord, another attorney, had the right to control what the worker did and to supervise the

Exhibit 2. Factors used to determine a worker's status under the common-law test

Factor	Worker is an employee if—	Worker is an independent contractor if—
Right to control	Employer controls details of the work	Worker controls details of the work
Type of business	Worker is not engaged in business or occupation distinct from employer's	Worker operates in business that is distinct from employer's business
Supervision	Employer supervises worker	Work is done without supervision
Skill level	Skill level need not be high or unique	Skill level is specialized, is unique, or requires substantial training
Tools and materials	Employer provides instrumentalities, tools, and location of workplace	Worker provides instrumentalities and tools of workplace and works at a site other than the employer's
Continuing relationship	Worker is employed for extended, continuous period	Worker is employed for specific project or for limited time
Method of payment	Worker is paid by the hour, or other computation based on time worked is used to determine pay	Worker is paid by the project
Integration	Work is part of employer's regular business	Work is not part of employer's regular business
Intent	Employer and worker intend to create an employer-employee relationship	Employer and worker do not intend to create an employer-employee relationship
Employment by more than one firm	Worker provides services only to one employer	Worker provides services to more than one business

method used to complete the work. John E. Walker rented office space from another attorney, Pliny Williamson, beginning in 1927 and was also hired by Williamson to perform legal services for a fixed monthly salary. In April 1938, the two attorneys established a new compensation arrangement under which Walker would pay his rent by providing legal services and would receive additional compensation when his services were valued at more than $100 per month. Upon reaching the age of 65 in 1938, Walker applied for Social Security benefits, including monthly insurance benefits, under the Social Security Act. Although the Social Security Administration initially paid Walker the insurance benefits on the basis of his representation that he was not an employee making more than $15 per month, the Agency subsequently ceased payments upon learning of Walker's arrangement with Williamson. The court found Walker to be an employee because, despite the change in the manner of compensation beginning in 1938, the kind of work that Walker did for Williamson did not change at all. Walker still performed work as an attorney at the direction of Williamson. That right to control was dispositive for the court.

Similarly, in *United States v. Polk*,[27] the U.S. Court of Appeals for the Ninth Circuit found that an employer could be convicted of a criminal offense for failure to pay FICA employment taxes, despite the employer's declaration that its workers were all subcontractors. Polk was notified by an IRS agent that he was required to establish a separate bank account to be used to deposit employees' tax withholdings. Prior to receiving this notice, Polk paid his workers on an hourly or weekly basis, had

them work fixed hours, supervised the workers, and supplied them with the tools and materials necessary to perform their work. Furthermore, with the exception of one individual, all of the workers worked exclusively for Polk. These conditions did not change after the IRS served Polk with notice that his workers were employees, but thereafter, Polk represented to the IRS that he no longer had employees and employed only subcontractors. Polk was convicted of a criminal offense for failure to withhold wages to pay FICA taxes. The appeals court sustained Polk's conviction, finding that the jury had properly considered, under the common-law test, the totality of the circumstances of the working relationship between Polk and his workers and also had properly focused on Polk's right to control the workers, both with respect to the product of the work and the means by which the product was produced.

To summarize, then, under the common-law test, an employee is a worker whose work process and work product are controlled by the employer. In determining who has the right to control in a particular case, courts look to such factors as supervision, skill level, method of payment, whether the relationship is ongoing, who supplies the tools and materials for the work, whether the relationship between the worker and the employer is exclusive, and the parties' intent, as well as other, related factors.

Economic realities test. The economic realities test, which is most significantly applied in the context of the Fair Labor Standards Act[28] governing minimum-wage and overtime obligations, focuses on the economic relationship between the worker

Exhibit 3. Factors used to determine a worker's status under the economic realities test

Factor	Worker is an employee if—	Worker is an independent contractor if—
Integration	Worker provides services that are a part of the employer's regular business	Worker provides services outside the regular business of the employer
Investment in facilities	Worker has no investment in the work facilities and equipment	Worker has a substantial investment in the work facilities and equipment
Right to control	Management retains a certain type and degree of control over the work	Management has no right to control the work process of the worker
Risk	Worker does not have the opportunity to make a profit or incur a loss	Worker has the opportunity to make a profit or incur a loss from the job
Skill	Work does not require any special or unique skills or judgment	Work requires a special skill, judgment, or initiative
Continuing relationship	Worker has a permanent or extended relationship with the business	Work relationship is for one project or a limited duration

and the employer. A worker is an employee under the test if the worker is economically dependent upon the employer for continued employment. The test examines the nature of the relationship in light of the fact that independent contractors would typically not rely on a sole employer for continued employment at any one time, but would work for, and be compensated by, many different employers, whereas most employees hold a single job and rely on that one employer for continued employment and for their primary source of income. The economic reality test is generally applied to laws whose purpose is to protect or benefit a worker, because courts view the protection of a worker who is financially dependent on a particular employer as important.[29] Because of its broader scope, the economic reality test has a greater likelihood of finding workers to be employees than does the common-law test. Accordingly, a worker could be classified as an employee for the purposes of dealing with one Federal law, such as the Fair Labor Standards Act, but as an independent contractor under another, like FICA. In evaluating whether a worker is an employee under the economic realities test, courts look to the factors listed in exhibit 3, some of which are similar to those considered under the common-law test.

In *Donovan* v. *DialAmerica Marketing, Inc.*,[30] the Third Circuit Court of Appeals demonstrated the precise application of the economic realities test, as well as the different results that can be reached regarding workers of the same corporation, even when just one legal test is applied. DialAmerica's principal business was the sale of magazine renewal subscriptions by telephone to persons whose subscriptions had expired or were nearing expiration. In pursuit of renewing subscriptions, the company hired workers to locate subscribers' phone numbers by looking names up in telephone books and calling directory assistance operators. In certain years, DialAmerica operated a program in which these workers were permitted to work from their homes. When they were hired, DialAmerica made the workers, called "home researchers," sign an "independent contractor's agreement" that supposedly established their status as

independent contractors. A worker would be given a box of 500 cards with names to be researched, and the company expected the cards to be returned within 1 week. The home researchers were free to choose the weeks and hours they worked; DialAmerica had little supervision over the workers, but placed certain conditions on how the work process was to be conducted, including stipulating the method for reporting back the results on each card and the ink to be used when doing so. DialAmerica also employed workers as "distributors," persons who gave the cards with names to the home researchers. The Department of Labor sued DialAmerica for paying the home researchers and distributors less than the minimum wage for the work they did, arguing that they were employees under the Fair Labor Standards Act.

The court of appeals ruled that, under the economic realities test, the home researchers were employees. First, the court found that the workers did not make a great investment in their work, they had little opportunity for profit or loss, and the work required little skill. Second, the court ruled that DialAmerica's lack of control over the manner in which the home researchers did their work did not support a finding that they were independent contractors, because the very nature of home work dictated that the times worked would be determined by the workers and they would be subjected to very little supervision when working. The fact that a person works from home does not, on its own, determine whether the person is an employee under the Fair Labor Standards Act, the court said. Third, the court found that the home researchers had a continuous working relationship with DialAmerica under which they did not work for other employers. Finally, the court held that the home researchers were an integral part of DialAmerica's business because they did the very work—locating phone numbers—that was essential to DialAmerica's ability to renew subscriptions, despite the fact that they located only approximately 4 percent to 5 percent of the number of phone numbers the company sought to be retrieved. After analyzing these factors, the court ruled that the

home researchers were economically dependent on Dial-America for continued employment and, therefore, were employees under the economic realities test.

In contrast, the appellate court held that the distributors of the research work were independent contractors under the Fair Labor Standards Act. The court found that DialAmerica exhibited minimal control over the distributors' work providing cards to the home researchers, because the distributors maintained records of the work and were permitted to recruit home researchers. The court also noted that the distributors risked financial loss if they did not manage the distribution network properly, because their transportation expenses could exceed their revenue. The transportation expenses also required the distributors to make an investment in the business, the court found. Finally, the distributors required somewhat specialized managerial skills in operating the distribution network, according to the court. Although the distributors were typically employed for a long period, the Court found that factor insufficient to overcome the weight of the remaining circumstances indicating that the distributors were independent contractors.

In *Brock* v. *Superior Care, Inc.*,[31] the U.S. Court of Appeals for the Second Circuit found that an employer had violated the Fair Labor Standard Act's overtime-pay protections by not paying overtime to nurses who were employees under the Act. Superior Care referred nurses for temporary assignments to hospitals, nursing homes, and individual patients. The company would assign nurses as work opportunities became available, and the nurses were free to refuse an assignment for any reason. If a nurse accepted an assignment, the nurse reported directly to the patient, and Superior Care provided minimal supervision through visits to job sites approximately once or twice a month. Patients contracted directly with Superior Care, which paid them an hourly wage. The nurses could hold other jobs, including jobs with other health care providers.

The court found that the nurses were employees under the economic realities test. As a preliminary matter, the court rejected the company's contention that the trial court had used evidence outside of the six factors that make up the test. Superior Care had two sets of payrolls, one for taxed employees and one for nontaxed employees, despite the fact that the nurses on both payrolls did exactly the same work. The workers on the nontaxed payroll did not receive overtime pay for their work. The trial court relied in part on that evidence in finding that those workers were not independent contractors. The appeals court noted that the factors of the economic reality test are not exclusive and that *any* relevant evidence can be considered as part of the totality of the circumstances surrounding the employment relationship. The court also stated that an employer's "self-serving" labeling of workers as independent contractors is not controlling. Turning to the application of the economic reality factors, the court found that (1) the nurses had no opportunity for profit or loss, because Superior Care set their wages and prohibited them from entering into privately paying contracts with patients, (2) the nursing services that were provided were the most integral part of Superior Cafe's business of providing health care personnel on request, and (3) despite a quantitatively calculated lack of visits by Superior Care supervisors, the com-

pany retained the right to supervise the nurses and exerted control over them in that regard. Although the nurses obviously were skilled workers and also had the opportunity to work for other health care employers besides Superior Care, the court found those factors nondispositive. According to the court, the weight of the evidence indicated that when all the circumstances of the employment relationship were considered, the nurses were employees and not independent contractors.

In *Brock* v. *Mr. W Fireworks, Inc.*,[32] the Court of Appeals for the Fifth Circuit found that operators of fireworks stands in south Texas were employees under the economic realities test, subject to the protections of the Fair Labor Standards Act, because (1) Mr. W controlled the method of selling fireworks and made a substantial investment in the business operations, (2) the operators lacked skill and independent initiative, and (3) the duration of the employment relationship was lengthy. According to the parties' testimony, Mr. W acquired land for fireworks stands, procured materials to build the stands, hired workers to construct the stands at its warehouse, recruited operators to run the stands during the two short periods in each year that Texas permits the sale of fireworks, employed workers to supply the stands with fireworks, and advertised the sale of fireworks through the stands. Mr. W paid the operators of the stands on a commission basis.

The appeals court rejected the trial court's finding that the operators were independent contractors, ruling that Mr. W exerted control over the operators by determining the location and size of the stands, by suggesting the retail price of the fireworks and preprinting price tags, by requiring operators to attend to the stands for 24 hours a day to avoid the loss of inventory, by providing display instructions that were almost uniformly followed by the operators, by supplying a substantial portion of advertising, and by determining how the operators would be paid. The court also found that the operators had little opportunity to determine their own profit or loss, because the commission for the sale of the fireworks was set by Mr. W; that the operators made little or no investment in the operation of the stands, whose construction was always financed by Mr. W; and that the operators, while good salespersons, did not exhibit a degree of independent skill or initiative sufficient to conclude that they were independent contractors. Finally, the fact that the fireworks stands were seasonal was simply an operational characteristic unique to the particular business, and the permanency of an employment relationship could accordingly be determined by whether the operators worked for the entire operative period of a particular season. Because the operators were economically dependent on Mr. W for their continued employment as sellers of fireworks, the operators were deemed employees under the economic realities test, entitled to the protections of the Fair Labor Standards Act.

In conclusion, the economic realities test, while similar to the common-law test, focuses on the ultimate concern of whether the economic reality, as illuminated by several factors, is that a worker depends on someone else's business for his or her continued employment, in which case the worker is an employee. If a worker operates an independent business, the worker is clas-

sified as an independent contractor under the economic realities test.

Hybrid test. The hybrid test combines elements of the common-law test and the economic realities test, in keeping with the accepted view of all courts that the totality of the circumstances surrounding the relationship between worker and employer should be examined to determine whether the worker is an employee or an independent contractor. In practice, the hybrid test considers the economic realities of the work relationship as a critical factor in the determination, but focuses on the employer's right to control the work process as a determinative factor.

The hybrid test is applied frequently in cases brought under Title VII of the Civil Rights Act of 1964, which prohibits employers from discriminating against employees on the basis of race, color, religion, sex, or national origin. For example, in *Diggs* v. *Harris Hospital—Methodist, Inc.*,[33] the U.S. Court of Appeals for the Fifth Circuit held that Jacqulyn Diggs, a black female physician, could not sustain a claim under Title VII for discrimination on the basis of race or sex or in retaliation for a prior charge of discrimination against the hospital. The court found that, although she was appointed to the hospital's provisional medical staff and enjoyed the privileges associated with that appointment, including the ability to treat patients through hospital facilities, Diggs was an independent contractor, not an employee, of the hospital under the hybrid test.

Noting first that the hybrid test takes into account both the economic realities of the working relationship and the extent to which the employer is able to control the details and means of the work being done, the court then specified additional factors to be considered under the test. Certain of those factors, including supervision, skill level, method of payment, who supplies the tools and materials, the duration of the employment relationship, the extent to which the work is integrated into the employer's business, and the intention of the parties, are considered under both the common-law test and the economic realities test. Beyond these factors, the court also considered the manner in which the work relationship was terminated (that is, by one or both parties and with or without notice or explanation), whether annual leave was provided to the workers, whether retirement benefits were provided to them, and whether the employer paid Social Security taxes for the workers.

In concluding that Diggs was not an employee, the court found that physicians' privileges at Harris Hospital were not necessary to Diggs' practice; that is, if Diggs were denied those privileges, her ability to obtain them at other area hospitals would not have been restricted. Focusing on the control factor, the court also found that, although the hospital both supplied the tools and materials to make it possible for Diggs to provide medical care and imposed standards of care upon those with privileges, the hospital did not, in fact, direct the manner or means by which medical care was to be provided by the physician. Diggs treated patients without direct supervision and merely required the presence of a sponsor during surgical procedures to attest to the physician's qualifications. Furthermore, the hospital did not pay a salary to Diggs, nor did it pay her li-

censing fees, professional dues, insurance premiums, taxes, or retirement benefits. These considerations cemented the court's conclusion that Diggs was an independent contractor who was not protected by Title VII.

The hybrid test seeks to combine the general and specific factors of both the common-law test and the economic realities test, recognizing that, in each legal determination of whether a worker is an employee or an independent contractor, a court may consider each and every circumstance of the employment relationship.

THE PROPER CLASSIFICATION OF A WORKER as an employee or independent contractor at the beginning of an employment relationship is important to both employers and workers with respect to their obligations and protections under Federal law. Although the classification does depend on the Federal law being applied, the overriding factor is who has the "right to control" the work process, and the relationship is based upon all of its characteristics, regardless of what label the employer applies to the worker.[34]

Notes

1. The figures reported are for the broadest of the Bureau's three measurements of the contingent workforce. For additional information, see the BLS news release, "Contingent and Alternative Work Arrangements," February 2001.
2. By the criteria of the survey, a worker may be in both a contingent and an alternative work arrangement, but is not automatically so, because contingent work is defined separately from alternative work arrangements.
3. *American Heritage Dictionary of the English Language*, 1978.
4. Henry Campbell Black, *Black's Law Dictionary* (St. Paul, MN, West Publishing Co, 1991), p. 363.
5. *Ibid.*, p. 530.
6. See, for example, Mark Diana and Robin H. Rome, "Beyond Traditional Employment: The Contingent Workforce," 196 APR, NJ Law 8, * 9 (April 1999).
7. 26 U.S.C. 3101 *et seq.*
8. 26 U.S.C. 3301 *et seq.*
9. 26 U.S.C. 3401 *et seq.*
10. In many cases, an independent contractor's true employer is the contracting agency, which would be subject to these Federal laws. In addition to the Federal laws that protect employees, additional State laws, including those which provide workers' compensation benefits, typically protect employees, but not independent contractors.
11. 29 U.S.C. 201 *et seq.*
12. 42 U.S.C. 2000(e) *et seq.*
13. 29 U.S.C. 621 *et seq.*
14. 29 U.S.C. 1001 *et seq.*
15. 42 U.S.C. 12101 *et seq.*
16. 29 U.S.C. 2601 *et seq.*
17. 29 U.S.C. 151 *et seq.*

18. Federal law provides employers with a safe-harbor provision to avoid a retroactive IRS reclassification of workers as employees where an employer had a "reasonable basis" for treating a worker as an independent contractor. An employer's good faith in making the determination is required for the safe harbor to apply.

19. The case has an extensive procedural history throughout the 1990s. For the opinion of the Ninth Circuit Court of Appeals regarding the status of the Microsoft workers focused on in this article, see 120 F.3d 1006.

20. The IRS used its "20-factor test" in making its determination regarding the employees' status. (For details of the test, see next section in the text.)

21. The District Court used the "common-law test" in making its determination regarding the employees' status. (For details of the test, see next section in the text.)

22. 490 U.S. 730 (1989).

23. *Black's Law Dictionary*, p. 62.

24. See IRS Revenue Ruling 87-41; see also "Summary of ms 20-Factor Test," from HRnext.com, on the Internet at **http://www.hrnext.com/tools/view.cfm?articles_id= 1470&tools_id=2**.

25. 112 S.Ct. 1344, 1348-49 (1992).

26. 137 F.2d 531 (2nd Circuit 1943).

27. 550 F.2d 566 (9th Cir. 1977).

28. The Fair Labor Standards Act uses the following uninformative definition of "employee" in the statutory language: "any individual employed by an employer." However, Congress and the courts have recognized that, because of its primary focus on protecting workers, the definition of "employee" under the Act is the broadest one used pursuant to the economic realities test.

29. See Myra H. Barron, "Who's an Independent Contractor? Who's an Employee?" 14 Lab. Law 457, 460 (winter/spring 1999).

30. 757 F.2d 1376 (3rd Cir. 1985).

31. 840 F.2d 1054 (2nd Cir. 1988).

32. 814 F.2d 1042 (5th Cir. 1987).

33. 847 F.2d 270 (9th Cir. 1988).

34. For additional discussions of the classification of workers as employees or independent contractors and the ramifications for employers, see John C. Fox, *Is That Worker an Independent Contractor or Your Employee?* (Palo Alto, CA, Fenwick and West, March 1997); Barron, "Who's an Independent Contractor?" Diana and Rome, *Beyond Traditional Employment*; and William D. Frumkin and Elliot D. Bernak, "Cost Savings from Hiring Contingent Workers May Be Lost if Their Status Is Challenged," *New York State Bar Journal*, special edition on labor and employment law, New York State Bar Association, September-October 1999.

Charles J. Muhl is an attorney in the firm of Goldberg, Kohn, Bell, Black, Rosenbloom & Moritz, Ltd., Chicago, Illinois. E-mail: charles.muhl@goldbergkohn.com

Strategizing for HR

A well-written business plan can earn you a seat at the table with top management.

By Kathryn Tyler

If you thought business plans, also called strategic plans, were only for CEOs and dot-com entrepreneurs, think again. Business plans can be a boon to HR departments as well. If you haven't already done so, now may be the time to develop your own HR business plan.

An HR plan can help you delineate your goals and your strategies for achieving them. It enables you to go beyond day-to-day tasks to see the larger purpose of your department and now it functions within the company. It helps you "align the resources and department to the broader needs of the organization," says Rogers Davis, assistant vice chancellor of human resources for the University of California, San Diego (UCSD).

Carol Asselta, SPHR, human resources manager for PECO Energy Company, a Philadelphia utility, says business plans help HR "think more holistically, to see systems rather than isolated elements. How does one thing impact another? How does everything fit?"

Having a plan also can aid communication within the department and with those outside HR, say experts interviewed for this article.

Davis, whose department is on its third strategic plan, says it "helps us communicate effectively what everyone is doing and know when progress is made." Asselta says having a business plan can help HR show executives the business rationale for its decisions by demonstrating how HR actions tie in to the company's overall goals.

By contrast, the absence of a business plan can leave an HR department adrift in a sea of uncertainty. "The alternative is a haphazard approach where you are constantly putting out fires, with no visions of where you should be or what you should be doing to get there," says Lee Hargrave, author of *Plan for Profitability!: How to Write a Strategic Business Plan* (Four Seasons Publishers, 1999).

Robert G. Stovall, principal of Robert G. Stovall Consulting, an HR solutions firm in Houston, asks, "If you don't have a plan, how do you know where you are going?"

What's a Business Plan?

"Most HR folks don't have a lot of training in how to do strategic planning," says Deborah Dwyer, PHR, associate professor and chair of the management department at the University of Toledo in Ohio. The first step, then, is to understand the difference between a companywide business plan and one geared specifically to the HR function.

A companywide business plan outlines the organization's current situation and where it intends to go. In its simplest form, the plan is a goal statement. But the plan also includes information on the issues facing the company—competition, opportunities, market conditions, industry changes and the company's strengths and weaknesses.

An HR plan describes what HR must do to help the company achieve the goals outlined in the business plan. An HR plan lists the action steps or milestones for meeting those goals, as well as target dates for completion and specific guidelines for measuring performance.

How far out should a plan project? It depends, says Hargrave, adding that "a typical company might have three to five years as the planning horizon."

The HR department at UCSD has a detailed two-year plan of short-term goals and a five-year plan of long-term goals, explains Davis. "We try to do plans longer than 12 months because the process is rather involved," he says.

Some question the value of making elaborate plans so far in advance, but Stovall says the planning process itself is worth the effort.

Investigating the facts and your assumptions about the future will give you new information that can help you react more quickly and with greater confidence, he says."

"It is important to ensure the HR business plan integrates well and supports the overall business plan of the company," says Hargrave. "The HR business plan should be an integral part."

Identify Goals and Action Steps

It is crucial that the HR plan is in alignment with the overall business plan. Almost every organization has a business planning and budgeting cycle—and HR must ensure its business plan is a part of that process, says David Ripley, a lecturer on HR management at the University of Canterbury in Christchurch, New Zealand. "If you're not a part of that [planning and budgeting] process," says Ripley, "your effort may just be a side show that nobody but you ever looks at." And, as a result, the HR and business plans may not align. Or, HR may not get the resources it needs.

Once you understand your company's goals, you must establish your own HR departmental goals. Ripley uses a simplified approach that focuses on five questions:

- Where am I now?
- Where do I want to go?
- What's the difference between where I am and where I want to go?
- How will I get there?
- How will I know if I'm succeeding?

He also recommends focusing on these three areas:

Operational excellence. How well are you conducting basic HR operations? This includes all functional areas, such as recruiting and compensation. To determine how well you are doing in these areas, you can conduct

employee surveys and review statistical data, such as turnover and absenteeism rates, in relation to industry averages.

For instance, Paychex Inc., a national provider of payroll, benefits and human resources services headquartered in Rochester, N.Y., wanted to improve its employee retention rates. "We recognized we needed a better reward package to retain people," says William G. Kuchta, vice-president of organizational development for Paychex.

The company decided that, in light of its consistently strong stock performance, it made sense to offer the employees stock options. Kuchta and his staff presented the proposal to upper management and the executives were so excited by the idea that they wanted to know how quickly the program could be implemented. The plan was "rolled out within eight days," says Kuchta.

The result? Turnover decreased, though Kuchta admits there are too many variables to claim that the stock options plan was the cause. But, he says, "There was a tremendous employee response and anecdotal evidence from employee comments, such as 'This solidifies my being here' and 'I really appreciate it.'"

Short-range objectives. Every business objective has a human content. Find out what it is and make sure it's addressed in your plan. HR must be seen as a contributor to the business. This will lead to HR practices that match current operational needs. For instance, Debra Schaefer, owner of the HR consulting firm Debra G. Schaefer & Associates LLC in Sylvania, Ohio, worked with Aeroquip-Vickars, a coupling manufacturer that is now part of Eaton Corporation. Aeroquip-Vickars acquired a business in Cincinnati, and Schaefer and her HR team immediately made plans to help the new employees transition into the company. "We prepared benefits and orientation kits for them to take home. We went down there and tried to answer their questions quickly. It was an opportunity to show how HR could be value-added in a business transaction," says Schaefer

Strategic organization building. This includes the things you do to help build the human capital that will enable the business unit to survive in the future. For example, about four years ago, Paychex discovered that its products—payroll services—were becoming much more complex, as a result of new government regulations and an increasing interest in 401(k) plans. To maintain alignment with the company's growth and marketing strategy, HR's business plan created a "three-pronged approach with regard to operations: a new systematic approach to recruiting, compensation changes and a multi-step training program. We had to train people to deal with a whole different set of products," says Kuchta. Within two years, HR had created dramatically different training and compensation programs and was working on changing the employment practices.

Extra Online Resources

For more information, consult the SHRM White Paper "Business/HR Alignment" by David E. Ripley, Ph.D., SPHR, at www.shrm.org/whitepapers/wplist.htm.

Dwyer gives another example of how to translate a company goal into an HR one: "If a company that makes business applications computer software decides it wants to get into the virtual gaming market, it will need to hire a lot of Visual Basic programmers. You will have to estimate the cost of recruiting and retaining them or of retraining the programmers you already have, as well as providing them with the hardware, software and other resources they need."

Once you complete these calculations, Dwyer suggests meeting with the finance department to do a cost/benefits or return on investment analysis. "If we invest in 10 more programmers at this cost, what would be [the] value added?" If it costs $600,000 to accomplish a goal that will yield only an additional $400,000 worth of revenue, the goal may have to be eliminated or reworked. The data you bring to the planning session is crucial in making this type of decision, she says.

How much detail should you include in your plan? "If the issue is critical to the business, sweat the details," says Ripley. Dwyer concurs, "The more detailed it is, the more likely you are to implement it." But Kuchta cautions against spending too much time crafting the language of the plan and not enough time executing it. "We don't bother with a lot of text. We only use bullets."

Ripley gives a litmus test: "Recruiting is a good example. You have critical skill positions—and you should be doing detailed planning related to those positions. However, you have other positions that can be filled easily and quickly, and everyone knows it—so don't ask line managers to make detailed projections about how many of those people they will need, by unit, for the next five years, or spend time working on detailed recruiting plans. A good way to have a plan lose credibility and be of little value is to try to get people to spend time developing incredibly detailed plans about things that don't warrant the time investment."

Once you have determined your goals and the action necessary to achieve them, then you must schedule target dates. Dwyer suggests doing "backward planning. You can say, 'We want X to be done by this date.' What tasks need to be done and what resources do we need in order to have this done by this date? Go backward to create a timeline." The HR department at Paychex also has done its planning this way. "You will see fairly quickly how big a problem

---

you've got, in terms of your deadline. If you have a problem, break out all the steps and start to look for places you can run things in parallel," says Ripley.

Who Should Be Involved

While HR planning usually is done by the head of the HR department, Dwyer says it is important to "consult with the people who will have to implement the plan, the people who are actually doing the work. They have information about what you need" to accomplish your goals.

Not at the Table?

Not privy to the company's overall business plan? Deborah Dwyer, PHR, associate professor and chair of the management department at the University of Toledo in Ohio, offers some suggestions for making your own plan more than just an exercise. First, "in order to write a plan, you must do an audit and analysis of your own functions." You need to analyze the information you do have, such as turnover and absenteeism rates, and survey your internal customers about how well you are meeting their needs.

For example, the HR department at UCSD conducts focus groups with internal customers, primarily academic departments, to ask what their service needs are and how HR can support them. Ask yourself, how can we improve our current products and services? How can we use new technology to make our services more convenient and efficient? What else could we do to attract and retain employees? Dwyer also recommends asking your senior manager for specific information regarding the overall business plan as it relates to your HR plan.

Interview your supervisor, suggests Carol Asselta, SPHR, human resources manager for PECO Energy Company, a Philadelphia utility. "Say, 'I could serve you better if I understood what your major goals are and what you want from me.' If you're not at the table, there are other ways to link in. Write a draft and get them to review it. It's a reverse way of doing it, but a lot of times you need to start with that to show that you understand the business."

—*Kathryn Tyler*

For example, Kuchta says that he usually selects a date several months in advance when

he and his six managers will go off-site for a day to focus on strategic planning. In the interim, those managers are to meet with their staffs and internal clients, asking them what they think are important HR goals for the coming year. Kuchta then creates an agenda that includes presentations on the top goals from each functional area, as well as some brainstorming time. Although most strategic planning takes place over a day once a year, Schaefer says, "Any plan is a living document that is continually evolving."

Stovall also says your plan should be "reviewed by someone outside of HR who knows the business." Good candidates for this are your primary internal customers because you want to be sure you will meet their needs.

One group outside HR you will need to work closely with is your organization's finance team. Unfortunately, most HR departments treat finance as a hurdle they must overcome, rather than a resource, says Kuchta. "Make them part of the planning team," he advises. "Don't bring them in after you're done."

And, he recommends, when it comes to crunching the numbers, "Don't use industry averages. Find out the numbers for your own company."

Financial information is the backbone of any business plan. Thus, HR professionals who do not have a background in reading financial statements should get trained, says

Dwyer. "They need to have some understanding of how the financial part of the business is operating."

Set Measurable Goals

Kuchta says that a plan, by itself, "means nothing. Only delivery counts." For every goal you create, you must have a way to measure performance. "Never set goals like 'develop,' 'increase' or 'improve' without a solid target, preferably with a number attached," he advises.

Ripley warns against falling into the activity trap. "Focus on outputs, not activity. You interviewed 1,000 applicants—so what? Measure accomplishments," he says. Even so-called soft goals, such as improved employee morale, can be quantified. For example, you can translate employee satisfaction surveys into numbers.

Asselta of PECO Energy adds, "Your deliverables must be quantifiable or qualifiable. Prove it in numbers. Businesspeople are numbers-driven."

Communicating After the Planning

Stovall recommends putting the plan "where all the relevant players can see it, review it

and measure against it. I always liked the idea of putting the plan on the bulletin board so everyone could see it. There are ways to reduce the plan to a few charts and graphs for 'public' consumption, then you can plot actual results versus the plan. Do it out in the open so all can see. It will gain you a lot of trust."

Kuchta agrees: "I take the plan to every meeting, and often lay it out on the table and see how far along we are."

Asselta adds, "If you don't have a business plan, you can't keep your whole team together. You don't know what your strategy is. A plan helps employees understand their purpose. It can energize people. They aren't just doing day-to-day work; they're progressing towards goals. Then HR isn't just a firefighter at a tactical level. You can escalate the value of HR in the organization by linking with the company's goals. Then, if you don't already have a seat at the table, you'll be worthy of one."

Kathryn Tyler, M.A., is a freelance writer and former HR generalist and trainer in Wixom, Mich. She may be contacted via her web site at http://www.kathryntyler.com.

managing in the new millennium

survivors of organizational downsizing

Patricia M. Buhler, D.B.A.

As the slowing economy has generated increased interest in the already popular downsizing strategy, more companies are addressing the problems of how to effectively implement the strategy. A flawed implementation results in a failed strategy.

Unfortunately, not even half of the firms that have downsized in the last decade were able to meet their objectives for cost reduction. The most ominous finding, however, is the spiral that downsizing begins—often leading to another round of lay-offs and yet another. And most of these again failing to meet their corporate objectives. As a "quick fix" of choice for management, downsizing generally fails to improve performance. Ironically enough, it usually has just the opposite effect—organizational performance suffers.

While downsizing itself may be an appropriate strategy, it is often the implementation that is flawed—resulting in a failure to meet objectives. This implementation involves both the planning before and after

the actual downsizing. The planning before includes deciding how the downsizing will be handled and the planning after includes how the leaner firm will operate. To be effective, this latter planning effort must include the survivors—those employees who remain with the firm.

This plan must clearly address several issues. These include how the downsizing will be communicated, the severance package for the downsized employees, the level of involvement of employees and the investment in the survivors.

There is significant emotional trauma associated with layoffs for all concerned management, those being laid off and those remaining with the firm. Regardless of the terminology, "rightsizing," "downsizing," "dumbsizing," "rebalancing of the skill sets," it is a response considered best for the company as a whole. This is the strategy selected to continue the operations of the organization. But to keep the firm operating becomes a function of the survivors. Failure to address the needs of the

survivors jeopardizes the health of the organization going forward.

"Survivor guilt" is the newly-coined phrase reflecting the emotional aspect of downsizing for those who remain with the company. While the future performance of the organization depends upon these people, some firms pay no attention to them. The downsizing plan must specifically address these survivors and how all the decisions made may impact these employees.

As operations continue in the leaner organization, the same production is usually required with fewer people. Or worse, fewer people must do more. The result is overworked employees. And many of these individuals are taking on new responsibilities and learning new skills.

The survivors must be given time to grieve. While in this period of grief, the company experiences declines in productivity and increases in the number of accidents. The company management must carefully acknowledge this period of grief and provide support to the survivors.

Ignoring this period of grief can magnify the negative cost sequences and prolong the period.

Providing employees with an early warning of the layoffs to come enables individuals to prepare and adjust. It is critical the reasons for the downsizing also be communicated. This helps people to better support the effort. Outlining all the steps of the downsizing effort enables people to prepare for the changes—and the possibility of layoff. The layoff policy should be in place and well communicated at this point.

Part of the information communicated organization-wide should include the specifics of how the downsized employees are being treated. Sharing information concerning the severance packages, insurance and outplacement are important to the survivors. Company newsletters, intranets or even special mailings to employees may be used to communicate vital information.

Managers MUST be very aware of their own behaviors. Jokes or light-hearted approaches to the downsizing must be avoided. Firms must be careful of very visible management perks (like newly decorated offices or new company cars) while other employees are losing their jobs. These perks communicate powerful non-verbal messages that are very negative to many in the organization. Discretion should be used to ensure the wrong message is not sent inadvertently.

Firms must be careful of the bunker mentality whereby management insulates itself—away from the survivors and their anxieties.

Management must maintain an open door policy. Communication becomes even more critical at this time. The survivors must feel management will listen—to their fears, their emotions, their anger and their anxiety. As their new roles may result in frustration as they feel overwhelmed and overworked, it is important for management to listen and respond to these emotions.

It is also important to manage the rumor mill. If the rumor mill tells the story (instead of the formal communication of the firm), morale and company loyalty may suffer. When organizations communicate too little, the rumor mill tends to work overtime to make up for the lack of formal communication. The rumor mill can be best managed by ensuring that formal communication is timely and honest. When the rumor mill is generating inaccurate information, this should be directly addressed in formal communication. Part of this should include a clear statement informing employees when the downsizing effort is really over.

If employees feel the layoffs were not fair, they will become less committed to the organization. Management can use discussion and information groups to inform employees of what is happening—and how it is being handled. Some larger organizations have even utilized hot lines for employees to obtain information. The key is to ensure the layoff policy is perceived as being fair and equitable.

Management must also be specific about their expectations—where the company is going, what role management will play and what they expect of the remaining employees. Downsizing is an emotional strategy that leaves everyone somewhat uncertain and insecure. Communicating clear expectations reduces some of this uncertainty thereby enabling people to think more in terms of what their new role is in the organization. That is, they should focus on how they will contribute to the organization's new objectives.

Severance Packages

There is a growing concern with the severance package being offered to employees who have been laid off in downsizing efforts. This severance package must be fair. And it is critical the organization thinks this issue through very carefully and that a formal, written policy is developed. This policy will usually include a requirement for length of service to be eligible (usually twelve months).

Larger companies average eight weeks of severance for middle mangers who have at least two years of experience with the firm.

Mid-size and smaller companies tend to pay an average of about two to four weeks of severance.

The general guideline used by the majority of firms is one month of severance pay for each year of service with the company. This is, however, totally at the discretion of the firm.

Some companies are even developing formulas similar to those used for early retirement packages (using experience and salary grade). In most cases, the severance package also contains a non-compete agreement.

The severance package is a good public relations tool. The reputation the company gains in handling severance can be instrumental in providing the reputation to make it easier to hire employees when the economy improves.

Those firms that were fair in the treatment of then-employees during downsizing will be more favorably perceived by job applicants when they begin to hire again.

Employee Involvement

Management must involve employees in the "new work" of the organization. Soliciting suggestions for how the work can be better performed is important. While management can provide the broad parameters (and communicate the vision of the company), the details can be left to the employees. This also makes them feel involved and valued in the new, leaner organization.

As the company involves people, they gain their employees' commitment. While the initial reaction of the firm is usually to centralize decision making, it is more effective in the long run to engage in participative decision making—enabling employ-

ees to become more involved in the very work they will be performing.

Some organizations have even found it extremely beneficial to allow employees to provide input in crafting the layoff strategy itself. This often achieves buy-in early in the process as those who are involved are more likely to support the effort they helped create.

Investing in the Survivors

Firms must be sure to recognize the contributions of the survivors in keeping the company going. Investing in the remaining workforce helps to ease feelings of uncertainty. It is natural for the survivors to think they are next. Providing training to the survivors prepares them to take over new responsibilities and communicates the company is willing to invest in them. This suggests the organization is planning to retain them—at least for a while.

The company can experience tremendous benefits in the programs they offer to support their survivors. Stress management programs show the firm cares about the employees remaining and provides coping skills to better manage the change process. Helping the survivors deal with their stress is also good business for the organization.

Most importantly, management must recognize the survivors are likely to leave if they do not feel valued. Even taking the time to discuss possible career paths (while costing the company nothing financially) can reap positive rewards. Management must be creative in their approach to recognizing the value of their employees—using a combination of financial and non-financial tools.

The downsizing strategy must be carefully managed if the firm is to realize any of the expected benefits. It requires particular attention be paid to the survivors and how decisions will impact these survivors. After all, the future success of the organization depends upon these survivors.

Strategic Human Resources Management in Government: Unresolved Issues

Jonathan Tompkins

The concept of strategic human resources management (SHRM) holds considerable promise for improving government performance. However, to realize this promise, it is necessary to invest the concept with clear meaning. This article explores unresolved issues regarding the meaning of SHRM and its relevance to public organizations. Arguing that the value of the concept is undermined by tying it too closely to strategic planning, the article offers an expanded, two-pronged understanding of SHRM. The personnel office, in addition to helping the agency implement strategic initiatives, also carries out an integrated personnel program guided by a coherent theory about what it should be doing and why.

The concept of strategic human resources management (SHRM) is well established in business literature.[1] It refers to ongoing efforts to align an organization's personnel policies and practices with its business strategy. The recent interest in SHRM reflects a growing awareness that human resources are the key to success in both public and private organizations. Yet, despite this growing awareness, the relevance of SHRM to public organizations is far from clear. Government agencies rarely operate in competitive markets and thus do not develop business strategies in the same sense that private organizations do. And because they function within larger systems of authority, they do not enjoy the same degree of autonomy that private organizations do to alter their personnel policies or provide performance-based incentives to employees. Given these inherent differences, SHRM cannot be transferred successfully from the private to the public sector without tailoring its design and implementation to the unique characteristics of public organizations.

At present there remain many unresolved issues about what modifications are required and the probabilities of their success.

If SHRM is to succeed in fundamentally altering the role of the personnel department and the practice of public personnel management, greater clarity is required regarding the concept of SHRM and how it is to be implemented in public organizations. Accordingly, this article examines unresolved issues regarding the relevance of SHRM for government agencies and closes with an argument for an expanded understanding of what it means to manage human resources strategically.

Procedural and Structural Prerequisites: Unresolved Issues

Figure 1 presents a conceptual framework representative of the kind found in the business literature. It depicts SHRM as a process that merges strategic planning and human resource management. Specifically, it views SHRM as a continuous process of determining mission-related objectives and aligning personnel policies and practices with those objectives. The personnel department plays a strategic role to the extent that its

Figure 1
SHRM: A Conceptual Framework

Analysis of Internal Environment				Analysis of External Environment	

Statement of Agency's Mission
and Strategic Objectives

VERTICAL
INTEGRATION

HR Objectives and Strategies

Function-Specific HR Policies and Practices

Classification & Pay	Recruitment & Selection	Training & Development	Employee Benefits	Performance Management	Employee & Labor Relations

HORIZONTAL INTEGRATION

policies and practices support accomplishment of the organization's objectives. Key components include analyzing the agency's internal and external environments, identifying the agency's strategic objectives, developing HR objectives and strategies consistent with the agency's goals (vertical integration), and aligning HR policies and practices with each other (horizontal integration). For this conceptual understanding of SHRM to be implemented successfully, certain structural and procedural requirements must be satisfied. These core requirements include the following:

1. An established strategic planning process.
2. Involvement of the HR director in the strategic planning process and full consideration of the personnel-related implications of the strategic objectives or initiatives under discussion.
3. A clear statement, written or unwritten, of each agency's mission and the strategic objectives to be achieved in pursuit of mission.
4. The vertical alignment of personnel policies and practices with an agency's mission and strategic objectives, and the horizontal integration of personnel policies and practices with each other.
5. A personnel office whose organizational role and structure are consistent with and contribute to the attainment of the agency's mission and strategic objectives.

These prerequisites capture what is required to integrate strategic planning with human resources management in a way that enhances organizational performance. Such an integration is difficult to achieve, for example, if there is no strategic planning process in place, no participation by the personnel director, and no subsequent development of personnel initiatives designed to support identified objectives. These prerequisites are explored

below, along with unresolved issues about how to fulfill them in governmental settings.

An Established Strategic Planning Process

The role of strategic planning is to provide agencies with a clear sense of direction by clarifying mission, setting priorities, and identifying goals and objectives. NAPA's *Guide for Effective Strategic Management of Human Resources* recommends a short and simple planning process, five to seven days in length, which establishes five or six key objectives to be accomplished during the next few years.[2] A short and simple process has the advantage of providing a clear sense of direction to line and staff officials without becoming an overly elaborate and ultimately hollow planning exercise.

Most federal agencies engage in strategic planning because they are required to do so by the Government Performance and Results Act of 1993. The extent of its use among state and local governments, although somewhat less clear, is indicated by the results of two studies. Of those responding to a national survey of state agencies conducted by Berry and Wechsler, 60 percent said they had strategic planning processes in place.[3] Similarly, in a study of municipalities with populations between 25,000 and 1,000,000, Poister and Streib found that 60 percent had adopted strategic planning in at least one department or program area.[4] These findings indicate that a large and growing number of state and local agencies are using strategic planning as a basic way of doing business.

One unresolved issue is whether the goals of SHRM are best achieved through a single, top-down, jurisdiction-wide strategic planning process or by separate agency-level planning processes. The business literature promotes strategic planning as a company-wide process in which top executives identify strategic objectives for the entire organization and managers de-

velop their operational plans accordingly. But however appropriate this may be in the private sector, it is less so in the public sector. The essential task of government agencies is to execute public law. Because each agency has a unique mission and set of mandates to carry out, a single, top-down strategic planning process is less appropriate for purposes of SHRM. As Poister and Streib observed in their study of municipal governments, strategic planning may be "more useful for major organizational units with a unified sense of mission rather than a highly diversified and fragmented municipal jurisdiction as a whole."[5] While it is true that states such as Oregon[6] and communities such as Rock Hill, South Carolina[7] have engaged in strategic planning, such efforts are typically short-term exercises designed to resolve jurisdiction-wide problems or policy issues rather than institutionalized processes designed to enhance agency performance. Enhanced performance is the purpose that SHRM is intended to serve. Because each agency has a unique mission and set of mandates, SHRM logically requires agency-level strategic planning processes guided by legislative intent as well as the chief executive's policy or political agenda. The subsequent integration of agency plans into a jurisdiction-wide strategic plan is not required for purposes of SHRM.

A second unresolved issue is whether SHRM requires a particular kind of strategic planning to deliver on its promise of enhanced organizational performance. Strategic planning may be practiced in a variety of ways.[8] It may be externally-oriented, bringing together a diverse range of stakeholders to resolve issues of mutual concern, or internally-oriented, bringing together a cross-functional team of agency officials to set internal priorities and objectives. It may be mandated from above for purposes of accountability, or adopted voluntarily by an agency to establish a clear sense of direction. It may comprise a temporary, problem-specific process that ends when the immediate problem has been resolved, or an ongoing, institutionalized process for goal setting and issues management. Lastly, it may follow the Harvard policy model and call for extensive analysis of the agency's internal and external environments, or it may avoid lengthy analyses, opting instead for simple goal-setting exercises.[9] Process characteristics are important because they affect how seriously strategic planning is taken by agency staff, its perceived value as a management tool, and how much it ultimately contributes to organizational performance.

Advocates of SHRM tend to assume an institutionalized, internally-oriented strategic planning process adopted by agencies to clarify their missions, set priorities, and decide upon strategic objectives. There are, however, two contrasting approaches in current use. Little attention has been given to which of these is best suited to SHRM. The **performance management approach**, which is typically mandated by law or executive order, aims to ensure accountability. Under this approach, strategic objectives are stated in terms of desired results, such as a ten percent increase in the number of criminal cases closed successfully, and appropriate performance measures are identified to track success in achieving identified objectives. Although touted as an important governmental reform by members of the managing-for-results movement,[10] this approach relies upon several problematic assumptions. Among

these are that agencies do not and will not pursue meaningful results on their own initiative, that rational planning models are appropriate for use in the public sector, that agencies can in fact translate their missions into measurable outcomes, and that agencies should be rewarded and sanctioned according to their degree of success in achieving their stated objectives. Despite the difficulties inherent in this approach, it has been mandated for use in the federal government as well as in many states. By contrast, the **issues management approach** is undertaken voluntarily to address emerging issues, internal or external to the agency, that are likely to affect its ability to carry out its mission.[11] Its primary purpose is adaptability rather than accountability. Under this approach, strategic objectives are stated in terms of the actions required to achieve a desired future state. Although the planning process is sometimes institutionalized and ongoing, in many cases it is undertaken on a limited basis to address emerging areas of concern. Examples of the latter include a federal agency seeking to maintain program quality in the face of budget cuts, a suburban school district wishing to explore educational reform initiatives, and a public library struggling to maintain employee morale as demand for its services continue to rise.[12] The issues management approach tends to emphasize political rationality (doing what is politically acceptable to powerful stakeholders) over formal rationality (utilizing objective criteria and cost-benefit calculations to determine how best to attain agency goals). Key stakeholders are often brought together to negotiate an agreement about what to do and how. This approach also tends to be more pragmatic than ideological, reflecting the assumption that strategic planning is a valuable management tool for adjusting an organization to its external environment and keeping it focused on desired future states. Although tracking success with quantitative measures is not excluded under this approach, emphasis is placed on addressing issues affecting the agency's ability to carry out its mission rather than managing performance through the use of outcome measures.

Although this issue remains unresolved, it is possible to cite three reasons why the performance management approach is less suited to the purposes of SHRM. First, its underlying assumptions are difficult to satisfy in practice, potentially leaving participants frustrated and undermining their commitment to the process. As Bryson and Roering have cautioned, "a strategic planning system characterized by substantial comprehensiveness, formal rationality in decision making, and tight control will work only in an organization that has a clear mission; clear goals and objectives; centralized authority; clear performance indicators; and information about actual performance available at reasonable cost. Few public-sector organizations—or functions or communities—operate under such conditions."[13] Second, performance management systems are usually mandated from above and monitored by budget and planning offices. The problems associated with mandating strategic planning for purposes of control are well established.[14] Such systems tend to create an underlying air of distrust, which undermines commitment to the process. They tend to skew goal statements, choice of performance measures, and actual behaviors towards those results that are easiest to achieve, whether or

not they truly enhance organizational performance. Third, the model of SHRM presented in Figure 1 calls for the alignment of personnel policies and practices with strategic initiatives designed to help the agency adapt to or cope with internal and external pressures. It does not call for their alignment with performance measures as such. Managing issues and measuring program results may be complementary processes, but planning for action and planning for control are two very different things. In the final analysis more research is required to determine whether the issues management approach is best suited to the purposes of SHRM or, alternatively, whether it is possible to integrate the two approaches successfully.

Involvement of the Personnel Director in Strategic Planning

SHRM as conceptualized in Figure 1 requires more than an established strategic planning process. It also requires the full involvement of the personnel director in that process. This is necessary to ensure that the strategic initiatives under discussion are evaluated in terms of their implications for human resources. When a new program initiative is under consideration, for example, the personnel director can offer an analysis of the gap between current human resources capabilities and projected needs. Similarly, if an agency wishes to adopt a customer-service orientation, the personnel director can explain the difficulties inherent in changing an organization's culture and the kinds of training and incentives required to accomplish it successfully. Involvement by the personnel director is also necessary so that the personnel staff can obtain a better and more complete understanding of the agency's mission and the issues confronting line managers.

Although examples of strategic partnerships are increasingly heralded in professional journals and at management conferences, many jurisdictions still do not include human resource professionals in strategic deliberations. An unresolved issue here is how to forge such a partnership. Traditionally, agency executives have tended to view the personnel office as a staff agency performing relatively routine functions and occupying a relatively low status in the organizational scheme of things. Consequently, they have not been inclined to involve personnel directors in strategic deliberations. At the same time many personnel directors have been slow to insist upon a strategic role because their professional training has not prepared them to perform such a role. Training in personnel management tends to emphasize the administration of personnel systems rather than general management or organizational development.

A Clear Statement of Strategic Objectives

Strategic goals and objectives, key products of the planning process, are often stated in a written plan. This plan provides a useful guide to the personnel office as it seeks to align existing policies and practices with strategic objectives. A written plan

is not, however, an essential requirement of SHRM. As noted in NAPA's *Guide for Effective Strategic Management of Human Resources*, "the absence of a written plan developed at the agency level does not mean that SHRM cannot exist. The HR office can develop its own plan for linking its goals to the agency's goals, or the staff can be reminded of the need to factor the agency's strategic goals into its daily operations."[15] For purposes of SHRM, all that is required is that members of the personnel staff know and understand the agency's strategic objectives so that they can contribute to their attainment.

Although this requirement appears straightforward enough, most discussions of strategic planning fail to define what the term strategy or strategic objective means in a public context. In private sector firms practicing SHRM, a business strategy is designed to give them a competitive edge over other firms in their industry. They have three basic strategies from which to choose.[16] The **innovation strategy** involves developing a unique product or service, or concentrating on a specific market niche; the **quality enhancement strategy** involves offering products or services that are superior in quality; and the **cost reduction** strategy involves reducing costs so that the firm can offer goods and services at the lowest possible price. Firms may also explore different growth strategies, such as those involving mergers and diversification. Once business strategies are selected, specific objectives are identified and the task of aligning personnel policies and practices begins.

Because public agencies are embedded in authority networks rather than economic markets, what it means to select a "business strategy" is much less clear. As Wechsler and Backoff have noted, the "strategies of public organizations, unlike business strategies, are produced in response to a variety of competing signals that emanate not from markets but from complex political, economic, legal, and organizational structures, processes, and relationships."[17] Whereas business executives are relatively unconstrained in making strategic decisions, the constraints encountered by public administrators often cause them to make strategic choices other than those they believe are best suited to mission attainment. Factors influencing choice of strategy include the political goals of elected officials, demands of powerful stakeholders, judicial mandates, budgetary constraints, the organization's capacities and resources, and its relationships with other organizations. Agencies are more likely to engage in strategic planning and more likely to succeed in implementing their intended objectives when they possess internal capacity for performance (adequate funding, personnel, and management systems), a supportive political environment, and a weak or divided external influence field. Conversely, strategies tend to be shaped by external demands rather than internal intentions when an agency experiences a hostile environment and low internal capacity.

An agency's strategy may be understood as the basic pattern reflected in its policy decisions and actions. Wechsler and Backoff's analysis of state agencies in Ohio revealed three basic patterns. **Developmental** strategies involve actions taken to enhance the agency's resources, status, influence, and capacity for future action, presumably as it relates to mission attainment. Developmental strategies are often products of a formal plan-

ning process in which strategists and planners deliberately seek to develop capacity so as to maintain internal control and enhance organizational performance. **Political** strategies involve actions taken either to balance competing stakeholder demands or to reward supporters of the administration by moving the agency in specific policy or programmatic directions. For example, control over internal operations may be tightened in order to further a specific political agenda. Such strategies are adopted where political and partisan pressures are high. **Protective** strategies involve actions designed to accommodate external pressures or appease external stakeholders while maintaining the organizational status quo. It is a reactive strategy more or less forced on an agency by an overtly hostile environment and weak internal capacity for strategic action. It is a pattern that is highly frustrating for agency staff.

Steeped in the rationalistic assumptions of planning theory, discussions of SHRM tend to envision agencies pursuing developmental, capacity-building strategies rather than political or protective strategies. In practice, however, a developmental strategy requires widely shared objectives, the capacity to plan and carry out strategic initiatives, extensive discretion, adequate resources, and relatively weak or divided external forces—conditions which often cannot be satisfied. Although Backoff and Wechsler do not address issues relating to SHRM, their analysis strongly suggests that SHRM may look very different in agencies engaged in political or protective strategies. Rather than helping an agency develop its capacity for mission attainment, the personnel office may be asked, for example, to help the agency secure the political loyalty of career civil servants, recruit and reward based on partisan or political criteria, or tighten control over employee performance. In short, although the concept of SHRM, with its emphasis on linking means and ends, strongly implies an institutionalized process utilized by agencies pursuing a developmental strategy, it must be kept in mind that agency performance can be defined in terms of political and protective objectives as well, and that SHRM, as it is generally understood, may be undermined or derailed as a result.

Alignment of HR Policies and Practices with Strategic Objectives

Although their mandates are set by external actors, agencies still must interpret their mandates, clarify their missions, and seek agreement among key stakeholders regarding how their missions will be carried out. Statements of strategic objectives, written or unwritten, emerge from these decision processes. The core requirement of SHRM is the alignment of personnel policies and practices with the agency's strategic objectives. Although many examples of alignment have been reported in the literature, no classification system has yet been proposed to capture how alignment is accomplished. In general, the reported examples tend to fall into one or more of the following categories:

1. Adapting to environmental change. This category includes actions taken by the personnel office in response to external events or trends, such as budget cuts, tight labor markets, changing demographic characteristics of workers, and new

technologies. During a period of retrenchment, for example, the personnel office can help managers communicate to staff members the reasons behind staff cutbacks and how they will be accomplished, develop and introduce an early retirement incentive program, counsel those who must be laid off about alternative job opportunities, provide stress management programs for those anxious about their jobs or struggling to cope with increased workloads, and explore the use of temporary or contract employees to ease workload burdens. Adaptive responses of this kind may or may not be guided by a formal statement of agency objectives.

2. Building human capacity to support strategic initiatives. Human resources planning is a traditional personnel function. It involves forecasting future staffing needs and taking steps to recruit new employees or train existing employees to meet the forecasted demands. What is unique in the context of SHRM is analysis of the gap between current and required capacity for each new strategic initiative. If an agency has decided to serve a new clientele group, expand services into new areas, or take on an entirely new program, the personnel office can play a strategic role by recruiting new employees with the requisite skills or enhancing the skills of existing personnel through training and development.

3. Changing organizational culture. Many public organizations have followed their private sector counterparts by reinventing and reengineering themselves. Major reform initiatives often require new organizational cultures, cultures driven by different values and requiring different behaviors. Adopting a "customer-service" orientation, for example, has become a common strategic objective in both the private and public sectors. The personnel office can help develop a shared commitment to service quality and customer satisfaction through its employee orientation sessions and training programs. It can also redesign performance appraisal and incentive systems so that employees are rewarded for emphasizing quality and customer service. The personnel office can undertake similar efforts in agencies seeking to move from a process-oriented to a results-oriented culture.[18]

4. Preparing employees for change. Staff members often resist the implementation of major reforms because of implicit or explicit threats to personal security. Thus, in addition to taking steps to develop a new organizational culture, the personnel office can also take steps to prepare employees for impending changes. It can, for example, encourage managers to involve employees in the design and implementation of the new program or reform initiative, help communicate the purposes behind the changes and the benefits to be derived from them, and provide additional training opportunities so that staff members are prepared to function successfully under the new order.

5. Supporting a specific "business strategy." This category, which overlaps with the preceding ones, is distinguished by the selection of a specific business strategy for success. Many of the examples of alignment in the business literature envision this kind of situation. When Marriott, for example, decided to gain a competitive advantage by being "the employer of choice," the personnel office altered its policies and practices so as to attract and retain the very best workers available.[19] An-

other business strategy is to become "a high commitment" organization. In this instance the personnel office is charged with altering its policies and practices to encourage employee development and empowerment. Indeed, some advocates tend to equate SHRM with the adoption of "progressive" policies designed to boost employee commitment and performance.[20] The common denominator in these business strategies is the belief that human resources are the key to organizational success.

These five kinds of actions are undertaken to achieve vertical integration. Vertical integration is a measure of how well personnel policies and practices, individually and collectively, contribute to organizational objectives. As indicated in Figure 1, horizontal integration is important as well. This is a measure of how well personnel policies mesh with each other in contributing to organizational objectives. The goal is to develop an integrated personnel program in which policies and practices in one functional area do not work at cross purposes with those in other areas.

Changing the Role and Structure of the Personnel Office

The first four requirements of SHRM cannot be satisfied unless the personnel office fundamentally alters the way it does business. An unresolved issue is how to do so. Advocates of SHRM have offered several recommendations in this regard. First, the personnel office must develop the capacity it needs to support strategic initiatives. This means it must develop staff expertise in job design, organizational development, change management, employee motivation, and human resource theory. The personnel staff must also develop knowledge of general management, agency mission, and the specific personnel problems facing managers. Whether this strategic role should be assigned to a special unit within the personnel office or should be expected of all personnel staff remains an unanswered question. Because the strategic and operational roles of the personnel office are contradictory in many respects, performing both roles in an integrated fashion will remain an ongoing challenge.

Second, the traditional control orientation must be superseded by a service orientation. The required line-staff partnership cannot be forged as long as the personnel office is perceived by agency managers as an enforcer of rules and a source of suffocating red tape. According to SHRM advocates, a service orientation can be established by assigning primary responsibility for human resource management to managers and creating service teams comprised of personnel generalists to assist managers in achieving mission-related objectives.[21] Under this proposal, personnel generalists are to perform a service-oriented role both when administering personnel systems such as classification and pay and when consulting with managers about specific personnel problems or objectives. Adopting a service orientation does not require that the personnel office abdicate its responsibility for safeguarding merit, employee rights, and equal employment opportunity. Rather, it means carrying out this responsibility as legal counselors rather than police officers. If the personnel office is to contribute more directly to an agency's mission, shifts in role orientation are important. For SHRM to be implemented successfully, according to NAPA, "the HR staff must believe that their mission is helping the agency accomplish its mission by assisting supervisors in managing their human resources."[22]

Lastly, many advocates of SHRM believe that highly centralized personnel systems must be decentralized and deregulated. Perry and Mesch argue, for example, that the implementation of SHRM is incompatible with highly centralized personnel systems.[23] Possessing unique missions and mandates, and facing unique situations, agencies must be able to tailor their personnel policies and practices to their strategic needs. Centralized personnel systems deny them the flexibility they need. Structural reforms may include reducing the number of centralized personnel regulations to the bare minimum needed to enforce statutory requirements, devolving responsibility for classification and applicant screening to the agency and bureau level, and delegating policy making authority downwards so that agencies can establish personnel policies suited to their individual needs. Advocates of structural reform believe that certain positive effects will follow, including greater flexibility and timeliness in personnel decision making and improved line-staff relations.

In fact, however, decentralization and deregulation may not be a prerequisite for the successful implementation of SHRM. Structural reform efforts tend to encounter serious obstacles and create new problems. For example, devolution of authority means that agency personnel must be trained to handle personnel transactions formerly handled by a central personnel office and new ways must be found to coordinate the efforts of all line and staff officials engaged in performing the personnel management function. Some of these obstacles may prove insurmountable, creating additional redundancies and waste and further undermining agency performance. From the perspective of SHRM, structural reform may not be necessary as long as each agency has sufficient authority and flexibility to align its personnel policies and practices with its strategic objectives. This, too, remains an unresolved issue.

An Expanded Understanding of SHRM

What it means to manage human resources strategically can be understood in more than one way. The difficulty with the understanding discussed above is that it lacks an integrated and sustained focus on the organization's human resources. Because it is closely tied to the practice of strategic planning, it envisions the personnel office taking only those actions necessary to support a specific strategic objective. In this instance the role of the personnel office may be strategic but it is also somewhat ad hoc and reactive. In actuality there is much the personnel office can do to advance an agency's strategic interests other than, or in addition to, supporting the initiatives that emerge from a strategic planning process.

An alternative understanding of what it means to manage human resources strategically has been suggested by Eugene McGregor.[24] The role of the personnel office, according to this

FIGURE 2 Human Resource Strategies

HR Strategies	Underlying Values	Desired Outcomes
Cost Containment Strategy. Containing labor costs by setting salaries at or below market levels, adopting wellness programs and managed care to reduce benefit costs, and using part-time, temporary, and contract employees whenever possible.	economy	cost-effective staffing
Performance Management Strategy. Setting measurable objectives for employees and making rewards contingent upon performance.	productivity	mission-related results
Involvement Strategy. Providing employees, individually or in teams, with considerable work autonomy, decision-making authority, and responsibility for a "complete" task.	empowerment	sense of ownership; enhanced motivation and contribution; employee commitment and retention
Retention Strategy. Providing the conditions necessary to retain valuable human resources, including generous benefit packages, pay that is at or above market, positive work environment, and family-friendly policies such as flextime and day care assistance.	need satisfaction	job satisfaction; employee commitment and retention
Investment Strategy. Increasing individual competence and organizational capacity by investing heavily in training and development.	human development	personal competence; agency adaptability; employee commitment and retention
Cohesion Strategy. Establishing a sense of community and strong social bonds through agency newsletters, picnics, and recreational activities, and by fostering open and trusting relationships between employees and managers and retention	comradeship; openness; trust.	job satisfaction; cooperative relations; employee commitment

understanding, is to help "manage strategic resources strategically." It begins from the premise that many, if not most, government jobs are knowledge-intensive, involving the creation of knowledge or the creation of "smart products" through the application of "trained intelligence." Where this is the case, the intellectual capital stored within the workers becomes the critical resource for the organization and must therefore be viewed as a strategic resource. Managing this strategic resource strategically involves determining essential knowledge, skills, and abilities; improving recruitment and selection methods; developing the capacities of all employees so that the agency can respond to any opportunity or threat appearing on the horizon; and fostering employee commitment so that human capital is not lost to other employers. In short, this alternative understanding envisions a personnel office pursuing an ongoing, integrated program for enhancing organizational performance by acquiring, developing, and managing human resources strategically.

With these observations in mind, it is possible to suggest an expanded, two-pronged approach to SHRM in which the personnel office, in addition to helping the agency implement strategic initiatives, also carries out an integrated personnel program guided by a coherent theory or philosophy about what it means to manage human resources strategically. A theory or philosophy of this kind specifies how human resources must be treated, how much money must be invested in developing human capital, the kind of culture and work climate that must be established, and the specific attitudes and behaviors that must be elicited if the agency is to achieve its vision of success.

That personnel offices are rarely guided by such a theory has been cited as the primary reason for their low institutional standing.[25] If the personnel office succeeds in developing such a theory in consultation with agency officials and legislative bodies, the next step is to identify and implement appropriate human resource strategies. Six human resource strategies are identified in Figure 2. Although these strategies are neither exhaustive nor mutually exclusive, they nonetheless serve to illustrate the connections between values and vision, desired outcomes, and the programmatic means by which to realize them.

The cost-containment strategy tends, in practice, to serve as a default strategy. Although it is antithetical to McGregor's understanding of what it means to manage strategic resources strategically, it is often the strategy of choice among elected officials concerned with holding the line on labor costs and budget increases. Where there is no agreed upon vision of success, nor any theory regarding the strategic importance of human resources to agency performance, other strategies tend to receive little attention. However, the convergence of several factors in recent years, including tighter labor markets, a growing proportion of high-skill and knowledge-intensive jobs, a better educated workforce with heightened growth needs, and political pressures to improve government performance, has turned attention to alternative strategies. The performance management strategy, for example, has been adopted in jurisdictions where the values and assumptions of the managing-for-results movement have gained sway.[26] Similarly, because most government employees are knowledge workers who can sell their intellectual capital on the open market, many agencies are turning to a combination of the investment, involvement, and retention strategies to attract, develop, and retain the human resources they need to provide knowledge intensive services in an ever changing environment. The investment strategy in particular reflects a growing awareness that human competence is the engine behind the creation of value.[27]

The strategies or combination of strategies chosen, if any, depends on situational factors such as the nature of the work performed by agency staff, the agency's capacity for pursuing excellence, and the priorities of its leaders. Political and practical factors often divert attention from developing a human resource philosophy or expending funds to put it into practice. Indeed, as McGregor has noted, "in the minds of many a case-hardened practitioner, the idea of strategic public-sector human resource management may well be an oxymoron."[28] But if the prospects for implementing SHRM in the public sector are uncertain, the concept itself represents a valuable goal toward which to strive.

Conclusion

The concept of SHRM as outlined above calls upon the personnel office to adopt a strategic role in addition to its operational roles as rule enforcer and guardian of the integrity of personnel systems. For the personnel staff, adopting a strategic role means being more responsive to agency goals by acting as consultants and service providers to line managers; supporting the attainment of the agency's strategic objectives; and carrying out an integrated, philosophy-driven personnel program. Although the concept of SHRM is steeped in problematic, rationalistic assumptions, it nonetheless holds considerable promise for enhancing government performance. Its success depends on whether the personnel office can integrate its strategic and operational roles successfully and whether it can satisfy the norms of political and formal rationality simultaneously. Too much is at stake for this potentially valuable concept to become a label for yet another failed management initiative.

Notes

1. Tichy, Noel M., Charles J. Fombrun, and Mary Anne Devanna, "Strategic Human Resource Management," *Sloan Management Review* 23 (Winter 1982): 47–61; Cynthia A. Lengnick-Hall and Mark L. Lengnick-Hall, "Strategic Human Resources Management: A Review of the Literature and a Proposed Typology," *Academy of Management Review* 13 (July 1988): 454–470; Randall Schuler, "Strategic Human Resource Management and Industrial Relations," *Human Relations* 42 (No. 2 1989):157–184.

2. National Academy of Public Administration (NAPA), *A Guide for Effective Strategic Management of Human Resources* (Washington D.C.: NAPA, 1996).

3. Berry, Frances Stokes and Barton Wechsler, "State Agencies' Experience with Strategic Planning: Findings from a National Survey," *Public Administration Review* 55 (March/April 1995): 159–168.

4. Poister, Theodore H. and Gregory Streib, "Management Tools in Municipal Government: Trends over the Past Decade," *Public Administration Review* 49 (May/June 1989): 240–248.

5. Poister and Streib, "Management Tools," 244.

6. Kissler, Gerald R., Karmen N. Fore, Willow S. Jacobson, William P. Kittredge, and Scott L. Stewart, "State Strategic Planning: Suggestions from the Oregon Experience," *Public Administration Review* 58 (July/August 1998): 353–359.

7. Wheeland, Craig M., "Citywide Strategic Planning: An Evaluation of Rock Hill's Empowering Vision," *Public Administration Review* 53 (January/February 1993): 65–72.

8. Bryson, John M., *Strategic Planning for Public and Nonprofit Organizations: A Guide to Strengthening and Sustaining Organizational Achievement* (San Francisco: Jossey-Bass, 1995).

9. Bryson, John M. and William D. Roering, "Applying Private-Sector Strategic Planning in the Public Sector," *Journal of the American Planning Association* 53 (Winter 1987): 9–22.

10. Osborne, David and Ted Gaebler, *Reinventing Government* (Reading, MA: Addison-Wesley, 1992).

11. Bryson, *Strategic Planning*; Paul C. Nutt and Robert W. Backoff, *Strategic Management of Public and Third Sector Organizations* (San Francisco: Jossey-Bass, 1992).

12. Bryson, *Strategic Planning*.

13. Bryson and Roering, "Applying Private-Sector Strategic Planning," 15.

14. Mintzberg, Henry, *The Rise and Fall of Strategic Planning* (New York: Free Press, 1994).

15. NAPA, *A Guide for Effective Strategic Management of Human Resources*, 17.

16. Porter, Michael E., *Competitive Strategy: Techniques for Analyzing Industries and Competitors* (New York: Free Press, 1980); Schuler, "Strategic Human Resource Management and Industrial Relations."

17. Wechsler, Barton and Robert W. Backoff, "The Dynamics of Strategy in Public Organizations," *Journal of the American Planning Association* 53 (Winter 1987): 34–43.

18. Popovich, Mark G. (ed.), *Creating High-Performance Government Organizations* (San Francisco: Jossey-Bass, 1998).

19. Ulrich, Dave, "Strategic and Human Resource Planning: Linking Customers and Employees," *Human Resource Planning* 15 (June 1992): 47+.

20. NAPA, *A Guide for Effective Strategic Management of Human Resources*.

21. Perry, James L. and Debra J. Mesch, "Strategic Human Resource Management," in *Public Personnel Management: Current Concerns, Future Challenges* edited by Carolyn Ban and Norma M. Riccucci (New York: Longman, 1997), 21–34.

22. NAPA, *A Guide for Effective Strategic Management of Human Resources*, 53.

23. Perry and Mesch, "Strategic Human Resource Management."

24. McGregor, Eugene B., *Strategic Management of Human Knowledge, Skills, and Abilities* (San Francisco: Jossey-Bass, 1991).

25. Christensen, Ralph, "Where is HR?" *Human Resource Management* 36 (Spring 1997): 81–84.

26. Lawler, Edward E., *Strategic Pay: Aligning Organizational Strategies and Pay Systems* (San Francisco: Jossey-Bass, 1990); Popovich, *Creating High-Performance Government Organizations*.

27. Christensen, "Where is HR?"; Lee Dyer and Gerald W. Holder, "A Strategic Perspective of Human Resource Management," in *Human Resource Management: Evolving Roles and Responsibilities* edited by Lee Dyer (Washington D.C.: Bureau of National Affairs, 1988): 1–46.

28. McGregor, *Strategic Management*, 33.

Jonathan Tompkins is Professor of Political Science at The University of Montana. His primary teaching responsibilities include courses in human resources management, strategic planning, and organization theory. He has published several articles relating to human resource management and a text entitled *Human Resource Management in Government*.

From *Public Personnel Management,* Spring 2002, pp. 95-110. © 2002 by the International Personnel Management Association (IPMA), 1617 Duke Street, Alexandria, VA 22314; www.ipma-hr.org.

DISABILITY DISCRIMINATION

A statute for liberty

Americans have had a comprehensive federal law on disability for more than a decade. What can their experience tell us about employing and retaining disabled people?

REPORT **PETER McGEER**

FOR ALMOST 30 YEARS, US LAWS HAVE BEEN IN PLACE to outlaw disability discrimination in employment, culminating in the Americans with Disabilities Act 1990 (ADA). Civil rights measures are reinforced by considerable government and voluntary sector support to help disabled Americans into employment. Despite this, statistics suggest that those with disabilities or long-term health problems are still not getting jobs, and when they do their income is half that of other people.

The UK has recently adopted similar measures to boost the employment prospects of disabled people, such as anti-discrimination legislation, a tax credit, the provision of financial and technical support to individuals in the workplace and welfare-to-work initiatives. We will no doubt be examining the effects of these in years to come.

Yet statistics must always be viewed with caution. There may be a simple reason for the static levels of employment for disabled people during the boom years of the past decade. In a debate between 150 labour economists and employment researchers at the Cornell Employment and Policy Institute in Washington, several participants said that adverse employment statistics

showed that the ADA was encouraging more people to declare disability as the reason for being unemployed. Incapacity benefit in the UK has had the same effect.

Despite this, US employers are still having difficulty hiring and accommodating disabled employees. For employers, attracting the right people is only part of the problem. According to research undertaken by Susanne Bruyère, director of the program on employment and disability at Cornell University, employers say the hardest tasks they face are changing the attitudes of co-workers and supervisors and adapting management systems.

In recent years Bruyère and her team have been researching employer policies in response to anti-discrimination legislation and in particular the functioning of HR professionals in the recruitment and retention of disabled employees.

Bruyère explains that there is a growing interest in absence management in the US, which is driving the development of disability management programmes in organisations. Research that she has carried out in the UK and the US suggests that the prospects of employing disabled people are improved when the organisation has a comprehensive

disability management strategy, allowing it to consult occupational health professionals, health and safety specialists, HR practitioners and employee representatives.

Disability management in the US is essentially about retaining employees who are in danger of leaving because of injury or onset of a disabling condition. However, Bruyère believes that integrated approaches to disability management will make it easier for organisations to recruit disabled people, since they will already have in place a substantial body of knowledge on how to accommodate their needs.

Pat Owens, a consultant and former vice-president of disability programmes with Unum Life Insurance Company in the US, says that disability management is about setting in place durable systems for accommodating such employees. The first principle of the accommodation process, she says, is to understand what people with disabilities can do rather than what they can't. "Everyone involved in the process should know what the requirements of the job are," she says.

Owens advises using simple job-analysis tools. "We need to look at where and how jobs are performed and what the job tasks are. If a person with a disability can perform the main tasks of a job, with or without adjustment, there is no excuse for their not being taken on."

In the UK, there is a strong tendency to measure an organisation's performance in the disability field by focusing on the numbers of disabled employees. This may be a hangover from the days of employment quotas, or part of the growing perception that disabled people are a substantial minority population, which needs to be reflected in workforce monitoring. But American experience shows us that focusing on numbers makes companies prone to quick fixes.

"Efforts specifically designed by organisations to increase the employment rates of people with disabilities really don't stand much of a long-term chance of success. People recruited under special initiatives do not last," says Craig Gray of the National Organisation on Disability (Nod) in the US.

Gray is director of Nod's Employ Ability Programs. He works with government, companies and major voluntary organisations to develop strategies to increase the employment of disabled people.

He argues that "hiring should go in tandem with a re-examination of business strategies and take advantage of the disabled community's potential market share."

Gray explains that often overworked managers don't have the time to understand what a "reasonable accommodation" is. (It is an adjustment that they are expected by law to make, in order to accommodate someone with disabilities.) Nor do they have the inclination to ensure that other employees understand their own role in accommodating a disabled team member.

He believes that HR will always play a key role in the employment of people with disabilities. "But it is not the HR managers who are running the front-line operations

of businesses," he says. "Surveys about the benefits of employing people with disabilities don't help in meeting production targets."

Yet HR can kick-start initiatives, bring people together and convince them that employing disabled people will be good for the organisation. HR has a key communications and project-management role.

Quick-fix solutions are clearly inappropriate, but on both sides of the Atlantic companies are beginning to concentrate on recruiting disabled people. Good examples are Centrica in the UK and Manpower in the US.

Centrica has successfully recruited over 140 long-term unemployed people, many with a disability, or with caring responsibilities, into its call centres. Richard Bide, group HR director, explains that the company did not start the project to demonstrate HR excellence or comply with legislation. "We needed to employ good people so we began by seeing this as a business issue."

Bide believes that traditional recruitment methods and bland equal opportunities statements will not help to attract significant numbers of disadvantaged people. "If you have a disability and have applied for numerous jobs in the past five years and received a standard rejection letter, are you going to trust someone who simply claims to be an equal opportunities employer?"

He believes that the first stage is removing the barriers that stop people from stepping forward and risking being turned down. Secondly, when a company has found disabled job applicants, many have been outside the job market for some time and must be given the opportunity to compete equally. For Centrica this can mean a two-day work preparation workshop before the interview.

Bide is keen to stress that Centrica has not lowered its recruitment standards and people brought into the company are of high calibre. "What we have done is determine their performance against our normal standards by thinking creatively about using competency-based questions," he says.

The company asks, for instance, about a time the candidate influenced someone to do something, rather than what they did in their previous job.

"You have to recognise that you are often dealing with people with quite different life experiences."

Centrica, together with the Employers' Forum on Disability, has recently published *Recruitment that works: enriching your organisation through partnership*, which outlines a project-led approach to finding practical solutions for disabled and disadvantaged people moving into work.

Manpower is the world's largest recruitment firm. It provided 2.7 million temporary workers worldwide in 2000. Terry Hueneke, chief executive for operations in the Americas, Australia, Japan and South-East Asia, explains that labour shortages in the US have given Manpower and its clients huge scope for recruiting America's underused pools of labour.

In 1998 Hueneke and his colleagues became aware of a major trend: growing numbers of Manpower's temporary

staff with disabilities were becoming permanent staff. "This gave us the incentive to be more proactive in recruiting from a number of areas such as people with disabilities, senior citizens and minority populations," he says.

Why did this happen? Studies by the Bendix Corporation, DuPont and the US Chamber of Commerce provide a clue. They show that disabled people's absentee rates are lower, productivity is higher or slightly above average and their safety record is much better.

The DuPont study revealed that 79 per cent of workers with a disability had better attendance, 91 per cent had "average or better" on-the-job performance and 96 per cent were rated better than the rest of the workforce on safety. There were no cases where disability contributed to instances where other workers were injured.

In Manpower's case, these advantages motivated the company to seek out individuals with disabilities and community organisations throughout the US.

Manpower's success in attracting and developing disabled employees is supported in a research study carried out by Peter Blanch at the University of Iowa—*The Emerging Role of the Staffing Industry in the Employment of Persons with Disabilities.*

The study found that the temporary-staffing industry provided a vital link to permanent, full-time employment for people with disabilities in the US.

Of the people studied, 60 per cent moved from no employment to permanent employment as a result of their work with Manpower. Annually, about 40 per cent of Manpower's workforce makes that move.

Neither Bide or Hueneke fears that the economic downturn, with its surplus labour, will erode their programmes on employment and disability. They both feel that the business case for employing disabled people is now firmly established in their organisations. Both say that line managers have learnt that disabled people contribute something extra, particularly when it comes to building relationships with customers.

Bide points out that in call centres, staff with disabilities tend to be older and more mature, bringing more balance to teams and a different style with customers.

Craig Gray agrees. "People with disabilities share a deep appreciation of diversity as often in our lives people have made judgments about our ability based on appearances. But we bring with us creativity, problem-solving skills and the ability to do things differently."

FURTHER READING

- *Implementation of the Americans with Disabilities Act in the US and the Disability Discrimination Act in the UK,* Susanne Bruyère, is available free at www.ilr.cornell.edu
- *Recruitment that works: Enriching your workforce through partnership,* is available from the Employers' Forum on Disability, (020 7403 3020).
- *The Emerging Role of the Staffing Industry in the Employment of Persons with Disabilities* is available free at www.its.uiowa.edu/law

Peter McGeer is an employment analyst with IRS and a freelance researcher and HR consultant. He can be contacted at include@dircon.co.uk

From *People Management,* January 2002, pp. 4-42. © 2002 by Peter McGreer. Reprinted by permission.

SEXUAL HARASSMENT

It Doesn't Go with the Territory

Conservative estimates are that one in two women and about one in 20 men have been sexually harrassed on the job.

By Rachel Thompson

Patricia Allen heard someone following her during her nightly patrol. She thought an inmate had escaped. Terrified, she informed her supervisors. Their response surprised her: it was just a coworker playing a 'prank.'

Allen wasn't amused. It wasn't the first time her safety had been compromised by co-workers. At a conference of the Law Union of Ontario earlier this year, Allen and other former guards broke their two-decade silence, describing acts of harassment that ranged from pornography strewn around the security office, to having their cars vandalized.

Statistics vary, but between 40 and 70 percent of Canadian women and around five percent of men report that they have experienced sexual harassment, usually from supervisors. All provincial legislatures and Parliament have enacted human rights statutes that prohibit sex discrimination, including sexual harassment. In law, sexual harassment focusses on behaviours: unwanted physical contact, sexual advances, requests for sexual favours, suggestive or offensive comments or gestures emphasizing sexuality, sexual identity or sexual orientation.

Its effects are far reaching. According to Constance Backhouse and Leah Cohen, authors of *The Secret Oppression: Sexual Harassment of Working Women*, "Sexual harassment can manifest itself physically and psychologically.... It can poison a woman's work environment to the extent that her livelihood is in danger."

Allen says she was told that she would be put into a cell to deal with any trouble with an inmate and that her male coworkers would not help. Another former guard, Julie Blair, told delegates that, "I actually found cells left open from the previous shift." Blair and Allen were hired in 1980 as part of a Corrections Canada project to bring female guards into federal men's prisons. Six years later, both of them quit.

Canadian courts and tribunals have established that employers must provide employees with a harassment-free workplace. If they don't, they can face significant financial penalties. The most common type of compensation is monetary, for lost wages or salary and pain and humiliation. Sexual harassment awards as high as $50,000 have been ordered by human rights commissions. However, the costs of harassment to workplaces go beyond the financial. Harassment also takes a toll on lost productivity, damages the image of the workplace and damages the overall working environment for employees.

Sexual harassment is not restricted to any one field, as a recent Canadian study confirmed. According to a Conference Board of Canada's June 2001 report, one third of female senior executives left their last job because of sexual harassment.

"We're not talking nervous entry-level graduates. We're talking ambitious, talented women," said Barbara Orser, author of the report. The study involved 350 women with senior posts in the public and private sectors. Respondents were also asked to predict when women would achieve equal representation in 10 key areas. Close to half predicted that discrimination in the workplace will always exist.

"Clearly we have work to do," observed Pamela Jeffrey, founder of the Toronto-based Women's Executive Network that commissioned the poll. Even the most optimistic respondents predicted that it would be more than 30 years before sexual harassment is wiped out.

In 1987, the Supreme Court of Canada unanimously ruled that employers are liable for the discriminatory acts of their employees in the course of their employment. In doing so, it overturned a Federal Court of Appeal which had ruled earlier that, while Bonnie Robichaud had been sexually harassed by her supervisor at the department of National Defence, the department was not liable for the contravention of her rights. The

Court ruled in Robichaud that the purpose of human rights legislation is to remove discrimination. As a result of the ruling, employers covered by the federal act are liable for the conduct of their employees.

Today, the Canadian military continues to see women leave en masse because of discrimination, harassment and sexual assault by their peers and supervisors. "Although increasing numbers of women are joining the navy, the attrition data indicates that a disproportionate number are leaving hard sea occupations," concluded a defence department review last year. This follows a 1988 *Maclean's* magazine investigation that revealed that cases of sexual assault in the military routinely went unpunished; an Armed Forces hotline was set up to register complaints.

Sexual harassment is more than a discrimination issue, a liability issue, a communication problem, an employee-relations problem or a productivity problem. According to a new book, *Sexual Harassment*, edited by philosophy professor Edmund Wall, sexual harassment represents a "serious moral problem."

Not according to Camille Paglia, who has published essays promoting the idea that women are harassed and physically abused by men due to natural forces. "Men," writes Paglia, the author of *Sex, Art, and American Culture*, "must quest, pursue, court or seize."

However, the fact that many men do not act this way speaks for itself, according to those who call sexual harassment a social, not a biological, problem.

"The idea is that biology cannot be questioned or changed, and is legitimate… " wrote Catharine A. McKinnon in her 1979 classic, *Sexual Harassment of Working Women: A Case of Sex Discrimination*. "In these cases, we are dealing with a male who is allegedly exercising his power as an employer, his power over a woman's material survival, and his sexual prerogatives as a man, to subject a woman sexually."

Ethicist Vaughana Macy Feary in her essay, "Sexual Harassment: Why the Corporate World Still Doesn't Get It," defends sexual harassment policies saying, "Even the most liberal moral theories acknowledge that harm to others is our strongest moral reason for restricting liberty." As Feary points out in *Sexual Harassment*, "Biological drives can be restrained and cultures, including corporate cultures, can be changed."

Beverly Suek, a Winnipeg-based harassment investigator agrees. "It's not about sex, it's about power and the misuse and abuse of power, even when it's between colleagues."

Suek is not surprised that the Conference Board study participants were so pessimistic about the chances of eradicating sexual harassment from the workplace. "Thirty years ago you were told to either 'Put up or shut up," she says. Today she sees a growing lack of acceptance of harassment. "I think we can consciously change corporate culture from one that is harassing to one that is respectful."

Sharron Gould, president of the Manitoba Association for Respectful Workplaces, concurs. "We're also seeing men verbalize their intolerance [for harassment] and when that happens, there is less harassment."

What Is It?

1. Unwanted or unsolicited sexual attention of a persistent or abusive nature made by a person who knew, or ought reasonably to know, that such attention is unwanted;

2. Implied or expressed promise of reward for complying with a sexually-oriented request;

3. Implied or expressed threat of reprisal in the form of actual reprisal or the denial of opportunity, for refusal to comply with a sexually-oriented request;

4. Any offensive, intimidating comments or behaviour concerning one's gender or sexual orientation that is sexually-oriented which may reasonably be perceived to create a negative psychological and emotional effect or environment.

Tips

1. Check with your human resources department or supervisor to see if there is a harassment or respectful workplace policy that outlines complaint handling.

2. Talk to your union to see if there is a policy against harassment or if there are other methods of resolving the complaint.

3. Contact your provincial or federal human rights commission to see if your situation is covered under its jurisdiction and policies.

4. Tell your harasser to stop the offending behaviour. Tell them that you are aware of your rights and intend to follow through with some action. If they refuse to stop, or you prefer not to confront them, continue to:

5. Document what has happened and keep any evidence.

6. Keep all documentation about your complaint, responses and any efforts to resolve it.

7. If all else fails, seek legal advice from a good labour lawyer.

One thing that researchers and human resource experts all agree on is that harassment escalates when there is lack of leadership among supervisors and administrators. For example, the military women were "not getting support from supervisors or administrators," according to the defence review. Confounding the issue is the fact that supervisors are often perpetrators, underlining the need for clear policies to protect employees from harassment as well as from retribution when they report harassment.

Five years ago, Theresa Vince, a Sears training administrator in Ontario, was shot and killed by her supervisor, Russell Davis. Vince, 54, was slated to take early retirement mere days after the shooting. Davis' fixation on his senior staffer was well known and the source of office jokes.

"He'd call her in [to his office] it seemed about every 20 minutes," one employee testified at her inquest, "for basically trivial stuff." Although Vince had complained to head office more than a year previously, nothing was done.

"Sexual harassment in the workplace is only there because the people at the top condone it and maybe practice it themselves," according to Jim Vince, Theresa Vince's widowed husband.

Although harassment is often persistent, a single event may constitute sexual harassment. In 1999, Brigadier-General Larry Smith was about to be promoted to deputy Inspector-General, a job that included investigating sexual harassment in the U.S. military. That prompted General Claudia Kennedy, a three-star general, to testify that she had been sexually harassed by Smith. His promotion was cancelled.

Criminal assaults are a clear form of harassment, but the more subtle clashes between the values of many men and women in the workplace are also a factor. "Women have quite different styles than men and some men do not value the difference," Suek says. "They prefer the women who have a style similar to theirs and therefore similar to the dominant male culture."

Organizations have personalities, just like people, says Suek. "In some, the management style, the policies, the overall corporate culture reinforces respect, dignity and caring. Much of that starts at the top with the senior executives and is reinforced by the management and unions.

"Others allow people to bully and don't stop it. Gossip is mean and hurtful. Minorities are not valued and those attitudes are supported by senior management or the union," says Suek.

Complicating these differences are sexist attitudes used by many men to justify their offensive behaviour. "There are myths that women like the attention, when most women don't," says Gould. "As long as we maintain these myths, we will have harassment."

Sexual harassment is a form of discrimination, even so called 'milder' forms. Writes Feary, "Pornography, sexual conversation, sexual and sexist jokes, girlie posters, and the like, are morally objectionable because they violate women's rights to enjoy fair equality of opportunity."

Investigating harassment is one of the specialities of Suek's firm, TLS Enterprises. After a complaint has been laid, Suek and her partners interview the parties involved, including the accused, the complainant and witnesses. Once the investigation is complete, they write a report explaining their conclusions and recommendations. It is up to the organization whether there will be any disciplinary actions or policy changes.

"The standard of proof is a 'balance of probabilities,'" Suek explains, "not 'beyond a reasonable doubt' as in criminal court. So we look to whether the circumstances are such that it 'probably' happened."

It may sound straightforward, but it rarely is. For example, there is often more than one complainant and more than one respondent. In such cases, an investigation reveals systemic sexual harassment is present, pointing to the need for further investigation or a larger organizational review.

Resolving specific complaints marks only the beginning—or the middle—of addressing the problem. "People who haven't been affected by harassment tend to think the issue is over once an investigation has taken place," explains Suek. "In fact, it is often a signal that the corporate culture has to be examined to determine how [harassment] can be prevented in the future.

Simply adopting a sexual harassment policy can give organizations a false sense of security. "Most often, they develop a policy and then forget about it until a crisis occurs," Suek observes.

Or they may say there isn't a problem because they haven't had a complaint. She describes how women in one organization who complained of harassment received dead rats in their mailboxes—for 'ratting-out' their fellow employees.

Working to change the culture of the organization is the only way to prevent harassment, experts agree. And that means developing policies on respectful workplaces and implementing mechanisms for dealing with complaints. When complaints have been resolved, management must communicate to the rest of the staff that the situation has been remedied. Training to deal with all kinds of conflict, including bullying, harassment or disrespect are also part of the solution. At the City of Winnipeg, 4,000 employees have completed the city's training on respectful workplace practices, boasts Gould, who handles harassment complaints as part of her job as the City of Winnipeg's employee relations consultant.

Many large corporations have taken a firm stand against sexual harassment. Dow Chemical fired 50 employees and disciplined 200 others last June for circulating pornographic images on company computers. Last year, Xerox fired 40 workers for spending work time surfing pornographic sites, and *The New York Times* fired 22 employees for circulating offensive e-mails. Last year, the Equal Employment Opportunity Commission in the U.S. filed the largest sexual harassment suit in its history against Mitsubishi, alleging harassment of 500 female employees.

Until problems surface, however, sexual harassment tends to be seen by managers as a 'soft issue,' not as important as something like finance. What they should remember, says Gould, "is that of the 100 most successful companies in Canada, the thing that sets apart the ones at the top is the time and effort spent on human capital." Treat employees well, respect them and your profit goes up.

"It sounds very simplistic, but the more that senior management models appropriate behaviour, the greater the likelihood that behaviour will be integrated into the workplace."

In smaller businesses, this may be difficult. Gould believes that the most vulnerable employees are those in small private companies. No union. No policies. No procedures. "It's often just them and the harasser," says Gould.

Unions are playing an increasingly important role in harassment protection. For example, the Canadian Union of Public Employees (CUPE) is developing contract language that includes all of the grounds covered by human rights legislation, including discrimination on the basis of sex and sexual orientation.

It wasn't always so. In the past, unions saw their duty of fair representation as a responsibility to defend only the person accused of harassment, says Maureen Morrison, a CUPE Equality Representative.

"Protecting the harasser under the guise of union solidarity allowed the boys to try to cover things up," she says. The increased participation of women in unions helped changed this practice, prompted by court cases that established that employers are responsible for maintaining a harassment-free workplace.

While union members accused of harassment are still represented by the unions, in keeping with the union's legal obligation, so are union members who make a harassment complaint. "This can be divisive," admits Morrison, "but it's part of a process of growth."

Today, union representatives like Morrison take the tack that "unions shouldn't try to protect people from their disrespectful behaviour."

At CUPE, negotiating policies on sexual harassment is part of a broader effort to support women-friendly policies including childcare, better family leave, better parental and maternity leave and pay equity.

When workplace grievance procedures are inadequate or nonexistent, sexual harassment complaints are made with human rights commissions (provincial or federal). A 17-year study of cases before the Canadian Human Rights Commission found that 75 percent of women who had filed complaints were no longer in their jobs. The study found that complainants often give up because the commission process can be time-consuming and often takes an emotional toll.

Another study found that the average sexual harassment complaint took more than two years to resolve. This points to another problem, namely that human rights commissions across the country tend to be hamstrung by a serious lack of funds.

"The people know what they are doing," Suek observes, "There just aren't enough of them or enough money."

Despite limited resources, the Manitoba Human Rights Commission 2000 annual report notes that the commission reduced the average time required to deal with complaints to 8.2 months. Nonetheless, harassment experts agree that the best way to stop harassment is to develop pro-active policies, rendering formal complaints a fail-safe measure of last resort.

Dealing with objectionable behaviour informally, through mediation or other workplace procedures, brings speedier results and can alleviate some of the stress on victims. A new federal government harassment policy extends beyond the legislated grounds of harassment of sex, race and sexual orientation to include personal harassment and abuse of authority. The policy encourages managers and employees to deal with conflicts at the outset.

Behaviour is one thing. Attitudes are another. That's why Gould stresses that "the remedy for harassment has to be substantive enough to have a positive change on the workplace culture."

The bottom line is that it is organizations' responsibility to ensure that managers "treat people with respect," says Gould, "You can't get any better than that."

Resources

Sexual Harassment in the Workplace, by Arjun Aggarwal and Madhu Gupta, June 2000. Published by Butterworths.

Talking from 9 to 5: How Women and Men's Conversational Styles Affect Who Gets Heard, Who Gets Credit and What Work Gets Done, by Debarah Tannen. William Morrow and Co. Inc, New York 1996.

Back Off!: How to Confront and Stop Sexual Harassment and Harassers, Martha J. Langelan. Published by Simon & Schuster, 1993.

The Canadian Human Rights Reporter http://www.cdn-hr-reporter.ca

What Is Sexual Harassment Produced by the Manitoba Human Rights Commission. http://www.gov.mb.ca/hrc/english/publications/sexhar.html

A Place for All: A Guide to Creating an Inclusive Workplace Download from the Web Site of the Canadian Human Rights Commission http://www.chrc-ccdp.ca

Sexual Harassment of Working Women: A Case of Sex Discrimination by Catharine A. McKinnon, 1979.

On-line news on sexual harassment cases in the U.S. http://www.now.org/nnt/03-97/sexual.html

Sexual Harassment, edited by Edmund Wall, Prometheus Books, Buffalo, New York. Second Edition.

Better Safe Than... A training manual for employers. English and French, 1993. Produced by the Ontario Women's Directorate.

A Time for Action on Sexual Harassment in the Workplace: Employer's Guide, 1993. Produced by the Ontario Women's Directorate, this guide is focussed on employers' responsibility.

Sexual Harassment: Working It Out, Manual and video, 1993. Produced by Ontario Women's Directorate and Ontario Federation of Labour, focuses on developing anti-harassment policies and methods of dealing with complaints.

This article was supported with a grant from the Manitoba Association for Respectful Workplaces.

Why 9/11 Didn't Change the Workplace

Despite news stories and advertising hype, studies show that the terrorist attacks have not brought massive changes to most American workplaces. HR professionals should monitor the specific needs of their employees, and keep the big picture in mind.

By Shari Caudron

On September 11, approximately 3,000 people were killed in the worst series of terrorist attacks this country has ever seen. The vast majority of victims had one characteristic, one major characteristic, in common: they were at work when they lost their lives. They were bond traders, chefs, firefighters, computer programmers, administrative assistants, custodians, vice presidents, and flight attendants. All were imperiled simply because they showed up for work that day.

In the weeks following the attacks, everyone in America—from hot-dog vendors standing beside their stainless-steel carts to the white-shirted Sunday news commentators—seemed to agree on one thing: that life in America would never be the same. The post-9/11 world and workplace would be radically different, they agreed. How could it *not* be?

The *Wall Street Journal* claimed, "The aftermath of the terrorist attacks posed an acid test for employers, often fundamentally changing the employer-employee relationship." Elie Wiesel, a Nobel laureate, was quoted in *Parade* magazine saying, "Now there is a before and after. Nothing will be the same." And business consultant Morrie Shechtman, chairman of The Shechtman Group, a consulting firm specializing in corporate culture, professed that "our belief that our institutions will somehow protect us has been shattered. That includes our nation, our local communities, and, yes, our workplaces."

But *is* the workplace so radically different today? Are workers more anxious and distracted? Are employees choosing family picnics over promotions? Has the radical shift predicted by prognosticators materialized?

While it's certainly true that Americans feel more vulnerable on American soil, and that the U.S. military has shifted its focus to terrorism, and that air travel has become much more cumbersome, the lingering impact of September 11 on most employers and working Americans has been, frankly speaking, quite negligible.

A study of 146 companies conducted by the Bureau of National Affairs in Washington, D.C., indicates that while employee anxiety did increase in three out of four firms after the attacks, employee concerns have not had an impact on productivity, absenteeism, tardiness, or the quality of work performed.

A study of 1,100 full-time workers by CareerBuilder found that productivity actually *rose* following the attacks, leading to

the conclusion that America's businesses managed to hum along quite nicely despite the horror.

This is not, however, what the media or consultants or vendors would have had you believe. In the wake of September 11, HR professionals were besieged by new reports and advertisements screaming about the desperate need for everything from heightened background checks, video monitoring, and executive security to enhanced EAP services, crisis planning, and teleconferencing technology.

What does all the talk about September 11 and the recession mean for HR professionals?
Are there any lessons to be learned?

Career counselors warned of a massive soul-searching among employees. Corporate psychologists discussed the inherent unpredictability of post-traumatic stress disorder. Diversity consultants advised managers to stay alert for increased discrimination. And why not? The country was in the midst of fearful uncertainty, and as Madison Avenue has long known, fear sells.

All of the concerns raised are valid, and should be considered, but the massive workplace changes predicted in September for the most part haven't materialized.

Granted, 36 percent of people responding to a national Red Cross survey claimed to be spending less time at work and more time with family and friends, but the desire for greater work/life balance isn't a new trend. Neither is the search for more meaningful work. In fact, the majority of supposedly "new" workplace concerns raised after September 11 are really just extensions of ongoing challenges.

Workplace security? That had been a concern because of perceptions about workplace violence. Video-conferencing and e-learning? They were already growing in popularity because of cost-savings. Multicultural awareness? This has been an issue at least since the Hudson Institute first released "Workplace 2000" in 1987.

"One of the mistakes made by the media and by some business presenters post-9/11 was the tendency to say that this or that has changed," says David Stum, president of Aon Consulting's Loyalty Institute in Ann Arbor, Michigan. "People may have been going to church more often or leaving work at 4 p.m. to hug their kids, but that doesn't mean true behavioral change has occurred. The only change we can state with assurance is that if a trend already existed before September 11, that trend has probably accelerated."

The other difficulty in trying to ferret out workplace changes is that it's hard to separate the events of that one day from the precipitous economic downturn that followed. Many of the adjustments and difficulties experimented by employers have more to do with downsizing, cost-cutting, and shrinking profit margins than they do with September 11.

Ilene Gochman, practice director, organization measurement, at Watson Wyatt Worldwide in Chicago, says, "The emo-

Exelon Experiences Subtle Changes
business results

Exelon Corporation is an electric utility company based in Chicago that provides power to some 5 million midwestern customers. In many ways, this company of 30,000 employees typifies the experiences of most American companies in dealing with the aftermath of the September 11 terrorist attacks.

On the day of the attacks, the company's downtown Chicago offices were evacuated and its nuclear plants went on high alert. The National Guard stepped in to provide additional monitoring and security. The next day, the company established procedures to help employees who wished to make blood donations or cash contributions to the victims. On September 13, letters were sent to workers reminding them of the services available through the company's EAP. Letters highlighting the importance of not discriminating against others because of religious beliefs quickly followed. Ten days after that, the company's HR department reviewed its military-leave policy and enhanced the benefits available to workers who might be called up.

But after the first two weeks of anxiety and action, the work life at Exelon pretty much returned to normal. According to S. Gary Snodgrass, senior vice president and chief HR officer, the workplace changes since that time have been subtle. "It's elusive and tough to get your arms around," Snodgrass says, "but employees and managers seem to show greater interest in getting to know more about each other. We've also seen employees reaffirming their wish to spend more time with family." Ironically, he adds, employees also seem to be more focused at work. "We provide a principal product and service to society. Our people have always had a fairly strong sense of purpose, but it seems higher now."

Are there any lessons that Snodgrass has personally learned from September 11? "The last few months have been a time of incredible personal reflection," he says. "I think the events helped all of us put our priorities in place and realize that at the end of the day, this is just work."

tional impact of September 11 and the recession are intertwined." And they are intertwined in some interesting ways.

The recession, for instance, has caused employees to feel much more uncertain about the future of their jobs, and for good reason. Last year, more than 2 million jobs were cut by U.S. companies, and unemployment leaped from 4.2 percent in January 2001 to 5.8 percent in December. Instead of job-hopping in the search for ever-greener pastures, today's employees are more likely to stay put and appreciate the work they have.

Lessons from September 11

business results

The terrorist attacks of September 11 have had little lasting impact on the workplaces of companies that were not directly affected. This doesn't mean, however, that there aren't HR lessons to be learned from the event. In fact, what the terrorist attacks did do was remind employers of the importance of taking care of certain basic HR issues, as well as being prepared for workplace emergencies. Some of the issues that have risen to the surface are:

1. Employee safety and security. "If employers don't pay attention to safety and security issues, there is the possibility for lawsuits regarding negligent hiring, supervision, and good old-fashioned negligence," says attorney Roger Brice, partner and head of the labor and employment group at Sonnenschein, Nath and Rosenthal in Chicago. "There is a general duty clause in OSHA that says that employers have to provide workplaces that are free of recognized hazards that could cause harm to employees. In light of 9/11, if employers don't take some heightened security precautions and bad things happen, they can be subject to liability."

Interestingly enough, when it comes to security, Brice believes that today's employees tend to be much more accepting of things they would have considered intrusions two years ago. This includes e-mail and voice-mail monitoring and the use of security badges and metal detectors.

2. Succession planning. The fact that so many people were killed on September 11 while at work underscores the importance of succession planning and the need for organizations to have already identified leaders who can step into key roles on short notice. "Companies cannot afford to have small numbers of people with skill sets that are not shared by others," says Paul Ofman, a consultant with RHR International in New York.

3. Policies regarding business travel. Employers have to determine what they will do with employees who are afraid to fly even though their jobs may require travel. If the fear is clinically based, it may be a covered disability under the ADA, and employers would have to make reasonable accommodations.

4. Military leave. HR must inform supervisors that employees have a right to military leave. By law, employees who are members of the military reserve must be granted leaves of absence on request. If the leaves of absence are for less than 91 days, the returning employees must be re-employed in the positions they would have had if the employment had not been interrupted by military service. If the leaves are longer, the returning employees must be reinstated to the positions they would have had *or* similar positions in terms of seniority, status, and pay.

5. Crisis planning. According to Arthur F. Silbergeld, a partner in the Los Angeles office of Proskauer Rose LLP, human resource departments should review and update their crisis and evacuation plans, and establish plans to provide employees with food and shelter for up to 72 hours in the event of a disaster that prevents them from leaving the premises.

6. Employee communication. In uncertain times—whether because of a terrorist attack or a declining economy—employees need communication from management more than ever. "HR executives need to be mindful that it is their job to connect the dots for employees," Ofman says. They have to demonstrate to employees why their jobs are still relevant in order to re-establish enthusiasm and commitment.

7. Employee-assistance plans. The counseling resources available through employee-assistance programs were used heavily in the weeks after September 11. According to a study by ComPsych, a company that manages workplace employee-assistance programs, one out of five employees who'd previously used their company's EAP used it following September 11, and an additional 11 percent of employees began to view EAP services with renewed respect.

One of the problems experienced by some companies with EAPs was that information about use of these services didn't always make it to the senior leaders who tend not to be well-informed about how people are feeling and reacting to crisis.

In just eight months last year, employee commitment as measured by Aon Consulting's Workplace Commitment Index jumped from a five-year low to a five-year high. This was due to anxiety and uncertainty caused by both the events of September 11 and the recession, Stum says. While employees in the late 1990s were looking for any good reason to leave a company, now they are looking for any good reason to stay, he says. "People have a tendency to hunker down and ride through crises as best they can."

Even though employees may appear to be more committed to their companies since September 11, Stum cautions that the jump represents a false loyalty. "We now have people who show up regularly and aren't looking for other opportunities," he says, "but they aren't bringing anything else to work either. No creativity, no commitment to customer service or quality, and no loyalty to the goals of the organization." Once the economy improves and September 11 gets further behind us, he predicts, employees will return to the job-hopping habits of the late 20th century. And with baby boomers retiring and demographic trends dramatically changing, there will be nothing to stop them.

"I liken it to the following analogy," Stum adds. "If there is only one airline that flies out of Detroit, that one airline will get an awful lot of false loyalty and repeat business from fliers. But

once someone opens a competitive airline next door, people aren't likely to be as loyal." It's the same thing with employment. Once the economy improves and companies start hiring, he says, anxiety levels and employee commitment are both likely to plummet.

So, what does all the talk about September 11 and the recession mean for HR professionals? Are there any lessons to be learned?

Although there were many reports about how September 11 was likely to affect companies, the actual effects—if they materialized at all—differed from one company to another.

If you step back from day-to-day concerns about downsizing, work/life issues, and employee commitment, and take a look at the big picture, several things become clear.

First, it apparently takes a lot more than terrorist attacks, however horrific, to disrupt the flow of American business. While it's been repeatedly stated that we live in an era of constant change, it's also true that fundamental workplace, business, and human concerns change very slowly, if at all. Sure, new issues crop up on a daily basis—such as coordinating military leave or providing employee grief counseling—but that doesn't mean you should take your eye off your company's long-term goals and objectives.

Second, although there were many reports about how September 11 was likely to affect companies, the actual effects—if they materialized at all—differed from one company to another. Instead of taking the generalized predictions of the media or consultants to heart, HR professionals should monitor the specific needs of their particular workforces. For example, instead of investing a great deal of money in teleconferencing technology because of widespread travel fear, companies should ask employees how they're feeling about travel and whether or not they would prefer teleconferencing.

The third lesson is that retention is still *the* key HR issue. Finding and keeping quality employees was an issue long before September 11, and even though unemployment has risen and downsizing receives a lot of press, HR professionals cannot be casual about the need to retain good employees. As Aon's Workplace Commitment Index indicates, employees are showing a desire to stay with their companies, but it's a desire born of fear. "HR directors should definitely still be thinking about the war for talent," Gochman says. "When you look at demographic trends, there simply aren't enough younger cohorts to take the place of retiring boomers."

Finally, the catastrophic events of September 11 underscore how the unexpected can happen at any time. No one could have predicted that 19 people could plan a terrorist attack of such immense and ingenious proportions. In the post-9/11 workplace, it is still the job of HR to help build a lasting sense of employee pride and commitment that can carry companies through all kinds of challenges.

Shari Caudron is a contributing editor based in Denver. To comment, e-mail editors@workforce.com.

DEALING WITH HR ISSUES FOLLOWING THE 9/11 TERRORIST ATTACKS

Robert W. Lincoln Jr.

In the aftermath of the September 11, 2001, terrorist attacks on U.S. citizens, our entire nation is grappling with the issues of safety and security in circumstances that were previously unimaginable. The attack on the World Trade Center in particular motivated many employers to change their processes and practices with regard to workplace safety and security in order to address both current and anticipated problems in these areas. Although these are the correct matters to pursue, they are not the only concerns. There are hosts of collateral human resources concerns that need to be discussed, revisited, reviewed, and resolved. Accordingly, the role of HR professionals is to work with the leadership of their companies to develop the people philosophies and strategies necessary for the implementation of short-term and long-term solutions to newly identified workplace problems.

THE CHALLENGE FOR HR

Like most things involving people and the HR function, the challenge is not to allow oneself to become overwhelmed with the scope of the problems and the complexity and costs of the solutions. Also, because there is such strong identification with the victims of the attack on the World Trade Center (every businessperson can identify with those flying in the doomed airplanes or just starting the work day in the offices destroyed during the attack), many people may develop a need to respond by "doing something." As a result, it is tempting to implement attack-related policies and programs that are valid to that particular situation, but might not be directly relevant to the needs of the specific company. Most of the people problems that have surfaced following the September 11 attacks are familiar to HR professionals. Employee benefits, counseling via employee assistance programs, selection, recruitment, change management, communications, recognition, and budget management are among the most pressing people issues to be addressed. Consequently, the first task of the HR professional should be to assess the needs of the organization, prioritize the response, and effectively implement solutions to problems. Granted, most of us have never had to deal with a human tragedy of this nature and magnitude, but if we can maintain poise and apply the tools that are part of the HR professional's trade, the exponential people issues resulting from the terrorist attack can be reduced to manageable clusters.

By organizing the HR issues into clusters, we can begin to realistically and objectively determine the impact of the attack on a particular organization and on particular individuals. In doing so, necessary human and financial resources can be aligned with specific people and groups based on known needs. There is also a subjective, emotional component that should be factored into every decision concerning the allocation of resources directed at solving the host of people problems, and this component is critical to the overall success of any implementation of HR programs created as the result of the attack.

MANAGEABLE CLUSTERS

Three clusters deal with both company-wide (macro) and individual (micro) people concerns. Contained within the clusters are a series of questions that articulate specific concerns, followed by the people issues that pertain to the questions. The answers to the questions will help determine whether any action should be taken on the people issues. The three cluster headings are:

1. The Impact on the Company (Internal Macro Issues). This relates to people issues that are general in nature but have an impact on the entire company. Solutions generated under this cluster give the HR professional a perspective on the strategic direction that the company wants to take.
2. The Impact on People within the Company (Internal Micro Issues). The company's strategic plan will help determine policies for addressing concerns of individuals and develop solutions.
3. The Impact on People Relevant to the Company (External Macro Issues). Here, the HR professional is working with the leadership of the company to determine the impact of the attack on customers and external clients, and what the appropriate response by the company will be.

Although it is possible to consider more than three clusters, the task of developing and implementing solu-

tions would become more difficult and less manageable. Working through the three clusters described in this article will be enough to get the HR professional headed in the right direction.

The details of the clusters are provided below:

1. Impact on the Company (Internal Macro Issues)

Was the company located in New York City?
People issues:
❑ Travel
❑ Administrative support
❑ Internal/external communications
❑ Budget revisions

Was the company located in the World Trade Center?
People issues:
❑ Employee benefits
❑ Office space
❑ Administrative support
❑ Internal/external communications
❑ Replacing departed or injured employees
❑ Counseling for surviving employees
❑ Budget revisions

2. Impact on People within the Company (Internal Micro Issues)

Were employees of the company killed or injured in the attack?
Issues affecting individuals:
❑ Employee benefits
  • Survivor benefits
  • Hardship loans for family members of the killed or injured employees
  • Financial planning for family members of the killed or injured employees
  • Counseling for family members of the killed or injured employees
❑ Internal/external communication
  • Possible memorials or other forms of remembrance and recognition
❑ Replacing departed or injured employees
❑ Budget revisions

Were family members of employees of the company killed or injured in the attack?
Issues affecting individuals:
❑ Employee benefits
  • Survivor benefits
  • Hardship loans for family members of the killed or injured family member
  • Financial planning for family members of the killed or injured family member
  • Counseling for family members of the killed or injured family member

❑ Time away from work (periodic and extended)
  Internal/external communications
  • Possible memorials or other forms of remembrance and recognition

Were friends of employees of the company killed or injured in the attack?
Issues affecting individuals:
❑ Employee counseling
❑ Time away from work (periodic and extended)

3. Impact on People Relevant to the Company (i.e., Customers/Clients (C/C) (External Macro Issues))

Was the C/C located in New York City?
C/C Issues:
❑ Suspended or delayed business activity
❑ Need for alternate suppliers

Was the C/C located in the World Trade Center?
C/C Issues:
❑ Suspended or delayed business activity
❑ Need for alternate suppliers

Was the C/C killed or injured in the attack?
C/C Issues:
❑ Suspended or delayed business activity
❑ Need for alternate suppliers
❑ Leaders/employees from the company taking the time to visit the C/C or attend memorials
❑ Donations for possible memorials of other forms of remembrance and recognition

Were employees of the C/C killed or injured in the attack?
❑ Leaders/employees from the company taking the time to visit the C/C or attend memorials
❑ Donations for possible memorials or other forms of remembrance and recognition

Were family members of the C/C killed or injured in the attack?
❑ Leaders/employees from the company taking the time to visit the C/C or attend memorials
❑ Donations for possible memorials or other forms of remembrance and recognition

Were friends of the C/C killed or injured in the attack?
❑ Donations for possible memorials or other forms of remembrance and recognition

Understandably some of the initial reactions to this process are "Who has the time to do all of this?" or "This seems more 'mechanical' than 'human'!" Clearly, HR has to be contemporaneously responsive and appropriately sensitive to the needs of people, and not come across as being bureaucratic and dispassionate. Utilization of such a process can help HR achieve this seemingly dissimilar

goal. Bear in mind that this "process" is a tool to be employed by HR or shared with a leadership team assigned with the responsibility for setting company policy during extreme business-related situations.

For example, companies have established (or reactivated) crisis-management teams. Teams comprising the CEO, head of security, CIO, HR, VP, and selected business VPs have been formed to develop a coordinated response to any future crisis that is outside the "business norm." It is conceivable that such a team, working at a high level on the crisis, would use the manageable cluster approach in order to distill issues and quickly set priorities for allocating human and financial resources.

Also, because of the emphasis on employee and survivor benefits, companies have seen the need to reinterpret and in some cases change the language in their policies. One large multinational had a provision in its policy that nullified any payout of life insurance benefits if an employee's death was the result of "an act of war." Because the September 11 attacks were characterized as an act of war against the United States, strict adherence to the language of the policy would have left the employees' survivors with no life insurance payout. However, the company chose to pay the insurance to the employees' survivors. Again, a tool like the above-mentioned checklists would assist a team in quickly gravitating toward this issue and resolving it. The company is now in the process of changing the language of the policy to make a distinction between "acts of terror" and "acts of war."

PERFORMANCE MEASUREMENTS

Appropriate metrics need to be developed in order to maintain perspective, pace, and focus on long- and short-term solutions. Complex performance measurements are not necessary; they simply need to be understandable and easily tracked. Performance indicators involving cycle time, costs, and client satisfaction should be established. Although specific measurements are going to vary based on the nature and number of people issues, there are several that serve as the building blocks for others. Examples of these metrics are

❏ Number of HR professionals assigned to address these issues
❏ Number of employees personally and directly impacted by these issues
❏ Service-satisfaction survey results from employees personally and directly affected by these issues
❏ Number and type of employee communications by management related to these issues
❏ Employee assistance program activity related to these issues

❏ Cost of employees assigned to address these issues
❏ Cost of employee benefits related to these issues
❏ Cost of contributions for memorials and donations related to these issues
❏ Cost of savings realized by suspended travel
❏ Cost of lost business resulting from suspended travel
❏ Cost of downsizing resulting from lost business
❏ Cost of hiring to replace departed or injured employees
❏ Cost of training new hires
❏ Cost of employee relocations

Human resources professionals at several companies affected by the World Trade Center attack were asked whether they were being constrained by costs to implement changes in people policies or practices and whether they were using any performance measurements. Consistently, the response of these HR managers was that they were told by senior management that "money was no object" in addressing employee needs resulting from the September 11 attacks. However, one senior HR executive admitted, "We really need to do this [monitor the financial impact of the policy changes and get a collective understanding by management] because we know that eventually it will become a business issue."

ADJUSTING TO NEW WORKPLACE ISSUES

Although the people issues created by the attack on the World Trade Center are familiar to the HR professionals, the cause and magnitude of the problems offer a different perspective on these issues. The approaches to solving these human problems will require the same skill and leadership necessitated by other workplace situations. HR professionals must rise to the challenge of quickly and effectively determining the course of action to solve a myriad of time-sensitive people problems. Solutions to problems will vary depending on company and management style, philosophy, and capabilities. While there are no "right" answers offered in this article, the templates and guidelines discussed will assist HR in helping management and employees get through the difficult times ahead.

Robert W. Lincoln Jr., JD, SPHR, has spent most of his career working with business presidents, function vice presidents, and executive management as their consultant on people issues. His experience in HR management involves recruitment and placement, succession planning, group facilitation, compensation, relocation, employee development, mergers and acquisitions, and people-strategy development and implementation. He worked for The Dow Chemical Company for 23 years, most recently as global HR director for chemicals and as the global HR task team director for the merger with Union Carbide. Currently, he heads Robert Lincoln Consulting LLC, a firm specializing in strategic HR planning, change management, and the coaching and counseling of executives and HR professionals. He may be reached via e-mail at rwlincjr@aol.com.

From *Employment Relations Today,* Winter 2002, pp. 1–7. © 2002 by Employment Relations Today.

UNIT 2
Meeting Human Resource Requirements

Unit Selections

Key Points to Consider

- Job requirements and working conditions have changed over the past several years. What new changes do you foresee in the workplace in the next 10 years? How do you see the impact of the 24/7 work schedule on employers and employees? What impact do you think telecommuting will have on the workplace? Do you think you will be working in the same kind of position as your parents?

- The first step in the process of working is getting hired. The last step is termination, whether for cause, leaving for a new job, retirement, or a "reduction in force." What trends do you see in the workforce concerning individuals and their careers? What do you think the impact of race or diversity in the workforce is? Do you see any changes coming?

- How do you see computerization being applied to human resources, and how will this change human resources?

 **Links: www.dushkin.com/online/**
These sites are annotated in the World Wide Web pages.

America's Job Bank
http://www.ajb.dni.us
National Center for the Workplace
http://socs.berkeley.edu/~iir/ncw/execsum.html

Organizations, whether profit or nonprofit, are more than collections of buildings, desks, and telephones. Organizations are made of people—people with their particular traits, habits, and idiosyncrasies that make them unique. Each individual has different needs and wants, and the employer and the worker must seek a reasonable compromise so that at least an adequate match may be found for both.

The importance of human resource planning is greater than ever and will probably be even more important in the future. As Thomas Peters and Robert Waterman have pointed out in their book *In Search of Excellence:*

> Quality and service, then, were invariable hallmarks of excellent firms. To get them, of course, everyone's cooperation is required, not just the mighty labors of the top 200. The excellent companies require and demand extraordinary performance from the average man. Dana's former chairman, Rene McPherson, says that neither the few destructive laggards nor the handful of brilliant performers are the key. Instead, he urges attention to the care, feeding and unshackling of the average man. We labeled it "productivity through people." All companies pay it lip service. Few deliver.

—Thomas Peters and Robert Waterman,
In Search of Excellence,
New York, Warner Books, 1987

In the future, organizations are going to have to pay more than just lip service to "productivity through people" if they want to survive and prosper. They will have to practice it by demonstrating an understanding of not only their clients' and customers' needs but also those of their employees. The only way they will be able to deliver the goods and services and achieve success is through those same employees. Companies are faced with the difficult task of finding the right people for the right jobs—a task that must be accomplished if the organization is going to have a future.

Organizations are trying to meet the needs of their employees by developing new and different approaches to workers' jobs. This means taking into account how society, the labor force, the family, and the nature of the jobs themselves have changed. Training and development will be key in meeting future human resource requirements. Employers will have to change the way they design their positions if they are to attract and keep good employees. They must consider how society has changed and how those changes have affected the labor force. They will have to consider how the labor force has changed and will change in the future, with fewer young people and more middle-aged employees as well as dual-career couples struggling to raise children and deal with aging parents. They will have to consider how the very nature of jobs has changed in society, especially from predominantly blue-collar to white-collar jobs, from "9 to 5" to "24/7," and "Using Telecommuting to Improve the Bottom Line."

Human resource planning, selection, and recruitment are going to be even more critical in the future. Companies will have to go to extraordinary lengths to attract and keep new employees. There is no mystery about the reasons for this situation. America

is aging, and there are fewer people in their late teens and early twenties to take the entry-level jobs that will be available in the future. Women, who for the past 20 years have been the major source of new employees, now represent almost half the workforce. As a result, new groups must be found, whether they are retirees, high school students, workers moonlighting on a second job, minority  group members, people with disabilities, or immigrants. One thing is certain: the workforce is changing and organizations will need to unlock the potential of all their employees. Other means of recruitment will need to be employed in the future. "Matching Colors" addresses this situation.

Another aspect of human resource planning involves both the selection process and the termination process. The days of working for only one company and then retiring with a gold watch and a pension are over. People are going to change jobs, if not companies, more frequently in the future, and many of the tasks they will be doing in the next 10, 15, or 20 years do not even exist today because of technological change. Midlife and midcareer changes are going to be far more common than they have been in the past, requiring people to change and adapt.

As seen in "A Wealth of Choice," human resources information systems offer important tools in managing human resources. The ability of computers to handle large amounts of data is now being applied to human resource management with very interesting results. These practices, applied to hiring and internal information management promise much greater automation of human resources in the future.

Meeting the human resource needs of any organization in the future is a difficult task. Assuming that the economy continues to grow at an acceptable rate, the need for workers will continue to increase, but many of the traditional sources of supply for new workers will be either exhausted or in decline. For example, human resource professionals know that there will be fewer workers available in the early twenties age group in the next 10 years because there are fewer teenagers today than 10 years ago. Management must plan for this shortage and consider alternative sources of potential employees. In turn, the individual employee must be ready to adapt quickly and efficiently to a changing environment. Job security is a thing of the past, and workers must remain flexible in order to cope with increased uncertainty.

Using TELECOMMUTING to IMPROVE the *Bottom Line*

THE BENEFITS DEFINITELY SEEM TO OUTWEIGH THE COSTS

By Jason A. Greer; Thomas E. Buttross, CMA, CPA; George Schmelzle, CPA

The first telecommuter on record was a Boston bank president who, in 1877, arranged to have a phone line strung from his office to his home in Somerville, Mass.[1] A century later, in 1973, rocket scientist Jack Nilles had endured Los Angeles gridlock one too many times. Fed up with his commute to and from a NASA satellite communications project, Nilles moved his work home, and modern "telecommuting" was born. Nilles was relaxed, had fewer interruptions, and saw his productivity rise. He went on to become a telecommuting advocate and wrote several books on the subject.

Telecommuting has taken off in the almost 30 years since Nilles's experiment. In 1978, Blue Cross/Blue Shield of South Carolina pioneered its "cottage keyer" project, which documented a 26% jump in productivity among telecommuting workers vs. their in-office counterparts. By 1986, many companies were starting small telecommuting programs for key employees or automating their sales force to reduce office overhead. In 1999, the Department of Labor reported that 28% of companies used telecommuting and estimated that by 2004 nearly a quarter of the American workforce could be doing so. Hundreds of Fortune 500 companies, including AT&T, Compaq, and IBM, plus other firms, such as Andersen and Pacific Bell, have instituted telecommuting programs in one form or another.

But how does a company make the transition to telecommuting? The potential benefits are enormous: increased employee productivity, reduced absenteeism, lower employee turnover, and an expanded labor pool. Telecommuting can improve recruitment, increase organizational flexibility, boost employee morale, and save on overhead expenses. Yet the organizational, cultural, and management challenges are equally daunting. How do managers weigh costs vs. benefits? What are the human resources issues? What are the security risks? How does management monitor expenses and productivity changes after implementation? As financial professionals assume more responsibility for internal consulting roles, they should be prepared to answer these questions.

Here's an inside look at the strategic issues one large company encountered in starting its telecommuting program.

THE CHALLENGE: PRODUCTIVITY, GROWTH, AND TELECOMMUTING

Widget Worldwide (the real company wanted anonymity) is a global organization based in the Midwest with billions in annual sales. Widget Worldwide's groundbreaking activity-based costing (ABC) program has dramatically reduced fixed and variable costs over the past few years. The company has grown steadily over the last four years and is facing a new dilemma: There's no more office space at corporate headquarters. Six years ago, Widget Worldwide began exploring how telecommuting might help them address their overcrowding problem.

In 1996, Widget Worldwide's CEO returned from a conference where one of the sessions highlighted the productivity gains of telecommuting. Inspired by what he saw, the CEO asked the Human Resources department to create a telecommuting program that would increase productivity and help the company deal with its growing pains. Employees are Widget Worldwide's most valuable asset, and the CEO recognized telecommuting as an opportunity to gain more value from that asset pool by making employees happier and more productive.

By the end of the year, HR had created a process and a set of policies for employees who wanted to work at home. HR and line management had to approve all requests to participate in the pilot. HR interviewed employees from several departments who had applied for the pilot and, a few months later, selected 10 to participate in the first experiment. The program was officially turned over to the Information Technology (IT) group in February 1998. IT's job was to oversee the setup and installation of telecommunication connections and computers and to manage the outside vendors and technology training courses for employees.

THE SOLUTION: EASIER SAID THAN DONE

Running a pilot program gave Widget Worldwide an opportunity to work out the kinks before rolling out the telecommuting program company-wide. The pilot proved to be a wise decision, considering the formidable technical challenges and vendor problems they encountered along the way.

One of the first issues was finding a vendor that could offer telecommuting services in the United States and the United Kingdom. Once the vendor had been selected, legal problems and delays set in. The vendor's contract didn't specify the number of employee installations, nor did it guarantee the vendor the longer-term contract for the program rollout. The vendor eventually realized there was going to be little profit, so it pulled back key resources, delaying the project three months. Fortunately, one of the vendor's project managers had a personal commitment to the pilot's success and performed most of the duties the vendor's entire team was supposed to provide.

Another delay came from having the Integrated Services Digital Network (ISDN) and phone lines installed by the local telephone company. The phone company's backlog of ISDN orders delayed installation for three to four weeks. And in some instances the telephone company had to come back to a telecommuter's home because the technician had cut the employee's personal phone line while installing the business line and ISDN. These incidents only added to the frustration and inconvenience of would-be telecommuters and turned up the pressure on IT to better manage the project and outside vendors.

Then there was a delay with home office furniture. Widget Worldwide had contracted with a reseller to provide the specially designed furniture for telecommuters' homes. A month after Widget Worldwide had selected the design, the furniture manufacturer shut down production for three weeks. When the furniture finally arrived, it was missing some parts—a situation compounded by the reseller's shoddy assembly. It took another two weeks for the reseller to reassemble the furniture. It would be five weeks before the telecommuters finally had their furniture.

To make matters worse, some of the computer equipment was delayed or defective—and sometimes both. The telecommuters' frustration grew with each delay and each new problem. Productivity was curbed. Equally important, the delays and problems undermined trust between telecommuters and IT—a significant issue for a project that relies so heavily on harmony of human and technological resources. The problems were eventually ironed out when the original telecommuting vendor was let go and replaced by a more reliable vendor. But the company learned some important lessons: Make sure you have reliable vendors. Cultivate trust. Be patient. Learn from your mistakes.

THE SELL: CORPORATE CULTURE AND TELECOMMUTING

Selling telecommuting within the established corporate culture was an unexpected challenge. To those accustomed to Widget Worldwide's traditional management culture, allowing employees to work from home seemed foolish. Managers scoffed that employees would disregard assignments, work shorter hours, and be hard to reach in an emergency. Anticipating this resistance, the HR department realized it had to market the program to line managers. Telecommuting, they argued, would increase employee productivity, reduce the number of sick days, and lower turnover. It would help with recruitment and offer managers flexibility in hiring and staffing. Employee morale would shoot up, and absenteeism would decline. And managers would save on overhead.

TELECOMMUTING, the HR department argued, would increase employee productivity, reduce the number of sick days, and lower turnover.

Telecommuting was an easy sell to employees. Within the first few weeks, over 50 employees volunteered to participate in the pilot. Some of the initial volunteers withdrew once HR stipulated that telecommuting could not be used in place of childcare. Still, the number of interested employees continued to grow even though telecommuters would be required to have daycare or a sitter for their children.

THE BOTTOM LINE: PRODUCTIVITY GAINS FROM TELECOMMUTING

Telecommuters are required to work an eight-hour day, just like their office-bound counterparts. Once the pilot was up and running, HR initiated informal feedback sessions with the telecommuters and their managers. All of the telecommuters reported increased productivity. One said, "I can perform an eight-hour day at the office in five hours at home." Another employee living in Florida and telecommuting to Midwest headquarters reported she could do eight hours of office work in four hours at home. More objectively, one telecommuter increased the number of insurance claims she could process from 25 per hour at her corporate office to 34 per hour at home.

Productivity increased so sharply, in fact, that HR began to worry that employees might become workaholics. Seeking moderation, HR created a telecommuter guide that incorporated the initial set of rules but also helped employees better understand the program—and how to set limits. This guide also explained how to work as a telecommuter and addressed frequently asked questions.

Only one of the 10 pilot members stopped telecommuting. (Her managers wanted her back in the office for more "hands-on" work assignments.) Overall, management has been delighted with the results.

THE SAVINGS: COST REDUCTIONS

Telecommuting proved to be an enormously successful cost-saving device for Widget Worldwide. The company saw a marked drop in its need for office space and realized significant cost savings in not housing employees at corporate headquarters. The average full cost of a standard employee office was around $9,800 per year—including all utilities, telecommunications, computer equipment, property taxes, etc. The first-time expenses of setting up a telecommuting employee were approximately $9,300 per person. As the number of telecommuters increases, the $9,300 first-year cost will decrease because some of the larger fixed costs will be spread over a larger number of people. Widget Worldwide provides the furniture, computer equipment, and the connectivity for the telecommuter, just like they would if the employee were on-site. The employee covers all other costs, including utilities, property taxes, and wear and tear on the house—all of which the company covers in traditional offices.

Telecommuting has allowed Widget Worldwide to expand without spending on new office space. At some point, current office space will become vacant, and the company may then reassign the space for productive use.

Down the road the company may rent out vacant space or dispose of it altogether—a savings either way. During the pilot, too few offices were vacated to allow consolidation and reallocation of space, so no actual savings occurred. But managers expect to realize savings of $500 per employee ($9,800 in-house vs. $9,300 telecommuting) after the program is rolled out company-wide.

TELECOMMUTING could provide an annual savings of $7,400 per telecommuter.

After the first year, the only recurring costs are the connectivity expenses—ISDN and phone line—which run around $200 per month per employee. Ignoring long-distance calls and computer upgrading every three to four years, telecommuting could provide an annual savings of $7,400 per telecommuter ($9,800 in-house vs. $2,400 telecommuting). These estimates are admittedly exaggerated since telecommuters come to the office once a week to attend meetings, pick up mail, etc.—which means they require temporary office space. Even if Widget Worldwide provided in-house office space for one-fifth of its telecommuters on any given workday, the company would incur traditional office expenses of only $1,960 per telecommuter ($9,800/5). This reduces the annual savings from $7,400 to $5,440 per telecommuter.

Given these savings, Widget Worldwide considered the pilot a success despite the initial setbacks. The cost was low—between $100,000 and $110,000—not including the soft costs of employee time, which are costs with or without telecommuting. Widget Worldwide is still considering a company-wide rollout and is working with a telecom provider to develop a strategy for all of its U.S. offices—another chapter, perhaps, in the story of telecommuting.

Note

1. *This brief history is shortened from http://www.hireability.com/ resourcetelecommuting.html.*

Jason A. Greer is a business integrator in Information Systems at the Midwest company upon which this article is based. Because the company doesn't want to be identified, no contact information is provided.

Thomas E. Buttross, Ph.D., CMA, CPA, is an assistant professor of accounting at Penn State Harrisburg. You can reach him by e-mail at teb11@psu.edu or by phone at (717) 948-6145.

George Schmelzle, Ph.D., CPA, is an assistant professor of accounting at Indiana University-Purdue University Fort Wayne. You can reach him by e-mail at SchmelzG@ipfw.edu or by phone at (219) 481-6468.

When good employees retire

No one said replacing long-time employees with new blood was going to be easy…

By Bridget McCrea, Contributing Editor

He was your right-hand man, the kind of employee you could trust to come in on weekends, deliver goods to customers in a snowstorm and be fiercely loyal to your company. He worked his way up through the ranks, starting out as a warehouse employee, moving into the outside sales force and finally up into the position of VP of sales. Along the way, he not only stuck with your distributorship through thick and thin, but he also racked up about 30 years of industry knowledge and experience.

Today he's 60 years old and ready to retire. As you run your finger along the edge of his official letter of resignation and wonder how in the world you're going to replace this valued employee, keep one thing in mind: you're not alone.

Nationwide, industrial distributors across all sectors are wondering the same thing. Replacing retiring workers has become quite a challenge with the unemployment rate hovering at a nationwide low of four percent. Today's employees change jobs frequently and don't have the company loyalty that existed 30 years ago when your valued employee was hired.

Distributorships are frequently family-run companies that employ long-time, experienced executives. Because of this, one would think that bringing in new blood would pose all sorts of problems. But according to Nella Barkley, president and founder of Crystal-Barkley Corp., a New York-based human resources and career consultancy for companies and individuals, it doesn't have to be a difficult process.

Put a succession plan in place

Barkley knows firsthand the woes distributors can experience when replacing retiring employees: her husband ran Cameron & Barkley, a Charleston, S.C., industrial distributor, for years, then retired recently due to health reasons. The company survived the changing of the guard and was recently purchased by Dutch conglomerate Hagemeyer.

Based on her experience in the industry and through her HR and career consulting, Barkley suggests a way to soften the blow of replacing retired employees in the industrial distribution business.

> **"Succession** *planning is vital*, **particularly in closely held companies, and** *needs to be considered* **years in advance."**
> — **Nella Barkley, Crystal-Barkley Corp.**

As long as the company has a good succession plan in place, the transition should be a smooth one. A what? That's right — a succession plan — something that the typical small business owner probably doesn't think about. But without that plan, Barkley says, just the simple act of losing one long-time employee could adversely affect a company.

"If the company doesn't have a good succession plan in place and is losing someone who has built very close customer contact relationships, then it will take a hit," says Barkley. "Succession planning is vital, particularly in closely held companies, and needs to be considered years in advance."

Barkley says the plan should include information about each employee and exactly which paths each would most prefer to travel as they move up through the ranks of the company. It's not just about company hierarchy, says Barkley, it's about identifying the employees' strengths and weaknesses, then creating a future plan that helps employees move into positions where they will grow and thrive.

Of course, even with a succession plan in place a distributor may still suffer hardships upon the loss of a key employee. In that case Barkley says one option is to let the retired employees cash in on their pension benefits, then their previous employers can make arrangements to invite them back on a consultant basis. "Very few people want to fully retire," she explains. "Men in particular miss the association terribly — it's like cutting off an arm."

Hire back retired employees

Mike Smeaton, president of Quad City Safety, Inc. in Davenport, Iowa, a 30-employee safety equipment distributor, knows the value of hiring back retired employees. With about 10 percent of his workforce nearing retirement, he says Quad City enjoys a "very low" turnover rate and hasn't been affected much by the low unemployment rate. "Most of our new employees come from leads provided by our current employees," he says. "They're usually the best new employee that we can hire."

But a few years back when one of Quad City's longtime warehouse employees wanted to retire, Smeaton realized there was no way he could replace the veteran's "intellectual capital." Instead of letting the employee's experience and work ethic walk out the door, Smeaton convinced him to stay on as a part-time employee. Smeaton says he even hired that employee's "retired" brother, also on a part-time basis, after learning that he, too, possessed the same traits — a good work ethic and customer-service focus — as his older brother.

> ## "Just because someone retires does not necessarily mean that they're out of a *company that they helped grow* to its current position"
> —Richard Milroy, Jr., R.A.M. Enterprise, Inc.

That setup has worked for three years, but will soon come to an end. "Soon I'll be faced with replacing both of them since there are no brothers left in that family," quips Smeaton, adding that another 40-year industry veteran who works in Quad City's customer service department has also been hinting about retirement. This time, Smeaton plans to seek out a qualified replacement, then train that person on the company's products, services and high customer service standard.

Quad City isn't the only distributorship that's trying to keep its retiring employees off the golf course. Richard A. Milroy, Jr., president of Portland, Ore.-based R.A.M. Enterprise, Inc., a 40-employee firm that specializes in sales

Ten ways to prepare for the big day

Sometimes, all of the planning in the world can't prepare you for the day when your best employee heads out of the office to a life of golf and RVs. We spoke with various experts and industry professionals for this article, and asked them to give us their best tips for preparing for the big day. Here are 10 tips to follow:

1. Keep in mind that critical shortages in talent resulting from retirement don't always have to be filled from the outside — look inside. Many organizations shortchange their internal resources. One human resources consultant says she often sees an average player become a star when given the opportunity to "get off the bench" and play.

2. Keep in mind that retirement doesn't mean "65" anymore. An organization shouldn't assume that they might lose their talent. Instead, ask what your company can do to entice a potential retiree to stay on. From there, there is also the option of using the retiree's services in a consulting capacity.

3. Similarly, one expert advises discussing options with the employee. Some like to walk away at retirement, others may want to leave for a while and come back part time, with limited hours at their comfort level —thus leading to a "slow" phase-out.

4. Involve the retiring employee as well as other staff members and non-employees like customers and vendors in the process of determining the criteria for the incoming employee.

5. Try placing employment ads in newspapers outside of your local area — preferably in an area with a higher unemployment rate, such as an area where a large plant or other facility may have recently shut down.

6. Tap into the minority and disabled populations. Several companies have gone so far as to purchase homes for several employees and their families, and have also provided them with transportation to and from work.

7. Keep the words "early identification" in mind and know who your key players are, even if you need to develop a five-year plan for each one. Over that time, bear in mind that you'll have to find someone within five years who will be able to fit into that position —whether they're homegrown or hired.

8. Communicate with other employees so they know what's going on during the retirement process, and ensure that they have a grasp of what the company is doing to make the transition as smooth as possible.

9. Think of the situation in terms of exactly what you need to do to attract a prospective employee to your company. Some firms are picking up closing costs on homes, while others offer relocation expenses, provide signing bonuses and include other perks they never would have thought of in the past.

10. Keep in mind that in the new millennium, for companies to be successful, they must take a different approach to employee hiring and retention, or risk being trampled by their competitors.

and service of flat and specialty conveyor belts, says about 10 percent of his workforce will be up for retirement in the next few years.

And one of R.A.M's key employees retired just over a year ago: Milroy's father, vice president of the company. With 42 years of industry experience the older Milroy was 65 at the time, and according to his son, quickly found himself "with nothing to do."

"In our industry, employees who have worked long hours typically haven't had the time to develop many other hobbies — all they did was work," says Milroy. The pair solved the boredom problem by signing up dad on a consulting basis. Today, he works several hours per month — more if certain projects demand it. He gets compensated as a 1099-based independent contractor, says Milroy, and has even established an apprentice program in which he trains groups of new workers on the "old trade."

"To me the next generation really needs to know that they have someone who can be a resource — someone to encourage them," says Milroy. "Besides, just because someone retires does not necessarily mean that they're out of a company that they helped grow to its current position."

Both distributors' strategy of bringing back retired employees to help cultivate the new regime is a smart move, according to Valerie Perez, managing partner at Morristown, Tenn.-based Design Management Alliance, a company that helps firms handle organizational and leadership development. She adds that establishing those mentoring relationships long before it's time for the employee to officially retire is the first step.

"Distributors should put those employees in mentoring-type relationships with other employees," says Perez, "where they are actually working with the newer hires and showing them the ropes."

But don't wait until your long-term employee hands you a two-week notice, warns Perez, adding that careful planning should start a year or more in advance of the big day. "Outside of the nuts and bolts, there's not much that can be passed on to the new employee in just a few weeks," she says.

In addition to just planning ahead, proper mentoring also requires an investment from the company itself. "You'll basically have two employees doing the same job for a period of time," Perez explains. "But that investment needs to be made if the company really wants to pass on those gems that the senior employees possess."

Whether distributors are willing to make that commitment or not is a purely individual choice, but the next time around Smeaton says he'll be following that advice. When asked if he'll be doing anything differently when the next letter of resignation lands on his desk he says simply: "I'll get replacements quicker."

A Dearth of Good Managers

DEMOGRAPHICS AND A NEED FOR NEW SKILL SETS HAVE CREATED A HIRING CRUNCH

BY MICHAEL A. VERESPEJ

WITH OVER ONE-HALF MILLION U.S. EMPLOYEES LAID OFF since December, the last thing you would suspect is that manufacturers are facing a shortage of managers.

Yet the reality is that there is a serious shortfall of managers at all levels—top executives to line managers. And, observes William Bigoness, associate dean and director of the school of executive education at Babson College, Wellesley, Mass., "There will be a crying need for management talent well into this century—and not just in the U.S. The major impediment China and other emerging economies face right now in achieving economic growth is a shortage of managerial talent."

Part of the reason is demographics. "People who historically have been good at managing are retiring. There just are not enough people behind the baby-boom generation [coming into the workplace] and fewer of them are good managers," asserts Neil Fox, chief information officer, Management Recruiters International Inc., Cleveland.

For example, in the U.S. alone, several demographic studies suggest that as many as half of the managers in manufacturing companies will be eligible to retire in the next five years. In addition, the U.S. unemployment rate is at its lowest level in 32 years, and the economy—despite the layoffs—is expected to create twice as many jobs as there are workers available.

That adds up to what Compaq Computer Corp. calculates as a 40% gap between need for and availability of managers. Another measurement of the problem is replacement rate for managers in manufacturing. According to a report released earlier this year by Towers Perrin and the Economist Intelligence Unit Ltd., that rate will be at least 60% over the next five years. "And the [recent] layoffs won't help ... because those are people who were in jobs that weren't necessary anymore either in their companies or others," says Stamford, Conn.-based Emmett Seaborn, leader of the global Total Rewards consulting group of Towers Perrin.

> ## "The business world is more demanding, and most of today's managers were trained for a world that doesn't exist anymore."
>
> **Edward E. Lawler III, director,**
> **Center for Effective Organizations,**
> **University of Southern California**

Exacerbating the situation are changing expectations of management duties. What's required to be a good manager today and what's considered to be acceptable managerial performance have changed dramatically.

"The business world is more demanding, and most of today's managers were trained for a world that doesn't exist anymore," explains Edward E. Lawler III, director of the Center for Effective Organizations at the University of Southern California's Marshall School of Business, Los Angeles. "You have more de-

manding stakeholders, completely new technologies that managers must understand, and an e-commerce environment."

In addition, because more decision-making has been pushed down in manufacturing companies, line managers—who previously only managed operations—now need to be as informed as senior managers about strategic business issues, as well as cultural, human-resource, and marketing issues. And there is a growing requirement for managers to have a global mind-set and manage across regions.

"There just are very few people with that combination of qualities," says Seaborn. "There is an enormous gap between what companies have and what they need."

Ironically, it's a shortage that manufacturers may have been able to prevent, suggests James M. Hunt, assistant professor of management at Babson. "The shortsighted nature of downsizings and layoffs a decade ago stripped manufacturers of their middle management and their bench strength," he says. "That meant not enough people had enough opportunities to learn on the job" over the last 10 years.

Make development a priority

THAT PARALLELS THE UNWILLINGNESS OF MOST COMPANIES to make manager development a top priority. Forty-five percent of the global organizations surveyed recently by human-resources consultants Watson Wyatt Worldwide said that they had no recruiting strategy at all. Another 11 % said that they only had a recruiting strategy in place for top management.

There are exceptions. Dell Computer Corp. and Intel Corp., suggests Lawler, have strong executive-development programs. In a similar vein, AlliedSignal, now a part of Honeywell International Inc., and General Electric Co. [which is acquiring Honeywell] have "tremendous track records" for moving people ahead every 18 to 24 months, notes Breck Ray, managing partner of executive-search firm Ray & Berndtson Inc., Fort Worth. And companies such as Sun Microsystems Inc. and Cisco Systems Inc. are recognized as leaders in facilitating career development for everyone in the company.

For the most part, companies have not made manager development a high priority. A case in point: Only 15% of the executives surveyed by McKinsey & Co. three years ago said improving the talent pool was a top priority, even though 75% of those same executives said that "a chronic shortage of talent" was one of the constraints on their companies' growth.

"We need to move to an era in which leadership becomes an organizational capability and not an individual characteristic that only a few people at the top … have," asserts USC's Lawler. Until manufacturers make a long-term commitment to "broadening the leadership talent … throughout the organization, the managerial talent shortage will continue," he warns.

The best approach: offer managers career development, challenging projects, internal and outside training, and opportunities for personal growth.

Manufacturing is at neither an advantage nor a disadvantage compared to new-economy or service-sector companies in attracting those workers. "Some people don't want to go into manufacturing because it is not as glamorous or as clean as the service sector," says John A. Challenger, CEO of outplacement firm Challenger, Gray & Christmas Inc., Chicago. "But the people systems and the culture still determine whether people go or don't go into certain industries. The companies that can provide opportunities and stability are the ones that have an advantage."

Which is why, says Lawler, a traditional, established manufacturer such as GE has an advantage over many companies in recruiting managers. "GE is not a new-economy company, but it has developed a reputation as a company that values human capital and leadership and is a good place to be a manager."

Thus, if a company is not attracting—or retaining—enough managers, it may need to look at its policies and management style, suggests Steve Leven, senior vice president and manager of worldwide human resources at Texas Instruments Inc., Dallas.

"Get an independent assessment of managers you have lost and find out why, because a lot of times people will say they leave for [more money] when there are really other reasons," says Leven. "It is easy to underestimate [from the inside] how hard it is sometimes for someone from the outside to join a company."

Matching Colors

Retail recruitment of minority executives is more than a matter of principle; it is a means of competitive survival.

BY DEBBY GARBATO STANKEVICH

At Home Depot's Villager's Hardware in Elizabeth, NJ, general store manager Tony Gonzalez is discussing a popular "langosta" dish with a customer perusing food processors. Gonzalez and his customer are natives of Puerto Rico and both prepare and enjoy the island's popular foods. Gonzalez thinks a certain model would be best for the job; a passing associate, one of many bilingual employees, agrees. The customer leaves the store with the appliance and a seafood recipe.

Such in-store interactions are becoming more commonplace throughout the retail industry as companies realize they need to establish and exploit the cultural and lingual bonds between their store associates and shoppers. What's more, an increasing number of retailers are adding diversity to their corporate ranks, from buyers to the corner office, in an effort to better understand the needs of the fastest growing segment of their customer base—the ethnic shopper.

Seventy percent of customers at the Villager's Hardware store in Elizabeth, NJ, are Hispanic, almost seven times the national average. The appointment of Gonzalez, an

18-year veteran of mainland U.S. retailing, is neither coincidence nor blind allegiance to political correctness. Rather, at Home Depot and other big-box chains, aggressive recruitment of Hispanic and African-American management is becoming an increasingly effective means of gaining market share and improving bottom line performance. It is also a way to take the first commandment in retailing a step further: Know thy customer by becoming that customer.

Hiring people from minority groups is just good business. "It's about the fact that there's money on the table," says Stephanie Springs, vice president of people and cultural diversity at Hoffman Estates, IL-based Sears, which has stepped up its own diversity initiative. "We're talking about a group which commands a good chunk of spending power. It's not just us saying it's politically correct."

True diversity involves more than hiring ethnic hourly associates. It means a retailer must aggressively recruit, mentor and promote African-Americans, Hispanics, Asians and other ethnic minorities from the

stores to positions of management on up through the district level and corporate offices. "If you're only going to look at it at point-of-sale you're going to be limited," says Springs, an African-American who joined Sears 27 years ago. "Diversity is broader than being serviced in a store by associates who speak my language and know what we like. The question is, Are we thinking through these customer perspectives in our corporate office?"

Chris Dowle, director of consumer industries and retail practice at A.T. Karney, a Chicago-based executive search firm, says Sears "has done one of the best jobs [of diversifying its workforce]. They have a very broad range of customers, and they have a tremendous amount to gain in providing the right goods. People talk about going to work there." Springs adds, "The company looks different than it did 27 years ago."

Bob Kenzer, chairman and CEO of New York-based Kenzer Corp., the country's 12th largest executive search firm, cites several retailers as having strong executive diversity programs. "Wal-Mart is doing a terrific job, along with Target and Kmart. So are some specialty chains,

like Ross Stores, Urban Brands and Charming Shoppes. Gap now has Bill Parker [an African-American executive who ran Kmart's home soft goods division for many years]. Dollar General and Family Dollar have done a good job, too."

Prejudicial barriers are falling, says Kenzer. "More retailers are becoming more committed to diversifying workforces and are sending messages on a daily basis," he says. "They're putting people in place who care about the customer. That's the name of any game you're in."

NO PLACE LIKE HOME DEPOT

Putting diversity into action in a chain's day-to-day business often involves combining the efforts of the corporate office with those of local store management. "I run this like it was my own store," notes Villager's Gonzalez. "They [corporate] have been very receptive to my input, a concept that translates across the company. I tell them area demands, from service levels to the way we can advertise." Villager's is a four-store housewares, hardware and home decor test concept from Atlanta-based Home Depot.

As mass retailers attempt to grow in an increasingly competitive environment, the type of micro-marketing utilized by minority management like Gonzalez at Home Depot is becoming more important and complex. This increases the need for management executives who are real experts in relating product to customer.

"Corporations are paying attention because it is all about numbers. Now more than ever, retailers are faced with increased competition," says Lafayette Jones, president/CEO of Winston-Salem, NC-based Segmented Marketing Services, which specializes in marketing consumer goods to ethnic groups. "They are looking for ways to make stores more attractive to customers. The competition is intense. America is over-stored and consumers have many options."

Jones, an African-American who worked for major packaged goods

TARGETING MINORITIES

Minority employees as a percentage of all employees in the following job categories.

	TARGET CORP.	U.S.	RETAIL INDUSTRY
Officials & Managers	18%	12%	14%
Professionals	16%	16%	14%
Sales Workers	35%	23%	26%
All Employees	33%	26%	27%

Compared with all U.S. companies, the retail industry employs a higher percentage of "sales workers" and a higher percentage of "officials and managers," but a lower percentage of "professionals." Target beats the industry average. With regard to senior management, a category not tracked by the Equal Employment Opportunity Council, Target says that 7% of its vice presidents and higher are ethnic minorities. Of middle management, 14% are minorities.

Source: Target.com

companies for several decades, says, "There were the various censuses—the 80s, 90s and 2000—showing ethnic markets are large, growing and influential beyond their communities. The search for margins and increased revenues has led retailers to do what McDonalds, Coca-Cola and beer marketers have done for three or four decades. Some retailers lag behind packaged goods, some do not."

While cultural diversity is nothing new in a country founded on immigration, retailing was much more fragmented in the first half of the 20th century. In the 1940s, for example, a Jewish deli, rather than a supermarket chain, may have been the only place to purchase Passover foods. "There weren't all these large retailers in the 30s, 40s or 50s," says Tracy Mullin, president and CEO of the Washington, DC-based National

Retail Federation, which, through the recent formation of a diversity council, has initiated the first industry-wide diversity initiative."

Those retailers that realize the importance of diversity also understand that the nature of retail makes diversity significant in ways that it may not be for some other industries. "Retail is one industry where the rubber meets the road," says Rolando de Aguiar, a Cuban-American and senior executive vice president at Ames Department Stores, which initiated an intense diversity program two years ago. "What's different is, say, an investment banker deals with a CEO for a very large part of his fee. I have to deal with 250 individual transactions to get my revenue. That really puts the emphasis on customer service."

Diversity is not a quota issue, says Aguiar, "It's making sure we use some of the assets we have, in the district office or home office. We try to address needs of certain folks and try not to adapt everybody to a monolithic style."

Diversity recruitment is also a means of educating the company at large. Roger Smith, an African-American district manager for 10 Ames stores in the Washington, DC, beltway area, says he supervises Anglo store managers whose customer base is African-American. "It works both ways," says Smith, who joined Ames in 1992 and has managed his territory for three years. "We've had several success stories. I had a store run by a white manager in a 100% black neighborhood. Not only did he increase sales, he reduced shrinkage. It all lies with the way people communicate. Is it easier for an African-American? Probably. But satisfying customers and being able to deal with any situation is a big part of business."

COLOR BLIND CEOs?

It is easy for a retailer to say it employs a diverse workforce. But for a diversity initiative to truly work in a cohesive way, the commitment has to come from the chief executive officer on down. In addition to identifying markets where micro-marketing is necessary and installing appropriate

executives, an effective initiative requires special advertising and promotions to minority communities; strong communication with non-ethnic buyers, DMMs and GMMS; as well as recruitment practices that seek out eligible candidates at both college and advanced levels.

"There is not a lot of diversity at the corporate level," says NRF's Mullin. A lot of women are being groomed for top jobs. I think minorities are right behind. Companies that are successful in recruiting minorities are companies where the CEO really wants to embrace this as an issue."

A.T. Karney's Dowdle describes Arthur Martinez, Sears' retired CEO, as having been very aggressive about the retailer's efforts. "He had the diversity executive reporting to him. He was very passionate about it." Springs says Sears even has a Chairman's Diversity Advisement Council that meets quarterly to work on diversity strategies.

Minneapolis-based Best Buy has stepped up diversity efforts over the past year. Cynthia Newsom, director of corporate human resources for the electronics chain, describes the CEO's role as the "driver" of the entire effort. "It backtracks all the way up to the corporate office. But while you have to have somebody help drive, the responsibility is everybody's. Before we started this intense effort, diversity was left up to folks to drive this on their own. Now, we have executive sponsorship and dedicated resources. We're working on increasing the mix in the buying office—not that it's totally white. I just don't think our corporate office is as we would like it."

At Ames, de Aguiar says true diversity requires support from the whole board of directors and other key executives. De Aguiar himself is part of Ames' top management. Still, the day-to-day details of diversity never escape him. He notices, for example, that populations shift and neighborhoods become "more Hispanic." He also conducts Spanish-language customer surveys and ensures that signage in Hispanic stores is bilingual. "This is becoming increasingly important as we open more stores in urban areas like Philadelphia and Chicago. I'm bilingual and bicultural and it's a perspective I live and feel—perhaps somebody not playing this role can't."

A STATE OF MIND

For some retailers, diversity is becoming a state of mind that calls for an open-mindedness to seek the best person for a job. He or she may not be the person with whom Anglo management may have the closest personal golf course bonds. "We try to make people understand diversity is part of everything we do," says Newsom of Best Buy.

San Francisco-based Gap, which runs Gap, Old Navy and Banana Republic, goes so far as to offer human resources personnel special classes that focus on diversity. Even the retailer's Web site has a section devoted to diversity hiring, says Jamie Edgerton, manager of corporate communications. "We have three reputable brands that speak to a diverse audience," he adds. "It's important to have diverse individuals in place from the sales floor on up that speak to our audience."

At Sears, Springs says the company initiated "Diversity Days" this past summer. The program, which plays off Sears Days, is a company-wide, educational undertaking designed to teach employees about diversity.

Best Buy conducts focus groups on diversity. "We've done a lot around understanding the topic," says Callie Camp, Best Buy's recruitment manager, who adds that the retailer has also added a Web site to attract potential candidates. Target also uses its Web site to publicize its diversity commitment.

At Atlanta-based Home Depot, Rosemary Munie, director of recruitment, says diversity has come to work hand-in-hand with the company's practice of managerial autonomy and decision-making. This combination fosters the spirit that went into Gonzalez' view of the Villager's store in Elizabeth as "his" store. "There is a greater awareness today to look for people of all backgrounds," she says.

"It's very entrepreneurial here, so you're not going to feel like you're just one of many people. There are a lot of companies that put up posters in the hall about values and have meetings about what's important. They don't necessarily live up to it," Munie adds.

At Walgreens, John Grant, an African-American district manager who oversees 28 stores in the Chicago Loop district, says since day one, the Deerfield, IL-based retailer has always had this attitude. Walgreens simply believed in developing talented, aggressive people—regardless of what they looked like.

Grant, who joined the company 27 years ago, believes Walgreens may historically have been an exception. "One thing I see in conversations with [ethnic] people at a certain level at other retailers is, 'This is as far as we can go.' These are people who have tried another retailer and have come to us."

At Ames, de Aguiar, who worked in the oil and gas industry for the first 10 years of his career, believes ethnic recruiting has evolved. "Twenty years ago, Hispanics going into management wasn't very common. Over time, acceptance grew. But you had to prove you were good and you had to prove you were as good as the folks that belong there. That is less evident."

Lionel Sosa, a partner at Garcia LKS in San Antonio, a Hispanic-oriented marketing, consulting and advertising agency, believes more changes are yet to come. "All industries are slow to react. Some can change quickly. Others are slower. In 25 or 30 years, nobody will be having this conversation," he says.

From *Retail Merchandiser* magazine, March 2001, p. 28. © 2001 by Retailer Merchandiser. Reprinted by permission.

MANAGEMENT

Playing e-Detective

STAFF SMARTS: CHECKING OUT APPLICANTS ONLINE CAN
SAVE YOU TROUBLE—AND GET YOU INTO IT

By Chris Penttila

WHEN SERGE KNYSTAUTAS IS CONSIDERING APPLICANTS FOR a job, he goes a step beyond reading cover letters and calling references. He uses Web search engines. "By the time we're down to five or 10 candidates and we're figuring out who to bring in for an interview, I'll spend 15 minutes searching [online]," says Knystautas, 28, founder and president of Loki Technologies Inc., a six-employee tech company in Bethesda, Maryland, with annual sales of about $1 million. "It's a good gut check."

Knystautas keeps his searches simple. He pulls up Web sites of former employers, does searches using the applicant's name, peruses university sites, and cruises news archives for postings to chat groups. If the applicant worked on a project with a notable name or has written source code, he might try to see if there's some history of it online.

Knystautas and entrepreneurs like him are trying to simplify and improve hiring processes by surfing the Web. If you know what you're looking for and how to search for it, the Web is the ultimate repository of public information. At least 20 states have already posted their criminal and property databases on the Web, with more to come.

But using the Internet for background checks raises some interesting questions. How seriously should you take the information you find? If you find a picture online of an applicant drinking beer at a party, for example, will that be enough to convince you not to hire that person? What if you're reading up on the wrong individual and you don't realize it?

"The real danger here is that you can take things way out of context," says Richard M. Smith, a Brookline, Massachusetts, Internet security and privacy consultant. "Someone who wants to do this should take [the information] with a grain of salt."

The Background Biz

That may be difficult for entrepreneurs afraid a hire they make will go terribly wrong—for example, say they find an applicant with a history of violence. It's those fears that are spurring more employers to do background checks, says Baxter Gillespie, assistant vice president of the Workplace Solutions division at Alpharetta, Georgia-based Choicepoint Inc., which performs background checks on job applicants for a fee. Choicepoint verifies identity and work experience, checks credit and criminal history, and can "uncover information [applicants] may not have reported to employers," he says.

The events of September. 11 have brought the importance of background checks into the limelight. "On the smaller [business] side, we've seen a significant increase in the number of customers," Gillespie says. Employers are expanding the scope of what they look for, searching for records in multiple states where an applicant has lived, for example.

Of the 378,000 background checks Choicepoint did during the first quarter of last year, 9,900 applicants were found to have some sort of criminal conviction they didn't mention on the application, including fraud, theft and forgery. About 1,000 candidates had been charged with assault and battery, 311 rape or other sex offenses, and 37 had faced murder charges.

Statistics like those are compelling, but Gillespie warns entrepreneurs using the Net on their own to be very careful because the Fair Credit and Reporting Act—which requires anyone handling consumer data to be impartial and protective of individuals' privacy—applies to pre-employment background screening. Ask applicants to sign a waiver if you plan on poking around—or risk a future lawsuit.

Careful and Consistent

Before you dig too deeply, make sure you've got policies for performing online background checks, says Jack Vonder Heide, president of Technology Briefing Centers Inc., a firm in Oakbrook Terrace, Illinois, that teaches companies how to do background checks on the Web. "It's important once you've got the information to double-check it," Vonder Heide says.

Knystautas doesn't take Web research at face value. "You can't be sure of the quality [of the information] you're getting," he says. "It's a fuzzy science." He backs up Web searches with phone calls and face-to-face meetings with applicants, where he can ask questions based in part on his online research. If he has nagging questions, he asks them. "Unless [what I find online] is something really bad, I don't worry about it too much," he says. So far, he hasn't found anything "really bad" online about ap-plicants, although he has avoided potential investors based on what he's read about them.

If you use the Web to check out job applicants, always confirm the information and don't let your final decision hinge on what you find out over the Internet. Also be prepared for questions about your own background because Internet searches are a two-way street these days. Says Smith, "I would expect that the person being interviewed for a job would also be 'Googling' the company and their future boss. 'Googling' works both directions."

CHRIS PENTTILA *is a freelance journalist in the Chapel Hill, North Carolina, area. Contact her at diris@sitting-duck.com or www.sitting-duck.com.*

Article 15

AGE DISCRIMINATION

LEARNING FROM EXPERIENCE

Clare Ranson and Elizabeth Raper explain how the USA and Australia have dealt with age discrimination issues facing the UK in the future

Once the age discrimination provisions of the European equal treatment directive become law, both direct and indirect discrimination, harassment, and victimisation on grounds of age will be prohibited. UK laws implementing it have to be in place by December 2006.

CAUTIONARY TALE

Age discrimination is big business in the US, as Ford Motor's recent high profile $10.5 million settlement demonstrated. Current and former employees claimed that a revised performance evaluation system, introduced by management in 2000, unfairly discriminated against older, white, male employees on grounds of age, race and sex by giving a disproportionate number of them lower grades, thereby removing their scope to obtain salary increases and promotions. Ford did not admit liability in the settlement.

Many UK organisations are unaware that US employees in UK subsidiaries "controlled" by a US parent company, or UK-based US employees still employed by a US company, will be covered by the Adea. Age discriminatory practices could create liability for them in attorneys' fees and compensatory damages.

Age discrimination legislation in the US is not new. The federal Age Discrimination in Employment Act (Adea) was introduced in 1967 to protect any individual (including job applicants) aged 40 or older from discrimination by an employer on the grounds of age.

The Adea makes it unlawful for employers to discriminate because of an individual's age in connection with any term, condition or privilege of employment, including hiring, firing, promotion, lay-off, compensation, benefits, job assignments and training. Victimisation ("retaliation" in the US) against any person opposing age discriminatory employment practices (for example, in a claim or as a witness in proceedings) is also expressly prohibited.

AGEING UNDER THE SUN

Age discrimination was first tackled in Australia through human rights legislation in 1990. There is still no uniform legislation governing it, but all states and territories prohibit age discrimination in employment, education and training, accommodation, and goods and services.

The main effect of this in employment has been the abolition of the compulsory retirement age, although there are exceptions. Most states compulsorily retire judges, for example, and in South Australia an industrial agreement may stipulate a compulsory retirement age. There are other significant variations between states. Victoria still maintains a small-firms' threshold of five employees or fewer, while most states have no such thresholds. The majority do have occupational requirement exemptions.

The impact of age discrimination on redundancy schemes remains contentious. All schemes use length of service as a criterion for selection. In some states, employers can also take age into account when offering voluntary redundancy packages. Other states are still trying to decide whether this is discriminatory. Case law is undecided and many provisions found to be discriminatory remain in collective agreements.

One reason for case law being so unsettled is having two different arenas within which employees may pursue a claim. They can either claim unlawful dismissal on the grounds of age discrimination in the federal Industrial Commission (like the UK employment tribunal) or bring a discrimination claim before the Human Rights and Equal Opportunity Commission. Both commissions have different jurisdictions and case law and are dissimilar in outlook.

The issue of junior wages has also been at the forefront of debate. Many collective agreements provide for junior rates of pay based solely on employees' age, usually graduated up to age 21. Such pay rates are exempt from anti-discrimination legislation. Whether this is discriminatory was the subject of a national inquiry. This concluded there were no feasible alternatives and junior rates of pay may be justified when protecting youth employment.
Elizabeth Raper

LEGAL CHECKLIST

SELF-EMPLOYED

Some employment law extends protection to workers described as "self-employed but not running their own business." This category fits between employment and genuinely independent contractors.

In **Byrne Brothers v Baird** (2002 IRLR 86 EAT) subcontractors' contracts stated they were self-employed. They had to give an indemnity against liability for negligence and correct substandard work. No work was guaranteed and they could refuse assignments. They were not entitled to holiday pay or collective agreement benefits, but were bound by the health and safety policy.

The EAT found they had personal service contracts even though they could send substitutes, because this could only happen with the client's permission. The workers were dependent on the employer, did not have an arm's length relationship with it and so fell into this in-between category. The EAT concluded they were entitled to paid leave under the Working Time Regulations.

RACE DISCRIMINATION

An employer is liable for all acts of discrimination committed by its employees in the course of their employment. In **Haringey Council v** Al-Azzawi (2002 IDS 703EAT), Al-Azzawi brought two race claims against the council. The tribunal accepted the second, a derogatory statement by another worker about "bloody Arabs", for which his colleague received a warning. This was overturned by the EAT. The council had a racial awareness policy, trained employees on it and disciplined wrongdoers. It could rely on the statutory defence of having taken all reasonably practicable steps to prevent the discriminatory act.

RESTRAINT CLAUSES

In **Ward Evans Financial Services v Fox** (2002 IRLR 120 CA) financial advisers' restraint clauses prevented them from inducing customers to leave the company. They intended to set up in competition and had purchased a dormant company. A client asked if it could transfer business to them. They said it could and this eventually happened.

The CA decided setting up a dormant company was not in breach. Trading commenced only after employment ceased, and the advisers had not solicited the client. But by saying they could undertake its business, they had failed to put their employer's interests first. They had to pay damages for this.

Compiled by the Aikin Driver Partnership

The courts and the US Equal Employment Opportunity Commission are responsible for policing the provisions of the Adea. Whether the UK will establish a separate age commission to monitor compliance with its new legislation is still under consideration.

Unlike the equal treatment directive, the Adea does not expressly include specific concepts of direct and indirect discrimination. Consequently, the federal courts have been left to clarify the act's exact scope. They are currently split across the districts about whether employees are protected from apparently neutral criteria that adversely affect older workers.

Most US employees used to retire between the ages of 45 and 55. Mandatory retirement ages are now generally prohibited under the Adea. Unless employers can show a fixed retirement age is due to a bona fide occupational qualification, or the employee is 65 or older, has been employed for two years or more in an "executive or policymaking position", and will retire on at least US $44,000 (£31,000) a year, enforced retirement at a specific age is discriminatory. The UK is likely to outlaw mandatory retirement ages, but will probably allow exceptions in prescribed circumstances.

Federal law in the US creates a basic minimum framework, and individual states are free to enact more expansive protection. They're chosen to do so on thresholds. With the exception of Louisiana and Mississippi, the threshold for triggering state anti-age discrimination protection is lower than the federal threshold of 20 employees. In many states it is five employees or fewer, or there is no threshold at all. The equal treatment directive has no thresholds but, like the US states, the UK could use derogations to exempt small employers (at least initially), as currently under the Disability Discrimination Act 1995, if it chooses.

Some states in the US, including Iowa, Kansas and Oregon, have reduced the qualifying age for protection from 40 to 18 years or older. Other state laws simply refer to "age", without specifying a qualifying requirement. Unlike the Adea, the equal treatment directive is not solely intended to protect older workers. We will have to wait and see whether the UK opts for a minimum age cut off.

Clare Ranson and Elizabeth Raper are employment lawyers with Baker & McKenzie in California and London

From *People Management*, March 7, 2002, pp. 20-21. © 2002 by Clare Ranson.

Teamwork Aids HRIS Decision Process

An HRIS rollout is too daunting a task to be left to one person.
Using teams to select and implement a system can ensure success.

By Frank Jossi

Last year, Camp Dresser & McKee Inc., a Cambridge, Mass.-based environmental consulting and engineering firm, decided it was time to relegate its human resource information system (HRIS) to the dustbin of history. After 12 years with the system, it was time to replace it with something a little more state-of-the-art. The company turned to Shawn Higgins, an HRIS specialist, to help lead the charge to select and install a new system. Higgins hired a consultant to move the process along and write a request for proposal (RFP). And, to assist him with this decision, Higgins created a team composed of all the major stakeholders in the software system, from information technology (IT) to finance, payroll to recruiting. He even brought to the team people he suspected would view with cynicism any new system the 3,500-employee firm purchased. He wound up with a team of 40 people. Higgins hopes that by making this a group effort, Camp Dresser will not only end up with the best HRIS to meet its needs (as this article goes to press, a final decision is expected shortly) but that there will be buy-in throughout the company, since every department played a role in selecting the software.

"In talking to people here and elsewhere I've found they don't understand the ramifications of these systems," says Higgins. "We wanted everyone's input to do something we believe will be a best-of-class system."

Members of the team have spent a great deal of time together, and apart, on the project. They met at least once a month, sometimes more often. They interviewed their own staffs to find out what they wanted in an HRIS package. They assisted the consultant in drafting the 65-page RFP, and they sat through days and days of presentations. Despite the enormous workload of managing a large team and the commitment required of its members, Higgins believes the effort will prove to be worth the trouble. Sure, it may have been an imperfect system— he concedes that if he had it to do over again the team's size would shrink dramatically—but, so far, it appears to be working.

Buying an HRIS solution can be among the most costly software decisions a company makes.

Increasing the Odds

Buying an HRIS solution can be among the most costly software decisions a company makes, and personnel will have to live with the decision for years to come. By forming a team to select the software (and, later, another for implementation), a company gains a level of buy-in from

leading stakeholders and creates a group of employees who can help their colleagues with training and support during and after implementation. Giving managers a voice will make them more comfortable with the final decision.

"If you get together a cross-functional group of various departments and get them involved in the process you have a greater chance of success," says Gene Sorbo, a former consultant and currently president and chief executive officer of Better Way Technologies Inc. in Fitchburg, Mass., which sells web-based HRIS services. "It's not going to be a good product if only HR is happy. If other groups aren't included it can be difficult."

The first challenge facing companies is finding the right person to serve as team leader. Too often, companies select a team leader who is more interested in advancing his or her career than choosing the right software. Sorbo recalls a client that selected a particularly aggressive manager to lead a software selection team. He took over the selection process with the idea he would use his success in that post to move forward in his company. Yet he did not have a great deal of technical expertise or HR experience, and, after a chorus of boos followed the implementation, the individual found "his head on a chopping block," says Sorbo.

A good leader, in contrast, will hold meetings on a regular basis that are not insufferably long, gently nudge team mem-

bers to gather information from their staffs and keep team members abreast of developments through e-mail or other means. Team leaders should lead the team to final choices as judiciously as possible and schedule vendor presentations as close to one another as possible before having the team move toward a final selection. Team leaders are part coaches, part nags and part traffic directors who must keep their eye on getting to the final choice in a timely manner.

Selecting the Team

The individual leading the HRIS selection process should assemble a team made up of representatives from such key departments as finance, payroll, benefits, IT, training and, of course, HR, says Sorbo. HRIS team leaders should seek employees with a technical understanding of software who may have been on selection committees in the past and who possess a keen understanding of the needs of their departments and of the organization as a whole, he says. The ideal is to have both functional and technical people involved.

"Creating an HRIS implementation team is really a competency management exercise," says Wayne Tarken, principal in Cherry Hill, N.J.-based HR Technology Group and a member of the Society for Human Resource Management HR Technology Management Committee. "You first identify the processes and stakeholders that will be impacted by the new technology and identify their program requirements and specifications. Then you identify and select those employees who have the competencies to work on the team, have knowledge of the technology issues and understand the requirements of the various stakeholders."

Once the members are chosen, teams can meet as frequently as once a week or as rarely as once a month, depending on the level of activity necessary to get the job done. In the early stages, teams typically meet once every week or two, says Sorbo, with frequent e-mail follow-ups to team members by the team leader.

When it comes to the size of the team, smaller usually is better. "Large teams just aren't very effective," says Tarken, who is also a member of the SHRM HR Technology X-Change advisory board. "You should identify everyone who is important and have them on the team, but you don't want more than 12 to 15 people because anything larger than that means nothing would get done."

In the initial meetings the team should document precisely how certain functions currently are handled in the organization, says Joe Collette, systems development manager at Boston-based Putnam Investments Inc. With that understanding, a team can better judge a new HRIS and how it might change the way payroll and benefits are administered, for example, and whether the company can adapt to new ways of doing business. Knowing the impact a system will have, and how it will transform the way a company does business, should lead to a more informed choice, Collette believes.

Making sure the managers of team members understand the level of commitment that will be demanded is important, says Lisa Plantamura, president of Phoenix Consulting Services in Mount Tabor, N.J. If the team leader is not getting what he needs out of members because of problems with managers, he should "make an issue out of it" on behalf of team members, says Plantamura. Steps should be taken to recognize team members' contributions and ensure that their performance reviews do not suffer because they took time away from their regular duties to aid in the HRIS selection process, she says.

Connecting with Consultants

Retaining the services of an outside consultant is crucial for the selection process to succeed, says Sorbo. Once the team establishes the attributes it wants in a system—usually a list long enough that no software could possibly fulfill each and every function—a consultant can bring the team back to reality by identifying the four or five core elements it really needs. Then, the consultant can speed the process by recommending four or five promising software packages out of the more than 100 HRIS programs available.

"In the selection phase a consultant can get the group to walk through the process in an advisory manner, and then the team makes the decision for itself," says Plantamura. "As a consultant, I suggest vendors, but I never say 'Use PeopleSoft.' I make them aware of the pitfalls, advantages and other experiences of people who have used various programs."

A consultant serves another important function, says Steve Chinn, director of compensation and benefits at Summit, N.J.-based Novartis Pharmaceuticals Corp. and leader of his company's HRIS selection team. Last year, Novartis hired a consultant who helped the HRIS team ask tough questions of vendors to discover whether their systems would actually work in the company's computing environment. The team and consultant asked what Windows versions the HRIS software was compatible with and what kind of upgrades were in store for clients. Chinn wanted a system capable of tracking with his company's transition to Windows 2000, a feature not all vendors could offer in a timely manner.

After a team has whittled down the number of systems being considered to two or three, Sorbo suggests the consultant or some team members make the effort to talk at length with references and visit them onsite to see how the software works. Any system for which references are not made available should be eliminated from consideration. When possible, the team members should find references within their own industry to see how the software is used under circumstances similar to their own, says Sorbo.

Once the selection is made, most of the non-technical team members can be excused from the team, with thanks. Many companies create a separate implementation team that includes members of the selection team with the appropriate expertise. At Novartis, Chinn asked five people from the nine-member selection team to serve on the implementation team. As Plantamura points out, implementation oversight requires the kind of detail work that sends non-techies heading for the door.

Ideally, the software selected should go through a rigorous review process conducted by the team.

The Real World

Ideally, the software selected should go through a rigorous review process conducted by the team, and the winning vendor will have the best product at the best price. The reality, however, is often much different. Many companies use teams to study vendors but often wind up choosing the product of a company with which they already have an established relationship. Chinn's team looked at six vendors before picking HR Perspective, from ADP Inc. in

Roseland, N.J. Novartis already used ADP's payroll software and liked it, giving that vendor a slight edge over the others.

Higgins says Camp Dresser is also leaning toward a software company with which it has an existing relationship. Camp Dresser resells Oracle software and serves as an Oracle partner. When Oracle heard Camp Dresser was in the market for an HRIS, it flew Camp Dresser executives to Silicon Valley to view Oracle Human Resources for a day. Oracle emphasized the existing relationship between the companies and offered a discount if an agreement could be reached quickly. While many on the software selection team were impressed by the PeopleSoft system, Higgins suspects that Oracle's outreach efforts will make it a shoo-in.

When the decision of a selection team is undermined or its conclusion pre-ordained, a company risks making the whole process look like a farce. "If you encourage a team to go out and do its own thing and make its own decisions and the ultimate result is something different, it's definitely demotivating," says Tarken. On the other hand, Chinn says no one left his team feeling their work was wasted since ADP's product, in the end, proved to be the best one for Novartis.

All the work can come to naught in other ways. Chinn's company is owned by a large Netherlands-based conglomerate, which recently instructed all subsidiaries that a common system, SAP, will be installed in 2002. HR/Perspective's reign as Novartis's HRIS package of choice will last less than three years. "I think the process would have worked even better if we didn't find out near the end of last year that all the facilities would go to a common system that would be SAP," Chinn laughs. "At least I get to keep this thing going until the year 2002."

Putting together an HRIS team will take some time, pull people away from other work and be a challenge to understand how systems will work in your environment. By choosing a diverse group of people who will be using the system, adding a consultant to the mix and keeping everyone focused on the result, you may pick a system nearly everyone likes. And if you suffer a few naysayers, at least you can remind them that all members of the HRIS team represented their constituencies and had a voice.

Frank Jossi is a freelance writer in St. Paul, Minn., specializing in technology, HR and business.

From *HR Magazine*, June 2001, pp. 165, 167, 169, 171-172 by Frank Jossi. © 2001 by Society for Human Resource Management, Alexandria, VA. Reprinted by permission.

A wealth of choice

Advances in human resource information technology and hosting models make solutions available for employers of all sizes.

By Craig Gunsauley

Widespread adoption of Internet-based technology is making it easier for employers of all sizes to implement human resource information systems (HRIS) that host employee data and give users the ability to conduct transactions.

The integration of data from separate systems made possible by client-server enterprise resource planning (ERP) systems is now available in Internet-based solutions through interfaces that are relatively easy to create and maintain.

For ERP clients, the change means that software formerly housed on the client desktop is now hosted by a server, either an internal system maintained by the client or an external system operated by an application service provider (ASP) and accessed through the Web.

Integrated systems that used to cost tens of millions of dollars and require platoons of consultants to convert data, customize applications and provide training can now be implemented in six to nine months, with all costs defined over the course of a three- to five-year service agreement.

As a result, ASP solutions originally designed to make systems affordable for medium-sized and small employers are being embraced by large organizations as well.

The advances in functionality of the Web-native systems are increasingly leading organizations away from expensive customized solutions. Baltimore-based software consulting and services organization Cedar, for example, finds that a large majority of respondents to a survey of 300 global organizations are moving away from customized solutions towards package-based, off-the-shelf products that can be implemented faster with lower total cost of ownership. More than 80% of the Cedar survey respondents say they plan to use a packaged application rather than an internally developed solution.

Organizations seeking to enable more employee and manager self-service find that Web-native systems can integrate data from several separate systems into a single point of access allowing in-depth information lookup and transactional capabilities.

As HR information systems house the data required to build these role-based portals, HR is increasingly taking the lead in driving corporate portal strategies, industry experts say. Cedar finds that 57% of North American respondents now have a portal strategy, up from 40% in 2000.

Client-server based ERP systems from vendors such as PeopleSoft, Oracle and SAP are evolving into Web-native systems that can be implemented without costly and time-consuming customization and training. These systems can be installed and maintained internally or delivered by ASPs through the Internet.

To oversee a successful technology strategy, HR must understand the value of the system and how it improves internal business processes, points out Cedar principal Helene Slowik.

These new systems often create new roles for HR and benefits staff and offer organizations the opportunity to streamline internal processes to fit the technology rather than attempting to customize the technology to adapt to established processes. The system should be able to deliver efficiencies such as reduced transaction costs and cycle times and improvements in employee satisfaction.

"More often companies look at application service providers in order to get out of conflicts with internal information technology departments," Slowik comments.

Many organizations seek to evaluate systems in terms of cost savings and staff reductions, when more significant returns can be realized through improved productivity of staff and business processes.

ASPs offer much quicker implementation if the organization can accept the functionality of the system. Because vendors host data from multiple organizations, systems cannot be easily customized for one client. However, these systems can be configured and modified to meet the needs of individual client organizations.

"If you're very content with it out of the box, the ASP model is attractive," Slowik observes. An ASP solution can be a temporary arrangement while the organization brings its internal resources up to date.

"Once you outsource the processes, you have to let go somewhat.

You move to a vendor management role, which is often a completely new role for HR," Slowik says. "HR is becoming more of a broker of services to employees rather than a provider of services."

In-house vs. outsourced

The choices that organizations face when evaluating HR and benefits systems are illustrated by the experiences of American Express and T. Rowe Price. Both organizations are upgrading their HR systems and seeking portal strategies to improve self-service.

American Express decided to outsource all health and welfare plan administration to Unifi Network, a Mellon Financial Corp. company. Implemented in six months, the arrangement provides employee self-service capabilities via the Web and through interactive voice response. Unifi also operates a service call center for American Express personnel.

"We wanted to take it more toward a self-service environment year-round," says Arlene Soto Baltrusitis, vice president of benefits at American Express. "As we looked at the various systems and how integrated they are, we realized that we could exit the administration of benefits."

This arrangement allowed American Express to significantly reduce benefits and HR staff. With some 60,000 active employees, the company has just five benefits personnel for health and welfare plans and seven staff for retirement plans.

Turnaround time for benefits transactions is now much faster because employees have immediate access to the data and transaction capabilities.

"When I came to American Express a little over two years ago, I was surprised at how paper-intensive we still were," Baltrusitis says.

The first year produced higher costs due to the implementation, but American Express will see a return on investment before the end of the five-year service agreement with Unifi Network.

"Our employees have received this extremely well," Baltrusitis comments. "More than 60% of our employees enrolled through the Web-based system the first year. Next year, we won't have the IVR options, so the total enrollment will be Web-based."

The switch has totally eliminated paper from the benefits administration and has directed all employee calls to Web sites and Unifi's service call center, Baltrusitis says. "For my team, it allows us to deal with the bigger strategic issues that need to be addressed. It has made us more effective."

Mutual fund company T. Rowe Price, on the other hand, recently began an upgrade from PeopleSoft 7.5 to the Internet-based 8.3. Begun in early March, the system should go live by mid-July in time for year-end processing in August, according to HRIS manager Karen Prehoda. Self-service capabilities for the firm's 3,600 employees will be implemented next year. Manager self-service, which costs extra, will be implemented in the latter stages of the project.

Because T. Rowe owns and operates the system, this upgrade will be overseen by a seven-member steering committee and involve 18 HR, six finance and six IT staffers plus one legal advisor and three Cedar consultants, Prehoda explains. The entire project will take about three years to complete, she adds.

Prehoda says that the implementation will eliminate many of the customized functions built in to the PeopleSoft system over the past 10 years. "A big focus is to go back to a vanilla PeopleSoft system."

Yearly maintenance fees for PeopleSoft 8.3 equal about 20% of the purchase cost, Prehoda states. "It's very costly to implement these systems and upgrade. It's a huge effort that includes a lot of people. It's not the technology that's complicated; it's the business process reorganization.

"It doesn't matter what system you choose, because you either have to change your processes or change the systems."

Training for HR and benefits staff, technical personnel and line managers will require a large effort, Prehoda predicts. "It's probably going to take three years to get where we want to be. We could probably forge ahead and do it faster, but ultimately we're conservative. We don't want to be on the bloody cutting edge. We'll let others take that lead and learn from their experiences."

Small choices

While large organizations debate the merits of internal systems versus outsource solutions, even small employers with 50 to 500 employees have a wealth of affordable HRIS choices to consider, says Richard Frantzreb, president of Advanced Personnel Systems, a publishing firm in Roseville, Calif.

Frantzreb notes there are more than 1,500 vendors of HR and benefits related software systems. He publishes a guidebook that examines the functionality of about 150 of these systems and recently released HR-Demo Rom: Inexpensive HR Information Systems. This includes specifications and demonstrations for 18 HR systems that cost $2,000 or less to purchase or $30 a month or less to access through an ASP.

Frantzreb says these systems include enough functionality out of the box to serve most of the needs of small and mid-sized employers. "Most buyers overlook most of their choices," he comments.

—C.G.

UNIT 3

Creating a Productive Work Environment

Unit Selections

Key Points to Consider

• What are some things you might do to motivate employees, especially in a downsizing environment? What are some of the things that motivate you?

• In today's environment, do you think people should be viewed more as partners or as workers?

• What strategies could you employ to communicate more effectively with your peers or your instructor? What things can destroy effective communication? What role does gender play in communication?

 **Links: www.dushkin.com/online/**
These sites are annotated in the World Wide Web pages.

Commission on the Future of Worker-Management Relations
   http://www.dol.gov/dol/_sec/public/media/reports/dunlop/dunlop.htm
The Downsizing of America
   http://www.nytimes.com/specials/downsize/glance.html
Employee Incentives and Career Development
   http://www.snc.edu/socsci/chair/336/group1.htm
Foundation for Enterprise Development
   http://www.fed.org/aboutus/aboutus.htm

Whenever anything is being accomplished, it is being done, I have learned, by a monomaniac with a mission.

—Peter Drucker

For years, management theorists have indicated that the basic functions of management are to plan, direct, organize, control, and staff organizations. Unfortunately, those five words only tell what the manager is to do. They do not tell the manager how to do it. Being a truly effective manager involves more than just those five tasks. It involves knowing what goals to set for the organization, pursuing those goals with more desire and determination than anyone else in the organization, communicating the goals once they have been established, and having other members of the organization adopt those goals as their own.

Motivation is one of the easiest concepts to understand, yet one of the most difficult to implement. Often the difference between successful and mediocre organizations is that people in successful organizations are motivated, and the management is engaged in going "The Extra Mile: Motivating Employees to Exceed Expectations," and have "A Plan for Keeping Employees Motivated." They are excited about the company, about what they do for the company, and about the company's products or services. Effective organizations build upon past successes, recognizing the truth of the old saying, "Nothing succeeds like success." If people feel good about themselves and good about their organization, then they are probably going to do a good job. Whether it is called morale, motivation, or enthusiasm, it still amounts to the same fragile concept—simple to understand, difficult to create and build, and very easy to destroy.

In order to maintain a motivated workforce for any task, it is necessary to establish an effective reward system. A truly motivated worker will respond much more effectively to a carrot than to a stick. Turned-on workers are having their needs met and are responding to the goals and objectives of the organization. They do an outstanding job because they want to, which results in an outstanding company. "Employees or Partners?" and "What Makes You Tick?" address some of the ways that organizations help motivate employees.

Perhaps the single most important skill for any manager, or, for that matter, any human being, is the ability to communicate. People work on this skill throughout their education in courses such as English and speech. They attempt to improve communication through an array of methods and media, which range from the printed word, e-mail, and television, to rumors and simple conversation. Yet managers often do not do a very good job of communicating with their employees or their customers. This is very unfortunate, because ineffective communication can often negate all of the other successes that a firm has enjoyed. "Enhancing Your Writing Skills" is something that a manager must strive for if you want to have people working together for a common goal. Managers and the firms they represent must hon-

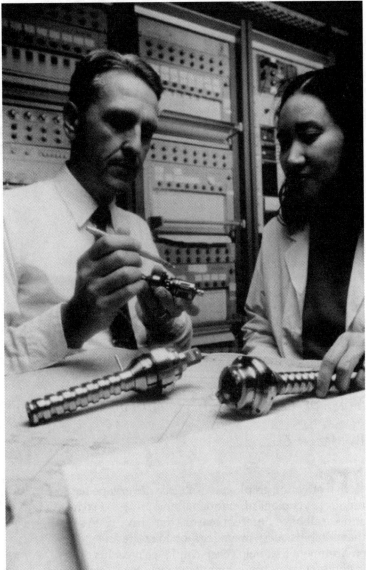

estly communicate their goals, as well as their instructions, to their employees, and this will often be in writing. If the manager does not do so, the employees will be confused and even distrustful, because they will not understand the rationale behind the instructions. If the manager is successful in honestly communicating the company's goals, ideals, and culture to the employees, and is able to build the motivation and enthusiasm that are necessary to successfully accomplish those goals, then he or she has become not just a manager but a leader, and that is indeed rare.

Creating a positive work environment is not easy. Communicating with and motivating people, whether employees, volunteers, citizens, or Boy Scouts, is difficult to do. Managers, however, are faced with the task of doing exactly that.

employees or partners?

You can win your staff's loyalty by treating them as associates, not subordinates.

By Milton Zall

otivating employees isn't easy. Everyone has unique psychological, emotional, and professional needs, and we all have different reasons that drive us to satisfy them. Yet it's every manager's job to create an environment that helps each employee meet his or her individual needs while simultaneously reaching bottom-line business objectives.

In his famous "Hierarchy of Needs" theory, sociologist Abraham Maslow showed the gradual escalation of workers' drives and motivations:

Physiological needs are at the bottom of the hierarchy and involve basic physical needs—the ability to acquire food, shelter, and clothing. These needs must be satisfied before an individual can progress up the hierarchical ladder.

Step two in the hierarchy involves safety needs. An individual requires a safe, nonthreatening workplace—job security, safe equipment, and a secure work environment.

Step three involves social needs. Once a person's basic needs are met, the individual can concentrate on his/her social needs—contact and friendship with fellow workers, social activities, and other opportunities.

As we move up the hierarchical ladder, we come to ego, which consists of external recognition, acknowledgment, and rewards.

The highest level of need is self-actualization—realizing our dreams and using our gifts, talents, and potential.

Progress through this hierarchy is the essential quality of human life. When people's basic needs are addressed and they feel secure, they begin to focus on internal motivation. Some individuals pursue material luxury, while others pursue their thirst for knowledge or artistic expression. Many are compelled by a desire to lead or help others, to play the hero, or to shine in society. A manager's challenge is to discern what makes each employee tick and to motivate each employee accordingly.

But external rewards work only temporarily. You and other managers need to create an environment where employees are committed to their jobs, their fellow workers, and their company. But this is a challenge. Although as a manager you can't play the role of psychologist or psychoanalyst, it benefits your company if you can discover who every worker is—get to know their drives, special gifts, abilities, hopes, and plans for the

future. If you take time to discover these attributes, you'll be able to find the best fit between employees and their jobs—a crucial step in building motivation.

ALIGNING BUSINESS OBJECTIVES AND EMPLOYEE MOTIVATION

Most organizations are doing away with traditional hierarchies, instead emphasizing teamwork and cooperation. For employees, this means fewer promotions and more collaboration. For employers, this means coming up with new ways to coax maximum versatility and productivity from all team members. Incentive plans are an increasingly popular strategy for aligning organizational and individual goals by treating employees as partners in both the risks and the successes of the business.

On a personal level, there are some common needs among all employees: the need for self-expression, the hope for professional development and career advancement, the desire to be accepted as a team member, the wish to be respected by management and to take pride in their work, and the need to be acknowledged, trusted, and rewarded. Through strategic communications, management's job is to communicate company goals; market, industry, and business information; and future plans—and to invite employee feedback. As a manager, you must learn how to place people in roles where they can use their abilities and make progress toward their personal goals. If you fail to do this, your company may experience substantial financial loss due to turnover, accidents, lawsuits, rebates, refunds, and loss of customers and sales.

Managers who encourage employees to use initiative and to set higher challenges for themselves achieve better results than managers who incite competition among employees.

You and other managers must learn how to create a corporate culture and a supportive work environment. This begins with strong leadership and excellent management. It continues with effective human resources strategies—positive discipline, fair and just treatment for all, clearly defined policies, and career and personal development training programs. It demands effective organizational communications, tools to facilitate communication, team assignments, reward programs, objective appraisals, adequate pay, and good benefits and company activities.

Because employees want personal recognition, it's important for them to know that management is aware of their existence and that managers recognize them, remember their names, and greet them. Individuals and departments need to be thanked for hard work and special feats, and they should be rewarded for unique contributions. Managers who encourage employees to use initiative and to set higher challenges for themselves achieve better results than managers who incite competition among employees. Gaining personal accomplishments at the expense of others undermines teamwork and threatens customer service. You can win the loyalty of your employees and get their best input by treating them as partners, by showing concern, by listening, and by sharing.

SOME PROGRESS HAS BEEN MADE

Over the past 25 years, as companies began experimenting with innovative workplace practices, two distinctly American high-performance models have emerged. The first is a U.S. version of lean production that relies on employee involvement. The second is a U.S. version of team production that relies on employee empowerment for performance gains. Productivity improves the most when work is reorganized so employees have the training, opportunity, and authority to participate effectively in decision making. Performance improves when employees know that they won't be punished for expressing unpopular ideas and won't lose their jobs if they help to improve productivity.

Employees want to receive a fair share of any performance gains—assurances that unionized workers in high-performance companies already enjoy. Attempts to improve performance by manipulating compensation packages have proven counterproductive. After all, it's far easier to design an incentive system that will do management's work than it is to reach consensus about goals and problems or to confront difficulties when they arise. The average life of an incentive system is about five years, and when the system stops paying off, employees turn against it. Soon precious attention, time, and money are expended on endless debates about the incentive system.

On the other hand, companies have seen remarkable gains in productivity and performance when workplace reorganizations make employees partners in the enterprise. The best efforts include employment security, gain sharing, and incentives to take part in training. In this sense, compensation packages are an important component of the human resource practices that are necessary to support high-performance work systems.

What can you and other managers do? You can focus on paying people equitably rather than using pay as an instrument of motivation. You should avoid coupling pay with yearly or quarterly performance and promote the top 10% to 15% of employees for outstanding long-term contributions. The poorest performers should be weeded

out, while the rest should be praised for good performance and recognized through other means.

THE MOTIVATING ORGANIZATION

A successful approach is often to carve employees into a share of the profit created by their part of the company. Profit should be defined in relevant cash-flow terms after covering the cost of all capital employed—a measure that Stern Stewart & Co. calls Economic Value Added (EVA). EVA provides employees with three clear incentives: to improve profitability, to grow profitability, and to withdraw resources from inefficient activities. EVA also directly ties decisions to the net present value of their enterprise.

More than 50 prominent companies have adopted the EVA approach to profit sharing. All key managers at Quaker Oats have been on an EVA sharing plan for several years, and Scott Paper Company introduced an EVA incentive program for all salaried employees at the beginning of 1993. Another example is Starbucks. Just as IBM is remembered by its strict dress code and Microsoft is known for its laid-back culture, Starbucks will be remembered for its innovative employee policies and its employee-focused management style. Although Starbucks is a multibillion dollar company, the company management structure is relatively flat. Howard Schultz, chairman and CEO, guides a team of about 10 other senior executives. Starbucks company power is divided under the control of three people or functional officers: the chief executive officer (Howard Schultz), the chief financial officer (Michael Casey), and the chief operations officer (Orin Smith). From there, a handful of regional managers oversee nearly 2,000 branch managers, who are responsible for all the partners in their own stores. Managers at the store level feel much closer to top executives. Store managers are encouraged to develop a career within the company, and the relatively flat management structure allows them to do so.

Intrinsic motivation—being motivated by challenge and enjoyment—is essential to creativity. But extrinsic motivation—being motivated by recognition and money—doesn't necessarily hurt. The most creative artists tend to be motivated more by challenge, but they also tend to be motivated by recognition. Can employee motivation be accomplished? Not easily, but if you plan it with sincerity and care and incorporate the notion of employee partnership, you'll succeed.

Milton Zall is a freelance writer who specializes in taxes, investments, and HR/business issues. He is a certified internal auditor and a registered investment advisor. You can reach him at miltzall@starpower.net.

From *Strategic Finance*, April 2001, pp. 62-65. © 2001 by Strategic Finance, published by Institute of Management Accountants, Montvale, NJ. Reprinted by permission.

The extra mile: Motivating employees to exceed expectations

David King

As business competition intensifies worldwide, companies must strive more than ever before to improve quality and production while controlling costs. How will they meet this challenge? While savvy management and continuing advances in technology can help, in the final analysis, the determining factor in a firm's success is its capacity for motivating employees to work together and exceed expectations.

How can you inspire your staff to go the extra mile? Beyond competitive compensation, strategic financial management professionals seek the opportunity to contribute their best and receive meaningful recognition for their efforts. Consider these tips for giving employees the incentive they need to rise to levels of truly extraordinary performance:

1. Invite open communication. You'll never be able to take full advantage of your staff's creativity unless you ensure they're comfortable expressing their ideas. By encouraging open discussion, you give employees a sense of ownership and pride in the business—a potent motivator. It signals that what they have to say really matters and that their contributions count.

Make sure every information exchange is a positive experience for all employees. Don't let even one innovative suggestion go to waste by allowing anyone to dismiss or make light of the ideas of another. Inviting team members to continually share their observations, concerns and recommendations will establish open communication as one of the defining elements of your department's culture.

2. Let your staff experiment. Don't just listen to employees' suggestions. Give them a chance to put their most promising ideas into action. Encourage alternative approaches to reaching common goals, and be prepared to accept honest mistakes along the way. While it's true that allowing staff to employ their own methods and make their own decisions is not entirely risk-free for either you or the organization, it's the only way to foster innovation and professional growth—and to motivate employees to go above and beyond expectations.

3. Communicate big-picture issues. For communication to be truly open, it must work both ways. You can't expect employees to communicate with you if you don't communicate with them. Not only should you listen to your team, it's also important for you to share your own knowledge of the company's overall strategies. Clearly convey your organization's vision, and clarify for each individual his or her role in accomplishing team objectives. Showing them how they fit into the big picture will significantly boost the quality of your employees' decisions and, in the process, their self-confidence and overall productivity.

4. Stress cross-functional teamwork. As the expertise of strategic financial management professionals becomes more sought after in interdepartmental teams, it's especially important for your staff to work well alongside employees with a variety of professional backgrounds and experience. Making the experience a motivational one rather than a chore requires some intervention by management.

Clarify the team's overall goals, and help them understand that these goals are more important than individual agendas. Encourage teammates to work together to come up with a solution—whether in a meeting or informally. If everyone participates on the team, especially in meetings, then employees feel a sense of ownership and responsibility, which can help move the project along. Help them see the value of sharing responsibility for project outcomes, and reward group accomplishments as much as you do individual achievement.

5. Recognize employees for their successes. Beyond financial rewards, perhaps the greatest motivator of all is for workers to simply know they're appreciated—that their contributions aren't going unnoticed. In fact, in a recent survey commissioned by RHI Management Resources, respondents revealed that lack of recognition is one of the primary reasons employees quit their jobs.

Make sure the everyday pressures of your job don't prevent you from taking the time to acknowledge the

outstanding efforts of your team. A simple "good job" inscribed on a particularly well-thought-out report—or a staff lunch at the conclusion of a major project—can go a long way toward reinforcing a sense of accomplishment and team spirit.

In an increasingly competitive business environment, a firm's success hinges on its ability to engage the talents and ideas of all of its employees. You can motivate your team of professionals to contribute their best work by creating an environment that is open to new ideas and continually celebrates outstanding performance.

David King is regional manager, Western Canada, for RHI Management Resources, North America's largest consulting services firm providing senior-level accounting and finance professionals on a project basis.

What makes you tick?

People are defined by the work they do. This is why leading psychologist Neil Conway is concerned that work/life policies fail to consider why we work at all. **Iona Bower** talks to him about his views on motivational theory

Although motivation gurus are a creation of the last 20 years, the subject is ages old. "The definition of motivation has been questioned ever since psychology began," says Neil Conway, a researcher in organisational psychology.

Conway's work for London University's Birkbeck College means that he is well aware that although motivation lies at the centre of much psychological study, it remains complicated.

For this reason, Conway suggests, work psychologists have defined motivation by studying five components: what initiates it, how the effort can be increased, how it can be sustained, what ends it and where it is directed.

These components could be looked at as different human drives, but what are the things that people want enough to begin and continue to be motivated by?

While many employers assume they are status or money, Conway says that we work because we have an intrinsic need to work.

"Certain approaches take the view that there are extrinsic and intrinsic motivators. Extrinsic factors are those which are 'out there' in your environment, such as benefits. They are also what are called hygiene factors [things like pay and job security which are extrinsic to the job and not motivating in themselves, but without which employees would feel demotivated].

"There are also intrinsic motivators," he says, "which are things you find personally rewarding or intrinsically motivating, such as the ability to express yourself within your work, have autonomy or a definite career path." He believes these intrinsic factors have the deepest effect on employee motivation. "Things that are much closer to your task such as your peers, or the nature of the task itself, are much more likely to determine how hard you are working," says Conway.

"Pay might be very important for someone doing a crappy job, because they might be doing it solely to get an income. For someone like me it's not so important because I like what I do"

Much of his work looks at the importance of improving job design and reward and development in order to achieve a successful HR strategy. "There is a lot of research being done into work design. Getting feedback from people you respect is very important—that is your own belief that you can do things. People generally like to feel that they are able to perform tasks, especially if they are part of their identity."

The concept of work as informing personal identity is central to finding out what motivates people at work.

"Research has found that if people won the lottery and were freed from the financial constraints of work, they would continue to work anyway," says Conway.

"It appears that work performs this identity function. It is the way you produce things, are creative, display your skills and your knowledge. Also it provides a structure to your day, and so organises your life outside work. It is generally found that one of the desirable qualities of work is in organising your time and your energy."

So, considering motivation in terms of job design could have a big influence on the way that people work and the tools employers use to motivate staff.

This also has an effect on the way employers might look at pay. "One of the difficult things about pay is that it tends to symbolise lots of other things as well," says Conway. He argues that while pay is a simple issue for employers, a pay rise can mean many more things to the employee: "It could mean their effort is more appreciated. To some, more pay can mean a higher status, or suggest you are going to be promoted later on."

Conway suggests that monetary reward is only a motivator for people that value extrinsic factors—often those for whom the task is not central to the fact of their working.

"Pay might be very important for someone doing a crappy job, because they might be doing it solely to get an income. For someone like me in the kind of job that doesn't give you many rewards in terms of pay, it's not so important because I like what I do."

However, while this may sound like good news for employers, it is unfortunately not as simple as that, and pay is still a sensitive issue—something that is not discussed with one's colleagues. Conway believes this is about equity—what an employee feels his or her pay is in relation to others, rather than whether the salary is considered to be a fair price for the job.

"Money probably isn't a very good motivator, but behind that there are many ideas about what money means to every individual. What does money mean in the context in which it is provided? Because if I am suddenly given more or less money than someone I work with, it could have an effect on the perceptions of equity within that group.

"So to say that pay is not important is also false as well. People have this idea now of basic thresholds of pay which cannot be violated. It has become a bit of a hygiene factor itself. You need it in place. Providing more will not necessarily be motivating, but if you try to retract it or provide pay which isn't reasonable within that employee's local market, then it will be demotivating."

If pay is only a motivating factor depending on your reference group and expectations, why is it so often used as a carrot?

Conway believes that as we are largely motivated by intrinsic factors connected with the task we are performing, the best way to motivate with money is to link pay to the task, thus making an intrinsic motivator.

"If you think of salespeople, pay is often commission-based and there is a very big increase in salary which can be achieved by working hard. So there is a very definite link between pay and the task itself."

Once again, though, he advises caution, because used in the wrong context, it can do more harm than good. "For most employees who are caught in performance systems, where at best you might get a bonus of only 4% or below over the course of a year, it doesn't really have much leverage as a motivator.

"It's almost insulting because the effort and reward are not comparable. This is why performance-related pay has come in for a lot of criticism; because it is not flexible enough."

Flexibility plays a big part in motivation, says Conway. Not so much in time off and flexitime arrangements, but in give and take. Offering motivators and rewards that are not part of the contract creates goodwill.

Three years ago Conway co-wrote, with David Guest, a report for the CIPD on what has become known as the *Psychological Contract*. While the term is largely associated with motivation and management techniques, Conway explains that it is all part of human psychology: "The psychological contract is a generic term, not just used for workplace situations. There is contract-making going on all the time. One of the situations in which this becomes most important is work, because you end up having quite close relationships with someone who isn't necessarily a friend or someone you would choose to spend time with."

Although the psychological contract is not binding as is a legal written contract, it is equally strong in what it means to employees and the power it has to motivate. "The psychological contract is unspoken," Conway continues. "An example might be that you expect appreciation from your line manager. Although it is not written down anywhere, if that doesn't happen you might think that if you are not appreciated, then you won't put so much effort in."

But where do these expectations come from?

There is a mixture of informing factors; "One will be your experience in previous jobs," Conway says. "Another is how the present relationship has developed over time. It can also be a comparative issue, for example, if you knew someone in the same position who got more than you did. Employees can also have low expectations developed, particularly by the HR function of the company: If you work for an organisation where there are pitiful human resource practices, the unspoken message is the organisation doesn't give a toss about its employees."

A vital part of this contract is keeping it unspoken: "There is that difficulty about formalising the psychological contract—you can create a rod for your own back, because it almost becomes a legal contract and

can be demotivational if not delivered upon."

"The difference between those two contracts is the relationship with trust. If I trust someone, I can kind of guarantee that contract in the long run, that even if I am not rewarded straight away, I know that it will all balance out in the end."

Formalising the contract may work for some companies, if their employees like to work that way, and Conway thinks it is vital to match reward structure to the culture of the company. "In a very bureaucratic culture, there are roles, which are highly specified. This leans towards a more formalised psychological contract, whereas in a more creative industry, you can allow people to work out of the box more, and so the psychological contract is more flexible, and more organic.

"I think work/life balance is a stupid idea. It doesn't explore your notion of occupational identity. It sees it as something different to the identity you have outside work. But work informs your life outside."

"If an employee has done a really great advertising campaign it wouldn't be rewarded in an ordinary bog-standard way which might pass as acceptable in a bureaucratic culture. If you are doing a creative job, you might expect to be rewarded in that way, whatever that might mean within that culture: perhaps to be publicly praised, or given commission. Certain people gravitate towards certain organisational cultures."

This recognition of the needs of the individual may change workplace culture in the next few years. While Conway accepts that the government's work/life balance policies have influenced jobs and put the needs of people at the centre of management practice, he thinks there have been oversights in failing to look at how work is intrinsic to who we are.

"That is why I think work/life balance is a stupid idea," he says. "It doesn't explore your notion of occupational identity. It sees it as something different to the identity you have outside work. But work informs your life outside work and the boundaries have a flexibility. I don't think it is helpful to draw the line between work and life outside work because it seems a very artificial distinction to me."

Conway believes that work/life balance, designed to motivate employees by making life easier, is breaking down motivation and is not something everyone is looking for: "Work/life balance is an individual thing. If you are wrapped up in work, you are not so worried about doing all the things you enjoy outside work."

The concept of work/life balance and the publicity it has received, however, have changed the things that are recognised as motivational factors.

"The idea of motivation has gone from the idea that employees just work for pay and it doesn't matter what they do, to people saying 'no, it does matter'. It is also about actualising oneself, using one's skills. We have this idea of a more complex individual now, an individual who is much more differentiated, motivated, and driven by autonomy with an expectation of progression and development."

This acceptance of the individual's career needs is something that Conway thinks might direct motivation theory over the next decade. The feelings of people and the way their feelings motivate them to act has a huge effect on the way they work—"look at people who kill their colleagues!" Conway points out.

"Emotion is pivotal to the way in which people perform. We get feedback from our emotions on how we perform in our jobs. If we have a goal that we are aiming for and we feel we are on track to achieve it then we feel content.

"Lots of employers don't worry about the emotional experience of their employees and this is an idiotic notion. Emotion intimately informs motivation, and management feedback makes us feel good about ourselves.

"Organisational psychology has started to look at behaviour more. We had a cognitive revolution and began to look at people's thoughts. I think the next big enquiry will be into emotions."

Dear Workforce:

A Plan for Keeping Employees Motivated

Dear *Workforce*:
We have an employee whose performance has dropped off after only a year in the position. How can we motivate him to excel?
—*Noncommissioned Officer in Charge,*
Virginia

Dear Distressed NCO:

For the answer, we talked to Matthew Goff, client development manager for SHL Canada in Toronto:

Providing personnel with the motivation to improve performance has to begin before these employees actually start work at the organization. Various well-designed human resource processes should be in place to ensure that when organizations recruit the best employees, they hold on to them.

These processes include a well-thought-out training and development plan that communicates how the organization values his or her skills and contributions, and that informs the person of personal development initiatives that are available for acquiring skills and competencies.

> A training and development plan can be linked to internal succession planning in which the new skills and competencies lead to other opportunities within the organization.

A training and development plan can be linked to internal succession planning in which the new skills and competencies lead to other opportunities within the organization. For example, an employee joins XYZ company in a role for which compe-

tencies and required levels of job performance have been fully communicated. Organizational structure also would have been communicated so that the employee fully recognizes opportunities within the company and is more likely to view the job as the start of a career, rather than just a job.

After a couple of years on the job, and perhaps after successful performance appraisals and personal development opportunities, the employee could be ready for further responsibility. If employees can see options ahead, it takes away the "no light at the end of the tunnel" syndrome often associated with 9-to-5 jobs.

Understanding the motivation of employees also is very important from a management perspective. Motivation is a complex phenomenon. It is far more complicated than just a consideration of factors such as material reward and status. Having a clear communication policy regarding a number of factors will help motivate your employees, and help you understand to what extent they are motivated by:

- Working under pressure and tight time frames
- Working in a competitive environment
- Work that requires commitment beyond normal working hours
- Opportunities for interaction with other people in their work
- The need to be able to uphold ideals and conform to high ethical standards

As with the flu, prevention is better than cure. Understanding what motivates employees very early on in their careers, and ensuring that you have clear training, development and succession planning systems in place, will help you retain your best employees—and keep their motivation at a high level.

Setting the Right Salary

Dear *Workforce*:

I am recruiting a highly desirable candidate for our technical development team, but there's one problem: we can only get him at a salary that's three to five times higher than that of the senior-most person on the team. The candidate has a comparable skill level but two years less experience than the senior staff member.

Do we go ahead and pay his asking price, thus giving rise to an imbalance in our pay structure? Or do we revise our senior technician's salary to offset the imbalance?

—*Betwixt and Between,*
senior executive-HR, software/services,
Mumbai, India

Dear HR Executive:

Here are some thoughts from Ron Elsdon, director, retention diagnostic services, at Drake Beam Morin in San Jose, California:

In the work world, we are moving into relationships with employees that have to be specific to each individual. That is why we have one-to-one relationships rather than one-to-many relationships. This provides the flexibility required to address the differing needs of each person. And this is the most effective way to attract and retain valued talent. With that in mind, it is important to negotiate compensation for your new recruit that matches his market value.

The significant difference between your new recruit's market value and that of your senior-most employee raises questions that should prompt an assessment to see if your compensation levels are competitive. A multiple three to five times higher seems excessive and also calls into question the claims of the new recruit.

Salary is only one part of the relationship with the employee. Employee bene-

fits, support for development, and recognition of flexibility in working arrangements can be equally important. For your existing employee, it will be important to understand which factors are of greatest importance and respond accordingly.

HR's Evolving Structure

Dear *Workforce:*
How should HR be structured today? Are there advantages and disadvantages to one organizational structure over another?

—*Wondering HR Rep,*
Software/Systems, Murray, Utah

Dear Wondering:

We had Andrew Geller, principal, Unifi Network, a subsidiary of Pricewaterhouse-Coopers, Teaneck, New Jersey, talk about the past and the present:

Trends in HR structure—a brief history

HR tasks developed in most large organizations as centralized staff functions, divided into specialty areas (compensation, benefits, staffing, etc.). There were representatives of HR (at the time usually called "personnel representatives") who were responsible for informing managers and employees about HR policies and programs, handling employee relations issues, and serving as a conduit to HR and line management for employee views and concerns.

As it became clear that different businesses needed and could afford different types of HR programs and benefits, even within the same corporation, HR began to decentralize, replicating the centralized HR structure at division levels. This had the advantage of supporting differentiated HR for each business, but its redundancies cost a lot of money and the specialist jobs got smaller (i.e., they supported smaller groups of employees) and thus attracted less capable or experienced people.

Two trends then emerged that drove HR toward the structure that is most typical today:

- Companies became more cost conscious, especially about staff functions.
- Senior executives began to realize that people really are a strategic asset, and that people strategy had to be linked to business strategy.

The resulting structure has three components:

1. Shared HR services for administrative and transactional functions, to create efficiencies and save money. This component reduced the redundancies of the previous, decentralized structure and focused on operational excellence.

2. Centers of Excellence, which are centralized units responsible for program development and consulting to businesses in highly specialized areas (compensation, OD, benefits planning, etc.). This leads to a critical mass in specialized areas, which attracts better people. The challenge is to ensure that the centers of excellence don't become ivory towers disconnected from business realities.

3. Decentralized HR business partners—personnel reps—whose responsibility is to understand the business issues and, as a member of a management team, to identify the HR implications and coordinate help from the appropriate center of excellence or outside vendors to deal with those implications. This new role, when played properly, enhances the strategic value of the people.

HR today—and future directions

This structure remains the paradigm for most large HR functions today. Compared to its predecessors, it is relatively efficient, and more business-focused. But most line managers, and even senior HR execs, will confess that their HR function is still too administrative, too expensive, and not equipped to deal with strategic people issues.

There is a new trend in HR, what I will call "distributed HR." It means that the design and delivery of HR functions is now done through multiple channels. The criterion is that it be done through the channel that delivers the HR service in a way that yields the greatest return (benefit and quality/cost) and/or has the most direct accountability for that HR activity.

What does this concept mean in practical terms? Several things:

- **Outsourcing of all administrative activities**. They are removed entirely from the internal HR organization and shifted to an outside vendor that can take advantage of greater economies of scale, has more ability to invest in new technologies, and can more easily focus on best practices. This has the advantage of reducing cost and allowing the internal HR function to move away from its transactional focus. It has the disadvantage of

providing less internal control and locking the company into a long-term commitment to one vendor.

- **Returning key elements of people-management back to the line**. This eliminates them from the HR function entirely. For example, while compensation program design remains a specialized activity that only HR or outside consultants can do, salary administration can be handled by line managers themselves, with the help of computer technology to provide the data and analytics that they need. This not only reduces HR function cost, but also gets the line to take responsibility for decisions that only they should make. They should be accountable for managing their own people. The approach has the disadvantage of taking up more line management time and, without proper advice and controls from the HR function, allows inexperienced managers to make inappropriate decisions.

- **Expecting employees to take more responsibility for their own HR management**. Examples include planning for development and career progression, and managing health-care expenditures. This empowers employees and makes them feel that the programs they help shape better fit their needs. The challenge is to ensure that employee empowerment is linked to business needs.

- **Reducing the number of "HR business partners."** But it should also be ensured that, freed from the administrative work they did in the past, these partners are truly strategic thinkers in both HR and business arenas, and are respected for these responsibilities by the line. The advantage is that businesses can finally begin to use their people as a source of competitive advantage. The challenge is to get the right HR people for these roles. Although the title "business partner" has been around for a while, there are few practitioners who really fit the mold.

- **Developing small teams of specialists**. These people function like SWAT teams who solve specialized HR problems. They are like centers of excellence of past times with two exceptions:

1) They are smaller and in many cases contain few permanent members, but recruit other internal or external consulting resources as a project requires.

2) They are not oriented to developing corporate-wide programs, but work more toward solving business-specific needs.

In summary, an organization with dispersed HR has a relatively small HR function. Although it may be organized along traditional lines (business partners, spe-

cialists, etc.), it works quite differently, playing a much more consultative role with its line clients. And much of the HR work gets done outside HR entirely—by employees, managers, and outsourcers.

The Right Way to Lay Off

Dear *Workforce*:

When performing a reduction in force of manufacturing employees, is it better to conduct terminations one by one or by group? We are concerned about violent reactions since no severance is being given, and we want to know if the group setting would inhibit or promote unwanted reactions.

—Safety & Training Facilitator,
manufacturing company,
Valencia, California

Dear Safety Facilitator:

We talked to Mark Gorkin, the "Stress Doc" of Washington, D.C., who says there's no contest:

One-by-one exit interviews acknowledge the psychological complexity of the termination process and respect the integrity of the soon-to-be former employee. Group termination avoids the issues and will fan the fires.

Advantages of one-on-one

Being forced to leave an organization is a trying experience for most people—especially if he or she has a long history there. A tight job market adds to the stress. Giving the employees no severance package may seem like salt on the wound. The human resources department should take the time on a one-on-one basis to note hard company economic realities and tough choices. And HR has to recognize that hard company choices won't negate the fact that people feel dissatisfied, angry, upset, and frightened.

One-by-one exit interviews acknowledge the psychological complexity of the termination process and respect the integrity of the soon-to-be former employee.

It's important to give the employees time and space to share how they feel about the reduction in force (RIF); that's the reason for the face-to-face meeting. As long as an employee does not become abusive or violent, some expression of anger is reasonable and healthy. (If an employee does become threatening, at least it's out in the open, and an appropriate safety response becomes a quick option.)

If the number of people being let go is very large, beyond HR's capacity for one-on-one administration, consider some pre-exit workshops led by trainers skilled in dealing with grief and termination. Consider employee assistance professionals or consultants with both a clinical and organizational training background.

Sometimes management cuts off this intimate termination process. Management may avoid this one-on-one venting because of feelings of guilt, which also is an understandable reaction. However, bringing out this array of emotions, though difficult, will likely reduce the chances of an outbreak of violence.

Dangers of a group meeting

A group meeting for the announcement of the RIF exacerbates the violence potential. Anger and feelings of abandonment or betrayal not vented or handled constructively lend themselves to reduction of individual responsibility for subsequent actions and could even lead to mob reaction.

Also, many people will not speak up in a group. For some of these individuals, anger will smolder inside. If such an individual finds this RIF threatening, has pre-existing emotional instability (especially a history of uncontrolled rage or premeditated belligerent or cruel behavior), then this person may be ripe for a violent reaction, even if a subsequent stress trigger seems trivial.

Finally, violence prevention should not be the sole purpose of one-on-one meetings. Hold them for such reasons as:

- Demonstrating respect for the employees
- Indicating appreciation for past contributions
- Showing that management is genuinely willing to tackle tough personnel issues
- Assuring surviving employees during a vulnerable period that management doesn't get rid of people on a whim
- Doing the right thing

This article is intended to provide useful information on the topic covered, but should not be construed as legal advice or a legal opinion. Also remember that state and foreign laws may differ from U.S. federal law.

Enhancing Your Writing Skills

By Max Messmer, Editor

Three weeks ago, your company's controller asked you to represent the accounting department on a cross-functional team charged with launching a sweeping new e-commerce initiative—uncharted territory for your firm. Rising to the challenge, you've already spent many 12-hour days and several weekends determining the resources required for the project and developing a cost/benefit analysis. Now it's time to formally communicate your findings to the rest of your team, most of whom have limited knowledge of accounting systems and procedures. Since writing has never been your strong suit, it occurs to you that the long hours you've put in thus far on the project may have been the easy part.

While it's true that writing can seem like more of an art that a science at times, there are steps you can take to improve your skills and confidence. In the process, you'll be increasing your value to your employer.

Even in our increasingly "e-enabled" business world, expertise in translating ideas into words is still critical. In fact, it's technology that's making these skills even more important than they've been in the past. Think about it. As technological advances such as e-mail allow us to communicate more rapidly, more often, and with greater numbers of people, writing is becoming a larger part of everyone's job.

That's not all. The number of projects taking accountants outside their departments to offer advice to senior management or serve on cross-functional teams is also amplifying the need to communicate persuasively. Writing skills, in particular, are no longer simply an advantage—they're a necessity.

Organization is the key

At the heart of effective writing is the ability to organize a series of thoughts. Like any assignment you tackle in your professional life, diving blindly into a writing project with no preparation or forethought is a recipe for disaster.

Start by identifying the objective of each memo or e-mail you write. Is your intent merely to inform, or do you want to create a call to action? Will you consider your communication a success if you've persuaded colleagues or managers to change their minds about a particular

issue? Or is your ultimate purpose to clarify a procedure that will help others work more efficiently with your department? The answer to these questions will guide the content of your document as well as its tone.

Once you've identified your true objective, take the time to list and prioritize the key points you want to make in support of it. For some, a formal outline works best since it allows them to visualize their thought process in detail. For others, simply jotting down the major elements they want to convey is more practical.

Write for your audience, not yourself

One of the most common mistakes inexperienced writers make is failing to consider the knowledge level of their audiences. While you may be your company's foremost expert on the intricacies of financial analysis or budgeting, you're unlikely to make a real connection with your readers who aren't accountants unless you write in terms they can understand easily. Don't assume that others will interpret a phrase a certain way just because you do. In particular, avoid "buzz" words or acronyms unless they're understood universally throughout your company.

Whenever possible, use plain English. Your readers will quickly lose patience with sentences they have to read several times just to determine what you're trying to say. While you don't want to "talk down" to your audience by oversimplifying or overexplaining concepts, few are impressed by unnecessarily formal or lengthy prose.

Get to the point

Present your primary message or call to action as quickly as possible. Few busy professionals today have the time to wade through long introductory paragraphs before coming to the point of a memo or narrative. Provide just enough to capture readers' attention and let them know what's being asked of them—ideally in no more than a page.

Master the mechanics

No matter how targeted and organized a written document is, if it contains spelling or grammatical errors,

it can lose most of its impact. Improper word usage can interfere with otherwise excellent communication. Even informal e-mail messages can create a bad impression if they contain grammatical mistakes.

If writing isn't your strong suit, consider taking a continuing education course or purchasing a business writing book. Then, whenever you write, keep your grammar guide within easy reach as a reference tool.

Polish by proofreading and editing

No matter how carefully you feel you've written a document, you should edit and proofread it before you submit it. Read back through a finished draft aloud to make sure the thoughts and word combinations flow smoothly. Check for redundancies, overuse of particular words or phrases, and sentences that could be misinterpreted by someone not familiar with your topic.

Proofreading a document for spelling and grammatical errors is best performed by re-reading it word by word. The spell-check function on your computer can help, but avoid depending on it entirely. Spell-check doesn't flag as errors omitted words or use of a wrong word spelled correctly.

Even in an age filled with technological advances that help accountants calculate, manage, and report information, proficiency in written communication is still highly valued. As you interact with colleagues throughout your firm and serve on more interdepartmental teams, your writing skills will become increasingly important. By carefully considering the objective and audience of each document you create and mastering some of the grammar basics, you'll be more comfortable with the written word. As an added benefit, the next time you're asked to prepare a detailed report, you'll have greater confidence in your ability. You may never learn to enjoy writing, but at least you'll know your efforts have made you a better communicator.

Max Messmer is chairman and CEO of Robert Half International Inc. (RHI), parent company of Robert Half®, Accountemps® and RHI Management Resources®. RHI is the world's first and largest specialized staffing firm placing accounting and finance professionals on a full-time, temporary and project basis. Messmer's most recent books are Managing Your Career For Dummies® *(IDG Books Worldwide),* Job Hunting For Dummies®, *2nd Edition (IDG Books Worldwide),* Human Resources Kit For Dummies® *(IDG Books Worldwide) and* The Fast Forward MBA in Hiring *(John Wiley & Sons).*

From *Strategic Finance*, January 2001, pp. 8-10. © 2001 by Strategic Finance, published by Institute of Management Accountants, Montvale, NJ. Reprinted by permission.

Harmony in the Workplace:
10 Positive Strategies
You Can Use

How do you and your coworkers interact? Your interactions can make your job easier or more difficult. Choosing a positive outlook and style can deflate most interpersonal tensions—and lead to better performance.

The key is developing good people skills. Fair, sensible, and ethical tactics encourage a productive, harmonious workplace. Negative tactics such as backstabbing, seizing undeserved credit, or starting malicious rumors hurt morale and teamwork.

To minimize negative interactions, try these strategies:

1. *Earn the respect of your peers and supervisor.* Don't just seek out plum assignments. Volunteer for some of those less desirable tasks most people avoid. Take advantage of opportunities that will allow you to demonstrate your skills, talents, and professionalism.

2. *Refrain from gossiping.* Gossip wastes company time. A person's career can be ruined by rumors. Stay out of the fray, and don't gossip. When co-workers complain to you about someone, suggest they discuss their concerns directly with the only person who can change the situation—the person they're complaining about.

3. *Don't be a critic.* Avoid criticizing your institution, management, or co-workers. It's unprofessional, and it diminishes you. Negativity lowers morale and encourages others to whine and complain. Also, some people are quick to report criticism. They won't hesitate to make others look bad so they can look good.

4. *Avoid pointing fingers.* Rather than making accusations, concentrate on suggesting a solution. Try to find out why the problem happened. Instead of saying "Sue messed up that account," say "We can fix the account, and here is what we need to do." If you must identify or question the person responsible for the problem, use sensitivity. Phrase your comments or questions so as to avoid embarrassing the person. People rarely make mistakes intentionally, and they usually feel remorseful already!

5. *Take credit for all that you do—and that means your mistakes, too.* If everyone is aware of your contributions and they know you are also willing to admit an error, you stand a much better chance of surviving a conflict. Keep your supervisor informed of what you're doing. When you have special challenges (for example, satisfying an irate customer), recap them in a brief e-mail or memo to your boss. Documenting your successes in finding solutions helps with performance reviews, too.

6. *Do PR for other people.* Publicize co-workers' accomplishments. When you do that, other people are less likely to see you as a threat. By giving credit where it's due, you gain respect and cooperation from colleagues. If a co-worker does an outstanding job on a special project, praise his or her achievement in a staff meeting or send a memo to his or her supervisor, copying your co-worker.

7. *Know when to be discreet.* Don't divulge private information. This includes personal problems, intimate details co-workers share, secrets you may have unintentionally discovered, and confidential business data. Direct all meddlers to the person in question. Of course, the exception is if you discover something illegal. You need to discuss that circumstance with your supervisor or security manager.

8. *Address negativity aimed at you.* If you find out that someone is complaining or gossiping about you, take the person aside and calmly tell what you heard. Be direct but polite, and state that you're open to discussing the issue. A courteous, professional demeanor helps disarm people. In a nice way, request that people talk to you directly anytime there's a problem.

9. *Put your negotiation skills to work.* Know when and how to compromise. Be willing to admit when you're wrong. Don't personalize problems; it's not about you, but about work. With flexibility and commitment on your part, you can learn to work with people you don't like and resolve interpersonal differences quickly.

10. *Don't hold grudges.* Once a problem is resolved, forget your anger. Let the problem be history and move on. Anytime you're angry with a co-worker, it tends to adversely affect your work. Demonstrate that your priority is to find feasible solutions. If you can do that, you'll win the respect of your peers, and what you say will carry more credibility.

HOW TO DEVELOP THE MIND OF A STRATEGIST

By James E.
Lukaszewski, APR

IMPORTANT BUSINESS KNOWLEDGE

One of the communications strategist's main values is to provide the boss with effective information with which to know and run the business. Bosses generally look for six kinds of feedback:

- Data feedback: Facts and information.
- Feeling feedback: Emotional intelligence about the states of minds of various constituencies.
- Intelligence of the old-fashioned kind: What is going on out there, what should he/she know about that no one else knows about, where is the edge?
- Advance information: Threats and exposure, unplanned visibility, organizational impact forecast.
- Real-time concerns: What are the things that executives should worry about today, tonight, and tomorrow morning; what can be deferred and why.
- Peer activities: Strategies, mistakes, and successes.

To act truly in the interests of the business by bringing in useful knowledge beyond that already known, the strategist faces tough personal questions:

- Can you separate yourself from your own predispositions, assumptions, and largely anti-management biases?
- Can you add positive energy to what management has to accomplish?
- Can you move different constituencies to listen and to act?
- Can you build the expectation of a strategic contribution from you, in management's eyes?
- Can you expect a call from the boss to help think things through?
- Can you assess, then clearly and quickly analyze the impact of bad news? Good news? No news?
- Can you fill management's blind spots and suggest ways to overcome management's limitations?
- Can you manage your ego throughout the process?
- Can you work successfully at a fairly substantial altitude and keep the bigger picture in mind?

FOCUS ON THE ULTIMATE OUTCOME

Strategy is a big-picture activity. It is always outcome focused. That's because strategy is virtually always about the fu-

ture. Strategy is a kind of magnetism that pushes, pulls, and adjusts the business in the larger context of its operations, but always in a forward direction.

Too often public relations and other staff functions get bogged down in what happened yesterday, last week, last month, or last budget cycle. We spend far too much time trying to figure out how we got to where we are.

Five years ago, I was working to resolve the differences and build a working relationship between five very disparate organizations—labor unions, religious organizations, non-government organizations (NGOs), activists, and a very large business. The result of their inability to get together was public bickering, arguing, demonstrations, and very dangerous, potentially explosive confrontations.

IF YOU OFFER VALUE, AND THE BOSS KNOWS OF THAT VALUE AND HAS RESPECT FOR YOUR THINKING, YOU WILL BE SOUGHT OUT.

At the suggestion of some very helpful people, one November day in 1995 we all wound up in the living room of a Presbyterian minister in East Brooklyn. That's just across the river from Manhattan. When we arrived, a very jovial, large man invited us into his comfortable living room where a roaring fire greeted us. When the six of us sat down—one labor leader, one religious leader, one NGO leader, two individuals from the company, and me—Reverend Smith laid down the only ground rule for the day. He said, "Today's discussion will be outcome focused. By that I mean that anything that happened this morning, yesterday afternoon, last week, last month, last year, the last decade, the last century is irrelevant to today's discussion. We will stay focused on what we can get done based on where we know we have to go. Should any of you feel you must move backwards, I will nudge you forward. If you cannot go forward, then I will invite you to leave so that my wife and I can have a pleasant Sunday afternoon."

This was an incredibly important meeting. After five years of painful, dangerous disagreement, in four and one-half hours we developed a one-page agreement, which was signed by everyone. All of these organizations are operating under this agreement to this day. I attribute amazing success to the notion of "outcome focus."

The strategist is informed by the past but chooses those lessons that help show direction to the future. This is what is known as "outcome focus."

Outcome-focused meetings are at least 50 percent shorter. Time is not wasted discussing what can't be changed. Forget the past. Recognize that everyone, from their own perspective, already owns some part of the past in ways we can never understand. Focus on the future, which no one owns and no one can forecast accurately. In strategy, we all come to the future completely equal with every other staff function or management advisor. Victory can only be designed when there is total focus on the future. It is very hard to go forward while looking and thinking backward. Achieving success and obtaining goals happens in the future, never in the past.

STRATEGY IS ALWAYS ABOUT THE FUTURE

You can be a successful strategist anywhere in your organization. Success does not require that you even be at the table. You do have to be sought out by the boss or someone the boss trusts. If you offer value, and the boss knows of that value and has respect for your thinking, you will be sought out. The person who is sought out is the person who can contribute something positive, useful, and of self-evident value, from the boss' perspective.

So what are the main lessons I'm trying to share about becoming and developing the mind of a strategist? I think there are three.

First, always think in terms of action options, including doing nothing. Doing nothing is the most challenging strategy to figure out unless the boss or lawyers mention it first. Then you will do nothing—for a while. If you want to be a strategist, you have to be first to mention doing nothing, then explaining, if you can, why other options are better, more acceptable, or will lead to victory. In its simplest form, doing nothing is often the most appealing strategy for most managers, at least in the beginning.

IF ALL YOU CAN THINK OF IS WHAT THE PRESS RELEASE OUGHT TO SAY, YOU'RE OF LITTLE VALUE IN STRATEGIC SITUATIONS.

Second, be a force for prompt, positive, forward thinking, outcome-focused incremental, constructive action. Avoid the negativity, defensiveness, and time-wasting whining executives, particularly those in difficult situations, tend to enjoy. Be reflective, but take only useful, positive lessons from the past.

Third, approach business problems from a business perspective. Use a management context. Separate yourself from the strictly media and the media relations solution. If all you can think of is what the press release ought to say, you're of very little value in strategic situations.

When it comes to being a strategist—a successful, counter intuitive, energetically positive thinker—your focus must remain on the success of the team, its leadership, and promptly achieving useful, important, positive goals.

Strategy is a tough challenge for tough-minded thinkers and relentlessly action-oriented doers.

It's like the apocryphal story of the young journalist interviewing Thomas Edison just after Edison successfully invented the light bulb. The enthusiastic young journalist said, "Mr. Edison, I understand it took you 6,000 attempts to perfect the light bulb." Mr. Edison replied, " That's probably correct." The reporter continued questioning, "Help me understand how a man of your obvious learning, knowledge, skill, ability, and creativity could make 6,000 mistaken attempts to make a simple light bulb. Isn't that embarrassing? Or aren't you as smart as your public relations people say you are?" Thomas Edison then reportedly replied, "Well, young man, I just ran out of ways to do it wrong."

If you can genuinely put yourself in the boss' shoes and look at things from an operational perspective, talk in the vocabulary of management, think and recommend using strategic management process approaches, then apply what you know how to do to that which management really needs done and what is truly important, you will have developed the mind of a strategist. You'll be sought out. Count on it.

See you at the table.

James E. Lukaszewski. APR, Fellow PRSA, is a U.S.-based public relations writer, teacher, and thinker. This article is the last in a three-part series, "How to Develop the Mind of a Strategist." You can contact Mr. Lukaszewski by E-mail at tlg@e911.com and visit his Web site at www.e911.com

UNIT 4

Developing Effective Human Resources

Unit Selections

Key Points to Consider

- Organizations spend a great deal of money on training and development. Why do many organizations feel it is necessary to provide courses in-house? Why do other organizations spend money on outside programs? Why might the training programs of some firms be inadequate, even though a great deal of money is spent on them? What are some of the questions organizations should be asking of their training and development operations?

- What are your career plans, and how do you plan to implement them? How has career development changed over the years? What do you think will be the impact of the Internet?

 **Links: www.dushkin.com/online/**
These sites are annotated in the World Wide Web pages.

Employment Interviews
http://www.snc.edu/socsci/chair/336/group3.htm

Feminist Majority Foundation
http://www.feminist.org

How to Do an Employee Appraisal
http://www.visitorinfo.com/gallery/howapp.htm

Human Resource Management
http://www.ozemail.com.au/~cyberwlf/3UB/main2.html

Every organization needs to develop its employees. This is accomplished through a number of activities, including formal corporate training, career development, and performance appraisal. Just as the society and the economy will continue to change, so will the human resource needs of organizations. Individuals and their employers must work together to achieve the effective use of human resources. They must plan together to make the maximum use of their abilities so as to meet the challenge of the changing environment in which they live.

American industry spends approximately the same amount of money each year on training and developing employees as is spent by all colleges and universities combined. It also trains roughly the same number of people as there are students in traditional postsecondary education. Corporate programs are often very elaborate and can involve months or even years of training. In fact, corporate training and development programs have been recognized by academia for their quality and excellence. The American Council for Education has a program designed to evaluate and make recommendations concerning corporate and government training programs for college credit. Corporations, themselves, have entered into the business of granting degrees that are recognized by regional accrediting agencies. For example, McDonald's grants an associate's degree from "Hamburger U." General Motors Institute (now Kettering University) offers the oldest formalized corporate degree-granting program in the United States, awarding a bachelor's in industrial management; Ernst and Young offers a master's in accountancy; and a Ph.D. program in policy analysis is available from the Rand Corporation. American industry is in the business of educating and training employees, not only as a simple introduction and orientation to the corporation, but as a continual and constant enterprise of lifelong learning so that both firms and employees can meet the challenges of an increasingly competitive world. Meeting these challenges depends on knowledge, not on sweat, and relies on the ability to adapt to and adopt technological, social, and economic changes faster than competitors do. But, for training to be truly effective and beneficial for the organization, then when "Creating a Learning Organization," management must be able to answer the questions posed by Mark McMaster, "Is Your Training a Waste of Money?"

There is an important difference between jobs and careers. Everyone who works, whether self-employed or employed by someone else, does a job. Although a career is made up of a series of jobs and positions over an individual's working life, it is more than that. It is a sense of direction, a purpose, and a knowledge of where one is going in one's professional life. Careers are shaped by individuals through the decisions they make concerning their own lives, not by organizations. It is the individual who must ultimately take the responsibility for what happens in his or her career. Organizations offer opportunities for advancement, and they fund training and development based on their own self-interest, not solely on workers' interest. Accordingly, the employee must understand that the responsibility for career development ultimately rests with him- or herself. In today's world of short job tenure, people will frequently change jobs and they must be prepared to do so at a moment's notice. Jobs are being lost, but they are also being created. "Choosing the Right Path" is every employee's concern.

One of the ways that organizations can assist in the career development of their employees is to engage in appropriate and effective performance appraisals. This process benefits both the employee and the employer. From the employer's perspective, it allows the organization to fine-tune the performance of the individual and to take appropriate action when the performance does not meet an acceptable standard. From the employee's perspective, appraisal allows the individual to evaluate his or her situation in the organization. Appraisal will indicate, in formal ways, how the individual is viewed by the organization. It is, for the employee, an opportunity to gauge the future.

To ignore the development of the potential of the employees of any organization is to court disaster—not only for the organization, but for the employee. People who have stopped developing themselves are cheating themselves and their employers. Both will be vulnerable to changes brought on by increased competition, but the workers will be the ones who join the statistics of the unemployed.

CREATING A learning organization

Creating a learning environment in the workplace is not only vital to keeping employees up to date on rapidly changing technology, but can also help to bring revenue to the company.

by Neal McChristy

JOE MILLER OWNS AN office supply store in a midsize town in the Midwest with a restaurant next door and a drugstore across the street. Joe is manager over a copier salesman, two clerks who handle requests for office supplies, and two technicians who work on the machines. When a customer comes in, Joe notices that he goes directly to Betty, one of his clerks, and starts asking her questions. In fact, at other times, Joe has noticed that when Georgette, his other clerk, is there alone, this customer will ask about when Betty will return so he can talk to her.

Joe notices that Betty listens with care to the customer and shows him two types of paper, he picks one and buys a box. This day, Joe asks the customer to come into his office saying, since he's a long-time customer, he'd like to ask him a few questions about customer service. The customer complies, and Joe asks him why he seems to prefer having Betty wait on him rather than Georgette, the newest employee of the two.

"She tells me everything I need about every product," the customer said. "I've asked her about paper, toner, pens—everything. She knows the latest about each product in the store—soup to nuts." Joe nodded.

"She just saved me money, too, by showing me a new type of paper that's processed chlorine free. Our company wants to try that to help the environment. She also knew where to find the partially recycled paper, and that's also something we're going towards. "She's the best salesman you have, Joe. She knows her stuff."

After the customer left, Joe brought Georgette into his office. "I'm going to see what I can do to help you learn about some of the supplies in this business. You're a good employee, but I think a little training will help you and the store even more."

It's likely that Georgette, in this fictional account, has already learned a lot in her years with the company by watching Betty and asking her questions, then doing it herself. This type of learning is one of the most effective learning tools available in the workplace.

Should Joe add a new employee, Georgette would likely find the new employee would bring new ideas and knowledge, maybe even challenging her own. And if Joe would face a complete shift in the office supplies or equipment he carries, his training process would need to be accelerated to accommodate a rapid, substantial change in how he does business. It's

all part of learning in the workplace, and visible managers like Joe need knowledge to stay ahead of the competition.

In spite of the crucial role of training in an industry changing as much as office equipment, service, and supplies, an owner looking at cost reduction often considers training expendable, especially in these times of recession. But providing a learning environment adds real dollars to the company. "I believe if your people are learning something every day, most of it will translate into better service for clients and that translates into revenue growth real quickly," says Warren Whitlock, president of Landmark Printer Service, Rialto, California.

Learning is critical

Learning is "absolutely vital" in the process of having loyal employees who will stay with a company, according to Ronelle Ingram, director of technical service for FKM Copier Products, Irvine. Calif. So how do you keep employees as motivated at work on Monday morning as Friday afternoon? Or, put another way, "Are they as motivated about work as what they do on Saturday?" asks Tim Con-

lon, Rochester, N.Y., chief learning officer for Xerox Corp.

Regardless of whether you are a multinational corporation or a small startup, educating and training employees remain a key element of your business' health and future.

"Nothing kills a learning plan quicker than some boring lecturer droning on about things people already know," says Paul Schwartz, president of CopierCareers.com, Minneapolis, Minn., which specializes in working with technicians and employers for copier-industry placement. "Dry, factual, elementary material delivered by uninspired instructors can put your brightest stars in a coma. Spice it up and it will sink in," he advises.

Various studies done in workplaces have shown that:

- learning new skills are crucial to keep employees on the job—not for helping them go somewhere else. Employees will gauge a large amount of job satisfaction on the training opportunities in a job. "There's a tremendous employee value associated with learning," says Conlon.
- employees learn more easily by interacting with each other than in classroom-type teaching. Schwartz suggests employees read, study, and report on materials that are proven winners, such as gurus in the training world, before undertaking training. "This exercise 'limbers up' the employees' minds, preparing them to receive the training you are paying for, thus making it eventually more effective," Schwartz says.
- people learn by doing much more readily than through traditional training. "Instructor-based training—one of our

traditional training methods—is not one of the best training modes," says Conlon.

Schwartz states that a learning plan must be tailored to the students. And, he says, ask which employees have "a fire in their belly to do the best by you, your customers, and their fellow employees. Those are the people who will benefit from the training you provide." You can't exactly discriminate against those who can't, or won't, learn and grow, but you don't have to throw good resources out the window, either.

"The bottom line is there are buffalo and there are steers," Schwarz says. "Buffalo roam the prairie, play in the snow, they have spirit and verve, and they thunder. Steers stand around munching and complaining."

Creating a future

Sometimes outcomes-based learning needs to be configured a different way in order to make it seem more attainable. Conlon uses the example of the person wanting to diet whose focus is on his or her weight. To turn this around, he says, the person could think about building a healthier lifestyle. Weight then becomes just one of the outcomes instead of the main drive for the diet. He calls this "creating a future instead of solving a problem."

Rapidly rising technology always creates a challenge that needs an immediate training solution. A majority of the office equipment and supplies training of late was first on the transition to digital sales and service and then the convergence of printers and copiers. "As many businesses look to transit from products to service to solutions," Conlon says, "this is where knowledge comes into play."

In the process of teaching people, Katherine Richard, regional director for the Kansas Small Business Development Center at Pittsburg State University, Pittsburg, Kan., says those training need to be aware that people have different traits and ways of learning; some learn by seeing, some by hearing, and some by doing. "Hands-on learning is really critical to making *what is learned* an every-

day part of our mode of operation," she says.

It's a truism that if someone needs something bad enough to survive in the workplace, they'll do it. "Real learning occurs," Conlon states, "at the point of need in the work you do."

Schwartz says any educational endeavor should be field-tested and proven before being applied internally. "One must get employees to collaborate, endorse, and embrace," he says, "and there must be real-time evaluation of effectiveness while the teaching happens, plus long-term measurement of tangible results."

Some employers have resisted training because they're afraid their trained employees will then seek work elsewhere. But FKM's Ingram says they've retained most of their employees who have gained new certifications. FKM service technicians who succeed at acquiring Microsoft Certified Systems Engineer (MCSE) or A+ certification status receive not only recognition and their name on the wall, but also bonuses and raises. FKM requires a signed one-year noncompete agreement, Ingram says, and "it works out well for everybody." And she says the accomplishment and recognition from their peers has been a powerful positive force for those who complete it. Of the 23 technicians who have taken A+ certification, only one has left, Ingram says.

Employees who internalize effective practices in the workplace will lead the business to productivity and profit and gain personal satisfaction, Schwartz says. "They have to make it something that lives in their guts 24/7," he says. "Passion isn't conjured: it's electrified by a mystical combination of the individual's predisposition to excellence and the organization's genius in nurturing, inspiring, and challenging individuals to higher levels of performance."

Lessons from larger companies

For larger companies, one of the ideas floating around is that teams meet the needs of people in the organization. Ron Armstrong, Hardy, Va., of R.V. Armstrong and Associ-

ates, says the top executive must make the commitment to such an organizational structure. Learning provided by the organization helps the team members perform and achieve at the level sought by management, according to Armstrong, and there's an accompanying return on the training investment by increasing productivity, quality, and customer satisfaction.

"Execs have more time for making strategic decisions," Armstrong states, "managers make better decisions regarding their functional responsibilities, and supervisors don't carry the burden of accountability for large groups of people (teams carry the responsibility, authority, and accountability for their performance) —they become the resource persons and the coaches; staff employees' expertise is needed; *and* clerical, production, and service employees develop a sense of self-worth, ownership, and satisfaction in their work."

Peter Senge, author of *The Fifth Discipline: The Art and Practice of the Learning Organization*, was suggested as a resource by both Whitlock and Conlon.

Senge advocates a learning structure that differs from what he calls the current assembly-line model of schools and emphasizes an organic-like learning process that creates, acquires, and transfers knowledge, changing with the acquisition of new knowledge.

Conlon says Xerox has done work with Senge's model as well as the Center for Creative Leadership (CCL) model. (The CCL overview Web page states, "… we believe leadership development is the cor-

nerstone of organizational effectiveness").

Much of the Xerox training has departed from classroom training toward e-learning, Conlon says, which gives everyone at Xerox access to training and feedback. In addition, mentors and chat rooms enhance the ability for employees to interact.

But Xerox's e-learning matrix doesn't have to be just for larger companies. An innovative manager or owner with a computer and access to the Internet has access to resources that can be used for learning, Conlon adds. "E-learning is available in a lot of different avenues out there."

Mom and pop need to stay current

Many of the old-timers who have owned stores in the copier and printer industry for 10–30 years are street savvy and don't necessarily have college training, Ingram says, and may not be as convinced of the value of teaching and training. "They've learned through the school of hard knocks," she says. But all that's changing as others join the office equipment area. Says Ingram, "The new generation is willing to learn, take the lead, and ask questions."

In the technical area such as Ingram's, the training is from within and uses a template. This is because of the task-oriented nature of office equipment service, she says. With competition for the customer as close as the nearest computer, Richard says there's a real need for mom-and-pop stores to stay current

on what's going on in their industry and how to compete with it. A lot of this is customer service, she says—staying abreast of current technology and what products the customer wants. She adds, "And if you don't have it, they'll go somewhere else."

Training opportunities are readily available through classes offered by junior colleges or vo-tech schools and from places such as small-business development centers throughout the United States, Richard says. The centers can offer in-store seminars on improving customer service.

Learning and training doesn't have to be formal. "Brown bag" lunches and sharing ideas among employees, making sure everyone participates in some way, are easily done. And such get-togethers foster not only education, but also interaction, which it seems is a vital conduit to learning.

Whatever the setting, think of training that has inspired and motivated in order to keep the attention of your audience and then do likewise, say experts on training.

"Learning plans should be full of real-life stories, emotional word pictures, and compelling and inspiring examples of what real people accomplished when they applied time-tested principles and practices," Schwartz says.

Neal McChristy is a freelance writer from Pittsburg, Kan. He may be contacted by e-mail at freelance9@kscable.com.

From *Office Solutions* magazine by Neil McChristy, February 2002, pp. 26-29. © 2002 by Office Solutions. Reprinted by permission.

Is Your Training a Waste of Money?

Companies spend more than ever on training their sales and marketing forces, but is the investment in learning producing more sales and better service? Often not, say many experts, and these nine all-too-common problems may be what keeps your training from producing results

by Mark McMaster

WE'VE ALL BEEN THERE: 30 minutes into a training session, it becomes painfully clear that your presence is little more than a gesture—the speaker's message is only somewhat relevant, and far too familiar, anyway. It reeks of stale lessons from the session you attended on the same topic three years ago. Worse, this is just the opening lecture of a two-day off-site training program, one which cost your company more than $1,000 per person and stole you away from clients and sales leads. As you stare blankly toward the front of the room, your mind drifts to the piles of paperwork now accumulating in your in-box and the calls you wish you could be making. You're on the receiving end of wasted training.

Guess what? At some point you've probably put your employees through the same experience. "Nine out of ten people who have been through training at an average company have been disappointed," estimates Skip Corsini, the national training manager for Shorenstein Realty Services in San Francisco. He's sat through plenty of such disappointments himself while attending training for Citibank, the Bank of America, and in the software industry. "I'm probably the best-trained person I've ever known, because I've gone through every cockamamie training program there is out there," he says. "Based on my experience, Corporate America is behind. What is important today will be taught ten years from now."

The problem isn't that training itself is unnecessary—a large portion of the $54 billion that American companies budgeted for training programs last year is spent on teaching crucial new skills for a changing economy. Now more than ever salespeople and marketers need to learn in order to compete, and thankfully, a hot economy has meant that many companies have added resources to invest in employee development. But ask many professionals in the training business, and they'll say that while companies are pouring increasing budgets into teaching soft skills and the latest sales methodologies, they're not taking the time to critically evaluate their teaching programs or strategically plan their employees' learning. At worst, training is applied as a quick fix for problems too deep to solve with a seminar. "*Panacea* is the word that comes to mind," says Brandon Hall, lead researcher at the e-learning specialist Brandon-Hall.com in Sunnyvale, California, about many managers' attitude toward training: "It's good for what ails 'ya," they think, but often, they aren't using the right medicine to cure the illness.

And therein lies the difficulty—because variables like knowledge and skills learned are nearly impossible to quantify, it's difficult to measure the ROI from training. Sales training is especially challenging to evaluate, because its obvious end goal—increased sales—is influenced by countless other variables. But that doesn't mean that managers should view training as a shot in the dark. Employee learning needs to be strategically planned and evaluated, says consultant Gerry Waller of the Productivity Resource Organization in Park Ridge, Illinois. "If [executives] thought of training as being similar to their advertising expenditures, for example, they're not going to throw

A TOUGH SELL: TRAINING THE SALESPERSON

FOR TRAINERS, salespeople can be one of the toughest audiences out there. "Part of the fun of being a hot-shot salesperson is being a little cocky and making fun of what's going on in front of the room," says Brandon Hall, lead researcher at the e-learning specialist Brandon-Hall.com in Sunny-vale, Cali-fornia. "Actually, one of the best bonding experiences I've had was subversive fun during training sessions." For a sales training meeting not to bomb, it's going to take more than a few motivational quotes and a Power-Point presentation. Sessions need to be geared to a salesperson's unique needs and attitudes.

"There are two elements in planning a successful program for salespeople," says Edward del Gaizo, a sales training consultant for Achieve-Global in Tampa, Florida. First, engage them by linking the training to their current workload. "Ask them to bring in one or two accounts that they're sitting on," he says. As they're going through the program, they can apply the lessons directly to their work at hand. It'll make the training immediately relevant, and the attendees will be using the knowledge as soon as they get back to work on those clients. It also gives the trainer an advantage: "By bringing their own accounts to training, it allows the trainer to examine how well salespeople have sold into the accounts," he says. "You've got hard numbers, which you can combine with interviews." Second, use a tool kit approach, that is, "simple forms that help the salespeople organize information and problem-solve.

Something that, if I know I'm going to be in a competitive situation, I can use to identify clients' needs quickly and easily," del Gaizo says.

Above all, avoid excessive reading material and theory. "Salespeople don't want to read during a meeting, and they're interested in skills, not theory," del Gaizo says. "They want practical information that they can use right away." Don't force an agenda on salespeople, but rather allow them to suggest what skills they'd like to learn. Most likely they already know what kinds of training might help their performance. And if participants help set the tone for the training session, it's less likely that they'll be back in a familiar scenario: goofing off at the table in back while the trainer lectures away.

ad dollars into a magazine that doesn't apply to their market," he says. "So why do they go off and do that for training programs?"

No simple recipe exists for an effective training curriculum, but—to further extend the medicinal metaphor—there are certainly symptoms of failure that can be easily diagnosed. By taking time to analyze training priorities and methods, suspect training programs can be identified and revised. Beware of the following nine problems that commonly plague training programs: If these situations sound familiar, your investment in training may be a waste of both time and money, not to mention a source of frustration to your employees.

1: Training can't solve the problem.

"NINETY-FIVE PERCENT of the time, when people think training is needed it isn't the whole solution," says Richard Chang, a training consultant in Irvine, California. Often, underlying problems exist that can't be fixed with training alone. One trainer recalls a client he worked with who was disappointed in the sales of recently introduced products. "The president of the company called me in and said, 'I want you to re-do all of our new product training.' Well, I've been in this business thirty years, and the way he said it didn't sit well with me. So I asked him, 'Could you share with me what's driving your concerns?' " says Dana Skiff, the president of Corporate Training Consultants in Shaumburg, Illinois. As it turns out, the company was founded on an original product, sales of which paid out a 25 percent commission. Newer ones got only 12 percent. "The answer

was that it was a commission problem, not a training problem," Skiff says, and his advice was to change the commission formula. Not surprisingly once the two commissions were equalized, "all of a sudden new products started taking off."

This situation happens all the time, if not as perceptibly as in this story, says Becky Nickol, the president of Team U-Turns, a consulting firm in Orlando, Florida. "Whenever someone wants me to do team building training, a red flag goes up immediately in my head," she says. "It's the same with many other organizational issues. In those cases you have to attack the infrastructure of the organization, not the symptoms. Sometimes it's a leader who is sabotaging the process. Usually it's changing beliefs and philosophy of business." She says she turns away clients that need to solve underlying problems before training can help.

"Everyone's looking for the quick fix, and the first reaction is, 'We'll do training,' " Waller says. To probe at the root cause of a problem, Hall says that companies should first do a needs analysis to determine if it's a training issue in the first place. "They should find someone they respect in their training department to go through a process of identifying the performance problem," and then determine what processes must change in order to solve it, he says.

2: Your busy, jaded employees aren't open to learning new skills.

WE'RE ALL VERY cynical about training," Hall says. "It goes back to our school days when we had to sit through class no matter what. It's also that we've experienced job training that's

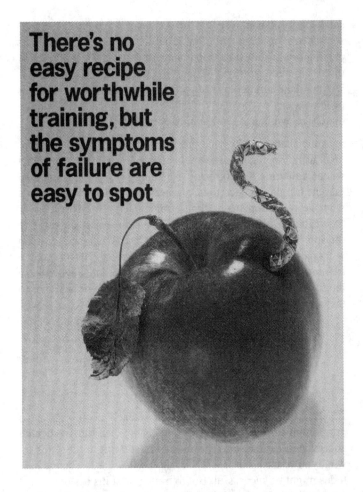

There's no easy recipe for worthwhile training, but the symptoms of failure are easy to spot

missed the mark." Sales professionals have a good excuse for being reluctant to attend time-consuming training programs: Their performance suffers when they are taken out of the field. Trainers say that salespeople are their most demanding customers, and the more training they receive, the less likely they're going to be wowed by new programs. "It's hard to impress these people because they've seen it all," says U-Turn's Nickol. That's a major impediment to learning, because if trainees aren't excited about what they're being trained in, they won't apply it in the workplace later.

That was part of the problem faced by Phyllis Misevich, a manager of training and organizational development at Spiegel, the catalog retailer based in Downers Grove, Illinois. "In the past we published a newsletter and a list of courses we offered every quarter. People could come and sign up, but attendance wasn't there," she says. Now Spiegel promotes its training program heavily—it even has its own logo. Managers are evaluated on how well they develop their employees, "and they're excited about that because now we have the tools to do it," Misevich says.

Jim Wall, a managing partner who supervises national sales training for Deloitte Consulting in Wilton, Connecticut, says that sales reps need to know how the training will help them make sales before they walk into the session. "Salespeople are out for the kill," he says. "They'll sign up for anything that's going to make them more effective at the kill. But it's got to be immediately applicable." Fred Lamparter, director of world-

wide training for Ogilvy & Mather advertising agency in New York, says that he doesn't always have the opportunity he would like to motivate employees and ensure their buy-in before a training session. "Very often, our [trainees] are assigned to us, and then it's usually a combination of management and human resources that determine who will go to what program," he says. Nevertheless, "I try to hype the programs and stress that it's going to be fun."

3: Managers don't support the training program.

IF THERE'S ONE problem that's the most insurmountable," says Lamparter, it's lack of cooperation from managers. Often, when trainees seem reluctant to learn a new technique it's because they're worried that it goes against their manager's methods. "You can tell that they're worried their boss won't let them do it," he says. "I certainly ask that the boss not undermine the techniques we're teaching. It's a real issue."

Joe Henderson, training director for business-to-business sales at New York–based AT&T, encounters the same problem often. "We find that managers don't view themselves as coaches, they view themselves as problem-solvers, so they don't reinforce what's taught in training," he says. "It's the perennial battle." He remembers one session on how salespeople could gain access to decision-makers, which managers were supportive of from the beginning. But even though they saw the need for the program, they weren't familiar with the curriculum, and they did nothing to reinforce or apply the skills taught after the training ended. "It just kind of died," he says, and salespeople gained little from the experience. For the next session Henderson organized, on teaming skills, he required sales managers to attend the training along with their reps, and he found that managers who attended were much more likely to coach their reps to develop these skills later.

Wendy Stone, who oversees sales training for the Lotus Development Corporation in Cambridge, Massachusetts, also found that the application of the company's newly taught sales methodology hinged on whether managers reinforced the use of its techniques at sales meetings. "So we started doing a push from the top down," she says. The vice president of sales speaks in terms of the methodology at leadership meetings, as do other high-level managers, and eventually it becomes ingrained in the sales culture of the organization.

4: Conflicting methods and philosophies are taught in each training session.

LOTUS SPENT MILLIONS of dollars developing tools and a training curriculum to reinforce the methodology mentioned above. But Stone noticed a problem: Outside speakers and trainers wouldn't present skills in a way that was consistent with the new sales practices. In addition, she found that new product training was more aligned with the old way of selling than the new. "It frustrated salespeople, because they're thinking, 'You made me spend all this time learning new material and then

Don't blame your trainer before you look at how your management affects learning

sales performance research at AchieveGlobal, a sales consulting firm in Tampa, Florida. Frontline managers' perceptions are important, but their input into sales training programs is often ignored, he says. When frontline managers aren't involved, the training may not correspond to the skills employees need on a day-to-day basis. Trainees can tell that it isn't immediately relevant, and the learning doesn't happen.

Anne Starobin, the vice president of professional development at Prudential Insurance in Newark, New Jersey, says that when evaluating her company's training program, "we learned that the training needed to be aligned with real work, and that's why we transitioned our focus from a centralized to a field-based focus." Whereas reps were once shipped off for training off-site, now each office has its own training associate who works in tandem with frontline managers. "Don't develop training in a vacuum," Starobin says. "I learned that lesson very long ago. Generic stuff doesn't work—it has to be relevant to the person at the time."

6: The training format doesn't fit the training need.

AMBITIOUS TRAINERS MAY attempt to teach a comprehensive program in a three-hour lecture, but chances are that in such an abbreviated format, the learning won't stick. It all depends on what you're trying to teach. "A half-day lecture to change attitudes might be successful. But to train new skills it's not," says AchieveGlobal's del Gaizo. Finding the correct format for a training session requires an analysis of "the blend of the topic, the audience, and the current work environment," Hall says. "If you've got a new product to introduce, and you've only got a half day to teach reps about it, you can do it. But if you've got new sales managers and they need training, that's not going to meet the mark," he says. Don't underestimate how long it takes to learn new skills. First the knowledge has to be absorbed, then trainees need time to practice the skills in a classroom environment. However, for training that focuses on knowledge rather than skills—for example, familiarization with new products—the classroom setting isn't necessary, and e-learning or self-directed study is more cost-efficient.

When developing an e-business sales training curriculum for IBM in Armonk, New York, vice president of e-business Ralph Senst almost made the decision to bring all of its 40,000 sales reps to a central location for classroom training. "There were weeks worth of understanding to transfer," he says. "It would have cost a heck of a lot of money. And by the time we'd completed the first wave, we'd have to start over again. It was like a vicious circle." Because the training dealt primarily with product familiarity and problem-solving, it could be taught efficiently with e-learning. So IBM developed a presentation software to convey the lessons over the Web. Senst estimates that the company saved $100 million by choosing e-learning over the classroom setting, and it also prevented taking weeks of the reps' field time each training cycle.

someone comes in and presents this product without answering the questions that I have learned how to ask,' " she says. "It's very destructive to the investment you've just made."

To overcome these discrepancies Stone made sure that each trainer was himself trained in the sales methodology, and even trained the entire marketing organization in its techniques as well. "We set up a rigorous set of requirements so that before they present to the sales force, they must show that the content uses the same vocabulary," Stone says.

5: The training isn't relevant to the company's pressing needs.

WHO MAKES THE decisions about training content? Too often, the wrong people do, says Edward del Gaizo, director of

To make
sure your reps are
learning skills they
can use, involve
them in training
decisions.

Training Effectiveness:
AN ROI CHECKLIST

IS YOUR TRAINING producing real value for your employees and your company? The Forum Corporation, a training consulting firm in Boston, looked at several decades of research on learning as well as its own consulting experience to gain an understanding about what makes training effective. Their report, *Achieving Business Results Through Training*, recommends that managers ask themselves the following questions to do a reality check on their training systems:

✓ Is your training linked to your strategic direction and business goals?

✓ Is it supported by strong leadership?

✓ Does it reflect the needs and values of your company's customers?

✓ Does it communicate your company's values?

✓ Does it help you address customer retention, acquisition, lower costs, less waste, higher speed, and greater innovation?

✓ Is it immediately relevant to your business?

✓ Can you clearly map an individual's path toward mastery?

✓ Does the environment empower employees to leverage what they learn?

✓ Does it lead to measurable results?

7: E-learning is overused, or used in the wrong situations.

COMPUTER-BASED TRAINING offers advantages in efficiency, but managers should make sure that it is the right medium for each training message. Take AT&T, for example: Two years ago few employees at the company were enthusiastic about its sales training program. "It just didn't engage them," Henderson says. Most of the curriculum was taught over the computer, and salespeople weren't relating to it. "Salespeople are gregarious, and they like human interaction," he says. Now, the company's program has been redesigned so that basics are taught through e-learning and more advanced skills are taught in the classroom.

Stone faced a similar problem at Lotus. Students didn't approach the company's electronic courses as seriously as their traditional training. "It's much easier to blow off an online class than not show up in a classroom," she says. "We built all these e-learning programs, but people didn't participate as much initially." One of the advantages to online learning—that it could be completed on the learner's own schedule—became a disadvantage. Because no set time was scheduled for learning, salespeople blew off the courses and dealt with other tasks piling up on their desks. The answer, not surprisingly, was to make managers more accountable for their salespeople's participation in

e-learning. "Once we got them on the tails of their reps and said, 'You've got to do this,' it took off," Stone says.

8: There's no follow-up after training.

SOME COMPANIES SPEND literally hundreds of millions of dollars on training," says Corporate Training Consultants' Skiff. "Then they wash their hands of it; people go back to work and there's no follow-up." It's crucial, Skiff says, that trainers or coaches continue working with trainees to ensure that the skills learned are applied in the workplace. Sue Bohle, the president of the Bohle Company, a public relations firm in Los Angeles, remembers her experience with training programs to which her former company sent her. "I'd go to these weekend courses, and two months later I'd find that my notes were still in a stack of papers on my desk and I'd eventually throw them out with the book from the training that I promised myself I'd read," she says. The lesson? When the learning isn't revisited after the training session ends, it won't stick.

PRO's Walker makes an analogy to sports training: Let's say you're a golfer and want to improve your swing. Before you

take classes, you're getting a certain handicap, but you know that you could play better. During the golf lessons a pro teaches you how to hold the club differently and swing in a way that's new to you. While you're in the session practicing, it actually begins to work. A week after the class you're back on the golf course, and the new swing isn't helping your game. "While you had the coach helping, it worked, but later it's completely new and you get lower results. If there's not a coach to help you get used to the new grip and swing, you're going to go back to your original form from before the training session," he says.

9: The trainer can't relate to your team.

THERE ARE FEW things more demoralizing than listening to a lecturer who flops. Ogilvy's Lamparter says that the worst training failures he has experienced were the result of underestimating the importance of an outside trainer's ability to connect to the audience. "Usually the mistake I made was that the trainer talked the agenda well, but didn't actually deliver the whole thing in real time until the day of the training, and just couldn't live up to it," he says. "The impromptu stuff—how you draw in the audience, and do live demos on situations and problems presented by the group—that's where supposedly good trainers fall down. I've had a couple of very expensive failures like that." Now, Lamparter asks to sit in on a similar session that the trainer leads for another company, or at least see a videotape of a live session. "Nothing short of that makes me confident," he says. "I've been burned enough that I need to see it in real time."

If there's one rule to hiring a sales trainer, it's to demand sales experience. If the person is in front of a class and can't tell his war stories and demonstrate that he understands sales culture, salespeople won't respect his methods, Henderson says. The biggest training flop he can remember was with a trainer that didn't have a career in sales. "He focused too much on the theory, not experience," he says. "He presented this great new theory for sales and then one of the students stood up and asked him for an example. He didn't have any. It was terrible. People actually got up and left."

If a training program faces one or more of these problems, it will need retooling before it can be effective. But if these situations ring familiar, that doesn't mean that you should ditch training altogether. Chances are your employees can benefit from new skills and knowledge. The answer is to take more time to look at the assumptions, methods, and outcomes of your training programs, and make sure that their ends meet your needs. Training manager Corsini agrees: Although he sees plenty of waste in most training programs, he admits that training is more than necessary—it's crucial. "I believe in education and the development of people," he says. "But I see what happens in our schools, and then I see what happens in companies, and I don't know who's dumber. The business world has nothing on the education world. Both sets of students are bored to death."

ASSOCIATE EDITOR MARK MCMASTER CAN BE REACHED AT MMCMASTER@SALESANDMARKETING.COM

From *Sales & Marketing Management*, January 2001, pp. 40-48. © 2001 by Sales & Marketing Management. Reprinted by permission of Mark McMaster

BRAND YOURSELF

WHETHER YOU WORK FOR A CORPORATION, RUN YOUR OWN BUSINESS, OR FREELANCE, USE YOUR NAME TO GAIN SIGNIFICANT POWER AND INFLUENCE

BY ANN BROWN

LITTLE DID TAVIS SMILEY KNOW that being fired, after five years, as the host and executive producer of Black Entertainment Television's (BET) *BET Tonight With Tavis Smiley*, would turn out to be a major career transition. In fact, it was the start of the branding of Tavis Smiley.

"I didn't realize my value because I hadn't gone outside [of BET] to find out," notes the author, lecturer, TV-radio personality, and political analyst. Even though Smiley had interviewed some of the world's top personalities, and snagged President Bill Clinton's first interview following the Monica Lewinsky incident, Smiley wasn't prepared for the flood of offers he received.

Within weeks after leaving BET, Smiley sealed an unprecedented trio of deals — as a correspondent on both ABC's *Good Morning America* and CNN's *Primetime Live*; and as host of a one-hour syndicated talk show for Buena Vista Television. "We did this all within eight to nine weeks," says Smiley. "And it only took that long because of all the paperwork."

The hot streak kept blazing. Smiley renewed his contract with ABC Radio Networks to continue his popular political commentaries on *The Tom Joyner Morning Show*, along with his syndicated spots, *The Smiley Report*, to air afternoons on black radio stations nationwide. National Public Radio tapped him for a daily one-hour morning show to air on 600 stations. Add to this, a two-book publishing deal with Doubleday and a product deal with Hay House Inc., a self-help book publishing company in Carlsbad, California. The result is a multimillion-dollar package of contracts.

Smiley made his name work for him and you can too. Whether you're a corporate exec, business owner, or freelancer, you can gain power and prestige by branding yourself. Branding means equating your name to a certain topic, product, or service. Through branding, your expertise is transformed into a valuable commodity. So brand yourself by following these steps:

STEP 1: FIND YOUR NICHE

First, you have to find your brand. Do this by "looking at the patterns of your life," says Norma Thompson Hollis, founder and CEO of Black Speakers Online (*www.blackspeakers.net*; 310-671-7136), which represents Smiley, success expert George Fraser, professional orator Patricia Russell-McCloud, and businessman Stedman Graham. "There are themes in your life that keep popping up." This could be your brand. Fraser, for example, used his love of networking to teach others how to schmooze with the best of them. Today, Fraser is considered one of the foremost authorities on networking and building effective relationships. His *SuccessGuide: The Networking Guide to Black Resources* has been self-published in 20 versions in nine cities.

Before presenting your brand image to the world, reassess your life, career, and what you want to achieve. "What are your strengths? What are you already known for? What are you passionate about?" asks Bob Baker, author of *Poor Richard's Branding Yourself Online: How to Use the Internet to Become a Celebrity or Expert in Your Field* (Top Floor Publishing, $29.95). "Done right, you'll be promoting your brand for many years, so make sure you choose an identity you'll be able to live with for a long time." But don't just pull an "identity" out of the air, cautions Baker. "Never look at the market, see a void, and then mold yourself into a personality that fills it."

Instead, your brand should be a natural extension of yourself — but not every aspect of yourself. A brand identity that displays your every interest rarely works. To pursue other interests, start a new brand, complete with a separate Website, newsletter, etc. That doesn't mean you have to change your name. Consider using a new business name.

Once you settle on an image, you'll want to describe it to others. "Create what I call a Brand Identity Statement (BIS),"

advises Baker. "A BIS spells out who you are and what you do. The ideal BIS should be short and specific, while indicating a clear benefit."

When choosing your brand, don't let your job describe you. "One mistake people make is that they identify their job title as who they are," notes professional executive coach Max D. Ellzey, Ed.D., owner of Culver City, California-based The Ellzey Group and president of the Los Angeles chapter of Professional Coaches and Mentors Association (*www.pcmaonline.com*). "Look at your purpose in life. What do you want to accomplish? What impact do you want to have on others? Once you are clearer about who you are and who you are becoming, you can move forward."

That's how Yvonne White started building her brand. Twenty-one years ago White catered events to make extra money during school breaks from the University of Colorado, where she majored in journalism. Now the 39-year-old entrepreneur puts on corporate functions for clients such as BMW, Ford Motor Company, Columbia Tristar Pictures, and MTV.

Although the Los Angeles-based Yvonne E. White & Co. (*www.YEWandCo.com*) was launched to provide catering services, along the way the company narrowed its focus and found its niche. "My godfather, Roy Schultz, a celebrity chef who counted Frank Sinatra as a client, got me started in catering, but I wanted to plan events; so today we do event planning and organizing parties. We do have a catering division," says White.

Throughout the years White focused the mission of her company even further. "I no longer do parties for under 100 people. I realized it was just as much work to throw a party for 20 as it was for 100," notes White, who employs 78 full- and part-time workers. White also stopped planning weddings and made her specialty in providing corporate affairs events with a twist. "I add a personal touch to events. I treat each event as if it [were] a party I was throwing in my own home. I do everything I can think of for the comfort of the guests. I even make sure the walking distance from the valet parking is convenient," she says. "The key to having a successful business to me is to find out what your competition is doing and provide something the competition isn't providing."

STEP 2: IS YOUR BRAND MARKETABLE?

OK. You've defined your brand, but is it marketable? Says Ellzey, "I ask my clients, 'What need can you satisfy better than anyone else, and how much are they willing to pay you for satisfying that need?' This question will determine how strong your brand is."

Look at the market. "Examine the environment and what's in demand," Hollis points out. "Currently, the entire country is looking for experts to help them deal with our changing times, experts on healing, financial advisors, etc." In fact, Hollis' most-recent presentation, "Be At Peace in Time of War," is very timely considering the post-September 11 tragedy. The topic is also very marketable. Speakers Etc. has organized special re-

treats, panel discussions, and symposiums on "helping people and organizations heal, rebuild, and achieve balance," she says.

Do your homework. "Go to a good search site and enter keywords related to your identity. Visit those sites that come up in the search," suggests Baker. "To have success branding yourself online, you must be able to identify a good number of highly traveled Websites, forums, and online publications that reach the people most likely to become your customers."

Listen to feedback. "Trust that if you have a desire to share your skills and/or knowledge, there will be immediate feedback about whether what you are sharing is valuable to others," says professional certified executive coach Dr. Barbara Walton of KTD Coaching Services (*www.knowthedifference.com*) in Lee's Summit, Missouri.

But, adds Hollis, don't try to appeal to everyone. "Focus on a niche market and narrow it down," she says. "The more you narrow down, the more of an expert you'll become on a specific topic." B. Smith used her fame as a successful restaurateur to become a culinary and lifestyle expert, and later turned that expertise into a business that includes products, books, and a magazine (that eventually folded). Her TV show currently airs in 187 markets (*www.bsmithwithstyle.com*).

Iyanla Vanzant, a self-made lecturer who used her life experiences to help others overcome obstacles, also used her popularity to launch speaking engagements, books, and now her own TV show.

For Smiley, whose passion for politics started at age 13, becoming a political-social commentator was a natural step. "I wanted to enlighten, encourage, and empower," says Smiley, who began his professional career as an aide to former Los Angeles Mayor Tom Bradley.

Test the market. When martial arts expert Billy Blanks decided he wanted to create a new form of exercise called Tae Bo (a combination of aerobics, martial arts, and boxing moves), he decided to try it out on his target market. After trying it out on his wife, he approached the workers and patrons of a beauty parlor near his martial arts school in Los Angeles and offered them free Tae Bo classes. After receiving positive feedback from women who took the classes, he knew an audience would pay for Tae Bo lessons.

STEP 3: SEEK PROFESSIONAL HELP

Throughout the branding process, you may need professional help. Career coaches can help formulate and promote your brand. Find a coach through the Professional Coaches and Mentors Association or the International Coach Federation (*www.coachfederation.com*). Their fees range from $200 to $1,000 monthly, or $100 an hour.

Black Speakers Online (*www.blackspeakers.net*) offers a consulting service for $125 an hour to help pinpoint your brand. And if speaking professionally is a goal, you may need to sign up with a speakers' bureau. "It will save you money in the long run," notes Hollis. "We package and market you by putting together a professional kit with your biography, audiotapes, videotapes, and print-marketing materials."

STEP 4: PROMOTION, PROMOTION, PROMOTION

Speak for free, advises Hollis. That's what Vanzant did. Using her life experiences as a platform, she began lecturing to women on public assistance for free. Locally, Vanzant became recognized and then published the first of her self-help books, *Tapping the Power Within: A Path to Self-Empowerment for Black Women* (Harlem River Press, out of print), in 1992.

"Test your skills and get feedback. It's also an opportunity to sell your product or services." Ellzey suggests. "Pick a topic that aligns with how you want to be branded, develop a speech or presentation that fits the category, and then volunteer to speak at a luncheon or some other event. You will begin to have more opportunities to speak, thus creating a tremendous amount of exposure." Speaking engagements that pay may soon follow. According to Hollis, speakers can earn from $5,000 on the low-end to $50,000 for celebrity speakers.

Look to the Web. "The Internet still offers a mountain of opportunity for sensible self-promoters who have a clear brand identity and a well-defined target audience," says Baker. "The low cost of entry makes it ideal for guerrilla marketers who prefer to use creativity instead of cash to promote themselves. The Internet allows you to use a wide range of tools to reach people — not only Websites and e-mail newsletters but also discussion forums, e-mail networking, online media coverage, e-books, free articles, digital file sharing, and more."

Tune in to local media. Following an unsuccessful bid for a spot on the Los Angeles City Council in 1988, Smiley needed to remain fresh in the public's mind because he had planned to run for office again. He created a 60-second political commentary show called *The Smiley Report*; he found sponsors and ran the spot on local black radio station KGFJ-AM. From there, the show went into syndication. Smiley developed a following, which led to a job as a commentator with Los Angeles' KABC-TV news in 1994. Smiley also co-hosted *Twentysomething Talk* for KABC-AM radio. BET and *The Tom Joyner Morning Show* would come next.

Through his segments on the Joyner show, which has more than seven million listeners daily, Smiley led several national on-air campaigns, including a calling on the carpet of CompUSA for its lack of advertising in black media. In August 1999, Joyner and Smiley began urging listeners to mail in sales receipts to prove that black consumers did, indeed, shop at CompUSA. Five boxes of these were sent to CompUSA without a reply. Smiley threatened to "take it to the next level" unless CompUSA responded.

Eventually, CompUSA agreed to an action plan that called for the company to advertise in black media outlets. Smiley's goal of becoming an advocate for black America had become a reality. Smiley got the word—and his brand— out by authoring several socially pointed books, five to date, with two more coming out this year.

STEP 5: BRANCHING YOUR BRAND

In order to take your brand into other arenas, make strategic alliances, says Smiley. That's what he did. "We've been very careful about how we brand Tavis Smiley, and who we make deals with," says Smiley, who launched The Smiley Group (*www.tavistalks.com*) as an umbrella company. "We turn down much more than we accept." One of his alliances is with Microsoft Corp. Smiley spoke on the "Build Your Business Tour," sponsored by the software giant. This year, Smiley will tour several cities with Microsoft Founder Bill Gates, doing a summit series on "BIT: Blacks in Technology," part of the Build Your Business Tour. Smiley has also developed a relationship with Wal-Mart, sponsors of *The Smiley Report*.

In 1999, Smiley launched the Tavis Smiley Foundation, which holds youth-leadership seminars and workshops, awards scholarships, and has a national mentorship program.

STEP 6: GOING BEYOND THE BRAND

Once your brand has become popular, look for ways for it to sell itself. According to Smiley, his product deal with Hay House will broaden the brand beyond his personality by packaging his speeches on audiotapes; distributing his gift products (i.e. Tavis Smiley empowerment cards), and direct-mail products. "The next phase in our development is that the brand flourishes without me having to be there," says Smiley. "So much now has to do with my taking part, and I can't be in 10 places at once." The Smiley Group's free, corporate-sponsored symposium series, which has grown to six a year and attracts 5,000-plus attendees per event, will be developed where Smiley doesn't necessarily have to take part personally.

Vanzant and B. Smith have expanded their brands. Vanzant launched her Inner Visions Worldwide Network Inc. and Bookstore (*www.innervisionsworldwide.com*) in Silver Spring, Maryland, which hosts personal growth classes and weekend workshops for men and women. And B. Smith added a pattern line to Vogue Patterns, while Oprah has *O* magazine and Harpo Productions, a TV and film production company in Chicago.

White, who has gotten all her clients through word of mouth, has never advertised or marketed her company—at least not yet. "I am going to create a video series on event/party planning," says White, relying on her staff to pick up any slack. "I've surrounded myself with a great group of people." If all goes as planned for White, her name will become synonymous worldwide with party planning.

Be careful, however, not to spread your brand too thin. There is such a thing as too much exposure, says Walton, especially if it isn't in alignment with your vision.

Career development and its practice: A historical perspective

Edwin L. Herr

The use of the term career development as descriptive of both the factors and the processes influencing individual career behavior and as synonymous with intervention in career behavior (e.g., the practice of career development) is relatively recent. As professional vocabulary evolves across time, so do the form and substance of career interventions and those to whom they are directed. At the beginning of the new millennium, this article reviews the legacy of the 20th century and considers selected theoretical and practical issues likely to be prominent in the practice of career development in the decades immediately ahead.

The term career development, as used in the title of the National Career Development Association, had increasingly come, at the end of the twentieth century, to describe both the total constellation of psychological, sociological, educational, physical, economic, and chance factors that combine to shape individual career behavior over the life span (Sears, 1982) and the interventions or practices that are used "to enhance a person's career development or to enable that person to make more effective career decisions" (Spokane, 1991, p. 22). Thus, inherent in the current usage of the term career development are two sets of theories, or conceptual categories, one that explains the development of career behavior across the life span and the other that describes how career behavior is changed by particular interventions.

This perspective about the contemporary use of the term career development is important simply to establish that terms, like professions, evolve. They are historical creations, the shape, substance, and labeling of which reflect social, polit-

ical, and economic change. Indeed, the term career was rarely used before the 1960s and the term development was rarely used before the 1950s. When the two terms were combined, they tended until the late 1960s to be described as vocational development or vocational psychology, not career development.

Against this context it is useful to consider the antecedent events that have led to the focus of this special issue: the practice of career development. Historical references to career development practice are more likely to use terms like vocational guidance or counseling, or career guidance or counseling, rather than career development practice, but all of these terms flow from the same roots.

Historical Perspectives

In this millennium issue of The Career Development Quarterly, it is useful to acknowledge that if one believes in evolution, rather than revolution, as the origin of career development practice, then the seeds of the future exist in the past and in the present. In such a view, the practice of career development in the twenty-first century will build on, be distributed more evenly across the world, and refine much of what has been learned and implemented in the twentieth century. If one discounts the interesting accounts (Dumont & Carson, 1995; Williamson, 1965) of the origins of career development practice that can be traced far into antiquity to demonstrate how various societies have helped persons choose their work, or, more likely, allocated work to people based on their class or caste, one can conclude that the theories and techniques that constitute current approaches to the practice of career development are

primarily creatures of the late nineteenth and early twentieth centuries.

Factors Influencing the Emergence of Vocational Guidance

The rise of what was first identified as vocational guidance in the United States in the late nineteenth and early twentieth centuries was directly associated with major shifts from a national economy that was primarily based in agriculture to an economy that was, as part of the industrial revolution that was spilling over from Europe to the United States, increasingly based in manufacturing and industrial processes. As the latter occurred, urbanization and occupational diversity increased, as did national concerns about strengthening vocational education and responding to the needs for information about how persons could identify and access emerging jobs. By the late 1800s, particularly in urban areas, such information was so differentiated and comprehensive that families or neighborhoods could no longer be the prime sources of occupational information or of the allocation of jobs; other more formal mechanisms, including rudimentary forms of vocational guidance, began to emerge in schools, in settlement houses, and in community centers.

A major factor in the rise of vocational guidance was the accelerating movement of large numbers of immigrants from nations with poor economic opportunities coming to the United States seeking new lives and options; a parallel phenomenon was occurring as people in the United States were migrating from rural to urban areas, spurred by the urbanization of jobs, particularly in the

concentrations of plants in major cities making steel, furniture, automobiles, and other large capital goods.

Cast against the processes of industrialization, urbanization, and immigration were many other issues that affected the development of vocational guidance. These issues included concerns about appropriate education for children and effective placement of adults into a rapidly changing occupational structure, about effective methods of distribution of immigrants across the spectrum of available occupations, and about the way to bridge the gap between schooling and the realities of the adult world. At the beginning of the twentieth century as at its end, many voices were raised in behalf of educational reform, arguing that schools were too "bookish," too college oriented, and with insufficient vocational education.

Other issues were also pervasive at the turn of the twentieth century. Among them were concerns about how to address changing family structures, the increasing proportion of girls and women entering the workplace rather than confining themselves to homemaking, diminished extended kinship systems, child labor, and the shifts in child rearing practices that were emerging in relation to migration and the consuming force of the industrial revolution. Moreover, as the social reformers and human rights activists were advocating, there was an emerging moral imperative that opposed child labor and argued that workers in the burgeoning economy of the early twentieth century needed to be seen not as the chattels of employers, not as property to be consumed and cast aside, but rather as persons of dignity with a right to determine their own destiny.

By any analysis, it is clear that the heritage of career development practice in the United States is rich, complex, and responsive to the social, political, and economic forces shaping the national context. Observers in and out of the professional ranks of career counselors and specialists in career guidance have reinforced the notion that the theories and practices that undergird and stimulate career development practice do not exist in a vacuum. Although, in any

period of social change, the force of certain personalities as articulators and visionaries, who advocate what needs to be done to convert ideas about career guidance or other processes into action, is critical; the historical moment—the political and social conditions—must be right for the seeds of change to take root and flourish. The last quarter of the nineteenth century and the first quarter of the twentieth century were such times.

One of the important chronicles of the rise of vocational guidance in the United States (Brewer, 1942) identified four conditions that were seen as major influences: the division of labor, the growth of technology, the extension of vocational education, and the spread of modern forms of democracy. Other observers elaborated on the connections between the rise and redirection of vocational guidance and counseling during the past 100 years and the effects of particular political or social phenomena—legislation, national crises, shifts in social values, the civil rights and women's liberation movements, and economic conditions.

Cremin (1964), a historian of education, contended that one of the associated outcomes of the Progressive Education movement in the late 1800s and the first 50 years of the twentieth century was the beginning of the guidance movement, particularly its emphasis on vocational guidance. He, like others, contended that the social reformism of the urban settlement workers was directly involved in the beginning of vocational guidance during the first years of the twentieth century and its subsequent implementation in the schools of Boston and other cities. Cremin argued that social reformers of the time believed [n]ot only that vocational counseling would lead to greater individual fulfillment; but that people suited to their job would tend to be active in the creation of more efficient and humane industrial systems … [therefore] the craft of vocational guidance would serve not only the youngsters who sought counsel, but the cause of social reform as well. (p. 12)

Cremin further contended that the effort to develop a science of education, also at the heart of the progressive movement, was reflected in

the major interest in tests and measurements that grew up in the United States immediately after the turn of the twentieth century. According to Cremin, it was in this context that "the idea developed of the guidance worker as a trained professional, wise in administering and interpreting scientific instruments for the prediction of vocational and educational success" (pp. 18-19).

Cremin's (1964) analysis of the impact of the Progressive Education era on vocational guidance and counseling is but one of the interesting interactions between educational reform and the rise of vocational guidance. Stephens (1970), also a historian, has argued that "the vocational education movement was an educational response to the general reform movement spawned by the industrialization of America" (p. xiii). More to the point of the origins of vocational guidance are Stephens's observations that [t]o many leaders of the vocational reform movement … it was apparent that vocational education was but the first part of a package of needed educational reforms. They argued that a school curriculum and educational goals that mirrored the occupational structure created merely a platform and impetus for launching youth into the world of work. What was clearly needed to consummate the launch were guidance mechanisms that would insure their safe and efficient arrival on the job. Without guidance experts it was argued, other efforts at reform would be aborted … Therefore, in the name of social and economic efficiency, the argument continued, the youth who has been carefully trained would also have to be carefully counseled into a suitable occupational niche. (p. xiv)

These analyses of the array of forces that shaped and defined the original antecedents to contemporary approaches to career guidance, career counseling, and to the practice of career development could be repeated from other vantage points. They would include extended discussions of persons and events that made significant conceptual and empirical contributions to the evolution of career development and its related career interventions. To do so would affirm the general applicability of

Borow's (1964) observations that the history of vocational guidance teaches two lessons:

(1) The growth of the movement must be evaluated against the Zeitgeist. Without an appreciation of the prevailing social and intellectual temper of the times, the interpretation of episodes in the sweep of professional history remains incomplete and often distorted; (2) Progress flows from seemingly small beginnings. (p. 47)

The Emergence of Vocational Guidance

The period to which the citations of Borow (1964), Brewer (1942), Cremin (1964), and Stephens (1970) spoke is considered the founding period of vocational guidance in the United States. It is the period when Parsons, generally conceded to be the father of the vocational guidance movement and, indeed, the architect of the vocational counseling process, wrote his classic book Choosing a Vocation, posthumously published in 1909. Trained as a civil engineer and a lawyer, Parsons spent most of his life dealing with social reform among the excesses of the free enterprise system as he saw them and the debasement of human nature, which he considered a result of the management of industrial organizations. He was at various times involved with activities of the settlement houses that had grown up in central Boston and in other cities along the northeastern seaboard.

Parsons in the later years of his life turned the focus of his attention to industrial education and vocational guidance in response to his feeling that too many people, especially the immigrants from Europe, were being wasted, both economically and socially, because of the haphazard way they got into the specialized world of the factory. Like so many others of his time, Parsons attacked the public schools for their specialization in book learning and advocated that "book work should be balanced with industrial education; and working children should spend part time in culture classes and industrial science" (Stephens, 1970, p. 39).

It was in response to the questions and issues inventoried here—those

dealing with human dignity, the effective matching of persons and jobs, educational and social reform—that the early models of vocational guidance and vocational counseling were created. The early vocational guidance procedures were seen as methods, both practical and humane, to help persons to be matched with the needs of the occupational structure in ways that both preserved the order and the rationality of such choices and the power of persons to make decisions about job options available to them rather than to be coerced or forced into whatever was immediately available. However, at the beginning of the twentieth century, although there was important research taking place about the measurement of individual differences and other counseling-relevant processes in university laboratories in Europe and the United States, there was essentially no scientific basis or theory on which to build models of vocational guidance or counseling. The practice of career development was emerging, but not yet career development theory.

To compensate for the lack of theory and applicable science—and the tools that counselors have come to depend on in career development practice (e.g., tests, dictionaries of occupational titles, The Occupational Outlook Handbook)—persons of conceptual genius in Europe and in the United States developed techniques and insights that began to create a knowledge base on which vocational counseling could be built.

Exemplary of such persons were Alfred Binet's work in France on intelligence testing; Spranger's work in Germany on types of personalities in relation to different types of jobs; Munsterberg's research in Germany on occupational choice and worker performance; the work of Jesse B. Davis and Eli Weaver in the United States on the educational and career problems of students; and, perhaps the preeminent contribution: the three-step paradigm of Parsons that guided the development of vocational guidance for at least the first 50 years of the twentieth century. Parsons, as part of his vision of the process, coined the term vocational guidance. In general, Parsons saw vocational guidance as a one-on-one

process, which he also called "vocational counseling" (Cremin, 1964; Parsons, 1909). In his concern about developing techniques by which school children, adolescent school leavers, and adults could come to true reasoning about jobs available to them, he proposed a tripartite set of concepts as a frame of reference for the use of techniques by a counselor. His classic three-step design included the following:

First, a clear understanding of yourself, aptitudes, abilities, interests, resources, limitations, and other qualities. Second, a knowledge of the requirements and conditions of success, advantages and disadvantages, compensation, opportunities, and prospects in different lines of work. Third, true reasoning on the relations of these two groups of facts. (Parsons, 1909, p. 5)

The techniques readily available for Parsons (1909) to use to implement his three-step process were limited. As a result, Parsons had his counselees read biographies and interview workers to learn about working environments and the occupational structure. In the absence of standardized tests of aptitudes or interest inventories, or directories of information about jobs or occupations, Parsons emphasized counselor observation of client characteristics and the coaching of the client in comprehensive self-study and in study of industrial opportunities available. He used extensive lists of questions for client self-study and sharing with the counselor. He offered techniques to assist clients to be introspective about their own likes and dislikes, successes and limitations, and to talk with the counselor about how to engage in true reasoning (decision making) related to the information they had. Although it is rarely noted, Parsons was expressly inclusive of, and tailored approaches to, both young men and young women. He assumed that many, but not all, of the vocational techniques he used were of equal value to boys and girls and men and women, and he provided special attention to information about industries open to women and how these positions could be accessed. He also provided statistics about occupations in which both men

and women were employed as well as those that employed primarily men. Some of the techniques Parsons pioneered are still used today, and some are incorporated into more sophisticated interventions for counselor use.

Although the history of the twentieth century has included fleshing out Parsons's model, adding steps to it (Salamone, 1988), providing scientific bases to each of the steps—identifying and measuring individual differences, documenting differences in occupational content and activity, and clarifying the elements of the decision-making process—the century's achievements go beyond the important contributions of Parsons's paradigm. Other theorists and practitioners have created an array of career development theories and practices that effectively intervene in the facilitation of career development, job choice and entry, work adjustment problems, unemployment, and underemployment. Still other theorists have advocated the differential perspectives and needs of women and men as well as of persons in racial and ethnic minority groups for career guidance (Gilligan, 1982; Leong, 1995; Pierce, 1933). As a result, the possible recipients of vocational guidance have become increasingly comprehensive in the range of problems that they present and in their ages and settings rather than being primarily adolescents in schools or settlement houses, as was true at the beginning of the twentieth century. Nevertheless, Parsons's paradigm continues to be a remarkable milestone in the evolution of career development practices.

Although there is much more that can be said about the important forces that shaped vocational guidance in the decades spanning the nineteenth and twentieth centuries, given the spatial limitations here, it is necessary to fast forward to the middle of the twentieth century to capture the growing conceptual changes that have shaped the final 50 years of the twentieth century. For a decade-by-decade compilation of major events shaping contemporary forms of career development practice, the reader is invited to examine the article later in this special issue titled "Selected Milestones in

the Evolution of Career Development Practices in the Twentieth Century" (Herr & Shahnasarian, 2001).

National Goals and Vocational Guidance

As the practice of career development unfolded in the twentieth century, a constant theme shaping its purposes was the impact of social, political, and economic influences, including national policy and legislation, on the growth and comprehensiveness of such practice. As national goals have changed since the beginning of the twentieth century in response to the needs of defense, economic depression, demographic changes in the population, and growth in new forms of industrial or information-based production, vocational or career guidance and counseling and other career development practices have been seen as making contributions to multiple national agendas: the facilitation of equality of access to education and training opportunities; educational reform; economic efficiency; creating human capital; matching persons and occupational opportunities; rehabilitating those on the margins of society by providing support and direction to their career development; and helping persons find dignity, purpose in, and adjustment to work.

Each of these goals has taken on more or less urgency, depending on events in the larger society that have arisen in different historical periods and that have varied markedly in their substance (Herr, 1997): for example, social reform interacting with the rise of the industrial revolution in the late 1800s; the cognizance of individual differences in the early 1900s; classification of military personnel and issues of national defense in the second decade of the 1900s; rising concern about persons with disabilities and the mentally ill in the 1920s; the economic exigencies and needs to match persons with available employment opportunities during the Great Depression of the 1930s; national defense in the 1940s and the 1950s; the democratization of education, civil rights, women's rights, and occupational opportunities in the Great Society programs of

the 1960s; concerns for equity and special needs populations in a climate of economic austerity in the 1970s; and the transformation from an industrial to an information-based global economy and from military to economic competition among nations in the 1980s and 1990s. Each of these historical periods spawned national social metaphors and rhetoric that ultimately pervaded policies and legislation, directly or indirectly affecting the practice of career development. In some instances, such legislation has identified particularly vulnerable populations (e.g., specific members of minority populations, persons in poverty and on welfare, single parents, the frail elderly) requiring specific forms of help to cope with changing social and economic conditions; in other legislation, the focus has been on groups of youth or adults who needed to be classified regarding their ability to perform specific jobs or to be provided with career direction relevant to national goals of finding personpower who could effectively serve the nation's military needs or its scientific needs.

A long inventory of national legislation, beginning in the first decades of the twentieth century and continuing to the present, has specifically advocated the importance of vocational and career guidance, shaped the practices and recipients of such interventions, and provided for the preparation and professionalization of counselors. As identified in the article on selected milestones [see *The Career Development Quarterly*, 49, pp. 225-232] (Herr & Shahnasarian, 2001), there have been many important landmark pieces of legislation that made significant contributions to the evolution of career guidance and counseling. A few examples of more recent legislation that have provided resources for, advocated career guidance as a policy imperative, and shaped the professional preparation of counselors would include the George Barden Act of 1946, the National Defense Education Act of 1958, the Career Education Incentive Act of 1976, the Carl D. Perkins Vocational Education Act of 1984 and subsequent amendments, and the School to Work Opportunities Act of 1994.

To cite only brief examples of the impact of these pieces of federal leg-

islation, the George Barden Act in 1946 paid the salaries and expenses of vocational counselors and made it possible to reimburse counselor training institutions. This legislation had many important effects. In addition to its statement about the importance of vocational counseling, it provided Harry Jager, then Head of the Occupational Information and Guidance Service of the U.S. Office of Education, resources to encourage the growth of state supervisors of guidance in state departments of education and to encourage these state supervisors to implement state certification processes for school counselors. At the time, one could be certified as a school counselor in many states with three credits of occupational information and three credits of principles of guidance. Jager and his colleagues in the U.S. Office of Education were concerned about the quality of vocational and school counselor preparation. At the time of the George Barden Act, there were approximately 80 institutions preparing counselors in the United States, 40 at the undergraduate level and 40 at the graduate level, compared with more than 400 graduate programs today. Jager, concerned about the need for more counselors and for improved quality and status for counselors, proclaimed that counselor preparation should be graduate preparation, not an undergraduate program. Between 1949 and 1952, Jager's unit in the U.S. Office of Education issued eight reports on counselor preparation, course content, in-service education, supervised practice by which to define "reimbursable counselor training courses," and course requirements for counselor certification (Hoyt, 1974). The result was a phaseout of most undergraduate programs of counselor preparation by the early 1950s and a growing concern with the professionalization of vocational and school counselors.

Shortly afterward, in 1958, the National Defense Education Act (NDEA) triggered the largest growth of secondary school counselors in the history of the nation. NDEA provided both the funds for schools to employ secondary school counselors and funds for higher education institutions to provide counselor education

programs, primarily in academic, yearlong institutes, typically leading to the master's degree. Although the major thrust of the NDEA legislation was on preparing secondary school counselors to identify, encourage, and counsel students who were academically talented in sciences and mathematics so that the United States could build its scientific capacity to compete with the Soviet Union in the "space race," a subtext of the legislation was the need for counselors to provide career development to students. Subsequently, the Carl D. Perkins Act of 1984 advanced the growing professionalization of counselors by asserting that the vocational guidance activities in the legislation should be implemented by "certified counselors." Although each of these pieces of legislation and the others cited deserve fuller treatment, the point is that national goals, policies, and legislation have been significant factors in advocating the importance of and the need for quality and comprehensive provisions of vocational and career guidance.

Changing Definitions of Vocational Guidance

In addition to the important role of federal legislation, a subset of major importance in affecting the practice of career development during the latter half of the twentieth century was the rise of theories of career development and the related redefinition of vocational guidance. A major milestone occurred in 1950, when Hoppock, then president of the National Vocational Guidance Association, observed that the traditional view of vocational guidance was "crumbling" (Hoppock, 1950). In 1951, following on Hoppock's observation, Super recommended that the traditional definition of vocational guidance that had stood since 1937 be revised. The 1937 definition stated that vocational guidance was "the process of assisting the individual to choose an occupation, prepare for it, enter upon it, and progress in it" (Super, 1951, p. 92). The definition proposed by Super (1951) and adopted by the National Vocational Guidance Association defined vocational guidance as [t]he process of helping a person to develop and accept an integrated and

adequate picture of himself [sic] and of his role in the world of work, to test this concept against reality, and to convert it into a reality, with satisfaction to himself and to society. (p. 89)

The latter definition changed the focus of vocational guidance from a concentration on what is to be chosen to increasing attention on the characteristics of the chooser. In the process, it diminished the emphasis on matching individual to job and on the provision of occupational information at a particular point in time. Instead, it emphasized the psychological nature of vocational choice, accented the developmental influences on career behavior across the life span, blended the personal and vocational dimensions of guidance into a whole, and elevated the importance of self-understanding and self-acceptance as the evaluative bases to which occupational and educational alternatives should be related.

Super's (1990) theoretical conceptions in the 1950s through the 1990s emphasized a life-span approach to career development, which describes changing career tasks and concerns in each of a series of life stages: growth, exploration, establishment, maintenance, and decline. He addressed both similar and different career patterns exhibited by men and women related to such physical and social phenomena as sex stereotyping, socialization, biological differences, and the opportunity structure. He made explicit the interaction of career development and personal development, the differential salience or meaning of work, how life roles and work roles affected individual career patterns, and the processes and elements related to career maturity and career adaptability.

During the 1950s and the 1960s, and subsequently, other major theories of career development were created and tested. The career theories of Roe (1956), Holland (1966), Krumboltz (1979), and others spawned additional paradigms of career behavior, based on interdisciplinary perspectives such as the psychodynamic effects of child-rearing practices on the development of occupational interests, the role of

behavioral style or personality type as the major influence in career choice, and the role of unique learning experiences reinforced by unfolding life events that affect individual preferences. The work of Roe, of Holland, of Krumboltz, and of Super (1957, 1990) led to the development of a large array of new assessment instruments (e.g., the Self-Directed Search, the Vocational Preference Inventory, the Adult Career Concerns Inventory, the Career Maturity Inventory, the Values Inventory, the Career Beliefs Inventory) and counseling interventions that operationalized the constructs embedded in the career theories. Theory building continued throughout the ensuing years of the twentieth century as had the creation of new tests and career interventions.

Of particular importance to theory building during the last quarter century of the twentieth century was the growing attention to the career development of women and of minority populations. Among such contributions are those of Astin's (1984) four constructs that address the possibility of gender differences in degree of career behavior rather than kind: motivation, sex role socialization, the structure of opportunity, and work expectations; the work of Betz and Hackett (1986) in examining the effects of level and strength of self-efficacy related to women's entrance into and performance in career-related processes; Farmer's (1985) analyses of influences on aspiration, mastery, and career commitment for men and women and her studies of diversity and women's career development from adolescence to adulthood (Farmer & Associates, 1997); Gilligan's (1982) efforts to describe women's sex role development leading to differences in the sexes in their expressions of intimacy and identity in relation to career behavior; and Hansen's work with her colleagues on creating career development curriculum designed to reflect the changing roles of young men and women in the workplace and in other life roles (Hansen & Minor, 1989) and her model of Integrative Life Planning (Hansen, 1997); and the work of Leong (1995) in describing the influences on career behavior of culturally different populations.

As the work of theory building and the legacy of ongoing work on individual differences, learning and development, trait-and-factor approaches, personality typologies, and interest measurement were assimilated into more comprehensive sets of constructs during the 1950s, 1960s, and 1970s, the language of vocational guidance and vocational counseling was subtly replaced by terms like career guidance and career counseling (Crites, 1981; Gysbers & Moore, 1971; Herr & Cramer, 1996; Wrenn, 1964) and by the emerging notions of the practice of career development. Assessment instruments were sometimes refined and renamed (e.g., the Vocational Maturity Inventory became the Career Maturity Inventory) and older theoretical models were reconceived and wedded to new constructs (e.g., trait-and-factor approaches seen as person-environment fit (Chartrand, 1991). The name of the National Vocational Guidance Association was changed to the National Career Development Association in 1985, suggesting that earlier views of the process of career development as the object of career interventions became instead synonymous with the practice of career development.

The latter decades of the twentieth century demonstrated the importance and the effectiveness of the practice of career development across a wide range of career issues, settings, and populations (e.g., Campbell, Connel, Boyle, & Bhaerman, 1983; Herr, 1997; Holland, Magoon, & Spokane, 1981; Hoyt, 1980; Oliver & Spokane, 1988; Spokane & Oliver, 1983). These decades also witnessed a consolidation of what is known about career behavior and how it can be used to guide planned programs of career interventions. In this sense, the practice of career development rests upon a legacy of concepts and practices that were developed and refined throughout the twentieth century (Herr, 1999; Savickas, 1999).

Insights Into the Future

Although it is not possible to be exhaustive in a brief retrospective view of the history of the practice of career development, it is clear, nevertheless, that there were major social, po-

litical, and economic changes throughout the twentieth century to which career theories and practices have been addressed. The history of the practice of career development is a record of conceptual growth and practical effects that is very positive in its contributions to individual purpose and productivity and to the economic health of the nation. However, this legacy of achievement is not yet complete.

Many of the questions and issues that precipitated the rise of vocational guidance and counseling in the late nineteenth and twentieth centuries, as the world began its transformation from a primarily agrarian economy to an industrial economy, are present in new guises as the nations of the world engage in the transformation from an industrial to a global, information-based economy. In the emerging world of the present and the future, career guidance and counseling, the practices of career development, are being constantly challenged to find new paradigms and new scientific bases as the important questions of individual choice and dignity are cast against a new and emerging set of questions that reflect the characteristics of a world occupational structure that is in considerable flux; that is increasingly affected by the pervasive influence of advanced technology on workplace procedures that reduce the need for workers' physical strength and increase their needs for knowledge and intellectual strength; and in which the opportunities to work, the language of work, the educational requirements to do work, and the organization of work are changing throughout the world. These conditions at the beginning of the twenty-first century are giving rise to such trends as the following.

Growth in the Practice of Career Development as a Worldwide Phenomenon

The practice of career development, career guidance and career counseling, and the other forms of career intervention were neither the same nor at the same level of development across the world at the end of the twentieth century. However, in the

twenty-first century, the practice of career development is likely to be more comprehensive in scope, more evenly distributed and accessible, and more indigenous as nations increasingly identify how the practice of career development will best meet their needs. Such national and cultural tailoring of the practice of career development to political, economic, and demographic characteristics will increase dramatically in the next several decades. So will the career theories and interventions that are invented and implemented in nations that differ substantially in their levels of educational and economic development. As such, career guidance, career counseling, and the practice of career development will become worldwide phenomena.

The Practice of Career Development as an Instrument of Individual Human Dignity

In a world that continues to struggle with conflicting desires to either degrade or enhance human dignity, assaults on human dignity continue to occur as a function of economic and workplace issues. They include the rise of, and the persistence of, high rates of unemployment in many nations; the permanent dislocation of persons from jobs because their skills are inadequate or because there are insufficient jobs; the procedures that bar people from work or occupational mobility because of ageism, racism, or sexism; the diminished feelings of personal identity and self-worth, affiliation, mastery, and economic independence that accompany organizational downsizing, unemployment and underemployment; the substitution of technology for people or the placing of persons in toxic work environments to produce economic gain. In these conditions, the practice of career development, among its other outcomes, serves as a mechanism to provide hope to people, the affirmation of their individual dignity and worth, and the support to establish new career directions. Without feelings of dignity and hope, it is unlikely that any individual can attain his or her full potential as a human being. Without personal dignity and hope, it is diffi-

cult to grant these things to others, to take personal responsibility for one's actions, to gain a sense of agency or self-efficacy, or to find alternatives to violence as an appropriate strategy to gain what one seeks.

The Practice of Career Development as an Instrument of Personal Flexibility

In the twenty-first century, career counselors and other career guidance specialists will be increasingly expected to assist persons to identify and learn the skills by which they can be more effective in planning for and choosing jobs, in making effective transitions and adjustments to work, in working cross-culturally and cross-nationally, and in managing their own careers and career transitions effectively. Scholars in the United States and in other regions of the world have argued that changes in the way that work is organized are resulting in new concepts about careers that are qualitatively different from the concepts that had prevailed through much of the twentieth century. New notions of career in many nations, including such implications as the changes taking place in the structure of employment opportunities, mean a widening diversity of career patterns and experiences ... more and different sorts of career transition will be taking place. One consequence may be that in the future more men will experience the kind of fragmented careers that many women have experienced (Arnold & Jackson, 1997, p. 428), more people will be working for small and medium-sized employers, and there will be more people who are self-employed. ... they highlight the need for lifelong learning and an appropriate strategy for career guidance to support people especially during career transitions ... (Arnold & Jackson, 1997, p. 429)

In a similar fashion, Hall and Associates (1996) speak to the rise of "protean careers." Accordingly, people's careers increasingly will become a succession of "ministages" (or short cycle learning stages) of exploration-trial-mastery-exit, as they move in and out of various product

areas, technologies, functions, organizations, and other work environments. (p. 33)

This protean form of career involves horizontal growth, expanding one's range of competencies and ways of connecting to work and other people, as opposed to the more traditional vertical growth of success (upward mobility). In the protean form of growth, the goal is learning, psychological success, and expansion of the identity. In the more traditional form, the goal was advancement, success and esteem in the eyes of others, and power. (p. 35)

Although it is not clear what proportion of the workforce will be affected by "new careers," personal flexibility in such contexts means that people in the twenty-first century need to know how to change with change, accept ambiguity and uncertainty, negotiate job or career changes multiple times in their working lifetimes, be able to plan and act on shifting career opportunities, develop technical and social skills as well as an ability to understand how and why such skills are used, modified, and supplemented, and to have the motivation to be career resilient—to persist in the face of change and unplanned-for problems and difficulties.

Career Counselors Will Take on Expanded Roles

Career counselors will increasingly take on roles as planners, applied behavioral scientists, and technologists as they tailor their career practices to the settings and populations that they serve. In addition to the role of the counselor or specialist in the practice of career development as one who seeks to keep hope alive in his or her clients, such professionals will increasingly assume other technical roles. As the twentieth century laid the base for the scientific knowledge of career behavior and documented the effectiveness of career interventions that facilitate or modify career behavior, the twenty-first century will undoubtedly witness major growth in knowledge related to the processes and techniques that work most effectively to resolve certain career problems with particular populations (e.g., women and men, the

affluent and the poor, majority and minority members) under specific conditions. Much of the new information in the field will come from cross-national studies and indigenous research in nations across the world. The expanded knowledge base in the theories of and the practice of career development will require career counselors, in their role as applied behavioral scientists, to become experts in how to facilitate positive career development across the life span and in its applications to particular settings and populations.

Flowing from a role as applied behavioral scientist, the career counselor of the twenty-first century will have an expanded role as a planner of structured programs. As is increasingly true in the present, among the major practices of career development will be the provision of workshops, modules, structured group programs, psychoeducational approaches, and career guidance curricula specifically planned to facilitate the types of career knowledge, skills, and behaviors that lead to personal flexibility and personal competence.

Furthermore, the career counselor of the twenty-first century will routinely be a technologist, able to plan and apply the use of computer-assisted career guidance systems, the Internet, CD-ROMs, and virtual reality approaches to experiencing possible work environments, games, self-assessment, international databases about educational and occupational opportunities, and other forms of technology to complement individual or group approaches to the practice of career development. Although the base for such roles had been initiated in the twentieth century, in the decades immediately ahead technology will be a core element of the practice of career development.

Conclusion

This article discusses in skeletal form the heritage that undergirds the practice of career development in the twenty-first century. The view here is that the early decades of the twenty-first century will witness a refinement of the conceptual perspectives and scientific knowledge that shaped career counseling and career guidance in the twentieth century. However, it is expected that the acceleration of the worldwide availability of career guidance and counseling in an international economy will be accompanied by a theoretical and research base that will develop from nations around the globe that are committed to developing their own indigenous models and practices of career development, rather than adopting those models and practices that originated in North America or Europe.

In such contexts, new theoretical and practical issues will continue to arise. They will include ensuring that the practice of career development is delivered in ways that are cost-effective and efficient; research that is devoted to understanding more fully the career behavior of the poor and the less educated; understanding more fully the pluralistic value and belief systems about the centrality of work among other life roles that dominate in different societies; career practice-career problem interactions; gender and racial factors in career behavior; methods of coaching and mentoring to stimulate career motivation and resilience that will bridge the chasms of despair, stress, and confusion that frequently accompany career transitions, poor person-job fit, underemployment or the loss of work; and new theories of work and practices of career development that address the growing number of temporary employees and persons unable to find permanent institutional employment around the world. As affirmed by the history of the twentieth century, the importance of the practice of career development in the twenty-first will grow as a worldwide, sociopolitical force designed to facilitate the economic health of nations and the purpose and productivity of individuals.

Edwin L. Herr is Distinguished Professor of Education (counselor education and counseling psychology) in the College of Education at The Pennsylvania State University, University Park.

References

Arnold, J., & Jackson, C. (1997). The new career: Issues and challenges. British Journal of Guidance and Counselling, 25, 427–434.

Astin, H. S. (1984). The meaning of work in women's lives: A sociopsychological model of career choice and work behavior. The Counseling Psychologist, 12, 117–126.

Betz, N. E., & Hackett, G. (1986). Applications of self-efficacy theory to understanding career choice behavior. Journal of Social and Clinical Psychology, 4, 279–289.

Borow, H. (Ed.). (1964). Man in a world at work. Boston: Houghton Mifflin.

Brewer, J. M. (1942). History of vocational guidance. New York: Harper & Brothers.

Campbell, R. E., Connel, J. B., Boyle, K. B., & Bhaerman, R. (1983). Enhancing career development. Recommendations for action. Columbus: The Ohio State University, The National Center for Research in Vocational Education.

Chartrand, J. M. (1991). The evolution of trait-and-factor career counseling. A person environment fit approach. Journal of Counseling & Development, 69, 518–524.

Cremin, L. A. (1964). The progressive heritage of the guidance movement. In F. Landy & L. Perry (Eds.), Guidance in American education: Background and prospects (pp. 11–19). Cambridge, MA: Harvard University Graduate School of Education.

Crites, J. O. (1981). Career counseling. Models, methods, and materials. New York: McGraw-Hill.

Dumont, F., & Carson, A. (1995). Precursors of vocational psychology in ancient civilizations. Journal of Counseling & Development, 73, 371–378.

Farmer, H. S. (1985). Model of career and achievement motivation for women and men. Journal of Counseling Psychology, 6, 12–14.

Farmer, H. S., & Associates. (1997). Diversity & women's career development: From adolescence to adulthood. Thousand Oaks, CA: Sage.

Gilligan, C. (1982). In a different voice. Cambridge, MA: Harvard University Press.

Gysbers, N. C., & Moore, E. J. (1971). Career development in the schools. In G. F. Law (Ed.), Contemporary concepts in vocational education (pp. 82–95). Washington, DC: American Vocational Association.

Hall, D. T., & Associates (Eds.). (1996). The career is dead—long live the career: A relational approach to careers. San Francisco: Jossey-Bass.

Hansen, L. S. (1997). Integrated life planning: Critical tasks for career development and changing life patterns. San Francisco: Jossey-Bass.

Hansen, L. S., & Minor, C. W. (1989). Work, family, and career development: Implications for persons, policies, and practices. Washington, DC: National Career Development Association.

Herr, E. L. (1997). Career counseling: A process in process. British Journal of Guidance and Counselling, 25, 81–93.

Herr, E. L. (1999, January). Career guidance and counseling in the 21st century: Continuity and change. Paper presented at the National Consultation on Career Development, Ottawa, Canada.

Herr, E. L., & Cramer, S. H. (1996). Career guidance and counseling through the lifespan. Systematic approaches (5th ed.). New York: HarperCollins.

Herr, E. L., & Shahnasarian, M. (2001). Selected milestones in the evolution of career development practices in the twentieth century. The Career Development Quarterly, 49, 225–232.

Holland, J. L. (1966). The psychology of vocational choice. Waltham, MA: Blaisdell.

Holland, J. L., Magoon, T. M., & Spokane, A. R. (1981). Counseling psychology: Career interventions, research, and theory. Annual Review of Psychology, 32, 279–300.

Hoppock, R. (1950). Presidential Address 1950. Occupations, 28, 497–499.

Hoyt, K. B. (1974). Professional preparation for vocational guidance. In E. L. Herr (Ed.), Vocational guidance and human development (pp. 502–528). Boston: Houghton Mifflin.

Hoyt, K. B. (1980). Evaluation of K–12 career education: A status report. Washington, DC: Office of Career Education.

Krumboltz, J. D. (1979). A social learning theory of career decision making. In A. M. Mitchell, G. B. Jones, & J. D. Krumboltz (Eds.), Social learning and career decision making (pp. 19–49). Cranston, RI: Carroll Press.

Leong, F. T. L. (Ed.). (1995). Career development and vocational behavior of ethnic minorities. Mahwah, NJ: Erlbaum.

Oliver, L. W., & Spokane, A. R. (1988). Career-intervention outcome: What contributes to client gain? Journal of Counseling Psychology, 35, 447–462. Dubuque, IA: Kendall/Hunt.

Parsons, F. (1909). Choosing a vocation. Boston: Houghton Mifflin.

Pierce, A. (1933). Vocations for women. New York: Macmillan.

Roe, A. (1956). The psychology of occupations. New York: Wiley.

Salamone, P. R. (1988). Career counseling: Steps and stages beyond Parsons. The Career Development Quarterly, 36, 218–221.

Savickas, M. L. (1999, May). Career development and public policy: The role of values, theory, and research. Paper presented at the International Symposium on Career Development and Public Policy, Ottawa, Canada.

Sears, S. (1982). A definition of career guidance terms: A national vocational guidance perspective. Vocational Guidance Quarterly, 31, 137–143.

Spokane, A. R. (1991). Career intervention. Englewood Cliffs, NJ: Prentice-Hall.

Spokane, A. R., & Oliver, L. W. (1983). The outcomes of vocational intervention. In S. H. Osipow & W. B. Walsh (Eds.), Handbook of vocational psychology (Vol. 2, pp. 99–136). Hillsdale, NJ: Erlbaum.

Stephens, W. R. (1970). Social reform and the origins of vocational guidance. Washington, DC: National Vocational Guidance Association.

Super, D. E. (1951). Vocational adjustment: Implementing a self-concept. Occupations, 30, 88–92.

Super, D. E. (1957). The psychology of careers. New York: Harper & Row.

Super, D. E. (1990). A life-span, life-span approach to career development. In D. Brown & L. Brook (Eds.), Career choice and development: Applying contemporary theories to practice (pp. 197–261). San Francisco: Jossey-Bass.

Williamson, E. G. (1965). Vocational counseling: Some historical, philosophical, and theoretical perspectives. New York: McGraw-Hill.

Wrenn, C. G. (1964). Human values and work in American life. In H. Borow (Ed.), Man in a world at work (pp. 24–44). Boston: Houghton Mifflin.

From *Career Development Quarterly*, March 2001, p. 196. © 2001 by Career Development Quarterly.

Choosing the Right Path

When you fail to plan, you plan to fail. Here's how to develop a career blueprint that will help you achieve your professional goals.

Cassandra Hayes

For some weary career warriors, Nancy Friedberg is a miracle worker. When the career coach met one of her clients—a librarian—he was stuck in a career rut. However, a year and eight counseling sessions later, Friedberg helped him make the switch from library science to technology consulting.

How did an English literature major end up as an SAP software consultant at one of the big four accounting firms? By working with a career coach and coming face-to-face with his personality, interests, and long-term goals. Friedberg helped him determine that consulting was his ideal career, and in today's computer-driven society, technology would be his conduit. But how?

Realizing that he was a quick study with excellent communication skills, a problem solver, and a strong relationship builder, she helped him develop a career plan that included first marketing those talents at a small firm. She also did a lot of work repositioning him—through his verbal presentation and résumé—to make him come across as a technology consultant rather than a librarian. Impressed, companies were willing to train him in the technology.

Today, poised to enter the next stage of his career-life plan, Friedberg's client recently joined a New Jersey pharmaceutical company. The move allows him to keep regular hours so that he can be home with his wife and new baby, as well as pursue an M.B.A. Over the past five years, Friedberg's client has not only paved

a rewarding and successful career path, but his salary also quadrupled into the six digits.

"It is so important to plan your career and not drift wherever the wind blows," says Friedberg, who is a New York-based career coach with the Five O'Clock Club, a national career-counseling organization, and has a private practice in the city. "You must do some careful long-term strategic assessment, think about what you might need at each stage of your life, commit to a plan, and accept the fact that there will be some trade-off along the way. Too often, people try to fit themselves into a job and end up patterning their lives around it. What they should do instead is find a job that fits them and fits into their lives."

It's no secret that many individuals resign themselves to lackluster careers, having never fully explored all their options. For example, peer or family influences force some into college when entrepreneurship or a technical or trade school education may have been better. Others choose college majors or fall into jobs based on the income potential and then later find themselves miserable.

In fact, a 1998 survey revealed that almost half of the 400 college-educated workers between the ages of 30 and 55 polled said they would choose a different major if they could do it over. The George Mason University and Potomac Knowledge Way survey further contends that the majority of college graduates have switched careers at least once, and about one in five expect to switch in

the future. Chalk it up to indecision, societal changes, or kismet, but more than likely it's because many didn't have a plan.

Let's face it. It's cheaper to do your homework up front than stay in the wrong job too long or change college majors halfway through school. Having a documented and well thought out plan early on helps you discover your career-related interests and abilities. It also helps you:

- Identify occupations that match your interests, competencies, and personality.
- Pinpoint corresponding fields of study for further education.
- Understand how you adjust to circumstances, people, and demands in your work environment, and whether these adjustments result in stress or satisfaction.
- Identify your communication and leadership style.
- Determine transferable skills and accomplishments.
- Find out who you are.

In charting your career path, you may find yourself needing professional assistance, a strategic plan, a viable network—or all three. Here, we'll show you how to use these elements to put together a plan that will help you get to the next step or transition in your career.

PUT ME IN, COACH

Whether it's a first career or a career change, many people have

sought out the services of a career counselor or coach. Referrals can be found at colleges and universities, through career-planning organizations such as the Five O'Clock Club, or through word of mouth.

"Find someone locally, with good credentials, who understands your area's job market and is experienced in helping people develop career plans," says Susan Urquhart-Brown, career counselor and principal at Career Steps Consulting in Oakland, California. "You can also locate career counselors and coaches who can help you implement your plan. The greatest benefit of having a counselor or coach is the other perspective they can provide." She notes, "You might be able to tune up your car, but a mechanic can probably do it faster and better."

Keep in mind that there aren't any universal requirements for career coaching. Depending on the state, some counselors must undergo rigorous state licensing requirements and have advanced degrees in counseling or social work. On the other hand, some coaches draw on years of work experience and simply hang out a shingle. Fees run the gamut, and can be as high as $200 an hour, depending on the experience of the counselor or coach.

The optimal career-planning process involves the use of various types of career tests, also known as assessments or inventories, such as the widely used Myers-Briggs Type Indicator (http://skepdic.com/myrsb.html) and the Campbell Interest and Skill Survey. These tests help you better understand your career interests, motivation, work style, personality, values, skills, and aptitudes. These and similar quantifying tests are also available online for nominal fees.

FOLLOW YOUR HEART

With or without the help of a career counselor, it's important to realistically assess how your interests and talents will transfer into the workplace. As a child, Javetta Boldes Robinson knew she wanted to have an impact on education and that she loved numbers. When she put the two together, they added up to a career in school finance. After getting a B.S. in accounting from California

State University at Sacramento in 1987, Robinson set her sights on becoming a school district CFO.

Robinson admits that the position she sought is not the most glamorous of accounting careers, especially when there are positions with big public accounting firms to take into consideration. Many tried to steer Robinson toward the corporate sector, but to no avail. "I had many job offers in those areas, but I didn't even consider them," recalls the 36-year-old Long Beach, California, resident. The career is also not one that many colleges focus on; therefore Robinson's plan included garnering much of her experience on the job. That meant getting her foot into the education unit of the California State Controllers Office.

But as life would have it, sometimes you have to be uncomfortable before you can be comfortable, and Robinson was turned down for two auditing positions. Undaunted, she took a detour in her career plan and accepted a job with the Department of Health. To her surprise, opportunity came sooner than she expected. On her first day at work, she was offered a position in her coveted controller's office, and she quit the Health Department on the spot. Although the auditor's position in the Women, Infants and Children's (WIC) unit of the controller's office wasn't her dream job, it got her that much closer to the education unit.

For a year and a half, she begged the education unit manager to hire her, but no positions were available. In the meantime Robinson broadened her auditing experience—a requirement for a higher-level position-and earned her CPA. In 1995, when the WIC unit's funding was in jeopardy, her entreaties paid off and she was transferred to the education unit. However, Robinson's plan was just getting started.

"I set a goal to be promoted every two to three years. If that didn't happen, then I asked why or began looking for opportunities elsewhere." Robinson learned everything she could as she chalked up the 1,000 hours of auditing experience required for her to advance in her career. " I would even do other people's work. I wanted to get all the experience I could get," says the president

of the western region of the National Association of Black Accountants (NABA).

Robinson befriended and tracked the accomplishments of many district CFOs. In 1997, after reading a newspaper article quoting the woman touted to be the best associate superintendent of business in the state (to whom a CFO generally reports), Robinson recruited her as her mentor. Soon after, a position opened in her mentor's district and Robinson was chosen.

At last, with five promotions in 12 years and unparalleled auditing, personnel management, and fiscal skills tucked beneath her belt, Robinson was promoted last year to chief financial officer of the Compton Unified School District. Reporting directly to the state administrator, she controls a budget of $327 million, with 100 employees and 23 schools under her financial management.

"Specializing helped my career tremendously. I knew there was a market and need for my skills, and moving around from company to company would not have gotten me to this point," says Robinson. "Being true to my plan has been instrumental in helping to further my career beyond those of my peers at public accounting firms."

GOAL SETTING FOR SUCCESS

Just as a map takes you where you're traveling on a highway, so your goals are a map for the road you're traveling in life. We've all set goals at one time or another that we failed to dedicate enough focus to in order to achieve them. That wasn't the case for Lance Moore.

"Throughout my career, I wanted to build a skill base that was marketable. My goal was to be able to go from company to company, build on those skills, and eventually own my own entity," says Moore, 39, for whom restaurant development and franchising has always been a long-term interest.

Moore's career path took off during college when he served a brief stint as a marketing representative at 3M in his hometown, Cleveland. After graduating from Stanford University in 1983, the economics

and English major joined IBM, where he not only honed his sales skills but also acquired retail experience working in the computer giant's product centers.

In 1990, a General Foods Brand Manager's Fellowship helped him earn an M.B.A. from Northwestern University's Kellogg School of Management—a school he chose specifically over Wharton because of its strong marketing curriculum.

After graduation, Moore jumped on the brand management track and joined his b-school benefactor, General Foods (now Kraft Foods Inc.). Five years later, Moore became a marketing manager for Omaha-based ConAgra Frozen Foods, a $27 billion food service supplier, where he was responsible for the popular Healthy Choice entrées. "The position allowed me to broaden my career path, go from sales to business analysis, and grow a business," says Moore. "I always focused on an upward growth curve and evaluated myself every quarter or annually to make sure that I was using all of my resources."

Throughout, Moore charted a career course that would give him the experience he needed to one day own his own business. "I worked in sales because it was like owning a business within a business. While at IBM, working with their product centers gave me retail experience. In my marketing roles at Kraft Foods, I had the opportunities to not only learn the food business but to also build brands and create new business," he says.

Today, Moore is a group vice president at Atlanta-based Blimpie International, the nation's No. 2 submarine sandwich chain and the only publicly traded one. With some 450 franchisees under his charge and a territory that covers 13 Western states, including Alaska, Hawaii, and Guam, Moore has entered the restaurant franchising business, realizing his original career goal.

KNOW ALL THERE IS TO KNOW

While Robinson prepared for a career within her organization, the same strategies apply when you're making a move outside of your current career or company. Regardless of where you are in your career, it's important to do informational interviews with people in the field or the company you want to enter. Also, expand your research to libraries and the Internet. "If you ask the average person to name the number of career opportunities available, most can only list about three dozen. However, there are about 20,000 job titles listed in the Bureau of Labor Statistics' Occupational Outlook Handbook," says Mark Patton, president of MGC Publications in Milwaukee and author of *Ultimate Careers and Businesses,* (MGC Publications; $12.95; 800-531-9874) a guide that provides information on nearly 500 associations, foundations, organizations, and periodicals. "You must expose yourself to other opportunities. Then you can plan your work and work your plan."

Clichéd as it might sound, networking is still an important key to getting the job you want. No college senior knows that better that Lydia Cutrer. Keen on making her mark as an investment banker, the 21-year-old Temple University senior majoring in accounting has made career inroads that many seasoned professionals would envy. "For me, it's been about building relationships," says Cutrer. "I thought that accounting would be a great foundation for entering the business world, and joined the student chapter of NABA to learn more about the career and get involved."

Not content with just one affiliation, the New Orleans native is also a member of the National Black M.B.A. Association and has done internships at AT&T and Chase. As one of the youngest members of the Next Generation Network, one of the many career programs offered by the Executive Leadership Council in

Washington, D.C., Cutrer has positioned herself to get the pick of plum jobs. Already, she has an offer from JP Morgan Chase and Co. to enter its two-year investment-banking program as an analyst after graduation this spring. Still in the early stages of her implementing her career plan, Cutrer plans to pursue her M.B.A. in two to three years and perhaps enter the fields of venture capitalism, urban revitalization, or management consulting. Conscious that she must continue to build and maintain her network, Cutrer regularly updates mentors and supporters on her progress via notes and e-mail, keeping herself in their minds should they become privy to a potential career or job opportunity.

WATCH FOR ROAD-BLOCKS AND HURDLES

Youthful bravado has a way of helping career dreams flourish, but somewhere along the way the implementation process gets stalled. It could be marriage, relocation, the birth of a child, getting too comfortable in a current job, a change in education plans, or a simple change of mind. "There is nothing wrong with doing the job you really want on the weekends or part-time," says Deborah Brown, president of D&B Consulting in Atlanta, who works with many attorneys who find themselves in career quagmires. "You can hold down the job that pays the bills and pursue your entrepreneurial or artistic goals during your off time until you determine how to do it full-time."

Career planning is an ongoing effort and never really ends. "Your goals should not just be in the present, but should also look ahead," says Urquhart-Brown. "Ask yourself, Where do I want to be in the next two to three years? It's very important that you don't stop your career planning once you get a job, even if it seems to be the ideal job today."

From *Black Enterprise* magazine, April 2001, p. 108. © 2001 by Black Enterprise. Reprinted by permission.

UNIT 5

Implementing Compensation, Beliefs, and Workplace Safety

Unit Selections

Key Points to Consider

- Companies are involved in worldwide competition, often with foreign organizations with much lower wage rates. What should management do to meet this competition? What do workers need to do to meet this competition?

- How would you implement a merit/incentive program in a staff department such as research and development or data processing? In a line department such as sales or production?

- Explain why you believe some senior executives might be overpaid. Do you feel some are underpaid? Cite examples and reasons for your conclusions.

- What strategies should employers implement to control the rising costs of benefits while still getting the maximum value for their employees? How would you address the health care crisis for an organization? A benefit not to be forgotten is Social Security, which is again a major issue. How would you suggest fixing it? Should it be privatized? Partially privatized?

- One of the problems facing American industry is an increase in violence. What can be done about it? What would you do about stress on the job?

 **Links: www.dushkin.com/online/**
These sites are annotated in the World Wide Web pages.

BenefitsLink: The National Employee Benefits Web Site
   http://www.benefitslink.com/index.php
Executive Pay Watch
   http://www.paywatch.org/paywatch/index.htm
Social Security Administration
   http://www.ssa.gov
WorkPlace Injury and Illness Statistics
   http://www.osha.gov/oshstats/work.html

Money makes the world go around … the world go around!

—From "Money" in the musical *Cabaret*

Individuals are usually paid what others perceive their work to be worth. This situation is not necessarily morally correct. In fact, it does not even have to be logical, but it is reality. Police officers and college instructors are often underpaid. They have difficult jobs, requiring highly specialized training, but these jobs do not pay well. Other professions pay better, and many illegal activities pay better than law enforcement or college teaching.

When a company is trying to determine the salary of individuals, two markets must be considered. The first is the internal structure of the firm, including the wages that the company pays for comparable jobs. If the organization brings a new employee on board, it must be careful not to set a pay rate for that individual that is inconsistent with those of other employees who are doing the same or similar jobs. The second market is the external market for employees. Salary information is available from many sources, including professional associations and the federal government. Of course, both current and prospective employees, as well as organizations, can easily gain access to this information. To ignore this information and justify pay rates only in terms of internal structure is to tempt fate. The company's top producers are the ones in whom the competition is the most interested, and no organization can afford a mass exodus of its top talent. Organizations must ask themselves, "What Are Employees Worth?"

One recent development in the area of compensation is a return to the concept of "pay for performance." Many firms are looking for ways to directly reward their top performers, as may be seen in "Pay and Employee Commitment: The Missing Link." As a result, the idea of merit pay has gained wide acceptance in both industry and government. Pay for performance has been used in industry for a long time, most commonly in the sales and marketing area, where employees have historically worked on commission plans based on their sales productivity. Organizations are constantly looking at these types of programs, as may be seen in "Should You Adjust Your Sales Compensation?"

Theoretically, merit pay and other types of pay for performance are effective, but they can easily be abused, and they are often difficult to administer because measuring performance accurately is difficult. Sales and production have numbers that are easily obtained, but research and development is a different situation. How does a firm measure the effectiveness of research and development for a particular year when such projects can often take several years for results to be achieved?

One issue that has evolved over the past several years is the question of pay for top executives, as seen in "Executive Pay," and "The Great CEO Pay Heist." During times of economic recession, most workers are asked to make sacrifices in the form of reduced raises, pay cuts, cuts in benefits, other compensation

reductions, or layoffs. Many of these sacrifices have not been applied to top management. Indeed, the compensation for top management has increased substantially during the past several years. When former president George Bush Sr. traveled to Japan with a number of top auto industry executives, this situation was highlighted. The auto industry in the United States had been doing very poorly, while the auto industry in Japan had been very successful—especially when compared to its U.S. counterpart. A comparison of the salaries of American auto executives with those of their Japanese rivals revealed that the Japanese executives receive only a fraction of the compensation of the Americans. This might lead one to question who is worth more—senior management of a successful Japanese firm or of a less successful American firm? Are chief executives overpaid, and if so, how did they get that way, and who should set their pay?

The fastest-growing aspect of employee compensation is benefits. Benefits are expensive to any firm, representing an ever-increasing burden to employers. As a result, many firms are reducing benefits and attempting to find more effective ways to spend their benefit dollars, as discussed in "Health-Care Costs: HR's Crisis Has Real Solutions" and "A New Model for Controlling Health-Care Costs." Also, the needs of the employees are changing. As our society ages, there is greater interest in health benefits and pensions, and less interest in maternity benefits. Another facet of the issue is that employees are seeking greater benefits in lieu of salary increases, because the benefits, with some exceptions, are not usually taxed.

Health and safety are also major concerns of employers and employees. The workplace has become more violent as workers act out against their employers for unfairness—whether real or imagined. Some firms have had to address the anger of employees and other problems, as seen in "Disengage the Rage: Defusing Employee Anger." The history of industrialization in the United States is filled with examples of industry's abuse of the safety and health of workers, as shown in "The Triangle Legacy, 90 Years After the Fire, Sweatshops Persist." To prevent this, there is now OSHA (the Occupational Safety and Health Administration) and there are child labor laws. Today, issues concerning safety and health in the workplace include AIDS, burnout, and substance abuse. These issues reflect not only changing social conditions but also a greater awareness of the threats presented by unsafe working conditions. An attempt to address some of these issues has been to practice what is essentially preventive medicine with wellness initiatives. While there was initially some doubt about their effectiveness, the results are now in, and wellness programs do work.

All in all, salaries, wages, and benefits represent a major expense and a time-consuming management task for most firms, and health and safety requirements are a potential area of significant loss, in terms of both dollars and lost production.

What are employees worth?

Companies and academics are working on ways to measure human capital. The bottom line so far? Your company's success is embedded in its people, and what's in their heads.

By Eilene Zimmerman

How is this possible? A company with a tiny share of a market niche, some rented office space, and a few computers goes public before it has profits, and after the IPO, it's valued in the hundreds of millions.

The answer may lie in what the company isn't telling us. Analysts and experts agree that nearly 75 percent of the sources of value in a company are never reported and we have yet to come up with an accounting system that can record it all. The hidden value in a company is usually lumped under "intangibles," thought of as soft, rather than hard, assets. But soft is a misnomer. High-tech business is what has driven our economic boom thus far, and what's truly valuable in a biotech, software, or telecommunications company isn't the networked computer system or the new lab equipment, but the minds behind it all.

"Value in this economy is increasingly being driven by employees and their ideas, as opposed to hard assets. So you not only have people creating a lot of value, but they are highly valued themselves, and switching jobs more frequently than ever," says Jonathan Low, a senior fellow at management and IT consulting firm Cap Gemini Ernst & Young (CGEY). Low specializes in the valuation of intangibles.

For the last year, he and other researchers at the CGEY Center for Business Innovation have interviewed institutional investors, pension fund and money managers—those responsible for most of the stock in the economy. They discovered that 35 to 40 percent of portfolio allocation decisions are based on nonfinancial information. "This was information not provided by the company, not found in the financial reports. That's revolutionary," says Low.

That information included things like how well a company executed its business plan, the morale of employees, corporate culture, and organizational structure. Very few companies provide information that relates to the human component of their organization; of those that do, many are European. Skandia, an international financial services company, is the one most often cited for its inclusion of human capital information in financial reports.

How Skandia Puts Employee Worth on Paper

In 1994, Skandia Group Worldwide decided to publish a supplement to its annual financial report focusing on its nonfinancial assets. The Intellectual Capital Supplement is now issued twice yearly, putting Skandia at the forefront of the trend toward valuing a company's human capital.

"In the old days, a country's GDP was created largely by agriculture and manufacturing companies. Their assets are accounted for in the traditional financial report, whereas employees, customer relationships, and product innovation isn't accounted for," says Jan Hoffmeister, vice president of intellectual capital management for Skandia. "Yet all of these information technology companies are creating a large part of countries' GDP now."

Because Skandia is in the business of financial services, the company felt it important to provide its own investors with as much information about the company as possible. "Everything we do has to do with knowledge,"says Hoffmeister. "People save up for their long-term retirement through Skandia and we need from other companies the same information we provide about ourselves, in order to invest money properly. We have more than a hundred billion dollars under management and have a keen interest in supporting initiatives to help companies report what creates value in the market."

Skandia tracks and compiles data about 40 different factors that affect its intellectual capital before writing an assessment of them in the annual report supplement. Those factors include things such as leadership, compensation, development, corporate culture, retention rates, satisfaction rates, and innovation. "We ask our stakeholders what is important to them in order for them to make their investment decisions. And we dialogue with our other stakeholders, like employees and customers," says Hoffmeister.

In its half-yearly report, Skandia breaks down human capital into five major components: competence, relationships, values, culture, and leadership. Some of these categories relate only to the individual, others to the entire organization.

Readers of the intellectual capital report are looking for indicators that reveal Skandia's potential for creating value in the future, says Hoffmeister. A trend of increasing employee satisfaction, comparatively low turnover, and product innovation, for example, would indicate a company moving in the right direction.

"A reader might look to see how successful sales from products created in the last 18 months were. Do we create new products on an ongoing basis? Are we keeping up and being innovative? This is the kind of thing our supplemental report provides to the public," he says.

What it doesn't provide, however, is an accounting of the return on investment Skandia gets for every dollar it invests in its people, or a dollar value on its human capital. "It's impossible to do that. You can account for the cost of expenses for employees and the total compensation package, but personally I don't think you can account for ROI," he says. "We're not there yet."

Since 1994, the company has reported on what it calls "intellectual capital"—its term for intangibles. "We do it because assets such as employees, customer relationships, and product solutions have become more and more important in creating future value to companies," says Jan Hoffmeister, vice president of intellectual capital management for Skandia Group Worldwide.

Hoffmeister says the fact that most companies are unable to account for intangibles is a huge problem. "How do you make investment decisions if you use an accounting system that doesn't really tell you very much about what creates value in the future?" he asks. Skandia provides the information about its employees through half-yearly reports that talk about compensation, training, leadership, and the like. Still, there's no line item in the report that puts a dollar value on human beings.

"The bottom line is, human capital matters when it comes to the bottom line."

That's because there simply isn't an accepted model for measuring it yet, says Margaret M. Blair, co-author of "Understanding Intangible Sources of Value," a Brookings Institution study released in November. "People talk about measuring the value of a life, but that's not what this is about. We want to know how you value the productivity and future benefit of additions to human capital, the special skills, talents, capabilities that are really embedded in the people," she says.

Blair defines human capital as part of a set of intangibles that a company simply cannot control. "Human capital gets on the elevator and walks out the door. The company can't directly control it. It's also things like the way employees work together, not just the sum of what an individual knows. There is a continuum of difficulty in finding ways to value this," she says. A study done by Baruch Lev at New York University has taken on that piece of the problem and Lev has released a model for valuing intangible assets. (www.stern.nyu.edu/-blev/)

Blair and her co-authors did find a convincing correlation between training—an investment in human capital—and strong corporate performance. Researchers at CGEY had similar results. Jonathan Low says CGEY looked at IPOs of companies that had gone public from 1986 to 1997 and found that about 50 percent of them had failed to either exceed or maintain the price of their stock when they went public. "The only statistically significant difference between those that succeeded at this and those that didn't was a nonfinancial factor," he says, "whether employees' interests were aligned with corporate strategy."

That alignment may come from giving lots of stock options to employees, heightening their stake in the company's success or failure. Another example, says Low, is more obvious. "Giving people a place where they are happy to come to work, respecting them."

Researchers at human resources consulting firm Watson Wyatt also found that good people practices overall increase a company's value. Watson Wyatt's first Human Capital Index study, completed late in 1999, found that scoring high in 30 key areas of human capital management relates to about 30 percentage points

Saratoga Institute's Top 10 Measures of Human Capital Management

The Saratoga Institute, now a part of Spherion's Human Capital Consulting Group, has been measuring the value of human capital for 20 years. Among the 250 different metrics used by the institute are revenue factors, profitability, and investment in a company's workforce. Using a number of formulae, researchers at the institute are able to quantify the value of human capital as well as its overall effectiveness, claims Robert Morgan, president of the Human Capital Consulting Group.

"One of the things we encourage companies to do is to take the top 10 metrics—not necessarily all 250—and measure themselves. Not every metric is important to a company. It depends how labor-intensive they are, if turnover is a problem, if they are in a knowledge industry, things like that."

Those 10 metrics were developed by Jack Fitz-enz, founder and chairman of the institute. Since there is no set standard of measurement that fits every company, Fitz-enz says, it's important to decide which of these apply to your company's situation. What is important to one firm, he says, might have little value to another.

1. Your Most Important Issues. These are the targets of all lower-level measures. Whether it be one or a few measures, make certain that you are focused on them and that your metrics lead in a direct line to them.

2. Human Capital Value Added. How do the people in your organization optimize themselves for the good of the company and for themselves? This is the prime measure of a person's contribution to profitability and shows that you can answer the question: "What are people worth?"

3. Human Capital ROI. This is the ratio of dollars spent on pay and benefits to an adjusted profit figure.

4. Separation Cost. It's important to know how many people are leaving and from which areas, but it's more important to know what that costs the organization. The average cost of separation for an employee is at least six months' equivalent of revenue per employee.

5. Voluntary Separation Rate. Loss of personnel represents potential lost opportunity, lost revenue, and more highly stressed employees who have to fill in the gaps. If you can cut the separation rate, you don't incur the cost of hiring for these positions or lose quality in your customer service.

6. Total Labor Cost Revenue Percent. This is total benefit and compensation cost as a percent of organizational revenue: the complete cost of human capital. In other words, this shows how much of what you are taking in through revenue goes to support the company's total labor cost (including temporary, seasonal, and contract or contingent workers. Thus, it accounts for all your W-2 and 1099 employees.

This metric is designed to help you track changes in your workforce. You can do this best by comparing this metric to your revenue factor, your compensation costs, your benefit costs, and your contingent off-payroll costs. If your Total Labor Cost Revenue Percent is increasing, you need to see if this is because your compensation costs or your benefit costs are increasing or if your revenue is decreasing. This will help you determine what actions to take based on your business objectives. Cutting costs may only help in the short-term if revenue is decreasing. Also, by looking at this number in comparison to your contingent off-payroll costs, you can analyze whether or not your contingent workforce is contributing to an increase or decrease in your total labor costs.

7. Total Compensation Revenue Percent. This is the percent of the organization's revenues that are allocated to the direct costs of the employees. This differs slightly from Total Labor Cost Percent; it does not include the costs for any off-payroll employees who receive a 1099. It only accounts for any on-payroll employees. Again, it is best to compare this measure to your Revenue Factor, your compensation costs, and your benefit costs to analyze what is happening with workers before creating strategies to address any concerns.

8. Training Investment Factor. Forces are in conflict within the workplace. There is a continuing invasion and distribution of technology aimed at improving individual productivity and a growing demand for better service. Yet many workers cannot read, write, do simple calculations or talk intelligently with customers. The organization must invest in bringing up basic skills.

9. Time to Start. With the ongoing shortage of talent, recruitment will be a major challenge. Monitoring the time from approval of a requisition until someone is on the job is a strategic indicator of revenue production.

10. Revenue Factor. This is the basic measure understood by managers.

---

in terms of market value or return to shareholders. The yearlong study was based on a comprehensive analysis of human resource practices at 405 publicly traded companies with at least three years of total returns to shareholders and a minimum of $100 million in revenue or market value.

"Historically, people have thought about people practices as a fuzzy, soft area. You're not sure that if you invest a dollar, you will get more than a dollar back. This study says very concretely that there is an empirical relationship between doing things for your people and getting a financial return," says John Parkington, practice director of organization effectiveness at Watson Wyatt.

Assessing the effectiveness of human capital is difficult, let alone trying to attach a dollar amount to it. Yet Robert Morgan, president of Spherion's Human Capital Consulting Group, says there is "absolutely a dollar amount you can put on a person. It's done in the boardroom now, not in HR."

www.workforce.com

For more
information on:

Employee worth
See how to calculate what your
employees are worth, go to
www.workforce.com/feature/
00/06/30

There is an enormous amount of work going on in this area, and various models for quantifying human capital abound. But Margaret Blair says the only way to come up with a definitive

Making Human Capital Measurements Add Up

Everyone wants to find a measurement system that works, but Pete Ramstead, executive vice president of strategy and finance for Personnel Decisions International in Minneapolis, says the emphasis should be on finding a sound logic to connect those measures to the business. "For example, [with] cost-to-hire and time-to-fill, without any way to measure how good the candidates are that you're hiring, you understand only efficiency, not effectiveness,"he says.

Frustrated with the lack of decision logic to go along with HR measurements, Ramstead teamed up five years ago with John Boudreau, director of Cornell University's Center for Advanced HR Studies, and created the Human Capital Bridge Framework, which enables companies to translate what employees do into financial capital.

Value is determined by measuring which talent pools are critical to a company's success, says Ramstead. "Think of it this way: a marketing department would never try to design an advertising program until they measured which customers are most important to them. Yet because HR is a propose-and-defend trap, they don't think strategically about issues of business."

Ramstead disagrees with companies like Skandia, which feels it necessary to include information in its annual report about human capital. "Nothing about the talent, like hours of training per employee, needs to be included in an annual report. If you want to communicate to shareholders how you're doing in human capital measures, you should explain how you're managing that capital and the measurements that show how you do it."

Ramstead and Boudreau suggest asking the following seven questions before designing or implementing a measurement system:

1. Are the connections between the human-capital metrics and the ultimate success of the organization clear and compelling?
2. When the organization's strategies change, do the measures identify where human capital strategies need to change?
3. Does the measurement system support the development of human capital strategies tailored to the organization's unique competitive advantage?
4. Will the measurement system drive distinctive human capital investments to the talent group that has the potential to create the greatest economic impact?
5. Can the measurement system support decisions about HR programs before they are implemented (rather than after)?
6. Can the measurement system reveal when HR programs should be discontinued?
7. Does the measurement framework identify how talent creates value within the organization in a way that is understandable and motivating to all employees?

method of evaluating that capital—and consequently properly evaluate companies—is through a coordinated effort. "Information is most valuable when it is shared in some commonly understood form. It's unlikely that these efforts will ever achieve their full potential unless they are coordinated," says the Brookings Institution report.

Blair is hopeful, though. "We are starting to ask the right questions," she says, "but we still have a long way to go."

Eilene Zimmerman is a freelance writer based in San Diego. To comment on this article, e-mail carroll@workforce.com.

From *Workforce*, February 2001, pp. 32-36. © 2001 by ACC Communications, Inc., Costa Mesa, CA. All rights reserved. Reprinted by permission.

GOING DOWN THE ROAD

Campaign for a Living Wage

JIM HIGHTOWER

If our so-called national leadership had not lost its shame gene, surely it would be red-faced over its failure to do some little something about the plummeting value of the minimum wage. Today's miserly minimum of $5.15 an hour delivers a sub-subsistence income of $10,700 a year, if you get full-time work. That's gross, in two meanings of the word. Millions of Americans—most of them adults and supporting families—are working either for this wage or are paid just a few coins more and have their poverty pay pegged to this wage floor.

There's been a longstanding proposal in Congress to raise the minimum wage by a buck, but stand there is all it has done, for neither party has moved it forward. There was a flurry of excitement a couple of years ago when House Speaker Dennis Hastert rose on his hind legs and gave an impassioned plea for Congress to help economically distressed people: "I am not crying crocodile tears, but they need to be able to have a life and provide for their family. They need to have a modest increase in their salary." Unfortunately, he was not talking about minimum-wage workers; rather he was speaking of the urgent need to raise the pay of members of Congress, which the members promptly did.

We progressives need to stop looking to Washington to do it for us and move our focus to the battleground where we have legitimate, lasting and growing power: America's grassroots. ACORN, an indefatigable organizer of low-income communities, and SEIU, the feisty

unionizer of the low-wage service industry, are two national groups that understand this. They've teamed up with churches, civil rights advocates, an array of unions, women's organizations and other local groups in cities, counties and states across America to pass not a minimum wage but living-wage laws. It is a sophisticated effort, including excellent research and support available through ACORN's Living Wage Resource Center (www.acorn.org). In less than eight years, these ground-level coalitions have won living-wage campaigns in seventy-nine places from coast to coast.

Tough Fight in the Big Easy

Their latest and most sweeping victory is in the Big Easy—New Orleans, the home of jazz, Mardi Gras, great food… and unconscionably low wages. The engine of the Crescent City's economy is the "hospitality" industry, including hotels, restaurants and clubs. These places rake in huge profits from the hundreds of millions of tourist dollars that flow through their doors every year, yet two-thirds of New Orleans service and retail workers are paid poverty wages. On average, full-time cooks there are paid 20 percent below the family poverty level, kitchen workers are 37 percent below poverty and housekeepers are 41 percent below. Yet, of America's twelve major tourist markets, New Orleans hotels enjoy the fourth-highest room rates, and its high-dollar restaurants are consistently packed. With such prodigious wealth be-

ing generated on the backs of such poorly paid workers, SEIU organizer Wade Rathke says of his city, "We're Jamaica without a beach."

Local pols were not going to do anything to right this disparity, so SEIU, ACORN and others decided to take it to the people. Their strategy was to propose a referendum: a simple one-buck increase over the federal minimum. This is lower than most living-wage ordinances (which go up to $12 an hour), but the New Orleans initiative throws by far the widest loop, applying the new $6.15-an-hour standard to practically all private-sector employees. The bottom line is that about 75,000 people—nearly a third of the city's working class—would get a boost of roughly $500 to $2,000 a year in their pay, depending on their current wage and the hours they work.

The New Orleans Campaign for a Living Wage (NOCLW) made another smart move: It appealed to small-business owners, especially in neighborhoods where low-wage workers live. Any extra bucks that these workers get tend to be spent in their own areas—getting the roof fixed, buying a used car, purchasing a few more groceries, etc.—so these are sales that ripple through the small-business community. It's classic percolate-up economics, recognizing that money is like manure: It works best if you spread it around.

But the opposition was not sleeping. It formed the Small Business Coalition to Save Jobs, an acronym that in plain English spells "Hokum." These so-

called small businesses were Marriott, Sheraton, Hyatt, Hilton and other global hotel chains, as well as such political powerhouses as the Chamber of Commerce, the Business Council and the Restaurant Association. They adopted a classic "the sky is falling" strategy, predicting mass layoffs, soaring prices and fleeing businesses.

But their real tactic was to do all they could to stop the vote, including rushing to the state legislature to ram a bill through that prohibits any city from enacting a minimum wage. With that done, they then asked the courts to quash the New Orleans initiative. But the state's highest appeals court finally ruled that the Hokum's lawsuit was moot, since the local law had not passed. If it did, then they could come back for a hearing. So the vote was on.

"Can you believe it," exclaimed Louisiana ACORN president Beulah Labostrie on election night, February 2. "Against all odds, we just gave a raise to 75,000 workers!" NOCLW's volunteers had made thousands of calls and gone door to door in a spirited shoe-leather campaign, getting 73,000 votes for the living wage and winning by a sweeping 63–37 margin.

The next day the corporate lawyers went running back to the courts, and a decision is due in the next few weeks on whether a trumped-up state law can overturn the voters' voice. Whichever way the decision goes, the people's sense of victory in New Orleans has been transforming. Rathke says that since the vote, "there's a step in people's walk that wasn't there before. They've learned that they have power, and their attitude is 'we can beat you again.' This is what the business guys are really worried about."

Rathke adds that the lesson for progressives is that "our base is really here. If we create coalitions and take our message to the people, we're gonna win. But we've got to be willing to put our vision of justice out there. Progressives can't be afraid to let people vote."

From *The Nation,* April 1, 2002, p. 8. © 2002 by The Nation. Reprinted by permission.

Pay and Employee Commitment: the missing link

BY OWEN PARKER AND LIZ WRIGHT

Pay accounts for one of the greatest investments an organization makes. Although a fair wage is the cornerstone of the contractual and implied agreements between employees and employers, the underlying assumption is that money can directly influence behaviour. Human resource theory and empirical evidence to the contrary, many employees and managers believe that simply increasing what people are paid will make them more motivated, productive or loyal. But, to what degree, if any, is such conventional wisdom correct?

Motivating factors and productivity issues have been the subjects of countless studies, books and papers. The influence of pay is an important ingredient in these discussions. Employee commitment, however, has only recently become a popular research topic. Yet, commitment is a critical issue for many executives, because of the need to attract, motivate and ultimately retain the right talent pool for a business to succeed.

Recently, Watson Wyatt developed an Employee Commitment Index and compared it to a number of organizational factors and activities. (Watson Wyatt Worldwide, *WorkCanada 2000: Change, Challenge and Commitment,* March, 2000) Using the findings of this survey, we will explore the connections between commitments and pay in this article.

THE VALUE OF COMMITMENT

The need to attract, motivate, develop and retain employees is critical to any organization's prosperity today. Creating an environment in which employees feel truly engaged—connected to the organization's goals and objectives, and satisfied with their jobs—has never been more crucial. The traditional costs involved in hiring and developing a new worker have always pointed to the importance of retaining employees. Recently, organizations have resorted to acquiring other companies to fill the talent gap, making retention a significant HR and business imperative. An essential element in any retention strategy is to ensure that employees remain committed to their organizations.

Recent academic research has found that employee commitment is a complex concept made up of a variety of elements. (John Meyer and Natalie Allen, *Commitment in the Workplace: Theory, Research and Application,* Sage Publications, Thousand Oaks, California, 1997) Although job and organizational satisfaction and corporate pride are essential facets of commitment, a host of other attitudes and attributes have an impact on whether employees remain truly committed to their employer. In its simplest form, however, commitment to an organization is the employee's perceived intention to stay with that organization.

RESEARCH OVERVIEW

Watson Wyatt polled over 1,600 Canadian employees at all job levels on their attitudes toward their workplace, jobs, managers and organizations. We asked people about specific functions, including:

• work organization

• communications

• overall work environment

• decision making

• supervision

• performance management

• career development/training

• leadership effectiveness

• compensation & benefits

• job content and satisfaction.

Respondents represented a cross-section of the Canadian working population, and came from organizations in various in-

dustries, including financial services, health care, technology, manufacturing, retail, professional services, utilities and government.

The Compensation-Satisfaction Index consisted of responses to people's satisfaction with their pay in comparison to others, with compensation for the work they do, and with their incentive packages. The Total Compensation Index focused on ascertaining the value of their total reward package and its links to the company's strategy, and their satisfaction with profit sharing or stock programs. The Pay-For-Performance Index included questions that asked respondents about the links between their performance, and pay or compensation.

Was our intuition correct? Did our research indicate that there is a link between employee commitment and compensation? As we describe below, our research does indicate that the compensation-related indices are linked to employee commitment, although the associations are stronger in some cases than others.

COMPENSATION AND COMMITMENT

As shown in Figure 1, a little less than half of the survey respondents said that they are committed to their employers. This finding should concern Canadian employers, because half of them are at risk of losing important segments of their workforces because of that lack of commitment.

Other respondents were either not committed or neutral. Those who are neutral present a unique challenge. They have the potential to effect a positive or negative change with relatively little inducement.

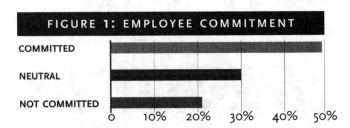

FIGURE 1: EMPLOYEE COMMITMENT

Similarly, fewer than half of the respondents indicated that they were satisfied with their compensation and total reward packages (see Figures 2 and 3). Perhaps more problematic, however, is the number of employees who said that they are dissatisfied. Approximately one-quarter of our sample expressed negative views about their compensation and total reward packages. Thus, an opportunity exists for executives and compensation specialists to provide innovative compensation solutions, and to effectively communicate the intent and details of these compensation packages.

The pay-for-performance index revealed the most negative result (see Figure 4). Only 19 percent of the respondents declared that they were satisfied with the pay-for-performance methods used by their employers; fully 60 percent were dissatisfied. This finding raises doubts about the effectiveness and appropriateness of today's pay-for-performance systems. Certainly, further investigation and understanding are needed

before conclusions can be finalized. However, these results point to an ever-decreasing satisfaction with how performance is being recognized and rewarded, and its link to employee commitment.

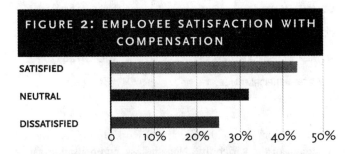

FIGURE 2: EMPLOYEE SATISFACTION WITH COMPENSATION

FIGURE 3: EMPLOYEE SATISFACTION WITH TOTAL REWARDS

There is another analytical approach that can be used to assess the relationship between commitment and compensation. Figure 5 displays the correlation among the various indices. Each cell in the table shows the correlation coefficient and the number of respondents included in the comparison. Although all of the correlations are statistically significant, most of the associations are relatively weak. However, there are moderately strong relationships between commitment and compensation satisfaction, and between total compensation and pay for performance. Thus, we can conclude that there is a direct relationship between satisfaction with compensation and employee commitment: The higher the satisfaction, the higher the commitment.

Added support for the link between compensation satisfaction and commitment appears when the underlying drivers of commitment are identified. These are shown in Figure 6.

When the statistical variance is addressed through a regression analysis, the combination of the major commitment drivers explains 63 percent of the employee commitment index. People awareness (i.e., the systems that organizations have for recruiting, retaining, work/life balance, flexible work arrangements, etc.) and job environment (i.e., the conditions related to

FIGURE 4: EMPLOYEE SATISFACTION WITH PAY FOR PERFORMANCE

FIGURE 5: CORRELATION BETWEEN COMMITMENT AND COMPENSATION INDICES

	COMMITMENT	COMPENSATION SATISFACTION	TOTAL REWARDS	PAY FOR PERFORMANCE
COMMITMENT	1.000 (1603)			
COMPENSATION SATISFACTION	.456* (1602)	1.000 (1603)		
TOTAL COMPENSATION	.390* (1487)	.371* (1487)	1.000 (1488)	
PAY FOR PERFORMANCE	.365* (1582)	.353* (1582)	.445* (1481)	1.000 (1583)

*COEFFICIENT STATISTICALLY SIGNIFICANT AT P<.01

job satisfaction, personal respect, and work stress) account for 35 percent of the variability. Nonetheless, compensation satisfaction remains an important commitment factor at nine percent. By addressing internal issues using these commitment drivers, including compensation satisfaction, organizations can influence their employees' commitment levels and possibly improve the rate at which they retain their human capital.

INCREASING COMPENSATION SATISFACTION (AND EMPLOYEE COMMITMENT)

Employee commitment remains a critical issue for many organizations. It is a primary factor in attracting and retaining the knowledge workers so necessary to corporate success. Compensation is a fundamental human resources and business lever but, until now, the connection between pay and commitment has not been assessed. What can we deduce from the connection in the preceding analysis?

Satisfaction with compensation is one of the drivers of employee commitment. For an employee to be satisfied with his/her pay, a few basic elements need to be present. People have to believe that the pay they earn is fair in relation to the work they do. They also must feel that their compensation, including salary, incentives and benefits, compares favourably with the realities of the market, especially in comparison to people doing the same work in similar circumstances.

Yet, only about half of Canadian workers expressed satisfaction with their compensation or total rewards program. Although part of the problem can be attributed to non-existent or ineffective compensation communication, organizations must recognize their responsibilities to foster greater compensation satisfaction. Executives, HR managers and compensation specialists must endeavour to introduce progressive and innovative compensation solutions.

Perhaps the greatest conundrum exists over pay for performance. For over a decade, pay for performance has been the foundation of many companies' compensation programs. While the concept is rational and practical, the results appear to be equivocal. Although highly successful in some environments, the application has not done what it was intended to do, espe-

cially from the perspective of employees. Unions don't endorse or use pay for performance; nevertheless, it still has a very low acceptance among a sizeable portion of salaried workers. Either the concept or its application has to be revisited and revised, or another approach has to be devised and used.

these practices exemplify the need to "walk the walk"

Findings from Watson Wyatt's Human Capital Index study (Watson Wyatt Worldwide, *Human Capital Index, Linking Human Capital and Value,* November, 1999) indicate that high-performing organizations tend to:

- offer stock plans to a large percentage of employees

- help poor performers improve and terminate those that perform unacceptably

FIGURE 6: KEY DRIVERS OF EMPLOYEE COMMITMENT

MANAGEMENT PERFORMANCE **A**　　JOB ENVIRONMENT **D**
COMPENSATION SATISFACTION **B**　　PEOPLE AWARENESS **E**
STRATEGIC COMMUNICATION **C**　　　　　　OTHER **F**

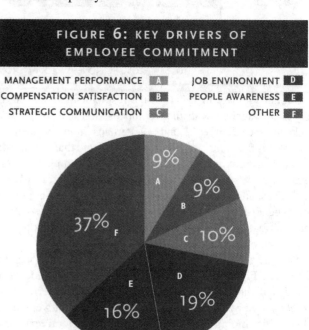

• pay top performers significantly more than average performers.

These practices exemplify the need to "walk the talk" and distinguish performance before effectively linking compensation to performance.

PROVEN STRATEGIES
FOR SUCCESS

One research clearly shows that there is an association between compensation and employee commitment. By enhancing compensation conditions and practices, commitment will likely improve. With improved commitment, retention will increase, turnover will decrease and employee morale will get stronger.

The challenge for HR managers in many organizations is to change executives' tendency to view compensation as an expense, and, instead, to regard it as an important human resource investment. An investment in people requires specific measures and focused processes to align people with business strategy. Successful organizations will recognize, distinguish and compensate true performance, and celebrate both individual and group accomplishments.

What compensation practices can an organization implement or alter to enhance organizational commitment? Certainly, accurate comparisons obtained by market compensation surveys are critical to ensure that wages are aligned with industry standards. In addition, some research has shown that companies paying above the industry standard can expect better financial outcomes (WW Human Capital Index). Such a strategy can add to an organization's reputation as an employer of choice. Being perceived as a leader in employee relations and rewards is critical in attracting, motivating and retaining employees.

Just as important, however, is a company's need to communicate its total reward package to its employees. It must emphasize not only the salary, bonuses, equity and benefits, but also other highly valued aspects of the employment deal. Some examples are flexible work arrangements and a culture that encourages teamwork.

Organizations in most industries are implementing innovative compensation approaches to differentiate themselves from other companies. In addition to standard wages, they offer stock options to employees other than their executives, provide generalized stock purchase programs and allow access to supplementary employee retirement programs.

Non-monetary benefits also have a role in compensation satisfaction. Intrinsic rewards have become essential differentiators in motivating people, especially as financial incentives become more homogeneous. Supporting life-work balance initiatives, flexible work arrangements and employee involvement in job design are examples of intrinsic rewards. These will be critical rewards that people want from their work.

Compensation remains a critical issue for organizations because of the financial investment in paying people. Likewise, fostering organizational commitment in employees is crucial to attracting, motivating and retaining the human capital necessary for corporate success. Although an association exists between compensation satisfaction and commitment, and is one of the drivers of commitment, it has to be considered as one of the pieces in a complex puzzle. Nevertheless, without a comprehensive and responsive compensation strategy, companies will fail to maximize the potential of their employees.

OWEN PARKER IS THE NATIONAL RESEARCH MANAGER FOR WATSON WYATT CANADA.
LIZ WRIGHT IS THE TORONTO, COMPENSATION LEADER FOR WATSON WYATT CANADA.

Should You Adjust Your Sales Compensation?

*A sagging economy may cause some HR professionals
to reconsider pay programs for sales personnel.*

By David Fiedler

For the woman working in travel sales at AAA of Western and Central New York, moving from inside sales to a position as an outside sales rep seemed wise. She would be trading the certainty of an hourly rate (plus bonus) for the risk of commission-only compensation, but a quick review of the previous year showed she would have come out farther ahead earning commissions.

She started her new job Sept. 4—one week before the terrorist attacks that brought the travel industry to its knees. "There are sales reps who didn't make any commission the whole month of October," says Hayley Schultz, HR manager at AAA.

Suddenly, commission-only compensation lost its luster for the new sales rep, who called Schultz to "complain that, as an employee, she must be paid at least minimum wage—even when she is not selling." Schultz pointed out that salespeople are exempt from New York's minimum wage requirements. "Naturally, she wasn't happy to hear that," says Schultz.

Schultz's situation is not uncommon. HR professionals across the country are struggling to determine if they should adjust their sales compensation plans in light of the events of the past few months. Does the combination of an already slumping economy, shaken further by the fallout from Sept. 11, warrant an examination of the way compensation is calculated and paid?

"Generally, we haven't seen a lot of companies changing their variable compensation plans," says Rob Bentley, senior consultant in sales force incentive design for Hewitt Associates LLC. "When companies suffer, it usually means salespeople do, too."

In fact, only 20 percent of companies plan to change the design of their incentive plans in any way, according to a November survey by Organization Resources Counselors Inc., a management and HR consulting firm headquartered in New York.

Take It Slow

Though sales reps may make a lot of noise about not achieving quotas, Bentley says companies should not adjust compensation for sales staff without a great deal of thought.

Mae Lon Ding agrees. "You should be very conservative in making changes to the compensation plan in mid-year," advises Ding, president of Personnel Systems Associates Inc., an Anaheim Hills, Calif., consulting firm that specializes in compensation and performance management.

Before making a move, consider the extent and depth of the downturn. "If it is short-term—a year or less—don't change a thing," says Ding. "When recovery is expected in the economy for the second half of 2002, why make changes in the sales comp plan now?"

To determine if pay plan changes are needed, Ding lists several steps HR professionals can take.

First, perform an analysis to see if the plan is working as intended. "Assess what percentage of the sales force will receive no bonus this year," she says. "If the company is profitable, at least 50 percent should make something in bonuses."

The reverse is also true—companies that aren't profitable shouldn't pay bonuses, says Ding. Doing so shows that sales goals are not aligned with company objectives.

Next, get a feel for what other companies in your field are doing. "You definitely need to remain competitive within your industry," says Ding.

Finally, don't overreact. A pay plan, says Ding, "is intended to recognize individual performance, but it is also a way for companies to share risks, to acknowledge that 'We're all in the same boat.'"

Know Whom You Are Dealing With

David Cichelli, senior vice president for the Alexander Group Inc., a Scottsdale, Ariz., management consulting firm, says HR professionals must take into account exactly the type of sales staff they have.

"There are two types of salespeople," Cichelli points out, "income producers and sales reps." The two roles serve different purposes, and their compensation should reflect that difference.

"For income producers, their compensation is purely commission—always," says Cichelli. "Their pay plans should not be adjusted because to do so runs counter to the basic principle that their income should be higher when times are good and lower when the economy is bad."

Extra Online Resources

For information on the elements that can weaken–or strengthen–a sales pay plan, see the online version of this article at www.shrm.org/hrmagazine.

The harsh reality is that an economic downturn should cause a reduction in the number of salespeople, says Cichelli.

Sales reps—who outnumber income producers—warrant more attention, says Cichelli. "A large component of their job is to represent the company and that product to the customer. The compensation equation for this group is created by the company and managed toward a targeted compensation level, achieved by combining a base salary with an incentive."

Cichelli recommends adjusting objectives so that 60 percent to 70 percent of sales reps achieve their quotas. If necessary, he says, employers should add guarantees to protect these employees. "You don't want sales reps to carry the uncertainty of the company."

When Changes Are Needed

Many options short of a full-blown overhaul can help increase the profitability of your company and keep your sales force moving forward.

"If anything, now is the time to make compensation richer and to increase the incentive opportunity," says Thomas McCoy, managing member of T.J. McCoy & Associates, a compensation consulting firm in Kansas City, Mo. "By reducing the base salary and increasing incentives, you are controlling cost to the company and encouraging sales staff to stay focused on what they need to be doing."

McCoy acknowledges the possibility that employees will react negatively to such a move. He suggests "using intensive communications to get people to buy into this action and to avoid negative perceptions. The real challenge to management is to be very visible, in touch and personable in implementing these changes."

Cutting base salary may seem drastic, but it might be the best move in some instances, says McCoy. "If the pain is severe, we have to take severe steps.

Minor Adjustments, Big Payoffs

Other less dramatic steps also can help salespeople focus on specific goals, says McCoy. "You can adjust targets and thresholds to make [them] more relevant and to get people to focus on what they need to do, rather than on things taking place outside their control."

McCoy points to special short-term incentive campaigns as another particularly effective tool. "These should be high-profile, high-visibility and short-term efforts. In your goals, you want something very specific, very basic and focused on driving and rewarding activity."

Bentley says companies should seize this chance to make long-needed changes. "Take advantage of the opportunity," he advises. "When the economy was great, companies often hesitated to make changes for fear of rocking the boat."

Bentley points particularly to the need for an administrative provision that allows employers to change the compensation plan when necessary. "Every company needs this type of clause," he says. "If you don't have this, now is the time to put it in."

Depending on the situation, Ding suggests offering a "consolation" bonus when sales goals are not met. "If the company will make money and salespeople have worked hard, I think this type of bonus is quite appropriate," says Ding. "It will not equal what they would have made, but it does still recognize their dedication and effort."

The Hard Facts

Risk is part of the sales equation and something that salespeople know up front, says Sherry Harsch-Porter, SPHR, founder/principal consultant at The Porter Bay Group, a compensation and rewards consulting firm in St. Louis.

"Especially when there is no cap on the money a person can make in the good times, why should the company pay up when they turn bad?" asks Harsch-Porter.

In some cases, offering additional compensation not tied to performance may harm the company's recovery from the slump. "As long as the goals are still accurate and achievable, they should be left in place," says Harsch-Porter. "It becomes a motivator for sales staff—they will work harder and longer to make up for the shortfall."

The main test of whether these goals are still valid is how they are perceived by the sales force. As long as the goals motivate the sales staff to keep pushing, these targets should remain unchanged.

In addition, these goals should have been established with input from the sales staff. As long as they believe the goals are realistic, providing additional compensation won't provide extra incentive.

David Fiedler is a St. Louis-based HR professional and freelance writer. He writes about a variety of topics, including compensation and technology/data privacy issues.

EXECUTIVE PAY

Many CEOs had a terrible year—but were still left with a mountain of wealth. *BusinessWeek's* 2001 survey gives the best picture yet of how much execs won and lost in the pay sweepstakes

For Lawrence J. Ellison, it was the best of years, it was the worst of years. Really. The Oracle Corp. chief executive earned a special place in the history of executive compensation last year with the $706 million he pocketed from exercising long-held stock options. It was an amount that far exceeds the gross domestic product of Grenada and constitutes the single biggest one-year haul of all time. But looked at another way, Ellison was also history's biggest loser. With Oracle stock off 57% for the year, the value of his option holdings fell by more than $2 billion.

Ellison's $706 million windfall is all the more remarkable considering that it occurred in a year when the nation's corporate elite experienced their first double-digit decline in pay in seven years, ending an extraordinary decade-long inflationary spiral that increased their average take by more than 550%. In a year when a slowing economy killed bonuses and plunged stock options under water at companies across the land, the average CEO's pay declined 16%, to $11 million, according to *BusinessWeek's* 52nd annual Executive Pay Scoreboard, compiled with Standard & Poor's EXECUCOMP. Take out Ellison's princely haul, and the drop in total pay was nearly 31%, to $9.1 million, a level not seen since 1997. "It was a sobering year, even for those who profited," says Patrick McGurn, director of corporate programs at proxy adviser Institutional Shareholder Services.

Nobody knows that better than Ellison. How could he record both the biggest gain and the biggest loss in one year? The answer points to a fundamental problem in the way executive pay is tallied. Most watchers, including *BusinessWeek*, count option gains in the year the exec cashes in, even though that value may have been building for a decade. Others estimate the future value of new options, sometimes miscalculating by hundreds of millions of dollars. Both methods miss an important change in executive compensation. For at least two decades now, compensation has been far more about wealth creation than pay for services rendered over the year. The engine

of change has been stock options, which have been handed out so lavishly they now make up 15% of shares outstanding.

To get a better reading on how much Corporate America really pays its CEOs, *BusinessWeek* is introducing a new measure that we call the change in pay-related wealth. It's based on the annual gain or loss in an executive's stock options, whether exercised or not, along with any salary, bonus, and stock grants for the year. We still rank executives based on how much they took home from options exercises, salary, and bonuses, but we believe that this new measure adds clarity to an increasingly complex and contentious topic.

Both the vast riches and the almost unimaginable losses recorded in the executive suite last year were a function of options, a perk that has come to represent a decade of corporate excess and greed. Compared with 2000, many more executives in the *BusinessWeek* Scoreboard took home less cash in 2001 and suffered losses in the value of their option holdings, just as shareholders suffered losses. What rankles critics is that many had enjoyed such enormous option gains in recent years that even big one-year losses left them with Everest-size mountains of stock-option wealth.

Some CEOs, of course, were punished for their companies' less-than-stellar results. Disney's Michael D. Eisner, JDS Uniphase's Jozef Straus, and Texas Instruments' Thomas J. Engibous all lost their bonuses. Straus and Adobe Systems' former CEO John E. Warnock received dramatically smaller option grants for the year. Others, including Archer Daniels Midland's G. Allen Andreas, were deprived of new grants entirely. Harry M. Jansen Kraemer Jr., CEO of Baxter International, voluntarily cut his bonus by 40%, even though his company's stock climbed by 20% in 2001. The reason: Defective Baxter dialysis machines were linked to the deaths of more than 50 people. Kraemer, who earned total cash compensation of $1.6 million plus a grant of 600,000 options, says somebody had to pay the price for the dialysis machine deaths: "Fifty people

THE TOP-PAID CHIEF EXECUTIVES...

		2001 SALARY & BONUS	LONG-TERM COMP†	TOTAL PAY
			MILLIONS	
1	LAWRENCE ELLISON ORACLE	$0	$706.1	$706.1
2	JOZEF STRAUS JDS UNIPHASE	0.5	150.3	150.8
3	HOWARD SOLOMON FOREST LABORATORIES	1.2	147.3	148.5
4	RICHARD FAIRBANK CAPITAL ONE FINANCIAL	0	142.2	142.2
5	LOUIS GERSTNER* IBM	10.1	117.3	127.4
6	CHARLES WANG** COMPUTER ASSOCIATES INTL.	1.0	118.1	119.1
7	RICHARD FULD JR. LEHMAN BROTHERS	4.8	100.4	105.2
8	JAMES McDONALD SCIENTIFIC-ATLANTA	2.1	84.7	86.8
9	STEVE JOBS*** APPLE COMPUTER	43.5	40.5	84.0
10	TIMOTHY KOOGLE**** YAHOO!	0.2	64.4	64.6
11	TONY WHITE APPLIED BIOSYSTEMS GROUP	1.7	60.2	61.9
12	DAVID RICKEY APPLIED MICRO CIRCUITS	0.9	58.6	59.5
13	JOHN GIFFORD MAXIM INTEGRATED PRODUCTS	0.3	57.7	58.0
14	PAUL FOLINO EMULEX	0.9	55.3	56.2
15	DOUGLAS DAFT COCA-COLA	5.1	49.9	55.0
16	GEOFFREY BIBLE PHILIP MORRIS	5.6	44.3	49.9
17	MICHAEL DEVLIN RATIONAL SOFTWARE	1.0	46.3	47.3
18	BRUCE KARATZ KB HOME	7.5	36.9	44.4
19	SANFORD WEILL CITIGROUP	18.7	23.9	42.6
20	MICKY ARISON CARNIVAL	2.2	38.3	40.5

†Long-term compensation includes exercised options, restricted shares, and long-term incentive payments; does not include the value of unexercised option grants.

*Retired as CEO March, 2002. **CEO until August, 2000. ***Amounts represent payments in fiscal 2001 toward purchase of aircraft given to Jobs as bonus in fiscal 2000. A $90 million bonus previously reported for the same plane was not made. ****Stepped down as CEO May, 2001.

Data: Standard & Poor's EXECUCOMP

... AND 10 WHO AREN'T CEOs

		2001 SALARY & BONUS	LONG-TERM COMP†	TOTAL PAY
1	STEPHEN CASE AOL TIME WARNER	$1.0	$127.3	$128.3
2	GREGORY DOUGHERTY***** JDS UNIPHASE	121.4	0	121.4
3	DONALD SCIFRES ***** JDS UNIPHASE	75.1	19.3	94.4
4	GREGORY ZEMAN CDW COMPUTER CENTERS	1.3	88.8	90.1
5	NIGEL MORRIS CAPITAL ONE FINANCIAL	0	89.5	89.5
6	JEFFREY HENLEY ORACLE	0.9	85.6	86.5
7	M. ZITA COBB JDS UNIPHASE	0.3	69.2	69.5
8	ROBERT HERBOLD ****** MICROSOFT	1.0	67.2	68.2
9	ROBERT PITTMAN AOL TIME WARNER	1.4	66.2	67.6
10	JEFFREY RAIKES MICROSOFT	0.7	57.3	58.0

†Long-term compensation includes exercised options, restricted shares, and long-term incentive payments; does not include the value of unexercised option grants.

***** Includes bonuses related to merger with SDL Inc. Joined company Feb. 13, 2001.
****** Retired as chief operating officer February, 2001.

Data: Standard & Poor's EXECUCOMP

ing the position of chairman. With Cisco Systems Inc.'s stock price down 72% in a year, CEO John T. Chambers last April requested that his annual base salary be reduced to $1. Instead, Chambers, who has pocketed $322.8 million over the past seven years as CEO, was awarded six million options.

A similar gargantuan option grant is how Ellison managed his $706 million miracle last year. In June, 1999, with Oracle stock trading at about $6, he agreed to trade four years of his salary and bonus in return for 10 million options, an almost unheard-of stockpile that escalated in value over the next 16 months as the stock hit a high of $46 in September, 2000. Proponents say that options align the chief executive's interests with those of shareholders, but that's not the way it worked at Oracle. By 2001, with the tech bubble bursting, Oracle stock was in a free fall. Rather than sit tight in a show of confidence, Ellison sold 29 million shares in a single week in January, flooding the market when investors already were jittery. He exercised 23 million options the same week for a gain of more than $706 million.

Within a month, Oracle stock had lost a third of its value, and the company was announcing that it would miss third-quarter earnings forecasts. That triggered further price declines and a rash of shareholder lawsuits alleging that Ellison engaged in "what appears to be the largest insider trading in the history of the U.S. financial market," according to one such suit. Ellison's stock sales were a factor in the sell-off that followed, says Henry Asher, president of Northstar Group Inc., which owns

died. If you have a problem, the buck stops somewhere, and it stops here."

As usual, though, many other CEOs were insulated from their companies' falling stock prices with new option grants or favorable repricings on their existing options. At Eastman Kodak Co., where the stock declined 23%, CEO Daniel A. Carp received 410,000 options, up from 100,000 the year before. A company spokesman said the option grant was small compared with other large companies' and intended to compensate Carp for assum-

GETTING A BETTER HANDLE ON TOTAL COMPENSATION

Figuring out how much a CEO really makes in any given year is a tricky task. It's not like the old days when pay consisted of a check in an envelope that you got every Friday afternoon. These days, the number for CEOs depends largely on how you value stock options, the most essential part of their compensation.

This year's poster child for executive-pay reform, Oracle Corp. founder Lawrence J. Ellison, either made the most ($706 million) or lost the most (a staggering $2 billion) last year. Which of these two numbers is more accurate and reasonable? It's an important question, because the answer could well alter the stormy debate over executive pay.

For years, *BusinessWeek* has reported all the gains from a stock-option exercise in a CEO's annual compensation. The reason: That income is taxable and reported to the Internal Revenue Service. Others, however, place a hypothetical value on a new stock-option grant in the year it is given. Even worse, some observers now do both, double-counting the same goodies so that the numbers look much larger than they actually are.

Sure, its' hard to work up any pity for someone making tens or hundreds of millions of dollars a year. But it's unfair and misleading to dump theoretical grant values or option gains in a single year's pay. Option gains are earned over a period as long as 10 years, while grant values are meant to predict an option's worth over its entire 10-year term.

As option income overwhelmed cash pay, this problem made it difficult to match pay to shareholder returns in a single year. "There are plenty of abuses going on in executive compensation, but saying there is no link between a CEO's total pay and performance is a wrong conclusion," says Fred Cook, founder of Fred-eric W. Cook & Co., a prominent pay consultant. "It's the measurement that's wrong."

For the first time, *BusinessWeek* is adding a new measurement called "pay-related wealth" to account for option gains and losses. It measures the change in value of all vested, unvested, and exercised stock options over the reported year. Added to this number is the executive's base salary, bonus, and the value of any restricted stock grants.

What the new methodology clearly demonstrates is that a CEO's financial health is directly related to his company's performance. When shareholders suffer, the CEOs almost always lose a big chunk. Last year, with the stock market in a tumble, the average CEO lost $15.4 million in pay-related wealth. Some 28 out of 365 CEOs in the *BusinessWeek* study, ranging from Merck & Co.'s Raymond V. Gilmartin to Colgate-Palmolive Co.'s Reuben Mark, lost more than $50 million each.

Of course, the only way a CEO can lose that much is to have a ton of options to begin with. Consider Cisco Systems Inc. CEO John T. Chambers. With shareholder return down 72% in fiscal 2001, Chambers lost $931.4 million in pay-related wealth, a drop of 85%. The $268,131 in cash he received could hardly offset the more than $950 million hit to his stock options. Even so, his in-the-money options were still worth $194.4 million at the end of the fiscal year.

Walt Disney Co.'s Michael D. Eisner, a perennial moneymaker in the CEO pay sweepstakes, lost nearly 100% of his pay-related wealth in the past fiscal year as shareholder return fell 51%. How can any executive lose almost all of his pay-related wealth? After drawing down a $1 million salary for the year, Eisner found that all his 21.4 million options were under water. But bear in mind that he already has taken home more than $1 billion in salary, bonus, and option exercises since becoming CEO of Disney in 1984.

The biggest winner on the pay-related wealth measure was Henry R. Silverman, CEO of Cendant Corp.

48,000 Oracle shares. "Was that a ringing endorsement for the company's short-term prospects?" asks Asher. "I don't think so." Oracle and Ellison declined to comment.

In a post-Enron world that has little tolerance for corporate financial maneuvers, Ellison's decision to cash out will likely add more fuel to the fiery debate over options, the perk that has sparked as much disdain for its overuse as the three-martini lunch of another era. Once a minor perk, options have come to account for 80% of the executive-compensation pie. Shareholder activists, institutional investors, and governance experts all viewed them as a way to turn managers into owners who would keep one eye trained on the stock price. Throughout the 1990s, boards gave out options with abandon, seeing them as a way not only to appease shareholder activists but also to compete in the increasingly tight market for top-flight talent. And best of all, they were free. Since accounting rules allow companies to grant options without treating them as a compensation expense on their income statements, options—unlike cash—have no impact on earnings. They were, and are, a license to print money.

But the increased use of stock options has created a host of problems. Many critics object to the sheer magnitude of the riches CEOs can now pocket. In 1950, when *BusinessWeek* first catalogued the pay of the nation's corporate elite, the highest-paid executive was General Motors Corp. President Charles E. Wilson, whose $652,156 pay package—$4.4 million in inflation-adjusted dollars—would make modern-day CEOs like Ellison laugh. Worse, the link between pay and performance that options are

His pay-related wealth jumped 64%, to $250.9 million. Shareholders aren't complaining, though: They saw returns of 104% on their investment in Cendant in the same period. IBM's Louis V. Gerstner Jr. was right up there

PAY-RELATED WEALTH: WINNERS & LOSERS

To judge more accurately how a chief executive fared in a single year, *BusinessWeek* is adopting a new measure called pay-related wealth. The measure includes the change in value of all the executive's outstanding stock options—exercised and not—for the year, along with cash compensation and restricted stock.

	EXECUTIVES		SHARE-HOLDERS
WINNERS	PAY-RELATED WEALTH 2001 MILLIONS	PERCENT CHANGE FROM 2000	TOTAL RETURN 2001*
1 HENRY SILVERMAN Cendant	$251.0	64%	104%
2 LOUIS GERSTNER JR. IBM	240.5	49	43
3 ROBERT FULD JR. Lehman Brothers	100.6	19	34
4 JEFFREY BARBAKOW Tenet Healthcare	96.9	204	78
5 HENRY DUQUES First Data	95.7	65	49
6 STEVE JOBS Apple Computer	83.4	9752	–40
7 HOWARD SOLOMAN Forest Laboratories	61.0	19	40
8 ANGELO MOZILO Countrywide Credit	60.1	334	93
9 ROBERT WALTER Cardinal Health	53.3	87	40
10 RICHARD BROWN Electronic Data Systems	52.7	226	20
LOSERS			
1 LAWRENCE ELLISON Oracle	–1970.1	–58	–57%
2 JOZEF STRAUS JDS Uniphase	–979.3	–87	–90
3 JOHN CHAMBERS Cisco Systems	–931.4	–85	–72
4 SCOTT MCNEALY Sun Microsystems	–587.7	–70	–65
5 MICHAEL EISNER Walt Disney	–265.8	–100	–51
6 DAN WARMENHOVEN Network Appliance	–243.7	–71	–77
7 IRWIN JACOBS Qualcomm	–216.3	–38	–33
8 DOUG BERTHIAUME Waters	–211.4	–61	–54
9 WILLIAM ROELANDTS Xilinx	–205.9	–65	–58
10 DAVID RICKEY Applied Micro Circuits	–203.3	–75	–78

*Total shareholder return is for the comparable fiscal-year pay period.
Data: Standard & Poor's EXECUCOMP, Bloomberg Financial Market

with Silverman. Gerstner's sum rose by 49% last year, to $240.5 million, as shareholders saw their returns increase 43%.

Our new measure has an added advantage: Many retiring CEOs wait to exercise their options until they no longer appear in the proxy statement. So they walk off with tens of millions of dollars of pay that never gets accounted for. This new methodology captures those gains throughout the CEO's tenure.

It also shows the dramatic leverage stock options give CEOs, particularly on the way up. When shares swing upward, CEOs reap vast rewards that often far outdistance those of investors. In a year when Tenet Healthcare Corp. shareholders enjoyed returns of 78%, CEO Jeffrey C. Barbakow's pay-related wealth shot up by 204%, to $96.9 million. At Electronic Data Systems Corp., investors had returns of 20%, but CEO Richard H. Brown had a 226% increase, to $52.7 million. But when stock prices decline, the CEO's fortunes tend to fall in line with those of shareholders, at least in percentage terms. Even Ellison's 58% decline in pay-related wealth was virtually equal to the 57% fall in shareholder return.

Why the big boost on the way up? It's largely in the math. If a stock climbs to $50 a share from $40, the shareholder return is 25%. But if a CEO's option is priced at $39, and the stock starts the year at $40 and ends the year at $50, his pay-related wealth increases by 1,000%. An analysis by consultants Michael P. Chavira and Beverly W. Aisenbrey with Cook & Co. found that options are typically leveraged at a multiple ranging from one to five times total shareholder return. It's another reason why boards need to be more stingy when they hand out grants.

By John A. Byrne in New York

supposed to provide is often subverted by compensation committees that ladle on more options when the company stock falls or swap the old underwater options for new, more valuable grants. Amazon.com Inc. and Lucent Technologies both repriced or swapped executive stock options. Says Peter Clapman, chief counsel for TIAA-CREF, the world's largest pension system with $275 billion in assets: "It's sort of heads you win, tails let's flip again."

Even worse for shareholders is the dilution problem. Every option granted makes the shares of every other stockholder less valuable. Investors are starting to catch on. This year, dozens of resolutions targeting exorbitant pay—at companies that include Boeing, Citigroup, and even General Electric—will be voted on by shareholders, and support for such proposals is on the rise. "We have

this kind of stock-option madness," says compensation consultant Alan Johnson. "The system is significantly broken."

Part of the problem is that while options decline in lockstep with stock prices, on the upside they offer far greater leverage. The gains in the fat years can provide a generous cushion during downturns. That's why some executives in our Scoreboard could suffer massive losses but unlike shareholders, still have lots left over. We believe our pay-related wealth measure provides a more complete look at this crucial component of CEO pay.

The results are eye-opening. Looking solely at cash compensation and option exercises, the nation's top executives had a bad year: 315 out of 730 in the *BusinessWeek* Scoreboard saw their total compensation decrease. But

PAY FOR PERFORMANCE: BOTH ENDS OF THE SCALE

To see how pay measures up to performance, *BusinessWeek* compares what the boss made over a three-year period with how he did for shareholders

EXECUTIVES WHO GAVE SHAREHOLDERS THE MOST FOR THEIR PAY...

		TOTAL PAY* MILLIONS OF DOLLARS	SHAREHOLDER RETURN**	RELATIVE INDEX
1	B. WAYNE HUGHES Public Storage	$0.3	47%	579
2	MARK LEVIN Millennium Pharmaceuticals	1.7	279	225
3	GEORGE PERLEGOS Atmel	1.3	92	150
4	DANE MILLER Biomet	1.2	75	143
5	IRWIN JACOBS Qualcomm	5.8	680	133

... AND THOSE WHO GAVE SHAREHOLDERS THE LEAST

1	LAWRENCE ELLISON Oracle	795.1	92	0.24
2	JOHN CHAMBERS Cisco Systems	279.3	-22	0.28
3	PETER KARMANOS JR. Compuware	93.9	-70	0.32
4	LOUIS GERSTNER IBM	303.2	33	0.44
5	L. DENNIS KIZLOWSKI Tyco Intl.	331.9	57	0.47

*Salary, bonus, and long-term compensation, including exercised stock options, for the 1999, 2000, and 2001 fiscal years
**Stock price on Dec. 31, 2001, plus dividends reinvested for three years, divided by stock price on Dec. 31, 1998
Data: Standard & Poor's EXECUCOMP

BusinessWeek's new measure of executive wealth reveals much steeper losses. In all, the plummeting value of stock-option holdings reduced pay-related wealth for the average executive by 43%, to $27.5 million. Of the 441 who either broke even or had holdings that increased in value, the average gain was 13%. Of the 216 who saw their wealth decline, the average loss totaled 60%. Indeed, at company after company, top executives with huge option stockpiles saw their wealth depleted by hundreds of millions of dollars. Cisco Systems' Chambers, Sun Microsystems' Scott G. McNealy, and Walt Disney's Eisner all took major hits to their wealth.

To be sure, not everyone was hurting. Howard Solomon, CEO of Forest Laboratories Inc., saw his salary increase nearly 13%, to $823,765, his bonus double to $400,000, and his take from option exercises top $147 million. In a year when Forest shareholders saw gains of 40%, compensation committee members felt he deserved every penny. Forest has enjoyed spectacular growth over the past five years. Solomon, who has been CEO since 1977, benefited enormously, since that growth sent the value of his options soaring. Says committee member Dan L. Goldwasser: "If a man is delivering substantial increases in shareholder value... it's only appropriate that he be rewarded for it."

Other CEO pay packages were harder to justify. Tyson Foods Inc. had a lousy year. Net income fell to $88 million from $151 million. Shareholder return was essentially flat—at a time when Tyson's peer-group companies doubled in value. And in December, a federal indictment in Tennessee accused the company and six managers of conspiring to smuggle illegal immigrants into the U.S. from Mexico to work in its poultry-processing plants, a charge the company denies. The upshot? CEO John H. Tyson received 200,000 new options and a $2.1 million bonus. The company says Tyson was rewarded for reducing debt by $86 million and negotiating the acquisition of meatpacker IBP. But others didn't see it that way. "I'm surprised the board would be so generous," says Charles M. Elson, director of the University of Delaware's Center for Corporate Governance. "It raises a lot of questions."

At other companies, boards quietly scaled back the tough performance targets executives needed to meet to win millions in rewards. At GM, CEO G. Richard Wagoner Jr. and other top executives who were entitled to a special performance bonus if the company's net-profit margin reached 5% by the end of 2003 will now be held to a less rigorous test. And at Coca-Cola Co., the goal line for CEO Douglas N. Daft to receive one million performance-based shares—20% annual earnings growth over five years—last year got a little bit closer. It's now 16%. With shares down 23%, his pay package totaled $55 million, including $5.1 million in salary and bonus and $49.9 million in option exercises.

Proponents say options align CEOs' interests with those of shareholders. That's not always the case.

Overall, though, the anemic economy skewed *BusinessWeek*'s pay-for-performance analysis sharply downward: CEOs with the best and worst shareholder returns relative to pay got less and posted sharply poorer returns than the executives in last year's analysis (table). The CEO who, dollar for dollar, gave the most this year was B. Wayne Hughes of Public Storage Inc. He delivered a 47% gain for stockholders for $254,300 in pay from 1999 through 2001—a pittance compared with last year's winner, David M. Rickey of Applied Micro Circuits Corp., who was paid $4.5 million for a staggering 4,751% return. At the bottom of the performance heap was Ellison, whose mammoth 2001 payday overshadowed his company's 92% three-year return for shareholders.

Companies that fared poorly in our pay-for-performance analysis took issue with our methodology. Oracle said it unfairly inflates pay by counting exercised options.

Cisco said it compares fiscal-year pay with calendar-year performance. In fact, calculating Cisco's return on a fiscal-year basis would result in a three-year return of 20% and move Chambers from the No. 2 slot to No. 3. Tyco said our methodology doesn't account for internal performance measures such as earnings, and IBM said it disregards nearly a decade of exceptional stock performance by Gerstner. Says IBM Vice-President Carol Makovich: "Mr. Gerstner's long-term leadership at IBM has produced outstanding results."

This year's survey of executive pay shows just how significantly CEO compensation has changed since Charles Wilson steered GM in the 1950s. Chief executives, once employees, have become owners. Salaries and bonuses are now afterthoughts compared with the potential wealth that options represent. Put another way, in a lousy year, Ellison took home almost three-quarters of a billion dollars. Imagine what he could make if Oracle shares turned around.

By Louis Lavelle, with Frederick F. Jespersen in New York and Michael Arndt in Chicago

---

COMPENSATION SCOREBOARD GLOSSARY

If the system worked perfectly, executive pay would rise when the boss delivered the goods for shareholders. And it would fall when corporate performance declined. But it doesn't always happen that way.

In this Scoreboard, *BusinessWeek*, along with Standard & Poor's EXECUCOMP, attempts to measure how closely pay matches performance. The study compares an executive's total compensation with the company's total return to shareholders in stock appreciation and dividends over three years. Three years of data are examined to minimize the impact of single-year windfalls. Each company is assigned to one of nine industry groups. Then, each executive's pay and the company's

total return to shareholders are measured against the others in the group.

This year, *BusinessWeek* also has added a new measure called pay-related wealth that takes into account increases or decreases in an executive's in-the-money stock options.

The Scoreboard companies boast market values that are among the 500 largest for which 2001 compensation data are available.

Performance ratings are given only when three years of data are available. On a scale of 5, 1 indicates the best performance; 5 is the worst. The top 15% of the sample receives a 1, 25% a 2, 30% a 3, 20% a 4, and 10% a 5.

2001 PAY-RELATED WEALTH

CHANGE IN PAY-RELATED WEALTH is 2001 salary, short- and long-term bonus, and the value of restricted stock grants plus the value of an executive's in-the-money stock options at yearend minus the value of options at the end of the previous year.

% CHANGE FROM 2000 represents the percentage increase or decrease in pay-related wealth compared with the previous year.

VALUE OF REMAINING OPTIONS is the yearend value of an executive's exercisable and unexercisable in-the-money stock options. It provides a glimpse of potential gains in the future.

PAY VS. SHAREHOLDER RETURN

TOTAL COMPENSATION is the sum of an executive's salary, bonus, and long-term compensation for the three years.

VALUE OF $100 INVESTED is the yearend 2001 value of a $100 investment in the company made three years earlier, including both share-price appreciation and dividends (reinvested).

RATING shows how an executive stacks up against peers, measured in terms of pay relative to total return to shareholders. The rating is based on an index in which the value of the investment is divided by total pay and then compared with other executives in the same industry.

Footnotes: †Indicates executive retired in 1999–2000 ‡May exclude option gains in earlier years e=estimated NA=not available NM=not meaningful

---

The great CEO pay heist

Executive compensation has become highway robbery—we all know that. But how did it happen? And why can't we stop it? The answers lie in the perverse interaction of CEOs, boards, consultants, even the feds.

BY GEOFFREY COLVIN

SANDY WEILL, WHO got a pay package worth some $151 million for running Citigroup last year, was a Brooklyn teenager back in the summer of 1950, preparing to return to Peekskill Military Academy. Jack Welch, whose pay for managing GE last year totaled about $125 million, was caddying at a golf course near his home in Massachusetts, having completed his freshman year at Salem High School. In Chicago, Larry Ellison—2000 pay as Oracle's chief: $92 million—was an ordinary 6-year-old. There's no reason any of them would have given the least bit of attention to events in Washington that summer, let alone suspected that what was going on there would change their lives and the life of virtually every future American CEO.

But that's what happened. After weeks of horsetrading, Congress sent President Truman the Revenue Act of 1950, and on Sept. 23 he signed it into law. Buried deep within that bill was a section amending the tax code. And that change, scarcely remarked upon at the time, made it legal and practical for companies to pay employees with an interesting form of currency called the stock option.

Thus began the madness. If you want to understand America's out-of-control CEO pay machine—including Steve Jobs' recent $872 million options grant, by far the largest ever—start there. The machine is worth understanding because it has begun churning out dollar amounts so mammoth that even hardened professionals grope for words. "Outrageous in many cases and unrelated to services rendered," says Charles Elson, a director of three publicly held corporations who runs the University of Delaware's Center for Corporate Governance. "In many cases, outside the charts," says Joseph Bachelder, the New York lawyer who has probably negotiated more top CEO pay contracts than anyone else. "Grossly high—astronomical," says Richard Koppes, a well-known governance expert with the Jones Day Reavis & Pogue law firm. "I've generally worried these guys weren't getting paid enough," says Harvard Business School professor Michael Jensen, who has written some of the most influential work on CEO pay. "But now even I'm troubled."

What they and many others find so stunning are recent gargantuan pay packages unlike any seen before. Maybe you recall being shocked by the numbers of about a decade ago, when Time Warner's Steve Ross got a $75 million package, and Heinz's Anthony O'Reilly received four million options worth some $40 million. Such amounts marked the top end of the scale through the boom times of the mid-'90s. But suddenly, in recent years, pay has ballooned into nine-figure totals, almost defying comprehension. Consider:

• The No. 1 earners in each of the past five years got packages valued cumulatively at nearly $1.4 billion (see chart), or $274 million on average. Yet far from delivering the superb results investors might have expected from the world's highest-priced management, four of the five companies have been marginal to horrible performers. They are Walt Disney, Cendant, Computer Associates, and Apple Computer.

• Apple's Steve Jobs got last year's mightiest pay package, valued by FORTUNE at $381 million. (For the purposes of calculating his 2000 package, we have valued his monstrous options grant at one-third the exercise price of the shares optioned. And, of course, we've included the $90 million Gulfstream the Apple board gave him.) How big is that? The last time the public got furious over CEO pay was in 1992, when reports of huge numbers for 1991 sparked a flurry of reform efforts. Yet the 14 highest-paid CEOs then, including such legendary mega-earners as Coca-Cola's Roberto Goizueta, Philip Morris' Hamish Maxwell, GE's Welch, and ITT's Rand Araskog, together earned less than Steve Jobs did last year all by himself (even without the plane!). Yes, it's true that Jobs has paid himself only $1 a year since he returned to Apple as CEO in 1997. And, yes, he deserves to be rewarded—handsomely—for bringing Apple back from the dead. But *still*...

• Dell CEO Michael Dell received more than 38 million options from 1996 through 1998, though as the company's sole

HIGHEST-PAID U.S. CEOs

"Compensation" in this article includes salary, bonus, restricted stock granted (regardless of when it vests), long-term payouts, "other" compensation, and an estimate of the present value of options grants. For that estimate, we have used a rule of thumb stipulating that the value of a standard ten-year option is one-third of the market price of the shares optioned. For options having shorter or longer terms, we have set valuations that depart from the one-third rule of thumb but are rationally related to it.

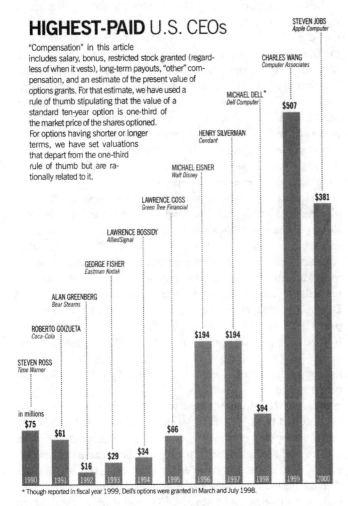

* Though reported in fiscal year 1999, Dell's options were granted in March and July 1998.

Fortune Chart/Source: Executive Compensation Advisory Services; Fortune

There's no simple explanation for the latest extraordinary pay figures. Today's roaring CEO pay machine is a giant device of many parts, built up over decades. Besides options, other important pieces have come from compensation consultants, economic developments, social trends, even government; indeed, the government's occasional attempts to restrain CEO pay have almost always had the opposite effect. What's so remarkable about the machine is that through all the ups and downs of business, the waxing and waning of corporate fortunes, it turns in only one direction—and faster all the time.

It wasn't always so. Through the '50s, the '60s, and part of the '70s, CEO pay actually grew more slowly than the pay of average workers. Most CEOs were publicly invisible and liked it that way. Adjusted for inflation, pay packages were much smaller than today's. They included options, though by modern standards the grants were pitiful; 20,000 shares were a big deal. Pay didn't seem tied particularly tightly to performance, yet stocks performed well: The S&P 500 advanced 11.3% a year on average in the low-inflation era from 1950 to 1964.

That golden age ended abruptly when stocks entered a long coma in 1964—and we soon began to see the early stirrings of today's opulent reward system. Since the market was going nowhere, options weren't paying off and substantial raises seemed hard to justify. So compensation consultants—yes, they were around back then—began cooking up the creative pay-enhancing gimmicks they have continued to devise ever since. Indeed, consultants play a critical role as the pay machine's expert mechanics. They understand every gear and sprocket and can always find a way to make the machine go faster. That's exactly what they do, in their utterly conflicted position—paid by management to advise management on how management should be paid.

The consultants' most inspired creation in the days of the stock market doldrums was a device called performance shares, which rewarded CEOs if they could increase earnings per share by a given amount in a given period—and never mind that EPS could be manipulated in a thousand unholy ways. What's important is the logic. You might have expected it to go like this: The stock isn't moving, so the CEO shouldn't be rewarded. But it was actually the opposite: The stock isn't moving, so we've got to find some other basis for rewarding the CEO. That difference, which persists to this day, is one of the keys to understanding megapay.

Another important element of today's CEO pay developed soon after. "An awful lot of CEOs should honor Curt Flood," says Michael Halloran of compensation firm SCA Consulting. Flood was the St. Louis Cardinals outfielder who in 1969 challenged the reserve clause in baseball players' contracts; though he lost his case in the Supreme Court, his quest inspired developments that made scores of players free agents by the late 1970s. Soon 20-year-old shortstops were making more than CEOs, and CEOs hated it. Surely they were worth more! And through that argument they started getting more. The counterargument—that athletes' pay, unlike CEOs', was determined in a brutally competitive open market—didn't get much airtime in the boardroom.

founder he already owned 353 million shares. Similarly, Oracle CEO Larry Ellison got a huge 20-million-share options grant, accounting for virtually all his pay last year, even though he already owned nearly 700 million company shares outright. What could possibly have been the point? "If they weren't already motivated enough to protect the owners' interests, then their shareholders are in worse trouble than they think," says shareholder activist Nell Minow.

The largest pay component in virtually all these cases is the stock option, which has mushroomed from modest use in the 1950s to a source of breathtaking CEO wealth today. A big reason for its runaway popularity is the insane way accounting authorities let companies treat options in financial statements—a way that's great for executives and awful for shareholders.

More broadly, pay is out of control because many board compensation committees, which set CEO pay, aren't doing their job. Why not? That's always been a bit of a mystery, because the comp committee code of silence is sort of like the Mob's *omertà*, only stricter. Nonetheless, FORTUNE's Carol Loomis persuaded some high-powered comp committee members to tell, anonymously, what goes on behind those doors. The picture isn't pretty.

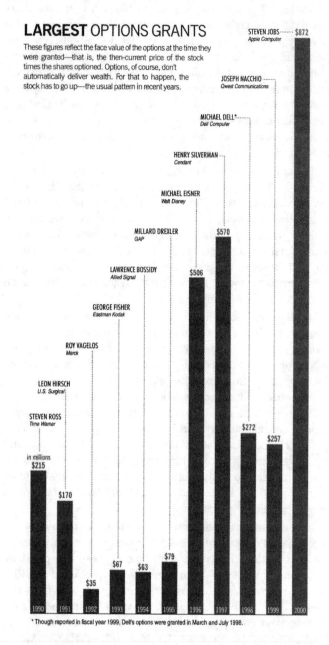

LARGEST OPTIONS GRANTS

These figures reflect the face value of the options at the time they were granted—that is, the then-current price of the stock times the shares optioned. Options, of course, don't automatically deliver wealth. For that to happen, the stock has to go up—the usual pattern in recent years.

STEVEN JOBS ········ $872
Apple Computer

JOSEPH NACCHIO ········
Qwest Communications

MICHAEL DELL* ········
Dell Computer

HENRY SILVERMAN ···
Cendant

MICHAEL EISNER
Walt Disney

MILLARD DREXLER ···
GAP $570

LAWRENCE BOSSIDY ···
Allied Signal $506

GEORGE FISHER
Eastman Kodak

ROY VAGELOS
Merck

LEON HIRSCH
U.S. Surgical

STEVEN ROSS
Time Warner

in millions
$215

$170

$35

$67

$63

$79

$272

$257

1990 1991 1992 1993 1994 1995 1996 1997 1998 1999 2000

* Though reported in fiscal year 1999, Dell's options were granted in March and July 1998.

Fortune Chart/Source: Executive Compensation Advisory Services; Fortune

Meanwhile, in a radical shift, CEOs were becoming celebrities. As business became glamorized in the 1980s, CEOs realized that being famous was more fun than being invisible. Compensation consultants who were around at the time report a startling phenomenon: Instead of being embarrassed by their appearance near the top of published CEO pay rankings, many CEOs began to consider it a badge of honor. That societal change is another key part of today's CEO pay machine.

Though stock options have been available since 1950, today's options culture began in the bull market of the 1980s. This makes perfect sense, of course; since stocks essentially went nowhere from 1964 to 1982, options during that era didn't exactly make a CEO's heart beat faster. But once stocks took off, options suddenly became an excellent vehicle for getting rich, and companies began delivering them in truckloads.

Besides, corporate raiders like Boone Pickens were arguing, rightly, that most CEOs didn't have enough skin in the game—they didn't own enough company stock to care about increasing the share price. Institutional investors and shareholder activists were pressing the same case. It was a classic demonstration that you should be careful what you wish for. Companies quickly responded by handing the CEO tons more options and restricted shares. Trouble was, that came on top of already generous cash pay—so the CEO's interest wasn't *really* aligned with that of the shareholders. Besides, if the stock went down, the CEO wouldn't lose money the way shareholders did. He or she simply wouldn't exercise the options.

We pause a moment now to recognize a couple of CEOs for historically significant roles. Michael Eisner signed on as Walt Disney's chief in 1984 with a contract that changed the game for all who followed. Written by Graef S. Crystal—then America's preeminent compensation consultant, now one of the most vehement critics of CEO pay—the contract offered huge rewards if Eisner delivered great profits. Crystal advised Disney's board that the contract could make Eisner the highest-paid CEO ever. Understood, said the board. Eisner then performed as hoped for, and his pay—$57 million in 1989, for example—ratcheted the numbers up a giant notch. (That contract has long since expired, and last year Eisner got big pay for poor performance.)

Eisner's fellow trailblazer was Roberto Goizueta, Coca-Cola's chief from 1981 until his death in 1997. He turned Coke into a champion performer, and because he was paid heavily in options and restricted stock, he apparently became the first executive billionaire: the first person to amass assets worth more than $1 billion as a hired hand, without having founded or financed a business. After that, CEOs could never think about their pay in the same way again.

The pay machine's newest pieces appeared in a flurry in the early 1990s. The forces of the previous decade—the bull market, the huge options grants, the Eisner-and-Goizueta effect—combined to produce a slew of mammoth pay packages. The public became furious—so furious that Washington had to act.

So in 1993 Congress created section 162(m) of the tax code, which prevents companies from taking a tax deduction for CEO salaries over $1 million a year; pay that varies on the basis of performance remains fully deductible. Compensation consultants agree that this change, far from restricting CEO pay, probably helped increase it. Many salaries that were below $1 million now rose to that level, since it was virtually government-endorsed.

Around the same time, the SEC required companies to report CEO pay in far greater detail, the better to inform shareholders. Ambitious CEOs now knew better than ever what their peers were getting—and could push for packages that were superior in every particular.

And with that, the main elements of today's megapay machine were in place. How does it work? Let's take a look:

1. A poorly performing company, under pressure from active investors, fires its CEO and seeks to bring in a highly touted outsider. The outsider has tons of options from his current em-

ployer that he'll forfeit if he leaves or joins a competitor. So the new employer has to make him whole by paying a massive signing bonus. Most egregious example: Conseco last year paid former GE Capital chief Gary Wendt a signing bonus of $45 million—cash—to forfeit his GE options and become CEO.

2. The ousted CEO was probably earning a lot—it's all public info—so the new guy argues, logically, that if the old CEO was getting so much for doing a lousy job, he, the presumed savior, should get a great deal more. He probably does, and the details are reported in the proxy statement.

3. The comp consultants duly enter that mammoth signing bonus and pay package into their databases, and the median pay in that industry jumps.

4. Every comp committee in that industry, when determining the chief's pay, is now looking at higher median levels. Since comp consultants report that virtually all committees believe their CEO ranks at the 75th percentile or above, they will almost certainly award packages that raise the median even further.

5. The typical underperforming CEO whose stock falls receives even more options and perhaps restricted stock. Inevitably, the publicly stated reason is that this gives him greater incentive to get the stock up. The actual logic is that since his old options are worthless—and because it would look profligate to take a tax hit by raising his salary above its current $1 million and a bonus increase would look terrible in light of recent poor performance—the only way to give him more money is to grant a big slug of new options at today's lower price, plus restricted stock, which will pay off no matter what.

6. Those mushrooming stock awards are cited by other comp committees as justification for handing lots more stock to their own CEOs.

7. When an underperformer finally gets canned, he leaves behind a formidable pay package, and the company may have to entice an outsider to give up his own giant package. Return to Step 1.

On and on this wondrous machine turns, cranking out bigger numbers with every revolution. Logical question: If all the machine's parts were installed by 1993, why is it only now that we're hearing such outrage over the results? Answer: The American public isn't angered by big pay. It's angered by perceived injustice. The last major outcry, in 1991 and 1992, arose from huge CEO pay at a time of recession and widespread lay-

offs. Pay kept right on rocketing after that, but when the economy got back on track and the stock markets caught fire, who cared? This time the backdrop is a dragging economy and a market collapse that hurt millions of people. Like the last crisis, this, too, shall pass.

And then what? Three facts combine to create the fuel that keeps the American CEO pay machine spinning at today's furious clip. First and most fundamental, the managers and directors, who control the corporation day by day, are not the owners, who bear the cost of what the managers and directors do. Shareholders may be incensed by their CEO's pay, but doing something about it is so cumbersome that it almost never happens. That separation of ownership from control, and the potential for mischief it creates, have been apparent for 70 years. We accept it because it's the price we pay for a system of broad-based capitalism that has enabled the funding of the world's largest and most successful enterprises.

Second, the American culture celebrates wealth and fame above almost all else. "Even if a CEO is worth it, should he take it?" asks Ken West of TIAA-CREF, America's largest private pension fund. In many countries a nine-figure pay package, and the attention it attracts, would be just too far outside social bounds. Not here.

Third, we're in a revolutionizing global economy where the difference between the right CEO and the wrong one is all the difference in the world. Many will fail. Demand for winners is huge, the supply small. In that environment the best CEOs will cost more than ever, and—who knows?—may be worth it.

Now, what are the odds that those facts will change anytime soon? Not good, it would seem. On the other hand, the chances that the economy will pick up and the public will feel better by next proxy season are excellent. That's why, despite this year's mind-blowing numbers and the outraged reaction they've provoked, a hard-headed realist would have to say that America's CEO pay machine looks well oiled and finely tuned, with a whole lot of life in it still.

REPORTER ASSOCIATES *Ann Harrington, Paola Hjelt*

FEEDBACK: *gcolvin@fortunemail.com*

Disengage the rage: Defusing employee anger

Expressing anger at a professional level... means not being abusive, and not using power to get even or to oppress.

By Phillip M. Perry

What would you do in this situation? You're moving back the deadline for a major staff project because of a mistake you made in your calendar. Now you're telling your employees they will have to stay late to get everything done. Bart, whose negative remarks about the company have always irritated you, suddenly explodes. With other staff members standing around, he tosses a stack of papers on the floor and yells at you: "If you knew how to manage, we wouldn't be stuck here after hours." You're thunderstruck. You feel anger welling up inside of you and...Whoa! Stop action! What will you do now?
Choice 1: Scream at Bart to shut up and get back to work.
Choice 2: Take a deep breath, then discuss the matter of staying after hours with Bart and the rest of your staff, addressing their concerns.
Choice 3: Inform Bart that he is out of line with his comments and ask him to come to your office at a specified time to discuss the matter. Which of the proposed responses is best?

Taking the High Road

If you've been managing for a while, you doubtless have encountered similar situations. The "Barts" of the world can be a special problem. Often, they perfect the practice of needling you without going so far that

they get fired. Their remarks can slowly generate anger inside you. Eventually, you come to a turning point such as the sudden explosion described above.

> ## Better Health through Anger (Expression)
>
> **W**hy not ignore anger, hoping it will go away on its own? This is a natural question, since often we feel guilty for our anger. We also can be tempted to repress anger to avoid harming a relationship, or of appearing to others to be out of control, or of creating a scene.
>
> But repressing anger can be dangerous. "It can cause headaches, high blood pressure, ulcers, heart problems, back pain, anxiety, depression and weight problems. It also can disrupt our relationships and affect our thinking," said Laura Boyd-Brown, president of Parker, Boyd-Brown and Associates, a consulting firm in Dartmouth, Nova Scotia. The tension between expressing and repressing can cause emotional turmoil that can damage relationships and careers. Too often, driving anger underground only results in an eventual blow-up.

What to do? If you're like most people, you feel the urge to yell back at Bart. Who wouldn't get some satisfaction from returning fire? Such re-

taliation, though, can damage your business and your reputation.

"When you get angry, the points you want to make are lost," said Lisa Costas, a psychologist with the Counseling Center for Human Development at the University of South Florida, Tampa. "You need to maintain a level of composure so your message is clear and is not buried in an emotional reaction." Expressing anger at a professional level, Costas said, means not being abusive, and not using power to get even or to oppress. That means addressing the outburst in a private meeting during which you can discuss the issues calmly.

So how do you handle Bart? Avoid escalating the conflict by addressing his personal comment in front of his peers at a time when both of you are upset. The group setting has another drawback: You want to discover what is really troubling Bart, who will be hesitant to communicate such information in front of his co-workers.

The best approach, Costas said, is to calm down (try counting to 10) and then set a time to discuss the matter. Costas suggests using a statement along these lines: "I'm sorry I made a mistake. We still have to stay late, and I will be here helping out. I would like to schedule a meeting with you this afternoon."

Sticks and Stones: When Employees Don't Perform

If you are feeling anger toward an employee who has not been performing well, or who has failed to carry out a promised duty, avoid the temptation to holler. Expressing anger by shouting or name-calling is counterproductive. "In the old days, intimidation was a fringe benefit of being a manager," said Ronald T. Potter-Efron, a partner and full-time chemical dependency/mental health therapist at First Things First, Ltd. in Eau Claire, Wis. "Those days are over. If you yell at a subordinate, you are liable to be fired yourself, or get sued for discrimination, or spark violence." At the very least, mistreated employees are much more likely to jump ship in this tight labor market."

"Angry outbursts put people on the defensive," added Laura Boyd-Brown, president of Parker, Boyd-Brown and Associates, a consulting firm in Dartmouth, Nova Scotia. "They cloud people's vision and make them much less open to solving problems." It's better to calm down and hold a meeting with the staff member. Boyd-Brown suggests saying something like this: "This is what I expected […] and this is what you did […]." Then show how the employee's actions harmed the team or the company: "Because of your actions, we didn't get the contract. I insist you get your work done on time in the future."

Prior to the meeting, investigate any failings you may have brought to the table. You need to be especially careful that personal factors do not enter into the formula. Always ask yourself this question: 'What's really going on here?'" Potter-Efron suggested. "You really need to be careful in your belief that the employee is messing up. Do you have unrealistic expectations toward people? Is there a problem with the system that may be setting up staff members for failure? Or is there something about you—perhaps you are a poor communicator or have an excessive need for control."

Anticipate the employee's possible reactions in a range of scenarios. if the worker has always become defensive when criticized, expect this to happen again, and have a ready response. "Very few people take criticism well," said Potter-Efron.

Avoid Name Calling

Tags such as lazy, useless and worthless are self-fulfilling," Potter-Efron added. "You get what you label." Communicate that you are angry at the performance of the employee, not at the employee as a person. When possible, involve the employee by offering an opportunity to correct the problem with a self-generated solution. Potter-Efron suggested asking something like this: "What are you going to do to change what you have done? And what help do you need?" The latter part should be added because sometimes the employee needs assistance in the form of altered work procedures or staff backup.

Allow the employee to save face by offering as much latitude as possible in generating solutions. Whether you are asking for a short-term fix or a long-term performance improvement, it's vital to insist on something that is both doable and measurable. "Set up a way to get feedback on the staff member's future performance," Potter-Efron recommended.

Workplaces with dysfunctional anger management have less efficient teams, increased sick time and lowered productivity. Further, a poor company image has a negative impact on hiring good staff. In contrast, a rational approach to anger management will bring your organization many benefits. "Employees function more effectively if they work in an anger-free work environment," Boyd-Brown said. "Then they can focus on what needs to get done. And that adds value to the bottom line."

Temper Your Temper

When preparing for the meeting, be sure to allow sufficient time. You will need to collect your thoughts and develop a plan. "Start by clarifying your own feelings of anger," suggested John Mayer, a University of New Hampshire psychologist who was one of the original formulators of the concept of emotional intelligence. "Enumerate the various things at its roots and figure out the best way of dealing with it based on where it's coming from." Following are some possible sources of your rage:

- Humiliation at being put down in front of your employees.
- Frustration at not having instructions carried out.
- Shame at failing to have your team pull through.

Be wary of carry-overs from your personal life. For example, does your anger stem partly from Bart's looks or mannerisms that resemble those of a family member you dislike? "Don't get into a kick-the-dog mentality," said Francis J. Friedman, president of Time & Place Strategies, a New York City-based consuiting firm. "You must leave family issues at home."

Be alert for another ingredient. "Anger always has a component of fear, and it can be multidimensional," Friedman added. "When we feel trapped, the only outlet is to be angry at the people who work for us." Do you fear the failure of missing your own performance goals or those of upper management? That you won't reach your own life goals? That you will be laughed at by peers or

family? Do you fear all of these to some extent?

Next step is to consider what may be going through Bart's mind. "Try to understand the individual who has expressed anger," said Laura Boyd-Brown, president of Parker, Boyd-Brown and Associates, a consulting firm in Dartmouth, Nova Scotia. What components might be involved?" Possibilities include:

- Ongoing frustrations that have erupted suddenly because of one final issue.
- Difficulties in his home life.
- Poor ability to communicate what resources he needs to get the job done.

Write down your analyses. If conditions permit, sleep on the problem prior to your meeting. It's important

to take time to think about the issue and what you want to say.

The Art of Listening

Your meeting with Bart should accomplish two goals. The first is to inform Bart that he must modify the way he expresses his displeasure. The second is to find out what is troubling him to reduce workplace friction down the road.

Start by communicating your anger about his behavior, but do it in a way that leads to productive interaction. A possible opener is: "I didn't appreciate the way you addressed me, especially in front of co-workers. I expect in the future, if you have a complaint, you will come to me personally, and we will discuss it."

Next, it is important to encourage Bart to open up with his feelings. "Your meeting with Bart is basically a negotiation," said Ian Jacobsen, president of Jacobsen Consulting Group, Sunnyvale, Calif. "One of the first rules of negotiation is you can't operate effectively unless you understand the other person's position." The best strategy is to listen until Bart has spilled everything. Jacobsen advises a statement such as this: "Okay, Bart, expand on what you have said about my management style. I want to know where you are coming from on this."

To help Bart open up, your demeanor should communicate genuine interest in his ideas rather than confrontation or accusation. "Monitor your tone of voice and body language," suggested Costas. "We don't have to like the people we work with, but we have to maintain professional relations so we can work together."

As Bart talks, jot down key words that you want to remember. When Bart has finished talking, he is ready to listen. At that point, Jacobsen suggests responding to Bart's main points. Avoid confronting Bart in an argumentative manner, or contradicting his statements. Your goal is to change his behavior so he is a productive staff member, not to change his mind or prove your worth. And Bart will feel freer to listen if he understands you are not trying to challenge his position.

Jacobsen suggests language such as this: "Bart, I understand these points you are making, and there is some validity to them. I take exception on these other points […] for these reasons […]. I'm not trying to get you to change your mind, but I want you to understand where I'm coming from."

Once you have laid out the scenario as to why the project schedule had to change, you can encourage more interaction by asking, "Okay Bart, if you were in my shoes, what would you do?"

"Maybe Bart has some good ideas," Jacobsen said. "Maybe he doesn't. But getting him to try to look at the problem from your perspective is important in terms of opening up his mind. At the same time, you are learning more about how to deal with him."

At the end of the discussion, restate and summarize Bart's key points to communicate to him that you really did listen and that you can empathize.

Handled properly, anger can improve workplace relationships. "Rather than feeling bad about your anger, recognize that it is a natural emotion, especially when you are challenged by a subordinate," Jacobsen said. "Realize that you have the ability to meet the challenge of anger in a constructive way. If you take time out to plan your response, you are much more apt to look back later and feel good about how you handled the situation."

Phillip M. Perry is a New York-based writer specializing in business management and legal issues. He maintains a Web site at http://pmperry.com.

How Safe Is *Your* Job?:

The Threat of
WORKPLACE VIOLENCE

"Changes in the American workplace have created fertile ground for breeding discontent and potential violence."

BY LAURENCE MILLER

"**A** DISGRUNTLED [pick one: postal worker, law client, insurance claimant, store customer, hospital patient, factory worker] stormed into a place of business yesterday, killing six people before turning the gun on himself. Film at 11." You've heard this one before. Often, the lead story is followed by interviews with coworkers or associates whose comments almost invariably follow one of two main themes:

"He was always a little strange, you know, quiet. Kept to himself a lot, didn't get along with too many people, but came in, did his job, and never caused any real trouble. Certainly, nobody figured him for the violent type. Man, we didn't see this one coming." Or: "Damnit, I knew it was just a matter of time till something like this happened. This guy was bad news, a ticking bomb, and we all knew it. But there were no precautions or any real kind of discipline at all. We tried to tell management, but they just got annoyed, said there was nothing they could do, and told us not to stir up trouble. When he finally snapped, we were sitting ducks."

Most traumas I deal with in my clinical and forensic psychology practice strike

suddenly and without warning or control. In those cases, the emphasis is on treating the victims, survivors, and their families after the fact. However, in virtually no other high-risk area is education, training, planning, and prevention so vital as in the case of workplace violence. In many cases, you *can* see this one coming and you *can* do something about it.

The National Institute of Occupational Safety and Health reports that homicide is the second-leading cause of death in the workplace. Murder is the number-one workplace killer of women and the third-leading cause of death for men, after motor vehicle accidents and machine-related fatalities. The majority of workplace homicides are committed by firearms. For every actual killing, there are anywhere from 10 to 100 sublethal acts of violence committed at work.

According to Michael Mantell and Steve Albrecht in *Ticking Bombs: Defusing Violence in the Workplace*, the cost of workplace violence for American businesses runs more than $4,000,000,000 annually, including lost work time, employee medical benefits, and legal expenses. Additional costs of workplace violence include replacing lost employees and retraining new ones, decreased

productivity, higher insurance premiums, raised security costs, bad publicity, lost business, and expensive litigation.

While demographics suggest that the majority of workplace violence is committed by strangers—robbers, disaffected clients and/or customers, etc.—the news media tend to focus attention on acts of lethal aggression committed by coworkers. That is because there is an almost visceral fear we all have of someone we see and talk with every day—someone *we thought we knew*—suddenly turning into a demon of destruction.

Joseph Kinney, executive director of the National Safe Workplace Institute, warns in *Violence at Work: How to Make Your Company Safer for Employees and Customers* that current and future generations of workers will continue to have less emotional maturity, greater feelings of unearned entitlement, poorer social skills, little experience in nonviolent conflict resolution, less respect for older generations, a lower attention span, poorer self-discipline, and higher rates of violence. The newly emerging young workforce is ill-equipped for the world of work, work culture, and work ethic. High turnover encouraged by low wages and poor man-

agement reinforces the impression that everyday work is for "chumps," and further denigrates loyalty and authority.

Kinney points out that, for the past 20 years, people have been bombarded by the egocentric message that all personal problems are caused by "society." Individuals are not responsible for their actions, and all blame is externalized. At the same time, there has been a breakdown in traditionally stabilizing institutions such as family, home, church, school, and community. Some workplace violence perpetrators have been quite up front in stating that they want to "strike back" and hurt as many people as they can, no matter who those people are, because of the supposed wrongs committed against them.

In practice, I've found that reported workplace threats actually vary widely in terms of their explicitness. A few threats are direct and unambiguous ("I'm gonna blow that SOB away"), while a far-greater number are nonspecific, falling into a gray zone ("You'll be sorry" or "He deserves whatever's coming to him") that makes it difficult for managers to take action against. Some threats may occur in the form of commiseration with violent news events ("Too bad about all those people, but I know how that restaurant shooter felt").

Indeed, glamorized violence is a staple of the entertainment media, and they have naturally taken an enormous interest in workplace violence, though they often misinterpret and misrepresent those events and the reasons behind them. The common conclusion of this sound-bite journalism is that the lethal perpetrator is either a "nut case" or else engaged in a crusade of "righteous" retribution against an unfair or even darkly conspiratorial employer. This may lead marginally disturbed viewers to "justify" their own future acts of violence.

Changes in the American workplace have created fertile ground for breeding discontent and potential violence. Levels of stress accumulate in many work settings as survivors of downsized corporations are made to take on extra work and fill multiple jobs. For the terminated, anger and hopelessness mount at the inability to replace lost jobs, compounded by the accompanying financial and family stresses. The sense of long-term common corporate purpose that once may have existed between managers and the rank and file has largely disappeared. The changed culture of resentment and entitlement in the workplace says that "This company *owes* me something, and if they don't give it to me, I'm gonna take it the hard way."

Managers and supervisors are increasingly unable or unwilling to use effective discipline or promote fair and effective management practices. Like dysfunctional families, dysfunctional workplaces share common characteristics, such as chronic labor-management disputes, frequent grievances filed by employees, excessive numbers of stress disability claims, persistent pilfering and/or tampering, understaffing and overwork, and a rigidly authoritarian and/or inconsistent management style.

According to forensic psychiatrist Robert Simon in *Bad Men Do What Good Men Dream*, satisfying work affords more than just an income. For most people, it provides stability, direction, security, a sense of achievement, self-worth, camaraderie, and a feeling of belonging. Most workers would regard losing a job as a traumatic event, but one they eventually come to resolve by picking up the pieces, going forward, and searching for new opportunities. However, for a small minority of vulnerable personalities, job loss—especially if perceived as "unfair"—is a devastating blow to the psyche, a mortal narcissistic wound. If the situation is further compounded by financial difficulties, health problems, family friction, and lack of personal support, the person may feel bereft of options.

For such individuals, job stress or job loss can trigger overwhelming rage. Blame is externalized, and vengeance brews as the worker begins to think, "Who do they think they are? I'll show them they can't do this to me and get away with ruining my life." For some, the intolerability of the job loss leads to hopelessness and suicidal intentions with a retaliatory sting: "If they wanna screw me, I can screw them back— big time. Why should other people go on living their happy lives, having what they want, when I can't? I may be going out, but I'm not going out alone." The idea percolates in the perpetrator's mind that, after he's gone, his Ramboesque exploits will be reported to millions around the world and his name will become a household word. Far from meekly slinking away, defeated and unnoticed, he will leave this world in a blaze of horror and glory—just like in the movies.

Preventing violence

While there will always be a few unstable, psychopathologically violence-prone individuals in any large organization, the current emphasis on "offender profiling" obscures a greater contributor to work-

place violence and general worker malaise, a set of factors that many companies might find far more difficult to address. These involve the twin evils of generally unfair management practices and lack of a specific workplace violence prevention and response plan.

While not every situation can be planned for, the absence of even the most rudimentary security measures and contingency plans in many organizations is appalling. The steps a firm takes to make its employees feel secure say a lot about corporate culture and workplace morale, and while no organization desires to operate under a fortress mentality, a few important measures can go a long way toward demonstrating concern for worker safety.

As deceptively simple as it sounds, the best way to avoid workplace violence is not to hire violent workers. Efforts in this regard include thorough application reviews and background checks, careful interviewing of prospective employees, and administering appropriate psychological screening measures.

Companies should have clear, strong, fair, and consistent written policies against violence and harassment, along with effective grievance procedures, efficient security programs, a reasonably supportive work environment, open channels of communication, and training in resolving conflicts through team building and negotiation skills. Plans should be in place that specify how threats are reported and to whom, as well as a protocol for investigating them.

The ideal goal of any disciplinary program is to strike a balance between an overly rigid and heavy-handed approach that presents management as hard and unreasonable, and a too-lax one that gives employees the impression of poor control in the organization. By identifying areas of agreement and disagreement, looking for alternatives, thinking creatively, and eventually finding solutions that have the support and commitment of all parties, a human resources manager is more likely to defuse the tension and resentment that may spark workplace violence. Discipline should occur in stages, with a clear policy and rationale, and with written documentation.

If it comes down to having no choice but to fire a worker, this should be done in a firm, but humane, manner. It should be made as clear as possible to the employee that the termination is for a specific reason, rather than for general "attitude" problems or personal reasons. The worker should understand that the termination action is final, and should be informed of any

counseling or other services offered by the company for the transition period.

An example of this approach that has been successfully applied to violence occurring in health care facilities is Robert Flannery's Assaulted Staff Action Program (ASAP). It provides a range of services, including individual critical incident debriefings of assaulted staff members and entire wards, a staff victims' support group, employee victim family debriefing and counseling, and referrals for follow-up psychotherapy as needed. The ASAP team structure is comprised of 15 direct-care staff volunteers, three supervisors, and the team director, who is responsible for administering the entire program and for ensuring that the quality of the services is maintained.

The program's developers claim that ASAP has proven useful in reducing the traumatic impact of patient assaults on employee victims and in significantly lowering the overall level of violence in facilities where it has been applied. More germane to the bottom line, ASAP saves the previously mentioned costs of workplace violence.

When violence happens

Sometimes, despite the best efforts at prevention, a dangerous situation begins to brew and a violent incident becomes a distinct possibility, or an incident just erupts explosively and personnel have to respond immediately. The nature of the response will depend on how thorough the pre-incident planning and training have been.

Warning signs may be observed hours, days, or weeks prior to a violent incident, and may be preceded by a history of work-related problems. In all too many cases, the sparks of a potentially violent reaction have been fanned into flames by abusive discipline, clumsily executed termination, or failure of management to address employee–employee grievances, causing the worker to "take matters into his own hands."

Plans and training for defusing violent episodes must be developed, put in place, and reviewed periodically. These include initial actions to take when a violent episode appears to be threatening, codes and

signals for summoning help, a chain of command for handling emergencies, appropriate use of verbal control tactics and body language, scene control and bystander containment, measures for dealing with weapons, and procedures for resolving hostage situations.

The crisis is not over when the police and TV crews leave. People may have been killed, others wounded, some held hostage, and many psychologically traumatized. Plans and policies for dealing with the aftermath of workplace violence are just as important as planning for the incident itself, and both may come under sharp scrutiny in later investigations, litigation, and corporate public relations. Companies should proactively set up policies and procedures for responding to the aftermath of a workplace violence incident. They should include mobilization of mental health services, media and public relations responses, family interventions, collaboration with law enforcement, physical security and cleanup, legal measures, postincident investigations, and plans for getting back to business. During the crisis and in its aftermath, the overriding question that will be asked by employees, their families, stakeholders and customers, the media, and the general public is: "What is this company doing to help its workers get through this?"

In this regard, commitment from the top of the management organization—"executive buy-in"—is crucial to determining how effectively such interventions will operate. In the worst case I can remember, a bank branch grudgingly arranged for a staff stress debriefing after a holdup, only because the service was mandated by their managed care contract. The branch managers clearly regarded the intervention as a waste of time that cut into employees' work hours. An uncomfortable backroom lunch and storage area was designated for the debriefing, which was frequently interrupted by people coming in and out to use the kitchen and bathroom. Some of those coworkers could be heard to make cracks about "free time." As a result, the participants wanted the whole thing over with as quickly as possible, and little therapeutic work was accomplished.

The best case I can remember (in terms of company support) involved a hostage and shooting crisis perpetrated by a disturbed customer of a medium-sized investment firm, resulting in two deaths and several injuries. The CEO immediately suspended business as usual, arranged for temps to cover the basic needs of the company, offered his home to be used for almost round-the-clock debriefings, and provided food, beverages, and, in a few cases, bed and board to employees who were too upset to drive home. He and the senior management staff offered help to survivors and their families, personally checked on proper funeral arrangements for the slain workers, frequently visited injured employees in the hospital, and generally shared in the grief and recovery of the members of their staff. Far more than any specific clinical services I could provide, this sincere and unselfish human response by senior management to tragedy within their ranks—a true expression of leadership—helped this firm to heal quickly and move on, always holding a place of respect for their slain comrades, but honoring their memories by productively continuing their work.

This brings us back to an earlier point: Bad things *do* happen to good companies—but they happen a lot less often than to bad ones. There will always be a few dangerously unstable people scattered among the workforce. However, businesses that treat their employees honorably, take the time and concern to implement safety measures, use firm but fair disciplinary procedures, and make it clear that harassment of its employees—by coworkers or management—will not be tolerated tend to have fewer violent incidents than less-well-run companies. Some workers may indeed have a short fuse, but fairly run and well-managed firms seem to know how to keep those fuses from being lit. This isn't just a safety issue—it's good business.

Laurence Miller, *a psychologist in Boca Raton, Fla., specializing in neuropsychology, business psychology, and corporate counseling, is the author of* Shocks to the System: Psychotherapy of Traumatic Disability Syndromes.

THE TRIANGLE LEGACY: 90 YEARS AFTER FIRE, SWEATSHOPS PERSIST

Scott Malone and Joanna Ramey

NEW YORK—Sunday will mark the 90th anniversary of the Triangle Shirtwaist fire, a disaster that claimed the lives of 146 women and started the drive to unionize the U.S. garment industry.

While the event should mark a point in time in a bygone era, it remains a symbolic reminder that the social and industrial factors that led to that tragedy are still alive today.

The infamous fire started late on a Saturday afternoon in 1911, in a cutting room at the Triangle factory, which occupied the top three floors of a 10-story building in Manhattan's Greenwich Village. But based on incidences that have occurred in recent years from El Monte, Calif., to Bangladesh, it could just as easily happen today. As the conflagration spread, fueled by rolls of fabric, some 500 workers discovered their easiest escape routes were blocked, as the factory's owners kept the doors locked to keep their mostly immigrant employees from leaving their sewing machines.

While some made it down the stairs or fled to the roof, the workers on the ninth floor were unable to force open the locked door. Many, their clothing afire, leapt from the windows. Their bodies, piled in the street, posed an obstacle for the fire trucks to battle the blaze.

A lot has changed in the apparel business over the last 90 years, as a result of that disaster. Labor laws now impose strict safety regulations on U.S. workplaces and with the flurry of publicity that sweatshops have attracted over the past decade, many retailers and wholesalers now require their suppliers around the world to sign agreements stating that they obey local labor laws and do not employ underage workers.

Nonetheless, sweatshops and dangerous working environments remain a fact of life for the apparel industry in major U.S. cities, most industry sources and observers believe. They're also one of the major exports of the U.S. apparel industry, case in point: the November blaze at a Bangladesh knitwear factory, which claimed the lives of 50 workers and hospitalized about 100 who were unable to escape the flames because the plant's main gates were locked.

Apparel executives, labor advocates and other industry observers said they believe that sweatshops are still very much a part of today's industry. Both in major U.S. urban centers—particularly New York and Los Angeles, which have substantial populations of illegal or undocumented immigrants—and abroad, plants continue to operate outside the law.

There are no clear numbers on how many sweatshops are in existence today, as illegal operations are inherently hard to track. In the mid-Nineties, the Clinton administration estimated that half of the 22,000 apparel contractors then operating in the U.S. were in violation of labor laws.

Opinions differ on how prevalent sweatshops remain in the U.S. today: While most sources said that the absolute number of sweatshops has likely dropped over the past two decades along with the overall falloff in manufacturing activity, some contended that over the past 10 years, sweatshops have come to represent a larger portion of the remaining operations.

Former Labor Secretary Robert Reich, who's now a professor at Brandeis University, said the increased attention paid to garment contractors over the last eight years has made the sweatshop situation in the U.S. "a bit better," but he added, "there is still a huge problem."

"Many manufacturers are working on very quick turnarounds. At the same time, everybody wants the cheapest merchandise possible. We also have an influx of immigrants, many undocumented, looking for work and we have unscrupulous subcontractors who link up with the two groups," said Reich, during whose tenure the notorious sweatshop in El Monte, Calif., which held 70 Thai immigrants in peonage, was discovered.

"We still don't have a comprehensive system in the U.S. getting major retailers and major manufacturers to inspect and control their subcontractors in a systematic way. We are inching closer to a system," Reich said. "Maybe this reflects a little bit of cynicism having [worked on this] issue for so many years, but I don't think we will get there unless major manufacturers and retailers face stiff liability" for using unscrupulous contractors.

In an industry characterized by razor-thin margins and intense competition at every step of the supply chain, observers said, it's all but inevitable that people will try to skirt the law if they think it will save a few bucks.

"Why do sweatshops continue to exist? Why do people keep trying to defraud the government by evading taxes?" Bud Konheim, chief executive officer of Nicole Miller, asked rhetorically, adding: "They think there is a great economic advantage to it. But there is not a great economic advantage to evading your taxes if you get caught."

Some observers argued that sweatshops have become more prevalent in the U.S. over the past few years, with their owners seizing the opportunity to take advantage of the waves of new immigrants coming to the U.S.

"In the apparel industry, we've seen a new growth of these very small shops in the big cities on the coasts," said Kate Bronfenbrenner, director of labor education at the New York State School of Industrial and Labor Relations at Cornell University in Ithaca, N.Y. "The operations are small and hidden from labor laws and they move constantly. Many of the workers there are working seven days a week for flat rates that can be $200 a week and they work 12 hours a day."

In the U.S., a sweatshop is defined by the Department of Labor as any factory with more than two violations of labor laws. That can include workers being paid less than the current minimum wage of $5.15 an hour or not being paid a higher rate for overtime, as well as safety violations.

"There is a tremendous lack of compliance with our labor standards in terms of minimum wages and overtime," claimed Linda Dworak, president of the New York-based Garment Industry Development Corp. "There are also many factories that operate under unsafe conditions. Fire exits are still locked in many factories."

Dworak said the GIDC believes that sweatshop operators mostly prey on illegal immigrants who are in less of a position to hold their employers accountable to the law.

"In the U.S., the worst conditions are in Los Angeles and New York, and that is where you have a large concentration of immigrant workers," she continued. "They're predominantly female and often have limited English, and if they're undocumented they're afraid to go to any kind of government enforcement agency."

Several observers said they believe that labor violations are an almost inevitable by-product of the highly competitive apparel environment.

"As we drive for lower prices every year, it's just impossible to be able to be completely in compliance with labor standards," said consultant Andrew Jassin, a partner in New York-based Jassin-O'Rourke Group. "It is driven by the retailers' constant need to have better margins and more sales. More sales come about through more promotion. We can't disregard the selling of product at discounts in the stores. That's a major factor. We need to think about where the product came from and how low they want to negotiate prices."

Indeed, the power that retailers exert over pricing leads even labor advocates to talk almost sympathetically about the plant managers who are often their adversaries.

"Contractors really have a very weak control over the economics of production," said Dworak. "Contractors are squeezed and squeezed and end up sometimes having to demand a lot of overtime from their employees."

A number of sources said that the contractor system, in which factory owners make a profit based on the cost of labor, but exercise little control over their pricing, tends to encourage sweatshops. That problem is exacerbated, they say, by the increasing reliance of retailers on private label merchandise.

"Some of them have codes of conduct, but they take an arm's-length position. Every guy blames the next guy," said Jay Mazur, president of UNITE—a descendant of the ILGWU, which rose to power after the Triangle Shirtwaist fire attracted attention to the dangerous conditions inside apparel factories.

Jassin agreed: "If you don't think about an issue, it's not an issue. Retailers first and foremost will say they abide by legal standards that are set and try to comply where possible. But because they're driving prices downward and they have middle people, they may not be as aware—purposely—of where those middle people get their products from. Maybe the retailers take, not a dim view, but an ostrich's point of view. As long as they get the price, quality and someone signs off on the compliance agreement, they may be happy."

The issue of whether retailers who sell private label merchandise should be considered manufacturers has become a key one on the labor front in recent years.

It is at the center of a debate in California over a state law passed last year that holds manufacturers and retailers jointly liable for the wages of apparel workers, if the contractors who employed them were unable to pay them. A draft version of regulations for enforcing that law, which may go into effect this spring, upset labor advocates because it exempted retailers.

Regardless of legal liability, labor advocates have taken their message to retailers' front doors, in an effort to place the blame for the use of sweatshops on a clear consumer target. NikeTown, Gap and Macy's are just three of the retailers that demonstrators have accused of using sweatshop labor over the past decade.

UNITE's Mazur said retailers "are major manufacturers, but they are unencumbered. They deny the fact they are manufacturers."

For their part, retailers insist that they are not manufacturers, but contend that they are taking the sweatshop issue seriously anyway.

"Retailers depend on manufacturers, and manufacturers have done a phenomenal job in addressing problems," said Steve Pfister, senior vice president of government relations with the National Retail Federation.

However, he strongly disagreed with the claim that retailers don't want to know what goes on at the plants where they do business. Rather, he contended, as the sweatshop issue has gained prominence,

retailers have paid ever-closer attention to the way the goods they sell are being made, by setting and maintaining vendor standards.

"For the retailer, their reputation is on the line," he said. "They are the name that the consumer sees and because of that, they have to take it seriously. If their reputation is going to be sullied, they will walk away from a factory. If anything, there is more interaction and oversight."

Retailers and vendors pointed to the industry's many efforts over the past few years to better manage labor standards at factories around the world—such as the Fair Labor Association, which grew out of a panel convened by the Clinton administration; and the Worldwide Responsible Apparel Production program, founded by the American Apparel Manufacturers Association, now known as the American Apparel and Footwear Association—as proof of their dedication to the issue.

"We are a very competitive industry, but we share a lot of information and best practices in this area," said Roberta Karp, senior vice president and general counsel at Liz Claiborne, who contended that apparel brands can no longer afford the risk of selling clothing made in sweatshop conditions.

"Our consumer cares very much" about the issue, she said. "They want to feel good about the product. They don't want to have a reason to feel bad about something."

While student protests about labor conditions have attracted a lot of attention, not all in the industry believe that concerns about labor issues really affect consumers' purchasing decisions.

One New York factory that industry sources cite as having high labor standards is the one operated in Chinatown by the Made in New York Group Inc., which produces the Lafayette 148 brand. While walking through the factory, Lafayette 148 president Deirdre Quinn pointed with pride to the six bright, airy, yet bustling, 10,000-square-foot production floors, which also turn out military uniforms and private label garments for high-end retailers.

However, she conceded that having a nice plant and content workers isn't much of a marketing advantage.

"We label our garments 'Made in New York City,' but I don't think it really makes a difference to the consumer," Quinn said. "The price has to be right. I'd like to think it makes a difference, but I don't really believe it."

The apparel industry is also dealing with a public suspicion that all garment factories are sweatshops. Aileen Dresner, executive vice president of Lafayette 148, said people often ask what the conditions in her factory are really like.

"We're in Chinatown. The first thing people say is, 'Is it a sweatshop?' And then, they give a little chuckle," she said. "And then, we take them in for a tour."

A sample room operated by designer Elie Tahari was the target of similar allegations last year, by a landlord who was trying to evict him from his space. In a somewhat unusual move, UNITE stepped in to back Tahari, claiming his shop was clean. The landlord, Chase Manhattan Bank, eventually backed down and sold the building to Tahari, who declined to comment on the issue for this story.

Over the past few years, apparel companies have struggled to explain to the public that the buying power of the dollar can be dramatically higher in other parts of the world.

In 1998, after reports of abusive conditions at some Vietnamese plants, Nike touted the findings of a Dartmouth University study that pointed out that while workers at two Nike-supplying plants earned about $550 a year, that far surpassed the $240 per capita income in that nation at the time.

Similarly, officials from Caribbean Basin nations have been trying to lure more apparel manufacturing jobs to their region. Henry Fransen, executive director of the Honduras Maquiladora Association, pointed out that over the past few years, the number of men working in his country's garment plants rose from about 5 percent to 28 percent—mainly because the men put their machismo behind them when they realized how much money they could make sewing clothes.

"Women were making more money than the men," he said.

Many people said they believe that the publicity surrounding the sweatshop issue has helped to improve working conditions in the U.S. and abroad. While they said that the industry can certainly reduce the prevalence of sweatshops, most held little hope that they'll ever be done away with entirely.

"Retailers don't want to be caught in a situation where they are getting bad publicity, and they are more and more concerned that the factories they are using are not sweatshops. Maybe I'm being optimistic, but I think things are changing a bit," said the GIDC's Dworak. Still, as to whether she thought the industry would ever be able to put an end to sweatshops, she said "that's going to be a big challenge."

Larry Martin, president of the AAFA, said that as the industry continues to globalize, it's going to become even harder to keep track of labor conditions around the world.

"There are places that are so remote that they probably wouldn't get found," he said. "But look, we haven't wiped out bank robbery, either. People are going to break the law and our job is to prosecute those who do."

Health-Care Costs:
HR's Crisis Has Real Solutions

**Health care costs will rise as much as 16 percent this year.
But by exposing employees to the cost consequences of their care, employers can rein in expenses.**

By Shari Caudron

In the United States, employers cover the cost of worker health care. If not exactly a right, then company-sponsored health benefits are certainly an expectation—so much so that employees are accustomed to having their companies not only pick up the entire health-care tab, but also make major decisions about providers, insurance carriers, and coverage areas. As a result, the average American worker is blissfully ignorant about the enormous complexity and staggering cost of the U.S. health-care system. This ignorance is expensive. Uninformed employees routinely choose higher-cost drugs without realizing it. They fail to manage chronic illnesses such as depression or diabetes, which leads to more costly medical care later on. They either head to the doctor at the first sign of a stomachache or neglect to go entirely. In the end, it's employers that pick up the tab for these ill-informed decisions. The era of the uninformed health-care consumer, however, may be rapidly drawing to a close. Why? Because spiraling costs mean that employers can no longer afford to accommodate employees who don't make wise health-care decisions.

How much are costs rising?

Nationwide, health costs are expected to rise between 13 and 16 percent in 2002, representing the fourth consecutive year of major cost hikes and the highest annual percentage increase in 10 years.

"For the next three to four years, there will be no other inflationary area of business that will affect an employer's bottom line as dramatically as the predicted 15 to 20 percent annual growth in health-insurance premiums," says John Word, managing partner of CaliforniaChoice, a small group health purchasing alliance based in Orange, California. In real numbers, a 15 percent increase on a $2,000 monthly premium will, over four years, raise that premium to $3,500. If the rate of increase is 20 percent, the monthly premium will more than double.

There are many things driving the meteoric rise in health costs. For starters, there's been a drastic escalation in prescription drug costs. Not only are there more drugs on the market, which naturally increases utilization, but consumers can also take more of these drugs in combination without side effects. Furthermore, direct-to-consumer marketing has been extremely successful in increasing demand for new drugs. "Today, about 70 percent of the people who go to the doctor and ask for a prescription because of an advertisement walk out with a prescription," says Randall Abbott, senior consultant with Watson Wyatt Worldwide in Philadelphia.

The continued development of life-saving technology also contributes to the rising health-care bill. Unlike other technology, health technology doesn't become less expensive over time, says Joe Luchok, communications manager of the Health Insurance Association of America, based in Washington, D.C. "Today, you can get a VCR for $99 that cost $1,000 20 years ago. That doesn't happen with MRIs."

America's aging population is another factor in escalating costs. Older people require more health care, and the health care

A Checklist of Other Cost-Saving Strategies

tools

Although the big news in health care is the shift toward making employees more accountable for the care they choose, companies are using many other strategies in an effort to contain costs. These include:

1. Wellness programs: corporate wellness efforts have been around for a long time but they've recently entered the Internet age. For example, companies such a 3Com, Chevron, and General Mills utilize an online health management program developed by WellMed to give employees immediate access to personalized health information. Giving employees access to health resources via home or work is another way that companies are encouraging employees to take responsibility for their own health management.

2. Disease management: Employers that contract with disease-management programs such as those offered by Milwaukee-based Innovative Resource Group are able to identify and manage the care of employees with chronic conditions such as asthma or diabetes. This helps to avoid the high costs associated with lost productivity and unmanaged medical conditions.

3. Absence management: Many companies are realizing that the cost of health insurance is only one piece of the puzzle. Such things as lost productivity and worker absences contribute to the hidden costs of health care. For this reason, more employers are starting to recognize that absences have to be managed more aggressively.

4. On-site primary care: Cleveland-based Whole Health Management, which provides on-site medical and fitness centers, recently started offering clients such as American Airlines on-site primary-care services. Geared to self-insured employers with at least 2,000 workers at a site, on-site primary care enables employees to obtain such things as physical exams and preventive health-care screenings without leaving the work site. According to Whole Health's calculations, employers receive a $5 return for every $1 spent.

5. Eliminating cost-inefficient plans: Companies are taking a closer look at health plans they currently offer and, by reviewing quality and financial factors, are beginning to eliminate those that aren't cost-effective.

6. Moving toward PPO: According to Hewitt Associates, employers are continuing to transition from point-of-service plans to preferred provider organization. PPOs offer lower administrative fees, competitive discounts, and greater freedom for employees, and can be relatively cost-neutral to organizations.

---

they receive is typically more expensive than that delivered to younger people.

Far from helping employers grapple with rising costs, the government has actually added to the burden through state insurance mandates that force employers to provide certain kinds of coverage. There are currently more than 1,400 mandates across the states that cover everything from alcoholism and infertility treatment to oral contraceptives and wigs, according to a study by Blue Cross/Blue Shield. "Many of these mandated coverage areas are over and above what is considered by employers to be basic protection against illness or injury," Abbott says.

The terrorist attacks of September 11—combined with the ensuing recession—have certainly not made the battle against rising health costs any easier. In fact, they may actually cause health-care benefit costs to rise faster than expected. There was a post-9/11 upswing in utilization of behavioral health and employee assistance plan services, as well as a rise in anti-anxiety and anti-depression prescription drug expenses. Layoffs are also contributing to escalating health costs by increasing the claim expense that companies face when their unemployed workers enroll for COBRA continuation coverage. "The dual effects of layoffs and the aftermath of September 11 will increase costs an additional 1 to 2 percent for companies nation-

wide, and 3 to 5 percent for metro New York companies," Abbott says.

For the last decade or so, employers have been able to keep the rise in health costs to a minimum by switching health plans, most notably from traditional indemnity coverage to some type of managed care, But managed care has reached a saturation point in its ability to save money through price discounts. "In recent years, most of the savings or flat costs in health care were because managed care has been able to evolve and cover more people," Abbott says. "But today, in most areas of the country, price discounts associated with managed care have been reached and the savings are over."

Employers are beginning to realize that the only way to effect longer-term changes in the cost of care is to get employees—the consumers of health care—more actively involved in purchasing and utilizing health-care services.

As a result, employers are beginning to realize that the only way to effect longer-term changes in the cost of care is to get em-

ployees—the *consumers* of health care—more actively involved in purchasing and utilizing health-care services. After all, one of the reasons medical costs keep rising is that consumers are separated from purchase decisions. Thus, there is no way to hold them accountable for utilization or costs. If companies are to have any hope of holding down cost increases, employees must be held more accountable for their health-care decisions. As Lou Cimini, senior vice president of HR and organizational performance for The Holmes Group, a manufacturer and distributor of small appliances in Milford, Massachusetts, explains: "The real change that has to occur is in the mind-set of employees from being passive to active consumers." As a result, employers are beginning to realize that the only way to affect longer-term changes in the cost of care is by getting employees—the consumers of health care—more actively involved in how they purchase and utilize healthcare services.

In fact, a recent survey by Hewitt Associates, a global management consulting firm, reveals that 61 percent of companies report being either somewhat or extremely comfortable with employees taking more responsibility for evaluating and selecting health plans, coverage levels, providers, and health-care services.

Building financial accountability

Employers are trying to increase employee accountability and at the same time reduce costs in a number of ways, the first of which is cost-sharing. Over the past three years, employers have taken a grin-and-bear-it approach to rising health costs. Instead of sharing a percentage of cost increases with employees, they absorbed the increases because they didn't want to risk alienating workers in a tight labor market.

Today, however, with unemployment rising and the economy in an official recession, employers are no longer willing to be so benevolent. According to a study by Watson Wyatt, a majority of employers (56 percent) report that employee contributions for health care—through such things as payroll deductions and co-pays—will increase this year. Furthermore, the amount of that increase is likely to be higher than the rate of inflation, as employers try to play catch-up for the last several years. "If costs go up 13.6 percent this year," Abbott says, "most employers will be increasing employee contributions by 20 to 25 percent."

Increasing employee contributions is not only a way for employers to relieve their cost burden, but also a way of encouraging employees to think harder about their health benefits. If they have to pay more for medical coverage, the hope is that employees may be prompted to move to less expensive coverage, to utilize spousal coverage through another company, to reduce their indiscriminate use of health services, and to choose lower-cost therapies.

Higher co-pays are also being applied to prescription drug coverage. Employers, if they haven't done so already, are migrating to pharmaceutical benefit plans that utilize drug formularies. Chris Robbins, principal, Arxcel, Inc., a consulting firm that helps employers manage prescription drug costs, says that formularies utilize a three-tier co-pay system. Employees pay

the highest co-pay for brand-name drugs, a lower co-pay for less expensive medication with the same effectiveness, and the smallest or no co-pay for generics. This forces employees to decide for themselves whether it's worth it to use, say, Pepcid for heartburn as opposed to the generic alternative.

How Does Your Company Compare?

trends

C&B Consulting Group, Inc., a New York-based employee benefits consulting firms, offers these facts:

- The average annual cost per employee for medical coverage is $5,266.29.

- On average, prescription drug claims represent 18.94 percent of total medical claims.

- The average percent of HMO premiums paid by employees is 17.25 percent for individual premiums, and 25.97 percent for family premiums.

- Preferred provider organizations remain the most widely offered type of medical plan.

- On average, employers spend 3.85 hours per week resolving claim problems.

- Almost 40 percent (38.66 percent) of employers cite service and administration as one of their top four concerns.

- Although more than 63 percent of employers list quality of medical services as one of their top four concerns, more than half of employers do not review quality-of-care issues with their carriers or third-party administrators.

The cost-savings that result from these strategies can be impressive. John E. Scully, senior vice president, human resources, for ABN AMRO North America, Inc., the holding company for LaSalle Bank in Chicago, saw his company's health costs rise an alarming 20 percent this year. By asking the 25,000 employees to contribute 3 percent more toward their health insurance costs—a jump from 21 to 24 percent—and by asking them to pay a higher co-pay for non-generic drugs, he anticipates saving $1.5 to $1.7 million this year.

Toward more consumer-driven health benefits

Two years ago, companies began debating the benefits of defined-contribution health plans, in which employers give workers vouchers that allow them to buy their own health care.

Employers quickly realized, however, that there were far too many obstacles in the way of defined-contribution plans becoming a reality: the vouchers would be taxable, the market infrastructure is not in place to allow individual consumers to buy medical insurance, and consumers are not very sophisticated when it comes to making decisions about health-care coverage. Still, employers liked the philosophy behind the defined-contribution model. They liked the idea of "defining," or capping, their annual per-employee health expenditures, and they liked fostering employee involvement in health-care decisions.

Fortunately, over the last couple of years, several alternative health-benefit approaches have hit the market that allow employers to do both these things without going so far as a defined-contribution voucher system. These approaches go by various names: consumer-driven health benefits, health-care asset management, and medical spending accounts. Providers include such company names as Definity, Lumenos, Vivius, and CareGain.

Despite the lack of a common lexicon, what these companies offer is similar: simplification of plans and administration, greater employee accountability, and more specific definition of health-care costs.

Definity, which is the best known of these new approaches, works with large self-insured companies like Minneapolis-based Woodward Governor Company, a provider of energy-control systems for industrial engines. Through Definity, Woodward purchased a high-deductible insurance plan for its employees. To help employees meet the cost of the deductible and purchase medical care throughout the year, Woodward established individual personal care accounts. Single employees, for example, received $1,000 per year with which to pay medical costs, whereas employees with families received $2,000.

Employees use these funds to pay for traditional medical care such as doctor visits and prescription drugs, as well as alternative therapies such as massage, chiropractic, and acupuncture. Whatever funds employees don't use during the year are rolled over to the next so that, over time, their health-care accounts grow in value. To discourage employees from avoiding health care altogether in an effort to save money, or choosing a face-lift instead of a pap smear, for example, the Definity plan provides 100 percent coverage of preventive health-care services. Furthermore, the personal care account is always maintained by Woodward. Employees don't have access to the funds for other uses.

If an employee's annual medical expenses do exceed the amount allotted to his personal care account, then insurance coverage kicks in. Employees will typically have to contribute an additional co-pay to reach the high deductible amount. Single employees, for example, who have $1,000 allotted to their personal care account, will have to pay an additional $500 out of pocket to meet the deductible. According to Chris Delaney, vice president of marketing for Definity, based in Minneapolis, 70 percent of employees will never reach the highest spending level.

To help employees make wise decisions about how to spend the dollars in their personal care accounts, Definity provides an extensive list of health and wellness information online. Em-

ployees at Woodward Governor, for example, can use the Definity site to search for providers in their region, check pricing for procedures, talk to nursing professinals, and determine the amount available in their personal care accounts. They also have online access to the consumer medical library at Johns Hopkins University.

"Getting consumers more involved and informed brings more pressure to bear on costs," Delaney says. Although the Definity approach is still in its infancy, self-insured employers such as Aon Corporation in Chicago and Medtronic, Inc., in Minneapolis, both of which have used Definity for the last year, saw employee utilization of services drop by 10 percent. If costs had held steady, that would represent a 10 percent decrease.

"This approach is about containing costs, and the only way we'll get there is if we keep the consumer involved, engaged, and concerned about their health-care benefit."

"This approach is about containing costs, and the only way we'll get there is if we keep the consumer involved, engaged, and concerned about their health-care benefit," Delaney adds.

CareGain, Inc., based in Princeton, New Jersey, offers a similar benefit for small and mid-sized employers. Under CareGain's "health care asset management" model, employers purchase high-deductible insurance plans for employees. The employers, however, require employees to pay only a small amount of the deductible. To fund the difference, employers establish personal accounts in each employee's name. This not only limits the employer's financial exposure but also provides a stop-loss mechanism for employees.

Amit Gupta, president and COO of CareGain, says that 75 to 80 percent of employees don't use health-care services worth more than $1,000 a year. At the end of the year, whatever is left in each employee's personal account is split between the employer and the employee. Unlike the Definity model, this allows employees to take their excess funds with them when they leave the company.

How much does the CareGain model save companies? "About 25 percent on average," Gupta says. He cites the example of one of their clients, a 100-person company that had a very generous health plan with premiums costing $800,000 per year. Going to a $2,500 deductible slashed premium costs to $490,000, a savings of $310,000. The company used $250,000 of that savings to fund the employee accounts so that each employee could have access to $2,500 for health expenses leading up to the deductible.

This represented a $60,000 savings right up front. If, over the course of the year, every employee used the $2,500 in his or her account, the net savings would still be $60,000. But chances are that the majority of employees will not even come close to that amount, creating a greater savings for the company by the end of the year. If only 30 percent of funds in the accounts is used, for example, the company would take the remaining 70 percent

and split it with employees. This equals an additional savings of $87,500.

Besides saving money, what CareGain, Definity, and the other new consumer-centric health plans have in common is that they encourage employees to think harder about what they are spending their money on and, in the process, to become more educated about the health-care delivery system. Both of these elements are necessary if employers are to have any hope of reducing the amount of health cost increases.

People have always looked at health-care purchases differently than other purchases because they've had no skin in the game. But by increasing payroll contributions and co-pays, and by giving employees accounts with which they can manage their own medical expenses, employers are hoping to change this model. Company provided health-care coverage may be an expectation in this country, but today's employers do have rights to a few expectations of their own.

---

workforce.com

For more info on: **Health Care**

Do you have questions about consumer-driven health care? Post them for an expert: workforce.com/community

---

Shari Caudron is a Workforce *contributing editor based in Denver. To comment, e-mail editors@workforce.com.*

A New Model for
Controlling
Health-Care Costs

Employers should consider bringing back some level of cost sharing.
When employees shop for some health services with their own money, they have reason to ask
"What will this cost?" and "Is this really necessary?"

By Mary S. Case

Consumer in the same phrase as *health care*? Right up there with jumbo shrimp on your list of favorite oxymorons? Perhaps it shouldn't be. Perhaps putting the consumer in the driver's seat is exactly what our health-care system needs.

Look at where we are today. Health plan purchasers—employers and others—are confronted with a significant resurgence of health-care inflation, with increases coming into 2001 nearing if not exceeding the double-digit barrier. HMO rates are far from immune to these cost increases, as they and other managed-care programs have been hit by soaring prescription drug costs and increasing provider fee pressures. A managed-care program is only as good as its provider network, and providers have strengthened both their resolve and negotiating power in their financial dealings with network managers.

Increases in the cost of care are compounded by growth in utilization and all of the other usual "trend" factors—expensive new technology, heightened demand from an aging population, and so on. Many of the much-ballyhooed care- and cost-management techniques have proven powerless against these trends, and have been abandoned by employers and some managed-care companies alike, because of a combination of questionable results and poor PR in the provider and patient communities.

Adding to cost pressures stemming from the health plans themselves, employers spend millions administering their complex structures of offerings, negotiating multiple sets of rates and benefits, and managing a myriad of network and plan rule variations. As for employees, well, they generally find more to hate than like about their health-care programs. And all of this comes at a time when a) the labor market is still tight, and b) corporate financial results are not what they once were.

How did we get here? It's the result of a series of efforts to "fix" what was perceived as "broken" in the health-care system (see chart below). In the 1970s, we began to move away from health "insurance" to health-care "management," abandoning most cost-sharing in favor of managed-care techniques. As each solution has generated its own set of issues, we have applied new fixes, ending up with the current array of plans, rules, and benefit expectations.

The Job of Managing Care

Employees today actually exercise choice and control one time each year—at open enrollment. By enrolling in a given managed-care plan, employees agree to submit to that plan's rules, with a trade-off of extremely high benefits (e.g., $10 co-payments for office visits and drugs, modest or no cost-sharing on other in-network care) that help make the rules palatable. Unfortunately, it has only recently dawned on us that much of managed care is not up to the job of managing care, particularly

Health Care Breaks and Fixes

Era	Prevalent Design(s)	Issues	"Fixes"
1970's	Base + major medical • "insurance" on high cost items • cost-sharing on routine	Excess inpatient use	Utilization review Comprehensive design
Early 1980's	Comprehensive • coinsurance on all • inpatient utilization review	Price inflation	HMOs Provider networks
Late 1980's/ Early 1990's	"Managed" indemnity/ PPO Co-pay based HMOs	Cost shift to outpatient HMO selection Push for provider choice	Point of service (POS) Capitation
Late 1990's	Co-pay based HMO and POS	Renewed inflation Plan proliferation Employee dissatisfaction Provider "pushback" Questionable results	Managed RX, formularies Some shift to PPO Vendor consolidation
Early 2000's	Co-pay based HMO, POS and PPO	Same old, same old • managed care benefits without managed care results • high administrative costs • legislative pressure for patients' rights • demand increases (technology, genomics, demographics)	Our current challenge

when the user is completely divorced from the financial consequences of use.

Our Current Challenge

Where do we go from here? Our current challenge is to change the demand curve for health care. It is generally accepted that about 65 cents of each health-care dollar is spent on "non-discretionary" care—treatment of heart disease, cancer, broken limbs, chronic disease. In these situations, most patients can exercise, and should generally be asked to exercise, very little control. The remaining 35 cents can be fairly considered "discretionary." This does not mean unnecessary; rather, it means that it is care over which the patient can and should exercise control. For this to begin to happen, we have to create a health-care consumer, at least partly by reinstating cost-sharing into the equation of health-care consumption, For a consumer model to work, the consumer must have some skin in the game,

to have a reason to ask, "What will this cost?" "Is this really necessary?" and "What alternatives are there that might cost less and be equally effective?"

As we move forward, we need to retain that which is good about managed care, and discard that which has not worked. Among its many successes, managed care has been effective at removing a great deal of inefficiency from the system, including excess hospital use and unchecked pricing. At its best, it has also been good at promoting preventive care and identifying high-quality providers. We all know that employees love not having to stockpile receipts and submit claims.

No new "fix" should abandon these gains, or create financial obstacles that hinder access to childhood immunizations, regular Pap smears, mammograms, and other desirable preventive measures. Any new fix should build on these gains. And any new fix should tap fully the power of the Internet to create the level of awareness—a mind-set of questioning rather than of passive acceptance—that is needed to turn patients into consumers.

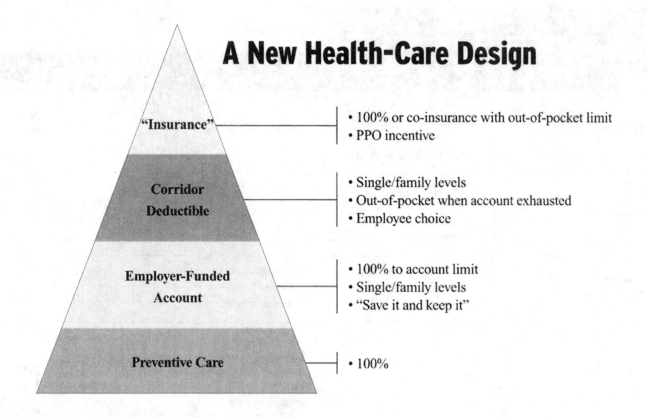

A New Health-Care Design

"Insurance"
- 100% or co-insurance with out-of-pocket limit
- PPO incentive

Corridor Deductible
- Single/family levels
- Out-of-pocket when account exhausted
- Employee choice

Employer-Funded Account
- 100% to account limit
- Single/family levels
- "Save it and keep it"

Preventive Care
- 100%

The New Design's Challenges

Design Issues	Defining covered preventive services
	Establishing cost-sharing parameters. • Out-of-pocket exposure (deductible/account level/corridor/coinsurance limits). • Demographic variations in cost-sharing (family status, pay, employee group).
	Determining eligible expenses (account, plan).
	Establishing extent/nature of employee choice in deductible levels/gap between deductible and account. • Pricing of choices (deductible variations, more "traditional" choices).
	Determining account accumulation rules (handling of unused amounts at termination, retirement).
Implementation challenges	Creating administrative (account/plan access and monitoring) and care management architecture.
	Ensuring network coverage for continued provider discounts and credentialing.
	Leveraging technology for ongoing employee education and self-service.
	Preparing for paradigm and culture shift and conducting employee education.

Rethinking Health Care

We have been working with some of our clients—and proselytizing others—to rethink today's health-care model. The basic design concept we are exploring involves four pieces (see "A New Health-Care Design").

• Forming the foundation of the pyramid, necessary *preventive care* is covered at a very high level (perhaps 100 percent) to ensure continued access to and use of these services.

• At the top of the pyramid, "insurance" (from the patient's perspective, irrespective of the actual funding mechanism) takes over, providing full reimbursement of necessary health care when a targeted cost-sharing level (an out-of-pocket limit) has been reached.

• The core of the pyramid is the core of the design concept: a high deductible combined with an employer-funded account that can be used toward satisfaction of that deductible. The high deductible creates the desired financial involvement on the part of the user; the account makes the high deductible acceptable in today's environment and budgetable for the user.

Key to the financial viability of the model is that there be a significant gap between deductible and account, a point at which employees will be out-of-pocket for their use of care. Also key to the financial and theoretical viability of the model is that the account belong to the employee, and that any unused funds from a given year's account allocation may be carried forward into the next year. Thus, although the employer provides funding toward satisfaction of the deductible, the employee is spending his or her own money, whether the money is from the account or out-of-pocket. Unused funds in the account can be accumulated and applied toward a following year's deductible or perhaps toward expenses in the longer-term future (e.g., retiree medical costs).

The design concept is analogous to the medical savings accounts that are currently available only to small employers and the self-employed. Here, the accounts are employer-funded and are earmarked specifically for health-care expenses. The "save it and keep it" idea behind the account is diametrically opposed to the "use it or lose it" idea behind today's flexible spending accounts. (The accounts in this model involve no employee pre-tax money and—we and others believe—are therefore exempt from cafeteria-plan rules that would require year-end forfeiture of unused amounts under current tax law.) And the design, which involves employee use of an accumulating account or out-of-pocket funds for significant up-front expenses, is diametrically opposed to today's co-payment design. As employees use their accounts, they will see what care costs, and they will begin to ask questions and change their utilization patterns.

Changes in design must be supported with technology that enables health-care consumers to tap into information about recommended care, possible providers of that care, and options. Consumers should also be able to monitor in "real-time" the status of their accounts, and see how their own management efforts yield results. To retain the convenience of (from the employee's perspective) paperless reimbursement from accounts or insurance, card-swipe (effectively debit card) technology should be in place at offices of physicians and other providers.

Building a New Paradigm

The design issues involved in a shift to this model are manifold, as are the implementation challenges (see chart, "The New Design's Challenges").

Perhaps the ultimate in consumer-based health care would be a shift to a "defined contribution" model, in which employees would use fixed allowances from their employers to shop for health-care insurance products from outside vendors. For a true DC model along these lines to become a reality, a great deal of change (in health-care markets, in employer and employee attitudes, in tax law) must take place. The model we describe here is a reality today, and we believe it can be a significant positive force in transforming today's health-care picture.

---

workforce.com
For more info on:
Health-Care Issues
Get ideas from your peers at the Benefits Forum workforce.com/community/benefits

---

Mary Case, a principal with Unifi Network, a subsidiary of PricewaterhouseCoopers, is a consultant in the firm's Flex/Health and Welfare practice. She works with employers on managing the full complement of health and welfare benefit plans, and her expertise lies primarily in strategy development for health care, total rewards/benefits design, and flex design and pricing.

From *Workforce*, July 2001, pp. 44-48. © 2001 by Crain Communications.

UNIT 6
Fostering Employee/ Management Relationships

Unit Selections

Key Points to Consider

- Unions have a special exemption under the antitrust laws. Do you think this is fair? Why or why not?

- Taking disciplinary action is often one of the most difficult and unpleasant activities that a manager must do. If you were a manager, how would you take disciplinary action? If you were the employee being disciplined, what would you do? What would you do about executives who have committed fraud? What do you think about the Enron scandal? What about the role Arthur Andersen played in the scandal?

- What are some of the advantages of hiring temporary employees? How would you feel about being one? For over a year?

- Should managers be concerned about ethics? Why or why not?

 **Links: www.dushkin.com/online/**
These sites are annotated in the World Wide Web pages.

Fair Measures: Legal Training for Managers
http://www.fairmeasures.com/asklawyer/archive/
Working Stiff Action Guide
http://www.pbs.org/weblab/workingstiff/action/

The American labor movement has a long history dating back to the start of the Industrial Revolution. That history has been marked by turmoil and violence as workers sought to press their demands on business owners, whether represented by managers or entrepreneurs. The American labor movement exists because working conditions, pay, and benefits were very poor during the early years of the Industrial Revolution in both the United States and the rest of the world. It should be remembered that the American labor movement is only a small part of a broader, worldwide labor movement that includes most Western European societies. The working conditions under which the first American industrial workers labored would be unacceptable today. Child labor was common. There are documented instances of 6- and 7-year-old children, chained to machines for 12 hours a day, 6 days a week, who threw themselves into the machines—choosing death over life in the dehumanized and mechanized existence of the early factory. Conditions in some factories in the North prior to the Civil War were so infamous that Southern congressmen used them as a justification for the institution of slavery. Slaves sometimes lived in better conditions than the factory workers of New England and many other Northern states.

Unions exist because workers sought a better working environment and a better standard of living. Companies often took advantage of employees, and the government sided with management and the owners, frequently quelling strikes and other forms of labor protest initiated by the workers. Such incidents as the Pullman Strike, the Hay-market Square Riot, and the Homestead Strike exemplify the struggle of the American labor movement to achieve recognition and success in the attempt to improve the lives of all workers, whether unionized or not. The victories of labor have been hard fought and hard won. During the past hundred years, the fortunes of the American labor movement have varied, and now their fortunes may be taking an even deeper downward turn with the revelations outlined in "A Black Eye for Labor."

Unions have been able to achieve their gains through the mechanism of collective bargaining. The individual has very little bargaining power when compared to a company, especially huge companies such as General Motors or AT&T. Collective bargaining allows workers to pool their collective resources and power to bargain with the corporation on a more equal footing. Unfortunately for the unions, many of the industries in which they are strongest are in decline. New leadership is necessary if the American labor movement is to survive and rebound in the next century and if it is to serve as a useful organ of society.

A union's ultimate weapon in contract negotiations, the strike, represents a complete breakdown of discipline from management's perspective. Disciplinary situations are almost always un-

pleasant, and today they can often lead to court cases, with all of the attendant legal questions and problems. A key to effective disciplinary action is documentation of employees' actions and the steps that were taken to correct them. Management needs to trust its employees, and if it does not, the work environment becomes untenable for both labor and management. Sometimes, however, it is the executive suite where the crimes take place and discipline needs to be administered, as seen in "Enough Is Enough."

The American labor movement has come a long way since the first strike by printers in Philadelphia in 1786. The journey, while difficult, has led to greater justice in the workplace and an increased standard of living for the nation as a whole. Unions have experienced both declines and increases in membership, but they have endured as a powerful social, political, and economic force. Whether or not they will again successfully "reinvent" themselves and adapt to a changing environment is a major question.

During the past 15 years, primarily as a result of the dislocations in the job market, temporary workers have become available to organizations. There are certain advantages to this situation for the employer as well as the employee, as discussed in "Temporary Solution."

There is also the issue of ethics. How companies treat their employees and their customers is going to be of increasing concern in the future. Ethical behavior will be at a premium, and managers know that it will be part of the job to be concerned with "Shades of Gray." New areas of concern are also arising with the recent revelations at Enron that has caused a "Crisis of Confidence" because of the "Dirty Rotten Numbers" Enron executives used, with the help of their auditors from Arthur Andersen, to defraud the public and the Enron employees.

The Workplace

COMMENTARY

A Black Eye for Labor

By Aaron Bernstein

The labor movement is being roiled by what could be one of its worst scandals in years. The controversy involves millions of dollars of profit taken by a dozen union leaders from selling stock of a labor-owned insurance company called ULLICO Inc. The gains came from a windfall the insurer earned from early investments in Global Crossing Holdings Ltd. The union officials got a disproportionate share of the profits, allegedly shortchanging their own unions, which own the bulk of ULLICO.

The profit-taking has attracted the interest of a Washington grand jury, which has subpoenaed ULLICO officials and others. It's not clear if there were illegal acts by the 30-plus union officials on ULLICO's board, including AFL-CIO President John J. Sweeney and the heads of about 12 unions—among them the carpenters' Douglas J. McCarron, the football players' Eugene Upshaw, and the hotel workers' John W. Wilhelm. While some, including Sweeney and Wilhelm, took no profits, most voted for the scheme, ULLICO documents show.

If labor's leaders don't try to clean up the mess, the entire labor movement could be tarnished. Already, critics inside labor are pushing Sweeney and the other union presidents to kick out those responsible for setting up the complex stock

plan. Their prime target: ULLICO CEO Robert A. Georgine, a former top AFL-CIO official for 26 years, who stood to make by far the most out of the transactions. Some are also insisting that the union leaders return much of their profit to the company. "Let's see them repay the money they ripped off," snaps one labor official who wasn't involved. "Unions shouldn't be doing this stuff, even if it was legal." ULLICO declined to comment, while Upshaw and Wilhelm didn't return phone calls.

To his credit, Sweeney knows labor's credibility as a critic of corporate greed is on the line. He has demanded a probe by an outsider, citing as a model the one William C. Powers, dean of the University of Texas law school, undertook at Enron Corp. On Mar. 21, Sweeney wrote to Georgine insisting on this after Georgine balked. One name floated: former Labor Secretary John T. Dunlop.

Labor must move fast to avoid big damage. If it doesn't, conservative groups could point fingers at unions as labor mounts campaigns in the fall congressional elections. Employers, too, could use the charges to campaign against unions in organizing drives at companies such as Honda Motor and Wal-Mart Stores Inc. Already, the mess has undercut the AFL-CIO's clout. It was gearing up to push for corporate-governance reforms

and had launched a campaign with the machinists' union to pressure Lockheed Martin Corp. not to renominate Enron director Frank Savage to its own board. The day the federation started getting media calls on ULLICO, though, AFL-CIO Secretary-Treasurer Richard L. Trumka pulled the plug, leaving machinists to lead the battle on their own. "He didn't want us to look like hypocrites," says one union official involved.

The chance for Georgine and others to profit arose because of the peculiar nature of ULLICO, the parent of Union Labor Life Insurance Co. The company, which sells insurance to union members, invested $7.6 million in seed money in Global Crossing in 1997. ULLICO sold about half its Global shares for a $335 million aftertax profit. But ULLICO is private, so its shares don't trade publicly. Instead, the company sets the price for the upcoming year every Dec. 31, based on its prior year's book value.

ULLICO directors gained handsomely from this procedure. On Dec. 17, 1999, Georgine offered to sell 4,000 shares to each of them at $54 apiece, the 1998 book value—even though ULLICO already knew its Global Crossing profits had lifted its stock value to $146. The union pension and general funds that own most of ULLICO's shares weren't given the same offer, or even told

about it, officials say. Georgine himself went from holding 8,868 shares in 1998 to 52,868 in 1999, according to ULLICO's proxies.

In 2000, ULLICO directors again took advantage of the lagging stock-valuation system to cash out. Before the Dec. 31 price adjustment that year, ULLICO offered to repurchase shares, as it had done annually since 1997. The tender, at $146, was limited to 205,000 shares out of 7.9 million outstanding. All shareholders could sell a prorated amount based on their total holding. Yet those with fewer than 10,000 shares—mostly the directors—could sell all their stock.

The result: Georgine and other directors, knowing the price would be cut to $75, were able to sell at $146, while the pension funds with much larger stakes were restricted in how much they could sell. Overall, ULLICO's directors sold 73,000 of their 120,000 shares, AFL-CIO officials say, giving them combined profits of at least $6.7 million.

It's not clear if the grand jury will find anything illegal about all this.

Damage Ahead

Several dozen union leaders who sit on the board of ULLICO Inc, a labor-owned insurer, are under fire for taking millions of dollars in stock gains from the company. Here's how the controversy could affect labor:

ELECTIONS
Conservative groups may use it against unions in the fall congressional races. Labor leaders also could be distracted trying to deal with the fallout.

POLITICS
Already, the AFL-CIO has pulled back from a reform campaign directed against Enron directors for fear of being attacked for similar behavior.

RECRUITMENT
Employers will be able to cite labor leaders' actions in organizing drives, when management frequently accuses unions of self-interest.

Data: *BusinessWeek*

One question is whether ULLICO's union directors breached fiduciary responsibilities to their union's pension and general funds. Even those who took little or nothing could have a problem if they merely approved the moves, insiders say. Still, unions hire Wall Street firms to manage their ULLICO holdings, which may insulate labor leaders from liability, legal experts say.

In scoring fat gains, union officials may have shortchanged the rank and file

---

Liable or not, ULLICO directors have damaged their credibility as union leaders. Nearly all of the insurer's capital comes from union members, which means these labor leaders have shortchanged the very people who voted them into office—at least politically.

Bernstein covers labor from Washington.

Labor law for supervisors: recent developments in employment testing

Mary-Kathryn Zachary

… employers have understandable concerns about employees performing their assigned work and about keeping company costs down and productivity up. Consequently, it is not surprising companies are increasingly taking advantage of developments in testing to screen applicants and employees interested in particular jobs. However, such testing may embroil companies in legal controversies, as recent cases involving nerve conduction tests and intelligence tests demonstrate.

Among the relatively recent developments in employee testing is the increasing use of evaluation tools such as nerve conduction tests, which can determine whether an individual is likely to suffer an injury related to carpal tunnel syndrome or cumulative trauma disorder. These injuries are of major concern to employers and to government agencies, such as OSHA. In fact, OSHA has been engaged for several years in developing guidelines for employers with respect to ergonomic issues. Because numerous employees today suffer from carpal tunnel syndrome or cumulative trauma disorder, companies are eager to avoid exacerbating existing medical conditions. Therefore, they may decide to use nerve conduction tests to determine which employees might be at risk of suffering such injuries if assigned to certain jobs. However, the EEOC has argued making employment decisions based on the use of such tests may violate the Americans with Disabilities Act.

As discussed last month, the Americans with Disabilities Act prohibits discrimination against qualified individuals with a disability, those with a record of a disability and those perceived as having a disability. To be successful in cases involving perceived disabilities, the aggrieved employees must demonstrate the employer believed the disabilities in question substantially limited the employees in the major life activity of working. In this context, substantially limited means significantly restricted in the ability to perform a class of jobs or a broad range of jobs in various classes as compared to the average person having comparable training, skills and abilities. Thus it refers to working in a general sense, not just the particular job in question. The EEOC has maintained applicants denied employment or current employees denied positions based on the results of nerve conduction or neurometry tests may be unlawful. In its view, these individuals are perceived as having a disability and thus fall within a protected class. In determining whether or not an individual is substantially limited in the major life activity of working, EEOC regulations call upon courts to consider the number and type of jobs using similar training, knowledge, skills or activities within the geographic area reasonably available to the individual from which the individual would also be excluded. The following recent cases provide examples of court handling of nerve conduction or neurometry testing.

In a pair of cases, the EEOC brought suit against an auto parts manufacturer in Northern Illinois and its successor employer over nerve conduction testing of job applicants. The tests were given to applicants who would be working in positions requiring repetitive or continuing motion or vibratory power tools. Individuals whom the test revealed to be susceptible to carpal tunnel syndrome or cumulative trauma disorder were rejected for employment in certain positions. The first case involved 72 rejected applicants; the second involved 16. The EEOC maintained these applicants fell under the provisions of the ADA because they were perceived as having impairments that substantially limited them in the major life activity of working. Ultimately, the cases failed because the EEOC did not successfully show that plaintiffs were substantially limited in employment generally, as opposed to those specific jobs. Inadequate information was made available to the court about the existence of

similar jobs in the region. Without such evidence, the plaintiffs could not establish they were disabled within the meaning of the statute. In one of the opinions written in these cases, the court noted it reached its decision "reluctantly" because it was possible such evidence could have been presented. On the other hand, it was also possible that such evidence was not presented because it did not exist. Mere speculation was not sufficient to warrant a ruling for the plaintiffs. EEOC v. Rockwell, 9 AD Cases 1092, 10 AD Cases 128 (N.D. 111. 1999). EEOC v. Cambridge Indus., Inc., 10 AD Cases 1747 (N.D. Ill. 2000).

In another case brought by the EEOC, a factory in Missouri producing foam pads for automobile seat covers conducted neurometry tests of job applicants for assembly line positions to ascertain whether or not they suffered from carpal tunnel syndrome or would have a high likelihood of developing it. Job offers to 19 applicants were revoked because of the test results. As in the previously discussed cases, the EEOC contended the applicants were discriminated against under the ADA because of perceived disabilities. However, the court concluded that whether or not the company's perception of the applicants as unqualified for the positions in question was justified, the perception did not apply to the employees' working in a broad range of other positions. The EEOC did not show the employer regarded the applicants as unable to work in any job requiring repetitive motions. Further, the court stated carpal tunnel syndrome was not usually regarded as a disability. Therefore, the applicants were not proven to be substantially limited in working, as required to invoke the protection of the ADA. EEOC v. Woodbridge Corp., No. 99-0370-CV-W-4 (W.D. Mo. 2000).

In addition to such evaluative tools as nerve conduction or neurometry tests, companies may employ psychological or intelligence tests to determine whether or not an individual should be placed in a particular position. Normally, high intelligence is considered an asset in a job search, not a liability. In fact, plaintiffs in age discrimination suits occasionally use as part of their cases they were informed they were "too qualified" for the job in terms of education, experience and/or intelligence. However, sometimes an employer can lawfully determine an employee is too intelligent for the job in question, as the following case reveals.

The 46-year old plaintiff in the case, as well as 500 other job applicants for police officer positions, went through a written screening process administered by a coalition of 14 cities and towns. The screening process included a test for cognitive ability. A manual accompanying the test warned test givers about the danger of making job decisions solely on the basis of top scores. Because employees who were overqualified for their positions could become bored and quit, the manual recommended scores for various occupations. The median score recommended for a police patrol officer

was 21. The plaintiff scored a 33 which was not only over the recommendation for a police patrol officer, but was over the median for any of the listed jobs.

When the plaintiff learned one of the cities in the coalition was hiring, he applied. However, he was informed he would not be interviewed because he did not fit the profile for the position. Because he suspected age discrimination, he filed an administrative complaint. The city responded he had been rejected because of his high score on the screening test. In order to prevent turnover,

---

IN A NUTSHELL

1. Although companies have available a variety of methods to evaluate the ability of an applicant or employee to perform a particular job, some types may raise legal issues.
2. The EEOC contends the use of nerve conduction tests to deny applicants certain jobs may constitute unlawful discrimination under the Americans with Disabilities Act.
3. For an applicant in a perceived disability case to be successful in challenging an employment decision based on a nerve conduction test, the applicant must show the employer believed the applicant was substantially limited in working generally, not just unable to perform the particular work in question.
4. Intelligence testing may sometimes be used to match employees to particular jobs. A public employer may overcome constitutional equal protection clause challenges and lawfully exclude an applicant from a position.
5. In testing, managers and other supervisory employees should be cautious in using testing to evaluate applicants for positions. Testing methods should be carefully studied to determine their applicability to particular types of positions.

---

the city stated, it had decided to only interview candidates who had scored between 20 and 27. The plaintiff then brought a civil rights action based on the equal protection clause of the Fourteenth Amendment of the U. S. Constitution and based on portions of the state constitution.

The Fourteenth Amendment prohibits governmental employers from denying the equal protection of the laws to a given classification of people. However, the district court found the plaintiff did not fall into a "suspect" category, such as race, that would require strict scrutiny of the city's decision. In cases involving suspect classes or fundamental rights, the courts apply a very high standard, with the government required to show a

compelling reason for treating an individual differently. Because the court held the city had demonstrated a rational basis for its decision, it granted summary judgment in favor of the defendants.

On appeal, the Second Circuit, in an unpublished decision, agreed the city's "upper cut" did not violate the equal protection clause. The appellate court noted there is no fundamental right to employment as a police officer. Because the city's policy did not involve "suspect" classifications, nor did it impinge upon a fundamental constitutional right, it had to be upheld if there was any reasonably conceivable state of facts that could provide a rational basis for the classification. Citing other cases, the Second Circuit stated governmental classifications need not be perfect, because the problems of government are practical ones. Therefore, the courts should not substitute their ideas of good economic or social policy for the government's approach, even if the latter's might seem illogical or unscientific in some instances.

The plaintiff had produced some evidence individuals who scored high on such tests do not actually experience more job dissatisfaction. However, the court downplayed the significance of that evidence by stating it did not matter whether or not the city was actually correct in its reasoning—what mattered was it was rational. Because the city could reasonably have relied on the manual accompanying the test, it was justified in using a high, as well as a low, score cutoff. Even if the policy was "unwise," in the words of the court, it was a rational decision intended to reduce job turnover, thereby lowering expenses associated with hiring and training police officers who did not stay long enough to warrant the costs, and, therefore, it was motivated by a legitimate government purpose. Jordan v. New London, 2000 U.S. LEXIS 22195 (2d Cir., unpublished opinion Aug. 23, 2000).

Workplace Disaster Proves Costly to Company in Many Ways

Workplace disasters can result in a variety of financial costs to companies. In addition to serious property loss, a company may face governmental fines and civil suits arising from major accidents that involve loss of life. The following case reveals the extent of this liability.

In 1999, an explosion and fire at a California refinery killed four contract workers. The accident occurred when workers cut through a line containing explosive liquid while performing maintenance work. A company involved has suffered substantial expenses arising out of the incident. It has provided 53,000 hours of training, spent more than $50 million on equipment inspections, repairs and replacements, paid out $1.75 million in fines and given $21 million to the families of three of the contract workers.

The above costs are not unusual in such cases. However, an additional cost was not as customary. In a separate lawsuit, a former ironworker foreman who sustained minor injuries during the explosion received $4 million in a settlement because witnessing the accident left him unable to work as an ironworker. The worker, who suffered from post traumatic stress disorder, tried for six months to return to work as an ironworker before his doctors advised him to quit trying. He is currently a maintenance worker at a university. Simoni v. Tosco Corp., No. C9900666 (Cal. Super. Ct., settled Aug. 10, 2000).

Union Rules in Nonunion Settings: The NLRB and Workplace Investigations

James F. Morgan, James M. Owens, and Glenn M. Gomes

Introduction

Employers increasingly have come to understand the importance of promptly investigating claims of wrongdoing by employees, especially in the area of sexual harassment. Recent developments in employment law, however, have created numerous new obstacles around which management must navigate when conducting workplace investigations. For example, firms using outside investigators must now comply with the disclosure provisions of the Fair Credit Reporting Act (Morgan, Owens & Gomes, 2000).

Even more surprising, the National Labor Relations Board (NLRB) ruled in July 2000 that nonunion workers are now entitled to have a coworker present at an investigatory interview that the employee reasonably believes might result in disciplinary action, a right heretofore reserved exclusively for unionized employees (*Epilepsy Foundation*, 2000). For employers contemplating (or actually conducting) workplace investigations, compliance with these new rulings will require an intimate understanding of the changes in the law and their implications for managing the investigatory process. Of course, noncompliance unnecessarily exposes employees to substantial risks and penalties.

This article first briefly reviews the heightened importance of conducting workplace investigations. We then focus on the latest development in the investigatory process, the reach of the NLRB into the nonunion workforce, and present suggestions to employers for dealing with the extension of certain rights heretofore reserved for union workers. In the final section, we discuss the need for changes in public policy in this area of employer-employee relations.

The Growing Importance of Workplace Investigations

Investigations of allegations of sexual harassment and other forms of workplace discrimination have received considerable attention recently (see, e.g., Morgan, Gomes & Owens, 2001; Gardner & Lewis, 2000). Moreover, in addition to reaffirming the principle that employers may be held liable for not establishing, disseminating, and consistently enforcing a policy that prohibits sexual harassment, recent U.S. Supreme Court decisions confirmed the need for employers to conduct a "reasonable" investigation if a complaint arises (*Burlington Industries*, 1998; *Faragher*, 1998). The Equal Employment Opportunity Commission subsequently issued revised enforcement guidelines emphasizing the importance of prompt, thorough, and impartial investigations conducted by well-trained investigators (EEOC, 1999). Given the Supreme Court's recent rulings and the EEOC's revised guidelines, there is a greater need now then ever before for an employer to conduct a vigorous and effective investigation when allegations of impropriety first arise. Indeed, the failure to investigate may very well be regarded as strong evidence that the employer approves, albeit implicitly, of the offending behavior.

Unfortunately, over-zealous employers may sanction an accused employee with termination before any type of "procedural due process" is provided. As a result, those accused of inappropriate behavior are also suing their employers for emotional distress, defamation, and wrongful discharge. To minimize the risk of such litigation, investigations conducted by employers should be perceived as fair and impartial, and merely adhering to the letter of the law may not guarantee such a perception (Dorfman, Cobb & Cox, 2000).

THE NLRB and Co-Employee Representation in Nonunion Settings

Consider, for a moment, the managerial and legal implications of the following not-so-far-fetched scenario:

> Gorby Gourmet, Inc. employs a sizable non-unionized workforce. Upon receiving a complaint of potential wrongdoing, management decides to investigate one of its employees, James Elgin, for an alleged violation of company policy. Management has requested that Mr. Elgin participate in an interview with appropriate company executives as part of the investigation. Suspecting that there may be disciplinary consequences arising from such an interview, Mr. Elgin demands to be accompanied by a fellow employee during the interview. How should Gorby Gourmet's management respond?

In an attempt to eliminate the "inequality of bargaining power between employees... and employers," Congress passed the National Labor Relations Act (the Act) in 1935. Most nonunion employers probably believe that if no union is attempting to organize the workplace, the Act does not apply to them. Because Section 1 of the Act encourages collective, not individual, bargaining as a means to reduce industrial strife, it would seem these employers would be correct. However, that is not the case. Section 7 of the Act provides that:

> [employees] shall have the right to self-organization, to form, join, or assist labor organizations... and to engage in *other concerted activities* for the purpose of collective bargaining or *other mutual aid or protection* (29 U.S.C. § 157, emphasis added).

The NLRB and the courts have found that "all" employees, both union and nonunion, have the right to engage in concerted activities for mutual aid or protection. Does this mean that James Elgin is entitled to protection when he made his request for a co-employee to witness the interview?

• The *Weingarten* Ruling and Its Confusing Legacy

In the early 1970s, the NLRB expanded Section 7 rights to include unionized employee requests to have a coworker present during meetings with their employers if disciplinary action might take place. While the courts did not enforce the initial Board decisions, in 1975 the U.S. Supreme Court decided in *NLRB v. J. Weingarten, Inc.* that Section 7 gives workers the right to have a union representative at the investigatory interview if disciplinary action is expected. This is now known as the "*Weingarten* right." The Court, however, did not address directly whether this right applied equally to nonunion workplaces.

In 1982, over the stern dissents of Chairman Van de Water and Member Hunter, a three-member Democratic majority of the NLRB extended the *Weingarten* right to nonunionized employees in the *Materials Research Corp.* decision. The majority believed "the rational enunciated in *Weingarten* compels the conclusion that unrepresented employees are entitled to the presence of a coworker at an investigatory interview." In its reasoning, the majority found that an employee's request to have a witness or representative at a meeting where disciplinary action is anticipated flows from the rights granted under Section 7 of the Act.

In 1985, the new Republican majority on the NLRB overruled *Material Research* in the decision of *Sears, Roebuck and Co.* By reversing itself, the majority essentially found that, in unionized settings, the *Weingarten* rule was entirely consistent with established principles of labor-management relations (see, e.g., Flack, 1986). The NLRB reasoned, however, that extending the Weingarten right to nonunion workers wreaked havoc with the fundamental provisions of the Act.

The NLRB revisited the issue no less than three more times in a series of decisions involving Dupont (see, e.g., Morris, 1989). Initially, in 1982, the NLRB followed the *Materials Research* decision (*DuPont,* 1982, commonly known as *DuPont I*). On appeal to the federal courts, the NLRB's decision was upheld (*DuPont,* 1984). By this time, the Reagan appointees had altered the composition of the NLRB, and they asked the court to vacate its opinion and remand the case for reconsideration. The NLRB subsequently followed the *Sears* rationale and held that *Weingarten* rights were not appropriate in a nonunion setting (*DuPont,* 1985, known as "*DuPont II*"). On appeal for the second time, the courts disagreed with the new NLRB majority that the Act "compels the conclusion" that nonunion employees are not entitled to *Weingarten* rights (*Slaughter,* 1986). Ultimately, in 1988, the NLRB once again ruled that *Weingarten* rights do not belong in a nonunion setting (*DuPont,* 1988, known as *DuPont III*).

• The *Epilepsy Foundation of Northeast Ohio* Decision

The decision in *Epilepsy Foundation of Northeast Ohio* (2000) involved a nonunion organization that provides services to persons affected by epilepsy. Two of Epilepsy's employees, Arnis Borgs and Ashraful Hasan, were involved in a research project concerning school-to-work transition for affected teenagers. In an attempt to remove their supervisor (Rick Berger) from the project, Borgs and Hasan wrote two memos to the executive director of Epilepsy Foundation, Christine Loehrke, stating that Berger was no longer needed on the project. After receiving the second memo, Loehrke directed Borgs to meet with her and the supervisor, but Borgs indicated he felt intimidated by the prospect of meeting with them be-

Table 1 Key Decisions and Principal Rulings

Decision	Year	Principal Ruling
NLRB v. Weingarten, Inc. 420 U.S. 251	1975	Section 7 of the National Labor Relations Act, which addresses "concerted activities" protects the right to be accompanied by a coworker at an investigatory meeting, but the right applies only to unionized workers.
Materials Research Corp. 262 NLRB 1010	1982	The right to be accompanied by a coworker at an investigatory meeting applies to both unionized and nonunionized workers.
Sears, Roebuck & Co. 274 NLRB 230	1985	Overrules *Materials Research*. The *Weingarten* decision is reinstated. Section 7 applies only when there is an exclusive bargaining representative.
E.I. DuPont de Nemours & Co. 289 NLRB 627	1988	Weingarten rights not applicable in nonunion settings.
Epilepsy Foundation of Northeast Ohio 331NLRB No. 92	2000	The principles of *Weingarten* should be extended to employees in nonunion workplaces, and such employees should be afforded the right to have a coworker present at an investigatory interview that the employee reasonably believes might result in disciplinary action.

cause of a prior reprimand he had received. Borgs asked if he could meet only with Loehrke, and upon being told no, he asked if his coworker, Hasan, could attend the meeting. Loehrke refused this request, and when Borgs refused to meet without Hasan, she sent Borgs home for the day. The next day Borgs met with Loehrke and the Director of Administration. At this meeting, Loehrke informed Borgs that he committed gross insubordination by refusing to meet with her and the supervisor the previous day and, as a result, was being terminated.

In a 3–2 decision, the Democratic majority in *Epilepsy Foundation* found that the employer had violated Section 8(a)(1) of the Act and ordered reinstatement and backpay for Borgs and Hasan. In deciding that *Weingarten* rights apply to the nonunionized sector, the majority decided that *Sears* and *DuPont* misconstrued the language of *Weingarten* and erroneously limited the *Weingarten* right to unionized settings. With this ruling, the NLRB changed 12 years of precedents (for a chronological summary of these decisions, see Table 1).

The Expanded *Weingarten* Right: A Necessarily Incomplete Primer

Any attempt to provide management in a nonunion environment with a definitive set of recommendations regarding compliance with the NLRB decision in *Epilepsy Foundation* will necessarily fall short because of the myriad differences between a union and a nonunion environment. Until greater clarity is achieved through further NLRB decisions, congressional action, or court

review, however, management must comply—as best they can—with the *Epilepsy Foundation's* unclear edict.

The rights and responsibilities which might flow from *Epilepsy Foundation* can be organized into two areas: (1) aspects of the *Weingarten* right that appear to transfer easily and unambiguously to the nonunion setting, and (2) aspects of the *Weingarten* right where the logic that supports their application is less clear in the absence of a union. In the latter case, management is left in significant peril, relying on nothing more than educated guesswork.

• Areas of Reasonable Certainty

Numerous basic aspects of the *Weingarten* doctrine appear applicable to the workplace regardless of whether a union is present. For example, the event that triggers the right of an employee to request a coworker's presence is independent of a union. The *Weingarten* right should attach to an employee when: (1) an employee is requested to meet individually with a member of management, (2) the employee invited to the meeting is being investigated for possible wrongdoing connected with work, and (3) the employee *reasonably believes* that discipline or other formal adverse consequences may result from what the employee says. Therefore, an employee accused of participating in a fraudulent transaction, insider trading, theft, or sexual harassment who is asked an "investigatory interview" may invoke the *Weingarten* right. Note, too, that investigations into absenteeism, poor attitude, or substandard work performance also would initiate this privilege.

Table 2 Commonly Asked Questions and Answers—Areas of Reasonable Certainty	
Does the manager have to notify an employee of the right to have a coworker present during an "investigatory interview?"	**No.** Unlike the *Miranda* warning provided to accused criminals, the employer is not required to notify an employee of the *Weingarten* right prior to or during the investigatory interview. Further, the employer need not post notices advertising the right.
Once the employee raises the *Weingarten* right, must the chosen co-employee receive compensation for the time spent preparing for the interview?	**No.** In a union setting, the accused employee's representative need not be paid for the time spent preparing for the interview. In fact, the pre-interview is not required to be conducted on "company time." It is unlikely the application of *Weingarten* to the nonunion environment would change these established rules.
Does the *Weingarten* right apply to meetings where particular disciplinary measures are announced?	**No.** A witness is allowed only at meetings where an employee is being investigated for wrongdoing. If the gathering is solely to declare discipline, the *Weingarten* right is not applicable.
If an employee demands a co-employee be present, what options are available to management?	**The employer may:** (1) Accede to the request from the employee; (2) Cancel the interview and proceed with the investigation without direct oral comments from the employee under investigation; or (3) Provide the employee with the choice of either not being interviewed or not having the co-employee present during the interview.

The *Weingarten* right is terminated by the completion of the investigation. Therefore, where the purpose of a conference is to mete out discipline, *Weingarten* does *not* require a coworker to be present. Management should understand, though, that if the meeting begins with a purpose of exacting discipline but then is transformed into a discussion regarding whether the employee committed a particular offense, the employee may ask for the presence of a coemployee (*Baton Rouge Water Works*, 1979). Further, once the right is asserted, employees are entitled to continued representation by a co-employee at subsequent meetings without separately reasserting such a request. Even if the employee fails to assert the *Weingarten* right at the first investigatory interview, the employee may invoke the right at any later investigatory meeting. These areas of relative certainty are summarized in Table 2.

Supervisors and employees often confuse the *Weingarten* right with a workplace-type of *Miranda* warning. The differences between these concepts, though, are considerable. The *Miranda* right provides, in part, that criminal suspects be apprised of their right to remain silent and have an attorney present during questioning (*Miranda*, 1966). In stark contrast, regardless of the workplace setting, the employer is under no obligation to inform an employee of the *Weingarten* right. Also, there is no right to an attorney during the questioning of an employee, according to the U.S. Supreme Court (*McLean Hospital*, 1982).

Finally, the options available to an employer when an employee requests the presence of a coworker should not change as *Weingarten* principles are applied in a nonunion setting. One option the employer may elect is simply to grant the request. While criticism has arisen from employer representatives that the presence of a coworker diminishes significantly the effectiveness of the investigatory interview, it is possible that an employer may view an employee representative as beneficial in conducting an effective examination. A second option available to the employer is to decide not to conduct the interview and to conclude the investigation without direct oral contributions from the employee being investigated. Depending on the type of offense and the amount of independent evidence available, there may be no need to ask specific questions of the person under investigation. The final option for an employer is to state to the employee being examined that he or she has a choice; if he or she desires a coworker be present, then no interview will occur or the employee can change his or her mind regarding the presence of a witness and proceed with the interview. This last option forces the employee to weight the strategic advantages associated with agreeing to the interview.

• Areas of Ambiguity and Confusion

While many similarities exist between union and nonunion workplaces, a closer examination of the application of *Weingarten* to the nonunion environment raises a host of unanswered questions, each of which may activate significant legal liability. Several of the more important areas of uncertainty are examined and summarized in Table 3.

Table 3 Commonly Asked Questions and Answers —Areas of Ambiguity and Confusion

Can an employer evade *Weingarten* by being vague regarding the purpose of the meeting?	**Unclear.** The right to a representative attaches once the employee possesses a reasonable belief that discipline might result. If the employer is unclear as to the reason for the meeting, an investigator may be able to make significant progress before the employee thinks about exercising the right.
What does *not* possess the right?	**Unclear.** In a union setting, the distinction between union and management is fairly clear. The *Weingarten* right is only applicable to union members. But in the nonunion environment, not only is the dichotomy far less severe, the rationale of protecting the integrity of a union is inapplicable.
Could an employee who was part of the impropriety being investigated serve as an employee representative?	**Yes, but...** This was, in fact, the request made by an employee in *Epilepsy Foundation*, and the majority of members on the NLRB found no difficulty with such a selection. One wonders, however, if permitting the attendance of an alleged wrongdoer's confederate adequately protects the entire workforce, or whether it merely protects the alleged wrongdoer.
When an employee asks for a co-employee but is then told that no interview will occur as a result of the request, how does an employer factor out of a decision discipline the fact that the individual was exercising the *Weingarten* right?	**Unclear.** While the employer may choose not to conduct an interview after the employee notifies the employer of the employee's desire to have a co-employee present, the employer will be found to have violated the National Labor Relations Act unless the employer can show that the employee's refusal to meet was not a "motivating factor" in the company's decision to discipline.

One area of confusion concerns whether a supervisor is eligible to serve as the co-employee. In the union setting, the bifurcated nature of the workplace into union and management sectors prevents supervisors from serving in this capacity. Functioning within this structure, the authority of the union remains intact because a union representative is presumed to be the appropriate co-employee. But in a nonunion environment, such a severe institutional division does not exist. In fact, it may be wise to allow a supervisor or someone else from management who possesses an understanding of the disciplinary process to serve in the co-employee role. The *Epilepsy Foundation* decision is not instructive on this point.

Myriad additional issues raise greater concerns regarding the application of *Weingarten* principles to the nonunion workplace. For instance, is it possible to select a co-employee who also may be under investigation for the same wrongdoing? Evidently, the answer is a qualified yes. This is the situation that occurred in *Epilepsy Foundation*. Borgs wanted to have Hasan, who sent with Borgs the memoranda regarding Berger to Loehrke, accompany him to the meeting with management. The majority of members on the NLRB in *Epilepsy Foundation* apparently found no fault with such an arrangement.

Similarly, could the employee choose an individual who is not currently available? In a unionized setting, the employer need not postpone the interview just because the chosen co-employee is unavailable. Instead, because another union representative is usually available, no harm to the employee's *Weingarten* right arises. But without a union, can the employee effectively postpone the investigative interview until it is convenient for the selected co-employee to participate? This could be an effective delaying tactic for the accused employee, creating a crisis for an employer where the investigation must concluded within a reasonable time (e.g., in allegations of sexual harassment). On the other hand, might the employer—not the employee—be able to choose the co-employee under *Epilepsy Foundation*? If this was possible, then the investigation could probably proceed expeditiously. Unfortunately, this approach might work against the employee under investigation should the employer pick someone who dislikes the individual who is the subject of the meeting.

Also, it is unclear exactly what role the co-employee plays in witnessing the investigatory interview. In the union arena, it is established that the employee's representative (often a union steward) cannot provide answers

for the employee or attempt to direct the proceedings. On the other hand, the employee's witness can ask questions of clarification and consult with the employee at any time (MacDougall, 2000). Given these established constraints on the activities of the coworkers, the co-employee witness may perform three important roles. First, the presence of an employee representative may serve to defuse a potentially emotional confrontation. Next, the witness provides another set of ears and eyes regarding the nature of the accusations by management. But most significantly, the *Weingarten* representative in a union setting usually brings a detailed understanding of the grievance procedure and pertinent provisions of the labor contract.

In a nonunion setting, these rationales are potentially less powerful. For example, union representatives are far more likely to be trained in conflict resolution than non-union workers. In addition, the person selected to accompany an employee to an interview may be inclined to contribute little to defuse emotional outbursts for fear of subtle retribution by the employer. Also, while the employee may garner some emotional support through the presence of the coworker, most individuals chosen for this role would have little understanding of the disciplinary process or the particular elements needed to support an accusation of employee misconduct. The union representative, on the other hand, would be quite conversant with this information. Moreover, in most nonunion enterprises, the disciplinary procedure is either not formalized or, if it is, does not rise to the level of sophistication associated with a unionized workforce. In other words, a person with some understanding of the employer's disciplinary procedure would probably add little.

Arguments Against Extending the *Weingarten* Right

In an interesting moment of eloquence, NLRB member Hurtgen wrote in dissent in the *Epilepsy Foundation* decision:

> By grafting the representational rights of the unionized setting onto the nonunion workplace, employers who are legitimately pursuing investigations of employee conduct will face an unknown trip-wire placed there by the Board... The workplace has become a garden of litigation and the Board is adding another cause of action to flower therein, but hiding in the weeds (p. 9).

We have shown that the extension of the *Weingarten* right to the nonunion workplace may raise more questions for employers than it answers, and that it may complicate or frustrate management's efforts to conduct reasonable investigations of allegations of misconduct. If the trip-wire is to be removed, and if the garden of litigation is to be restored to its prior and less cluttered condition, what would be the major arguments in favor of limiting the *Weingarten* right to unionized settings?

• Retaining Managerial Prerogatives

The most obvious criticism of the NLRB's majority opinion in the *Epilepsy Foundation* decision is that it inappropriately skews the historical and longstanding delicate balance between the legitimate rights and privileges of both employers and employees. The decision takes away from the nonunion employer the previously unfettered right of such an employer to deal with its employees as individuals rather than as members of a group. The granting of rights heretofore reserved to employees in the collective bargaining context creates an additional exception to longstanding employment-at-will principles. While the provisions of Section 7 of the Act may at most protect an employee's right to seek the assistance of a co-worker in an investigatory interview, the employer should be obligated to comply with that request, and, therefore, should be allowed to discipline the employee for insubordination if the employee refuses to be interviewed without a coworker being present. To effectively balance the conflicting interests of management and labor, and in the absence of a collective bargaining agreement, the employer must retain the prerogative to make judgments about whether or not a legitimate investigation would be assisted or hindered by the presence of a third party.

Similarly, the extension of the *Weingarten* right to non-union settings confers a specific "right to representation" in a particular situation (i.e., investigations reasonably believed to result in disciplinary action) despite the fact that these same employees have declined to elect a union to represent them in any other relationships with management. This curious asymmetry gives employees unbargained-for leverage at the expense of their employers. Under the traditions of employment-at-will principle, however, the employer's freedom to deal individually with employees extends to all of the terms and conditions of employment, including decisions about discipline.

• Resolving Collective versus Individual Interests

While shop stewards are charged with protecting the interests of the group under a collective bargaining agreement, there is no guarantee that an invited coworker in a nonunion setting will safeguard the interests of the employees as a group; indeed, it is assumed that the coworker invited to attend an investigatory interview has been invited by the interviewee precisely to assist the employee's individual interests. The invited coworker would be under no obligation to act on behalf of any group.

• Recognizing Different "Due Process" Dynamics

It can be further argued that, in contrast to a union steward, a coworker in a nonunion setting would be less able to exercise vigilant oversight regarding any potential unjust imposition of sanctions by an employer because there would be no established framework for due process (as

there would be in a collective bargaining agreement). Access to reliable information regarding how other employees have been treated by the employer under similar circumstances in the past would not exist. An invited coworker probably would not have the knowledge, skills, and experience of union stewards; moreover, it is highly likely that the invited coworker may have some emotional involvement with the interviewee (or, worse, some involvement in the alleged wrongdoing). In a union setting, a union representative in an investigatory interview may serve a useful purpose by making contributions that would head off formal grievances; in the nonunion workplace, however, enforceable formal grievance procedures typically do not exist.

• Precluding a Hobson's Choice

The extension of the *Weingarten* right to the nonunion workplace may work to the disadvantage of the very employees it was designed to assist. If the employer chose to forego an investigatory interview rather than conduct it with the interviewee's coworker in attendance, the prospective interviewee will lose a chance to provide the employer with his or her side of the story. Given the choice between being given a chance to provide your side of the story without a coworker present, or being precluded from telling your side of the story because you insisted on the presence of a coworker, what would be your decision?

Conclusion

For 25 years the *Weingarten* right has aided the unionized work environment as a means of balancing the interests of the union member and management. However, with the extension of the *Weingarten* right to the approximately 85% of the private sector workforce not represented by a union, many are wondering wether important interests of both individual employers under investigation and management are properly served.

Practical problems exist in attempting to apply the *Weingarten* right—which appears to be premised, according to the U.S. Supreme Court, on the presence of a collective bargaining environment—to a nonunion environment bereft of a knowledgeable union steward serving as the employee's representative. Moreover, there are serious theoretical concerns whether the decision impinges unnecessarily on the right of nonunion employers to deal with employees as individuals rather than as members of a group. Finally, unless a compelling rationale can be offered in support of changing a well established rule of law, societal interests in a stable legal environment—and not political party affiliations on the NLRB—should prevail.

With the growing importance of workplace investigations, employers and employees deserve a legal landscape that accurately describes a set of due process rights applicable to the workplace. And no place within that landscape is more emotionally charged or critical to effectively dealing with potential legal liability than the investigatory interview of one accused with wrongdoing. Unfortunately, as a result of the *Epilepsy Foundation* decision, practical and conceptual uncertainties abound. The American workplace deserves better.

REFERENCES

Baton Rouge Water Works, 246 NLRB 995 (1979).

Burlington Industries, Inc. v. Ellerth, 118 S. Ct. 2257 (1998).

Dorfman, P. W., Cobb, A. T., & Cox, R. (2000). Investigations of sexual harassment allegations: Legal means fair—or does it? *Human Resources Management, 39* (1), 33–49.

EEOC (1999). Enforcement Guidance on Vicarious Employer Liability for Unlawful Harassment by Supervisors, *EEOC Compliance Manual,* No. 915.002 (June 18, 1999), at www.eeoc.gov/docs/harassment.html.

E. I. DuPont de Nemours & Co., 262 N.L.R.B. 1028 (1982) [*DuPont I*].

E. I. DuPont de Nemours & Co., 274 N.L.R.B. 1104 (1985) [*DuPont II*].

E. I. DuPont de Nemours & Co., 289 N.L.R.B. 627 (1988) [*DuPont III*].

E. I. DuPont de Nemours & Co. v NLRB, 724 F.2d 1061, vacated, 733 F.2d 296 (3d Cir. 1984).

Epilepsy Foundation of Northeast Ohio, 331 NLRB, No. 92 (July 10, 2000).

Faragher v. City of Boca Raton, 118 S.Ct. 2275 (1998).

Flack, J. D. (1986). Note: Limiting the *Weingarten* Right in the Nonunion Setting: The Implications of *Sears, Roebuck and Co., Catholic University Law Review* 35, 1033–1059.

Gardner, S., & Lewis, K. (2000). Sexual harassment investigations: A portrait of contradictions. *SAM Advanced Management Journal, 65* (4), 29–36.

MacDougall, H. L. (2000). *Epilepsy Foundation of Northeast Ohio:* NLRB's tripwire for nonunion employers. *Labor Law Journal, 59* (3), 59–69.

Materials Research Corporation, 262 NLRB 1010 (1982).

McLean Hospital, 264 NLRB 459 (1982).

Miranda v. Arizona, 86 S. Ct. 1602 (1966).

Morgan, J. F., Gomes, G. M., & Owens, J. M. (2001). Outsourcing investigations of sexual harassment: The unexpected consequences of good intentions. *Employment Relations Today, 27* (4), 65–78.

Morgan, J. F., Owens, J. M., & Gomes, G. M. (2000). Investigating workplace discrimination: The impact of the Fair Credit Reporting Act. *Journal of Employment Discrimination Law, 2* (4), 324–331.

Morris, C. J. (1989). NLRB protection in the nonunion workplace: A glimpse at a General Theory of Section 7 Conduct. *University of Pennsylvania Law Review*, 137, 1673–1754.

National Labor Relations Act. 29 U.S.C. 151 et seq. (2001).

National Labor Relations Board v. J. Weingarten, Inc., 95 S. Ct. 959 (1975).

Sears, Roebuck and Co. and International Union of Electrical, Radio and Machine Workers, AFL-CIO-CLC, 274 NLRB 230 (1985).

Slaughter v. NLRB, 794 F.2d 120 (3d Cir. 1986).

Dr. Morgan, College of Business, California State University, Chico, a Professor of Management and an attorney, specializes in employment laws and has published a number of articles on workplace issues. Dr. Owens, College of Business, California State University, Chico, also an attorney and teacher of management, recently co-authored a textbook on business law. Dr. Gomes, College of Business, California State University, Chico, a Professor of Management, specializes in strategic management and business policy.

From *SAM Advanced Management Journal*, Vol. 67, No. 1, Winter 2002, pp. 22–40. © 2002 by SAM Advanced Management Journal (SAM AMJ). Reprinted by permission.

It's either greed or need.

Why Employees Commit Fraud

BY JOSEPH T. WELLS

It is important for CPAs to understand what motivates people to commit fraud so they can better assess risk and assist employers or clients in implementing appropriate preventive and detective measures. One element common to most occupational fraud offenders, from the CEO to the rank-and-file employee, is that almost none of them took their jobs for the purpose of committing fraud—they are typically first-time offenders.

Facing that fact, one must ask the logical question: How do good people go bad? An obvious answer is greed. But many so-called greedy people do not lie, cheat and steal to get what they want. There are two separate but related theories about why employees commit fraud. The first is based on a 20-year-old Hollinger and Clark study of 12,000 employees in the workforce. It found that nearly 90% engaged in "workplace deviance," which included behavior such as goldbricking, workplace slowdowns, sick time abuses and pilferage. On top of that, an astonishing *one-third* of employees actually had stolen money or merchandise on the job. (Remember: Even top executives are "employees.")

WAGES IN KIND

The researchers concluded the most common reason employees committed fraud had little to do with opportunity, but more with motivation—the more dissatisfied the employee, the more likely he or she was to engage in criminal behavior. One criminologist described the phenomenon as "wages in kind." All of us have a sense of our own worth; if we believe we are not being fairly treated or adequately compensated, statistically we are at much higher risk of trying to balance the scales.

A second theory about why employees commit fraud is related to financial pressures. In the late 1940s, criminologist Donald R. Cressey interviewed nearly 200 incarcerated embezzlers, including convicted executives. He found the great majority committed fraud to meet their financial obligations. Cressey observed that two other factors had to be present for employees to commit fraud. They must perceive an opportunity to commit and conceal their crimes, and be able to rationalize their offenses as something other than criminal activity.

Here are just two examples of situations in which it would have been beneficial to know what pressures were behind the fraud.

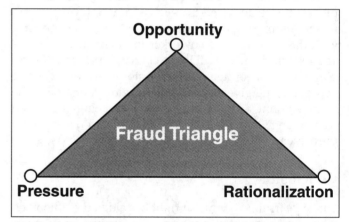

Source: Reprinted from "Occupational Fraud and Abuse," by Joseph T. Wells, Obsidian Publishing Co. 1997

• An investor spent his life savings gaining control of a 100-year-old public company that manufactured vacuum cleaners. After installing himself as CEO, the investor introduced a completely new product line. But the new vacuums were vastly inferior to the old ones, and consumers returned them to the factory in droves. Rather than credit the inventory account for returns, the CEO simply rented off-site space to store the junk vacuums. When the scheme got too big to control, the executive saw the futility of continuing the scheme, so he confessed to the authorities. Inventory was overstated by $40 million. The independent auditors were sued for malpractice, and the business folded. The CEO went to jail. Investors lost everything. The CEO's motivation? He had hocked everything he owned to acquire the company. The auditors hadn't—and couldn't have—known that.

• According to legend, a loyal bookkeeper for a company was denied a $100 monthly raise. The bookkeeper was incensed, so he methodically stole for the next 20 years, until he retired. His replacement discovered an amazing fact: The retired bookkeeper had pilfered exactly $100 a month—the precise sum of the raise he had requested.

When "Yes" is a Red Flag

SAS no. 82. *Consideration of Fraud in a Financial Statement Audit,* describes some of the characteristics that may influence employees to commit financial statement frauds and asset misappropriations. The more "yes" answers to the questions below, the more likely it will be auditors will find motivations exist for fraud.

Financial Statement Frauds

- Is management compensation tied closely to company value?
- Is management dominated by a single person or a small group?
- Does management display a significant disregard for regulations or controls?
- Has management restricted the auditor's access to documents or personnel?
- Has management set unrealistic financial goals?
- Does management have any past history of illegal conduct?

Asset Misappropriations

- Is an employee obviously dissatisfied?
- Does that employee have a past history of dishonesty or illegal conduct?
- Does that employee have known financial pressures, such as excessive debt, bad credit or tax liens?
- Has that employee's lifestyle or behavior changed significantly?

OPPORTUNITY IS KEY

The lesson in these stories is that fraud does not occur in isolation. All crime is a combination of *motive* and *opportunity*. The opportunity to commit fraud is typically addressed through internal controls—if the proper checks and balances exist, it is more difficult (though still not impossible) to defraud an organization.

To deter opportunity, divide responsibility. If one person controls both the books *and* the assets, the ability to commit fraud is limited only by that person's imagination. But if another employee shares a task, it is less likely a perpetrator can succeed. Furthermore, if an employee needs help to defraud an organization, opportunity is greatly reduced. It is one thing to commit a fraud by yourself, quite another to ask someone to aid in your scheme.

Some argue that internal controls are simply not enough to deter fraud. They cite two reasons: First, con-
trols are supposed to provide only reasonable assurance. Second, there are few controls that cannot be overridden or circumvented by people with sufficient motivation.

The body of research into why "good" employees turn to fraud can be distilled into at least two important concepts. Employees and executives who feel unfairly treated sometimes believe they can right the scales by committing occupational fraud and abuse. Workplace conditions are therefore a major risk factor in predicting fraud. Also, employees faced with embarrassing financial difficulties pose a significant problem. The simple moral to the auditor is to pay attention to what goes on outside the books, too. So while you're looking at the numbers, keep one eye and both ears open for disgruntled or financially strapped employees. It may mean all the difference in detecting fraud.

CASE STUDY: HOW A CFO PLOWED HIMSELF UNDER

Tractors—that's what brought McKinley down. The simple but vital machines were the main reason McKinley stole $150,000 from the bank where he worked as a chief financial officer.

McKinley's tale of woe actually had begun years earlier. He was an honor graduate from a prestigious Tennessee college with a degree in accounting. McKinley came from the right family, made a good marriage, attended the right church and went to work for the right bank. He earned his CPA. His future looked bright, but in McKinley's opinion, not bright enough. It seems that his lineage didn't come with a lot of money. So like many of us, McKinley decided to regularly invest a portion of his paycheck, hoping the investment would eventually bring him financial security.

Then McKinley did a very un-accountant-like thing. He put all his money in a local tractor dealership. On top of that, he borrowed all the money he could from his own employer and threw it on the pile. McKinley bragged to his co-workers about his new acquisition as evidence of his business acumen. But before long, McKinley's investment soured. He was then faced with a dilemma: The CFO would have to tell the bank president the truth—that even though he was in charge of the bank's money, he could not manage his own finances. The thought of admitting that, to acknowledge that he, the hot-shot CFO, wasn't all that savvy, was unthinkable to McKinley. So he concocted a scheme.

McKINLEY'S BIG IDEA

First, McKinley had to raise nearly $10,000 to get his bank note out of default. Since he helped install the bank's system of internal control, he knew there was a simple way to override it. Specifically, as the bank's CFO, he was the ultimate authority on journal entries. He not only reviewed the entries of other employees, but also could

make them himself. Other than the bank's regulators and external auditors, no one saw the numbers after McKinley.

To cover the money he needed, McKinley made a journal entry. The debit was to a bank correspondent account, a clearing account with lots of volume. That way, the entry was more likely to be lost in the shuffle. The credit was to McKinley's own personal checking account at the bank. Then he made a second entry, crediting the bank's correspondent account and debiting one of the bank's expense accounts: consulting, advertising or other "soft" expenses.

The trick worked. McKinley got the money to cover his past due bank payments, and no one was the wiser. It may have been that the technique was a little too easy, because the next time McKinley needed money, he reverted to the same method. In just over a year, he embezzled $150,000, using some of the money to cover his debts.

McKINLEY DID *WHAT?*

Greed being what it is, McKinley became very much addicted to stealing money. And like so many other addicts, he somehow lost the ability to reason. That is the only explanation for what occurred next. One of the bank's customers accidentally paid the same note twice. When the second check came in, it was forwarded to McKinley for handling. The $6,000 check sat on McKinley's desk for a week. All he needed to do was return it to the customer. But then, during a weak moment, McKinley stamped the bank's endorsement on the back of the check, *signed his own name* below, and deposited the proceeds directly into *his own checking account.*

When the check was returned to the customer, he quickly noticed the duplicate payment and called the bank. Since McKinley was out, the customer talked to the bank's internal auditor. Although the auditor could hardly believe her ears, she obtained a copy of the check and then promptly notified management, which authorized a full fraud examination that documented McKinley's thefts. He pled guilty and served three years in federal prison. His CPA license was revoked.

LESSONS LEARNED

The bank's external auditors did not detect McKinley's thefts. The $150,000 loss was not material to the financial statements as a whole, so there was no responsibility for the auditors to find the defalcation. Still, this incident proved embarrassing; the bank lost faith in the audit firm for not detecting the embezzlement and changed auditors as a result. Even though the original auditors were not required to detect such a fraud, most of us want to get the best service possible. And sometimes, as in this case, cli-

ents don't really want to hear the limits of an audit; they want to affix blame.

> It would have been helpful if the auditors had asked each employee one simple question: Do you suspect any fraud within this organization?

Could the auditors have seen any of the indications of fraud? Perhaps. Considering all the circumstances, the outcome might have been better had the auditors taken a different approach. First, there were clues in the books. Some were well-hidden; others were not. Embezzlers frequently prefer to hide their thefts in high-volume accounts. Had the auditors known this fact, perhaps they would have looked more carefully at the correspondent accounts. Another accounting clue was that McKinley eventually hid his thefts in "soft" expenses. Finally, auditors for financial institutions have access to the checking accounts of officers and employees. Had McKinley's account been examined, the auditors would have noticed that the former CPA had deposited all his ill-gotten gain in his own checking account at his own bank. This is not a smart move, but for some inexplicable reason, almost every embezzler does exactly the same thing.

A VERY SIMPLE QUESTION

It would also have been helpful if the auditors had stepped back from the books long enough to privately ask each employee they worked with a powerful but simple question: *Do you suspect any fraud within this organization?* Had they done so, the auditors might have learned that employees were already suspicious of McKinley. Even though he had started out well regarded at the bank, McKinley's life changed when he began stealing. He started becoming moody and irritable, and it was clear to the other employees that he was living well beyond his means. McKinley thought he was doing a good job covering his tracks, but his ill-fated tractor investment and his family troubles were well known to many of the bank's fifty-plus employees.

Why didn't any of these employees tell what they knew? Because no one asked. A CPA firm that asks the right questions can become a hero for a client. It can also prevent embarrassment from defalcations it isn't required to uncover but that were caught because the auditors were on the alert.

JOSEPH T. WELLS, CPA, CFE, is founder and chairman of the Association of Certified Fraud Examiners, Austin, Texas. His e-mail address is: joe@cfenet.com.

ENOUGH IS ENOUGH

WHITE-COLLAR CRIMINALS: THEY LIE THEY CHEAT THEY STEAL AND THEY'VE BEEN GETTING AWAY WITH IT FOR TOO LONG

BY CLIFTON LEAF

Arthur Levitt, the tough-talking former chairman of the Securities and Exchange Commission, spoke of a "multitude of villains." Red-faced Congressmen hurled insults, going so far as to compare the figures at the center of the Enron debacle unfavorably to carnival hucksters. The Treasury Secretary presided over a high-level working group aimed at punishing negligent CEOs and directors. Legislators from all but a handful of states threatened to sue the firm that bollixed up the auditing, Arthur Andersen. There was as much handwringing, proselytizing, and bloviating in front of the witness stand as there was shredding behind it.

It took a late-night comedian, though, to zero in on the central mystery of this latest corporate shame. After a parade of executives from Enron and Arthur Andersen flashed on the television monitor, Jon Stewart, anchor of *The Daily Show*, turned to the camera and shouted, "Why aren't all of you in jail? And not like white-guy jail—*jail* jail. With people by the weight room going, 'Mmmmm.'"

It was a pitch-perfect question. And, sadly, one that was sure to get a laugh.

Not since the savings-and-loan scandal a decade ago have high crimes in the boardroom provided such rich television entertainment. But that's not for any lack of malfeasance. Before Enronitis inflamed the public, gigantic white-collar swindles were rolling through the business world and the legal system with their customary regularity. And though they displayed the full creative range of executive thievery, they had one thing in common: Hardly anyone ever went to prison.

Regulators alleged that divisional managers at investment firm Credit Suisse First Boston participated in a "pervasive" scheme to siphon tens of millions of dollars of their customers' trading profits during the Internet boom of 1999 and early 2000 by demanding excessive trading fees. (For one 1999 quarter the backdoor bonuses amounted to as much as a fifth of the firm's total commissions.) Those were the facts, as outlined by the SEC and the National Association of Securities Dealers in a high-profile news conference earlier this year. But the January news conference wasn't to announce an indictment. It was to herald a settlement, in which CSFB neither admitted nor denied wrongdoing. Sure, the SEC concluded that the investment bank had failed to observe "high standards of commercial honor," and the company paid $100 million in fines and "disgorgement," and CSFB itself punished 19 of its employees with fines ranging from $250,000 to $500,000. But whatever may or may not have happened, no one was charged with a crime. The U.S. Attorney's office in Manhattan dropped its investigation when the case was settled. Nobody, in other words, is headed for the hoosegow.

A month earlier drugmaker ICN Pharmaceuticals actually pleaded guilty to one count of criminal fraud for intentionally misleading investors—over many years, it now seems—about the FDA approval status of its flagship drug, ribavirin. The result of a five-year grand jury investigation? A $5.6 million fine and the company's accession to a three-year "probationary" period. Prosecutors said that not only had the company deceived investors, but its chairman, Milan Panic, had also made more than a million dollars off the fraud as he hurriedly sold shares. He was never charged with insider trading or any other criminal act. The SEC is taking a firm stand, though, "seeking to bar Mr. Panic from serving as a director or officer of any publicly traded company." Tough luck.

And who can forget those other powerhouse scandals, Sunbeam and Waste Management? The notorious Al "Chainsaw" Dunlap, accused of zealously fabricating Sunbeam's financial statements when he was chief executive, is facing only civil, not criminal, charges. The SEC charged that Dunlap and his minions made use of every accounting fraud in the book, from "channel stuffing" to "cookie jar reserves." The case is now in the discovery phase of trial and likely to be settled; he has denied wrongdoing. (Earlier Chainsaw rid himself of a class-

Schemers and scams: a brief history of bad business

It takes some pretty spectacular behavior to get busted in this country for a white-collar crime. But the business world has had a lot of overachievers willing to give it a shot.

by Ellen Florian

1920:
The Ponzi scheme

Charles Ponzi planned to arbitrage postal coupons—buying them from Spain and selling them to the U.S. Postal Service at a profit. To raise capital, he outlandishly promised investors a 50% return in 90 days. They naturally swarmed in, and he paid the first with cash collected from those coming later. He was imprisoned for defrauding 40,000 people of $15 million.

1929:
Albert Wiggin

In the summer of 1929, Wiggin, head of Chase National Bank, cashed in by shorting 42,000 shares of his company's stock. His trades, though legal, were counter to the interests of his shareholders and led to passage of a law prohibiting executives from shorting their own stock.

1930:
Ivar Krueger, the Match King

Heading companies that made two-thirds of the world's matches, Krueger ruled—until the Depression. To keep going, he employed 400 off-the-books vehicles that only he understood, scammed his bankers, and forged signatures. His empire collapsed when he had a stroke.

1938:
Richard Whitney

Ex-NYSE president Whitney propped up his liquor business by tapping a fund for widows and orphans of which he was trustee and stealing from the New York Yacht Club and a relative's estate. He did three years' time.

1961:
The electrical cartel

Executives of GE, Westinghouse, and other big-name companies conspired to serially win bids on federal projects. Seven served time—among the first imprisonments in the 70-year history of the Sherman Antitrust Act.

1962:
Billie Sol Estes

A wheeler-dealer out to corner the West Texas fertilizer market, Estes built up capital by mortgaging nonexistent farm gear. Jailed in 1965 and paroled in 1971, he did the mortgage bit again, this time with nonexistent oil equipment. He was re-jailed in 1979 for tax evasion and did five years.

1970:
Cornfeld and Vesco

Bernie Cornfeld's Investors Overseas Service, a fund-of-funds outfit, tanked in 1970, and Cornfeld was jailed in Switzerland. Robert Vesco "rescued" IOS with $5 million and then absconded with an estimated $250 million, fleeing the U.S. He's said to be in Cuba serving time for unrelated crimes.

1983:
Marc Rich

Fraudulent oil trades in 1980–1981 netted Rich and his partner, Pincus Green, $105 million, which they moved to offshore subsidiaries. Expecting to be indicted by U.S. Attorney Rudy Giuliani for evading taxes, they fled to Switzerland, where tax evasion is not an extraditable crime. Clinton pardoned Rich in 2001.

1986:
Boesky and Milken and Drexel Burnham Lambert

The Feds got Wall Streeter Ivan Boesky for insider trading, and then Boesky's testimony helped them convict Drexel's Michael Milken for market manipulation. Milken did two years in prison, Boesky 22 months. Drexel died.

1989:
Charles Keating and the collapse of Lincoln S&L

Keating was convicted of fraudulently marketing junk bonds and making sham deals to manufacture profits. Sentenced to 12½ years, he served less than five. Cost to taxpayers: $3.4 billion, a sum making this the most expensive S&L failure.

(continued)

Schemers and Scams (continued)

1991: BCCI	1991: Salomon Brothers	1995: Nick Leeson and Barings Bank	1995: Bankers Trust	1997: Walter Forbes
The Bank of Credit & Commerce International got tagged the "Bank for Crooks & Criminals International" after it came crashing down in a money-laundering scandal that disgraced, among others, Clark Clifford, advisor to four Presidents.	Trader Paul Mozer violated rules barring one firm from bidding for more than 35% of the securities offered at a Treasury auction. He did four months' time. Salomon came close to bankruptcy. Chairman John Gutfreund resigned.	A 28-year-old derivatives trader based in Singapore, Leeson brought down 233-year-old Barings by betting Japanese stocks would rise. He hid his losses—$1.4 billion—for a while but eventually served more than three years in jail.	Derivatives traders misled clients Gibson Greetings and Procter & Gamble about the risks of exotic contracts they entered into. P&G sustained about $200 million in losses but got most of it back from BT. The Federal Reserve sanctioned the bank.	Only months after Cendant was formed by the merger of CUC and HFS, cooked books that created more than $500 million in phony profits showed up at CUC. Walter Forbes, head of CUC, has been indicted on fraud charges and faces trial this year.
1997: Columbia/HCA	**1998: Waste Management**	**1998: Al Dunlap**	**1999: Martin Frankel**	**2000: Sotheby's and Al Taubman**
This Nashville company became the target of the largest-ever federal investigation into healthcare scams and agreed in 2000 to an $840 million Medicare-fraud settlement. Included was a criminal fine—rare in corporate America—of $95 million.	Fighting to keep its reputation as a fast grower, the company engaged in aggressive accounting for years and then tried straight-out books cooking. In 1998 it took a massive charge, restating years of earnings.	He became famous as "Chainsaw Al" by firing people. But he was then axed at Sunbeam for illicitly manufacturing earnings. He loved overstating revenues—booking sales, for example, on grills neither paid for nor shipped.	A financier who siphoned off at least $200 million from a series of insurance companies he controlled, Frankel was arrested in Germany four months after going on the lam. Now jailed in Rhode Island—no bail for this guy—he awaits trial on charges of fraud and conspiracy.	The world's elite were ripped off by years of price-fixing on the part of those supposed bitter competitors, auction houses Sotheby's and Christie's. Sotheby's chairman, Taubman, was found guilty of conspiracy last year. He is yet to be sentenced.

action shareholder suit for $15 million, without admitting culpability.) Whatever the current trial's outcome, Dunlap will still come out well ahead. Sunbeam, now under bankruptcy protection, gave him $12.7 million in stock and salary during 1998 alone. And if worse comes to worst, he can always tap the stash he got from the sale of the disemboweled Scott Paper to Kimberly-Clark, which by Dunlap's own estimate netted him a $100 million bonanza.

Sunbeam investors, naturally, didn't fare as well. When the fraud was discovered internally, the company was forced to restate its earnings, slashing half the reported profits from fiscal 1997. After that embarrassment, Sunbeam shares fell from $52 to $7 in just six months—a loss of $3.8 billion in market cap. Sound familiar?

The auditor in that case, you'll recall, was Arthur Andersen, which paid $110 million to settle a civil action. According to an SEC release in May, an Andersen partner authorized unqualified audit opinions even though "he was aware of many of the company's accounting improprieties and disclosure failures." The opinions were false and misleading. But nobody is going to jail.

At Waste Management, yet another Andersen client, income reported over six years was overstated by $1.4 billion. Andersen coughed up $220 million to shareholders to wipe its hands clean. The auditor, agreeing to the SEC's first antifraud injunction against a major firm in more than 20 years, also paid a $7 million fine to close the complaint. Three partners were assessed fines, ranging from $30,000 to $50,000, as well. (You guessed it. Not even home detention.) Concedes one former regulator familiar with the case: "Senior people at Andersen got off when we felt we had the goods." Andersen did not respond to a request for comment.

The list goes on—from phony bookkeeping at the former Bankers Trust (now part of Deutsche Bank) to allegations of insider trading by a former Citigroup vice president. One employee of California tech firm nVidia admitted that he cleared

The Incredible Shrinking Fraudster

The white-collar inmate population has actually shrunk in proportional terms—from 2.8% of the total in 1985 to 0.6% today. Much of that is due to mandatory drug-sentencing laws.

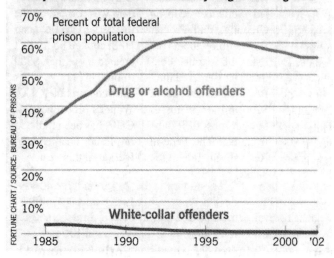

nearly half a million dollars in a single day in March 2000 from an illegal insider tip. He pleaded guilty to criminal charges, paid fines, and got a 12-month grounding at home.

The problem will not go away until white-collar thieves face a consequence they're actually scared of: time in jail.

While none of those misbehaviors may rise to Enronian proportions, at least in terms of salacious detail, taken en masse they say something far more distressing. The double standard in criminal justice in this country is starker and more embedded than many realize. Bob Dylan was right: Steal a little, and they put you in jail. Steal a lot, and you're likely to walk away with a lecture and a court-ordered promise not to do it again.

Far beyond the pure social inequity—and that would be bad enough, we admit—is a very real dollar-and-cents cost, a doozy of a recurring charge that ripples through the financial markets. As the Enron case makes abundantly clear, white-collar fraud is not a victimless crime. In this age of the 401(k), when the retirement dreams of middle-class America are tied to the integrity of the stock market, crooks in the corner office are everybody's problem. And the problem will not go away until white-collar thieves face a consequence they're actually scared of: time in jail.

The U.S. regulatory and judiciary systems, however, do little if anything to deter the most damaging Wall Street crimes. Interviews with some six dozen current and former federal prosecutors, regulatory officials, defense lawyers, criminologists, and high-ranking corporate executives paint a disturbing picture. The already stretched "white-collar" task forces of the FBI focus on wide-ranging schemes like Internet, insurance, and Medicare fraud, abandoning traditional securities and accounting offenses to the SEC. Federal securities regulators, while determined and well trained, are so understaffed that they often have to let good cases slip away. Prosecutors leave scores of would-be criminal cases referred by the SEC in the dustbin, declining to prosecute more than half of what comes their way. State regulators, with a few notable exceptions, shy away from the complicated stuff. So-called self-regulatory organizations like the National Association of Securities Dealers are relatively toothless; trade groups like the American Institute of Certified Public Accountants stubbornly protect their own. And perhaps worst of all, corporate chiefs often wink at (or nod off to) overly aggressive tactics that speed along the margins of the law.

LET'S START WITH THE NUMBERS. WALL STREET, AFTER ALL, IS about numbers, about playing the percentages. And that may be the very heart of the problem. Though securities officials like to brag about their enforcement records, few in America's top-floor suites and corporate boardrooms fear the local sheriff. They know the odds of getting caught.

The U.S. Attorneys' Annual Statistical Report is the official reckoning of the Department of Justice. For the year 2000, the most recent statistics available, federal prosecutors say they charged 8,766 defendants with what they term white-collar crimes, convicting 6,876, or an impressive 78% of the cases brought. Not bad. Of that number, about 4,000 were sentenced to prison—nearly all of them for less than three years. (The average time served, experts say, is closer to 16 months.)

But that 4,000 number isn't what you probably think it is. The Justice Department uses the white-collar appellation for virtually every kind of fraud, says Henry Pontell, a leading criminologist at the University of California at Irvine, and co-author of *Big-Money Crime: Fraud and Politics in the Savings and Loan Crisis*. "I've seen welfare frauds labeled as white-collar crimes," he says. Digging deeper into the Justice Department's 2000 statistics, we find that only 226 of the cases involved securities or commodities fraud.

And guess what: Even those are rarely the highfliers, says Kip Schlegel, chairman of the department of criminal justice at Indiana University, who wrote a study on Wall Street lawbreaking for the Justice Department's research wing. Many of the government's largest sting operations come from busting up cross-state Ponzi schemes, "affinity" investment scams (which prey on the elderly or on particular ethnic or religious groups), and penny-stock boiler rooms, like the infamous Stratton Oakmont and Sterling Foster. They are bad seeds, certainly. But let's not kid ourselves: They are not corporate-officer types or high-level Wall Street traders and bankers—what we might call *starched*-collar criminals. "The criminal sanction is generally reserved for the losers," says Schlegel, "the scamsters, the low-rent crimes."

Statistics from the Federal Bureau of Prisons, up to date as of October 2001, make it even clearer how few white-collar criminals are behind bars. Of a total federal inmate population of

The SEC's Impressive Margins

Did someone say "resource problem"? The SEC is, in fact, a moneymaking machine. The U.S. Treasury keeps fees and penalties. Disgorgements go into a fund for fraud victims.

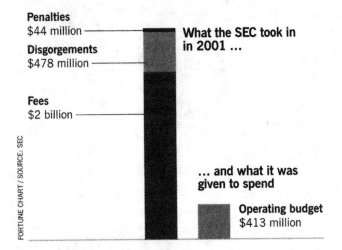

Penalties
$44 million

Disgorgements
$478 million

Fees
$2 billion

What the SEC took in in 2001 ...

... and what it was given to spend

Operating budget
$413 million

FORTUNE CHART / SOURCE: SEC

156,238, prison authorities say only 1,021 fit the description—which includes everyone from insurance schemers to bankruptcy fraudsters, counterfeiters to election-law tamperers to postal thieves. Out of those 1,000 or so, well more than half are held at minimum-security levels—often privately managed "Club Feds" that are about two steps down the comfort ladder from Motel 6.

And how many of them are the starched-collar crooks who commit securities fraud? The Bureau of Prisons can't say precisely. The Department of Justice won't say either—but the answer lies in its database.

Susan Long, a professor of quantitative methods at the school of management at Syracuse University, co-founded a Web data clearinghouse called TRAC, which has been tracking prosecutor referrals from virtually every federal agency for more than a decade. Using a barrage of Freedom of Information Act lawsuits, TRAC has been able to gather data buried in the Justice Department's own computer files (minus the individual case numbers that might be used to identify defendants). And the data, which follow each matter from referral to the prison steps, tell a story the Justice Department doesn't want you to know.

In the full ten years from 1992 to 2001, according to TRAC data, SEC enforcement attorneys referred 609 cases to the Justice Department for possible criminal charges. Of that number, U.S. Attorneys decided what to do on about 525 of the cases—declining to prosecute just over 64% of them. Of those they did press forward, the feds obtained guilty verdicts in a respectable 76%. But even then, some 40% of the convicted starched-collars didn't spend a day in jail. In case you're wondering, here's the magic number that did: 87.

FIVE-POINT TYPE IS SMALL PRINT, SO TINY THAT ALMOST everyone who remembers the Bay of Pigs or the fall of Saigon will need bifocals to read it. For those who love pulp fiction or

the crime blotters in their town weeklies, however, there is no better place to look than in the small print of the *Wall Street Journal*'s B section. Once a month, buried in the thick folds of newsprint, are bullet reports of the NASD's disciplinary actions. February's disclosures about alleged misbehavior, for example, range from the unseemly to the lurid—from an Ohio bond firm accused of systematically overcharging customers and fraudulently marking up trades to a California broker who deposited a client's $143,000 check in his own account. Two senior VPs of a Pittsburgh firm, say NASD officials, cashed out of stock, thanks to timely inside information they received about an upcoming loss; a Dallas broker reportedly converted someone's 401(k) rollover check to his personal use.

In all, the group's regulatory arm received 23,753 customer complaints against its registered reps between the years 1997 and 2000. After often extensive investigations, the NASD barred "for life" during this period 1,662 members and suspended another 1,000 or so for violations of its rules or of laws on the federal books. But despite its impressive 117-page *Sanction Guidelines*, the NASD can't do much of anything to its miscreant broker-dealers other than throw them out of the club. It has no statutory right to file civil actions against rule breakers, it has no subpoena power, and from the looks of things it can't even get the bums to return phone calls. Too often the disciplinary write-ups conclude with a boilerplate "failed to respond to NASD requests for information."

"That's a good thing when they default," says Barry Goldsmith, executive vice president for enforcement at NASD Regulation. "It gives us the ability to get the wrongdoers out quickly to prevent them from doing more harm."

Goldsmith won't say how many cases the NASD passes on to the SEC or to criminal prosecutors for further investigation. But he does acknowledge that the securities group refers a couple of hundred suspected insider-trading cases to its higher-ups in the regulatory chain.

Thus fails the first line of defense against white-collar crime: self-policing. The situation is worse, if anything, among accountants than it is among securities dealers, says John C. Coffee Jr., a Columbia Law School professor and a leading authority on securities enforcement issues. At the American Institute of Certified Public Accountants, he says, "no real effort is made to enforce the rules." Except one, apparently. "They have a rule that they do not take action against auditors until all civil litigation has been resolved," Coffee says, "because they don't want their actions to be used against their members in a civil suit." Lynn E. Turner, who until last summer was the SEC's chief accountant and is now a professor at Colorado State University, agrees. "The AICPA," he says, "often failed to discipline members in a timely fashion, if at all. And when it did, its most severe remedy was just to expel the member from the organization."

Al Anderson, senior VP of AICPA, says the criticism is unfounded. "We have been and always will be committed to enforcing the rules," he says. The next line of defense after the professional associations is the SEC. The central role of this independent regulatory agency is to protect investors in the financial markets by making sure that publicly traded companies

The Odds Against Doing Time

Regulators like to talk tough, but when it comes to actual punishment, all but a handful of Wall Street cheats get off with a slap on the wrist.

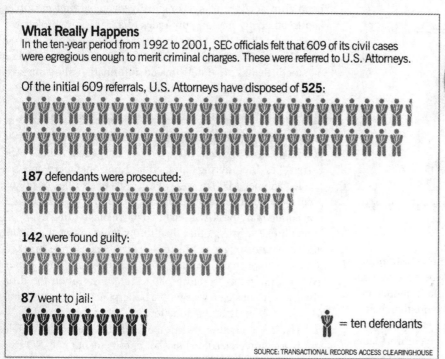

What Really Happens
In the ten-year period from 1992 to 2001, SEC officials felt that 609 of its civil cases were egregious enough to merit criminal charges. These were referred to U.S. Attorneys.

Of the initial 609 referrals, U.S. Attorneys have disposed of **525**:

187 defendants were prosecuted:

142 were found guilty:

87 went to jail:

= ten defendants

SOURCE: TRANSACTIONAL RECORDS ACCESS CLEARINGHOUSE

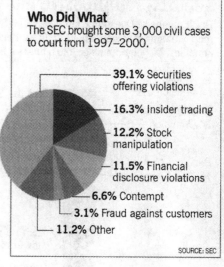

Who Did What
The SEC brought some 3,000 civil cases to court from 1997–2000.

- **39.1%** Securities offering violations
- **16.3%** Insider trading
- **12.2%** Stock manipulation
- **11.5%** Financial disclosure violations
- **6.6%** Contempt
- **3.1%** Fraud against customers
- **11.2%** Other

SOURCE: SEC

A Look at Self-Policing
Few complaints received last year by the NASD resulted in serious sanctions.

Registered reps	675,821
Customer complaints received	5,155
Individuals barred	466
Individuals suspended	346

SOURCE: NASD REGULATION

play by the rules. With jurisdiction over every constituent in the securities trade, from brokers to mutual funds to accountants to corporate filers, it would seem to be the voice of Oz. But the SEC's power, like that of the Wizard, lies more in persuasion than in punishment. The commission can force companies to comply with securities rules, it can fine them when they don't, it can even charge them in civil court with violating the law. But it can't drag anybody off to prison. To that end, the SEC's enforcement division must work with federal and state prosecutors—a game that often turns into weak cop/bad cop.

Nevertheless, the last commission chairman, Arthur Levitt, did manage to shake the ground with the power he had. For the 1997–2000 period, for instance, attorneys at the agency's enforcement division brought civil actions against 2,989 respondents. That figure includes 487 individual cases of alleged insider trading, 365 for stock manipulation, 343 for violations of laws and rules related to financial disclosure, 196 for contempt of the regulatory agency, and another 94 for fraud against customers. In other words, enough bad stuff to go around. What would make them civil crimes, vs. actual handcuff-and-fingerprint ones? Evidence, says one SEC regional director. "In a civil case you need only a preponderance of evidence that there was an intent to defraud," she says. "In a criminal case you have to prove that intent beyond a reasonable doubt."

When the SEC does find a case that smacks of criminal intent, the commission refers it to a U.S. Attorney. And that is where the second line of defense often breaks down. The SEC has the expertise to sniff out such wrongdoing but not the big stick of prison to wave in front of its targets. The U.S. Attorney's office has the power to order in the SWAT teams but often lacks the expertise—and, quite frankly, the inclination—to deconstruct a complex financial crime. After all, it is busy pursuing drug kingpins and terrorists.

And there is also the key issue of institutional kinship, say an overwhelming number of government authorities. U.S. Attorneys, for example, have kissing-cousin relationships with the agencies they work with most, the FBI and DEA. Prosecutors and investigators often work together from the start and know the elements required on each side to make a case stick. That is hardly true with the SEC and all but a handful of U.S. Attorneys around the country. In candid conversations, current and former regulators cited the lack of warm cooperation between the law-enforcement groups, saying one had no clue about how the other worked.

THIRTEEN BLOCKS FROM WALL STREET IS A DIFFERENT KIND of ground zero. Here, in the shadow of the imposing Federalist-style courthouses of lower Manhattan, is a nine-story stone fortress of indeterminate color, somewhere in the unhappy genus of waiting-room beige. As with every federal building these days, there are reminders of the threat of terrorism, but this particular outpost has taken those reminders to the status of a four-bell alarm. To get to the U.S. Attorney's office, a visitor must wind his way through a phalanx of blue police barricades, stop

by a kiosk manned by a U.S. marshal, enter a giant white tent with police and metal detectors, and proceed to a bulletproof visitors desk, replete with armed guards. Even if you make it to the third floor, home of the Securities and Commodities Fraud Task Force, Southern District of New York, you'll need an electronic passkey to get in.

This, the office which Rudy Giuliani led to national prominence with his late-1980s busts of junk-bond king Michael Milken, Ivan Boesky, and the Drexel Burnham insider-trading ring, is one of the few outfits in the country that even know how to prosecute complex securities crimes. Or at least one of the few willing to take them on. Over the years it has become the favorite (and at times lone) repository for the SEC's enforcement hit list.

And how many attorneys are in this office to fight the nation's book cookers, insider traders, and other Wall Street thieves? Twenty-five—including three on loan from the SEC. The unit has a fraction of the paralegal and administrative help of even a small private law firm. Assistant U.S. Attorneys do their own copying, and in one recent sting it was Sandy—one of the unit's two secretaries—who did the records analysis that broke the case wide open.

Even this office declines to prosecute more than half the cases referred to it by the SEC. Richard Owens, the newly minted chief of the securities task force and a six-year veteran of the unit, insists that it is not for lack of resources. There are plenty of legitimate reasons, he says, why a prosecutor would choose not to pursue a case—starting with the possibility that there may not have been true criminal intent.

But many federal regulators scoff at such bravado. "We've got too many crooks and not enough cops," says one. "We could fill Riker's Island if we had the resources."

And Owens' office is as good as it gets in this country. In other cities, federal and state prosecutors shun securities cases for all kinds of understandable reasons. They're harder to pull off than almost any other type of case—and the payoff is rarely worth it from the standpoint of local political impact. "The typical state prosecution is for a standard common-law crime," explains Philip A. Feigin, an attorney with Rothgerber Johnson & Lyons in Denver and a former commissioner of the Colorado Securities Division. "An ordinary trial will probably last for five days, it'll have 12 witnesses, involve an act that occurred in one day, and was done by one person." Now hear the pitch coming from a securities regulator thousands of miles away. "Hi. We've never met, but I've got this case I'd like you to take on. The law that was broken is just 158 pages long. It involves only three years of conduct—and the trial should last no more than three months. What do you say?" The prosecutor has eight burglaries or drug cases he could bring in the time it takes to prosecute a single white-collar crime. "It's a completely easy choice," says Feigin.

That easy choice, sadly, has left a glaring logical—and moral—fallacy in the nation's justice system: Suite thugs don't go to jail because street thugs have to. And there's one more thing on which many crime experts are adamant. The double standard makes no sense whatsoever when you consider the damage done by the offense. Sociologist Pontell and his col-

leagues Kitty Calavita, at U.C. Irvine, and Robert Tillman, at New York's St. John's University, have demonstrated this in a number of compelling academic studies. In one the researchers compared the sentences received by major players (that is, those who stole $100,000 or more) in the savings-and-loan scandal a decade ago with the sentences handed to other types of nonviolent federal offenders. The starched-collar S&L crooks got an average of 36.4 months in the slammer. Those who committed burglary—generally swiping $300 or less—got 55.6 months; car thieves, 38 months; and first-time drug offenders, 64.9 months. Now compare the costs of the two kinds of crime: The losses from all bank robberies in the U.S. in 1992 *totaled* $35 million, according to the FBI's Uniform Crime Reports. That's about 1% of the estimated cost of Charles Keating's fraud at Lincoln Savings & Loan.

"Nobody writes an e-mail that says, 'Gee, I think I'll screw the public today.' There's never been a fraud of passion."

"OF ALL THE FACTORS THAT LEAD TO CORPORATE CRIME, NONE comes close in importance to the role top management plays in tolerating, even shaping, a culture that allows for it," says William Laufer, the director of the Zicklin Center for Business Ethics Research at the Wharton School. Laufer calls it "winking." And with each wink, nod, and nudge-nudge, instructions of a sort are passed down the management chain. Accounting fraud, for example, often starts in this way. "Nobody writes an e-mail that says, 'Gee, I think I'll screw the public today,'" says former regulator Feigin. "There's never been a fraud of passion. These things take years." They breed slowly over time.

So does the impetus to fight them. Enron, of course, has stirred an embarrassed Administration and Congress to action. But it isn't merely Enron that worries legislators and the public—it's *another* Enron. Every day brings news of one more accounting gas leak that for too long lay undetected. Wariness about Lucent, Rite Aid, Raytheon, Tyco, and a host of other big names has left investors not only rattled but also questioning the very integrity of the financial reporting system.

And with good reason. Two statistics in particular suggest that no small degree of executive misconduct has been brewing in the corporate petri dish. In 1999 and 2000 the SEC demanded 96 restatements of earnings or other financial statements—a figure that was more than in the previous nine years combined. Then, in January, the Federal Deposit Insurance Corp. announced more disturbing news. The number of publicly traded companies declaring bankruptcy shot up to a record 257, a stunning 46% over the prior year's total, which itself had been a record. These companies shunted $259 billion in assets into protective custody—that is, away from shareholders. And a record 45 of these losers were biggies, companies with assets greater than $1 billion. That might all seem normal in a time of burst

bubbles and economic recession. But the number of nonpublic bankruptcies has barely risen. Regulators and plaintiffs lawyers say both restatements and sudden public bankruptcies often signal the presence of fraud.

The ultimate cost could be monumental. "Integrity of the markets, and the willingness of people to invest, are critical to us," says Harvey J. Goldschmid, a professor of law at Columbia since 1970 and soon to be an SEC commissioner. "Widespread false disclosure would be incredibly dangerous. People could lose trust in corporate filings altogether."

So will all this be enough to spark meaningful changes in the system? Professor Coffee thinks the Enron matter might move Congress to take action. "I call it the phenomenon of crash-then-law," he says. "You need three things to get a wave of legislation and litigation: a recession, a stock market crash, and a true villain." For instance, Albert Wiggin, head of Chase National Bank, cleaned up during the crash of 1929 by short-selling his own company stock. "From that came a new securities law, Section 16(b), that prohibits short sales by executives," Coffee says.

But the real issue isn't more laws on the books—it's enforcing the ones that are already there. And that, says criminologist Kip Schlegel, is where the government's action falls far short of the rhetoric. In his 1994 study on securities lawbreaking for the Justice Department, Schlegel found that while officials were talking tough about locking up insider traders, there was little evidence to suggest that the punishments imposed—either the incarceration rates or the sentences themselves—were more severe. "In fact," he says, "the data suggest the opposite trend. The government lacks the will to bring these people to justice."

DENNY CRAWFORD SAYS THERE'S AN ALL-TOO-SIMPLE REASON for this. The longtime commissioner of the Texas Securities Board, who has probably put away more bad guys than any other state commissioner, says most prosecutors make the crimes too complicated. "You've got to boil it down to lying, cheating, and stealing," she says, in a warbly voice that sounds like pink lemonade. "That's all it is—the best way to end securities fraud is to put every one of these crooks in jail."

Reprinted from the March 18, 2002 issue of *Fortune*, pp. 62-65 by special permission. © 2002 by Time, Inc.

Temporary Solution

CHRISSY KADLECK

Temp workers are enjoying the flexibility of a thriving industry.

For more than 20 years, Dana Hart has refused to be a starving artist. Hart, now a full-time actor, has worked off and on as a temporary employee at businesses across the country, at first shoveling coal and later graduating to administrative-assistant positions.

"I started with Manpower in the 1970s, when I was an apprentice at the Cleveland Play House," Hart says. The Berea resident continues his relationship with Manpower Inc., an international staffing agency, to supplement his income between acting contracts.

In fact, Hart's situation reflects a large segment of the temp industry. "About 38 percent of the people who come through the staffing industry are truly doing it because they do not want traditional full-time employment," says Nicki Artese, former vice president of communications for The Reserves Network, who recently moved to Chicago to work for a similar company. "They just want to work when they want to work."

A booming economy and a tight labor market with record-low unemployment are offering greater flexibility for temporary workers to pursue career and personal goals, says Rob Searson, president of RKS & Associates in Lyndhurst.

"People can find jobs relatively easily, and employers are having a hard time filling positions," says Searson, an employee resource and general business consultant. "So employers are more open to alternative ways to employ the talent that they need."

And many individuals want more control over the time they spend at work. "They don't want to make a long-term commitment because in many cases, they're working toward some other goal," he adds.

The relationship between a temp worker and employer comes with a unique set of challenges for both sides.

For Hart, limited hours worked through the agency resulted in a span of six jobs without health benefits.

Yet employers, such as Joseph Sikora, vice president of administration and human resources at Cleveland-based NuDi Products Co. Inc., consider not having to offer benefits to temps as a plus. Sikora's company, which manufactures test harnesses and other test-specific devices for the transportation industry, uses temporary agencies to help with overflow from large orders.

"We're very much a custom house; we can have a lot of jobs at one time," Sikora says, adding that he has needed up to 40 temps at one time. "We can increase and decrease our work force without increasing additional expenses like paying benefits and unemployment."

In fact, Searson says, temp workers employed by the agency don't even register on the company's payroll. "We want to be fair to our people," Sikora says, noting that the company is able to meet its production needs without having to hire new employees and then lay them off during slow times.

"Businesses that utilize temporary staffing are very savvy businesspeople, because they realize the moral issues" of hiring people and then laying them off when the work is completed, says Kathie Hartman, owner and president of Personnel Services Inc. in Mentor.

But make no mistake: An employer shouldn't automatically expect a particular temp worker to fit perfectly with their company. "A lot of these people do not have a work ethic," says Sikora. "And we have a great deal of turnover."

Thus, training new employees can pose a problem. "Unless it is very defined, structured work—like data entry and word processing—there is always a learning curve involved," Searson says. "So a company may go through a learning process with a person, then discover it's not working and then have to start all over. And you could go through this cycle several times before you get someone to your liking."

For that reason, Dean Henry, graphics production manager at Moen Inc., tries to recruit temporary designers who already have worked with his department. Moen, which uses graphic designers about

three times a year for catalogs and product-specific sell sheets—projects that last one week to several months—"can ask for a production artist all the way up to an art director," he says. Henry even has asked for particular designers by name to cut down the learning curve.

Likewise, agency workers can decline any placement or request a transfer without any penalty or blemish on their work history.

Cheryl Wagner of Jefferson says the flexibility that temp work affords her fits perfectly into her balancing act of raising a family and tailoring her schedule around her husband's vacations and time off.

"You can pick when and where you want to work," she says. "I like it because you get a variety of jobs, but the downside is the pay." Wagner says she might eventually consider accepting a full-time position, but she says her employment through Mentor-based Hartman Personnel Services "looks good on a resume and shows that there is still some stability," even though she works in a variety of offices.

As a newcomer to the area, Carol Dow-Richards of Madison says she uses her temporary assignments as a vehicle to meet new people, learn the area and make some extra money. Dow-Richards and her family moved to Northeast Ohio in fall 2000 when her husband, an executive with Eaton Corp., was transferred from a position in Perrysburg.

"I don't want the constraints of a fulltime job," she says. Six years ago her son, now 16, suffered a stroke and was left with severe disabilities. He attends a boarding school, in which Dow-Richards is very involved. And when he is home, she devotes all her time and energy to caring for him. "You just can't have a job and say I have something that is close to my heart and it requires me to leave for extended periods of time."

Dow-Richards says she's not "a typical temporary employee." She has run her own business designing and marketing children's wear, which she closed after her son's stroke. She was a sales director with Mary Kay and has worked as a substitute teacher.

"What I am being paid is next to nothing," she says, but quickly adds that she isn't really doing the work for the money. Right now, she says her work future is in limbo. She's even toying with restarting her business.

"I'm just riding the wave right now," Dow-Richards says.

The ebb and flow of work orders at Thermagon Inc. keeps Kathy Rhubart, human-resources manager, busy coordinating temporary placements to round out her work force.

The Cleveland company, which manufacturers thermally conductive material for electronics, has grown from 10 employees in 1996 to more than 100 to date and uses temporary placements to screen for potential full-time hires.

"Oftentimes we just need a lot of people really fast, and we can build our staffing more quickly with just a call, rather than going through the interview process," Rhubart says. "We also have a chance to see how they are going to work out. We tend to look at them as a potential permanent employee."

But she says there is also a downside to sidestepping the interview process.

"When you are hiring, you are also looking at the person, not only the skills, and trying to get a read on whether they will fit in," she says. For permanent employees, we also do background investigations and drug testing. We don't do that with temporary help unless we are considering them for full-time employment, so we don't know a lot about the person the way we do with permanent employees."

Shades of Gray

Universal codes of ethics cannot be overlaid in every sector of the world, or in every market. Internal auditors—especially those who work in multinational organizations—must understand the mix of ethical behaviors and how they impact corporate codes of ethics.

BY JERRY G. KREUZE, ZAHIDA LUQMANI, AND MUSHTAQ LUQMANI

Well-developed corporate codes of ethics help organizations foster ethical environments, deter unethical behavior, and cope with problems and ethical dilemmas. The codes establish the ground rules by which the organization operates and evaluates.

By its very nature, however, the zone of business ethics can be amorphous. It can be pervaded by many shades of gray, even in environments that are quite similar. When the environments are clearly diverse, boilerplate codes of ethics will not be relevant or effective.

Complex cultural, individual, and market-based forces influence ethical behavior in different parts of the world. For example, the ethical demands placed on companies operating in intensively competitive, ethically hostile environments are significantly different from those of companies operating in regulated, highly stable environments.

As more companies engage in international trade and expand their operations across national boundaries, understanding the factors that drive ethical decision-making becomes increasingly important. Internal auditors should be aware of all the elements that impact ethical behavior and how they interact.

THE IMPACT OF CULTURE AND COMPETITION

Two key forces—the culture and the competitive intensity of the market—have great impact on ethical behavior. Although these dynamic components must ultimately be considered jointly, each must also be understood separately.

CULTURAL FACTORS People from different cultures generally do not have the same values. Because values are linked to ethical beliefs, codes of ethics must consider these divergent value systems.

Cultural ethical issues were addressed to some extent in the U.S. Foreign Corrupt Practices Act of 1977. This legislation makes it a crime for U.S. based multinationals to make "sensitive payments," or bribes, to officials of foreign governments. The act implies that U.S. ethical standards should apply to business activities both inside and outside its boundaries, thereby establishing a clear example of moral absolutism, where one universally acceptable set of moral views and behavior is defined. Additionally, the Organisation for Economic Co-operation and Development's Convention on Combating Bribery of Foreign Public Officials in International Business Transactions, obliges signatories to adopt national legislation that makes it a crime to bribe foreign public officials.

Yet, societies can vary along several cultural dimensions; and ethical behavior is not absolute in all nations. If issues are not clearly immoral, such as murder, then cultural relativism argues that no one culture's ethical standards are any more or less moral than those of other cultures. Culture-based codes of ethics must consider each country's views with regard to moral absolutism. Internal auditors must not only be aware of these differences; they should also be cognizant that in some countries a universally imposed code of ethics could be in opposition to deeply held beliefs.

Assessing an Organization's Ethical Climate

As a creation of a society, every organization—whether economic or political, private or public—has primary, overarching responsibilities to that society to be obedient, benevolent, and accountable. The organization uses various legal forms, structures, strategies, and procedures to ensure that it complies with society's legal and regulatory rules; satisfies the generally accepted business norms, ethical precepts, and social expectations of society; provides overall benefit to society and enhances the interests of the specific stakeholders in both the short- and long-term; and reports fully and truthfully to its owners, regulators, other stakeholders, and general public to ensure accountability for its decisions, actions, conduct, and performance.

At a minimum, the internal audit activity should periodically assess the state of the ethical climate of the organization and the effectiveness of its strategies, tactics, communications, and other processes in achieving the desired level of legal and ethical compliance. Internal auditors should evaluate the effectiveness of the following features of an enhanced, highly effective ethical culture:

- Formal code of conduct, which is clear and understandable, and related statements, policies (including procedures covering fraud and corruption), and other expressions of aspiration.
- Frequent communications and demonstrations of expected ethical attitudes and behavior by the influential leaders of the organization.
- Explicit strategies to support and enhance the ethical culture with regular programs to update and renew the organization's commitment to an ethical culture.

- Several easily accessible ways for people to confidentially report alleged violations of the code, policies, and other acts of misconduct.
- Regular declarations by employees, suppliers, and customers that they are aware of the requirements for ethical behavior in transacting the organization's affairs.
- Clear delegation of responsibilities to ensure that ethical consequences are evaluated, confidential counseling is provided, allegations of misconduct are investigated, and case findings are properly reported.
- Easy access to learning opportunities to enable all employees to be ethics advocates.
- Positive personnel practices that encourage every employee to contribute to the ethical climate of the organization.
- Regular surveys of employees, suppliers, and customers to determine the state of the ethical culture of the organization.
- Regular reviews of the formal and informal processes within the organization that could potentially create pressures and biases that would undermine the ethical culture.
- Regular reference and background checks as part of the hiring procedures, including integrity tests, drug screening, and similar measures.

Excerpted from Practice Advisory 2130-1: Role of the Internal Audit Activity and Internal Auditor in the Ethical Culture of an Organization, an Interpretation of *Standard 2130* from the *Standards for the Professional Practice of Internal Auditing*.

G. Hofstede, author of *Culture's Consequences: International Differences in Work-related Values*, suggests that societies differ along four cultural dimensions: individualism/collectivism, power, masculinity/femininity, and uncertainty avoidance:

- INDIVIDUALISM/COLLECIVSM. In societies where individuals are primarily concerned with their own interests and the interests of their immediate families, individualism is emphasized. Collectivism, on the other hand, views individuals as members of a group, and group norms supplant individual morals.

   In the United States, for example, the tendency is toward individualism, and many codes

emphasize individual conduct issues. Those codes should be reevaluated, however, when a corporation operates in countries such as India that emphasize collectivism. Codes that emphasize policies for the "good of the company" may not be effective in countries that stress individualism, but they are well-positioned for collectivism cultures.

- POWER. Societies vary to the extent that they accept inequality in power and consider inequality to be normal. Great disparity in pay and benefits among worker groups may create incentives for the less advantaged to cheat on hours worked and to borrow corporate assets. Large executive compen-

sation and benefit packages tend to create significant hostility and resentment in some countries.

   Conversely, policies calling for significant equities among workers may also create conflict. The idea that less powerful individuals in society should regard inequity as normal is widely accepted in some societies.

- MASCULINE/FEMININE. Masculinity-based cultures accept assertiveness, competitiveness, and the accumulation of material wealth. In feminine societies, relationships are perceived to be of great importance; and the role of each sex is seen as essentially equal. Cultures favoring femininity would advo-

cate equal pay for equal work and favor benefits for working parents, for example.

- AVOIDING UNCERTAINTY. The level of frustration brought on by unstructured, unpredictable situations varies from one environment to another. Some societies, such as Greece, tend to be intolerant of personal risk, whereas citizens in the United States generally accept greater uncertainty and personal risk. Codes of ethics that are very detailed and attempt to mandate specific behavior may cause frustration for individuals who thrive in unstructured, unpredictable situations, but they would be well-received in societies intolerant of personal risk.

Internal auditors must be fully aware of the dynamics culture creates in corporations and in their codes of ethics. Auditors' assessments and recommendations will be far more meaningful if they reflect and incorporate these understandings.

PERFECT VS. IMPERFECT MARKETS

Market-based factors can create powerful incentives and impediments for corporations. In perfect markets there are no significant barriers to entry, meaning there are no significant capital expenditures or government regulations. In such markets where numerous businesses compete vigorously with each other for customers, companies may be inclined to violate even minimally imposed legal standards. These companies operate according to a survival mentality, as customers typically hold no loyalty to a particular business and product, and the company is operating with razor-thin profit margins.

Perfect markets require firms to act smartly, but they do not induce them to act ethically. In fact, perfect markets frequently are imperfect in their enforcement of business morality. Moreover, anonymity inherent in these markets further fosters unethical behavior.

In competitive markets, codes of ethics must be closely monitored. In the short run, the internal auditor should determine whether employee behavior is at the level minimally re-

quired by laws and regulations. In the long run, a commitment by management to a high ethical standing must be effectively transmitted and modeled to employees.

Imperfect markets dominated by large companies constitute a sizable segment of today's organized business activity. These oligopolistic market structures are created by numerous factors, including technological innovations, information asymmetry, large capital requirements, and government regulations. Reputation, industry stature, repeat business, and customer loyalty are key elements.

In theory, organizations in imperfect markets do not face the severe price constraints of intensively competitive markets and may be able to generate above-average profits. Consequently, these companies tend to behave more ethically than companies operating in intensively competitive environments. Their large-scale operations require collective action, with each individual contributing little in relationship to the whole. As a result, collective ethical morals replace individual beliefs, or, at least, they tend to influence individual beliefs to a great extent.

In such environments, corporate codes of ethics are usually more effective and controlled. Internal auditors should respond accordingly by helping to develop effective codes of ethics and ensuring employee awareness and adherence to those guidelines for behavior.

MELDING CULTURAL AND MARKET-BASED FACTORS

Unethical business conduct occurs in large and small firms, in perfect and imperfect markets, and in good and bad times. Thus, ethical behavior can be linked to a mix of cultural and market-based factors. The following framework can be used to assess the effectiveness and appropriateness of the corporate code of conduct. Such assessments can be critical as auditors determine the extent of substantive tests of the records and form an opinion of the reliability of the financial system. The framework is divided into four sectors based on competitive/industry factors.

SECTOR A: ETHICALLY HOSTILE ENVIRONMENTS

Although ethically hostile environments could occur anywhere, most of them likely lie in emerging regions where a common ethical framework and legal constraints on corporate behavior might be lacking. Many corporations in Sector A environments are strictly profit maximizers. Individual ethics, although present, do not make a significant impact on the culture.

The environment creates competitiveness, rather than cooperation, among individuals. Culture-based ethics can help neutralize the situation in the long-term. On the other hand, strong culture-based ethics can complement corporate codes, especially when the codes are strong. Nonetheless, behavioral changes may be slow and require constant monitoring.

In highly competitive and entrepreneurial environments, such as in start-up companies and the e-commerce industry, a sense of individualism is created. Individual ethics, and the culture-based ethics creating them, dominate.

In Sector A environments, initial emphasis should be placed on compliance with minimum legal requirements. Over the long-term, corporate codes can constrain corporate behavior to create an environment that fosters ethical behavior beyond the legal minimums. In this environment, corporate codes of ethics must be fully communicated to employees and be consistent with the ethical aspects of culture-based ethical standards. Behavior must be continually monitored and compared to the code of ethics. Sanctions for unethical behavior must be strictly enforced to encourage adherence to the code of ethics.

Internal and External Factors Influencing Ethical Behavior

IMPORTANCE OF CULTURE-BASED ETHICS

HIGH

SECTOR A
Ethically Hostile Environment
- Strong corporate codes are needed.
- Individual ethics lack power.
- Culture-based ethics can minimize environmental impacts.

SECTOR B
Highly Competitive and Entrepreneurial Environment
- Ethics are best controlled on an individual basis.
- Professional ethics may be more influential than corporate ethics.
- Culture-based ethics remain important.

LOW   **HIGH**

SECTOR D
High Growth in Economic Activity Environment
- Culture-based ethics are evolving.
- Weaker individual ethics exist since individuals are less loyal to professions.
- Strong corporate codes are needed.

SECTOR C
Regulated or Highly Stable and Mature Environment
- Industry is already in compliance with culture-based ethics.
- Individuals remain loyal to company and professions.
- Corporate codes maintain order.

IMPORTANCE OF INDIVIDUALS' ETHICS

LOW

The upper half of the framework, Sectors A and B, represent environments where the influence of culture-based ethics is significant. In fact, culture-based ethics in these environments tend to overshadow corporate codes. Conversely, in the bottom half of the framework, culture-based ethics play a much smaller role. Similarly, the left half of the framework presents environments where strong codes are necessary, because individual ethics lack power and tend to be weak. Individual ethics, on the other hand, are dominant in environments on the right half of the framework.

NOTE. This framework is based on a model that was developed by S. Sethi and L. Sama and published in the *Business Ethics Quarterly*.

SECTOR B: HIGHLY COMPETITIVE AND ENTREPRENEURIAL ENVIRONMENTS

In highly competitive and entrepreneurial environments, such as in start-up companies and the e-commerce industry, a sense of individualism is created. Individual ethics, and the culture-based ethics creating them, dominate.

Individuals in Sector B environments may have a closer alliance to their professional organizations than to the company. Because professional organizations may, therefore, have more impact than corporate codes on ethical behavior, management will likely want to encourage employee participation in professional organizations with strong codes of ethics. The professional organizations become the police force, with corporate codes filling in the gaps and shortcomings of the professional codes of ethics.

Culture-based ethics remain important, because they are ingrained in individuals, singularly and collectively. These ethics serve as a foundation for professional and corporate ethics. If the codes of ethics of professional organizations are to have credence, however, they must be consistent with the culture-based ethics of the vast majority of its members—and so must corporate codes of ethics.

SECTOR C: REGULATED OR HIGHLY STABLE AND MATURE ENVIRONMENTS

Regulated or highly stable and mature environments, such as utilities, mining, and railroads, may be the most ethical. The maturity of the industry suggests that culture-based ethics already are consistent with corporate policies. Also, the typical stability of employment in Sector C companies promotes more loyalty to the company, rather than to professional organizations.

Effective codes of ethics are perhaps most important in Sector C,

however. Older, well-established companies should already be in compliance with culture-based ethics, but as demographics change, the culture-based ethics become fluid. Corporate codes of ethics must adjust to these shifts where necessary.

Professional and corporate codes of ethics continue to be important deterrents to unethical behavior in Sector C environments. Corporate codes are an effective way of maintaining order, and they should effectively complement professional, culture-based, and individual codes of ethics.

SECTOR D: HIGH GROWTH ECONOMIC ACTIVITY

Dramatic, rapid changes cause stress on culture-based ethics, frequently modifying these ethics to conform to the new order. Individuals in Sector D corporations often experience confusion and inconsistencies, weakening the impact of individual, professional, and organizational codes of ethics. The environment becomes the pri-

mary focus, supplanting professional loyalties.

Effective, fully communicated corporate codes can be an important element in adding stability and consistency. Modifications in these codes may be required as the industry evolves and matures. In this environment, internal auditors must primarily rely on the corporate code of ethics to drive ethical behavior.

GUIDING CORPORATE BEHAVIOR

Effective codes of ethics are vital to organizations on many levels. At a practical level, they can also dramatically affect internal audit practice. In situations where unethical behavior is suspected, the lack of a code of ethics multiplies the internal auditors' required tests and significantly lessens the validity of any assurances rendered.

In their evaluations, internal auditors must acknowledge, assess, and consider jointly all the elements that act as powerful incentives and impediments in guiding corporate ethical behavior. Auditors must differentiate among the shades of gray and recognize that "one size fits all" cannot be applied to corporate codes of ethics.

JERRY G. KREUZE, PhD, MBA, CPA, is professor of accounting at Western Michigan University in Kalamazoo.

ZAHIDA LUQMANI, MBA, is an instructor of marketing at Western Michigan University.

MUSHTAQ LUQMANI, PhD, MBA, is professor of marketing at Western Michigan University.

From *Internal Auditor*, April 2001, p. 48. © 2001 with permission by The Institute of Internal Auditors, Inc.

LESSONS FROM THE DARK SIDE

WHAT CAN AN UPSTANDING MBA LEARN FROM A CROOK? PLENTY.

BY MICHAEL KAPLAN AND SETH STEVENSON

*Names of the three principle subjects and some identifying details have been changed.

There are two economies in this country. There's the one that's out in the open, that you hear about on the news, that Alan Greenspan obsesses over, that is tracked and watched and poked and prodded and scrutinized and studied. Then there's the other economy—the one that transacts its business at night, in bars, back alleys, and other shady spots just out of the public view. By some estimates the underground economy generates hundreds of billions annually in the United States. And while businesses like bookmaking, drug dealing, and ticket scalping may not be legally or morally defensible, they are businesses much like any other. To explore the ins and outs of some less celebrated, less respected expressions of American commerce, *MBA Jungle* sat down with a handful of, shall we say, extra-legal entrepreneurs. Then we ran their business practices past a few carefully selected analysts, with an eye toward finding points of similarity between those ventures you read about in the business section and those that show up on the police blotter. Let's just say they've got more in common than you might think.

JEFFREY*, BOOKIE, DES MOINES

It's a Sunday morning in November, just a few minutes before 10, and Jeffrey, 42, stares at a pair of six-line phones on his desk. Rangy and blond, in chinos and a pale yellow polo shirt, he savors each moment of silence in the basement office of his split-level home. Once the clock strikes 10, his phone lines will start ringing furiously. Fast-talking bettors will want to know the line, or point spread, on the Giants game, and fellow bookies will look to lay off a few of their lopsided bets. Jeffrey must remain cool while taking action and continually shuffling point spreads. Between calls, with the hold lights flashing like strobes, Jeffrey—who can clear as much as $30,000 on a good weekend—explains the finer points of his chosen vocation.

CUSTOMER SERVICE

Jeffrey realizes he's in a service-oriented line of work. Top customers get monogrammed golf balls and bottles of single malt for Christmas, invites to attend his annual Final Four party, and occasional loans if needed. If they want to bet more than he is comfortable with, Jeffrey brokers their bets to bigger bookies (rather than run the risk of losing business); and, if need be, he takes bets on weekday afternoons so customers' families won't know they're gambling. For general convenience—his and his players'—he puts a recording of the next day's line on his answering machine every Saturday night. "A lot of it just comes down to being personable, to relating to them in a way that goes beyond the betting," says Jeffrey. "I ask how they're doing; I know their wives and girlfriends. It should be like they're calling someone who is a friend as well as a business associate. I make sure they don't feel like they're negotiating with AT&T when they call me."

COLIN CAMERER, PROFESSOR OF ECONOMICS, CALIFORNIA INSTITUTE OF TECHNOLOGY: "To put it in cold terms, you want to make the customer feel guilty if he breaks off the business, because he thinks he's your pal. You create an emotional umbilical cord. Like any high-level salesman, his job is to make 100 guys each feel like one of his five best friends. When these guys are losing, it's his job to make them feel like this is no big deal, that it's just fun between friends."

ACCOUNTS RECEIVABLE

The downside for a bookie is that he always pays off when he loses but sometimes gets stiffed when he wins. In the old days, Jeffrey says, you were able to get a leg breaker to loosen the wallets of short-

fingered clients. These days a move like that is liable to result in police involvement—not good when you're committing dozens of misdemeanors and felonies every week. "If they don't make good on their losses, we're pretty toothless. A guy tells me that his car broke down, that his kid had to go to the doctor, that he's got no money…" His voice trails off, and he shrugs. "If we don't get paid in a week or two, we know we won't get paid at all. That's when we write it off as a cost of doing business." Still, there are a few options: "I'll try to make it difficult for him around town, by warning other bookies. And I'll call the guy who referred the deadbeat, and he'll usually make one call on my behalf to try to get the money."

CAMERER: "This is like offshore banking. Standard legal mechanisms don't apply, so you need to rely on a kind of reputational collateral. Deals in countries where there is poor patent protection get done like this all the time. One thing he could do is come down harder on the guy who gave the referral, tell him he should pay part of what this guy skipped out on. But if the original guy is a good customer, you wouldn't want to alienate him over this."

GETTING THE BUSINESS

Traditionally, bookies have maintained low profiles. But Jeffrey is a new-school operator. He lets people know what he does and sees no shame in it. Jeffrey imagines himself a low priority for the local police, characterizing his profession's status as "not 100 percent legal." This casual attitude affords the effusive Jeffrey the freedom to hand out business cards and network with the enthusiasm of a glad-handing real estate broker. He calls most people "Sir." "Some of my new customers come to me through referrals," he says, adding that he loves to chat about sports. "Other times, if I'm out in public, say, at a strip joint, and I hear people talking about a game, I ask them if they like to bet on football. They tell me they do, but they don't know who to bet with. I say, 'You're talking to him.'"

CAMERER: "He runs his business like somebody who's putting together exotic, potentially shady investment packages. And like anybody who gets between you and your money in a gray area, where the rules are not clear and the law will not help you, he needs to have a personality that makes people want to trust him and take a leap of faith."

DUE DILIGENCE

Gamblers tend to talk big, boasting about corporations they've launched, shopping malls they've built, and annuities they've received. But Jeffrey isn't easily impressed. When it comes to betting, he won't take an untried player at his word. Whenever possible, he vets new gamblers by asking for references (bookies they previously bet with, mutual friends) and sets initial wagering limits of $500 per weekend. "If somebody wants to bet much more, I ask him to put the money up; if he can't or won't, then something is wrong," he explains.

CAMERER: "He's operating exactly like a credit card company. He's doing as much of a credit check as he can, then giving the customer a chance to develop his credit rating so that he can be trusted with ever-increasing sums. And making somebody lay down the money up front is just like collateralizing a card for an iffy client. In that regard, he is practicing basic conservative banking."

HEDGING

A few football seasons ago, Jeffrey had a less than happy Thanksgiving. Starting on Turkey Day afternoon, all the favorites were kicking butt—a problem, as most gamblers like to bet on favorites. By that Sunday night, he found himself $30,000 in the hole. During the next few weeks, players doubled up their bets and things went from bad to worse; he sold his car and took out a second mortgage in order to keep paying off—doing anything else would have been tantamount to going out of business. He claims to have finished the year "a little bit in the red—my only losing season ever." That said, he figures that normally only 5 or 10 of his 105 players make it to Super Bowl Sunday on the plus side.

Jeffrey now pays more attention to keeping his bets balanced. "When it gets up to $5,000 on one side over the other, I'll lay off $4,000 with a bigger bookie," he admits, acknowledging that he maintains a bankroll of at least $100,000 to cover payouts. He receives a 10 percent fee on every bet and moves point spreads to balance wagers. "Once I figure out the public's trend, I make my adjustments to the line. Sure, if you give nine points while everybody else is giving seven, you can get rich as shit. But you risk winning the world or losing it," he says.

CAMERER: "Point spreads are like interest rates; one has to do with a sporting event, the other has to do with present

economy vs. future economy. Bookies and bankers like to keep everything balanced so that they can reap commissions without taking risks. It rarely works out perfectly, but the good banks try to get as close to that perfect balance as possible. Furthermore, part of what the bank sells to its customers is a certain assurance and trust, a guarantee that it will always be there, even if there is a rush on their money. Same thing with Jeffrey. People bet with him because they believe that even if he takes a beating, he will still pay off."

SANDY, ECSTASY DEALER, BOSTON

Sandy's not a flashy dealer in a sweatsuit and chains tapping your shoulder on the dance floor. He's a small businessman with a mortgage to pay. At 26, he's working his way through school and gunning for a legit job when he graduates. Sandy's got a steady girlfriend and two cats. He's articulate and polite, neatly attired, and a conscientious neighbor. Drug dealing isn't a cool lifestyle to him; it's a living, and a good one at that. Sandy sits on his leather couch, surveying a living room full of expensive electronics, and fields questions between answering his ceaselessly ringing cell phone and peering out his closed blinds (looking, of course, for a guy who owes him money). One more thing you should know about Sandy—he's a B-school student. Dean's list, in fact.

"I used to go up to people at clubs, hoping the next person wasn't an undercover cop. It was incredibly stressful."

VIRTUAL DEALING

Sandy barely touches the ecstasy pills he distributes. Instead, he quickly turns them over to a handpicked team of salesmen. "I used to go up to people at clubs, hoping the next person wasn't an undercover cop," he says. "It was incredibly stressful. I think I lost hair that way." Now he's strictly a middleman. He's only scared when he picks up a load of pills to bring them back to his place and bag them up for distribu-

tion. "That's when people get caught. They pull you over for not signaling a left turn, and then they search your car," Sandy explains. The pills generally leave his hands very soon after he gets home. For the most part, Sandy sells simply by making a few phone calls. He doesn't even have to leave his house. Sometimes, he never touches the pills at all—he just picks up the phone, puts the right people together… and takes a cut, of course.

"When there's a really hot ticket, we go stand in line, cut in line, buy our limits, then get back in line."

ANONYMOUS PROFESSOR, COLUMBIA BUSINESS SCHOOL: "It sounds like he's almost a 'virtual drug dealer.' A virtual business is when you don't manufacture and don't hold inventory—you just orchestrate. This is an evolving business structure, especially popular in semiconductors. You might contract out work based on a design, outsource the manufacturing, and mostly just orchestrate. Cisco does some of this, contracting out much of the hardware design, delivery, and packaging—it's virtual manufacturing."

BUYING ON CONSIGNMENT

Sandy gets "cuffed" 300 pills or more each week from a guy one rung above him on the dealing chain. Cuffed means the pills are on consignment—Sandy pays the guy back only after he's sold everything. If he doesn't sell out, he returns the leftover pills and doesn't pay for them. But it goes further: Sandy cuffs his pills in turn to several salesmen under him. He buys at $12 a pill and sells at $15. His salesmen sell to the actual users for $18 to $20 a pill.

PROFESSOR: "Buying on consignment happens when you have a high level of inventory that needs to be financed, so the supplier finances your inventory. Wholesaler to wholesaler, you generally don't expect to get the product back, but in retail, however, you can often actually return the product if you don't sell it. A common example is greeting-card stores. The wholesaler expects a certain fraction will be sold, and the markup is so huge and the cost of production is so low that it makes it okay if the retailer returns some of the product."

BROAD MARKETS

Sandy's customers range from shaggy kids at rock concerts to curious college types to party-happy yuppy workers. He sells to black people, white people, men and women. He doesn't discriminate and doesn't narrowly target: All are welcome to buy.

PROFESSOR: "At least he has a marketing strategy. He's got a clear focus in that he's chosen a broad market target."

QUALITY CONTROL

"The one thing that could really upset me about dealing," says Sandy, "is if I sold a bad bunch of pills and some kid died. I couldn't live with that on my conscience. But I've done research on the Web about the pills I have been getting, matching them up with batches that have been coming through the area, and all the pills have been pure MDMA so far. I think I'm getting good stuff."

PROFESSOR: "If you can guarantee quality, you can charge a higher price. With uncertain quality, your market can fall apart. Really, it's a matter of branding. For example, the name Sheraton assures you a certain level of service at a hotel, so you're willing to pay a certain price for that service. He's doing a similar thing."

DISPUTE RESOLUTION

"I'm always in control, so I could use my savings if something really went wrong and I needed to make a payment," says Sandy. "But the guys I buy from introduced me to this crazy dude they use when people owe them money. I only had to meet him once. Very big, very intimidating. I've heard stories about how he shot a guy, how he'll break your arms. He also drives a very nice car."

PROFESSOR: "In business, we call this guy a lawyer. It's just the chosen method of enforcing a deal."

GEORGE, TICKET SCALPER, NEW YORK CITY

All week long, George, 38, tall and skinny with a shock of blond hair, has been hustling Mariah Carey tickets— and the profits have been steady. The downside of his business, however, will soon become obvious. Crossing the parking lot of an East Coast sports arena, where Carey fans will squeal most of the night, George groans. "Tonight has the potential to be a disaster," he says. "The

box office is selling tickets for a show that was supposed to be sold out"—putting last-minute tickets on sale is an increasingly common tactic employed by promoters to thwart scalpers—"and now nobody wants to pay a premium. I stand to lose more than a thousand dollars tonight." Three members of his scalping team are fanned out around the arena, hustling hard. George stands near the box office, trying to poach people off the official ticket line by offering his tickets at mild discounts. By the time Carey hits the stage, George has dumped most of his tickets—at a loss. "Damned promoters," he grumbles. "They screwed us good tonight. I'm $1,800 in the hole." Don't feel bad for George, though. At a Knicks game a couple of nights later, he makes it all back—and then some.

BUILDING INVENTORY

When the Stone Temple Pilots announced a surprise show in a small nightclub, George beat other scalpers to the box office. With a crew of 10, he managed to corner the market, eventually holding more than half the tickets to the show, which sold out within a couple of hours, and clearing a substantial profit. His MO was pretty standard: "When there's a really hot ticket, we go stand in line, cut in line, buy our limits, and get back into the line; we ask all the people around us if they could get extra tickets for us," he says, leaving the impression that it's a fan-to-fan transaction rather than fan-to-scalper. "Afterward we put ads in the paper to buy and sell tickets, check with the ticket agencies, try to match buyers with sellers. At the event, we buy and sell, laying out our own money and buying as many tickets as we think we can sell at a profit. On the night of the event, I'm always looking for people who need to unload tickets but aren't pros. Ideally, it's a guy who'll give me a nice spread between what he'll sell to me for and what I know somebody else will pay."

ASWATH DAMODARAN, PROFESSOR OF FINANCE, NYU STERN: "The analogy for this is an IPO. If it's set below a fair value, you want to get as many shares of it as possible—just as they want to get their hands on as many tickets as they can, as long as the price is right. You can ask for more shares, but the problem is, like the one a ticket scalper faces, you may not find people who want to pay your price. Then you need to sell at a loss."

PRICING STRATEGY

A ticket's face value is irrelevant to George. "We determine the value based on supply and demand," he says. George watches public demand on the days immediately following a sale and uses that to set a base price. "Madonna is $250 for a mediocre seat," he says. "But I get phone calls from people who are willing to pay $350 apiece. At that point I might say to them that I can't do it for less than $400. If there are 10 people willing to pay $350, why not raise the price to meet the demand? But still, the tickets are outrageously priced and that creates risk. If you buy 100 tickets, you're laying out $25,000. Even for Madonna that's too much. She might add a night, which will put twice as many seats on the market—I think of it like stock splitting—and then the bad tickets will suddenly become worth a lot less. The good news is that I can go to a show like that with a few hundred bucks, start buying, selling, and get something going for myself."

DAMODARAN: "A portfolio manager's advantage is that the market does the dirty work of finding demand. If there was a sanctioned market for scalpers, there would be a room with a screen showing what people are paying. The interesting thing is that this is what eBay does. When you go on eBay and see World Series tickets up for sale, you see what people are willing to pay. It's the equivalent of traders looking at order books. If I were a ticket scalper, I would carry a Palm with Internet capability and gauge what tickets are selling for before setting my price."

TIMING THE MARKET

As show time nears, George monitors the flow of business. He watches the peaks and valleys and tries to predict when prices will dip for the last time. That, says George, is a skill that comes with experience. "A lot of people get into this business and lose money because they don't know when to stop buying," he explains. "If you get greedy and buy tickets that would have been profitable an hour ago—but prove tough to sell now—you will lose more than you win. I try to invest as little as possible at any given moment. I need enough inventory so that I can do business, but I try to avoid holding so many seats that I'm liable to get stuck with them after the show starts."

DAMODARAN: "Right here, George is operating in a manner that is similar to a market maker on the floor of a stock exchange. Sometimes a market maker will take a position on a stock and let his inventory build up. George does something similar when he sees, say, the parking lot filling with cars driven by fans who have no tickets."

BLACK SUNDAY?

The 2000 Super Bowl in Atlanta looked like a disaster. The city was hit by a surprise ice storm, flights were canceled, ticket prices plummeted. Scalpers were left with two possible decisions: "Start dumping at a loss or else ride it out, hold on to your tickets, and hope for an upswing in the price," says George. The positive tick came on Sunday morning when the skies cleared, planes landed, and ticket prices skyrocketed from less than $800 to $1,500 or more. "By Sunday morning there were a lot of people who wished they had held onto their tickets. Of course, though, it could have easily gone the other way and gotten even worse."

DAMODARAN: "There is a point in time when you need to unload, or else what you're holding on to will be worth zero. You might have a margin call coming, which would be the equivalent of a blizzard hitting and your ticket value going to nearly nothing. George is a lot like a stock trader: preferring to tell you about the ones he caught rather than the ones that did not work out."

From *MBA Jungle*, February 2002, pp. 60-65. © 2002 by MBA Jungle.

Crisis of confidence

In the first of two special reports on Enron's demise, we look at how it has shaken the nerves of many of the UK's 4.5 million employee shareholders

REPORT **ZOË ROBERTS**

ASK ANY REWARDS EXPERT ABOUT the Enron pensions disaster that followed the collapse of the US energy giant and the first thing they will tell you is that it could not happen in the UK.

More than 20,000 Enron employees in the US lost up to a billion dollars because their pension scheme was invested in Enron's own stock. The company had been matching employee contributions to the pension plan with Enron stock, but when the company started to go down, employees were prevented by Enron management from selling any of their shares, while executives were allowed to sell theirs.

The collapse has sparked a US pension regulations review.

But Graeme Nuttall, a member of the Treasury's employee ownership advisory group and managing director of share plans team Equity Incentives, told *PM*: "In the UK things have always been organised very differently, because pension and share plans are kept separate."

He pointed out that share schemes in the UK are designed to be incentive-based programmes rather than act as pension plans.

"The problem in America is that share schemes are so associated with pension systems and so much pension money can be invested in one company. This cannot be done in the UK," Nutall explained.

In the UK, pension schemes cannot invest more than 5 per cent in a single company. Nevertheless, there are concerns that the media focus on recent high-profile crashes in which employees have lost money, could spark a lack of confidence in share schemes.

"The share crashes of Marconi, Railtrack and Enron have not helped encourage employees to become shareholders in the companies where they work," said Roy Burdett, a senior consultant at New Bridge Street Consultants, specialists in share schemes and pensions.

Duncan Brown, European practice leader for performance and reward at pay consultancy Towers Perrin and incoming CIPD assistant director general, believes that, unless the company's shares are 'swimming underwater', employees will be savvy enough to ride out fluctuations in the market.

But he added: "These high-profile collapses may have a marginal effect, and employers could see a bit of reticence among employees to take part in some schemes".

David Hanratty, director of investment planning at company advisers Nelson Investment Planning, advises employees on schemes when they are launched and what to do with shares once schemes finish. He admits there is currently a degree of nervousness among staff.

"There are certainly some doubts after these incidents, particularly on the back of Railtrack," he said. "However, these fears are largely misinformed and unfounded."

Hanratty said the problem lies with what employees are doing with investments after a share scheme matures. "At Railtrack, the problem was not with the employee share scheme," he said. "It was what happened after the share scheme had ended. Many employees just sat on their shares. If you sit on £ 20,000 of shares in one company you are taking a big risk, regardless of which company it is."

The message now being delivered to companies is that good communication with employees on share schemes is essential to restoring confidence.

Robert Postlethwaite, partner in the law firm Pinsent Curtis Biddle's share schemes division, advised employers to ensure that staff have sound financial advice on the pros and cons of share schemes.

"It is important for companies to be very clear about what they are doing—whether they are providing pensions or access to share-based incentive plans," he said.

According to Hanratty, as UK pensions are 'watered down', with the shift from defined benefit (whereby the employer bears the investment risk and guarantees a final pension) to defined contribution (whereby the employee buys their own pension), employees will increasingly rely on share schemes to provide their retirement 'nest eggs'. This is a move seen in a number of companies, most recently frozen food retailer Iceland.

"These share schemes will be critical for employees, who in the future will need to create their own wealth," he said.

This means educating employees on how to get the most from their matured share schemes.

Hanratty explained: "Three or four years ago, encouraging employees to buy shares in other companies was anathema, but there has been a massive change in attitude as these employers are realising that it is a vital part of the incentive package."

Pro Share, which advises on the start-up of investment clubs, recently gave awards to water company United Utilities for the way it provides financial education to employees and offers innovative share schemes. Eighty-one per cent of United Utilities employees are involved in share schemes.

"We have a comprehensive maturity pack to advise our employees on what to do at the end of a scheme," said Rob Briers, secretariat manager responsible for share schemes at the company.

Briers also believes it is one of the only companies in the UK to offer employees a multi-stock ISA on maturity of schemes, which encourages them to diversify their share ownership.

From *People Management,* February 21, 2002 , pp. 14-15. © by People Management, Personal Publications Ltd. Reprinted by permission.

Dirty *rotten* numbers

Enron has made us shine a light on the books of America's public companies. Now, if your company carries even a hint of bad accounting, the stock will be savaged.

By Andy Serwer

In E.B. White's classic children's book *Charlotte's Web*, there's a scene in which Templeton the rat has just stuffed himself with the garbage left behind after a fair. "What a night," he says. "What feasting and carousing. Never have I seen such leavings, and everything well ripened and seasoned with the passage of time and the heat of the day. Oh it was rich, my friends, rich." That's what happens at the end of a fair or a carnival. After all the crowds and the excitement, what remains is nothing more than half-eaten cotton candy and assorted other trash. And so it is with the 1990s bull market. The tech-stock hawkers, mindless speculators, and clueless dot-commers have pulled up their stakes, and what we're left with is a bunch of smelly debris. The problem is, our digestive tracts aren't like Templeton's. We can't eat this stuff.

There's something terribly rotten with American business right now, and it's making a lot of us sick. All the new-economy lying and cheating that went on back in the '90s has come back to bite us in the you-know-what. And now it's judgment day. No more excuses. No more extended deadlines, extra lines of credit, or skeevy numbers. No more "just trust us." No more b.s. Even as Wall Street gazes hopefully at signs of a recovery, the market is ruthlessly separating the haves (as in, your numbers are on the level) from the have-nots (your numbers stink!). "It's sell first and ask questions later on anything that doesn't look clean," says Steve Galbraith, chief investment officer at Morgan Stanley.

Obviously, the trigger event here was the Enron scandal, which would give even Templeton the rat indigestion. Yes, Enron may have been a rogue operation, but its collapse has forced us to shine a halogen light on the books of America's public companies, and what we're seeing sure ain't pretty. In the last couple of days of January alone, stocks of Tyco, Cen-

dant, Williams Cos., PNC, Elan, and Anadarko were brutally punished for alleged or acknowledged accounting problems.

The price we, the public, pay for all this is absolutely mind-boggling. Former SEC chief accountant Lynn Turner, who's now teaching at Colorado State University, estimates that over the past six years, the cost to investors—in terms of stock market losses—of financial restatements is well over $100 billion. And that doesn't include Enron, which is in a league of its own. As Turner points out, the cost of Enron's failure is roughly six times the $15 billion loss suffered from Hurricane Andrew.

But the ultimate cost could be much larger. If Wall Street's growing anxiety about the quality of corporate earnings leads to lower multiples, CEOs will face increased pressure to maintain earnings by cutting back on things like capital spending, dealing a potentially lethal blow to the recovery. "I'm deeply worried about the effect of Enron on business confidence," says the CEO of a major technology company.

It is an environment that disturbs even the most seasoned Wall Street hands. "It's hard for me not to be angry," says Goldman Sachs' CEO, Hank Paulson, with regard to Enron and others that cross the line. "It's an issue of reputational impairment. Accounting is the lifeblood of our capital markets system, and we have a great need for improvement." Arthur Levitt, former head of the SEC, is even blunter: "America's investors have been ripped off as massively as a bank being held up by a guy with a gun and mask."

So what's going on here? Have we entered a new era of corporate moral decay? Why is this happening now? And what in the world can be done to fix this mess?

First, understand that dodgy accounting, or bad numbers, or whatever you want to call it, covers a multitude of sins. There are companies that, with or without the help of auditors, commit out-and-out fraud. Less egregious but almost as deadly to share-

---

The system's broke. Here are a few good suggestions on how to fix it.

Arthur Levitt

The former SEC chairman, who's now a senior consultant to the Carlyle Group in Washington, D.C., has never been shy about speaking his mind when it comes to questionable accounting. Levitt says that during his tenure the accounting profession lobbied against reforms that could have prevented some of the problems currently vexing investors. He favors establishing an independent oversight board that has real teeth and calls for diminishing the power of the AICPA, the accounting profession's trade group. The worst-case scenario? Doing nothing, he says. That could erode investors' confidence in the market and drive stock prices down.

Jack Ciesielski

From his offices in downtown Baltimore, Ciesielski publishes the deeply penetrating *Analyst's Accounting Observer*. And for an accounting newsletter, it's a good read. For the past five years Ciesielski has published an unscientific year-in-review history of accounting, including major blow-ups. As you might imagine, the number of black eyes has grown, from two in 1997 to 22 last year. What should be done? "One thing would be to make companies file their 10-Qs and earnings press release with pro forma numbers at the same time; that way investors could compare pro forma numbers with GAAP numbers." That would prevent companies from focusing investor attention on squishy pro forma numbers and away from GAAP.

Harvey Goldschmid

He's been a professor of law at Columbia University in New York since 1970, and he's counsel at Weil Goltshal & Manges. Goldschmid worked in Arthur Levitt's SEC as general counsel and special senior advisor. He's keenly aware of the pressure CEOs now face when it comes to making the stock of their company go up and stay up. "Previously the CEO's job was much more secure. Today, with CEOs that much more accountable for their stocks' performance, they are under greater pressure to keep the share price up." Like Levitt, he favors a new independent accountancy board for auditors. Goldschmid has been recommended by Sen. Tom Daschle to be appointed an SEC commissioner.

Warren Buffett

Three years ago the Berkshire Hathaway CEO proposed three questions any audit committee should ask auditors: (1) If the auditor were solely responsible for preparation of the company's financial statements, would they have been done differently, in either material or nonmaterial ways? If differently, the auditor should explain both management's argument and his own. (2) If the auditor were an investor, would he have received the information essential to understanding the company's financial performance during the reporting period? (3) Is the company following the same internal audit procedure the auditor would if he were CEO? If not, what are the differences and why? Damn good questions.

---

holders are companies that screw up unintentionally and are forced to restate their numbers. And then there are companies—and this is the largest club, including many of America's bluest of blue chips—that bend and stretch accounting rules to make their numbers prettier. It's not fraud—it's even legal—but it's deceptive.

No one can calculate how many companies are playing loosey-goosey with their books right now. We can only count them when they get caught, or when they restate earnings, or when a journalist or an analyst (God forbid!) raises a red flag. What's clear, however, is that there is more bad accounting out there than ever before. According to Michael Young, a lawyer at Willkie Farr & Gallagher, 116 companies needed to correct or restate their financial statements in 1997. By 2000 that number had more than doubled, to 233. Last year was probably worse. In a separate, confidential survey of big-company CFOs, some two-thirds said they had been pressured by their bosses to misrepresent financial statements. Only 55% said they had successfully resisted.

How did things get so wiggy? Declining corporate ethics definitely plays a role. "Today is significantly different from the 1950s," says Berkshire Hathaway CEO Warren Buffett, who has long been critical of accounting ruses. "Back then there was less disclosure, but the disclosure you had was accurate. In the 1960s you started to have more games being played. Conglomerates were trying to pump up their stock to use it as currency in takeovers, but old-line America didn't do it. It was still the good guys vs. the bad guys. It's not like today, where too often otherwise high-grade companies start with a number [for quarterly earnings] and work backward. Situational ethics has reared its ugly head."

Changes in the bean-counting business certainly haven't helped matters. In the late 1970s the federal government pushed the accounting profession to abandon a code of conduct that prevented accounting firms from undercutting one another on price or even soliciting a company that used another of the Big Eight (now Big Five) firms. The FTC said this was anticompetitive (which it was), but it also protected accounting firms from

CFOs who didn't like being told no. Under the new rules, if the auditor doesn't play ball with an aggressive CFO, it is much easier for the company to tell the auditor bye-bye.

But the single biggest reason behind the recent spate of God-awful accounting has got to be the rise of the cult of the shareholder. Simply put, over time so much focus has been placed on levitating companies' stock prices that many executives will do almost anything—legal or otherwise—to make it happen.

The cult of the shareholder began during the takeover and LBO boom of the 1980s, when corporate raiders forced CEOs to "maximize shareholder value." The explosion of stock options in the 1990s created millions of employee shareholders dependent on rising stock values. Then there are retirement accounts. (God love them!) Newfangled 401(k)s often became loaded up with company stock, making the daily gyrations of share prices a nationwide infatuation.

Let's not forget about senior management, which was increasingly paid in stock and options, and often compensated based on the performance of its stock or the company's earnings growth. Says Harvey Goldschmid, a Columbia Law School professor who worked with Levitt at the SEC: "Previously the CEO's job was much more secure. Today, with CEOs that much more accountable for their stocks' performance, they are under greater pressure to keep the share price up." And for one group of acquisitive companies, a high stock price was even more important. Cisco, Tyco, and others bought dozens of companies in the late 1990s, almost always with stock. The higher the stock price, the more companies they could swallow.

Of course Wall Street was a willing accomplice in all this. Analysts' reports became compromised by the banking side of their firms, looking to protect lucrative relationships with clients. According to Frank Partnoy, a law professor at the University of San Diego, as late as October 2001, 16 of 17 securities analysts covering Enron rated it a strong buy or a buy. Scary stuff.

The earnings guidance game, of course, is another facet of the corruption of independent analysis. Companies guide the analysts to a number and then magically beat it by a penny. The most adroit at this technique was Cisco, which until recently "beat" the Street estimate by 1 cent, quarter after quarter. That brings us back to what Buffett said about backing into quarterly earnings. If your company did 23 cents in Q1 '98, and you told the Street you were growing at 17%, then you damn well better hit 27 cents in Q1 '99! To Buffett this practice practically necessitates cheating. "No large company can grow earnings 15% quarter after quarter like that," he says. "It isn't the way business works."

Companies under the gun

Tyco It's impossible to tell from the financial statements just how much of the conglomerate's earnings growth is being generated from its continual stream of acquisitions—and how much is actually sustainable.

Williams Cos. Management admits it's in a fog about how to account for more than $2 billion in debts owed by a former subsidiary. No sign yet of a fourth-quarter earnings release.

J.P. Morgan Chase Investors are only now discovering that the bank may lose billions from its dealings with Enron. The company's financial statements provide no mention of the exotic offshore vehicles that it used to do business with the fallen energy company.

Calpine Last year the SEC instructed it to change the way it presents Ebitda in its annual report.

RSA Security In 2001 the company began booking sales as soon as its software was shipped to distributors—why wait until an end user actually purchased it? The SEC is investigating whether the change was adequately disclosed to investors.

And so to keep those earnings gains coming, executives have resorted to various gambits. One familiar one is trade loading, or borrowing from next quarter's sales, as Gillette once practiced—shoving razorblades into the channel in quantities that exceeded consumer demand. Or a company tries to book sales that may occur down the road. Some suggest that Verisign, which registers domain names, employs this practice. "You get a domain name for 29 bucks for a year, and then the company asks you if you want to re-up," says a hedge fund manager who has shorted the stock. "Even if you don't pay for the next year, Verisign books your next year's fee as deferred revenue, assuming you will come back." Verisign says it books roughly half of those fees.

ADDITIONAL REPORTING BY *Janice Revell and Julia Boorstin*

UNIT 7

International Human Resource Management

Unit Selections

Key Points to Consider

- How does the smaller world affect the practice of human resource management?

- What are some considerations of transnational firms in the human resource area?

- How would you expect organizations in the future to view the market for potential employees?

- How would you expect organizations to view compensation of international employees?

- How do you think the union movement outside the United States is going to react to multinational corporations?

 **Links: www.dushkin.com/online/**
These sites are annotated in the World Wide Web pages.

Globalization and Human Resource Management
www.cic.sfu.ca/forum/adler.html

Labor Relations and the National Labor Relations Board
http://www.snc.edu/socsci/chair/336/group2.htm

The world is changing and getting smaller all the time. At the beginning of the twentieth century, the Wright brothers flew at Kitty Hawk, and some 25 years later, Charles Lindbergh flew from New York to Paris alone, nonstop. In 1969 the spacecraft Eagle One landed on the moon, and Neil Armstrong said, "One small step for man, one giant leap for mankind."

Indeed, the giant leaps have become smaller. The world has shrunk due to transportation and communication. Communication is virtually instantaneous—not as it was during the early part of the 1800s, when the Battle of New Orleans was fought several weeks after the peace treaty for the War of 1812 had been signed. For centuries, travel was limited to the speed of a horse or a ship. During the nineteenth century, however, speeds of 60 or even 100 miles an hour were achieved by railroad trains. Before the twentieth century was half over, the speed of sound had been exceeded, and in the 15 years that followed, humans circled the globe in 90 minutes. Less than 10 years later, human beings broke free from Earth's gravity and walked on the Moon. The exotic became commonplace. Societies and cultures that had been remote from each other are now close, and people must now live with a diversity unknown in the past.

A shrinking world also means an expanding economy, a global economy, because producers and their raw materials and markets are now much closer to each other than they once were. People, and the organizations they represent, often do business all over the world, and their representatives are often members of foreign societies and cultures. Human resource management in just the domestic arena is an extremely difficult task; when the rest of the world is added to the effort, it becomes a monumental undertaking.

Workers in the United States are competing directly with workers in other parts of the world. Companies often hold out for the lowest bidder in a competition for wage rates. This often forces the wage rates down for higher-paying countries, while only marginally bringing up the wages of the lower-paying societies—a development that is bound to have a direct impact on the standard of living in all of the developed countries of the world.

As more firms become involved in world trade, they must begin to hire foreign workers. Some of these people are going to stay with the firm and become members of the corporate cadre. In the global economy, it is not uncommon for Indian employees to find themselves working for American or European multinational corporations in, say, Saudi Arabia. This presents the human resource professional with a problem of blending the three cultures into a successful mix. In this example, the ingredients are a well-educated Asian, working in a highly traditional Middle Eastern society, for a representative of Western technology and culture. The situation involves three different sets of values, three different points of view, and three different sets of expectations on how people should act and be treated. "Cross-Cultural Awareness" is just one piece of the puzzle.

American industry does not have a monopoly on new ideas in human resources. Other societies have successfully dealt with many of the same problems. While U.S. firms certainly will not adopt every idea (lifetime employment as practiced in Japan seems the most obvious noncandidate), they can learn much from organizations outside the United States. Human resource managers need to think globally, if they are going to meet the needs of their employees and contribute to the success of the corporation.

Faster and better communication and transportation are leading to a more closely knit social, cultural, and economic world, where people's global abilities can make the difference between the success or failure of an organization.

Article 51

Personnel Demands Attention Overseas

NEW YORK--Human resource considerations should be paramount when investment companies consider going global, and yet usually, they are given the lowest priority, according to Sheryl Colyer, global head of human resources at Citigroup Asset Management of New York. Colyer spoke at the National Investment Company Service Association east coast regional meeting held here earlier this month. The priority given human resources could be decisive in a company's success or failure abroad, she said.

Staffing is one of the critical issues for a company when entering new markets, according to Colyer. A company's approach depends on whether it is expanding overseas by acquiring an existing company or by building ones own, new operation, she said. Citigroup has both formed several joint ventures and made acquisitions in Latin America while it has created its own operations in Asia.

Regardless of whether a company chooses to build its own or acquire existing operations, companies must decide if they are going to hire locally or send workers from existing offices and pay expatriate costs, according to Colyer.

"We really need to think about this hard and fast and consider it up front," said Colyer. When going into other markets, there are certain skills needed, she said. In some cases, those skills will not be found locally. If some people have the necessary skills, there can be stiff competition for them and a company will probably pay a premium for the skills.

Companies should have specific plans with regard to expatriate issues, she said. When Citigroup reviewed its expatriate costs, it found that many people were "career expatriates," meaning they and their families lived abroad permanently, according to Colyer. That is not the best system because it does not make the best use of workers' experiences and because expatriate employees are, in general, more expensive than people hired locally, she said.

"What we've learned from this is to certainly have an exit strategy in terms of sending someone over to do specific things," said Colyer. "The plan is to train and transfer the skill and knowledge to someone in the other country or [to] rotate them out. We now look at the expatriate situation to be something not more than a 3-year assignment."

When a company buys an existing overseas operation, retention of the existing employees is a key concern. When doing a cost/benefit analysis and determining whether it is advantageous to go into another country, companies must figure in the cost of retention packages, according to Colyer. "Often we don't [do this] and we have found that it is a significant cost to retain," she said. "We try to phase that in over time." Usually, it can be paid out over a two-year period, she said.

"What we have found is that if you're not careful with your comp and benefit packages and how you staff your leadership in these countries, you become the recruiting ground or training ground for other firms," Colyer said. "It's important to note that, if a company is entering that country, they will pay a premium for that skill that you have spent many hours and dollars training."

Furthermore, with regard to compensation, companies need to determine which jobs are global, meaning they require certain compensation regardless of location, according to Colyer. The majority of jobs are not like that. "A one-size-fits all philosophy won't work," she said. "A pay scale out of New York may not be appropriate in Taiwan. Complications around a global pay scale severely disrupts the pay practices when you have other businesses in those countries."

Understanding what resources are available and at what cost, specifically with regard to human capital, is critical before moving into new markets, according to Sanjay Vatsa, vice president of global operations and business strategies and solutions at Merill Lynch Investment Managers of New York. "In some countries, people are less expensive than gas and water," said Vatsa.

"You have to understand the data mix in that country before you can adopt a process and implement a system."

While it is always important for companies to be explicit with regard to how they measure performance, it is particularly important when working globally because of the independence global offices are given, according to Colyer."

It is so important to be clear on the success criteria in terms of how you are going to measure the employee that you have across the world," said Colyer. "I can't overemphasize this. We don't do a good job, in general, of being clear with the success criteria—how will you be measured? What are the goals? We [at Citigroup] don't do it well when they're sitting in the same office, never mind when operating around the globe. This becomes critical because of the way compensation is perceived [and regulated] differently around the world."

For example, Citigroup has encountered situations in Latin America in which an employee's pay and title are associated with what type of car they can receive, and in Japan, where regulations impede a company from offering stock options at the same time as salary. It is imperative to make it absolutely clear what benefits come with any given position, she said.

Having a clearly defined organizational strategy is also important when going into new markets, said Colyer. Companies can either have a functional structure, where employees report back to the central office, a regional structure, where they report to a regional business manager, or a combination of both, said Colyer. Citigroup uses a combination of the two. In Asia, Latin America and Europe, it has regional business managers to whom wholesalers and people with other functions report, but these people have a direct connection with and report back to the home office as well. Having that dual approach can be complicated, she said.

"There can be a lot of misunderstanding around who makes final decisions about things," she said. "In our structure, because we do this combination, it appears as if we are decentralized, when in essence we are very centralized because a lot of our decisions are really out of New York. We like to think we are making them in a decentralized fashion, but… the regions around the globe really are not as strong in decision-making as we would like them to be."

The goal is to make decision-making regional, but this has to be achieved gradually, she said."

You want to get the decision-making to where the work is actually being done because you can certainly find yourself in this U.S.- centric thinking that does not hold true across the world," she said.

Culture is another critical factor, but is often overlooked because it is not tangible, according to Colyer. For example, when Citigroup Asset Management merged with an insurance company in Taiwan and got a part of its asset management business, the local Citigroup office was changed to the local name. That caused unexpected problems, according to Colyer.

"It was perceived [by employees] that it was better to work for a non-local entity and so the Citigroup name was important and [local workers] joined because of that," said Colyer. "When the name was going away and the local entity name would now be the name of the company, we ran into some severe retention issues because the employees identified with the name Citigroup as opposed to the local company, and they did not want to work for that local entity even though we would still be part of it. Don't underestimate or over-estimate the brand name of your entity around what that means from an organizational cultural standpoint. And certainly when you're doing marketing to your customers, understand the implications to your employees."

Employees and resources need to be specifically dedicated to human resources when expanding globally, said Colyer.

Andrew Brent

Cross-cultural awareness

*Effective managers can recognize and adapt to
different work styles and cultures.*

By Lee Gardenswartz and Anita Rowe

Getting work done through others requires a free flow of accurate information and open, productive relationships with employees. But that's easier said than done in a diverse workplace where many cultures collide.

Many a manager has been frustrated by the employee who nods in apparent understanding of a direction, then does just the opposite. Or there are the staff members who grow cold and distant after receiving feedback on their work, as well as the team members who clam up at meetings when asked for suggestions.

But culture is behind our behavior on the job. Often without our realization, culture influences how close we stand, how loud we speak, how we deal with conflict—even how we participate in a meeting.

While many cultural norms influence a manager's behavior and subsequent reactions, five particularly important ones are hierarchy and status, groups vs. individual orientation, time consciousness, communication and conflict resolution. By failing to understand how culture impacts individual needs and preferences, managers often misinterpret behaviors.

Nurturing a Safe, Inclusive Climate

When we ask people to describe a desirable work climate, we tend to hear very similar answers—regardless of geography or industry. Responses include words such as "high trust," "collaborative," "accountable," "feeling connected," "effective problem solving"and "feeling valued." But trying to create a climate in which complex work groups feel the same way about these matters is not easy.

Consider the norm of hierarchy and status. If you want all people to feel valued

and to participate in problem solving or decision making, differences in this norm could be inhibiting. An employee who has been taught deference to age, gender or title, might—out of respect—shy away from being honest or offering ideas because offering suggestions to an elder or a boss might appear to be challenging authority.

---

*To get the information and
effective communication
you need, you have to find
alternative approaches.*

The manager also may need to structure a climate that balances preferences for group and individual work. The employee who can't or won't subordinate individual needs or desires for the good of the group may perform better working alone.

A culturally competent manager will create opportunities for individuals to take some risks and explore projects that don't require coordinating with others. Doing so can encourage employees with a strong individualist bent to draw attention to important matters, such as policies or procedures that don't work.

On the other hand, when managers place too high a premium on avoiding workplace discord, even individualistic employees may be discouraged from providing potentially constructive feedback.

Time-conscious managers may see people whose cultures take a more relaxed view toward deadlines as being less committed to team goals, as well as less dependable, accountable and reliable. Or, consider the employee who nods "yes" but doesn't mean it. Both individuals are not only operating according to their own rules of communication, but they also are inter-

preting each other's behavior through that lens.

If you are a direct communicator, you probably expect a "tell it like it is," response from the employee. But the employee may be an indirect communicator who expects you to read the contextual clues to understand his response. His cultural background might require you to pick up on nonverbal cues to understand that his nodding and affirmative response is a polite, face-saving gesture, not an indication of agreement or understanding.

What happens with the team that clams up? Your egalitarian approach and individualistic orientation expects teamwork between manager and employees; you expect people to think and speak for themselves. But for staff members with a more hierarchical and group orientation, taking the initiative to make suggestions to an authority figure would be awkward for all involved. They may expect you as the manager to demonstrate your leadership by making decisions and giving directions.

Recognizing the Role of Culture

So what can you do? First, recognize the role culture plays in interactions and try to identify the critical elements of the cultures involved. What are your preferences and expectations, and what are the norms and preferences of your employee? Second, don't interpret their behavior through your cultural background. Most employees don't intend to be deceptive, difficult or unproductive; they are simply adhering to their cultural programming.

However, to get the information and effective communication you need, you have to find alternative approaches that are more in line with the employee's culture. Here are some suggestions:

- Avoid yes/no questions such as "Is that clear?" or "Do you understand?" Give the employee options from which to choose. Ask for specific information, such as "Which step will you do first with this new procedure?"

- If time allows, perform the task along with the employee or watch to see how well he understands your directions.

- Try using passive language that focuses on the situation or behavior, rather than the individual. For example, "Calls must be answered by the third ring" or "All requests need accurate charge codes in order to be processed."

- Give employees enough lead time to collect their thoughts before a meeting so they can feel prepared to bring input.

- Have employees work in small groups, generating ideas through discussion and presenting input as a group.

Developing Employees

One of the most important functions of a manager is developing and grooming employees for promotion. Cross-cultural norms have a huge impact on this job because of the underlying assumptions a manager might make about an employee's potential.

A manager who is aware of different cultural norms is less likely to incorrectly interpret behaviors.

To determine promotion potential, managers consider such questions as: How is initiative demonstrated? What behaviors show commitment? How much is high potential determined by accomplishing the task and how much is determined by good interpersonal skills? How do employees get to use and showcase their unique talents?

In answering these questions, a manager aware of the influence of hierarchy, time consciousness, communication and group orientation will make fewer assumptions about the motivations and drive of certain employees.

Initiative won't necessarily be defined as acting without waiting for directions but seen perhaps through the lens of a good team member who kept the group moving, made some contribution and helped preserve harmony in the face of expected differences.

Commitment may not be defined in terms of meeting deadlines but also as encouraging further exploration of an issue, and thus more creative or flexible in striving to get a best outcome. Perhaps an employee will never openly challenge ideas at a meeting but instead will offer back-door suggestions that can influence the direction of a project.

A manager who is aware of different cultural norms is less likely to incorrectly interpret behaviors and prescribe ineffective courses of action when developing people. Toward this end, here are some suggestions for managers to consider:

- Teach employees to interpret the culture of the organization by pointing out factors such as how people dress, recreational patterns and the formality or informality of communication. Employees can make effective choices when they clearly understand the informal rules of the organizational culture.

- Help employees understand the difference between deadlines that are non-negotiable and those that are more elastic. Get an accurate sense of the person's planning and organizational skills. Then, set clear expectations that help the employee perform better and build in followup sessions.

- Coach employees who are uncomfortable acknowledging their own individual work to talk about accomplishments through work group performance. As employees try to move up, the need to sell oneself in an unassuming way as part of a work group is a comfortable way to show one's part in a group's accomplishment.

- Focus on relationship building. An employee can learn that giving a manager feedback is an act of loyalty and help. But this is a paradigm shift that requires rapport, safety and trust.

Conflict: Dealing with Differences

Conflict is difficult to manage for most of us, and it becomes more so when employees and managers have different rules about how to handle it. Along with conflicts about schedules, work projects or assignments, differences in approach can spark conflicts. Some employees will prefer direct discussion of differences. Others will find this approach upsetting and disruptive to smooth work relationships. In addition, differences in attitudes toward status may influence how people deal with conflict.

Begin the awareness process by helping employees recognize these differences and share their preferences with one another. This proactive approach helps avoid unnecessary rubs by building a common base of understanding about the best ways to deal with each other. Beyond understanding, taking specific steps to resolve conflict in culturally appropriate ways is critical.

Here are some suggestions:

- Hold team development sessions where employees can learn more about their own and each other's conflict styles and preferences.

- In one-on-one sessions, help employees understand cultural differences that may underlie the conflicts they are experiencing.

- Consider using a third-party intermediary to help resolve conflict in a face-saving manner.

- Create a norm that says conflict is a normal part of any workplace and that resolving it requires give and take on all sides.

- Work to create solution strategies that meet both your objectives and those of your employee.

Lee Gardenswartz and Anita Rowe are partners in the management consulting firm of Gardenswartz & Rowe of Los Angeles. Both hold doctorates of human behavior from the United States International University.

Safe Haven

Accommodating the needs of employees
and families in hostile environments can
increase expenses and alter tax liability.

*By Barbara Hanrehan
and Donald R. Bentivoglio*

Family members accompanying employees assigned to foreign work sites always have been a major focus of international HR (IHR) programs, and the Sept. 11 terrorist attacks and the conflict in Afghanistan have increased concerns for their safety. Anecdotal evidence indicates that assignees in at-risk areas are not requesting an early return home, but some workers are asking employers to send their family members home or move them to a more secure environment.

Many employers are trying to accommodate these requests, but such a change in the family's residence raises a number of human resources and international assignment program (IAP) issues, some of which have a potential tax impact.

If the assignee's family is relocated from the international work location to their home or another location, the organization must decide whether to allow increased home leave for the assignee. This may appear to be strictly an IHR issue, but the organization and the assignee also face tax implications of more frequent trips home, as well as the costs of maintaining dual households.

Home Is Where the Work Is

Under the Internal Revenue Code (IRC), the tax home of a taxpayer is the primary business location, although that may not be where the family lives. That means that if the assignee's family returns to the United States, and the assignee is eligible for increased home leave trips, the costs of those visits are equivalent to taxable home leave. However, if the trips are coordinated with business meetings near the family location, they may not be considered taxable home leave, so HR should consider this cost-savings strategy.

Regardless of the tax implications, HR managers must determine the number and duration of reimbursable home leave tips they will provide. Prior to Sept. 11, most North American-based companies allowed one trip home per year, but that policy generally assumed that the family would be traveling together.

Paying for additional home trips may be significantly more costly to the company if the assignee is tax-equalized i.e., the company would generally assume the assignee's additional tax costs of the reimbursed extra trips in addition to the actual costs of the trip. If the assignee is not tax-equalized, the company could deduct these travel expenses as a normal compensation expense, but any travel reimbursements to the assignee would be considered taxable income to them. A third alternative would be for the assignee to absorb all expenses related to the additional home leave with the company simply providing the additional time away from the assignment. In this case, there are no taxable events to either party.

On another note, if an employee had been on a long-term assignment and the family moved back home prior to the end of the assignment, which had less than one year to run, the assignment is still considered long-term. But home leave trips do not qualify as deductible business trips if the assignment is for less than one year.

Middle Ground

Alternatively, some families many not return to the United States but instead may relocate to a country that is considered safer than the work site. Normally, if the assignee maintains a second household, only the expenses related to the household nearest the work assignment can be used in computing the housing cost allowance. However, in certain situations (for example, when the second foreign home is necessary due to dangerous or adverse conditions) individuals may include these doubled housing expenses (i.e., the expenses of maintaining a second home for a spouse and dependents) in computing the housing cost exclusion, according to Section 911 of the IRC.

U.S.-based assignees sometimes feel threatened by events near the work site and choose to relocate their families to areas that are more pro-American. Such adverse conditions could include war or civil insurrection. For example, if the assignee was originally in Pakistan and the family has relocated to Hong Kong for safety, the IRS would allow the housing cost exclusion to include the costs of both households. However, that would not change the tax home for the assignee, and the company's reimbursements for the assignee's travel expenses for trips to the second household would be taxable as compensation.

HR also must consider the taxability of moving expenses when the family relocates but the employee remains. Are costs of relocating the family a deductible (i.e., non-taxable) moving expense? For moving expenses to be deductible, the primary business location must change. If only the family moves, the primary business location has not changed, so the expenses are not deductible. If the employer pays moving costs, that would be considered taxable income to the assignee.

Protecting Employees

If the assignee (and family) remains in a potentially unsafe work location, the company may be required to re-evaluate and upgrade security arrangements, which could increase expenses. For example, providing a car and driver to certain employees would normally be taxed as ordinary income, because employees cannot normally deduct commuting expenses. However, under the IRC section that governs working condition fringe provisions, an employer may provide specialized tax-free transportation for employees whose security is threatened. Because many businesses have legitimate safety concerns when employees commute in certain foreign locations (including traveling to and from business meetings and business sites), employers may provide a driver and a specially equipped vehicle (for example, bulletproof), with the value being excluded from the assignee's gross income. However, the normal cost of commuting still remains nondeductible, and, if provided to an employee, it would be a taxable benefit.

A company must meet the following conditions to deduct the costs of improving employees' security:

- The company must establish a formal security program for its employees. The 24-hour plan must apply to the work location, the commute and the home environment.
- The company must provide a chauffeur or driver trained in evasive driving techniques. If the driver is not a professionally trained security driver, then no part is excluded from income.
- The overall security plan must apply to all aspects of the employee's daily life. If the workplace has been secured and the home has not been secured, the program fails to meet the overall security plan requirement. In addition, the plan must cover not only the assignee but also his or her spouse and dependents.

Similar rules apply to employer-provided aircraft if the assignee uses it in remote and/or large geographic areas.

Barbara Hanrehan is a tax partner with Deloitte & Touche's International Assignment Services. Donald R. Bentivoglio is a senior manager with Deloitte & Touche's International Assignment Services specializing in international human resources.

NOTES

Index

Index

Test Your Knowledge Form

We encourage you to photocopy and use this page as a tool to assess how the articles in *Annual Editions* expand on the information in your textbook. By reflecting on the articles you will gain enhanced text information. You can also access this useful form on a product's book support Web site at *http://www.dushkin.com/online/*.

NAME:

DATE:

TITLE AND NUMBER OF ARTICLE:

BRIEFLY STATE THE MAIN IDEA OF THIS ARTICLE:

LIST THREE IMPORTANT FACTS THAT THE AUTHOR USES TO SUPPORT THE MAIN IDEA:

WHAT INFORMATION OR IDEAS DISCUSSED IN THIS ARTICLE ARE ALSO DISCUSSED IN YOUR TEXTBOOK OR OTHER READINGS THAT YOU HAVE DONE? LIST THE TEXTBOOK CHAPTERS AND PAGE NUMBERS:

LIST ANY EXAMPLES OF BIAS OR FAULTY REASONING THAT YOU FOUND IN THE ARTICLE:

LIST ANY NEW TERMS/CONCEPTS THAT WERE DISCUSSED IN THE ARTICLE, AND WRITE A SHORT DEFINITION:

We Want Your Advice

ANNUAL EDITIONS revisions depend on two major opinion sources: one is our Advisory Board, listed in the front of this volume, which works with us in scanning the thousands of articles published in the public press each year; the other is you—the person actually using the book. Please help us and the users of the next edition by completing the prepaid article rating form on this page and returning it to us. Thank you for your help!

ANNUAL EDITIONS: Human Resources 03/04

ARTICLE RATING FORM

Here is an opportunity for you to have direct input into the next revision of this volume.
We would like you to rate each of the articles listed below, using the following scale:

1. **Excellent: should definitely be retained**
2. **Above average: should probably be retained**
3. **Below average: should probably be deleted**
4. **Poor: should definitely be deleted**

Your ratings will play a vital part in the next revision.
Please mail this prepaid form to us as soon as possible.
Thanks for your help!

RATING	ARTICLE
	1. HR Outsourcing—A Money-Saving Strategy
	2. What Is an Employee? The Answer Depends on the Federal Law
	3. Strategizing for HR
	4. Managing in the New Millennium: Survivors of Organizational Downsizing
	5. Strategic Human Resources Management in Government: Unresolved Issues
	6. A Statute for Liberty
	7. Sexual Harassment: It Doesn't Go With the Territory
	8. Why 9/11 Didn't Change the Workplace
	9. Dealing With HR Issues Following the 9/11 Terrorist Attacks
	10. Using Telecommuting to Improve the Bottom Line
	11. When Good Employees Retire
	12. A Dearth of Good Managers
	13. Matching Colors
	14. Playing e-Detective
	15. Learning From Experience
	16. Teamwork Aids HRIS Decision Process
	17. A Wealth of Choice
	18. Employees or Partners?
	19. The Extra Mile: Motivating Employees to Exceed Expectations
	20. What Makes You Tick?
	21. A Plan for Keeping Employees Motivated
	22. Enhancing Your Writing Skills
	23. Harmony in the Workplace: 10 Positive Strategies You Can Use
	24. How to Develop the Mind of a Strategist
	25. Creating a Learning Organization
	26. Is Your Training a Waste of Money?
	27. Brand Yourself
	28. Career Development and Its Practice: A Historical Perspective
	29. Choosing the Right Path
	30. What Are Employees Worth?
	31. Going Down the Road: Campaign for a Living Wage
	32. Pay and Employee Commitment: The Missing Link

RATING	ARTICLE
	33. Should You Adjust Your Sales Compensation?
	34. Executive Pay
	35. The Great CEO Pay Heist
	36. Disengage the Rage: Defusing Employee Anger
	37. How Safe Is Your Job? The Threat of Workplace Violence
	38. The Triangle Legacy: 90 Years After Fire, Sweatshops Persist
	39. Health-Care Costs: HR's Crisis Has Real Solutions
	40. A New Model for Controlling Health-Care Costs
	41. A Black Eye for Labor
	42. Labor Law for Supervisors: Recent Developments in Employment Testing—Part II
	43. Union Rules in Nonunion Settings: The NLRB and Workplace Investigations
	44. Why Employees Commit Fraud
	45. Enough Is Enough
	46. Temporary Solution
	47. Shades of Gray
	48. Lessons From the Darkside
	49. Crisis of Confidence
	50. Dirty Rotten Numbers
	51. Personnel Demands Attention Overseas
	52. Cross-Cultural Awareness
	53. Safe Haven

(Continued on next page)

BUSINESS REPLY MAIL
FIRST-CLASS MAIL PERMIT NO. 84 GUILFORD CT

POSTAGE WILL BE PAID BY ADDRESSEE

McGraw-Hill/Dushkin
530 Old Whitfield Street
Guilford, Ct 06437-9989

ABOUT YOU

Name _____   Date _____

Are you a teacher? ☐   A student? ☐
Your school's name
_____

Department
_____

Address _____ City _____ State _____ Zip _____

School telephone # _____

YOUR COMMENTS ARE IMPORTANT TO US!

Please fill in the following information:
For which course did you use this book?
_____

Did you use a text with this ANNUAL EDITION? ☐ yes ☐ no
What was the title of the text?
_____

What are your general reactions to the *Annual Editions* concept?
_____

Have you read any pertinent articles recently that you think should be included in the next edition? Explain.
_____

Are there any articles that you feel should be replaced in the next edition? Why?
_____

Are there any World Wide Web sites that you feel should be included in the next edition? Please annotate.
_____

May we contact you for editorial input? ☐ yes ☐ no
May we quote your comments? ☐ yes ☐ no

GO FAR...WITHOUT GOING FAR FROM HOME.
Nearby colleges want to hear from you!

Peterson's Regional College Survey lets you show colleges in your geographic area what makes you a great applicant. Complete the survey online at www.petersons.com/studentnetworks or return this completed form by mail, indicating which colleges interest you.

Enter Peterson's $5000 scholarship giveaway!
No purchase necessary to win.
Review the official rules at www.petersons.com/promo/code/scholarship_rules.asp.

*❑ I have read and agree to the 2007 $5000 Peterson's Scholarship Rules.
(Box must be checked to be eligible to participate in the Regional College Survey Program and the $5000 scholarship drawing)
*All fields marked with an asterisk are required.

West

*Name: _____

*Address: _____

*City: _____ *State: _____ *Zip: _____

Student Home Phone: _____

Student Mobile Phone: _____

Student E-mail: _____

Parent/Guardian E-mail: _____

Preferred method of contact: ❑ E-mail ❑ Home Ph. ❑ Mobile Ph. ❑ US Mail

*DOB (mm/dd/yyyy): _____ Gender: ❑ Male ❑ Female

Race/ethnic background—U.S. citizens and permanent residents only (optional):

❑ American Indian or Aleut   ❑ Asian or Pacific Islander
❑ Black or African American   ❑ Caucasian
❑ Latin American or Hispanic ❑ Mexican American or Chicano
❑ Puerto Rican   ❑ Other

School & Scores
Name and location of your high school:

High School Name: _____

City: _____ State: _____

*Expected year of high school graduation: _____

Estimated Current GPA: (4.0 = A) _____

PSAT Scores: Critical Reading _____ Math _____ Writing _____

SAT Scores: Critical Reading _____ Math _____ Writing _____

PLAN Score: _____ ACT Score: _____

Please indicate your top choice for field of study (Mark only one choice):

❑ Architecture   ❑ Dance   ❑ Music
❑ Art   ❑ Education   ❑ Physical Sciences
❑ Biology   ❑ Engineering   ❑ Prelaw Studies
❑ Business   ❑ Health Science   ❑ Premedical Studies
❑ Communications   ❑ Humanities/   ❑ Social Sciences
❑ Computer and   Humanistic Studies ❑ Undecided
  Information Sciences   ❑ Mathematics

For each item, mark an "X" on the appropriate line if you participate in this activity in high school or expect to participate in it in college.

	HIGH SCHOOL	COLLEGE
Academic interest groups	____	____
Arts	____	____
Community service	____	____
Debate	____	____
Drama and theatrical productions	____	____
Intramural sports	____	____
Junior varsity and varsity athletics	____	____
Music, including chorus, band, and orchestra	____	____
National Honor Society	____	____
Political/social issues group	____	____
Religious groups	____	____
School spirit organization	____	____
Student government	____	____
Student publications (newspaper, yearbook)	____	____

❑ Check here to receive information about relevant products and services from Peterson's and its partners.

*Please mark below the colleges you find most appealing and from which you would like to receive catalogs, viewbooks, and other admission/financial aid material.

CALIFORNIA
❑ University of La Verne

HAWAII
❑ Hawai'i Pacific University

NEW MEXICO
❑ St. John's College

OREGON
❑ George Fox University
❑ Linfield College

WASHINGTON
❑ Gonzaga University
❑ Seattle University

WYOMING
❑ University of Wyoming

This out-of-area school also wants to hear from you.

NEW YORK
❑ Eugene Lang College The New School for Liberal Arts

*All fields marked with an asterisk are required.

PETERSON'S
A COMPANY

BUSINESS REPLY MAIL
FIRST-CLASS MAIL   PERMIT NO. 4764   TRENTON, NJ

POSTAGE WILL BE PAID BY ADDRESSEE

REGIONAL COLLEGES CONSORTIUM
PETERSON'S
PRINCETON PIKE CORPORATE CENTER
2000 LENOX DRIVE
LAWRENCEVILLE, NJ 08648-9913

▲   Fold here to return (do not detach)   ▲

Please tape closed to mail
▼

PETERSON'S
COLLEGES IN THE WEST

2008

PETERSON'S

A nelnet COMPANY

PETERSON'S

A ⓝelnet COMPANY

About Peterson's, a Nelnet company

Peterson's (www.petersons.com) is a leading provider of education information and advice, with books and online resources focusing on education search, test preparation, and financial aid. Its Web site offers searchable databases and interactive tools for contacting educational institutions, online practice tests and instruction, and planning tools for securing financial aid. Peterson's serves 110 million education consumers annually.

For more information, contact Peterson's, 2000 Lenox Drive, Lawrenceville, NJ 08648; 800-338-3282; or find us on the World Wide Web at www.petersons.com/about.

Editor: Fern A. Oram; Production Editor: Mark D. Snider; Copy Editors: Bret Bollmann, Michael Haines, Brooke James, Sally Ross, Pam Sullivan, Valerie Bolus Vaughan; Research Project Manager: Daniel Margolin; Research Associate: Mary Penniston; Programmer: Phyllis Johnson; Manufacturing Manager: Ray Golaszewski; Composition Manager: Linda M. Williams; Client Relations Representatives: Janet Garwo, Mimi Kaufman, Karen D. Mount, Danielle Vreeland

ISSN 1525-3813
ISBN-13: 978-0-7689-2420-6
ISBN-10: 0-7689-2420-0

Printed in the United States of America

10 9 8 7 6 5 4 3 2 1   09 08 07

Twenty-second Edition

CONTENTS

A Note from the Peterson's Editors

Welcome to the world of college decision making. You are probably considering at least one college that is relatively near your home. It may surprise you to learn that the majority of all students go to college within a 300-mile radius of where they live. Because of that factor, we publish this series of college guides that focuses on the colleges in each of six regions of the country so that students can easily compare the colleges in their own area. (Two-year public and proprietary colleges are not included because their admission patterns are significantly different from other colleges.)

For advice and guidance in the college search and selection process, just turn the page. "Surviving Standardized Tests" describes the most frequently used tests and lists test dates for 2007–08. Of course, part of the college selection process involves visiting the schools themselves and "The Whys and Whats of College Visits" is just the planner you need to make those trips well worth your while. Next, "Applying 101" provides advice on how best to approach the application phase of the process. If you've got questions about transferring, "Successful Transfer" has got the answers you need. "Who's Paying for This? Financial Aid Basics" and the "Financial Aid Programs for Schools in the West" articles provide you with the essential information on how to meet your education expenses. "Searching for Four-Year Colleges Online" gives you all the tips you'll need to integrate the Web into your college search. Lastly, you'll want to read through "How to Use This Guide" and learn how to use all the information presented in this volume.

Following these articles are the **Profiles of Colleges** sections. The **Profiles** are easy to read and should give you a good sense of whether a college meets your basic needs and should be considered further. This consistently formatted collection of data can provide a balance to the individual mailings you are likely to receive from colleges. The **Profiles** appear in geographical order by state.

In a number of the **Profiles** (those marked with a *Sponsor* icon), you will find helpful information about social life, academic life, campus visits, and interviews. These **Special Messages to Students** are written in each case by a college admissions office staff member. You will find valuable insights into what each writer considers special about his or her institution (both socially and academically), what is expected of you during your interview at that college, and how important the interview is there. You will also be alerted to outstanding attractions on campus or nearby so you can plan a productive visit. In many cases, travel information (nearest commercial airport and nearest interstate highway) that will be of help on your campus visit is included.

And if you still thirst for even more information, look for the two-page narrative descriptions appearing in the **Close-Ups of Colleges** sections of the book. These descriptions are written by admissions deans and provide great detail about each college. They are edited to provide a consistent format across entries for your ease of comparison.

The **Indexes** at the back of the book ("Majors and Degrees," "Athletic Programs and Scholarships," and "ROTC Programs") enable you to pinpoint colleges listed in the **Profiles** according to their specific offerings. In addition, there is an "Alphabetical Listing of Colleges and Universities" to enable you to quickly find a school that you may have already determined meets your criteria.

We hope you will find this information helpful. Our advice is to relax, enjoy high school, and do as well as you can in your courses. Give yourself enough time during the early stages of your search to think about what kind of person you are and what you want to become so you can choose colleges for the right reasons. Read all college materials with an open mind, and visit as many campuses as you can. Plan ahead so you do not rush through your applications. Try to remember that admission directors are as interested in you and the possibility of your attending their college as you are in the possibility of applying. They spend most of their time reaching out to students, explaining their colleges' programs and policies, and simplifying the application process whenever they can. If you think of them as people who like students and if you can picture them taking the time to carefully provide the information in this book for you, it might help to lessen any anxiety you are feeling about applying. In fact, the admission people whose names you will find in this book hope to hear from you.

We welcome any comments or suggestions you may have about this publication and invite you to complete our online survey at **www.petersons.com/booksurvey**. Or you can fill out the survey at the back of this book, tear it out, and mail it to us at:

Publishing Department
Peterson's, a Nelnet company
2000 Lenox Drive
Lawrenceville, NJ 08648

Your feedback will help us make your education dreams possible.

The editors at Peterson's wish you success and happiness wherever you enroll.

The College Admissions Process

Surviving Standardized Tests

WHAT ARE STANDARDIZED TESTS?

Colleges and universities in the United States use tests to help evaluate applicants' readiness for admission or to place them in appropriate courses. The tests that are most frequently used by colleges are the ACT of American College Testing, Inc., and the College Board's SAT. In addition, the Educational Testing Service (ETS) offers the TOEFL test, which evaluates the English-language proficiency of nonnative speakers. The tests are offered at designated testing centers located at high schools and colleges throughout the United States and U.S. territories and at testing centers in various countries throughout the world. The ACT and SAT are each taken by more than a million students each year. The TOEFL test is taken by more than 800,000 students each year.

Upon request, special accommodations for students with documented visual, hearing, physical, or learning disabilities are available. Examples of special accommodations include tests in Braille or large print and such aids as a reader, recorder, magnifying glass, or sign language interpreter. Additional testing time may be allowed in some instances. Contact the appropriate testing program or your guidance counselor for details on how to request special accommodations.

College Board SAT Program

Currently, the SAT Program consists of the SAT and the SAT Subject Tests. The SAT is a 3-hour 45-minute test made up of ten sections, primarily multiple-choice, that focuses on college success skills of writing, critical reading, and mathematics. The writing component measures grammar and usage and includes a short, student-written essay. The critical reading sections test verbal reasoning and critical reading skills. Emphasis is placed on reading passages, which are 400–850 words in length. Some reading passages are paired; the second opposes, supports, or in some way complements the point of view expressed in the first. The three mathematics sections test a student's ability to solve problems involving arithmetic, Algebra I and II, and geometry. They include questions that require students to produce their own responses, in addition to questions with four or five answer choices from which students can choose. Calculators may be used on the SAT mathematics sections.

The SAT Subject Tests are 1-hour tests, primarily multiple-choice, in specific subjects that measure students' knowledge of these subjects and their ability to apply that knowledge. Some colleges may require or recommend these tests for placement, or even admission. The Subject Tests measure a student's academic achievement in high school and may indicate readiness for certain college programs. Tests offered include Literature, U.S. History, World History, Mathematics Level 1, Mathematics Level 2, Biology E/M (Ecological/Molecular), Chemistry, Physics, French, German, Modern Hebrew, Italian, Latin, and Spanish, as well as Foreign Language Tests with Listening in Chinese, French, German, Japanese, Korean, and Spanish. The Mathematics Level 1 and 2 tests require the use of a scientific calculator.

SAT scores are automatically sent to each student who has taken the test. On average, they are mailed about three weeks after the test. Students may request that the scores be reported to their high schools or to the colleges to which they are applying.

DON'T FORGET TO . . .

- Take the SAT or ACT before application deadlines.
- Note that test registration deadlines precede test dates by about six weeks.
- Register to take the TOEFL test if English is not your native language and you are planning on studying at a North American college.
- Practice your test-taking skills with **Peterson's Master the SAT, Peterson's Ultimate ACT Tool Kit, The Real ACT Prep Guide** (published by Peterson's), and **Peterson's Master TOEFL Reading Skills, Peterson's Master TOEFL Vocabulary,** and **Peterson's Master TOEFL Writing Skills.**
- Contact the College Board or American College Testing, Inc., in advance if you need special accommodations when taking tests.

ACT Program

The ACT Program is a comprehensive data collection, processing, and reporting service designed to assist in educational and career planning. The ACT instrument consists of four academic tests, taken under timed conditions, and a Student Profile Section and Interest Inventory, completed when students register for the ACT.

The academic tests cover four areas—English, mathematics, reading, and science reasoning. The ACT consists of 215 multiple-choice questions and takes approximately 3 hours and 30 minutes to complete with breaks (testing time is actually 2 hours and 55 minutes). They are designed to assess the student's educational development and readiness to handle college-level work. The minimum standard score is 1, the maximum is 36, and the national average is 21. Students should note that an optional writing test is also offered.

The Student Profile Section requests information about each student's admission and enrollment plans, academic and out-of-class high school achievements and aspirations, and high school course work. The student is also asked to supply biographical data and self-reported high school grades in the four subject-matter areas covered by the academic tests.

The ACT has a number of career planning services, including the ACT Interest Inventory, which is designed to measure six major dimensions of student interests–business contact, business operations, technical, science, arts, and social service. Results are used to compare the student's interests with those of college-bound students who later majored in each of a wide variety of areas. Inventory results are also used to help students compare their work-activity preferences with work activities that characterize twenty-three "job families."

Because the information resulting from the ACT Program is used in a variety of educational settings, American College Testing, Inc., prepares three reports for each student: the Student Report, the High School Report, and the College Report. The Student Report normally is sent to the student's high school, except after the June test date, when it is sent directly to the student's home address. The College Report is sent to the colleges the student designates.

Early in the school year, American College Testing, Inc., sends registration packets to high schools across the country that contain all the information a student needs to register for the ACT. High school guidance offices also receive a supply of *Preparing for the ACT*, a booklet that contains a complete practice test, an answer key, and general information about preparing for the test.

Test of English as a Foreign Language (TOEFL)

The TOEFL is used by various organizations, such as colleges and universities, to determine English proficiency.

2007–08 ACT AND SAT TEST DATES

ACT

September 15, 2007*
October 27, 2007
December 8, 2007
February 9, 2008**
April 12, 2008
June 14, 2008

All test dates fall on a Saturday. Tests are also given on the Sundays following the Saturday test dates for students who cannot take the test on Saturday because of religious reasons. The basic ACT registration fee for 2006–07 was $29 ($49 outside of the U.S.). The optional writing test is $14 and is refundable for students who are absent on test day.

*The September test is available only in Arizona, California, Florida, Georgia, Illinois, Indiana, Maryland, Nevada, North Carolina, Pennsylvania, South Carolina, Texas, and Washington.

**The February test date is not available in New York.

SAT

October 16, 2007 (SAT and SAT Subject Tests)
November 3, 2007 (SAT, SAT Subject Tests, and Language Tests with Listening*)
December 1, 2007 (SAT and SAT Subject Tests)
January 26, 2008 (SAT, SAT Subject Tests, and ELPT)
March 1, 2008 (SAT only)**
May 3, 2008 (SAT and SAT Subject Tests)
June 7, 2008 (SAT and SAT Subject Tests)

For the 2006–07 academic year, the basic fee for the SAT was $41.50. The basic fee for the SAT Subject Tests was $18, $19 for the Language Tests with Listening, and $8 each for all other Subject Tests. Students can take up to three SAT Subject Tests on a single date, and an $18 basic registration and reporting fee should be added for each test date. Tests are also given on the Sundays following the Saturday test dates for students who cannot take the test on Saturday because of religious reasons. Fee waivers are available to juniors and seniors who cannot afford test fees.

*Language Tests with Listening are only offered in November. See the Registration Bulletin for details.

**The March test date is only available in the U.S. and its territories.

The test is offered in different formats depending on the test taker's location. The TOEFL iBT tests students in the areas of speaking, listening, reading, and writing in an Internet-based format.

The TOEFL PBT (paper-based test) tests students in the areas of listening, structure, reading comprehension, and writing. Score requirements are set by individual institutions. For more information on TOEFL, and to obtain a copy of the Information Bulletin, contact the Educational Testing Service.

The Whys and Whats of College Visits

Dawn B. Sova, Ph.D.

The campus visit should not be a passive activity for you and your parents. Take the initiative and gather information beyond that provided in the official tour. You will see many important indicators during your visit that will tell you more about the true character of a college and its students than the tour guide will reveal. Know what to look for and how to assess the importance of such indicators.

WHAT SHOULD YOU ASK AND WHAT SHOULD YOU LOOK FOR?

Your first stop on a campus visit is the visitor center or admissions office, where you will probably have to wait to meet with a counselor. Colleges usually plan to greet visitors later than the appointed time in order to give them the opportunity to review some of the campus information that is liberally scattered throughout the visitor waiting room. Take advantage of the time to become even more familiar with the college by arriving 15 to 30 minutes before your appointment to observe the behavior of staff members and to browse through the yearbooks and student newspapers that will be available.

If you prepare in advance, you will have already reviewed the college catalog and map of the campus. These materials familiarize you with the academic offerings and the physical layout of the campus, but the true character of the college and its students emerges in other ways.

Begin your investigation with the visitor center staff members. As a student's first official contact with the college, they should make every effort to welcome prospective students and project a friendly image.

- How do they treat you and other prospective students who are waiting? Are they friendly and willing to speak with you, or do they try their hardest to avoid eye contact and conversation?
- Are they friendly with each other and with students who enter the office, or are they curt and unwilling to help?
- Does the waiting room have a friendly feeling or is it cold and sterile?

If the visitor center staff members seem indifferent to *prospective* students, there is little reason to believe that they will be warm and welcoming to current students. View such behavior as a warning to watch very carefully the interaction of others with you during the tour. An indifferent or unfriendly reception in the admissions office may be simply the first of many signs that attending this college will not be a pleasant experience.

Look through several yearbooks and see the types of activities that are actually photographed, as opposed to the activities that colleges promise in their promotional literature. Some questions are impossible to answer if the college is very large, but for small and moderately sized colleges the yearbook is a good indicator of campus activity.

- Has the number of clubs and organizations increased or decreased in the past five years?
- Do the same students appear repeatedly in activities?
- Do sororities and fraternities dominate campus activities?
- Are participants limited to one sex or one ethnic group, or is there diversity?
- Are all activities limited to the campus, or are students involved in activities in the community?

Use what you observe in the yearbooks as a means of forming a more complete understanding of the college, but don't base your entire impression on just one facet. If time permits, look through several copies of the school newspaper, which should reflect the major concerns and interests of the students. The paper is also a good way to learn about the campus social life.

- Does the paper contain a mix of national and local news?
- What products or services are advertised?
- How assertive are the editorials?
- With what topics are the columnists concerned?
- Are movies and concerts that meet your tastes advertised or reviewed?
- What types of ads appear in the classified section?

The newspaper should be a public forum for students, and, as such, should reflect the character of the campus and of

the student body. A paper that deals only with seemingly safe and well-edited topics on the editorial page and in regular feature columns might indicate administrative censorship. A lack of ads for restaurants might indicate either a lack of good places to eat or that area restaurants do not welcome student business. A limited mention of movies, concerts, or other entertainment might reveal a severely limited campus social life. Even if ads and reviews are included, you should still balance how such activities reflect your tastes.

You will have only a limited amount of time to ask questions during your initial meeting with the admissions counselor, for very few schools include a formal interview in the initial campus visit or tour. Instead, this brief meeting is often just a nicety that allows the admissions office to begin a file for the student and to record some initial impressions. Save your questions for the tour guide and for students on campus you meet along the way.

HOW CAN YOU ASSESS THE TRUE CHARACTER OF A COLLEGE AND ITS STUDENTS?

Colleges do not train their tour guides to deceive prospective students, but they do caution guides to avoid unflattering topics and campus sites. Does this mean that you are consigned to see only a sugarcoated version of life on a particular college campus? Not at all, especially not if you are observant.

Most organized campus visits include such campus facilities as dormitories, dining halls, libraries, student activity and recreation centers, and the health and student services centers. Some may only be pointed out, while you will walk through others. Either way, you will find that many signs of the true character of the college emerge if you keep your eyes open.

Bulletin boards in dormitories and student centers contain a wealth of information about campus activities, student concerns, and campus groups. Read the posters, notices, and messages to learn what *really* interests students. Unlike ads in the school newspaper, posters put up by students advertise both on- and off-campus events, so they will give you an idea of what is also available in the surrounding community.

Review the notices, which may cover either campuswide events or events that concern only small groups of students. The catalog may not mention a performance group, but an individual dormitory with its own small theater may offer regular productions. Poetry readings, jam sessions, writers' groups, and other activities may be announced and show diversity of student interests.

Even the brief bulletin board messages offering objects for sale and noting objects that people want to purchase reveal a lot about a campus. Are most of the items computer related? Or do the messages specify CDs, audio equipment, or musical instruments? Are offers to trade goods or services posted? Don't ignore the "ride wanted" messages. Students who want to share rides home during a break may specify widely diverse geographical locations. If so, then you know that the student body is not limited to only the immediate area or one locale. Other messages can also enhance your knowledge of the true character of the campus and its students.

As you walk through various buildings, examine their condition carefully.

- Is the paint peeling, and do the exteriors look worn?
- Are the exteriors and interiors of the building clean?
- Is the equipment in the classrooms up-to-date or outdated?

Pay particular attention to the dormitories, especially to factors that might affect your safety. Observe the appearance of the structure, and ask about the security measures in and around the dormitories.

- Are the dormitories noisy or quiet?
- Do they seem crowded?
- How good is the lighting around each dormitory?
- Are the dormitories spread throughout the campus or are they clustered in one main area?
- Who has access to the dormitories in addition to students?
- How secure are the means by which students enter and leave the dormitory?

While you are on the subject of dormitory safety, you should also ask about campus safety. Don't expect that the guide will rattle off a list of crimes that have been committed in the past year. To obtain that information, access the recent year of issues of *The Chronicle of Higher Education* and locate its yearly report on campus crime. Also ask the guide about safety measures that the campus police take and those that students have initiated.

- Can students request escorts to their residences late at night?
- Do campus shuttle buses run at frequent intervals all night?
- Are "blue-light" telephones liberally placed throughout the campus for students to use to call for help?
- Do the campus police patrol the campus regularly?

If the guide does not answer your questions satisfactorily, wait until after the tour to contact the campus police or traffic office for answers.

Campus tours usually just point out the health services center without taking the time to walk through. Even if you don't see the inside of the building, you should take a close look at the location of the health services center and ask the guide questions about services.

- How far is the health center from the dormitories?
- Is a doctor always on call?
- Does the campus transport sick students from their dormitories or must they walk?
- What are the operating hours of the health center?
- Does the health center refer students to a nearby hospital?

If the guide can't answer your questions, visit the health center later and ask someone there.

Most campus tours take pride in showing students their activities centers, which may contain snack bars, game rooms, workout facilities, and other means of entertainment. Should you scrutinize this building as carefully as the rest? Of course. Outdated and poorly maintained activity equipment contributes to your total impression of the college. You should also ask about the hours, availability, and cost (no, the activities are usually *not* free) of using the bowling alleys, pool tables, air hockey tables, and other ammenities.

As you walk through campus with the tour, also look carefully at the appearance of the students who pass. The way in which both men and women groom themselves, the way they dress, and even their physical bearing communicate a lot more than any guidebook can. If everyone seems to conform to the same look, you might feel that you would be uncomfortable at the college, however nonconformist that look might be. On the other hand, you might not feel comfortable on a campus that stresses diversity of dress and behavior, and your observations now can save you discomfort later.

- Does every student seem to wear a sorority or fraternity t-shirt or jacket?
- Is everyone of your sex sporting the latest fad haircut?
- Do all of the men or the women seem to be wearing expensive name-brand clothes?
- Do most of the students seem to be working hard to look outrageous with regards to clothing, hair color, and body art?
- Would you feel uncomfortable in a room full of these students?

Is appearance important to you? If it is, then you should consider very seriously if you answer *yes* to any of the above questions. You don't have to be the same as everyone else on campus, but standing out too much may make you unhappy.

As you observe the physical appearance of the students, also listen to their conversations as you pass them? What

are they talking about? How are they speaking? Are their voices and accents all the same, or do you hear diversity in their speech? Are you offended by their language? Think how you will feel if surrounded by the same speech habits and patterns for four years.

WHERE SHOULD YOU VISIT ON YOUR OWN?

Your campus visit is not over when the tour ends because you will probably have many questions yet to be answered and many places to still be seen. Where you go depends upon the extent to which the organized tour covers the campus. Your tour should take you to view residential halls, health and student services centers, the gymnasium or field house, dining halls, the library, and recreational centers. If any of the facilities on this list have been omitted, visit them on your own and ask questions of the students and staff members you meet. In addition, you should step off campus and gain an impression of the surrounding community. You will probably become bored with life on campus and spend at least some time off campus. Make certain that you know what the surrounding area is like.

The campus tour leaves little time to ask impromptu questions of current students, but you can do so after the tour. Eat lunch in one of the dining halls. Most will allow visitors to pay cash to experience a typical student meal. Food may not be important to you now while you are living at home and can simply take anything you want from the refrigerator at any time, but it will be when you are away at college with only a meal ticket to feed you.

- How clean is the dining hall? Consider serving tables, floors, and seating.
- What is the quality of the food?
- How big are the portions?
- How much variety do students have at each meal?
- How healthy are the food choices?

While you are eating, try to strike up a conversation with students and tell them that you are considering attending their college. Their reactions and advice can be eye-opening. Ask them questions about the academic atmosphere and the professors.

- Are the classes large or small?
- Do the majority of the professors only lecture or are tutorials and seminars common?
- Is the emphasis of the faculty career-oriented or abstract?
- Are the teaching methods innovative and stimulating or boring and dull?
- Is the academic atmosphere pressured, lax, or somewhere in between?
- Which are the strong majors? The weak majors?

- Is the emphasis on grades or social life or a mix of both at the college?
- How hard do students have to work to receive high grades?

Current students can also give you the inside line on the true nature of the college social life. You may gain some idea through looking in the yearbook, in the newspaper, and on the bulletin boards, but students will reveal the true highs and lows of campus life. Ask them about drug use, partying, dating, drinking, and anything else that may affect your life as a student.

- Which are the most popular club activities?
- What do students do on weekends? Do most go home?
- How frequently do concerts occur on campus? Who has recently performed?
- How can you become involved in specific activities (name them)?
- How strictly are campus rules enforced and how severe are penalties?
- What counseling services are available?
- Are academic tutoring services available?
- Do they feel that the faculty really cares about students, especially freshmen?

You will receive the most valuable information from current students, but you will only be able to speak with them after the tour is over. And you might have to risk rejection as you try to initiate conversations with students who might not want to reveal how they feel about the campus. Still, the value of this information is worth the chance.

If you have the time, you should also visit the library to see just how accessible research materials are and to observe the physical layout. The catalog usually specifies the days and hours of operation, as well as the number of volumes contained in the library and the number of periodicals to which it subscribes. A library also requires accessibility, good lighting, an adequate number of study carrels, and lounge areas for students. Many colleges have created 24-hour study lounges for students who find the residence halls too noisy for studying, although most colleges claim that they designate areas of the residences as "quiet study" areas. You may not be interested in any of this information, but when you are a student you will have to make frequent use of the campus library so you should know what is available. You should at least ask how extensive their holdings are in your proposed major area. If they have virtually nothing, you will have to spend a lot of time ordering items via interlibrary loan or making copies, which can become expensive. The ready answer of students that they will obtain their information from the Internet is unpleasantly countered by professors who demand journal articles with documentation.

Make a point of at least driving through the community surrounding the college because you will be spending time there shopping, dining, working in a part-time job, or attending events. Even the largest and best-stocked campus will not meet all of your social and personal needs. If you can spare the time, stop in several stores to see if they welcome college students.

- Is the surrounding community suburban, urban, or rural?
- Does the community offer stores of interest, such as bookstores, craft shops, and boutiques?
- Do the businesses employ college students?
- Does the community have a movie or stage theater?
- Are there several types of interesting restaurants?
- Do there seem to be any clubs that court a college clientele?
- Is the center of activity easy to walk to, or do you need other transportation?

You might feel that a day is not enough to answer all of your questions, but even answering some questions will provide you with a stronger basis for choosing a college. Many students visit a college campus several times before making their decision. Keep in mind that for the rest of your life you will be associated with the college that you attend. You will spend four years of your life at this college. The effort of spending several days to obtain the information to make your decision is worthwhile.

Dawn B. Sova, Ph.D., is a former newspaper reporter and columnist, as well as the author of more than eight books and numerous magazine articles. She teaches creative and research writing, as well as scientific and technical writing, newswriting, and journalism.

Applying 101

The words "applying yourself" have several important meanings in the college application process. One meaning refers to the fact that you need to keep focused during this important time in your life, keep your priorities straight, and know the dates that your applications are due so you can apply on time. The phrase might also refer to the person who is really responsible for your application—you.

You are the only person who should compile your college application. You need to take ownership of this process. The guidance counselor is not responsible for completing your applications, and neither are your parents. College applications must be completed in addition to your normal workload at school, college visits, and SAT, ACT, or TOEFL testing.

THE APPLICATION

The application is your way of introducing yourself to a college admissions office. As with any introduction, you want to make a good first impression. The first thing you should do in presenting your application is to find out what the college or university needs from you. Read the application carefully to find out the application fee and deadline, required standardized tests, number of essays, interview requirements, and anything else you can do or submit to help improve your chances for acceptance.

Completing college applications yourself helps you learn more about the schools to which you are applying. The information a college asks for in its application can tell you much about the school. State university applications often tell you how they are going to view their applicants. Usually, they select students based on GPAs and test scores. Colleges that request an interview, ask you to respond to a few open-ended questions, or require an essay are interested in a more personal approach to the application process and may be looking for different types of students than those sought by a state school.

In addition to submitting the actual application, there are several other items that are commonly required. You will be responsible for ensuring that your standardized test scores and your high school transcript arrive at the colleges to which you apply. Most colleges will ask that you submit teacher recommendations as well. Select teachers who know you and your abilities well and allow them plenty of time to complete the recommendations. When all portions of the application have been completed and sent in, whether

---

FOLLOW THESE TIPS WHEN FILLING OUT YOUR APPLICATION

- **Follow the directions to the letter.** You don't want to be in a position to ask an admissions officer for exceptions due to your inattentiveness.
- **Proofread all parts of your application,** including your essay. Again, the final product indicates to the admissions staff how meticulous and careful you are in your work.
- **Submit your application as early as possible,** provided all of the pieces are available. If there is a problem with your application, this will allow you to work through it with the admissions staff in plenty of time. If you wait until the last minute, it not only takes away that cushion but also reflects poorly on your sense of priorities.
- **Keep a copy** of the completed application, whether it is a photocopy or a copy saved on your computer.

---

electronically or by mail, make sure you follow up with the college to ensure their receipt.

THE APPLICATION ESSAY

Whereas the other portions of your application—your transcript, test scores, and involvement in extracurricular activities—are a reflection of what you've accomplished up to this point, your application essay is an opportunity to present yourself in the here and now. The essay shows your originality and verbal skills and is very important. Test scores and grades may represent your academic results, but your essay shows how you approach a topic or problem and express your opinion.

Some colleges may request one essay or a combination of essays and short-answer topics to learn more about who you are and how well you can communicate your thoughts. Common essay topics cover such simple themes as writing about yourself and your experiences or why you want to attend that particular school. Other colleges will ask that you show your imaginative or creative side by writing about a favorite author, for instance, or commenting on a hypothetical situation. In such cases, they will be looking at your thought processes and level of creativity.

Admissions officers, particularly those at small or mid-size colleges, use the essay to determine how you, as a

student, will fit into life at that college. The essay, therefore, is a critical component of the application process. Here are some tips for writing a winning essay:

- Colleges are looking for an honest representation of who you are and what you think. Make sure that the tone of the essay reflects enthusiasm, maturity, creativity, the ability to communicate, talent, and your leadership skills.

- Be sure you set aside enough time to write the essay, revise it, and revise it *again*. Running "spell check" will only detect a fraction of the errors you probably made on your first pass at writing it. Take a break and then come back to it and reread it. You will probably notice other style, content, and grammar problems—and ways that you can improve the essay overall.

- Always answer the question that is being asked, making sure that you are specific, clear, and true to your personality.

- Enlist the help of reviewers who know you well—friends, parents, teachers—since they are likely to be the most honest and will keep you on track in the presentation of your true self.

THE PERSONAL INTERVIEW

Although it is relatively rare that a personal interview is required, many colleges recommend that you take this opportunity for a face-to-face discussion with a member of the admissions staff. Read through the application materials to determine whether or not a college places great emphasis on the interview. If they strongly recommend that you have one, it may work against you to forego it.

In contrast to a group interview and some alumni interviews, which are intended to provide information about a college, the personal interview is viewed both as an information session and as further evaluation of your skills and strengths. You will meet with a member of the admissions staff who will be assessing your personal qualities, high school preparation, and your capacity to contribute to undergraduate life at the institution. On average, these meetings last about 45 minutes—a relatively short amount of time in which to gather information and leave the desired impression—so here are some suggestions on how to make the most of it.

Scheduling Your Visit

Generally, students choose to visit campuses in the summer or fall of their senior year. Both times have their advantages. A summer visit, when the campus is not in session, generally allows for a less hectic visit and interview. Visiting in the fall, on the other hand, provides the opportunity to see

what campus life is like in full swing. If you choose the fall, consider arranging an overnight trip so that you can stay in one of the college dormitories. At the very least, you should make your way around campus to take part in classes, athletic events, and social activities. Always make an appointment and avoid scheduling more than two college interviews on any given day. Multiple interviews in a single day hinder your chances of making a good impression, and your impressions of the colleges will blur into each other as you hurriedly make your way from place to place.

Preparation

Know the basics about the college before going for your interview. Read the college viewbook or catalog in addition to this guide. You will be better prepared to ask questions that are not answered in the literature and that will give you a better understanding of what the college has to offer. You should also spend some time thinking about your strengths and weaknesses and, in particular, what you are looking for in a college education. You will find that as you get a few interviews under your belt, they will get easier. You might consider starting with a college that is not a top contender on your list, so that the stakes are not as high.

Asking Questions

Inevitably, your interviewer will ask you, "Do you have any questions?" Not having one may suggest that you're unprepared or, even worse, not interested. When you do ask questions, make sure that they are ones that matter to you and that have a bearing on your decision about whether or not to attend that college. The questions that you ask will give the interviewer some insight into your personality and priorities. Avoid asking questions that are answered in the college literature—again, a sign of unpreparedness. Although the interviewer will undoubtedly pose questions to you, the interview should not be viewed merely as a question-and-answer session. If a conversation evolves out of a particular question, so much the better. Your interviewer can learn a great deal about you from how you sustain a conversation. Similarly, you will be able to learn a great deal about the college in a conversational format.

Separate the Interview from the Interviewer

Many students base their feelings about a college solely on their impressions of the interviewer. Try not to characterize a college based only on your personal reaction, however, since your impressions can be skewed by whether you and your interviewer hit it off. Pay lots of attention to everything

else that you see, hear, and learn about a college. Once on campus, you may never see your interviewer again.

In the end, remember to relax and be yourself. Your interviewer will expect you to be somewhat nervous, which will relieve some of the pressure. Don't drink jitters-producing caffeinated beverages prior to the interview, and suppress nervous fidgets like leg-wagging, finger-drumming, or bracelet-jangling. Consider your interview an opportunity to put forth your best effort and to enhance everything that the college knows about you up to this point.

THE FINAL DECISION

Once you have received your acceptance letters, it is time to go back and look at the whole picture. Provided you received more than one acceptance, you are now in a position to compare your options. The best way to do this is to compare your original list of important college-ranking criteria with what you've discovered about each college along the way. In addition, you and your family will need to factor in the financial aid component. You will need to look beyond these cost issues and the quantifiable pros and cons of each college, however, and know that you have a good feeling about your final choice. Before sending off your acceptance letter, you need to feel confident that the college will feel like home for the next four years. Once the choice is made, the only hard part will be waiting for an entire summer before heading off to college!

Successful Transfer

Adrienne Aaron Rulnick

Transfer students need and deserve detailed and accurate information but often lack direction as to where it can be obtained. Few general college guides offer information about transfer deadlines and required minimum grade point averages for transfer admission. College catalogs are not always clear about the specific requirements and procedures for transfer students who may be confused about whether they need to present high school records, SAT or ACT scores, or a guidance counselor's recommendation, particularly if they have been out of high school for several years. Transfer advisers are not available to those enrolled at a baccalaureate institution; at community and junior colleges, the transfer advising function may be performed by a designated transfer counselor or by a variety of college advisers who are less clearly identified.

The challenge for transfer students is to determine what they need to know in order to make good, informed decisions and identify the individuals and resources that can provide that information. An organized research process is very much at the heart of a successful transfer.

HOW TO BEGIN

Perhaps the most important first step in this process is one of self-analysis. Adopting a consumer approach is appropriate—higher education is a formidable purchase, no matter how it is financed. The reputation of the college from which you obtain your degree may open doors to future jobs and careers; friendships and contacts you make at college can provide a significant network for lifelong social and professional relationships. The environment of a transfer school may be the perfect opportunity for you to test out urban living or the joys of country life, explore a different area of the country, experience college residential living for the first time, or move out of the family nest into your first apartment. Like any major purchase in your life, there are costs and benefits to be weighed. Trade-offs include cost, distance, rigor of academic work, extra time in school required by a cooperative education program, and specific requirements, such as foreign language competence at a liberal arts institution or courses in religion at an institution with a denominational affiliation.

USE EXPERIENCE AS A GUIDE

The wise consumer reflects on his or her own experience with a product (i.e., your initial college or colleges) and then seeks out people who have firsthand experience with the new product being considered. Talk to friends and family members who have attended the colleges you are considering; ask college faculty members you know to tell you about the colleges they attended and how they view these schools. Talk to people engaged in the careers you are considering: What are their impressions of the best programs and schools in their field? Make sure you sample a variety of opinions, but beware of dated experiences. An engineering department considered top-notch when Uncle Joe attended college twenty years ago might be very different today!

THE NITTY-GRITTY

Once your list is reduced to a manageable number of schools, it is important to identify academic requirements, requisite grade point averages for admission, and deadline dates. Most schools admit for both the fall and spring semesters; those on a trimester system may have winter and summer admissions as well. Some schools have rolling admission policies and will process applications as they are received; others, particularly the more selective colleges, have firm deadlines because their admission process involves a committee review, and decisions are made on a competitive basis. It is helpful to know how many transfer students are typically accepted for the semester you wish to begin, whether the minimum grade point average is indicative of the actual average of accepted students (this can vary widely), and whether the major you are seeking has special prerequisites and admission procedures. For example, fine arts programs admission procedures usually require portfolios or auditions. For engineering, computer science, and some business majors, there are specific requirements in mathematics that must be met before a student is considered for admission. Many specialized health-care programs, including nursing, may only admit once a year. Some schools have different standards for sophomore and junior transfers or for in-state and out-of-state students.

Other criteria that you should identify include whether college housing and financial aid are available for transfer students. Some colleges have special transfer scholarships that require separate applications and references, while others simply award aid based on applications that indicate a high grade point average or membership in a nationally recognized junior and community college honor society, such as Phi Theta Kappa. There are also scholarships for

transfer students who demonstrate accomplishment in specified academic and performance areas; the latter may be based on talent competitions or accomplishment evidenced in a portfolio or audition.

NONTRADITIONAL STUDENTS

For the nontraditional student, usually defined as anyone beyond the traditional college age range of 18 to 23, there may be additional aspects to investigate. Some colleges award credit based on demonstrated life experience; many colleges grant credit for qualifying scores on the CLEP exams or for participation in the DANTES program. Experience in industry may yield college credit as well. If you are ready and able to pursue further college work but are not in a position to attend regular classes, there are a variety of distance learning options at fully accredited colleges. Other colleges provide specialized support services for nontraditional students and may allow students the opportunity to attend part-time if they have family and work responsibilities. In some cases, usually at large universities, there may be married student housing or family housing available. More and more schools have established day-care facilities, although the waiting lists are often very long.

APPLYING

Once you have identified the schools that meet the needs you have established as priorities, it is time to begin the application process. Make sure you observe all the indicated deadlines. It never hurts to have everything in early, as there can be consequences, such as closed-out majors and the loss of housing and financial aid, if you submit your application late. Make appointments with faculty members and others who are providing references; make sure they understand what is required of them and when and where their references must be sent. It is your responsibility to follow through to make sure all of your credentials are received, including transcripts from all colleges previously attended, even if you only took one summer course or

attended for less than a semester. If you have not yet had the opportunity to visit the schools to which you are applying, now is the time to do so. Arrange interviews wherever possible, and make sure to include a tour of the campus and visits to the department and career offices to gain a picture of the facilities and future opportunities. If you have questions about financial aid, schedule an appointment in the financial aid office, and make sure you are aware of all the deadlines and requirements and any scholarship opportunities for which you are eligible.

MAKING YOUR CHOICE

Congratulations! You have been accepted at the colleges of your choice. Now what? Carefully review the acceptance of your previous college credit and how it has been applied. You are entitled to know how many transfer credits you have received and your expected date of graduation. Compare financial aid packages and housing options. The best choice should emerge from this review process. Then, send a note to the schools you will not be attending. Acknowledge your acceptance, but indicate that you have chosen to attend elsewhere. Carefully read everything you have received from the college of your choice. Return required deposits within the deadline, reserve time to attend transfer orientation, arrange to have your final transcript sent from the college you currently attend, and review the financial picture. This is the time to finalize college loan applications and make sure you are in a position to meet all the costs entailed at this college. Don't forget to include the costs of travel and housing.

You've done it! While many transfer students reflect on how much work was involved in the transfer admission process, those who took the time to follow all of the steps outlined report a sense of satisfaction with their choices and increased confidence in themselves.

Adrienne Aaron Rulnick was formerly a Transfer Counselor at Berkshire Community College.

Who's Paying for This? Financial Aid Basics

A college education can be expensive—costing more than $150,000 for four years at some of the higher priced private colleges and universities. Even at the lower cost state colleges and universities, the cost of a four-year education can approach $60,000. Determining how you and your family will come up with the necessary funds to pay for your education requires planning, perseverance, and learning as much as you can about the options that are available to you. But before you get discouraged, recent College Board statistics show that 42 percent of full-time students attend four-year public and private colleges with tuition and fees less than $6000, while 13 percent attend colleges that have tuition and fees more than $24,000. College costs tend to be less in the western states and higher in New England.

Paying for college should not be looked at as a four-year financial commitment. For many families, paying the total cost of a student's college education out of current income and savings is usually not realistic. For families that have planned ahead and have financial savings established for higher education, the burden is a lot easier. But for most, meeting the cost of college requires the pooling of current income and assets and investing in longer-term loan options. These family resources, together with financial assistance from state, federal, and institutional sources, enable millions of students each year to attend the institution of their choice.

FINANCIAL AID PROGRAMS

There are three types of financial aid:

1. Gift-aid—Scholarships and grants are funds that do not have to be repaid.
2. Loans—Loans must be repaid, usually after graduation; the amount you have to pay back is the total you've borrowed plus any accrued interest. This is considered a source of self-help aid.
3. Student employment—Student employment is a job arranged for you by the financial aid office. This is another source of self-help aid.

The federal government has four major grant programs— the Federal Pell Grant, the Federal Supplemental Educational Opportunity Grant, Academic Competitiveness Grants (ACG), and SMART grants. ACG and SMART grants are limited to students who qualify for a Pell grant and are awarded to a select group of students. Overall, these grants are targeted to low-to-moderate income families with significant financial need. The federal government also sponsors a student employment program called the Federal Work-Study Program, which offers jobs both on and off campus; and several loan programs, including those for students and for parents of undergraduate students.

There are two types of student loan programs: subsidized and unsubsidized. The subsidized Federal Stafford Student Loan and the Federal Perkins Loan are need-based, government-subsidized loans. Students who borrow through these programs do not have to pay interest on the loan until after they graduate or leave school. The unsubsidized Federal Stafford Student Loan and the Parent Loan Program are not based on need, and borrowers are responsible for the interest while the student is in school. There are different methods on how these loans are administered. Once you choose your college, the financial aid office will guide you through this process.

After you've submitted your financial aid application and you've been accepted for admission, each college will send you a letter describing your financial aid award. Most award letters show estimated college costs, how much you and your family are expected to contribute, and the amount and types of aid you have been awarded. Most students are awarded aid from a combination of sources and programs. Hence, your award is often called a financial aid "package."

SOURCES OF FINANCIAL AID

More than 12 million students and family apply for financial aid each year. Financial aid from all sources exceeds $152 billion per year. The largest single source of aid is the federal government, which awarded more than $94 billion during 2005–06.

The next largest source of financial aid is found in the college and university community. Institutions award an estimated $24.4 billion to students each year. Most of this aid is awarded to students who have a demonstrated need based on the Federal Methodology. Some institutions use a

different formula, the Institutional Methodology (IM), to award their own funds in conjunction with other forms of aid. Institutional aid may be either need-based or non-need based. Aid that is not based on need is usually awarded for a student's academic performance (merit awards), specific talents or abilities, or to attract the type of students a college seeks to enroll.

Another source of financial aid is from state government, awarding more than $6.8 billion per year. All states offer grant and/or scholarship aid, most of which is need-based. However, more and more states are offering substantial merit-based aid programs. Most state programs award aid only to students attending college in their home state.

Other sources of financial aid include:

- Private agencies
- Foundations
- Corporations
- Clubs
- Fraternal and service organizations
- Civic associations
- Unions
- Religious groups that award grants, scholarships, and low-interest loans
- Employers that provide tuition reimbursement benefits for employees and their children

More information about these different sources of aid is available from high school guidance offices, public libraries, college financial aid offices, directly from the sponsoring organizations, and on the Web at www.petersons.com and www.finaid.org.

HOW NEED-BASED FINANCIAL AID IS AWARDED

When you apply for aid, your family's financial situation is analyzed using a government-approved formula called the Federal Methodology. This formula looks at five items:

1. Demographic information of the family
2. Income of the parents
3. Assets of the parents
4. Income of the student
5. Assets of the student

This analysis determines the amount you and your family are expected to contribute toward your college expenses, called your Expected Family Contribution or EFC. If the EFC is equal to or more than the cost of attendance at a particular college, then you do not demonstrate financial need. However, even if you don't have financial need, you may still qualify for aid, as there are grants, scholarships, and loan programs that are not need-based.

If the cost of your education is greater than your EFC, then you do demonstrate financial need and qualify for assistance. The amount of your financial need that can be met varies from school to school. Some are able to meet your full need, while others can only cover a certain percentage of need. Here's the formula:

Cost of Attendance
– Expected Family Contribution

= Financial Need

The EFC remains constant, but your need will vary according to the costs of attendance at a particular college. In general, the higher the tuition and fees at a particular college, the higher the cost of attendance will be. Expenses for books and supplies, room and board, transportation, and other miscellaneous items are included in the overall cost of attendance. It is important to remember that you do not have to be "needy" to qualify for financial aid. Many middle and upper-middle income families qualify for need-based financial aid.

APPLYING FOR FINANCIAL AID

Every student must complete the Free Application for Federal Student Aid (FAFSA) to be considered for financial aid. The FAFSA is available from your high school guidance office, many public libraries, colleges in your area, or directly from the U.S. Department of Education.

Students are encouraged to apply for federal student aid on the Web. The electronic version of the FAFSA can be accessed at http://www.fafsa.ed.gov. Both the student and at least one parent must apply for a federal pin number at http://www.pin.ed.gov. The pin number serves as your electronic signature when applying for aid on the Web.

To award their own funds, some colleges require an additional application, the Financial Aid PROFILE® form. The PROFILE asks supplemental questions that some colleges and awarding agencies feel provide a more accurate assessment of the family's ability to pay for college. It is up to the college to decide whether it will use only the FAFSA or both the FAFSA and the PROFILE. PROFILE applications are available from the high school guidance office and on the Web. Both the paper application and the Web site list those colleges and programs that require the PROFILE application.

If Every College You're Applying to for Fall 2008 Requires the FAFSA

. . . then it's pretty simple: Complete the FAFSA after January 1, 2008, being certain to send it in before any college-imposed deadlines. (You are not permitted to send

in the 2008–09 FAFSA before January 1, 2008.) Most college FAFSA application deadlines are in February or early March. It is easier if you have all your financial records for the previous year available, but if that is not possible, you are strongly encouraged to use estimated figures.

After you send in your FAFSA, either with the paper application or electronically, you'll receive a Student Aid Report (SAR) that includes all of the information you reported and shows your EFC. If you provided an e-mail address, the SAR is sent to you electronically; otherwise, you will receive a paper copy in the mail. Be sure to review the SAR, checking to see if the information you reported is accurately represented. If you used estimated numbers to complete the FAFSA, you may have to resubmit the SAR with any corrections to the data. The college(s) you have designated on the FAFSA will receive the information you reported and will use that data to make their decision. In many instances, the colleges you've applied to will ask you to send copies of your and your parents' federal income tax returns for 2007, plus any other documents needed to verify the information you reported.

If a College Requires the PROFILE

Step 1: Register for the Financial Aid PROFILE in the fall of your senior year in high school.

You can apply for the PROFILE online at http://profileonline.collegeboard.com/index.jsp. Registration information with a list of the colleges that require the PROFILE are available in most high school guidance offices. There is a fee for using the Financial Aid PROFILE application ($23 for the first college and $18 for each additional college). You must pay for the service by credit card when you register. If you do not have a credit card, you will be billed. A limited number of fee waivers are automatically granted to first-time applicants based on the financial information provided on the PROFILE.

Step 2: Fill out your customized Financial Aid PROFILE.

Once you register, your application will be immediately available online and will have questions which all students must complete, questions which must be completed by the student's parents (unless the student is independent and the colleges or programs selected do not require parental information), and *may* have supplemental questions needed by one or more of your schools or programs. If required, those will be found in Section Q of the application.

In addition to the PROFILE Application you complete online, you may also be required to complete a Business/Farm Supplement via traditional paper format. Completion of this form is not a part of the online process. If this form is required, instructions on how to download and print the supplemental form are provided. If your biological or adoptive parents are separated or divorced and your colleges and programs require it, your noncustodial parent may be asked to complete the Noncustodial PROFILE.

Once you complete and submit your PROFILE Application, it will be processed and sent directly to your requested colleges and programs.

IF YOU DON'T QUALIFY FOR NEED-BASED AID

If you are not eligible for need-based aid, you can still find ways to lessen the burden on your parents.

Here are some suggestions:

- Search for merit scholarships. You can start at the initial stages of your application process. College merit awards are becoming increasingly important as more and more colleges award these grants to students they especially want to attract. As a result, applying to a college at which your qualifications put you at the top of the entering class may give you a larger merit award. Another source of aid to look for is private scholarships that are given for special skills and talents. Additional information can be found at www.petersons.com and at www.finaid.org.

- Seek employment during the summer and the academic year. The student employment office at your college can help you locate a school-year job. Many colleges and local businesses have vacancies remaining after they have hired students who are receiving Federal Work-Study Program financial aid.

- Borrow through the unsubsidized Federal Stafford Student Loan programs. These are generally available to all students. The terms and conditions are similar to the subsidized loans. The biggest difference is that the borrower is responsible for the interest while still in college, although most lenders permit students to delay paying the interest right away and add the accrued interest to the total amount owed. You must file the FAFSA to be considered.

- After you've secured what you can through scholarships, working, and borrowing, your parents will be expected to meet their share of the college bill (the Expected Family Contribution). Many colleges offer monthly payment plans that spread the cost over the academic year. If the monthly payments are too high, parents can borrow through the Federal Parent Loan for Undergraduate Students (Federal PLUS Program), through one of the many private education loan programs available, or through home equity loans and lines of credit. Families seeking assistance in financing college

expenses should inquire at the financial aid office about what programs are available at the college. Some families seek the advice of professional financial advisers and tax consultants.

HOW IS YOUR EXPECTED FAMILY CONTRIBUTION CALCULATED?

The chart on the next page makes the following assumptions:

- two parent family where age of older parent is 45
- lower income families (under $30,000) will file the 1040A or 1040EZ tax form

- student income is less than $2300
- there are no student assets
- there is only one family member attending college

All figures are estimates and may vary when the complete FAFSA or PROFILE application is submitted.

Approximate Expected Family Contribution

ASSETS		INCOME BEFORE TAXES								
		$20,000	30,000	40,000	50,000	60,000	70,000	80,000	90,000	100,000
$ 20,000										
FAMILY SIZE	3	$ 0	160	1,800	3,500	5,800	9,100	12,600	14,100	17,400
	4	0	0	850	2,500	4,400	7,100	10,600	12,000	15,300
	5	0	0	0	1,600	3,300	5,500	8,600	10,100	13,400
	6	0	0	0	600	2,200	4,100	6,600	7,900	11,200
$ 30,000										
FAMILY SIZE	3	$ 0	160	1,800	3,500	5,800	9,100	12,600	14,100	17,400
	4	0	0	850	2,500	4,400	7,100	10,600	12,000	15,300
	5	0	0	0	1,600	3,300	5,500	8,600	10,100	13,400
	6	0	0	0	600	2,200	4,100	6,600	7,900	11,200
$ 40,000										
FAMILY SIZE	3	$ 0	160	1,800	3,500	5,800	9,100	12,600	14,100	17,400
	4	0	0	850	2,500	4,400	7,100	10,600	12,000	15,300
	5	0	0	0	1,600	3,300	5,500	8,600	10,100	13,400
	6	0	0	0	600	2,200	4,100	6,600	7,900	11,200
$ 50,000										
FAMILY SIZE	3	$ 0	340	2,000	3,800	6,200	9,500	13,000	14,500	17,800
	4	0	0	1,100	2,700	4,700	7,400	11,000	12,400	15,700
	5	0	0	0	1,800	3,500	5,800	9,000	10,400	13,750
	6	0	0	0	800	2,400	4,300	6,900	8,300	11,600
$ 60,000										
FAMILY SIZE	3	$ 0	600	2,300	4,100	6,600	10,000	13,600	15,000	18,300
	4	0	0	1,300	3,000	5,000	8,000	11,500	13,000	16,300
	5	0	0	400	2,050	3,800	6,200	9,600	11,000	14,300
	6	0	0	0	1,000	2,700	4,600	7,400	8,800	12,150
$ 80,000										
FAMILY SIZE	3	$ 0	1,130	2,800	4,800	7,600	11,200	14,700	16,150	19,500
	4	0	170	1,800	3,600	5,900	9,100	9,600	14,100	17,400
	5	0	0	900	2,600	4,500	7,200	10,700	12,100	15,450
	6	0	0	0	1,600	3,200	5,400	8,500	10,000	13,300
$ 100,000										
FAMILY SIZE	3	$ 0	1,660	3,400	5,600	8,800	12,300	15,900	17,300	20,600
	4	0	700	2,400	4,200	6,800	10,250	13,800	15,200	18,500
	5	0	0	1,400	3,100	5,300	8,300	11,800	13,300	16,600
	6	0	0	400	2,100	3,900	6,300	9,700	11,100	14,400
$ 120,000										
FAMILY SIZE	3	$ 0	2,190	4,000	6,500	9,900	13,400	17,000	18,400	21,700
	4	0	1,220	3,000	4,900	7,800	11,400	14,900	16,350	19,650
	5	0	310	2,000	3,700	6,100	9,500	13,000	14,400	17,700
	6	0	0	1,000	2,600	4,600	7,300	10,800	12,200	15,550
$ 140,000										
FAMILY SIZE	3	$ 0	2,700	4,700	7,500	11,000	13,400	18,100	19,500	22,850
	4	0	1,750	3,500	5,700	9,000	12,500	16,000	17,750	20,800
	5	0	850	2,500	4,400	7,100	10,500	14,100	15,500	18,850
	6	0	0	1,500	3,200	5,300	8,400	11,900	13,350	16,650

Financial Aid Programs for Schools in the West

Each state government has established one or more state-administered financial aid programs for qualified students. The state programs may be restricted to legal residents of the state, or they also may be available to out-of-state students who are attending public or private colleges or universities within the state. In addition, other qualifications may apply.

The programs are described below in alphabetical order, along with information about how to determine eligibility and how to apply. The information refers to awards for 2006–07, unless otherwise stated. Students should write to the address given for each program to request that award details for 2007–08 be sent to them as soon as they are available.

ALASKA

GEAR UP Alaska Scholarship. Scholarship provides up to $7000 each year for up to four years of undergraduate study (up to $3500 each year for half-time study). Applicant must be an Alaska high school senior or have an diploma or GED. Must be under the age of 22 years. For more details visit: http://www.eed.state.ak.us/gearup/scholarship.html. *Award:* Scholarship for use in freshman, sophomore, junior, or senior year; not renewable. Award amount: $3500–$7000. Number of awards: varies. *Eligibility Requirements:* Applicant must be high school student; age 22 or under; planning to enroll or expecting to enroll full- or part-time at a two-year or four-year institution or university and resident of Alaska. Available to U.S. citizens. *Application Requirements:* Application, financial need analysis, references, transcript. *Deadline:* May 31. **Contact:** Scholarship Committee, Alaska State Department of Education, 801 West 10th Street, Suite 200, PO Box 110500, Juneau, AK 99811-0500. E-mail: customer_service@acpe.state.ak.us. Phone: 907-465-2800. Fax: 907-465-4156. Web site: www.eed.state.ak.us.

ARIZONA

Arizona Private Postsecondary Education Student Financial Assistance Program. Provides grants to financially needy Arizona Community College graduates, to attend a private postsecondary baccalaureate degree-granting institution. *Award:* Forgivable loan for use in freshman, sophomore, junior, or senior year; renewable. Award amount: $1000–$1500. Number of awards: varies. *Eligibility Requirements:* Applicant must be enrolled or expecting to enroll full-time at a four-year institution or university; resident of Arizona and studying in Arizona. Available to U.S. citizens. *Application Requirements:* Application, financial need analysis, transcript, promissory note. *Deadline:* June 30. **Contact:** Danny Lee, PFAP Program Manager, Arizona Commission for Postsecondary Education, 2020 North Central Avenue, Suite 550, Phoenix, AZ 85004-4503. E-mail: dan_lee@azhighered.org. Phone: 602-258-2435 Ext. 103. Fax: 602-258-2483. Web site: www.azhighered.gov.

Leveraging Educational Assistance Partnership. Grants to financially needy students, who enroll in and attend postsecondary education or training in Arizona schools. Program was formerly known as the State Student Incentive Grant or SSIG Program. *Award:* Grant for use in freshman, sophomore, junior, senior, or graduate year; not renewable. Award amount: $700–$2500. Number of awards: varies. *Eligibility Requirements:* Applicant must be enrolled or expecting to enroll full- or part-time at a two-year, four-year, or technical institution or university; resident of Arizona and studying in Arizona. Available to U.S. citizens. *Application Requirements:* Application, financial need analysis. *Deadline:* April 30. **Contact:** Mila A. Zaporteza, Business Manager and LEAP Financial Aid Manager, Arizona Commission for Postsecondary Education, 2020 North Central Avenue, Suite 550, Phoenix, AZ 85004-4503. E-mail: mila@azhighered.org. Phone: 602-258-2435 Ext. 102. Fax: 602-258-2483. Web site: www.azhighered.gov.

CALIFORNIA

Cal Grant C. Award for California residents who are enrolled in a short-term vocational training program. Program must lead to a recognized degree or certificate. Course length must be a minimum of 4 months and no longer than 24 months. Students must be attending an approved California institution and show financial need. *Award:* Grant for use in freshman or sophomore year; renewable. Award amount: $576–$3168. Number of awards: up to 7761. *Eligibility Requirements:* Applicant must be enrolled or expecting to enroll full- or part-time at a two-year or technical institution; resident of California and studying in California. Available to U.S. citizens. *Application Requirements:* Application, financial need analysis, GPA verification. *Deadline:* March 2. **Contact:** Student Support Services Branch, California Student Aid Commission, PO Box 419027, Rancho Cordova, CA 95741-9027. E-mail: custsvcs@csac.ca.gov. Phone: 916-526-7590. Fax: 916-526-8002. Web site: www.csac.ca.gov.

Child Development Teacher and Supervisor Grant Program. Award is for those students pursuing an approved course of study leading to a Child Development Permit issued by the California Commission on Teacher Credentialing. In exchange for each year funding is received, recipients agree to provide one year of service in a licensed childcare center. *Academic Fields/Career Goals:* Education. *Award:* Grant for use in freshman, sophomore, junior, senior, or graduate year; renewable. Award amount: $1000–$2000. Number of awards: up to 300. *Eligibility Requirements:* Applicant must be enrolled or expecting to enroll full- or part-time at a two-year or four-year institution or university; resident of California and studying in California. Applicant or parent of applicant must have employment or volunteer experience in teaching. Available to U.S. citizens. *Application Requirements:* Application, financial need analysis, references, GPA verification. *Deadline:* June 30. **Contact:** Diana Fuentes-Michel, Executive Director, California Student Aid Commission, PO Box 419027, Rancho Cordova, CA 95741-9027. E-mail: studentsupport@csac.ca.gov. Phone: 916-526-7268. Fax: 916-526-8002. Web site: www.csac.ca.gov.

Competitive Cal Grant A. Award for California residents who are not recent high school graduates attending an approved college or university within the state. Must show financial need and meet minimum 3.0 GPA requirement. *Award:* Grant for use in freshman, sophomore, junior, or senior year; renewable. Award amount: $2772–$6636. Number of awards: 22,500. *Eligibility Requirements:* Applicant must be enrolled or expecting to enroll full- or part-time at a two-year or four-year institution or university; resident of California and studying in California. Applicant must have 3.0 GPA or higher. Available to U.S. citizens. *Application Requirements:* Application, financial need analysis, GPA verification. *Deadline:* March 2. **Contact:** Student Support Services Branch, California Student Aid Commission, PO Box

419027, Rancho Cordova, CA 95741-9027. E-mail: custsvcs@csac.ca.gov. Phone: 916-526-7590. Fax: 916-526-8002. Web site: www.csac.ca.gov.

Cooperative Agencies Resources for Education Program. Renewable award available to California resident attending a two-year California community college. Must have no more than 70 degree-applicable units, currently receive CALWORKS/TANF, and have at least one child under fourteen years of age. Must be in EOPS, single head of household, and 18 or older. Contact local college EOPS-CARE office. *Award:* Grant for use in freshman or sophomore year; renewable. Award amount: varies. Number of awards: 10,000–11,000. *Eligibility Requirements:* Applicant must be age 18 and over; enrolled or expecting to enroll full-time at a two-year institution; single; resident of California and studying in California. Available to U.S. citizens. *Application Requirements:* Application, financial need analysis, test scores, transcript. *Deadline:* varies. **Contact:** Cheryl Fong, CARE Coordinator, California Community Colleges, 1102 Q Street, Sacramento, CA 95814-6511. E-mail: cfong@cccco.edu. Phone: 916-323-5954. Fax: 916-327-8232. Web site: www.cccco.edu.

Entitlement Cal Grant B. Provide grant funds for access costs for low-income students in an amount not to exceed $1551. Must be California residents and enroll in an undergraduate academic program of not less than one academic year at a qualifying postsecondary institution. Must show financial need and meet the minimum 2.0 GPA requirement. *Award:* Grant for use in freshman, sophomore, junior, or senior year; renewable. Award amount: $700–$1551. Number of awards: varies. *Eligibility Requirements:* Applicant must be age 23 or under; enrolled or expecting to enroll full- or part-time at a two-year, four-year, or technical institution or university; resident of California and studying in California. Available to U.S. citizens. *Application Requirements:* Application, financial need analysis. *Deadline:* March 2. **Contact:** Student Support Services Branch, California Student Aid Commission, PO Box 419027, Rancho Cordova, CA 95741-9027. E-mail: custsvcs@csac.ca.gov. Phone: 916-526-7590. Fax: 916-526-8002. Web site: www.csac.ca.gov.

Law Enforcement Personnel Dependents Scholarship. Provides college grants to needy dependents of California law enforcement officers, officers and employees of the Department of Corrections and Department of Youth Authority, and firefighters killed or disabled in the line of duty. *Award:* Grant for use in freshman, sophomore, junior, or senior year; renewable. Award amount: $100–$11,259. Number of awards: varies. *Eligibility Requirements:* Applicant must be enrolled or expecting to enroll full- or part-time at a two-year or four-year institution or university; resident of California and studying in California. Applicant or parent of applicant must have employment or volunteer experience in police/firefighting. Available to U.S. citizens. *Application Requirements:* Application, financial need analysis, transcript, birth certificate, death certificate of parents or spouse, police report. *Deadline:* continuous. **Contact:** Specialized Programs Operations Branch, California Student Aid Commission, PO Box 419029, Rancho Cordova, CA 95741-9027. E-mail: custsvcs@csac.ca.gov. Phone: 916-526-7590. Fax: 916-526-8002. Web site: www.csac.ca.gov.

COLORADO

American Legion Auxiliary Department of Colorado Department President's Scholarship for Junior Member. Open to children, spouses, grandchildren, great-grandchildren of veterans, and veterans who served in the armed forces during eligibility dates for membership in the American Legion. Applicants must be Colorado residents who have been accepted by an accredited school in Colorado. *Award:* Scholarship for use in freshman year; not renewable. Award amount: up to $500. Number of awards: 1–2. *Eligibility Requirements:* Applicant must be high school student; planning to enroll or expecting to enroll full- or part-time at a four-year institution or university and resident of Colorado. Available to U.S. citizens. Applicant must have general military experience. *Application Requirements:* Application, essay, references, transcript. *Deadline:* April 15. **Contact:** Jean Lennie, Department Secretary And Treasurer, American Legion Auxiliary, Department

of Colorado, 7465 East First Avenue, Suite D, Denver, CO 80230. E-mail: ala@coloradolegion.org. Phone: 303-367-5388. Fax: 303-367-0688. Web site: www.coloradolegion.org.

American Legion Auxiliary Department of Colorado Past President Parley Nurses Scholarship. Open to children, spouses, grandchildren, great-grandchildren of veterans, and veterans who served in the armed forces during eligibility dates for membership in the American Legion. Applicants must be Colorado residents who have been accepted by an accredited school of nursing in Colorado. *Academic Fields/Career Goals:* Nursing. *Award:* Scholarship for use in freshman, sophomore, junior, senior, or graduate year; not renewable. Award amount: up to $500. Number of awards: 3–5. *Eligibility Requirements:* Applicant must be enrolled or expecting to enroll full- or part-time at a four-year institution or university; resident of Colorado and studying in Colorado. Applicant or parent of applicant must be member of American Legion or Auxiliary. Available to U.S. citizens. Applicant or parent must meet one or more of the following requirements: general military experience; retired from active duty; disabled or killed as a result of military service; prisoner of war; or missing in action. *Application Requirements:* Application, essay, financial need analysis, references. *Deadline:* April 1. **Contact:** Department of Colorado, American Legion Auxiliary, Department of Colorado, 7465 East First Avenue, Suite D, Denver, CO 80230. E-mail: ala@coloradolegion.org. Phone: 303-367-5388. Web site: www.coloradolegion.org.

Colorado Student Grant. Assists Colorado residents attending eligible public, private, or vocational institutions within the state. Application deadlines vary by institution. Renewable award for undergraduates. Contact the financial aid office at the college/institution for more information and an application. *Award:* Grant for use in freshman, sophomore, junior, or senior year; renewable. Award amount: $1500–$5000. Number of awards: varies. *Eligibility Requirements:* Applicant must be enrolled or expecting to enroll full- or part-time at a two-year, four-year, or technical institution or university; resident of Colorado and studying in Colorado. Available to U.S. citizens. *Application Requirements:* Application, financial need analysis. *Deadline:* varies. **Contact:** Tobin Bliss, Financial Aid Director, Colorado Commission on Higher Education, 1380 Lawrence Street, Suite 1200, Denver, CO 80204-2059. E-mail: tobin.bliss@cche.state.co.us. Phone: 303-866-2723. Web site: www.state.co.us/cche.

Colorado Undergraduate Merit Scholarships. Renewable awards for students attending Colorado state-supported institutions at the undergraduate level. Must demonstrate superior scholarship or talent. Contact college financial aid office for complete information and deadlines. *Award:* Scholarship for use in freshman, sophomore, junior, or senior year; renewable. Award amount: $1230. Number of awards: 10,823. *Eligibility Requirements:* Applicant must be enrolled or expecting to enroll full- or part-time at a two-year, four-year, or technical institution or university; resident of Colorado and studying in Colorado. Applicant must have 3.0 GPA or higher. Available to U.S. citizens. *Application Requirements:* Application, test scores, transcript. *Deadline:* varies. **Contact:** Tobin Bliss, Financial Aid Director, Colorado Commission on Higher Education, 1380 Lawrence Street, Suite 1200, Denver, CO 80204-2059. E-mail: tobin.bliss@cche.state.co.us. Phone: 303-866-2723. Web site: www.state.co.us/cche.

Governor's Opportunity Scholarship. Scholarship available for the most needy first-time freshman whose parents' adjusted gross income is less than $26,000. Must be U.S. citizen or permanent legal resident. Work-study is part of the program. *Award:* Scholarship for use in freshman year; renewable. Award amount: up to $10,700. Number of awards: 250. *Eligibility Requirements:* Applicant must be high school student; planning to enroll or expecting to enroll full-time at a two-year, four-year, or technical institution or university; resident of Colorado and studying in Colorado. Available to U.S. citizens. *Application Requirements:* Application, financial need analysis, test scores, transcript. *Deadline:* continuous. **Contact:** Tobin Bliss, Financial Aid Director, Colorado Commission on Higher Education, 1380 Law-

rence Street, Suite 1200, Denver, CO 80204-2059. E-mail: tobin.bliss@cche.state.co.us. Phone: 303-866-2723. Web site: www.state.co.us/cche.

Western Undergraduate Exchange (WUE) Program. Students can enroll in designated two- and four-year undergraduate programs at public institutions in participating states at reduced tuition level. Students can apply directly to the admissions office at participating institution, and should indicate he/she want to be considered as a WUE student. *Award:* Scholarship for use in freshman, sophomore, junior, or senior year; renewable. Award amount: varies. Number of awards: varies. *Eligibility Requirements:* Applicant must be enrolled or expecting to enroll full- or part-time at a two-year or four-year institution; resident of Alaska, Arizona, California, Colorado, Hawaii, Idaho, Montana, Nevada, New Mexico, North Dakota, Oregon, South Dakota, Utah, Washington, or Wyoming and studying in Alaska, Arizona, California, Colorado, Hawaii, Idaho, Montana, Nevada, New Mexico, North Dakota, Oregon, or South Dakota. Available to U.S. citizens. *Application Requirements:* Application. *Deadline:* varies. **Contact:** Margo Schultz, Program Coordinator, Western Interstate Commission for Higher Education, PO Box 9752, Boulder, CO 80301-9752. E-mail: info-sep@wiche.edu. Phone: 303-541-0270. Web site: www.wiche.edu.

HAWAII

Hawaii State Student Incentive Grant. Grants are given to residents of Hawaii who are enrolled in a participating Hawaiian state school. Funds are for undergraduate tuition only. Applicants must submit a financial need analysis. *Award:* Grant for use in freshman, sophomore, junior or senior year; renewable. Award amount: $200–$2000. Number of awards: 470. *Eligibility Requirements:* Applicant must be enrolled or expecting to enroll full- or part-time at a two-year, four-year, or technical institution or university; resident of Hawaii and studying in Hawaii. Available to U.S. citizens. *Application Requirements:* Application, financial need analysis. *Deadline:* continuous. **Contact:** Janine Oyama, Financial Aid Specialist, Hawaii State Postsecondary Education Commission, University of Hawaii, Honolulu, HI 96822. Phone: 808-956-6066.

Robert C. Byrd Honors Scholarship-Hawaii. Scholarship is available to students planning to attend college. The scholarship is federally funded, state-administered and recognizes exceptional high school seniors who show promise of continued excellence in the postsecondary educational system. Must have a minimum GPA of 3.2 and 1270 SAT. Applicant must be a legal resident of the State of Hawaii. Hawaii residents who are attending high school in another state are eligible to apply. Deadline: March 17. *Award:* Scholarship for use in freshman, sophomore, junior, or senior year; renewable. Award amount: $1500. Number of awards: 28. *Eligibility Requirements:* Applicant must be high school student; planning to enroll or expecting to enroll full-time at a two-year, four-year, or technical institution or university and resident of Hawaii. Available to U.S. citizens. *Application Requirements:* Application, transcript, community service. *Deadline:* March 17. **Contact:** Deanna Helber, Education Specialist, Hawaii Department of Education, 641 18th Avenue, Building V, Room 201, Honolulu, HI 96816-4444. E-mail: dee_helber@notes.k12.hi.us. Phone: 808-735-6222. Fax: 808-733-9890. Web site: doe.k12.hi.us.

IDAHO

Education Incentive Loan Forgiveness Contract-Idaho. Renewable award assists Idaho residents enrolling in teacher education or nursing programs within the state. Must rank in top 15 percent of high school graduating class, have a 3.0 GPA or above, and agree to work in Idaho for two years. Deadlines vary. Contact financial aid office at institution of choice. *Academic Fields/Career Goals:* Education; Nursing. *Award:* Forgivable loan for use in freshman year; renewable. Award amount: varies. Number of awards: 13–45. *Eligibility Requirements:* Applicant must be high school student; planning to enroll or expecting to enroll full-time at a two-year or four-year institution or university; resident of Idaho and studying in Idaho.

Applicant must have 3.0 GPA or higher. Available to U.S. citizens. *Application Requirements:* Application, test scores, transcript. *Deadline:* varies. **Contact:** Dana Kelly, Program Manager, Idaho State Board of Education, PO Box 83720, Boise, ID 83720-0037. E-mail: dana.kelly@osbe.idaho.gov. Phone: 208-332-1574. Web site: www.boardofed.idaho.gov.

Freedom Scholarship. Scholarship for children of Idaho citizens determined by the federal government to have been prisoners of war, missing in action, or killed in action or died of injuries or wounds sustained in action in southeast Asia, including Korea, or who shall become so hereafter, in any area of armed conflicts. Applicant must attend an Idaho public college or university and meet all requirements for regular admission. The award value and the number of awards granted varies. Deadline: January 15. *Award:* Scholarship for use in freshman, sophomore, junior, senior, graduate, or postgraduate years; not renewable. Award amount: varies. Number of awards: varies. *Eligibility Requirements:* Applicant must be enrolled or expecting to enroll full- or part-time at a two-year, four-year, or technical institution or university; resident of Idaho and studying in Idaho. Available to U.S. citizens. Applicant or parent must meet one or more of the following requirements: general military experience; retired from active duty; disabled or killed as a result of military service; prisoner of war; or missing in action. *Application Requirements:* Application. *Deadline:* January 15. **Contact:** Dana Kelly, Program Manager, Idaho State Board of Education, PO Box 83720, Boise, ID 83720-0037. E-mail: dana.kelly@osbe.idaho.gov. Phone: 208-332-1574. Web site: www.boardofed.idaho.gov.

Idaho Minority and "At Risk" Student Scholarship. Renewable award for Idaho residents who are disabled or members of a minority group and have financial need. Must attend one of eight postsecondary institutions in the state for undergraduate study. Deadlines vary by institution. Must be a U.S. citizen and be a graduate of an Idaho high school. Contact college financial aid office. *Award:* Scholarship for use in freshman, sophomore, junior, or senior year; renewable. Award amount: $3000. Number of awards: 35–40. *Eligibility Requirements:* Applicant must be American Indian/Alaska Native, Asian/Pacific Islander, Black (non-Hispanic), or Hispanic; enrolled or expecting to enroll full-time at a two-year, four-year, or technical institution or university; resident of Idaho and studying in Idaho. Applicant must be hearing impaired, physically disabled, or visually impaired. Available to U.S. citizens. *Application Requirements:* Application, financial need analysis, transcript. *Deadline:* varies. **Contact:** Dana Kelly, Program Manager, Idaho State Board of Education, PO Box 83720, Boise, ID 83720-0037. E-mail: dana.kelly@osbe.idaho.gov. Phone: 208-332-1574. Web site: www.boardofed.idaho.gov.

Idaho Promise Category A Scholarship Program. Renewable award available to Idaho residents who are graduating high school seniors. Must attend an approved Idaho institute of higher education on full-time basis. Must have a cumulative GPA of 3.5 or above and an ACT score of 28 or above. Scholarship value is $3000. Deadline: January 15. *Award:* Scholarship for use in freshman year; renewable. Award amount: $3000. Number of awards: 25. *Eligibility Requirements:* Applicant must be high school student; planning to enroll or expecting to enroll full-time at a two-year, four-year, or technical institution or university; resident of Idaho and studying in Idaho. Applicant must have 3.5 GPA or higher. Available to U.S. citizens. *Application Requirements:* Application, applicant must enter a contest, test scores. *Deadline:* January 15. **Contact:** Lynn Humphrey, Manager, Student Aid Programs, Idaho State Board of Education, PO Box 83720, Boise, ID 83720-0037. E-mail: lhumphre@osbe.state.id.us. Phone: 208-334-2270. Fax: 208-334-2632. Web site: www.boardofed.idaho.gov.

Idaho Promise Category B Scholarship Program. Available to Idaho residents entering college for the first time prior to the age of 22. Must have completed high school or its equivalent in Idaho and have a minimum GPA of 3.0 or an ACT score of 20 or higher. Scholarship limited to two years or four semesters. *Award:* Scholarship for use in freshman or sophomore year; renewable. Award amount: $500. Number of awards: varies. *Eligibility Requirements:* Applicant must be age 21 or under; enrolled or expecting to enroll full-time at a two-year, four-

year, or technical institution or university; resident of Idaho and studying in Idaho. Applicant must have 3.0 GPA or higher. Available to U.S. citizens. *Application Requirements:* Application, transcript. *Deadline:* continuous. **Contact:** Lynn Humphrey, Manager, Student Aid Programs, Idaho State Board of Education, PO Box 83720, Boise, ID 83720-0037. Phone: 208-334-2270. Fax: 208-334-2632. Web site: www.boardofed.idaho.gov.

Leveraging Educational Assistance State Partnership Program (LEAP). One-time award assists students attending participating Idaho trade schools, colleges, and universities majoring in any field except theology or divinity. Must be U.S. citizen or permanent resident, and show financial need. Deadlines vary by institution. *Award:* Grant for use in freshman, sophomore, junior, senior, or graduate year; not renewable. Award amount: $400–$5000. Number of awards: varies. *Eligibility Requirements:* Applicant must be enrolled or expecting to enroll full- or part-time at a two-year, four-year, or technical institution or university; resident of Idaho and studying in Idaho. Available to U.S. citizens. *Application Requirements:* Application, financial need analysis, self-addressed stamped envelope. *Deadline:* varies. **Contact:** Lynn Humphrey, Manager, Student Aid Programs, Idaho State Board of Education, PO Box 83720, Boise, ID 83720-0037. Phone: 208-334-2270. Fax: 208-334-2632. Web site: www.boardofed.idaho.gov.

Public Safety Officer Dependent Scholarship. Scholarship for dependents of full-time Idaho public safety officers who were killed or disabled in the line of duty. Recipients will attend an Idaho postsecondary institution with a full waiver of fees. Scholarship value is $500. Deadline: January 15. *Award:* Scholarship for use in freshman year; renewable. Award amount: up to $500. Number of awards: varies. *Eligibility Requirements:* Applicant must be enrolled or expecting to enroll full- or part-time at a two-year or four-year institution or university; resident of Idaho and studying in Idaho. Applicant or parent of applicant must have employment or volunteer experience in police/firefighting. Available to U.S. citizens. Applicant must have general military experience. *Application Requirements:* Application. *Deadline:* January 15. **Contact:** Dana Kelly, Program Manager, Idaho State Board of Education, PO Box 83720, Boise, ID 83720-0037. E-mail: dana.kelly@osbe.idaho.gov. Phone: 208-332-1574. Web site: www.boardofed.idaho.gov.

MONTANA

Montana Higher Education Opportunity Grant. This grant is awarded based on need to undergraduate students attending either part-time or full-time who are residents of Montana and attending participating Montana schools. Awards are limited to the most needy students. A specific major or program of study is not required. This grant does not need to be repaid, and students may apply each year. Apply by filing FAFSA by March 1 and contacting the financial aid office at the admitting college. *Award:* Grant for use in freshman, sophomore, junior, or senior year; not renewable. Award amount: $400–$600. Number of awards: up to 800. *Eligibility Requirements:* Applicant must be enrolled or expecting to enroll full- or part-time at a two-year or four-year institution or university; resident of Montana and studying in Montana. Available to U.S. citizens. *Application Requirements:* Application, financial need analysis, resume, FAFSA. *Deadline:* March 1. **Contact:** Janice Kirkpatrick, Grants and Scholarship Coordinator, Montana Guaranteed Student Loan Program, Office of Commissioner of Higher Education, PO Box 203101, Helena, MT 59620-3101. E-mail: jkirkpatrick@mgslp.state.mt.us. Phone: 406-444-0638. Fax: 406-444-1869. Web site: www.mgslp.state.mt.us.

Montana Tuition Assistance Program-Baker Grant. Need-based grant for Montana residents attending participating Montana schools who have earned at least $2575 during the previous calendar year. Must be enrolled full time. Grant does not need to be repaid. Award covers the first undergraduate degree or certificate. Apply by filing FAFSA by March 1 and contacting the financial aid office at the admitting college. *Award:* Grant for use in freshman, sophomore, junior, or senior year; not renewable. Award amount: $100–$1000. Number of awards: 1000–3000. *Eligibility Requirements:* Applicant must

be enrolled or expecting to enroll full-time at a two-year or four-year institution or university; resident of Montana and studying in Montana. Available to U.S. citizens. *Application Requirements:* Application, financial need analysis, resume, FAFSA. *Deadline:* March 1. **Contact:** Janice Kirkpatrick, Grants and Scholarship Coordinator, Montana Guaranteed Student Loan Program, Office of Commissioner of Higher Education, PO Box 203101, Helena, MT 59620-3101. E-mail: jkirkpatrick@mgslp.state.mt.us. Phone: 406-444-0638. Fax: 406-444-1869. Web site: www.mgslp.state.mt.us.

Montana University System Honor Scholarship. Scholarship will be awarded annually to high school seniors graduating from accredited Montana high schools. The MUS Honor Scholarship is a four year renewable scholarship that waives the tuition and registration fee at one of the Montana University System campuses or one of the three community colleges (Flathead Valley in Kalispell, Miles in Miles City or Dawson in Glendive). The scholarship must be used within 9 months after high school graduation. Deadline: January 31. *Award:* Scholarship for use in freshman, sophomore, junior, or senior year; renewable. Award amount: varies. Number of awards: varies. *Eligibility Requirements:* Applicant must be high school student; planning to enroll or expecting to enroll full- or part-time at a two-year or four-year institution or university; resident of Montana and studying in Montana. Applicant must have 3.5 GPA or higher. Available to U.S. citizens. *Application Requirements:* Application, test scores, transcript. *Deadline:* January 31. **Contact:** Janice Kirkpatrick, Grant and Scholarship Coordinator, Montana Guaranteed Student Loan Program, Office of Commissioner of Higher Education, PO Box 203101, Helena, MT 59620-3101. E-mail: jkirkpatrick@mgslp.state.mt.us. Phone: 406-444-0638. Fax: 406-444-1869. Web site: www.mgslp.state.mt.us.

NEVADA

Governor Guinn Millennium Scholarship. Scholarship for high school graduates with a diploma from a Nevada public or private high school in the graduating class of the year 2000 or later. Must complete high school with at least 3.25 GPA. *Award:* Scholarship for use in freshman, sophomore, junior, or senior year; not renewable. Award amount: $10,000. Number of awards: 1. *Eligibility Requirements:* Applicant must be enrolled or expecting to enroll full-time at a two-year or four-year institution and resident of Nevada. Available to U.S. citizens. *Application Requirements:* Application. *Deadline:* varies. **Contact:** Christy Thurston, Office Assistant, Nevada Office of the State Treasurer, 555 East Washington Avenue, Suite 4600, Las Vegas, NV 89101. E-mail: info@nevadatreasurer.gov. Phone: 702-486-3383. Fax: 702-486-3246. Web site: www.nevadatreasurer.gov.

Nevada Student Incentive Grant. Grants awarded to undergraduate and graduate students who are Nevada residents pursuing their first degree. Recipients must be enrolled at least halftime and have financial need. Awards may range from $200 to $4000. Any field of study eligible. High school students may not apply. *Award:* Grant for use in freshman, sophomore, junior, senior, or graduate year; not renewable. Award amount: $200–$4000. Number of awards: 400–800. *Eligibility Requirements:* Applicant must be enrolled or expecting to enroll full- or part-time at a two-year, four-year, or technical institution or university; resident of Nevada and studying in Nevada. Available to U.S. citizens. *Application Requirements:* Application, financial need analysis. *Deadline:* continuous. **Contact:** Bill Arensdorf, Director, Nevada Department of Education, 700 East Fifth Street, Carson City, NV 89701. E-mail: warensdorf@doe.nv.gov. Phone: 775-687-9200. Fax: 775-687-9101. Web site: www.doe.nv.gov.

University and Community College System of Nevada NASA Space Grant and Fellowship Program. The grant provides graduate fellowships and undergraduate scholarship to qualified student majoring in aerospace science, technology and related fields. Must be Nevada resident studying at a Nevada college/university. Minimum 2.5 GPA required. *Academic Fields/Career Goals:* Aviation/Aerospace; Chemical Engineering; Computer Science/Data Processing; Engineering/Technology; Physical Sciences and Math. *Award:* Scholarship for use in freshman, sophomore, junior, senior, or graduate year; not renew-

able. Award amount: $2500–$30,000. Number of awards: 1–20. *Eligibility Requirements:* Applicant must be enrolled or expecting to enroll full-time at a two-year or four-year institution or university; resident of Nevada and studying in Nevada. Applicant must have 3.0 GPA or higher. Available to U.S. citizens. *Application Requirements:* Application, autobiography, essay, resume, references, transcript, project proposal, budget. *Deadline:* April 13. **Contact:** Cindy Routh, Program Coordinator, NASA Nevada Space Grant Consortium, 2215 Raggio Parkway, Reno, NV 89512. E-mail: nvsg@dri.edu. Phone: 775-673-7674. Fax: 775-673-7485. Web site: www.unr.edu/spacegrant.

NEW MEXICO

Allied Health Student Loan Program-New Mexico. Award to increase the number if physician assistants in areas of the state which have experienced shortages of health practitioners, by making educational loans to students seeking certification/licensers in an eligible health field. As a condition of each loan, the student shall declare his/her intent to practice as a health professional in a designated shortage area. For every year of service, a portion of the loan will be forgiven. *Academic Fields/Career Goals:* Dental Health/Services; Health and Medical Sciences; Nursing; Social Sciences; Therapy/Rehabilitation. *Award:* Forgivable loan for use in freshman, sophomore, junior, or senior year; renewable. Award amount: up to $12,000. Number of awards: 1–40. *Eligibility Requirements:* Applicant must be enrolled or expecting to enroll full- or part-time at a four-year institution or university; resident of New Mexico and studying in New Mexico. Available to U.S. citizens. *Application Requirements:* Application, financial need analysis, transcript, FAFSA. *Deadline:* July 1. **Contact:** Ofelia Morales, Director of Financial Aid, New Mexico Commission on Higher Education, 1068 Cerrillos Road, Santa Fe, NM 87505. E-mail: ofelia.morales@state.nm.us. Phone: 505-476-6506. Fax: 505-476-6511. Web site: www.hed.state.nm.us.

Amigo Scholars Program for Non-residents. Scholarship for non-resident high school graduates. Applicant must have high school GPA of 3.5 or higher, ACT composite score of 23 or SAT of 1060. Must be a U.S. citizen. Deadline: May 1. *Award:* Scholarship for use in freshman year; renewable. Award amount: varies. Number of awards: varies. *Eligibility Requirements:* Applicant must be high school student and planning to enroll or expecting to enroll full- or part-time at a four-year institution or university. Available to U.S. citizens. *Application Requirements:* Application, resume. *Deadline:* May 1. **Contact:** Robert Romero, Financial Aid Advisor, University of New Mexico, Mesa Vista Hall, Room 3019, Albuquerque, NM 87131. E-mail: schol@unm.edu. Phone: 505-277-6090. Fax: 505-277-5325. Web site: www.unm.edu.

Children of Deceased Veterans Scholarship-New Mexico. Award for New Mexico residents who are children of veterans killed or disabled as a result of service, prisoner of war, or veterans missing in action. Must be between ages of 16 to 26. For use at New Mexico schools for undergraduate study. Should submit parent's death certificate and DD form 214. *Award:* Scholarship for use in freshman, sophomore, junior, or senior year; renewable. Award amount: $300. Number of awards: varies. *Eligibility Requirements:* Applicant must be age 16-26; enrolled or expecting to enroll full- or part-time at a two-year or four-year institution or university; resident of New Mexico and studying in New Mexico. Available to U.S. citizens. Applicant or parent must meet one or more of the following requirements: general military experience; retired from active duty; disabled or killed as a result of military service; prisoner of war; or missing in action. *Application Requirements:* Application, transcript, death certificate or notice of casualty, DD form 214. *Deadline:* continuous. **Contact:** Alan Martinez, Director, State Benefits Division, New Mexico Veterans Service Commission, Bataan Memorial Building, 300 Galisteo, Room 142, Santa Fe, NM 87504. E-mail: alan.martinez@state.nm.us. Phone: 505-827-6300. Fax: 505-827-6372. Web site: www.dvs.state.nm.us.

College Affordability Grant. The purpose of the grant is to encourage New Mexico students with financial need, who do not qualify for other state grants and scholarships, to attend and complete educational programs at a New Mexico public college or university. Student must have unmet need after all other financial aid has been awarded. Student may not be receiving any other state grants or scholarships. Renewable upon satisfactory academic progress. Grant value is $1000. Deadline: continuous. *Award:* Grant for use in freshman, sophomore, junior, or senior year; renewable. Award amount: up to $1000. Number of awards: varies. *Eligibility Requirements:* Applicant must be enrolled or expecting to enroll full- or part-time at a two-year or four-year institution or university; resident of New Mexico and studying in New Mexico. Available to U.S. citizens. *Application Requirements:* Financial need analysis. *Deadline:* continuous. **Contact:** Ofelia Morales, Director of Financial Aid, New Mexico Commission on Higher Education, 1068 Cerrillos Road, Santa Fe, NM 87505. Phone: 505-476-6506. Web site: www.hed.state.nm.us.

Legislative Endowment Scholarships. Renewable scholarships to provide aid for undergraduate students with substantial financial need who are attending public postsecondary institutions in New Mexico. Four-year schools may award up to $2500 per academic year, two-year schools may award up to $1000 per academic year. Deadlines: set by each institution. *Award:* Scholarship for use in freshman, sophomore, junior, or senior year; renewable. Award amount: $1000–$2500. Number of awards: varies. *Eligibility Requirements:* Applicant must be enrolled or expecting to enroll full- or part-time at a two-year or four-year institution or university; resident of New Mexico and studying in New Mexico. Available to U.S. citizens. *Application Requirements:* Application, financial need analysis, FAFSA. *Deadline:* varies. **Contact:** Ofelia Morales, Director of Financial Aid, New Mexico Commission on Higher Education, 1068 Cerrillos Road, Santa Fe, NM 87505. E-mail: ofelia.morales@state.nm.us. Phone: 505-476-6506. Fax: 505-476-6511. Web site: www.hed.state.nm.us.

Lottery Success Scholarships. Renewable Scholarship for New Mexico high school graduates or GED recipients who plan to attend an eligible New Mexico public college or university. Must be enrolled full-time and maintain 2.5 GPA. *Award:* Scholarship for use in freshman, sophomore, junior, or senior year; renewable. Award amount: varies. Number of awards: 1. *Eligibility Requirements:* Applicant must be high school student; planning to enroll or expecting to enroll full-time at a four-year institution or university; resident of New Mexico and studying in New Mexico. Applicant must have 2.5 GPA or higher. Available to U.S. citizens. *Application Requirements:* Application, FAFSA. *Deadline:* varies. **Contact:** Ofelia Morales, Director of Financial Aid, New Mexico Commission on Higher Education, 1068 Cerrillos Road, Santa Fe, NM 87505. E-mail: ofelia.morales@state.nm.us. Phone: 505-476-6506. Fax: 505-476-6511. Web site: www.hed.state.nm.us.

New Mexico Competitive Scholarship. Scholarships for non-resident or non-citizen of the United States to encourage out-of-state students, who have demonstrated high academic achievement in high school, to enroll in public four-year universities in New Mexico. Renewable for up to four years. High School GPA and ACT varies. For details visit: http://fin.hed.state.nm.us. *Award:* Scholarship for use in freshman, sophomore, junior, or senior year; renewable. Award amount: varies. Number of awards: varies. *Eligibility Requirements:* Applicant must be high school student; planning to enroll or expecting to enroll full-time at a four-year institution or university and studying in New Mexico. Available to Canadian and non-U.S. citizens. *Application Requirements:* Application, essay, references, test scores. *Deadline:* varies. **Contact:** Ofelia Morales, Director of Financial Aid, New Mexico Commission on Higher Education, 1068 Cerrillos Road, Santa Fe, NM 87505. E-mail: ofelia.morales@state.nm.us. Phone: 505-476-6506. Fax: 505-476-6511. Web site: www.hed.state.nm.us.

New Mexico Scholars' Program. Renewable award program created to encourage New Mexico high school students to attend public postsecondary institutions or the following private colleges in New Mexico: College of Santa Fe, St. John's College, College of the Southwest. For details visit: http://fin.hed.state.nm.us. Deadlines: set by each institution. *Award:* Scholarship for use in freshman, sophomore, junior, or senior year; renewable. Award amount: varies. Number of

awards: 1. *Eligibility Requirements:* Applicant must be age 21 or under; enrolled or expecting to enroll full-time at a two-year or four-year institution; resident of New Mexico and studying in New Mexico. Available to U.S. citizens. *Application Requirements:* Application, financial need analysis, test scores, FAFSA. *Deadline:* varies. **Contact:** Ofelia Morales, Director of Financial Aid, New Mexico Commission on Higher Education, 1068 Cerrillos Road, Santa Fe, NM 87505. E-mail: ofelia.morales@state.nm.us. Phone: 505-476-6506. Fax: 505-476-6511. Web site: www.hed.state.nm.us.

New Mexico Student Incentive Grant. Grant created to provide aid for undergraduate students with substantial financial need who are attending public colleges or universities or the following eligible colleges in New Mexico: College of Santa Fe, St. John's College, College of the Southwest, Institute of American Indian Art, Crownpoint Institute of Technology, Dine College and Southwestern Indian Polytechnic Institute. Part-time students are eligible for pro-rated awards. *Award:* Grant for use in freshman, sophomore, junior, or senior year; not renewable. Award amount: $200–$2500. Number of awards: varies. *Eligibility Requirements:* Applicant must be enrolled or expecting to enroll full- or part-time at a two-year, four-year, or technical institution or university; resident of New Mexico and studying in New Mexico. Available to U.S. citizens. *Application Requirements:* Application, financial need analysis. *Deadline:* varies. **Contact:** Ofelia Morales, Director of Financial Aid, New Mexico Commission on Higher Education, 1068 Cerrillos Road, Santa Fe, NM 87505. E-mail: ofelia.morales@state.nm.us. Phone: 505-476-6506. Fax: 505-476-6511. Web site: www.hed.state.nm.us.

New Mexico Vietnam Veteran Scholarship. Award for Vietnam veterans who are New Mexico residents for minimum of ten years and attending state funded postsecondary schools. Must have been awarded the Vietnam Campaign medal. Must submit DD 214 and discharge papers. *Award:* Scholarship for use in freshman, sophomore, junior, or senior year; renewable. Award amount: varies. Number of awards: varies. *Eligibility Requirements:* Applicant must be enrolled or expecting to enroll full- or part-time at a two-year, four-year, or technical institution or university; resident of New Mexico and studying in New Mexico. Available to U.S. citizens. Applicant must have general military experience. *Application Requirements:* Application, copy of DD214. *Deadline:* continuous. **Contact:** Alan Martinez, Director, State Benefits Division, New Mexico Veterans Service Commission, Bataan Memorial Building, 300 Galisteo, Room 142, Santa Fe, NM 87504. E-mail: alan.martinez@state.nm.us. Phone: 505-827-6300. Fax: 505-827-6372. Web site: www.dvs.state.nm.us.

Nursing Student Loan-For-Service Program. Award to increase the number of nurses in areas of the state which have experienced shortages by making educational loans to students entering nursing programs. As a condition of each loan, the student shall declare his/her intent to practice as a health professional in a designated shortage area. For every year of service, a portion of the loan will be forgiven. Deadline: July 1. *Academic Fields/Career Goals:* Nursing. *Award:* Forgivable loan for use in freshman, sophomore, junior, or senior year; renewable. Award amount: up to $12,000. Number of awards: varies. *Eligibility Requirements:* Applicant must be enrolled or expecting to enroll full- or part-time at a four-year institution or university; resident of New Mexico and studying in New Mexico. Available to U.S. citizens. *Application Requirements:* Application, financial need analysis, transcript, FAFSA. *Deadline:* July 1. **Contact:** Ofelia Morales, Director of Financial Aid, New Mexico Commission on Higher Education, 1068 Cerrillos Road, Santa Fe, NM 87505. E-mail: ofelia.morales@state.nm.us. Phone: 505-476-6506. Fax: 505-476-6511. Web site: www.hed.state.nm.us.

Vietnam Veterans' Scholarship Program. Renewable scholarship program created to provide aid for Vietnam veterans who are undergraduate and graduate students attending public postsecondary institutions or select private colleges in New Mexico. College includes: College of Santa Fe, St. John's College and College of the Southwest. *Award:* Scholarship for use in freshman, sophomore, junior, senior, or graduate year; renewable. Award amount: varies. Number of awards:

1. *Eligibility Requirements:* Applicant must be enrolled or expecting to enroll full-time at a two-year or four-year institution; resident of New Mexico and studying in New Mexico. Available to U.S. citizens. Applicant must have general military experience. *Application Requirements:* Application, certification by the NM Veteran's commission. *Deadline:* varies. **Contact:** Ofelia Morales, Director of Financial Aid, New Mexico Commission on Higher Education, 1068 Cerrillos Road, Santa Fe, NM 87505. E-mail: ofelia.morales@state.nm.us. Phone: 505-476-6506. Fax: 505-476-6511. Web site: www.hed.state.nm.us.

OREGON

American Ex-Prisoner of War Scholarships: Peter Connacher Memorial Scholarship. Renewable award for American prisoners-of-war and their descendants. Written proof of prisoner-of-war status and discharge papers from the U.S. Armed Forces must accompany application. Statement of relationship between applicant and former prisoner-of-war is required. See Web site at http://www.osac.state.or.us for details. *Award:* Scholarship for use in freshman, sophomore, junior, or senior year; renewable. Award amount: varies. Number of awards: varies. *Eligibility Requirements:* Applicant must be enrolled or expecting to enroll full-time at a two-year or four-year institution and resident of Oregon. Available to U.S. citizens. Applicant or parent must meet one or more of the following requirements: general military experience; retired from active duty; disabled or killed as a result of military service; prisoner of war; or missing in action. *Application Requirements:* Application, essay, financial need analysis, transcript, activities chart. *Deadline:* March 1. **Contact:** Director of Grant Programs, Oregon Student Assistance Commission, 1500 Valley River Drive, Suite 100, Eugene, OR 97401-7020. Phone: 800-452-8807 Ext. 7395. Web site: www.osac.state.or.us.

Children, Adult, and Family Services Scholarship. Award for graduating high school seniors currently in foster care or participating in Independent Living Program (ILP) or GED recipients or continuing college students formerly in foster care. Only for Oregon public colleges. Visit Web site: http://www.osac.state.or.us for more details. *Award:* Scholarship for use in freshman, sophomore, junior, senior, or graduate year; renewable. Award amount: varies. Number of awards: varies. *Eligibility Requirements:* Applicant must be enrolled or expecting to enroll full-time at a two-year or four-year institution or university; resident of Oregon and studying in Oregon. Available to U.S. citizens. *Application Requirements:* Application, essay, financial need analysis, references, transcript, activity chart. *Deadline:* March 1. **Contact:** Director of Grant Programs, Oregon Student Assistance Commission, 1500 Valley River Drive, Suite 100, Eugene, OR 97401-7020. Phone: 800-452-8807 Ext. 7395. Web site: www.osac.state.or.us.

Dorothy Campbell Memorial Scholarship. Renewable award for female Oregon high school graduates with a minimum 2.75 GPA. Must submit essay describing strong, continuing interest in golf and the contribution that sport has made to applicant's development. *Award:* Scholarship for use in freshman, sophomore, junior, or senior year; renewable. Award amount: varies. Number of awards: varies. *Eligibility Requirements:* Applicant must be enrolled or expecting to enroll full-time at a four-year institution; female; resident of Oregon; studying in Oregon and must have an interest in golf. Available to U.S. citizens. *Application Requirements:* Application, essay, financial need analysis, transcript, activity chart. *Deadline:* March 1. **Contact:** Director of Grant Programs, Oregon Student Assistance Commission, 1500 Valley River Drive, Suite 100, Eugene, OR 97401-7020. Phone: 800-452-8807 Ext. 7395. Web site: www.osac.state.or.us.

Glenn Jackson Scholars Scholarships (OCF). Award for graduating high school seniors who are dependents of employees or retirees of Oregon Department of Transportation or Parks and Recreation Department. Employees must have worked in their department at least three years as of the March 1 scholarship deadline. Award for maximum twelve undergraduate quarters or six quarters at a two-year institution. Visit Web site http://www.osac.state.or.us for more details. *Award:* Scholarship for use in freshman, sophomore, junior, or senior year; renewable. Award amount: varies. Number of awards: varies. *Eligibility

Requirements: Applicant must be high school student; planning to enroll or expecting to enroll full- or part-time at a four-year institution and resident of Oregon. Applicant or parent of applicant must be affiliated with Oregon Department of Transportation Parks and Recreation. Applicant or parent of applicant must have employment or volunteer experience in designated career field. Available to U.S. citizens. *Application Requirements:* Application, essay, financial need analysis, references, transcript, activity chart. *Deadline:* March 1. **Contact:** Director of Grant Programs, Oregon Student Assistance Commission, 1500 Valley River Drive, Suite 100, Eugene, OR 97401-7020. Phone: 800-452-8807 Ext. 7395. Web site: www.osac.state.or.us.

Lawrence R. Foster Memorial Scholarship. One-time award to students enrolled or planning to enroll in a public health degree program. First preference given to those working in the public health field and those pursuing a graduate degree in public health. Undergraduates entering junior or senior year health programs may apply if seeking a public health career, and not private practice. Prefer applicants from diverse cultures. Must provide three references. Additional essay required. Must be resident of Oregon. *Academic Fields/Career Goals:* Health and Medical Sciences. *Award:* Scholarship for use in junior, senior, graduate, or postgraduate years; renewable. Award amount: varies. Number of awards: varies. *Eligibility Requirements:* Applicant must be enrolled or expecting to enroll full- or part-time at a four-year institution and resident of Oregon. Available to U.S. citizens. *Application Requirements:* Application, essay, financial need analysis, references, transcript, activity chart. *Deadline:* March 1. **Contact:** Director of Grant Programs, Oregon Student Assistance Commission, 1500 Valley River Drive, Suite 100, Eugene, OR 97401-7020. Phone: 800-452-8807 Ext. 7395. Web site: www.osac.state.or.us.

Oregon Occupational Safety and Health Division Workers Memorial Scholarship. Available to Oregon residents who are high school graduates or GED recipients, and either who are the dependents or spouses of an Oregon worker who was killed or permanently disabled on the job. Submit essay of 500 words or less titled, "How has the injury or death of your parent or spouse affected or influenced your decision to further your education?ö. *Award:* Scholarship for use in freshman, sophomore, junior, senior, or graduate year; renewable. Award amount: varies. Number of awards: varies. *Eligibility Requirements:* Applicant must be enrolled or expecting to enroll full-time at a four-year institution or university and resident of Oregon. Applicant or parent of applicant must have employment or volunteer experience in designated career field. Available to U.S. citizens. *Application Requirements:* Application, essay, financial need analysis, test scores, transcript, social security number or workers compensation claim. *Deadline:* March 1. **Contact:** Director of Grant Programs, Oregon Student Assistance Commission, 1500 Valley River Drive, Suite 100, Eugene, OR 97401-7020. Phone: 800-452-8807 Ext. 7395. Web site: www.osac.state.or.us.

Oregon Scholarship Fund Community College Student Award. Scholarship open to Oregon residents enrolled or planning to enroll in Oregon community college programs. May apply for one additional year. *Award:* Scholarship for use in freshman or sophomore year; renewable. Award amount: varies. Number of awards: varies. *Eligibility Requirements:* Applicant must be enrolled or expecting to enroll full-time at a two-year institution; resident of Oregon and studying in Oregon. Available to U.S. citizens. *Application Requirements:* Application, essay, financial need analysis, transcript, activity chart. *Deadline:* March 1. **Contact:** Director of Grant Programs, Oregon Student Assistance Commission, 1500 Valley River Drive, Suite 100, Eugene, OR 97401-7020. Phone: 800-452-8807 Ext. 7395. Web site: www.osac.state.or.us.

Oregon Scholarship Fund Transfer Student Award. Award open to Oregon residents who are currently enrolled in their second year at a community college and are planning to transfer to a four-year college in Oregon. Prior recipients may apply for one additional year. *Award:* Scholarship for use in sophomore or junior year; renewable. Award amount: varies. Number of awards: varies. *Eligibility Requirements:* Applicant must be enrolled or expecting to enroll full-time at a two-

year or four-year institution; resident of Oregon and studying in Oregon. Available to U.S. citizens. *Application Requirements:* Application, essay, financial need analysis, transcript, activity chart. *Deadline:* March 1. **Contact:** Director of Grant Programs, Oregon Student Assistance Commission, 1500 Valley River Drive, Suite 100, Eugene, OR 97401-7020. Phone: 800-452-8807 Ext. 7395. Web site: www.osac.state.or.us.

Oregon Student Assistance Commission Employee and Dependent Scholarship. Award for current permanent employees of the OSAC, who are past initial trial service or legally dependent children of current permanent employees at the time of the March 1 scholarship deadline or legally dependent children of an employee who retires, is permanently disabled, or deceased directly from employment at OSAC. Dependents must enroll full-time and employees must enroll at least half-time. Must reapply each year for up to four years. *Award:* Scholarship for use in freshman, sophomore, junior, or senior year; not renewable. Award amount: varies. Number of awards: 1. *Eligibility Requirements:* Applicant must be enrolled or expecting to enroll full- or part-time at a four-year institution and resident of Oregon. Available to U.S. citizens. *Application Requirements:* Application, essay, transcript, activities chart. *Deadline:* March 1. **Contact:** Director of Grant Programs, Oregon Student Assistance Commission, 1500 Valley River Drive, Suite 100, Eugene, OR 97401-7020. Phone: 800-452-8807 Ext. 7395. Web site: www.osac.state.or.us.

Oregon Trucking Association Safety Council Scholarship. One-time award available to a child of an Oregon Trucking Association member, or child of employee of member. Applicants must be Oregon residents who are graduating high school seniors from an Oregon high school. *Award:* Scholarship for use in freshman year; not renewable. Award amount: varies. Number of awards: 4. *Eligibility Requirements:* Applicant must be high school student; planning to enroll or expecting to enroll full-time at a four-year institution and resident of Oregon. Applicant or parent of applicant must be affiliated with Oregon Trucking Association. Applicant or parent of applicant must have employment or volunteer experience in designated career field. Available to U.S. citizens. *Application Requirements:* Application, essay, financial need analysis, references, transcript, activity chart. *Deadline:* March 1. **Contact:** Director of Grant Programs, Oregon Student Assistance Commission, 1500 Valley River Drive, Suite 100, Eugene, OR 97401-7020. Phone: 800-452-8807 Ext. 7395. Web site: www.osac.state.or.us.

Oregon Veterans' Education Aid. To be eligible, veteran must have served in U.S. armed forces 90 days and been discharged under honorable conditions. Must be U.S. citizen and Oregon resident. Korean War veteran or received campaign or expeditionary medal or ribbon awarded by U.S. armed forces for services after June 30, 1958. Full-time students receive $50 per month, and part-time students receive $35 per month. *Award:* Grant for use in freshman, sophomore, junior, senior, graduate, or postgraduate years; not renewable. Award amount: $150. Number of awards: up to 100. *Eligibility Requirements:* Applicant must be enrolled or expecting to enroll full-time at a two-year, four-year, or technical institution or university; resident of Oregon and studying in Oregon. Available to U.S. citizens. Applicant or parent must meet one or more of the following requirements: general military experience; retired from active duty; disabled or killed as a result of military service; prisoner of war; or missing in action. *Application Requirements:* Application, certified copy of DD Form 214. *Deadline:* continuous. **Contact:** Loriann Sheridan, Educational Aid Coordinator, Oregon Department of Veterans Affairs, 700 Summer Street, NE, Salem, OR 97301-1289. E-mail: sheridl@odva.state.or.us. Phone: 503-373-2085. Fax: 503-373-2393. Web site: www.odva.state.or.us.

Robert C. Byrd Honors Scholarship-Oregon. Renewable award available to Oregon high school seniors with a GPA of at least 3.85 or a GED score of 3300 and ACT scores of at least 29 or SAT combined math and critical reading scores of 1300. See Web site: http://www.osac.state.or.us for more information. Deadline: March 1. *Award:* Scholarship for use in freshman, sophomore, junior, or senior year; renewable. Award amount: varies. Number of awards: 15–75. *Eligibil-*

ity Requirements: Applicant must be high school student; planning to enroll or expecting to enroll full-time at a two-year or four-year institution and resident of Oregon. Available to U.S. citizens. *Application Requirements:* Application, essay, financial need analysis, test scores, transcript, activity chart. *Deadline:* March 1. **Contact:** Scholarship and Access Programs, Oregon Student Assistance Commission, 1500 Valley River Drive, Suite 100, Eugene, OR 97401-7020. Phone: 541-687-7395. Web site: www.osac.state.or.us.

UTAH

New Century Scholarship. Scholarship for qualified high school graduates of Utah. Must attend Utah state-operated college. Award depends on number of hours student enrolled. Please contact for further eligibility requirements. Eligible recipients receive an award equal to 75 percent of tuition for 60 credit hours toward the completion of a bachelor's degree. For more details see Web site: http://www.utahsbr.edu. *Award:* Scholarship for use in freshman, sophomore, junior, or senior year; renewable. Award amount: $1300–$3400. Number of awards: 1. *Eligibility Requirements:* Applicant must be enrolled or expecting to enroll full- or part-time at a four-year institution or university; resident of Utah and studying in Utah. Available to U.S. citizens. *Application Requirements:* Application, transcript, GPA/copy of enrollment verification from an eligible Utah 4-year institution, verification from registrar of completion of requirements for associates degree. *Deadline:* continuous. **Contact:** Charles Downer, Compliance Officer, Utah State Board of Regents, Board of Regents Building, The Gateway, 60 South 400 West, Salt Lake City, UT 84101-1284. E-mail: cdowner@utahsbr.edu. Phone: 801-321-7221. Fax: 801-366-8470. Web site: www.utahsbr.edu.

Terrill H. Bell Teaching Incentive Loan. Designed to provide financial assistance to outstanding Utah students pursuing a degree in education. The incentive loan funds full-time tuition and general fees for eight semesters. After graduation/certification the loan may be forgiven if the recipient teaches in a Utah public school or accredited private school (K-12). Dollar value varies. Loan forgiveness is done on a year-for-year basis. For more details see Web site: http://www.utahsbr.edu. *Academic Fields/Career Goals:* Education. *Award:* Forgivable loan for use in freshman, sophomore, junior, senior, or graduate year; renewable. Award amount: varies. Number of awards: 365. *Eligibility Requirements:* Applicant must be enrolled or expecting to enroll full-time at a two-year or four-year institution or university; resident of Utah and studying in Utah. Available to U.S. citizens. *Application Requirements:* Application, essay, references, test scores, transcript. *Deadline:* varies. **Contact:** Charles Downer, Compliance Officer, Utah State Board of Regents, Board of Regents Building, The Gateway, 60 South 400 West, Salt Lake City, UT 84101-1284. E-mail: cdowner@utahsbr.edu. Phone: 801-321-7221. Fax: 801-366-8470. Web site: www.utahsbr.edu.

T.H. Bell Teaching Incentive Loan-Utah. Renewable awards for Utah residents who are high school seniors wishing to pursue teaching careers. The award value varies depending upon tuition and fees at a Utah institution. Must agree to teach in a Utah public school or pay back loan through monthly installments. Must be a U.S. citizen. Deadline: April 27. *Academic Fields/Career Goals:* Education; Special Education. *Award:* Forgivable loan for use in freshman year; renewable. Award amount: varies. Number of awards: 25–50. *Eligibility Requirements:* Applicant must be high school student; planning to enroll or expecting to enroll full-time at a four-year institution or university; resident of Utah and studying in Utah. Available to U.S. citizens. *Application Requirements:* Application, essay, test scores, transcript. *Deadline:* April 27. **Contact:** Diane DeMan, Executive Secretary, Utah State Office of Education, 250 East 500 South, PO Box 144200, Salt Lake City, UT 84111. Phone: 801-538-7741. Fax: 801-538-7973. Web site: www.schools.utah.gov.

Utah Centennial Opportunity Program for Education. The award is available to students with substantial financial need for use at any of the participating Utah institutions. The student must be a Utah resident. Contact the financial aid office of the participating institution for requirements and deadlines. *Award:* Grant for use in freshman, sophomore, junior, or senior year; not renewable. Award amount: $300–$5000. Number of awards: up to 2102. *Eligibility Requirements:* Applicant must be enrolled or expecting to enroll full- or part-time at a two-year, four-year, or technical institution or university; resident of Utah and studying in Utah. Available to U.S. citizens. *Application Requirements:* Financial need analysis. *Deadline:* continuous. **Contact:** Ms. Lynda L. Reid, Student Aid Specialist III, Utah Higher Education Assistance Authority, 60 South 400 West, The Board of Regents Building, The Gateway, Salt Lake City, UT 84101-1284. E-mail: lreid@utahsbr.edu. Phone: 801-321-7207. Fax: 801-366-8470. Web site: www.uheaa.org.

Utah Leveraging Educational Assistance Partnership. The award is available to students with substantial financial need for use at any of the participating Utah institutions. The student must be a Utah resident. Contact the financial aid office of the participating institution for requirements and deadlines. *Award:* Grant for use in freshman, sophomore, junior, or senior year; not renewable. Award amount: $300–$2500. Number of awards: 1–3886. *Eligibility Requirements:* Applicant must be enrolled or expecting to enroll full- or part-time at a two-year, four-year, or technical institution or university; resident of Utah and studying in Utah. Available to U.S. citizens. *Application Requirements:* Financial need analysis. *Deadline:* continuous. **Contact:** Ms. Lynda L. Reid, Student Aid Specialist III, Utah Higher Education Assistance Authority, 60 South 400 West, The Board of Regents Building, The Gateway, Salt Lake City, UT 84101-1284. E-mail: lreid@utahsbr.edu. Phone: 801-321-7207. Fax: 801-366-8470. Web site: www.uheaa.org.

WASHINGTON

American Indian Endowed Scholarship. Awarded to financially needy undergraduate and graduate students with close social and cultural ties with a Native-American community. Must be Washington resident, enrolled full-time at Washington school. Deadline: May 15. *Award:* Scholarship for use in freshman, sophomore, junior, senior, or graduate year; renewable. Award amount: $500–$2000. Number of awards: 15. *Eligibility Requirements:* Applicant must be American Indian/Alaska Native; enrolled or expecting to enroll full-time at a two-year, four-year, or technical institution or university; resident of Washington and studying in Washington. Available to U.S. citizens. *Application Requirements:* Application, financial need analysis. *Deadline:* May 15. **Contact:** Ann Lee, Program Manager, Washington Higher Education Coordinating Board, 917 Lakeridge Way, PO Box 43430, Olympia, WA 98504-3430. E-mail: annl@hecb.wa.gov. Phone: 360-755-7843. Fax: 360-753-7808. Web site: www.hecb.wa.gov.

Educational Opportunity Grant. Annual grants of $2500 to encourage financially needy, placebound students to complete bachelor's degree. Must be unable to continue education due to family or work commitments, health concerns, financial needs or other similar factors. Must be Washington residents, and have completed two years of college. Grants can only be used at eligible four-year colleges in Washington. Applications are accepted from the beginning of April through the following months until funds are depleted. *Award:* Grant for use in junior or senior year; renewable. Award amount: $2500. Number of awards: 1300. *Eligibility Requirements:* Applicant must be enrolled or expecting to enroll full-time at a four-year institution; resident of Washington and studying in Washington. Available to U.S. citizens. *Application Requirements:* Application, financial need analysis. *Deadline:* continuous. **Contact:** Dawn Cypriano-McAferty, Program Manager, Washington Higher Education Coordinating Board, 917 Lakeridge Way, PO Box 43430, Olympia, WA 98504-3430. E-mail: eog@hecb.wa.gov. Phone: 360-753-7800. Fax: 360-753-7808. Web site: www.hecb.wa.gov.

Future Teachers Conditional Scholarship and Loan Repayment Program. The program is designed to encourage outstanding students and paraprofessionals to become teachers. Participants must agree to teach in Washington K-12 schools, in return for conditional scholarships or loan repayments. Additional consideration is given to individu-

als seeking certification or additional endorsements in teacher subject shortage areas, as well as to individuals with demonstrated bilingual ability. Must be residents of Washington and attend an institution in Washington. *Academic Fields/Career Goals:* Education. *Award:* Forgivable loan for use in freshman, sophomore, junior, or senior year; renewable. Award amount: $2600–$5800. Number of awards: 50. *Eligibility Requirements:* Applicant must be enrolled or expecting to enroll full- or part-time at a two-year or four-year institution or university; resident of Washington and studying in Washington. Available to U.S. citizens. *Application Requirements:* Application, essay, references, transcript, bilingual verification (if applicable). *Deadline:* October 15. **Contact:** Mary Knutson, Program Coordinator, Washington Higher Education Coordinating Board, 917 Lakeridge Way, PO Box 43430, Olympia, WA 98504-3430. E-mail: futureteachers@hecb.wa.gov. Phone: 360-753-7845. Fax: 360-753-7808. Web site: www.hecb.wa.gov.

Health Professional Scholarship Program. The program was created to attract and retain health professionals, to serve in critical shortage areas in Washington state. Must sign a promissory note agreeing to serve for a minimum of three years in a designated shortage area in Washington state or pay back funds at double penalty with the interest. *Academic Fields/Career Goals:* Health and Medical Sciences. *Award:* Forgivable loan for use in junior, senior, or graduate year; renewable. Award amount: varies. Number of awards: varies. *Eligibility Requirements:* Applicant must be enrolled or expecting to enroll full- or part-time at a four-year institution or university. Available to U.S. citizens. *Application Requirements:* Application, references, transcript. *Deadline:* April 30. **Contact:** Kathy McVay, Program Administrator, Washington Higher Education Coordinating Board, PO Box 47834, Olympia, WA 98504-7834. E-mail: kathy.mcvay@doh.wa.gov. Phone: 360-236-2816. Web site: www.hecb.wa.gov.

Robert C. Byrd Honors Scholarship-Washington. Scholarship for high school seniors who demonstrate outstanding academic achievement and show promise of continued academic excellence. Must be Washington residents. *Award:* Scholarship for use in freshman, sophomore, junior, or senior year; not renewable. Award amount: $1500–$6000. Number of awards: varies. *Eligibility Requirements:* Applicant must be high school student; planning to enroll or expecting to enroll full-time at a four-year institution or university and resident of Washington. Available to U.S. citizens. *Application Requirements:* Application, transcript. *Deadline:* varies. **Contact:** Kara Larson, Superintendent of Public Instruction, Washington Higher Education Coordinating Board, PO Box 47200, Olympia, WA 98504-7200. E-mail: kara.larson@k12.wa.us. Phone: 360-725-6225. Web site: www.hecb.wa.gov.

State Need Grant. The program helps Washington's lowest-income undergraduate students to pursue degrees, hone skills, or retrain for new careers. Students with family incomes equal to or less than 50 percent of the state median are eligible for up to 100 percent of the maximum grant. Students with family incomes between 51 percent and 65 percent of the state median are eligible for up to 75 percent of the maximum grant. *Award:* Grant for use in freshman, sophomore, junior, or senior year; renewable. Award amount: $553–$5156. Number of awards: 55,000. *Eligibility Requirements:* Applicant must be enrolled or expecting to enroll full- or part-time at a two-year or four-year institution or university; resident of Washington and studying in Washington. Available to U.S. citizens. *Application Requirements:* Application, financial need analysis, FAFSA. *Deadline:* continuous. **Contact:** Karola Longoria, Administrative Assistant, Student Financial Assist, Washington Higher Education Coordinating Board, 917 Lakeridge Way, PO Box 43430, Olympia, WA 98504-3430. E-mail: karolal@hecb.wa.gov. Phone: 360-753-7850. Fax: 360-753-7808. Web site: www.hecb.wa.gov.

Washington Award for Vocational Excellence. Award for students who are currently a state resident enrolled in a Washington State high school, skills center, or public community or technical college. Recipients of this annual award receive monetary grants, based on availability of funds. *Award:* Grant for use in freshman or sophomore year; renewable. Award amount: varies. Number of awards: 147. *Eligibil-*

ity Requirements: Applicant must be enrolled or expecting to enroll full- or part-time at a two-year, four-year, or technical institution or university; resident of Washington and studying in Washington. Available to U.S. and non-U.S. citizens. *Application Requirements:* Application, essay, references. *Deadline:* March 2. **Contact:** Lee Williams, Program Administrator, Washington State Workforce Training and Education Coordinating Board, 128 Tenth Avenue, SW, PO Box 43105, Olympia, WA 98504-3105. E-mail: lwilliams@wtb.wa.gov. Phone: 360-586-3321. Fax: 360-586-5862. Web site: www.wtb.wa.gov.

Washington Award for Vocational Excellence (WAVE). Award to honor vocational students from the districts of Washington. Grants for up to two years of undergraduate resident tuition. Must be enrolled in Washington high school, skills center, or technical college at time of application. Must complete 360 hours in single vocational program in high school or one year at technical college. Contact principal or guidance counselor for more information. *Award:* Grant for use in freshman, sophomore, junior, or senior year; renewable. Award amount: $2586–$5887. Number of awards: 147. *Eligibility Requirements:* Applicant must be enrolled or expecting to enroll full-time at a two-year, four-year, or technical institution or university; resident of Washington and studying in Washington. Available to U.S. citizens. *Application Requirements:* Application. *Deadline:* February 16. **Contact:** Ann Lee, Program Manager, Washington Higher Education Coordinating Board, 917 Lakeridge Way, PO Box 43430, Olympia, WA 98504-3430. E-mail: annl@hecb.wa.gov. Phone: 360-753-7843. Fax: 360-753-7808. Web site: www.hecb.wa.gov.

Washington Scholars Program. Awards high school students from the legislative districts of Washington. Must be enrolled in college or university in Washington. Scholarships equal up to four years of full-time resident undergraduate tuition and fees. Contact principal or guidance counselor for more information. *Award:* Grant for use in freshman, sophomore, junior, or senior year; renewable. Award amount: $2586–$5887. Number of awards: 147. *Eligibility Requirements:* Applicant must be high school student; planning to enroll or expecting to enroll full-time at a four-year institution or university; resident of Washington and studying in Washington. Available to U.S. citizens. *Application Requirements:* Application. *Deadline:* continuous. **Contact:** Ann Lee, Program Manager, Washington Higher Education Coordinating Board, 917 Lakeridge Way, PO Box 43430, Olympia, WA 98504-3430. E-mail: annl@hecb.wa.gov. Phone: 360-753-7843. Fax: 360-753-7808. Web site: www.hecb.wa.gov.

WICHE Professional Student Exchange. Scholarship for students at senior year of undergraduate degree or above. Must be residents of Washington. Must return to Washington and serve for a minimum of four years. Deadline: October 15. *Award:* Scholarship for use in senior, graduate, or postgraduate years; renewable. Award amount: $13,600–$17,000. Number of awards: 14. *Eligibility Requirements:* Applicant must be enrolled or expecting to enroll full-time at an institution or university; resident of Washington and studying in Washington. Available to U.S. citizens. *Application Requirements:* Application, financial need analysis, transcript. *Deadline:* October 15. **Contact:** Dawn McAferty, Program Manager, Washington Higher Education Coordinating Board, 917 Lakeridge Way, PO Box 43430, Olympia, WA 98504. E-mail: dawnc@hecb.wa.gov. Phone: 360-753-7846. Fax: 360-704-6246. Web site: www.hecb.wa.gov.

WYOMING

Douvas Memorial Scholarship. Available to Wyoming residents who are first-generation Americans. Must be between 18 and 22 years old. Must be used at any Wyoming public institution of higher education for study in freshman year. *Award:* Scholarship for use in freshman year; not renewable. Award amount: $500. Number of awards: 1. *Eligibility Requirements:* Applicant must be age 18-22; enrolled or expecting to enroll full- or part-time at a two-year or four-year institution or university; resident of Wyoming and studying in Wyoming. Available to U.S. citizens. *Application Requirements:* Application. *Deadline:* March 24. **Contact:** Gerry Maas, Director, Health and Safety, Wyoming Department of Education, 2300 Capitol Avenue, Hathaway

Building, Second Floor, Cheyenne, WY 82002-0050. E-mail: gmaas@educ.state.wy.us. Phone: 307-777-6282. Fax: 307-777-6234.

Hathaway Scholarship. Scholarship for Wyoming students to pursue postsecondary education within the state. *Award:* Scholarship for use in freshman, sophomore, junior, or senior year; not renewable. Award amount: $1000. Number of awards: 1. *Eligibility Requirements:* Applicant must be enrolled or expecting to enroll full-time at a two-year or four-year institution or university and resident of Wyoming. Available to U.S. citizens. *Application Requirements:* Application. *Deadline:* varies. **Contact:** Gerry Maas, Director, Health and Safety, Wyoming Department of Education, 2300 Capitol Avenue, Hathaway Building, Second Floor, Cheyenne, WY 82002-0050. E-mail: gmaas@educ.state.wy.us. Phone: 307-777-6282. Fax: 307-777-6234.

Superior Student in Education Scholarship-Wyoming. Scholarship available each year to sixteen new Wyoming high school graduates who plan to teach in Wyoming. The award covers costs of undergraduate tuition at the University of Wyoming or any Wyoming community college. *Academic Fields/Career Goals:* Education. *Award:* Scholarship for use in freshman, sophomore, junior, or senior year; renewable. Award amount: varies. Number of awards: 16. *Eligibility Requirements:* Applicant must be high school student; planning to enroll or expecting to enroll full-time at a four-year institution or university; resident of Wyoming and studying in Wyoming. Applicant must have 3.0 GPA or higher. Available to U.S. citizens. *Application Requirements:* Application, references, test scores, transcript. *Deadline:* October 31. **Contact:** Joel Anne Berrigan, Assistant Director, Scholarships, State of Wyoming, administered by University of Wyoming, Student Financial Aid, Department 3335, 1000 East University Avenue, Laramie, WY 82071-3335. E-mail: finaid@uwyo.edu. Phone: 307-766-2117. Fax: 307-766-3800. Web site: www.uwyo.edu/scholarships.

Vietnam Veterans Award-Wyoming. Scholarship available to Wyoming residents who served in the armed forces between August 5, 1964, and May 7, 1975, and received a Vietnam service medal. *Award:* Scholarship for use in freshman, sophomore, junior, or senior year; renewable. Award amount: varies. Number of awards: varies. *Eligibility Requirements:* Applicant must be enrolled or expecting to enroll full- or part-time at a two-year or four-year institution or university and resident of Wyoming. Available to U.S. citizens. Applicant must have general military experience. *Application Requirements:* Application. *Deadline:* continuous. **Contact:** Joel Anne Berrigan, Assistant Director, Scholarships, State of Wyoming, administered by University of Wyoming, Student Financial Aid, Department 3335, 1000 East University Avenue, Laramie, WY 82071-3335. E-mail: finaid@uwyo.edu. Phone: 307-766-2117. Fax: 307-766-3800. Web site: www.uwyo.edu/scholarships.

Searching for Four-Year Colleges Online

The Internet can be a great tool for gathering information about four-year colleges and universities. There are many worthwhile sites that are ready to help guide you through the various aspects of the selection process, including Peterson's College Search at www.petersons.com.

HOW PETERSON'S COLLEGE SEARCH CAN HELP

Peterson's College Search is a comprehensive information resource that will help you make sense of the college admissions process and is a great place to start your college search-and-selection journey—it's as easy as these three steps:

1. Decide what's important
2. Define your criteria
3. Get results

Decide What's Important

There's no such thing as a best college—there's only the best college *for you*! Peterson's College Search site is organized into various sections and offers you enhanced search criteria—and it's easy to use! You can find colleges by name or keyword for starters, or do a detailed search based on the following:

- The Basics (location, setting, size, cost, type, religious and ethnic affiliation)
- Student Body (male-female ratio, diversity, in-state vs. out-of-state)
- Getting In (selectivity, GPA)
- Academics (degree type, majors, special programs and services)
- Campus Life (sports, clubs, fraternities and sororities, housing)

Define Your Criteria

Now it's time to take to define your criteria by taking a closer look at some more specific details. Here you are able to answer questions about what is important to you, skip questions that aren't important, and click for instant results. You'll be prompted to think about criteria such as:

- Where do you want to study?
- What range of tuition are you willing to consider?
- How many people do you want to go to school with?
- What kinds of clubs and activities are you looking for?

Get Results

Once you have gotten your results, simply click on any school to get information about the institution, including school type, setting, degrees offered, comprehensive cost, entrance difficulty, application deadline, undergraduate student population, minority breakdown, international population, housing info, freshman, faculty, majors, academic programs, student life, athletics, facilities/endowment, costs, financial aid, and applying. Keep reading but take a peek at all the great info you'll see on Petersons.com on the next page!

Get Free Info

If, after looking at the information provided on Peterson's College Search, you still have questions, you can send an e-mail directly to the admissions department of the school. Just click on the "Get Free Info" button and send your message!

Visit School Site

For institutions that have provided information about their Web sites, simply click on the "Visit School Site" button and you will be taken directly to that institution's Web page. Once you arrive at the school's Web site, look around and get a feel for the place. Often, schools offer virtual tours of the campus, complete with photos and commentary.

Close-Up

If the schools you are interested in have provided Peterson's with a **Close-Up,** you can do a keyword search on that description. Here, schools are given the opportunity to communicate unique features of their programs to prospective students.

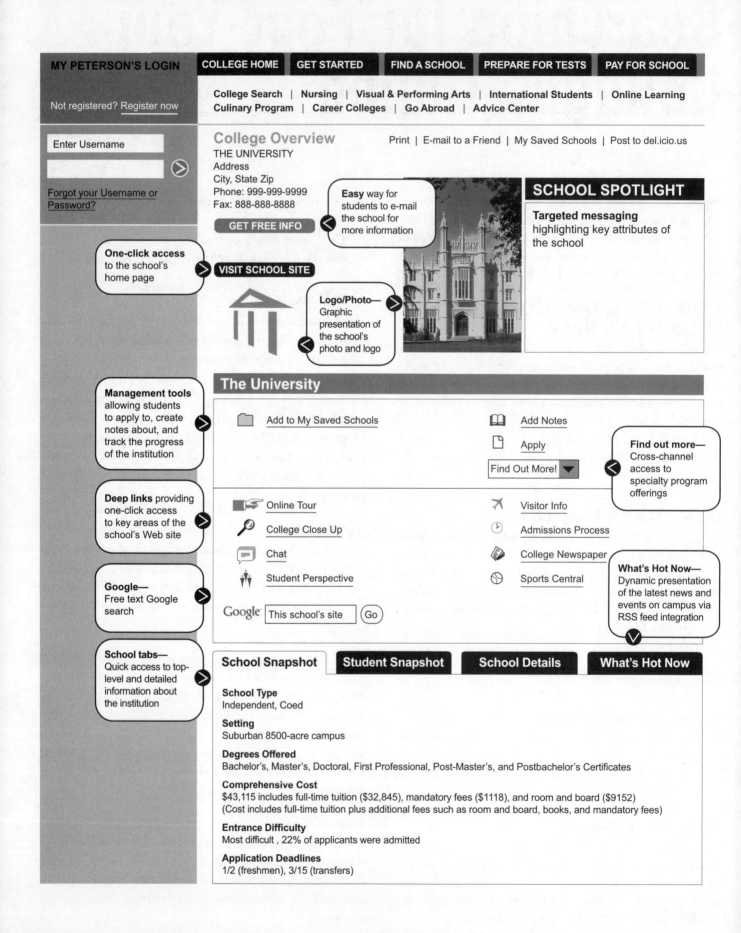

Add to My Saved Schools/Add Notes/Apply

The "Add to My Saved Schools" features are designed to help you with your college planning with management tools to create notes about and track the school. The Apply link gives you the ability to directly apply to the school online.

WRITE ADMISSIONS ESSAYS

This year, 500,000 college applicants will write 500,000 different admissions essays. Half will be rejected by their first-choice school, while only 11 percent will gain admission to the nation's most selective colleges. With acceptance rates at all-time lows, setting yourself apart requires more than just blockbuster SAT scores and impeccable transcripts—it requires the perfect application essay. Named "the world's premier application essay editing service" by the *New York Times* Learning Network and "one of the best essay services on the Internet" by the *Washington Post*, EssayEdge (www.essayedge.com) has helped more applicants write successful personal statements than any other company in the world. Learn more about EssayEdge and how it can give you an edge over hundreds of applicants with comparable academic credentials.

PRACTICE FOR YOUR TEST

At Peterson's, we understand that the college admissions process can be very stressful. With the stakes so high and the competition getting tighter every year, it's easy to feel like the process is out of your control. Fortunately, preparing for college admissions tests, like the PSAT/NMSQT, SAT, and ACT, helps you exert some control over the options you will have available to you. You can visit Peterson's Prep Central to learn more about how Peterson's can help you maximize your scores—and your options.

USE THE TOOLS TO YOUR ADVANTAGE

Choosing a college is an involved and complicated process. The tools available to you on www.petersons.com can help you to be more productive in this process. So, what are you waiting for? Fire up your computer; your future alma mater may be just a click away!

How to Use This Guide

This article provides an outline of the **Profile** format, describing the items covered. All college information presented was supplied to Peterson's by the colleges themselves. Any item that does not apply to a particular college or for which no current information was supplied may be omitted from that college's **Profile**. Colleges that were unable to supply usable data in time for publication are listed by name and, if available, Web address.

PROFILES OF COLLEGES IN THE WEST

This section presents pertinent factual and statistical data for each college in a standard format for easy comparison.

General Information

The first paragraph gives a brief introduction to the college, covering the following elements.

Type of student body: The categories are *men's* (100 percent of the student body), *primarily men's, women's* (100 percent of the student body), *primarily women's*, and *coed*. A few schools are designated as *undergraduate: women only; graduate: coed* or *undergraduate: men only; graduate: coed*. A college may also be designated as coordinate with another institution, indicating that there are separate colleges or campuses for men and women, but facilities, courses, and institutional governance are shared.

Institutional control: A *public* college receives its funding wholly or primarily from the federal, state, and/or local government. The term *private* indicates an independent, nonprofit institution, that is, one whose funding comes primarily from private sources and tuition. This category includes independent, religious colleges, which may also specify a particular religious denomination or church affiliation. Profit-making institutions are designated as *proprietary*.

Institutional type: A *two-year college* awards associate degrees and/or offers the first two years of a bachelor's degree program. A *primarily two-year college* awards bachelor's degrees, but the vast majority of students are enrolled in two-year programs. A *four-year college* awards bachelor's degrees and may also award associate degrees, but it does not offer graduate (postbachelor's) degree programs. A *five-year college* offers a five-year bachelor's program in a professional field such as architecture or pharmacy but does not award graduate degrees. An *upper-level institution* awards bachelor's degrees, but entering students must have at least two years of previous college-level credit; it may also offer graduate degree programs. A *comprehensive institution* awards

bachelor's degrees and may also award associate degrees; graduate degree programs are offered primarily at the master's, specialist's, or professional level, although one or two doctoral programs may also be offered. A *university* offers four years of undergraduate work plus graduate degrees through the doctorate in more than two academic and/or professional fields.

Founding date: This is the year the college came into existence or was chartered, reflecting the period during which it has existed as an educational institution, regardless of subsequent mergers or other organizational changes.

Degree levels: An *associate* degree program may consist of either a college-transfer program, equivalent to the first two years of a bachelor's degree, or a one- to three-year terminal program that provides training for a specific occupation. A *bachelor's* degree program represents a three- to five-year liberal arts, science, professional, or preprofessional program. A *master's* degree is the first graduate degree in the liberal arts and sciences and certain professional fields and usually requires one to two years of full-time study. A *doctoral* degree is the highest degree awarded in research-oriented academic disciplines and usually requires from three to six years of full-time graduate study; the *first professional* degrees in such fields as law and medicine are also at the doctoral level. For colleges that award degrees in one field only, such as art or music, the field of specialization is indicated.

Campus setting: This indicates the size of the campus in acres or hectares and its location.

Academic Information

This paragraph contains information on the following items.

Faculty: The number of full-time and part-time faculty members is given, followed by the percentage of the full-time faculty members who hold doctoral, first professional, or terminal degrees, and then the student-faculty ratio. (Not all colleges calculate the student-faculty ratio in the same way; Peterson's prints the ratio provided by the college.)

Library holdings: The numbers of books, serials, and audiovisual materials in the college's collections are listed.

Special programs: *Academic remediation for entering students* consists of instructional courses designed for students deficient in the general competencies necessary for a regular postsecondary curriculum and educational setting. *Services for LD students* include special help for learning-disabled students with resolvable difficulties, such as dyslexia. *Honors programs* are any special programs for very able students,

offering the opportunity for educational enrichment, independent study, acceleration, or some combination of these. *Cooperative (co-op) education programs* are formal arrangements with off-campus employers, allowing students to combine work and study in order to gain degree-related experience, usually extending the time required to complete a degree. *Study abroad* is an arrangement by which a student completes part of the academic program studying in another country. A college may operate a campus abroad or it may have a cooperative agreement with other U.S. institutions or institutions in other countries. *Advanced placement* gives credit toward a degree awarded for acceptable scores on College Board Advanced Placement tests. *Accelerated degree programs* allow students to earn a bachelor's degree in three academic years. *Freshmen honors college* is a separate academic program for talented freshmen. *English as a second language (ESL)* is a course of study designed specifically for students whose native language is not English. *Double major* consists of a program of study in which a student concurrently completes the requirements of two majors. *Independent study* consists of academic work, usually undertaken outside the regular classroom structure, chosen or designed by the student with departmental approval and instructor supervision. *Distance learning* consists of credit courses that can be accessed off campus via cable television, the Internet, satellite, videotapes, correspondence courses, or other media. *Self-designed major* is a program of study based on individual interests, designed by the student with the assistance of an adviser. *Summer session for credit* includes summer courses through which students may make up degree work or accelerate their program. *Part-time degree programs* offer students the ability to earn a degree through part-time enrollment in regular session (daytime) classes or evening, weekend, or summer classes. *External degree programs* are programs of study in which students earn credits toward a degree through a combination of independent study, college courses, proficiency examinations, and personal experience. External degree programs require minimal or no classroom attendance. *Adult/continuing education programs* are courses offered for nontraditional students who are currently working or are returning to formal education. *Internships* are any short-term, supervised work experience, usually related to a student's major field, for which the student earns academic credit. The work can be full- or part-time, on or off campus, paid or unpaid. *Off-campus study* is a formal arrangement with one or more domestic institutions under which students may take courses at the other institution(s) for credit.

Most popular majors: The most popular field or fields of study at the college, in terms of the number of undergraduate degrees conferred in 2006, are listed.

Student Body Statistics

Enrollment: The total number of students, undergraduates, and freshmen (or entering students for an upper-level institution) enrolled in degree programs as of fall 2006 are given.

With reference to the undergraduate enrollment for fall 2006, the percentages of women and men and the number of states and countries from which students hail are listed. The following percentages are also provided: in-state students, international students, and the percentage of last year's graduating class who went on to graduate and professional schools.

Expenses

Costs are given in each profile according to the most up-to-date figures available from each college for the 2006–07 or 2007–08 academic year.

Annual expenses may be expressed as a comprehensive fee (includes full-time tuition, mandatory fees, and college room and board) or as separate figures for full-time tuition, fees, room and board, and/or room only. For public institutions where tuition differs according to residence, separate figures are given for area and/or state residents and for nonresidents. Part-time tuition and fees are expressed in terms of a per-unit rate (per credit, per semester hour, etc.) as specified by the college.

The tuition structure at some institutions is complex in that freshmen and sophomores may be charged a different rate from that for juniors and seniors; a professional or vocational division may have a different fee structure from the liberal arts division of the same institution; or part-time tuition may be prorated on a sliding scale according to the number of credit hours taken. In all of these cases, the average figures are given along with an explanation of the basis for the variable rate. For colleges that report that room and board costs vary according to the type of accommodation and meal plan, the average costs are given. The phrase *no college housing* indicates that the college does not own or operate any housing facilities for its undergraduate students.

Financial Aid

This paragraph contains information on the following items.

Forms of financial aid: The categories of college-administered aid available to undergraduates are listed. College-administered means that the college itself determines the recipient and amount of each award. The types of aid covered are *non-need scholarships*, *need-based scholarships*, *athletic grants*, and *part-time jobs*.

Financial aid: This item pertains to undergraduates who enrolled full-time in a four-year college in 2005 or 2006. The figures given are the dollar amount of the average financial aid package, including scholarships, grants, loans, and part-time jobs, received by such undergraduates.

Financial aid application deadline: This deadline may be given as a specific date, as continuous processing up to a specific date or until all available aid has been awarded, or as a priority date rather than a strict deadline, meaning that students are encouraged to apply by that date in order to have the best chance of obtaining aid.

Freshman Admission

The supporting data that a student must submit when applying for freshman admission are grouped into three categories: *required for all*, *recommended*, and *required for some*. They may include an essay, a high school transcript, letters of recommendation, an interview on campus or with local alumni, standardized test scores, and, for certain types of schools or programs, special requirements such as a musical audition or an art portfolio.

The most commonly required standardized tests are the ACT and the College Board's SAT and SAT Subject Tests. TOEFL (Test of English as a Foreign Language) is for international students whose native language is not English.

The application deadline for admission is given as either a specific date or *rolling*. Rolling means that applications are processed as they are received, and qualified students are accepted as long as there are openings. The application deadline for out-of-state students is indicated if it differs from the date for state residents. *Early decision* and *early action* deadlines are also given when applicable. Early decision is a program whereby students may apply early, are notified of acceptance or rejection well in advance of the usual notification date, and agree to accept an offer of admission, the assumption being that only one early application has been made. Early action is the same as early decision except that applicants are not obligated to accept an offer of admission.

Transfer Admission

This paragraph gives the application requirements and application deadline for a student applying for admission as a transfer from another institution. In addition to the requirements previously listed for freshman applicants, requirements for transfers may also include a college transcript and a minimum college grade point average (expressed as a number on a scale of 0 to 4.0, where 4.0 equals A, 3.0 equals B, etc.). The name of the person to contact for additional transfer information is also given if it is different from the person listed in **For Further Information**.

Entrance Difficulty

This paragraph contains the college's own assessment of its *entrance difficulty* level, including notation of an *open admission policy* where applicable. Open admission means that virtually all applicants are accepted without regard to standardized test scores, grade average, or class rank. A college may indicate that open admission is limited to a certain category of applicants, such as state residents, or does not apply to certain selective programs, often those in the health professions.

The five levels of entrance difficulty are *most difficult*, *very difficult*, *moderately difficult*, *minimally difficult*, and *noncompetitive*.

The final item in this paragraph is the percentage of applicants accepted for the fall 2006 freshman (or entering) class.

For Further Information

The name, title, and mailing address of the person to contact for more information on application and admission procedures are given at the end of the **Profile**. A telephone number, fax number, e-mail address, and Web site are also included in this paragraph for **Profiles** that do not contain this information in the paragraph on interviews and campus visits.

SPECIAL MESSAGE TO STUDENTS

In addition, a number of college admissions office staff members, as part of a major information-dissemination effort, have supplemented their **Profile** with special descriptive information on four topics of particular interest to students.

Social Life: This paragraph conveys a feeling for life on campus by addressing such questions as: What are the most popular activities? Are there active fraternities and sororities? What is the role of student government? Do most students live on campus or commute? Does the college have a religious orientation?

Academic Highlights: This paragraph describes some of the special features and characteristics of the college's academic program, such as special degree programs and opportunities for study abroad or internships.

Interviews and Campus Visits: Colleges that conduct on-campus admission interviews describe the importance of an interview in their admission process and what they try to learn about a student through the interview. For those colleges that do not interview applicants individually, there is information on how a student interested in the college can visit the campus to meet administrators, faculty members,

and currently enrolled students as well as on what the prospective applicant should try to accomplish through such a visit. This paragraph may also include a list of the most noteworthy places or things to see during a campus visit and the location, telephone number (including toll-free numbers if available), and business hours of the office to contact for information about appointments and campus visits. Also included, when available, is travel information, specifically the nearest commercial airport and the nearest interstate highway, with the appropriate exit.

For Further Information: The name and mailing address of the person and/or office to contact for more information on the school are included in this paragraph. A telephone number, fax number, e-mail address, and Web site may also be included.

CLOSE-UPS OF COLLEGES IN THE WEST

Two-page narrative descriptions appear in this section, providing an inside look at colleges and universities, shifting the focus to a variety of other factors, some of them intangible, that should also be considered. The descriptions presented in this section provide a wealth of statistics that are crucial components in the college decision-making equation—components such as tuition, financial aid, and major fields of study. Prepared exclusively by college officials, the descriptions are designed to help give students a better sense of the individuality of each institution, in terms that include campus environment, student activities, and lifestyle. Such quality-of-life intangibles can be the deciding factors in the college selection process.

The absence from this section of any college or university does not constitute an editorial decision on the part of Peterson's. In essence, this section is an open forum for colleges and universities, on a voluntary basis, to communicate their particular message to prospective college students. The colleges included have paid a fee to Peterson's to provide this information. The descriptions are edited to provide a consistent format across entries for your ease of comparison and are presented alphabetically by the official name of the institution.

PROFILES AND CLOSE-UPS OF OTHER COLLEGES TO CONSIDER

Do you know that schools sometimes target specific areas of the country for student recruitment, even if those states are not part of a specific region? In this section, you'll find **Profiles** and **Close-Ups** of schools outside the region of this guide looking to recruit students like you. The format

of both the **Profiles** and the **Close-Ups** in this section matches the format in the previous sections.

INDEXES

Majors and Degrees

This index lists hundreds of undergraduate major fields of study that are currently offered most widely. The majors appear in alphabetical order, each followed by an alphabetical list of the colleges that report offering a program in that field and the degree levels (*A* for associate, *B* for bachelor's) available. The majors represented here are based on the National Center for Education Statistics (NCES) 2000 Classification of Instructional Programs (CIP). The CIP is a taxonomic coding scheme that contains titles and descriptions of instructional programs, primarily at the postsecondary level. CIP was originally developed to facilitate NCES's collection and reporting of postsecondary degree completions, by major field of study, using standard classifications that capture the majority of program activity. The CIP is the accepted federal government reporting standard for classifying instructional programs. However, although the term "major" is used in this guide, some colleges may use other terms, such as "concentration," "program of study," or "field."

Athletic Programs and Scholarships

This index lists the colleges that report offering intercollegiate athletic programs, listed alphabetically. An *M* or *W* following the college name indicates that the sport is offered for men or women, respectively. An *s* in parentheses following an *M* or *W* indicates that athletic scholarships (or grants-in-aid) are offered by the college for men or women, respectively, in that sport.

ROTC Programs

This index lists the colleges that report offering Reserve Officers' Training Corps programs in one or more branches of the armed services, as indicated by letter codes following the college name: *A* for Army, *N* for Navy, and *AF* for Air Force. A *c* in parentheses following the branch letter code indicates that the program is offered through a cooperative arrangement on another college's campus.

Alphabetical Listing of Colleges and Universities

This index gives the page locations of various entries for all the colleges and universities in this book. The page numbers for the **Profiles** are printed in regular type, those for **Profiles**

with **Special Messages** in *italic* type, and those for **Close-Ups** in **boldface** type. When there is more than one number in **boldface** type, it indicates that the institution has more than one **Close-Up**.

DATA COLLECTION PROCEDURES

The data contained in the **Profiles** and **Indexes** were researched between fall 2006 and spring 2007 through *Peterson's Annual Survey of Undergraduate Institutions* and *Peterson's Annual Survey of Undergraduate Financial Aid.* Questionnaires were sent to the more than 2,100 colleges and universities that met the outlined inclusion criteria. All data included in this edition have been submitted by officials (usually admissions and financial aid officers, registrars, or institutional research personnel) at the colleges. In addition, many of the institutions that submitted data were contacted directly by the Peterson's research staff to verify unusual figures, resolve discrepancies, or obtain additional data. All usable information received in time for publication has been included. The omission of any particular item from an index or profile listing signifies that the information is either not applicable to that institution or not available. Because of Peterson's comprehensive editorial review and because all material comes directly from college officials, we believe that the information presented in this guide is accurate. You should check with a specific college or university at the time of application to verify such figures as tuition and fees, which may have changed since the publication of this volume.

CRITERIA FOR INCLUSION IN THIS BOOK

The term "four-year college" is the commonly used designation for institutions that grant the baccalaureate degree. Four years is the expected amount of time required to earn this degree, although some bachelor's degree programs may be completed in three years, others require five years, and part-time programs may take considerably longer. Upper-level institutions offer only the junior and senior years and accept only students with two years of college-level credit. Therefore, "four-year college" is a conventional term that accurately describes most of the institutions included in this guide, but it should not be taken literally in all cases.

To be included in this guide, an institution must have full accreditation or be a candidate for accreditation (preaccreditation) status by an institutional or specialized accrediting body recognized by the U.S. Department of Education or the Council for Higher Education Accreditation (CHEA). Institutional accrediting bodies, which review each institution as a whole, include the six regional associations of schools and colleges (Middle States, New England, North Central, Northwest, Southern, and Western), each of which is responsible for a specified portion of the United States and its territories. Other institutional accrediting bodies are national in scope and accredit specific kinds of institutions (e.g., Bible colleges, independent colleges, and rabbinical and Talmudic schools). Program registration by the New York State Board of Regents is considered to be the equivalent of institutional accreditation, since the board requires that all programs offered by an institution meet its standards before recognition is granted. There are recognized specialized or professional accrediting bodies in more than forty different fields, each of which is authorized to accredit institutions or specific programs in its particular field. For specialized institutions that offer programs in one field only, we designate this to be the equivalent of institutional accreditation. A full explanation of the accrediting process and complete information on recognized, institutional (regional and national) and specialized accrediting bodies can be found online at www.chea.org or at www.ed.gov/admins/finaid/accred/index.html.

Profiles of Colleges in the West

Map of the West

This map provides a general perspective on the West and shows the major metropolitan areas and capital of each state.

Alaska

ALASKA BIBLE COLLEGE

Glennallen, Alaska

Alaska Bible College is a coed, private, nondenominational, four-year college, founded in 1966, offering degrees at the associate and bachelor's levels. It has an 80-acre campus in Glennallen.

Academic Information The faculty has 7 members (43% full-time), 14% with terminal degrees. The student-faculty ratio is 7:1. The library holds 30,764 titles and 105 serial subscriptions. Special programs include academic remediation, advanced placement credit, double majors, self-designed majors, part-time degree programs (daytime), and internships. The most frequently chosen baccalaureate field is theology and religious vocations.
Student Body Statistics The student body is made up of 38 undergraduates (6 freshmen). 29 percent are women and 71 percent are men. Students come from 15 states and territories. 41 percent are from Alaska. 40 percent of the 2006 graduating class went on to graduate and professional schools.
Expenses for 2007–08 *Application fee:* $35. *Comprehensive fee:* $11,500 includes full-time tuition ($6500) and college room and board ($5000). *Part-time tuition:* $285 per credit hour.
Financial Aid Forms of aid include need-based and non-need-based scholarships and part-time jobs. The application deadline for financial aid is July 1 with a priority deadline of July 1.
Freshman Admission Alaska Bible College requires an essay, a high school transcript, a minimum 2.0 high school GPA, 2 recommendations, an interview, SAT or ACT scores, and TOEFL scores for international students. The application deadline for regular admission is July 1.
Transfer Admission The application deadline for admission is July 1.
Entrance Difficulty Alaska Bible College assesses its entrance difficulty level as minimally difficult. For the fall 2006 freshman class, 86 percent of the applicants were accepted.
For Further Information Contact Mrs. Carol C. Ridley, Director of Admissions, Alaska Bible College, Box 289, 200 College Road, Glennallen, AK 99588-0289. *Telephone:* 907-822-3201 or 800-478-7884 (toll-free). *Fax:* 907-822-5027. *E-mail:* info@akbible.edu. *Web site:* http://www.akbible.edu/.

ALASKA PACIFIC UNIVERSITY

Anchorage, Alaska

Alaska Pacific University is a coed, private, comprehensive institution, founded in 1959, offering degrees at the associate, bachelor's, and master's levels. It has a 170-acre campus in Anchorage.

Academic Information The faculty has 110 members (41% full-time), 37% with terminal degrees. The undergraduate student-faculty ratio is 9:1. The library holds 788,708 titles and 3,434 serial subscriptions. Special programs include academic remediation, services for learning-disabled students, study abroad, advanced placement credit, accelerated degree programs, double majors, independent study, distance learning, self-designed majors, summer session for credit, part-time degree programs (daytime, evenings, weekends, summer), adult/continuing education programs, and internships. The most frequently chosen baccalaureate fields are education, natural resources/environmental science, parks and recreation.
Student Body Statistics The student body totals 733, of whom 510 are undergraduates (58 freshmen). 66 percent are women and 34 percent are men. Students come from 21 states and territories and 3 other countries. 63 percent are from Alaska. 0.6 percent are international students.
Expenses for 2007–08 *Application fee:* $25. *Comprehensive fee:* $26,610 includes full-time tuition ($19,500), mandatory fees ($110), and college room and board ($7000). *Part-time tuition:* $650 per semester hour. *Part-time mandatory fees:* $55 per term.

Financial Aid Forms of aid include need-based and non-need-based scholarships and part-time jobs. The priority application deadline for financial aid is April 15.
Freshman Admission Alaska Pacific University requires an essay, a high school transcript, a minimum 2.5 high school GPA, 2 recommendations, SAT or ACT scores, and TOEFL scores for international students. An interview is required for some. The application deadline for regular admission is August 15.
Transfer Admission The application deadline for admission is August 15.
Entrance Difficulty Alaska Pacific University assesses its entrance difficulty level as moderately difficult. For the fall 2006 freshman class, 93 percent of the applicants were accepted.
For Further Information Contact Mr. Michael Warner, Director of Admissions, Alaska Pacific University, 4101 University Drive, Anchorage, AK 99508. *Telephone:* 907-564-8248 or 800-252-7528 (toll-free). *Fax:* 907-564-8317. *E-mail:* admissions@alaskapacific.edu. *Web site:* http://www.alaskapacific.edu/.

See page 154 for the College Close-Up.

CHARTER COLLEGE

Anchorage, Alaska

http://www.chartercollege.org/

SHELDON JACKSON COLLEGE

Sitka, Alaska

http://www.sj-alaska.edu/

UNIVERSITY OF ALASKA ANCHORAGE

Anchorage, Alaska

University of Alaska Anchorage is a coed, public, comprehensive unit of University of Alaska System, founded in 1954, offering degrees at the associate, bachelor's, and master's levels. It has a 428-acre campus in Anchorage.

Academic Information The faculty has 1,199 members (47% full-time). The undergraduate student-faculty ratio is 18:1. The library holds 894,080 titles and 3,833 serial subscriptions. Special programs include academic remediation, services for learning-disabled students, an honors program, cooperative (work-study) education, study abroad, advanced placement credit, accelerated degree programs, ESL programs, double majors, independent study, distance learning, self-designed majors, summer session for credit, part-time degree programs (daytime, evenings, weekends, summer), adult/continuing education programs, internships, and arrangement for off-campus study with members of the National Student Exchange, Western Interstate Commission for Higher Education, Western Undergraduate Exchange.
Student Body Statistics The student body totals 17,023, of whom 16,242 are undergraduates (1,719 freshmen). 60 percent are women and 40 percent are men. Students come from 50 states and territories and 41 other countries. 98 percent are from Alaska. 1.8 percent are international students.
Expenses for 2006–07 *Application fee:* $40. *State resident tuition:* $3600 full-time, $120 per credit hour part-time. *Nonresident tuition:* $11,970 full-time, $399 per credit hour part-time. Both full-time and part-time tuition varies according to course level. *College room and board:* $8030. Room and board charges vary according to board plan and housing facility.
Financial Aid Forms of aid include need-based and non-need-based scholarships, athletic grants, and part-time jobs. The application deadline for financial aid is August 1 with a priority deadline of April 1.
Freshman Admission University of Alaska Anchorage requires a minimum 2.0 high school GPA, SAT or ACT scores, and TOEFL scores for international students. A high school transcript is required for some. The application deadline for regular admission is July 1.
Entrance Difficulty University of Alaska Anchorage assesses its entrance difficulty level as noncompetitive; minimally difficult for transfers;

University of Alaska Anchorage (continued)

minimally difficult for bachelor's degree programs. For the fall 2006 freshman class, 77 percent of the applicants were accepted.

For Further Information Contact Enrollment Services, University of Alaska Anchorage, PO Box 141629, 3901 Old Seward Highway, Anchorage, AK 99508-8046. *Telephone:* 907-786-1480. *Fax:* 907-786-4888. *E-mail:* enroll@uaa.alaska.edu. *Web site:* http://www.uaa.alaska.edu/.

UNIVERSITY OF ALASKA FAIRBANKS

Fairbanks, Alaska

University of Alaska Fairbanks is a coed, public unit of University of Alaska System, founded in 1917, offering degrees at the associate, bachelor's, master's, and doctoral levels. It has a 2,250-acre campus in Fairbanks.

Academic Information The faculty has 658 members (48% full-time). The undergraduate student-faculty ratio is 13:1. The library holds 620,760 titles, 144,583 serial subscriptions, and 729,494 audiovisual materials. Special programs include academic remediation, services for learning-disabled students, an honors program, cooperative (work-study) education, study abroad, advanced placement credit, accelerated degree programs, double majors, independent study, distance learning, self-designed majors, summer session for credit, part-time degree programs (daytime, evenings, weekends, summer), external degree programs, internships, and arrangement for off-campus study with National Student Exchange. The most frequently chosen baccalaureate fields are business/marketing, biological/life sciences, engineering.

Student Body Statistics The student body totals 8,341, of whom 7,274 are undergraduates (887 freshmen). 60 percent are women and 40 percent are men. Students come from 51 states and territories and 34 other countries. 85 percent are from Alaska. 1.7 percent are international students.

Expenses for 2007–08 *Application fee:* $40. *State resident tuition:* $3600 full-time, $128 per credit part-time. *Nonresident tuition:* $11,970 full-time, $407 per credit part-time. *Mandatory fees:* $708 full-time, $7.56 per credit part-time, $48 per term part-time. *College room and board:* $6030. *College room only:* $3440.

Financial Aid Forms of aid include need-based and non-need-based scholarships, athletic grants, and part-time jobs. The average aided 2006–07 undergraduate received an aid package worth an estimated $8905. The priority application deadline for financial aid is February 15.

Freshman Admission University of Alaska Fairbanks requires a high school transcript, a minimum 2.0 high school GPA, SAT or ACT scores, and TOEFL scores for international students. The application deadline for regular admission is July 1 and for nonresidents it is July 1.

Transfer Admission The application deadline for admission is July 1.

Entrance Difficulty University of Alaska Fairbanks assesses its entrance difficulty level as minimally difficult. For the fall 2006 freshman class, 74 percent of the applicants were accepted.

For Further Information Contact Ms. Nancy Dix, Director, Admissions, University of Alaska Fairbanks, PO Box 757480, Fairbanks, AK 99775-7480. *Telephone:* 907-474-7500 or 800-478-1823 (toll-free). *Fax:* 907-474-5379. *E-mail:* fyapply@uaf.edu. *Web site:* http://www.uaf.edu/.

See page 198 for the College Close-Up.

UNIVERSITY OF ALASKA SOUTHEAST

Juneau, Alaska

University of Alaska Southeast is a coed, public, comprehensive unit of University of Alaska System, founded in 1972, offering degrees at the associate, bachelor's, and master's levels. It has a 198-acre campus in Juneau.

Academic Information The faculty has 239 members (49% full-time), 25% with terminal degrees. The undergraduate student-faculty ratio is 12:1. The library holds 176,312 titles and 438 serial subscriptions. Special programs include academic remediation, services for learning-disabled students, cooperative (work-study) education, study abroad, advanced

placement credit, independent study, distance learning, self-designed majors, summer session for credit, part-time degree programs (daytime, evenings, weekends, summer), adult/continuing education programs, internships, and arrangement for off-campus study with National Student Exchange. The most frequently chosen baccalaureate fields are business/marketing, biological/life sciences, liberal arts/general studies.

Student Body Statistics The student body totals 2,965, of whom 2,753 are undergraduates (183 freshmen). 64 percent are women and 36 percent are men. Students come from 44 states and territories and 5 other countries. 84 percent are from Alaska. 3.5 percent are international students.

Expenses for 2006–07 *Application fee:* $40. *State resident tuition:* $3600 full-time, $120 per credit hour part-time. *Nonresident tuition:* $11,970 full-time, $399 per credit hour part-time. *Mandatory fees:* $796 full-time. Full-time tuition and fees vary according to course level and course load. Part-time tuition varies according to course level and course load. *College room and board:* $5790. Room and board charges vary according to housing facility.

Financial Aid Forms of aid include need-based and non-need-based scholarships and part-time jobs. The average aided 2005–06 undergraduate received an aid package worth $6967. The priority application deadline for financial aid is June 1.

Freshman Admission University of Alaska Southeast requires a high school transcript, a minimum 2.0 high school GPA, SAT or ACT scores, and TOEFL scores for international students. An essay is required for some. The application deadline for regular admission is rolling.

Transfer Admission The application deadline for admission is rolling.

Entrance Difficulty University of Alaska Southeast has an open admission policy.

For Further Information Contact Ms. Deema Ferguson, Admissions Clerk, University of Alaska Southeast, 11120 Glacier Highway, Juneau, AK 99801-8625. *Telephone:* 877-465-4827 Ext. 6100 or 877-796-4827 (toll-free). *Fax:* 907-796-6365. *E-mail:* admissions@uas.alaska.edu. *Web site:* http://www.uas.alaska.edu/.

See page 200 for the College Close-Up.

Arizona

AIBT INTERNATIONAL INSTITUTE OF THE AMERICAS

See International Institute of the Americas.

AL COLLINS GRAPHIC DESIGN SCHOOL

See Collins College: A School of Design and Technology.

AMERICAN INDIAN COLLEGE OF THE ASSEMBLIES OF GOD, INC.

Phoenix, Arizona

http://www.aicag.edu/

ARGOSY UNIVERSITY, PHOENIX

Phoenix, Arizona

http://www.argosyu.edu/

ARIZONA STATE UNIVERSITY

Tempe, Arizona

Arizona State University is a coed, public unit of Arizona State University, founded in 1885, offering degrees at the bachelor's, master's, doctoral, and first professional levels and post-master's and postbachelor's certificates. It has an 814-acre campus in Tempe near Phoenix.

Academic Information The faculty has 1,974 members (90% full-time), 86% with terminal degrees. The undergraduate student-faculty ratio is 23:1. The library holds 4 million titles, 30,839 serial subscriptions, and 2 million audiovisual materials. Special programs include academic remediation, services for learning-disabled students, an honors program, cooperative (work-study) education, study abroad, advanced placement credit, accelerated degree programs, Freshman Honors College, double majors, independent study, distance learning, summer session for credit, part-time degree programs (daytime, evenings, summer), adult/continuing education programs, internships, and arrangement for off-campus study with University of Arizona, Northern Arizona University. The most frequently chosen baccalaureate fields are business/marketing, communications/journalism, interdisciplinary studies.

Student Body Statistics The student body totals 51,234, of whom 41,815 are undergraduates (7,894 freshmen). 51 percent are women and 49 percent are men. Students come from 52 states and territories and 96 other countries. 75 percent are from Arizona. 2.6 percent are international students.

Expenses for 2006–07 *Application fee:* $25, $50 for nonresidents. *State resident tuition:* $4591 full-time, $240 per credit part-time. *Nonresident tuition:* $15,750 full-time, $656 per credit part-time. *Mandatory fees:* $97 full-time. Full-time tuition and fees vary according to location and program. Part-time tuition varies according to location and program. *College room and board:* $6900. *College room only:* $4200. Room and board charges vary according to board plan, housing facility, and location.

Financial Aid Forms of aid include need-based and non-need-based scholarships, athletic grants, and part-time jobs. The average aided 2005–06 undergraduate received an aid package worth $8649. The priority application deadline for financial aid is March 1.

Freshman Admission Arizona State University requires a high school transcript, a minimum 3.0 high school GPA, SAT or ACT scores, and TOEFL scores for international students. The application deadline for regular admission is rolling.

Transfer Admission The application deadline for admission is rolling.

Entrance Difficulty Arizona State University assesses its entrance difficulty level as moderately difficult; very difficult for engineering, computer science, business programs. For the fall 2006 freshman class, 92 percent of the applicants were accepted.

For Further Information Contact Martha Byrd, Dean of Undergraduate Admissions, Arizona State University, Box 870112, Tempe, AZ 85287-0112. *Telephone:* 480-965-7788. *Fax:* 480-965-3610. *E-mail:* ugradinq@asu.edu. *Web site:* http://www.asu.edu/.

ARIZONA STATE UNIVERSITY AT THE DOWNTOWN PHOENIX CAMPUS

Phoenix, Arizona

http://www.asu.edu/downtownphoenix/

ARIZONA STATE UNIVERSITY AT THE POLYTECHNIC CAMPUS

Mesa, Arizona

Arizona State University at the Polytechnic Campus is a coed, public, comprehensive unit of Arizona State University, founded in 1995, offering degrees at the bachelor's and master's levels. It has a 600-acre campus in Mesa near Phoenix.

Academic Information The faculty has 158 members (100% full-time), 77% with terminal degrees. The undergraduate student-faculty ratio is 23:1. The library holds 4 million titles, 33,122 serial subscriptions, and 100,838 audiovisual materials. Special programs include services for learning-disabled students, an honors program, study abroad, advanced placement credit, accelerated degree programs, double majors, independent study, distance learning, self-designed majors, summer session for credit, part-time degree programs (daytime, evenings, weekends, summer), and internships. The most frequently chosen baccalaureate fields are business/marketing, agriculture, education.

Student Body Statistics The student body totals 6,545, of whom 5,589 are undergraduates (236 freshmen). 54 percent are women and 46 percent are men. Students come from 44 states and territories and 45 other countries. 88 percent are from Arizona. 1.6 percent are international students.

Expenses for 2006–07 *Application fee:* $50. *State resident tuition:* $4400 full-time, $229 per credit hour part-time. *Nonresident tuition:* $15,750 full-time, $656 per credit hour part-time. *Mandatory fees:* $48 full-time. Full-time tuition and fees vary according to degree level, location, and program. Part-time tuition varies according to course load, degree level, location, and program. *College room and board:* $5100. *College room only:* $3200. Room and board charges vary according to board plan, housing facility, location, and student level.

Financial Aid Forms of aid include need-based and non-need-based scholarships, athletic grants, and part-time jobs. The average aided 2005–06 undergraduate received an aid package worth $8439. The priority application deadline for financial aid is March 1.

Freshman Admission Arizona State University at the Polytechnic Campus requires a high school transcript and TOEFL scores for international students. A minimum 3.0 high school GPA and SAT or ACT scores are recommended. An essay and an interview are required for some. The application deadline for regular admission is rolling and for early action it is November 1.

Transfer Admission The application deadline for admission is rolling.

Entrance Difficulty Arizona State University at the Polytechnic Campus assesses its entrance difficulty level as moderately difficult. For the fall 2006 freshman class, 87 percent of the applicants were accepted.

For Further Information Contact Wadell Blackwell, Student Recruitment/Retention Specialist, Arizona State University at the Polytechnic Campus, 7001 East Williams Field Road #350, Mesa, AZ 85212. *Telephone:* 480-727-1165. *Fax:* 480-727-1008. *E-mail:* asueast@au.edu. *Web site:* http://www.poly.asu.edu/.

ARIZONA STATE UNIVERSITY AT THE WEST CAMPUS

Phoenix, Arizona

Arizona State University at the West campus is a coed, public, comprehensive unit of Arizona State University, founded in 1984, offering degrees at the bachelor's and master's levels and postbachelor's certificates. It has a 300-acre campus in Phoenix.

Academic Information The faculty has 462 members (50% full-time), 57% with terminal degrees. The undergraduate student-faculty ratio is 21:1. The library holds 348,697 titles and 2,422 serial subscriptions. Special programs include services for learning-disabled students, an honors program, study abroad, advanced placement credit, Freshman Honors College, double majors, independent study, distance learning, self-designed majors, summer session for credit, part-time degree programs (daytime, evenings), adult/continuing education programs, and internships. The most frequently chosen baccalaureate fields are business/marketing, education, security and protective services.

Student Body Statistics The student body totals 8,211, of whom 6,941 are undergraduates (539 freshmen). 65 percent are women and 35 percent are men. Students come from 37 states and territories and 15 other countries. 95 percent are from Arizona. 0.5 percent are international students.

Expenses for 2006–07 *Application fee:* $25. *State resident tuition:* $4400 full-time, $229 per credit hour part-time. *Nonresident tuition:* $15,750 full-time, $656 per credit hour part-time. *Mandatory fees:* $44 full-time. Part-time tuition varies according to course load. *College room only:* $4200.

Arizona State University at the West campus (continued)

Financial Aid Forms of aid include need-based and non-need-based scholarships and part-time jobs. The application deadline for financial aid is March 1 with a priority deadline of February 15.

Freshman Admission Arizona State University at the West campus requires a high school transcript, SAT or ACT scores, and TOEFL scores for international students. A minimum 3.0 high school GPA is recommended. The application deadline for regular admission is rolling.

Transfer Admission The application deadline for admission is rolling.

Entrance Difficulty Arizona State University at the West campus assesses its entrance difficulty level as moderately difficult. For the fall 2006 freshman class, 60 percent of the applicants were accepted.

For Further Information Contact Mr. Thomas Cabot, Registrar, Arizona State University at the West campus, PO Box 37100, 4701 West Thunderbird Road, Phoenix, AZ 85069-7100. *Telephone:* 602-543-8134. *Fax:* 602-543-8312. *E-mail:* cabot@asu.edu. *Web site:* http://www.west.asu.edu/.

ARIZONA STATE UNIVERSITY EAST

See Arizona State University at the Polytechnic Campus.

THE ART CENTER DESIGN COLLEGE

Tucson, Arizona

The Art Center Design College is a coed, proprietary, four-year college, founded in 1983, offering degrees at the associate and bachelor's levels.

For Further Information Contact Ms. Colleen Gimbel-Froebe, Director of Enrollment Management, The Art Center Design College, 2525 North Country Club Road, Tucson, AZ 85716-2505. *Telephone:* 520-325-0123 or 800-825-8753 (toll-free). *Fax:* 520-325-5535. *E-mail:* cgf@theartcenter.edu. *Web site:* http://www.theartcenter.edu/.

THE ART INSTITUTE OF PHOENIX

Phoenix, Arizona

The Art Institute of Phoenix is a coed, proprietary, four-year college of Education Management Corporation, founded in 1995, offering degrees at the associate and bachelor's levels. It has a 3-acre campus in Phoenix.

Academic Information The faculty has 83 members (47% full-time). The student-faculty ratio is 17:1. The library holds 13,463 titles and 150 serial subscriptions. Special programs include academic remediation, services for learning-disabled students, an honors program, cooperative (work-study) education, advanced placement credit, independent study, distance learning, summer session for credit, and internships.

Student Body Statistics The student body is made up of 1,055 undergraduates (328 freshmen). 51 percent are women and 49 percent are men. Students come from 30 states and territories and 9 other countries. 69 percent are from Arizona. 0.4 percent are international students.

Expenses for 2006–07 *Application fee:* $50. *One-time mandatory fee:* $100. *Tuition:* $18,576 full-time, $387 per credit hour part-time. Both full-time and part-time tuition varies according to course load. *College room only:* $6028.

Financial Aid Forms of aid include need-based scholarships and part-time jobs. The application deadline for financial aid is continuous.

Freshman Admission The Art Institute of Phoenix requires an essay, a high school transcript, an interview, and TOEFL scores for international students. A minimum 2.0 high school GPA is recommended. The application deadline for regular admission is rolling.

Transfer Admission The application deadline for admission is rolling.

Entrance Difficulty The Art Institute of Phoenix assesses its entrance difficulty level as minimally difficult. For the fall 2006 freshman class, 64 percent of the applicants were accepted.

For Further Information Contact Mr. Jerry Driskill, Director of Admissions, The Art Institute of Phoenix, 2233 West Dunlap Avenue, Phoenix, AZ 85021. *Telephone:* 602-331-7500 or 800-474-2479 (toll-free). *Fax:* 602-331-5302. *E-mail:* aipxadm@aii.edu. *Web site:* http://www.aipx.artinstitutes.edu/.

CHAPARRAL COLLEGE

Tucson, Arizona

http://www.chap-col.edu/

COLLEGE OF THE HUMANITIES AND SCIENCES, HARRISON MIDDLETON UNIVERSITY

Tempe, Arizona

http://www.chumsci.edu/

COLLINS COLLEGE: A SCHOOL OF DESIGN AND TECHNOLOGY

Tempe, Arizona

Collins College: A School of Design and Technology is a coed, proprietary, four-year college of Career Education Corporation, founded in 1978, offering degrees at the associate and bachelor's levels. It has a 3-acre campus in Tempe near Phoenix.

Academic Information The faculty has 102 members (75% full-time). The student-faculty ratio is 30:1. The library holds 1,000 titles.

Student Body Statistics The student body is made up of 1,690 undergraduates. 23 percent are women and 77 percent are men. Students come from 50 states and territories. 25 percent are from Arizona.

Expenses for 2006–07 *Application fee:* $50. *Tuition:* $24,250 full-time. Full-time tuition varies according to class time, course level, course load, degree level, location, program, reciprocity agreements, and student level. *Part-time tuition:* varies with class time, course level, course load, degree level, reciprocity agreements, student level. *College room only:* $4600.

Financial Aid Forms of aid include need-based and non-need-based scholarships and part-time jobs. The average aided 2005–06 undergraduate received an aid package worth $11,500. The application deadline for financial aid is continuous.

Freshman Admission Collins College: A School of Design and Technology requires an essay, a high school transcript, and an interview. SAT or ACT scores are recommended. The application deadline for regular admission is rolling.

Transfer Admission The application deadline for admission is rolling.

Entrance Difficulty Collins College: A School of Design and Technology has an open admission policy.

For Further Information Contact Admissions Department, Collins College: A School of Design and Technology, 1140 South Priest, Tempe, AZ 85281. *Telephone:* 480-966-3000 or 800-876-7070 (toll-free out-of-state). *Fax:* 480-966-2599. *E-mail:* contact@collinscollege.edu. *Web site:* http://www.collinscollege.edu/.

DeVRY UNIVERSITY

Mesa, Arizona

http://www.devry.edu/

DeVRY UNIVERSITY
Phoenix, Arizona

DeVry University is a coed, proprietary, comprehensive unit of DeVry University, founded in 1967, offering degrees at the associate, bachelor's, and master's levels and postbachelor's certificates. It has an 18-acre campus in Phoenix.

Academic Information The faculty has 70 members (56% full-time). The undergraduate student-faculty ratio is 18:1. The library holds 22,500 titles and 7,230 serial subscriptions. Special programs include academic remediation, services for learning-disabled students, advanced placement credit, accelerated degree programs, distance learning, summer session for credit, part-time degree programs (daytime, evenings, weekends, summer), and adult/continuing education programs. The most frequently chosen baccalaureate fields are business/marketing, computer and information sciences, engineering technologies.

Student Body Statistics The student body totals 1,185, of whom 1,006 are undergraduates (271 freshmen). 22 percent are women and 78 percent are men. Students come from 41 states and territories and 4 other countries. 95 percent are from Arizona. 1.4 percent are international students.

Expenses for 2007–08 *Application fee:* $50. *Tuition:* $12,900 full-time, $490 per credit part-time. *Mandatory fees:* $320 full-time.

Financial Aid Forms of aid include need-based and non-need-based scholarships. The application deadline for financial aid is continuous.

Freshman Admission DeVry University requires a high school transcript, an interview, and TOEFL scores for international students. The application deadline for regular admission is rolling.

Transfer Admission The application deadline for admission is rolling.

Entrance Difficulty DeVry University assesses its entrance difficulty level as minimally difficult; moderately difficult for electronics engineering technology program.

For Further Information Contact Admissions Office, DeVry University, 2149 West Dunlap Avenue, Phoenix, AZ 85021-2995. *Telephone:* 602-870-9222. *Web site:* http://www.devry.edu/.

EDUCATION AMERICA, TEMPE CAMPUS
See Remington College–Tempe Campus.

EMBRY-RIDDLE AERONAUTICAL UNIVERSITY
Prescott, Arizona

Embry-Riddle Aeronautical University is a coed, private, comprehensive institution, founded in 1978, offering degrees at the bachelor's and master's levels. It has a 547-acre campus in Prescott.

Academic Information The faculty has 124 members (81% full-time), 58% with terminal degrees. The undergraduate student-faculty ratio is 14:1. Special programs include academic remediation, services for learning-disabled students, an honors program, cooperative (work-study) education, study abroad, advanced placement credit, accelerated degree programs, ESL programs, double majors, independent study, distance learning, self-designed majors, summer session for credit, part-time degree programs, adult/continuing education programs, and internships. The most frequently chosen baccalaureate fields are engineering, social sciences, transportation and materials moving.

Student Body Statistics The student body totals 1,674, of whom 1,630 are undergraduates (403 freshmen). 17 percent are women and 83 percent are men. Students come from 52 states and territories and 29 other countries. 21 percent are from Arizona. 3.5 percent are international students. 20 percent of the 2006 graduating class went on to graduate and professional schools.

Expenses for 2007–08 *Application fee:* $50. *Comprehensive fee:* $33,344 includes full-time tuition ($25,400), mandatory fees ($730), and college room and board ($7214). *College room only:* $3990. *Part-time tuition:* $1060 per credit hour.

Financial Aid Forms of aid include need-based and non-need-based scholarships and part-time jobs. The average aided 2006–07 undergraduate received an aid package worth an estimated $15,248. The application deadline for financial aid is continuous.

Freshman Admission Embry-Riddle Aeronautical University requires a high school transcript, a minimum 2.0 high school GPA, SAT or ACT scores, and TOEFL scores for international students. An essay, recommendations, and an interview are recommended. A minimum 3.0 high school GPA and medical examination for flight students are required for some. The application deadline for regular admission is rolling.

Transfer Admission The application deadline for admission is rolling.

Entrance Difficulty Embry-Riddle Aeronautical University assesses its entrance difficulty level as moderately difficult. For the fall 2006 freshman class, 88 percent of the applicants were accepted.

For Further Information Contact Mr. Bill Thompson, Director of Admissions, Embry-Riddle Aeronautical University, 3700 Willow Creek Road, Prescott, AZ 86301-3720. *Telephone:* 928-777-6600 or 800-888-3728 (toll-free). *Fax:* 928-777-6606. *E-mail:* pradmit@erau.edu. *Web site:* http://www.embryriddle.edu/.

See page 166 for the College Close-Up.

EVEREST COLLEGE
Phoenix, Arizona

Everest College is a coed, proprietary, primarily two-year college of Corinthian Colleges, Inc., founded in 1982, offering degrees at the associate and bachelor's levels.

Academic Information The faculty has 77 members (19% full-time), 32% with terminal degrees. The student-faculty ratio is 23:1. The library holds 17,515 titles, 48 serial subscriptions, and 514 audiovisual materials. Special programs include academic remediation, services for learning-disabled students, study abroad, double majors, independent study, distance learning, and adult/continuing education programs.

Student Body Statistics The student body is made up of 1,187 undergraduates (527 freshmen). 83 percent are women and 17 percent are men. Students come from 29 states and territories. 76 percent are from Arizona. 0.3 percent are international students. 7 percent of the 2006 graduating class went on to four-year colleges.

Expenses for 2007–08 *Application fee:* $0. *Tuition:* $13,056 full-time, $272 per quarter hour part-time. *Mandatory fees:* $100 full-time, $25 per term part-time.

Financial Aid Forms of aid include need-based scholarships.

Freshman Admission Everest College requires a high school transcript, a minimum 2.0 high school GPA, and an interview. An essay is required for some. The application deadline for regular admission is rolling.

Entrance Difficulty Everest College assesses its entrance difficulty level as noncompetitive. For the fall 2006 freshman class, 78 percent of the applicants were accepted.

For Further Information Contact Mr. Jim Askins, Director of Admissions, Everest College, 10400 North 25th Avenue, Suite 190, Phoenix, AZ 85021. *Telephone:* 602-942-4141. *Fax:* 602-943-0960. *E-mail:* jaskins@cci.edu. *Web site:* http://www.everest-college.com/.

GRAND CANYON UNIVERSITY
Phoenix, Arizona

Grand Canyon University is a coed, private, Southern Baptist, comprehensive institution, founded in 1949, offering degrees at the bachelor's and master's levels. It has a 90-acre campus in Phoenix.

Academic Information The faculty has 1,683 members (5% full-time), 35% with terminal degrees. The undergraduate student-faculty ratio is 17:1. Special programs include academic remediation, an honors program, cooperative (work-study) education, study abroad, advanced placement credit, accelerated degree programs, Freshman Honors College, ESL programs, double majors, independent study, distance learning, summer session for credit, part-time degree programs, adult/continuing education programs, internships, and arrangement for off-campus study with Coalition for Christian Colleges and Universities.

Grand Canyon University (continued)

Student Body Statistics The student body totals 10,297, of whom 2,693 are undergraduates (441 freshmen). 69 percent are women and 31 percent are men. Students come from 53 states and territories and 10 other countries. 36 percent are from Arizona. 1.5 percent are international students.

Expenses for 2007–08 *Application fee:* $100. *Comprehensive fee:* $21,920 includes full-time tuition ($13,920), mandatory fees ($500), and college room and board ($7500). *Part-time tuition:* $580 per credit. *Part-time mandatory fees:* $250 per term.

Financial Aid Forms of aid include need-based and non-need-based scholarships, athletic grants, and part-time jobs. The application deadline for financial aid is continuous.

Freshman Admission Grand Canyon University requires a high school transcript, SAT or ACT scores, and TOEFL scores for international students. A minimum 2.0 high school GPA is recommended. An essay, a minimum 2.0 high school GPA, 3 recommendations, an interview, SAT scores, ACT scores, SAT or ACT scores, SAT and SAT Subject Test or ACT scores, SAT Subject Test scores, are required for some. The application deadline for regular admission is rolling.

Transfer Admission The application deadline for admission is rolling.

Entrance Difficulty Grand Canyon University assesses its entrance difficulty level as moderately difficult. For the fall 2006 freshman class, 88 percent of the applicants were accepted.

For Further Information Contact Enrollment, Grand Canyon University, 3300 West Camelback Road, PO Box 11097, Phoenix, AZ 86017-3030. *Telephone:* 800-486-7085 or 800-800-9776 (toll-free in-state). *Fax:* 602-589-2580. *E-mail:* admissionsonline@gcu.edu. *Web site:* http://www.gcu.edu/.

HIGH-TECH INSTITUTE

Phoenix, Arizona

http://www.high-techinstitute.com/

INTERNATIONAL BAPTIST COLLEGE

Tempe, Arizona

International Baptist College is a coed, private, Baptist, comprehensive institution, founded in 1980, offering degrees at the associate, bachelor's, master's, and doctoral levels. It has a 12-acre campus in Tempe near Phoenix.

Expenses for 2006–07 *Application fee:* $35. *Comprehensive fee:* $10,870 includes full-time tuition ($6000), mandatory fees ($570), and college room and board ($4300). *Part-time tuition:* $250 per credit. *Part-time mandatory fees:* $9 per credit.

For Further Information Contact Ms. Rebecca M. Stertzbach, Director of Recruitment, International Baptist College, 2150 East Southern Avenue, Tempe, AZ 85282. *Telephone:* 480-838-7070 Ext. 262 or 800-422-4858 (toll-free). *Fax:* 480-505-3299. *E-mail:* jeff.caupp@ibconline.edu. *Web site:* http://www.tri-citybaptist.org/ibc/.

INTERNATIONAL IMPORT-EXPORT INSTITUTE

Phoenix, Arizona

International Import-Export Institute is a coed, proprietary, upper-level institution, founded in 1995.

For Further Information Contact Dr. Donald N. Burton, International Import-Export Institute, 2432 West Peoria Avenue, Suite 1026, Phoenix, AZ 85029. *Telephone:* 602-648-5750 or 800-474-8013 (toll-free). *Fax:* 602-648-5755. *E-mail:* director@expandglobal.com. *Web site:* http://www.iiei.edu/.

INTERNATIONAL INSTITUTE OF THE AMERICAS

Mesa, Arizona

International Institute of the Americas is a coed, private, primarily two-year college, founded in 1982, offering degrees at the associate and bachelor's levels.

Academic Information The faculty has 15 members (40% full-time), 20% with terminal degrees. The student-faculty ratio is 10:1. Special programs include distance learning and part-time degree programs.

Student Body Statistics The student body is made up of 145 undergraduates.

Expenses for 2007–08 *Application fee:* $200. *Tuition:* $9850 full-time. *Mandatory fees:* $200 full-time.

Freshman Admission International Institute of the Americas requires an interview. The application deadline for regular admission is rolling and for nonresidents it is rolling.

Transfer Admission The application deadline for admission is rolling.

Entrance Difficulty International Institute of the Americas assesses its entrance difficulty level as noncompetitive.

For Further Information Contact Mr. Todd Olehausen, Campus Director, International Institute of the Americas, 925 South Gilbert Road, Suite 201, Mesa, AZ 84204-4448. *Telephone:* 480-545-8755 or 888-886-2428 (toll-free). *Fax:* 480-926-1371. *E-mail:* wging@iia.edu. *Web site:* http://www.iia-online.com/site/.

INTERNATIONAL INSTITUTE OF THE AMERICAS

Phoenix, Arizona

International Institute of the Americas is a coed, private, primarily two-year college, founded in 1979, offering degrees at the associate and bachelor's levels.

Academic Information The faculty has 34 members (56% full-time), 21% with terminal degrees. The student-faculty ratio is 12:1. Special programs include distance learning and part-time degree programs.

Student Body Statistics The student body is made up of 424 undergraduates.

Expenses for 2007–08 *Application fee:* $200. *Tuition:* $9850 full-time. *Mandatory fees:* $200 full-time.

Freshman Admission International Institute of the Americas requires an interview and TOEFL scores for international students. The application deadline for regular admission is rolling and for nonresidents it is rolling.

Transfer Admission The application deadline for admission is rolling.

Entrance Difficulty International Institute of the Americas has an open admission policy.

For Further Information Contact Mr. Lynn McConnell, Campus Director, International Institute of the Americas, 6049 North 43rd Avenue, Phoenix, AZ 85019. *Telephone:* 602-242-6265 or 800-793-2428 (toll-free). *Fax:* 602-973-2572. *E-mail:* lmcconnell@iia.edu. *Web site:* http://www.iia-online.com/site/.

INTERNATIONAL INSTITUTE OF THE AMERICAS

Tucson, Arizona

International Institute of the Americas is a coed, private, primarily two-year college, founded in 1979, offering degrees at the associate and bachelor's levels.

Academic Information The faculty has 26 members (54% full-time), 12% with terminal degrees. The student-faculty ratio is 10:1. Special programs include distance learning and part-time degree programs.

Student Body Statistics The student body is made up of 267 undergraduates.

Expenses for 2007–08 *Application fee:* $200. *Tuition:* $9850 full-time. *Mandatory fees:* $200 full-time.

Freshman Admission International Institute of the Americas requires an interview. The application deadline for regular admission is rolling and for nonresidents it is rolling.

Transfer Admission The application deadline for admission is rolling.

Entrance Difficulty International Institute of the Americas assesses its entrance difficulty level as noncompetitive.

For Further Information Contact Ms. Leigh Anne Pechota, Campus Director, International Institute of the Americas, 5441 East 22nd Street, Sutie 125, Tucson, AZ 85711. *Telephone:* 520-748-9799 or 888-292-2428 (toll-free). *Fax:* 520-748-9355. *E-mail:* lpechota@iia.edu. *Web site:* http://www.iia-online.com/site/.

ITT TECHNICAL INSTITUTE

Phoenix, Arizona

http://www.itt-tech.edu/

ITT TECHNICAL INSTITUTE

Tempe, Arizona

ITT Technical Institute is a proprietary, four-year college, founded in 1963, offering degrees at the associate and bachelor's levels.

Expenses for 2006–07 *Application fee:* $100. Contact school for program costs.

Freshman Admission ITT Technical Institute requires a high school transcript, an interview, and Wonderlic aptitude test. Recommendations are recommended. The application deadline for regular admission is rolling.

Transfer Admission The application deadline for admission is rolling.

For Further Information Contact Ms. Patti Moberly, Director of Recruitment, ITT Technical Institute, 5005 South Wendler Drive, Tempe, AZ 85282. *Telephone:* 602-437-7500 or 800-879-4881 (toll-free). *Fax:* 602-437-7505. *Web site:* http://www.itt-tech.edu/.

ITT TECHNICAL INSTITUTE

Tucson, Arizona

ITT Technical Institute is a coed, proprietary, primarily two-year college of ITT Educational Services, Inc, founded in 1984, offering degrees at the associate and bachelor's levels. It has a 3-acre campus in Tucson.

Expenses for 2006–07 *Application fee:* $100. Contact school for program costs.

Financial Aid Forms of aid include need-based scholarships and part-time jobs. The application deadline for financial aid is continuous.

Freshman Admission ITT Technical Institute requires a high school transcript, an interview, TOEFL scores for international students, and Wonderlic aptitude test. Recommendations are recommended. The application deadline for regular admission is rolling.

Transfer Admission The application deadline for admission is rolling.

Entrance Difficulty ITT Technical Institute assesses its entrance difficulty level as minimally difficult.

For Further Information Contact Ms. Linda Lemken, Director of Recruitment, ITT Technical Institute, 1455 West River Road, Tucson, AZ 85704. *Telephone:* 520-408-7488 or 800-870-9730 (toll-free). *Fax:* 520-292-9899. *Web site:* http://www.itt-tech.edu/.

MIDWESTERN UNIVERSITY, GLENDALE CAMPUS

Glendale, Arizona

Midwestern University, Glendale Campus is a coed, private, upper-level institution, founded in 1996, offering degrees at the bachelor's, master's, and doctoral levels and postbachelor's certificates.

For Further Information Contact Mr. James Walters, Director of Admissions, Midwestern University, Glendale Campus, 19555 North 59th Avenue, Glendale, AZ 85308. *Telephone:* 623-572-3340, 888-247-9277 (toll-free in-state), or 888-247-9271 (toll-free out-of-state). *Fax:* 623-572-3229. *E-mail:* admissionaz@midwestern.edu. *Web site:* http://www.midwestern.edu/.

NORTHCENTRAL UNIVERSITY

Prescott, Arizona

http://www.ncu.edu/

NORTHERN ARIZONA UNIVERSITY

Flagstaff, Arizona

Northern Arizona University is a coed, public unit of Arizona State University, founded in 1899, offering degrees at the bachelor's, master's, doctoral, and first professional levels and post-master's and postbachelor's certificates. It has a 730-acre campus in Flagstaff.

Academic Information The faculty has 1,492 members (51% full-time), 57% with terminal degrees. The undergraduate student-faculty ratio is 16:1. The library holds 687,456 titles, 29,526 serial subscriptions, and 34,118 audiovisual materials. Special programs include services for learning-disabled students, an honors program, cooperative (work-study) education, study abroad, advanced placement credit, accelerated degree programs, Freshman Honors College, ESL programs, double majors, independent study, distance learning, summer session for credit, part-time degree programs (daytime, evenings, summer), internships, and arrangement for off-campus study with National Student Exchange. The most frequently chosen baccalaureate fields are business/marketing, education, visual and performing arts.

Student Body Statistics The student body totals 20,562, of whom 14,526 are undergraduates (2,846 freshmen). 60 percent are women and 40 percent are men. Students come from 56 states and territories and 66 other countries. 83 percent are from Arizona. 2.3 percent are international students. 43 percent of the 2006 graduating class went on to graduate and professional schools.

Expenses for 2006–07 *Application fee:* $25. *State resident tuition:* $4376 full-time, $270 per credit hour part-time. *Nonresident tuition:* $13,316 full-time, $596 per credit hour part-time. *Mandatory fees:* $170 full-time. Full-time tuition and fees vary according to program. Part-time tuition varies according to program. *College room and board:* $6260. *College room only:* $3452. Room and board charges vary according to board plan and housing facility.

Financial Aid Forms of aid include need-based and non-need-based scholarships, athletic grants, and part-time jobs. The average aided 2006–07 undergraduate received an aid package worth an estimated $7885. The priority application deadline for financial aid is February 14.

Freshman Admission Northern Arizona University requires a high school transcript, a minimum 3.00 high school GPA, and SAT or ACT scores. A minimum 3.0 high school GPA is recommended. Recommendations are required for some. The application deadline for regular admission is rolling.

Transfer Admission The application deadline for admission is rolling.

Northern Arizona University (continued)

Entrance Difficulty Northern Arizona University assesses its entrance difficulty level as moderately difficult. For the fall 2006 freshman class, 32 percent of the applicants were accepted.

For Further Information Contact Ms. Janet Heinrichs, Assistant Director, Northern Arizona University, PO Box 4084, Flagstaff, AZ 86011. *Telephone:* 928-523-6006 or 888-MORE-NAU (toll-free). *Fax:* 928-523-0226. *E-mail:* undergraduate.admissions@nau.edu. *Web site:* http://www.nau.edu/.

See page 180 for the College Close-Up.

PRESCOTT COLLEGE

Prescott, Arizona

Prescott College is a coed, private, comprehensive institution, founded in 1966, offering degrees at the bachelor's, master's, and doctoral levels and postbachelor's certificates. It has a 4-acre campus in Prescott.

Academic Information The faculty has 77 members (53% full-time), 40% with terminal degrees. The undergraduate student-faculty ratio is 7:1. The library holds 26,169 titles and 248 serial subscriptions. Special programs include services for learning-disabled students, advanced placement credit, double majors, independent study, self-designed majors, summer session for credit, external degree programs, adult/continuing education programs, internships, and arrangement for off-campus study with Four Corners School of Outdoor Education, Grand Canyon Field Institute. The most frequently chosen baccalaureate fields are education, natural resources/environmental science, psychology.

Student Body Statistics The student body totals 1,053, of whom 758 are undergraduates (56 freshmen). 61 percent are women and 39 percent are men. Students come from 47 states and territories. 43 percent are from Arizona.

Expenses for 2006–07 *Application fee:* $25. *One-time mandatory fee:* $800. *Tuition:* $18,576 full-time, $516 per credit hour part-time. *Mandatory fees:* $135 full-time. Full-time tuition and fees vary according to course load and degree level. *College room only:* $1560.

Financial Aid Forms of aid include need-based scholarships and part-time jobs. The application deadline for financial aid is continuous.

Freshman Admission Prescott College requires a high school transcript, 2 recommendations, SAT or ACT scores, and TOEFL scores for international students. An essay and an interview are required for some. The application deadline for regular admission is August 15 and for nonresidents it is August 15.

Transfer Admission The application deadline for admission is August 15.

Entrance Difficulty Prescott College assesses its entrance difficulty level as moderately difficult. For the fall 2006 freshman class, 82 percent of the applicants were accepted.

For Further Information Contact Mr. Timothy Robison, Director of Resident Degree Program Admissions, Prescott College, 220 Grove Avenue, Prescott, AZ 86301. *Telephone:* 877-350-2100 or 800-628-6364 (toll-free). *Fax:* 928-776-5242. *E-mail:* admissions@prescott.edu. *Web site:* http://www.prescott.edu/.

See page 184 for the College Close-Up.

REMINGTON COLLEGE–TEMPE CAMPUS

Tempe, Arizona

http://www.remingtoncollege.edu/

RHODES COLLEGE

See Everest College.

SOUTHWESTERN COLLEGE

Phoenix, Arizona

http://www.swcaz.edu/

TOHONO O'ODHAM COMMUNITY COLLEGE

Sells, Arizona

http://www.tocc.cc.az.us/

UNIVERSITY OF ADVANCING TECHNOLOGY

Tempe, Arizona

University of Advancing Technology is a coed, proprietary, comprehensive institution, founded in 1983, offering degrees at the associate, bachelor's, and master's levels.

Academic Information The faculty has 64 members. The undergraduate student-faculty ratio is 19:1. The library holds 27,500 titles, 92 serial subscriptions, and 1,200 audiovisual materials. Special programs include cooperative (work-study) education, double majors, independent study, distance learning, summer session for credit, and internships.

Student Body Statistics The student body totals 1,227, of whom 1,178 are undergraduates (188 freshmen). 6 percent are women and 94 percent are men. Students come from 39 states and territories. 39 percent are from Arizona. 1.2 percent are international students.

Expenses for 2007–08 *Application fee:* $0. *Comprehensive fee:* $24,800 includes full-time tuition ($16,300), mandatory fees ($100), and college room and board ($8400). *College room only:* $6360.

Financial Aid Forms of aid include need-based and non-need-based scholarships and part-time jobs. The application deadline for financial aid is continuous.

Freshman Admission University of Advancing Technology requires an essay, a high school transcript, and TOEFL scores for international students. A minimum 2.5 high school GPA, SAT scores, ACT scores, and SAT or ACT scores are required for some. The application deadline for regular admission is rolling.

For Further Information Contact Admissions Office, University of Advancing Technology, 2625 West Baseline Road, Tempe, AZ 85283-1042. *Telephone:* 602-383-8228, 602-383-8228 (toll-free in-state), or 800-658-5744 (toll-free out-of-state). *Fax:* 602-383-8222. *E-mail:* admissions@uat.edu. *Web site:* http://www.uat.edu/.

See page 196 for the College Close-Up.

THE UNIVERSITY OF ARIZONA

Tucson, Arizona

The University of Arizona is a coed, public unit of Arizona Board of Regents, founded in 1885, offering degrees at the bachelor's, master's, doctoral, and first professional levels and postbachelor's certificates. It has a 362-acre campus in Tucson.

Academic Information The faculty has 1,455 members (97% full-time), 98% with terminal degrees. The undergraduate student-faculty ratio is 19:1. The library holds 4 million titles, 23,790 serial subscriptions, and 51,136 audiovisual materials. Special programs include services for learning-disabled students, an honors program, study abroad, advanced placement credit, Freshman Honors College, ESL programs, double majors, independent study, distance learning, summer session for credit, part-time degree programs (daytime, evenings, summer), adult/continuing education programs, and internships. The most frequently chosen baccalaureate fields are business/marketing, communications/journalism, social sciences.

Student Body Statistics The student body totals 36,805, of whom 28,442 are undergraduates (6,009 freshmen). 53 percent are women and 47

percent are men. Students come from 27 states and territories and 135 other countries. 67 percent are from Arizona. 2.5 percent are international students.

Expenses for 2006–07 *Application fee:* $25. *State resident tuition:* $4594 full-time, $290 per credit hour part-time. *Nonresident tuition:* $14,800 full-time, $667 per credit hour part-time. *Mandatory fees:* $172 full-time. Full-time tuition and fees vary according to course load. Part-time tuition varies according to course load. *College room and board:* $7850. *College room only:* $4350. Room and board charges vary according to board plan and housing facility.

Financial Aid Forms of aid include need-based and non-need-based scholarships and part-time jobs. The average aided 2005–06 undergraduate received an aid package worth $8078.

Freshman Admission The University of Arizona requires a high school transcript and TOEFL scores for international students. SAT or ACT scores are recommended. A minimum 3.0 high school GPA, recommendations, and an interview are required for some. The application deadline for regular admission is April 1.

Transfer Admission The application deadline for admission is June 1.

Entrance Difficulty The University of Arizona assesses its entrance difficulty level as moderately difficult; very difficult for architecture, engineering, allied health, pharmacy, nursing, business, public administration, education programs. For the fall 2006 freshman class, 80 percent of the applicants were accepted.

For Further Information Contact Ms. Lori Goldman, Director of Admissions, The University of Arizona, PO Box 210040, Tucson, AZ 85721-0040. *Telephone:* 520-621-3237. *Fax:* 520-621-9799. *E-mail:* appinfo@arizona.edu. *Web site:* http://www.arizona.edu/.

UNIVERSITY OF PHOENIX ONLINE CAMPUS

Phoenix, Arizona

University of Phoenix Online Campus is a coed, proprietary, comprehensive institution, founded in 1989, offering degrees at the associate, bachelor's, master's, and doctoral levels and post-master's and postbachelor's certificates.

Academic Information The faculty has 6,237 members, 29% with terminal degrees. The undergraduate student-faculty ratio is 16:1. The library holds 1,759 titles and 692 serial subscriptions. Special programs include services for learning-disabled students, advanced placement credit, accelerated degree programs, independent study, distance learning, external degree programs, and adult/continuing education programs. The most frequently chosen baccalaureate fields are business/marketing, computer and information sciences, health professions and related sciences.

Student Body Statistics The student body totals 160,150, of whom 113,387 are undergraduates (11,518 freshmen). 64 percent are women and 36 percent are men. 5.7 percent are international students.

Expenses for 2006–07 *Application fee:* $45. *Tuition:* $14,180 full-time, $473 per credit part-time. Full-time tuition varies according to program.

Financial Aid Forms of aid include need-based and non-need-based scholarships. The average aided 2005–06 undergraduate received an aid package worth $3846. The application deadline for financial aid is continuous.

Freshman Admission University of Phoenix Online Campus requires 1 recommendation. A high school transcript is required for some. The application deadline for regular admission is rolling.

Transfer Admission The application deadline for admission is rolling.

Entrance Difficulty University of Phoenix Online Campus has an open admission policy.

For Further Information Contact Ms. Beth Barilla, Associate Vice President, Student Admissions and Services, University of Phoenix Online Campus, 4615 East Elwood Street, Mail Stop AA-K101, Phoenix, AZ 85040-1958. *Telephone:* 480-317-6000, 800-776-4867 (toll-free in-state), or 800-228-7240 (toll-free out-of-state). *Fax:* 480-894-1758. *E-mail:* beth.barilla@phoenix.edu. *Web site:* http://www.uopxonline.com/.

UNIVERSITY OF PHOENIX–PHOENIX CAMPUS

Phoenix, Arizona

University of Phoenix–Phoenix Campus is a coed, proprietary, comprehensive institution, founded in 1976, offering degrees at the bachelor's and master's levels and post-master's and postbachelor's certificates.

Academic Information The faculty has 784 members (2% full-time), 24% with terminal degrees. The undergraduate student-faculty ratio is 9:1. The library holds 1,759 titles and 692 serial subscriptions. Special programs include services for learning-disabled students, advanced placement credit, accelerated degree programs, independent study, distance learning, external degree programs, and adult/continuing education programs. The most frequently chosen baccalaureate fields are business/marketing, computer and information sciences, health professions and related sciences.

Student Body Statistics The student body totals 8,497, of whom 4,910 are undergraduates (144 freshmen). 57 percent are women and 43 percent are men. 5.4 percent are international students.

Expenses for 2006–07 *Application fee:* $45. *Tuition:* $9630 full-time.

Financial Aid Forms of aid include need-based and non-need-based scholarships. The average aided 2005–06 undergraduate received an aid package worth $4921. The application deadline for financial aid is continuous.

Freshman Admission University of Phoenix–Phoenix Campus requires 1 recommendation and TOEFL scores for international students. A high school transcript is required for some. The application deadline for regular admission is rolling.

Transfer Admission The application deadline for admission is rolling.

Entrance Difficulty University of Phoenix–Phoenix Campus has an open admission policy.

For Further Information Contact Ms. Beth Barilla, Associate Vice President, Student Admissions and Services, University of Phoenix–Phoenix Campus, 4615 East Elwood Street, Mail Stop AA-K101, Phoenix, AZ 85040-1958. *Telephone:* 480-317-6000, 800-776-4867 (toll-free in-state), or 800-228-7240 (toll-free out-of-state). *Fax:* 480-894-1758. *E-mail:* beth.barilla@phoenix.edu. *Web site:* http://www.phoenix.edu/.

UNIVERSITY OF PHOENIX–SOUTHERN ARIZONA CAMPUS

Tucson, Arizona

University of Phoenix–Southern Arizona Campus is a coed, proprietary, comprehensive institution, founded in 1979, offering degrees at the bachelor's and master's levels and post-master's certificates.

Academic Information The faculty has 610 members (4% full-time), 28% with terminal degrees. The undergraduate student-faculty ratio is 8:1. The library holds 1,759 titles and 692 serial subscriptions. Special programs include services for learning-disabled students, advanced placement credit, accelerated degree programs, independent study, distance learning, external degree programs, and adult/continuing education programs. The most frequently chosen baccalaureate fields are business/marketing, computer and information sciences, health professions and related sciences.

Student Body Statistics The student body totals 2,839, of whom 2,096 are undergraduates (52 freshmen). 60 percent are women and 40 percent are men. 10.8 percent are international students.

Expenses for 2006–07 *Application fee:* $45. *Tuition:* $9990 full-time, $333 per credit part-time.

Financial Aid Forms of aid include need-based and non-need-based scholarships. The average aided 2005–06 undergraduate received an aid package worth $4838. The application deadline for financial aid is continuous.

Freshman Admission University of Phoenix–Southern Arizona Campus requires 1 recommendation and TOEFL scores for international students. A high school transcript is required for some. The application deadline for regular admission is rolling.

University of Phoenix–Southern Arizona Campus (continued)

Transfer Admission The application deadline for admission is rolling.
Entrance Difficulty University of Phoenix–Southern Arizona Campus has an open admission policy.
For Further Information Contact Ms. Beth Barilla, Associate Vice President, Student Admissions and Services, University of Phoenix–Southern Arizona Campus, 4615 East Elwood Street, Mail Stop AA-K101, Phoenix, AZ 85040-1958. *Telephone:* 480-317-6000, 800-776-4867 (toll-free in-state), or 800-228-7240 (toll-free out-of-state). *Fax:* 480-894-1758. *E-mail:* beth.barilla@phoenix.edu. *Web site:* http://www.phoenix.edu/.

WESTERN INTERNATIONAL UNIVERSITY

Phoenix, Arizona

Western International University is a coed, proprietary, comprehensive institution, founded in 1978, offering degrees at the associate, bachelor's, and master's levels. It has a 4-acre campus in Phoenix.

Academic Information The faculty has 385 members, 22% with terminal degrees. The undergraduate student-faculty ratio is 10:1. The library holds 7,500 titles and 125 serial subscriptions. Special programs include academic remediation, an honors program, study abroad, advanced placement credit, accelerated degree programs, ESL programs, double majors, independent study, distance learning, summer session for credit, part-time degree programs, and adult/continuing education programs.
Student Body Statistics The student body totals 2,229, of whom 1,649 are undergraduates (23 freshmen). 67 percent are women and 33 percent are men. Students come from 48 states and territories and 52 other countries. 68 percent are from Arizona. 2 percent are international students.
Expenses for 2006–07 *Application fee:* $85. *Tuition:* $7992 full-time, $333 per credit part-time. Both full-time and part-time tuition varies according to location.
Freshman Admission Western International University requires a high school transcript, a minimum 2.5 high school GPA, an interview, and TOEFL scores for international students. 3 recommendations are recommended. 3 recommendations are required for some. The application deadline for regular admission is rolling.
Transfer Admission The application deadline for admission is rolling.
Entrance Difficulty Western International University assesses its entrance difficulty level as moderately difficult.
For Further Information Contact Ms. Karen Janitell, Director of Enrollment, Western International University, 9215 North Black Canyon Highway, Phoenix, AZ 85021. *Telephone:* 602-943-2311 Ext. 1063. *E-mail:* karen.janitell@apollogrp.edu. *Web site:* http://www.wintu.edu/.

California

ACADEMY OF ART UNIVERSITY

San Francisco, California

Academy of Art University is a coed, proprietary, comprehensive institution, founded in 1929, offering degrees at the associate, bachelor's, and master's levels. It has a 3-acre campus in San Francisco.

Academic Information The faculty has 1,047 members (14% full-time). The undergraduate student-faculty ratio is 12:1. The library holds 36,000 titles, 476 serial subscriptions, and 3,500 audiovisual materials. Special programs include academic remediation, services for learning-disabled students, ESL programs, independent study, distance learning, summer session for credit, part-time degree programs, adult/continuing education programs, and internships. The most frequently chosen baccalaureate field is visual and performing arts.
Student Body Statistics The student body totals 9,483, of whom 7,438 are undergraduates (984 freshmen). 51 percent are women and 49 percent are men. Students come from 56 states and territories and 75 other countries. 74 percent are from California. 14.5 percent are international students. 7 percent of the 2006 graduating class went on to graduate and professional schools.
Expenses for 2007–08 *Application fee:* $100. *Comprehensive fee:* $27,280 includes full-time tuition ($14,400), mandatory fees ($280), and college room and board ($12,600). *Part-time tuition:* $600 per credit.
Financial Aid Forms of aid include need-based scholarships and part-time jobs. The average aided 2005–06 undergraduate received an aid package worth $5875. The priority application deadline for financial aid is March 2.
Freshman Admission Academy of Art University requires a high school transcript and TOEFL scores for international students. A minimum 2.0 high school GPA, an interview, and a portfolio are recommended. The application deadline for regular admission is rolling.
Transfer Admission The application deadline for admission is rolling.
Entrance Difficulty Academy of Art University has an open admission policy. It assesses its entrance difficulty as minimally difficult for transfers.
For Further Information Contact Mr. John Meurer, Vice President, Admissions, Academy of Art University, 79 New Montgomery Street, San Francisco, CA 94105. *Telephone:* 415-263-2219 or 800-544-ARTS (toll-free). *Fax:* 415-263-4130. *E-mail:* info@academyart.edu. *Web site:* http://www.academyart.edu/.

See page 152 for the College Close-Up.

ALLIANT INTERNATIONAL UNIVERSITY

San Diego, California

Alliant International University is a coed, private unit of Alliant International University, founded in 1952, offering degrees at the bachelor's, master's, and doctoral levels and postbachelor's certificates. It has a 60-acre campus in San Diego.

Academic Information The faculty has 288 members (45% full-time), 100% with terminal degrees. The undergraduate student-faculty ratio is 15:1. The library holds 212,394 titles and 674 serial subscriptions. Special programs include academic remediation, services for learning-disabled students, an honors program, study abroad, advanced placement credit, ESL programs, independent study, distance learning, summer session for credit, part-time degree programs (daytime, evenings), adult/continuing education programs, and internships. The most frequently chosen baccalaureate fields are business/marketing, psychology, public administration and social services.
Student Body Statistics The student body totals 3,521, of whom 178 are undergraduates. 52 percent are women and 48 percent are men. Students come from 15 states and territories and 38 other countries. 90 percent are from California. 30.3 percent are international students. 15 percent of the 2006 graduating class went on to graduate and professional schools.
Expenses for 2007–08 *Application fee:* $45. *Tuition:* $14,400 full-time, $530 per unit part-time. *Mandatory fees:* $370 full-time.
Financial Aid Forms of aid include need-based and non-need-based scholarships, athletic grants, and part-time jobs. The average aided 2006–07 undergraduate received an aid package worth an estimated $16,250. The priority application deadline for financial aid is March 2.
Freshman Admission Alliant International University requires a high school transcript and TOEFL scores for international students. The application deadline for regular admission is rolling.
For Further Information Contact Ms. Susan Topham, Alliant International University, 10455 Pomerado Road, San Diego, CA 92131-1799. *Telephone:* 858-635-4772 or 866-825-5426 (toll-free). *Fax:* 858-635-4739. *E-mail:* admissions3@alliant.edu. *Web site:* http://www.alliant.edu/.

AMERICAN ACADEMY OF DRAMATIC ARTS/HOLLYWOOD

Hollywood, California

http://www.aada.org/

THE AMERICAN COLLEGE

See American InterContinental University.

AMERICAN INTERCONTINENTAL UNIVERSITY

Los Angeles, California

http://www.aiuniv.edu/

ANTIOCH UNIVERSITY LOS ANGELES

Culver City, California

Antioch University Los Angeles is a coed, private, upper-level unit of Antioch University, founded in 1972, offering degrees at the bachelor's and master's levels and post-master's and postbachelor's certificates. It has a 1-acre campus in Culver City near Los Angeles.

Academic Information The faculty has 172 members (12% full-time), 52% with terminal degrees. The undergraduate student-faculty ratio is 14:1. Special programs include academic remediation, services for learning-disabled students, cooperative (work-study) education, advanced placement credit, accelerated degree programs, double majors, independent study, distance learning, self-designed majors, summer session for credit, part-time degree programs (daytime, evenings, weekends, summer), external degree programs, adult/continuing education programs, and internships.
Student Body Statistics The student body totals 495, of whom 139 are undergraduates. 68 percent are women and 32 percent are men. Students come from 1 state or territory.
Expenses for 2007–08 *Application fee:* $60. *Tuition:* $15,498 full-time, $501 per credit part-time.
Transfer Admission Antioch University Los Angeles requires a college transcript. Standardized test scores are required for some. The application deadline for admission is August 1.
Entrance Difficulty Antioch University Los Angeles assesses its entrance difficulty level as moderately difficult. For the fall 2006 entering class, 90 percent of the applicants were accepted.
For Further Information Contact Judith Magee, Director of Admissions and Financial Aid, Antioch University Los Angeles, 400 Corporate Pointe, Culver City, CA 90230. *Telephone:* 310-578-1080 Ext. 217 or 800-7ANTIOCH (toll-free). *Fax:* 310-822-4824. *E-mail:* admissions@antiochla.edu. *Web site:* http://www.antiochla.edu/.

ANTIOCH UNIVERSITY SANTA BARBARA

Santa Barbara, California

Antioch University Santa Barbara is a coed, private, upper-level unit of Antioch University, founded in 1977, offering degrees at the bachelor's and master's levels. It is located in Santa Barbara near Los Angeles.

Academic Information The faculty has 71 members (23% full-time). The undergraduate student-faculty ratio is 15:1. Special programs include academic remediation, accelerated degree programs, double majors, independent study, self-designed majors, summer session for credit, part-time degree programs, adult/continuing education programs, and internships. The most frequently chosen baccalaureate field is liberal arts/general studies.
Student Body Statistics The student body totals 284, of whom 94 are undergraduates. 69 percent are women and 31 percent are men. 1.1 percent are international students.
Expenses for 2006–07 *Application fee:* $60. *Tuition:* $13,935 full-time, $465 per unit part-time. *Mandatory fees:* $48 full-time.
Financial Aid Forms of aid include need-based scholarships and part-time jobs. The application deadline for financial aid is continuous.

Transfer Admission Antioch University Santa Barbara requires a college transcript and a minimum 2.0 college GPA. The application deadline for admission is rolling.
For Further Information Contact Ankara M. McPherson, Director of Admissions, Antioch University Santa Barbara, 801 Garden Street, Suite 101, Santa Barbara, CA 93101-1580. *Telephone:* 805-962-8179. *Fax:* 805-962-4786. *E-mail:* admissions@antiochsb.edu. *Web site:* http://www.antiochsb.edu/.

ARGOSY UNIVERSITY, INLAND EMPIRE

San Bernardino, California

http://www.argosyu.edu/inlandempire/

ARGOSY UNIVERSITY, ORANGE COUNTY

Santa Ana, California

Argosy University, Orange County is a coed, proprietary university, offering degrees at the associate, bachelor's, master's, and doctoral levels. It is located in Santa Ana near Los Angeles and San Diego.

Academic Information The faculty has 81 members (14% full-time), 90% with terminal degrees. The undergraduate student-faculty ratio is 22:1. The library holds 1,200 titles and 50 serial subscriptions. Special programs include academic remediation, services for learning-disabled students, distance learning, and part-time degree programs (daytime, evenings, weekends, summer).
Student Body Statistics The student body totals 646, of whom 81 are undergraduates. 59 percent are women and 41 percent are men.
Financial Aid Forms of aid include need-based and non-need-based scholarships and part-time jobs.
Freshman Admission The application deadline for regular admission is rolling.
Transfer Admission The application deadline for admission is rolling.
Entrance Difficulty Argosy University, Orange County assesses its entrance difficulty level as moderately difficult.
For Further Information Contact Director of Admissions, Argosy University, Orange County, 3501 West Sunflower Avenue, Suite 110, Santa Ana, CA 92704. *Telephone:* 714-338-6200 or 800-716-9598 (toll-free). *E-mail:* auocadmissions@argosyu.edu. *Web site:* http://www.argosyu.edu/.

ARGOSY UNIVERSITY, SAN DIEGO

San Diego, California

Argosy University, San Diego is a coed, proprietary, upper-level institution, offering degrees at the associate level.

For Further Information Contact Admissions Director, Argosy University, San Diego, 7650 Mission Valley Road, San Diego, CA 92108. *Telephone:* 858-598-1900 or 866-505-0333 (toll-free). *E-mail:* auadmissions@argosyu.edu. *Web site:* http://www.argosyu.edu/sandiego/.

ARGOSY UNIVERSITY, SAN FRANCISCO BAY AREA

Point Richmond, California

Argosy University, San Francisco Bay Area is a coed, proprietary, upper-level institution, founded in 1998, offering degrees at the bachelor's, master's, and doctoral levels. It is located in Point Richmond near Oakland and San Francisco.

Academic Information The faculty has 11 members (9% full-time), 100% with terminal degrees. The undergraduate student-faculty ratio is 10:1. The library holds 6,500 titles, 95 serial subscriptions, and 950 audiovisual materials. Special programs include services for learning-disabled students, independent study, distance learning, summer session for

Argosy University, San Francisco Bay Area (continued)
credit, part-time degree programs, adult/continuing education programs, and internships. The most frequently chosen baccalaureate field is psychology.

Student Body Statistics The student body totals 670, of whom 44 are undergraduates. 86 percent are women and 14 percent are men. Students come from 1 state or territory and 2 other countries. 95 percent are from California. 50 percent of the 2006 graduating class went on to graduate and professional schools.

Expenses for 2007–08 *Application fee:* $50. *Tuition:* $13,650 full-time, $475 per credit part-time. *Mandatory fees:* $360 full-time.

Financial Aid Forms of aid include need-based and non-need-based scholarships and part-time jobs. The application deadline for financial aid is continuous.

Transfer Admission The application deadline for admission is rolling.

Entrance Difficulty Argosy University, San Francisco Bay Area assesses its entrance difficulty level as minimally difficult for transfers. For the fall 2006 entering class, 85 percent of the applicants were accepted.

For Further Information Contact Mr. John Stofan, Argosy University, San Francisco Bay Area, 999 Canal Boulevard, Suite A, Point Richmond, CA 94804. *Telephone:* 510-837-3709, 866-215-2777 Ext. 205 (toll-free in-state), or 866-215-2777 (toll-free out-of-state). *Fax:* 510-215-0299. *E-mail:* jstofan@argosyu.edu. *Web site:* http://www.argosyu.edu/.

ARGOSY UNIVERSITY, SANTA MONICA
Santa Monica, California

Argosy University, Santa Monica is a coed, proprietary university, offering degrees at the associate level.

For Further Information Contact Admissions Director, Argosy University, Santa Monica, 2900 31st Street, Santa Monica, CA 90405. *Telephone:* 310-866-4000 or 866-505-0332 (toll-free). *E-mail:* auadmissions@argosyu.edu. *Web site:* http://www.argosyu.edu/santamonica/.

ART CENTER COLLEGE OF DESIGN
Pasadena, California

Art Center College of Design is a coed, private, comprehensive institution, founded in 1930, offering degrees at the bachelor's and master's levels. It has a 175-acre campus in Pasadena near Los Angeles.

Academic Information The faculty has 407 members (16% full-time). The undergraduate student-faculty ratio is 12:1. The library holds 93,038 titles and 450 serial subscriptions. Special programs include advanced placement credit, accelerated degree programs, independent study, summer session for credit, adult/continuing education programs, and internships.

Student Body Statistics The student body totals 1,631, of whom 1,485 are undergraduates (55 freshmen). 40 percent are women and 60 percent are men. Students come from 31 states and territories and 28 other countries. 67 percent are from California. 16.2 percent are international students.

Expenses for 2006–07 *Application fee:* $45. *Tuition:* $27,710 full-time. *Mandatory fees:* $200 full-time.

Financial Aid Forms of aid include need-based and non-need-based scholarships and part-time jobs. The average aided 2005–06 undergraduate received an aid package worth $13,708. The priority application deadline for financial aid is March 1.

Freshman Admission Art Center College of Design requires an essay, a high school transcript, a portfolio, and TOEFL scores for international students. A minimum 3.0 high school GPA and an interview are recommended. SAT or ACT scores are required for some. The application deadline for regular admission is rolling.

Transfer Admission The application deadline for admission is rolling.

Entrance Difficulty Art Center College of Design assesses its entrance difficulty level as very difficult. For the fall 2006 freshman class, 71 percent of the applicants were accepted.

For Further Information Contact Ms. Kit Baron, Vice President of Admissions, Art Center College of Design, 1700 Lida Street, Pasadena, CA 91103-1999. *Telephone:* 626-396-2373. *Fax:* 626-795-0578. *E-mail:* admissions@artcenter.edu. *Web site:* http://www.artcenter.edu/.

THE ART INSTITUTE OF CALIFORNIA–INLAND EMPIRE
San Bernardino, California

The Art Institute of California–Inland Empire is a coed, proprietary, four-year college, offering degrees at the bachelor's level.

Academic Information The library holds 6,000 titles, 84 serial subscriptions, and 550 audiovisual materials. Special programs include services for learning-disabled students, cooperative (work-study) education, summer session for credit, part-time degree programs, and internships.

Student Body Statistics The student body is made up of 93 undergraduates (59 freshmen). 45 percent are women and 55 percent are men. Students come from 1 state or territory. 98 percent are from California.

Expenses for 2006–07 *Application fee:* $150. *Tuition:* $21,024 full-time, $428 per credit part-time. *Mandatory fees:* $1200 full-time.

Freshman Admission The Art Institute of California–Inland Empire requires an essay, a high school transcript, and an interview. SAT or ACT scores are recommended. Recommendations are required for some. The application deadline for regular admission is October 1 and for nonresidents it is October 1.

Entrance Difficulty The Art Institute of California–Inland Empire assesses its entrance difficulty level as noncompetitive. For the fall 2006 freshman class, 100 percent of the applicants were accepted.

For Further Information Contact Admissions Office, The Art Institute of California–Inland Empire, 630 East Brier Drive, San Bernadino, CA 92408. *Telephone:* 909-915-2100 or 800-353-0812 (toll-free out-of-state). *Fax:* 909-915-2130. *E-mail:* mjeffs@aii.edu. *Web site:* http://www.artinstitutes.edu/inlandempire/.

THE ART INSTITUTE OF CALIFORNIA–LOS ANGELES
Santa Monica, California

The Art Institute of California–Los Angeles is a coed, proprietary, four-year college of Education Management Corporation, offering degrees at the associate and bachelor's levels.

Academic Information The faculty has 120 members (48% full-time), 4% with terminal degrees. The student-faculty ratio is 19:1. The library holds 45,478 titles, 375 serial subscriptions, and 4 audiovisual materials. Special programs include academic remediation, services for learning-disabled students, an honors program, study abroad, advanced placement credit, independent study, distance learning, summer session for credit, adult/continuing education programs, and internships. The most frequently chosen baccalaureate fields are personal and culinary services, visual and performing arts.

Student Body Statistics The student body is made up of 2,068 undergraduates (328 freshmen). 34 percent are women and 66 percent are men. Students come from 21 states and territories and 22 other countries. 3 percent are international students.

Expenses for 2007–08 *Application fee:* $50. *Tuition:* $21,840 full-time, $455 per credit part-time. *College room only:* $10,652.

Freshman Admission The Art Institute of California–Los Angeles requires an essay, a high school transcript, an interview, and TOEFL scores for international students. A minimum 2.5 high school GPA, recommendations, and a portfolio are required for some. The application deadline for regular admission is rolling.

Transfer Admission The application deadline for admission is rolling.

Entrance Difficulty The Art Institute of California–Los Angeles has an open admission policy.
For Further Information Contact Assistant Director of Admissions, The Art Institute of California–Los Angeles, 2900 31st Street, Santa Monica, CA 90405-3035. *Telephone:* 310-752-4700 or 888-646-4610 (toll-free). *Fax:* 310-752-4708. *E-mail:* ailaadm@aii.edu. *Web site:* http://www.aicala. artinstitutes.edu/.

THE ART INSTITUTE OF CALIFORNIA–ORANGE COUNTY

Santa Ana, California

The Art Institute of California–Orange County is a coed, proprietary, four-year college of Education Management Corporation, founded in 2000, offering degrees at the associate and bachelor's levels. It is located in Santa Ana near Orange County, Los Angeles.

Academic Information The faculty has 100 members (51% full-time). The student-faculty ratio is 19:1. The library holds 7,260 titles, 114 serial subscriptions, and 1,712 audiovisual materials. Special programs include academic remediation, services for learning-disabled students, cooperative (work-study) education, study abroad, advanced placement credit, independent study, distance learning, and internships.
Student Body Statistics The student body is made up of 1,637 undergraduates (258 freshmen). 39 percent are women and 61 percent are men. Students come from 20 states and territories.
Expenses for 2006–07 *Application fee:* $0. *Comprehensive fee:* $33,304 includes full-time tuition ($21,024), mandatory fees ($1680), and college room and board ($10,600). *Part-time tuition:* $428 per quarter hour.
Financial Aid Forms of aid include need-based scholarships and part-time jobs. The priority application deadline for financial aid is March 2.
Freshman Admission The Art Institute of California–Orange County requires an essay, a high school transcript, and an interview. A minimum 2.0 high school GPA and recommendations are recommended. A minimum 2.5 high school GPA, recommendations, and a portfolio are required for some. The application deadline for regular admission is rolling.
Transfer Admission The application deadline for admission is rolling.
Entrance Difficulty For the fall 2006 freshman class, 53 percent of the applicants were accepted.
For Further Information Contact Mr. Steve Rickard, The Art Institute of California–Orange County, 3601 West Sunflower Avenue, Santa Ana, CA 92704. *Telephone:* 714-830-0200 or 888-549-3055 (toll-free). *Fax:* 714-556-3055. *E-mail:* srickard@aii.edu. *Web site:* http://www.aicaoc.artinstitutes. edu/.

THE ART INSTITUTE OF CALIFORNIA–SAN DIEGO

San Diego, California

The Art Institute of California–San Diego is a coed, proprietary, four-year college of Education Management Corporation, founded in 1981, offering degrees at the associate and bachelor's levels.

Academic Information The faculty has 126 members (49% full-time), 100% with terminal degrees. The student-faculty ratio is 22:1. The library holds 12,009 titles, 1,668 serial subscriptions, and 1,449 audiovisual materials. Special programs include services for learning-disabled students, cooperative (work-study) education, double majors, summer session for credit, and internships. The most frequently chosen baccalaureate fields are business/marketing, visual and performing arts.
Student Body Statistics The student body is made up of 2,386 undergraduates. Students come from 26 states and territories. 64 percent are from California. 1.3 percent are international students.
Expenses for 2006–07 *Application fee:* $50. *Tuition:* $21,024 full-time, $438 per credit part-time. *College room only:* $9200.

Financial Aid Forms of aid include need-based and non-need-based scholarships and part-time jobs. The application deadline for financial aid is continuous.
Freshman Admission The Art Institute of California–San Diego requires an essay, a high school transcript, an interview, minimum GPA of 2.5 and portfolio required for GAD students, and TOEFL scores for international students. A minimum 2.0 high school GPA is recommended. Recommendations and SAT or ACT scores are required for some. The application deadline for regular admission is rolling.
Transfer Admission The application deadline for admission is rolling.
Entrance Difficulty The Art Institute of California–San Diego assesses its entrance difficulty level as minimally difficult.
For Further Information Contact The Art Institute of California-San Diego, The Art Institute of California–San Diego, 7650 Mission Valley Road, San Diego, CA 92108. *Telephone:* 858-598-1399 or 800-591-2422 Ext. 3117 (toll-free in-state). *Fax:* 619-291-3206. *E-mail:* info@aii.edu. *Web site:* http://www.aica.artinstitutes.edu/.

THE ART INSTITUTE OF CALIFORNIA–SAN FRANCISCO

San Francisco, California

The Art Institute of California–San Francisco is a coed, proprietary, four-year college of Education Management Corporation, founded in 1939, offering degrees at the associate and bachelor's levels.

Academic Information The faculty has 108 members (20% full-time). The student-faculty ratio is 16:1. The library holds 11,185 titles, 52 serial subscriptions, and 2,514 audiovisual materials. Special programs include academic remediation, services for learning-disabled students, an honors program, cooperative (work-study) education, study abroad, advanced placement credit, accelerated degree programs, distance learning, summer session for credit, part-time degree programs (daytime, evenings, summer), internships, and arrangement for off-campus study.
Student Body Statistics The student body is made up of 1,624 undergraduates. 46 percent are women and 54 percent are men. Students come from 5 states and territories and 32 other countries. 80 percent are from California. 3.5 percent are international students.
Expenses for 2006–07 *Application fee:* $50. *Tuition:* $20,640 full-time. *College room only:* $7851.
Financial Aid Forms of aid include need-based and non-need-based scholarships and part-time jobs. The priority application deadline for financial aid is March 2.
Freshman Admission The Art Institute of California–San Francisco requires an essay, a high school transcript, an interview, and TOEFL scores for international students. A minimum 2.0 high school GPA is recommended. Recommendations are required for some. The application deadline for regular admission is rolling and for nonresidents it is rolling.
Transfer Admission The application deadline for admission is rolling.
Entrance Difficulty The Art Institute of California–San Francisco assesses its entrance difficulty level as moderately difficult; minimally difficult for out-of-state applicants; minimally difficult for transfers. For the fall 2006 freshman class, 99 percent of the applicants were accepted.
For Further Information Contact Mr. Clark Dawood, Dean of Student Affairs, The Art Institute of California–San Francisco, 1170 Market Street, San Francisco, CA 94102-4908. *Telephone:* 415-276-1004 or 888-493-3261 (toll-free). *Fax:* 415-863-6344. *E-mail:* aisfadm@aii.edu. *Web site:* http:// www.aicasf.artinstitutes.edu/.

ART INSTITUTE OF SOUTHERN CALIFORNIA

See Laguna College of Art & Design.

ART INSTITUTES INTERNATIONAL AT SAN FRANCISCO

See The Art Institute of California–San Francisco.

AZUSA PACIFIC UNIVERSITY

Azusa, California

Azusa Pacific University is a coed, private, nondenominational, comprehensive institution, founded in 1899, offering degrees at the bachelor's, master's, doctoral, and first professional levels. It has a 60-acre campus in Azusa near Los Angeles.

Academic Information The faculty has 334 members (90% full-time). The undergraduate student-faculty ratio is 11:1. The library holds 185,708 titles and 14,031 serial subscriptions. Special programs include academic remediation, services for learning-disabled students, an honors program, cooperative (work-study) education, study abroad, advanced placement credit, accelerated degree programs, Freshman Honors College, ESL programs, double majors, independent study, distance learning, summer session for credit, part-time degree programs (daytime), adult/continuing education programs, internships, and arrangement for off-campus study.

Student Body Statistics The student body totals 8,128, of whom 4,722 are undergraduates (870 freshmen). 63 percent are women and 37 percent are men. Students come from 48 states and territories and 47 other countries. 73 percent are from California. 2.5 percent are international students.

Expenses for 2006–07 *Application fee:* $45. *Comprehensive fee:* $31,078 includes full-time tuition ($23,050), mandatory fees ($700), and college room and board ($7328). *College room only:* $3690. Full-time tuition and fees vary according to course load. Room and board charges vary according to board plan, housing facility, and student level. *Part-time tuition:* $960 per unit. Part-time tuition varies according to course load.

Financial Aid Forms of aid include need-based and non-need-based scholarships, athletic grants, and part-time jobs. The average aided 2005–06 undergraduate received an aid package worth $19,785. The application deadline for financial aid is July 1 with a priority deadline of March 2.

Freshman Admission Azusa Pacific University requires an essay, a high school transcript, a minimum 2.8 high school GPA, 2 recommendations, SAT or ACT scores, and TOEFL scores for international students. An interview is required for some. The application deadline for regular admission is June 1 and for early action it is December 1.

Transfer Admission The application deadline for admission is June 1.

Entrance Difficulty Azusa Pacific University assesses its entrance difficulty level as moderately difficult. For the fall 2006 freshman class, 74 percent of the applicants were accepted.

For Further Information Contact Mr. Dave Burke, Dean of Enrollment, Azusa Pacific University, 901 East Alosta Avenue, PO Box 7000, Azusa, CA 91702-7000. *Telephone:* 626-812-3016 or 800-TALK-APU (toll-free). *E-mail:* admissions@apu.edu. *Web site:* http://www.apu.edu/.

See page 158 for the College Close-Up.

BETHANY UNIVERSITY

Scotts Valley, California

Bethany University is a coed, private, Assemblies of God, comprehensive institution, founded in 1919, offering degrees at the associate, bachelor's, and master's levels. It has a 40-acre campus in Scotts Valley near San Francisco and San Jose.

Academic Information The faculty has 72 members (38% full-time), 26% with terminal degrees. The undergraduate student-faculty ratio is 11:1. The library holds 59,453 titles and 858 serial subscriptions. Special programs include academic remediation, services for learning-disabled students, advanced placement credit, accelerated degree programs, independent study, distance learning, summer session for credit, part-time degree programs, external degree programs, adult/continuing education programs, and internships.

Student Body Statistics The student body totals 547, of whom 474 are undergraduates (70 freshmen). 59 percent are women and 41 percent are men. Students come from 20 states and territories and 5 other countries. 85 percent are from California. 1.5 percent are international students.

Expenses for 2007–08 *Application fee:* $35. *Comprehensive fee:* $24,035 includes full-time tuition ($16,400), mandatory fees ($875), and college room and board ($6760). *College room only:* $3360. *Part-time tuition:* $685 per unit. *Part-time mandatory fees:* $250 per term.

Financial Aid Forms of aid include need-based and non-need-based scholarships, athletic grants, and part-time jobs. The priority application deadline for financial aid is March 2.

Freshman Admission Bethany University requires an essay, a high school transcript, a minimum 2.0 high school GPA, 2 recommendations, Christian commitment, SAT or ACT scores, and TOEFL scores for international students. The application deadline for regular admission is July 31.

Transfer Admission The application deadline for admission is July 31.

Entrance Difficulty Bethany University assesses its entrance difficulty level as minimally difficult. For the fall 2006 freshman class, 54 percent of the applicants were accepted.

For Further Information Contact Ms. Sharon Anderson, Vice President of Student Life and Enrollment, Bethany University, 800 Bethany Drive, Scotts Valley, CA 95066-2820. *Telephone:* 831-438-3800 Ext. 3900 or 800-843-9410 (toll-free). *Fax:* 831-438-4517. *E-mail:* info@bethany.edu. *Web site:* http://www.bethany.edu/.

BETHESDA CHRISTIAN UNIVERSITY

Anaheim, California

http://www.bcu.edu/

BIOLA UNIVERSITY

La Mirada, California

Biola University is a coed, private, interdenominational university, founded in 1908, offering degrees at the bachelor's, master's, doctoral, and first professional levels. It has a 95-acre campus in La Mirada near Los Angeles.

Academic Information The faculty has 444 members (45% full-time). The undergraduate student-faculty ratio is 17:1. The library holds 301,956 titles, 17,876 serial subscriptions, and 18,712 audiovisual materials. Special programs include academic remediation, services for learning-disabled students, an honors program, cooperative (work-study) education, study abroad, advanced placement credit, accelerated degree programs, ESL programs, double majors, independent study, summer session for credit, part-time degree programs, adult/continuing education programs, internships, and arrangement for off-campus study with Council for Christian Colleges and Universities. The most frequently chosen baccalaureate fields are business/marketing, physical sciences, psychology.

Student Body Statistics The student body totals 5,752, of whom 3,924 are undergraduates (807 freshmen). 60 percent are women and 40 percent are men. Students come from 49 states and territories and 42 other countries. 75 percent are from California. 3.5 percent are international students.

Expenses for 2007–08 *Application fee:* $45. *Comprehensive fee:* $32,513 includes full-time tuition ($24,988), mandatory fees ($155), and college room and board ($7370). *College room only:* $3850. *Part-time tuition:* $1068 per unit.

Financial Aid Forms of aid include need-based and non-need-based scholarships and part-time jobs. The application deadline for financial aid is continuous.

Freshman Admission Biola University requires an essay, a high school transcript, 2 recommendations, SAT or ACT scores, and TOEFL scores for international students. A minimum 3.0 high school GPA and an interview are recommended. An interview is required for some. The application deadline for regular admission is March 1 and for early action it is December 1.

Transfer Admission The application deadline for admission is March 1.

Entrance Difficulty Biola University assesses its entrance difficulty level as moderately difficult. For the fall 2006 freshman class, 80 percent of the applicants were accepted.

For Further Information Contact Mr. Andre Stephens, Director of Enrollment Management, Biola University, 13800 Biola Avenue, La Mirada, CA 90639. *Telephone:* 562-903-4752 or 800-652-4652 (toll-free). *Fax:* 562-903-4709. *E-mail:* admissions@biola.edu. *Web site:* http://www.biola.edu/.

BROOKS INSTITUTE OF PHOTOGRAPHY
Santa Barbara, California
http://www.brooks.edu/

BROWN MACKIE COLLEGE–LOS ANGELES
See Argosy University, Santa Monica.

BROWN MACKIE COLLEGE–SAN DIEGO
See Argosy University, San Diego.

CALIFORNIA BAPTIST UNIVERSITY
Riverside, California

California Baptist University is a coed, private, Southern Baptist, comprehensive institution, founded in 1950, offering degrees at the bachelor's and master's levels. It has a 110-acre campus in Riverside near Los Angeles.

Academic Information The faculty has 285 members (42% full-time), 30% with terminal degrees. The undergraduate student-faculty ratio is 20:1. The library holds 180,946 titles, 11,166 serial subscriptions, and 3,633 audiovisual materials. Special programs include an honors program, study abroad, advanced placement credit, accelerated degree programs, ESL programs, double majors, independent study, distance learning, summer session for credit, part-time degree programs (daytime, evenings, weekends, summer), adult/continuing education programs, internships, and arrangement for off-campus study with Council for Christian Colleges and Universities. The most frequently chosen baccalaureate fields are liberal arts/general studies, business/marketing, psychology.

Student Body Statistics The student body totals 3,409, of whom 2,623 are undergraduates (439 freshmen). 64 percent are women and 36 percent are men. Students come from 34 states and territories and 27 other countries. 95 percent are from California. 2.6 percent are international students.

Expenses for 2006–07 *Application fee:* $45. *Comprehensive fee:* $25,710 includes full-time tuition ($17,680), mandatory fees ($1220), and college room and board ($6810). *College room only:* $2800. Full-time tuition and fees vary according to class time and program. Room and board charges vary according to board plan and housing facility. *Part-time tuition:* $680 per semester hour. *Part-time mandatory fees:* $170 per term. Part-time tuition and fees vary according to class time and program.

Financial Aid Forms of aid include need-based and non-need-based scholarships, athletic grants, and part-time jobs. The average aided 2005–06 undergraduate received an aid package worth $11,670. The priority application deadline for financial aid is March 2.

Freshman Admission California Baptist University requires an essay, a high school transcript, a minimum 2.0 high school GPA, 2 recommendations, SAT or ACT scores, and TOEFL scores for international students. An interview is recommended. The application deadline for regular admission is rolling; for nonresidents it is rolling; and for early action it is December 1.

Transfer Admission The application deadline for admission is rolling.

Entrance Difficulty California Baptist University assesses its entrance difficulty level as minimally difficult. For the fall 2006 freshman class, 69 percent of the applicants were accepted.

For Further Information Contact Mr. Allen Johnson, Director, Undergraduate Admissions, California Baptist University, 8432 Magnolia Avenue, Riverside, CA 92504-3297. *Telephone:* 951-343-4212 or 877-228-8866 (toll-free). *Fax:* 951-343-4525. *E-mail:* admissions@calbaptist.edu. *Web site:* http://www.calbaptist.edu/.

CALIFORNIA CHRISTIAN COLLEGE
Fresno, California

California Christian College is a coed, private, four-year college, offering degrees at the associate and bachelor's levels. It has a 5-acre campus in Fresno near Fresno.

Academic Information The faculty has 10 members (40% full-time), 30% with terminal degrees. The student-faculty ratio is 3:1. The library holds 13,154 titles, 7 serial subscriptions, and 430 audiovisual materials. Special programs include academic remediation, cooperative (work-study) education, accelerated degree programs, independent study, summer session for credit, and part-time degree programs (daytime, evenings, summer).

Student Body Statistics The student body is made up of 32 undergraduates (4 freshmen). 38 percent are women and 63 percent are men. Students come from 3 states and territories.

Expenses for 2006–07 *Application fee:* $40. *Tuition:* $9500 full-time, $4750 per term part-time.

Financial Aid Forms of aid include need-based scholarships and part-time jobs. The priority application deadline for financial aid is March 2.

Freshman Admission California Christian College requires an essay, a high school transcript, a minimum 2.0 high school GPA, 2 recommendations, statement of faith, moral/ethical statement, TOEFL scores for international students, and standardized Bible content tests. An interview and SAT or ACT scores are recommended. The application deadline for regular admission is rolling.

Transfer Admission The application deadline for admission is rolling.

Entrance Difficulty California Christian College has an open admission policy.

For Further Information Contact Mr. Brian Henderer, Director of Admissions and Recruitment, California Christian College, 4881 East University Avenue, Fresno, CA 93703. *Telephone:* 559-251-4215 Ext. 5571. *Fax:* 559-251-4231. *E-mail:* cccfresno@aol.com. *Web site:* http://www.calchristiancollege.org/.

CALIFORNIA COAST UNIVERSITY
Santa Ana, California
http://www.calcoast.edu/

CALIFORNIA COLLEGE
San Diego, California
http://www.cc-sd.edu

CALIFORNIA COLLEGE OF THE ARTS
San Francisco, California

California College of the Arts is a coed, private, comprehensive institution, founded in 1907, offering degrees at the bachelor's and master's levels. It has a 4-acre campus in San Francisco.

Academic Information The faculty has 375 members (9% full-time), 62% with terminal degrees. The undergraduate student-faculty ratio is 15:1. The library holds 39,000 titles and 340 serial subscriptions. Special programs include academic remediation, services for learning-disabled

California College of the Arts (continued)

students, an honors program, cooperative (work-study) education, study abroad, advanced placement credit, double majors, independent study, self-designed majors, summer session for credit, internships, and arrangement for off-campus study with Mills College, Holy Names College, AICAD Mobility Program, University of San Francisco.

Student Body Statistics The student body totals 1,622, of whom 1,310 are undergraduates (184 freshmen). 59 percent are women and 41 percent are men. Students come from 39 states and territories and 26 other countries. 65 percent are from California. 6.9 percent are international students.

Expenses for 2006–07 *Application fee:* $50. *Comprehensive fee:* $36,529 includes full-time tuition ($27,624), mandatory fees ($290), and college room and board ($8615). Full-time tuition and fees vary according to course load. Room and board charges vary according to housing facility. *Part-time tuition:* $1151 per unit. Part-time tuition varies according to course load.

Financial Aid Forms of aid include need-based and non-need-based scholarships and part-time jobs. The average aided 2006–07 undergraduate received an aid package worth an estimated $19,275. The priority application deadline for financial aid is March 1.

Freshman Admission California College of the Arts requires an essay, a high school transcript, a minimum 2.0 high school GPA, 2 recommendations, a portfolio, and TOEFL scores for international students. An interview is required for some. The application deadline for regular admission is February 1.

Transfer Admission The application deadline for admission is rolling.

Entrance Difficulty California College of the Arts assesses its entrance difficulty level as moderately difficult. For the fall 2006 freshman class, 78 percent of the applicants were accepted.

For Further Information Contact Ms. Robynne Royster, Director of Admissions, California College of the Arts, 1111 Eighth Street at 16th and Wisconsin, San Francisco, CA 94107. *Telephone:* 415-703-9523 Ext. 9532 or 800-447-1ART (toll-free). *Fax:* 415-703-9539. *E-mail:* enroll@cca.edu. *Web site:* http://www.cca.edu/.

CALIFORNIA DESIGN COLLEGE

Los Angeles, California

California Design College is a coed, proprietary, four-year college of Education Management Corporation, founded in 1992, offering degrees at the associate and bachelor's levels.

Academic Information The faculty has 59 members (20% full-time). The student-faculty ratio is 27:1. The library holds 3,200 titles and 124 serial subscriptions. Special programs include academic remediation, cooperative (work-study) education, study abroad, advanced placement credit, distance learning, part-time degree programs (daytime, evenings, weekends, summer), and adult/continuing education programs.

Student Body Statistics The student body is made up of 635 undergraduates (190 freshmen). 82 percent are women and 18 percent are men. Students come from 39 states and territories and 6 other countries. 67 percent are from California. 1 percent of the 2006 graduating class went on to graduate and professional schools.

Expenses for 2007–08 *Application fee:* $50. *Comprehensive fee:* $30,462 includes full-time tuition ($21,024), mandatory fees ($150), and college room and board ($9288). *Part-time tuition:* $438 per credit.

Financial Aid Forms of aid include need-based scholarships and part-time jobs. The application deadline for financial aid is continuous.

Freshman Admission California Design College requires an essay, a high school transcript, and an interview. Recommendations and a portfolio are required for some. The application deadline for regular admission is rolling.

Transfer Admission The application deadline for admission is rolling.

For Further Information Contact Ms. Melissa Romero, Director of Admissions, California Design College, 3440 Wilshire Boulevard, Tenth Floor, Los Angeles, CA 90010. *Telephone:* 213-251-3636 Ext. 153, 213-251-3636 (toll-free in-state), or 877-468-6232 (toll-free out-of-state). *Fax:* 213-385-3545. *E-mail:* aicdcinfo@aii.edu. *Web site:* http://www.cdc.edu/.

CALIFORNIA INSTITUTE OF INTEGRAL STUDIES

San Francisco, California

California Institute of Integral Studies is a coed, private, upper-level institution, founded in 1968, offering degrees at the bachelor's, master's, and doctoral levels.

Expenses for 2006–07 *Application fee:* $65. *Tuition:* $16,130 full-time, $610 per unit part-time. *Mandatory fees:* $480 full-time. The full-time tuition and fees reflects the cost for three semesters per year for the Bachelor's program.

For Further Information Contact Admissions Department./Student Worker, California Institute of Integral Studies, 1453 Mission Street, San Francisco, CA 94103. *Telephone:* 415-575-6156. *Fax:* 415-575-1268. *E-mail:* info@ciis.edu. *Web site:* http://www.ciis.edu/.

CALIFORNIA INSTITUTE OF TECHNOLOGY

Pasadena, California

California Institute of Technology is a coed, private university, founded in 1891, offering degrees at the bachelor's, master's, and doctoral levels. It has a 124-acre campus in Pasadena near Los Angeles.

Academic Information The faculty has 311 members (94% full-time), 95% with terminal degrees. The undergraduate student-faculty ratio is 3:1. The library holds 3 million titles and 3,500 serial subscriptions. Special programs include services for learning-disabled students, cooperative (work-study) education, study abroad, ESL programs, double majors, independent study, self-designed majors, and arrangement for off-campus study with Occidental College, Scripps College, Art Center College of Design.

Student Body Statistics The student body totals 2,086, of whom 864 are undergraduates (214 freshmen). 29 percent are women and 71 percent are men. Students come from 46 states and territories and 28 other countries. 31 percent are from California. 8 percent are international students.

Expenses for 2007–08 *Application fee:* $60. *Comprehensive fee:* $42,375 includes full-time tuition ($29,940), mandatory fees ($2895), and college room and board ($9540). *College room only:* $5370.

Financial Aid Forms of aid include need-based and non-need-based scholarships and part-time jobs. The average aided 2006–07 undergraduate received an aid package worth an estimated $25,923. The priority application deadline for financial aid is January 15.

Freshman Admission California Institute of Technology requires an essay, a high school transcript, 2 recommendations, SAT or ACT scores, and SAT Subject Test in Math Level II C and either physics, chemistry, or biology. TOEFL scores for international students are recommended. The application deadline for regular admission is January 1 and for early action it is November 1.

Transfer Admission The application deadline for admission is February 15.

Entrance Difficulty California Institute of Technology assesses its entrance difficulty level as most difficult. For the fall 2006 freshman class, 17 percent of the applicants were accepted.

For Further Information Contact Mr. Rick T. Bischoff, Director of Admissions, California Institute of Technology, 1200 East California Boulevard, Pasadena, CA 91125-0001. *Telephone:* 626-395-6341. *Fax:* 626-683-3026. *E-mail:* ugadmissions@caltech.edu. *Web site:* http://www.caltech.edu/.

CALIFORNIA INSTITUTE OF THE ARTS

Valencia, California

California Institute of the Arts is a coed, private, comprehensive institution, founded in 1961, offering degrees at the bachelor's and master's levels and postbachelor's certificates. It has a 60-acre campus in Valencia near Los Angeles.

Academic Information The faculty has 287 members (51% full-time), 10% with terminal degrees. The undergraduate student-faculty ratio is 7:1. The library holds 98,415 titles and 324 serial subscriptions. Special programs include services for learning-disabled students, cooperative (work-study) education, study abroad, advanced placement credit, independent study, self-designed majors, and internships. The most frequently chosen baccalaureate field is visual and performing arts.
Student Body Statistics The student body totals 1,349, of whom 839 are undergraduates (156 freshmen). 43 percent are women and 57 percent are men. Students come from 50 states and territories and 33 other countries. 33 percent are from California.
Expenses for 2007–08 *Application fee:* $70. *Comprehensive fee:* $39,855 includes full-time tuition ($31,290), mandatory fees ($565), and college room and board ($8000). *College room only:* $4530.
Financial Aid Forms of aid include need-based and non-need-based scholarships and part-time jobs. The average aided 2006–07 undergraduate received an aid package worth an estimated $27,631. The priority application deadline for financial aid is March 2.
Freshman Admission California Institute of the Arts requires an essay, a high school transcript, 2 recommendations, portfolio or audition, and TOEFL scores for international students. An interview is required for some. The application deadline for regular admission is January 5.
Transfer Admission The application deadline for admission is January 5.
Entrance Difficulty California Institute of the Arts assesses its entrance difficulty level as very difficult. For the fall 2006 freshman class, 31 percent of the applicants were accepted.
For Further Information Contact Director of Admissions, California Institute of the Arts, 24700 McBean Parkway, Valencia, CA 91355. *Telephone:* 661-255-1050 or 800-545-2787 (toll-free). *Fax:* 661-253-7710. *E-mail:* admiss@calarts.edu. *Web site:* http://www.calarts.edu/.

CALIFORNIA LUTHERAN UNIVERSITY
Thousand Oaks, California

California Lutheran University is a coed, private, Lutheran, comprehensive institution, founded in 1959, offering degrees at the bachelor's, master's, and doctoral levels and post-master's and postbachelor's certificates. It has a 290-acre campus in Thousand Oaks near Los Angeles.

Academic Information The faculty has 283 members (47% full-time), 60% with terminal degrees. The undergraduate student-faculty ratio is 15:1. The library holds 132,744 titles and 1,497 serial subscriptions. Special programs include an honors program, cooperative (work-study) education, study abroad, advanced placement credit, accelerated degree programs, double majors, independent study, self-designed majors, summer session for credit, part-time degree programs (daytime, evenings, weekends, summer), adult/continuing education programs, internships, and arrangement for off-campus study with Wagner College, American University (Washington Semester). The most frequently chosen baccalaureate fields are business/marketing, communications/journalism, social sciences.
Student Body Statistics The student body totals 3,298, of whom 2,128 are undergraduates (403 freshmen). 53 percent are women and 47 percent are men. Students come from 40 states and territories and 21 other countries. 78 percent are from California. 2.6 percent are international students. 45 percent of the 2006 graduating class went on to graduate and professional schools.
Expenses for 2007–08 *Application fee:* $45. *Comprehensive fee:* $35,220 includes full-time tuition ($25,790), mandatory fees ($200), and college room and board ($9230). *Part-time tuition:* $830 per unit.
Financial Aid Forms of aid include need-based and non-need-based scholarships and part-time jobs.
Freshman Admission California Lutheran University requires an essay, a high school transcript, a minimum 2.8 high school GPA, 1 recommendation, SAT or ACT scores, and TOEFL scores for international students. A minimum 3.0 high school GPA and an interview are recommended.

Entrance Difficulty California Lutheran University assesses its entrance difficulty level as moderately difficult. For the fall 2006 freshman class, 66 percent of the applicants were accepted.
For Further Information Contact Mr. Matthew Ward, Dean of Undergraduate Enrollment, California Lutheran University, Office of Admission, #1350, Thousand Oaks, CA 91360. *Telephone:* 805-493-3135 or 877-258-3678 (toll-free). *Fax:* 805-493-3114. *E-mail:* cluadm@clunet.edu. *Web site:* http://www.callutheran.edu/.

CALIFORNIA MARITIME ACADEMY
Vallejo, California

California Maritime Academy is a coed, public, four-year college of California State University System, founded in 1929, offering degrees at the bachelor's level. It has a 64-acre campus in Vallejo near San Francisco.

Academic Information The student-faculty ratio is 22:1. The library holds 28,377 titles and 273 serial subscriptions. Special programs include academic remediation, advanced placement credit, distance learning, summer session for credit, and internships.
Student Body Statistics The student body is made up of 792 undergraduates. 22 percent are women and 78 percent are men. Students come from 18 states and territories and 16 other countries. 87 percent are from California. 1 percent of the 2006 graduating class went on to graduate and professional schools.
Expenses for 2006–07 *Application fee:* $55. *State resident tuition:* $0 full-time. *Nonresident tuition:* $10,170 full-time. *Mandatory fees:* $3476 full-time. Full-time tuition and fees vary according to program and student level. *College room and board:* $7460. *College room only:* $3480. Room and board charges vary according to board plan and housing facility.
Financial Aid Forms of aid include need-based and non-need-based scholarships and part-time jobs. The priority application deadline for financial aid is March 3.
Freshman Admission California Maritime Academy requires a high school transcript, a minimum 2.0 high school GPA, a health form, SAT or ACT scores, and TOEFL scores for international students.
Entrance Difficulty California Maritime Academy assesses its entrance difficulty level as moderately difficult. For the fall 2006 freshman class, 62 percent of the applicants were accepted.
For Further Information Contact Tim Harrison, Assistant Director of Admission, California Maritime Academy, 200 Maritime Academy Drive, Vallejo, CA 94590-0644. *Telephone:* 707-654-1330 or 800-561-1945 (toll-free). *Fax:* 707-654-1336. *E-mail:* admission@csum.edu. *Web site:* http://www.csum.edu/.

CALIFORNIA NATIONAL UNIVERSITY FOR ADVANCED STUDIES
Northridge, California

California National University for Advanced Studies is a coed, proprietary, comprehensive institution, founded in 1993, offering degrees at the bachelor's and master's levels and postbachelor's certificates.

Expenses for 2006–07 *Application fee:* $75. *Tuition:* $4860 full-time, $270 per unit part-time. *Mandatory fees:* $175 full-time. Part-time tuition varies according to course level and course load.
For Further Information Contact Ms. Stephanie Smith, Registrar, California National University for Advanced Studies, California National University Admissions, 8550 Balboa Boulevard, Suite 210, Northridge, CA 91325. *Telephone:* 818-830-2411, 800-744-2822 (toll-free in-state), or 800-782-2422 (toll-free out-of-state). *Fax:* 818-830-2418. *E-mail:* cnuadms@mail.cnuas.edu. *Web site:* http://www.cnuas.edu/.

CALIFORNIA POLYTECHNIC STATE UNIVERSITY, SAN LUIS OBISPO

San Luis Obispo, California

California Polytechnic State University, San Luis Obispo is a coed, public, comprehensive unit of California State University System, founded in 1901, offering degrees at the bachelor's and master's levels. It has a 6,000-acre campus in San Luis Obispo.

Academic Information The faculty has 1,170 members (60% full-time), 53% with terminal degrees. The undergraduate student-faculty ratio is 20:1. The library holds 763,651 titles and 5,529 serial subscriptions. Special programs include academic remediation, services for learning-disabled students, an honors program, cooperative (work-study) education, study abroad, advanced placement credit, ESL programs, double majors, independent study, distance learning, summer session for credit, part-time degree programs, external degree programs, internships, and arrangement for off-campus study with other units of the California State University System. The most frequently chosen baccalaureate fields are business/marketing, agriculture, engineering.

Student Body Statistics The student body totals 18,722, of whom 17,777 are undergraduates (3,668 freshmen). 43 percent are women and 57 percent are men. Students come from 46 states and territories and 39 other countries. 93 percent are from California. 1.1 percent are international students. 15 percent of the 2006 graduating class went on to graduate and professional schools.

Expenses for 2006–07 *Application fee:* $55. *State resident tuition:* $0 full-time. *Nonresident tuition:* $14,520 full-time, $226 per unit part-time. *Mandatory fees:* $4350 full-time, $982 per term part-time. Both full-time and part-time tuition and fees vary according to course load and program. *College room and board:* $8453. *College room only:* $4766. Room and board charges vary according to board plan and housing facility.

Financial Aid Forms of aid include need-based and non-need-based scholarships and part-time jobs. The average aided 2005–06 undergraduate received an aid package worth $7456. The application deadline for financial aid is June 30 with a priority deadline of March 1.

Freshman Admission California Polytechnic State University, San Luis Obispo requires a high school transcript, SAT or ACT scores, and TOEFL scores for international students. The application deadline for regular admission is November 30 and for early decision it is October 31.

Transfer Admission The application deadline for admission is November 30.

Entrance Difficulty California Polytechnic State University, San Luis Obispo assesses its entrance difficulty level as moderately difficult; most difficult for business, electronic engineering, electrical engineering, aeronautical engineering, architecture, architectural engineering programs. For the fall 2006 freshman class, 47 percent of the applicants were accepted.

For Further Information Contact Mr. James Maraviglia, Director of Admissions and Evaluations, California Polytechnic State University, San Luis Obispo, 1 Grand Avenue, San Luis Obispo, CA 93407. *Telephone:* 805-756-2311. *Fax:* 805-756-5400. *E-mail:* admissions@calpoly.edu. *Web site:* http://www.calpoly.edu/.

CALIFORNIA SCHOOL OF PROFESSIONAL PSYCHOLOGY

See Alliant International University.

CALIFORNIA STATE POLYTECHNIC UNIVERSITY, POMONA

Pomona, California

California State Polytechnic University, Pomona is a coed, public, comprehensive unit of California State University System, founded in 1938, offering degrees at the bachelor's and master's levels. It has a 1,400-acre campus in Pomona near Los Angeles.

Academic Information The faculty has 1,289 members (53% full-time), 54% with terminal degrees. The undergraduate student-faculty ratio is 23:1. The library holds 748,154 titles, 4,603 serial subscriptions, and 6,062 audiovisual materials. Special programs include academic remediation, services for learning-disabled students, an honors program, cooperative (work-study) education, study abroad, advanced placement credit, ESL programs, double majors, summer session for credit, part-time degree programs, adult/continuing education programs, internships, and arrangement for off-campus study with other units of the California State University System, Desert Studies Consortium, Southern California Ocean Studies Consortium. The most frequently chosen baccalaureate fields are business/marketing, engineering, liberal arts/general studies.

Student Body Statistics The student body totals 20,510, of whom 18,650 are undergraduates (2,879 freshmen). 43 percent are women and 57 percent are men. Students come from 45 states and territories and 46 other countries. 98 percent are from California. 5.3 percent are international students.

Expenses for 2006–07 *Application fee:* $55. *State resident tuition:* $0 full-time. *Nonresident tuition:* $10,170 full-time, $226 per unit part-time. *Mandatory fees:* $3015 full-time, $657 per term part-time. *College room and board:* $7908. Room and board charges vary according to board plan and housing facility.

Financial Aid Forms of aid include need-based and non-need-based scholarships, athletic grants, and part-time jobs. The application deadline for financial aid is continuous.

Freshman Admission California State Polytechnic University, Pomona requires a high school transcript, a minimum 2.0 high school GPA, SAT or ACT scores, and TOEFL scores for international students. The application deadline for regular admission is November 30.

Transfer Admission The application deadline for admission is November 30.

Entrance Difficulty California State Polytechnic University, Pomona assesses its entrance difficulty level as moderately difficult; minimally difficult for exceptional admit, Educational Opportunity Program applicants. For the fall 2006 freshman class, 72 percent of the applicants were accepted.

For Further Information Contact Dr. George R. Bradshaw, Director, Admissions and Outreach, California State Polytechnic University, Pomona, 3801 West Temple Avenue, Pomona, CA 91768-2557. *Telephone:* 909-869-3427. *Fax:* 909-869-4529. *E-mail:* admissions@csupomona.edu. *Web site:* http://www.csupomona.edu/.

CALIFORNIA STATE UNIVERSITY, BAKERSFIELD

Bakersfield, California

California State University, Bakersfield is a coed, public, comprehensive unit of California State University System, founded in 1970, offering degrees at the bachelor's and master's levels. It has a 575-acre campus in Bakersfield.

For Further Information Contact Dr. Kendyl Magnuson, Associate Dean of Admissions and Records, California State University, Bakersfield, 9001 Stockdale Highway, Balersfield, CA 93311-1099. *Telephone:* 661-664-3036 or 800-788-2782 (toll-free in-state). *E-mail:* admissions@csub.edu. *Web site:* http://www.csubak.edu/.

CALIFORNIA STATE UNIVERSITY CHANNEL ISLANDS

Camarillo, California

California State University Channel Islands is a coed, public, comprehensive unit of California State University System, founded in 2002, offering degrees at the bachelor's and master's levels and postbachelor's certificates.

Academic Information The faculty has 227 members (37% full-time). The undergraduate student-faculty ratio is 19:1. Special programs include

academic remediation, services for learning-disabled students, study abroad, advanced placement credit, and double majors. The most frequently chosen baccalaureate fields are business/marketing, liberal arts/general studies, psychology.

Student Body Statistics The student body totals 3,123, of whom 2,868 are undergraduates (464 freshmen). 61 percent are women and 39 percent are men. Students come from 4 states and territories and 3 other countries. 100 percent are from California.

Expenses for 2006–07 *Application fee:* $50. *Nonresident tuition:* $10,170 full-time, $339 per unit part-time. *Mandatory fees:* $2980 full-time. *College room and board:* $9800. *College room only:* $7000.

Freshman Admission California State University Channel Islands requires a high school transcript, a minimum 2.0 high school GPA, and SAT or ACT scores. A minimum 3.0 high school GPA is recommended.

Entrance Difficulty California State University Channel Islands assesses its entrance difficulty level as noncompetitive. For the fall 2006 freshman class, 45 percent of the applicants were accepted.

For Further Information Contact Ms. Ginger Reyes, California State University Channel Islands, One University Drive, Camarillo, CA 93012. *Telephone:* 805-437-8520. *Fax:* 805-437-8519. *E-mail:* prospective.student@csuci.edu. *Web site:* http://www.csuci.edu/.

CALIFORNIA STATE UNIVERSITY, CHICO
Chico, California

California State University, Chico is a coed, public, comprehensive unit of California State University System, founded in 1887, offering degrees at the bachelor's and master's levels and post-master's and postbachelor's certificates. It has a 119-acre campus in Chico.

Academic Information The faculty has 965 members (55% full-time), 59% with terminal degrees. The undergraduate student-faculty ratio is 21:1. The library holds 957,181 titles, 24,244 serial subscriptions, and 28,500 audiovisual materials. Special programs include academic remediation, services for learning-disabled students, an honors program, cooperative (work-study) education, study abroad, advanced placement credit, ESL programs, double majors, independent study, distance learning, self-designed majors, summer session for credit, part-time degree programs (daytime, evenings), external degree programs, adult/continuing education programs, and internships. The most frequently chosen baccalaureate fields are business/marketing, liberal arts/general studies, social sciences.

Student Body Statistics The student body totals 16,250, of whom 14,927 are undergraduates (2,477 freshmen). 53 percent are women and 47 percent are men. Students come from 42 states and territories and 36 other countries. 97 percent are from California. 1.8 percent are international students. 27 percent of the 2006 graduating class went on to graduate and professional schools.

Expenses for 2006–07 *Application fee:* $55. *State resident tuition:* $0 full-time. *Nonresident tuition:* $12,690 full-time, $339 per unit part-time. *Mandatory fees:* $3412 full-time, $446 per term part-time. Part-time tuition and fees vary according to course load. *College room and board:* $8314. *College room only:* $5772. Room and board charges vary according to board plan and housing facility.

Financial Aid Forms of aid include need-based and non-need-based scholarships, athletic grants, and part-time jobs. The average aided 2005–06 undergraduate received an aid package worth $8508. The application deadline for financial aid is continuous.

Freshman Admission California State University, Chico requires a high school transcript, GPA of 10th and 11th grade college prep courses only, SAT or ACT scores, and TOEFL scores for international students. A minimum 2.0 high school GPA is required for some. The application deadline for regular admission is November 30.

Transfer Admission The application deadline for admission is November 30.

Entrance Difficulty California State University, Chico assesses its entrance difficulty level as moderately difficult; minimally difficult for

transfers; very difficult for nursing, recording arts. For the fall 2006 freshman class, 90 percent of the applicants were accepted.

For Further Information Contact Dr. John F. Swiney, Director of Admissions, California State University, Chico, 400 West First Street, Chico, CA 95929-0722. *Telephone:* 800-542-4426 or 800-542-4426 (toll-free). *Fax:* 530-898-6456. *E-mail:* info@csuchico.edu. *Web site:* http://www.csuchico.edu/.

CALIFORNIA STATE UNIVERSITY, DOMINGUEZ HILLS
Carson, California

California State University, Dominguez Hills is a coed, public, comprehensive unit of California State University System, founded in 1960, offering degrees at the bachelor's and master's levels. It has a 350-acre campus in Carson near Los Angeles.

Academic Information The faculty has 687 members (39% full-time), 47% with terminal degrees. The undergraduate student-faculty ratio is 21:1. The library holds 428,840 titles, 49,130 serial subscriptions, and 4,999 audiovisual materials. Special programs include academic remediation, an honors program, cooperative (work-study) education, study abroad, advanced placement credit, ESL programs, self-designed majors, summer session for credit, part-time degree programs, external degree programs, adult/continuing education programs, internships, and arrangement for off-campus study with other institutions of the California State University System, National Student Exchange. The most frequently chosen baccalaureate fields are business/marketing, health professions and related sciences, liberal arts/general studies.

Student Body Statistics The student body totals 12,068, of whom 8,925 are undergraduates (1,058 freshmen). 69 percent are women and 31 percent are men. Students come from 20 states and territories and 46 other countries. 99 percent are from California. 0.9 percent are international students.

Expenses for 2007–08 *Application fee:* $55. *State resident tuition:* $0 full-time. *Nonresident tuition:* $13,221 full-time, $339 per unit part-time. *Mandatory fees:* $3051 full-time. *College room and board:* $8690. *College room only:* $5990.

Financial Aid Forms of aid include need-based and non-need-based scholarships, athletic grants, and part-time jobs. The average aided 2005–06 undergraduate received an aid package worth $8239. The application deadline for financial aid is April 15 with a priority deadline of March 2.

Freshman Admission California State University, Dominguez Hills requires a high school transcript, SAT or ACT scores, and TOEFL scores for international students. The application deadline for regular admission is rolling.

Transfer Admission The application deadline for admission is rolling.

Entrance Difficulty California State University, Dominguez Hills assesses its entrance difficulty level as moderately difficult. For the fall 2006 freshman class, 65 percent of the applicants were accepted.

For Further Information Contact Information Center, California State University, Dominguez Hills, 1000 East Victoria Street, Carson, CA 90747-0001. *Telephone:* 310-243-3696. *Web site:* http://www.csudh.edu/.

CALIFORNIA STATE UNIVERSITY, EAST BAY
Hayward, California

California State University, East Bay is a coed, public, comprehensive unit of California State University System, founded in 1957, offering degrees at the bachelor's and master's levels and postbachelor's certificates. It has a 343-acre campus in Hayward near San Francisco.

Expenses for 2007–08 *Application fee:* $55. *State resident tuition:* $0 full-time. *Nonresident tuition:* $8136 full-time. *Mandatory fees:* $2916 full-time. *College room and board:* $8939.

For Further Information Contact Mr. Dave Vasquez, Director of Admissions, California State University, East Bay, 25800 Carlos Bee Boulevard, Hayward, CA 94542-3035. *Telephone:* 510-885-3248. *Fax:* 510-885-3816. *E-mail:* adminfo@csuhayward.edu. *Web site:* http://www.csueastbay.edu/.

CALIFORNIA STATE UNIVERSITY, FRESNO
Fresno, California

California State University, Fresno is a coed, public, comprehensive unit of California State University System, founded in 1911, offering degrees at the bachelor's, master's, and doctoral levels. It has a 1,410-acre campus in Fresno.

Academic Information The faculty has 1,251 members (52% full-time), 56% with terminal degrees. The library holds 2,617 serial subscriptions. Special programs include academic remediation, services for learning-disabled students, an honors program, cooperative (work-study) education, study abroad, advanced placement credit, accelerated degree programs, Freshman Honors College, ESL programs, double majors, independent study, distance learning, self-designed majors, summer session for credit, part-time degree programs (daytime, evenings, summer), adult/continuing education programs, internships, and arrangement for off-campus study with other units of the California State University System.

Student Body Statistics The student body totals 22,098, of whom 18,951 are undergraduates (2,602 freshmen). 58 percent are women and 42 percent are men. Students come from 50 states and territories and 69 other countries. 98 percent are from California. 1.8 percent are international students.

Expenses for 2006–07 *Application fee:* $55. *State resident tuition:* $0 full-time. *Nonresident tuition:* $13,209 full-time, $339 per unit part-time. *Mandatory fees:* $3039 full-time, $990 per term part-time. *College room and board:* $6880. *College room only:* $3700.

Financial Aid Forms of aid include need-based and non-need-based scholarships, athletic grants, and part-time jobs. The average aided 2006–07 undergraduate received an aid package worth an estimated $6762. The priority application deadline for financial aid is March 2.

Freshman Admission California State University, Fresno requires a high school transcript, a minimum 2.00 high school GPA, SAT or ACT scores, and TOEFL scores for international students. The application deadline for regular admission is April 1.

Entrance Difficulty California State University, Fresno assesses its entrance difficulty level as minimally difficult; very difficult for physical therapy, athletic training programs. For the fall 2006 freshman class, 69 percent of the applicants were accepted.

For Further Information Contact Ms. Yolanda Deleon, Admissions Officer, California State University, Fresno, 5150 North Maple Avenue, M/S JA 57, Fresno, CA 93740-8026. *Telephone:* 559-278-6115. *Fax:* 559-278-4812. *E-mail:* donna_mills@csufresno.edu. *Web site:* http://www.csufresno.edu/.

CALIFORNIA STATE UNIVERSITY, FULLERTON
Fullerton, California

California State University, Fullerton is a coed, public, comprehensive unit of California State University System, founded in 1957, offering degrees at the bachelor's and master's levels. It has a 225-acre campus in Fullerton near Los Angeles.

Academic Information The faculty has 2,031 members (37% full-time). The undergraduate student-faculty ratio is 24:1. The library holds 1 million titles and 29,888 serial subscriptions. Special programs include academic remediation, services for learning-disabled students, an honors program, cooperative (work-study) education, study abroad, advanced placement credit, Freshman Honors College, ESL programs, double

majors, independent study, distance learning, self-designed majors, summer session for credit, part-time degree programs (daytime, evenings, summer), adult/continuing education programs, internships, and arrangement for off-campus study with other institutions of the California State University System. The most frequently chosen baccalaureate fields are business/marketing, communications/journalism, education.

Student Body Statistics The student body totals 35,921, of whom 30,606 are undergraduates (3,851 freshmen). 58 percent are women and 42 percent are men. Students come from 42 states and territories and 58 other countries. 98 percent are from California. 3.7 percent are international students.

Expenses for 2006–07 *Application fee:* $55. *State resident tuition:* $0 full-time. *Nonresident tuition:* $10,170 full-time, $339 per unit part-time. *Mandatory fees:* $3030 full-time, $987 per term part-time. Both full-time and part-time tuition and fees vary according to course load. *College room only:* $4408.

Financial Aid Forms of aid include need-based and non-need-based scholarships, athletic grants, and part-time jobs. The average aided 2006–07 undergraduate received an aid package worth an estimated $6675. The priority application deadline for financial aid is March 2.

Freshman Admission California State University, Fullerton requires a high school transcript, a minimum 2.0 high school GPA, SAT or ACT scores, and TOEFL scores for international students. The application deadline for regular admission is November 30.

Transfer Admission The application deadline for admission is rolling.

Entrance Difficulty California State University, Fullerton assesses its entrance difficulty level as moderately difficult; very difficult for out-of-state applicants; minimally difficult for transfers. For the fall 2006 freshman class, 61 percent of the applicants were accepted.

For Further Information Contact Ms. Nancy J. Dority, Assistant Vice President of Enrollment Services, California State University, Fullerton, Office of Admissions and Records, PO Box 6900, 800 North State College Boulevard, Fullerton, CA 92834-6900. *Telephone:* 714-278-2350. *Web site:* http://www.fullerton.edu/.

CALIFORNIA STATE UNIVERSITY, HAYWARD

See California State University, East Bay.

CALIFORNIA STATE UNIVERSITY, LONG BEACH
Long Beach, California

California State University, Long Beach is a coed, public, comprehensive unit of California State University System, founded in 1949, offering degrees at the bachelor's and master's levels and postbachelor's certificates. It has a 320-acre campus in Long Beach near Los Angeles.

Academic Information The faculty has 2,227 members (46% full-time), 52% with terminal degrees. The undergraduate student-faculty ratio is 20:1. The library holds 1 million titles and 18,749 serial subscriptions. Special programs include academic remediation, services for learning-disabled students, an honors program, study abroad, advanced placement credit, accelerated degree programs, ESL programs, double majors, independent study, distance learning, self-designed majors, summer session for credit, part-time degree programs (daytime, evenings, summer), adult/continuing education programs, internships, and arrangement for off-campus study with other institutions of the California State University System. The most frequently chosen baccalaureate fields are business/marketing, liberal arts/general studies, visual and performing arts.

Student Body Statistics The student body totals 35,574, of whom 29,576 are undergraduates (4,464 freshmen). 60 percent are women and 40 percent are men. Students come from 46 states and territories and 85 other countries. 99 percent are from California. 4.7 percent are international students.

Expenses for 2007–08 *Application fee:* $55. *State resident tuition:* $0 full-time. *Nonresident tuition:* $10,170 full-time, $339 per unit part-time. *Mandatory fees:* $3116 full-time, $904 per term part-time. *College room and board:* $7536.

Financial Aid Forms of aid include need-based and non-need-based scholarships, athletic grants, and part-time jobs. The priority application deadline for financial aid is March 2.

Freshman Admission California State University, Long Beach requires a high school transcript, SAT or ACT scores, and TOEFL scores for international students. A minimum 2.0 high school GPA and minimum GPA of 2.4 for nonresidents are required for some. The application deadline for regular admission is November 30.

Transfer Admission The application deadline for admission is November 30.

Entrance Difficulty California State University, Long Beach assesses its entrance difficulty level as moderately difficult. For the fall 2006 freshman class, 52 percent of the applicants were accepted.

For Further Information Contact Mr. Thomas Enders, Director of Enrollment Services, California State University, Long Beach, Brotman Hall, 1250 Bellflower Boulevard, Long Beach, CA 90840. *Telephone:* 562-985-4641. *Web site:* http://www.csulb.edu/.

CALIFORNIA STATE UNIVERSITY, LOS ANGELES

Los Angeles, California

California State University, Los Angeles is a coed, public, comprehensive unit of California State University System, founded in 1947, offering degrees at the bachelor's, master's, and doctoral levels. It has a 173-acre campus in Los Angeles.

Academic Information The faculty has 1,184 members (48% full-time). The undergraduate student-faculty ratio is 20:1. The library holds 1 million titles, 31,366 serial subscriptions, and 2,545 audiovisual materials. Special programs include academic remediation, services for learning-disabled students, an honors program, cooperative (work-study) education, study abroad, advanced placement credit, accelerated degree programs, ESL programs, double majors, independent study, distance learning, self-designed majors, summer session for credit, part-time degree programs, adult/continuing education programs, internships, and arrangement for off-campus study with other units of the California State University System. The most frequently chosen baccalaureate fields are business/marketing, education, security and protective services.

Student Body Statistics The student body totals 20,565, of whom 15,352 are undergraduates (1,689 freshmen). 62 percent are women and 38 percent are men. Students come from 35 states and territories and 64 other countries. 94 percent are from California. 6.1 percent are international students.

Expenses for 2006–07 *Application fee:* $55. *State resident tuition:* $0 full-time. *Nonresident tuition:* $11,216 full-time, $226 per unit part-time. *Mandatory fees:* $3080 full-time, $673.75 per unit part-time. Both full-time and part-time tuition and fees vary according to course level. *College room and board:* $7866.

Financial Aid Forms of aid include need-based and non-need-based scholarships and part-time jobs. The average aided 2006–07 undergraduate received an aid package worth an estimated $7672. The priority application deadline for financial aid is March 2.

Freshman Admission California State University, Los Angeles requires a high school transcript and TOEFL scores for international students. SAT or ACT scores are required for some. The application deadline for regular admission is June 15.

Transfer Admission The application deadline for admission is June 15.

Entrance Difficulty California State University, Los Angeles assesses its entrance difficulty level as moderately difficult; minimally difficult for transfers. For the fall 2006 freshman class, 61 percent of the applicants were accepted.

For Further Information Contact Mr. Vince Lopez, Director of Outreach and Recruitment, California State University, Los Angeles, 5151 State University Drive, Los Angeles, CA 90032-8530. *Telephone:* 323-343-3839. *E-mail:* admission@calstatela.edu. *Web site:* http://www.calstatela.edu/.

CALIFORNIA STATE UNIVERSITY, MONTEREY BAY

Seaside, California

California State University, Monterey Bay is a coed, public, comprehensive unit of California State University System, founded in 1994, offering degrees at the bachelor's and master's levels and postbachelor's certificates. It has a 1,500-acre campus in Seaside near San Jose.

Academic Information The faculty has 291 members (46% full-time). The undergraduate student-faculty ratio is 20:1. The library holds 65,000 titles, 3,800 serial subscriptions, and 1,250 audiovisual materials. Special programs include academic remediation, services for learning-disabled students, cooperative (work-study) education, study abroad, double majors, independent study, distance learning, self-designed majors, summer session for credit, part-time degree programs (daytime, evenings, summer), external degree programs, adult/continuing education programs, and internships.

Student Body Statistics The student body totals 3,577, of whom 3,376 are undergraduates (534 freshmen). 56 percent are women and 44 percent are men. Students come from 39 states and territories and 19 other countries. 97 percent are from California. 0.8 percent are international students.

Expenses for 2007–08 *Application fee:* $55. *State resident tuition:* $0 full-time. *Nonresident tuition:* $10,170 full-time, $339 per credit part-time. *Mandatory fees:* $3035 full-time, $973 per term part-time. *College room and board:* $7696. *College room only:* $5196.

Financial Aid Forms of aid include need-based and non-need-based scholarships and part-time jobs. The priority application deadline for financial aid is March 2.

Freshman Admission California State University, Monterey Bay requires a high school transcript, a minimum 2.0 high school GPA, and SAT or ACT scores. The application deadline for regular admission is rolling.

Transfer Admission The application deadline for admission is rolling.

Entrance Difficulty California State University, Monterey Bay assesses its entrance difficulty level as minimally difficult. For the fall 2006 freshman class, 75 percent of the applicants were accepted.

For Further Information Contact Admissions and Recruitment, California State University, Monterey Bay, 100 Campus Center, Seaside, CA 93955-8001. *Telephone:* 831-582-3738. *Fax:* 831-582-3738. *E-mail:* admissions@csumb.edu. *Web site:* http://csumb.edu/.

CALIFORNIA STATE UNIVERSITY, NORTHRIDGE

Northridge, California

California State University, Northridge is a coed, public, comprehensive unit of California State University System, founded in 1958, offering degrees at the bachelor's and master's levels. It has a 356-acre campus in Northridge near Los Angeles.

Academic Information The faculty has 1,941 members (41% full-time). The undergraduate student-faculty ratio is 23:1. The library holds 1 million titles, 1,779 serial subscriptions, and 10,046 audiovisual materials. Special programs include academic remediation, services for learning-disabled students, study abroad, advanced placement credit, accelerated degree programs, ESL programs, double majors, independent study, distance learning, self-designed majors, summer session for credit, part-time degree programs, adult/continuing education programs, internships, and arrangement for off-campus study with other units of the California State University System, National Student Exchange. The most frequently chosen baccalaureate fields are business/marketing, psychology, social sciences.

Student Body Statistics The student body totals 34,560, of whom 28,281 are undergraduates (3,695 freshmen). 59 percent are women and 41 percent are men. Students come from 40 states and territories and 7 other countries. 99 percent are from California. 5.1 percent are international students. 100 percent of the 2006 graduating class went on to graduate and professional schools.

California State University, Northridge (continued)

Expenses for 2006–07 *Application fee:* $55. *State resident tuition:* $0 full-time. *Nonresident tuition:* $11,178 full-time, $339 per unit part-time. *Mandatory fees:* $3042 full-time, $1521 per term part-time. *College room and board:* $9328. *College room only:* $5155. Room and board charges vary according to board plan and housing facility.

Financial Aid Forms of aid include need-based and non-need-based scholarships, athletic grants, and part-time jobs. The average aided 2005–06 undergraduate received an aid package worth $8382. The priority application deadline for financial aid is March 2.

Freshman Admission California State University, Northridge requires a high school transcript, SAT or ACT scores, and TOEFL scores for international students. The application deadline for regular admission is November 30.

Transfer Admission The application deadline for admission is November 30.

Entrance Difficulty California State University, Northridge assesses its entrance difficulty level as moderately difficult; very difficult for out-of-state applicants. For the fall 2006 freshman class, 70 percent of the applicants were accepted.

For Further Information Contact Ms. Mary Baxton, Associate Director of Admissions and Records, California State University, Northridge, 18111 Nordhoff Street, Northridge, CA 91330-8207. *Telephone:* 818-677-3777. *Fax:* 818-677-3766. *E-mail:* admissions.records@csun.edu. *Web site:* http://www.csun.edu/.

CALIFORNIA STATE UNIVERSITY, SACRAMENTO

Sacramento, California

California State University, Sacramento is a coed, public, comprehensive unit of California State University System, founded in 1947, offering degrees at the bachelor's, master's, and doctoral levels. It has a 300-acre campus in Sacramento.

Academic Information The faculty has 1,719 members (47% full-time), 52% with terminal degrees. The undergraduate student-faculty ratio is 20:1. The library holds 1 million titles, 2,918 serial subscriptions, and 23,880 audiovisual materials. Special programs include academic remediation, services for learning-disabled students, an honors program, cooperative (work-study) education, study abroad, advanced placement credit, accelerated degree programs, ESL programs, double majors, independent study, distance learning, self-designed majors, summer session for credit, part-time degree programs (daytime, evenings, weekends, summer), internships, and arrangement for off-campus study with other units of the California State University System. The most frequently chosen baccalaureate fields are business/marketing, public administration and social services, social sciences.

Student Body Statistics The student body totals 28,529, of whom 23,615 are undergraduates (2,655 freshmen). 57 percent are women and 43 percent are men. Students come from 35 states and territories and 142 other countries. 99 percent are from California. 1.3 percent are international students.

Expenses for 2006–07 *Application fee:* $55. *State resident tuition:* $0 full-time. *Nonresident tuition:* $12,690 full-time, $339 per unit part-time. *Mandatory fees:* $3284 full-time, $276 per term part-time. *College room and board:* $7966. *College room only:* $5250. Room and board charges vary according to board plan.

Financial Aid Forms of aid include need-based and non-need-based scholarships and part-time jobs. The average aided 2005–06 undergraduate received an aid package worth $8354. The priority application deadline for financial aid is March 2.

Freshman Admission California State University, Sacramento requires a minimum 2.0 high school GPA and TOEFL scores for international students. A high school transcript and SAT or ACT scores are required for some. The application deadline for regular admission is August 1 and for early action it is November 30.

Transfer Admission The application deadline for admission is July 1.

Entrance Difficulty California State University, Sacramento assesses its entrance difficulty level as moderately difficult; very difficult for out-of-state applicants. For the fall 2006 freshman class, 62 percent of the applicants were accepted.

For Further Information Contact Mr. Emiliano Diaz, Director of University Outreach Services, California State University, Sacramento, 6000 J Street, Lassen Hall, Sacramento, CA 95819-6048. *Telephone:* 916-278-3901. *Fax:* 916-278-5603. *E-mail:* admissions@csus.edu. *Web site:* http://www.csus.edu/.

CALIFORNIA STATE UNIVERSITY, SAN BERNARDINO

San Bernardino, California

California State University, San Bernardino is a coed, public, comprehensive unit of California State University System, founded in 1965, offering degrees at the bachelor's and master's levels. It has a 430-acre campus in San Bernardino near Los Angeles.

Academic Information The faculty has 633 members (71% full-time). The undergraduate student-faculty ratio is 21:1. The library holds 731,259 titles and 2,028 serial subscriptions. Special programs include services for learning-disabled students, an honors program, cooperative (work-study) education, study abroad, accelerated degree programs, double majors, independent study, distance learning, self-designed majors, summer session for credit, part-time degree programs (daytime, evenings, weekends, summer), adult/continuing education programs, internships, and arrangement for off-campus study with National Student Exchange. The most frequently chosen baccalaureate fields are business/marketing, liberal arts/general studies, social sciences.

Student Body Statistics The student body totals 16,479, of whom 12,926 are undergraduates (1,845 freshmen). 65 percent are women and 35 percent are men. Students come from 37 states and territories and 43 other countries. 99 percent are from California. 2.8 percent are international students.

Expenses for 2006–07 *Application fee:* $55. *State resident tuition:* $0 full-time. *Nonresident tuition:* $8136 full-time, $226 per unit part-time. *Mandatory fees:* $3398 full-time. Part-time tuition varies according to course load. *College room and board:* $5886. *College room only:* $4376. Room and board charges vary according to board plan and housing facility.

Financial Aid Forms of aid include need-based and non-need-based scholarships, athletic grants, and part-time jobs. The average aided 2006–07 undergraduate received an aid package worth an estimated $7648. The priority application deadline for financial aid is March 2.

Freshman Admission California State University, San Bernardino requires a high school transcript, a minimum 2.0 high school GPA, SAT or ACT scores, and TOEFL scores for international students. The application deadline for regular admission is rolling.

Transfer Admission The application deadline for admission is rolling.

Entrance Difficulty California State University, San Bernardino assesses its entrance difficulty level as moderately difficult. For the fall 2006 freshman class, 63 percent of the applicants were accepted.

For Further Information Contact Ms. Cynthia Olivo, Associate Director, California State University, San Bernardino, 5500 University Parkway, University Hall, Room 107, San Bernardino, CA 92407-2397. *Telephone:* 909-537-5188. *Fax:* 909-537-7034. *E-mail:* moreinfo@mail.csusb.edu. *Web site:* http://www.csusb.edu/.

CALIFORNIA STATE UNIVERSITY, SAN MARCOS

San Marcos, California

California State University, San Marcos is a coed, public, comprehensive unit of California State University System, founded in 1990, offering degrees at the bachelor's and master's levels. It has a 304-acre campus in San Marcos near San Diego.

Academic Information The faculty has 501 members (37% full-time). The undergraduate student-faculty ratio is 24:1. The library holds 233,445 titles and 2,043 serial subscriptions. Special programs include academic remediation, services for learning-disabled students, study abroad, advanced placement credit, ESL programs, double majors, independent study, distance learning, self-designed majors, summer session for credit, part-time degree programs, adult/continuing education programs, internships, and arrangement for off-campus study with San Diego State University, Palomar College, Mira Costa College.
Student Body Statistics The student body totals 6,956, of whom 6,327 are undergraduates (804 freshmen). 61 percent are women and 39 percent are men. 99 percent are from California. 3 percent are international students.
Expenses for 2006–07 *Application fee:* $55. *State resident tuition:* $0 full-time. *Nonresident tuition:* $8136 full-time, $339 per unit part-time. *Mandatory fees:* $3092 full-time. Part-time tuition varies according to course load. *College room only:* $5600. Room charges vary according to housing facility.
Financial Aid Forms of aid include need-based and non-need-based scholarships, athletic grants, and part-time jobs. The priority application deadline for financial aid is March 2.
Freshman Admission California State University, San Marcos requires a high school transcript, a minimum 3.12 high school GPA, and TOEFL scores for international students. SAT or ACT scores are required for some. The application deadline for regular admission is November 30.
Transfer Admission The application deadline for admission is November 30.
Entrance Difficulty California State University, San Marcos assesses its entrance difficulty level as moderately difficult. For the fall 2006 freshman class, 44 percent of the applicants were accepted.
For Further Information Contact Ms. Cherine Heckman, Director of Admissions, California State University, San Marcos, 333 South Twin Oaks Valley Road, San Marcos, CA 92096-0001. *Telephone:* 760-750-4848. *Fax:* 760-750-3248. *E-mail:* apply@csusm.edu. *Web site:* http://www.csusm.edu/.

CALIFORNIA STATE UNIVERSITY, STANISLAUS
Turlock, California

California State University, Stanislaus is a coed, public, comprehensive unit of California State University System, founded in 1957, offering degrees at the bachelor's and master's levels. It has a 228-acre campus in Turlock.

Academic Information The faculty has 511 members (57% full-time), 56% with terminal degrees. The undergraduate student-faculty ratio is 19:1. The library holds 369,047 titles, 17,612 serial subscriptions, and 4,593 audiovisual materials. Special programs include academic remediation, services for learning-disabled students, an honors program, cooperative (work-study) education, study abroad, advanced placement credit, ESL programs, double majors, independent study, distance learning, self-designed majors, summer session for credit, part-time degree programs (daytime, evenings, summer), adult/continuing education programs, internships, and arrangement for off-campus study with other units of the California State University System. The most frequently chosen baccalaureate fields are business/marketing, liberal arts/general studies, social sciences.
Student Body Statistics The student body totals 8,374, of whom 6,671 are undergraduates (946 freshmen). 66 percent are women and 34 percent are men. Students come from 20 states and territories and 46 other countries. 99 percent are from California. 1.4 percent are international students. 17.8 percent of the 2006 graduating class went on to graduate and professional schools.
Expenses for 2006–07 *Application fee:* $55. *State resident tuition:* $0 full-time. *Nonresident tuition:* $10,170 full-time, $339 per unit part-time. *Mandatory fees:* $3043 full-time, $862 per term part-time. *College room and board:* $7178. *College room only:* $4278. Room and board charges vary according to board plan and housing facility.
Financial Aid Forms of aid include need-based and non-need-based scholarships, athletic grants, and part-time jobs. The average aided

2006–07 undergraduate received an aid package worth an estimated $7923. The priority application deadline for financial aid is March 2.
Freshman Admission California State University, Stanislaus requires a high school transcript and TOEFL scores for international students. A minimum 3.0 high school GPA is recommended. An interview, SAT or ACT scores, and ELM/EPT, TOEFL are required for some. The application deadline for regular admission is July 1 and for early action it is October 1.
Transfer Admission The application deadline for admission is July 1.
Entrance Difficulty For the fall 2006 freshman class, 93 percent of the applicants were accepted.
For Further Information Contact Student Outreach, California State University, Stanislaus, 801 West Monte Vista Avenue, Turlock, CA 95382. *Telephone:* 209-667-3122 or 800-300-7420 (toll-free in-state). *Fax:* 209-667-3788. *E-mail:* outreach_help_desk@csustan.edu. *Web site:* http://www.csustan.edu/.

CHAPMAN UNIVERSITY
Orange, California

Chapman University is a coed, private, comprehensive institution, founded in 1861, affiliated with the Christian Church (Disciples of Christ), offering degrees at the bachelor's, master's, and first professional levels and postbachelor's certificates. It has a 76-acre campus in Orange near Los Angeles.

Academic Information The faculty has 538 members (52% full-time). The undergraduate student-faculty ratio is 16:1. The library holds 220,759 titles and 1,731 serial subscriptions. Special programs include academic remediation, services for learning-disabled students, an honors program, study abroad, advanced placement credit, ESL programs, double majors, independent study, distance learning, self-designed majors, summer session for credit, part-time degree programs (daytime, evenings, summer), adult/continuing education programs, and internships. The most frequently chosen baccalaureate fields are business/marketing, communications/journalism, visual and performing arts.
Student Body Statistics The student body totals 5,908, of whom 4,086 are undergraduates (957 freshmen). 59 percent are women and 41 percent are men. Students come from 50 states and territories and 32 other countries. 77 percent are from California. 1.8 percent are international students.
Expenses for 2006–07 *Application fee:* $55. *Comprehensive fee:* $41,248 includes full-time tuition ($29,900), mandatory fees ($848), and college room and board ($10,500). Room and board charges vary according to board plan and housing facility. *Part-time tuition:* $920 per credit. Part-time tuition varies according to course load.
Financial Aid Forms of aid include need-based and non-need-based scholarships and part-time jobs. The average aided 2005–06 undergraduate received an aid package worth $20,421. The priority application deadline for financial aid is March 2.
Freshman Admission Chapman University requires an essay, a high school transcript, 1 recommendation, SAT or ACT scores, and TOEFL scores for international students. An interview and SAT Subject Test scores are recommended. The application deadline for regular admission is January 31 and for early action it is November 30.
Transfer Admission The application deadline for admission is March 15.
Entrance Difficulty Chapman University assesses its entrance difficulty level as moderately difficult. For the fall 2006 freshman class, 53 percent of the applicants were accepted.
For Further Information Contact Mr. Michael Drummy, Assistant Vice President of Enrollment Services and Chief Admission Officer, Chapman University, One University Drive, Orange, CA 92866. *Telephone:* 714-997-6711 or 888-CUAPPLY (toll-free). *Fax:* 714-997-6713. *E-mail:* admit@chapman.edu. *Web site:* http://www.chapman.edu/.

See page 160 for the College Close-Up.

CHARLES R. DREW UNIVERSITY OF MEDICINE AND SCIENCE

Los Angeles, California

Charles R. Drew University of Medicine and Science is a coed, private, comprehensive institution, founded in 1966, offering degrees at the associate, bachelor's, master's, and doctoral levels.

Expenses for 2006–07 *Application fee:* $35. *Tuition:* $10,000 full-time, $250 per unit part-time. *Mandatory fees:* $100 full-time, $100 per year part-time. Both full-time and part-time tuition and fees vary according to course load and program.

For Further Information Contact Ms. Maranda Montgomery, Director, Student Affairs, Charles R. Drew University of Medicine and Science, 1731 East 120th Street, Keck Building, Los Angeles, CA 90059. *Telephone:* 323-357-3638. *Fax:* 323-563-4923. *E-mail:* mmmontgo@cdrewu.edu. *Web site:* http://www.cdrewu.edu/.

CHRISTIAN HERITAGE COLLEGE

See San Diego Christian College.

CLAREMONT McKENNA COLLEGE

Claremont, California

Claremont McKenna College is a coed, private, four-year college of The Claremont Colleges Consortium, founded in 1946, offering degrees at the bachelor's level. It has a 50-acre campus in Claremont near Los Angeles.

Academic Information The faculty has 146 members (77% full-time), 92% with terminal degrees. The student-faculty ratio is 9:1. The library holds 2 million titles and 6,028 serial subscriptions. Special programs include services for learning-disabled students, an honors program, study abroad, advanced placement credit, accelerated degree programs, double majors, independent study, self-designed majors, internships, and arrangement for off-campus study with 5 members of The Claremont Colleges, Haverford College, Colby College, Spelman College, Morehouse College.

Student Body Statistics The student body is made up of 1,153 undergraduates (296 freshmen). 46 percent are women and 54 percent are men. Students come from 44 states and territories and 25 other countries. 44 percent are from California. 3.6 percent are international students. 20 percent of the 2006 graduating class went on to graduate and professional schools.

Expenses for 2006–07 *Application fee:* $60. *Comprehensive fee:* $45,590 includes full-time tuition ($33,000), mandatory fees ($1850), and college room and board ($10,740). *College room only:* $5420. Full-time tuition and fees vary according to reciprocity agreements. Room and board charges vary according to board plan and housing facility. *Part-time tuition:* varies with reciprocity agreements.

Financial Aid Forms of aid include need-based and non-need-based scholarships and part-time jobs. The average aided 2006–07 undergraduate received an aid package worth an estimated $28,191.

Freshman Admission Claremont McKenna College requires an essay, a high school transcript, a minimum 3.0 high school GPA, 3 recommendations, SAT or ACT scores, and TOEFL scores for international students. An interview and SAT Subject Test scores are recommended. The application deadline for regular admission is January 2; for early decision plan 1 it is November 15; and for early decision plan 2 it is January 2.

Transfer Admission The application deadline for admission is April 1.

Entrance Difficulty Claremont McKenna College assesses its entrance difficulty level as most difficult; very difficult for transfers. For the fall 2006 freshman class, 22 percent of the applicants were accepted.

For Further Information Contact Mr. Richard C. Vos, Vice President/Dean of Admission and Financial Aid, Claremont McKenna College, 890 Columbia Avenue, Claremont, CA 91711. *Telephone:* 909-621-8088. *Fax:* 909-621-8516. *E-mail:* admission@claremontmckenna.edu. *Web site:* http://www.claremontmckenna.edu/.

CLEVELAND CHIROPRACTIC COLLEGE-LOS ANGELES CAMPUS

Los Angeles, California

Cleveland Chiropractic College-Los Angeles Campus is a coed, private, upper-level institution, founded in 1911, offering degrees at the associate, bachelor's, and first professional levels.

Academic Information The faculty has 38 members (68% full-time), 97% with terminal degrees. The undergraduate student-faculty ratio is 7:1. The library holds 23,937 titles, 152 serial subscriptions, and 2,323 audiovisual materials. Special programs include cooperative (work-study) education, advanced placement credit, accelerated degree programs, double majors, distance learning, summer session for credit, part-time degree programs (evenings, summer), and adult/continuing education programs. The most frequently chosen baccalaureate field is health professions and related sciences.

Student Body Statistics The student body totals 379, of whom 108 are undergraduates. 34 percent are women and 66 percent are men. Students come from 3 states and territories and 2 other countries. 98 percent are from California. 1.9 percent are international students.

Expenses for 2006–07 *Application fee:* $35. *Tuition:* $5520 full-time, $230 per credit part-time. *Mandatory fees:* $200 full-time, $200 per year part-time. Both full-time and part-time tuition and fees vary according to course level.

Transfer Admission The application deadline for admission is September 29.

Entrance Difficulty Cleveland Chiropractic College-Los Angeles Campus has an open admission policy.

For Further Information Contact Ms. Theresa Moore, Director of Multicampus Admissions, Cleveland Chiropractic College-Los Angeles Campus, 590 North Vermont Avenue, Los Angeles, CA 90004-2196. *Telephone:* 323-906-2031 or 800-446-CCLA (toll-free). *Fax:* 323-906-2094. *E-mail:* la.admissions@cleveland.edu. *Web site:* http://www.clevelandchiropractic.edu/.

COGSWELL POLYTECHNICAL COLLEGE

Sunnyvale, California

Cogswell Polytechnical College is a coed, primarily men's, private, four-year college of Foundation for Educational Achievement, San Diego, founded in 1887, offering degrees at the bachelor's level. It has a 2-acre campus in Sunnyvale near San Francisco and San Jose.

Academic Information The faculty has 46 members (28% full-time), 13% with terminal degrees. The student-faculty ratio is 8:1. The library holds 10,069 titles, 102 serial subscriptions, and 8,181 audiovisual materials. Special programs include advanced placement credit, double majors, distance learning, summer session for credit, part-time degree programs (daytime, evenings, summer), external degree programs, adult/continuing education programs, and internships.

Student Body Statistics The student body is made up of 287 undergraduates (32 freshmen). 15 percent are women and 85 percent are men. Students come from 15 states and territories. 82 percent are from California. 2 percent of the 2006 graduating class went on to graduate and professional schools.

Expenses for 2006–07 *Application fee:* $55. *Tuition:* $14,904 full-time, $621 per credit part-time. *Mandatory fees:* $80 full-time. Full-time tuition and fees vary according to course load. Part-time tuition varies according to course load. *College room only:* $3000. Room charges vary according to housing facility.

Financial Aid Forms of aid include need-based and non-need-based scholarships and part-time jobs. The priority application deadline for financial aid is March 1.

Freshman Admission Cogswell Polytechnical College requires an essay, a high school transcript, a minimum 2.5 high school GPA, and TOEFL scores for international students. Recommendations, an interview, and a portfolio are required for some. The application deadline for regular admission is June 1.

Transfer Admission The application deadline for admission is June 1.

Entrance Difficulty Cogswell Polytechnical College assesses its entrance difficulty level as moderately difficult. For the fall 2006 freshman class, 71 percent of the applicants were accepted.

For Further Information Contact Bill Souza, Admissions Coordinator, Cogswell Polytechnical College, 1175 Bordeaux Drive, Sunnyvale, CA 94089. *Telephone:* 408-541-0100 Ext. 155 or 800-264-7955 (toll-free). *Fax:* 408-747-0764. *E-mail:* info@cogswell.edu. *Web site:* http://www.cogswell.edu/.

THE COLBURN SCHOOL CONSERVATORY OF MUSIC

Los Angeles, California

The Colburn School Conservatory of Music is a coed, private, four-year college, founded in 1980, offering degrees at the bachelor's level and postbachelor's certificates. It is located in Los Angeles near Los Angeles.

Academic Information The faculty has 22 members. Special programs include ESL programs.

Student Body Statistics The student body is made up of 30 undergraduates (8 freshmen). 57 percent are women and 43 percent are men. Students come from 8 states and territories and 6 other countries.

Expenses for 2006–07 *Application fee:* $100. *Tuition:* $0 full-time. *Mandatory fees:* $1500 full-time. All students receive monetary support which covers tuition, room and board.

Freshman Admission The Colburn School Conservatory of Music requires an essay, a high school transcript, 2 recommendations, an interview, and TOEFL score required for all non-native English speakers. SAT or ACT scores are recommended. The application deadline for regular admission is January 15.

Transfer Admission The application deadline for admission is January 15.

Entrance Difficulty For the fall 2006 freshman class, 12 percent of the applicants were accepted.

For Further Information Contact Mr. Hank Mou, Admissions Specialist, The Colburn School Conservatory of Music, 200 South Grand Avenue, Los Angeles, CA 90012. *Telephone:* 213-621-2200. *Fax:* 213-621-2110. *E-mail:* admissions@colburnschool.edu. *Web site:* http://www.colburnschool.edu/.

COLEMAN COLLEGE

San Diego, California

http://www.coleman.edu/

COLEMAN COLLEGE

San Marcos, California

http://www.coleman.edu/

COLLEGE OF NOTRE DAME

See Notre Dame de Namur University.

COLUMBIA COLLEGE HOLLYWOOD

Tarzana, California

Columbia College Hollywood is a coed, private, four-year college, founded in 1952, offering degrees at the associate and bachelor's levels. It has a 1-acre campus in Tarzana.

Academic Information The faculty has 52 full-time members. The library holds 9,000 titles, 23 serial subscriptions, and 3,000 audiovisual materials. Special programs include accelerated degree programs, summer session for credit, part-time degree programs (daytime, weekends, summer), and adult/continuing education programs.

Student Body Statistics The student body is made up of 301 undergraduates. 26 percent are women and 74 percent are men. 48 percent are from California. 5 percent of the 2006 graduating class went on to graduate and professional schools.

Expenses for 2006–07 *Application fee:* $50. *Comprehensive fee:* $19,539 includes full-time tuition ($11,985), mandatory fees ($1110), and college room and board ($6444). *Part-time tuition:* $337.50 per unit. *Part-time mandatory fees:* $150 per term.

Financial Aid Forms of aid include need-based scholarships and part-time jobs. The application deadline for financial aid is continuous.

Freshman Admission Columbia College Hollywood requires an essay, a high school transcript, a minimum 2.0 high school GPA, 2 recommendations, an interview, and TOEFL scores for international students. A portfolio is recommended. The application deadline for regular admission is rolling.

Entrance Difficulty Columbia College Hollywood assesses its entrance difficulty level as minimally difficult; moderately difficult for cinema program. For the fall 2006 freshman class, 60 percent of the applicants were accepted.

For Further Information Contact Carmen Munoz, Admissions Director, Columbia College Hollywood, 18618 Oxnard Street, Tarzana, CA 91356. *Telephone:* 818-345-8414 or 800-785-0585 (toll-free in-state). *Fax:* 818-345-9053. *E-mail:* admissions@columbiacollege.edu. *Web site:* http://www.columbiacollege.edu/.

CONCORDIA UNIVERSITY

Irvine, California

Concordia University is a coed, private, comprehensive unit of The Concordia University System, founded in 1972, affiliated with the Lutheran Church–Missouri Synod, offering degrees at the bachelor's and master's levels and postbachelor's certificates (associate's degree for international students only). It has a 70-acre campus in Irvine near Los Angeles.

Academic Information The faculty has 199 members (44% full-time), 42% with terminal degrees. The undergraduate student-faculty ratio is 15:1. The library holds 80,300 titles, 7,144 serial subscriptions, and 1,365 audiovisual materials. Special programs include an honors program, cooperative (work-study) education, study abroad, advanced placement credit, accelerated degree programs, ESL programs, double majors, independent study, distance learning, self-designed majors, summer session for credit, part-time degree programs (daytime, evenings, summer), external degree programs, adult/continuing education programs, internships, and arrangement for off-campus study with San Diego and Temecula Degree Completion Satellite Campuses. The most frequently chosen baccalaureate fields are business/marketing, education, liberal arts/general studies.

Student Body Statistics The student body totals 2,317, of whom 1,348 are undergraduates (247 freshmen). 62 percent are women and 38 percent are men. Students come from 28 states and territories and 10 other countries. 82 percent are from California. 1.9 percent are international students.

Expenses for 2006–07 *Application fee:* $50. *Comprehensive fee:* $28,190 includes full-time tuition ($21,130) and college room and board ($7060). *College room only:* $4380. Room and board charges vary according to board plan. *Part-time tuition:* $600 per unit. Part-time tuition varies according to course load.

Financial Aid Forms of aid include need-based and non-need-based scholarships, athletic grants, and part-time jobs. The average aided 2006–07 undergraduate received an aid package worth an estimated $20,751. The application deadline for financial aid is April 1 with a priority deadline of March 2.

Freshman Admission Concordia University requires a high school transcript, 2 recommendations, SAT or ACT scores, and TOEFL scores for international students. A minimum 2.8 high school GPA and an interview are recommended. The application deadline for regular admission is rolling.

Transfer Admission The application deadline for admission is rolling.

Concordia University (continued)

Entrance Difficulty For the fall 2006 freshman class, 66 percent of the applicants were accepted.
For Further Information Contact Ms. Lori McDonald, Executive Director of Enrollment Services, Concordia University, 1530 Concordia West, Irvine, CA 92612-3299. *Telephone:* 949-854-8002 Ext. 1170 or 800-229-1200 (toll-free). *Fax:* 949-854-6894. *E-mail:* admission@cui.edu. *Web site:* http://www.cui.edu/.

DEEP SPRINGS COLLEGE
Deep Springs, California

Deep Springs College is a men's, private, two-year college, founded in 1917, offering degrees at the associate level. It has a 3,000-acre campus in Deep Springs.

Expenses for 2007–08 *Application fee:* $0. Contact the college directly for admission/tuition details.
For Further Information Contact Dr. Louis Fantasia, President, Deep Springs College, HC 72, Box 45001, Dyer, NV 89010-9803. *Telephone:* 760-872-2000. *Fax:* 760-872-4466. *E-mail:* apcom@deepsprings.edu. *Web site:* http://www.deepsprings.edu/.

DESIGN INSTITUTE OF SAN DIEGO
San Diego, California

http://www.disd.edu/

DeVRY UNIVERSITY
Elk Grove, California

http://www.devry.edu/

DeVRY UNIVERSITY
Fremont, California

DeVry University is a coed, proprietary, comprehensive unit of DeVry University, founded in 1998, offering degrees at the associate, bachelor's, and master's levels and postbachelor's certificates. It has a 17-acre campus in Fremont near San Francisco.

Academic Information The faculty has 124 members (40% full-time). The undergraduate student-faculty ratio is 16:1. The library holds 40,000 titles and 3,060 serial subscriptions. Special programs include academic remediation, services for learning-disabled students, advanced placement credit, accelerated degree programs, distance learning, summer session for credit, part-time degree programs (daytime, evenings, weekends, summer), and adult/continuing education programs. The most frequently chosen baccalaureate fields are business/marketing, computer and information sciences, engineering technologies.
Student Body Statistics The student body totals 1,581, of whom 1,421 are undergraduates (261 freshmen). 29 percent are women and 71 percent are men. Students come from 25 states and territories and 9 other countries. 98 percent are from California. 0.9 percent are international students.
Expenses for 2007–08 *Application fee:* $50. *Tuition:* $14,320 full-time, $525 per credit part-time. *Mandatory fees:* $320 full-time.
Financial Aid Forms of aid include need-based and non-need-based scholarships and part-time jobs. The application deadline for financial aid is continuous.
Freshman Admission DeVry University requires a high school transcript, an interview, and TOEFL scores for international students. The application deadline for regular admission is rolling.
Transfer Admission The application deadline for admission is rolling.

Entrance Difficulty DeVry University assesses its entrance difficulty level as minimally difficult; moderately difficult for electronics engineering technology program.
For Further Information Contact Director of Admissions, DeVry University, 6600 Dumbarton Circle, Fremont, CA 94555-3615. *Telephone:* 510-574-1100. *Web site:* http://www.devry.edu/.

DeVRY UNIVERSITY
Irvine, California

http://www.devry.edu/

DeVRY UNIVERSITY
Long Beach, California

DeVry University is a coed, proprietary, comprehensive unit of DeVry University, founded in 1984, offering degrees at the associate, bachelor's, and master's levels and postbachelor's certificates. It has a 23-acre campus in Long Beach near Los Angeles.

Academic Information The faculty has 94 members (30% full-time). The undergraduate student-faculty ratio is 15:1. The library holds 15,500 titles and 85 serial subscriptions. Special programs include academic remediation, services for learning-disabled students, advanced placement credit, accelerated degree programs, distance learning, summer session for credit, part-time degree programs (daytime, evenings, weekends, summer), and adult/continuing education programs. The most frequently chosen baccalaureate fields are business/marketing, computer and information sciences, engineering technologies.
Student Body Statistics The student body totals 1,098, of whom 892 are undergraduates (160 freshmen). 30 percent are women and 70 percent are men. Students come from 23 states and territories and 11 other countries. 99 percent are from California. 0.1 percent are international students.
Expenses for 2007–08 *Application fee:* $50. *Tuition:* $13,700 full-time, $500 per credit part-time. *Mandatory fees:* $320 full-time.
Financial Aid Forms of aid include need-based and non-need-based scholarships and part-time jobs. The application deadline for financial aid is continuous.
Freshman Admission DeVry University requires a high school transcript, an interview, and TOEFL scores for international students. The application deadline for regular admission is rolling.
Transfer Admission The application deadline for admission is rolling.
Entrance Difficulty DeVry University assesses its entrance difficulty level as minimally difficult; moderately difficult for electronics engineering technology program.
For Further Information Contact Admissions Office, DeVry University, 3880 Kilroy Airport Way, Long Beach, CA 90806-2449. *Telephone:* 562-427-0861. *Web site:* http://www.devry.edu/.

DeVRY UNIVERSITY
Pomona, California

DeVry University is a coed, proprietary, comprehensive unit of DeVry University, founded in 1983, offering degrees at the associate, bachelor's, and master's levels and postbachelor's certificates. It has a 15-acre campus in Pomona near Los Angeles.

Academic Information The faculty has 93 members (38% full-time). The undergraduate student-faculty ratio is 21:1. The library holds 17,000 titles and 77 serial subscriptions. Special programs include academic remediation, services for learning-disabled students, advanced placement credit, accelerated degree programs, distance learning, summer session for credit, part-time degree programs (daytime, evenings, weekends, summer), and adult/continuing education programs. The most frequently chosen baccalaureate fields are business/marketing, computer and information sciences, engineering technologies.

Student Body Statistics The student body totals 1,706, of whom 1,541 are undergraduates (227 freshmen). 28 percent are women and 72 percent are men. Students come from 25 states and territories and 19 other countries. 99 percent are from California. 0.9 percent are international students.

Expenses for 2007–08 *Application fee:* $50. *Tuition:* $13,700 full-time, $500 per credit part-time. *Mandatory fees:* $320 full-time.

Financial Aid Forms of aid include need-based and non-need-based scholarships and part-time jobs. The application deadline for financial aid is continuous.

Freshman Admission DeVry University requires a high school transcript, an interview, and TOEFL scores for international students. The application deadline for regular admission is rolling.

Transfer Admission The application deadline for admission is rolling.

Entrance Difficulty DeVry University assesses its entrance difficulty level as minimally difficult; moderately difficult for electronics engineering technology program.

For Further Information Contact Admissions Office, DeVry University, 901 Corporate Center Drive, University Center, Pomona, CA 91768-2642. *Telephone:* 909-622-8866. *Web site:* http://www.devry.edu/.

DeVRY UNIVERSITY
San Diego, California
http://www.devry.edu/

DeVRY UNIVERSITY
San Francisco, California
http://www.devry.edu/

DeVRY UNIVERSITY
Sherman Oaks, California

DeVry University is a coed, proprietary, comprehensive institution, offering degrees at the associate, bachelor's, and master's levels and postbachelor's certificates.

Academic Information The faculty has 93 members (16% full-time). The undergraduate student-faculty ratio is 10:1. Special programs include accelerated degree programs and distance learning.

Student Body Statistics The student body totals 635, of whom 525 are undergraduates (80 freshmen). 24 percent are women and 76 percent are men. 99 percent are from California. 1.1 percent are international students.

Expenses for 2007–08 *Application fee:* $50. *Tuition:* $13,700 full-time, $500 per credit part-time. *Mandatory fees:* $320 full-time.

Freshman Admission The application deadline for regular admission is rolling.

Transfer Admission The application deadline for admission is rolling.

For Further Information Contact Admissions Office, DeVry University, 15301 Ventura Boulevard, D-100, Sherman Oaks, CA 91403. *Telephone:* 888-610-0800 or 888-610-0800 (toll-free). *Web site:* http://www.devry.edu/.

DeVRY UNIVERSITY
West Hills, California

DeVry University is a coed, proprietary, comprehensive unit of DeVry University, founded in 1999, offering degrees at the associate, bachelor's, and master's levels and postbachelor's certificates. It has a 20-acre campus in West Hills.

Expenses for 2006–07 *Application fee:* $50. *Tuition:* $12,340 full-time, $465 per credit part-time. *Mandatory fees:* $310 full-time, $200 per year part-time. Both full-time and part-time tuition and fees vary according to course load.

For Further Information Contact Admissions Office, DeVry University, 22801 Roscoe Boulevard, West Hills, CA 91304-3200. *Telephone:* 818-932-3001 or 888-610-0800 (toll-free). *Web site:* http://www.devry.edu/.

DOMINICAN SCHOOL OF PHILOSOPHY AND THEOLOGY
Berkeley, California

Dominican School of Philosophy and Theology is a coed, private, Roman Catholic, upper-level institution, founded in 1932, offering degrees at the bachelor's, master's, and first professional levels. It is located in Berkeley near San Francisco.

Academic Information The faculty has 24 members (50% full-time), 92% with terminal degrees. The undergraduate student-faculty ratio is 4:1. The library holds 409,592 titles and 1,466 serial subscriptions. Special programs include services for learning-disabled students, study abroad, double majors, independent study, part-time degree programs (daytime), and arrangement for off-campus study with University of California, Berkeley, Graduate Theological Union, Mills College, Holy Names College.

Student Body Statistics The student body totals 89, of whom 5 are undergraduates. 40 percent are women and 60 percent are men. 98 percent are from California.

Expenses for 2007–08 *Application fee:* $40. *Tuition:* $11,616 full-time, $484 per credit part-time. *Mandatory fees:* $50 full-time, $50 per year part-time.

Transfer Admission Dominican School of Philosophy and Theology requires a minimum 2.5 college GPA and a college transcript. The application deadline for admission is rolling.

Entrance Difficulty Dominican School of Philosophy and Theology assesses its entrance difficulty level as moderately difficult.

For Further Information Contact Mr. John D. Knutsen, Dominican School of Philosophy and Theology, 2301 Vine Street, Berkeley, CA 94708. *Telephone:* 510-883-2073. *Fax:* 510-849-1372. *E-mail:* admissions@dspt.edu. *Web site:* http://www.dspt.edu/.

DOMINICAN UNIVERSITY OF CALIFORNIA
San Rafael, California

Dominican University of California is a coed, private, comprehensive institution, founded in 1890, affiliated with the Roman Catholic Church, offering degrees at the bachelor's and master's levels and postbachelor's certificates. It has an 80-acre campus in San Rafael near San Francisco.

Academic Information The faculty has 306 members (25% full-time), 48% with terminal degrees. The undergraduate student-faculty ratio is 11:1. The library holds 93,207 titles, 415 serial subscriptions, and 2,011 audiovisual materials. Special programs include academic remediation, services for learning-disabled students, an honors program, study abroad, advanced placement credit, ESL programs, double majors, independent study, self-designed majors, summer session for credit, part-time degree programs (daytime, evenings, weekends, summer), external degree programs, adult/continuing education programs, internships, and arrangement for off-campus study with University of California, Berkeley, Aquinas College, St. Thomas Aquinas College, Barry University. The most frequently chosen baccalaureate fields are health professions and related sciences, liberal arts/general studies, social sciences.

Student Body Statistics The student body totals 2,045, of whom 1,468 are undergraduates (267 freshmen). 76 percent are women and 24 percent are men. Students come from 25 states and territories and 16 other countries. 93 percent are from California. 2.3 percent are international students.

Dominican University of California (continued)

Expenses for 2007–08 *Application fee:* $40. *Comprehensive fee:* $42,780 includes full-time tuition ($30,480), mandatory fees ($300), and college room and board ($12,000). *College room only:* $6980. *Part-time tuition:* $1270 per unit. *Part-time mandatory fees:* $150 per term.

Financial Aid Forms of aid include need-based and non-need-based scholarships, athletic grants, and part-time jobs. The average aided 2005–06 undergraduate received an aid package worth $20,605. The priority application deadline for financial aid is March 2.

Freshman Admission Dominican University of California requires an essay, a high school transcript, a minimum 2.5 high school GPA, 1 recommendation, SAT or ACT scores, and TOEFL scores for international students. SAT Subject Test scores are recommended. An interview is required for some. The application deadline for regular admission is August 1.

Transfer Admission The application deadline for admission is rolling.

Entrance Difficulty Dominican University of California assesses its entrance difficulty level as moderately difficult; noncompetitive for evening, weekend programs. For the fall 2006 freshman class, 52 percent of the applicants were accepted.

For Further Information Contact Mr. Art Criss, Director of Undergraduate Admissions, Dominican University of California, 50 Acacia Avenue, San Rafael, CA 94901-2298. *Telephone:* 415-485-3204 or 888-323-6763 (toll-free). *Fax:* 415-485-3214. *E-mail:* enroll@dominican.edu. *Web site:* http://www.dominican.edu/.

EDUCATION AMERICA UNIVERSITY

See Remington College–San Diego Campus.

EMMANUEL BIBLE COLLEGE

Pasadena, California

http://www.emmanuelbiblecollege.edu/

FIDM/THE FASHION INSTITUTE OF DESIGN & MERCHANDISING, LOS ANGELES CAMPUS

Los Angeles, California

FIDM/The Fashion Institute of Design & Merchandising, Los Angeles Campus is a coed, proprietary, primarily two-year college of Fashion Institute of Design and Merchandising, founded in 1969, offering degrees at the associate and bachelor's levels (also includes Orange County Campus).

Academic Information The faculty has 292 members (21% full-time). The student-faculty ratio is 14:1. The library holds 21,099 titles and 462 serial subscriptions. Special programs include academic remediation, services for learning-disabled students, cooperative (work-study) education, study abroad, advanced placement credit, ESL programs, independent study, distance learning, summer session for credit, part-time degree programs (daytime, evenings, weekends, summer), adult/continuing education programs, and internships.

Student Body Statistics The student body is made up of 4,143 undergraduates (1,045 freshmen). 90 percent are women and 10 percent are men. Students come from 4 states and territories and 25 other countries. 81 percent are from California. 6.8 percent are international students.

Expenses for 2007–08 *Application fee:* $225. *Tuition:* $18,285 full-time. *Mandatory fees:* $500 full-time.

Financial Aid Forms of aid include need-based scholarships and part-time jobs. The application deadline for financial aid is continuous.

Freshman Admission FIDM/The Fashion Institute of Design & Merchandising, Los Angeles Campus requires an essay, a high school transcript, 3 recommendations, an interview, major-determined project, and

Wonderlic Aptitude Test. 3 recommendations and major-determined project are required for some. The application deadline for regular admission is rolling.

Transfer Admission The application deadline for admission is rolling.

Entrance Difficulty FIDM/The Fashion Institute of Design & Merchandising, Los Angeles Campus assesses its entrance difficulty level as moderately difficult.

For Further Information Contact Ms. Susan Aronson, Director of Admissions, FIDM/The Fashion Institute of Design & Merchandising, Los Angeles Campus, FIDM LA, 919 South Grand Avenue, Los Angeles, CA 90015. *Telephone:* 213-624-1200 Ext. 5400 or 800-624-1200 (toll-free). *Fax:* 213-624-4799. *E-mail:* info@fidm.com. *Web site:* http://www.fidm.edu/.

FOUNDATION COLLEGE

San Diego, California

For Information Write to Foundation College, San Diego, CA 92108-1306.

FRESNO PACIFIC UNIVERSITY

Fresno, California

Fresno Pacific University is a coed, private, comprehensive institution, founded in 1944, affiliated with the Mennonite Brethren Church, offering degrees at the associate, bachelor's, and master's levels. It has a 42-acre campus in Fresno.

Academic Information The faculty has 238 members (35% full-time), 31% with terminal degrees. The undergraduate student-faculty ratio is 16:1. The library holds 196,000 titles and 16,000 serial subscriptions. Special programs include services for learning-disabled students, cooperative (work-study) education, study abroad, advanced placement credit, accelerated degree programs, ESL programs, double majors, independent study, distance learning, self-designed majors, summer session for credit, part-time degree programs (daytime, evenings, weekends, summer), adult/continuing education programs, internships, and arrangement for off-campus study with California State University, Fresno; Mennonite Brethren Biblical Seminary; San Joaquin College of Law. The most frequently chosen baccalaureate fields are business/marketing, education, theology and religious vocations.

Student Body Statistics The student body totals 2,324, of whom 1,565 are undergraduates (201 freshmen). 68 percent are women and 32 percent are men. Students come from 18 states and territories and 36 other countries. 96 percent are from California. 2.3 percent are international students.

Expenses for 2006–07 *Application fee:* $40. *Comprehensive fee:* $26,780 includes full-time tuition ($20,550), mandatory fees ($240), and college room and board ($5990). *College room only:* $3400. Full-time tuition and fees vary according to program. Room and board charges vary according to board plan and housing facility. *Part-time tuition:* $735 per unit. Part-time tuition varies according to program.

Financial Aid Forms of aid include need-based and non-need-based scholarships and part-time jobs. The average aided 2005–06 undergraduate received an aid package worth $16,270. The priority application deadline for financial aid is March 2.

Freshman Admission Fresno Pacific University requires an essay, a high school transcript, 1 recommendation, SAT and SAT Subject Test or ACT scores, and TOEFL scores for international students. A minimum 3.10 high school GPA is recommended. The application deadline for regular admission is rolling.

Transfer Admission Fresno Pacific University requires a college transcript and a minimum 2.40 college GPA. Standardized test scores are recommended. The application deadline for admission is rolling.

Entrance Difficulty Fresno Pacific University assesses its entrance difficulty level as moderately difficult. For the fall 2006 freshman class, 68 percent of the applicants were accepted.
For Further Information Contact Ms. Yamilette Rodriguez, Fresno Pacific University, 1717 South Chestnut Avenue, #2005, Fresno, CA 93727. *Telephone:* 800-600-6089 or 800-660-6089 (toll-free in-state). *Fax:* 559-453-2007. *E-mail:* ugadmis@fresno.edu. *Web site:* http://www.fresno.edu/.

See page 168 for the College Close-Up.

GOLDEN GATE UNIVERSITY
San Francisco, California

Golden Gate University is a coed, private university, founded in 1901, offering degrees at the bachelor's, master's, doctoral, and first professional levels.

Expenses for 2006–07 *Application fee:* $55. *Tuition:* $11,520 full-time, $1440 per course part-time.
For Further Information Contact Ms. Cherron Hoppes, Director of Admission, Golden Gate University, 536 Mission Street, San Francisco, CA 94105-2968. *Telephone:* 415-442-7800 or 800-448-4968 (toll-free). *Fax:* 415-442-7807. *E-mail:* info@ggu.edu. *Web site:* http://www.ggu.edu/.

HARVEY MUDD COLLEGE
Claremont, California

Harvey Mudd College is a coed, private, four-year college of The Claremont Colleges Consortium, founded in 1955, offering degrees at the bachelor's and master's levels. It has a 33-acre campus in Claremont near Los Angeles.

Academic Information The faculty has 89 members (87% full-time), 99% with terminal degrees. The undergraduate student-faculty ratio is 9:1. The library holds 3 million titles and 16,308 serial subscriptions. Special programs include services for learning-disabled students, study abroad, advanced placement credit, double majors, self-designed majors, internships, and arrangement for off-campus study with other members of The Claremont Colleges, Swarthmore College, Rensselaer Polytechnic Institute. The most frequently chosen baccalaureate fields are engineering, computer and information sciences, physical sciences.
Student Body Statistics The student body is made up of 729 undergraduates (180 freshmen). 29 percent are women and 71 percent are men. Students come from 43 states and territories and 20 other countries. 49 percent are from California. 3.7 percent are international students. 43 percent of the 2006 graduating class went on to graduate and professional schools.
Expenses for 2007–08 *Application fee:* $50. *Comprehensive fee:* $46,082 includes full-time tuition ($34,670) and college room and board ($11,412). *College room only:* $5729.
Financial Aid Forms of aid include need-based and non-need-based scholarships and part-time jobs. The average aided 2006–07 undergraduate received an aid package worth an estimated $27,752. The application deadline for financial aid is February 1.
Freshman Admission Harvey Mudd College requires an essay, a high school transcript, 3 recommendations, SAT or ACT scores, SAT and SAT Subject Test scores, and SAT Subject Test in Math 2C and second exam of choice (Math 1C is not accepted). An interview and TOEFL scores for international students are recommended. The application deadline for regular admission is January 15 and for early decision it is November 15.
Transfer Admission The application deadline for admission is April 1.
Entrance Difficulty Harvey Mudd College assesses its entrance difficulty level as most difficult. For the fall 2006 freshman class, 30 percent of the applicants were accepted.
For Further Information Contact Mr. Peter Osgood, Interim Vice President and Dean of Admissions and Financial Aid, Harvey Mudd College, 301 Platt Boulevard, Claremont, CA 91711. *Telephone:* 909-621-8011. *Fax:* 909-607-7046. *E-mail:* admission@hmc.edu. *Web site:* http://www.hmc.edu/.

HEALD COLLEGE-CONCORD
Concord, California

Heald College-Concord is a coed, private, two-year college, founded in 1863, offering degrees at the associate level. It has a 5-acre campus in Concord near San Francisco.

Expenses for 2006–07 *Application fee:* $40. *Tuition:* $10,275 full-time.
For Further Information Contact Keith Woodman, Director of Admissions, Heald College-Concord, 5130 Commercial Circle, Concord, CA 94520. *Telephone:* 925-288-5800 or 800-755-3550 (toll-free in-state). *Fax:* 925-288-5896. *E-mail:* kwoodman@heald.edu. *Web site:* http://www.heald.edu/.

HEALD COLLEGE-FRESNO
Fresno, California

Heald College-Fresno is a coed, private, two-year college, founded in 1863, offering degrees at the associate level. It has a 3-acre campus in Fresno.

Expenses for 2006–07 *Application fee:* $40. *Tuition:* $10,275 full-time.
For Further Information Contact Ms. Tina Mathis, Director of Admissions, Heald College-Fresno, 255 West Bullard Avenue, Fresno, CA 93704-1706. *Telephone:* 559-438-4222 or 800-755-3550 (toll-free in-state). *Fax:* 209-438-6368. *E-mail:* tmathis@heald.edu. *Web site:* http://www.heald.edu/.

HEALD COLLEGE-HAYWARD
Hayward, California

Heald College-Hayward is a coed, private, two-year college, founded in 1863, offering degrees at the associate level. It is located in Hayward near San Francisco.

Expenses for 2006–07 *Application fee:* $40. *Tuition:* $10,275 full-time. Full-time tuition varies according to class time, course load, and program. *Part-time tuition:* varies with class time, course load, program.
For Further Information Contact Mrs. Barbara Gordon, Director of Admissions, Heald College-Hayward, 25500 Industrial Boulevard, Hayward, CA 94545. *Telephone:* 510-783-2100 or 800-755-3550 (toll-free in-state). *Fax:* 510-783-3287. *E-mail:* bgordon@heald.edu. *Web site:* http://www.heald.edu/.

HEALD COLLEGE-RANCHO CORDOVA
Rancho Cordova, California

Heald College-Rancho Cordova is a coed, private, two-year college, founded in 1863, offering degrees at the associate level. It has a 1-acre campus in Rancho Cordova near Sacramento.

Expenses for 2006–07 *Application fee:* $40. *Tuition:* $10,275 full-time.
For Further Information Contact Director of Admissions, Heald College-Rancho Cordova, 2910 Prospect Park Drive, Rancho Cordova, CA 95670-6005. *Telephone:* 916-638-1616 or 800-755-3550 (toll-free in-state). *Fax:* 916-853-8282. *E-mail:* info@heald.edu. *Web site:* http://www.heald.edu/.

HEALD COLLEGE-ROSEVILLE
Roseville, California

Heald College-Roseville is a coed, private, two-year college, founded in 1863, offering degrees at the associate level. It has a 5-acre campus in Roseville.

Heald College-Roseville (continued)

Expenses for 2006–07 *Application fee:* $40. *Tuition:* $10,275 full-time.
For Further Information Contact Kristi Culpepper, Director of Admissions, Heald College-Roseville, 7 Sierra Gate Plaza, Roseville, CA 95678. *Telephone:* 916-789-8600 or 800-755-3550 (toll-free in-state). *E-mail:* kculpepp@heald.edu. *Web site:* http://www.heald.edu/.

HEALD COLLEGE-SALINAS
Salinas, California

Heald College-Salinas is a coed, private, two-year college, founded in 1863, offering degrees at the associate level. It is located in Salinas near San Jose.

Expenses for 2006–07 *Application fee:* $40. *Tuition:* $10,275 full-time.
For Further Information Contact Mr. Jason Ferguson, Director of Admissions, Heald College-Salinas, 1450 North Main Street, Salinas, CA 93906. *Telephone:* 831-443-1700 or 800-755-3550 (toll-free in-state). *Fax:* 831-443-1050. *E-mail:* jferguso@heald.edu. *Web site:* http://www.heald.edu/.

HEALD COLLEGE-SAN FRANCISCO
San Francisco, California

Heald College-San Francisco is a coed, private, two-year college, founded in 1863, offering degrees at the associate level.

Expenses for 2006–07 *Application fee:* $40. *Tuition:* $10,275 full-time.
For Further Information Contact Ms. Jennifer Dunckel, Director of Admissions, Heald College-San Francisco, 350 Mission Street, San Francisco, CA 94105. *Telephone:* 415-808-3000 or 800-755-3550 (toll-free in-state). *Fax:* 415-808-3003. *E-mail:* jennifer_dunckel@heald.edu. *Web site:* http://www.heald.edu/.

HEALD COLLEGE-SAN JOSE
Milpitas, California

Heald College-San Jose is a coed, private, two-year college, founded in 1863, offering degrees at the associate level. It has a 5-acre campus in Milpitas near San Jose.

Expenses for 2006–07 *Application fee:* $40. *Tuition:* $10,275 full-time.
For Further Information Contact Clarence Hardiman, Director of Admissions, Heald College-San Jose, 341 Great Mall Parkway, Milpitas, CA 95035. *Telephone:* 408-934-4900 or 800-755-3550 (toll-free in-state). *Fax:* 408-934-7777. *E-mail:* chardima@heald.edu. *Web site:* http://www. heald.edu/.

HEALD COLLEGE-STOCKTON
Stockton, California

Heald College-Stockton is a coed, private, two-year college, founded in 1863, offering degrees at the associate level.

Expenses for 2006–07 *Application fee:* $40. *Tuition:* $10,275 full-time.
For Further Information Contact Director of Admissions, Heald College-Stockton, 1605 East March Lane, Stockton, CA 95210. *Telephone:* 209-473-5200 or 800-755-3550 (toll-free in-state). *Fax:* 209-477-2739. *E-mail:* info@heald.edu. *Web site:* http://www.heald.edu/.

HOLY NAMES UNIVERSITY
Oakland, California

Holy Names University is a coed, primarily women's, private, Roman Catholic, comprehensive institution, founded in 1868, offering degrees at the bachelor's and master's levels and postbachelor's certificates. It has a 60-acre campus in Oakland near San Francisco.

Academic Information The faculty has 136 members (24% full-time), 54% with terminal degrees. The undergraduate student-faculty ratio is 13:1. The library holds 109,297 titles, 8,003 serial subscriptions, and 5,078 audiovisual materials. Special programs include academic remediation, services for learning-disabled students, study abroad, advanced placement credit, accelerated degree programs, ESL programs, double majors, independent study, distance learning, self-designed majors, summer session for credit, part-time degree programs (evenings, weekends), adult/continuing education programs, and internships. The most frequently chosen baccalaureate fields are business/marketing, health professions and related sciences, psychology.
Student Body Statistics The student body totals 1,048, of whom 620 are undergraduates (86 freshmen). 75 percent are women and 25 percent are men. Students come from 15 states and territories and 13 other countries. 92 percent are from California. 3.6 percent are international students.
Expenses for 2006–07 *Application fee:* $50. *Comprehensive fee:* $30,710 includes full-time tuition ($22,470), mandatory fees ($240), and college room and board ($8000). *College room only:* $4200. Full-time tuition and fees vary according to course load. Room and board charges vary according to board plan. *Part-time tuition:* $750 per unit. *Part-time mandatory fees:* $120 per term.
Financial Aid Forms of aid include need-based and non-need-based scholarships, athletic grants, and part-time jobs. The average aided 2006–07 undergraduate received an aid package worth an estimated $15,554. The application deadline for financial aid is June 30 with a priority deadline of March 2.
Freshman Admission Holy Names University requires an essay, a high school transcript, SAT or ACT scores, and TOEFL scores for international students. An interview is required for some. The application deadline for regular admission is August 1.
Transfer Admission Standardized test scores are required for some. The application deadline for admission is August 1.
Entrance Difficulty Holy Names University assesses its entrance difficulty level as moderately difficult. For the fall 2006 freshman class, 63 percent of the applicants were accepted.
For Further Information Contact Mr. Michael Miller, Vice President for Student Affairs, Holy Names University, 3500 Mountain Boulevard, Oakland, CA 94619. *Telephone:* 510-436-1351 or 800-430-1321 (toll-free). *Fax:* 510-436-1325. *E-mail:* admissions@hnu.edu. *Web site:* http://www.hnu. edu/.

HOPE INTERNATIONAL UNIVERSITY
Fullerton, California

Hope International University is a coed, private, comprehensive institution, founded in 1928, affiliated with the Christian Churches and Churches of Christ, offering degrees at the associate, bachelor's, and master's levels. It has a 16-acre campus in Fullerton near Los Angeles.

Academic Information The faculty has 211 members (13% full-time), 50% with terminal degrees. The undergraduate student-faculty ratio is 16:1. The library holds 100,000 titles and 500 serial subscriptions. Special programs include academic remediation, study abroad, advanced placement credit, accelerated degree programs, ESL programs, double majors, independent study, distance learning, summer session for credit, part-time degree programs (daytime, evenings), adult/continuing education programs, internships, and arrangement for off-campus study with California State University, Fullerton. The most frequently chosen baccalaureate fields are family and consumer sciences, business/marketing, theology and religious vocations.
Student Body Statistics The student body totals 903, of whom 660 are undergraduates (83 freshmen). 52 percent are women and 48 percent are men. Students come from 26 states and territories and 22 other countries. 76 percent are from California. 2.9 percent are international students. 40 percent of the 2006 graduating class went on to graduate and professional schools.

Expenses for 2006–07 *Application fee:* $40. *Comprehensive fee:* $26,070 includes full-time tuition ($18,400), mandatory fees ($420), and college room and board ($7250). *College room only:* $4200. Full-time tuition and fees vary according to program. Room and board charges vary according to board plan. *Part-time tuition:* $685 per unit. Part-time tuition varies according to program.

Financial Aid Forms of aid include need-based and non-need-based scholarships and part-time jobs. The priority application deadline for financial aid is March 2.

Freshman Admission Hope International University requires an essay, a high school transcript, a minimum 2.5 high school GPA, 2 recommendations, rank in upper 50% of high school class, SAT or ACT scores, and TOEFL scores for international students. SAT scores are recommended. An interview is required for some. The application deadline for regular admission is June 1.

Transfer Admission The application deadline for admission is June 1.

Entrance Difficulty Hope International University assesses its entrance difficulty level as moderately difficult. For the fall 2006 freshman class, 67 percent of the applicants were accepted.

For Further Information Contact Ms. Midge Madden, Office Manager, Hope International University, 2500 East Nutwood Avenue, Fullerton, CA 92831-3138. *Telephone:* 714-879-3901 or 800-762-1294 (toll-free). *Fax:* 714-526-0231. *E-mail:* mfmadden@hiu.edu. *Web site:* http://www.hiu.edu/.

HSI LAI UNIVERSITY

See University of the West.

HUMBOLDT STATE UNIVERSITY

Arcata, California

Humboldt State University is a coed, public, comprehensive unit of California State University System, founded in 1913, offering degrees at the bachelor's and master's levels. It has a 161-acre campus in Arcata.

Academic Information The faculty has 551 members (52% full-time), 56% with terminal degrees. The undergraduate student-faculty ratio is 18:1. The library holds 1 million titles, 1,737 serial subscriptions, and 20,962 audiovisual materials. Special programs include academic remediation, services for learning-disabled students, an honors program, cooperative (work-study) education, study abroad, advanced placement credit, ESL programs, double majors, independent study, distance learning, self-designed majors, summer session for credit, part-time degree programs (daytime, summer), adult/continuing education programs, internships, and arrangement for off-campus study with members of the National Student Exchange, California State University System.

Student Body Statistics The student body totals 7,435, of whom 6,466 are undergraduates (958 freshmen). 54 percent are women and 46 percent are men. Students come from 47 states and territories and 12 other countries. 87 percent are from California. 0.7 percent are international students.

Expenses for 2007–08 *Application fee:* $55. *Nonresident tuition:* $339 per unit part-time.

Financial Aid Forms of aid include need-based and non-need-based scholarships and part-time jobs. The priority application deadline for financial aid is March 2.

Freshman Admission Humboldt State University requires a high school transcript, a minimum 2.0 high school GPA, and TOEFL scores for international students. SAT or ACT scores are required for some. The application deadline for regular admission is November 30.

Transfer Admission The application deadline for admission is November 30.

Entrance Difficulty Humboldt State University assesses its entrance difficulty level as moderately difficult; very difficult for out-of-state applicants. For the fall 2006 freshman class, 80 percent of the applicants were accepted.

For Further Information Contact Ms. Rebecca Kalal, Assistant Director of Admissions, Humboldt State University, 1 Harpst Street, Arcata, CA 95521-8299. *Telephone:* 707-826-6221. *Fax:* 707-826-6190. *E-mail:* hsuinfo@laurel.humboldt.edu. *Web site:* http://www.humboldt.edu/.

HUMPHREYS COLLEGE

Stockton, California

http://www.humphreys.edu/

INSTITUTE OF COMPUTER TECHNOLOGY

See LA College International.

INTERIOR DESIGNERS INSTITUTE

Newport Beach, California

http://www.idi.edu/

INTERNATIONAL TECHNOLOGICAL UNIVERSITY

Santa Clara, California

http://www.itu.edu/

ITT TECHNICAL INSTITUTE

Anaheim, California

ITT Technical Institute is a coed, proprietary, primarily two-year college of ITT Educational Services, Inc, founded in 1982, offering degrees at the associate and bachelor's levels. It has a 5-acre campus in Anaheim near Los Angeles.

Expenses for 2006–07 *Application fee:* $100. Contact school for program costs.

Financial Aid Forms of aid include need-based scholarships and part-time jobs. The application deadline for financial aid is continuous.

Freshman Admission ITT Technical Institute requires a high school transcript, an interview, TOEFL scores for international students, and Wonderlic aptitude test. Recommendations are recommended. The application deadline for regular admission is rolling.

Transfer Admission The application deadline for admission is rolling.

Entrance Difficulty ITT Technical Institute assesses its entrance difficulty level as minimally difficult.

For Further Information Contact Ms. Sheryl Schulgen, Director of Recruitment, ITT Technical Institute, 525 North Muller Avenue, Anaheim, CA 92801. *Telephone:* 714-535-3700. *Fax:* 714-535-1802. *Web site:* http://www.itt-tech.edu/.

ITT TECHNICAL INSTITUTE

Clovis, California

ITT Technical Institute is a coed, proprietary, four-year college, founded in 2005, offering degrees at the associate and bachelor's levels.

Expenses for 2006–07 Contact school directly for program costs.

For Further Information Contact Ms. Linda Stolling, Director of Recruitment, ITT Technical Institute, 362 North Clovis Avenue, Clovis, NM 93612. *Telephone:* 559-325-5400. *Fax:* 559-325-5499. *Web site:* http://www.itt-tech.edu/campus/school.cfm?lloc_num=61.

ITT TECHNICAL INSTITUTE

Lathrop, California

ITT Technical Institute is a coed, proprietary, primarily two-year college of ITT Educational Services, Inc, founded in 1997, offering degrees at the associate and bachelor's levels.

ITT Technical Institute (continued)

Expenses for 2006–07 *Application fee:* $100. Contact school for program costs.

Financial Aid Forms of aid include need-based scholarships and part-time jobs. The application deadline for financial aid is continuous.

Freshman Admission ITT Technical Institute requires a high school transcript, an interview, and Wonderlic aptitude test. Recommendations are recommended. The application deadline for regular admission is rolling.

Transfer Admission The application deadline for admission is rolling.

Entrance Difficulty ITT Technical Institute assesses its entrance difficulty level as minimally difficult.

For Further Information Contact Ms. Kathy Paradis, Director of Recruitment, ITT Technical Institute, 16916 South Harlan Road, Lathrop, CA 95330. *Telephone:* 209-858-0077 or 800-346-1786 (toll-free in-state). *Fax:* 209-858-0277. *Web site:* http://www.itt-tech.edu/.

ITT TECHNICAL INSTITUTE
Oxnard, California

ITT Technical Institute is a coed, proprietary, primarily two-year college of ITT Educational Services, Inc, founded in 1993, offering degrees at the associate and bachelor's levels. It is located in Oxnard near Los Angeles.

Expenses for 2006–07 *Application fee:* $100. Contact school for program costs.

Financial Aid Forms of aid include need-based scholarships and part-time jobs. The application deadline for financial aid is continuous.

Freshman Admission ITT Technical Institute requires a high school transcript, an interview, and Wonderlic aptitude test. Recommendations are recommended. The application deadline for regular admission is rolling.

Transfer Admission The application deadline for admission is rolling.

Entrance Difficulty ITT Technical Institute assesses its entrance difficulty level as minimally difficult.

For Further Information Contact Milo Hager, Director of Recruitment, ITT Technical Institute, 2051 Solar Drive, Building B, Oxnard, CA 93036. *Telephone:* 805-988-0143 or 800-530-1582 (toll-free in-state). *Fax:* 805-988-1813. *Web site:* http://www.itt-tech.edu/.

ITT TECHNICAL INSTITUTE
Rancho Cordova, California

ITT Technical Institute is a coed, proprietary, primarily two-year college of ITT Educational Services, Inc, founded in 1954, offering degrees at the associate and bachelor's levels. It has a 5-acre campus in Rancho Cordova.

Expenses for 2006–07 *Application fee:* $100. Contact school for program costs.

Financial Aid Forms of aid include need-based scholarships and part-time jobs. The application deadline for financial aid is continuous.

Freshman Admission ITT Technical Institute requires a high school transcript, an interview, TOEFL scores for international students, and Wonderlic aptitude test. Recommendations are recommended. The application deadline for regular admission is rolling.

Transfer Admission The application deadline for admission is rolling.

Entrance Difficulty ITT Technical Institute assesses its entrance difficulty level as minimally difficult.

For Further Information Contact Mr. Vance Klinke, Director of Recruitment, ITT Technical Institute, 10863 Gold Center Drive, Rancho Cordova, CA 95670. *Telephone:* 916-851-3900 or 800-488-8466 (toll-free). *Fax:* 916-851-9225. *Web site:* http://www.itt-tech.edu/.

ITT TECHNICAL INSTITUTE
San Bernardino, California

ITT Technical Institute is a coed, proprietary, primarily two-year college of ITT Educational Services, Inc, founded in 1987, offering degrees at the associate and bachelor's levels. It is located in San Bernardino near Los Angeles.

Expenses for 2006–07 *Application fee:* $100. Contact school for program costs.

Financial Aid Forms of aid include need-based scholarships and part-time jobs. The application deadline for financial aid is continuous.

Freshman Admission ITT Technical Institute requires a high school transcript, an interview, TOEFL scores for international students, and Wonderlic aptitude test. Recommendations are recommended. The application deadline for regular admission is rolling.

Transfer Admission The application deadline for admission is rolling.

Entrance Difficulty ITT Technical Institute assesses its entrance difficulty level as minimally difficult.

For Further Information Contact Director of Recruitment, ITT Technical Institute, 670 East Carnegie Drive, San Bernardino, CA 92408. *Telephone:* 909-806-4600 or 800-888-3801 (toll-free in-state). *Fax:* 909-806-4699. *Web site:* http://www.itt-tech.edu/.

ITT TECHNICAL INSTITUTE
San Diego, California

ITT Technical Institute is a coed, proprietary, primarily two-year college of ITT Educational Services, Inc, founded in 1981, offering degrees at the associate and bachelor's levels.

Expenses for 2006–07 *Application fee:* $100. Contact school for program costs.

Financial Aid Forms of aid include need-based scholarships and part-time jobs. The application deadline for financial aid is continuous.

Freshman Admission ITT Technical Institute requires a high school transcript, an interview, and Wonderlic aptitude test. Recommendations are recommended. The application deadline for regular admission is rolling.

Transfer Admission The application deadline for admission is rolling.

Entrance Difficulty ITT Technical Institute assesses its entrance difficulty level as minimally difficult.

For Further Information Contact Ron Begora, Director of Recruitment, ITT Technical Institute, 9680 Granite Ridge Drive, San Diego, CA 92123. *Telephone:* 858-571-8500 or 800-883-0380 (toll-free in-state). *Fax:* 858-571-1277. *Web site:* http://www.itt-tech.edu/.

ITT TECHNICAL INSTITUTE
San Dimas, California

ITT Technical Institute is a coed, proprietary, primarily two-year college of ITT Educational Services, Inc, founded in 1982, offering degrees at the associate and bachelor's levels. It has a 4-acre campus in San Dimas near Los Angeles.

Expenses for 2006–07 *Application fee:* $100. Contact school for program costs.

Financial Aid Forms of aid include need-based scholarships and part-time jobs. The application deadline for financial aid is continuous.

Freshman Admission ITT Technical Institute requires a high school transcript, an interview, TOEFL scores for international students, and Wonderlic aptitude test. Recommendations are recommended. The application deadline for regular admission is rolling.

Transfer Admission The application deadline for admission is rolling.

Entrance Difficulty ITT Technical Institute assesses its entrance difficulty level as minimally difficult.

For Further Information Contact Ms. Laura Brozeck, Director of Recruitment, ITT Technical Institute, 650 West Cienega Avenue, San Dimas, CA 91773. *Telephone:* 909-971-2300 or 800-414-6522 (toll-free in-state). *Fax:* 626-337-5271. *Web site:* http://www.itt-tech.edu/.

ITT TECHNICAL INSTITUTE
Sylmar, California

ITT Technical Institute is a coed, proprietary, primarily two-year college of ITT Educational Services, Inc, founded in 1982, offering degrees at the associate and bachelor's levels. It is located in Sylmar near Los Angeles.

Expenses for 2006–07 *Application fee:* $100. Contact school for program costs.
Financial Aid Forms of aid include need-based scholarships and part-time jobs. The application deadline for financial aid is continuous.
Freshman Admission ITT Technical Institute requires a high school transcript, an interview, and Wonderlic aptitude test. Recommendations are recommended. The application deadline for regular admission is rolling.
Transfer Admission The application deadline for admission is rolling.
Entrance Difficulty ITT Technical Institute assesses its entrance difficulty level as minimally difficult.
For Further Information Contact Ms. Kelly Christensen, Director of Recruitment, ITT Technical Institute, 12669 Encinitas Avenue, Sylmar, CA 91342. *Telephone:* 818-364-5151 or 800-363-2086 (toll-free in-state). *Fax:* 818-364-5150. *Web site:* http://www.itt-tech.edu/.

ITT TECHNICAL INSTITUTE
Torrance, California

ITT Technical Institute is a coed, proprietary, primarily two-year college of ITT Educational Services, Inc, founded in 1987, offering degrees at the associate and bachelor's levels. It is located in Torrance near Los Angeles.

Expenses for 2006–07 *Application fee:* $100. Contact school for program costs.
Financial Aid Forms of aid include need-based scholarships and part-time jobs. The application deadline for financial aid is continuous.
Freshman Admission ITT Technical Institute requires a high school transcript, an interview, TOEFL scores for international students, and Wonderlic aptitude test. Recommendations are recommended. The application deadline for regular admission is rolling.
Transfer Admission The application deadline for admission is rolling.
Entrance Difficulty ITT Technical Institute assesses its entrance difficulty level as minimally difficult.
For Further Information Contact Mr. Freddie Polk, Director of Recruitment, ITT Technical Institute, 20050 South Vermont Avenue, Torrance, CA 90502. *Telephone:* 310-380-1555. *Fax:* 310-380-1557. *Web site:* http://www.itt-tech.edu/.

JOHN F. KENNEDY UNIVERSITY
Pleasant Hill, California
http://www.jfku.edu/

THE KING'S COLLEGE AND SEMINARY
Van Nuys, California
http://www.kingscollege.edu/

LA COLLEGE INTERNATIONAL
Los Angeles, California

LA College International is a coed, proprietary, four-year college, founded in 1981, offering degrees at the associate and bachelor's levels.

Academic Information The faculty has 28 members, 4% with terminal degrees. The student-faculty ratio is 15:1. The library holds 2,000 titles. Special programs include advanced placement credit, independent study, and internships.
Student Body Statistics The student body is made up of 137 undergraduates (124 freshmen). 45 percent are women and 55 percent are men. Students come from 1 state or territory and 3 other countries.
Expenses for 2006–07 *Application fee:* $75. *Tuition:* $12,566 full-time. *Mandatory fees:* $506 full-time.
Financial Aid Forms of aid include need-based and non-need-based scholarships. The application deadline for financial aid is continuous.
Freshman Admission LA College International requires a high school transcript and an interview. CPAt is required for some.
Entrance Difficulty LA College International has an open admission policy.
For Further Information Contact Director of Admissions, LA College International, 3200 Wilshire Boulevard 4th Floor, Los Angeles, CA 90010. *Telephone:* 213-381-3333 or 800-57 GO ICT (toll-free in-state). *Fax:* 213-383-9369. *Web site:* http://www.lac.edu/.

LAGUNA COLLEGE OF ART & DESIGN
Laguna Beach, California
http://www.lagunacollege.edu/

LA SIERRA UNIVERSITY
Riverside, California

La Sierra University is a coed, private, Seventh-day Adventist, comprehensive institution, founded in 1922, offering degrees at the bachelor's, master's, and doctoral levels and post-master's and postbachelor's certificates. It has a 100-acre campus in Riverside near Los Angeles.

Academic Information The faculty has 178 members (52% full-time), 43% with terminal degrees. The undergraduate student-faculty ratio is 14:1. The library holds 261,629 titles, 1,072 serial subscriptions, and 10,702 audiovisual materials. Special programs include academic remediation, services for learning-disabled students, an honors program, study abroad, advanced placement credit, accelerated degree programs, ESL programs, double majors, independent study, self-designed majors, summer session for credit, part-time degree programs (daytime, evenings, summer), adult/continuing education programs, internships, and arrangement for off-campus study with Loma Linda University. The most frequently chosen baccalaureate fields are biological/life sciences, business/marketing, liberal arts/general studies.
Student Body Statistics The student body totals 1,896, of whom 1,578 are undergraduates (323 freshmen). 56 percent are women and 44 percent are men. Students come from 23 states and territories and 27 other countries. 86 percent are from California. 9.8 percent are international students.
Expenses for 2007–08 *Application fee:* $30. *Comprehensive fee:* $28,176 includes full-time tuition ($21,060), mandatory fees ($786), and college room and board ($6330). *Part-time tuition:* $585 per unit.
Financial Aid Forms of aid include need-based and non-need-based scholarships and part-time jobs. The average aided 2005–06 undergraduate received an aid package worth $15,006.
Freshman Admission La Sierra University requires an essay, a high school transcript, a minimum 2.5 high school GPA, 2 recommendations, SAT or ACT scores, and TOEFL scores for international students. An interview is required for some. The application deadline for regular admission is rolling.
Transfer Admission The application deadline for admission is rolling.
Entrance Difficulty La Sierra University assesses its entrance difficulty level as moderately difficult. For the fall 2006 freshman class, 33 percent of the applicants were accepted.
For Further Information Contact Bobby Brown, Director of Admissions, La Sierra University, 45 Riverwalk Parkway, Riverside, CA 92515. *Telephone:* 951-785-2176 or 800-874-5587 (toll-free). *Fax:* 951-785-2901. *E-mail:* ivy@lasierra.edu. *Web site:* http://www.lasierra.edu/.

LEE COLLEGE AT THE UNIVERSITY OF JUDAISM

See University of Judaism.

LIFE PACIFIC COLLEGE

San Dimas, California

Life Pacific College is a coed, private, four-year college, founded in 1923, affiliated with the International Church of the Foursquare Gospel, offering degrees at the associate and bachelor's levels. It has a 9-acre campus in San Dimas near Los Angeles.

For Further Information Contact Ms. Gina Nicodemus, Director of Admissions, Life Pacific College, 1100 Covina Boulevard, San Dimas, CA 91773-3298. *Telephone:* 909-599-5433 Ext. 314 or 877-886-5433 Ext. 314 (toll-free). *Fax:* 909-706-3070. *E-mail:* adm@lifepacific.edu. *Web site:* http://www.lifepacific.edu/.

LINCOLN UNIVERSITY

Oakland, California

Lincoln University is a coed, private, comprehensive institution, founded in 1919, offering degrees at the bachelor's and master's levels. It has a 2-acre campus in Oakland.

Academic Information The faculty has 35 members (23% full-time). The undergraduate student-faculty ratio is 14:1. The library holds 17,752 titles and 762 serial subscriptions. Special programs include advanced placement credit, ESL programs, summer session for credit, and internships.
Student Body Statistics The student body totals 227, of whom 54 are undergraduates (28 freshmen). 50 percent are women and 50 percent are men. 68 percent of the 2006 graduating class went on to graduate and professional schools.
Expenses for 2007–08 *Application fee:* $75. *Tuition:* $7320 full-time, $305 per unit part-time. *Mandatory fees:* $400 full-time.
Freshman Admission Lincoln University requires a high school transcript, a minimum 2.0 high school GPA, and TOEFL scores for international students. An essay, recommendations, and an interview are required for some. The application deadline for regular admission is August 22.
Transfer Admission The application deadline for admission is August 22.
Entrance Difficulty Lincoln University assesses its entrance difficulty level as minimally difficult. For the fall 2006 freshman class, 90 percent of the applicants were accepted.
For Further Information Contact Toni Ong, Student Service Coordinator, Lincoln University, 401 15th Street, Oakland, CA 94612-2801. *Telephone:* 510-628-8010. *Fax:* 510-628-8012. *E-mail:* studentservices@lincolnuca.edu. *Web site:* http://www.lincolnuca.edu/.

LOMA LINDA UNIVERSITY

Loma Linda, California

Loma Linda University is a coed, private, Seventh-day Adventist, upper-level institution, founded in 1905, offering degrees at the associate, bachelor's, master's, doctoral, and first professional levels and postbachelor's certificates (associate degree and nursing students may enter at the sophomore level). It is located in Loma Linda near Los Angeles.

Academic Information The faculty has 155 members (70% full-time), 72% with terminal degrees. The undergraduate student-faculty ratio is 8:1. The library holds 338,418 titles and 1,671 serial subscriptions. Special programs include ESL programs, independent study, distance learning, internships, and arrangement for off-campus study. The most frequently chosen baccalaureate field is health professions and related sciences.
Student Body Statistics The student body totals 3,972, of whom 1,212 are undergraduates. 75 percent are women and 25 percent are men.

Students come from 29 states and territories and 30 other countries. 87 percent are from California. 6.6 percent are international students.
Expenses for 2007–08 *Application fee:* $60. *Tuition:* $25,860 full-time, $485 per unit part-time. *Mandatory fees:* $1460 full-time, $430 per term part-time. *College room only:* $2460.
Financial Aid Forms of aid include need-based scholarships and part-time jobs. The priority application deadline for financial aid is March 2.
For Further Information Contact Admissions Office, Loma Linda University, Loma Linda, CA 92350. *Telephone:* 909-558-1000. *Web site:* http://www.llu.edu/.

LOYOLA MARYMOUNT UNIVERSITY

Los Angeles, California

Loyola Marymount University is a coed, private, Roman Catholic, comprehensive institution, founded in 1911, offering degrees at the bachelor's, master's, doctoral, and first professional levels and postbachelor's certificates. It has a 128-acre campus in Los Angeles.

Academic Information The faculty has 1,154 members (41% full-time). The undergraduate student-faculty ratio is 11:1. The library holds 495,920 titles and 10,057 serial subscriptions. Special programs include services for learning-disabled students, an honors program, cooperative (work-study) education, study abroad, advanced placement credit, accelerated degree programs, double majors, independent study, self-designed majors, summer session for credit, part-time degree programs (daytime, evenings, summer), adult/continuing education programs, and internships.
Student Body Statistics The student body totals 8,903, of whom 5,746 are undergraduates (1,264 freshmen). 58 percent are women and 42 percent are men. Students come from 51 states and territories and 38 other countries. 74 percent are from California. 1.9 percent are international students.
Expenses for 2006–07 *Application fee:* $50. *Comprehensive fee:* $41,124 includes full-time tuition ($29,198), mandatory fees ($636), and college room and board ($11,290). *College room only:* $7890. Room and board charges vary according to board plan and housing facility. *Part-time tuition:* $1216 per unit. Part-time tuition varies according to course load.
Financial Aid Forms of aid include need-based and non-need-based scholarships, athletic grants, and part-time jobs. The application deadline for financial aid is July 30 with a priority deadline of February 15.
Freshman Admission Loyola Marymount University requires an essay, a high school transcript, 2 recommendations, SAT or ACT scores, and TOEFL scores for international students. An interview is recommended. The application deadline for regular admission is January 15.
Transfer Admission The application deadline for admission is June 1.
Entrance Difficulty Loyola Marymount University assesses its entrance difficulty level as very difficult. For the fall 2006 freshman class, 54 percent of the applicants were accepted.
For Further Information Contact Mr. Matthew X. Fissinger, Director of Admissions, Loyola Marymount University, 1 LMU Drive Suite 100, Los Angeles, CA 90045-8350. *Telephone:* 310-338-2750 or 800-LMU-INFO (toll-free). *E-mail:* admissions@lmu.edu. *Web site:* http://www.lmu.edu/.

MARYMOUNT COLLEGE, PALOS VERDES, CALIFORNIA

Rancho Palos Verdes, California

Marymount College, Palos Verdes, California is a coed, private, Roman Catholic, two-year college, founded in 1932, offering degrees at the associate level. It has a 26-acre campus in Rancho Palos Verdes near Los Angeles.

Academic Information The faculty has 91 members (46% full-time), 35% with terminal degrees. The student-faculty ratio is 16:1. The library holds 42,104 titles and 328 serial subscriptions. Special programs include academic remediation, services for learning-disabled students, an honors program, study abroad, advanced placement credit, ESL programs,

independent study, summer session for credit, part-time degree programs (daytime, weekends, summer), adult/continuing education programs, and internships.

Student Body Statistics The student body is made up of 652 undergraduates (305 freshmen). 54 percent are women and 46 percent are men. Students come from 26 states and territories and 21 other countries. 77 percent are from California. 10.3 percent are international students.

Expenses for 2007–08 *Application fee:* $35. *Comprehensive fee:* $31,445 includes full-time tuition ($21,230), mandatory fees ($321), and college room and board ($9894). *Part-time tuition:* $700 per unit.

Financial Aid Forms of aid include need-based scholarships and part-time jobs. The priority application deadline for financial aid is March 2.

Freshman Admission Marymount College, Palos Verdes, California requires a high school transcript. A minimum 2.0 high school GPA, SAT or ACT scores, and TOEFL scores for international students are recommended. An essay, recommendations, and an interview are required for some. The application deadline for regular admission is July 1.

Transfer Admission The application deadline for admission is August 15.

Entrance Difficulty Marymount College, Palos Verdes, California assesses its entrance difficulty level as minimally difficult. For the fall 2006 freshman class, 66 percent of the applicants were accepted.

For Further Information Contact Ms. Nina Lococo, Dean of Admission and Financial Aid, Marymount College, Palos Verdes, California, 30800 Palos Verdes Drive East, Rancho Palos Verdes, CA 90815. *Telephone:* 310-377-5501. *Fax:* 310-265-0962. *E-mail:* admissions@marymountpv.edu. *Web site:* http://www.marymountpv.edu/.

THE MASTER'S COLLEGE AND SEMINARY
Santa Clarita, California

The Master's College and Seminary is a coed, private, nondenominational, comprehensive institution, founded in 1927, offering degrees at the bachelor's, master's, doctoral, and first professional levels and first professional certificates. It has a 110-acre campus in Santa Clarita near Los Angeles.

Academic Information The faculty has 188 members (38% full-time), 52% with terminal degrees. The undergraduate student-faculty ratio is 10:1. The library holds 178,337 titles, 12,867 serial subscriptions, and 7,413 audiovisual materials. Special programs include academic remediation, services for learning-disabled students, cooperative (work-study) education, study abroad, advanced placement credit, accelerated degree programs, double majors, independent study, summer session for credit, part-time degree programs (daytime, evenings, weekends), external degree programs, adult/continuing education programs, and internships. The most frequently chosen baccalaureate fields are business/marketing, education, philosophy and religious studies.

Student Body Statistics The student body totals 1,521, of whom 1,130 are undergraduates (189 freshmen). 50 percent are women and 50 percent are men. Students come from 43 states and territories and 24 other countries. 66 percent are from California. 2.8 percent are international students. 11 percent of the 2006 graduating class went on to graduate and professional schools.

Expenses for 2006–07 *Application fee:* $40. *Comprehensive fee:* $27,670 includes full-time tuition ($20,770) and college room and board ($6900). *College room only:* $3860. Full-time tuition varies according to course load, degree level, and program. Room and board charges vary according to board plan. *Part-time tuition:* $870 per credit hour. Part-time tuition varies according to course load, degree level, and program.

Financial Aid Forms of aid include need-based and non-need-based scholarships, athletic grants, and part-time jobs. The average aided 2005–06 undergraduate received an aid package worth $15,054. The priority application deadline for financial aid is March 2.

Freshman Admission The Master's College and Seminary requires an essay, a high school transcript, a minimum 2.50 high school GPA, 2 recommendations, an interview, SAT or ACT scores, and TOEFL scores for international students. The application deadline for for early action it is November 15.

Transfer Admission The application deadline for admission is March 2.

Entrance Difficulty The Master's College and Seminary assesses its entrance difficulty level as moderately difficult. For the fall 2006 freshman class, 29 percent of the applicants were accepted.

For Further Information Contact Ms. Hollie Gorsh, Director of Admissions, The Master's College and Seminary, 21726 Placerita Canyon Road, Santa Clarita, CA 91321. *Telephone:* 661-259-3540 Ext. 3369 or 800-568-6248 (toll-free). *Fax:* 661-288-1037. *E-mail:* admissions@masters.edu. *Web site:* http://www.masters.edu/.

MENLO COLLEGE
Atherton, California

Menlo College is a coed, private, four-year college, founded in 1927, offering degrees at the bachelor's level. It has a 45-acre campus in Atherton near San Francisco.

Academic Information The faculty has 71 members (32% full-time), 38% with terminal degrees. The student-faculty ratio is 18:1. The library holds 64,700 titles and 175 serial subscriptions. Special programs include academic remediation, services for learning-disabled students, an honors program, cooperative (work-study) education, study abroad, advanced placement credit, accelerated degree programs, double majors, independent study, self-designed majors, summer session for credit, part-time degree programs (daytime, evenings, summer), adult/continuing education programs, and internships. The most frequently chosen baccalaureate fields are business/marketing, communications/journalism, liberal arts/general studies.

Student Body Statistics The student body is made up of 769 undergraduates (183 freshmen). 40 percent are women and 60 percent are men. Students come from 24 states and territories and 34 other countries. 82 percent are from California. 9.6 percent are international students.

Expenses for 2006–07 *Application fee:* $40. *Comprehensive fee:* $36,020 includes full-time tuition ($25,920), mandatory fees ($300), and college room and board ($9800). Full-time tuition and fees vary according to program. Room and board charges vary according to housing facility. *Part-time tuition:* $1080 per unit. Part-time tuition varies according to course load and program.

Financial Aid Forms of aid include need-based and non-need-based scholarships and part-time jobs. The average aided 2006–07 undergraduate received an aid package worth an estimated $19,677. The priority application deadline for financial aid is March 2.

Freshman Admission Menlo College requires an essay, a high school transcript, 1 recommendation, SAT or ACT scores, and TOEFL scores for international students. A minimum 3.0 high school GPA and an interview are recommended. The application deadline for regular admission is rolling; for nonresidents it is rolling; and for early action it is December 1.

Transfer Admission The application deadline for admission is rolling.

Entrance Difficulty Menlo College assesses its entrance difficulty level as moderately difficult. For the fall 2006 freshman class, 69 percent of the applicants were accepted.

For Further Information Contact Mr. Ken Bowman, Director of Admission, Menlo College, 1000 El Camino Real, Atherton, CA 94027. *Telephone:* 650-543-3932 or 800-556-3656 (toll-free). *Fax:* 650-543-4496. *E-mail:* admissions@menlo.edu. *Web site:* http://www.menlo.edu/.

MILLS COLLEGE
Oakland, California

Mills College is an undergraduate: women only; graduate: coed, private, comprehensive institution, founded in 1852, offering degrees at the bachelor's, master's, and doctoral levels and postbachelor's certificates. It has a 135-acre campus in Oakland near San Francisco.

Academic Information The faculty has 189 members (47% full-time). The undergraduate student-faculty ratio is 11:1. The library holds 254,351 titles, 13,211 serial subscriptions, and 7,640 audiovisual materials. Special programs include services for learning-disabled students, an honors program, study abroad, advanced placement credit, double majors, independent study, self-designed majors, adult/continuing education programs, internships, and arrangement for off-campus study with

Mills College (continued)

University of California, Berkeley, California State University, Hayward, Sonoma State University, 9 other California colleges, American University, Agnes Scott College, Barnard College, Fisk University, Hollins College, Howard University, Manhattanville College, Mount Holyoke College, Simmons College, Spelman College, Swarthmore College, Wellesley College, Wheaton College. The most frequently chosen baccalaureate fields are English, social sciences, visual and performing arts.

Student Body Statistics The student body totals 1,410, of whom 927 are undergraduates (200 freshmen). 100 percent are women. Students come from 35 states and territories and 6 other countries. 71 percent are from California. 3.5 percent are international students.

Expenses for 2006–07 *Application fee:* $40. *Comprehensive fee:* $43,264 includes full-time tuition ($30,300), mandatory fees ($2724), and college room and board ($10,240). *College room only:* $5460. Full-time tuition and fees vary according to course load. Room and board charges vary according to board plan and housing facility. *Part-time tuition:* $5090 per course. Part-time tuition varies according to course load.

Financial Aid Forms of aid include need-based and non-need-based scholarships and part-time jobs. The average aided 2005–06 undergraduate received an aid package worth $24,002. The application deadline for financial aid is February 15 with a priority deadline of February 15.

Freshman Admission Mills College requires a high school transcript, 3 recommendations, essay or graded paper, SAT or ACT scores, and TOEFL scores for international students. An interview and SAT Subject Test scores are recommended. The application deadline for regular admission is May 1 and for early action it is November 15.

Transfer Admission The application deadline for admission is March 1.

Entrance Difficulty Mills College assesses its entrance difficulty level as moderately difficult. For the fall 2006 freshman class, 65 percent of the applicants were accepted.

For Further Information Contact Ms. Giulietta Aquino, Vice President of Enrollment Management, Mills College, 5000 MacArthur Boulevard, Oakland, CA 94613-1301. *Telephone:* 510-430-2135 or 800-87-MILLS (toll-free). *Fax:* 510-430-3314. *E-mail:* admission@mills.edu. *Web site:* http://www.mills.edu/.

MOUNT ST. MARY'S COLLEGE

Los Angeles, California

Mount St. Mary's College is a coed, primarily women's, private, Roman Catholic, comprehensive institution, founded in 1925, offering degrees at the associate, bachelor's, and master's levels and postbachelor's certificates. It has a 71-acre campus in Los Angeles.

Academic Information The faculty has 327 members (24% full-time), 24% with terminal degrees. The undergraduate student-faculty ratio is 19:1. The library holds 140,000 titles and 750 serial subscriptions. Special programs include academic remediation, services for learning-disabled students, an honors program, study abroad, advanced placement credit, accelerated degree programs, Freshman Honors College, ESL programs, double majors, independent study, self-designed majors, summer session for credit, part-time degree programs, adult/continuing education programs, internships, and arrangement for off-campus study with University of Southern California, University of California, Los Angeles, Sisters of Saint Joseph College Consortium. The most frequently chosen baccalaureate fields are health professions and related sciences, business/marketing, social sciences.

Student Body Statistics The student body totals 2,384, of whom 1,921 are undergraduates (411 freshmen). 94 percent are women and 6 percent are men. Students come from 13 states and territories. 96 percent are from California. 0.2 percent are international students. 30 percent of the 2006 graduating class went on to graduate and professional schools.

Expenses for 2006–07 *Application fee:* $40. *Comprehensive fee:* $32,897 includes full-time tuition ($23,380), mandatory fees ($770), and college room and board ($8747). *Part-time tuition:* $900 per unit.

Financial Aid Forms of aid include need-based and non-need-based scholarships and part-time jobs. The application deadline for financial aid is May 15 with a priority deadline of March 2.

Freshman Admission Mount St. Mary's College requires an essay, a high school transcript, a minimum 2.0 high school GPA, 1

recommendation, SAT or ACT scores, and TOEFL scores for international students. A minimum 3.0 high school GPA, an interview, and SAT scores are recommended. The application deadline for regular admission is February 15 and for early action it is December 1.

Transfer Admission The application deadline for admission is March 15.

Entrance Difficulty Mount St. Mary's College assesses its entrance difficulty level as moderately difficult; minimally difficult for associate degree programs. For the fall 2006 freshman class, 86 percent of the applicants were accepted.

For Further Information Contact Mr. Dean Kilgour, Dean of Admissions, Mount St. Mary's College, 12001 Chalon Road, Los Angeles, CA 90049-1599. *Telephone:* 310-954-4252 or 800-999-9893 (toll-free). *E-mail:* admissions@msmc.la.edu. *Web site:* http://www.msmc.la.edu/.

MT. SIERRA COLLEGE

Monrovia, California

http://www.mtsierra.edu/

MUSICIANS INSTITUTE

Hollywood, California

http://www.mi.edu/

THE NATIONAL HISPANIC UNIVERSITY

San Jose, California

http://www.nhu.edu/

NATIONAL UNIVERSITY

La Jolla, California

National University is a coed, private, comprehensive unit of National University System, founded in 1971, offering degrees at the associate, bachelor's, and master's levels and postbachelor's certificates.

Academic Information The faculty has 3,195 members (6% full-time), 30% with terminal degrees. The undergraduate student-faculty ratio is 16:1. The library holds 250,000 titles, 18,889 serial subscriptions, and 17,884 audiovisual materials. Special programs include services for learning-disabled students, advanced placement credit, accelerated degree programs, ESL programs, double majors, independent study, distance learning, summer session for credit, part-time degree programs (daytime, evenings, summer), adult/continuing education programs, internships, and arrangement for off-campus study with Servicemembers Opportunity Colleges. The most frequently chosen baccalaureate fields are business/marketing, interdisciplinary studies, psychology.

Student Body Statistics The student body totals 25,992, of whom 7,068 are undergraduates (757 freshmen). 58 percent are women and 42 percent are men. Students come from 46 states and territories and 76 other countries. 93 percent are from California. 1 percent are international students.

Expenses for 2006–07 *Application fee:* $60. *Tuition:* $9072 full-time, $1134 per course part-time. *Mandatory fees:* $60 full-time. Full-time tuition and fees vary according to course load. Part-time tuition varies according to course load.

Financial Aid Forms of aid include need-based and non-need-based scholarships. The average aided 2005–06 undergraduate received an aid package worth $9389. The application deadline for financial aid is continuous.

Freshman Admission National University requires a high school transcript, a minimum 2.0 high school GPA, an interview, and TOEFL scores for international students. An essay is required for some. The application deadline for regular admission is rolling.

Transfer Admission The application deadline for admission is rolling.

Entrance Difficulty National University has an open admission policy.
For Further Information Contact Mr. Dominick Giovanniello, Associate Regional Dean, San Diego, National University, 11255 North Torrey Pines Road, La Jolla, CA 92037. *Telephone:* 800-628-8648 Ext. 7701 or 800-NAT-UNIV (toll-free). *Fax:* 858-642-8709. *E-mail:* advisor@nu.edu. *Web site:* http://www.nu.edu/.

NEW COLLEGE OF CALIFORNIA
San Francisco, California

New College of California is a coed, private, comprehensive institution, founded in 1971, offering degrees at the bachelor's and master's levels and postbachelor's certificates.

Academic Information The faculty has 192 members (64% full-time). The undergraduate student-faculty ratio is 15:1. The library holds 24,000 titles and 50 serial subscriptions. Special programs include academic remediation, cooperative (work-study) education, study abroad, accelerated degree programs, independent study, self-designed majors, part-time degree programs (daytime, evenings, weekends, summer), and internships.
Student Body Statistics The student body totals 1,316, of whom 681 are undergraduates (363 freshmen). 50 percent are women and 50 percent are men. 0.4 percent are international students. 22 percent of the 2006 graduating class went on to graduate and professional schools.
Expenses for 2007–08 *Application fee:* $50. *Tuition:* $13,390 full-time. *Mandatory fees:* $140 full-time.
Financial Aid Forms of aid include part-time jobs.
Freshman Admission New College of California requires an essay, a high school transcript, and TOEFL scores for international students. An interview is recommended. 2 recommendations are required for some. The application deadline for regular admission is rolling.
Transfer Admission The application deadline for admission is rolling.
Entrance Difficulty New College of California has an open admission policy.
For Further Information Contact Ms. JoHanna Coash, Admissions Inquiry Office, New College of California, 777 Valencia Street, San Francisco, CA 94110. *Telephone:* 415-437-3420 or 888-437-3460 (toll-free). *Fax:* 415-865-2636. *E-mail:* admissions@newcollege.edu. *Web site:* http://www.newcollege.edu/.

NEWSCHOOL OF ARCHITECTURE & DESIGN
San Diego, California
http://www.newschoolarch.edu/

NORTHWESTERN POLYTECHNIC UNIVERSITY
Fremont, California

Northwestern Polytechnic University is a coed, private, comprehensive institution, founded in 1984, offering degrees at the bachelor's, master's, and doctoral levels. It has a 2-acre campus in Fremont near San Francisco and San Jose.

Academic Information The faculty has 56 members (11% full-time), 46% with terminal degrees. The undergraduate student-faculty ratio is 12:1. The library holds 12,000 titles and 200 serial subscriptions. Special programs include advanced placement credit, ESL programs, distance learning, summer session for credit, part-time degree programs (evenings, weekends, summer), adult/continuing education programs, and internships.
Student Body Statistics The student body totals 439, of whom 132 are undergraduates (10 freshmen). 38 percent are women and 62 percent are men. Students come from 7 states and territories and 10 other countries.

93 percent are from California. 61 percent are international students. 40 percent of the 2006 graduating class went on to graduate and professional schools.
Expenses for 2006–07 *Application fee:* $60. *Tuition:* $6600 full-time, $275 per unit part-time. *Mandatory fees:* $140 full-time, $70 per term part-time. Both full-time and part-time tuition and fees vary according to course load. *College room only:* $3600. Room charges vary according to housing facility.
Freshman Admission Northwestern Polytechnic University requires a high school transcript and a minimum 2.0 high school GPA. An interview, SAT scores, and TOEFL scores for international students are recommended. An essay and an interview are required for some. The application deadline for regular admission is September 10 and for nonresidents it is September 10.
Transfer Admission The application deadline for admission is September 10.
Entrance Difficulty For the fall 2006 freshman class, 100 percent of the applicants were accepted.
For Further Information Contact Ms. Catherine Meng, Admission Officer, Northwestern Polytechnic University, 47671 Westinghouse Drive, Fremont, CA 94539. *Telephone:* 510-657-5913. *Fax:* 510-657-8975. *E-mail:* admission@npu.edu. *Web site:* http://www.npu.edu/.

NOTRE DAME DE NAMUR UNIVERSITY
Belmont, California

Notre Dame de Namur University is a coed, private, Roman Catholic, comprehensive institution, founded in 1851, offering degrees at the bachelor's and master's levels. It has an 80-acre campus in Belmont near San Francisco.

Academic Information The faculty has 156 members (35% full-time). The undergraduate student-faculty ratio is 12:1. The library holds 90,702 titles, 15,000 serial subscriptions, and 9,122 audiovisual materials. Special programs include academic remediation, services for learning-disabled students, cooperative (work-study) education, study abroad, advanced placement credit, accelerated degree programs, ESL programs, double majors, independent study, self-designed majors, summer session for credit, part-time degree programs (daytime, evenings, summer), adult/continuing education programs, internships, and arrangement for off-campus study with Trinity College (DC), Emmanuel College (MA). The most frequently chosen baccalaureate fields are business/marketing, liberal arts/general studies, public administration and social services.
Student Body Statistics The student body totals 1,583, of whom 857 are undergraduates (138 freshmen). 64 percent are women and 36 percent are men. Students come from 24 states and territories and 11 other countries. 64 percent are from California. 3.6 percent are international students.
Expenses for 2007–08 *Application fee:* $40. *Comprehensive fee:* $35,230 includes full-time tuition ($24,450), mandatory fees ($200), and college room and board ($10,580). *College room only:* $7000. *Part-time tuition:* $545 per unit. *Part-time mandatory fees:* $30 per term.
Financial Aid Forms of aid include need-based and non-need-based scholarships and part-time jobs. The priority application deadline for financial aid is March 2.
Freshman Admission Notre Dame de Namur University requires an essay, a high school transcript, recommendations, audition is required for music programs, SAT or ACT scores, and TOEFL scores for international students. An interview is required for some. The application deadline for regular admission is rolling.
Transfer Admission The application deadline for admission is rolling.
Entrance Difficulty Notre Dame de Namur University assesses its entrance difficulty level as minimally difficult. For the fall 2006 freshman class, 97 percent of the applicants were accepted.
For Further Information Contact Mr. Joseph Romano, Associate Director for Undergraduate Admission, Notre Dame de Namur University, 1500 Ralston Avenue, Belmont, CA 94002-1908. *Telephone:* 650-508-3589 or 800-263-0545 (toll-free). *Fax:* 650-508-3426. *E-mail:* jromano@ndnu.edu. *Web site:* http://www.ndnu.edu.

OCCIDENTAL COLLEGE

Los Angeles, California

Occidental College is a coed, private, comprehensive institution, founded in 1887, offering degrees at the bachelor's and master's levels. It has a 120-acre campus in Los Angeles.

Academic Information The faculty has 220 members (68% full-time). The undergraduate student-faculty ratio is 10:1. The library holds 497,161 titles and 903 serial subscriptions. Special programs include services for learning-disabled students, an honors program, study abroad, advanced placement credit, double majors, independent study, self-designed majors, summer session for credit, internships, and arrangement for off-campus study with California Institute of Technology, Art Center College of Design, Morehouse College, Spelman College. The most frequently chosen baccalaureate fields are social sciences, psychology, visual and performing arts.

Student Body Statistics The student body totals 1,825, of whom 1,804 are undergraduates (458 freshmen). 56 percent are women and 44 percent are men. Students come from 46 states and territories and 21 other countries. 49 percent are from California. 2.5 percent are international students. 30 percent of the 2006 graduating class went on to graduate and professional schools.

Expenses for 2007–08 *Application fee:* $50. *Comprehensive fee:* $44,833 includes full-time tuition ($34,400), mandatory fees ($933), and college room and board ($9500). *Part-time tuition:* $1435 per credit.

Financial Aid Forms of aid include need-based and non-need-based scholarships and part-time jobs. The average aided 2005–06 undergraduate received an aid package worth $29,089. The application deadline for financial aid is February 1 with a priority deadline of February 1.

Freshman Admission Occidental College requires an essay, a high school transcript, 2 recommendations, SAT or ACT scores, and TOEFL scores for international students. An interview and SAT Subject Test scores are recommended. The application deadline for regular admission is January 10 and for early decision it is November 15.

Transfer Admission The application deadline for admission is March 15.

Entrance Difficulty Occidental College assesses its entrance difficulty level as very difficult. For the fall 2006 freshman class, 42 percent of the applicants were accepted.

For Further Information Contact Mr. Vince Cuseo, Dean of Admission, Occidental College, 1600 Campus Road, Los Angeles, CA 90041. *Telephone:* 323-259-2700 or 800-825-5262 (toll-free). *Fax:* 323-341-4875. *E-mail:* admission@oxy.edu. *Web site:* http://www.oxy.edu/.

OTIS COLLEGE OF ART AND DESIGN

Los Angeles, California

Otis College of Art and Design is a coed, private, comprehensive institution, founded in 1918, offering degrees at the bachelor's and master's levels. It has a 5-acre campus in Los Angeles.

Academic Information The faculty has 257 members (23% full-time), 33% with terminal degrees. The undergraduate student-faculty ratio is 8:1. The library holds 42,000 titles and 150 serial subscriptions. Special programs include academic remediation, an honors program, cooperative (work-study) education, study abroad, advanced placement credit, Freshman Honors College, ESL programs, independent study, summer session for credit, adult/continuing education programs, internships, and arrangement for off-campus study with The Consortium of East Coast Art Schools. The most frequently chosen baccalaureate fields are architecture, visual and performing arts.

Student Body Statistics The student body totals 1,125, of whom 1,073 are undergraduates (161 freshmen). 67 percent are women and 33 percent are men. Students come from 21 states and territories and 13 other countries. 76 percent are from California. 12.5 percent are international students. 5 percent of the 2006 graduating class went on to graduate and professional schools.

Expenses for 2007–08 *Application fee:* $50. *Tuition:* $27,796 full-time, $945 per credit part-time. *Mandatory fees:* $550 full-time.

Financial Aid Forms of aid include need-based and non-need-based scholarships and part-time jobs. The average aided 2005–06 undergraduate received an aid package worth $19,067.

Freshman Admission Otis College of Art and Design requires an essay, a high school transcript, a minimum 2.5 high school GPA, a portfolio, SAT or ACT scores, and TOEFL scores for international students. 1 recommendation and an interview are recommended. The application deadline for regular admission is rolling.

Transfer Admission The application deadline for admission is rolling.

Entrance Difficulty Otis College of Art and Design assesses its entrance difficulty level as moderately difficult; very difficult for transfer students in toy design, digital media programs. For the fall 2006 freshman class, 56 percent of the applicants were accepted.

For Further Information Contact Mr. Marc D. Meredith, Dean of Admissions, Otis College of Art and Design, 9045 Lincoln Boulevard, Los Angeles, CA 90045-9785. *Telephone:* 310-665-6820 or 800-527-OTIS (toll-free). *Fax:* 310-665-6821. *E-mail:* admissions@otis.edu. *Web site:* http://www.otis.edu/.

PACIFIC OAKS COLLEGE

Pasadena, California

Pacific Oaks College is a coed, primarily women's, private, upper-level institution, founded in 1945, offering degrees at the bachelor's and master's levels and post-master's and postbachelor's certificates. It has a 2-acre campus in Pasadena near Los Angeles.

Academic Information The faculty has 125 members (22% full-time). The undergraduate student-faculty ratio is 22:1. The library holds 36,000 titles, 87 serial subscriptions, and 125 audiovisual materials. Special programs include independent study, distance learning, summer session for credit, part-time degree programs (daytime, evenings, weekends, summer), adult/continuing education programs, internships, and arrangement for off-campus study with Four College Consortium.

Student Body Statistics The student body totals 1,028, of whom 257 are undergraduates (55 in entering class). 96 percent are women and 4 percent are men.

Expenses for 2007–08 *Application fee:* $55. *Tuition:* $19,080 full-time, $795 per unit part-time. *Mandatory fees:* $60 full-time, $30 per term part-time.

Financial Aid Forms of aid include need-based scholarships and part-time jobs.

Transfer Admission Pacific Oaks College requires a college transcript. Standardized test scores are required for some. The application deadline for admission is June 1.

Entrance Difficulty Pacific Oaks College assesses its entrance difficulty level as noncompetitive for transfers. For the fall 2006 entering class, 77 percent of the applicants were accepted.

For Further Information Contact Ms. Augusta Pickens, Office of Admissions, Pacific Oaks College, 5 Westmoreland Place, Pasadena, CA 91103. *Telephone:* 626-397-1349 or 800-684-0900 (toll-free). *Fax:* 626-666-1220. *E-mail:* admissions@pacificoaks.edu. *Web site:* http://www.pacificoaks.edu/.

PACIFIC STATES UNIVERSITY

Los Angeles, California

Pacific States University is a coed, private, comprehensive institution, founded in 1928, offering degrees at the bachelor's and master's levels. It has a 1-acre campus in Los Angeles.

Academic Information The faculty has 16 members (25% full-time), 62% with terminal degrees. The undergraduate student-faculty ratio is 20:1. The library holds 15,000 titles and 108 serial subscriptions. Special programs include study abroad, accelerated degree programs, ESL programs, independent study, self-designed majors, summer session for credit, and adult/continuing education programs.

Student Body Statistics The student body totals 68, of whom 44 are undergraduates (22 freshmen). 18 percent are women and 82 percent are men. 90 percent are from California. 20 percent of the 2006 graduating class went on to graduate and professional schools.

Expenses for 2006–07 *Application fee:* $100. *Tuition:* $8400 full-time, $195 per unit part-time. *Mandatory fees:* $460 full-time. Full-time tuition and fees vary according to course load. Part-time tuition varies according to course load.
Freshman Admission Pacific States University requires an essay, a high school transcript, a minimum 2.5 high school GPA, and TOEFL scores for international students. The application deadline for regular admission is September 21.
Transfer Admission The application deadline for admission is October 27.
Entrance Difficulty Pacific States University has an open admission policy.
For Further Information Contact Ms. Marina Miller, Assistant Director of Admissions, Pacific States University, 1516 South Western Avenue, Los Angeles, CA 90006. *Telephone:* 323-731-2383 or 888-200-0383 (toll-free). *Fax:* 323-731-7276. *E-mail:* admission@psuca.edu. *Web site:* http://www.psuca.edu/.

PACIFIC UNION COLLEGE
Angwin, California

Pacific Union College is a coed, private, Seventh-day Adventist, comprehensive institution, founded in 1882, offering degrees at the associate, bachelor's, and master's levels. It has a 200-acre campus in Angwin near San Francisco.

Academic Information The faculty has 95 members (85% full-time), 53% with terminal degrees. The undergraduate student-faculty ratio is 15:1. The library holds 173,839 titles and 812 serial subscriptions. Special programs include academic remediation, services for learning-disabled students, an honors program, cooperative (work-study) education, study abroad, advanced placement credit, double majors, independent study, distance learning, self-designed majors, summer session for credit, part-time degree programs (daytime, summer), adult/continuing education programs, internships, and arrangement for off-campus study. The most frequently chosen baccalaureate fields are education, health professions and related sciences, mathematics.
Student Body Statistics The student body totals 1,397, of whom 1,394 are undergraduates (265 freshmen). 54 percent are women and 46 percent are men. Students come from 40 states and territories and 24 other countries. 81 percent are from California. 6.8 percent are international students.
Expenses for 2006–07 *Application fee:* $30. *Comprehensive fee:* $25,917 includes full-time tuition ($20,130), mandatory fees ($135), and college room and board ($5652). *College room only:* $3447. Full-time tuition and fees vary according to course load. *Part-time tuition:* $584 per quarter hour. *Part-time mandatory fees:* $45 per term. Part-time tuition and fees vary according to course load.
Financial Aid Forms of aid include need-based and non-need-based scholarships and part-time jobs. The average aided 2006–07 undergraduate received an aid package worth an estimated $10,958. The priority application deadline for financial aid is March 2.
Freshman Admission Pacific Union College requires a high school transcript, a minimum 2.3 high school GPA, 3 recommendations, SAT or ACT scores, and TOEFL scores for international students. The application deadline for regular admission is rolling.
Transfer Admission The application deadline for admission is rolling.
Entrance Difficulty Pacific Union College assesses its entrance difficulty level as moderately difficult. For the fall 2006 freshman class, 41 percent of the applicants were accepted.
For Further Information Contact Mr. Darren Hagen, Director of Enrollment Services, Pacific Union College, Enrollment Services, One Angwin Avenue, Angwin, CA 94508. *Telephone:* 707-965-6425 or 800-862-7080 (toll-free). *Fax:* 707-965-6432. *E-mail:* enroll@puc.edu. *Web site:* http://www.puc.edu/.

PATTEN UNIVERSITY
Oakland, California

Patten University is a coed, private, interdenominational, comprehensive institution, founded in 1944, offering degrees at the associate, bachelor's, and master's levels and postbachelor's certificates. It has a 5-acre campus in Oakland near San Francisco.

Academic Information The faculty has 95 members (18% full-time), 35% with terminal degrees. The undergraduate student-faculty ratio is 14:1. The library holds 35,000 titles and 250 serial subscriptions. Special programs include services for learning-disabled students, an honors program, advanced placement credit, accelerated degree programs, double majors, distance learning, summer session for credit, part-time degree programs, adult/continuing education programs, and internships.
Student Body Statistics The student body totals 791, of whom 734 are undergraduates (46 freshmen). 39 percent are women and 61 percent are men. Students come from 12 states and territories. 95 percent are from California. 80 percent of the 2006 graduating class went on to graduate and professional schools.
Expenses for 2007–08 *Application fee:* $30. *Comprehensive fee:* $18,230 includes full-time tuition ($11,880) and college room and board ($6350). *Part-time tuition:* $495 per unit.
Financial Aid Forms of aid include need-based and non-need-based scholarships and part-time jobs. The priority application deadline for financial aid is May 31.
Freshman Admission Patten University requires an essay, a high school transcript, a minimum 2.5 high school GPA, 2 recommendations, SAT or ACT scores, and TOEFL scores for international students. An interview is recommended. The application deadline for regular admission is July 31.
Transfer Admission The application deadline for admission is rolling.
Entrance Difficulty Patten University has an open admission policy.
For Further Information Contact Ms. Kim Guerra, Patten University, 2433 Coolidge Avenue, Oakland, CA 94601. *Telephone:* 510-261-8500 Ext. 7763. *Fax:* 510-534-4344. *E-mail:* kim.guerra@patten.edu. *Web site:* http://www.patten.edu/.

PEPPERDINE UNIVERSITY
Malibu, California

Pepperdine University is a coed, private university, founded in 1937, affiliated with the Church of Christ, offering degrees at the bachelor's, master's, doctoral, and first professional levels and post-master's certificates. It has an 830-acre campus in Malibu near Los Angeles.

Academic Information The faculty has 707 members (56% full-time), 97% with terminal degrees. The undergraduate student-faculty ratio is 12:1. The library holds 1 million titles and 103,654 serial subscriptions. Special programs include an honors program, study abroad, advanced placement credit, double majors, independent study, self-designed majors, summer session for credit, part-time degree programs (daytime, evenings), and internships. The most frequently chosen baccalaureate fields are business/marketing, communications/journalism, social sciences.
Student Body Statistics The student body totals 7,593, of whom 3,297 are undergraduates (706 freshmen). 57 percent are women and 43 percent are men. Students come from 50 states and territories and 61 other countries. 50 percent are from California. 6 percent are international students. 63 percent of the 2006 graduating class went on to graduate and professional schools.
Expenses for 2006–07 *Application fee:* $65. *Comprehensive fee:* $42,240 includes full-time tuition ($32,620), mandatory fees ($120), and college room and board ($9500). Room and board charges vary according to board plan and housing facility. *Part-time tuition:* $1010 per unit.
Financial Aid Forms of aid include need-based and non-need-based scholarships, athletic grants, and part-time jobs. The average aided 2005–06 undergraduate received an aid package worth $30,991. The application deadline for financial aid is February 15 with a priority deadline of February 15.
Freshman Admission Pepperdine University requires an essay, a high school transcript, 2 recommendations, SAT or ACT scores, and TOEFL scores for international students. An interview is recommended. The application deadline for regular admission is January 15.

Pepperdine University (continued)

Transfer Admission The application deadline for admission is January 15.

Entrance Difficulty Pepperdine University assesses its entrance difficulty level as very difficult. For the fall 2006 freshman class, 28 percent of the applicants were accepted.

For Further Information Contact Mr. Paul A. Long, Dean of Admission and Enrollment Management, Pepperdine University, 24255 Pacific Coast Highway, Malibu, CA 90263-4392. *Telephone:* 310-506-4392. *Fax:* 310-506-4861. *E-mail:* admission-seaver@pepperdine.edu. *Web site:* http://www.pepperdine.edu/.

PITZER COLLEGE

Claremont, California

Pitzer College is a coed, private, four-year college of The Claremont Colleges Consortium, founded in 1963, offering degrees at the bachelor's level. It has a 35-acre campus in Claremont near Los Angeles.

Academic Information The faculty has 95 members (72% full-time), 95% with terminal degrees. The student-faculty ratio is 11:1. The library holds 2 million titles and 16,000 serial subscriptions. Special programs include services for learning-disabled students, an honors program, cooperative (work-study) education, study abroad, advanced placement credit, ESL programs, double majors, independent study, self-designed majors, summer session for credit, part-time degree programs (daytime, evenings, summer), adult/continuing education programs, internships, and arrangement for off-campus study with The Claremont Colleges, Colby College, Haverford College, Spelman College, Morehouse College. The most frequently chosen baccalaureate fields are psychology, social sciences, visual and performing arts.

Student Body Statistics The student body is made up of 958 undergraduates (229 freshmen). 59 percent are women and 41 percent are men. Students come from 42 states and territories and 8 other countries. 58 percent are from California. 2.3 percent are international students. 24 percent of the 2006 graduating class went on to graduate and professional schools.

Expenses for 2006–07 *Application fee:* $50. *Comprehensive fee:* $43,708 includes full-time tuition ($31,000), mandatory fees ($3038), and college room and board ($9670). *College room only:* $6120. Full-time tuition and fees vary according to course load. Room and board charges vary according to board plan. *Part-time tuition:* $3875 per course. Part-time tuition varies according to course load.

Financial Aid Forms of aid include need-based and non-need-based scholarships and part-time jobs. The average aided 2006–07 undergraduate received an aid package worth an estimated $30,802. The application deadline for financial aid is February 1.

Freshman Admission Pitzer College requires an essay, a high school transcript, 3 recommendations, and TOEFL scores for international students. An interview is recommended. SAT or ACT scores are required for some. The application deadline for regular admission is January 1.

Transfer Admission The application deadline for admission is April 15.

Entrance Difficulty Pitzer College assesses its entrance difficulty level as moderately difficult. For the fall 2006 freshman class, 37 percent of the applicants were accepted.

For Further Information Contact Anna Burkhalter, Associate Directors of Admission, Pitzer College, 1050 North Mills Avenue, Claremont, CA 91711-6101. *Telephone:* 909-621-8129 or 800-748-9371 (toll-free). *Fax:* 909-621-8770. *E-mail:* admission@pitzer.edu. *Web site:* http://www.pitzer.edu/.

PLATT COLLEGE

Huntington Beach, California

http://www.plattcollege.edu/

PLATT COLLEGE SAN DIEGO

San Diego, California

Platt College San Diego is a coed, proprietary, primarily two-year college, founded in 1879, offering degrees at the associate and bachelor's levels. It is located in San Diego near San Diego.

Academic Information The faculty has 37 members (19% full-time), 3% with terminal degrees. The student-faculty ratio is 15:1. The library holds 750 titles, 27 serial subscriptions, and 403 audiovisual materials. Special programs include academic remediation, cooperative (work-study) education, and adult/continuing education programs. The most frequently chosen baccalaureate field is visual and performing arts.

Student Body Statistics The student body is made up of 264 undergraduates (130 freshmen). 27 percent are women and 73 percent are men. Students come from 4 states and territories. 95 percent are from California. 90 percent of the 2006 graduating class went on to four-year colleges.

Expenses for 2007–08 *Application fee:* $110. *Tuition:* $19,214 full-time. *Mandatory fees:* $110 full-time.

Freshman Admission Platt College San Diego requires a high school transcript, an interview, and Wonderlic aptitude test. An essay and TOEFL scores for international students are recommended.

For Further Information Contact Mr. Craig Hinson, Admissions Representative, Platt College San Diego, 6250 El Cajon Boulevard, San Diego, CA 92115-3919. *Telephone:* 619-265-0107 or 866-752-8826 (toll-free). *Fax:* 619-265-8655. *E-mail:* chinson@platt.edu. *Web site:* http://www.platt.edu/.

POINT LOMA NAZARENE UNIVERSITY

San Diego, California

Point Loma Nazarene University is a coed, private, Nazarene, comprehensive institution, founded in 1902, offering degrees at the bachelor's and master's levels. It has an 88-acre campus in San Diego.

Academic Information The faculty has 145 full-time members. The undergraduate student-faculty ratio is 15:1. The library holds 152,377 titles and 25,505 serial subscriptions. Special programs include academic remediation, services for learning-disabled students, an honors program, study abroad, advanced placement credit, double majors, independent study, summer session for credit, part-time degree programs (daytime, evenings, summer), internships, and arrangement for off-campus study with American University, Coalition for Christian Colleges and Universities. The most frequently chosen baccalaureate fields are business/marketing, liberal arts/general studies, psychology.

Student Body Statistics The student body totals 3,437, of whom 2,383 are undergraduates (538 freshmen). 61 percent are women and 39 percent are men. Students come from 40 states and territories and 14 other countries. 79 percent are from California. 0.8 percent are international students.

Expenses for 2007–08 *Application fee:* $50. *Comprehensive fee:* $31,200 includes full-time tuition ($23,200), mandatory fees ($530), and college room and board ($7470). *Part-time tuition:* $900 per unit. *Part-time mandatory fees:* $20 per unit.

Financial Aid Forms of aid include non-need-based scholarships and athletic grants. The average aided 2006–07 undergraduate received an aid package worth an estimated $16,100. The priority application deadline for financial aid is March 2.

Freshman Admission Point Loma Nazarene University requires an essay, a high school transcript, a minimum 2.8 high school GPA, 2 recommendations, SAT or ACT scores, and TOEFL scores for international students. SAT scores are recommended. An interview is required for some. The application deadline for regular admission is March 1 and for early action it is December 1.

Transfer Admission The application deadline for admission is rolling.

Entrance Difficulty Point Loma Nazarene University assesses its entrance difficulty level as moderately difficult. For the fall 2006 freshman class, 65 percent of the applicants were accepted.

For Further Information Contact Mr. Chip Killingsworth, Director of Admissions, Point Loma Nazarene University, 3900 Lomaland Drive, San Diego, CA 92106. *Telephone:* 619-849-2273 or 800-733-7770 (toll-free). *Fax:* 619-849-2601. *E-mail:* admissions@pointloma.edu. *Web site:* http://www.pointloma.edu/.

POMONA COLLEGE

Claremont, California

Pomona College is a coed, private, four-year college of The Claremont Colleges Consortium, founded in 1887, offering degrees at the bachelor's level. It has a 140-acre campus in Claremont near Los Angeles.

Academic Information The faculty has 203 members (87% full-time), 91% with terminal degrees. The student-faculty ratio is 8:1. The library holds 2 million titles. Special programs include services for learning-disabled students, study abroad, advanced placement credit, double majors, independent study, self-designed majors, internships, and arrangement for off-campus study with other members of The Claremont Colleges, Swarthmore College, Colby College, Smith College, Spelman College.

Student Body Statistics The student body is made up of 1,545 undergraduates (379 freshmen). 50 percent are women and 50 percent are men. Students come from 49 states and territories and 31 other countries. 32 percent are from California. 2.6 percent are international students. 33 percent of the 2006 graduating class went on to graduate and professional schools.

Expenses for 2006–07 *Application fee:* $60. *Comprehensive fee:* $43,156 includes full-time tuition ($31,580), mandatory fees ($285), and college room and board ($11,291). Room and board charges vary according to board plan.

Financial Aid Forms of aid include need-based scholarships and part-time jobs. The average aided 2006–07 undergraduate received an aid package worth an estimated $32,100. The application deadline for financial aid is February 1.

Freshman Admission Pomona College requires an essay, a high school transcript, 2 recommendations, SAT and SAT Subject Test or ACT scores, and TOEFL scores for international students. A minimum 3.0 high school GPA, an interview, and portfolio or tapes for art and performing arts programs are recommended. The application deadline for regular admission is January 2; for early decision plan 1 it is November 15; and for early decision plan 2 it is December 28.

Transfer Admission The application deadline for admission is March 15.

Entrance Difficulty Pomona College assesses its entrance difficulty level as most difficult. For the fall 2006 freshman class, 18 percent of the applicants were accepted.

For Further Information Contact Mr. Bruce Poch, Vice President and Dean of Admissions, Pomona College, 333 North College Way, Claremont, CA 91711. *Telephone:* 909-621-8134. *Fax:* 909-621-8952. *E-mail:* admissions@pomona.edu. *Web site:* http://www.pomona.edu/.

PROFESSIONAL GOLFERS CAREER COLLEGE

Temecula, California

http://www.golfcollege.edu/

QUEEN OF THE HOLY ROSARY COLLEGE

Mission San Jose, California

Queen of the Holy Rosary College is a coed, primarily women's, private, Roman Catholic, two-year college, founded in 1930, offering degrees at the associate level. It has a 37-acre campus in Mission San Jose near San Jose.

Academic Information The faculty has 17 members, 12% with terminal degrees. The student-faculty ratio is 5:1. The library holds 24,937 titles, 150 serial subscriptions, and 502 audiovisual materials. Special programs include academic remediation, ESL programs, summer session for credit, part-time degree programs (daytime, summer), and adult/continuing education programs.

Student Body Statistics The student body is made up of 195 undergraduates. 97 percent are women and 3 percent are men.

Freshman Admission Queen of the Holy Rosary College requires an essay, a high school transcript, and a minimum 2.0 high school GPA. A minimum 3.0 high school GPA, an interview, and SAT scores are recommended. The application deadline for regular admission is July 1.

Transfer Admission The application deadline for admission is July 1.

Entrance Difficulty Queen of the Holy Rosary College has an open admission policy.

For Further Information Contact Sr. Mary Paul Mehegan, Dean of the College, Queen of the Holy Rosary College, 43326 Mission Boulevard, PO Box 3908, Mission San Jose, CA 94539. *Telephone:* 510-657-2468. *Fax:* 510-657-1734. *Web site:* http://www.msjdominicans.org/QHRC/index.html.

REDSTONE COLLEGE–LOS ANGELES

Inglewood, California

http://www.redstone.edu/

REMINGTON COLLEGE–SAN DIEGO CAMPUS

San Diego, California

http://www.remingtoncollege.edu/

SAINT MARY'S COLLEGE OF CALIFORNIA

Moraga, California

Saint Mary's College of California is a coed, private, Roman Catholic, comprehensive institution, founded in 1863, offering degrees at the bachelor's, master's, and doctoral levels. It has a 420-acre campus in Moraga near San Francisco.

Academic Information The faculty has 539 members (37% full-time). The undergraduate student-faculty ratio is 11:1. The library holds 220,337 titles, 15,000 serial subscriptions, and 5,670 audiovisual materials. Special programs include an honors program, study abroad, advanced placement credit, double majors, independent study, self-designed majors, part-time degree programs (daytime, evenings, weekends), adult/continuing education programs, internships, and arrangement for off-campus study with members of the January Interim Program. The most frequently chosen baccalaureate fields are business/marketing, communications/journalism, social sciences.

Student Body Statistics The student body totals 3,962, of whom 2,835 are undergraduates (610 freshmen). 63 percent are women and 37 percent are men. Students come from 40 states and territories and 28 other countries. 89 percent are from California. 1.8 percent are international students. 50 percent of the 2006 graduating class went on to graduate and professional schools.

Expenses for 2006–07 *Application fee:* $55. *Comprehensive fee:* $39,616 includes full-time tuition ($28,900), mandatory fees ($150), and college room and board ($10,566). *College room only:* $5926. Full-time tuition and fees vary according to course load. Room and board charges vary according to board plan and housing facility. *Part-time tuition:* $3615 per course. Part-time tuition varies according to course load.

Financial Aid Forms of aid include need-based and non-need-based scholarships, athletic grants, and part-time jobs. The average aided 2006–07 undergraduate received an aid package worth an estimated $21,717. The priority application deadline for financial aid is February 15.

Freshman Admission Saint Mary's College of California requires an essay, a high school transcript, a minimum 2.0 high school GPA, 1

Saint Mary's College of California (continued)

recommendation, SAT or ACT scores, and TOEFL scores for international students. A minimum 3.0 high school GPA is recommended. A minimum 3.0 high school GPA and an interview are required for some. The application deadline for regular admission is January 15 and for early action it is November 15.

Transfer Admission The application deadline for admission is July 1.

Entrance Difficulty Saint Mary's College of California assesses its entrance difficulty level as moderately difficult. For the fall 2006 freshman class, 70 percent of the applicants were accepted.

For Further Information Contact Ms. Dorothy Jones, Dean of Admissions, Saint Mary's College of California, PO Box 4800, Moraga, CA 94556-4800. *Telephone:* 925-631-4224 or 800-800-4SMC (toll-free). *Fax:* 925-376-7193. *E-mail:* smcadmit@stmarys-ca.edu. *Web site:* http://www.stmarys-ca.edu/.

SALVATION ARMY COLLEGE FOR OFFICER TRAINING

See The Salvation Army College for Officer Training at Crestmont.

THE SALVATION ARMY COLLEGE FOR OFFICER TRAINING AT CRESTMONT
Rancho Palos Verdes, California

The Salvation Army College for Officer Training at Crestmont is a coed, private, two-year college, founded in 1878, offering degrees at the associate level. It has a 44-acre campus in Rancho Palos Verdes near Los Angeles.

Expenses for 2006–07 *Application fee:* $15. *Comprehensive fee:* $10,600 includes full-time tuition ($1500), mandatory fees ($850), and college room and board ($8250).

For Further Information Contact Capt. Kevin Jackson, Director of Curriculum, The Salvation Army College for Officer Training at Crestmont, 30840 Hawthorne Boulevard, Rancho Palos Verdes, CA 90275. *Telephone:* 310-544-6442 or 310-544-6440 (toll-free in-state). *Fax:* 310-265-6520. *E-mail:* kevin_jackson@usw.salvationarmy.org. *Web site:* http://www.crestmont.edu/.

SAMUEL MERRITT COLLEGE
Oakland, California

Samuel Merritt College is a coed, primarily women's, private, upper-level institution, founded in 1909, offering degrees at the bachelor's, master's, doctoral, and first professional levels (bachelor's degree offered jointly with Saint Mary's College of California). It has a 1-acre campus in Oakland near San Francisco.

Academic Information The faculty has 171 members (37% full-time), 30% with terminal degrees. The undergraduate student-faculty ratio is 10:1. The library holds 36,995 titles, 2,970 serial subscriptions, and 1,947 audiovisual materials. Special programs include academic remediation, services for learning-disabled students, cooperative (work-study) education, advanced placement credit, accelerated degree programs, independent study, distance learning, summer session for credit, part-time degree programs (daytime, evenings, summer), internships, and arrangement for off-campus study with Saint Mary's College of California. The most frequently chosen baccalaureate field is health professions and related sciences.

Student Body Statistics The student body totals 1,178, of whom 403 are undergraduates (16 in entering class). 88 percent are women and 12 percent are men. Students come from 3 states and territories and 1 other country. 99 percent are from California. 0.3 percent are international students.

Expenses for 2006–07 *Application fee:* $35. *Tuition:* $29,220 full-time, $1214 per unit part-time. *Mandatory fees:* $356 full-time, $356 per year part-time. Both full-time and part-time tuition and fees vary according to degree level and program. *College room only:* $5903.

Financial Aid Forms of aid include need-based scholarships and part-time jobs. The priority application deadline for financial aid is March 2.

Transfer Admission The application deadline for admission is March 1.

Entrance Difficulty Samuel Merritt College assesses its entrance difficulty level as moderately difficult.

For Further Information Contact Ms. Anne Seed, Director of Admissions, Samuel Merritt College, 570 Hawthorne Avenue, Oakland, CA 94609. *Telephone:* 510-869-6610 or 800-607-MERRITT (toll-free). *Fax:* 510-869-6525. *E-mail:* admission@samuelmerritt.edu. *Web site:* http://www.samuelmerritt.edu/.

SAN DIEGO CHRISTIAN COLLEGE
El Cajon, California

San Diego Christian College is a coed, private, nondenominational, four-year college, founded in 1970, offering degrees at the bachelor's level and postbachelor's certificates. It has a 55-acre campus in El Cajon near San Diego.

Academic Information The faculty has 49 members (59% full-time), 31% with terminal degrees. The student-faculty ratio is 12:1. The library holds 111,702 titles, 11,250 serial subscriptions, and 1,342 audiovisual materials. Special programs include academic remediation, an honors program, study abroad, advanced placement credit, ESL programs, double majors, independent study, self-designed majors, summer session for credit, part-time degree programs (daytime, evenings, summer), adult/continuing education programs, and internships. The most frequently chosen baccalaureate fields are family and consumer sciences, interdisciplinary studies, psychology.

Student Body Statistics The student body totals 543, of whom 502 are undergraduates (120 freshmen). 54 percent are women and 46 percent are men. Students come from 15 states and territories and 7 other countries. 90 percent are from California. 2 percent are international students. 36 percent of the 2006 graduating class went on to graduate and professional schools.

Expenses for 2007–08 *Application fee:* $25. *Comprehensive fee:* $26,426 includes full-time tuition ($18,220), mandatory fees ($666), and college room and board ($7540). *Part-time tuition:* $607 per credit. *Part-time mandatory fees:* $250 per term.

Financial Aid Forms of aid include need-based and non-need-based scholarships, athletic grants, and part-time jobs. The average aided 2005–06 undergraduate received an aid package worth $14,547. The priority application deadline for financial aid is March 2.

Freshman Admission San Diego Christian College requires an essay, a high school transcript, 2 recommendations, SAT or ACT scores, and TOEFL scores for international students. A minimum 2.75 high school GPA and an interview are recommended. The application deadline for regular admission is July 1.

Transfer Admission The application deadline for admission is July 1.

Entrance Difficulty San Diego Christian College assesses its entrance difficulty level as moderately difficult. For the fall 2006 freshman class, 72 percent of the applicants were accepted.

For Further Information Contact Ms. Rene Inman, Associate Director of Admissions, San Diego Christian College, 2100 Greenfield Drive, El Cajon, CA 92019-1157. *Telephone:* 619-588-7747 or 800-676-2242 (toll-free). *Fax:* 619-590-1739. *E-mail:* chadm@sdcc.edu. *Web site:* http://www.sdcc.edu/.

SAN DIEGO STATE UNIVERSITY
San Diego, California

San Diego State University is a coed, public unit of California State University System, founded in 1897, offering degrees at the bachelor's, master's, and doctoral levels and post-master's and postbachelor's certificates. It has a 300-acre campus in San Diego.

Academic Information The faculty has 1,725 members (57% full-time). The undergraduate student-faculty ratio is 19:1. The library holds 1 million titles and 8,245 serial subscriptions. Special programs include academic remediation, services for learning-disabled students, an honors program, study abroad, advanced placement credit, ESL programs, double majors, independent study, distance learning, self-designed majors, summer session for credit, part-time degree programs (daytime, evenings, summer), internships, and arrangement for off-campus study with other units of the California State University System.

Student Body Statistics The student body totals 34,305, of whom 28,527 are undergraduates (5,124 freshmen). 58 percent are women and 42 percent are men. Students come from 51 states and territories and 64 other countries. 95 percent are from California. 2.3 percent are international students.

Expenses for 2006–07 *Application fee:* $55. *State resident tuition:* $0 full-time. *Nonresident tuition:* $10,170 full-time, $339 per unit part-time. *Mandatory fees:* $3160 full-time, $1033 per term part-time. Full-time tuition and fees vary according to degree level. Part-time tuition and fees vary according to course load and degree level. *College room and board:* $10,093. Room and board charges vary according to board plan and housing facility.

Financial Aid Forms of aid include need-based and non-need-based scholarships, athletic grants, and part-time jobs. The average aided 2006–07 undergraduate received an aid package worth an estimated $7300. The application deadline for financial aid is March 2.

Freshman Admission San Diego State University requires a high school transcript, a minimum 2.0 high school GPA, 2.5 GPA for non-California residents, SAT or ACT scores, and TOEFL scores for international students. The application deadline for regular admission is November 30.

Transfer Admission The application deadline for admission is November 30.

Entrance Difficulty San Diego State University assesses its entrance difficulty level as moderately difficult. For the fall 2006 freshman class, 48 percent of the applicants were accepted.

For Further Information Contact Ms. Beverly Arata, Director of Admissions, San Diego State University, 5500 Campanile Drive, San Diego, CA 92182-0771. *Telephone:* 619-594-6336. *E-mail:* admissions@sdsu.edu. *Web site:* http://www.sdsu.edu/.

SAN FRANCISCO ART INSTITUTE

San Francisco, California

San Francisco Art Institute is a coed, private, comprehensive institution, founded in 1871, offering degrees at the bachelor's and master's levels and postbachelor's certificates. It has a 3-acre campus in San Francisco.

Academic Information The faculty has 121 members (14% full-time). The undergraduate student-faculty ratio is 11:1. The library holds 35,500 titles, 210 serial subscriptions, and 1,250 audiovisual materials. Special programs include academic remediation, services for learning-disabled students, cooperative (work-study) education, study abroad, advanced placement credit, ESL programs, double majors, independent study, summer session for credit, part-time degree programs (daytime, evenings, weekends, summer), adult/continuing education programs, internships, and arrangement for off-campus study with Association of Independent Colleges of Art and Design; Akademie Vytvarnych Umenr, Prague, Czech Republic; Bezalel Academy of Arts and Design, Jerusalem, Israel; Chelsea College of Art and Design, London, England; Ecole Nationale Superieure des Beaux-Arts, Paris, France; Glasgow School of Art, Glasgow, Scotland; Gerritt-Rietveld Academie, Amsterdam, Holland; Valand School of Fine Arts, Goteborg, Sweden. The most frequently chosen baccalaureate field is visual and performing arts.

Student Body Statistics The student body totals 652, of whom 420 are undergraduates (69 freshmen). 50 percent are women and 50 percent are men. Students come from 34 states and territories and 12 other countries. 74 percent are from California. 7.8 percent are international students.

Expenses for 2006–07 *Application fee:* $65. *Tuition:* $27,200 full-time, $1175 per unit part-time. *Mandatory fees:* $35 full-time, $175. Part-time tuition and fees vary according to course load. *College room only:* $7200. Room charges vary according to housing facility.

Financial Aid Forms of aid include need-based and non-need-based scholarships and part-time jobs. The average aided 2006–07 undergraduate received an aid package worth an estimated $24,880. The application deadline for financial aid is continuous.

Freshman Admission San Francisco Art Institute requires an essay, a high school transcript, recommendations, a portfolio, SAT or ACT scores, and TOEFL scores for international students. An interview is recommended. The application deadline for regular admission is rolling.

Transfer Admission The application deadline for admission is rolling.

Entrance Difficulty San Francisco Art Institute assesses its entrance difficulty level as moderately difficult. For the fall 2006 freshman class, 26 percent of the applicants were accepted.

For Further Information Contact Office of Admissions, San Francisco Art Institute, 800 Chestnut Street, San Francisco, CA 94133. *Telephone:* 415-749-4500 or 800-345-SFAI (toll-free). *E-mail:* admissions@sfai.edu. *Web site:* http://www.sfai.edu/.

See page 190 for the College Close-Up.

SAN FRANCISCO CONSERVATORY OF MUSIC

San Francisco, California

San Francisco Conservatory of Music is a coed, private, comprehensive institution, founded in 1917, offering degrees at the bachelor's and master's levels. It has a 2-acre campus in San Francisco.

Academic Information The faculty has 104 members (27% full-time), 18% with terminal degrees. The undergraduate student-faculty ratio is 7:1. The library holds 60,000 titles, 80 serial subscriptions, and 15 audiovisual materials. Special programs include academic remediation, advanced placement credit, independent study, part-time degree programs (daytime), and internships.

Student Body Statistics The student body totals 374, of whom 220 are undergraduates (43 freshmen). 52 percent are women and 48 percent are men. 26.5 percent are international students.

Expenses for 2007–08 *Application fee:* $100. *Tuition:* $29,700 full-time, $1320 per credit part-time. *Mandatory fees:* $280 full-time, $140 per term part-time.

Financial Aid Forms of aid include need-based and non-need-based scholarships and part-time jobs. The priority application deadline for financial aid is February 17.

Freshman Admission San Francisco Conservatory of Music requires an essay, a high school transcript, 2 recommendations, and audition. SAT or ACT scores are recommended. The application deadline for regular admission is December 1 and for nonresidents it is December 1.

Transfer Admission The application deadline for admission is December 1.

Entrance Difficulty San Francisco Conservatory of Music assesses its entrance difficulty level as moderately difficult. For the fall 2006 freshman class, 52 percent of the applicants were accepted.

For Further Information Contact Alexander Brose, San Francisco Conservatory of Music, 50 Oak Street, San Francisco, CA 94102. *Telephone:* 800-899-7326. *Fax:* 415-503-6299. *E-mail:* admit@sfcm.edu. *Web site:* http://www.sfcm.edu/.

SAN FRANCISCO STATE UNIVERSITY

San Francisco, California

San Francisco State University is a coed, public, comprehensive unit of California State University System, founded in 1899, offering degrees at the bachelor's, master's, and doctoral levels and postbachelor's certificates. It has a 90-acre campus in San Francisco.

Academic Information The faculty has 1,807 members (49% full-time), 51% with terminal degrees. The undergraduate student-faculty ratio is 21:1. The library holds 1 million titles, 15,644 serial subscriptions, and 192,862 audiovisual materials. Special programs include academic remediation, services for learning-disabled students, an honors program,

San Francisco State University (continued)

cooperative (work-study) education, study abroad, advanced placement credit, accelerated degree programs, ESL programs, double majors, independent study, distance learning, self-designed majors, summer session for credit, part-time degree programs (daytime, evenings, weekends, summer), adult/continuing education programs, internships, and arrangement for off-campus study with The San Francisco Consortium, 18 other institutions of the California State University System. The most frequently chosen baccalaureate fields are business/marketing, social sciences, visual and performing arts.

Student Body Statistics The student body totals 29,628, of whom 23,843 are undergraduates (3,258 freshmen). 59 percent are women and 41 percent are men. Students come from 46 states and territories and 129 other countries. 99 percent are from California. 5.6 percent are international students.

Expenses for 2006–07 *Application fee:* $55. *State resident tuition:* $0 full-time. *Nonresident tuition:* $10,170 full-time, $339 per unit part-time. *Mandatory fees:* $3166 full-time, $323 per term part-time. Both full-time and part-time tuition and fees vary according to degree level. *College room and board:* $9544. *College room only:* $6202. Room and board charges vary according to board plan and housing facility.

Financial Aid Forms of aid include need-based scholarships, athletic grants, and part-time jobs. The average aided 2006–07 undergraduate received an aid package worth an estimated $8441. The priority application deadline for financial aid is March 2.

Freshman Admission San Francisco State University requires a high school transcript and TOEFL scores for international students. SAT or ACT scores are required for some. The application deadline for regular admission is rolling.

Entrance Difficulty San Francisco State University assesses its entrance difficulty level as moderately difficult; very difficult for out-of-state applicants. For the fall 2006 freshman class, 66 percent of the applicants were accepted.

For Further Information Contact Admissions Officer, San Francisco State University, 1600 Holloway Avenue, San Francisco, CA 94132. *Telephone:* 415-338-1113. *Fax:* 415-338-7196. *E-mail:* ugadmit@sfsu.edu. *Web site:* http://www.sfsu.edu/.

SAN JOAQUIN VALLEY COLLEGE
Visalia, California

San Joaquin Valley College is a coed, private, two-year college, founded in 1977, offering degrees at the associate level.

Expenses for 2006–07 *Tuition:* $11,475 full-time, $348 per unit part-time.

For Further Information Contact Mr. Joseph Holt, Director of Marketing and Admissions, San Joaquin Valley College, 3828 West Caldwell Avenue, Suite A, Visalia, CA 93277. *Telephone:* 559-651-2500. *Fax:* 559-734-9048. *E-mail:* josephh@sjvc.edu. *Web site:* http://www.sjvc.edu.

SAN JOSE CHRISTIAN COLLEGE

See William Jessup University.

SAN JOSE STATE UNIVERSITY
San Jose, California

San Jose State University is a coed, public, comprehensive unit of California State University System, founded in 1857, offering degrees at the bachelor's and master's levels. It has a 104-acre campus in San Jose.

Academic Information The library holds 2 million titles, 35,390 serial subscriptions, and 32,270 audiovisual materials. Special programs include academic remediation, services for learning-disabled students, an honors program, cooperative (work-study) education, study abroad, advanced placement credit, accelerated degree programs, ESL programs, double majors, independent study, distance learning, self-designed majors, summer

session for credit, part-time degree programs (daytime, evenings, summer), adult/continuing education programs, internships, and arrangement for off-campus study with other institutions of the California State University System. The most frequently chosen baccalaureate fields are business/marketing, engineering, visual and performing arts.

Student Body Statistics The student body totals 29,604, of whom 22,521 are undergraduates (2,722 freshmen). 51 percent are women and 49 percent are men. 3.1 percent are international students.

Expenses for 2006–07 *Application fee:* $55. *Nonresident tuition:* $10,170 full-time, $339 per unit part-time. *Mandatory fees:* $3296 full-time. Full-time tuition and fees vary according to course load. Part-time tuition varies according to course load. *College room and board:* $9096. *College room only:* $5640. Room and board charges vary according to board plan and housing facility.

Financial Aid Forms of aid include need-based and non-need-based scholarships. The average aided 2005–06 undergraduate received an aid package worth $9822.

Freshman Admission San Jose State University requires a high school transcript and TOEFL scores for international students. SAT or ACT scores are required for some. The application deadline for regular admission is November 30.

Transfer Admission The application deadline for admission is rolling.

Entrance Difficulty For the fall 2006 freshman class, 65 percent of the applicants were accepted.

For Further Information Contact San Jose State University, One Washington Square, San Jose, CA 95192-0001. *Telephone:* 408-283-7500. *Fax:* 408-924-2050. *E-mail:* contact@sjsu.edu. *Web site:* http://www.sjsu.edu/.

SANTA CLARA UNIVERSITY
Santa Clara, California

Santa Clara University is a coed, private, Roman Catholic (Jesuit) university, founded in 1851, offering degrees at the bachelor's, master's, doctoral, and first professional levels and post-master's, first professional, and postbachelor's certificates. It has a 106-acre campus in Santa Clara near San Francisco and San Jose.

Academic Information The faculty has 766 members (62% full-time), 76% with terminal degrees. The undergraduate student-faculty ratio is 12:1. The library holds 786,360 titles, 4,459 serial subscriptions, and 10,493 audiovisual materials. Special programs include services for learning-disabled students, an honors program, cooperative (work-study) education, study abroad, advanced placement credit, double majors, independent study, self-designed majors, summer session for credit, and internships. The most frequently chosen baccalaureate fields are business/marketing, engineering, social sciences.

Student Body Statistics The student body totals 7,952, of whom 4,613 are undergraduates (1,339 freshmen). 54 percent are women and 46 percent are men. Students come from 38 states and territories and 21 other countries. 55 percent are from California. 2.6 percent are international students. 17.2 percent of the 2006 graduating class went on to graduate and professional schools.

Expenses for 2006–07 *Application fee:* $55. *Comprehensive fee:* $41,280 includes full-time tuition ($30,900) and college room and board ($10,380). Room and board charges vary according to board plan, housing facility, and student level. *Part-time tuition:* $1030 per unit. Part-time tuition varies according to course load.

Financial Aid Forms of aid include need-based and non-need-based scholarships, athletic grants, and part-time jobs. The average aided 2006–07 undergraduate received an aid package worth an estimated $19,689. The priority application deadline for financial aid is February 1.

Freshman Admission Santa Clara University requires an essay, a high school transcript, 1 recommendation, SAT or ACT scores, and TOEFL scores for international students. The application deadline for regular admission is January 15 and for early action it is November 1.

Transfer Admission The application deadline for admission is May 1.

Entrance Difficulty Santa Clara University assesses its entrance difficulty level as moderately difficult; very difficult for transfer students in business programs. For the fall 2006 freshman class, 66 percent of the applicants were accepted.

For Further Information Contact Ms. Sandra Hayes, Dean of Undergraduate Admissions, Santa Clara University, 500 El Camino Real, Santa Clara, CA 95053. *Telephone:* 408-554-4700. *Fax:* 408-554-5255. *E-mail:* ugadmissions@scu.edu. *Web site:* http://www.scu.edu/.

SCRIPPS COLLEGE

Claremont, California

Scripps College is a women's, private, four-year college of The Claremont Colleges Consortium, founded in 1926, offering degrees at the bachelor's level and postbachelor's certificates. It has a 30-acre campus in Claremont near Los Angeles.

Academic Information The faculty has 95 members (71% full-time), 97% with terminal degrees. The student-faculty ratio is 11:1. The library holds 3 million titles, 35,033 serial subscriptions, and 3,578 audiovisual materials. Special programs include study abroad, advanced placement credit, accelerated degree programs, double majors, independent study, self-designed majors, part-time degree programs (daytime, evenings), internships, and arrangement for off-campus study with 5 members of The Claremont Colleges, Colby College, Haverford College, Spelman College, California Institute of Technology, American University (Washington Semester), Drew University, George Washington University. The most frequently chosen baccalaureate fields are area and ethnic studies, social sciences, visual and performing arts.

Student Body Statistics The student body totals 890, of whom 869 are undergraduates (223 freshmen). Students come from 41 states and territories and 6 other countries. 42 percent are from California. 1.2 percent are international students. 21 percent of the 2006 graduating class went on to graduate and professional schools.

Expenses for 2006–07 *Application fee:* $50. *Comprehensive fee:* $43,800 includes full-time tuition ($33,506), mandatory fees ($194), and college room and board ($10,100). *College room only:* $5400. Full-time tuition and fees vary according to program. Room and board charges vary according to board plan. *Part-time tuition:* $4188 per course. Part-time tuition varies according to program.

Financial Aid Forms of aid include need-based and non-need-based scholarships and part-time jobs. The average aided 2006–07 undergraduate received an aid package worth an estimated $29,642.

Freshman Admission Scripps College requires an essay, a high school transcript, 3 recommendations, a graded writing sample, SAT or ACT scores, and TOEFL scores for international students. A minimum 3.0 high school GPA and an interview are recommended. The application deadline for regular admission is January 1; for early decision plan 1 it is November 1; and for early decision plan 2 it is January 1.

Transfer Admission The application deadline for admission is April 1.

Entrance Difficulty Scripps College assesses its entrance difficulty level as very difficult. For the fall 2006 freshman class, 45 percent of the applicants were accepted.

For Further Information Contact Ms. Patricia F. Goldsmith, Dean of Admission and Financial Aid, Scripps College, 1030 Columbia Avenue, Claremont, CA 91711. *Telephone:* 909-621-8149 or 800-770-1333 (toll-free). *Fax:* 909-607-7508. *E-mail:* admission@scrippscollege.edu. *Web site:* http://www.scrippscollege.edu.

SHASTA BIBLE COLLEGE

Redding, California

Shasta Bible College is a coed, private, nondenominational, comprehensive institution, founded in 1971, offering degrees at the associate, bachelor's, and master's levels. It has a 25-acre campus in Redding.

Academic Information The faculty has 34 members (29% full-time), 29% with terminal degrees. The undergraduate student-faculty ratio is 5:1. The library holds 30,321 titles and 103 serial subscriptions. Special programs include academic remediation, cooperative (work-study) education, accelerated degree programs, double majors, independent study, distance learning, summer session for credit, part-time degree programs, and adult/continuing education programs.

Student Body Statistics The student body totals 109, of whom 94 are undergraduates (10 freshmen). 52 percent are women and 48 percent are men. Students come from 9 states and territories and 3 other countries. 75 percent are from California. 4.3 percent are international students.

Expenses for 2007–08 *Application fee:* $35. *Tuition:* $7200 full-time, $225 per unit part-time. *Mandatory fees:* $380 full-time, $380 per year part-time. *College room only:* $1650.

Financial Aid Forms of aid include need-based and non-need-based scholarships and part-time jobs. The average aided 2005–06 undergraduate received an aid package worth $5544. The application deadline for financial aid is continuous.

Freshman Admission Shasta Bible College requires an essay, a high school transcript, a minimum 2.0 high school GPA, 4 recommendations, and TOEFL scores for international students. An interview is required for some. The application deadline for regular admission is August 27.

Transfer Admission The application deadline for admission is August 27.

Entrance Difficulty Shasta Bible College has an open admission policy.

For Further Information Contact Mr. Mark A. Mueller, Registrar, Shasta Bible College, 2951 Goodwater Avenue, Redding, CA 96002. *Telephone:* 530-221-4275 Ext. 206, 800-800-45BC (toll-free in-state), or 800-800-6929 (toll-free out-of-state). *Fax:* 530-221-6929. *E-mail:* admissions@shasta.edu. *Web site:* http://www.shasta.edu/.

SILICON VALLEY UNIVERSITY

San Jose, California

http://www.svuca.edu/

SIMPSON UNIVERSITY

Redding, California

Simpson University is a coed, private, comprehensive institution, founded in 1921, affiliated with The Christian and Missionary Alliance, offering degrees at the associate, bachelor's, and master's levels. It has a 92-acre campus in Redding.

Academic Information The faculty has 104 members (35% full-time), 54% with terminal degrees. The undergraduate student-faculty ratio is 17:1. The library holds 116,871 titles, 12,235 serial subscriptions, and 2,548 audiovisual materials. Special programs include services for learning-disabled students, an honors program, study abroad, advanced placement credit, accelerated degree programs, double majors, independent study, distance learning, self-designed majors, summer session for credit, part-time degree programs (daytime, evenings, weekends, summer), adult/continuing education programs, internships, and arrangement for off-campus study with Coalition for Christian Colleges and Universities. The most frequently chosen baccalaureate fields are liberal arts/general studies, psychology, theology and religious vocations.

Student Body Statistics The student body totals 1,015, of whom 862 are undergraduates (164 freshmen). 64 percent are women and 36 percent are men. Students come from 24 states and territories and 5 other countries. 82 percent are from California. 1.4 percent are international students.

Expenses for 2007–08 *Application fee:* $20. *Comprehensive fee:* $25,000 includes full-time tuition ($18,600) and college room and board ($6400).

Financial Aid Forms of aid include need-based and non-need-based scholarships, athletic grants, and part-time jobs. The average aided 2005–06 undergraduate received an aid package worth $7750.

Freshman Admission Simpson University requires an essay, a high school transcript, 2 recommendations, Christian commitment, SAT or ACT scores, and TOEFL scores for international students. An interview is required for some. The application deadline for regular admission is rolling.

Transfer Admission The application deadline for admission is rolling.

Simpson University (continued)

Entrance Difficulty Simpson University assesses its entrance difficulty level as moderately difficult. For the fall 2006 freshman class, 55 percent of the applicants were accepted.

For Further Information Contact Mr. James Herberger, Director of Enrollment Management, Simpson University, 2211 College View Drive, Redding, CA 96003. *Telephone:* 530-224-5600 or 800-598-2493 (toll-free). *Fax:* 530-226-4861. *E-mail:* admissions@simpsonuniversity.edu. *Web site:* http://www.simpsonuniversity.edu/.

SOKA UNIVERSITY OF AMERICA
Aliso Viejo, California

Soka University of America is a coed, private, four-year college, founded in 2001, offering degrees at the bachelor's and master's levels. It has a 103-acre campus in Aliso Viejo.

Academic Information The faculty has 55 members (69% full-time), 82% with terminal degrees. The undergraduate student-faculty ratio is 8:1. The library holds 63,806 titles and 11,141 serial subscriptions. Special programs include academic remediation, services for learning-disabled students, study abroad, independent study, and internships. The most frequently chosen baccalaureate field is liberal arts/general studies.

Student Body Statistics The student body totals 380, of whom 360 are undergraduates (86 freshmen). 62 percent are women and 38 percent are men. Students come from 18 states and territories and 32 other countries. 19 percent are from California. 34.2 percent are international students. 40 percent of the 2006 graduating class went on to graduate and professional schools.

Expenses for 2007–08 *Application fee:* $45. *Comprehensive fee:* $30,708 includes full-time tuition ($22,108) and college room and board ($8600). *Part-time tuition:* $922 per credit.

Freshman Admission Soka University of America requires an essay, a high school transcript, 2 recommendations, SAT or ACT scores, and ACT Writing Test. The application deadline for regular admission is January 6; for nonresidents it is January 6; and for early action it is October 15.

Entrance Difficulty Soka University of America assesses its entrance difficulty level as moderately difficult. For the fall 2006 freshman class, 40 percent of the applicants were accepted.

For Further Information Contact Ms. Marilyn Grove, Director of Student Recruitment Programs, Soka University of America, Enrollment Services, 1 University Drive, Aliso Viejo, CA 92656. *Telephone:* 949-480-4131, 949-480-4150 (toll-free in-state), or 888-600-SOKA (toll-free out-of-state). *Fax:* 949-480-4151. *E-mail:* admission@soka.edu. *Web site:* http://www.soka.edu/.

SONOMA STATE UNIVERSITY
Rohnert Park, California

Sonoma State University is a coed, public, comprehensive unit of California State University System, founded in 1960, offering degrees at the bachelor's and master's levels. It has a 280-acre campus in Rohnert Park near San Francisco.

Academic Information The faculty has 542 members. The undergraduate student-faculty ratio is 23:1. The library holds 636,613 titles and 21,115 serial subscriptions. Special programs include academic remediation, services for learning-disabled students, an honors program, cooperative (work-study) education, study abroad, advanced placement credit, accelerated degree programs, ESL programs, double majors, independent study, distance learning, self-designed majors, summer session for credit, part-time degree programs (daytime, evenings), adult/continuing education programs, internships, and arrangement for off-campus study with other units of the California State University System, National Student Exchange, Mills College.

Student Body Statistics The student body totals 7,749, of whom 6,599 are undergraduates (1,053 freshmen). 63 percent are women and 37 percent are men. Students come from 40 states and territories and 29 other countries. 98 percent are from California. 1.1 percent are international students.

Expenses for 2006–07 *Application fee:* $55. *State resident tuition:* $0 full-time. *Nonresident tuition:* $10,170 full-time. *Mandatory fees:* $3648 full-time.

Financial Aid Forms of aid include need-based and non-need-based scholarships, athletic grants, and part-time jobs. The average aided 2005–06 undergraduate received an aid package worth $9971. The priority application deadline for financial aid is January 31.

Freshman Admission Sonoma State University requires a high school transcript, SAT or ACT scores, and TOEFL scores for international students. The application deadline for regular admission is rolling.

Transfer Admission The application deadline for admission is rolling.

Entrance Difficulty Sonoma State University assesses its entrance difficulty level as moderately difficult; very difficult for out-of-state applicants. For the fall 2006 freshman class, 66 percent of the applicants were accepted.

For Further Information Contact Mr. Gustavo Flores, Interim Director of Admissions, Sonoma State University, 1801 East Cotati Avenue, Rohnert Park, CA 94928. *Telephone:* 707-664-2778. *Fax:* 707-664-2060. *E-mail:* csumentor@sonoma.edu. *Web site:* http://www.sonoma.edu/.

SOUTHERN CALIFORNIA COLLEGE

See Vanguard University of Southern California.

SOUTHERN CALIFORNIA INSTITUTE OF ARCHITECTURE
Los Angeles, California

Southern California Institute of Architecture is a coed, private, comprehensive institution, founded in 1972, offering degrees at the bachelor's, master's, and first professional levels.

Academic Information The faculty has 80 members. The undergraduate student-faculty ratio is 15:1. The library holds 30,000 titles and 109 serial subscriptions. Special programs include academic remediation, cooperative (work-study) education, study abroad, advanced placement credit, ESL programs, summer session for credit, and internships.

Student Body Statistics The student body totals 438, of whom 232 are undergraduates (11 freshmen). 32 percent are women and 68 percent are men. Students come from 33 states and territories and 18 other countries. 70 percent are from California. 15.5 percent are international students. 10 percent of the 2006 graduating class went on to graduate and professional schools.

Expenses for 2007–08 *Application fee:* $60. *Tuition:* $10,636 full-time. *Mandatory fees:* $60 full-time.

Financial Aid Forms of aid include need-based and non-need-based scholarships and part-time jobs. The average aided 2005–06 undergraduate received an aid package worth $11,946. The priority application deadline for financial aid is March 2.

Freshman Admission Southern California Institute of Architecture requires an essay, a high school transcript, a minimum 2.0 high school GPA, 3 recommendations, a portfolio, SAT or ACT scores, and TOEFL scores for international students. An interview is recommended. The application deadline for regular admission is February 1.

Transfer Admission The application deadline for admission is rolling.

Entrance Difficulty Southern California Institute of Architecture assesses its entrance difficulty level as moderately difficult. For the fall 2006 freshman class, 58 percent of the applicants were accepted.

For Further Information Contact Mr. J.J. Jackman, Admissions Director, Southern California Institute of Architecture, Freight Yard, 960 East 3rd Street, Los Angeles, CA 90013. *Telephone:* 213-613-2200 Ext. 321 or 800-774-7242 (toll-free). *Fax:* 213-613-2260. *E-mail:* jj@sciarc.edu. *Web site:* http://www.sciarc.edu/.

SOUTHERN CALIFORNIA INSTITUTE OF TECHNOLOGY

Anaheim, California

http://www.scitcollege.com/

SOUTHERN CALIFORNIA SEMINARY

El Cajon, California

http://www.socalsem.edu/

STANFORD UNIVERSITY

Stanford, California

Stanford University is a coed, private university, founded in 1891, offering degrees at the bachelor's, master's, doctoral, and first professional levels. It has an 8,180-acre campus in Stanford near San Francisco.

Academic Information The faculty has 1,041 members (98% full-time), 98% with terminal degrees. The undergraduate student-faculty ratio is 6:1. The library holds 8 million titles, 75,000 serial subscriptions, and 2 million audiovisual materials. Special programs include services for learning-disabled students, an honors program, study abroad, advanced placement credit, double majors, independent study, self-designed majors, summer session for credit, internships, and arrangement for off-campus study with Howard University; Hopkins Marine Station; Spelman College; Morehouse College, Dartmouth College. The most frequently chosen baccalaureate fields are interdisciplinary studies, engineering, social sciences.

Student Body Statistics The student body totals 17,747, of whom 6,422 are undergraduates (1,646 freshmen). 48 percent are women and 52 percent are men. Students come from 52 states and territories and 68 other countries. 66 percent are from California. 6.1 percent are international students. 35 percent of the 2006 graduating class went on to graduate and professional schools.

Expenses for 2006–07 *Application fee:* $75. *Comprehensive fee:* $43,361 includes full-time tuition ($32,994) and college room and board ($10,367). *College room only:* $5571. Room and board charges vary according to board plan.

Financial Aid Forms of aid include need-based scholarships, athletic grants, and part-time jobs. The average aided 2005–06 undergraduate received an aid package worth $29,234. The priority application deadline for financial aid is February 15.

Freshman Admission Stanford University requires an essay, a high school transcript, 2 recommendations, and SAT or ACT scores. SAT Subject Test scores and TOEFL scores for international students are recommended. The application deadline for regular admission is December 15 and for early action it is November 1.

Transfer Admission The application deadline for admission is March 15.

Entrance Difficulty Stanford University assesses its entrance difficulty level as most difficult. For the fall 2006 freshman class, 11 percent of the applicants were accepted.

For Further Information Contact Rick Shaw, Dean of Undergraduate Admissions and Financial Aid, Stanford University, Montag Building, 355 Galvez Street, Stanford, CA 94305-3020. *Telephone:* 650-723-2091. *Fax:* 650-723-6050. *E-mail:* admission@stanford.edu. *Web site:* http://www.stanford.edu/.

THOMAS AQUINAS COLLEGE

Santa Paula, California

Thomas Aquinas College is a coed, private, Roman Catholic, four-year college, founded in 1971, offering degrees at the bachelor's level. It has a 170-acre campus in Santa Paula near Los Angeles.

Academic Information The faculty has 37 members (84% full-time), 65% with terminal degrees. The student-faculty ratio is 11:1. The library holds 62,000 titles and 85 serial subscriptions. Special programs include cooperative (work-study) education. The most frequently chosen baccalaureate field is liberal arts/general studies.

Student Body Statistics The student body is made up of 351 undergraduates (104 freshmen). 50 percent are women and 50 percent are men. Students come from 43 states and territories and 8 other countries. 42 percent are from California. 7.7 percent are international students. 36 percent of the 2006 graduating class went on to graduate and professional schools.

Expenses for 2007–08 *Application fee:* $0. *Comprehensive fee:* $27,000 includes full-time tuition ($20,400) and college room and board ($6600).

Financial Aid Forms of aid include need-based scholarships and part-time jobs. The average aided 2006–07 undergraduate received an aid package worth an estimated $16,202. The application deadline for financial aid is March 2.

Freshman Admission Thomas Aquinas College requires an essay, a high school transcript, 3 recommendations, and SAT or ACT scores. A minimum 3.0 high school GPA and TOEFL scores for international students are recommended. An interview is required for some. The application deadline for regular admission is rolling.

Entrance Difficulty Thomas Aquinas College assesses its entrance difficulty level as very difficult. For the fall 2006 freshman class, 83 percent of the applicants were accepted.

For Further Information Contact Mr. Jonathan P. Daly, Director of Admissions, Thomas Aquinas College, 10000 North Ojai Road, Santa Paula, CA 93060-9621. *Telephone:* 805-525-4417 Ext. 361 or 800-634-9797 (toll-free). *Fax:* 805-525-9342. *E-mail:* admissions@thomasaqinas.edu. *Web site:* http://www.thomasaquinas.edu/.

TOURO UNIVERSITY INTERNATIONAL

Cypress, California

Touro University International is a coed, private university, offering degrees at the bachelor's, master's, and doctoral levels and postbachelor's certificates (offers only online degree programs).

Academic Information The faculty has 213 members (24% full-time), 99% with terminal degrees. The undergraduate student-faculty ratio is 18:1. The library holds 30,692 titles and 1,500 serial subscriptions. Special programs include distance learning, summer session for credit, part-time degree programs (daytime, evenings, weekends, summer), and adult/continuing education programs.

Student Body Statistics The student body is made up of 2,743 undergraduates (183 freshmen). 35 percent are women and 65 percent are men. Students come from 50 states and territories and 14 other countries. 10 percent are from California.

Expenses for 2007–08 *Application fee:* $0. *Tuition:* $8000 full-time, $250 per credit part-time.

Freshman Admission Touro University International requires a high school transcript, a minimum 3.0 high school GPA, and TOEFL scores for international students. An interview is recommended. An essay is required for some. The application deadline for regular admission is rolling.

Entrance Difficulty Touro University International has an open admission policy.

For Further Information Contact Wei Ren-Finaly, Registrar, Touro University International, 5336 Plaza Drive, 3rd Floor, Cypress, CA 90630. *Telephone:* 714-816-0366. *Fax:* 714-827-7407. *E-mail:* registration@tourou.edu. *Web site:* http://www.tourou.edu/.

TRINITY LIFE BIBLE COLLEGE

Sacramento, California

http://www.tlbc.edu/

UNITED STATES INTERNATIONAL UNIVERSITY

See Alliant International University.

UNIVERSITY OF CALIFORNIA, BERKELEY

Berkeley, California

University of California, Berkeley is a coed, public unit of University of California System, founded in 1868, offering degrees at the bachelor's, master's, doctoral, and first professional levels. It has a 1,232-acre campus in Berkeley near San Francisco.

Academic Information The faculty has 2,026 members (76% full-time), 98% with terminal degrees. The undergraduate student-faculty ratio is 15:1. The library holds 15 million titles, 192,030 serial subscriptions, and 125,734 audiovisual materials. Special programs include services for learning-disabled students, an honors program, study abroad, advanced placement credit, accelerated degree programs, ESL programs, double majors, independent study, distance learning, self-designed majors, summer session for credit, adult/continuing education programs, internships, and arrangement for off-campus study with Holy Names College, Mills College, Dominican College, John F. Kennedy University, San Francisco State University, Sonoma State University, California State University, Hayward. The most frequently chosen baccalaureate fields are biological/life sciences, engineering, social sciences.

Student Body Statistics The student body totals 33,933, of whom 23,863 are undergraduates (4,157 freshmen). 54 percent are women and 46 percent are men. Students come from 53 states and territories and 87 other countries. 89 percent are from California. 3.2 percent are international students.

Expenses for 2006–07 *Application fee:* $60. *State resident tuition:* $0 full-time. *Nonresident tuition:* $18,684 full-time. *Mandatory fees:* $6654 full-time. Full-time tuition and fees vary according to program. *College room and board:* $13,074. Room and board charges vary according to board plan and housing facility.

Financial Aid Forms of aid include need-based and non-need-based scholarships, athletic grants, and part-time jobs. The average aided 2006–07 undergraduate received an aid package worth an estimated $15,710. The application deadline for financial aid is March 2 with a priority deadline of March 2.

Freshman Admission University of California, Berkeley requires an essay, a high school transcript, SAT or ACT scores, SAT Subject Test scores, and TOEFL scores for international students. The application deadline for regular admission is November 30.

Transfer Admission The application deadline for admission is November 30.

Entrance Difficulty University of California, Berkeley assesses its entrance difficulty level as very difficult; most difficult for out-of-state applicants; most difficult for some engineering programs. For the fall 2006 freshman class, 24 percent of the applicants were accepted.

For Further Information Contact Mr. Walter Robinson, Office of Undergraduate Admissions, University of California, Berkeley, Berkeley, CA 94720-1500. *Telephone:* 510-642-3175. *Fax:* 510-642-7333. *E-mail:* ouars@uclink.berkeley.edu. *Web site:* http://www.berkeley.edu/.

UNIVERSITY OF CALIFORNIA, DAVIS

Davis, California

University of California, Davis is a coed, public unit of University of California System, founded in 1905, offering degrees at the bachelor's, master's, doctoral, and first professional levels and post-master's and postbachelor's certificates. It has a 5,993-acre campus in Davis near San Francisco.

Academic Information The faculty has 1,888 members (84% full-time), 95% with terminal degrees. The undergraduate student-faculty ratio is 19:1. The library holds 4 million titles, 44,020 serial subscriptions, and 14,944 audiovisual materials. Special programs include academic remediation, services for learning-disabled students, an honors program, study abroad, advanced placement credit, Freshman Honors College, ESL programs, double majors, independent study, self-designed majors, summer session for credit, part-time degree programs, adult/continuing education programs, and internships. The most frequently chosen baccalaureate fields are biological/life sciences, engineering, social sciences.

Student Body Statistics The student body totals 29,628, of whom 23,458 are undergraduates (5,528 freshmen). 55 percent are women and 45 percent are men. Students come from 48 states and territories and 101 other countries. 98 percent are from California. 1.8 percent are international students. 38 percent of the 2006 graduating class went on to graduate and professional schools.

Expenses for 2006–07 *Application fee:* $60. *State resident tuition:* $0 full-time. *Nonresident tuition:* $18,168 full-time. *Mandatory fees:* $7593 full-time. *College room and board:* $11,354.

Financial Aid Forms of aid include need-based and non-need-based scholarships and part-time jobs. The average aided 2005–06 undergraduate received an aid package worth $11,697. The priority application deadline for financial aid is March 2.

Freshman Admission University of California, Davis requires an essay, a high school transcript, a minimum 2.8 high school GPA, high school subject requirements, SAT or ACT scores, SAT Subject Test scores, and TOEFL scores for international students. The application deadline for regular admission is November 30.

Transfer Admission The application deadline for admission is November 30.

Entrance Difficulty University of California, Davis assesses its entrance difficulty level as moderately difficult. For the fall 2006 freshman class, 68 percent of the applicants were accepted.

For Further Information Contact Pamela Burnett, Director of Undergraduate Admissions, University of California, Davis, Undergraduate Admission and Outreach Services, 178 Mrak Hall, Davis, CA 95616. *Telephone:* 530-752-1011. *Fax:* 530-752-1280. *E-mail:* freshmanadmissions@ucdavis.edu. *Web site:* http://www.ucdavis.edu/.

UNIVERSITY OF CALIFORNIA, IRVINE

Irvine, California

University of California, Irvine is a coed, public unit of University of California System, founded in 1965, offering degrees at the bachelor's, master's, doctoral, and first professional levels and postbachelor's certificates. It has a 1,477-acre campus in Irvine near Los Angeles.

Academic Information The faculty has 1,925 members (74% full-time), 93% with terminal degrees. The undergraduate student-faculty ratio is 19:1. Special programs include academic remediation, services for learning-disabled students, an honors program, study abroad, accelerated degree programs, ESL programs, double majors, independent study, distance learning, summer session for credit, and internships. The most frequently chosen baccalaureate fields are biological/life sciences, psychology, social sciences.

Student Body Statistics The student body totals 25,229, of whom 20,719 are undergraduates (4,836 freshmen). 51 percent are women and 49 percent are men. 97 percent are from California. 2 percent are international students.

Expenses for 2006–07 *Application fee:* $60. *State resident tuition:* $0 full-time. *Nonresident tuition:* $18,684 full-time. *Mandatory fees:* $6141 full-time. *College room and board:* $9815.

Financial Aid Forms of aid include need-based and non-need-based scholarships, athletic grants, and part-time jobs. The average aided 2006–07 undergraduate received an aid package worth an estimated $13,221. The application deadline for financial aid is May 1 with a priority deadline of March 2.

Freshman Admission University of California, Irvine requires an essay, a high school transcript, a minimum 2.8 high school GPA, SAT and SAT Subject Test or ACT scores, and TOEFL scores for international students. The application deadline for regular admission is November 30.

Transfer Admission The application deadline for admission is November 30.

Entrance Difficulty For the fall 2006 freshman class, 60 percent of the applicants were accepted.

For Further Information Contact Ms. Marguerite Bonous-Hammarth, Director of Admissions and Relations with Schools, University of California, Irvine, 204 Administration, Irvine, CA 92697-1075. *Telephone:* 949-824-6703. *Web site:* http://www.uci.edu/.

UNIVERSITY OF CALIFORNIA, LOS ANGELES

Los Angeles, California

University of California, Los Angeles is a coed, public unit of University of California System, founded in 1919, offering degrees at the bachelor's, master's, doctoral, and first professional levels. It has a 419-acre campus in Los Angeles.

Academic Information The faculty has 2,505 members (75% full-time), 98% with terminal degrees. The undergraduate student-faculty ratio is 17:1. The library holds 8 million titles, 77,509 serial subscriptions, and 291,664 audiovisual materials. Special programs include services for learning-disabled students, an honors program, study abroad, advanced placement credit, Freshman Honors College, ESL programs, double majors, independent study, distance learning, self-designed majors, summer session for credit, adult/continuing education programs, internships, and arrangement for off-campus study. The most frequently chosen baccalaureate fields are psychology, biological/life sciences, social sciences.

Student Body Statistics The student body totals 38,218, of whom 25,432 are undergraduates (4,811 freshmen). 56 percent are women and 44 percent are men. Students come from 49 states and territories and 59 other countries. 98 percent are from California. 3.8 percent are international students.

Expenses for 2006–07 *Application fee:* $60. *State resident tuition:* $0 full-time. *Nonresident tuition:* $18,827 full-time. *Mandatory fees:* $7143 full-time. *College room and board:* $11,141. Room and board charges vary according to board plan and housing facility.

Financial Aid Forms of aid include need-based and non-need-based scholarships, athletic grants, and part-time jobs. The average aided 2006–07 undergraduate received an aid package worth an estimated $14,329. The application deadline for financial aid is continuous.

Freshman Admission University of California, Los Angeles requires an essay, SAT or ACT scores, SAT Subject Test scores, and TOEFL scores for international students. The application deadline for regular admission is November 30.

Transfer Admission University of California, Los Angeles requires standardized test scores. The application deadline for admission is November 30.

Entrance Difficulty University of California, Los Angeles assesses its entrance difficulty level as very difficult. For the fall 2006 freshman class, 26 percent of the applicants were accepted.

For Further Information Contact Dr. Vu T. Tran, Director of Undergraduate Admissions, University of California, Los Angeles, 405 Hilgard Avenue, Box 951436, Los Angeles, CA 90095-1436. *Telephone:* 310-825-3101. *E-mail:* ugadm@saonet.ucla.edu. *Web site:* http://www.ucla.edu/.

UNIVERSITY OF CALIFORNIA, RIVERSIDE

Riverside, California

University of California, Riverside is a coed, public unit of University of California System, founded in 1954, offering degrees at the bachelor's, master's, and doctoral levels. It has a 1,200-acre campus in Riverside near Los Angeles.

Academic Information The faculty has 857 members (85% full-time), 98% with terminal degrees. The undergraduate student-faculty ratio is 18:1. The library holds 2 million titles, 29,941 serial subscriptions, and 27,313 audiovisual materials. Special programs include academic remediation, services for learning-disabled students, an honors program, cooperative (work-study) education, study abroad, advanced placement credit, accelerated degree programs, ESL programs, double majors,

independent study, self-designed majors, summer session for credit, adult/continuing education programs, internships, and arrangement for off-campus study with University of California, Santa Barbara, University of California, Davis, University of California, Los Angeles. The most frequently chosen baccalaureate fields are business/marketing, biological/life sciences, social sciences.

Student Body Statistics The student body totals 16,875, of whom 14,792 are undergraduates (3,594 freshmen). 52 percent are women and 48 percent are men. Students come from 27 states and territories and 26 other countries. 99 percent are from California. 1.9 percent are international students. 26 percent of the 2006 graduating class went on to graduate and professional schools.

Expenses for 2006–07 *Application fee:* $60. *State resident tuition:* $0 full-time. *Nonresident tuition:* $18,684 full-time. *Mandatory fees:* $6591 full-time. *College room and board:* $10,200. Room and board charges vary according to board plan and housing facility.

Financial Aid Forms of aid include need-based and non-need-based scholarships, athletic grants, and part-time jobs. The average aided 2006–07 undergraduate received an aid package worth an estimated $13,933. The application deadline for financial aid is March 2 with a priority deadline of March 2.

Freshman Admission University of California, Riverside requires an essay, a high school transcript, a minimum 2.8 high school GPA, SAT or ACT scores, and TOEFL scores for international students. The application deadline for regular admission is November 30.

Transfer Admission The application deadline for admission is November 30.

Entrance Difficulty University of California, Riverside assesses its entrance difficulty level as very difficult. For the fall 2006 freshman class, 83 percent of the applicants were accepted.

For Further Information Contact Emily Engelschall, Director, Undergraduate Recruitment, University of California, Riverside, 1120 Hinderaker Hall, Riverside, CA 92521. *Telephone:* 951-827-4531. *Fax:* 951-827-6344. *E-mail:* discover@ucr.edu. *Web site:* http://www.ucr.edu/.

UNIVERSITY OF CALIFORNIA, SAN DIEGO

La Jolla, California

University of California, San Diego is a coed, public unit of University of California System, founded in 1959, offering degrees at the bachelor's, master's, doctoral, and first professional levels. It has a 1,976-acre campus in La Jolla near San Diego.

Academic Information The faculty has 1,149 members (84% full-time), 98% with terminal degrees. The undergraduate student-faculty ratio is 19:1. The library holds 3 million titles, 28,104 serial subscriptions, and 405,266 audiovisual materials. Special programs include services for learning-disabled students, an honors program, cooperative (work-study) education, study abroad, advanced placement credit, accelerated degree programs, Freshman Honors College, ESL programs, double majors, independent study, self-designed majors, summer session for credit, internships, and arrangement for off-campus study with Dartmouth College, Spelman College, Morehouse College. The most frequently chosen baccalaureate fields are engineering, psychology, social sciences.

Student Body Statistics The student body totals 26,465, of whom 21,369 are undergraduates (4,589 freshmen). 52 percent are women and 48 percent are men. 97 percent are from California. 40 percent of the 2006 graduating class went on to graduate and professional schools.

Expenses for 2006–07 *Application fee:* $60. *State resident tuition:* $0 full-time. *Nonresident tuition:* $18,684 full-time. *Mandatory fees:* $6,685 full-time. Full-time tuition and fees vary according to location. *College room and board:* $9657. Room and board charges vary according to board plan and location.

Financial Aid Forms of aid include need-based and non-need-based scholarships and part-time jobs. The average aided 2006–07 undergraduate received an aid package worth an estimated $13,745. The priority application deadline for financial aid is March 2.

Freshman Admission University of California, San Diego requires an essay, a high school transcript, a minimum 2.8 high school GPA, SAT or ACT scores, SAT Subject Test scores, TOEFL scores for international students, and 3 SAT Subject Tests (including SAT Writing Test). A

University of California, San Diego (continued)

minimum 3.4 high school GPA is required for some. The application deadline for regular admission is November 30.

Transfer Admission The application deadline for admission is November 30.

Entrance Difficulty University of California, San Diego assesses its entrance difficulty level as very difficult; most difficult for out-of-state applicants. For the fall 2006 freshman class, 44 percent of the applicants were accepted.

For Further Information Contact Mr. Randell Hernandez, Associate Director of Admissions and Relations with Schools, University of California, San Diego, 9500 Gilman Drive, 0021, La Jolla, CA 92093-0021. *Telephone:* 858-534-4831. *E-mail:* admissionsinfo@ucsd.edu. *Web site:* http://www.ucsd.edu/.

UNIVERSITY OF CALIFORNIA, SANTA BARBARA
Santa Barbara, California

University of California, Santa Barbara is a coed, public unit of University of California System, founded in 1909, offering degrees at the bachelor's, master's, and doctoral levels and first professional certificates. It has a 989-acre campus in Santa Barbara.

Academic Information The faculty has 1,067 members (86% full-time), 100% with terminal degrees. The undergraduate student-faculty ratio is 17:1. The library holds 3 million titles, 36,902 serial subscriptions, and 125,324 audiovisual materials. Special programs include services for learning-disabled students, an honors program, cooperative (work-study) education, study abroad, advanced placement credit, accelerated degree programs, ESL programs, double majors, independent study, distance learning, self-designed majors, summer session for credit, internships, and arrangement for off-campus study with other campuses of the University of California System.

Student Body Statistics The student body totals 21,062, of whom 18,212 are undergraduates (4,096 freshmen). 55 percent are women and 45 percent are men. Students come from 51 states and territories and 112 other countries. 96 percent are from California. 1.3 percent are international students. 31 percent of the 2006 graduating class went on to graduate and professional schools.

Expenses for 2006–07 *Application fee:* $60. *State resident tuition:* $0 full-time. *Nonresident tuition:* $18,684 full-time. *Mandatory fees:* $7277 full-time. *College room and board:* $11,178. *College room only:* $8798.

Financial Aid Forms of aid include need-based and non-need-based scholarships, athletic grants, and part-time jobs. The average aided 2005–06 undergraduate received an aid package worth $13,437. The priority application deadline for financial aid is March 2.

Freshman Admission University of California, Santa Barbara requires an essay, a high school transcript, SAT or ACT scores, SAT Subject Test scores, and TOEFL scores for international students. An interview is required for some. The application deadline for regular admission is November 30.

Transfer Admission The application deadline for admission is November 30.

Entrance Difficulty University of California, Santa Barbara assesses its entrance difficulty level as very difficult. For the fall 2006 freshman class, 53 percent of the applicants were accepted.

For Further Information Contact Office of Admissions, University of California, Santa Barbara, 1210 Cheadle Hall, Santa Barbara, CA 93106-2014. *Telephone:* 805-893-2881. *Fax:* 805-893-2676. *E-mail:* admissions@sa.ucsb.edu. *Web site:* http://www.ucsb.edu/.

UNIVERSITY OF CALIFORNIA, SANTA CRUZ
Santa Cruz, California

University of California, Santa Cruz is a coed, public unit of University of California System, founded in 1965, offering degrees at the bachelor's, master's, and doctoral levels and postbachelor's certificates. It has a 2,000-acre campus in Santa Cruz near San Francisco and San Jose.

Academic Information The faculty has 759 members (72% full-time), 98% with terminal degrees. The undergraduate student-faculty ratio is 19:1. The library holds 1 million titles, 25,486 serial subscriptions, and 36,585 audiovisual materials. Special programs include academic remediation, services for learning-disabled students, cooperative (work-study) education, study abroad, advanced placement credit, Freshman Honors College, ESL programs, double majors, independent study, self-designed majors, summer session for credit, part-time degree programs, adult/continuing education programs, internships, and arrangement for off-campus study with other campuses of the University of California System, University of New Hampshire, University of New Mexico. The most frequently chosen baccalaureate fields are biological/life sciences, social sciences, visual and performing arts.

Student Body Statistics The student body totals 15,364, of whom 13,961 are undergraduates (3,350 freshmen). 53 percent are women and 47 percent are men. Students come from 45 states and territories and 12 other countries. 98 percent are from California. 0.7 percent are international students.

Expenses for 2006–07 *Application fee:* $60. *State resident tuition:* $0 full-time. *Nonresident tuition:* $18,168 full-time. *Mandatory fees:* $7962 full-time. *College room and board:* $11,805. Room and board charges vary according to board plan and housing facility.

Financial Aid Forms of aid include need-based and non-need-based scholarships. The average aided 2006–07 undergraduate received an aid package worth an estimated $14,422. The application deadline for financial aid is June 1 with a priority deadline of March 17.

Freshman Admission University of California, Santa Cruz requires an essay, a high school transcript, SAT or ACT scores, TOEFL scores for international students, and SAT Subject Tests required in two different areas: history/social science, English literature, mathematics, laboratory science, or language other than English. The application deadline for regular admission is November 30.

Transfer Admission The application deadline for admission is November 30.

Entrance Difficulty University of California, Santa Cruz assesses its entrance difficulty level as very difficult. For the fall 2006 freshman class, 80 percent of the applicants were accepted.

For Further Information Contact Kevin Browne, Executive Director of Admissions and University Registrar, University of California, Santa Cruz, Admissions Office, Cook House, Santa Cruz, CA 95064. *Telephone:* 831-459-5779. *Fax:* 831-459-4452. *E-mail:* admissions@ucsc.edu. *Web site:* http://www.ucsc.edu/.

UNIVERSITY OF JUDAISM
Bel Air, California

University of Judaism is a coed, private, Jewish, comprehensive institution, founded in 1947, offering degrees at the bachelor's and master's levels. It has a 28-acre campus in Bel Air near Los Angeles.

Academic Information The faculty has 91 members (21% full-time), 42% with terminal degrees. The undergraduate student-faculty ratio is 7:1. The library holds 110,000 titles, 400 serial subscriptions, and 20 audiovisual materials. Special programs include academic remediation, services for learning-disabled students, cooperative (work-study) education, study abroad, advanced placement credit, double majors, independent study, self-designed majors, summer session for credit, part-time degree programs, internships, and arrangement for off-campus study with Mount Saint Mary's College, Cedars-Sinai Medical Center, University of California, Los Angeles.

Student Body Statistics The student body totals 291, of whom 115 are undergraduates (18 freshmen). 49 percent are women and 51 percent are men. Students come from 10 states and territories and 3 other countries. 70 percent are from California. 70 percent of the 2006 graduating class went on to graduate and professional schools.

Expenses for 2006–07 *Application fee:* $35. *Comprehensive fee:* $31,078 includes full-time tuition ($19,440), mandatory fees ($860), and college room and board ($10,778). Room and board charges vary according to board plan. *Part-time tuition:* $810 per credit.

Financial Aid Forms of aid include need-based and non-need-based scholarships and part-time jobs. The average aided 2006–07 undergraduate received an aid package worth an estimated $19,860. The priority application deadline for financial aid is March 2.

Freshman Admission University of Judaism requires an essay, a high school transcript, 2 recommendations, SAT or ACT scores, and TOEFL scores for international students. A minimum 3.3 high school GPA and an interview are recommended. An interview is required for some. The application deadline for regular admission is rolling and for early decision it is December 31.

Transfer Admission The application deadline for admission is rolling.

Entrance Difficulty University of Judaism assesses its entrance difficulty level as moderately difficult; very difficult for President's Scholars Program.

For Further Information Contact Mr. Matt Davidson, Director of Undergraduate Admissions, University of Judaism, 15600 Mulholland Drive, Los Angeles, CA 90077-1519. *Telephone:* 310-476-9777 Ext. 250 or 888-853-6763 (toll-free). *Fax:* 310-471-3657. *E-mail:* admissions@uj.edu. *Web site:* http://www.uj.edu/.

UNIVERSITY OF LA VERNE

La Verne, California

SPONSOR
See Front Insert for Details!

University of La Verne is a coed, private university, founded in 1891, offering degrees at the associate, bachelor's, master's, doctoral, and first professional levels and post-master's and postbachelor's certificates (also offers continuing education program with significant enrollment not reflected in profile). It has a 38-acre campus in La Verne near Los Angeles.

Academic Information The faculty has 402 members (48% full-time), 38% with terminal degrees. The undergraduate student-faculty ratio is 12:1. The library holds 195,488 titles, 531,006 serial subscriptions, and 1,720 audiovisual materials. Special programs include academic remediation, services for learning-disabled students, an honors program, study abroad, advanced placement credit, accelerated degree programs, Freshman Honors College, ESL programs, double majors, independent study, distance learning, self-designed majors, summer session for credit, part-time degree programs (daytime, evenings, weekends, summer), adult/continuing education programs, internships, and arrangement for off-campus study with Elizabethtown College, Juniata College, McPherson College, Bridgewater College, Manchester College. The most frequently chosen baccalaureate fields are business/marketing, liberal arts/general studies, social sciences.

Student Body Statistics The student body totals 3,876, of whom 1,685 are undergraduates (319 freshmen). 64 percent are women and 36 percent are men. Students come from 13 states and territories and 5 other countries. 98 percent are from California. 1.7 percent are international students.

Expenses for 2007–08 *Application fee:* $50. *Comprehensive fee:* $35,340 includes full-time tuition ($25,590) and college room and board ($9750). *College room only:* $5100. *Part-time tuition:* $720 per unit.

Financial Aid Forms of aid include need-based and non-need-based scholarships and part-time jobs. The average aided 2006–07 undergraduate received an aid package worth an estimated $20,615.

Freshman Admission University of La Verne requires an essay, a high school transcript, 2 recommendations, SAT or ACT scores, and TOEFL scores for international students. An interview is recommended. The application deadline for regular admission is February 1.

Transfer Admission The application deadline for admission is April 1.

Entrance Difficulty University of La Verne assesses its entrance difficulty level as moderately difficult. For the fall 2006 freshman class, 60 percent of the applicants were accepted.

SPECIAL MESSAGE TO STUDENTS

Social Life The University of La Verne (ULV) students participate in activities such as intercollegiate and intramural sports; fraternities and sororities; cultural, political, or religious clubs; student government; campus publications; and theater. Three residence halls house a culturally and ethnically diverse student body.

Academic Highlights The University comprises the College of Arts and Sciences, College of Business and Public Management, College of Education and Organizational Leadership, College of Law, and the Regional Campus Administration. ULV offers bachelor's, master's, and doctoral degrees. Students are encouraged to take advantage of the study-abroad program to expand and enhance their lives.

Interviews and Campus Visits The University of La Verne invites students and their families to take a closer look at the campus. Located in Miller Hall, the Office of Admission is open from 8 to 5, Monday through Friday. To schedule a campus visit or interview, students should call the Office of Admission at 909-392-2800 or 800-876-4858 (toll-free) or via e-mail at admissions@ulv.edu. The nearest commercial airport is Ontario International.

For Further Information Write to Office of Admission, University of La Verne, 1950 Third Street, La Verne, CA 91750. *Fax:* 909-392-2714. *E-mail:* admissions@ulv.edu. *Web site:* http://www.ulv.edu.

UNIVERSITY OF PHOENIX–BAY AREA CAMPUS

Pleasanton, California

University of Phoenix–Bay Area Campus is a coed, proprietary, comprehensive institution, offering degrees at the associate, bachelor's, and master's levels.

Academic Information The faculty has 1,426 members (1% full-time), 27% with terminal degrees. The undergraduate student-faculty ratio is 7:1. The library holds 1,759 titles and 692 serial subscriptions. Special programs include services for learning-disabled students, advanced placement credit, accelerated degree programs, independent study, distance learning, external degree programs, and adult/continuing education programs. The most frequently chosen baccalaureate fields are business/ marketing, computer and information sciences, public administration and social services.

Student Body Statistics The student body totals 3,139, of whom 2,249 are undergraduates (68 freshmen). 61 percent are women and 39 percent are men. 11.3 percent are international students.

Expenses for 2006–07 *Application fee:* $45. *Tuition:* $13,390 full-time, $446 per credit part-time.

Financial Aid Forms of aid include need-based and non-need-based scholarships. The average aided 2005–06 undergraduate received an aid package worth $3866. The application deadline for financial aid is continuous.

Freshman Admission University of Phoenix–Bay Area Campus requires 1 recommendation and TOEFL scores for international students. A high school transcript is required for some. The application deadline for regular admission is rolling.

Transfer Admission The application deadline for admission is rolling.

Entrance Difficulty University of Phoenix–Bay Area Campus has an open admission policy.

For Further Information Contact Ms. Beth Barilla, Associate Vice President, Student Admissions and Services, University of Phoenix–Bay Area Campus, 4615 East Elwood Street, Mail Stop AA-K101, Phoenix, AZ 85040-1958. *Telephone:* 480-317-6000 or 877-4-STUDENT (toll-free). *Fax:* 480-594-1758. *E-mail:* beth.barilla@phoenix.edu. *Web site:* http://www. phoenix.edu/.

UNIVERSITY OF PHOENIX–CENTRAL VALLEY CAMPUS

Fresno, California

University of Phoenix–Central Valley Campus is a coed, proprietary, comprehensive institution, founded in 2004, offering degrees at the bachelor's and master's levels and postbachelor's certificates.

Academic Information The faculty has 652 members (6% full-time), 12% with terminal degrees. The undergraduate student-faculty ratio is 9:1. The library holds 1,759 titles and 692 serial subscriptions. Special programs include services for learning-disabled students, advanced placement credit, accelerated degree programs, independent study, distance learning, external degree programs, and adult/continuing education programs. The most frequently chosen baccalaureate fields are business/marketing, computer and information sciences, public administration and social services.
Student Body Statistics The student body totals 2,145, of whom 1,780 are undergraduates (53 freshmen). 68 percent are women and 32 percent are men. 4.2 percent are international students.
Expenses for 2006–07 *Application fee:* $45. *Tuition:* $12,350 full-time, $412 per credit part-time. Full-time tuition varies according to program.
Financial Aid Forms of aid include need-based and non-need-based scholarships. The application deadline for financial aid is continuous.
Freshman Admission University of Phoenix–Central Valley Campus requires 1 recommendation. A high school transcript is required for some. The application deadline for regular admission is rolling.
Transfer Admission The application deadline for admission is rolling.
Entrance Difficulty University of Phoenix–Central Valley Campus has an open admission policy.
For Further Information Contact Ms. Beth Barilla, Associate Vice President, Student Admissions and Services, University of Phoenix–Central Valley Campus, 4615 East Elwood Street, Mail Stop AA-K101, Phoenix, AZ 85040-1958. *Telephone:* 480-317-6000, 888-776-4867 (toll-free in-state), or 888-228-7240 (toll-free out-of-state). *Fax:* 480-643-1521. *E-mail:* beth.barilla@phoenix.edu. *Web site:* http://www.phoenix.edu/.

UNIVERSITY OF PHOENIX–SACRAMENTO VALLEY CAMPUS

Sacramento, California

University of Phoenix–Sacramento Valley Campus is a coed, proprietary, comprehensive institution, founded in 1993, offering degrees at the bachelor's and master's levels.

Academic Information The faculty has 1,303 members (3% full-time), 18% with terminal degrees. The undergraduate student-faculty ratio is 7:1. The library holds 1,759 titles and 692 serial subscriptions. Special programs include services for learning-disabled students, advanced placement credit, accelerated degree programs, independent study, distance learning, external degree programs, and adult/continuing education programs. The most frequently chosen baccalaureate fields are business/marketing, computer and information sciences, health professions and related sciences.
Student Body Statistics The student body totals 4,585, of whom 3,480 are undergraduates (117 freshmen). 66 percent are women and 34 percent are men. 15.1 percent are international students.
Expenses for 2006–07 *Application fee:* $45. *Tuition:* $12,900 full-time.
Financial Aid Forms of aid include need-based and non-need-based scholarships. The average aided 2005–06 undergraduate received an aid package worth $4481. The application deadline for financial aid is continuous.
Freshman Admission University of Phoenix–Sacramento Valley Campus requires 1 recommendation and TOEFL scores for international students. A high school transcript is required for some. The application deadline for regular admission is rolling.
Transfer Admission The application deadline for admission is rolling.

Entrance Difficulty University of Phoenix–Sacramento Valley Campus has an open admission policy.
For Further Information Contact Ms. Beth Barilla, Associate Vice President, Student Admissions and Services, University of Phoenix–Sacramento Valley Campus, 4615 East Elwood Street, Mail Stop AA-K101, Phoenix, AZ 85040-1958. *Telephone:* 480-317-6000, 800-776-4867 (toll-free in-state), or 800-228-7240 (toll-free out-of-state). *Fax:* 480-894-1758. *E-mail:* beth.barilla@phoenix.edu. *Web site:* http://www.phoenix.edu/.

UNIVERSITY OF PHOENIX–SAN DIEGO CAMPUS

San Diego, California

University of Phoenix–San Diego Campus is a coed, proprietary, comprehensive institution, founded in 1988, offering degrees at the bachelor's and master's levels.

Academic Information The faculty has 978 members (4% full-time), 34% with terminal degrees. The undergraduate student-faculty ratio is 9:1. The library holds 1,759 titles and 692 serial subscriptions. Special programs include services for learning-disabled students, advanced placement credit, accelerated degree programs, independent study, distance learning, external degree programs, and adult/continuing education programs. The most frequently chosen baccalaureate fields are business/marketing, computer and information sciences, health professions and related sciences.
Student Body Statistics The student body totals 3,781, of whom 2,780 are undergraduates (37 freshmen). 55 percent are women and 45 percent are men. 10.1 percent are international students.
Expenses for 2006–07 *Application fee:* $45. *Tuition:* $12,450 full-time.
Financial Aid Forms of aid include need-based and non-need-based scholarships. The average aided 2005–06 undergraduate received an aid package worth $4180. The application deadline for financial aid is continuous.
Freshman Admission University of Phoenix–San Diego Campus requires 1 recommendation and TOEFL scores for international students. A high school transcript is required for some. The application deadline for regular admission is rolling.
Transfer Admission The application deadline for admission is rolling.
Entrance Difficulty University of Phoenix–San Diego Campus has an open admission policy.
For Further Information Contact Ms. Beth Barilla, Associate Vice President, Student Admissions and Services, University of Phoenix–San Diego Campus, 4615 East Elwood Street, Mail Stop AA-K101, Phoenix, AZ 85040-1958. *Telephone:* 480-317-6000, 888-776-4867 (toll-free in-state), or 888-228-7240 (toll-free out-of-state). *Fax:* 480-894-1758. *E-mail:* beth.barilla@phoenix.edu. *Web site:* http://www.phoenix.edu/.

UNIVERSITY OF PHOENIX–SOUTHERN CALIFORNIA CAMPUS

Costa Mesa, California

University of Phoenix–Southern California Campus is a coed, proprietary, comprehensive institution, founded in 1980, offering degrees at the bachelor's and master's levels.

Academic Information The faculty has 3,228 members (1% full-time), 30% with terminal degrees. The undergraduate student-faculty ratio is 10:1. The library holds 1,759 titles and 692 serial subscriptions. Special programs include services for learning-disabled students, advanced placement credit, accelerated degree programs, independent study, distance learning, external degree programs, and adult/continuing education programs. The most frequently chosen baccalaureate fields are business/marketing, computer and information sciences, public administration and social services.
Student Body Statistics The student body totals 14,760, of whom 11,166 are undergraduates (244 freshmen). 65 percent are women and 35 percent are men. 9.3 percent are international students.

Expenses for 2006–07 *Application fee:* $45. *Tuition:* $13,710 full-time.
Financial Aid Forms of aid include need-based and non-need-based scholarships. The average aided 2005–06 undergraduate received an aid package worth $4394. The application deadline for financial aid is continuous.
Freshman Admission University of Phoenix–Southern California Campus requires 1 recommendation and TOEFL scores for international students. A high school transcript is required for some. The application deadline for regular admission is rolling.
Transfer Admission The application deadline for admission is rolling.
Entrance Difficulty University of Phoenix–Southern California Campus has an open admission policy.
For Further Information Contact Ms. Beth Barilla, Associate Vice President, Student Admissions and Services, University of Phoenix–Southern California Campus, 4615 East Elwood Street, Mail Stop AA-K101, Phoenix, AZ 85040-1958. *Telephone:* 480-317-6000, 800-776-4867 (toll-free in-state), or 800-228-7240 (toll-free out-of-state). *Fax:* 480-894-1758. *E-mail:* beth.barilla@phoenix.edu. *Web site:* http://www.phoenix.edu/.

UNIVERSITY OF REDLANDS
Redlands, California

University of Redlands is a coed, private, comprehensive institution, founded in 1907, offering degrees at the bachelor's and master's levels and post-master's and postbachelor's certificates. It has a 140-acre campus in Redlands near Los Angeles.

Academic Information The faculty has 316 members (52% full-time), 58% with terminal degrees. The undergraduate student-faculty ratio is 12:1. The library holds 268,387 titles, 11,800 serial subscriptions, and 7,134 audiovisual materials. Special programs include academic remediation, services for learning-disabled students, an honors program, study abroad, advanced placement credit, Freshman Honors College, double majors, independent study, self-designed majors, adult/continuing education programs, internships, and arrangement for off-campus study with members of the Association for Innovation in Higher Education, American University. The most frequently chosen baccalaureate fields are business/marketing, liberal arts/general studies, social sciences.
Student Body Statistics The student body totals 2,407, of whom 2,313 are undergraduates (613 freshmen). 57 percent are women and 43 percent are men. Students come from 43 states and territories and 10 other countries. 68 percent are from California. 1.6 percent are international students. 45 percent of the 2006 graduating class went on to graduate and professional schools.
Expenses for 2006–07 *Application fee:* $45. *Comprehensive fee:* $38,136 includes full-time tuition ($28,476), mandatory fees ($300), and college room and board ($9360). *College room only:* $5221. Room and board charges vary according to board plan and housing facility. *Part-time tuition:* $890 per credit. *Part-time mandatory fees:* $150 per term. Part-time tuition and fees vary according to course load.
Financial Aid Forms of aid include need-based and non-need-based scholarships and part-time jobs. The average aided 2006–07 undergraduate received an aid package worth an estimated $25,693. The priority application deadline for financial aid is February 15.
Freshman Admission University of Redlands requires an essay, a high school transcript, 2 recommendations, SAT or ACT scores, and TOEFL scores for international students. An interview is recommended. The application deadline for regular admission is March 1.
Transfer Admission The application deadline for admission is May 1.
Entrance Difficulty University of Redlands assesses its entrance difficulty level as moderately difficult. For the fall 2006 freshman class, 65 percent of the applicants were accepted.
For Further Information Contact Mr. Paul Driscoll, Dean of Admissions, University of Redlands, PO Box 3080, Redlands, CA 92373-0999. *Telephone:* 909-748-8159 or 800-455-5064 (toll-free). *Fax:* 909-335-4089. *E-mail:* admissions@redlands.edu. *Web site:* http://www.redlands.edu/.

UNIVERSITY OF SAN DIEGO
San Diego, California

University of San Diego is a coed, private, Roman Catholic university, founded in 1949, offering degrees at the bachelor's, master's, doctoral, and first professional levels and post-master's, first professional, and postbachelor's certificates. It has a 180-acre campus in San Diego.

Academic Information The faculty has 723 members (50% full-time), 90% with terminal degrees. The undergraduate student-faculty ratio is 15:1. The library holds 714,082 titles and 10,451 serial subscriptions. Special programs include services for learning-disabled students, an honors program, study abroad, advanced placement credit, ESL programs, double majors, independent study, summer session for credit, part-time degree programs (daytime, evenings, summer), and internships. The most frequently chosen baccalaureate fields are business/marketing, communications/journalism, social sciences.
Student Body Statistics The student body totals 7,483, of whom 4,962 are undergraduates (1,106 freshmen). 60 percent are women and 40 percent are men. Students come from 50 states and territories. 64 percent are from California. 2 percent are international students.
Expenses for 2007–08 *Application fee:* $55. *Comprehensive fee:* $43,524 includes full-time tuition ($32,300), mandatory fees ($264), and college room and board ($10,960). *Part-time tuition:* $1115 per unit. *Part-time mandatory fees:* $56 per term.
Financial Aid Forms of aid include need-based and non-need-based scholarships, athletic grants, and part-time jobs. The average aided 2005–06 undergraduate received an aid package worth $20,558. The priority application deadline for financial aid is February 20.
Freshman Admission University of San Diego requires an essay, a high school transcript, 1 recommendation, SAT or ACT scores, and TOEFL scores for international students. The application deadline for regular admission is January 15 and for early action it is November 15.
Transfer Admission The application deadline for admission is March 1.
Entrance Difficulty University of San Diego assesses its entrance difficulty level as very difficult; moderately difficult for transfers. For the fall 2006 freshman class, 46 percent of the applicants were accepted.
For Further Information Contact Mr. Stephen Pultz, Director of Admission, University of San Diego, 5998 Alcala Park, San Diego, CA 92110. *Telephone:* 619-260-4506 or 800-248-4873 (toll-free). *Fax:* 619-260-6836. *E-mail:* admissions@sandiego.edu. *Web site:* http://www.sandiego.edu/.

UNIVERSITY OF SAN FRANCISCO
San Francisco, California

University of San Francisco is a coed, private, Roman Catholic (Jesuit) university, founded in 1855, offering degrees at the bachelor's, master's, doctoral, and first professional levels and post-master's certificates. It has a 55-acre campus in San Francisco near in San Francisco.

Academic Information The faculty has 871 members (41% full-time), 77% with terminal degrees. The undergraduate student-faculty ratio is 14:1. The library holds 1 million titles and 5,560 serial subscriptions. Special programs include academic remediation, services for learning-disabled students, an honors program, cooperative (work-study) education, study abroad, advanced placement credit, ESL programs, double majors, distance learning, self-designed majors, summer session for credit, part-time degree programs (daytime, evenings, weekends, summer), external degree programs, adult/continuing education programs, internships, and arrangement for off-campus study with American University, Jackson State University.
Student Body Statistics The student body totals 8,549, of whom 5,384 are undergraduates (1,078 freshmen). 64 percent are women and 36 percent are men. Students come from 49 states and territories and 62 other countries. 76 percent are from California. 6.7 percent are international students. 42 percent of the 2006 graduating class went on to graduate and professional schools.
Expenses for 2007–08 *Application fee:* $55. *Comprehensive fee:* $41,910 includes full-time tuition ($30,840), mandatory fees ($340), and college room and board ($10,730). *College room only:* $7230. *Part-time tuition:* $1060 per unit. *Part-time mandatory fees:* $340 per year.

University of San Francisco (continued)

Financial Aid Forms of aid include need-based and non-need-based scholarships, athletic grants, and part-time jobs. The average aided 2006–07 undergraduate received an aid package worth an estimated $22,062. The priority application deadline for financial aid is February 15.

Freshman Admission University of San Francisco requires an essay, a high school transcript, a minimum 2.8 high school GPA, 1 recommendation, SAT or ACT scores, and TOEFL scores for international students. A minimum 3.0 high school GPA is recommended. An interview is required for some. The application deadline for regular admission is February 1 and for early action it is November 15.

Transfer Admission The application deadline for admission is rolling.

Entrance Difficulty University of San Francisco assesses its entrance difficulty level as moderately difficult. For the fall 2006 freshman class, 72 percent of the applicants were accepted.

For Further Information Contact Mr. Michael Hughes, Director, University of San Francisco, 2130 Fulton Street, San Francisco, CA 94117-1080. *Telephone:* 415-422-6563, 415-422-6563 (toll-free in-state), or 800-CALL USF (toll-free out-of-state). *Fax:* 415-422-2217. *E-mail:* admissions@usfca.edu. *Web site:* http://www.usfca.edu/.

UNIVERSITY OF SARASOTA, CALIFORNIA CAMPUS

See Argosy University, Orange County.

UNIVERSITY OF SOUTHERN CALIFORNIA
Los Angeles, California

University of Southern California is a coed, private university, founded in 1880, offering degrees at the bachelor's, master's, doctoral, and first professional levels and post-master's, first professional, and postbachelor's certificates. It has a 155-acre campus in Los Angeles.

Academic Information The faculty has 2,570 members (61% full-time), 77% with terminal degrees. The undergraduate student-faculty ratio is 10:1. The library holds 4 million titles, 60,718 serial subscriptions, and 59,824 audiovisual materials. Special programs include services for learning-disabled students, an honors program, cooperative (work-study) education, study abroad, advanced placement credit, accelerated degree programs, Freshman Honors College, ESL programs, double majors, independent study, distance learning, self-designed majors, summer session for credit, part-time degree programs (daytime, evenings), internships, and arrangement for off-campus study with Hebrew Union College–Jewish Institute of Religion, Howard University, American University. The most frequently chosen baccalaureate fields are business/marketing, social sciences, visual and performing arts.

Student Body Statistics The student body totals 33,389, of whom 16,729 are undergraduates (2,763 freshmen). 50 percent are women and 50 percent are men. Students come from 60 states and territories and 114 other countries. 62 percent are from California. 9.1 percent are international students.

Expenses for 2006–07 *Application fee:* $65. *Comprehensive fee:* $44,036 includes full-time tuition ($33,314), mandatory fees ($578), and college room and board ($10,144). *College room only:* $5580. Full-time tuition and fees vary according to program. Room and board charges vary according to board plan and housing facility. *Part-time tuition:* $1121 per term. *Part-time mandatory fees:* $289 per term. Part-time tuition and fees vary according to course load and program.

Financial Aid Forms of aid include need-based and non-need-based scholarships, athletic grants, and part-time jobs. The average aided 2005–06 undergraduate received an aid package worth $29,641. The priority application deadline for financial aid is January 20.

Freshman Admission University of Southern California requires an essay, a high school transcript, SAT or ACT scores, and TOEFL scores for international students. Recommendations and an interview are recommended. Recommendations are required for some. The application deadline for regular admission is January 10.

Transfer Admission The application deadline for admission is February 1.

Entrance Difficulty University of Southern California assesses its entrance difficulty level as most difficult. For the fall 2006 freshman class, 25 percent of the applicants were accepted.

For Further Information Contact Katharine L. Harrington, Dean/Director of Admission, University of Southern California, University Park Campus, Los Angeles, CA 90089. *Telephone:* 213-740-1111. *Fax:* 213-740-6364. *E-mail:* admitusc@usc.edu. *Web site:* http://www.usc.edu/.

UNIVERSITY OF THE PACIFIC
Stockton, California

University of the Pacific is a coed, private university, founded in 1851, offering degrees at the bachelor's, master's, doctoral, and first professional levels. It has a 175-acre campus in Stockton near Sacramento.

Academic Information The faculty has 656 members (61% full-time), 84% with terminal degrees. The undergraduate student-faculty ratio is 14:1. The library holds 373,759 titles, 1,826 serial subscriptions, and 10,755 audiovisual materials. Special programs include academic remediation, services for learning-disabled students, an honors program, cooperative (work-study) education, study abroad, advanced placement credit, accelerated degree programs, ESL programs, double majors, independent study, self-designed majors, summer session for credit, part-time degree programs (daytime, evenings, summer), adult/continuing education programs, and internships. The most frequently chosen baccalaureate fields are biological/life sciences, business/marketing, engineering.

Student Body Statistics The student body totals 6,251, of whom 3,535 are undergraduates (878 freshmen). 56 percent are women and 44 percent are men. Students come from 36 states and territories and 18 other countries. 85 percent are from California. 2.9 percent are international students.

Expenses for 2006–07 *Application fee:* $60. *Comprehensive fee:* $36,050 includes full-time tuition ($26,920), mandatory fees ($430), and college room and board ($8700). *College room only:* $4350. Room and board charges vary according to board plan and housing facility. *Part-time tuition:* $930 per unit. Part-time tuition varies according to course load.

Financial Aid Forms of aid include need-based and non-need-based scholarships, athletic grants, and part-time jobs. The average aided 2006–07 undergraduate received an aid package worth an estimated $24,110.

Freshman Admission University of the Pacific requires an essay, a high school transcript, a minimum 2.5 high school GPA, 1 recommendation, SAT or ACT scores, and TOEFL scores for international students. A minimum 3.0 high school GPA is recommended. Audition for music program is required for some. The application deadline for regular admission is January 15 and for early action it is November 15.

Transfer Admission University of the Pacific requires standardized test scores, a college transcript, and a minimum 2.5 college GPA. A minimum 3.0 college GPA is recommended. The application deadline for admission is June 1.

Entrance Difficulty University of the Pacific assesses its entrance difficulty level as moderately difficult. For the fall 2006 freshman class, 69 percent of the applicants were accepted.

For Further Information Contact Mr. Marc McGee, Director of Admissions, University of the Pacific, 3601 Pacific Avenue, Stockton, CA 95211. *Telephone:* 209-946-2211 or 800-959-2867 (toll-free). *Fax:* 209-946-2413. *E-mail:* admissions@pacific.edu. *Web site:* http://www.pacific.edu/.

See page 202 for the College Close-Up.

UNIVERSITY OF THE WEST
Rosemead, California

University of the West is a coed, private, comprehensive institution, founded in 1991, offering degrees at the bachelor's, master's, doctoral, and first professional levels and post-master's certificates. It has a 10-acre campus in Rosemead.

Academic Information The faculty has 26 members (31% full-time), 38% with terminal degrees. The library holds 60,000 titles and 6,000 serial subscriptions. Special programs include cooperative (work-study) education, accelerated degree programs, ESL programs, double majors, independent study, summer session for credit, part-time degree programs, adult/continuing education programs, and internships.

Expenses for 2007–08 *Application fee:* $50. *Comprehensive fee:* $16,956 includes full-time tuition ($9000), mandatory fees ($270), and college room and board ($7686). *College room only:* $4788. *Part-time tuition:* $300 per unit. *Part-time mandatory fees:* $170 per year.

Financial Aid Forms of aid include need-based and non-need-based scholarships and part-time jobs. The application deadline for financial aid is continuous.

Freshman Admission University of the West requires an essay, a high school transcript, a minimum 2.0 high school GPA, and 3 recommendations. TOEFL scores for international students and TOEFL are recommended. The application deadline for regular admission is June 1.

For Further Information Contact Ms. Grace Hsiao, Admissions Officer, University of the West, 1409 North Walnut Grove Avenue, Rosemead, CA 91770. *Telephone:* 626-571-8811 Ext. 120. *Fax:* 626-571-4413. *E-mail:* graceh@uwest.edu. *Web site:* http://www.uwest.edu/.

VANGUARD UNIVERSITY OF SOUTHERN CALIFORNIA

Costa Mesa, California

Vanguard University of Southern California is a coed, private, comprehensive institution, founded in 1920, affiliated with the Assemblies of God, offering degrees at the bachelor's and master's levels. It has a 38-acre campus in Costa Mesa near Los Angeles.

Academic Information The faculty has 204 members (32% full-time), 41% with terminal degrees. The undergraduate student-faculty ratio is 14:1. The library holds 157,500 titles, 2,000 serial subscriptions, and 6,900 audiovisual materials. Special programs include services for learning-disabled students, study abroad, advanced placement credit, accelerated degree programs, double majors, independent study, summer session for credit, part-time degree programs (evenings, weekends, summer), external degree programs, adult/continuing education programs, internships, and arrangement for off-campus study with Council for Christian Colleges and Universities, Los Angeles Film Studies Center. The most frequently chosen baccalaureate fields are business/marketing, education, psychology.

Student Body Statistics The student body totals 2,146, of whom 1,854 are undergraduates (396 freshmen). 63 percent are women and 37 percent are men. Students come from 2 states and territories and 17 other countries. 85 percent are from California. 1 percent are international students.

Expenses for 2006–07 *Application fee:* $45. *One-time mandatory fee:* $70. *Tuition:* $21,094 full-time, $879 per credit hour part-time. *Mandatory fees:* $470 full-time, $35 per term part-time. Both full-time and part-time tuition and fees vary according to course load. *College room only:* $3568. Room charges vary according to housing facility.

Financial Aid Forms of aid include need-based and non-need-based scholarships, athletic grants, and part-time jobs. The average aided 2006–07 undergraduate received an aid package worth an estimated $19,883. The application deadline for financial aid is March 2.

Freshman Admission Vanguard University of Southern California requires an essay, a high school transcript, a minimum 2.8 high school GPA, 2 recommendations, SAT or ACT scores, and TOEFL scores for international students. An interview is required for some. The application deadline for regular admission is December 1.

Transfer Admission The application deadline for admission is December 1.

Entrance Difficulty Vanguard University of Southern California assesses its entrance difficulty level as moderately difficult. For the fall 2006 freshman class, 83 percent of the applicants were accepted.

For Further Information Contact Amberley Wolf, Director of Undergraduate Admissions, Vanguard University of Southern California, 55 Fair Drive, Costa Mesa, CA 92626. *Telephone:* 714-556-3610 Ext. 4120 or 800-722-6279 (toll-free). *Fax:* 714-966-5471. *E-mail:* admissions@vanguard.edu. *Web site:* http://www.vanguard.edu/.

WESTERN CAREER COLLEGE

Emeryville, California

http://www.westerncollege.edu/

WESTERN CAREER COLLEGE

Fremont, California

http://www.westerncollege.edu/

WESTERN CAREER COLLEGE

San Jose, California

http://www.westerncollege.edu/

WESTERN CAREER COLLEGE

Walnut Creek, California

http://www.westerncollege.edu/campus_locations/antioch_campus.html

WESTMONT COLLEGE

Santa Barbara, California

Westmont College is a coed, private, nondenominational, four-year college, founded in 1937, offering degrees at the bachelor's level and postbachelor's certificates. It has a 133-acre campus in Santa Barbara near Los Angeles.

Academic Information The faculty has 142 members (63% full-time). The student-faculty ratio is 12:1. The library holds 174,246 titles, 380 serial subscriptions, and 11,375 audiovisual materials. Special programs include academic remediation, services for learning-disabled students, an honors program, study abroad, advanced placement credit, accelerated degree programs, double majors, self-designed majors, summer session for credit, internships, and arrangement for off-campus study with 13 members of the Christian College Consortium, 90 members of the Christian Colleges and Universities, American University (Washington Semester). The most frequently chosen baccalaureate fields are communications/journalism, biological/life sciences, English.

Student Body Statistics The student body totals 1,337, of whom 1,332 are undergraduates (329 freshmen). 60 percent are women and 40 percent are men. Students come from 39 states and territories and 10 other countries. 65 percent are from California. 0.8 percent are international students. 69 percent of the 2006 graduating class went on to graduate and professional schools.

Expenses for 2006–07 *Application fee:* $50. *Comprehensive fee:* $38,702 includes full-time tuition ($28,700), mandatory fees ($770), and college room and board ($9232). *College room only:* $5672. Room and board charges vary according to board plan.

Financial Aid Forms of aid include need-based and non-need-based scholarships, athletic grants, and part-time jobs. The average aided 2006–07 undergraduate received an aid package worth an estimated $20,266. The priority application deadline for financial aid is March 1.

Freshman Admission Westmont College requires an essay, a high school transcript, 1 recommendation, SAT or ACT scores, and TOEFL scores for

Westmont College (continued)
international students. An interview is recommended. An interview and TOEFL are required for some. The application deadline for regular admission is February 15 and for early action it is November 1.

Transfer Admission The application deadline for admission is March 1.

Entrance Difficulty Westmont College assesses its entrance difficulty level as moderately difficult. For the fall 2006 freshman class, 65 percent of the applicants were accepted.

For Further Information Contact Mrs. Joyce Luy, Dean of Admission, Westmont College, 955 La Paz Road, Santa Barbara, CA 93108. *Telephone:* 805-565-6200 or 800-777-9011 (toll-free). *Fax:* 805-565-6234. *E-mail:* admissions@westmont.edu. *Web site:* http://www.westmont.edu/.

WESTWOOD COLLEGE–ANAHEIM

Anaheim, California

Westwood College–Anaheim is a coed, proprietary, primarily two-year college, offering degrees at the associate and bachelor's levels. It is located in Anaheim near Los Angeles.

For Further Information Contact Mr. Paul Sallenbach, Director of Admissions, Westwood College–Anaheim, 1551 South Douglass Road, Anaheim, CA 92806. *Telephone:* 714-704-2721 or 877-650-6050 (toll-free in-state). *Fax:* 714-704-2735. *E-mail:* info@westwood.edu. *Web site:* http://www.westwood.edu/.

WESTWOOD COLLEGE–INLAND EMPIRE

Upland, California

Westwood College–Inland Empire is a coed, proprietary, primarily two-year college, offering degrees at the associate and bachelor's levels. It is located in Upland near Los Angeles.

For Further Information Contact Mr. Lyle Seavers, Director of Admissions, Westwood College–Inland Empire, 20 West 7th Street, Upland, CA 91786-7148. *Telephone:* 909-931-7550 or 866-288-9488 (toll-free in-state). *Fax:* 909-931-9195. *E-mail:* info@westwood.edu. *Web site:* http://www.westwood.edu/.

WESTWOOD COLLEGE–LOS ANGELES

Los Angeles, California

Westwood College–Los Angeles is a coed, proprietary, primarily two-year college, offering degrees at the associate and bachelor's levels.

For Further Information Contact Mr. Ron Milman, Director of Admissions, Westwood College–Los Angeles, 3250 Wilshire Boulevard, 4th Floor, Los Angeles, CA 90010. *Telephone:* 213-739-9999 or 877-377-4600 (toll-free in-state). *Fax:* 213-382-2468. *E-mail:* info@westwood.edu. *Web site:* http://www.westwood.edu/.

WESTWOOD COLLEGE–LOS ANGELES

See Redstone College–Los Angeles.

WESTWOOD COLLEGE–SOUTH BAY CAMPUS

Long Beach, California

Westwood College–South Bay Campus is a coed, proprietary, primarily two-year college of AITU Colleges, founded in 2002, offering degrees at the associate and bachelor's levels. It has a 1-acre campus in Long Beach near Los Angeles.

For Further Information Contact Jesse Kamekona, Director of Admissions, Westwood College–South Bay Campus, 19700 South Vermont Avenue, Suite 100, Torrance, CA 90502. *Telephone:* 310-965-0888 or 888-403-3308 (toll-free). *Fax:* 310-965-0881. *Web site:* http://www.westwood.edu.

WHITTIER COLLEGE

Whittier, California

http://www.whittier.edu/

WILLIAM JESSUP UNIVERSITY

Rocklin, California

William Jessup University is a coed, private, nondenominational, four-year college, founded in 1939, offering degrees at the associate and bachelor's levels and postbachelor's certificates. It has a 156-acre campus in Rocklin near Sacramento.

Academic Information The faculty has 91 members (23% full-time), 32% with terminal degrees. The student-faculty ratio is 12:1. The library holds 52,294 titles and 247 serial subscriptions. Special programs include academic remediation, services for learning-disabled students, advanced placement credit, accelerated degree programs, double majors, independent study, summer session for credit, part-time degree programs (daytime, evenings), adult/continuing education programs, and internships. The most frequently chosen baccalaureate fields are business/marketing, psychology, theology and religious vocations.

Student Body Statistics The student body totals 592, of whom 581 are undergraduates (50 freshmen). 56 percent are women and 44 percent are men. Students come from 9 states and territories and 2 other countries. 93 percent are from California. 0.5 percent are international students.

Expenses for 2006–07 *Application fee:* $35. *Comprehensive fee:* $24,016 includes full-time tuition ($17,238) and college room and board ($6778). *Part-time tuition:* $730 per semester hour.

Financial Aid Forms of aid include need-based and non-need-based scholarships, athletic grants, and part-time jobs. The priority application deadline for financial aid is June 1.

Freshman Admission William Jessup University requires an essay, a high school transcript, a minimum 2.0 high school GPA, 2 recommendations, SAT or ACT scores, and TOEFL scores for international students. The application deadline for regular admission is August 1.

Transfer Admission The application deadline for admission is August 1.

Entrance Difficulty William Jessup University assesses its entrance difficulty level as noncompetitive. For the fall 2006 freshman class, 48 percent of the applicants were accepted.

For Further Information Contact Mr. Vance Pascua, Director of Admission, William Jessup University, 333 Sunset Boulevard, Rocklin, CA 95765. *Telephone:* 408-577-2222 or 800-355-7522 (toll-free). *Fax:* 916-577-2220. *E-mail:* admissions@jessup.edu. *Web site:* http://www.jessup.edu/.

WOODBURY UNIVERSITY

Burbank, California

Woodbury University is a coed, private, comprehensive institution, founded in 1884, offering degrees at the bachelor's and master's levels. It has a 22-acre campus in Burbank near Los Angeles.

Academic Information The faculty has 237 members (19% full-time). The undergraduate student-faculty ratio is 12:1. The library holds 69,515 titles, 363 serial subscriptions, and 2,035 audiovisual materials. Special programs include academic remediation, services for learning-disabled students, study abroad, advanced placement credit, accelerated degree programs, double majors, independent study, summer session for credit, part-time degree programs (daytime, evenings, weekends, summer), adult/continuing education programs, and internships. The most frequently chosen baccalaureate fields are architecture, business/marketing, visual and performing arts.

Student Body Statistics The student body totals 1,485, of whom 1,310 are undergraduates (135 freshmen). 56 percent are women and 44 percent are men. Students come from 14 states and territories and 39 other countries. 80 percent are from California. 5.7 percent are international students.

Expenses for 2006–07 *Application fee:* $35. *Comprehensive fee:* $31,676 includes full-time tuition ($23,232), mandatory fees ($340), and college room and board ($8104). *College room only:* $4952. Full-time tuition and fees vary according to program. Room and board charges vary according to board plan and housing facility. *Part-time tuition:* $758 per unit. *Part-time mandatory fees:* $340 per term. Part-time tuition and fees vary according to class time, course load, and program.

Financial Aid Forms of aid include need-based and non-need-based scholarships and part-time jobs. The average aided 2005–06 undergraduate received an aid package worth $16,591. The application deadline for financial aid is continuous.

Freshman Admission Woodbury University requires a high school transcript, a minimum 2.0 high school GPA, SAT or ACT scores, and TOEFL scores for international students. An essay, a minimum 3.0 high school GPA, 2 recommendations, and an interview are recommended. A portfolio is required for some. The application deadline for regular admission is rolling.

Transfer Admission The application deadline for admission is rolling.

Entrance Difficulty Woodbury University assesses its entrance difficulty level as moderately difficult. For the fall 2006 freshman class, 77 percent of the applicants were accepted.

For Further Information Contact Ms. Sabrina Taylor, Director of Admissions, Woodbury University, 7500 Glenoaks Boulevard, Burbank, CA 91510-7846. *Telephone:* 800-784-9663 or 800-784-WOOD (toll-free). *Fax:* 818-767-0032. *E-mail:* admissions@woodbury.edu. *Web site:* http://www.woodbury.edu/.

YESHIVA OHR ELCHONON CHABAD/WEST COAST TALMUDICAL SEMINARY

Los Angeles, California

For Information Write to Yeshiva Ohr Elchonon Chabad/West Coast Talmudical Seminary, Los Angeles, CA 90046-7660.

Colorado

ADAMS STATE COLLEGE

Alamosa, Colorado

Adams State College is a coed, public, comprehensive institution, founded in 1921, offering degrees at the associate, bachelor's, and master's levels. It has a 90-acre campus in Alamosa.

Academic Information The faculty has 217 members (49% full-time), 36% with terminal degrees. The undergraduate student-faculty ratio is 14:1. The library holds 469,783 titles, 19,979 serial subscriptions, and 2,576 audiovisual materials. Special programs include academic remediation, services for learning-disabled students, study abroad, advanced placement credit, accelerated degree programs, double majors, independent study, distance learning, self-designed majors, summer session for credit,

part-time degree programs (daytime, evenings, weekends, summer), adult/continuing education programs, internships, and arrangement for off-campus study with members of the Consortium of State Colleges in Colorado. The most frequently chosen baccalaureate fields are business/marketing, liberal arts/general studies, social sciences.

Student Body Statistics The student body totals 4,899, of whom 2,308 are undergraduates (513 freshmen). 57 percent are women and 43 percent are men. Students come from 34 states and territories and 2 other countries. 89 percent are from Colorado.

Expenses for 2006–07 *Application fee:* $20. *State resident tuition:* $2030 full-time, $92 per credit hour part-time. *Nonresident tuition:* $8456 full-time, $384 per credit hour part-time. *Mandatory fees:* $895 full-time, $33 per credit hour part-time. Full-time tuition and fees vary according to course load and student level. Part-time tuition and fees vary according to course load. *College room and board:* $6160. *College room only:* $3290. Room and board charges vary according to board plan and housing facility. The Colorado College Opportunity Fund stipend has been applied to instate tuition.

Financial Aid Forms of aid include need-based and non-need-based scholarships, athletic grants, and part-time jobs. The average aided 2005–06 undergraduate received an aid package worth $6865. The application deadline for financial aid is continuous.

Freshman Admission Adams State College requires a high school transcript, a minimum 2.0 high school GPA, audition for music majors, SAT or ACT scores, and TOEFL scores for international students. An essay, a high school transcript, recommendations, and an interview are required for some. The application deadline for regular admission is August 1.

Transfer Admission The application deadline for admission is August 1.

Entrance Difficulty Adams State College assesses its entrance difficulty level as moderately difficult. For the fall 2006 freshman class, 62 percent of the applicants were accepted.

For Further Information Contact Mr. Eric Carpio, Director of Admissions, Adams State College, 208 Edgemont Boulevard, Alamosa, CO 81102. *Telephone:* 719-587-7712 or 800-824-6494 (toll-free). *Fax:* 719-587-7522. *E-mail:* ascadmit@adams.edu. *Web site:* http://www.adams.edu/.

AMERICAN SENTINEL UNIVERSITY

Englewood, Colorado

http://www.americansentinel.edu/

ARGOSY UNIVERSITY, DENVER

Denver, Colorado

Argosy University, Denver is a coed, proprietary university, offering degrees at the associate level.

For Further Information Contact Admissions Director, Argosy University, Denver, 1200 Lincoln Street, Denver, CO 80203. *Telephone:* 303-248-2700 or 866-431-5981 (toll-free). *E-mail:* auadmissions@argosyu.edu. *Web site:* http://www.argosyu.edu/.

THE ART INSTITUTE OF COLORADO

Denver, Colorado

The Art Institute of Colorado is a coed, proprietary, four-year college of Education Management Corporation, founded in 1952, offering degrees at the associate and bachelor's levels.

Academic Information The faculty has 137 members (53% full-time), 20% with terminal degrees. The student-faculty ratio is 19:1. The library holds 13,100 titles, 200 serial subscriptions, and 500 audiovisual materials. Special programs include academic remediation, services for learning-disabled students, study abroad, advanced placement credit, independent study, distance learning, part-time degree programs (daytime, evenings,

The Art Institute of Colorado (continued)

weekends, summer), external degree programs, adult/continuing education programs, and internships. The most frequently chosen baccalaureate fields are education, personal and culinary services.

Student Body Statistics The student body is made up of 2,765 undergraduates (524 freshmen). 51 percent are women and 49 percent are men. Students come from 33 states and territories and 5 other countries. 50 percent are from Colorado. 3 percent of the 2006 graduating class went on to graduate and professional schools.

Expenses for 2007–08 *Application fee:* $50. *Tuition:* $419 per credit part-time.

Financial Aid Forms of aid include need-based and non-need-based scholarships and part-time jobs. The application deadline for financial aid is continuous.

Freshman Admission The Art Institute of Colorado requires an essay, a high school transcript, an interview, and TOEFL scores for international students. The application deadline for regular admission is rolling.

Transfer Admission The application deadline for admission is rolling.

Entrance Difficulty The Art Institute of Colorado assesses its entrance difficulty level as minimally difficult.

For Further Information Contact Mr. Brian Parker, Director of Admissions, The Art Institute of Colorado, 1200 Lincoln Street, Denver, CO 80203. *Telephone:* 303-837-0825 Ext. 4729 or 800-275-2420 (toll-free). *Fax:* 303-860-8520. *E-mail:* aicinfo@aii.edu. *Web site:* http://www.aic.artinstitutes.edu/.

ASPEN UNIVERSITY

Denver, Colorado

http://www.aspen.edu/

BOULDER COLLEGE OF MASSAGE THERAPY

Boulder, Colorado

Boulder College of Massage Therapy is a coed, private, two-year college, founded in 1975, offering degrees at the associate level.

Student Body Statistics The student body is made up of 220 undergraduates.

Expenses for 2006–07 *Application fee:* $75. *Tuition:* $13,860 full-time.

Entrance Difficulty Boulder College of Massage Therapy assesses its entrance difficulty level as noncompetitive.

For Further Information Contact Admissions Office, Boulder College of Massage Therapy, 6255 Longbow Drive, Boulder, CO 80301. *Telephone:* 303-530-2100 or 800-442-5131 (toll-free out-of-state). *Fax:* 303-530-2204. *E-mail:* 6255 Longbow Drive. *Web site:* http://www.bcmt.org/.

CAMBRIDGE COLLEGE

Aurora, Colorado

Cambridge College is a private, two-year college, offering degrees at the associate level.

Student Body Statistics The student body is made up of 578 undergraduates.

Expenses for 2006–07 *Application fee:* $50. *Tuition:* $26,224 per degree program.

Entrance Difficulty Cambridge College assesses its entrance difficulty level as noncompetitive.

For Further Information Contact Admissions Office, Cambridge College, 350 Blackhawk Street, Aurora, CO 80011. *Telephone:* 720-859-7900 or 800-322-4132 (toll-free in-state). *Web site:* http://www.cambridgecollege.com/.

COLLEGEAMERICA–COLORADO SPRINGS

Colorado Spring, Colorado

CollegeAmerica–Colorado Springs is a coed, proprietary, primarily two-year college, offering degrees at the associate and bachelor's levels.

For Further Information Contact Admissions Office, CollegeAmerica–Colorado Springs, 3645 Citadel Drive South, Colorado Springs, CO 80909. *Telephone:* 719- 637-0600. *E-mail:* crenya@collegeamerica.edu. *Web site:* http://www.collegeamerica.com/.

COLLEGEAMERICA–DENVER

Denver, Colorado

CollegeAmerica–Denver is a coed, proprietary, primarily two-year college, founded in 1962, offering degrees at the associate and bachelor's levels.

Student Body Statistics The student body is made up of 444 undergraduates.

Financial Aid Forms of aid include need-based scholarships. The application deadline for financial aid is continuous.

Entrance Difficulty CollegeAmerica–Denver assesses its entrance difficulty level as noncompetitive.

For Further Information Contact Admissions Office, CollegeAmerica–Denver, 1385 South Colorado Boulevard, Denver, CO 80222. *Telephone:* 303-691-9756 or 800-97-SKILLS (toll-free in-state). *Fax:* 303-695-6059. *E-mail:* collegeamerica@aol.com. *Web site:* http://www.collegeamerica.com/.

COLLEGEAMERICA–FORT COLLINS

Fort Collins, Colorado

http://www.collegeamerica.edu/

COLORADO CHRISTIAN UNIVERSITY

Lakewood, Colorado

Colorado Christian University is a coed, private, interdenominational, comprehensive institution, founded in 1914, offering degrees at the associate, bachelor's, and master's levels. It has a 26-acre campus in Lakewood near Denver.

Academic Information The faculty has 46 members (93% full-time), 72% with terminal degrees. The undergraduate student-faculty ratio is 21:1. The library holds 71,565 titles and 1,192 serial subscriptions. Special programs include academic remediation, services for learning-disabled students, an honors program, cooperative (work-study) education, study abroad, advanced placement credit, accelerated degree programs, double majors, independent study, distance learning, self-designed majors, summer session for credit, part-time degree programs (daytime, evenings, weekends, summer), adult/continuing education programs, internships, and arrangement for off-campus study with Colorado Institute of Art, Metropolitan State College, University of Colorado at Denver, Red Rocks Community College. The most frequently chosen baccalaureate fields are business/marketing, computer and information sciences, education.

Student Body Statistics The student body totals 2,221, of whom 1,897 are undergraduates (225 freshmen). 61 percent are women and 39 percent are men. Students come from 45 states and territories and 9 other countries. 44 percent are from Colorado. 0.5 percent are international students.

Expenses for 2007–08 *Application fee:* $50. *Comprehensive fee:* $25,975 includes full-time tuition ($18,200), mandatory fees ($150), and college room and board ($7625). *College room only:* $4415.

Financial Aid Forms of aid include need-based and non-need-based scholarships, athletic grants, and part-time jobs. The priority application deadline for financial aid is March 15.

Freshman Admission Colorado Christian University requires an essay, a high school transcript, 2 recommendations, an interview, SAT or ACT scores, and TOEFL scores for international students. A minimum 2.8 high school GPA, 3 recommendations, and an interview are required for some. The application deadline for regular admission is August 21.

Entrance Difficulty Colorado Christian University assesses its entrance difficulty level as moderately difficult. For the fall 2006 freshman class, 65 percent of the applicants were accepted.

For Further Information Contact Mr. Jeff Cazer, Associate, Colorado Christian University, 180 South Garrison Street, Lakewood, CO 80226. *Telephone:* 303-963-3200 or 800-44-FAITH (toll-free). *Fax:* 303-963-3201. *E-mail:* admission@ccu.edu. *Web site:* http://www.ccu.edu/.

THE COLORADO COLLEGE
Colorado Springs, Colorado

The Colorado College is a coed, private, comprehensive institution, founded in 1874, offering degrees at the bachelor's and master's levels (master's degree in education only). It has a 90-acre campus in Colorado Springs near Denver.

Academic Information The faculty has 195 members (81% full-time). The undergraduate student-faculty ratio is 10:1. The library holds 532,793 titles, 4,649 serial subscriptions, and 22,830 audiovisual materials. Special programs include services for learning-disabled students, study abroad, advanced placement credit, ESL programs, double majors, independent study, self-designed majors, summer session for credit, internships, and arrangement for off-campus study with American University, Associated Colleges of the Midwest Programs. The most frequently chosen baccalaureate fields are biological/life sciences, social sciences, visual and performing arts.

Student Body Statistics The student body totals 1,998, of whom 1,970 are undergraduates (492 freshmen). 55 percent are women and 45 percent are men. Students come from 49 states and territories and 17 other countries. 27 percent are from Colorado. 1.8 percent are international students. 25 percent of the 2006 graduating class went on to graduate and professional schools.

Expenses for 2006–07 *Application fee:* $50. *Comprehensive fee:* $40,176 includes full-time tuition ($32,124) and college room and board ($8052). *College room only:* $4368. Room and board charges vary according to board plan.

Financial Aid Forms of aid include need-based and non-need-based scholarships, athletic grants, and part-time jobs. The average aided 2006–07 undergraduate received an aid package worth an estimated $29,982. The application deadline for financial aid is February 15 with a priority deadline of February 15.

Freshman Admission The Colorado College requires an essay, a high school transcript, 3 recommendations, SAT or ACT scores, and TOEFL scores for international students. An interview is recommended. The application deadline for regular admission is January 15 and for early action it is November 15.

Transfer Admission The application deadline for admission is March 1.

Entrance Difficulty The Colorado College assesses its entrance difficulty level as very difficult. For the fall 2006 freshman class, 34 percent of the applicants were accepted.

For Further Information Contact Mr. Matt Bonser, Associate Director of Admission, The Colorado College, 900 Block North Cascade, West, Colorado Springs, CO 80903-3294. *Telephone:* 719-389-6344 or 800-542-7214 (toll-free). *Fax:* 719-389-6816. *E-mail:* admission@coloradocollege.edu. *Web site:* http://www.coloradocollege.edu/.

COLORADO SCHOOL OF MINES
Golden, Colorado

Colorado School of Mines is a coed, public university, founded in 1874, offering degrees at the bachelor's, master's, doctoral, and first professional levels. It has a 373-acre campus in Golden near Denver.

Academic Information The faculty has 299 members (65% full-time), 72% with terminal degrees. The undergraduate student-faculty ratio is 15:1. The library holds 150,000 titles and 4,883 serial subscriptions. Special programs include academic remediation, services for learning-disabled students, an honors program, cooperative (work-study) education, study abroad, advanced placement credit, accelerated degree programs, ESL programs, double majors, independent study, summer session for credit, and internships. The most frequently chosen baccalaureate fields are computer and information sciences, engineering, physical sciences.

Student Body Statistics The student body totals 4,056, of whom 3,223 are undergraduates (787 freshmen). 22 percent are women and 78 percent are men. Students come from 44 states and territories and 52 other countries. 80 percent are from Colorado. 4.3 percent are international students. 15 percent of the 2006 graduating class went on to graduate and professional schools.

Expenses for 2006–07 *Application fee:* $45. *State resident tuition:* $8088 full-time, $300 per semester hour part-time. *Nonresident tuition:* $20,624 full-time, $687 per semester hour part-time. *Mandatory fees:* $922 full-time, $60. Part-time tuition and fees vary according to course load. *College room and board:* $6880. *College room only:* $3600. Room and board charges vary according to board plan and housing facility.

Financial Aid Forms of aid include need-based and non-need-based scholarships, athletic grants, and part-time jobs. The average aided 2006–07 undergraduate received an aid package with an estimated $14,800. The priority application deadline for financial aid is March 1.

Freshman Admission Colorado School of Mines requires a high school transcript, SAT or ACT scores, and TOEFL scores for international students. Rank in upper one-third of high school class is recommended. An essay, recommendations, and an interview are required for some. The application deadline for regular admission is June 1.

Transfer Admission The application deadline for admission is June 1.

Entrance Difficulty Colorado School of Mines assesses its entrance difficulty level as very difficult. For the fall 2006 freshman class, 84 percent of the applicants were accepted.

For Further Information Contact Ms. Heather Boyd, Associate Director of Enrollment Management, Colorado School of Mines, Student Center, 1600 Maple Street, Golden, CO 80401. *Telephone:* 303-273-3227 or 800-446-9488 Ext. 3220 (toll-free out-of-state). *Fax:* 303-273-3509. *E-mail:* admit@mines.edu. *Web site:* http://www.mines.edu/.

COLORADO STATE UNIVERSITY
Fort Collins, Colorado

Colorado State University is a coed, public unit of Colorado State University System, founded in 1870, offering degrees at the bachelor's, master's, doctoral, and first professional levels. It has a 579-acre campus in Fort Collins near Denver.

Academic Information The faculty has 892 members (96% full-time), 99% with terminal degrees. The undergraduate student-faculty ratio is 18:1. The library holds 2 million titles, 31,372 serial subscriptions, and 5,932 audiovisual materials. Special programs include services for learning-disabled students, an honors program, cooperative (work-study) education, study abroad, advanced placement credit, accelerated degree programs, ESL programs, double majors, independent study, distance learning, summer session for credit, part-time degree programs, internships, and arrangement for off-campus study with Aims Community College. The most frequently chosen baccalaureate fields are business/marketing, family and consumer sciences, social sciences.

Student Body Statistics The student body totals 26,723, of whom 21,283 are undergraduates (4,093 freshmen). 52 percent are women and 48 percent are men. Students come from 53 states and territories and 50 other countries. 82 percent are from Colorado. 1.2 percent are international students.

Expenses for 2006–07 *Application fee:* $50. *State resident tuition:* $3466 full-time, $192.55 per credit hour part-time. *Nonresident tuition:* $14,994 full-time, $833 per credit hour part-time. *Mandatory fees:* $1251 full-time, $33.11 per term part-time. Both full-time and part-time tuition and fees vary according to course load. *College room and board:* $6602. *College room only:* $2980. Room and board charges vary according to board plan and housing facility.

Financial Aid Forms of aid include need-based and non-need-based scholarships, athletic grants, and part-time jobs. The average aided

Colorado State University (continued)

2005–06 undergraduate received an aid package worth $8455. The priority application deadline for financial aid is March 1.

Freshman Admission Colorado State University requires a high school transcript, SAT or ACT scores, and TOEFL scores for international students. An essay and recommendations are recommended. The application deadline for regular admission is July 1.

Transfer Admission The application deadline for admission is July 1.

Entrance Difficulty Colorado State University assesses its entrance difficulty level as moderately difficult; very difficult for engineering, technical journalism, business, landscape architecture, art, computer and science programs. For the fall 2006 freshman class, 86 percent of the applicants were accepted.

For Further Information Contact Ms. Mary Ontiveros, Executive Director of Admissions, Colorado State University, Spruce Hall, Fort Collins, CO 80523-0015. *Telephone:* 970-491-6909. *Fax:* 970-491-7799. *E-mail:* admissions@colostate.edu. *Web site:* http://www.colostate.edu/.

See page 162 for the College Close-Up.

COLORADO STATE UNIVERSITY-PUEBLO

Pueblo, Colorado

Colorado State University-Pueblo is a coed, public, comprehensive unit of Colorado State University System, founded in 1933, offering degrees at the bachelor's and master's levels. It has a 275-acre campus in Pueblo near Colorado Springs.

Academic Information The faculty has 315 members (53% full-time). The undergraduate student-faculty ratio is 16:1. The library holds 265,062 titles, 8,404 serial subscriptions, and 12,902 audiovisual materials. Special programs include academic remediation, services for learning-disabled students, an honors program, cooperative (work-study) education, study abroad, advanced placement credit, accelerated degree programs, ESL programs, double majors, independent study, distance learning, summer session for credit, part-time degree programs (daytime, evenings, weekends, summer), external degree programs, adult/continuing education programs, internships, and arrangement for off-campus study with Adams State College, Colorado State University, University of Colorado at Denver.

Student Body Statistics The student body totals 6,205, of whom 5,087 are undergraduates (671 freshmen). 60 percent are women and 40 percent are men. Students come from 43 states and territories and 22 other countries. 90 percent are from Colorado. 2.9 percent are international students.

Expenses for 2006–07 *Application fee:* $25. *State resident tuition:* $2975 full-time, $124 per credit hour part-time. *Nonresident tuition:* $13,543 full-time, $564 per credit hour part-time. *Mandatory fees:* $1215 full-time, $40 per credit hour part-time. *College room and board:* $5810. *College room only:* $2960.

Financial Aid Forms of aid include need-based and non-need-based scholarships, athletic grants, and part-time jobs. The average aided 2006–07 undergraduate received an aid package worth an estimated $7693. The priority application deadline for financial aid is March 1.

Freshman Admission Colorado State University-Pueblo requires a high school transcript, a minimum 2.0 high school GPA, SAT or ACT scores, and TOEFL scores for international students. An essay, a high school transcript, and recommendations are required for some. The application deadline for regular admission is August 1.

Transfer Admission Standardized test scores are required for some. The application deadline for admission is August 1.

Entrance Difficulty Colorado State University-Pueblo assesses its entrance difficulty level as moderately difficult; minimally difficult for transfers; very difficult for nursing program. For the fall 2006 freshman class, 96 percent of the applicants were accepted.

For Further Information Contact Ms. Jennifer Jensen, Associate Director of Admissions and Records, Colorado State University-Pueblo, 2200 Bonforte Blvd., Pueblo, CO 81001. *Telephone:* 719-549-2434. *Fax:* 719-549-2419. *E-mail:* jennifer.jensen@colostate-pueblo.edu. *Web site:* http://www.colostate-pueblo.edu/.

COLORADO TECHNICAL UNIVERSITY

Colorado Springs, Colorado

http://www.coloradotech.edu

COLORADO TECHNICAL UNIVERSITY DENVER CAMPUS

Greenwood Village, Colorado

http://www.coloradotech.edu/

DENVER INSTITUTE OF TECHNOLOGY

See Westwood College–Denver North.

DENVER TECHNICAL COLLEGE AT COLORADO SPRINGS

See DeVry University.

DeVRY UNIVERSITY

Broomfield, Colorado

http://www.devry.edu/

DeVRY UNIVERSITY

Colorado Springs, Colorado

DeVry University is a coed, proprietary, comprehensive unit of DeVry University, founded in 2001, offering degrees at the associate, bachelor's, and master's levels. It has a 9-acre campus in Colorado Springs.

Expenses for 2006–07 *Application fee:* $50. *Tuition:* $12,340 full-time, $465 per credit part-time. *Mandatory fees:* $310 full-time, $200 per year part-time. Both full-time and part-time tuition and fees vary according to course load.

For Further Information Contact Admissions Office, DeVry University, 1175 Kelly Johnson Boulevard, Colorado Springs, CO 80920. *Telephone:* 303-329-0955 or 866-338-7934 (toll-free). *Fax:* 719-632-1909. *Web site:* http://www.devry.edu/.

DeVRY UNIVERSITY

Westminster, Colorado

DeVry University is a coed, proprietary, four-year college, founded in 1945, offering degrees at the associate, bachelor's, and master's levels and postbachelor's certificates. It has a 3-acre campus in Westminster near Denver.

Academic Information The faculty has 36 members (50% full-time). The undergraduate student-faculty ratio is 19:1. The library holds 500,000 titles and 27 serial subscriptions. Special programs include academic remediation, accelerated degree programs, distance learning, summer session for credit, and adult/continuing education programs. The most frequently chosen baccalaureate fields are business/marketing, computer and information sciences, engineering technologies.

Student Body Statistics The student body totals 710, of whom 626 are undergraduates (99 freshmen). 36 percent are women and 64 percent are men. 97 percent are from Colorado.

Expenses for 2007–08 *Application fee:* $50. *Tuition:* $13,700 full-time, $500 per credit part-time. *Mandatory fees:* $320 full-time.

Financial Aid Forms of aid include need-based and non-need-based scholarships and part-time jobs. The application deadline for financial aid is continuous.
Freshman Admission DeVry University requires a high school transcript and TOEFL scores for international students. An essay and an interview are required for some. The application deadline for regular admission is rolling.
Transfer Admission The application deadline for admission is rolling.
Entrance Difficulty DeVry University has an open admission policy.
For Further Information Contact Admissions Office, DeVry University, 1870 West 122nd Avenue, Suite 316, Westminster, CO 80234-2010. *Telephone:* 303-280-7400. *Web site:* http://www.devry.edu/.

EDUCATION AMERICA, COLORADO SPRINGS CAMPUS

See Remington College–Colorado Springs Campus.

EDUCATION AMERICA, DENVER CAMPUS

See Remington College–Denver Campus.

FORT LEWIS COLLEGE
Durango, Colorado

Fort Lewis College is a coed, public, four-year college, founded in 1911, offering degrees at the bachelor's level. It has a 350-acre campus in Durango.

Academic Information The faculty has 240 members (75% full-time), 61% with terminal degrees. The student-faculty ratio is 18:1. The library holds 187,642 titles, 17,551 serial subscriptions, and 4,046 audiovisual materials. Special programs include academic remediation, services for learning-disabled students, an honors program, cooperative (work-study) education, study abroad, advanced placement credit, accelerated degree programs, ESL programs, double majors, independent study, distance learning, self-designed majors, summer session for credit, part-time degree programs (daytime, evenings, summer), adult/continuing education programs, and internships. The most frequently chosen baccalaureate fields are business/marketing, liberal arts/general studies, social sciences.
Student Body Statistics The student body is made up of 3,907 undergraduates (910 freshmen). 48 percent are women and 52 percent are men. Students come from 46 states and territories and 10 other countries. 72 percent are from Colorado. 0.9 percent are international students. 14 percent of the 2006 graduating class went on to graduate and professional schools.
Expenses for 2006–07 *Application fee:* $30. *State resident tuition:* $5102 full-time, $210 per credit hour part-time. *Nonresident tuition:* $13,190 full-time, $659 per credit hour part-time. *Mandatory fees:* $871 full-time, $44.25 per credit hour part-time. Full-time tuition and fees vary according to reciprocity agreements. Part-time tuition and fees vary according to course load and reciprocity agreements. *College room and board:* $6468. *College room only:* $3420. Room and board charges vary according to board plan and housing facility.
Financial Aid Forms of aid include need-based and non-need-based scholarships, athletic grants, and part-time jobs. The average aided 2005–06 undergraduate received an aid package worth $7142. The priority application deadline for financial aid is February 15.
Freshman Admission Fort Lewis College requires a high school transcript, a minimum 2.0 high school GPA, SAT or ACT scores, and TOEFL scores for international students. An essay, recommendations, and an interview are recommended. The application deadline for regular admission is August 1.
Transfer Admission The application deadline for admission is rolling.

Entrance Difficulty Fort Lewis College assesses its entrance difficulty level as moderately difficult. For the fall 2006 freshman class, 73 percent of the applicants were accepted.
For Further Information Contact Ms. Bridget Irish, Coordinator of First Year Programs, General Education and Enrichment Experience, Fort Lewis College, 1000 Rim Drive, Durango, CO 81301. *Telephone:* 970-247-7157. *Fax:* 970-247-7190. *E-mail:* irish_b@fortlewis.edu. *Web site:* http://www.fortlewis.edu/.

INTERNATIONAL UNIVERSITY

See Jones International University.

ITT TECHNICAL INSTITUTE
Thornton, Colorado

ITT Technical Institute is a coed, proprietary, primarily two-year college of ITT Educational Services, Inc, founded in 1984, offering degrees at the associate and bachelor's levels. It has a 2-acre campus in Thornton near Denver.

Expenses for 2006–07 *Application fee:* $100. Contact school for program costs.
Financial Aid Forms of aid include need-based scholarships and part-time jobs. The application deadline for financial aid is continuous.
Freshman Admission ITT Technical Institute requires a high school transcript, an interview, TOEFL scores for international students, and Wonderlic aptitude test. Recommendations are recommended. The application deadline for regular admission is rolling.
Transfer Admission The application deadline for admission is rolling.
Entrance Difficulty ITT Technical Institute assesses its entrance difficulty level as minimally difficult.
For Further Information Contact Ms. Tracy Arnett, Director of Recruitment, ITT Technical Institute, 500 East 84th Avenue, Thornton, CO 80229. *Telephone:* 303-288-4488 or 800-395-4488 (toll-free). *Fax:* 303-288-8166. *Web site:* http://www.itt-tech.edu/.

JOHNSON & WALES UNIVERSITY
Denver, Colorado

Johnson & Wales University is a coed, private, four-year college, founded in 1993, offering degrees at the associate and bachelor's levels.

Academic Information The faculty has 78 members (63% full-time). The student-faculty ratio is 25:1. The library holds 30,000 titles, 210 serial subscriptions, and 1,170 audiovisual materials. Special programs include academic remediation, services for learning-disabled students, an honors program, cooperative (work-study) education, advanced placement credit, accelerated degree programs, summer session for credit, part-time degree programs (daytime, evenings), adult/continuing education programs, and internships. The most frequently chosen baccalaureate fields are family and consumer sciences, history, parks and recreation.
Student Body Statistics The student body is made up of 1,543 undergraduates (404 freshmen). 52 percent are women and 48 percent are men. Students come from 51 states and territories and 22 other countries. 44 percent are from Colorado. 2.9 percent are international students.
Expenses for 2007–08 *Application fee:* $0. *Comprehensive fee:* $30,012 includes full-time tuition ($20,478), mandatory fees ($984), and college room and board ($8550). *Part-time tuition:* $379 per quarter hour.
Financial Aid Forms of aid include need-based and non-need-based scholarships and part-time jobs. The average aided 2005–06 undergraduate received an aid package worth $12,710. The application deadline for financial aid is continuous.
Freshman Admission Johnson & Wales University requires a high school transcript and TOEFL scores for international students. A minimum 2.0 high school GPA and SAT or ACT scores are

Johnson & Wales University (continued)

recommended. An essay, a minimum 2.75 high school GPA, an interview, and SAT or ACT scores are required for some. The application deadline for regular admission is rolling.

Transfer Admission The application deadline for admission is rolling.

Entrance Difficulty Johnson & Wales University assesses its entrance difficulty level as minimally difficult. For the fall 2006 freshman class, 80 percent of the applicants were accepted.

For Further Information Contact Kim Ostrowski, Director of Admissions, Johnson & Wales University, 7150 Montview Boulevard, Denver, CO 80220. *Telephone:* 977-598-3368 or 877-598-3368 (toll-free). *Fax:* 303-256-9333. *E-mail:* den.admissions@jwu.edu. *Web site:* http://www.jwu.edu/.

JONES INTERNATIONAL UNIVERSITY
Centennial, Colorado

Jones International University is a coed, proprietary, comprehensive institution, founded in 1995, offering degrees at the bachelor's and master's levels (offers only online degree programs).

Expenses for 2006–07 *Application fee:* $50. *Tuition:* $9720 full-time, $1215 per course part-time. *Mandatory fees:* $480 full-time, $60 per course part-time.

For Further Information Contact Ms. Candace Morrissey, Associate Director of Admissions, Jones International University, 9697 East Mineral Avenue, Centennial, CO 80112. *Telephone:* 303-784-8904 or 800-811-5663 (toll-free). *Fax:* 303-799-0966. *E-mail:* admissions@international.edu. *Web site:* http://www.jonesinternational.edu/.

MESA STATE COLLEGE
Grand Junction, Colorado

Mesa State College is a coed, public, comprehensive unit of State Colleges in Colorado, founded in 1925, offering degrees at the associate, bachelor's, and master's levels. It has a 42-acre campus in Grand Junction.

Academic Information The faculty has 396 members (52% full-time). The undergraduate student-faculty ratio is 19:1. The library holds 260,784 titles, 31,992 serial subscriptions, and 12,248 audiovisual materials. Special programs include academic remediation, services for learning-disabled students, an honors program, cooperative (work-study) education, study abroad, advanced placement credit, accelerated degree programs, double majors, independent study, distance learning, self-designed majors, summer session for credit, part-time degree programs (daytime, evenings, summer), adult/continuing education programs, internships, and arrangement for off-campus study with members of the Consortium of State Colleges in Colorado, National Student Exchange Program. The most frequently chosen baccalaureate fields are business/marketing, social sciences, visual and performing arts.

Student Body Statistics The student body totals 5,938, of whom 5,854 are undergraduates (1,240 freshmen). 59 percent are women and 41 percent are men. Students come from 45 states and territories. 90 percent are from Colorado. 0.3 percent are international students.

Expenses for 2007–08 *Application fee:* $30. *State resident tuition:* $3614 full-time, $139.02 per hour part-time. *Nonresident tuition:* $11,193 full-time, $430.50 per hour part-time. *Mandatory fees:* $226 full-time, $8.15 per hour part-time. *College room and board:* $7214. *College room only:* $3708.

Financial Aid Forms of aid include need-based and non-need-based scholarships, athletic grants, and part-time jobs. The average aided 2006–07 undergraduate received an aid package worth an estimated $7081. The priority application deadline for financial aid is March 1.

Freshman Admission Mesa State College requires a high school transcript and SAT or ACT scores. An essay, 2 recommendations, and TOEFL scores for international students are recommended. The application deadline for regular admission is rolling.

Transfer Admission The application deadline for admission is rolling.

Entrance Difficulty Mesa State College has an open admission policy for Associate degree programs. It assesses its entrance difficulty as moderately

difficult for out-of-state applicants; moderately difficult for transfers; very difficult for nursing, allied health, education, science, engineering programs.

For Further Information Contact Mr. Rance Larsen, Director of Admission, Mesa State College, 1100 North Avenue, Grand Junction, CO 81501. *Telephone:* 970-248-1875 or 800-982-MESA (toll-free). *Fax:* 970-248-1973. *E-mail:* rlarsen@mesastate.edu. *Web site:* http://www.mesastate.edu/.

METROPOLITAN STATE COLLEGE OF DENVER
Denver, Colorado
http://www.mscd.edu/

NAROPA UNIVERSITY
Boulder, Colorado

Naropa University is a coed, private, comprehensive institution, founded in 1974, offering degrees at the bachelor's, master's, and first professional levels. It has a 12-acre campus in Boulder near Denver.

Academic Information The faculty has 206 members (26% full-time), 31% with terminal degrees. The undergraduate student-faculty ratio is 9:1. The library holds 27,500 titles and 75 serial subscriptions. Special programs include services for learning-disabled students, cooperative (work-study) education, study abroad, advanced placement credit, double majors, independent study, distance learning, self-designed majors, summer session for credit, part-time degree programs (daytime), adult/continuing education programs, and internships. The most frequently chosen baccalaureate fields are interdisciplinary studies, psychology, visual and performing arts.

Student Body Statistics The student body totals 1,136, of whom 473 are undergraduates (55 freshmen). 59 percent are women and 41 percent are men. Students come from 46 states and territories and 7 other countries. 26 percent are from Colorado. 3.1 percent are international students.

Expenses for 2006–07 *Application fee:* $50. *Comprehensive fee:* $26,320 includes full-time tuition ($19,426) and college room and board ($6894). *College room only:* $4050. Full-time tuition varies according to course load. Room and board charges vary according to board plan. *Part-time tuition:* $630 per semester hour. *Part-time mandatory fees:* $288 per term. Part-time tuition and fees vary according to course load.

Financial Aid Forms of aid include need-based scholarships and part-time jobs. The average aided 2006–07 undergraduate received an aid package worth an estimated $21,838. The priority application deadline for financial aid is March 1.

Freshman Admission Naropa University requires an essay, a high school transcript, 2 recommendations, an interview, and TOEFL scores for international students. SAT or ACT scores are recommended. The application deadline for regular admission is January 15.

Transfer Admission The application deadline for admission is rolling.

Entrance Difficulty Naropa University assesses its entrance difficulty level as moderately difficult. For the fall 2006 freshman class, 91 percent of the applicants were accepted.

For Further Information Contact Ms. Amy Kopkin, Admissions Counselor, Naropa University, 2130 Arapahoe Avenue, Boulder, CO 80302. *Telephone:* 303-546-5285 or 800-772-0410 (toll-free out-of-state). *Fax:* 303-546-3583. *E-mail:* admissions@naropa.edu. *Web site:* http://www.naropa.edu/.

NATIONAL AMERICAN UNIVERSITY
Colorado Springs, Colorado
http://www.national.edu/

NATIONAL AMERICAN UNIVERSITY
Denver, Colorado

National American University is a coed, proprietary, four-year college, founded in 1974, offering degrees at the associate, bachelor's, and master's levels.

Academic Information The faculty has 35 members. The undergraduate student-faculty ratio is 10:1. The library holds 400 titles and 33 serial subscriptions. Special programs include academic remediation, advanced placement credit, accelerated degree programs, ESL programs, double majors, independent study, distance learning, summer session for credit, part-time degree programs (daytime, evenings, weekends, summer), adult/continuing education programs, and internships.
Student Body Statistics The student body totals 206, of whom 200 are undergraduates. 42 percent are women and 59 percent are men.
Expenses for 2007–08 *Application fee:* $25. *Tuition:* $9720 full-time, $270 per quarter hour part-time.
Financial Aid Forms of aid include need-based and non-need-based scholarships and part-time jobs. The application deadline for financial aid is continuous.
Freshman Admission National American University requires a high school transcript, an interview, and TOEFL scores for international students. The application deadline for regular admission is rolling.
Transfer Admission The application deadline for admission is rolling.
Entrance Difficulty National American University has an open admission policy.
For Further Information Contact Jacklyn Haack, Director of Admissions, National American University, 1325 South Colorado Blvd, Suite 100, Denver, CO 80222. *Telephone:* 303-876-7112. *Fax:* 303-876-7105. *E-mail:* jhaack@national.edu. *Web site:* http://www.national.edu/.

NAZARENE BIBLE COLLEGE
Colorado Springs, Colorado

Nazarene Bible College is a coed, private, four-year college, founded in 1967, affiliated with the Church of the Nazarene, offering degrees at the associate and bachelor's levels. It has a 64-acre campus in Colorado Springs near Denver.

Academic Information The faculty has 79 members (18% full-time), 68% with terminal degrees. The student-faculty ratio is 10:1. The library holds 64,651 titles, 1,756 serial subscriptions, and 8,580 audiovisual materials. Special programs include academic remediation, double majors, independent study, distance learning, summer session for credit, part-time degree programs (daytime, evenings, summer), and internships. The most frequently chosen baccalaureate field is theology and religious vocations.
Student Body Statistics The student body is made up of 808 undergraduates (21 freshmen). 37 percent are women and 63 percent are men. Students come from 50 states and territories and 1 other country. 45 percent are from Colorado. 0.5 percent are international students.
Expenses for 2007–08 *Application fee:* $0. *Tuition:* $8100 full-time, $300 per credit hour part-time. *Mandatory fees:* $300 full-time.
Financial Aid Forms of aid include need-based and non-need-based scholarships and part-time jobs. The application deadline for financial aid is continuous.
Freshman Admission Nazarene Bible College requires an essay, a high school transcript, 2 recommendations, and TOEFL scores for international students. The application deadline for regular admission is July 31.
Transfer Admission The application deadline for admission is July 31.
Entrance Difficulty Nazarene Bible College has an open admission policy.
For Further Information Contact Dr. Laurel Matson, Director of Admissions/Public Relations, Nazarene Bible College, 1111 Academy Park Loop, Colorado Springs, CO 80910-3704. *Telephone:* 719-884-5061 or 800-873-3873 (toll-free). *Fax:* 719-884-5199. *Web site:* http://www.nbc.edu/.

PLATT COLLEGE
Aurora, Colorado

http://www.plattcolorado.edu/

REGIS UNIVERSITY
Denver, Colorado

Regis University is a coed, private, Roman Catholic (Jesuit), comprehensive institution, founded in 1877, offering degrees at the bachelor's, master's, and doctoral levels. It has a 90-acre campus in Denver.

Academic Information The faculty has 1,342 members (17% full-time), 27% with terminal degrees. The undergraduate student-faculty ratio is 9:1. The library holds 350,000 titles and 20,800 serial subscriptions. Special programs include academic remediation, services for learning-disabled students, an honors program, cooperative (work-study) education, study abroad, advanced placement credit, accelerated degree programs, Freshman Honors College, double majors, independent study, distance learning, self-designed majors, summer session for credit, part-time degree programs (daytime, evenings, weekends, summer), external degree programs, adult/continuing education programs, internships, and arrangement for off-campus study with other Jesuit colleges and universities.
Student Body Statistics The student body totals 16,004, of whom 8,119 are undergraduates (529 freshmen). 63 percent are women and 37 percent are men. Students come from 40 states and territories. 77 percent are from Colorado. 0.9 percent are international students. 15 percent of the 2006 graduating class went on to graduate and professional schools.
Expenses for 2007–08 *Application fee:* $40. *Comprehensive fee:* $35,730 includes full-time tuition ($26,600), mandatory fees ($300), and college room and board ($8830). *College room only:* $5050. *Part-time tuition:* $831 per hour. *Part-time mandatory fees:* $240 per year.
Financial Aid Forms of aid include need-based and non-need-based scholarships, athletic grants, and part-time jobs. The average aided 2005–06 undergraduate received an aid package worth $17,572. The priority application deadline for financial aid is March 1.
Freshman Admission Regis University requires an essay, a high school transcript, a minimum 2.5 high school GPA, 1 recommendation, SAT or ACT scores, and TOEFL scores for international students. SAT Subject Test scores are recommended. 2 recommendations and an interview are required for some. The application deadline for regular admission is rolling and for nonresidents it is rolling.
Transfer Admission The application deadline for admission is rolling.
Entrance Difficulty Regis University assesses its entrance difficulty level as moderately difficult. For the fall 2006 freshman class, 25 percent of the applicants were accepted.
For Further Information Contact Mr. Vic Davolt, Director of Admission, Regis University, 3333 Regis Boulevard, Denver, CO 80221-1099. *Telephone:* 303-458-4905 or 800-388-2366 Ext. 4900 (toll-free). *Fax:* 303-964-5534. *E-mail:* regisadm@regis.edu. *Web site:* http://www.regis.edu/.

See page 186 for the College Close-Up.

REMINGTON COLLEGE–COLORADO SPRINGS CAMPUS
Colorado Springs, Colorado

Remington College–Colorado Springs Campus is a coed, proprietary, four-year college, offering degrees at the associate and bachelor's levels. It has a 3-acre campus in Colorado Springs.

Academic Information The faculty has 12 members (50% full-time). The student-faculty ratio is 11:1. The library holds 4,370 titles, 67 serial subscriptions, and 322 audiovisual materials. Special programs include cooperative (work-study) education and distance learning.
Student Body Statistics The student body is made up of 65 undergraduates (39 freshmen). 69 percent are women and 31 percent are men.
Expenses for 2007–08 *Tuition:* $18,480 full-time.

Remington College–Colorado Springs Campus (continued)

Entrance Difficulty Remington College–Colorado Springs Campus assesses its entrance difficulty level as noncompetitive. For the fall 2006 freshman class, 100 percent of the applicants were accepted.

For Further Information Contact Ms. Shirley McCray, Campus President, Remington College–Colorado Springs Campus, 6050 Erin Park Drive, #250, Colorado Springs, CO 80918. *Telephone:* 769-532-1234. *Fax:* 719-264-1234. *Web site:* http://www.remingtoncollege.edu/.

REMINGTON COLLEGE–DENVER CAMPUS
Lakewood, Colorado
http://www.remingtoncollege.edu/

ROCKY MOUNTAIN COLLEGE OF ART & DESIGN
Lakewood, Colorado

Rocky Mountain College of Art & Design is a coed, proprietary, four-year college, founded in 1963, offering degrees at the bachelor's level. It has a 23-acre campus in Lakewood.

Academic Information The faculty has 65 members (38% full-time). The student-faculty ratio is 11:1. The library holds 6,287 titles and 65 serial subscriptions. Special programs include academic remediation, cooperative (work-study) education, study abroad, advanced placement credit, accelerated degree programs, double majors, independent study, summer session for credit, part-time degree programs (daytime, summer), and internships. The most frequently chosen baccalaureate fields are communication technologies, education, visual and performing arts.

Student Body Statistics The student body is made up of 454 undergraduates (83 freshmen). 59 percent are women and 41 percent are men. Students come from 37 states and territories and 3 other countries. 67 percent are from Colorado. 0.9 percent are international students. 5 percent of the 2006 graduating class went on to graduate and professional schools.

Expenses for 2007–08 *Application fee:* $35. *Tuition:* $823 per credit part-time.

Financial Aid Forms of aid include need-based and non-need-based scholarships and part-time jobs. The priority application deadline for financial aid is April 1.

Freshman Admission Rocky Mountain College of Art & Design requires a high school transcript, a minimum 2.0 high school GPA, an interview, and a portfolio. TOEFL scores for international students are recommended. The application deadline for regular admission is rolling.

Transfer Admission The application deadline for admission is rolling.

Entrance Difficulty Rocky Mountain College of Art & Design assesses its entrance difficulty level as moderately difficult. For the fall 2006 freshman class, 100 percent of the applicants were accepted.

For Further Information Contact Ms. Angela Carlson, Director of Admissions and Marketing, Rocky Mountain College of Art & Design, 1600 Pierce Street, Lakewood, CO 80214. *Telephone:* 303-753-6046 or 800-888-ARTS (toll-free). *Fax:* 303-759-4970. *E-mail:* admit@rmcad.edu. *Web site:* http://www.rmcad.edu/.

TEIKYO LORETTO HEIGHTS UNIVERSITY
Denver, Colorado
http://www.tlhu.edu/

UNITED STATES AIR FORCE ACADEMY
Colorado Springs, Colorado

United States Air Force Academy is a coed, primarily men's, public, four-year college, founded in 1954, offering degrees at the bachelor's level. It has an 18,000-acre campus in Colorado Springs near Denver.

Academic Information The faculty has 563 members (100% full-time), 49% with terminal degrees. The student-faculty ratio is 8:1. The library holds 445,379 titles and 1,693 serial subscriptions. Special programs include academic remediation, study abroad, advanced placement credit, ESL programs, double majors, independent study, self-designed majors, summer session for credit, internships, and arrangement for off-campus study with other United States service academies.

Student Body Statistics The student body is made up of 4,524 undergraduates (1,266 freshmen). 18 percent are women and 82 percent are men. Students come from 52 states and territories and 14 other countries. 6 percent are from Colorado. 1.3 percent are international students. 7.6 percent of the 2006 graduating class went on to graduate and professional schools.

Expenses for 2006–07 *Application fee:* $0. Tuition, room and board, and medical and dental care are provided by the U.S. government. Each cadet receives a salary from which to pay for uniforms, supplies, and personal expenses. Entering freshmen are required to deposit $2500 to defray the initial cost of uniforms and equipment.

Freshman Admission United States Air Force Academy requires an essay, a high school transcript, a minimum 2.0 high school GPA, an interview, authorized nomination, SAT or ACT scores, and TOEFL scores for international students. The application deadline for regular admission is January 31.

Transfer Admission The application deadline for admission is January 31.

Entrance Difficulty United States Air Force Academy assesses its entrance difficulty level as most difficult. For the fall 2006 freshman class, 14 percent of the applicants were accepted.

For Further Information Contact Mr. Rolland Stoneman, Associate Director of Admissions/Selections, United States Air Force Academy, HQ USAFA/RR, 2304 Cadet Drive, Suite 2300, USAF Academy, CO 80840-5025. *Telephone:* 719-333-2520 or 800-443-9266 (toll-free). *Fax:* 719-333-3012. *E-mail:* rr_webmail@usafa.af.mil. *Web site:* http://www.usafa.edu/.

UNIVERSITY OF COLORADO AT BOULDER
Boulder, Colorado

University of Colorado at Boulder is a coed, public unit of University of Colorado System, founded in 1876, offering degrees at the bachelor's, master's, doctoral, and first professional levels. It has a 600-acre campus in Boulder near Denver.

Academic Information The faculty has 1,845 members (68% full-time), 73% with terminal degrees. The undergraduate student-faculty ratio is 16:1. The library holds 4 million titles, 26,152 serial subscriptions, and 450,928 audiovisual materials. Special programs include services for learning-disabled students, an honors program, cooperative (work-study) education, study abroad, advanced placement credit, accelerated degree programs, Freshman Honors College, ESL programs, double majors, independent study, distance learning, self-designed majors, summer session for credit, part-time degree programs (daytime, evenings, summer), adult/continuing education programs, internships, and arrangement for off-campus study with other units of the University of Colorado System. The most frequently chosen baccalaureate fields are business/marketing, communications/journalism, social sciences.

Student Body Statistics The student body totals 31,399, of whom 26,163 are undergraduates (5,645 freshmen). 47 percent are women and 53 percent are men. Students come from 53 states and territories and 115 other countries. 69 percent are from Colorado. 1.7 percent are international students. 38 percent of the 2006 graduating class went on to graduate and professional schools.

Expenses for 2006–07 *Application fee:* $50. *State resident tuition:* $4554 full-time. *Nonresident tuition:* $22,450 full-time. *Mandatory fees:* $1089 full-time. Full-time tuition and fees vary according to program. *College room and board:* $8300. Room and board charges vary according to board plan, location, and student level.

Financial Aid Forms of aid include need-based and non-need-based scholarships, athletic grants, and part-time jobs. The average aided 2006–07 undergraduate received an aid package worth an estimated $10,362.

Freshman Admission University of Colorado at Boulder requires a high school transcript, a minimum 2.0 high school GPA, SAT or ACT scores,

and TOEFL scores for international students. An essay, a minimum 3.0 high school GPA, and recommendations are recommended. Audition for music program is required for some. The application deadline for regular admission is January 15.

Transfer Admission The application deadline for admission is April 1.

Entrance Difficulty University of Colorado at Boulder assesses its entrance difficulty level as moderately difficult; very difficult for engineering programs. For the fall 2006 freshman class, 88 percent of the applicants were accepted.

For Further Information Contact Admissions Office, University of Colorado at Boulder, Regent Administrative Center 125, 552 UCB, Boulder, CO 80309. *Telephone:* 303-492-6301. *Fax:* 303-492-7115. *E-mail:* apply@colorado.edu. *Web site:* http://www.colorado.edu/.

UNIVERSITY OF COLORADO AT COLORADO SPRINGS

Colorado Springs, Colorado

University of Colorado at Colorado Springs is a coed, public, comprehensive institution, founded in 1965, offering degrees at the bachelor's, master's, and doctoral levels and postbachelor's certificates. It has a 400-acre campus in Colorado Springs near Denver.

Academic Information The faculty has 556 members (36% full-time), 36% with terminal degrees. The undergraduate student-faculty ratio is 18:1. The library holds 391,638 titles and 2,201 serial subscriptions. Special programs include services for learning-disabled students, cooperative (work-study) education, advanced placement credit, accelerated degree programs, double majors, independent study, distance learning, summer session for credit, part-time degree programs (daytime, evenings, weekends, summer), and internships. The most frequently chosen baccalaureate fields are business/marketing, communications/journalism, social sciences.

Student Body Statistics The student body totals 8,583, of whom 6,296 are undergraduates (755 freshmen). 59 percent are women and 41 percent are men. Students come from 44 states and territories and 26 other countries. 80 percent are from Colorado. 0.3 percent are international students.

Expenses for 2006–07 *Application fee:* $50. *State resident tuition:* $5490 full-time. *Nonresident tuition:* $22,950 full-time. *Mandatory fees:* $1047 full-time. *College room and board:* $7662.

Financial Aid Forms of aid include need-based and non-need-based scholarships and part-time jobs. The average aided 2005–06 undergraduate received an aid package worth $6456. The priority application deadline for financial aid is April 1.

Freshman Admission University of Colorado at Colorado Springs requires a high school transcript, SAT or ACT scores, and TOEFL scores for international students. The application deadline for regular admission is July 1.

Transfer Admission The application deadline for admission is July 1.

Entrance Difficulty University of Colorado at Colorado Springs assesses its entrance difficulty level as moderately difficult; very difficult for business, engineering, nursing programs. For the fall 2006 freshman class, 63 percent of the applicants were accepted.

For Further Information Contact Mr. James Tidwell, Assistant Admissions Director, University of Colorado at Colorado Springs, PO Box 7150, Colorado Springs, CO 80933-7150. *Telephone:* 719-262-3383 or 800-990-8227 Ext. 3383 (toll-free). *Fax:* 719-262-3116. *E-mail:* admrec@mail.uccs.edu. *Web site:* http://www.uccs.edu/.

UNIVERSITY OF COLORADO AT DENVER AND HEALTH SCIENCES CENTER

Denver, Colorado

University of Colorado at Denver and Health Sciences Center is a coed, public unit of University of Colorado System, founded in 1912, offering degrees at the bachelor's, master's, doctoral, and first professional levels and post-master's certificates. It has a 171-acre campus in Denver.

Academic Information The faculty has 1,362 members (43% full-time), 57% with terminal degrees. The undergraduate student-faculty ratio is 15:1. The library holds 927,468 titles, 88,134 serial subscriptions, and 15,366 audiovisual materials. Special programs include services for learning-disabled students, an honors program, cooperative (work-study) education, study abroad, advanced placement credit, accelerated degree programs, ESL programs, double majors, independent study, distance learning, self-designed majors, summer session for credit, part-time degree programs (daytime, evenings, weekends, summer), adult/continuing education programs, internships, and arrangement for off-campus study with Metropolitan State College, Community College of Denver. The most frequently chosen baccalaureate fields are business/marketing, health professions and related sciences, social sciences.

Student Body Statistics The student body totals 19,766, of whom 10,387 are undergraduates (808 freshmen). 57 percent are women and 43 percent are men. Students come from 51 states and territories and 57 other countries. 96 percent are from Colorado. 1.5 percent are international students.

Expenses for 2007–08 *Application fee:* $50. *State resident tuition:* $4330 full-time. *Nonresident tuition:* $16,200 full-time. *Mandatory fees:* $847 full-time.

Financial Aid Forms of aid include need-based and non-need-based scholarships and part-time jobs. The priority application deadline for financial aid is April 1.

Freshman Admission University of Colorado at Denver and Health Sciences Center requires a high school transcript, a minimum 2.5 high school GPA, SAT or ACT scores, and TOEFL scores for international students. The application deadline for regular admission is July 22 and for nonresidents it is July 22.

Transfer Admission The application deadline for admission is July 22.

Entrance Difficulty University of Colorado at Denver and Health Sciences Center assesses its entrance difficulty level as moderately difficult; very difficult for engineering, business programs. For the fall 2006 freshman class, 69 percent of the applicants were accepted.

For Further Information Contact Ms. Barbara Edwards, Director of Admissions, University of Colorado at Denver and Health Sciences Center, PO Box 173354, Campus Box 167, Denver, CO 80217. *Telephone:* 303-556-3287. *Fax:* 303-556-4838. *E-mail:* admissions@castle.cudenver.edu. *Web site:* http://www.ucdhsc.edu/.

UNIVERSITY OF DENVER

Denver, Colorado

University of Denver is a coed, private university, founded in 1864, offering degrees at the bachelor's, master's, doctoral, and first professional levels. It has a 125-acre campus in Denver.

Academic Information The faculty has 1,050 members (46% full-time). The undergraduate student-faculty ratio is 11:1. The library holds 1 million titles and 6,283 serial subscriptions. Special programs include services for learning-disabled students, an honors program, cooperative (work-study) education, study abroad, advanced placement credit, accelerated degree programs, Freshman Honors College, ESL programs, double majors, independent study, self-designed majors, summer session for credit, part-time degree programs (daytime, evenings, weekends, summer), adult/continuing education programs, and internships. The most frequently chosen baccalaureate fields are business/marketing, communications/journalism, social sciences.

Student Body Statistics The student body totals 10,374, of whom 4,877 are undergraduates (1,103 freshmen). 55 percent are women and 45 percent are men. Students come from 52 states and territories and 54 other countries. 50 percent are from Colorado. 3.9 percent are international students. 24 percent of the 2006 graduating class went on to graduate and professional schools.

Expenses for 2006–07 *Application fee:* $50. *Comprehensive fee:* $39,600 includes full-time tuition ($29,628), mandatory fees ($744), and college room and board ($9228). *College room only:* $5676. Full-time tuition and fees vary according to class time, course load, and program. Room and

University of Denver (continued)

board charges vary according to board plan and housing facility. *Part-time tuition:* $823 per quarter hour. Part-time tuition varies according to class time, course load, and program.

Financial Aid Forms of aid include need-based and non-need-based scholarships, athletic grants, and part-time jobs. The average aided 2005–06 undergraduate received an aid package worth $20,757. The priority application deadline for financial aid is March 1.

Freshman Admission University of Denver requires an essay, a high school transcript, 2 recommendations, an interview, and SAT or ACT scores. TOEFL scores for international students are recommended. A minimum 2.0 high school GPA is required for some. The application deadline for regular admission is January 15 and for early action it is November 1.

Transfer Admission The application deadline for admission is rolling.

Entrance Difficulty University of Denver assesses its entrance difficulty level as moderately difficult. For the fall 2006 freshman class, 82 percent of the applicants were accepted.

For Further Information Contact Mr. Todd Rinehart, Assistant Vice Chancellor for Enrollment, University of Denver, University Park, Denver, CO 80208. *Telephone:* 303-871-2036 or 800-525-9495 (toll-free out-of-state). *Fax:* 303-871-3301. *E-mail:* admission@du.edu. *Web site:* http://www.du.edu/.

UNIVERSITY OF NORTHERN COLORADO
Greeley, Colorado

University of Northern Colorado is a coed, public university, founded in 1890, offering degrees at the bachelor's, master's, and doctoral levels (specialist). It has a 240-acre campus in Greeley near Denver.

Academic Information The faculty has 632 members (65% full-time). The undergraduate student-faculty ratio is 24:1. The library holds 1 million titles and 3,417 serial subscriptions. Special programs include academic remediation, services for learning-disabled students, an honors program, cooperative (work-study) education, study abroad, advanced placement credit, ESL programs, double majors, independent study, distance learning, self-designed majors, summer session for credit, part-time degree programs (daytime, evenings, weekends, summer), external degree programs, adult/continuing education programs, internships, and arrangement for off-campus study with National Student Exchange. The most frequently chosen baccalaureate fields are business/marketing, interdisciplinary studies, social sciences.

Student Body Statistics The student body totals 12,981, of whom 10,799 are undergraduates (2,521 freshmen). 61 percent are women and 39 percent are men. Students come from 48 states and territories. 91 percent are from Colorado. 0.5 percent are international students. 11.6 percent of the 2006 graduating class went on to graduate and professional schools.

Expenses for 2006–07 *Application fee:* $40. *State resident tuition:* $3276 full-time, $136.50 per credit hour part-time. *Nonresident tuition:* $11,858 full-time, $494 per credit hour part-time. *Mandatory fees:* $674 full-time, $33.70 per credit hour part-time. Both full-time and part-time tuition and fees vary according to program. *College room and board:* $6832. *College room only:* $3260. Room and board charges vary according to board plan and housing facility.

Financial Aid Forms of aid include need-based and non-need-based scholarships, athletic grants, and part-time jobs. The average aided 2005–06 undergraduate received an aid package worth $10,075. The priority application deadline for financial aid is March 1.

Freshman Admission University of Northern Colorado requires a high school transcript, a minimum 2.9 high school GPA, and SAT or ACT scores. An interview is required for some. The application deadline for regular admission is August 1.

Transfer Admission University of Northern Colorado requires a college transcript and a minimum 2.0 college GPA. Standardized test scores are required for some. The application deadline for admission is rolling.

Entrance Difficulty University of Northern Colorado assesses its entrance difficulty level as moderately difficult. For the fall 2006 freshman class, 80 percent of the applicants were accepted.

For Further Information Contact Mr. Chris Dowen, Interim Director of Admissions, University of Northern Colorado, Campus Box 10, Carter Hall 3006, Greeley, CO 80639. *Telephone:* 970-351-2881 or 888-700-4UNC (toll-free in-state). *Fax:* 970-351-2984. *E-mail:* admissions.help@unco.edu. *Web site:* http://www.unco.edu/.

UNIVERSITY OF PHOENIX–DENVER CAMPUS
Lone Tree, Colorado

University of Phoenix–Denver Campus is a coed, proprietary, comprehensive institution, offering degrees at the bachelor's and master's levels and post-master's certificates.

Academic Information The faculty has 955 members (5% full-time), 23% with terminal degrees. The undergraduate student-faculty ratio is 9:1. The library holds 1,759 titles and 692 serial subscriptions. Special programs include services for learning-disabled students, advanced placement credit, accelerated degree programs, independent study, distance learning, external degree programs, and adult/continuing education programs. The most frequently chosen baccalaureate fields are business/marketing, computer and information sciences, health professions and related sciences.

Student Body Statistics The student body totals 2,948, of whom 1,645 are undergraduates (39 freshmen). 61 percent are women and 39 percent are men. 9.4 percent are international students.

Expenses for 2006–07 *Application fee:* $45. *Tuition:* $9750 full-time.

Financial Aid Forms of aid include need-based and non-need-based scholarships. The average aided 2005–06 undergraduate received an aid package worth $4347. The application deadline for financial aid is continuous.

Freshman Admission University of Phoenix–Denver Campus requires 1 recommendation and TOEFL scores for international students. A high school transcript is required for some. The application deadline for regular admission is rolling.

Transfer Admission The application deadline for admission is rolling.

Entrance Difficulty University of Phoenix–Denver Campus has an open admission policy.

For Further Information Contact Ms. Beth Barilla, Associate Vice President, Student Admissions and Services, University of Phoenix–Denver Campus, 4615 East Elmwood Street, Mail Stop AA-KK101, Phoenix, AZ 85040-1958. *Telephone:* 480-317-6000, 800-776-4867 (toll-free in-state), or 800-228-7240 (toll-free out-of-state). *Fax:* 480-894-1758. *E-mail:* beth.barilla@phoenix.edu. *Web site:* http://www.phoenix.edu/.

UNIVERSITY OF PHOENIX–SOUTHERN COLORADO CAMPUS
Colorado Springs, Colorado

University of Phoenix–Southern Colorado Campus is a coed, proprietary, comprehensive institution, founded in 1999, offering degrees at the bachelor's and master's levels.

Academic Information The faculty has 431 members, 21% with terminal degrees. The undergraduate student-faculty ratio is 8:1. The library holds 1,759 titles and 692 serial subscriptions. Special programs include services for learning-disabled students, advanced placement credit, accelerated degree programs, independent study, distance learning, external degree programs, and adult/continuing education programs. The most frequently chosen baccalaureate fields are business/marketing, computer and information sciences, security and protective services.

Student Body Statistics The student body totals 1,090, of whom 618 are undergraduates (17 freshmen). 54 percent are women and 46 percent are men. 19.9 percent are international students.

Expenses for 2006–07 *Application fee:* $45. *Tuition:* $9750 full-time.

Financial Aid Forms of aid include need-based and non-need-based scholarships. The average aided 2005–06 undergraduate received an aid package worth $4814. The application deadline for financial aid is continuous.

Freshman Admission University of Phoenix–Southern Colorado Campus requires 1 recommendation and TOEFL scores for international students. A high school transcript is required for some. The application deadline for regular admission is rolling.

Transfer Admission The application deadline for admission is rolling.

Entrance Difficulty University of Phoenix–Southern Colorado Campus has an open admission policy.

For Further Information Contact Ms. Beth Barilla, Associate Vice President, Student Admissions and Services, University of Phoenix–Southern Colorado Campus, 4615 East Elwood Street, Mail Stop AA-K101, Phoenix, AZ 85040-1958. *Telephone:* 480-317-6000, 800-776-4867 (toll-free in-state), or 800-228-7240 (toll-free out-of-state). *Fax:* 480-894-1758. *E-mail:* beth.barilla@phoenix.edu. *Web site:* http://www.phoenix.edu/.

UNIVERSITY OF SOUTHERN COLORADO

See Colorado State University-Pueblo.

WESTERN STATE COLLEGE OF COLORADO
Gunnison, Colorado

Western State College of Colorado is a coed, public, four-year college, founded in 1901, offering degrees at the bachelor's level. It has a 381-acre campus in Gunnison.

Academic Information The faculty has 146 members (75% full-time), 62% with terminal degrees. The student-faculty ratio is 18:1. The library holds 158,698 titles and 719 serial subscriptions. Special programs include services for learning-disabled students, an honors program, cooperative (work-study) education, study abroad, advanced placement credit, accelerated degree programs, double majors, self-designed majors, summer session for credit, part-time degree programs (summer), adult/continuing education programs, internships, and arrangement for off-campus study with State Colleges of Colorado, National Student Exchange. The most frequently chosen baccalaureate fields are business/marketing, parks and recreation, visual and performing arts.

Student Body Statistics The student body is made up of 2,094 undergraduates (515 freshmen). 38 percent are women and 62 percent are men. Students come from 50 states and territories. 70 percent are from Colorado. 12 percent of the 2006 graduating class went on to graduate and professional schools.

Expenses for 2006–07 *Application fee:* $30. *State resident tuition:* $2553 full-time, $106 per credit hour part-time. *Nonresident tuition:* $11,112 full-time, $463 per credit hour part-time. *Mandatory fees:* $796 full-time. Full-time tuition and fees vary according to course load. Part-time tuition varies according to course load. *College room and board:* $6976. *College room only:* $3794. Room and board charges vary according to board plan and housing facility.

Financial Aid Forms of aid include need-based and non-need-based scholarships, athletic grants, and part-time jobs. The average aided 2005–06 undergraduate received an aid package worth $8800. The priority application deadline for financial aid is April 1.

Freshman Admission Western State College of Colorado requires a high school transcript, SAT or ACT scores, and TOEFL scores for international students. A minimum 2.5 high school GPA is recommended. An essay, 2 recommendations, and an interview are required for some. The application deadline for regular admission is August 1.

Entrance Difficulty Western State College of Colorado assesses its entrance difficulty level as moderately difficult. For the fall 2006 freshman class, 63 percent of the applicants were accepted.

For Further Information Contact Mr. Timothy Albers, Director of Admissions, Western State College of Colorado, Western State College of Colorado, 6 Admission Office, Gunnison, CO 81231. *Telephone:* 970-943-2119 or 800-876-5309 (toll-free). *Fax:* 970-943-2212. *E-mail:* discover@western.edu. *Web site:* http://www.western.edu/.

WESTWOOD COLLEGE–DENVER NORTH
Denver, Colorado

Westwood College–Denver North is a coed, proprietary, primarily two-year college, founded in 1953, offering degrees at the associate and bachelor's levels. It has an 11-acre campus in Denver.

Expenses for 2006–07 *Application fee:* $100. *Tuition:* $12,300 full-time, $467 per credit part-time. *Mandatory fees:* $510 full-time, $120 per term part-time. Both full-time and part-time tuition and fees vary according to course load and program.

For Further Information Contact Ms. Dianne Hopkins, New Student Coordinator, Westwood College–Denver North, 7350 North Broadway, Denver, CO 80221-3653. *Telephone:* 303-650-5050 Ext. 325 or 800-992-5050 (toll-free). *Fax:* 303-487-0214. *Web site:* http://www.westwood.edu/.

WESTWOOD COLLEGE–DENVER SOUTH
Denver, Colorado

Westwood College–Denver South is a coed, proprietary, primarily two-year college, offering degrees at the associate and bachelor's levels. It is located in Denver near Denver, CO.

For Further Information Contact Mr. Ron DeJong, Director of Admissions, Westwood College–Denver South, 3150 South Sheridan Boulevard, Denver, CO 80227-5548. *Telephone:* 303-934-2790 or 800-281-2978 (toll-free). *Fax:* 303-934-2583. *E-mail:* info@westwood.edu. *Web site:* http://www.westwood.edu/.

YESHIVA TORAS CHAIM TALMUDICAL SEMINARY
Denver, Colorado

For Information Write to Yeshiva Toras Chaim Talmudical Seminary, Denver, CO 80204-1415.

Hawaii

ARGOSY UNIVERSITY, HAWAI'I
Honolulu, Hawaii

http://www.argosyu.edu/honolulu/

BRIGHAM YOUNG UNIVERSITY–HAWAII
Laie, Hawaii

Brigham Young University–Hawaii is a coed, private, Latter-day Saints, four-year college, founded in 1955, offering degrees at the associate and bachelor's levels and postbachelor's certificates. It has a 60-acre campus in Laie near Honolulu.

Academic Information The faculty has 184 members (64% full-time), 40% with terminal degrees. The student-faculty ratio is 15:1. The library holds 321,400 titles and 11,325 serial subscriptions. Special programs include academic remediation, services for learning-disabled students, an honors program, cooperative (work-study) education, advanced placement credit, accelerated degree programs, Freshman Honors College, ESL programs, double majors, summer session for credit, part-time degree programs (daytime, evenings, summer), adult/continuing education programs, internships, and arrangement for off-campus study.

Hawaii

Brigham Young University–Hawaii (continued)

Student Body Statistics The student body is made up of 2,473 undergraduates (221 freshmen). 57 percent are women and 43 percent are men. Students come from 47 states and territories and 67 other countries. 33 percent are from Hawaii. 47.9 percent are international students.

Expenses for 2006–07 *Application fee:* $30. *Comprehensive fee:* $8210 includes full-time tuition ($3040) and college room and board ($5170). Full-time tuition varies according to course load. Room and board charges vary according to board plan and housing facility. *Part-time tuition:* $190 per credit.

Financial Aid Forms of aid include need-based and non-need-based scholarships, athletic grants, and part-time jobs. The average aided 2006–07 undergraduate received an aid package worth an estimated $11,000. The application deadline for financial aid is March 31 with a priority deadline of March 1.

Freshman Admission Brigham Young University–Hawaii requires an essay, a high school transcript, a minimum 3.0 high school GPA, resume of activities, ecclesiastical endorsement, SAT or ACT scores, and TOEFL scores for international students. ACT scores are recommended. Recommendations are required for some. The application deadline for regular admission is February 15.

Transfer Admission The application deadline for admission is March 15.

Entrance Difficulty Brigham Young University–Hawaii assesses its entrance difficulty level as moderately difficult. For the fall 2006 freshman class, 19 percent of the applicants were accepted.

For Further Information Contact Mr. Arapata P. Meha, Brigham Young University–Hawaii, 55-220 Kulanui Street, BYUH 1973, Laie, Oahu, HI 96762. *Telephone:* 808-293-3731. *Fax:* 808-293-3741. *E-mail:* admissions@byuh.edu. *Web site:* http://www.byuh.edu/.

CHAMINADE UNIVERSITY OF HONOLULU

Honolulu, Hawaii

Chaminade University of Honolulu is a coed, private, Roman Catholic, comprehensive institution, founded in 1955, offering degrees at the associate, bachelor's, and master's levels and postbachelor's certificates. It has a 62-acre campus in Honolulu.

Expenses for 2006–07 *Application fee:* $50. *Comprehensive fee:* $24,340 includes full-time tuition ($14,820), mandatory fees ($140), and college room and board ($9380). *College room only:* $4980. *Part-time tuition:* $494 per credit.

For Further Information Contact Martin Motooka, Admissions Counselor, Chaminade University of Honolulu, 3140 Waialae Avenue, Honolulu, HI 96816-1578. *Telephone:* 808-735-4735 or 800-735-3733 (toll-free out-of-state). *Fax:* 808-739-4647. *E-mail:* admissions@chaminade.edu. *Web site:* http://www.chaminade.edu/.

EDUCATION AMERICA, HONOLULU CAMPUS

See Remington College–Honolulu Campus.

HAWAII BUSINESS COLLEGE

Honolulu, Hawaii

http://www.hbc.edu/

HAWAI'I PACIFIC UNIVERSITY

Honolulu, Hawaii

SPONSOR See Front Insert for Details!

Hawai'i Pacific University is a coed, private, comprehensive institution, founded in 1965, offering degrees at the associate, bachelor's, and master's levels and post-master's and postbachelor's certificates. It has a 140-acre campus in Honolulu.

Academic Information The faculty has 618 members (43% full-time), 46% with terminal degrees. The undergraduate student-faculty ratio is 16:1. The library holds 162,000 titles, 12,000 serial subscriptions, and 8,700 audiovisual materials. Special programs include academic remediation, services for learning-disabled students, an honors program, cooperative (work-study) education, study abroad, advanced placement credit, accelerated degree programs, Freshman Honors College, ESL programs, double majors, independent study, distance learning, self-designed majors, summer session for credit, part-time degree programs (daytime, evenings, weekends, summer), adult/continuing education programs, internships, and arrangement for off-campus study with Carroll College, Creighton University, Samuel Merritt College, Southern California University of Health Sciences. The most frequently chosen baccalaureate fields are business/marketing, computer and information sciences, health professions and related sciences.

Student Body Statistics The student body totals 8,080, of whom 6,856 are undergraduates (661 freshmen). 61 percent are women and 39 percent are men. Students come from 53 states and territories and 103 other countries. 48 percent are from Hawaii. 9.6 percent are international students. 56 percent of the 2006 graduating class went on to graduate and professional schools.

Expenses for 2007–08 *Application fee:* $50. *Comprehensive fee:* $23,640 includes full-time tuition ($13,000), mandatory fees ($80), and college room and board ($10,560). *Part-time tuition:* $254 per credit.

Financial Aid Forms of aid include need-based and non-need-based scholarships, athletic grants, and part-time jobs. The average aided 2006–07 undergraduate received an aid package worth an estimated $12,326. The priority application deadline for financial aid is March 1.

Freshman Admission Hawai'i Pacific University requires a high school transcript, a minimum 2.5 high school GPA, and SAT or ACT scores. An essay, 2 recommendations, and TOEFL scores for international students are recommended. An interview is required for some. The application deadline for regular admission is rolling.

Transfer Admission The application deadline for admission is rolling.

Entrance Difficulty Hawai'i Pacific University assesses its entrance difficulty level as moderately difficult. For the fall 2006 freshman class, 80 percent of the applicants were accepted.

SPECIAL MESSAGE TO STUDENTS

Social Life Student life at Hawai'i Pacific University (HPU) is designed to meet students' needs at both the commuter campus in downtown Honolulu and windward Hawai'i Loa campus. Student government and a variety of clubs and organizations—representing student interest in professional, service, cultural, and sports activities—offer opportunities for leadership development. Students participate in an array of intramural sports, including basketball, soccer, tennis, and volleyball. With its culturally diverse student body and faculty, HPU is rich in exciting and stimulating experiences, both in and out of the classroom.

Academic Highlights Career Services is central to the philosophy at HPU. The Cooperative Education and Internship Program offers students the option of paid work experience and up to 12 semester hours of credit for that work. International programs are offered in the context of Hawai'i's multicultural society and also provide opportunities to study abroad. The marine science program involves extensive fieldwork aboard the University's 42-foot research vessel *Kaholo*. Four summer sessions are available during which a student may earn credit equivalent to a regular academic semester.

Interviews and Campus Visits HPU believes a visit to the campus by prospective students and their parents to be of great value. The

University encourages students to make arrangements for a full campus tour. Admissions coordinators are available to review academic and cocurricular programs and to answer any questions. A visit can be arranged by phone, e-mail, or fax or via regular mail to suit the convenience of students and parents. Visitors to HPU should visit both the downtown campus and the windward Hawai'i Loa campus. The two are located 8 miles apart and are connected by a free intercampus shuttle. At the downtown campus, visitors should see Meader Library, the Learning Assistance Center, the Frear Center, and the Career Services Center. On the windward campus, visitors should see the Atherton Learning Center and the residence halls. For information about appointments and campus visits, prospective students should call the Office of Admissions at 808-544-0238 or 866–CALL–HPU (toll-free), Monday through Friday, 8 a.m. to 5 p.m. The fax number is 808-544-1136. The office is located at 1164 Bishop Street, Suite 200, on campus. The nearest commercial airport is Honolulu International.

For Further Information Write to the Office of Admissions, Hawai'i Pacific University, 1164 Bishop Street, Suite 200, Honolulu, HI 96813. *E-mail:* admissions@hpu.edu/jump. *Web site:* http://www.hpu.edu/jump.

See page 172 for the College Close-Up.

HAWAI'I THEOLOGICAL SEMINARY

Honolulu, Hawaii

http://www.icgshawaii.org/

HAWAII TOKAI INTERNATIONAL COLLEGE

Honolulu, Hawaii

Hawaii Tokai International College is a coed, private, two-year college of Tokai University Educational System (Japan), founded in 1992, offering degrees at the associate level.

Expenses for 2006–07 *Application fee:* $50. *Tuition:* $375 per credit part-time.
For Further Information Contact Mr. Derrick Kerr, Director, Student Services, Hawaii Tokai International College, 2241 Kapiolani Boulevard, Honolulu, HI 96826. *Telephone:* 808-983-4154. *Fax:* 808-983-4107. *E-mail:* htic@tokai.edu. *Web site:* http://www.tokai.edu/.

HEALD COLLEGE–HONOLULU

Honolulu, Hawaii

Heald College-Honolulu is a coed, private, two-year college, founded in 1863, offering degrees at the associate level.

Expenses for 2006–07 *Application fee:* $40. *Tuition:* $10,275 full-time.
For Further Information Contact Wendy Nishimura, Director of Admissions, Heald College-Honolulu, 1500 Kapiolani Boulevard, Suite 201, Honolulu, HI 96814. *Telephone:* 808-955-1500 or 800-755-3550 (toll-free in-state). *Fax:* 808-955-6964. *E-mail:* wnishimu@heald.edu. *Web site:* http://www.heald.edu/.

INTERNATIONAL COLLEGE AND GRADUATE SCHOOL

See Hawai'i Theological Seminary.

REMINGTON COLLEGE–HONOLULU CAMPUS

Honolulu, Hawaii

http://www.remingtoncollege.edu/

TRANSPACIFIC HAWAII COLLEGE

Honolulu, Hawaii

TransPacific Hawaii College is a coed, primarily women's, private, two-year college, founded in 1977, offering degrees at the associate level (majority of students are from outside of U.S. and participate in intensive ESL program in preparation for transfer to a 4-year institution).

Expenses for 2006–07 *Application fee:* $50. *Tuition:* $16,250 full-time.
For Further Information Contact Dr. John Norris, President, TransPacific Hawaii College, 5257 Kalanianaole Highway, Honolulu, HI 96821. *Telephone:* 808-377-5402 Ext. 313. *Fax:* 808-373-4754. *E-mail:* jnorris@transpacific.org. *Web site:* http://www.transpacific.org/.

UNIVERSITY OF HAWAII AT HILO

Hilo, Hawaii

University of Hawaii at Hilo is a coed, public, comprehensive unit of University of Hawaii System, founded in 1970, offering degrees at the bachelor's and master's levels and postbachelor's certificates. It has a 115-acre campus in Hilo.

Academic Information The faculty has 377 members (63% full-time), 47% with terminal degrees. The undergraduate student-faculty ratio is 11:1. The library holds 250,000 titles and 2,500 serial subscriptions. Special programs include services for learning-disabled students, an honors program, study abroad, advanced placement credit, ESL programs, double majors, independent study, distance learning, self-designed majors, summer session for credit, part-time degree programs (daytime, evenings, summer), internships, and arrangement for off-campus study with members of the National Student Exchange.
Student Body Statistics The student body totals 3,507, of whom 3,276 are undergraduates (470 freshmen). 60 percent are women and 40 percent are men. Students come from 50 states and territories and 38 other countries. 59 percent are from Hawaii. 9.3 percent are international students.
Expenses for 2006–07 *Application fee:* $50. *State resident tuition:* $3000 full-time, $125 per credit hour part-time. *Nonresident tuition:* $9552 full-time, $398 per credit hour part-time. *Mandatory fees:* $148 full-time, $40.50 per term part-time. Full-time tuition and fees vary according to reciprocity agreements. Part-time tuition and fees vary according to course load. *College room and board:* $6292. *College room only:* $3190. Room and board charges vary according to board plan and housing facility.
Financial Aid Forms of aid include need-based and non-need-based scholarships, athletic grants, and part-time jobs. The average aided 2006–07 undergraduate received an aid package worth an estimated $6555. The priority application deadline for financial aid is March 1.
Freshman Admission University of Hawaii at Hilo requires a high school transcript and SAT or ACT scores. A minimum 3.0 high school GPA and TOEFL scores for international students are recommended. Recommendations are required for some. The application deadline for regular admission is July 1.
Transfer Admission The application deadline for admission is July 1.
Entrance Difficulty University of Hawaii at Hilo assesses its entrance difficulty level as moderately difficult. For the fall 2006 freshman class, 51 percent of the applicants were accepted.
For Further Information Contact Mr. James Cromwell, Student Services Specialist/Director of Admissions, University of Hawaii at Hilo, 200 West Kawili Street, Hilo, HI 96720-4091. *Telephone:* 808-974-7414, 808-974-7414 (toll-free in-state), or 800-897-4456 (toll-free out-of-state). *Fax:* 808-933-0861. *E-mail:* uhhao@hawaii.edu. *Web site:* http://www.uhh.hawaii.edu/.

UNIVERSITY OF HAWAII AT MANOA
Honolulu, Hawaii

University of Hawaii at Manoa is a coed, public university, founded in 1907, offering degrees at the bachelor's, master's, doctoral, and first professional levels and postbachelor's certificates. It has a 300-acre campus in Honolulu.

Academic Information The faculty has 1,272 members (93% full-time), 87% with terminal degrees. The undergraduate student-faculty ratio is 11:1. The library holds 3 million titles, 28,705 serial subscriptions, and 63,942 audiovisual materials. Special programs include services for learning-disabled students, an honors program, cooperative (work-study) education, study abroad, advanced placement credit, accelerated degree programs, ESL programs, double majors, independent study, distance learning, self-designed majors, summer session for credit, part-time degree programs (daytime, evenings, summer), internships, and arrangement for off-campus study with members of the National Student Exchange. The most frequently chosen baccalaureate fields are business/marketing, education, social sciences.

Student Body Statistics The student body totals 20,357, of whom 14,037 are undergraduates (1,775 freshmen). 55 percent are women and 45 percent are men. 74 percent are from Hawaii. 5.5 percent are international students.

Expenses for 2007–08 *Application fee:* $50. *State resident tuition:* $5136 full-time, $214 per credit hour part-time. *Nonresident tuition:* $14,400 full-time, $600 per credit hour part-time. *Mandatory fees:* $254 full-time. *College room and board:* $7185. *College room only:* $4527.

Financial Aid Forms of aid include need-based and non-need-based scholarships, athletic grants, and part-time jobs. The average aided 2006–07 undergraduate received an aid package worth an estimated $7573. The priority application deadline for financial aid is March 1.

Freshman Admission University of Hawaii at Manoa requires a high school transcript, a minimum 2.8 high school GPA, minimum SAT score of 510 for verbal, math and writing sections, SAT or ACT scores, and TOEFL scores for international students. The application deadline for regular admission is May 1.

Transfer Admission The application deadline for admission is May 1.

Entrance Difficulty University of Hawaii at Manoa assesses its entrance difficulty level as moderately difficult. For the fall 2006 freshman class, 68 percent of the applicants were accepted.

For Further Information Contact Ms. Janice Heu, Interim Director of Admissions and Records, University of Hawaii at Manoa, 2600 Campus Road, Room 001, Honolulu, HI 96822. *Telephone:* 808-956-8975 or 800-823-9771 (toll-free). *Fax:* 808-956-4148. *E-mail:* ar-info@hawaii.edu. *Web site:* http://www.uhm.hawaii.edu/.

UNIVERSITY OF HAWAII–WEST OAHU
Pearl City, Hawaii

University of Hawaii–West Oahu is a coed, public, upper-level unit of University of Hawaii System, founded in 1976, offering degrees at the bachelor's level. It is located in Pearl City near Honolulu.

Academic Information The faculty has 53 members (53% full-time), 81% with terminal degrees. The student-faculty ratio is 13:1. The library holds 25,000 titles and 132 serial subscriptions. Special programs include services for learning-disabled students, study abroad, advanced placement credit, double majors, distance learning, summer session for credit, part-time degree programs (daytime, evenings, weekends, summer), and arrangement for off-campus study with Windwood Community College; University of Hawaii Centers at Maui, Kauai and West Hawaii. The most frequently chosen baccalaureate fields are business/marketing, psychology, social sciences.

Student Body Statistics The student body is made up of 866 undergraduates. 69 percent are women and 31 percent are men. 92 percent are from Hawaii. 0.2 percent are international students.

Expenses for 2007–08 *Application fee:* $50. *State resident tuition:* $3216 full-time, $134 per credit part-time. *Nonresident tuition:* $10,176 full-time, $424 per credit part-time. *Mandatory fees:* $10 full-time, $5 per term part-time.

Financial Aid Forms of aid include need-based and non-need-based scholarships and part-time jobs. The priority application deadline for financial aid is April 1.

Transfer Admission University of Hawaii–West Oahu requires a minimum 2.0 college GPA and a college transcript. The application deadline for admission is August 1.

Entrance Difficulty University of Hawaii–West Oahu assesses its entrance difficulty level as moderately difficult. For the fall 2006 entering class, 87 percent of the applicants were accepted.

For Further Information Contact Terri Ota, Registrar, University of Hawaii–West Oahu, 96-129 Ala Ike Street, Pearl City, HI 96782. *Telephone:* 808-454-4700 or 808-454 Ext. 4700 (toll-free in-state). *Fax:* 808-453-6075. *E-mail:* tota@hawaii.edu. *Web site:* http://www.uhwo.hawaii.edu/.

UNIVERSITY OF PHOENIX–HAWAII CAMPUS
Honolulu, Hawaii

University of Phoenix–Hawaii Campus is a coed, proprietary, comprehensive institution, offering degrees at the bachelor's and master's levels (courses conducted at 121 campuses and learning centers in 25 states).

Academic Information The faculty has 430 members (3% full-time), 31% with terminal degrees. The undergraduate student-faculty ratio is 6:1. The library holds 1,759 titles and 692 serial subscriptions. Special programs include services for learning-disabled students, advanced placement credit, accelerated degree programs, independent study, distance learning, external degree programs, and adult/continuing education programs. The most frequently chosen baccalaureate fields are business/marketing, computer and information sciences, public administration and social services.

Student Body Statistics The student body totals 1,730, of whom 796 are undergraduates (14 freshmen). 68 percent are women and 32 percent are men. 31.4 percent are international students.

Expenses for 2006–07 *Application fee:* $45. *Tuition:* $11,700 full-time.

Financial Aid Forms of aid include need-based and non-need-based scholarships. The average aided 2005–06 undergraduate received an aid package worth $4557. The application deadline for financial aid is continuous.

Freshman Admission University of Phoenix–Hawaii Campus requires 1 recommendation and TOEFL scores for international students. A high school transcript is required for some. The application deadline for regular admission is rolling.

Transfer Admission The application deadline for admission is rolling.

Entrance Difficulty University of Phoenix–Hawaii Campus has an open admission policy.

For Further Information Contact Ms. Beth Barilla, Associate Vice President, Student Admissions and Services, University of Phoenix–Hawaii Campus, 4615 East Elwood Street, Mail Stop AA-K101, Phoenix, AZ 85040-1958. *Telephone:* 480-317-6000, 800-776-4867 (toll-free in-state), or 800-228-7240 (toll-free out-of-state). *Fax:* 480-894-1758. *E-mail:* beth.barilla@phoenix.edu. *Web site:* http://www.phoenix.edu/.

Idaho

ALBERTSON COLLEGE OF IDAHO
Caldwell, Idaho

Albertson College of Idaho is a coed, private, comprehensive institution, founded in 1891, offering degrees at the bachelor's and master's levels. It has a 50-acre campus in Caldwell.

Academic Information The faculty has 93 members (81% full-time), 54% with terminal degrees. The undergraduate student-faculty ratio is 9:1.

The library holds 183,308 titles and 703 serial subscriptions. Special programs include services for learning-disabled students, an honors program, cooperative (work-study) education, study abroad, advanced placement credit, double majors, independent study, self-designed majors, part-time degree programs (daytime), internships, and arrangement for off-campus study with Northwest Nazarene University. The most frequently chosen baccalaureate fields are business/marketing, history, social sciences.

Student Body Statistics The student body totals 822, of whom 793 are undergraduates (211 freshmen). 59 percent are women and 41 percent are men. Students come from 28 states and territories and 9 other countries. 72 percent are from Idaho. 1.4 percent are international students. 22 percent of the 2006 graduating class went on to graduate and professional schools.

Expenses for 2007–08 *Application fee:* $50. *Comprehensive fee:* $24,005 includes full-time tuition ($17,000), mandatory fees ($680), and college room and board ($6325). *College room only:* $2850.

Financial Aid Forms of aid include need-based scholarships and athletic grants. The average aided 2006–07 undergraduate received an aid package worth an estimated $14,850.

Freshman Admission Albertson College of Idaho requires an essay, a high school transcript, 1 recommendation, SAT or ACT scores, and TOEFL scores for international students. An interview is recommended. The application deadline for regular admission is June 1 and for early action it is December 15.

Transfer Admission The application deadline for admission is rolling.

Entrance Difficulty Albertson College of Idaho assesses its entrance difficulty level as moderately difficult. For the fall 2006 freshman class, 74 percent of the applicants were accepted.

For Further Information Contact Ms. Charlene Brown, Assistant Director of Admissions, Albertson College of Idaho, 2112 Cleveland Boulevard, Caldwell, ID 83605-4494. *Telephone:* 208-459-5689 or 800-244-3246 (toll-free). *Fax:* 208-459-5151. *E-mail:* admission@albertson.edu. *Web site:* http://www.albertson.edu/.

See page 156 for the College Close-Up.

BOISE BIBLE COLLEGE

Boise, Idaho

Boise Bible College is a coed, private, nondenominational, four-year college, founded in 1945, offering degrees at the associate and bachelor's levels. It has a 17-acre campus in Boise.

Academic Information The faculty has 16 members (50% full-time), 19% with terminal degrees. The student-faculty ratio is 16:1. The library holds 29,431 titles and 115 serial subscriptions. Special programs include academic remediation, advanced placement credit, double majors, independent study, distance learning, part-time degree programs (daytime, evenings), adult/continuing education programs, and internships.

Student Body Statistics The student body is made up of 184 undergraduates (59 freshmen). 51 percent are women and 49 percent are men. Students come from 9 states and territories and 3 other countries. 45 percent are from Idaho. 2.3 percent are international students.

Expenses for 2006–07 *Application fee:* $25. *Comprehensive fee:* $11,730 includes full-time tuition ($6840), mandatory fees ($90), and college room and board ($4800). Room and board charges vary according to student level. *Part-time tuition:* $288 per credit. *Part-time mandatory fees:* $3 per credit, $10 per semester hour.

Financial Aid Forms of aid include need-based and non-need-based scholarships and part-time jobs. The priority application deadline for financial aid is February 15.

Freshman Admission Boise Bible College requires an essay, a high school transcript, a minimum 2.0 high school GPA, 3 recommendations, SAT or ACT scores, and TOEFL scores for international students. An interview is recommended. The application deadline for regular admission is August 1.

Transfer Admission The application deadline for admission is August 1.

Entrance Difficulty Boise Bible College assesses its entrance difficulty level as minimally difficult. For the fall 2006 freshman class, 99 percent of the applicants were accepted.

For Further Information Contact Mr. Martin Flaherty, Director of Admissions, Boise Bible College, 8695 Marigold Street, Boise, ID 83704. *Telephone:* 208-376-7731 or 800-893-7755 (toll-free). *Fax:* 208-376-7743. *E-mail:* martinf@boisebible.edu. *Web site:* http://www.boisebible.edu/.

BOISE STATE UNIVERSITY

Boise, Idaho

Boise State University is a coed, public, comprehensive unit of Idaho System of Higher Education, founded in 1932, offering degrees at the associate, bachelor's, master's, and doctoral levels. It has a 175-acre campus in Boise.

Academic Information The faculty has 1,073 members (58% full-time), 60% with terminal degrees. The undergraduate student-faculty ratio is 18:1. The library holds 838,932 titles, 5,575 serial subscriptions, and 58,047 audiovisual materials. Special programs include academic remediation, services for learning-disabled students, an honors program, cooperative (work-study) education, study abroad, advanced placement credit, Freshman Honors College, ESL programs, double majors, independent study, distance learning, self-designed majors, summer session for credit, part-time degree programs (daytime, evenings, weekends, summer), adult/continuing education programs, internships, and arrangement for off-campus study with National Student Exchange. The most frequently chosen baccalaureate fields are business/marketing, education, health professions and related sciences.

Student Body Statistics The student body totals 188,265, of whom 17,040 are undergraduates (2,560 freshmen). 54 percent are women and 46 percent are men. Students come from 35 states and territories and 47 other countries. 89 percent are from Idaho. 1.2 percent are international students. 25 percent of the 2006 graduating class went on to graduate and professional schools.

Expenses for 2006–07 *Application fee:* $40. *State resident tuition:* $2670 full-time, $143 per credit part-time. *Nonresident tuition:* $7778 full-time, $143 per credit part-time. *Mandatory fees:* $1484 full-time, $68 per credit part-time. Full-time tuition and fees vary according to reciprocity agreements. Part-time tuition and fees vary according to course load. *College room and board:* $5778. Room and board charges vary according to board plan and housing facility.

Financial Aid Forms of aid include need-based and non-need-based scholarships, athletic grants, and part-time jobs. The average aided 2006–07 undergraduate received an aid package worth an estimated $8003. The application deadline for financial aid is June 1 with a priority deadline of February 15.

Freshman Admission Boise State University requires TOEFL scores for international students. A high school transcript is recommended. A high school transcript, a minimum 2.0 high school GPA, and SAT or ACT scores are required for some. The application deadline for regular admission is July 12.

Transfer Admission The application deadline for admission is July 12.

Entrance Difficulty Boise State University assesses its entrance difficulty level as minimally difficult; moderately difficult for transfers; moderately difficult for nursing program. For the fall 2006 freshman class, 90 percent of the applicants were accepted.

For Further Information Contact Ms. Barbara Fortin, Dean of Admissions, Boise State University, Enrollment Services, 1910 University Drive, Boise, ID 83725. *Telephone:* 208-426-1177, 800-632-6586 (toll-free in-state), or 800-824-7017 (toll-free out-of-state). *E-mail:* bsuinfo@boisestate.edu. *Web site:* http://www.boisestate.edu/.

BRIGHAM YOUNG UNIVERSITY–IDAHO

Rexburg, Idaho

Brigham Young University–Idaho is a coed, private, two-year college, founded in 1888, affiliated with The Church of Jesus Christ of Latter-day Saints, offering degrees at the associate level. It has a 255-acre campus in Rexburg.

Brigham Young University–Idaho (continued)

Academic Information The faculty has 420 members. The student-faculty ratio is 25:1. The library holds 134,423 titles, 889 serial subscriptions, and 34,556 audiovisual materials. Special programs include academic remediation, services for learning-disabled students, an honors program, advanced placement credit, accelerated degree programs, summer session for credit, part-time degree programs (daytime, evenings, summer), adult/continuing education programs, and internships.

Student Body Statistics The student body is made up of 11,443 undergraduates. Students come from 50 states and territories. 36 percent are from Idaho. 90 percent of the 2006 graduating class went on to four-year colleges.

Expenses for 2006–07 *Application fee:* $30. *Comprehensive fee:* $7440 includes full-time tuition ($2890) and college room and board ($4550). Full-time tuition varies according to program. Room and board charges vary according to board plan, housing facility, and location. *Part-time tuition:* $1440 per term. Part-time tuition varies according to course load. Non-Latter Day Saints' full year tuition is $5,780.

Financial Aid Forms of aid include need-based scholarships and part-time jobs. The application deadline for financial aid is continuous.

Freshman Admission Brigham Young University–Idaho requires an essay, a high school transcript, an interview, SAT or ACT scores, and TOEFL scores for international students. The application deadline for regular admission is February 15.

Transfer Admission The application deadline for admission is March 15.

Entrance Difficulty Brigham Young University–Idaho assesses its entrance difficulty level as moderately difficult; very difficult for nursing program. For the fall 2006 freshman class, 95 percent of the applicants were accepted.

For Further Information Contact Mr. Steven Davis, Assistant Director of Admissions, Brigham Young University–Idaho, 120 Kimball, Rexburg, ID 83460-1615. *Telephone:* 208-356-1026. *Fax:* 208-356-1220. *E-mail:* daviss@byui.edu. *Web site:* http://www.byui.edu/.

IDAHO STATE UNIVERSITY
Pocatello, Idaho

Idaho State University is a coed, public university, founded in 1901, offering degrees at the bachelor's, master's, doctoral, and first professional levels and post-master's, first professional, and postbachelor's certificates. It has a 972-acre campus in Pocatello.

Academic Information The faculty has 908 members (72% full-time), 43% with terminal degrees. The undergraduate student-faculty ratio is 15:1. The library holds 1 million titles, 444 serial subscriptions, and 2,204 audiovisual materials. Special programs include academic remediation, services for learning-disabled students, an honors program, study abroad, advanced placement credit, ESL programs, double majors, independent study, distance learning, self-designed majors, summer session for credit, part-time degree programs (daytime, evenings, summer), external degree programs, adult/continuing education programs, internships, and arrangement for off-campus study with University of Idaho, National Student Exchange.

Student Body Statistics The student body totals 12,679, of whom 10,640 are undergraduates (1,331 freshmen). 56 percent are women and 44 percent are men. Students come from 46 states and territories and 65 other countries. 95 percent are from Idaho. 1.9 percent are international students.

Expenses for 2007–08 *Application fee:* $40. *State resident tuition:* $2689 full-time, $214 per credit hour part-time. *Nonresident tuition:* $10,959 full-time, $329 per credit hour part-time. *Mandatory fees:* $1501 full-time. *College room and board:* $4950. *College room only:* $2250.

Financial Aid Forms of aid include need-based and non-need-based scholarships, athletic grants, and part-time jobs. The average aided 2005–06 undergraduate received an aid package worth $5731. The application deadline for financial aid is continuous.

Freshman Admission Idaho State University requires a high school transcript, a minimum 2.0 high school GPA, SAT or ACT scores, and TOEFL scores for international students. ACT scores are recommended. The application deadline for regular admission is August 1.

Transfer Admission The application deadline for admission is August 1.

Entrance Difficulty Idaho State University has an open admission policy. It assesses its entrance difficulty as noncompetitive for applicants over 21 with GED.

For Further Information Contact Ms. Alison Crane, Interim Director of Recruitment, Idaho State University, PO Box 8270, 741 South 7th, Pocatello, ID 83209. *Telephone:* 208-373-1706. *Fax:* 208-282-4511. *E-mail:* info@isu.edu or cranali@isu.edu. *Web site:* http://www.isu.edu/.

ITT TECHNICAL INSTITUTE
Boise, Idaho

ITT Technical Institute is a coed, proprietary, primarily two-year college of ITT Educational Services, Inc, founded in 1906, offering degrees at the associate and bachelor's levels. It has a 1-acre campus in Boise.

Expenses for 2006–07 *Application fee:* $100. Contact school for program costs.

Financial Aid Forms of aid include need-based scholarships and part-time jobs. The application deadline for financial aid is continuous.

Freshman Admission ITT Technical Institute requires a high school transcript, an interview, TOEFL scores for international students, and Wonderlic aptitude test. Recommendations are recommended. The application deadline for regular admission is rolling.

Transfer Admission The application deadline for admission is rolling.

Entrance Difficulty ITT Technical Institute assesses its entrance difficulty level as minimally difficult.

For Further Information Contact Ms. Jennifer Kandler, Director of Recruitment, ITT Technical Institute, 12302 West Explorer Drive, Boise, IA 83713. *Telephone:* 208-322-8844 or 800-666-4888 (toll-free in-state). *Fax:* 208-322-0173. *Web site:* http://www.itt-tech.edu/.

LEWIS-CLARK STATE COLLEGE
Lewiston, Idaho

Lewis-Clark State College is a coed, public, four-year college, founded in 1893, offering degrees at the associate and bachelor's levels. It has a 44-acre campus in Lewiston.

Academic Information The faculty has 155 full-time members. The student-faculty ratio is 15:1. The library holds 139,499 titles and 1,612 serial subscriptions. Special programs include academic remediation, services for learning-disabled students, an honors program, cooperative (work-study) education, study abroad, advanced placement credit, accelerated degree programs, ESL programs, double majors, independent study, distance learning, self-designed majors, summer session for credit, part-time degree programs (daytime, evenings, weekends, summer), external degree programs, adult/continuing education programs, internships, and arrangement for off-campus study. The most frequently chosen baccalaureate fields are business/marketing, education, health professions and related sciences.

Student Body Statistics The student body is made up of 3,394 undergraduates (482 freshmen). 62 percent are women and 38 percent are men. Students come from 37 states and territories and 31 other countries. 85 percent are from Idaho. 3.9 percent are international students.

Expenses for 2006–07 *Application fee:* $35. *State resident tuition:* $3897 full-time, $194 per credit part-time. *Nonresident tuition:* $10,841 full-time, $194 per credit part-time. Full-time tuition varies according to course load and reciprocity agreements. *College room and board:* $4670. *College room only:* $2200. Room and board charges vary according to board plan and housing facility.

Financial Aid Forms of aid include need-based and non-need-based scholarships, athletic grants, and part-time jobs. The average aided 2005–06 undergraduate received an aid package worth $5445. The priority application deadline for financial aid is March 1.

Freshman Admission Lewis-Clark State College requires a high school transcript, a minimum 2.0 high school GPA, and TOEFL scores for international students. An interview, SAT or ACT scores, and ACT COMPASS are required for some. The application deadline for regular admission is rolling.

Transfer Admission Lewis-Clark State College requires a college transcript and a minimum 2.0 college GPA. Standardized test scores are required for some. The application deadline for admission is rolling.
Entrance Difficulty Lewis-Clark State College assesses its entrance difficulty level as minimally difficult; moderately difficult for nursing program, international students. For the fall 2006 freshman class, 62 percent of the applicants were accepted.
For Further Information Contact Soo Lee Bruce-Smith, Coordinator of New Student Recruitment, Lewis-Clark State College, 500 8th Avenue, Lewiston, ID 83501. *Telephone:* 208-792-2210 or 800-933-LCSC Ext. 2210 (toll-free). *Fax:* 208-792-2876. *E-mail:* admissions@lcsc.edu. *Web site:* http://www.lcsc.edu/.

NEW SAINT ANDREWS COLLEGE
Moscow, Idaho

New Saint Andrews College is a coed, proprietary, four-year college, founded in 1993.

Academic Information The faculty has 15 members (53% full-time), 27% with terminal degrees. The student-faculty ratio is 10:1. The library holds 58,500 titles, 40 serial subscriptions, and 400 audiovisual materials. Special programs include advanced placement credit, independent study, summer session for credit, and part-time degree programs.
Student Body Statistics The student body is made up of 157 undergraduates (60 freshmen). 54 percent are women and 46 percent are men. Students come from 33 states and territories and 5 other countries. 10 percent are from Idaho. 7 percent are international students. 36 percent of the 2006 graduating class went on to graduate and professional schools.
Expenses for 2007–08 *Application fee:* $25. *Tuition:* $7800 full-time, $725 per course part-time.
Freshman Admission New Saint Andrews College requires an essay, a high school transcript, recommendations, and SAT or ACT scores. An interview is required for some. The application deadline for regular admission is February 15 and for early action it is December 1.
Transfer Admission The application deadline for admission is February 15.
Entrance Difficulty New Saint Andrews College assesses its entrance difficulty level as moderately difficult; very difficult for transfers. For the fall 2006 freshman class, 75 percent of the applicants were accepted.
For Further Information Contact Aaron Rench, Director of Admissions, New Saint Andrews College, PO Box 9025, Moscow, ID 83843. *Telephone:* 208-882-1566. *Fax:* 208-882-4293. *E-mail:* info@nsa.edu. *Web site:* http://www.nsa.edu/.

NORTHWEST NAZARENE UNIVERSITY
Nampa, Idaho

Northwest Nazarene University is a coed, private, comprehensive institution, founded in 1913, affiliated with the Church of the Nazarene, offering degrees at the bachelor's and master's levels. It has an 85-acre campus in Nampa.

Academic Information The faculty has 93 members (96% full-time), 72% with terminal degrees. The undergraduate student-faculty ratio is 13:1. The library holds 100,966 titles and 821 serial subscriptions. Special programs include academic remediation, services for learning-disabled students, an honors program, cooperative (work-study) education, study abroad, advanced placement credit, accelerated degree programs, Freshman Honors College, independent study, self-designed majors, summer session for credit, part-time degree programs (daytime, evenings, summer), adult/continuing education programs, internships, and arrangement for off-campus study with CCCU Exchange programs. The most frequently chosen baccalaureate fields are business/marketing, education, theology and religious vocations.
Student Body Statistics The student body totals 1,749, of whom 1,225 are undergraduates (292 freshmen). 60 percent are women and 40 percent are men. Students come from 32 states and territories and 7 other countries. 40 percent are from Idaho. 0.8 percent are international students.

Expenses for 2007–08 *Application fee:* $25. *Comprehensive fee:* $25,270 includes full-time tuition ($19,700), mandatory fees ($270), and college room and board ($5300). *Part-time tuition:* $853 per credit.
Financial Aid Forms of aid include need-based and non-need-based scholarships, athletic grants, and part-time jobs. The average aided 2006–07 undergraduate received an aid package worth an estimated $13,180. The priority application deadline for financial aid is March 1.
Freshman Admission Northwest Nazarene University requires an essay, a high school transcript, a minimum 2.5 high school GPA, 2 recommendations, minimum ACT score of 18, SAT or ACT scores, and TOEFL scores for international students. An interview is required for some. The application deadline for regular admission is August 15 and for early action it is December 15.
Entrance Difficulty Northwest Nazarene University assesses its entrance difficulty level as moderately difficult. For the fall 2006 freshman class, 54 percent of the applicants were accepted.
For Further Information Contact Stacey Berggren, Director of Admissions, Northwest Nazarene University, 623 Holly Street, Admissions Welcome Center, Nampa, ID 83686. *Telephone:* 208-467-8000 or 877-668-4968 (toll-free). *Fax:* 208-467-8645. *E-mail:* admissions@nnu.edu. *Web site:* http://www.nnu.edu/.

STEVENS-HENAGER COLLEGE
Boise, Idaho
http://www.stevenshenager.edu/

UNIVERSITY OF IDAHO
Moscow, Idaho

University of Idaho is a coed, public university, founded in 1889, offering degrees at the bachelor's, master's, doctoral, and first professional levels and post-master's certificates. It has a 1,450-acre campus in Moscow.

Academic Information The faculty has 590 members (93% full-time), 82% with terminal degrees. The undergraduate student-faculty ratio is 20:1. The library holds 1 million titles, 14,230 serial subscriptions, and 8,717 audiovisual materials. Special programs include academic remediation, services for learning-disabled students, an honors program, cooperative (work-study) education, study abroad, advanced placement credit, accelerated degree programs, double majors, independent study, distance learning, self-designed majors, summer session for credit, part-time degree programs (daytime, evenings, summer), adult/continuing education programs, internships, and arrangement for off-campus study with National Student Exchange. The most frequently chosen baccalaureate fields are business/marketing, education, engineering.
Student Body Statistics The student body totals 11,739, of whom 9,127 are undergraduates (1,621 freshmen). 45 percent are women and 55 percent are men. Students come from 52 states and territories and 73 other countries. 74 percent are from Idaho. 1.8 percent are international students.
Expenses for 2006–07 *Application fee:* $40. *State resident tuition:* $0 full-time. *Nonresident tuition:* $9600 full-time, $140 per credit part-time. *Mandatory fees:* $4200 full-time, $200 per credit part-time. Full-time tuition and fees vary according to degree level and program. Part-time tuition and fees vary according to course load, degree level, and program. *College room and board:* $5696. Room and board charges vary according to board plan and housing facility.
Financial Aid Forms of aid include need-based and non-need-based scholarships, athletic grants, and part-time jobs. The average aided 2005–06 undergraduate received an aid package worth $9471. The priority application deadline for financial aid is February 15.
Freshman Admission University of Idaho requires a high school transcript, a minimum 2.2 high school GPA, SAT or ACT scores, and TOEFL scores for international students. SAT scores are recommended. An essay is required for some. The application deadline for regular admission is August 1.
Transfer Admission The application deadline for admission is rolling.

University of Idaho (continued)

Entrance Difficulty University of Idaho assesses its entrance difficulty level as moderately difficult. For the fall 2006 freshman class, 53 percent of the applicants were accepted.

For Further Information Contact Mr. Dan Davenport, Director of Admissions, University of Idaho, PO Box 444264, Moscow, ID 83844-4264. *Telephone:* 208-885-6326 or 888-884-3246 (toll-free). *Fax:* 208-885-9119. *E-mail:* admappl@uidaho.edu. *Web site:* http://www.uidaho.edu/.

UNIVERSITY OF PHOENIX–IDAHO CAMPUS

Meridian, Idaho

University of Phoenix–Idaho Campus is a coed, proprietary, comprehensive institution, offering degrees at the bachelor's and master's levels.

Academic Information The faculty has 113 members (3% full-time), 19% with terminal degrees. The undergraduate student-faculty ratio is 6:1. The library holds 1,759 titles and 692 serial subscriptions. Special programs include services for learning-disabled students, advanced placement credit, accelerated degree programs, independent study, distance learning, external degree programs, and adult/continuing education programs. The most frequently chosen baccalaureate fields are business/marketing, computer and information sciences, security and protective services.

Student Body Statistics The student body totals 659, of whom 532 are undergraduates (4 freshmen). 53 percent are women and 47 percent are men. 27.8 percent are international students.

Expenses for 2006–07 *Application fee:* $45. *Tuition:* $10,200 full-time, $340 per credit part-time.

Financial Aid Forms of aid include need-based and non-need-based scholarships. The average aided 2005–06 undergraduate received an aid package worth $4067. The application deadline for financial aid is continuous.

Freshman Admission University of Phoenix–Idaho Campus requires 1 recommendation and TOEFL scores for international students. A high school transcript is required for some. The application deadline for regular admission is rolling.

Transfer Admission The application deadline for admission is rolling.

Entrance Difficulty University of Phoenix–Idaho Campus has an open admission policy.

For Further Information Contact Ms. Beth Barilla, Associate Vice President, Student Admissions and Services, University of Phoenix–Idaho Campus, 4615 East Elwood Street, Mail Stop AA-K101, Phoenix, AZ 85040-1958. *Telephone:* 480-317-6000, 800-776-4867 (toll-free in-state), or 800-228-7240 (toll-free out-of-state). *Fax:* 480-894-1758. *E-mail:* beth.barilla@phoenix.edu. *Web site:* http://www.phoenix.edu/.

Montana

BLACKFEET COMMUNITY COLLEGE

Browning, Montana

http://www.bfcc.org/

CARROLL COLLEGE

Helena, Montana

Carroll College is a coed, private, Roman Catholic, four-year college, founded in 1909, offering degrees at the associate and bachelor's levels. It has a 64-acre campus in Helena.

Expenses for 2006–07 *Application fee:* $35. *Comprehensive fee:* $24,760 includes full-time tuition ($18,110), mandatory fees ($300), and college room and board ($6350). Full-time tuition and fees vary according to course load. Room and board charges vary according to board plan and housing facility. *Part-time tuition:* varies with course load.

For Further Information Contact Ms. Cynthia Thornquist, Director of Admissions and Enrollment, Carroll College, 1601 North Benton Avenue, Helena, MT 59625-0002. *Telephone:* 406-447-4384 or 800-992-3648 (toll-free). *Fax:* 406-447-4533. *E-mail:* enroll@carroll.edu. *Web site:* http://www.carroll.edu/.

CHIEF DULL KNIFE COLLEGE

Lame Deer, Montana

Chief Dull Knife College is a coed, private, two-year college, founded in 1975, offering degrees at the associate level. It has a 3-acre campus in Lame Deer.

Academic Information The faculty has 30 members (27% full-time). The library holds 10,000 titles and 128 serial subscriptions. Special programs include academic remediation, services for learning-disabled students, cooperative (work-study) education, summer session for credit, part-time degree programs (daytime, evenings, weekends), adult/continuing education programs, internships, and arrangement for off-campus study with members of the American Indian Higher Education Consortium.

Student Body Statistics The student body is made up of 460 undergraduates. 50 percent of the 2006 graduating class went on to four-year colleges.

Expenses for 2006–07 *Application fee:* $0. *State resident tuition:* $2260 full-time.

Financial Aid Forms of aid include need-based scholarships and part-time jobs. The application deadline for financial aid is continuous.

Freshman Admission Chief Dull Knife College requires a high school transcript. The application deadline for regular admission is rolling.

Transfer Admission The application deadline for admission is rolling.

Entrance Difficulty Chief Dull Knife College has an open admission policy.

For Further Information Contact Mr. William L. Wertman, Registrar and Director of Admissions, Chief Dull Knife College, PO Box 98, 1 College Drive, Lame Deer, MT 59043-0098. *Telephone:* 406-477-6215. *Fax:* 406-477-6219. *Web site:* http://www.cdkc.edu/.

DULL KNIFE MEMORIAL COLLEGE

See Chief Dull Knife College.

LITTLE BIG HORN COLLEGE

Crow Agency, Montana

Little Big Horn College is a coed, private, two-year college, founded in 1980, offering degrees at the associate level. It has a 5-acre campus in Crow Agency.

Academic Information The faculty has 12 members (92% full-time). The student-faculty ratio is 25:1. Special programs include part-time degree programs (daytime) and arrangement for off-campus study with members of the American Indian Higher Education Consortium.

Student Body Statistics The student body is made up of 317 undergraduates. Students come from 1 state or territory.

Expenses for 2006–07 *State resident tuition:* $2780 full-time.

Financial Aid Forms of aid include part-time jobs.

Freshman Admission Little Big Horn College requires a high school transcript. The application deadline for regular admission is rolling.

Transfer Admission The application deadline for admission is rolling.

Entrance Difficulty Little Big Horn College has an open admission policy.

For Further Information Contact Ms. Ann Bullis, Dean of Student Services, Little Big Horn College, Box 370, 1 Forest Lane, Crow Agency, MT 59022-0370. *Telephone:* 406-638-2228 Ext. 50. *Web site:* http://www.lbhc.cc.mt.us/.

MONTANA STATE UNIVERSITY

Bozeman, Montana

Montana State University is a coed, public unit of Montana University System, founded in 1893, offering degrees at the bachelor's, master's, and doctoral levels and post-master's certificates. It has a 1,170-acre campus in Bozeman.

Academic Information The faculty has 805 members (68% full-time), 67% with terminal degrees. The undergraduate student-faculty ratio is 17:1. The library holds 712,241 titles, 8,757 serial subscriptions, and 9,346 audiovisual materials. Special programs include academic remediation, services for learning-disabled students, an honors program, study abroad, advanced placement credit, ESL programs, double majors, independent study, distance learning, self-designed majors, summer session for credit, part-time degree programs (daytime, evenings, summer), adult/continuing education programs, internships, and arrangement for off-campus study with members of the National Student Exchange. The most frequently chosen baccalaureate fields are business/marketing, engineering, visual and performing arts.

Student Body Statistics The student body totals 12,338, of whom 10,832 are undergraduates (2,216 freshmen). 46 percent are women and 54 percent are men. Students come from 50 states and territories and 69 other countries. 70 percent are from Montana. 1.4 percent are international students.

Expenses for 2006–07 *Application fee:* $30. *State resident tuition:* $5673 full-time. *Nonresident tuition:* $15,522 full-time. Full-time tuition varies according to course load. *College room and board:* $6450. Room and board charges vary according to board plan and housing facility.

Financial Aid Forms of aid include need-based and non-need-based scholarships, athletic grants, and part-time jobs. The average aided 2005–06 undergraduate received an aid package worth $7444.

Freshman Admission Montana State University requires a high school transcript, a minimum 2.5 high school GPA, SAT or ACT scores, and TOEFL scores for international students. The application deadline for regular admission is rolling.

Transfer Admission The application deadline for admission is rolling.

Entrance Difficulty Montana State University assesses its entrance difficulty level as moderately difficult. For the fall 2006 freshman class, 66 percent of the applicants were accepted.

For Further Information Contact Ms. Ronda Russell, Director of New Student Services, Montana State University, PO Box 172190, Bozeman, MT 59717-2190. *Telephone:* 406-994-2452 or 888-MSU-CATS (toll-free). *Fax:* 406-994-1923. *E-mail:* admissions@montana.edu. *Web site:* http://www.montana.edu/.

MONTANA STATE UNIVERSITY–BILLINGS

Billings, Montana

Montana State University–Billings is a coed, public, comprehensive unit of Montana University System, founded in 1927, offering degrees at the associate, bachelor's, and master's levels and post-master's and postbachelor's certificates. It has a 92-acre campus in Billings.

Academic Information The faculty has 286 members (60% full-time). The undergraduate student-faculty ratio is 19:1. The library holds 488,004 titles and 3,276 serial subscriptions. Special programs include academic remediation, services for learning-disabled students, an honors program, cooperative (work-study) education, study abroad, advanced placement credit, accelerated degree programs, ESL programs, double majors, independent study, distance learning, summer session for credit, part-time degree programs (daytime, evenings, summer), external degree programs, adult/continuing education programs, internships, and arrangement for off-campus study. The most frequently chosen baccalaureate fields are business/marketing, education, liberal arts/general studies.

Student Body Statistics The student body totals 4,799, of whom 4,312 are undergraduates (759 freshmen). 63 percent are women and 37 percent are men. Students come from 45 states and territories and 18 other countries. 92 percent are from Montana. 0.8 percent are international students. 8 percent of the 2006 graduating class went on to graduate and professional schools.

Expenses for 2006–07 *Application fee:* $30. *State resident tuition:* $3951 full-time, $141 per credit hour part-time. *Nonresident tuition:* $13,305 full-time, $371 per credit hour part-time. *Mandatory fees:* $1104 full-time. Full-time tuition and fees vary according to course load, degree level, and location. Part-time tuition varies according to course load, degree level, and location. *College room and board:* $4310. Room and board charges vary according to board plan and housing facility.

Financial Aid Forms of aid include need-based and non-need-based scholarships, athletic grants, and part-time jobs. The average aided 2005–06 undergraduate received an aid package worth $9363. The priority application deadline for financial aid is March 1.

Freshman Admission Montana State University–Billings requires a high school transcript, a minimum 2.5 high school GPA, SAT or ACT scores, and TOEFL scores for international students. The application deadline for regular admission is July 1.

Transfer Admission The application deadline for admission is rolling.

Entrance Difficulty Montana State University–Billings assesses its entrance difficulty level as moderately difficult. For the fall 2006 freshman class, 100 percent of the applicants were accepted.

For Further Information Contact Ms. Shelly Andersen, Associate Director of Admissions, Montana State University–Billings, 1500 University Drive, Billings, MT 59101. *Telephone:* 406-657-2158 or 800-565-6782 (toll-free). *Fax:* 406-657-2302. *E-mail:* sandersen@msubillings.edu. *Web site:* http://www.msubillings.edu/.

MONTANA STATE UNIVERSITY–NORTHERN

Havre, Montana

http://www.msun.edu/

MONTANA TECH OF THE UNIVERSITY OF MONTANA

Butte, Montana

Montana Tech of The University of Montana is a coed, public, comprehensive unit of Montana University System, founded in 1895, offering degrees at the associate, bachelor's, and master's levels and postbachelor's certificates. It has a 56-acre campus in Butte.

Academic Information The faculty has 149 members (74% full-time), 44% with terminal degrees. The undergraduate student-faculty ratio is 16:1. The library holds 165,734 titles and 20,233 serial subscriptions. Special programs include academic remediation, services for learning-disabled students, cooperative (work-study) education, advanced placement credit, double majors, independent study, distance learning, self-designed majors, summer session for credit, part-time degree programs (daytime, evenings, summer), adult/continuing education programs, and internships. The most frequently chosen baccalaureate fields are engineering, business/marketing, health professions and related sciences.

Student Body Statistics The student body totals 2,951, of whom 2,850 are undergraduates (463 freshmen). 43 percent are women and 57 percent are men. Students come from 33 states and territories and 18 other countries. 88 percent are from Montana. 14 percent of the 2006 graduating class went on to graduate and professional schools.

Expenses for 2006–07 *Application fee:* $30. *State resident tuition:* $5605 full-time, $270 per credit hour part-time. *Nonresident tuition:* $14,766 full-time, $651 per credit hour part-time. *Mandatory fees:* $50 per credit part-time, $58. Full-time tuition varies according to course level, course load, and degree level. Part-time tuition and fees vary according to course

Montana Tech of The University of Montana (continued)

level, course load, and degree level. *College room and board:* $5594. *College room only:* $2410. Room and board charges vary according to board plan.

Financial Aid Forms of aid include need-based and non-need-based scholarships, athletic grants, and part-time jobs. The average aided 2006–07 undergraduate received an aid package worth an estimated $7000. The priority application deadline for financial aid is March 1.

Freshman Admission Montana Tech of The University of Montana requires a high school transcript, a minimum 2.5 high school GPA, proof of immunization, standardized test scores, SAT or ACT scores, and TOEFL scores for international students. The application deadline for regular admission is rolling.

Transfer Admission The application deadline for admission is rolling.

Entrance Difficulty Montana Tech of The University of Montana has an open admission policy for students attending the College of Technology.

For Further Information Contact Mr. Tony Campeau, Director of Admissions, Montana Tech of The University of Montana, 1300 West Park Street, Butte, MT 59701-8997. *Telephone:* 406-496-4178 or 800-445-TECH Ext. 1 (toll-free). *Fax:* 406-496-4170. *E-mail:* admissions@mtech.edu. *Web site:* http://www.mtech.edu/.

ROCKY MOUNTAIN COLLEGE

Billings, Montana

Rocky Mountain College is a coed, private, interdenominational, comprehensive institution, founded in 1878, offering degrees at the associate, bachelor's, and master's levels. It has a 60-acre campus in Billings.

Academic Information The faculty has 112 members (43% full-time), 33% with terminal degrees. The undergraduate student-faculty ratio is 13:1. The library holds 100,078 titles, 378 serial subscriptions, and 1,359 audiovisual materials. Special programs include academic remediation, services for learning-disabled students, an honors program, study abroad, advanced placement credit, accelerated degree programs, ESL programs, double majors, independent study, distance learning, self-designed majors, summer session for credit, part-time degree programs (daytime, evenings, summer), adult/continuing education programs, and internships. The most frequently chosen baccalaureate fields are business/marketing, education, health professions and related sciences.

Student Body Statistics The student body totals 912, of whom 863 are undergraduates (156 freshmen). 55 percent are women and 45 percent are men. Students come from 37 states and territories and 15 other countries. 64 percent are from Montana. 5 percent are international students. 19 percent of the 2006 graduating class went on to graduate and professional schools.

Expenses for 2006–07 *Application fee:* $25. *Comprehensive fee:* $22,250 includes full-time tuition ($16,389), mandatory fees ($253), and college room and board ($5608). *College room only:* $2550. Full-time tuition and fees vary according to course load and program. Room and board charges vary according to board plan and housing facility. *Part-time tuition:* $674 per credit. *Part-time mandatory fees:* $67 per term. Part-time tuition and fees vary according to course load and program.

Financial Aid Forms of aid include need-based and non-need-based scholarships, athletic grants, and part-time jobs. The priority application deadline for financial aid is April 1.

Freshman Admission Rocky Mountain College requires a high school transcript, a minimum 2.5 high school GPA, SAT or ACT scores, and TOEFL scores for international students. An essay, 2 recommendations, and an interview are required for some. The application deadline for regular admission is rolling.

Transfer Admission Rocky Mountain College requires standardized test scores, a college transcript, and a minimum 3.0 college GPA. The application deadline for admission is rolling.

Entrance Difficulty Rocky Mountain College assesses its entrance difficulty level as moderately difficult. For the fall 2006 freshman class, 72 percent of the applicants were accepted.

For Further Information Contact Ms. Laurie Rodriguez, Director of Admissions, Rocky Mountain College, 1511 Poly Drive, Billings, MT 59102. *Telephone:* 406-657-1026 or 800-877-6259 (toll-free). *Fax:* 406-259-9751. *E-mail:* admissions@rocky.edu. *Web site:* http://www.rocky.edu/.

SALISH KOOTENAI COLLEGE

Pablo, Montana

Salish Kootenai College is a coed, private, primarily two-year college, founded in 1977, offering degrees at the associate and bachelor's levels. It has a 4-acre campus in Pablo.

Academic Information The faculty has 80 members (56% full-time). The library holds 24,000 titles and 200 serial subscriptions. Special programs include academic remediation, services for learning-disabled students, cooperative (work-study) education, summer session for credit, part-time degree programs, adult/continuing education programs, and arrangement for off-campus study with members of the American Indian Higher Education Consortium.

Student Body Statistics The student body is made up of 1,088 undergraduates (108 freshmen). 61 percent are women and 39 percent are men. Students come from 3 states and territories.

Expenses for 2006–07 *Area resident tuition:* $2664 full-time, $74 per credit part-time. *State resident tuition:* $4572 full-time, $127 per credit part-time. *Nonresident tuition:* $9144 full-time, $254 per credit part-time. *Mandatory fees:* $789 full-time, $95 per credit part-time. Both full-time and part-time tuition and fees vary according to course load. *College room and board:* $6975.

Financial Aid Forms of aid include need-based scholarships and part-time jobs. The application deadline for financial aid is continuous.

Freshman Admission Salish Kootenai College requires a high school transcript, proof of immunization, tribal enrollment, and TABE. The application deadline for regular admission is rolling.

Transfer Admission The application deadline for admission is rolling.

Entrance Difficulty Salish Kootenai College has an open admission policy.

For Further Information Contact Ms. Jackie Moran, Admissions Officer, Salish Kootenai College, 52000 Highway 93, PO Box 70, Pablo, MT 59855. *Telephone:* 406-275-4866. *Fax:* 406-275-4810. *E-mail:* jackie_moran@skc.edu. *Web site:* http://www.skc.edu/.

STONE CHILD COLLEGE

Box Elder, Montana

Stone Child College is a coed, private, two-year college, founded in 1984, offering degrees at the associate level.

Academic Information The faculty has 22 members (45% full-time).

Student Body Statistics The student body is made up of 240 undergraduates.

Expenses for 2006–07 *Application fee:* $10. *State resident tuition:* $2370 full-time.

Financial Aid Forms of aid include need-based scholarships and part-time jobs. The application deadline for financial aid is continuous.

Freshman Admission Stone Child College requires a high school transcript.

Entrance Difficulty Stone Child College has an open admission policy.

For Further Information Contact Mr. Ted Whitford, Director of Admissions/Registrar, Stone Child College, RR1, Box 1082, Box Elder, MT 59521. *Telephone:* 406-395-4313. *Fax:* 406-395-4836. *E-mail:* uanet337@quest.ocsc.montana.edu. *Web site:* http://www.montana.edu/wwwscc/.

UNIVERSITY OF GREAT FALLS

Great Falls, Montana

University of Great Falls is a coed, private, Roman Catholic, comprehensive institution, founded in 1932, offering degrees at the associate, bachelor's, and master's levels. It has a 40-acre campus in Great Falls.

Academic Information The faculty has 103 members (33% full-time), 30% with terminal degrees. The undergraduate student-faculty ratio is 11:1. The library holds 108,926 titles, 457 serial subscriptions, and 1,620 audiovisual materials. Special programs include academic remediation,

services for learning-disabled students, cooperative (work-study) education, advanced placement credit, double majors, independent study, distance learning, summer session for credit, part-time degree programs (daytime, evenings, weekends, summer), external degree programs, adult/continuing education programs, internships, and arrangement for off-campus study with Flathead Valley Community College; Bellevue University, NE. The most frequently chosen baccalaureate fields are education, psychology, public administration and social services.

Student Body Statistics The student body totals 716, of whom 632 are undergraduates (121 freshmen). 69 percent are women and 31 percent are men. Students come from 25 states and territories and 3 other countries. 82 percent are from Montana. 1.4 percent are international students. 12 percent of the 2006 graduating class went on to graduate and professional schools.

Expenses for 2007–08 *Application fee:* $35. *Comprehensive fee:* $22,150 includes full-time tuition ($15,450), mandatory fees ($900), and college room and board ($5800). *College room only:* $2700. *Part-time tuition:* $490 per credit. *Part-time mandatory fees:* $30 per credit.

Financial Aid Forms of aid include need-based and non-need-based scholarships, athletic grants, and part-time jobs. The average aided 2006–07 undergraduate received an aid package worth an estimated $11,886.

Freshman Admission University of Great Falls requires a high school transcript and TOEFL scores for international students. An essay, an interview, and SAT or ACT scores are recommended. The application deadline for regular admission is August 1 and for nonresidents it is August 1.

Transfer Admission The application deadline for admission is August 1.

Entrance Difficulty University of Great Falls has an open admission policy.

For Further Information Contact Paula Highlander, Director of Admissions, University of Great Falls, 1301 20th Street South, Great Falls, MT 59405. *Telephone:* 406-791-5200 or 800-856-9544 (toll-free). *Fax:* 406-791-5209. *E-mail:* enroll@ugf.edu. *Web site:* http://www.ugf.edu/.

THE UNIVERSITY OF MONTANA
Missoula, Montana

The University of Montana is a coed, public unit of Montana University System, founded in 1893, offering degrees at the associate, bachelor's, master's, doctoral, and first professional levels and post-master's certificates. It has a 220-acre campus in Missoula.

Academic Information The library holds 1 million titles, 7,279 serial subscriptions, and 56,866 audiovisual materials. Special programs include academic remediation, services for learning-disabled students, an honors program, cooperative (work-study) education, study abroad, advanced placement credit, Freshman Honors College, ESL programs, double majors, independent study, distance learning, summer session for credit, part-time degree programs, external degree programs, adult/continuing education programs, internships, and arrangement for off-campus study with members of the National Student Exchange. The most frequently chosen baccalaureate fields are business/marketing, communications/journalism, social sciences.

Student Body Statistics The student body totals 13,558, of whom 11,431 are undergraduates. Students come from 52 states and territories and 61 other countries. 77 percent are from Montana. 1.5 percent are international students. 28 percent of the 2006 graduating class went on to graduate and professional schools.

Expenses for 2006–07 *Application fee:* $30. *State resident tuition:* $3686 full-time, $164 per credit part-time. *Nonresident tuition:* $13,193 full-time, $573 per credit part-time. *Mandatory fees:* $1291 full-time, $40 per credit part-time. Full-time tuition and fees vary according to degree level, location, program, reciprocity agreements, and student level. Part-time tuition and fees vary according to course load, degree level, location, and student level. *College room and board:* $5860. *College room only:* $2660. Room and board charges vary according to board plan and housing facility.

Financial Aid Forms of aid include need-based and non-need-based scholarships, athletic grants, and part-time jobs. The average aided 2005–06 undergraduate received an aid package worth $7866. The priority application deadline for financial aid is February 15.

Freshman Admission The University of Montana requires a high school transcript, a minimum 2.5 high school GPA, SAT 1540 (M-V-Wr) or ACT 22; and SAT Math 420 or ACT Math 17, SAT or ACT scores, and TOEFL scores for international students. ACT ASSET or ACT COMPASS is required for some. The application deadline for regular admission is rolling.

Transfer Admission The application deadline for admission is rolling.

Entrance Difficulty The University of Montana assesses its entrance difficulty level as moderately difficult; most difficult for Davidson Honors College. For the fall 2006 freshman class, 93 percent of the applicants were accepted.

For Further Information Contact Ms. Juana Alcala, Manager, Enrollment Services, The University of Montana, Missoula, MT 59812-0002. *Telephone:* 406-243-6266 or 800-462-8636 (toll-free). *Fax:* 406-243-5711. *E-mail:* admiss@umontana.edu. *Web site:* http://www.umt.edu/.

THE UNIVERSITY OF MONTANA–WESTERN
Dillon, Montana

The University of Montana–Western is a coed, public, four-year college of Montana University System, founded in 1893, offering degrees at the associate and bachelor's levels. It has a 36-acre campus in Dillon.

Academic Information The faculty has 85 members (71% full-time), 60% with terminal degrees. The student-faculty ratio is 16:1. The library holds 137,258 titles, 8,345 serial subscriptions, and 3,338 audiovisual materials. Special programs include academic remediation, services for learning-disabled students, an honors program, cooperative (work-study) education, advanced placement credit, accelerated degree programs, double majors, independent study, distance learning, self-designed majors, summer session for credit, part-time degree programs (daytime, evenings, weekends, summer), adult/continuing education programs, internships, and arrangement for off-campus study. The most frequently chosen baccalaureate fields are business/marketing, education, social sciences.

Student Body Statistics The student body is made up of 1,176 undergraduates (245 freshmen). 57 percent are women and 43 percent are men. Students come from 10 states and territories and 4 other countries. 80 percent are from Montana. 0.7 percent are international students. 12 percent of the 2006 graduating class went on to graduate and professional schools.

Expenses for 2007–08 *Application fee:* $30. *State resident tuition:* $3355 full-time, $148 per credit part-time. *Nonresident tuition:* $11,675 full-time, $487 per credit part-time. *Mandatory fees:* $857 full-time. *College room and board:* $5250. *College room only:* $2080.

Financial Aid Forms of aid include need-based and non-need-based scholarships, athletic grants, and part-time jobs. The priority application deadline for financial aid is March 1.

Freshman Admission The University of Montana–Western requires a high school transcript, a minimum 2.5 high school GPA, immunization record, 2 doses of MMR, SAT or ACT scores, and TOEFL scores for international students. The application deadline for regular admission is rolling.

Transfer Admission The application deadline for admission is rolling.

Entrance Difficulty The University of Montana–Western assesses its entrance difficulty level as minimally difficult. For the fall 2006 freshman class, 98 percent of the applicants were accepted.

For Further Information Contact Admissions, The University of Montana–Western, 710 South Atlantic, Dillon, MT 59725. *Telephone:* 406-683-7331, 866-869-6668 (toll-free in-state), or 877-683-7493 (toll-free out-of-state). *Fax:* 406-683-7493. *E-mail:* admissions@umwestern.edu. *Web site:* http://www.umwestern.edu/.

WESTERN MONTANA COLLEGE
See The University of Montana–Western.

Nevada

THE ART INSTITUTE OF LAS VEGAS

Henderson, Nevada

The Art Institute of Las Vegas is a coed, proprietary, four-year college of Education Management Corporation, founded in 2002, offering degrees at the associate and bachelor's levels.

Academic Information The faculty has 79 members (34% full-time), 9% with terminal degrees. The student-faculty ratio is 19:1. Special programs include services for learning-disabled students, an honors program, study abroad, distance learning, and summer session for credit. The most frequently chosen baccalaureate field is visual and performing arts.
Student Body Statistics The student body is made up of 1,046 undergraduates (134 freshmen). 46 percent are women and 54 percent are men. 77 percent are from Nevada.
Expenses for 2007–08 *Application fee:* $50. *Tuition:* $19,872 full-time, $414 per credit part-time. *Mandatory fees:* $1000 full-time. *College room only:* $5850.
Freshman Admission The Art Institute of Las Vegas requires an essay, a high school transcript, and an interview. A minimum X high school GPA is recommended. The application deadline for regular admission is rolling.
Transfer Admission The application deadline for admission is rolling.
Entrance Difficulty The Art Institute of Las Vegas has an open admission policy. It assesses its entrance difficulty as minimally difficult for transfers.
For Further Information Contact Mr. Dewey McGuirk, The Art Institute of Las Vegas, 2350 Corporate Circle, Henderson, NV 89074. *Telephone:* 702-369-9944. *Fax:* 702-992-8494. *E-mail:* dmcguirk@aii.edu. *Web site:* http://www.ailv.artinstitutes.edu/.

DeVRY UNIVERSITY

Henderson, Nevada

DeVry University is a coed, proprietary, comprehensive unit of DeVry University, offering degrees at the associate, bachelor's, and master's levels and postbachelor's certificates.

Academic Information The faculty has 1 members. The undergraduate student-faculty ratio is 71:1. Special programs include academic remediation, services for learning-disabled students, advanced placement credit, accelerated degree programs, distance learning, summer session for credit, part-time degree programs (daytime, evenings, weekends, summer), and adult/continuing education programs. The most frequently chosen baccalaureate field is business/marketing.
Student Body Statistics The student body totals 149, of whom 97 are undergraduates (21 freshmen). 41 percent are women and 59 percent are men. 95 percent are from Nevada. 2.1 percent are international students.
Expenses for 2007–08 *Application fee:* $50. *Tuition:* $12,900 full-time, $490 per credit part-time. *Mandatory fees:* $120 full-time.
Freshman Admission DeVry University requires a high school transcript and an interview. The application deadline for regular admission is rolling.
Transfer Admission The application deadline for admission is rolling.
Entrance Difficulty DeVry University assesses its entrance difficulty level as minimally difficult.
For Further Information Contact Admissions Office, DeVry University, 2490 Paseo Verde Parkway, Suite 150, Henderson, NV 89074. *Telephone:* 702-933-9700. *Web site:* http://www.devry.edu/.

GREAT BASIN COLLEGE

Elko, Nevada

Great Basin College is a coed, public, primarily two-year college of University and Community College System of Nevada, founded in 1967, offering degrees at the associate and bachelor's levels. It has a 45-acre campus in Elko.

Academic Information The faculty has 210 members (32% full-time). The library holds 38,765 titles and 2,635 audiovisual materials. Special programs include academic remediation, services for learning-disabled students, cooperative (work-study) education, ESL programs, independent study, distance learning, summer session for credit, part-time degree programs (daytime, evenings, weekends, summer), external degree programs, and adult/continuing education programs.
Student Body Statistics The student body is made up of 3,349 undergraduates (546 freshmen). 65 percent are women and 35 percent are men. Students come from 13 states and territories. 97 percent are from Nevada.
Expenses for 2007–08 *Application fee:* $5. *State resident tuition:* $1,642 full-time. *Nonresident tuition:* $4335 full-time. *College room and board:* $4520. *College room only:* $1900.
Financial Aid Forms of aid include need-based scholarships and part-time jobs. The priority application deadline for financial aid is May 13.
Freshman Admission Great Basin College requires a high school transcript. The application deadline for regular admission is rolling.
Transfer Admission The application deadline for admission is rolling.
Entrance Difficulty Great Basin College has an open admission policy except for nursing program. It assesses its entrance difficulty as moderately difficult for nursing program.
For Further Information Contact Ms. Julie Byrnes, Director of Enrollment Management, Great Basin College, 1500 College Parkway, Elko, NV 89801-3348. *Telephone:* 775-753-2271. *Fax:* 775-753-2311. *E-mail:* stdsvc@gbcnv.edu. *Web site:* http://www.gbcnv.edu/.

ITT TECHNICAL INSTITUTE

Henderson, Nevada

ITT Technical Institute is a coed, proprietary, primarily two-year college of ITT Educational Services, Inc, founded in 1997, offering degrees at the associate and bachelor's levels.

Expenses for 2006–07 *Application fee:* $100. Contact school for program costs.
Financial Aid Forms of aid include need-based scholarships and part-time jobs. The application deadline for financial aid is continuous.
Freshman Admission ITT Technical Institute requires a high school transcript, an interview, and Wonderlic aptitude test. Recommendations are recommended. The application deadline for regular admission is rolling.
Transfer Admission The application deadline for admission is rolling.
Entrance Difficulty ITT Technical Institute assesses its entrance difficulty level as minimally difficult.
For Further Information Contact Ms. Anne Buzak, Director of Recruitment, ITT Technical Institute, 168 North Gibson Road, Henderson, NV 89014. *Telephone:* 702-558-5404 or 800-488-8459 (toll-free in-state). *Fax:* 702-558-5412. *Web site:* http://www.itt-tech.edu/.

MORRISON UNIVERSITY

Reno, Nevada

Morrison University is a coed, proprietary, comprehensive institution, founded in 1902, offering degrees at the associate, bachelor's, and master's levels. It has a 2-acre campus in Reno.

Academic Information The faculty has 25 members (60% full-time). The library holds 6,000 titles and 20 serial subscriptions. Special programs include academic remediation, accelerated degree programs, ESL programs, summer session for credit, part-time degree programs (daytime, evenings, summer), adult/continuing education programs, and internships.
Student Body Statistics The student body totals 136, of whom 114 are undergraduates (23 freshmen). 53 percent are women and 47 percent are men. Students come from 8 states and territories and 5 other countries. 2 percent of the 2006 graduating class went on to graduate and professional schools.
Expenses for 2007–08 *Application fee:* $25. *Tuition:* $8000 full-time, $800 per course part-time. *Mandatory fees:* $25 full-time.
Financial Aid Forms of aid include need-based and non-need-based scholarships. The application deadline for financial aid is continuous.

Freshman Admission Morrison University requires a high school transcript and an interview. CPAt of 160 for paralegal program is recommended. An essay is required for some.

Entrance Difficulty Morrison University has an open admission policy.

For Further Information Contact Mr. Charles Timinsky, Director of Enrollment, Morrison University, 10315 Professional Circle, Suite 201, Reno, NV 89521. *Telephone:* 775-850-0700 Ext. 101 or 800-369-6144 (toll-free). *Fax:* 775-850-0711. *E-mail:* ctiminsky@morrison.neumont.edu. *Web site:* http://www.morrison.neumont.edu/.

NEVADA STATE COLLEGE AT HENDERSON
Henderson, Nevada

Nevada State College at Henderson is a coed, public, four-year college of Nevada System of Higher Education, founded in 2002, offering degrees at the bachelor's level. It has a 520-acre campus in Henderson near Las Vegas.

Academic Information The faculty has 141 members (37% full-time), 18% with terminal degrees. The student-faculty ratio is 9:1. The library holds 6,800 titles and 80 audiovisual materials. Special programs include academic remediation, services for learning-disabled students, cooperative (work-study) education, advanced placement credit, accelerated degree programs, ESL programs, double majors, independent study, distance learning, self-designed majors, summer session for credit, part-time degree programs, adult/continuing education programs, internships, and arrangement for off-campus study.

Student Body Statistics The student body is made up of 1,959 undergraduates (249 freshmen). 72 percent are women and 28 percent are men. 96 percent are from Nevada.

Expenses for 2007–08 *Application fee:* $30. *State resident tuition:* $0 full-time. *Nonresident tuition:* $7437 full-time, $87 per credit part-time. *Mandatory fees:* $1992 full-time, $83 per credit part-time.

Freshman Admission Nevada State College at Henderson requires a high school transcript and a minimum 2.0 high school GPA. SAT or ACT scores are recommended. The application deadline for regular admission is August 20.

Transfer Admission The application deadline for admission is August 20.

Entrance Difficulty For the fall 2006 freshman class, 39 percent of the applicants were accepted.

For Further Information Contact Ms. Patricia Ring, Registrar, Nevada State College at Henderson, 1125 Nevada State Drive, Henderson, NV 89107. *Telephone:* 702-992-2114. *Fax:* 702-992-2111. *E-mail:* patricia.ring@nsc.nevada.edu. *Web site:* http://www.nsc.nevada.edu/.

SIERRA NEVADA COLLEGE
Incline Village, Nevada

Sierra Nevada College is a coed, private, comprehensive institution, founded in 1969, offering degrees at the bachelor's and master's levels. It has a 20-acre campus in Incline Village near Reno.

Academic Information The faculty has 75 members (25% full-time). The undergraduate student-faculty ratio is 10:1. The library holds 35,000 titles and 175 serial subscriptions. Special programs include academic remediation, services for learning-disabled students, an honors program, cooperative (work-study) education, study abroad, advanced placement credit, accelerated degree programs, double majors, independent study, summer session for credit, part-time degree programs (daytime, evenings), adult/continuing education programs, and internships.

Student Body Statistics The student body totals 492, of whom 302 are undergraduates (67 freshmen). 51 percent are women and 49 percent are men. Students come from 32 states and territories and 5 other countries. 29 percent are from Nevada. 3 percent are international students.

Expenses for 2007–08 *Application fee:* $0. *Tuition:* $976 per unit part-time.

Financial Aid Forms of aid include need-based and non-need-based scholarships, athletic grants, and part-time jobs. The priority application deadline for financial aid is June 1.

Freshman Admission Sierra Nevada College requires an essay, a high school transcript, a minimum 2.0 high school GPA, SAT or ACT scores, and TOEFL scores for international students. An interview is recommended. Recommendations and school report form for high school seniors are required for some. The application deadline for regular admission is rolling.

Transfer Admission The application deadline for admission is rolling.

Entrance Difficulty Sierra Nevada College assesses its entrance difficulty level as moderately difficult. For the fall 2006 freshman class, 68 percent of the applicants were accepted.

For Further Information Contact Matt Delekta, James McMaster, Dean of Enrollment Services and Registrar, Sierra Nevada College, 999 Tahoe Boulevard, Incline Village, NV 89451. *Telephone:* 866-412-4636 or 775-831-1314 (toll-free in-state). *Fax:* 775-831-6223. *E-mail:* admissions@sierranevada.edu. *Web site:* http://www.sierranevada.edu/.

UNIVERSITY OF NEVADA, LAS VEGAS
Las Vegas, Nevada

University of Nevada, Las Vegas is a coed, public unit of Nevada System of Higher Education, founded in 1957, offering degrees at the bachelor's, master's, doctoral, and first professional levels and post-master's and postbachelor's certificates. It has a 358-acre campus in Las Vegas.

Academic Information The faculty has 1,677 members (57% full-time). The undergraduate student-faculty ratio is 18:1. The library holds 1 million titles, 18,568 serial subscriptions, and 14,235 audiovisual materials. Special programs include academic remediation, services for learning-disabled students, an honors program, cooperative (work-study) education, study abroad, advanced placement credit, accelerated degree programs, ESL programs, double majors, independent study, distance learning, self-designed majors, summer session for credit, part-time degree programs (daytime, evenings, weekends, summer), adult/continuing education programs, internships, and arrangement for off-campus study with National Student Exchange, Western Interstate Commission for Higher Education, Western Undergraduate Exchange. The most frequently chosen baccalaureate fields are business/marketing, communications/journalism, education.

Student Body Statistics The student body totals 27,933, of whom 21,853 are undergraduates (2,768 freshmen). 56 percent are women and 44 percent are men. Students come from 51 states and territories and 54 other countries. 79 percent are from Nevada. 4.1 percent are international students. 9 percent of the 2006 graduating class went on to graduate and professional schools.

Expenses for 2007–08 *Application fee:* $60. *State resident tuition:* $3,622 full-time, $116.75 per credit hour part-time. *Nonresident tuition:* $14,432 full-time, $245.25 per credit hour part-time. *Mandatory fees:* $544 full-time. *College room and board:* $8857. *College room only:* $5600.

Financial Aid Forms of aid include need-based and non-need-based scholarships, athletic grants, and part-time jobs. The average aided 2005–06 undergraduate received an aid package worth $6416.

Freshman Admission University of Nevada, Las Vegas requires a high school transcript, a minimum 2.5 high school GPA, and TOEFL scores for international students. SAT or ACT scores are recommended. 2 recommendations and SAT or ACT scores are required for some. The application deadline for regular admission is February 1.

Transfer Admission The application deadline for admission is April 1.

Entrance Difficulty University of Nevada, Las Vegas assesses its entrance difficulty level as moderately difficult. For the fall 2006 freshman class, 75 percent of the applicants were accepted.

For Further Information Contact Ms. Kristi Rodriguez, Director for Undergraduate Recruitment, University of Nevada, Las Vegas, 4505 Maryland Parkway, Box 451021, Las Vegas, NV 89154-1021. *Telephone:* 702-774-8001. *Fax:* 702-774-8008. *E-mail:* undergraduate.recruitment@unlv.edu. *Web site:* http://www.unlv.edu/.

UNIVERSITY OF NEVADA, RENO

Reno, Nevada

University of Nevada, Reno is a coed, public unit of Nevada System of Higher Education, founded in 1874, offering degrees at the bachelor's, master's, doctoral, and first professional levels and post-master's, first professional, and postbachelor's certificates. It has a 200-acre campus in Reno.

Academic Information The faculty has 988 members (51% full-time), 66% with terminal degrees. The undergraduate student-faculty ratio is 19:1. The library holds 1 million titles, 19,058 serial subscriptions, and 49,433 audiovisual materials. Special programs include academic remediation, services for learning-disabled students, an honors program, study abroad, advanced placement credit, ESL programs, double majors, independent study, distance learning, summer session for credit, part-time degree programs (daytime, evenings, summer), adult/continuing education programs, internships, and arrangement for off-campus study with National Student Exchange. The most frequently chosen baccalaureate fields are business/marketing, education, health professions and related sciences.

Student Body Statistics The student body totals 16,663, of whom 13,134 are undergraduates (2,357 freshmen). 54 percent are women and 46 percent are men. Students come from 45 states and territories and 48 other countries. 82 percent are from Nevada. 2.7 percent are international students.

Expenses for 2006–07 *Application fee:* $60. *State resident tuition:* $3,278 full-time, $109.25 per credit part-time. *Nonresident tuition:* $13,188 full-time, $225 per credit part-time. *Mandatory fees:* $218 full-time. Full-time tuition and fees vary according to course load. Part-time tuition varies according to course load. *College room and board:* $8199. *College room only:* $4400. Room and board charges vary according to board plan and housing facility.

Financial Aid Forms of aid include need-based and non-need-based scholarships, athletic grants, and part-time jobs. The priority application deadline for financial aid is February 1.

Freshman Admission University of Nevada, Reno requires a high school transcript, a minimum 2.75 high school GPA, and TOEFL scores for international students. The application deadline for regular admission is rolling and for early action it is November 15.

Transfer Admission The application deadline for admission is rolling.

Entrance Difficulty University of Nevada, Reno assesses its entrance difficulty level as moderately difficult. For the fall 2006 freshman class, 86 percent of the applicants were accepted.

For Further Information Contact Dr. Melisa Choroszy, Associate Vice President of Enrollment Services, University of Nevada, Reno, Mail Stop 120, Reno, NV 89557. *Telephone:* 775-784-4700 or 866-263-8232 (toll-free). *Fax:* 775-784-4283. *E-mail:* asknevada@unr.edu. *Web site:* http://www.unr.edu/.

UNIVERSITY OF PHOENIX–LAS VEGAS CAMPUS

Las Vegas, Nevada

University of Phoenix–Las Vegas Campus is a coed, proprietary, comprehensive institution, founded in 1994, offering degrees at the bachelor's and master's levels and post-master's certificates.

Academic Information The faculty has 668 members (3% full-time), 26% with terminal degrees. The undergraduate student-faculty ratio is 11:1. The library holds 1,759 titles and 692 serial subscriptions. Special programs include services for learning-disabled students, advanced placement credit, accelerated degree programs, independent study, distance learning, external degree programs, and adult/continuing education programs. The most frequently chosen baccalaureate fields are business/marketing, computer and information sciences, security and protective services.

Student Body Statistics The student body totals 3,484, of whom 2,379 are undergraduates (76 freshmen). 64 percent are women and 36 percent are men. 9.9 percent are international students.

Expenses for 2006–07 *Application fee:* $45. *Tuition:* $10,200 full-time.

Financial Aid Forms of aid include need-based and non-need-based scholarships. The average aided 2005–06 undergraduate received an aid package worth $4273. The application deadline for financial aid is continuous.

Freshman Admission University of Phoenix–Las Vegas Campus requires 1 recommendation and TOEFL scores for international students. A high school transcript is required for some. The application deadline for regular admission is rolling.

Transfer Admission The application deadline for admission is rolling.

Entrance Difficulty University of Phoenix–Las Vegas Campus has an open admission policy.

For Further Information Contact Ms. Beth Barilla, Associate Vice President, Student Admissions and Services, University of Phoenix–Las Vegas Campus, 4615 East Elwood Street, Mail Stop AA-K101, Phoenix, AZ 85040-1958. *Telephone:* 480-317-6000, 800-776-4867 (toll-free in-state), or 800-228-7240 (toll-free out-of-state). *Fax:* 480-894-1758. *E-mail:* beth.barilla@phoenix.edu. *Web site:* http://www.phoenix.edu/.

New Mexico

COLLEGE OF SANTA FE

Santa Fe, New Mexico

College of Santa Fe is a coed, private, comprehensive institution, founded in 1947, offering degrees at the associate, bachelor's, and master's levels. It has a 100-acre campus in Santa Fe near Albuquerque.

Academic Information The faculty has 267 members (24% full-time). The undergraduate student-faculty ratio is 7:1. Special programs include academic remediation, services for learning-disabled students, cooperative (work-study) education, study abroad, advanced placement credit, accelerated degree programs, double majors, independent study, distance learning, self-designed majors, summer session for credit, part-time degree programs (daytime, evenings, weekends, summer), adult/continuing education programs, internships, and arrangement for off-campus study with Great Lakes Colleges Association, New York City Arts Program. The most frequently chosen baccalaureate fields are business/marketing, education, visual and performing arts.

Student Body Statistics The student body totals 2,004, of whom 1,362 are undergraduates (155 freshmen). 55 percent are women and 45 percent are men. Students come from 48 states and territories. 27 percent are from New Mexico. 0.8 percent are international students.

Expenses for 2007–08 *Application fee:* $35. *Comprehensive fee:* $33,657 includes full-time tuition ($24,872), mandatory fees ($1200), and college room and board ($7585). *College room only:* $3692. *Part-time tuition:* $795 per credit hour. *Part-time mandatory fees:* $25 per credit hour.

Financial Aid Forms of aid include need-based and non-need-based scholarships, athletic grants, and part-time jobs. The average aided 2005–06 undergraduate received an aid package worth $18,934. The priority application deadline for financial aid is March 15.

Freshman Admission College of Santa Fe requires an essay, a high school transcript, 2 recommendations, an interview, SAT or ACT scores, and TOEFL scores for international students. A minimum 3.0 high school GPA is recommended. Portfolio or audition for visual and performing arts programs is required for some. The application deadline for regular admission is rolling.

Transfer Admission The application deadline for admission is rolling.

Entrance Difficulty College of Santa Fe assesses its entrance difficulty level as moderately difficult; very difficult for performing arts, moving image arts, creative writing. For the fall 2006 freshman class, 78 percent of the applicants were accepted.

For Further Information Contact Mr. Jeff Miller, Dean of Enrollment, College of Santa Fe, 1600 Saint Michael's Drive, Santa Fe, NM 87505-7634. *Telephone:* 505-473-6133 or 800-456-2673 (toll-free). *Fax:* 505-473-6129. *E-mail:* admissions@csf.edu. *Web site:* http://www.csf.edu.

COLLEGE OF THE SOUTHWEST

Hobbs, New Mexico

College of the Southwest is a coed, private, comprehensive institution, founded in 1962, offering degrees at the bachelor's and master's levels. It has a 162-acre campus in Hobbs.

Academic Information The faculty has 90 members (32% full-time), 31% with terminal degrees. The undergraduate student-faculty ratio is 12:1. The library holds 76,217 titles and 287 serial subscriptions. Special programs include services for learning-disabled students, advanced placement credit, double majors, distance learning, summer session for credit, part-time degree programs (daytime, evenings, summer), external degree programs, adult/continuing education programs, and internships.

Student Body Statistics The student body totals 741, of whom 608 are undergraduates (90 freshmen). 62 percent are women and 38 percent are men. Students come from 11 states and territories and 11 other countries. 74 percent are from New Mexico. 4.4 percent are international students.

Expenses for 2006–07 *Application fee:* $25. *Comprehensive fee:* $15,900 includes full-time tuition ($10,500) and college room and board ($5400). Full-time tuition varies according to course load. Room and board charges vary according to housing facility. *Part-time tuition:* $350 per hour. Part-time tuition varies according to course load.

Financial Aid Forms of aid include need-based and non-need-based scholarships, athletic grants, and part-time jobs. The average aided 2006–07 undergraduate received an aid package worth an estimated $8390. The application deadline for financial aid is August 1 with a priority deadline of April 1.

Freshman Admission College of the Southwest requires a high school transcript, a minimum 2.0 high school GPA, and SAT or ACT scores. TOEFL scores for international students are recommended. The application deadline for regular admission is rolling.

Transfer Admission The application deadline for admission is rolling.

Entrance Difficulty College of the Southwest assesses its entrance difficulty level as moderately difficult; noncompetitive for transfers. For the fall 2006 freshman class, 46 percent of the applicants were accepted.

For Further Information Contact Dr. Steve Hill, Dean of Recruitment, College of the Southwest, 6610 Lovington Highway, Hobbs, NM 88240. *Telephone:* 505-392-6563 or 800-530-4400 (toll-free). *Fax:* 505-392-6006. *E-mail:* shill@csw.edu. *Web site:* http://www.csw.edu/.

CROWNPOINT INSTITUTE OF TECHNOLOGY

Crownpoint, New Mexico

http://www.citech.edu/academics.htm

EASTERN NEW MEXICO UNIVERSITY

Portales, New Mexico

Eastern New Mexico University is a coed, public, comprehensive unit of Eastern New Mexico University System, founded in 1934, offering degrees at the associate, bachelor's, and master's levels. It has a 240-acre campus in Portales.

Academic Information The faculty has 263 members (57% full-time), 52% with terminal degrees. The undergraduate student-faculty ratio is 17:1. The library holds 305,108 titles and 7,621 serial subscriptions. Special programs include academic remediation, services for learning-disabled students, an honors program, cooperative (work-study) education, study abroad, advanced placement credit, accelerated degree programs, ESL programs, double majors, distance learning, self-designed majors, summer session for credit, part-time degree programs (daytime, evenings, summer), external degree programs, adult/continuing education programs, and internships. The most frequently chosen baccalaureate fields are business/marketing, education, liberal arts/general studies.

Student Body Statistics The student body totals 4,033, of whom 3,291 are undergraduates (567 freshmen). 56 percent are women and 44 percent are men. Students come from 37 states and territories and 16 other countries. 81 percent are from New Mexico. 1 percent are international students.

Expenses for 2006–07 *Application fee:* $0. *State resident tuition:* $2136 full-time, $89 per credit hour part-time. *Nonresident tuition:* $7692 full-time, $320.50 per credit hour part-time. *Mandatory fees:* $828 full-time, $34.50 per credit hour part-time. *College room and board:* $4568. *College room only:* $2178. Room and board charges vary according to housing facility.

Financial Aid Forms of aid include need-based and non-need-based scholarships and part-time jobs. The priority application deadline for financial aid is March 1.

Freshman Admission Eastern New Mexico University requires a high school transcript, a minimum 2.0 high school GPA, SAT or ACT scores, and TOEFL scores for international students. The application deadline for regular admission is rolling.

Transfer Admission The application deadline for admission is rolling.

Entrance Difficulty Eastern New Mexico University assesses its entrance difficulty level as minimally difficult. For the fall 2006 freshman class, 65 percent of the applicants were accepted.

For Further Information Contact Ms. Donna Kittrell, Director, Eastern New Mexico University, Station #7 ENMU, Portales, NM 88130. *Telephone:* 505-562-2178 or 800-367-3668 (toll-free). *Fax:* 505-562-2118. *E-mail:* donna.kittrell@enmu.edu. *Web site:* http://www.enmu.edu/.

INSTITUTE OF AMERICAN INDIAN ARTS

Santa Fe, New Mexico

http://www.iaia.edu/

INTERNATIONAL INSTITUTE OF THE AMERICAS

Albuquerque, New Mexico

International Institute of the Americas is a coed, private, primarily two-year college, offering degrees at the associate and bachelor's levels.

Academic Information The faculty has 15 members (47% full-time), 27% with terminal degrees. The student-faculty ratio is 12:1. Special programs include distance learning and part-time degree programs.

Student Body Statistics The student body is made up of 185 undergraduates. 89 percent are women and 11 percent are men.

Expenses for 2007–08 *Application fee:* $200. *Tuition:* $9850 full-time. *Mandatory fees:* $200 full-time.

Freshman Admission International Institute of the Americas requires an interview. The application deadline for regular admission is rolling.

Transfer Admission The application deadline for admission is rolling.

Entrance Difficulty International Institute of the Americas assesses its entrance difficulty level as noncompetitive.

For Further Information Contact Campus Director, International Institute of the Americas, 4201 Central Avenue NW, Suite J, Albuquerque, NM 87105-1649. *Telephone:* 505-880-2877 or 888-660-2428 (toll-free). *Fax:* 505-352-0199. *E-mail:* esigman@iia.edu. *Web site:* http://www.iia-online.com/site/.

ITT TECHNICAL INSTITUTE

Albuquerque, New Mexico

ITT Technical Institute is a coed, proprietary, primarily two-year college of ITT Educational Services, Inc, founded in 1989, offering degrees at the associate and bachelor's levels.

Expenses for 2006–07 *Application fee:* $100. Contact school for program costs.

Financial Aid Forms of aid include need-based scholarships and part-time jobs. The application deadline for financial aid is continuous.

ITT Technical Institute (continued)

Freshman Admission ITT Technical Institute requires a high school transcript, an interview, and Wonderlic aptitude test. Recommendations are recommended. The application deadline for regular admission is rolling.
Transfer Admission The application deadline for admission is rolling.
Entrance Difficulty ITT Technical Institute assesses its entrance difficulty level as minimally difficult.
For Further Information Contact Mr. John Crooks, Director of Recruitment, ITT Technical Institute, 5100 Masthead Street, NE, Albuquerque, NM 87109. *Telephone:* 505-828-1114 or 800-636-1114 (toll-free in-state). *Fax:* 505-828-1849. *Web site:* http://www.itt-tech.edu/.

NATIONAL AMERICAN UNIVERSITY

Albuquerque, New Mexico

http://www.national.edu/

NATIONAL COLLEGE OF MIDWIFERY

Taos, New Mexico

http://www.midwiferycollege.org/

NEW MEXICO HIGHLANDS UNIVERSITY

Las Vegas, New Mexico

New Mexico Highlands University is a coed, public, comprehensive institution, founded in 1893, offering degrees at the associate, bachelor's, and master's levels. It has a 120-acre campus in Las Vegas.

Academic Information The faculty has 109 members (67% full-time), 80% with terminal degrees. The undergraduate student-faculty ratio is 25:1. The library holds 386,489 titles and 740 serial subscriptions. Special programs include academic remediation, services for learning-disabled students, an honors program, cooperative (work-study) education, advanced placement credit, accelerated degree programs, double majors, independent study, distance learning, summer session for credit, part-time degree programs, internships, and arrangement for off-campus study with San Juan Community College, Santa Fe Community College, NMHU Center at Roswell; NMHU Center at Rio Rancho. The most frequently chosen baccalaureate fields are education, business/marketing, health professions and related sciences.
Student Body Statistics The student body totals 3,750, of whom 1,986 are undergraduates (236 freshmen). 62 percent are women and 38 percent are men. Students come from 19 states and territories and 3 other countries. 92 percent are from New Mexico. 0.4 percent are international students.
Expenses for 2006–07 *Application fee:* $15. *State resident tuition:* $2424 full-time, $101 per credit hour part-time. *Nonresident tuition:* $3636 full-time, $101 per credit hour part-time. *Mandatory fees:* $20 full-time. Full-time tuition and fees vary according to course load and location. Part-time tuition varies according to course load and location. *College room and board:* $4476. *College room only:* $2056. Room and board charges vary according to board plan and housing facility.
Financial Aid Forms of aid include need-based and non-need-based scholarships, athletic grants, and part-time jobs. The priority application deadline for financial aid is March 1.
Freshman Admission New Mexico Highlands University requires a high school transcript, a minimum 2.0 high school GPA, and TOEFL scores for international students. 2 recommendations and an interview are required for some. The application deadline for regular admission is rolling.
Transfer Admission The application deadline for admission is rolling.

Entrance Difficulty New Mexico Highlands University assesses its entrance difficulty level as minimally difficult. For the fall 2006 freshman class, 69 percent of the applicants were accepted.
For Further Information Contact Ms. Judy Cordova, Vice President for Student Affairs, New Mexico Highlands University, Box 9000, Las Vegas, NM 87701. *Telephone:* 505-454-3566 or 800-338-6648 (toll-free). *Fax:* 505-454-3552. *E-mail:* judycordova@nmhu.edu. *Web site:* http://www.nmhu.edu/.

NEW MEXICO INSTITUTE OF MINING AND TECHNOLOGY

Socorro, New Mexico

New Mexico Institute of Mining and Technology is a coed, public university, founded in 1889, offering degrees at the associate, bachelor's, master's, and doctoral levels. It has a 320-acre campus in Socorro near Albuquerque.

Academic Information The faculty has 147 members (85% full-time), 86% with terminal degrees. The undergraduate student-faculty ratio is 11:1. The library holds 321,829 titles and 884 serial subscriptions. Special programs include services for learning-disabled students, cooperative (work-study) education, advanced placement credit, accelerated degree programs, double majors, independent study, distance learning, self-designed majors, summer session for credit, part-time degree programs (daytime), and internships. The most frequently chosen baccalaureate fields are engineering, computer and information sciences, physical sciences.
Student Body Statistics The student body totals 1,846, of whom 1,336 are undergraduates (282 freshmen). 33 percent are women and 67 percent are men. Students come from 24 states and territories and 29 other countries. 87 percent are from New Mexico. 2.1 percent are international students. 16 percent of the 2006 graduating class went on to graduate and professional schools.
Expenses for 2006–07 *Application fee:* $15. *State resident tuition:* $3439 full-time, $143.41 per hour part-time. *Nonresident tuition:* $10,873 full-time, $453.04 per hour part-time. *Mandatory fees:* $532 full-time. Part-time tuition varies according to course load. *College room and board:* $5090. *College room only:* $2290. Room and board charges vary according to board plan and housing facility.
Financial Aid Forms of aid include need-based and non-need-based scholarships and part-time jobs. The priority application deadline for financial aid is June 1.
Freshman Admission New Mexico Institute of Mining and Technology requires a high school transcript, a minimum 2.5 high school GPA, SAT or ACT scores, and TOEFL scores for international students. An interview and ACT scores are recommended. 2 recommendations are required for some. The application deadline for regular admission is August 1.
Transfer Admission The application deadline for admission is August 1.
Entrance Difficulty New Mexico Institute of Mining and Technology assesses its entrance difficulty level as moderately difficult. For the fall 2006 freshman class, 61 percent of the applicants were accepted.
For Further Information Contact Mr. Mike Kloeppel, Director of Admissions, New Mexico Institute of Mining and Technology, 801 Leroy Place, Socorro, NM 87801. *Telephone:* 505-835-5424 or 800-428-TECH (toll-free). *Fax:* 505-835-5989. *E-mail:* admission@admin.nmt.edu. *Web site:* http://www.nmt.edu/.

NEW MEXICO STATE UNIVERSITY

Las Cruces, New Mexico

New Mexico State University is a coed, public unit of New Mexico State University System, founded in 1888, offering degrees at the associate, bachelor's, master's, and doctoral levels and post-master's certificates. It has a 900-acre campus in Las Cruces near El Paso.

Academic Information The faculty has 908 members (72% full-time), 66% with terminal degrees. The undergraduate student-faculty ratio is 19:1. The library holds 2 million titles, 2,890 serial subscriptions, and 4,332 audiovisual materials. Special programs include academic

remediation, services for learning-disabled students, an honors program, cooperative (work-study) education, study abroad, advanced placement credit, accelerated degree programs, double majors, independent study, distance learning, self-designed majors, summer session for credit, part-time degree programs (daytime, evenings, weekends, summer), adult/continuing education programs, internships, and arrangement for off-campus study with members of the National Student Exchange, other units of the New Mexico State University System. The most frequently chosen baccalaureate fields are business/marketing, education, engineering.

Student Body Statistics The student body totals 16,415, of whom 13,210 are undergraduates (1,946 freshmen). 56 percent are women and 44 percent are men. Students come from 50 states and territories and 39 other countries. 84 percent are from New Mexico. 0.8 percent are international students.

Expenses for 2006–07 *Application fee:* $15. *State resident tuition:* $3164 full-time, $163.25 per credit part-time. *Nonresident tuition:* $12,738 full-time, $550.25 per credit part-time. *Mandatory fees:* $1066 full-time. *College room and board:* $5576. *College room only:* $3226. Room and board charges vary according to board plan and gender.

Financial Aid Forms of aid include need-based and non-need-based scholarships, athletic grants, and part-time jobs. The average aided 2006–07 undergraduate received an aid package worth an estimated $7438. The priority application deadline for financial aid is March 1.

Freshman Admission New Mexico State University requires a high school transcript, a minimum 2.0 high school GPA, SAT or ACT scores, and TOEFL scores for international students. The application deadline for regular admission is August 19.

Transfer Admission The application deadline for admission is August 14.

Entrance Difficulty New Mexico State University assesses its entrance difficulty level as moderately difficult. For the fall 2006 freshman class, 87 percent of the applicants were accepted.

For Further Information Contact Mr. Tyler Pruett, Director of Admissions, New Mexico State University, Box 30001, MSC 3A, Las Cruces, NM 88003-8001. *Telephone:* 505-646-3121 or 800-662-6678 (toll-free). *Fax:* 505-646-6330. *E-mail:* admssions@nmsu.edu. *Web site:* http://www.nmsu.edu/.

NORTHERN NEW MEXICO COLLEGE
Española, New Mexico

Northern New Mexico College is a coed, public, primarily two-year college of New Mexico Commission on Higher Education, founded in 1909, offering degrees at the associate and bachelor's levels. It has a 35-acre campus in Española.

Academic Information The faculty has 253 members (18% full-time), 8% with terminal degrees. The library holds 18,065 titles and 222 serial subscriptions. Special programs include academic remediation, services for learning-disabled students, advanced placement credit, distance learning, summer session for credit, and part-time degree programs (daytime, evenings, weekends, summer).

Student Body Statistics The student body is made up of 2,272 undergraduates. Students come from 5 states and territories. 99 percent are from New Mexico.

Expenses for 2006–07 *Application fee:* $0. *State resident tuition:* $1080 full-time, $36 per credit part-time. *Nonresident tuition:* $2550 full-time, $85 per credit part-time. *Mandatory fees:* $156 full-time, $6.50 per credit part-time. Both full-time and part-time tuition and fees vary according to course level.

Financial Aid Forms of aid include need-based scholarships and part-time jobs. The priority application deadline for financial aid is March 1.

Freshman Admission Northern New Mexico College requires a high school transcript and TOEFL scores for international students. The application deadline for regular admission is rolling.

Transfer Admission The application deadline for admission is rolling.

Entrance Difficulty Northern New Mexico College has an open admission policy.

For Further Information Contact Mr. Mike L. Costello, Registrar, Northern New Mexico College, 921 Paseo de Oñate, Española, NM 87532. *Telephone:* 505-747-2193. *Fax:* 505-747-2191. *E-mail:* dms@nnmc.edu. *Web site:* http://www.nnmc.edu/.

ST. JOHN'S COLLEGE
Santa Fe, New Mexico

SPONSOR See Front Insert for Details!

St. John's College is a coed, private, comprehensive institution, founded in 1964, offering degrees at the bachelor's and master's levels. It has a 250-acre campus in Santa Fe.

Academic Information The faculty has 72 members (96% full-time), 78% with terminal degrees. The undergraduate student-faculty ratio is 8:1. The library holds 65,000 titles and 140 serial subscriptions. Special programs include summer session for credit, internships, and arrangement for off-campus study with St. John's College (MD).

Student Body Statistics The student body totals 520, of whom 434 are undergraduates (120 freshmen). 44 percent are women and 56 percent are men. Students come from 46 states and territories and 7 other countries. 5 percent are from New Mexico. 1.8 percent are international students. 23 percent of the 2006 graduating class went on to graduate and professional schools.

Expenses for 2007–08 *Application fee:* $0. *Comprehensive fee:* $45,280 includes full-time tuition ($36,346), mandatory fees ($250), and college room and board ($8684).

Financial Aid Forms of aid include need-based and non-need-based scholarships and part-time jobs. The average aided 2006–07 undergraduate received an aid package worth an estimated $24,858. The application deadline for financial aid is February 15.

Freshman Admission St. John's College requires an essay, a high school transcript, 2 recommendations, and TOEFL scores for international students. 3 recommendations and an interview are recommended. An interview and SAT or ACT scores are required for some. The application deadline for regular admission is rolling.

Transfer Admission The application deadline for admission is rolling.

Entrance Difficulty St. John's College assesses its entrance difficulty level as very difficult. For the fall 2006 freshman class, 80 percent of the applicants were accepted.

SPECIAL MESSAGE TO STUDENTS

Social Life St John's College offers popular student activities including search and rescue, skiing, backpacking, rafting, fencing, Karate Do, Jiu-jitsu, dancing, community service, drama, student government, newspaper, and intramural sports. Santa Fe is a sophisticated, multicultural, historic, and artistic community, offering great coffee shops, bookstores, cinema, and performing arts. At 7,000 feet, the campus is nestled in the Rocky Mountains, where the air is fresh and clear, and the sun always shines.

Academic Highlights Reading and discussing the Great Books—seminal works in philosophy, literature, political theory, history, mathematics, science, economics, theology, music—from Homer to Freud, Euclid to Einstein—studying in a curriculum common to all, creates a cohesive intellectual community. Small seminar-style classes generate an active, conversational mode of learning, requiring students to make sense of important ideas for themselves. The atmosphere is cooperative and intellectual, and the workload is demanding. Student progress is monitored through oral evaluations and largely based on daily participation in class as well as written papers. There are no midterm or final examinations.

Interviews and Campus Visits The application process is partially self-selective, and the interview and campus visit are ways to demonstrate knowledge of and interest in the Great Books Program. Both are strongly encouraged due to the College's uncommon program and methods of learning. Interviews are normally conducted on campus and are offered to interested juniors and seniors throughout the year. The campus visits are comprehensive, lasting 24 hours, and incorporate observing several classes, conversing informally with faculty members and students, sleeping in student housing, eating in the dining hall, and interviewing with both a member of the faculty and an admissions

St. John's College (continued)
counselor. For more information, prospective students should call the Office of Admission at 800-331-5232 (toll-free) or 505-984-6060, e-mail at admissions@sjcsf.edu, or visit http://www.stjohnscollege.edu. The nearest commercial airport is Albuquerque International Sunport.

For Further Information Write to Mr. Larry Clendenin, Director of Admissions, St. John's College, 1160 Camino Cruz Blanca, Santa Fe, NM 87505. *E-mail:* admissions@sjcsf.edu. *Web site:* http://www.stjohnscollege.edu.

See page 188 for the College Close-Up.

UNIVERSITY OF NEW MEXICO
Albuquerque, New Mexico

University of New Mexico is a coed, public university, founded in 1889, offering degrees at the associate, bachelor's, master's, doctoral, and first professional levels and post-master's certificates. It has an 875-acre campus in Albuquerque near Albuquerque.

Academic Information The faculty has 1,411 members (63% full-time), 70% with terminal degrees. The undergraduate student-faculty ratio is 19:1. The library holds 3 million titles and 592,243 serial subscriptions. Special programs include academic remediation, services for learning-disabled students, an honors program, cooperative (work-study) education, study abroad, advanced placement credit, accelerated degree programs, ESL programs, double majors, independent study, distance learning, self-designed majors, summer session for credit, part-time degree programs (daytime, evenings, weekends, summer), adult/continuing education programs, internships, and arrangement for off-campus study with National Student Exchange, Western Undergraduate Exchange, Western Interstate Commission for Higher Education, International Student Exchange. The most frequently chosen baccalaureate fields are business/marketing, education, health professions and related sciences.
Student Body Statistics The student body totals 26,172, of whom 18,725 are undergraduates (3,091 freshmen). 58 percent are women and 42 percent are men. Students come from 52 states and territories and 67 other countries. 89 percent are from New Mexico. 0.7 percent are international students.
Expenses for 2006–07 *Application fee:* $20. *State resident tuition:* $4,336 full-time, $180.65 per credit hour part-time. *Nonresident tuition:* $14,177 full-time. Part-time tuition varies according to course load. *College room and board:* $6680. *College room only:* $3900. Room and board charges vary according to board plan and housing facility.
Financial Aid Forms of aid include need-based and non-need-based scholarships, athletic grants, and part-time jobs. The priority application deadline for financial aid is March 1.
Freshman Admission University of New Mexico requires a high school transcript, a minimum 2.25 high school GPA, SAT or ACT scores, and TOEFL scores for international students. An essay and recommendations are required for some. The application deadline for regular admission is June 15.
Transfer Admission The application deadline for admission is June 15.
Entrance Difficulty University of New Mexico assesses its entrance difficulty level as moderately difficult. For the fall 2006 freshman class, 73 percent of the applicants were accepted.
For Further Information Contact Ms. Robin Ryan, Associate Director of Admissions, University of New Mexico, Office of Admissions, PO Box 4895, Albuquerque, NM 87196-4895. *Telephone:* 505-277-2446 or 800-CALLUNM (toll-free in-state). *Fax:* 505-277-6686. *E-mail:* apply@unm.edu. *Web site:* http://www.unm.edu/.

UNIVERSITY OF NEW MEXICO–GALLUP
Gallup, New Mexico

University of New Mexico–Gallup is a coed, public, primarily two-year college of New Mexico Commission on Higher Education, founded in 1968, offering degrees at the associate and bachelor's levels. It has an 80-acre campus in Gallup.

Academic Information The faculty has 159 members (47% full-time). The student-faculty ratio is 25:1. The library holds 36,172 titles and 354 serial subscriptions. Special programs include academic remediation, services for learning-disabled students, an honors program, cooperative (work-study) education, advanced placement credit, self-designed majors, summer session for credit, part-time degree programs (daytime, evenings, weekends, summer), adult/continuing education programs, and internships.
Student Body Statistics The student body is made up of 2,858 undergraduates. Students come from 10 states and territories and 4 other countries. 0.2 percent are international students. 10 percent of the 2006 graduating class went on to four-year colleges.
Expenses for 2006–07 *Application fee:* $15. *State resident tuition:* $1344 full-time. *Nonresident tuition:* $3096 full-time.
Financial Aid Forms of aid include need-based scholarships and part-time jobs. The priority application deadline for financial aid is March 1.
Freshman Admission University of New Mexico–Gallup requires TOEFL scores for international students. A high school transcript, SAT scores, and ACT scores are required for some. The application deadline for regular admission is rolling.
Transfer Admission The application deadline for admission is rolling.
Entrance Difficulty University of New Mexico–Gallup has an open admission policy. It assesses its entrance difficulty as minimally difficult for associate of arts programs.
For Further Information Contact Ms. Pearl A. Morris, Admissions Representative, University of New Mexico–Gallup, 200 College Road, Gallup, NM 87301-5603. *Telephone:* 505-863-7500. *Fax:* 505-863-7610. *E-mail:* pmorris@gallup.unm.edu. *Web site:* http://www.gallup.unm.edu/.

UNIVERSITY OF PHOENIX–NEW MEXICO CAMPUS
Albuquerque, New Mexico

University of Phoenix–New Mexico Campus is a coed, proprietary, comprehensive institution, offering degrees at the bachelor's and master's levels.

Academic Information The faculty has 658 members (5% full-time), 23% with terminal degrees. The undergraduate student-faculty ratio is 10:1. The library holds 1,759 titles and 692 serial subscriptions. Special programs include services for learning-disabled students, advanced placement credit, accelerated degree programs, independent study, distance learning, external degree programs, and adult/continuing education programs. The most frequently chosen baccalaureate fields are business/marketing, computer and information sciences, public administration and social services.
Student Body Statistics The student body totals 4,586, of whom 3,537 are undergraduates (150 freshmen). 63 percent are women and 37 percent are men. 11.1 percent are international students.
Expenses for 2006–07 *Application fee:* $45. *Tuition:* $9750 full-time.
Financial Aid Forms of aid include need-based and non-need-based scholarships. The average aided 2005–06 undergraduate received an aid package worth $5497. The application deadline for financial aid is continuous.
Freshman Admission University of Phoenix–New Mexico Campus requires 1 recommendation and TOEFL scores for international students. A high school transcript is required for some. The application deadline for regular admission is rolling.
Transfer Admission The application deadline for admission is rolling.
Entrance Difficulty University of Phoenix–New Mexico Campus has an open admission policy.
For Further Information Contact Ms. Beth Barilla, Associate Vice President, Student Admissions and Services, University of Phoenix–New Mexico Campus, 4615 East Elwood Street, Mail Stop AA-K101, Phoenix, AZ 85040-1958. *Telephone:* 480-317-6000, 800-776-4867 (toll-free in-state), or 800-228-7240 (toll-free out-of-state). *Fax:* 480-894-1758. *E-mail:* beth.barilla@phoenix.edu. *Web site:* http://www.phoenix.edu/.

WESTERN NEW MEXICO UNIVERSITY
Silver City, New Mexico
http://www.wnmu.edu/

Oregon

THE ART INSTITUTE OF PORTLAND
Portland, Oregon

The Art Institute of Portland is a coed, proprietary, four-year college of Education Management Corporation, founded in 1963, offering degrees at the associate and bachelor's levels. It has a 1-acre campus in Portland.

Academic Information The faculty has 104 members (26% full-time), 25% with terminal degrees. The student-faculty ratio is 16:1. The library holds 26,078 titles and 208 serial subscriptions. Special programs include academic remediation, services for learning-disabled students, an honors program, study abroad, advanced placement credit, independent study, distance learning, summer session for credit, part-time degree programs (daytime, evenings, weekends, summer), and internships. The most frequently chosen baccalaureate field is visual and performing arts.
Student Body Statistics The student body is made up of 1,614 undergraduates (221 freshmen). 53 percent are women and 47 percent are men. Students come from 21 states and territories and 14 other countries. 63 percent are from Oregon.
Expenses for 2006–07 *Application fee:* $50. *Comprehensive fee:* $26,880 includes full-time tuition ($18,630) and college room and board ($8250). *College room only:* $5550. *Part-time tuition:* $414 per credit hour.
Financial Aid Forms of aid include need-based and non-need-based scholarships and part-time jobs. The average aided 2006–07 undergraduate received an aid package worth an estimated $8002.
Freshman Admission The Art Institute of Portland requires an essay, a high school transcript, an interview, and TOEFL scores for international students. Recommendations are recommended. Placement exam is required for some. The application deadline for regular admission is rolling.
Transfer Admission The application deadline for admission is rolling.
Entrance Difficulty The Art Institute of Portland assesses its entrance difficulty level as minimally difficult. For the fall 2006 freshman class, 59 percent of the applicants were accepted.
For Further Information Contact Kelly Alston, Director of Admissions, The Art Institute of Portland, 1122 NW Davis Street, Portland, OR 97209-2911. *Telephone:* 503-228-6528 or 888-228-6528 (toll-free). *Fax:* 503-227-1945. *E-mail:* aipdadm@aii.edu. *Web site:* http://www.aipd.artinstitutes.edu/.

BASSIST COLLEGE
See The Art Institute of Portland.

BIRTHINGWAY COLLEGE OF MIDWIFERY
Portland, Oregon
http://www.birthingway.edu/

CASCADE COLLEGE
Portland, Oregon

Cascade College is a coed, private, four-year college, founded in 1994, affiliated with the Church of Christ, offering degrees at the bachelor's level. It has a 13-acre campus in Portland.

Academic Information The faculty has 35 members (40% full-time), 37% with terminal degrees. The student-faculty ratio is 14:1. The library holds 30,232 titles and 86 serial subscriptions. Special programs include academic remediation, services for learning-disabled students, study abroad, advanced placement credit, accelerated degree programs, double majors, independent study, summer session for credit, internships, and arrangement for off-campus study with Mt. Hood Community College. The most frequently chosen baccalaureate fields are education, business/marketing, interdisciplinary studies.
Student Body Statistics The student body is made up of 295 undergraduates (68 freshmen). 55 percent are women and 45 percent are men. Students come from 23 states and territories and 6 other countries. 36 percent are from Oregon. 3.4 percent are international students. 8 percent of the 2006 graduating class went on to graduate and professional schools.
Expenses for 2006–07 *Application fee:* $25. *Comprehensive fee:* $18,920 includes full-time tuition ($12,200), mandatory fees ($600), and college room and board ($6120). Full-time tuition and fees vary according to course load. *Part-time tuition:* $510 per semester hour. Part-time tuition varies according to course load.
Financial Aid Forms of aid include need-based and non-need-based scholarships, athletic grants, and part-time jobs. The average aided 2005–06 undergraduate received an aid package worth $11,825. The application deadline for financial aid is August 15 with a priority deadline of May 15.
Freshman Admission Cascade College requires a high school transcript, recommendations, and TOEFL scores for international students. The application deadline for regular admission is rolling.
Transfer Admission The application deadline for admission is rolling.
Entrance Difficulty Cascade College has an open admission policy.
For Further Information Contact Ms. Rebecca Lewis, Student Life Office, Cascade College, 9101 East Burnside, Portland, OR 97216-1515. *Telephone:* 503-257-1202 or 800-550-7678 (toll-free). *Fax:* 503-257-1222. *E-mail:* rlewis@cascade.edu. *Web site:* http://www.cascade.edu/.

CONCORDIA UNIVERSITY
Portland, Oregon

Concordia University is a coed, private, comprehensive unit of Concordia University System, founded in 1905, affiliated with the Lutheran Church–Missouri Synod, offering degrees at the associate, bachelor's, and master's levels and postbachelor's certificates. It has a 13-acre campus in Portland.

Academic Information The faculty has 114 members (39% full-time), 39% with terminal degrees. The undergraduate student-faculty ratio is 20:1. The library holds 74,326 titles, 22,150 serial subscriptions, and 2,430 audiovisual materials. Special programs include academic remediation, study abroad, advanced placement credit, accelerated degree programs, ESL programs, double majors, self-designed majors, summer session for credit, part-time degree programs (evenings, weekends, summer), adult/continuing education programs, internships, and arrangement for off-campus study with Oregon Independent Colleges Association, Concordia University System. The most frequently chosen baccalaureate fields are business/marketing, education, psychology.
Student Body Statistics The student body totals 1,598, of whom 1,083 are undergraduates (183 freshmen). 65 percent are women and 35 percent are men. Students come from 26 states and territories and 12 other countries. 42 percent are from Oregon. 1.1 percent are international students.
Expenses for 2007–08 *Application fee:* $20. *Comprehensive fee:* $27,360 includes full-time tuition ($20,900), mandatory fees ($190), and college room and board ($6270). *College room only:* $2980. *Part-time tuition:* $650 per credit.
Financial Aid Forms of aid include need-based and non-need-based scholarships, athletic grants, and part-time jobs. The application deadline for financial aid is continuous.
Freshman Admission Concordia University requires an essay, a high school transcript, a minimum 2.5 high school GPA, 1 recommendation, SAT or ACT scores, and TOEFL scores for international students. An interview is recommended. An interview is required for some. The application deadline for regular admission is rolling.

Concordia University (continued)

Transfer Admission The application deadline for admission is rolling.
Entrance Difficulty Concordia University assesses its entrance difficulty level as moderately difficult; minimally difficult for transfers. For the fall 2006 freshman class, 64 percent of the applicants were accepted.
For Further Information Contact Ms. Bobi Swan, Dean of Admission, Concordia University, 2811 Northeast Holman, Portland, OR 97211-6099. *Telephone:* 503-493-6526 or 800-321-9371 (toll-free). *Fax:* 503-280-8531. *E-mail:* admissions@portland.edu. *Web site:* http://www.cu-portland.edu/.

CORBAN COLLEGE
Salem, Oregon

Corban College is a coed, private, four-year college, founded in 1935, offering degrees at the associate, bachelor's, and master's levels. It has a 107-acre campus in Salem near Portland.

Academic Information The faculty has 104 members (35% full-time), 25% with terminal degrees. The undergraduate student-faculty ratio is 13:1. The library holds 98,700 titles, 600 serial subscriptions, and 5,000 audiovisual materials. Special programs include services for learning-disabled students, an honors program, study abroad, advanced placement credit, accelerated degree programs, Freshman Honors College, double majors, independent study, distance learning, self-designed majors, summer session for credit, adult/continuing education programs, internships, and arrangement for off-campus study with Oregon Independent Colleges Association, Council of Christian Colleges and Universities. The most frequently chosen baccalaureate fields are business/marketing, education, family and consumer sciences.
Student Body Statistics The student body totals 900, of whom 847 are undergraduates (188 freshmen). 60 percent are women and 40 percent are men. Students come from 28 states and territories and 2 other countries. 68 percent are from Oregon. 0.2 percent are international students.
Expenses for 2006–07 *Application fee:* $40. *Comprehensive fee:* $26,364 includes full-time tuition ($19,084), mandatory fees ($210), and college room and board ($7070). Room and board charges vary according to board plan. *Part-time tuition:* $795 per credit. Part-time tuition varies according to course load.
Financial Aid Forms of aid include need-based and non-need-based scholarships, athletic grants, and part-time jobs. The average aided 2005–06 undergraduate received an aid package worth $12,148. The priority application deadline for financial aid is February 15.
Freshman Admission Corban College requires an essay, a high school transcript, a minimum 2.5 high school GPA, 3 recommendations, SAT or ACT scores, and TOEFL scores for international students. The application deadline for regular admission is August 1.
Transfer Admission The application deadline for admission is August 1.
Entrance Difficulty Corban College assesses its entrance difficulty level as moderately difficult. For the fall 2006 freshman class, 79 percent of the applicants were accepted.
For Further Information Contact Ms. Heidi Stowman, Director of Admissions, Corban College, 5000 Deer Park Drive, SE, Salem, OR 97301-9392. *Telephone:* 503-375-7115 or 800-845-3005 (toll-free out-of-state). *Fax:* 503-585-4316. *E-mail:* admissions@corban.edu. *Web site:* http://www.corban.edu/.

DeVRY UNIVERSITY
Portland, Oregon

DeVry University is a coed, proprietary, comprehensive unit of DeVry University, offering degrees at the bachelor's and master's levels and postbachelor's certificates.

Academic Information The faculty has 4 members. The undergraduate student-faculty ratio is 46:1. Special programs include academic remediation, services for learning-disabled students, advanced placement credit, accelerated degree programs, distance learning, summer session for credit, part-time degree programs (daytime, evenings, weekends, summer), and adult/continuing education programs. The most frequently chosen baccalaureate field is business/marketing.

Student Body Statistics The student body totals 105, of whom 63 are undergraduates (10 freshmen). 25 percent are women and 75 percent are men. 73 percent are from Oregon.
Expenses for 2007–08 *Application fee:* $50. *Tuition:* $12,900 full-time, $490 per credit part-time. *Mandatory fees:* $120 full-time.
Freshman Admission DeVry University requires a high school transcript and an interview. The application deadline for regular admission is rolling.
Transfer Admission The application deadline for admission is rolling.
Entrance Difficulty DeVry University assesses its entrance difficulty level as minimally difficult.
For Further Information Contact Admissions Office, DeVry University, 9755 SW Barnes Road, Suite 150, Portland, OR 97225-6651. *Telephone:* 503-296-7468. *Web site:* http://www.devry.edu/.

EASTERN OREGON UNIVERSITY
La Grande, Oregon

Eastern Oregon University is a coed, public, comprehensive unit of Oregon University System, founded in 1929, offering degrees at the bachelor's and master's levels. It has a 121-acre campus in La Grande.

Academic Information The faculty has 117 members (87% full-time), 56% with terminal degrees. The undergraduate student-faculty ratio is 23:1. The library holds 329,942 titles and 998 serial subscriptions. Special programs include services for learning-disabled students, an honors program, cooperative (work-study) education, study abroad, advanced placement credit, ESL programs, double majors, independent study, distance learning, self-designed majors, summer session for credit, part-time degree programs, external degree programs, adult/continuing education programs, internships, and arrangement for off-campus study with National Student Exchange.
Student Body Statistics The student body totals 3,425, of whom 3,038 are undergraduates (359 freshmen). 61 percent are women and 39 percent are men. Students come from 43 states and territories and 31 other countries. 69 percent are from Oregon. 2.6 percent are international students.
Expenses for 2006–07 *Application fee:* $50. *State resident tuition:* $4500 full-time, $100 per credit hour part-time. *Nonresident tuition:* $4500 full-time. *Mandatory fees:* $1329 full-time. Full-time tuition and fees vary according to course load. Part-time tuition varies according to course load. *College room and board:* $7776. Room and board charges vary according to board plan and housing facility.
Financial Aid Forms of aid include need-based and non-need-based scholarships, athletic grants, and part-time jobs. The application deadline for financial aid is continuous.
Freshman Admission Eastern Oregon University requires a high school transcript, a minimum 3.0 high school GPA, SAT or ACT scores, and TOEFL scores for international students. An essay and 2 recommendations are required for some. The application deadline for regular admission is September 1 and for early action it is December 1.
Entrance Difficulty Eastern Oregon University assesses its entrance difficulty level as moderately difficult; minimally difficult for transfers. For the fall 2006 freshman class, 43 percent of the applicants were accepted.
For Further Information Contact Mr. Jaime Contreras, Director, Admissions, Eastern Oregon University, 1 University Boulevard, La Grande, OR 97850-2899. *Telephone:* 541-962-3393, 800-452-8639 (toll-free in-state), or 800-452-3393 (toll-free out-of-state). *Fax:* 541-962-3418. *E-mail:* admissions@eou.edu. *Web site:* http://www.eou.edu/.

EUGENE BIBLE COLLEGE
Eugene, Oregon

Eugene Bible College is a coed, private, four-year college, founded in 1925, affiliated with the Open Bible Standard Churches, offering degrees at the bachelor's level. It has a 40-acre campus in Eugene.

Academic Information The faculty has 24 members (58% full-time), 29% with terminal degrees. The student-faculty ratio is 10:1. The library holds 35,000 titles and 251 serial subscriptions. Special programs include

academic remediation, cooperative (work-study) education, advanced placement credit, double majors, independent study, distance learning, summer session for credit, part-time degree programs (daytime), and internships. The most frequently chosen baccalaureate field is theology and religious vocations.

Student Body Statistics The student body is made up of 222 undergraduates (61 freshmen). 44 percent are women and 56 percent are men. Students come from 16 states and territories and 2 other countries. 55 percent are from Oregon. 0.9 percent are international students. 20 percent of the 2006 graduating class went on to graduate and professional schools.

Expenses for 2006–07 *Application fee:* $30. *Comprehensive fee:* $13,525 includes full-time tuition ($7800), mandatory fees ($920), and college room and board ($4805).

Financial Aid Forms of aid include need-based and non-need-based scholarships, athletic grants, and part-time jobs. The average aided 2006–07 undergraduate received an aid package worth an estimated $8900. The application deadline for financial aid is September 1 with a priority deadline of March 1.

Freshman Admission Eugene Bible College requires an essay, a high school transcript, a minimum 2.0 high school GPA, 2 recommendations, SAT or ACT scores, and TOEFL scores for international students. The application deadline for regular admission is September 1.

Transfer Admission The application deadline for admission is September 1.

Entrance Difficulty Eugene Bible College assesses its entrance difficulty level as minimally difficult. For the fall 2006 freshman class, 46 percent of the applicants were accepted.

For Further Information Contact Mr. Trent Combs, Director of Admissions, Eugene Bible College, 2155 Bailey Hill Road, Eugene, OR 97405. *Telephone:* 541-485-1780 Ext. 3115 or 800-322-2638 (toll-free). *Fax:* 541-343-5801. *E-mail:* admissions@ebc.edu. *Web site:* http://www.ebc.edu/.

GEORGE FOX UNIVERSITY

Newberg, Oregon

SPONSOR
See Front Insert
for Details!

George Fox University is a coed, private, Friends university, founded in 1891, offering degrees at the bachelor's, master's, doctoral, and first professional levels and postbachelor's certificates. It has an 85-acre campus in Newberg near Portland.

Academic Information The faculty has 324 members (49% full-time), 47% with terminal degrees. The undergraduate student-faculty ratio is 12:1. The library holds 208,048 titles, 3,900 serial subscriptions, and 6,335 audiovisual materials. Special programs include academic remediation, services for learning-disabled students, an honors program, study abroad, advanced placement credit, accelerated degree programs, ESL programs, double majors, independent study, self-designed majors, summer session for credit, part-time degree programs (evenings, weekends), adult/continuing education programs, internships, and arrangement for off-campus study with members of the Christian College Consortium, Coalition for Christian Colleges and Universities, Oregon Independent Colleges Association. The most frequently chosen baccalaureate fields are business/marketing, history, interdisciplinary studies.

Student Body Statistics The student body totals 3,252, of whom 1,864 are undergraduates (416 freshmen). 61 percent are women and 39 percent are men. Students come from 25 states and territories and 13 other countries. 68 percent are from Oregon. 1.7 percent are international students. 24 percent of the 2006 graduating class went on to graduate and professional schools.

Expenses for 2007–08 *Application fee:* $40. *Comprehensive fee:* $31,390 includes full-time tuition ($23,470), mandatory fees ($320), and college room and board ($7600). *College room only:* $4280. *Part-time tuition:* $730 per hour.

Financial Aid Forms of aid include need-based and non-need-based scholarships and part-time jobs. The average aided 2006–07 undergraduate received an aid package worth an estimated $16,709.

Freshman Admission George Fox University requires an essay, a high school transcript, 2 recommendations, and SAT or ACT scores. An interview and TOEFL scores for international students are recommended.

An interview is required for some. The application deadline for regular admission is February 1 and for early action it is December 1.

Transfer Admission The application deadline for admission is June 1.

Entrance Difficulty George Fox University assesses its entrance difficulty level as moderately difficult. For the fall 2006 freshman class, 86 percent of the applicants were accepted.

SPECIAL MESSAGE TO STUDENTS

Social Life Student organizations at George Fox provide opportunities for the development of leadership qualities and interpersonal relationships. They are designed to supplement classroom work with practical experience and to provide wholesome and profitable recreation. Many activities are available, including campus government, NCAA Division III athletics, intramurals, music, drama, publications, social and religious organizations, and various special-interest groups.

Academic Highlights In order to enrich the intercultural and international awareness of the campus community, George Fox University offers the Juniors Abroad program, a transportation-subsidized overseas course of approximately three weeks, to qualified juniors. To enhance the learning and research of students, the University developed Computers Across the Curriculum, which provides every freshman with a computer that is his or hers to keep after graduation.

Interviews and Campus Visits Students interested in enrolling at George Fox are encouraged to visit the campus, preferably while classes are in session. A visit provides an opportunity to observe classes, see the campus facilities, and talk with current students and professors. Visits should be arranged five days in advance through the admissions office. Bounded on three sides by a residential area, the George Fox campus borders Hess Creek, a natural setting with tall trees, ferns, and wildflowers. The spacious 85-acre, century-old campus features a large grass academic quadrangle and a mix of modern and historic buildings. For information about appointments and campus visits, prospective students should call the Office of Undergraduate Admissions at 800-765-4369 (toll-free), Monday through Friday, 8 to 5. The office is located in the Edward F. Stevens Center. The nearest commercial airport is Portland International.

For Further Information Write to the Office of Undergraduate Admissions, George Fox University, 414 North Meridian, Newberg, OR 97132-2697.

See page 170 for the College Close-Up.

GUTENBERG COLLEGE

Eugene, Oregon

Gutenberg College is a coed, private, four-year college, offering degrees at the bachelor's level.

Academic Information The faculty has 10 members (70% full-time), 50% with terminal degrees. The student-faculty ratio is 6:1.

Student Body Statistics The student body is made up of 48 undergraduates (20 freshmen). 54 percent are women and 46 percent are men. Students come from 12 states and territories and 2 other countries. 46 percent are from Oregon. 4.2 percent are international students.

Expenses for 2007–08 *Application fee:* $20. *Comprehensive fee:* $15,673 includes full-time tuition ($10,568), mandatory fees ($650), and college room and board ($4455). *Part-time tuition:* $350 per quarter hour.

Freshman Admission Gutenberg College requires an essay, a high school transcript, 2 recommendations, an interview, and SAT scores. The application deadline for regular admission is April 1.

Transfer Admission Gutenberg College requires standardized test scores and a college transcript.

Gutenberg College (continued)

Entrance Difficulty Gutenberg College has an open admission policy.
For Further Information Contact Mr. Terry Stollar, Director of Admissions and Development, Gutenberg College, 1883 University Street, Eugene, OR 97403. *Telephone:* 541-736-9071. *Fax:* 541-683-6997. *E-mail:* tstollar@gutenberg.edu. *Web site:* http://www.gutenberg.edu/.

HEALD COLLEGE-PORTLAND

Portland, Oregon

Heald College-Portland is a coed, private, two-year college, founded in 1863, offering degrees at the associate level.

Expenses for 2006–07 *Application fee:* $40. *Tuition:* $10,275 full-time.
For Further Information Contact Director of Admissions, Heald College-Portland, 625 Southwest Broadway, 4th Floor, Portland, OR 97205. *Telephone:* 503-229-0492 or 800-755-3550 (toll-free in-state). *Fax:* 503-229-0498. *E-mail:* info@heald.edu. *Web site:* http://www.heald.edu/.

ITT TECHNICAL INSTITUTE

Portland, Oregon

ITT Technical Institute is a coed, proprietary, primarily two-year college of ITT Educational Services, Inc, founded in 1971, offering degrees at the associate and bachelor's levels. It has a 4-acre campus in Portland.

Expenses for 2006–07 *Application fee:* $100. Contact school for program costs.
Financial Aid Forms of aid include need-based scholarships and part-time jobs. The application deadline for financial aid is continuous.
Freshman Admission ITT Technical Institute requires a high school transcript, an interview, TOEFL scores for international students, and Wonderlic aptitude test. Recommendations are recommended. The application deadline for regular admission is rolling.
Transfer Admission The application deadline for admission is rolling.
Entrance Difficulty ITT Technical Institute assesses its entrance difficulty level as minimally difficult.
For Further Information Contact Mr. Greg Lester, Director of Recruitment, ITT Technical Institute, 6035 Northeast 78th Court, Portland, OR 97218. *Telephone:* 503-255-6500 or 800-234-5488 (toll-free). *Fax:* 503-255-8381. *Web site:* http://www.itt-tech.edu/.

LEWIS & CLARK COLLEGE

Portland, Oregon

Lewis & Clark College is a coed, private, comprehensive institution, founded in 1867, offering degrees at the bachelor's, master's, doctoral, and first professional levels and post-master's certificates. It has a 137-acre campus in Portland.

Academic Information The faculty has 376 members (57% full-time), 69% with terminal degrees. The undergraduate student-faculty ratio is 13:1. The library holds 227,609 titles, 7,477 serial subscriptions, and 11,586 audiovisual materials. Special programs include services for learning-disabled students, an honors program, study abroad, advanced placement credit, accelerated degree programs, ESL programs, double majors, independent study, self-designed majors, summer session for credit, part-time degree programs (daytime, summer), internships, and arrangement for off-campus study with Oregon Independent Colleges Association. The most frequently chosen baccalaureate fields are psychology, biological/life sciences, social sciences.
Student Body Statistics The student body totals 3,641, of whom 1,985 are undergraduates (509 freshmen). 61 percent are women and 39 percent are men. Students come from 49 states and territories and 44 other countries. 23 percent are from Oregon. 4 percent are international students. 19 percent of the 2006 graduating class went on to graduate and professional schools.

Expenses for 2006–07 *Application fee:* $50. *One-time mandatory fee:* $3876. *Comprehensive fee:* $37,820 includes full-time tuition ($29,556), mandatory fees ($216), and college room and board ($8048). *College room only:* $4172. *Part-time tuition:* $1489 per credit hour.
Financial Aid Forms of aid include need-based and non-need-based scholarships and part-time jobs. The average aided 2006–07 undergraduate received an aid package worth an estimated $25,018. The priority application deadline for financial aid is March 1.
Freshman Admission Lewis & Clark College requires an essay, a high school transcript, a minimum 2.0 high school GPA, 2 recommendations, TOEFL scores for international students, and SAT, ACT, or academic portfolio. A minimum 3.0 high school GPA and an interview are recommended. 4 recommendations, portfolio applicants must submit samples of graded work, and SAT or ACT scores are required for some. The application deadline for regular admission is February 1 and for early action it is November 15.
Transfer Admission The application deadline for admission is July 1.
Entrance Difficulty Lewis & Clark College assesses its entrance difficulty level as very difficult. For the fall 2006 freshman class, 58 percent of the applicants were accepted.
For Further Information Contact Mr. Michael Sexton, Dean of Admissions, Lewis & Clark College, 0615 SW Palatine Hill Road, Portland, OR 97219-7899. *Telephone:* 503-768-7040 or 800-444-4111 (toll-free). *Fax:* 503-768-7055. *E-mail:* admissions@lclark.edu. *Web site:* http://www.lclark.edu/.

See page 174 for the College Close-Up.

LINFIELD COLLEGE

McMinnville, Oregon

SPONSOR
See Front Insert
for Details!

Linfield College is a coed, private, American Baptist Churches in the USA, four-year college, founded in 1849, offering degrees at the bachelor's level. It has a 193-acre campus in McMinnville near Portland.

Academic Information The faculty has 181 members (57% full-time), 67% with terminal degrees. The student-faculty ratio is 13:1. The library holds 179,098 titles, 1,268 serial subscriptions, and 33,203 audiovisual materials. Special programs include services for learning-disabled students, study abroad, advanced placement credit, ESL programs, double majors, independent study, distance learning, self-designed majors, summer session for credit, part-time degree programs (daytime, evenings, summer), external degree programs, adult/continuing education programs, internships, and arrangement for off-campus study with American Baptist Colleges and Universities. The most frequently chosen baccalaureate fields are business/marketing, education, social sciences.
Student Body Statistics The student body is made up of 1,754 undergraduates (449 freshmen). 54 percent are women and 46 percent are men. Students come from 26 states and territories and 21 other countries. 57 percent are from Oregon. 2.4 percent are international students. 20 percent of the 2006 graduating class went on to graduate and professional schools.
Expenses for 2006–07 *Application fee:* $40. *Comprehensive fee:* $31,254 includes full-time tuition ($23,930), mandatory fees ($244), and college room and board ($7080). *College room only:* $3760. Room and board charges vary according to board plan and housing facility. *Part-time tuition:* $745 per credit. *Part-time mandatory fees:* $72 per term. Part-time tuition and fees vary according to course load.
Financial Aid Forms of aid include need-based and non-need-based scholarships and part-time jobs. The average aided 2006–07 undergraduate received an aid package worth an estimated $18,300. The priority application deadline for financial aid is February 1.
Freshman Admission Linfield College requires an essay, a high school transcript, 1 recommendation, SAT or ACT scores, and TOEFL scores for international students. An interview is recommended. The application deadline for regular admission is February 15 and for early action it is November 15.
Transfer Admission The application deadline for admission is April 15.
Entrance Difficulty Linfield College assesses its entrance difficulty level as moderately difficult. For the fall 2006 freshman class, 73 percent of the applicants were accepted.

SPECIAL MESSAGE TO STUDENTS

Social Life As a residential college, Linfield emphasizes on-campus activities. Linfield's student government sponsors programs and entertainment each weekend, charters almost forty student-interest clubs, publishes a weekly newspaper, operates an FCC-licensed radio station, and coordinates a popular intramural agenda. With the College located near Portland and the coast, students have off-campus options as well.

Academic Highlights Linfield has made a commitment to provide students with an international experience while enrolled. The environment for students encourages exploration and unity in an increasingly global society. The College offers semester options in Austria, China, Costa Rica, England, France, Galapagos, Ireland, Japan, Korea, Mexico, and Norway. In addition, there are numerous travel-study programs available during January term. The student-faculty ratio is 12:1. The professors are accessible, provide help outside the classroom, and challenge students to excel and grow. Research and internships are generated through professors and advisers as well as through the career and counseling center. Linfield's new 56,000-square-foot library combines traditional print collections and wireless electronic technology to provide access to the Web and Web-based databases. Other new facilities on campus include a new theater, fine arts center, and music center.

Interviews and Campus Visits Students are encouraged to visit the campus during the academic year. Overnight stays, appointments to meet with faculty members and coaches, and visits to classes can be arranged in advance. Students guide tours twice a day, Monday through Saturday. Lunch is provided for students. Student-guided tours are available during the summer, but meals and housing are not provided then. For information about appointments and campus visits, students should go online to http://www.linfield.edu/ or stop by or call the Office of Admission at 800-640-2287, Monday through Friday, 7:30 to 5:30. The office is located in the Michelbook House on campus. The nearest commercial airport is Portland International; the nearest highway is Highway 99W.

For Further Information Write to the Office of Admission, Linfield College, 900 South Baker Street, McMinnville, OR 97128. *E-mail:* admission@linfield.edu. *Web site:* http://www.linfield.edu.

See page 176 for the College Close-Up.

MARYLHURST UNIVERSITY

Marylhurst, Oregon

Marylhurst University is a coed, private, Roman Catholic, comprehensive institution, founded in 1893, offering degrees at the bachelor's and master's levels and postbachelor's certificates. It has a 73-acre campus in Marylhurst near Portland.

Academic Information The faculty has 228 members (18% full-time). Special programs include services for learning-disabled students, study abroad, advanced placement credit, accelerated degree programs, ESL programs, double majors, independent study, distance learning, self-designed majors, summer session for credit, part-time degree programs (daytime, evenings, weekends, summer), adult/continuing education programs, internships, and arrangement for off-campus study with members of the Oregon Independent Colleges Association. The most frequently chosen baccalaureate fields are business/marketing, communications/journalism, visual and performing arts.
Student Body Statistics The student body totals 1,249, of whom 855 are undergraduates (13 freshmen). 73 percent are women and 27 percent are men. 88 percent are from Oregon. 1.4 percent are international students.
Expenses for 2006–07 *Application fee:* $20. *Tuition:* $13,860 full-time, $323 per credit part-time. *Mandatory fees:* $360 full-time, $8 per credit

part-time. Both full-time and part-time tuition and fees vary according to course load, degree level, and program.
Financial Aid Forms of aid include need-based scholarships and part-time jobs. The application deadline for financial aid is continuous.
Freshman Admission Marylhurst University requires a high school transcript, recommendations, and an interview. A minimum 2.0 high school GPA and TOEFL scores for international students are recommended.
Transfer Admission The application deadline for admission is rolling.
Entrance Difficulty Marylhurst University has an open admission policy except for some programs.
For Further Information Contact Admissions, Marylhurst University, 17600 Pacific Highway (Highway 43), PO Box 261, Marylhurst, OR 97036. *Telephone:* 503-636-8141 or 800-634-9982 (toll-free). *Fax:* 503-635-6585. *E-mail:* admissions@marylhurst.edu. *Web site:* http://www.marylhurst.edu/.

MOUNT ANGEL SEMINARY

Saint Benedict, Oregon

http://www.mtangel.edu/Seminary/Seminary.htm

MULTNOMAH BIBLE COLLEGE AND BIBLICAL SEMINARY

Portland, Oregon

Multnomah Bible College and Biblical Seminary is a coed, private, interdenominational, comprehensive institution, founded in 1936, offering degrees at the bachelor's, master's, and first professional levels and postbachelor's certificates. It has a 22-acre campus in Portland.

Academic Information The faculty has 62 members (50% full-time), 44% with terminal degrees. The undergraduate student-faculty ratio is 19:1. The library holds 108,297 titles, 378 serial subscriptions, and 1,662 audiovisual materials. Special programs include academic remediation, services for learning-disabled students, advanced placement credit, double majors, summer session for credit, part-time degree programs (daytime, summer), adult/continuing education programs, and internships. The most frequently chosen baccalaureate field is theology and religious vocations.
Student Body Statistics The student body totals 827, of whom 593 are undergraduates (75 freshmen). 45 percent are women and 55 percent are men. Students come from 28 states and territories and 4 other countries. 45 percent are from Oregon. 0.7 percent are international students.
Expenses for 2006–07 *Application fee:* $40. *Comprehensive fee:* $17,790 includes full-time tuition ($12,450) and college room and board ($5340). Full-time tuition varies according to course load. Room and board charges vary according to board plan and housing facility. *Part-time tuition:* $515 per semester hour. Part-time tuition varies according to course load.
Financial Aid Forms of aid include need-based and non-need-based scholarships and part-time jobs. The priority application deadline for financial aid is March 1.
Freshman Admission Multnomah Bible College and Biblical Seminary requires an essay, a high school transcript, a minimum 2.5 high school GPA, 4 recommendations, SAT or ACT scores, and TOEFL scores for international students. The application deadline for regular admission is July 15.
Transfer Admission The application deadline for admission is July 15.
Entrance Difficulty Multnomah Bible College and Biblical Seminary assesses its entrance difficulty level as moderately difficult. For the fall 2006 freshman class, 87 percent of the applicants were accepted.
For Further Information Contact Ms. Nancy Gerecz, Admissions Assistant, Multnomah Bible College and Biblical Seminary, 8435 Northeast Glisan Street, Portland, OR 97220-5898. *Telephone:* 503-255-0332 Ext. 373 or 800-275-4672 (toll-free). *Fax:* 503-254-1268. *E-mail:* admiss@multnomah.edu. *Web site:* http://www.multnomah.edu/.

See page 178 for the College Close-Up.

NORTHWEST CHRISTIAN COLLEGE
Eugene, Oregon

Northwest Christian College is a coed, private, Christian, comprehensive institution, founded in 1895, offering degrees at the associate, bachelor's, and master's levels and postbachelor's certificates. It has an 8-acre campus in Eugene near Portland.

Academic Information The faculty has 80 members (26% full-time), 26% with terminal degrees. The undergraduate student-faculty ratio is 9:1. The library holds 60,250 titles and 261 serial subscriptions. Special programs include academic remediation, services for learning-disabled students, cooperative (work-study) education, study abroad, advanced placement credit, accelerated degree programs, ESL programs, double majors, independent study, distance learning, self-designed majors, summer session for credit, part-time degree programs (daytime, evenings), adult/continuing education programs, internships, and arrangement for off-campus study with University of Oregon, Lane Community College. The most frequently chosen baccalaureate fields are business/marketing, education, psychology.

Student Body Statistics The student body totals 480, of whom 387 are undergraduates (66 freshmen). 62 percent are women and 38 percent are men. Students come from 13 states and territories. 90 percent are from Oregon.

Expenses for 2006–07 *Application fee:* $0. *Comprehensive fee:* $26,314 includes full-time tuition ($19,890) and college room and board ($6424). *College room only:* $2800. Full-time tuition varies according to course load and program. Room and board charges vary according to board plan and housing facility. *Part-time tuition:* $663 per credit. Part-time tuition varies according to course load and program.

Financial Aid Forms of aid include need-based and non-need-based scholarships, athletic grants, and part-time jobs. The average aided 2006–07 undergraduate received an aid package worth an estimated $16,807.

Freshman Admission Northwest Christian College requires an essay, a high school transcript, a minimum 2.5 high school GPA, 2 recommendations, SAT or ACT scores, and TOEFL scores for international students. An interview is recommended. SAT Subject Test scores are required for some. The application deadline for regular admission is rolling.

Transfer Admission The application deadline for admission is rolling.

Entrance Difficulty Northwest Christian College assesses its entrance difficulty level as moderately difficult. For the fall 2006 freshman class, 61 percent of the applicants were accepted.

For Further Information Contact Director of Admissions, Northwest Christian College, 828 East 11th Avenue, Eugene, OR 97401-3745. *Telephone:* 541-684-7201 or 877-463-6622 (toll-free). *Fax:* 541-684-7317. *E-mail:* admissions@nwcc.edu. *Web site:* http://www.nwcc.edu/.

OREGON COLLEGE OF ART & CRAFT
Portland, Oregon

Oregon College of Art & Craft is a coed, private, four-year college, founded in 1907, offering degrees at the bachelor's level and postbachelor's certificates. It has an 11-acre campus in Portland.

Academic Information The faculty has 23 members (43% full-time), 87% with terminal degrees. The student-faculty ratio is 9:1. The library holds 9,000 titles and 90 serial subscriptions. Special programs include advanced placement credit, double majors, independent study, part-time degree programs (daytime, evenings), adult/continuing education programs, internships, and arrangement for off-campus study with AICAD Mobility Program. The most frequently chosen baccalaureate field is visual and performing arts.

Student Body Statistics The student body is made up of 153 undergraduates (8 freshmen). 59 percent are women and 41 percent are men. Students come from 26 states and territories and 2 other countries. 53 percent are from Oregon.

Expenses for 2006–07 *Application fee:* $35. *Tuition:* $16,900 full-time, $2214 per course part-time. *Mandatory fees:* $1000 full-time, $50 per course part-time. *College room only:* $3600.

Financial Aid Forms of aid include need-based and non-need-based scholarships and part-time jobs. The average aided 2005–06 undergraduate received an aid package worth $18,130. The priority application deadline for financial aid is March 1.

Freshman Admission Oregon College of Art & Craft requires an essay, a high school transcript, a minimum 2.5 high school GPA, 2 recommendations, a portfolio, and TOEFL scores for international students. SAT scores and ACT scores are recommended. An interview is required for some. The application deadline for regular admission is rolling.

Transfer Admission The application deadline for admission is rolling.

Entrance Difficulty Oregon College of Art & Craft assesses its entrance difficulty level as minimally difficult. For the fall 2006 freshman class, 82 percent of the applicants were accepted.

For Further Information Contact Ms. Debrah Spencer, Interim Director of Admissions, Oregon College of Art & Craft, 8245 Southwest Barnes Road, Portland, OR 97225-6349. *Telephone:* 503-297-5544 Ext. 129 or 800-390-0632 Ext. 129 (toll-free). *Fax:* 503-297-9651. *E-mail:* admissions@ocac.edu. *Web site:* http://www.ocac.edu/.

OREGON HEALTH & SCIENCE UNIVERSITY
Portland, Oregon

Oregon Health & Science University is a coed, public, upper-level institution, founded in 1974, offering degrees at the bachelor's, master's, doctoral, and first professional levels and post-master's, first professional, and postbachelor's certificates. It has a 116-acre campus in Portland.

Academic Information The faculty has 836 members (60% full-time). The library holds 200,771 titles and 2,110 serial subscriptions. Special programs include advanced placement credit, distance learning, summer session for credit, part-time degree programs (daytime, evenings, summer), and arrangement for off-campus study with other members of the Oregon University System. The most frequently chosen baccalaureate field is health professions and related sciences.

Student Body Statistics The student body totals 2,418, of whom 597 are undergraduates. 85 percent are women and 15 percent are men. Students come from 31 states and territories and 3 other countries. 89 percent are from Oregon. 0.8 percent are international students.

Expenses for 2006–07 *Application fee:* $125. *State resident tuition:* $8880 full-time, $185 per credit part-time. *Nonresident tuition:* $20,688 full-time, $431 per credit part-time. *Mandatory fees:* $2660 full-time, $1644 per year part-time.

Financial Aid Forms of aid include need-based and non-need-based scholarships and part-time jobs. The average aided 2006–07 undergraduate received an aid package worth an estimated $11,238.

Transfer Admission Oregon Health & Science University requires a college transcript. Standardized test scores and a minimum 2.5 college GPA are required for some. The application deadline for admission is February 1.

Entrance Difficulty Oregon Health & Science University assesses its entrance difficulty level as moderately difficult.

For Further Information Contact Jennifer Anderson, Registrar and Director of Financial Aid, Oregon Health & Science University, 3181 Southwest Sam Jackson Park Road, Mail Code: 337A/SNADM, Portland, OR 97201-3098. *Telephone:* 503-494-0647. *Fax:* 503-494-4350. *E-mail:* andersje@ohsu.edu. *Web site:* http://www.ohsu.edu/.

OREGON INSTITUTE OF TECHNOLOGY
Klamath Falls, Oregon

Oregon Institute of Technology is a coed, public, four-year college of Oregon University System, founded in 1947, offering degrees at the associate, bachelor's, and master's levels. It has a 173-acre campus in Klamath Falls.

Academic Information The faculty has 223 members (60% full-time). The undergraduate student-faculty ratio is 14:1. The library holds 90,389 titles and 1,764 serial subscriptions. Special programs include academic

remediation, services for learning-disabled students, cooperative (work-study) education, study abroad, advanced placement credit, double majors, distance learning, summer session for credit, part-time degree programs (daytime, evenings, summer), external degree programs, internships, and arrangement for off-campus study with Portland State University.
Student Body Statistics The student body totals 3,146, of whom 3,134 are undergraduates (296 freshmen). 49 percent are women and 51 percent are men. Students come from 37 states and territories and 13 other countries. 85 percent are from Oregon. 0.9 percent are international students.
Expenses for 2006–07 *Application fee:* $50. *State resident tuition:* $4590 full-time, $102 per credit part-time. *Nonresident tuition:* $14,760 full-time, $102 per credit part-time. *Mandatory fees:* $1329 full-time. *College room and board:* $6480. *College room only:* $3195.
Financial Aid Forms of aid include need-based and non-need-based scholarships, athletic grants, and part-time jobs. The priority application deadline for financial aid is March 1.
Freshman Admission Oregon Institute of Technology requires a high school transcript, a minimum 3.0 high school GPA, SAT or ACT scores, and TOEFL scores for international students. Recommendations are required for some. The application deadline for regular admission is October 1.
Transfer Admission The application deadline for admission is February 1.
Entrance Difficulty Oregon Institute of Technology assesses its entrance difficulty level as moderately difficult. For the fall 2006 freshman class, 88 percent of the applicants were accepted.
For Further Information Contact Mr. Palmer Muntz, Director of Admissions, Oregon Institute of Technology, 3201 Campus Drive, Klamath Falls, OR 97601. *Telephone:* 541-885-1150, 800-422-2017 (toll-free in-state), or 800-343-6653 (toll-free out-of-state). *Fax:* 541-885-1115. *E-mail:* oit@oit.edu. *Web site:* http://www.oit.edu/.

OREGON STATE UNIVERSITY
Corvallis, Oregon

Oregon State University is a coed, public unit of Oregon University System, founded in 1868, offering degrees at the bachelor's, master's, doctoral, and first professional levels and postbachelor's certificates. It has a 422-acre campus in Corvallis near Portland.

Academic Information The faculty has 1,166 members (66% full-time), 65% with terminal degrees. The undergraduate student-faculty ratio is 19:1. The library holds 689,119 titles and 12,254 serial subscriptions. Special programs include academic remediation, services for learning-disabled students, an honors program, cooperative (work-study) education, study abroad, advanced placement credit, accelerated degree programs, Freshman Honors College, ESL programs, double majors, independent study, distance learning, self-designed majors, summer session for credit, part-time degree programs, external degree programs, internships, and arrangement for off-campus study with members of the National Student Exchange, members of the Western Interstate Commission for Higher Education. The most frequently chosen baccalaureate fields are business/marketing, engineering, family and consumer sciences.
Student Body Statistics The student body totals 19,362, of whom 15,829 are undergraduates (2,945 freshmen). 47 percent are women and 53 percent are men. Students come from 50 states and territories and 100 other countries. 86 percent are from Oregon. 1.4 percent are international students.
Expenses for 2006–07 *Application fee:* $50. *State resident tuition:* $4320 full-time, $120 per credit part-time. *Nonresident tuition:* $16,236 full-time, $451 per credit part-time. *Mandatory fees:* $1323 full-time. Part-time tuition varies according to course load. *College room and board:* $7344. Room and board charges vary according to board plan and housing facility.
Financial Aid Forms of aid include need-based and non-need-based scholarships, athletic grants, and part-time jobs. The average aided 2005–06 undergraduate received an aid package worth $9022. The application deadline for financial aid is May 1 with a priority deadline of February 28.
Freshman Admission Oregon State University requires an essay, a high school transcript, a minimum 3.0 high school GPA, SAT or ACT scores,

and TOEFL scores for international students. SAT Subject Test scores are required for some. The application deadline for regular admission is September 1 and for early action it is November 1.
Transfer Admission The application deadline for admission is May 1.
Entrance Difficulty Oregon State University assesses its entrance difficulty level as moderately difficult. For the fall 2006 freshman class, 92 percent of the applicants were accepted.
For Further Information Contact Ms. Michele Sandlin, Director of Admissions, Oregon State University, Corvallis, OR 97331. *Telephone:* 541-737-4411 or 800-291-4192 (toll-free in-state). *E-mail:* osuadmit@orst.edu. *Web site:* http://oregonstate.edu/.

See page 182 for the College Close-Up.

OREGON STATE UNIVERSITY–CASCADES
Bend, Oregon

http://www.osucascades.edu

PACIFIC NORTHWEST COLLEGE OF ART
Portland, Oregon

Pacific Northwest College of Art is a coed, private, four-year college, founded in 1909, offering degrees at the bachelor's level. It has a 2-acre campus in Portland.

Expenses for 2006–07 *Application fee:* $35. *Comprehensive fee:* $24,508 includes full-time tuition ($17,480), mandatory fees ($728), and college room and board ($6300). Full-time tuition and fees vary according to course load. Room and board charges vary according to housing facility. *Part-time tuition:* $728 per semester hour. *Part-time mandatory fees:* $28 per semester hour. Part-time tuition and fees vary according to course load.
For Further Information Contact Ms. Rebecca Haas, Director of Admissions, Pacific Northwest College of Art, 1241 NW Johnson Street, Portland, OR 97209. *Telephone:* 503-821-8972. *Fax:* 503-821-8978. *E-mail:* admissions@pnca.edu. *Web site:* http://www.pnca.edu/.

PACIFIC UNIVERSITY
Forest Grove, Oregon

Pacific University is a coed, private, comprehensive institution, founded in 1849, offering degrees at the bachelor's, master's, doctoral, and first professional levels. It has a 60-acre campus in Forest Grove near Portland.

Academic Information The faculty has 119 members (75% full-time), 66% with terminal degrees. The undergraduate student-faculty ratio is 13:1. The library holds 206,198 titles, 20,908 serial subscriptions, and 8,580 audiovisual materials. Special programs include services for learning-disabled students, cooperative (work-study) education, study abroad, advanced placement credit, ESL programs, double majors, independent study, summer session for credit, internships, and arrangement for off-campus study with United Church of Christ related colleges and universities. The most frequently chosen baccalaureate fields are biological/life sciences, business/marketing, education.
Student Body Statistics The student body totals 2,790, of whom 1,347 are undergraduates (360 freshmen). 61 percent are women and 39 percent are men. Students come from 49 states and territories and 16 other countries. 49 percent are from Oregon. 0.1 percent are international students. 35 percent of the 2006 graduating class went on to graduate and professional schools.
Expenses for 2007–08 *Application fee:* $40. *Comprehensive fee:* $33,840 includes full-time tuition ($25,830), mandatory fees ($840), and college room and board ($7170). *College room only:* $3720. *Part-time tuition:* $1016 per credit hour.
Financial Aid Forms of aid include need-based and non-need-based scholarships and part-time jobs. The average aided 2005–06 undergraduate received an aid package worth $17,492. The priority application deadline for financial aid is February 15.

Pacific University (continued)

Freshman Admission Pacific University requires an essay, a high school transcript, a minimum 3.0 high school GPA, 1 recommendation, SAT or ACT scores, and TOEFL scores for international students. An interview is recommended. The application deadline for regular admission is August 15.

Transfer Admission The application deadline for admission is rolling.

Entrance Difficulty Pacific University assesses its entrance difficulty level as moderately difficult. For the fall 2006 freshman class, 82 percent of the applicants were accepted.

For Further Information Contact Ms. Karen Dunston, Director of Undergraduate Admission, Pacific University, 2043 College Way, Forest Grove, OR 97116-1797. *Telephone:* 503-352-2218 or 877-722-8648 (toll-free). *Fax:* 503-352-2975. *E-mail:* admissions@pacificu.edu. *Web site:* http://www.pacificu.edu/.

PIONEER PACIFIC COLLEGE

Wilsonville, Oregon

Pioneer Pacific College is a coed, proprietary, primarily two-year college, founded in 1981, offering degrees at the associate and bachelor's levels. It is located in Wilsonville near Portland.

Academic Information The faculty has 119 members (41% full-time), 8% with terminal degrees. The student-faculty ratio is 15:1. The library holds 2,500 titles. Special programs include an honors program, accelerated degree programs, and internships.

Student Body Statistics The student body is made up of 986 undergraduates (94 freshmen). 77 percent are women and 23 percent are men. 94 percent are from Oregon.

Expenses for 2007–08 *Application fee:* $50. *Tuition:* $9750 full-time, $228 per credit hour part-time. *Mandatory fees:* $400 full-time.

Financial Aid Forms of aid include need-based scholarships. The application deadline for financial aid is continuous.

Freshman Admission Pioneer Pacific College requires a high school transcript, an interview, TOEFL scores for international students, and CPAt. The application deadline for regular admission is rolling.

Entrance Difficulty Pioneer Pacific College has an open admission policy.

For Further Information Contact Ms. Kristin Lynn, Director of Admissions, Pioneer Pacific College, 27501 Southwest Parkway Avenue, Wilsonville, OR 97070. *Telephone:* 866-772-4636 or 866-PPC-INFO (toll-free in-state). *Fax:* 503-682-1514. *E-mail:* inquiries@pioneerpacific.edu. *Web site:* http://www.pioneerpacific.edu/.

PIONEER PACIFIC COLLEGE-EUGENE/SPRINGFIELD BRANCH

Springfield, Oregon

http://www.pioneerpacificcollege.com/

PORTLAND STATE UNIVERSITY

Portland, Oregon

Portland State University is a coed, public unit of Oregon University System, founded in 1946, offering degrees at the bachelor's, master's, and doctoral levels and postbachelor's certificates. It has a 49-acre campus in Portland.

Academic Information The faculty has 1,260 members (59% full-time), 53% with terminal degrees. The undergraduate student-faculty ratio is 17:1. The library holds 2 million titles and 10,308 serial subscriptions. Special programs include academic remediation, services for learning-disabled students, an honors program, cooperative (work-study) education, study abroad, advanced placement credit, accelerated degree programs, Freshman Honors College, ESL programs, double majors, independent study, distance learning, summer session for credit, part-time degree programs (daytime, evenings, weekends, summer), adult/continuing

education programs, internships, and arrangement for off-campus study with other members of the Oregon University System. The most frequently chosen baccalaureate fields are business/marketing, liberal arts/general studies, social sciences.

Student Body Statistics The student body totals 24,254, of whom 17,998 are undergraduates (1,460 freshmen). 54 percent are women and 46 percent are men. Students come from 55 states and territories and 79 other countries. 80 percent are from Oregon. 3.6 percent are international students.

Expenses for 2006–07 *Application fee:* $50. *One-time mandatory fee:* $150. *State resident tuition:* $4320 full-time, $96 per credit part-time. *Nonresident tuition:* $16,155 full-time, $96 per credit part-time. *Mandatory fees:* $1280 full-time, $23 per credit part-time, $58.50 per term part-time. Full-time tuition and fees vary according to program. *College room and board:* $8940. *College room only:* $6300. Room and board charges vary according to board plan and housing facility.

Financial Aid Forms of aid include need-based and non-need-based scholarships and part-time jobs. The average aided 2006–07 undergraduate received an aid package worth an estimated $7762. The application deadline for financial aid is continuous.

Freshman Admission Portland State University requires a high school transcript, a minimum 3.0 high school GPA, SAT or ACT scores, and TOEFL scores for international students. The application deadline for regular admission is rolling.

Transfer Admission The application deadline for admission is rolling.

Entrance Difficulty Portland State University assesses its entrance difficulty level as moderately difficult. For the fall 2006 freshman class, 91 percent of the applicants were accepted.

For Further Information Contact Ms. Jennifer Cardenas, Director of New Student Programs, Portland State University, PO Box 751, Portland, OR 97207-0751. *Telephone:* 503-725-3511 or 800-547-8887 (toll-free). *Fax:* 503-725-5525. *E-mail:* jcardenas@pdx.edu. *Web site:* http://www.pdx.edu/.

REED COLLEGE

Portland, Oregon

Reed College is a coed, private, comprehensive institution, founded in 1908, offering degrees at the bachelor's and master's levels. It has a 110-acre campus in Portland.

Academic Information The faculty has 132 members (90% full-time), 89% with terminal degrees. The undergraduate student-faculty ratio is 10:1. The library holds 564,598 titles, 23,290 serial subscriptions, and 21,538 audiovisual materials. Special programs include services for learning-disabled students, cooperative (work-study) education, study abroad, advanced placement credit, double majors, independent study, part-time degree programs (daytime), internships, and arrangement for off-campus study with Oregon Independent Colleges Association, Pacific Northwest College of Art. The most frequently chosen baccalaureate fields are biological/life sciences, English, social sciences.

Student Body Statistics The student body totals 1,436, of whom 1,407 are undergraduates (376 freshmen). 55 percent are women and 45 percent are men. Students come from 49 states and territories and 39 other countries. 13 percent are from Oregon. 5.3 percent are international students.

Expenses for 2006–07 *Application fee:* $40. *Comprehensive fee:* $43,530 includes full-time tuition ($34,300), mandatory fees ($230), and college room and board ($9000). *College room only:* $4660. Room and board charges vary according to board plan and housing facility. *Part-time tuition:* $5800 per course. Part-time tuition varies according to course load.

Financial Aid Forms of aid include need-based scholarships and part-time jobs. The average aided 2006–07 undergraduate received an aid package worth an estimated $27,257. The application deadline for financial aid is February 1 with a priority deadline of January 15.

Freshman Admission Reed College requires an essay, a high school transcript, 2 recommendations, SAT or ACT scores, and TOEFL scores for international students. An interview and SAT Subject Test scores are recommended. The application deadline for regular admission is January 15 and for early decision plan 1 it is November 15.

Transfer Admission The application deadline for admission is March 1.

Entrance Difficulty Reed College assesses its entrance difficulty level as most difficult. For the fall 2006 freshman class, 40 percent of the applicants were accepted.

For Further Information Contact Mr. Paul Marthers, Dean of Admission, Reed College, 3203 Southeast Woodstock Boulevard, Portland, OR 97202-8199. *Telephone:* 503-777-7511 or 800-547-4750 (toll-free out-of-state). *Fax:* 503-777-7553. *E-mail:* admission@reed.edu. *Web site:* http://www.reed.edu/.

SOUTHERN OREGON UNIVERSITY
Ashland, Oregon

Southern Oregon University is a coed, public, comprehensive unit of Oregon University System, founded in 1926, offering degrees at the bachelor's and master's levels and postbachelor's certificates. It has a 175-acre campus in Ashland.

Academic Information The faculty has 289 members (67% full-time). The undergraduate student-faculty ratio is 22:1. The library holds 315,000 titles, 1,949 serial subscriptions, and 7,800 audiovisual materials. Special programs include academic remediation, services for learning-disabled students, an honors program, cooperative (work-study) education, study abroad, advanced placement credit, accelerated degree programs, Freshman Honors College, ESL programs, double majors, independent study, distance learning, self-designed majors, summer session for credit, part-time degree programs, adult/continuing education programs, internships, and arrangement for off-campus study with National Student Exchange, other members of the Oregon University System. The most frequently chosen baccalaureate fields are business/marketing, communications/journalism, social sciences.

Student Body Statistics The student body totals 4,675, of whom 4,130 are undergraduates (762 freshmen). 58 percent are women and 42 percent are men. Students come from 45 states and territories and 33 other countries. 78 percent are from Oregon. 1.9 percent are international students.

Expenses for 2006–07 *Application fee:* $50. *State resident tuition:* $4986 full-time, $108 per credit part-time. *Nonresident tuition:* $14,691 full-time, $108 per credit part-time. *Mandatory fees:* $25 per credit part-time. *College room and board:* $6468.

Financial Aid Forms of aid include need-based and non-need-based scholarships, athletic grants, and part-time jobs. The average aided 2006–07 undergraduate received an aid package worth an estimated $8196. The priority application deadline for financial aid is March 1.

Freshman Admission Southern Oregon University requires a high school transcript, 2.75 high school GPA or minimum SAT score of 1010, SAT or ACT scores, and TOEFL scores for international students. An essay, recommendations, and SAT Subject Test scores are required for some. The application deadline for regular admission is rolling.

Transfer Admission The application deadline for admission is rolling.

Entrance Difficulty Southern Oregon University assesses its entrance difficulty level as moderately difficult. For the fall 2006 freshman class, 93 percent of the applicants were accepted.

For Further Information Contact Ms. Mara Affre, Director of Admissions, Southern Oregon University, 1250 Siskiyou Boulevard, Ashland, OR 97520. *Telephone:* 541-552-6411 or 800-482-7672 (toll-free in-state). *Fax:* 541-552-6614. *E-mail:* admissions@sou.edu. *Web site:* http://www.sou.edu/.

See page 194 for the College Close-Up.

UNIVERSITY OF OREGON
Eugene, Oregon

University of Oregon is a coed, public unit of Oregon University System, founded in 1872, offering degrees at the bachelor's, master's, doctoral, and first professional levels and post-master's and postbachelor's certificates. It has a 295-acre campus in Eugene.

Academic Information The faculty has 1,129 members (70% full-time), 96% with terminal degrees. The undergraduate student-faculty ratio is 18:1. The library holds 3 million titles, 18,826 serial subscriptions, and 443,827 audiovisual materials. Special programs include academic remediation, services for learning-disabled students, an honors program, study abroad, advanced placement credit, accelerated degree programs, Freshman Honors College, ESL programs, double majors, independent study, distance learning, self-designed majors, summer session for credit, part-time degree programs (daytime, evenings, weekends, summer), adult/continuing education programs, internships, and arrangement for off-campus study with National Student Exchange. The most frequently chosen baccalaureate fields are business/marketing, communications/journalism, social sciences.

Student Body Statistics The student body totals 20,348, of whom 16,529 are undergraduates (3,423 freshmen). 53 percent are women and 47 percent are men. Students come from 52 states and territories and 87 other countries. 75 percent are from Oregon. 4.6 percent are international students. 22 percent of the 2006 graduating class went on to graduate and professional schools.

Expenses for 2006–07 *Application fee:* $50. *State resident tuition:* $4341 full-time, $107 per credit hour part-time. *Nonresident tuition:* $16,755 full-time, $433 per credit hour part-time. *Mandatory fees:* $1497 full-time. Full-time tuition and fees vary according to class time, course load, program, and reciprocity agreements. Part-time tuition varies according to class time, course load, program, and reciprocity agreements. *College room and board:* $7827. Room and board charges vary according to board plan and housing facility.

Financial Aid Forms of aid include need-based and non-need-based scholarships, athletic grants, and part-time jobs. The average aided 2005–06 undergraduate received an aid package worth $7671. The priority application deadline for financial aid is March 1.

Freshman Admission University of Oregon requires a high school transcript, a minimum 3 high school GPA, SAT or ACT scores, and TOEFL scores for international students. An essay and 2 recommendations are required for some. The application deadline for regular admission is January 15 and for early action it is November 1.

Transfer Admission The application deadline for admission is May 15.

Entrance Difficulty University of Oregon assesses its entrance difficulty level as moderately difficult; very difficult for architecture, Honors College programs. For the fall 2006 freshman class, 88 percent of the applicants were accepted.

For Further Information Contact Ms. Martha Pitts, Assistant Vice President for Enrollment Services and Director of Admissions, University of Oregon, 1217 University of Oregon, Eugene, OR 97403-1217. *Telephone:* 541-346-3201 or 800-232-3825 (toll-free in-state). *Fax:* 541-346-5815. *E-mail:* uoadmit@uoregon.edu. *Web site:* http://www.uoregon.edu/.

UNIVERSITY OF PHOENIX–OREGON CAMPUS
Tigard, Oregon

University of Phoenix–Oregon Campus is a coed, proprietary, comprehensive institution, founded in 1976, offering degrees at the bachelor's and master's levels.

Academic Information The faculty has 495 members (4% full-time), 20% with terminal degrees. The undergraduate student-faculty ratio is 7:1. The library holds 1,759 titles and 692 serial subscriptions. Special programs include services for learning-disabled students, advanced placement credit, accelerated degree programs, independent study, distance learning, external degree programs, and adult/continuing education programs. The most frequently chosen baccalaureate fields are business/marketing, computer and information sciences, public administration and social services.

Student Body Statistics The student body totals 1,836, of whom 1,481 are undergraduates (26 freshmen). 53 percent are women and 47 percent are men. 6.9 percent are international students.

Expenses for 2006–07 *Application fee:* $45. *Tuition:* $10,770 full-time.

Financial Aid Forms of aid include need-based and non-need-based scholarships. The average aided 2005–06 undergraduate received an aid package worth $4213. The application deadline for financial aid is continuous.

University of Phoenix–Oregon Campus (continued)

Freshman Admission University of Phoenix–Oregon Campus requires 1 recommendation and TOEFL scores for international students. A high school transcript is required for some. The application deadline for regular admission is rolling.

Transfer Admission The application deadline for admission is rolling.

Entrance Difficulty University of Phoenix–Oregon Campus has an open admission policy.

For Further Information Contact Ms. Beth Barilla, Associate Vice President, Student Admissions and Services, University of Phoenix–Oregon Campus, 4615 East Elwood Street, Mail Stop AA-K101, Phoenix, AZ 85040-1958. *Telephone:* 480-317-6000, 800-776-4867 (toll-free in-state), or 800-228-7240 (toll-free out-of-state). *Fax:* 480-894-1758. *E-mail:* beth.barilla@phoenix.edu. *Web site:* http://www.phoenix.edu/.

UNIVERSITY OF PORTLAND

Portland, Oregon

University of Portland is a coed, private, Roman Catholic, comprehensive institution, founded in 1901, offering degrees at the bachelor's and master's levels and post-master's certificates. It has a 125-acre campus in Portland.

Academic Information The faculty has 306 members (64% full-time), 60% with terminal degrees. The undergraduate student-faculty ratio is 12:1. The library holds 350,000 titles, 1,400 serial subscriptions, and 11,044 audiovisual materials. Special programs include services for learning-disabled students, an honors program, study abroad, advanced placement credit, double majors, independent study, summer session for credit, part-time degree programs, adult/continuing education programs, internships, and arrangement for off-campus study. The most frequently chosen baccalaureate fields are business/marketing, engineering, health professions and related sciences.

Student Body Statistics The student body totals 3,478, of whom 2,907 are undergraduates (725 freshmen). 63 percent are women and 37 percent are men. Students come from 39 states and territories and 19 other countries. 42 percent are from Oregon. 1.4 percent are international students. 10 percent of the 2006 graduating class went on to graduate and professional schools.

Expenses for 2006–07 *Application fee:* $50. *Comprehensive fee:* $34,240 includes full-time tuition ($26,000), mandatory fees ($390), and college room and board ($7850). *College room only:* $3925. Full-time tuition and fees vary according to program. Room and board charges vary according to board plan and housing facility. *Part-time tuition:* $822 per credit hour. Part-time tuition varies according to program.

Financial Aid Forms of aid include need-based and non-need-based scholarships, athletic grants, and part-time jobs. The average aided 2005–06 undergraduate received an aid package worth $21,821. The priority application deadline for financial aid is March 1.

Freshman Admission University of Portland requires an essay, a high school transcript, 1 recommendation, SAT or ACT scores, and TOEFL scores for international students. The application deadline for regular admission is June 1.

Transfer Admission The application deadline for admission is June 1.

Entrance Difficulty University of Portland assesses its entrance difficulty level as moderately difficult; very difficult for business, computer, engineering programs. For the fall 2006 freshman class, 65 percent of the applicants were accepted.

For Further Information Contact Mr. Jason McDonald, Dean of Admissions, University of Portland, 5000 North Willamette Boulevard, Portland, OR 97203. *Telephone:* 503-943-7147 or 888-627-5601 (toll-free out-of-state). *Fax:* 503-943-7315. *E-mail:* admissions@up.edu. *Web site:* http://www.up.edu/.

WARNER PACIFIC COLLEGE

Portland, Oregon

Warner Pacific College is a coed, private, comprehensive institution, founded in 1937, affiliated with the Church of God, offering degrees at the associate, bachelor's, and master's levels and postbachelor's certificates. It has a 15-acre campus in Portland.

Academic Information The faculty has 35 members (100% full-time). The undergraduate student-faculty ratio is 14:1. The library holds 54,000 titles and 400 serial subscriptions. Special programs include academic remediation, services for learning-disabled students, an honors program, cooperative (work-study) education, study abroad, advanced placement credit, accelerated degree programs, double majors, independent study, self-designed majors, summer session for credit, part-time degree programs (evenings), adult/continuing education programs, internships, and arrangement for off-campus study with Mt. Hood Community College, Concordia College (OR), Oregon Independent Colleges Association.

Student Body Statistics The student body totals 740, of whom 720 are undergraduates (76 freshmen). 65 percent are women and 35 percent are men. Students come from 20 states and territories and 6 other countries. 71 percent are from Oregon. 1.4 percent are international students.

Expenses for 2006–07 *Application fee:* $50. *Comprehensive fee:* $28,148 includes full-time tuition ($20,480), mandatory fees ($1928), and college room and board ($5740). Full-time tuition and fees vary according to course load, location, and reciprocity agreements. Room and board charges vary according to board plan and housing facility. *Part-time tuition:* varies with course load, location, reciprocity agreements.

Financial Aid Forms of aid include need-based and non-need-based scholarships, athletic grants, and part-time jobs. The average aided 2006–07 undergraduate received an aid package worth an estimated $19,963. The application deadline for financial aid is continuous.

Freshman Admission Warner Pacific College requires an essay, a high school transcript, a minimum 2.5 high school GPA, SAT or ACT scores, and TOEFL scores for international students. A minimum 3.0 high school GPA, an interview, and SAT Subject Test scores are recommended. 1 recommendation and an interview are required for some. The application deadline for regular admission is rolling.

Transfer Admission The application deadline for admission is rolling.

Entrance Difficulty Warner Pacific College assesses its entrance difficulty level as moderately difficult. For the fall 2006 freshman class, 56 percent of the applicants were accepted.

For Further Information Contact Mrs. Shannon Mackey, Executive Director of Enrollment Management, Warner Pacific College, 2219 Southeast 68th Avenue, Portland, OR 97215. *Telephone:* 503-517-1020, 800-582-7885 (toll-free in-state), or 800-804-1510 (toll-free out-of-state). *Fax:* 503-517-1352. *E-mail:* admiss@warnerpacific.edu. *Web site:* http://www.warnerpacific.edu/.

See page 206 for the College Close-Up.

WESTERN BAPTIST COLLEGE

See Corban College.

WESTERN OREGON UNIVERSITY

Monmouth, Oregon

Western Oregon University is a coed, public, comprehensive unit of Oregon University System, founded in 1856, offering degrees at the associate, bachelor's, and master's levels and postbachelor's certificates. It has a 157-acre campus in Monmouth near Portland.

Academic Information The faculty has 312 members (56% full-time), 52% with terminal degrees. The undergraduate student-faculty ratio is 19:1. The library holds 227,707 titles, 2,158 serial subscriptions, and 8,010 audiovisual materials. Special programs include academic remediation, services for learning-disabled students, an honors program, study abroad, advanced placement credit, Freshman Honors College, ESL programs, double majors, independent study, distance learning, self-designed majors, summer session for credit, part-time degree programs, adult/continuing education programs, internships, and arrangement for off-campus study with other members of the Oregon University System. The most frequently chosen baccalaureate fields are education, business/marketing, social sciences.

Student Body Statistics The student body totals 4,885, of whom 4,183 are undergraduates (805 freshmen). 59 percent are women and 41 percent

are men. Students come from 29 states and territories and 12 other countries. 91 percent are from Oregon. 2.1 percent are international students.

Expenses for 2006–07 *Application fee:* $50. *State resident tuition:* $3510 full-time, $192 per credit part-time. *Nonresident tuition:* $13,650 full-time, $237 per credit part-time. *Mandatory fees:* $1173 full-time. *College room and board:* $7030. Room and board charges vary according to board plan and housing facility.

Financial Aid Forms of aid include need-based and non-need-based scholarships, athletic grants, and part-time jobs. The average aided 2006–07 undergraduate received an aid package worth an estimated $6902. The priority application deadline for financial aid is March 1.

Freshman Admission Western Oregon University requires a high school transcript, a minimum 2.75 high school GPA, general college prep program completion, SAT or ACT scores, and TOEFL scores for international students. The application deadline for regular admission is rolling.

Transfer Admission The application deadline for admission is rolling.

Entrance Difficulty Western Oregon University assesses its entrance difficulty level as moderately difficult. For the fall 2006 freshman class, 88 percent of the applicants were accepted.

For Further Information Contact Mr. Rob Findtner, Assistant Director of Admissions, Western Oregon University, 345 North Monmouth Avenue, Monmouth, OR 97361. *Telephone:* 503-838-8211 or 877-877-1593 (toll-free). *Fax:* 503-838-8067. *E-mail:* wolfgram@wou.edu. *Web site:* http://www.wou.edu/.

WILLAMETTE UNIVERSITY

Salem, Oregon

Willamette University is a coed, private, United Methodist, comprehensive institution, founded in 1842, offering degrees at the bachelor's, master's, and first professional levels and first professional and postbachelor's certificates. It has a 72-acre campus in Salem near Portland.

Academic Information The faculty has 312 members (69% full-time). The undergraduate student-faculty ratio is 10:1. The library holds 317,000 titles and 1,400 serial subscriptions. Special programs include services for learning-disabled students, cooperative (work-study) education, study abroad, advanced placement credit, accelerated degree programs, double majors, independent study, self-designed majors, part-time degree programs (daytime), internships, and arrangement for off-campus study with American University, Urban Life Center (Chicago). The most frequently chosen baccalaureate fields are foreign languages and literature, biological/life sciences, social sciences.

Student Body Statistics The student body totals 2,747, of whom 2,055 are undergraduates (482 freshmen). 56 percent are women and 44 percent are men. Students come from 38 states and territories and 18 other countries. 40 percent are from Oregon. 0.7 percent are international students. 25 percent of the 2006 graduating class went on to graduate and professional schools.

Expenses for 2006–07 *Application fee:* $50. *Comprehensive fee:* $37,268 includes full-time tuition ($30,018) and college room and board ($7250). Full-time tuition varies according to course load. Room and board charges vary according to board plan and housing facility. *Part-time tuition:* $3753 per course. Part-time tuition varies according to course load.

Financial Aid Forms of aid include need-based and non-need-based scholarships and part-time jobs. The average aided 2006–07 undergraduate received an aid package worth an estimated $26,640. The priority application deadline for financial aid is February 1.

Freshman Admission Willamette University requires an essay, a high school transcript, a minimum 2.0 high school GPA, 1 recommendation, SAT or ACT scores, and TOEFL scores for international students. An interview is recommended. An interview is required for some. The application deadline for regular admission is February 1 and for early action it is December 1.

Transfer Admission The application deadline for admission is February 1.

Entrance Difficulty Willamette University assesses its entrance difficulty level as very difficult. For the fall 2006 freshman class, 74 percent of the applicants were accepted.

For Further Information Contact Dr. Robin Brown, Vice President for Enrollment, Willamette University, 900 State Street, Salem, OR 97301. *Telephone:* 877-LIBARTS or 877-542-2787 (toll-free). *Fax:* 503-375-5363. *E-mail:* libarts@willamette.edu. *Web site:* http://www.willamette.edu/.

Utah

BRIGHAM YOUNG UNIVERSITY

Provo, Utah

Brigham Young University is a coed, private unit of Church Education System (CES) of The Church of Jesus Christ of Latter-day Saints, founded in 1875, affiliated with The Church of Jesus Christ of Latter-day Saints, offering degrees at the bachelor's, master's, doctoral, and first professional levels. It has a 557-acre campus in Provo near Salt Lake City.

Academic Information The faculty has 1,759 members (75% full-time), 63% with terminal degrees. The undergraduate student-faculty ratio is 21:1. The library holds 4 million titles and 27,161 serial subscriptions. Special programs include academic remediation, services for learning-disabled students, an honors program, cooperative (work-study) education, study abroad, advanced placement credit, accelerated degree programs, Freshman Honors College, ESL programs, double majors, independent study, distance learning, summer session for credit, part-time degree programs (daytime, evenings, summer), external degree programs, adult/continuing education programs, internships, and arrangement for off-campus study with BYU Salt Lake Center. The most frequently chosen baccalaureate fields are business/marketing, education, visual and performing arts.

Student Body Statistics The student body totals 34,185, of whom 30,480 are undergraduates (4,606 freshmen). 49 percent are women and 51 percent are men. Students come from 56 states and territories and 125 other countries. 32 percent are from Utah. 2.2 percent are international students.

Expenses for 2007–08 *Application fee:* $30. *Comprehensive fee:* $14,140 includes full-time tuition ($7680) and college room and board ($6460). Latter Day Saints full-time student $3840 per year.

Financial Aid Forms of aid include need-based and non-need-based scholarships, athletic grants, and part-time jobs. The average aided 2005–06 undergraduate received an aid package worth $4067. The priority application deadline for financial aid is April 20.

Freshman Admission Brigham Young University requires an essay, a high school transcript, 1 recommendation, an interview, ACT scores, and TOEFL scores for international students. The application deadline for regular admission is February 1.

Transfer Admission The application deadline for admission is March 1.

Entrance Difficulty Brigham Young University assesses its entrance difficulty level as moderately difficult. For the fall 2006 freshman class, 70 percent of the applicants were accepted.

For Further Information Contact Mr. Tom Gourley, Dean of Admissions and Records, Brigham Young University, A-153 Abraham Smoot Building, Provo, UT 84602. *Telephone:* 801-422-2507. *Fax:* 801-422-0005. *E-mail:* admissions@byu.edu. *Web site:* http://www.byu.edu/.

CALIFORNIA COLLEGE FOR HEALTH SCIENCES

Salt Lake City, Utah

http://www.cchs.edu/

DIXIE STATE COLLEGE OF UTAH
St. George, Utah

Dixie State College of Utah is a coed, public, primarily two-year college of Utah System of Higher Education, founded in 1911, offering degrees at the associate and bachelor's levels. It has a 117-acre campus in St. George.

Academic Information The faculty has 337 members (34% full-time). The student-faculty ratio is 22:1. The library holds 94,747 titles and 263 serial subscriptions. Special programs include academic remediation, services for learning-disabled students, an honors program, cooperative (work-study) education, advanced placement credit, ESL programs, independent study, distance learning, summer session for credit, part-time degree programs (daytime, evenings, summer), adult/continuing education programs, and arrangement for off-campus study.
Student Body Statistics The student body is made up of 5,704 undergraduates (1,329 freshmen). 54 percent are women and 46 percent are men. Students come from 42 states and territories and 14 other countries. 93 percent are from Utah. 0.5 percent are international students.
Expenses for 2007–08 *Application fee:* $35. *State resident tuition:* $2292 full-time. *Nonresident tuition:* $9024 full-time. *Mandatory fees:* $442 full-time.
Financial Aid Forms of aid include need-based scholarships and part-time jobs. The priority application deadline for financial aid is April 1.
Freshman Admission Dixie State College of Utah requires a high school transcript and TOEFL scores for international students. The application deadline for regular admission is rolling.
Entrance Difficulty Dixie State College of Utah has an open admission policy.
For Further Information Contact Ms. Darla Rollins, Admissions Coordinator, Dixie State College of Utah, 225 South 700 East Street, St. George, UT 84770-3876. *Telephone:* 435-652-7702 or 888-GO2DIXIE (toll-free). *Fax:* 435-656-4005. *E-mail:* rollins@dixie.edu. *Web site:* http://www.dixie.edu/.

ITT TECHNICAL INSTITUTE
Murray, Utah

ITT Technical Institute is a coed, proprietary, primarily two-year college of ITT Educational Services, Inc, founded in 1984, offering degrees at the associate and bachelor's levels. It has a 3-acre campus in Murray near Salt Lake City.

Expenses for 2006–07 *Application fee:* $100. Contact school for program costs.
Financial Aid Forms of aid include need-based scholarships and part-time jobs. The application deadline for financial aid is continuous.
Freshman Admission ITT Technical Institute requires a high school transcript, an interview, TOEFL scores for international students, and Wonderlic aptitude test. Recommendations are recommended. The application deadline for regular admission is rolling.
Transfer Admission The application deadline for admission is rolling.
Entrance Difficulty ITT Technical Institute assesses its entrance difficulty level as minimally difficult.
For Further Information Contact Gabrielle Roh, Director of Recruitment, ITT Technical Institute, 920 West Levoy Drive, Murray, UT 84123. *Telephone:* 801-263-3313 or 800-365-2136 (toll-free). *Fax:* 801-263-3497. *Web site:* http://www.itt-tech.edu/.

LDS BUSINESS COLLEGE
Salt Lake City, Utah

LDS Business College is a coed, private, two-year college of Latter-day Saints Church Educational System, founded in 1886, affiliated with The Church of Jesus Christ of Latter-day Saints, offering degrees at the associate level.

Academic Information The faculty has 102 members (21% full-time), 3% with terminal degrees. The student-faculty ratio is 20:1. The library holds 24,000 titles and 130 serial subscriptions. Special programs include academic remediation, advanced placement credit, summer session for credit, part-time degree programs (daytime, evenings, weekends, summer), adult/continuing education programs, and internships.
Student Body Statistics The student body is made up of 1,317 undergraduates (339 freshmen). 54 percent are women and 46 percent are men. Students come from 40 states and territories and 50 other countries. 47 percent are from Utah. 22.2 percent are international students.
Expenses for 2007–08 *Application fee:* $25. *Comprehensive fee:* $7180 includes full-time tuition ($2600) and college room and board ($4580). *Part-time tuition:* $108 per credit hour.
Financial Aid Forms of aid include need-based scholarships. The application deadline for financial aid is continuous.
Freshman Admission LDS Business College requires a high school transcript, an interview, and TOEFL scores for international students. SAT or ACT scores are recommended. The application deadline for regular admission is rolling.
Transfer Admission The application deadline for admission is rolling.
Entrance Difficulty LDS Business College has an open admission policy.
For Further Information Contact Mr. Matt D. Tittle, Assistant Dean of Students, LDS Business College, 411 East South Temple, Salt Lake City, UT 84111-1392. *Telephone:* 801-524-8146 or 800-999-5767 (toll-free). *Fax:* 801-524-1900. *E-mail:* md-tittle@ldsbc.edu. *Web site:* http://www.ldsbc.edu/.

MIDWIVES COLLEGE OF UTAH
Orem, Utah

Midwives College of Utah is a women's, private, comprehensive institution, founded in 1980, offering degrees at the bachelor's and master's levels.

Expenses for 2006–07 Annual tuition for the Associate's program is $10,000; the Bachelor's program is $15,000.
For Further Information Contact Ms. Jodie Fisher, President, Midwives College of Utah, 560 South State Street, Suite B2, Orem, UT 84058. *Telephone:* 801-764-9068 or 866-764-9068 (toll-free). *Fax:* 775-245-4255. *E-mail:* office@midwifery.edu. *Web site:* http://www.midwifery.edu/.

NEUMONT UNIVERSITY
Salt Lake City, Utah

Neumont University is a coed, primarily men's, proprietary, four-year college, founded in 2002, offering degrees at the bachelor's level.

Academic Information The faculty has 30 members (83% full-time), 17% with terminal degrees. The student-faculty ratio is 5:1. Special programs include accelerated degree programs.
Student Body Statistics The student body is made up of 300 undergraduates. 8 percent are women and 92 percent are men. Students come from 40 states and territories and 10 other countries. 68 percent are from Utah.
Expenses for 2007–08 *Application fee:* $35. *Tuition:* $27,000 full-time. *College room only:* $3600.
Freshman Admission Neumont University requires an essay, a high school transcript, 2 recommendations, an interview, SAT or ACT scores, and TOEFL scores for international students. The application deadline for regular admission is rolling.
Transfer Admission The application deadline for admission is rolling.
For Further Information Contact Mr. Scott Sainsbury, Director of Admissions, Neumont University, 10701 South Riverfront Parkway, Suite 300, South Jordan, UT 84095. *Telephone:* 801-302-2800 or 866-622-3448 (toll-free). *Fax:* 801-733-2811. *E-mail:* act@northface.edu. *Web site:* http://www.neumont.edu/.

SOUTHERN UTAH UNIVERSITY
Cedar City, Utah

Southern Utah University is a coed, public, comprehensive unit of Utah System of Higher Education, founded in 1897, offering degrees at the associate, bachelor's, and master's levels. It has a 113-acre campus in Cedar City.

Academic Information The faculty has 285 members (77% full-time), 63% with terminal degrees. The undergraduate student-faculty ratio is 23:1. The library holds 180,424 titles, 6,165 serial subscriptions, and 13,352 audiovisual materials. Special programs include academic remediation, services for learning-disabled students, an honors program, cooperative (work-study) education, advanced placement credit, ESL programs, double majors, independent study, distance learning, summer session for credit, part-time degree programs, adult/continuing education programs, and internships. The most frequently chosen baccalaureate fields are business/marketing, communications/journalism, education.
Student Body Statistics The student body totals 7,029, of whom 6,601 are undergraduates (1,269 freshmen). 58 percent are women and 42 percent are men. Students come from 40 states and territories and 14 other countries. 86 percent are from Utah. 1.1 percent are international students.
Expenses for 2006–07 *Application fee:* $40. *State resident tuition:* $3,564 full-time. *Nonresident tuition:* $10,602 full-time. *Mandatory fees:* $504 full-time. *College room and board:* $4154. Room and board charges vary according to board plan and housing facility.
Financial Aid Forms of aid include need-based and non-need-based scholarships, athletic grants, and part-time jobs. The average aided 2005–06 undergraduate received an aid package worth $5471. The application deadline for financial aid is continuous.
Freshman Admission Southern Utah University requires a high school transcript, a minimum 2.0 high school GPA, SAT or ACT scores, and TOEFL scores for international students. The application deadline for regular admission is August 1.
Transfer Admission The application deadline for admission is rolling.
Entrance Difficulty Southern Utah University assesses its entrance difficulty level as moderately difficult. For the fall 2006 freshman class, 80 percent of the applicants were accepted.
For Further Information Contact Mr. Dale S. Orton, Director of Admissions, Southern Utah University, 351 West University Boulevard, Cedar City, UT 84720. *Telephone:* 435-586-7740. *Fax:* 435-865-8223. *E-mail:* admininfo@suu.edu. *Web site:* http://www.suu.edu/.

STEVENS-HENAGER COLLEGE
Ogden, Utah
http://www.stevenshenager.edu/

UNIVERSITY OF PHOENIX–UTAH CAMPUS
Salt Lake City, Utah

University of Phoenix–Utah Campus is a coed, proprietary, comprehensive institution, founded in 1984, offering degrees at the bachelor's and master's levels.

Academic Information The faculty has 761 members (7% full-time), 24% with terminal degrees. The undergraduate student-faculty ratio is 10:1. The library holds 1,759 titles and 692 serial subscriptions. Special programs include services for learning-disabled students, advanced placement credit, accelerated degree programs, independent study, distance learning, external degree programs, and adult/continuing education programs. The most frequently chosen baccalaureate fields are business/marketing, computer and information sciences, public administration and social services.
Student Body Statistics The student body totals 3,986, of whom 2,559 are undergraduates (50 freshmen). 45 percent are women and 55 percent are men. 2 percent are international students.
Expenses for 2006–07 *Application fee:* $45. *Tuition:* $10,200 full-time.

Financial Aid Forms of aid include need-based and non-need-based scholarships. The average aided 2005–06 undergraduate received an aid package worth $4810. The application deadline for financial aid is continuous.
Freshman Admission University of Phoenix–Utah Campus requires TOEFL scores for international students. A high school transcript is required for some. The application deadline for regular admission is rolling.
Transfer Admission The application deadline for admission is rolling.
Entrance Difficulty University of Phoenix–Utah Campus has an open admission policy.
For Further Information Contact Ms. Beth Barilla, Associate Vice President, Student Admissions and Services, University of Phoenix–Utah Campus, 4615 East Elwood Street, Mail Stop AA-K101, Phoenix, AZ 85040-1958. *Telephone:* 480-317-6000, 800-776-4867 (toll-free in-state), or 800-228-7240 (toll-free out-of-state). *Fax:* 480-894-1758. *E-mail:* beth.barilla@phoenix.edu. *Web site:* http://www.phoenix.edu/.

UNIVERSITY OF UTAH
Salt Lake City, Utah

University of Utah is a coed, public unit of Utah System of Higher Education, founded in 1850, offering degrees at the bachelor's, master's, doctoral, and first professional levels and post-master's and postbachelor's certificates. It has a 1,500-acre campus in Salt Lake City.

Academic Information The faculty has 1,758 members (69% full-time), 70% with terminal degrees. The undergraduate student-faculty ratio is 14:1. The library holds 6 million titles, 33,517 serial subscriptions, and 74,731 audiovisual materials. Special programs include academic remediation, services for learning-disabled students, an honors program, cooperative (work-study) education, study abroad, advanced placement credit, accelerated degree programs, Freshman Honors College, ESL programs, double majors, independent study, distance learning, self-designed majors, summer session for credit, part-time degree programs (daytime, evenings, weekends, summer), internships, and arrangement for off-campus study with members of the National Student Exchange. The most frequently chosen baccalaureate fields are business/marketing, communications/journalism, social sciences.
Student Body Statistics The student body totals 28,619, of whom 22,155 are undergraduates (2,838 freshmen). 45 percent are women and 55 percent are men. Students come from 55 states and territories and 104 other countries. 84 percent are from Utah. 2.5 percent are international students.
Expenses for 2006–07 *Application fee:* $35. *State resident tuition:* $3972 full-time. *Nonresident tuition:* $13,902 full-time. *Mandatory fees:* $691 full-time. Full-time tuition and fees vary according to course level, course load, degree level, and program. *College room and board:* $5828. *College room only:* $3016. Room and board charges vary according to board plan and housing facility. Contact university directly for part-time tuition costs.
Financial Aid Forms of aid include need-based and non-need-based scholarships, athletic grants, and part-time jobs. The average aided 2005–06 undergraduate received an aid package worth $8086.
Freshman Admission University of Utah requires a high school transcript, a minimum 2.6 high school GPA, SAT or ACT scores, and TOEFL scores for international students. A minimum 3.0 high school GPA and ACT scores are recommended. Recommendations are required for some. The application deadline for regular admission is April 1.
Transfer Admission The application deadline for admission is April 1.
Entrance Difficulty University of Utah assesses its entrance difficulty level as moderately difficult. For the fall 2006 freshman class, 84 percent of the applicants were accepted.
For Further Information Contact Ms. Suzanne Espinoza, Director of High School Services, University of Utah, 250 South Student Services Building, 201 South, 1460 E Room 206, Salt Lake City, UT 84112. *Telephone:* 801-581-8761 or 800-444-8638 (toll-free). *Fax:* 801-585-3257. *E-mail:* u-info@sa.utah.edu. *Web site:* http://www.utah.edu/.

UTAH STATE UNIVERSITY

Logan, Utah

Utah State University is a coed, public unit of Utah System of Higher Education, founded in 1888, offering degrees at the associate, bachelor's, master's, and doctoral levels and post-master's and postbachelor's certificates. It has a 456-acre campus in Logan.

Academic Information The faculty has 739 members (94% full-time). The undergraduate student-faculty ratio is 18:1. The library holds 2 million titles, 12,369 serial subscriptions, and 16,504 audiovisual materials. Special programs include academic remediation, services for learning-disabled students, an honors program, cooperative (work-study) education, study abroad, advanced placement credit, accelerated degree programs, Freshman Honors College, ESL programs, double majors, independent study, distance learning, self-designed majors, summer session for credit, part-time degree programs (daytime, evenings, summer), adult/continuing education programs, internships, and arrangement for off-campus study with Weber State University. The most frequently chosen baccalaureate fields are business/marketing, education, engineering.

Student Body Statistics The student body totals 14,444, of whom 12,779 are undergraduates (2,562 freshmen). 48 percent are women and 52 percent are men. Students come from 53 states and territories and 52 other countries. 73 percent are from Utah. 3 percent are international students. 23 percent of the 2006 graduating class went on to graduate and professional schools.

Expenses for 2006–07 *Application fee:* $40. *State resident tuition:* $3378 full-time. *Nonresident tuition:* $10,878 full-time. *Mandatory fees:* $571 full-time. Full-time tuition and fees vary according to course load and student level. *College room and board:* $4400. *College room only:* $1550. Room and board charges vary according to board plan and housing facility.

Financial Aid Forms of aid include need-based and non-need-based scholarships, athletic grants, and part-time jobs. The average aided 2006–07 undergraduate received an aid package worth an estimated $6455. The application deadline for financial aid is continuous.

Freshman Admission Utah State University requires a high school transcript, SAT or ACT scores, and TOEFL scores for international students. A minimum 2.75 high school GPA is recommended. The application deadline for regular admission is rolling.

Transfer Admission The application deadline for admission is rolling.

Entrance Difficulty Utah State University assesses its entrance difficulty level as moderately difficult. For the fall 2006 freshman class, 97 percent of the applicants were accepted.

For Further Information Contact Ms. Jenn Putnam, Director, Admissions Office, Utah State University, 0160 Old Main Hill, Logan, UT 84322-0160. *Telephone:* 435-797-1079 or 800-488-8108 (toll-free). *Fax:* 435-797-3708. *E-mail:* admit@usu.edu. *Web site:* http://www.usu.edu/.

UTAH VALLEY STATE COLLEGE

Orem, Utah

Utah Valley State College is a coed, public, four-year college of Utah System of Higher Education, founded in 1941, offering degrees at the associate and bachelor's levels. It has a 200-acre campus in Orem near Salt Lake City.

Academic Information The faculty has 1,256 members (33% full-time), 18% with terminal degrees. The student-faculty ratio is 22:1. The library holds 173,000 titles and 6,000 serial subscriptions. Special programs include academic remediation, services for learning-disabled students, an honors program, cooperative (work-study) education, study abroad, advanced placement credit, accelerated degree programs, ESL programs, double majors, independent study, distance learning, self-designed majors, summer session for credit, part-time degree programs (daytime, evenings, weekends, summer), internships, and arrangement for off-campus study with UVSC Wasatch Campus; Heber City, University Mall, North Lehi Valley Ed Center, Spanish Fork Ed. Center. The most frequently chosen baccalaureate fields are business/marketing, health professions and related sciences, liberal arts/general studies.

Student Body Statistics The student body is made up of 23,305 undergraduates (3,157 freshmen). 43 percent are women and 57 percent

are men. Students come from 50 states and territories and 78 other countries. 86 percent are from Utah. 0.4 percent are international students.

Expenses for 2006–07 *Application fee:* $30. *State resident tuition:* $2812 full-time, $110 per credit part-time. *Nonresident tuition:* $9842 full-time, $344 per credit part-time. *Mandatory fees:* $496 full-time, $248 per term part-time. Part-time tuition and fees vary according to course load.

Financial Aid Forms of aid include need-based scholarships, athletic grants, and part-time jobs.

Freshman Admission Utah Valley State College requires TOEFL scores for international students. A high school transcript is recommended. The application deadline for regular admission is rolling.

Transfer Admission The application deadline for admission is rolling.

Entrance Difficulty Utah Valley State College has an open admission policy.

For Further Information Contact Mrs. Liz Childs, Director of Admissions, Utah Valley State College, 800 West University Parkway, Orem, UT 84058-5999. *Telephone:* 801-863-8460. *Fax:* 801-225-4677. *E-mail:* info@uvsc.edu. *Web site:* http://www.uvsc.edu/.

WEBER STATE UNIVERSITY

Ogden, Utah

Weber State University is a coed, public, comprehensive unit of Utah System of Higher Education, founded in 1889, offering degrees at the associate, bachelor's, and master's levels and postbachelor's certificates. It has a 526-acre campus in Ogden near Salt Lake City.

Academic Information The faculty has 909 members (51% full-time), 33% with terminal degrees. The undergraduate student-faculty ratio is 22:1. The library holds 734,487 titles and 19,881 audiovisual materials. Special programs include academic remediation, services for learning-disabled students, an honors program, cooperative (work-study) education, study abroad, advanced placement credit, accelerated degree programs, Freshman Honors College, ESL programs, double majors, independent study, distance learning, self-designed majors, summer session for credit, part-time degree programs (daytime, evenings, summer), external degree programs, adult/continuing education programs, internships, and arrangement for off-campus study with Utah State University, Southern Utah University, Dixie College, Utah Valley State College, Salt Lake Community College. The most frequently chosen baccalaureate fields are business/marketing, education, health professions and related sciences.

Student Body Statistics The student body totals 18,303, of whom 17,849 are undergraduates (2,456 freshmen). 51 percent are women and 49 percent are men. Students come from 52 states and territories and 37 other countries. 97 percent are from Utah. 0.6 percent are international students. 46 percent of the 2006 graduating class went on to graduate and professional schools.

Expenses for 2006–07 *Application fee:* $30. *State resident tuition:* $2793 full-time, $115 per credit hour part-time. *Nonresident tuition:* $9776 full-time, $401 per credit hour part-time. *Mandatory fees:* $640 full-time. Part-time tuition varies according to course load. *College room and board:* $5328. *College room only:* $2142. Room and board charges vary according to board plan and housing facility.

Financial Aid Forms of aid include need-based scholarships, athletic grants, and part-time jobs. The priority application deadline for financial aid is March 1.

Freshman Admission Weber State University requires a high school transcript. TOEFL scores for international students are recommended. SAT or ACT scores are required for some. The application deadline for regular admission is August 22.

Transfer Admission The application deadline for admission is rolling.

Entrance Difficulty Weber State University has an open admission policy.

For Further Information Contact Mr. John Allred, Admissions Advisor, Weber State University, 1137 University Circle, Ogden, UT 84408-1137. *Telephone:* 801-626-6050, 800-634-6568 (toll-free in-state), or 800-848-7770 (toll-free out-of-state). *Fax:* 801-626-6744. *E-mail:* admissions@weber.edu. *Web site:* http://weber.edu/.

WESTERN GOVERNORS UNIVERSITY

Salt Lake City, Utah

http://www.wgu.edu/

WESTMINSTER COLLEGE

Salt Lake City, Utah

Westminster College is a coed, private, comprehensive institution, founded in 1875, offering degrees at the bachelor's and master's levels and postbachelor's certificates. It has a 27-acre campus in Salt Lake City.

Academic Information The faculty has 246 members (48% full-time), 45% with terminal degrees. The undergraduate student-faculty ratio is 11:1. The library holds 154,069 titles, 695 serial subscriptions, and 7,350 audiovisual materials. Special programs include academic remediation, services for learning-disabled students, an honors program, cooperative (work-study) education, study abroad, advanced placement credit, accelerated degree programs, double majors, independent study, self-designed majors, summer session for credit, part-time degree programs (daytime, evenings, weekends, summer), external degree programs, and internships. The most frequently chosen baccalaureate fields are business/marketing, health professions and related sciences, psychology.

Student Body Statistics The student body totals 2,479, of whom 1,959 are undergraduates (375 freshmen). 58 percent are women and 42 percent are men. Students come from 38 states and territories and 29 other countries. 86 percent are from Utah. 1 percent are international students. 25 percent of the 2006 graduating class went on to graduate and professional schools.

Expenses for 2006–07 *Application fee:* $40. *Comprehensive fee:* $27,170 includes full-time tuition ($20,640), mandatory fees ($390), and college room and board ($6140). Full-time tuition and fees vary according to course load. Room and board charges vary according to board plan. *Part-time tuition:* $860 per credit hour. *Part-time mandatory fees:* $220 per term.

Financial Aid Forms of aid include need-based and non-need-based scholarships, athletic grants, and part-time jobs. The average aided 2005–06 undergraduate received an aid package worth $15,651.

Freshman Admission Westminster College requires an essay, a high school transcript, a minimum 2.5 high school GPA, 1 recommendation, SAT or ACT scores, and TOEFL scores for international students. An essay and an interview are recommended. The application deadline for regular admission is rolling and for nonresidents it is rolling.

Transfer Admission The application deadline for admission is rolling.

Entrance Difficulty Westminster College assesses its entrance difficulty level as moderately difficult. For the fall 2006 freshman class, 79 percent of the applicants were accepted.

For Further Information Contact Ms. Bonnie Sofarelli, Director of Admissions, Westminster College, 1840 South 1300 East, Salt Lake City, UT 84105-3697. *Telephone:* 801-832-2210 or 800-748-4753 (toll-free out-of-state). *Fax:* 801-832-3101. *E-mail:* bsofarelli@westminstercollege.edu. *Web site:* http://www.westminstercollege.edu/.

See page 208 for the College Close-Up.

Washington

ANTIOCH UNIVERSITY SEATTLE

Seattle, Washington

http://www.antiochsea.edu/

ARGOSY UNIVERSITY, SEATTLE

Seattle, Washington

http://www.argosyu.edu/

THE ART INSTITUTE OF SEATTLE

Seattle, Washington

The Art Institute of Seattle is a coed, proprietary, four-year college of Education Management Corporation, founded in 1982, offering degrees at the associate and bachelor's levels.

Academic Information The faculty has 144 members (44% full-time), 1% with terminal degrees. The student-faculty ratio is 20:1. The library holds 19,787 titles, 295 serial subscriptions, and 2,685 audiovisual materials. Special programs include academic remediation, services for learning-disabled students, an honors program, study abroad, advanced placement credit, distance learning, summer session for credit, part-time degree programs (daytime, evenings, weekends, summer), adult/continuing education programs, and internships.

Student Body Statistics The student body is made up of 2,352 undergraduates (452 freshmen). 51 percent are women and 49 percent are men. Students come from 46 states and territories and 28 other countries. 83 percent are from Washington. 5.7 percent are international students.

Expenses for 2007–08 *Application fee:* $50. *Tuition:* $19,968 full-time, $416 per credit part-time. *College room only:* $9156.

Financial Aid Forms of aid include need-based scholarships and part-time jobs. The application deadline for financial aid is continuous.

Freshman Admission The Art Institute of Seattle requires an essay, a high school transcript, a minimum 2.0 high school GPA, an interview, and TOEFL scores for international students. 3 recommendations, SAT scores, and ACT scores are recommended. 2.5 GPA required for Bachelor degree applicants is required for some. The application deadline for regular admission is rolling.

Transfer Admission The application deadline for admission is rolling.

Entrance Difficulty The Art Institute of Seattle assesses its entrance difficulty level as moderately difficult. For the fall 2006 freshman class, 94 percent of the applicants were accepted.

For Further Information Contact Mr. Michael Reese, Registrar, The Art Institute of Seattle, 2323 Elliott Avenue, Seattle, WA 98121. *Telephone:* 206-239-2284 or 800-275-2471 (toll-free). *Fax:* 206-269-0275. *E-mail:* mreese@aii.edu. *Web site:* http://www.ais.artinstitutes.edu/.

BASTYR UNIVERSITY

Kenmore, Washington

Bastyr University is a coed, private, upper-level institution, founded in 1978, offering degrees at the bachelor's, master's, and first professional levels and post-master's, first professional, and postbachelor's certificates. It has a 50-acre campus in Kenmore near Seattle.

Academic Information The faculty has 151 members (36% full-time), 90% with terminal degrees. The undergraduate student-faculty ratio is 12:1. The library holds 14,000 titles and 265 serial subscriptions. Special programs include cooperative (work-study) education, double majors, independent study, summer session for credit, part-time degree programs (daytime, summer), and internships. The most frequently chosen baccalaureate fields are health professions and related sciences, interdisciplinary studies, psychology.

Student Body Statistics The student body totals 1,126, of whom 263 are undergraduates (128 in entering class). 81 percent are women and 19 percent are men. Students come from 16 states and territories and 8 other countries. 60 percent are from Washington. 4.2 percent are international students.

Expenses for 2007–08 *Application fee:* $60. *Tuition:* $14,625 full-time, $325 per credit part-time. *Mandatory fees:* $1740 full-time. *College room only:* $3650.

Bastyr University (continued)

Financial Aid Forms of aid include need-based and non-need-based scholarships and part-time jobs. The average aided 2006–07 undergraduate received an aid package worth an estimated $17,600. The priority application deadline for financial aid is May 1.

Transfer Admission Bastyr University requires a college transcript and a minimum 2.25 college GPA. Standardized test scores are required for some. The application deadline for admission is March 15.

Entrance Difficulty For the fall 2006 entering class, 80 percent of the applicants were accepted.

For Further Information Contact Mr. Ted Olsen, Director of Admissions, Bastyr University, 14500 Juanita Drive NE, Kenmore, WA 98028-4966. *Telephone:* 425-602-3101. *Fax:* 425-602-3090. *E-mail:* admiss@bastyr.edu. *Web site:* http://www.bastyr.edu/.

CENTRAL WASHINGTON UNIVERSITY
Ellensburg, Washington

Central Washington University is a coed, public, comprehensive institution, founded in 1891, offering degrees at the bachelor's and master's levels and postbachelor's certificates. It has a 380-acre campus in Ellensburg.

Academic Information The faculty has 579 members (68% full-time), 65% with terminal degrees. The undergraduate student-faculty ratio is 21:1. The library holds 434,424 titles and 1,469 serial subscriptions. Special programs include academic remediation, services for learning-disabled students, an honors program, cooperative (work-study) education, study abroad, advanced placement credit, ESL programs, double majors, independent study, distance learning, self-designed majors, summer session for credit, part-time degree programs (daytime, evenings, summer), adult/continuing education programs, internships, and arrangement for off-campus study with National Student Exchange. The most frequently chosen baccalaureate fields are business/marketing, education, security and protective services.

Student Body Statistics The student body totals 10,688, of whom 10,145 are undergraduates (1,480 freshmen). 53 percent are women and 47 percent are men. Students come from 35 states and territories and 46 other countries. 96 percent are from Washington. 1.6 percent are international students.

Expenses for 2006–07 *Application fee:* $50. *State resident tuition:* $4392 full-time, $146 per credit part-time. *Nonresident tuition:* $13,347 full-time, $445 per credit part-time. *Mandatory fees:* $846 full-time. Part-time tuition varies according to course load. *College room and board:* $7140. Room and board charges vary according to board plan and housing facility.

Financial Aid Forms of aid include need-based and non-need-based scholarships, athletic grants, and part-time jobs. The average aided 2005–06 undergraduate received an aid package worth $7775. The priority application deadline for financial aid is March 1.

Freshman Admission Central Washington University requires a high school transcript, a minimum 2.0 high school GPA, SAT or ACT scores, and TOEFL scores for international students. An essay, recommendations, and an interview are required for some. The application deadline for regular admission is April 1.

Transfer Admission The application deadline for admission is April 1.

Entrance Difficulty Central Washington University assesses its entrance difficulty level as moderately difficult; very difficult for Douglas Honors College. For the fall 2006 freshman class, 75 percent of the applicants were accepted.

For Further Information Contact Ms. Lisa Garcia-Hanson, Director of Admissions, Central Washington University, 400 East University Way, Ellensburg, WA 98926-7463. *Telephone:* 509-963-1211 or 866-298-4968 (toll-free). *Fax:* 509-963-3022. *E-mail:* cwuadmis@cwu.edu. *Web site:* http://www.cwu.edu/.

CITY UNIVERSITY
Bellevue, Washington

City University is a coed, private, comprehensive institution, founded in 1973, offering degrees at the associate, bachelor's, and master's levels and postbachelor's certificates. It is located in Bellevue near Seattle.

Expenses for 2006–07 *Application fee:* $80. *Tuition:* $8040 full-time, $268 per credit hour part-time. *Mandatory fees:* $120 full-time, $40 per term part-time.

For Further Information Contact Student Services Center, City University, 11900 NE First Street, Bellevue, WA 98005. *Telephone:* 888-422-4898 or 888-42-CITYU (toll-free). *Fax:* 425-709-5361. *E-mail:* info@cityu.edu. *Web site:* http://www.cityu.edu/.

CORNISH COLLEGE OF THE ARTS
Seattle, Washington

Cornish College of the Arts is a coed, private, four-year college, founded in 1914, offering degrees at the bachelor's level. It has a 4-acre campus in Seattle.

Expenses for 2006–07 *Application fee:* $35. *Tuition:* $22,350 full-time, $950 per credit part-time. *Mandatory fees:* $400 full-time.

For Further Information Contact Ms. Sharron Starling, Associate Director of Admissions, Cornish College of the Arts, 1000 Lenora Street, Seattle, WA 98121. *Telephone:* 206-726-5017 or 800-726-ARTS (toll-free). *Fax:* 206-720-1011. *E-mail:* admissions@cornish.edu. *Web site:* http://www.cornish.edu/.

CROWN COLLEGE
Tacoma, Washington

Crown College is a coed, proprietary, primarily two-year college, founded in 1969, offering degrees at the associate and bachelor's levels (bachelor's degree in public administration only). It is located in Tacoma near Seattle.

Expenses for 2006–07 *Application fee:* $135. *Tuition:* $7500 full-time. *Mandatory fees:* $385 full-time.

For Further Information Contact Mrs. Jesica McMullin, Crown College, 8739 South Hosmer, Tacoma, WA 98444. *Telephone:* 253-531-3123, 800-755-9525 (toll-free in-state), or 888-689-3688 (toll-free out-of-state). *Fax:* 253-531-3521. *E-mail:* admissions@crowncollege.edu. *Web site:* http://www.crowncollege.edu/.

DeVRY UNIVERSITY
Bellevue, Washington

http://www.devry.edu/

DeVRY UNIVERSITY
Federal Way, Washington

DeVry University is a coed, proprietary, comprehensive unit of DeVry University, founded in 2001, offering degrees at the associate, bachelor's, and master's levels and postbachelor's certificates. It has a 12-acre campus in Federal Way.

Academic Information The faculty has 62 members (52% full-time). The undergraduate student-faculty ratio is 14:1. The library holds 6,021 titles and 6,807 serial subscriptions. Special programs include academic remediation, services for learning-disabled students, advanced placement credit, accelerated degree programs, distance learning, summer session for credit, part-time degree programs (daytime, evenings, weekends, summer),

and adult/continuing education programs. The most frequently chosen baccalaureate fields are business/marketing, computer and information sciences, engineering technologies.

Student Body Statistics The student body totals 812, of whom 730 are undergraduates (129 freshmen). 27 percent are women and 73 percent are men. 0.6 percent are international students.

Expenses for 2007–08 *Application fee:* $50. *Tuition:* $14,320 full-time, $525 per credit part-time. *Mandatory fees:* $320 full-time.

Financial Aid Forms of aid include need-based and non-need-based scholarships and part-time jobs. The application deadline for financial aid is continuous.

Freshman Admission DeVry University requires a high school transcript, an interview, and TOEFL scores for international students. The application deadline for regular admission is rolling.

Transfer Admission The application deadline for admission is rolling.

Entrance Difficulty DeVry University assesses its entrance difficulty level as minimally difficult; moderately difficult for electronics engineering technology.

For Further Information Contact Admissions Department, DeVry University, 3600 South 344th Way, Federal Way, WA 98001-9558. *Telephone:* 253-943-2800. *Fax:* 253-943-2800. *Web site:* http://www.devry.edu/.

DIGIPEN INSTITUTE OF TECHNOLOGY

Redmond, Washington

DigiPen Institute of Technology is a coed, proprietary, comprehensive institution, founded in 1988, offering degrees at the associate, bachelor's, and master's levels. It has a 1-acre campus in Redmond.

Academic Information The faculty has 56 members (64% full-time). The undergraduate student-faculty ratio is 14:1. The library holds 2,117 titles, 52 serial subscriptions, and 277 audiovisual materials. Special programs include academic remediation, services for learning-disabled students, advanced placement credit, independent study, summer session for credit, and internships.

Student Body Statistics The student body totals 783, of whom 745 are undergraduates. 8 percent are women and 92 percent are men. 37 percent are from Washington.

Expenses for 2007–08 *Application fee:* $75. *Tuition:* $16,720 full-time, $414 per credit part-time. *Mandatory fees:* $160 full-time, $80 per term part-time.

Freshman Admission DigiPen Institute of Technology requires an essay, a high school transcript, a minimum 2.5 high school GPA, 2 recommendations, SAT or ACT scores, and TOEFL scores for international students. Art portfolio is recommended. Art portfolio is required for some. The application deadline for regular admission is rolling and for nonresidents it is rolling.

Transfer Admission The application deadline for admission is rolling.

Entrance Difficulty DigiPen Institute of Technology assesses its entrance difficulty level as moderately difficult. For the fall 2006 freshman class, 46 percent of the applicants were accepted.

For Further Information Contact Ms. Angela Kugler, Admissions Manager, DigiPen Institute of Technology, 5001 150th Avenue NE, Redmond, WA 98052. *Telephone:* 425-895-4438. *Fax:* 425-558-0378. *E-mail:* akugler@digipen.edu. *Web site:* http://digipen.edu/.

EASTERN WASHINGTON UNIVERSITY

Cheney, Washington

Eastern Washington University is a coed, public, comprehensive institution, founded in 1882, offering degrees at the bachelor's, master's, and doctoral levels. It has a 335-acre campus in Cheney.

Academic Information The undergraduate student-faculty ratio is 20:1. The library holds 852,186 titles, 6,429 serial subscriptions, and 31,832 audiovisual materials. Special programs include academic remediation, services for learning-disabled students, an honors program, cooperative (work-study) education, study abroad, advanced placement credit, ESL programs, double majors, independent study, distance learning, self-

designed majors, summer session for credit, part-time degree programs (daytime, evenings, weekends, summer), internships, and arrangement for off-campus study with Intercollegiate Center for Nursing. The most frequently chosen baccalaureate fields are business/marketing, education, health professions and related sciences.

Student Body Statistics The student body is made up of 11,161 undergraduates. Students come from 46 states and territories and 34 other countries. 92 percent are from Washington. 1.5 percent are international students.

Expenses for 2006–07 *Application fee:* $50. *State resident tuition:* $4278 full-time, $143 per credit part-time. *Nonresident tuition:* $13,335 full-time, $444 per credit part-time. *Mandatory fees:* $287 full-time, $95 per term part-time. Both full-time and part-time tuition and fees vary according to course load. *College room and board:* $6182. Room and board charges vary according to board plan and housing facility.

Financial Aid Forms of aid include need-based and non-need-based scholarships, athletic grants, and part-time jobs. The priority application deadline for financial aid is February 15.

Freshman Admission Eastern Washington University requires a high school transcript, a minimum 2.0 high school GPA, SAT or ACT scores, and TOEFL scores for international students. A minimum 3.0 high school GPA is recommended. An essay, recommendations, and an interview are required for some. The application deadline for regular admission is September 15.

Transfer Admission The application deadline for admission is rolling.

Entrance Difficulty Eastern Washington University assesses its entrance difficulty level as moderately difficult. For the fall 2006 freshman class, 83 percent of the applicants were accepted.

For Further Information Contact Ms. Shannon Carr, Director of Admissions, Eastern Washington University, 526 Fifth Street, SUT 101, Cheney, WA 99004-2447. *Telephone:* 509-359-6582. *Fax:* 509-359-6692. *E-mail:* admissions@mail.ewu.edu. *Web site:* http://www.ewu.edu/.

See page 164 for the College Close-Up.

THE EVERGREEN STATE COLLEGE

Olympia, Washington

The Evergreen State College is a coed, public, comprehensive unit of Washington State Public Institution, founded in 1967, offering degrees at the bachelor's and master's levels. It has a 1,000-acre campus in Olympia near Seattle.

Academic Information The faculty has 232 members (68% full-time), 73% with terminal degrees. The undergraduate student-faculty ratio is 21:1. The library holds 471,406 titles, 12,579 serial subscriptions, and 89,195 audiovisual materials. Special programs include services for learning-disabled students, cooperative (work-study) education, study abroad, advanced placement credit, accelerated degree programs, double majors, independent study, self-designed majors, summer session for credit, part-time degree programs (daytime, evenings, weekends, summer), internships, and arrangement for off-campus study with University of Washington. The most frequently chosen baccalaureate field is liberal arts/general studies.

Student Body Statistics The student body totals 4,416, of whom 4,124 are undergraduates (583 freshmen). 55 percent are women and 45 percent are men. Students come from 54 states and territories and 7 other countries. 77 percent are from Washington. 0.4 percent are international students. 28 percent of the 2006 graduating class went on to graduate and professional schools.

Expenses for 2006–07 *Application fee:* $50. *State resident tuition:* $4371 full-time, $145.70 per quarter hour part-time. *Nonresident tuition:* $14,562 full-time, $485.30 per quarter hour part-time. *Mandatory fees:* $490 full-time, $7.85 per quarter hour part-time, $42 per term part-time. Both full-time and part-time tuition and fees vary according to course load and degree level. *College room and board:* $7140. *College room only:* $4620. Room and board charges vary according to board plan, housing facility, and student level.

Financial Aid Forms of aid include need-based and non-need-based scholarships and part-time jobs. The priority application deadline for financial aid is March 15.

The Evergreen State College (continued)

Freshman Admission The Evergreen State College requires a high school transcript, a minimum 2.0 high school GPA, SAT or ACT scores, and TOEFL scores for international students. An essay is recommended. The application deadline for regular admission is rolling.

Transfer Admission The application deadline for admission is rolling.

Entrance Difficulty The Evergreen State College assesses its entrance difficulty level as moderately difficult. For the fall 2006 freshman class, 95 percent of the applicants were accepted.

For Further Information Contact Mr. Doug Scrima, Director of Admissions, The Evergreen State College, 2700 Evergreen Parkway NW, Olympia, WA 98505. *Telephone:* 360-867-6170. *Fax:* 360-867-6576. *E-mail:* admissions@evergreen.edu. *Web site:* http://www.evergreen.edu/.

GONZAGA UNIVERSITY

Spokane, Washington

SPONSOR See Front Insert for Details!

Gonzaga University is a coed, private, Roman Catholic, comprehensive institution, founded in 1887, offering degrees at the bachelor's, master's, doctoral, and first professional levels and post-master's certificates. It has a 94-acre campus in Spokane.

Academic Information The faculty has 639 members (52% full-time). The undergraduate student-faculty ratio is 12:1. The library holds 305,517 titles and 32,106 serial subscriptions. Special programs include services for learning-disabled students, an honors program, study abroad, advanced placement credit, accelerated degree programs, ESL programs, double majors, independent study, summer session for credit, part-time degree programs (daytime, evenings, weekends, summer), adult/continuing education programs, internships, and arrangement for off-campus study with American University. The most frequently chosen baccalaureate fields are business/marketing, engineering, social sciences.

Student Body Statistics The student body totals 6,610, of whom 4,275 are undergraduates (977 freshmen). 54 percent are women and 46 percent are men. Students come from 50 states and territories and 36 other countries. 51 percent are from Washington. 1.1 percent are international students.

Expenses for 2006–07 *Application fee:* $45. *Comprehensive fee:* $32,232 includes full-time tuition ($24,590), mandatory fees ($422), and college room and board ($7220). *College room only:* $3560. Room and board charges vary according to board plan and housing facility. *Part-time tuition:* $715 per credit. *Part-time mandatory fees:* $45 per term.

Financial Aid Forms of aid include need-based and non-need-based scholarships, athletic grants, and part-time jobs. The average aided 2005–06 undergraduate received an aid package worth $18,004. The priority application deadline for financial aid is February 1.

Freshman Admission Gonzaga University requires an essay, a high school transcript, a minimum 3.0 high school GPA, 1 recommendation, SAT or ACT scores, and TOEFL scores for international students. An interview is recommended. The application deadline for regular admission is February 1 and for early action it is November 15.

Transfer Admission Gonzaga University requires a college transcript. Standardized test scores are required for some. The application deadline for admission is June 1.

Entrance Difficulty Gonzaga University assesses its entrance difficulty level as moderately difficult. For the fall 2006 freshman class, 67 percent of the applicants were accepted.

SPECIAL MESSAGE TO STUDENTS

Social Life Because personal growth is as important as intellectual development, Gonzaga University (GU) places great emphasis on student life outside of class. As a residential community, 98 percent of freshmen and 43 percent of the total student body live on campus in GU's seventeen residence halls and seven apartment complexes. Residence halls range in size from 35 people in a single-sex hall to 361

in Gonzaga's largest coed hall. In addition, students are encouraged to participate in more than 100 different clubs and organizations, including NCAA Division I athletics, intramural sports, a nationally ranked debate team, a nationally recognized mock trials team, and a variety of service clubs. As a testament to its students' commitment to service, Gonzaga provides the greatest number of service hours in the entire city of Spokane.

Academic Highlights All undergraduates complete Gonzaga's core curriculum emphasizing a comprehensive liberal arts and sciences education. GU offers more than seventy-five areas of study in arts and sciences, business (accounting and business administration with various concentrations), education (physical, special, teacher certification, and sport management), engineering and applied science (civil, computer, electrical, general, and mechanical engineering; computer science; and a joint M.B.A. program), and professional studies (exercise science, general studies, and nursing). GU offers qualified students the opportunity to study abroad through programs in Australia, Brazil, British West Indies, China, Costa Rica, El Salvador, England, France, Ireland, Italy, Japan, Mexico, and Spain.

Interviews and Campus Visits All interested students are encouraged to visit the campus through Gonzaga's Visit Office. Personalized schedules may include a financial aid session, an interview with an admission counselor, and a campus tour through the Foley Center Library, the Martin Centre athletic facility (with its state-of-the-art student fitness center), the Jundt Art Center and Museum, and many other facilities. Students may also sit in on classes, meet with professors, and stay overnight in a residence hall on a space-available basis. For appointments, students should call the Office of Admission at 800-322-2584 Ext. 6531 (toll-free), Monday through Friday, 8 to 4 (Pacific time), at least two weeks prior to visiting. The office is located in Gonzaga's Administration Building, 502 East Boone Avenue. The nearest commercial airport, Spokane International, is about 15 minutes from the campus.

For Further Information Write to Julie McCulloh, Dean of Admission, Gonzaga University, 502 East Boone Avenue, Spokane, WA 99258-0102. *E-mail:* admissions@gonzaga.edu.

HERITAGE UNIVERSITY

Toppenish, Washington

Heritage University is a coed, private, comprehensive institution, founded in 1982, offering degrees at the associate, bachelor's, and master's levels and postbachelor's certificates. It has a 10-acre campus in Toppenish.

Expenses for 2006–07 *Application fee:* $0. *Tuition:* $9600 full-time, $320 per credit hour part-time. *Mandatory fees:* $45 full-time.

For Further Information Contact Ms. Leticia Garcia, Director of Admissions and Recruitment, Heritage University, 3240 Fort Road, Toppenish, WA 98948-9599. *Telephone:* 509-865-8508 or 888-272-6190 (toll-free in-state). *Fax:* 509-865-4469. *E-mail:* garcia_l@heritage.edu. *Web site:* http://www.heritage.edu/.

ITT TECHNICAL INSTITUTE

Bothell, Washington

ITT Technical Institute is a coed, proprietary, primarily two-year college of ITT Educational Services, Inc, founded in 1993, offering degrees at the associate and bachelor's levels.

Expenses for 2006–07 *Application fee:* $100. Contact school for program costs.

Financial Aid Forms of aid include need-based scholarships and part-time jobs. The application deadline for financial aid is continuous.

Freshman Admission ITT Technical Institute requires a high school transcript, an interview, and Wonderlic aptitude test. Recommendations are recommended. The application deadline for regular admission is rolling.

Transfer Admission The application deadline for admission is rolling.

Entrance Difficulty ITT Technical Institute assesses its entrance difficulty level as minimally difficult.

For Further Information Contact Mr. Brad Tmavsky, Director of Recruitment, ITT Technical Institute, 1615 75th Street SW, Everett, WA 98203. *Telephone:* 425-583-0200 or 800-272-3791 (toll-free in-state). *Fax:* 425-485-3438. *Web site:* http://www.itt-tech.edu/.

ITT TECHNICAL INSTITUTE
Seattle, Washington

ITT Technical Institute is a coed, proprietary, primarily two-year college of ITT Educational Services, Inc, founded in 1932, offering degrees at the associate and bachelor's levels.

Expenses for 2006–07 *Application fee:* $100. Contact school for program costs.

Financial Aid Forms of aid include need-based scholarships and part-time jobs. The application deadline for financial aid is continuous.

Freshman Admission ITT Technical Institute requires a high school transcript, an interview, TOEFL scores for international students, and Wonderlic aptitude test. Recommendations are recommended. The application deadline for regular admission is rolling.

Transfer Admission The application deadline for admission is rolling.

Entrance Difficulty ITT Technical Institute assesses its entrance difficulty level as minimally difficult.

For Further Information Contact Mr. David Thompson, Director of Recruitment, ITT Technical Institute, 12720 Gateway Drive, Seattle, WA 98168. *Telephone:* 206-244-3300 or 800-422-2029 (toll-free). *Fax:* 206-246-7635. *Web site:* http://www.itt-tech.edu/.

ITT TECHNICAL INSTITUTE
Spokane, Washington

ITT Technical Institute is a coed, proprietary, primarily two-year college of ITT Educational Services, Inc, founded in 1985, offering degrees at the associate and bachelor's levels. It has a 3-acre campus in Spokane.

Expenses for 2006–07 *Application fee:* $100. Contact school for program costs.

Financial Aid Forms of aid include need-based scholarships and part-time jobs. The application deadline for financial aid is continuous.

Freshman Admission ITT Technical Institute requires a high school transcript, an interview, TOEFL scores for international students, and Wonderlic aptitude test. Recommendations are recommended. The application deadline for regular admission is rolling.

Transfer Admission The application deadline for admission is rolling.

Entrance Difficulty ITT Technical Institute assesses its entrance difficulty level as minimally difficult.

For Further Information Contact Mr. Gregory L. Alexander, Director of Recruitment, ITT Technical Institute, 13518 East Indiana Avenue, Spokane Valley, WA 99216. *Telephone:* 509-926-2900 or 800-777-8324 (toll-free). *Fax:* 509-926-2908. *Web site:* http://www.itt-tech.edu/.

NORTHWEST COLLEGE OF ART
Poulsbo, Washington

Northwest College of Art is a coed, proprietary, four-year college, founded in 1982, offering degrees at the bachelor's level. It has a 26-acre campus in Poulsbo near Seattle.

Academic Information Special programs include double majors, summer session for credit, and internships.

Financial Aid Forms of aid include need-based and non-need-based scholarships. The application deadline for financial aid is May 1.

Freshman Admission Northwest College of Art requires an essay, a high school transcript, a minimum 2.5 high school GPA, 3 recommendations, an interview, a portfolio, and TOEFL scores for international students. The application deadline for regular admission is June 1.

Transfer Admission The application deadline for admission is June 1.

Entrance Difficulty Northwest College of Art assesses its entrance difficulty level as moderately difficult.

For Further Information Contact Mr. Mark Stoddard, Admissions, Northwest College of Art, 16464 State Highway 305, Poulsbo, WA 98370. *Telephone:* 360-779-9993 or 800-769-ARTS (toll-free). *Fax:* 360-779-9933. *E-mail:* mstoddard@nca.edu. *Web site:* http://www.nca.edu/.

NORTHWEST SCHOOL OF WOODEN BOATBUILDING
Port Hadlock, Washington

http://www.nwboatschool.org/

NORTHWEST UNIVERSITY
Kirkland, Washington

Northwest University is a coed, private, comprehensive institution, founded in 1934, affiliated with the Assemblies of God, offering degrees at the associate, bachelor's, and master's levels. It has a 56-acre campus in Kirkland near Seattle.

Academic Information The faculty has 97 members (56% full-time), 36% with terminal degrees. The undergraduate student-faculty ratio is 20:1. The library holds 120,226 titles, 11,454 serial subscriptions, and 4,216 audiovisual materials. Special programs include academic remediation, cooperative (work-study) education, study abroad, advanced placement credit, accelerated degree programs, ESL programs, double majors, independent study, summer session for credit, part-time degree programs, adult/continuing education programs, and internships. The most frequently chosen baccalaureate fields are business/marketing, psychology, theology and religious vocations.

Student Body Statistics The student body totals 1,265, of whom 1,141 are undergraduates (170 freshmen). 61 percent are women and 39 percent are men. Students come from 26 states and territories and 13 other countries. 83 percent are from Washington. 1.7 percent are international students.

Expenses for 2007–08 *Application fee:* $30. *Comprehensive fee:* $26,340 includes full-time tuition ($19,520), mandatory fees ($242), and college room and board ($6578). *Part-time tuition:* $820 per credit. *Part-time mandatory fees:* $242 per year.

Financial Aid Forms of aid include need-based and non-need-based scholarships, athletic grants, and part-time jobs. The average aided 2006–07 undergraduate received an aid package worth an estimated $12,826. The application deadline for financial aid is August 1 with a priority deadline of March 1.

Freshman Admission Northwest University requires an essay, a high school transcript, a minimum 2.3 high school GPA, 2 recommendations, SAT or ACT scores, and TOEFL scores for international students. An interview is required for some. The application deadline for regular admission is August 1.

Transfer Admission The application deadline for admission is August 1.

Entrance Difficulty Northwest University assesses its entrance difficulty level as moderately difficult. For the fall 2006 freshman class, 75 percent of the applicants were accepted.

For Further Information Contact Mr. Ben Thomas, Director of Admissions, Northwest University, PO Box 579, Kirkland, WA 98083-0579. *Telephone:* 425-889-5212 or 800-669-3781 (toll-free). *Fax:* 425-889-5224. *E-mail:* admissions@northwestu.edu. *Web site:* http://www.northwestu.edu/.

PACIFIC LUTHERAN UNIVERSITY

Tacoma, Washington

Pacific Lutheran University is a coed, private, comprehensive institution, founded in 1890, affiliated with the Evangelical Lutheran Church in America, offering degrees at the bachelor's and master's levels and post-master's and postbachelor's certificates. It has a 126-acre campus in Tacoma near Seattle.

Academic Information The faculty has 266 members (83% full-time), 89% with terminal degrees. The undergraduate student-faculty ratio is 15:1. The library holds 350,750 titles, 3,433 serial subscriptions, and 12,954 audiovisual materials. Special programs include services for learning-disabled students, cooperative (work-study) education, study abroad, advanced placement credit, ESL programs, double majors, independent study, self-designed majors, summer session for credit, part-time degree programs (daytime, summer), adult/continuing education programs, and internships. The most frequently chosen baccalaureate fields are business/marketing, education, social sciences.

Student Body Statistics The student body totals 3,640, of whom 3,340 are undergraduates (670 freshmen). 64 percent are women and 36 percent are men. Students come from 43 states and territories and 25 other countries. 80 percent are from Washington. 5.1 percent are international students.

Expenses for 2006–07 *Application fee:* $40. *Comprehensive fee:* $30,590 includes full-time tuition ($23,450) and college room and board ($7140). *College room only:* $3510. Full-time tuition varies according to course load. Room and board charges vary according to board plan and housing facility. *Part-time tuition:* $731 per semester hour. Part-time tuition varies according to course load.

Financial Aid Forms of aid include need-based and non-need-based scholarships and part-time jobs. The average aided 2006–07 undergraduate received an aid package worth an estimated $23,185. The priority application deadline for financial aid is March 1.

Freshman Admission Pacific Lutheran University requires an essay, a high school transcript, 1 recommendation, SAT or ACT scores, and TOEFL scores for international students. A minimum 2.5 high school GPA is recommended. An interview is required for some. The application deadline for regular admission is rolling.

Transfer Admission The application deadline for admission is rolling.

Entrance Difficulty Pacific Lutheran University assesses its entrance difficulty level as moderately difficult. For the fall 2006 freshman class, 74 percent of the applicants were accepted.

For Further Information Contact Dr. Laura Majovski, Vice President for Admissions and Student Life, Pacific Lutheran University, Tacoma, WA 98447. *Telephone:* 253-535-7151 or 800-274-6758 (toll-free). *Fax:* 253-536-5136. *E-mail:* admission@plu.edu. *Web site:* http://www.plu.edu/.

SAINT MARTIN'S UNIVERSITY

Lacey, Washington

Saint Martin's University is a coed, private, Roman Catholic, comprehensive institution, founded in 1895, offering degrees at the bachelor's and master's levels and postbachelor's certificates. It has a 300-acre campus in Lacey near Tacoma.

Expenses for 2006–07 *Application fee:* $35. *Comprehensive fee:* $27,365 includes full-time tuition ($20,675), mandatory fees ($290), and college room and board ($6400). *College room only:* $3000. *Part-time tuition:* $689 per credit. *Part-time mandatory fees:* $145 per term.

For Further Information Contact Mr. Todd Abbott, Director of Admission, Saint Martin's University, 5300 Pacific Avenue, SE, Lacey, WA 98503-1297. *Telephone:* 360-438-4590 or 800-368-8803 (toll-free). *Fax:* 360-412-6189. *E-mail:* admissions@stmartin.edu. *Web site:* http://www.stmartin.edu/.

SEATTLE PACIFIC UNIVERSITY

Seattle, Washington

Seattle Pacific University is a coed, private, Free Methodist, comprehensive institution, founded in 1891, offering degrees at the bachelor's, master's, and doctoral levels and post-master's certificates. It has a 35-acre campus in Seattle.

Academic Information The faculty has 364 members (50% full-time), 49% with terminal degrees. The undergraduate student-faculty ratio is 14:1. The library holds 191,807 titles, 1,230 serial subscriptions, and 4,408 audiovisual materials. Special programs include academic remediation, services for learning-disabled students, an honors program, cooperative (work-study) education, study abroad, advanced placement credit, ESL programs, double majors, independent study, distance learning, self-designed majors, summer session for credit, part-time degree programs (daytime, evenings, weekends, summer), external degree programs, adult/continuing education programs, internships, and arrangement for off-campus study with 13 members of the Coalition for Christian Colleges and Universities. The most frequently chosen baccalaureate fields are business/marketing, family and consumer sciences, health professions and related sciences.

Student Body Statistics The student body totals 3,830, of whom 2,979 are undergraduates (622 freshmen). 67 percent are women and 33 percent are men. Students come from 46 states and territories and 24 other countries. 66 percent are from Washington. 0.7 percent are international students. 12 percent of the 2006 graduating class went on to graduate and professional schools.

Expenses for 2006–07 *Application fee:* $45. *Comprehensive fee:* $31,209 includes full-time tuition ($23,055), mandatory fees ($336), and college room and board ($7818). *College room only:* $4212. Room and board charges vary according to board plan and housing facility. *Part-time tuition:* $641 per credit. Part-time tuition varies according to course load.

Financial Aid Forms of aid include need-based and non-need-based scholarships, athletic grants, and part-time jobs. The average aided 2006–07 undergraduate received an aid package worth an estimated $19,709.

Freshman Admission Seattle Pacific University requires an essay, a high school transcript, a minimum 2.5 high school GPA, 2 recommendations, SAT or ACT scores, and TOEFL scores for international students. SAT scores are recommended. The application deadline for regular admission is February 1 and for early action it is November 15.

Transfer Admission The application deadline for admission is August 1.

Entrance Difficulty Seattle Pacific University assesses its entrance difficulty level as moderately difficult. For the fall 2006 freshman class, 80 percent of the applicants were accepted.

For Further Information Contact Mr. Jobe Nice, Acting Director of Admissions, Seattle Pacific University, 3307 3rd Avenue, W, Seattle, WA 98119-1997. *Telephone:* 206-281-2021 or 800-366-3344 (toll-free). *Fax:* 206-281-2669. *E-mail:* admissions@spu.edu. *Web site:* http://www.spu.edu/.

SEATTLE UNIVERSITY

Seattle, Washington

SPONSOR See Front Insert for Details!

Seattle University is a coed, private, Roman Catholic, comprehensive institution, founded in 1891, offering degrees at the bachelor's, master's, doctoral, and first professional levels and post-master's, first professional, and postbachelor's certificates. It has a 46-acre campus in Seattle.

Academic Information The faculty has 594 members (68% full-time), 73% with terminal degrees. The undergraduate student-faculty ratio is 13:1. The library holds 141,478 titles, 2,701 serial subscriptions, and 5,649 audiovisual materials. Special programs include services for learning-disabled students, an honors program, study abroad, advanced placement credit, accelerated degree programs, Freshman Honors College, ESL programs, double majors, independent study, self-designed majors, summer session for credit, part-time degree programs, adult/continuing education programs, internships, and

arrangement for off-campus study with Photographic Center Northwest. The most frequently chosen baccalaureate fields are business/marketing, health professions and related sciences, psychology.

Student Body Statistics The student body totals 7,226, of whom 4,160 are undergraduates (787 freshmen). 61 percent are women and 39 percent are men. Students come from 47 states and territories and 76 other countries. 60 percent are from Washington. 6.4 percent are international students.

Expenses for 2006–07 *Application fee:* $45. *Comprehensive fee:* $32,118 includes full-time tuition ($24,615) and college room and board ($7503). *College room only:* $4818. Full-time tuition varies according to course load. Room and board charges vary according to board plan. *Part-time tuition:* $547 per credit. Part-time tuition varies according to course load.

Financial Aid Forms of aid include need-based and non-need-based scholarships, athletic grants, and part-time jobs. The average aided 2006–07 undergraduate received an aid package worth an estimated $23,740. The priority application deadline for financial aid is February 1.

Freshman Admission Seattle University requires an essay, a high school transcript, a minimum 2.5 high school GPA, 2 recommendations, SAT or ACT scores, and TOEFL scores for international students. The application deadline for regular admission is rolling.

Transfer Admission The application deadline for admission is August 15.

Entrance Difficulty Seattle University assesses its entrance difficulty level as moderately difficult; very difficult for upper-level nursing, engineering, diagnostic ultrasound, honors programs. For the fall 2006 freshman class, 65 percent of the applicants were accepted.

SPECIAL MESSAGE TO STUDENTS

Social Life Opportunities for involvement outside of class are extensive, varied, and as diverse as the students who attend Seattle University. The school is within walking distance of the major cultural and athletic facilities of one of America's finest cities. Therefore, most campus activities focus upon taking advantage of this major metropolis and on promoting student community and cohesiveness. There are more than eighty-five clubs, which include Hui o'Nani (the Hawaiian Student Organization), Earth Action Coalition, the National Society of Black Engineers, Forensics, and the Hiyu Coulee Hiking Club. There are twelve NCAA Division II athletic teams (men's and women's basketball, soccer, swimming, cross-country and track, and women's softball and volleyball) as well as a variety of intramural and club sports, such as tennis, cycling, skiing, and ice hockey. Service and leadership are central to Seattle University. Campus ministry plays a major role in student life as reflected by the Peace and Social Justice Center, involvement in Habitat for Humanity, and the student-run "Street Feed." Seattle University has the only Calcutta Club on any campus in the nation, and annually students travel to India to perform volunteer work. Approximately 1,600 of Seattle University's 4,135 undergraduates live on campus in three residence halls and in campus garden apartments.

Academic Highlights Seattle University is the only classically urban institute in the Northwest—accordingly, a firm academic foundation is established on campus, and the city is used as an extension of the classroom. Internship and part-time employment opportunities abound for students in all majors. Seattle University is noted as a fine liberal arts institution as well as for incorporating three professional schools, which produce leaders respected throughout the Puget Sound region. Major corporate, industrial, government, and health-care leaders assist students as professional mentors as well as actively serving on specific business, nursing, and science and engineering advisory boards. The University is distinctive for the significant percentage of women teaching in fields such as business, the sciences, and engineering; the prevalence of writing requirements throughout the curriculum; and its strong emphasis on students acquiring experience working on academic projects as teams.

Interviews and Campus Visit Seattle University is a short ride from Seatac International Airport, and its location at the juncture of Broadway and Madison Street is convenient to Interstates 5 and 90. Visitors find themselves within walking distance of major museums, the

symphony, theater district, the Pike Place Market, the International District, historic Pioneer Square, and eclectic Capitol Hill. Interviews are strongly encouraged, though not required. Appointments are typically available 9 to 5, Monday and Tuesday, and 9 to 3, Wednesday through Friday, with interviews available 9 to 1 many Saturdays. Campus tours are offered several times a day during the week and during the Saturdays the Admissions Office is open. During the week, admissions visits can be combined with appointments with financial aid and athletics, and students may also visit classes. Students should call 206-296-2000 or 800-426-7123 (toll-free) two weeks in advance to schedule an appointment to allow the best possible service.

For Further Information Write to Mr. Michael K. McKeon, Dean, Admissions Office, Seattle University, 901 12th Avenue, Seattle, WA 98122-1090. *E-mail:* admissions@seattleu.edu. *Web site:* http://www.seattleu.edu.

See page 192 for the College Close-Up.

TRINITY LUTHERAN COLLEGE
Issaquah, Washington

Trinity Lutheran College is a coed, private, Lutheran, four-year college, founded in 1944, offering degrees at the associate and bachelor's levels and postbachelor's certificates. It has a 46-acre campus in Issaquah near Seattle.

Academic Information The faculty has 28 members (46% full-time). The library holds 31,000 titles and 217 serial subscriptions. Special programs include academic remediation, services for learning-disabled students, study abroad, advanced placement credit, ESL programs, double majors, independent study, part-time degree programs (daytime, evenings), internships, and arrangement for off-campus study with Concordia University (OR).

Student Body Statistics The student body is made up of 115 undergraduates. Students come from 13 states and territories and 6 other countries. 90 percent are from Washington. 8 percent of the 2006 graduating class went on to graduate and professional schools.

Expenses for 2006–07 *Application fee:* $30. *Comprehensive fee:* $19,748 includes full-time tuition ($13,720) and college room and board ($6028). *Part-time tuition:* $490 per credit hour.

Financial Aid Forms of aid include need-based and non-need-based scholarships and part-time jobs. The priority application deadline for financial aid is March 1.

Freshman Admission Trinity Lutheran College requires a high school transcript, a minimum 2.0 high school GPA, 2 recommendations, SAT or ACT scores, and TOEFL scores for international students. An interview is required for some. The application deadline for regular admission is September 15.

Transfer Admission The application deadline for admission is September 15.

Entrance Difficulty Trinity Lutheran College assesses its entrance difficulty level as minimally difficult. For the fall 2006 freshman class, 51 percent of the applicants were accepted.

For Further Information Contact Jon Olson, Director of Admissions, Trinity Lutheran College, 4221 228th Avenue, SE, Issaquah, WA 98029-9299. *Telephone:* 425-961-5516 or 800-843-5659 (toll-free). *Fax:* 425-392-0404. *E-mail:* admission@tlc.edu. *Web site:* http://www.tlc.edu/.

UNIVERSITY OF PHOENIX–EASTERN WASHINGTON CAMPUS
Spokane Valley, Washington

University of Phoenix–Eastern Washington Campus is a coed, proprietary, comprehensive institution, founded in 2003, offering degrees at the bachelor's and master's levels.

Academic Information The faculty has 121 members (15% full-time), 26% with terminal degrees. The undergraduate student-faculty ratio is 4:1.

University of Phoenix–Eastern Washington Campus (continued)

The library holds 1,759 titles and 692 serial subscriptions. Special programs include services for learning-disabled students, advanced placement credit, accelerated degree programs, independent study, distance learning, external degree programs, and adult/continuing education programs. The most frequently chosen baccalaureate field is business/marketing.

Student Body Statistics The student body totals 294, of whom 254 are undergraduates (14 freshmen). 56 percent are women and 44 percent are men. 28 percent are international students.

Expenses for 2006–07 *Application fee:* $45. *Tuition:* $10,260 full-time, $342 per credit part-time.

Financial Aid Forms of aid include need-based and non-need-based scholarships. The average aided 2005–06 undergraduate received an aid package worth $4005. The application deadline for financial aid is continuous.

Freshman Admission University of Phoenix–Eastern Washington Campus requires 1 recommendation. A high school transcript is required for some. The application deadline for regular admission is rolling.

Transfer Admission The application deadline for admission is rolling.

Entrance Difficulty University of Phoenix–Eastern Washington Campus has an open admission policy.

For Further Information Contact Ms. Beth Barilla, Associate Vice President, Student Admissions and Services, University of Phoenix–Eastern Washington Campus, 4615 East Elwood Street, Mail Stop AA-K101, Phoenix, AZ 85040-1958. *Telephone:* 480-894-1758, 800-697-8223 (toll-free in-state), or 800-228-7240 (toll-free out-of-state). *Fax:* 480-643-1521. *E-mail:* beth.barilla@phoenix.edu. *Web site:* http://www.phoenix.edu/.

UNIVERSITY OF PHOENIX–WASHINGTON CAMPUS

Seattle, Washington

University of Phoenix–Washington Campus is a coed, proprietary, comprehensive institution, founded in 1997, offering degrees at the bachelor's and master's levels.

Academic Information The faculty has 258 members (6% full-time), 31% with terminal degrees. The undergraduate student-faculty ratio is 9:1. The library holds 1,759 titles and 692 serial subscriptions. Special programs include services for learning-disabled students, advanced placement credit, accelerated degree programs, independent study, distance learning, external degree programs, and adult/continuing education programs. The most frequently chosen baccalaureate fields are business/marketing, computer and information sciences, public administration and social services.

Student Body Statistics The student body totals 1,758, of whom 1,430 are undergraduates (19 freshmen). 57 percent are women and 43 percent are men. 3.6 percent are international students.

Expenses for 2006–07 *Application fee:* $45. *Tuition:* $11,190 full-time.

Financial Aid Forms of aid include need-based and non-need-based scholarships. The average aided 2005–06 undergraduate received an aid package worth $3681. The application deadline for financial aid is continuous.

Freshman Admission University of Phoenix–Washington Campus requires 1 recommendation and TOEFL scores for international students. A high school transcript is required for some. The application deadline for regular admission is rolling.

Transfer Admission The application deadline for admission is rolling.

Entrance Difficulty University of Phoenix–Washington Campus has an open admission policy.

For Further Information Contact Ms. Beth Barilla, Associate Vice President, Student Admissions and Services, University of Phoenix–Washington Campus, 4615 East Elwood Street, Mail Stop AA-K101, Phoenix, AZ 85040-1958. *Telephone:* 480-317-6000, 800-776-4867 (toll-free in-state), or 800-228-7240 (toll-free out-of-state). *Fax:* 480-894-1758. *E-mail:* beth.barilla@phoenix.edu. *Web site:* http://www.phoenix.edu/.

UNIVERSITY OF PUGET SOUND

Tacoma, Washington

University of Puget Sound is a coed, private, comprehensive institution, founded in 1888, offering degrees at the bachelor's, master's, and first professional levels and post-master's certificates. It has a 97-acre campus in Tacoma near Seattle.

Academic Information The faculty has 274 members (81% full-time), 78% with terminal degrees. The undergraduate student-faculty ratio is 12:1. The library holds 364,662 titles, 20,008 serial subscriptions, and 16,868 audiovisual materials. Special programs include an honors program, cooperative (work-study) education, study abroad, advanced placement credit, double majors, independent study, self-designed majors, summer session for credit, part-time degree programs (daytime, evenings, summer), and internships. The most frequently chosen baccalaureate fields are business/marketing, social sciences, visual and performing arts.

Student Body Statistics The student body totals 2,819, of whom 2,539 are undergraduates (678 freshmen). 58 percent are women and 42 percent are men. Students come from 47 states and territories and 13 other countries. 30 percent are from Washington. 0.4 percent are international students. 36 percent of the 2006 graduating class went on to graduate and professional schools.

Expenses for 2006–07 *Application fee:* $40. *Comprehensive fee:* $37,730 includes full-time tuition ($29,870), mandatory fees ($190), and college room and board ($7670). *College room only:* $4190. Full-time tuition and fees vary according to course load. Room and board charges vary according to board plan and housing facility. *Part-time tuition:* $3770 per unit. Part-time tuition varies according to course load.

Financial Aid Forms of aid include need-based and non-need-based scholarships and part-time jobs. The average aided 2006–07 undergraduate received an aid package worth an estimated $22,740. The priority application deadline for financial aid is February 1.

Freshman Admission University of Puget Sound requires an essay, a high school transcript, 2 recommendations, SAT or ACT scores, and TOEFL scores for international students. A minimum 3.0 high school GPA and an interview are recommended. The application deadline for regular admission is February 1; for early decision plan 1 it is November 15; and for early decision plan 2 it is December 15.

Transfer Admission The application deadline for admission is July 1.

Entrance Difficulty University of Puget Sound assesses its entrance difficulty level as moderately difficult. For the fall 2006 freshman class, 65 percent of the applicants were accepted.

For Further Information Contact Dr. George Mills, Vice President for Enrollment, University of Puget Sound, 1500 North Warner Street, Tacoma, WA 98416-1062. *Telephone:* 253-879-3211 or 800-396-7191 (toll-free). *Fax:* 253-879-3993. *E-mail:* admission@ups.edu. *Web site:* http://www.ups.edu/.

UNIVERSITY OF WASHINGTON

Seattle, Washington

University of Washington is a coed, public university, founded in 1861, offering degrees at the bachelor's, master's, doctoral, and first professional levels and first professional certificates. It has a 703-acre campus in Seattle.

Academic Information The faculty has 3,617 members (81% full-time), 93% with terminal degrees. The undergraduate student-faculty ratio is 11:1. The library holds 6 million titles and 50,245 serial subscriptions. Special programs include academic remediation, services for learning-disabled students, an honors program, cooperative (work-study) education, study abroad, advanced placement credit, accelerated degree programs, ESL programs, double majors, independent study, distance learning, self-designed majors, summer session for credit, part-time degree programs, adult/continuing education programs, and internships. The most frequently chosen baccalaureate fields are business/marketing, education, social sciences.

Student Body Statistics The student body totals 39,524, of whom 27,836 are undergraduates (5,475 freshmen). 52 percent are women and 48

percent are men. Students come from 52 states and territories and 59 other countries. 86 percent are from Washington. 3.6 percent are international students.

Expenses for 2006–07 *Application fee:* $50. *State resident tuition:* $5988 full-time. *Nonresident tuition:* $21,286 full-time. Full-time tuition varies according to course load. *College room and board:* $6561. Room and board charges vary according to board plan and housing facility.

Financial Aid Forms of aid include need-based and non-need-based scholarships, athletic grants, and part-time jobs. The average aided 2006–07 undergraduate received an aid package worth an estimated $12,000. The priority application deadline for financial aid is February 28.

Freshman Admission University of Washington requires an essay, a minimum 2.0 high school GPA, SAT or ACT scores, and TOEFL scores for international students. A high school transcript is required for some. The application deadline for regular admission is January 15.

Transfer Admission The application deadline for admission is February 15.

Entrance Difficulty University of Washington assesses its entrance difficulty level as moderately difficult; very difficult for transfers. For the fall 2006 freshman class, 68 percent of the applicants were accepted.

For Further Information Contact Admissions Office, University of Washington, 1410 NE Campus Parkway, Box 355852, Seattle, WA 98195-5852. *Telephone:* 206-543-9686. *Fax:* 206-685-3655. *Web site:* http://www.washington.edu/.

UNIVERSITY OF WASHINGTON, BOTHELL
Bothell, Washington

University of Washington, Bothell is a coed, public, upper-level unit of University of Washington, founded in 1990, offering degrees at the bachelor's and master's levels. It has a 128-acre campus in Bothell.

Academic Information The faculty has 103 members (71% full-time), 92% with terminal degrees. The undergraduate student-faculty ratio is 14:1. The library holds 73,749 titles, 720 serial subscriptions, and 6,100 audiovisual materials. Special programs include services for learning-disabled students, an honors program, cooperative (work-study) education, study abroad, advanced placement credit, double majors, independent study, summer session for credit, part-time degree programs, adult/continuing education programs, and internships. The most frequently chosen baccalaureate fields are business/marketing, health professions and related sciences, interdisciplinary studies.

Student Body Statistics The student body totals 1,683, of whom 1,441 are undergraduates. 55 percent are women and 45 percent are men. Students come from 7 states and territories and 5 other countries. 98 percent are from Washington. 0.8 percent are international students.

Expenses for 2006–07 *Application fee:* $50. *State resident tuition:* $5859 full-time. *Nonresident tuition:* $21,157 full-time.

Entrance Difficulty University of Washington, Bothell assesses its entrance difficulty level as moderately difficult. For the fall 2006 entering class, 76 percent of the applicants were accepted.

For Further Information Contact Lindsey Kattenhorn, Assistant Director of Admissions, University of Washington, Bothell, 18115 Campus Way NE, Bothell, WA 98011-8246. *Telephone:* 425-352-5000. *Fax:* 425-352-5455. *E-mail:* freshmen@uwb.edu. *Web site:* http://www.uwb.edu.

UNIVERSITY OF WASHINGTON, TACOMA
Tacoma, Washington

University of Washington, Tacoma is a coed, public, upper-level unit of University of Washington, founded in 1990, offering degrees at the bachelor's, master's, and first professional levels and postbachelor's certificates. It has a 46-acre campus in Tacoma.

Academic Information The faculty has 142 members (73% full-time). The undergraduate student-faculty ratio is 14:1. The library holds 6 million titles, 44,608 serial subscriptions, and 107,408 audiovisual materials. Special programs include academic remediation, services for learning-disabled students, an honors program, cooperative (work-study) education, study abroad, advanced placement credit, accelerated degree programs,

double majors, independent study, distance learning, summer session for credit, part-time degree programs, adult/continuing education programs, and internships. The most frequently chosen baccalaureate fields are business/marketing, health professions and related sciences, interdisciplinary studies.

Student Body Statistics The student body totals 2,292, of whom 1,856 are undergraduates (562 in entering class). 60 percent are women and 40 percent are men. Students come from 18 states and territories and 4 other countries. 96 percent are from Washington. 0.8 percent are international students.

Expenses for 2007–08 *Application fee:* $50. *State resident tuition:* $5898 full-time, $923 per course part-time. *Nonresident tuition:* $21,198 full-time, $3532 per course part-time. *Mandatory fees:* $429 full-time, $15 per credit part-time.

Entrance Difficulty For the fall 2006 entering class, 35 percent of the applicants were accepted.

For Further Information Contact Ms. Wanda Curtis, Director, Admissions, University of Washington, Tacoma, 1900 Commerce Street, Tacoma, WA 98402. *Telephone:* 253-692-4400 or 800-736-7750 (toll-free out-of-state). *Fax:* 253-692-4414. *E-mail:* wandaec@u.washington.edu. *Web site:* http://www.tacoma.washington.edu/.

WALLA WALLA COLLEGE
College Place, Washington

Walla Walla College is a coed, private, Seventh-day Adventist, comprehensive institution, founded in 1892, offering degrees at the associate, bachelor's, and master's levels. It has a 77-acre campus in College Place.

Academic Information The faculty has 181 members (63% full-time), 51% with terminal degrees. The undergraduate student-faculty ratio is 13:1. The library holds 178,450 titles and 1,105 serial subscriptions. Special programs include academic remediation, services for learning-disabled students, an honors program, cooperative (work-study) education, study abroad, advanced placement credit, Freshman Honors College, ESL programs, double majors, independent study, summer session for credit, part-time degree programs (daytime, evenings, summer), and internships.

Student Body Statistics The student body totals 1,876, of whom 1,635 are undergraduates (323 freshmen). 48 percent are women and 52 percent are men. Students come from 41 states and territories and 19 other countries. 60 percent are from Washington. 1 percent are international students.

Expenses for 2006–07 *Application fee:* $40. *Comprehensive fee:* $25,724 includes full-time tuition ($20,810), mandatory fees ($204), and college room and board ($4710). *College room only:* $2547. *Part-time tuition:* $516 per credit.

Financial Aid Forms of aid include need-based and non-need-based scholarships and part-time jobs. The average aided 2005–06 undergraduate received an aid package worth $17,608. The application deadline for financial aid is continuous.

Freshman Admission Walla Walla College requires a high school transcript, a minimum 2.0 high school GPA, 3 recommendations, SAT scores, SAT or ACT scores, and TOEFL scores for international students. The application deadline for regular admission is rolling and for nonresidents it is September 30.

Transfer Admission The application deadline for admission is rolling.

Entrance Difficulty Walla Walla College assesses its entrance difficulty level as moderately difficult. For the fall 2006 freshman class, 94 percent of the applicants were accepted.

For Further Information Contact Mr. Dallas Weis, Director of Admissions, Walla Walla College, 204 South College Avenue, College Place, WA 99324. *Telephone:* 509-527-2327 or 800-541-8900 (toll-free). *Fax:* 509-527-2397. *E-mail:* info@wwc.edu. *Web site:* http://www.wwc.edu/.

WASHINGTON STATE UNIVERSITY
Pullman, Washington

Washington State University is a coed, public university, founded in 1890, offering degrees at the bachelor's, master's, doctoral, and first

Washington State University (continued)

professional levels and post-master's and postbachelor's certificates. It has a 620-acre campus in Pullman.

Academic Information The faculty has 1,501 members (72% full-time), 79% with terminal degrees. The undergraduate student-faculty ratio is 14:1. The library holds 2 million titles, 31,590 serial subscriptions, and 417,538 audiovisual materials. Special programs include services for learning-disabled students, an honors program, study abroad, advanced placement credit, accelerated degree programs, ESL programs, double majors, independent study, distance learning, self-designed majors, summer session for credit, part-time degree programs (daytime, summer), external degree programs, internships, and arrangement for off-campus study with University of Idaho, Education Abroad, National Student Exchange. The most frequently chosen baccalaureate fields are business/marketing, communications/journalism, social sciences.

Student Body Statistics The student body totals 23,655, of whom 19,554 are undergraduates (2,856 freshmen). 52 percent are women and 48 percent are men. Students come from 50 states and territories and 51 other countries. 89 percent are from Washington. 2.4 percent are international students.

Expenses for 2006–07 *Application fee:* $50. *State resident tuition:* $5432 full-time, $294 per credit part-time. *Nonresident tuition:* $15,072 full-time, $776 per credit part-time. *Mandatory fees:* $1015 full-time. Part-time tuition varies according to course load. *College room and board:* $6890. *College room only:* $3390. Room and board charges vary according to board plan, housing facility, and location.

Financial Aid Forms of aid include need-based and non-need-based scholarships, athletic grants, and part-time jobs. The average aided 2005–06 undergraduate received an aid package worth $9929. The priority application deadline for financial aid is March 1.

Freshman Admission Washington State University requires an essay, a high school transcript, a minimum 2.0 high school GPA, SAT or ACT scores, and TOEFL scores for international students. 3 recommendations are required for some.

Entrance Difficulty Washington State University assesses its entrance difficulty level as moderately difficult. For the fall 2006 freshman class, 77 percent of the applicants were accepted.

For Further Information Contact Ms. Wendy Peterson, Director of Admissions, Washington State University, PO Box 641067, Pullman, WA 99164-1067. *Telephone:* 509-335-5586 or 888-468-6978 (toll-free). *Fax:* 509-335-4902. *E-mail:* admiss2@wsu.edu. *Web site:* http://www.wsu.edu/.

WESTERN WASHINGTON UNIVERSITY
Bellingham, Washington

Western Washington University is a coed, public, comprehensive institution, founded in 1893, offering degrees at the bachelor's and master's levels and postbachelor's certificates. It has a 223-acre campus in Bellingham near Seattle and Vancouver.

Academic Information The faculty has 651 members (75% full-time), 71% with terminal degrees. The undergraduate student-faculty ratio is 19:1. The library holds 1 million titles and 5,236 serial subscriptions. Special programs include services for learning-disabled students, an honors program, cooperative (work-study) education, study abroad, advanced placement credit, accelerated degree programs, ESL programs, double majors, independent study, distance learning, self-designed majors, summer session for credit, internships, and arrangement for off-campus study with National Student Exchange. The most frequently chosen baccalaureate fields are business/marketing, English, social sciences.

Student Body Statistics The student body totals 14,035, of whom 12,838 are undergraduates (2,425 freshmen). 55 percent are women and 45 percent are men. Students come from 44 states and territories and 29 other countries. 94 percent are from Washington. 0.2 percent are international students. 14 percent of the 2006 graduating class went on to graduate and professional schools.

Expenses for 2006–07 *Application fee:* $50. *State resident tuition:* $3894 full-time, $145 per credit part-time. *Nonresident tuition:* $14,441 full-time, $497 per credit part-time. *Mandatory fees:* $1,108 full-time. Full-time tuition and fees vary according to location. Part-time tuition varies

according to location. *College room and board:* $6785. *College room only:* $4409. Room and board charges vary according to board plan and housing facility.

Financial Aid Forms of aid include need-based and non-need-based scholarships, athletic grants, and part-time jobs. The average aided 2006–07 undergraduate received an aid package worth an estimated $9310. The priority application deadline for financial aid is February 15.

Freshman Admission Western Washington University requires a high school transcript, SAT or ACT scores, TOEFL scores for international students, and TOEFL for International Students. An essay is recommended. The application deadline for regular admission is March 1.

Transfer Admission The application deadline for admission is April 1.

Entrance Difficulty Western Washington University assesses its entrance difficulty level as moderately difficult. For the fall 2006 freshman class, 74 percent of the applicants were accepted.

For Further Information Contact Ms. Karen Copetas, Director of Admissions, Western Washington University, 516 High Street, Bellingham, WA 98225-9009. *Telephone:* 360-650-3440. *Fax:* 360-650-7369. *E-mail:* admit@wwu.edu. *Web site:* http://www.wwu.edu/.

WHITMAN COLLEGE
Walla Walla, Washington

Whitman College is a coed, private, four-year college, founded in 1859, offering degrees at the bachelor's level. It has a 117-acre campus in Walla Walla.

Academic Information The faculty has 191 members (62% full-time), 83% with terminal degrees. The student-faculty ratio is 9:1. The library holds 395,841 titles, 12,843 serial subscriptions, and 7,565 audiovisual materials. Special programs include services for learning-disabled students, an honors program, cooperative (work-study) education, study abroad, advanced placement credit, accelerated degree programs, double majors, independent study, self-designed majors, and arrangement for off-campus study with American University, Associated Colleges of the Midwest, Great Lakes Colleges Association, Columbia University. The most frequently chosen baccalaureate fields are biological/life sciences, social sciences, visual and performing arts.

Student Body Statistics The student body is made up of 1,455 undergraduates (366 freshmen). 54 percent are women and 46 percent are men. Students come from 43 states and territories and 25 other countries. 41 percent are from Washington. 3.4 percent are international students.

Expenses for 2006–07 *Application fee:* $45. *Comprehensive fee:* $38,646 includes full-time tuition ($30,530), mandatory fees ($276), and college room and board ($7840). *College room only:* $3600. Room and board charges vary according to board plan and housing facility. *Part-time tuition:* $1280 per credit.

Financial Aid Forms of aid include need-based and non-need-based scholarships and part-time jobs. The average aided 2006–07 undergraduate received an aid package worth an estimated $22,300. The application deadline for financial aid is February 1 with a priority deadline of November 15.

Freshman Admission Whitman College requires an essay, a high school transcript, 1 recommendation, SAT or ACT scores, and TOEFL scores for international students. An interview is recommended. The application deadline for regular admission is January 15 and for early decision plan 1 it is November 15.

Transfer Admission The application deadline for admission is January 15.

Entrance Difficulty Whitman College assesses its entrance difficulty level as very difficult. For the fall 2006 freshman class, 47 percent of the applicants were accepted.

For Further Information Contact Mr. Tony Cabasco, Dean of Admission and Financial Aid, Whitman College, 515 Boyer Avenue, Walla Walla, WA 99362-2083. *Telephone:* 509-527-5176 or 877-462-9448 (toll-free). *Fax:* 509-527-4967. *E-mail:* admission@whitman.edu. *Web site:* http://www.whitman.edu/.

WHITWORTH UNIVERSITY

Spokane, Washington

Whitworth University is a coed, private, Presbyterian, comprehensive institution, founded in 1890, offering degrees at the bachelor's and master's levels. It has a 200-acre campus in Spokane.

Academic Information The faculty has 291 members (41% full-time). The undergraduate student-faculty ratio is 13:1. The library holds 17,982 titles and 773 serial subscriptions. Special programs include services for learning-disabled students, cooperative (work-study) education, study abroad, advanced placement credit, ESL programs, double majors, independent study, self-designed majors, summer session for credit, part-time degree programs, adult/continuing education programs, internships, and arrangement for off-campus study with 3 members of the Intercollegiate Center for Nursing, 2 members of the Intercollegiate Language Study Consortium. The most frequently chosen baccalaureate fields are business/marketing, education, visual and performing arts.

Student Body Statistics The student body totals 2,504, of whom 2,256 are undergraduates (470 freshmen). 61 percent are women and 39 percent are men. Students come from 31 states and territories and 25 other countries. 58 percent are from Washington. 0.9 percent are international students. 20 percent of the 2006 graduating class went on to graduate and professional schools.

Expenses for 2007–08 *Application fee:* $0. *Comprehensive fee:* $32,986 includes full-time tuition ($25,382), mandatory fees ($310), and college room and board ($7294).

Financial Aid Forms of aid include need-based and non-need-based scholarships and part-time jobs. The average aided 2006–07 undergraduate received an aid package worth an estimated $17,200. The priority application deadline for financial aid is March 1.

Freshman Admission Whitworth University requires an essay, a high school transcript, recommendations, and TOEFL scores for international students. An interview and SAT or ACT scores are required for some. The application deadline for regular admission is March 1 and for early action it is November 30.

Transfer Admission The application deadline for admission is July 1.

Entrance Difficulty Whitworth University assesses its entrance difficulty level as very difficult; moderately difficult for transfers. For the fall 2006 freshman class, 63 percent of the applicants were accepted.

For Further Information Contact Ms. Marianne Hansen, Director of Admission, Whitworth University, 300 West, Hawthorne Road, Spokane, WA 99251. *Telephone:* 509-777-4348 or 800-533-4668 (toll-free out-of-state). *Fax:* 509-777-3758. *E-mail:* admission@whitworth.edu. *Web site:* http://www.whitworth.edu/.

See page 210 for the College Close-Up.

Wyoming

UNIVERSITY OF WYOMING

Laramie, Wyoming

University of Wyoming is a coed, public university, founded in 1886, offering degrees at the bachelor's, master's, doctoral, and first professional levels and post-master's certificates. It has a 785-acre campus in Laramie.

Academic Information The faculty has 720 members (92% full-time), 83% with terminal degrees. The undergraduate student-faculty ratio is 10:1. The library holds 2 million titles, 11,668 serial subscriptions, and 9,961 audiovisual materials. Special programs include services for learning-disabled students, an honors program, study abroad, advanced placement credit, accelerated degree programs, ESL programs, double majors, independent study, distance learning, self-designed majors, summer session for credit, part-time degree programs (daytime, evenings, summer), external degree programs,

internships, and arrangement for off-campus study. The most frequently chosen baccalaureate fields are business/marketing, education, engineering.

Student Body Statistics The student body totals 13,203, of whom 9,468 are undergraduates (1,574 freshmen). 52 percent are women and 48 percent are men. Students come from 53 states and territories and 57 other countries. 73 percent are from Wyoming. 1.8 percent are international students. 18 percent of the 2006 graduating class went on to graduate and professional schools.

Expenses for 2007–08 *Application fee:* $40. *State resident tuition:* $2820 full-time, $94 per credit hour part-time. *Nonresident tuition:* $9660 full-time, $322 per credit hour part-time. *Mandatory fees:* $734 full-time, $176 per term part-time. *College room and board:* $7274. *College room only:* $3158.

Financial Aid Forms of aid include need-based and non-need-based scholarships, athletic grants, and part-time jobs. The average aided 2005–06 undergraduate received an aid package worth $7012. The priority application deadline for financial aid is February 1.

Freshman Admission University of Wyoming requires a high school transcript, a minimum 2.75 high school GPA, SAT or ACT scores, and TOEFL scores for international students. A high school transcript and a minimum 3.0 high school GPA are required for some. The application deadline for regular admission is August 10.

Transfer Admission The application deadline for admission is August 10.

Entrance Difficulty University of Wyoming assesses its entrance difficulty level as moderately difficult.

SPECIAL MESSAGE TO STUDENTS

Social Life The University of Wyoming, known as UW, offers more than 200 campus clubs and organizations so students have plenty of opportunities to get involved. Students may join a fraternity or sorority, run for a student government office, or participate in an honor or professional society. Be it writing for a campus publication, voicing political views, or joining student religious organizations, UW's opportunities are as diverse as its student body. Musical performances and concerts, plays, comedians, and other fun events are featured on campus every semester. Students also enjoy nearly sixty different intramural and club sports and all the outdoor adventure the Rocky Mountains can supply.

Academic Highlights UW students enjoy small classes that average just 29 students each, and the 16:1 student-faculty ratio means that individual attention from professors is part of the UW way of life. Fully 89 percent of the courses are taught by professors, not graduate assistants. This outstanding academic environment allows for relationships to develop between students and their professors in all six colleges: Agriculture, Arts and Sciences, Business, Education, Engineering, and Health Sciences. At UW, academic excellence is evident. UW proudly claims 2 Rhodes, 6 Truman, and 10 Goldwater scholarship winners just in the last thirteen years. Senior agriculture students routinely score in the top quartile nationwide against all other seniors completing the ACT-comprehensive exams. The College of Arts and Sciences, UW's largest, offers more than 50 percent of all majors, including a self-designed major. The debate team has recently won two national championships, and the theater and dance students routinely perform in a national competition at the Kennedy Center in Washington, D.C. Senior business students consistently score in the top 10 percent against all other business students completing the Major Field Achievement Test in Business. The NEA ranked UW's College of Education as one of the top seven teacher-preparation programs in the nation. Senior engineering students consistently score higher on their national examinations, Fundamentals of Engineering Exam, and their engineering honor society was recently voted as the most outstanding chapter in the nation. The College of Health Sciences also boasts nearly 100 percent job placement within six months after graduation. Also, the UW honors program has been cited as one of the best in the nation for its innovative courses, award-winning faculty, and lively and supportive atmosphere.

University of Wyoming (continued)

Interviews and Campus Visits Since seeing is believing, UW strongly encourages prospective students to visit the campus. It is the easiest way to determine if UW is the right choice. With advance notice, UW visits include a tour with a current student, individual meetings with professors or department staff members, and a visit with an admissions representative. There are also opportunities to speak with representatives from financial aid, residence life, varsity sports, and the honors program. To schedule a visit, prospective students can call 307-766-5160 or 800-DIAL-WYO (toll-free) or visit the Web site at http://www.uwyo.edu. The nearest commercial airport is Laramie Regional.

For Further Information Write to the Admissions Office, University of Wyoming, Department 3435, 1000 East University Avenue, Laramie, WY 82071-3435. *E-mail:* why-wyo@uwyo.edu.

See page 204 for the College Close-Up.

Close-Ups of Colleges in the West

ACADEMY OF ART UNIVERSITY
SAN FRANCISCO, CALIFORNIA

The University

In 1929, Academy of Art University founder Richard S. Stephens, who was the advertising creative director of *Sunset* magazine, acted on his belief that "aspiring artists and designers, given proper instruction, hard work, and dedication, can learn the skills needed to become successful professionals." His new school of advertising art consisted of 46 students meeting in one room on San Francisco's Kearny Street. The instructors, who were professional artists, brought real-world problems, situations, solutions, and practical experience to the students. Thus was born the school's philosophy by the founder: Hire today's best practicing professionals to teach the art and design professionals of tomorrow. At that time, advertising consisted primarily of illustrations, photos, and copy. Consequently, it became necessary to teach beginning students the fundamentals of drawing, painting, color, light, and photography as well as layout and typography.

When Richard A. Stephens succeeded his father as president in 1951, the Foundations Department was added, ensuring all students comprehended the basic principles of traditional art and design. Illustration soon expanded to include fine arts (drawing, painting, sculpture, and printmaking), and advertising design spawned the Graphic Design Department. Fashion (design, textiles, and merchandising) and Interior Design Departments were also added. In 1966, the Academy officially became a college, and in a decade, the Master of Fine Arts degree was offered. Five more buildings were purchased, and by 1992, there were more than 2,500 students. The leadership of the Academy was then turned over to the third generation, Elisa Stephens, granddaughter of the school's founder. She quickly determined that the school's small Computer Arts Department had enormous potential to prepare students for multimedia careers when allied with such companies as Silicon Graphics, Pixar, Adobe, and Walt Disney Productions. It is now one of the largest departments at the Academy.

Today, Academy of Art University is the largest private accredited art and design school in the nation with an enrollment of more than 9,500 students from nearly every country in the world. More than one third of the student body is made up of international students. The Academy has more than twenty facilities that house classrooms, studios, galleries, and dormitories. The students, who are admitted through an open-enrollment policy, aspire to earn either an A.A., a B.F.A., or a certificate in one of thirteen design majors. The school maintains a fleet of buses to connect the different points of the campus, all of which are located within the city limits of San Francisco, one of the world's most vibrant and beautiful cities. The faculty, which is 80 percent part-time and made up of working art and design professionals, is recruited from all across the nation and is drawn to the creative and intellectual center that is the Bay Area. Extensive senior-year internship programs allow students to gain valuable experience and develop strong portfolios in their chosen field before graduation.

Academy of Art University offers an M.F.A. program in architecture.

Location

The city of San Francisco is one of the great cultural centers of the world; a melting pot of diversity, ethnicity, and creativity that has spawned major museums and galleries, world-class opera and theaters, dance companies, film production and recording studios, technological innovation, performing artists ranging from classical to popular music, and numerous other cultural opportunities. The city's status as a tourist mecca located on the Pacific Rim ensures that one encounters people from all corners of the world. The climate is moderate and offers kaleidoscopic blends of sunshine and fog nine months of the year. The Northpoint campus is located at world-famous Pier 39; one can view Alcatraz Island from classroom windows. Four other buildings are two blocks from historic Union Square

in the commercial heart of the city. Three other buildings are located near the Financial District. The city offers myriad locations for field trips and studio visits. World-renowned artists display their creations in the Academy's four nonprofit art galleries, which are open to the public. The University is an urban institution that both draws upon and contributes to the cultural wealth of the community in which it resides.

Majors and Degrees

Academy of Art University offers A.A. and B.F.A. degrees and certificates in the following majors: advertising (account planning, art direction, copywriting, and television commercials), animation/visual effects (background painting/layout design, character development, game design, storyboard art, VFX/compositing, visual development, and 3-D modeling), computer arts/new media (computer graphics, digital imaging, new media, and Web design), digital arts and communications (client and service-side Internet design creative programming, information architecture, interactive information graphics, interactive modeling, prototyping/testing, and usability), fashion (fashion design, fashion illustration, knitwear, merchandising, and textiles), fine art (ceramics, metal arts, painting/drawing, printmaking, and sculpture), graphic design (corporate and brand identity, motion graphics, multimedia, package design, print and collateral, and Web site design), illustration (cartooning, children's books, editorial, feature film animation, and 2-D animation), industrial design (furniture, product, toy, and transportation), interior architecture and design (commercial, furniture, and residential), motion pictures and television (acting, advertising/director–camera, cinematography, directing, editing, producing, production design, screenwriting, and special effects), and photography (advertising, digital photography, documentary, fine art, photo illustration, and photojournalism).

Academic Programs

A total of 132 credit units are required to earn a Bachelor of Fine Arts degree, consisting of 18 units of foundations courses, 60 units in the major, 12 units of art electives, and 42 units of liberal arts/art history courses. First-year students must complete six foundations courses before the end of the year. Fundamental courses are related specifically to students' majors to prepare them to begin intense focus courses in their field by the sophomore year. All major courses of study are structured so the student builds upon skills learned the previous semester and advances to the next level of technical or creative proficiency. Some related major courses may be taken concurrently. Each course is worth 3 credits. Liberal arts courses teach practical applications for forging a professional career in art and design. International students who come from countries where English is not the primary language may take additional ESL classes, as determined by English language proficiency testing. Students are advised to meet with departmental directors at least once during the academic year to have their progress assessed. Portfolios are reviewed before the junior year to determine whether or not a student has progressed sufficiently to continue study at the Academy.

Academic Facilities

The Academy's facilities reflect its commitment to training students for careers in art and design; not only do students have access to some of the most advanced facilities in the nation, but the Academy continually invests in new equipment to ensure that it remains on the cutting edge of technology. By learning on industry-standard equipment, students gain valuable professional skills that make them highly employable.

The Academy's eight-story Digital Arts Center offers students from the Computer Arts/New Media, Digital Arts and Communications, Animation-Visual Effects, Motion Pictures and Television, Advertising, and Fashion Departments access to an incredible array of tech-

nology. The center has a multitude of computer workstations, including Silicon Graphics, Adobe Premier, and autoCAD workstations. Students also have the use of Avid digital-editing suites, multitrack sound-editing studios, a dedicated green-screen studio, and various other video equipment, including Bosch Telecine equipment.

The Photography Department occupies its own building, which houses individual studios and a wide range of equipment, including full-length shooting studios; Hasselblad, Mamyia, Canon, and Sinar cameras; Broncolor, Norman, and Speedotron strobe systems; black-and-white darkrooms; a color lab facility with single-print stations; and the latest technology, such as Macintosh G5 computers for digital imaging and output. In addition, the Academy's modern, professional studio is one of the largest of any photography school in the nation and is ideal for shooting automobiles, motorcycles, and large sets.

The Fine Art Department has been relocated to one of the Academy's newest buildings, and is solely dedicated to painting, drawing, and printmaking. There are five floors occupied by studio space and labs fully equipped for silkscreen, lithography, book arts, etching/intaglio, and relief painting.

The Academy's Fine Art/Sculpture Center is a 58,000-square-foot facility that houses state-of-the-art studios for figure, ceramic, neon/illumination, bronze, metal fabrication, and mold-making sculpture. Students also have use of an off-site bronze-casting facility and foundry. When students graduate from the Academy, they have the opportunity to exhibit in one of the three non-profit galleries located in the heart of downtown San Francisco's premier gallery district. These street-level facilities are an excellent way for students to promote and sell their work and to gain networking experience.

The Library houses more than 30,000 books and magazines, as well as 375 CD titles, 150,000 slides, and 2,000 videos. Computers with Internet access are available to students, as well as an online catalog, color scanners, and color and black-and-white copiers. Workshops and electronic study guides are also available. The Academy Resource Center offers all students free learning support services that include study hall, tutoring, mentoring, mid-point review and study-skills workshops, a writing lab, a state-of-the-art multimedia language lab, an English for Art Program, and a Conversation Partner Program.

Costs

Tuition is $600 per credit unit for undergraduates. Full-time students carry either 12 or 15 units per semester. There is a nonrefundable $140 registration fee—$100 is applicable toward tuition. Lab fees run from $25 to $400 per semester, depending on the class. Tuition and fees are subject to change at any time. Art supplies can run from $250 to $500 per semester, depending on the major. The Academy has most of the expensive technical equipment available for students to borrow or use in a lab.

Academy of Art University operates more than thirteen campus housing facilities within the city. Several housing options are offered, and costs vary from $6600 to $10,000 per academic year (fall and spring semesters). For further information, students may contact the Academy Housing Office directly at 415-618-6335 or via e-mail at housing@academyart.edu.

Financial Aid

The Academy offers financial aid packages consisting of grants, loans, and work-study to eligible students with a demonstrated need. Low-interest loans are available to all eligible students, regardless of need. As financial aid programs, procedures, and eligibility requirements change frequently, applicants should contact the Financial Aid Office for current requirements at the University's address or phone number.

Faculty

The Academy averages nearly 500 faculty members each semester, most of whom are full-time art and design professionals and part-time teachers. The student-teacher ratio for undergraduate classes averages 18:1.

Student Government

Although there is no formal student government, each department has between 2 and 3 student representatives who meet with the president as needed throughout the semester to discuss any student issues.

Admission Requirements

Applicants for the B.F.A. program must have a high school diploma or GED equivalent. There is no portfolio requirement for the A.A. and B.F.A. programs. International students take written and speech tests to determine which ESL classes may have to be completed. Most ESL classes can be taken in conjunction with art and design classes. All foundations classes offer specialized ESL sections with instructors trained for language assistance. The application fee is $100 for undergraduates. A $500 tuition deposit applies to international applicants.

Application and Information

Students may apply to enter the Academy at the beginning of the spring, fall, or summer semesters. Information in this profile is subject to change. Students should contact Academy of Art University for current information or visit its Web site.

For further information and a catalog, students may contact:

Prospective Student Services
Academy of Art University
79 New Montgomery Street
San Francisco, California 94105
Phone: 415-274-2222
        800-544-2787 (toll-free)
Fax: 415-618-6287
E-mail: info@academyart.edu
Web site: http://academyart.edu

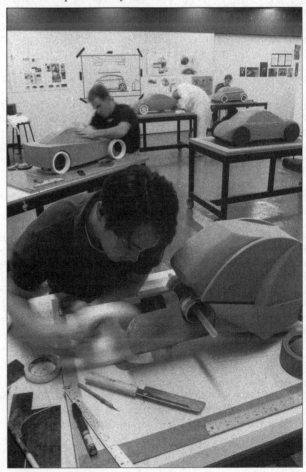
Students working at Academy of Art University.

ALASKA PACIFIC UNIVERSITY
ANCHORAGE, ALASKA

The University

Alaska Pacific University (APU) believes that how a student learns is as important as what a student learns. Alaska Pacific University employs an active learning philosophy that transcends the traditional classroom and the conventional format of lecture and examination. APU students—through projects, self-directed study, collaborative study, internships, research, field study, and study abroad—are prepared for leadership and self-direction in their careers, professions, or graduate school. All undergraduate students are involved in internships and project-based learning from the first year forward, a process that culminates in each student's senior project. Upon graduation, every APU student will have learned and demonstrated the ability to apply their education to real world situations.

APU's 387 undergraduate students currently represent thirty-four states and four countries. Minority students make up a growing portion of APU's undergraduate enrollment, which is strengthened by close working relationships between Native Alaskan communities and the University. Small classes; lively interaction among students, faculty members, and staff members; and personal academic advising are special benefits of the Alaska Pacific experience. APU is proud of its 11:1 student-faculty ratio, and that 97 percent of classes consist of less than 20 students. Class size is deliberately kept small to maintain Alaska Pacific's commitment to individualized learning and the freedom necessary for its students to create an expressive and meaningful relationship with their academic interests.

All freshmen are required to live on campus during their first year. APU's residence halls are centrally located, offering breathtaking views of the Chugach Mountains and convenient access to the dining facility, sports center, and classes. The residence halls offer one-, two-, and three-bedroom suites, while upperclassmen and graduate students have the opportunity to live in alternative housing on campus. A fall 2007 opening is planned for a new apartment-style dorm that can house up to 24 students.

Alaska Pacific University has a world-class Nordic ski team that trains in Alaska and competes in national, international, and Olympic events. The Nordic ski team has a summer Nordic ski facility on Eagle Glacier, where the American Olympic Team trains, along with other world-class skiers. Downhill skiers and snowboarders take advantage of two major ski resorts, each within an hour's drive of the campus, offering some of the most challenging, exciting, and varied ski conditions in the world.

Alaska Pacific students are encouraged to take a high degree of initiative in organizing and participating in campus activities. Extracurricular activities range from intramural club sports such as ice-skating, snowshoe softball, volleyball, Nordic skiing, and basketball to participation in the various student government–sponsored activities, such as the student newspaper and yearbook. APU offers a wide variety of programs for all ability levels, including the use of the indoor climbing wall, kayaking, ice climbing, and weekend camping and hiking trips. Students are also encouraged to take advantage of the extensive collection of recreational equipment offered through the Moseley Sports Center, including, but not limited to, backpacks, tents, sleeping bags, kayaks, canoes, skis, and snowshoes.

Graduate programs include a certification-only program for K–8 education, the Master of Business Administration (M.B.A.), M.B.A. in telecommunications management, M.B.A. in global finance, M.B.A. in health services administration, Master of Arts, Master of Science in Counseling Psychology, Master of Science in Environmental Science, and the Master of Science in Outdoor and Environmental Education.

Location

Alaska Pacific University is located on a 170-acre campus in suburban Anchorage. It is unquestionably one of the most beautiful campuses in the United States. Expansive lawns, woods, and University Lake frame nearly 3 miles of campus trails that lead bikers, hikers, in-line skaters, skiers, and runners into an extensive regional trail system that stretches from the ocean waters of Cook Inlet throughout the city and into the mountains to the east. The campus is a world unto itself, with no through roads or traffic; it has an atmosphere appropriate to the dynamic, student-centered, personal style of education for which APU is known.

Anchorage is an outdoor enthusiast's dream. In spring and summer, opportunities for fishing, hiking, mountain climbing, biking, sea kayaking, and camping abound. Winter sports activities include downhill and cross-country skiing, hockey, broomball, and sled-dog racing.

Anchorage's resident population has a strong interest in arts and entertainment. Cultural facilities and organizations in the Anchorage community include the Anchorage Museum of History and Art, the Alaskan Center for the Performing Arts, the Anchorage Symphony Orchestra, the Anchorage Concert Association, and the Anchorage Opera. APU's Grant Hall Theatre is the scene of a variety of student-sponsored and local productions, concerts, and lectures. With a population of 263,000, Anchorage offers a multitude of malls, cafés, clubs, and restaurants.

Majors and Degrees

Alaska Pacific University offers eight undergraduate programs with majors in business administration, education (with K–8 certification), environmental policy and planning, environmental science, liberal studies, marine biology, outdoor studies, and psychology.

Academic Programs

Alaska Pacific University's undergraduate curriculum is designed to integrate a comprehensive background in the liberal arts and in-depth study within each major. APU structures its classes around its active, hands-on learning philosophy. The curriculum emphasizes personal growth through student-centered, experiential education using Alaska, the Arctic, the Pacific Rim, and study abroad as active laboratories for learning.

APU focuses on developing student leadership skills for active service to society by encouraging openness to positive change, innovation, and individual initiative. Central to the philosophy of education at APU is the block-and-session semester format. In addition to two traditional sessions, three times per year students may take a block class—a one-month intensive course allowing students to focus entirely on a specific subject. Block

courses enable students and faculty members to travel together to different parts of Alaska and the world to pursue internships and self-directed studies. Block courses regularly travel to such locations as rural Alaska, Russia, England, Italy, Costa Rica, Mexico, and the Pacific Rim.

Academic Facilities

The Consortium Library serves University students and faculty members. It is operated through an agreement between APU and the University of Alaska, Anchorage. Centrally located, the library contains more than 384,000 bound volumes, including original government documents, sheet music, nonprint media, and a special Alaskana collection. The Academic Support Center located in Atwood Center has up-to-date technology and offers Internet access and e-mail accounts for all APU students. The Atwood Center also contains an excellent climbing wall, exercise room, ski team facilities, bookstore, art center, and photo lab alongside the cafeteria and two residence halls. Grant Hall houses the community theater, coffee shop, art gallery, numerous faculty offices, classrooms, and computer labs. The Carr-Gottstein Building features seminar and conference rooms, lecture halls, a computer lab, and an art exhibition area.

Costs

Undergraduate tuition for 2006–07 was $19,500 for all students. Room and board charges were $6700 per year. The year's activity fees for full-time students were $110, and books and miscellaneous supplies were estimated at $1000. Incoming first-year students were guaranteed no tuition increases for up to five years; transfer students receive the same guarantee, prorated.

Financial Aid

The primary purpose of student financial assistance at Alaska Pacific University is to provide financial resources to students who would otherwise be unable to pursue their educational goals. Most assistance is available on the basis of demonstrated need, although some funds are specifically allocated for the recognition of academic excellence and special talents. APU offers supplemental aid in the form of grants, loans, work opportunities, and scholarships. In order to be considered for assistance, students are required to first submit the Free Application for Federal Student Aid (FAFSA) and then complete the APU Supplemental Aid form. APU's FAFSA reporting code is #001061. Funds are also available for international students.

Faculty

Alaska Pacific University is a teaching university, not a research university. Members of the full-time faculty are selected for their teaching abilities and are encouraged to involve their students in their research and professional activities. Seventy-seven percent hold a Ph.D. or terminal degree in their fields, and many are in demand as consultants in areas such as international business, environmental quality, telecommunications, and multicultural education. The University's faculty-student ratio of 1:11 allows frequent and meaningful faculty-student interaction, resulting in a learning environment of the highest quality.

Student Government

The Associated Students of Alaska Pacific University (ASAPU) is the student-elected governance responsible for campus leadership. ASAPU initiates and sponsors many student activities, including student orientation events, student banquets, sports events, cultural activities, special awards, and student assemblies. All campus clubs and organizations work through ASAPU for formal recognition and funding. Student representatives sit on most major University committees and task forces.

Admission Requirements

In admitting students, Alaska Pacific University considers each student's grade point average, SAT or ACT scores, essay, letters of recommendation, and extracurricular activities. In general, APU recognizes that some students may flourish for the first time within APU's distinctive approach to education. APU welcomes diversity, uniqueness, and personal integrity. To apply, a candidate for first-year admission must submit an application for admission, two letters of recommendation, a personal essay, an official high school transcript, SAT or ACT scores, and a $25 application fee. Transfer applicants must submit an application for admission, transcripts from all colleges or universities they have attended, a personal essay, and a $25 application fee. International students must meet all of the above requirements, as well as submit evidence of financial support and obtain a minimum score of 550 on the paper-based TOEFL or 79 on the Internet-based version.

Application and Information

Although there is no application deadline, applications for fall that are received by February 1 receive financial aid priority.

All inquiries and application material should be directed to:

Office of Admissions
Alaska Pacific University
4101 University Drive
Anchorage, Alaska 99508-4672
Phone: 907-564-8248
        800-252-7528 (toll-free)
E-mail: admissions@alaskapacific.edu
Web site: http://www.alaskapacific.edu

ALBERTSON COLLEGE OF IDAHO

CALDWELL, IDAHO

The College

Founded in 1891, Albertson College of Idaho (ACI) is Idaho's oldest four-year institution of higher education. The school offers a personalized education through small classes, close faculty-student interaction, and a tight-knit campus community. It is consistently ranked with the best liberal arts colleges in the nation. It is ranked twelfth in all of U.S. higher education by the Princeton Review's *America's Best Value Colleges* for "best values" and eleventh in the nation for "professors bringing material to life." Intel ranked ACI second among the nation's liberal arts colleges and first in the Northwest in wireless technology.

The 793 undergraduate and 29 graduate students come from twenty-one states and territories. More than half of all Albertson College students live on campus. Students have their choice of five residence halls, which include individual heating and cooling in every room, computer labs in each hall, and meeting areas and kitchen facilities. Every room is connected to the Internet and e-mail. Upperclass students have the option of living in the Village, which offers an apartment-style living environment on campus.

Albertson College of Idaho is full of surprises—the varsity athletics program is one of them. Coyote athletic teams compete in the National Association of Intercollegiate Athletics (NAIA) and the Cascade Collegiate Conference (CCC). The men's and women's ski teams have won thirty-four national championships in the last twenty-seven years. The men's baseball team has qualified for postseason play every year since 1987, winning the national championship in 1998. ACI sponsors intercollegiate athletic competition for men in baseball, basketball, cross-country, golf, skiing, soccer, swimming, and track. Women compete in basketball, cross-country, golf, skiing, soccer, softball, swimming, tennis, track, and volleyball. In addition to varsity sports, Albertson College of Idaho also has strong intramural and club sports programs, including an outdoor program. Outdoor program activities include backcountry skiing, backpacking, camping, fly fishing, hiking, inner tubing, kayaking, rafting, rock climbing, snowshoeing, stargazing, and winter camping.

More than fifty student clubs and organizations represent some of the best ways to get involved and make friends. Whether volunteering with the Potter's Clay group to build low-income housing in Mexico or writing articles for the student newspaper, all students are encouraged to engage with the community on and off campus. Best of all, the College's size means every student can have a meaningful impact.

Location

Albertson College of Idaho's nationally ranked residential campus is located in Caldwell, Idaho, just 30 minutes from Boise, the state capital, and within an hour of spectacular wilderness. Caldwell, a picturesque town of 30,000, offers a number of shops and services for students. It is also in the heart of Idaho's beautiful wine country, where wineries host music and cultural events throughout the year.

Majors and Degrees

Albertson College of Idaho offers thirty-two majors, thirty-seven minors, and seventeen collaborative programs through sixteen academic departments. All of the programs of study are flexible enough to allow for personalized study and various concentrations and for students to create their own majors.

Departmental majors include accounting, anthropology/art, biology, business–business and the arts, business–international political economy, business–language and culture, chemistry, creative writing, English, environmental studies, exercise science, health sciences, history, international political economy, mathematics, mathematics–physics, music, philosophy, physical education, political economy, pre-engineering, psychology, religion, Spanish; sport and fitness management; teacher certification (five-year program), and theater.

One of Albertson College of Idaho's strengths is in the area of premedicine and preparation for professions in the health sciences. Thanks to collaborative programs between ACI and other institutions, students can spend three to four years at ACI and two to three years at the cooperating university, earning degrees from both. Collaborative programs in health professions include clinical lab science, nursing, occupational therapy, physical therapy, physician assistant studies, pharmaceutical science and public health, pharmacy, and speech-language pathology and audiology.

In addition, Albertson College offers collaborative programs in engineering, including agricultural, biological systems, biomedical, chemical, civil, computer, earth and environmental, electrical, geological, industrial, manufacturing, materials, mechanical, and metallurgical and mining. There is also a collaborative program in math–computer science.

Academic Programs

With an average class size of just 9.6, students receive a great deal of attention and support from their professors. One of the many innovative aspects of the academic program at Albertson College of Idaho is the First Year Experience. Through this unique program, all first-year students are divided into small groups, or cohorts. Students enroll in courses and participate in group activities with members of their cohorts. This program is designed to connect students personally, academically, and socially with their peers and with the College.

To earn a bachelor's degree, students must complete a minimum of 124 semester credits, at least 40 of which must be in upper-division course work. Some type of independent work at the upper-division level is also required for graduation. This requirement can be met by honors study, courses designated by departments, or internships.

The Gipson Scholar Program allows students to work closely with a panel of advisers to create an interdisciplinary major tailored specifically for them. In addition, many departments offer an honors program with independent studies and projects for a more in-depth study of a student's major.

Off-Campus Programs

Albertson College of Idaho's Center for Experiential Learning helps students find world-class internships and job opportunities. In addition, opportunities for independent work are available through all College departments. The center also helps students to realize their employment and/or graduate

school goals through developmental activities that start in freshman year and end with senior transition meetings.

Students can participate in off-campus internships, as well as study abroad. Internships are planned, structured, supervised experiences that enable students to develop skills for organizing information and solving routine problems expected of professionals in a given discipline. They are offered every term, including summer. Communication, teamwork, and leadership skills are often tested and honed within an internship/employment setting. Some internships are already established, and students can design others.

Albertson College of Idaho has a unique six-week Winter Term, during which students are offered innovative classes and exciting travel courses led by the College's professors. Traveling in a small group, students are completely immersed in the subject. Recent programs include Australian Biology; London History and Art History; Economics and French Literature; Costa Rican Biology; German Business, Economy, and Culture; the Cuba Experience; and Thailand and Vietnam: Globalization in Three Dimensions.

Academic Facilities

Campus facilities include the McCain Student Center, which houses a bookstore, coffee house, movie theater, snack bar, and dining area plus a TV lounge and student government offices; the J. A. Albertson Activities Center, a 75,000-square-foot activities center that contains a large gymnasium, a swimming pool, and weight and aerobics rooms; the Orma J. Smith Museum of Natural History; and the Whittenberger Planetarium.

Terteling Library contains 183,756 bound volumes, 75,000 government documents, 27,535 microform items, 797 periodical subscriptions, and 1,117 audiotapes, videotapes, records, and CDs. It provides search services for the collections of 45,402 other libraries through WorldCat.

The $6-million Langroise Performing and Fine Arts Center houses the College's music, theater, dance, and visual arts departments. The 54,000-square-foot facility includes a 188-seat recital hall and a 140-seat studio theater. Jewett Auditorium is an 850-seat auditorium used for concerts, lectures, symposia, and meetings that require a large capacity and a full stage. Rosenthal Gallery of Art hosts a half-dozen art shows each academic year, including four or five touring exhibits. It also contains a stage that is used for intimate performances and readings.

Costs

Full-time tuition is $17,000 and mandatory fees are $680. Room and board costs vary according to board plan and housing facility but range from approximately $5900 to $7800. Part-time tuition is $625 per credit.

Financial Aid

The average cost of attending ACI is significantly lower than for comparable four-year liberal arts colleges. From the beginning of the admissions process, prospective students are provided with information on the range of financial aid they can expect. This allows parents and prospective students to realistically assess the cost of an ACI education early in the decision process. ACI awards merit-, performance-, and need-based aid.

Faculty

The heart of the Albertson College of Idaho education is the interaction of students and faculty members. Selected for their academic achievements and teaching ability, ACI professors are renowned for unlocking the potential of their students. The student-faculty ratio is 11:1, and no classes are taught by graduate assistants. There are 66 faculty members, 86 percent of whom are full-time. Seventy-nine percent of the faculty members hold terminal degrees.

Student Government

The Associated Students of Albertson College of Idaho (ASACI) comprises the Executive Council, the Student Senate, and the Program Council. The Executive Council includes the student body president, vice president, secretary, treasurer, and program council director. The Student Senate, governed by the ASACI Vice President, has been actively involved with passing student legislation since its inception. Senators are elected to represent each residence hall and to represent students living off campus. All students are encouraged to run for Senate offices. The Program Council consists of elected directors and a group of volunteers who plan campuswide social events. Traditional events sponsored by Program Council have been midnight movies, midnight breakfasts, Winterfest, Casino Night, and Spring Fling.

In 2006, Albertson College of Idaho students, led by the student body president, developed a comprehensive, student-run Honor Code System. The Honor Code System consists of two complementary parts: An Academic Honor Code that focuses on upholding academic integrity and proscribing lying, cheating, and stealing in matters pertaining to college business, and a Student Life Honor Code that deals with all other aspects of the student experience.

Admission Requirements

In order to be considered for admission to Albertson College of Idaho, all applicants must submit the application for admission (dated and signed with application fee), official transcripts from high school and/or all colleges attended or proof of GED, official scores from the ACT or SAT, and a $50 nonrefundable application fee for paper application or $20 nonrefundable application fee for the online application. A personal essay and a teacher/counselor recommendation are also required. Additional letters may be submitted. An interview is recommended but not required. The application deadline is May 1 for freshmen, and there is rolling admissions for transfer students.

Application and Information

Charlene Brown, Director of Admission
Albertson College of Idaho
2112 Cleveland Boulevard
Caldwell, Idaho 83605-4494
Phone: 208-459-5305
        800-244-3246 (toll-free)
Fax: 208-459-5757
E-mail: admission@albertson.edu
Web site: http://www.albertson.edu

AZUSA PACIFIC UNIVERSITY

AZUSA, CALIFORNIA

The University

Celebrating more than 100 years of excellence in Christian higher education, Azusa Pacific University (APU) is a comprehensive university that was founded in 1899. Azusa Pacific earned university status in 1981. Committed to the goal of each student's personal, spiritual, and academic growth, APU provides extensive opportunities for student development with academic emphases in liberal arts and professional studies.

The University is divided into one college and six schools: the College of Liberal Arts and Sciences and the Schools of Music, Nursing, Education, Behavioral and Applied Sciences, Business and Management, and Theology.

On-campus residential living is a distinctive feature of student life at APU, with several areas from which to choose. Each differs in size, location, structure, type, and activities. Each area sponsors individual and large-group events, academic and social activities, spiritual and cultural experiences, indoor and outdoor recreational opportunities, and both highly structured and spontaneous activities.

The University's 8,346 students (4,602 of whom are undergraduates) come from forty-six states and seventy-one nations and represent forty-nine religious denominations. APU students are strong academically, entering with an average GPA of 3.67 and a combined SAT score of 1114. They are often leaders in their high schools, churches, and communities. Azusa Pacific offers excellent leadership development programs that teach students how to be positive contributors to their communities, jobs, and society.

Twenty-one master's degree programs and six doctorates are offered in addition to the fifty undergraduate programs.

Location

Azusa Pacific University is located in the foothills of the San Gabriel Valley communities of Azusa and Glendora, 26 miles northeast of Los Angeles. APU is only an hour's drive from beaches, amusement parks, mountains, ski resorts, and cultural centers. The climate is moderate, mostly warm and dry throughout the school year.

Majors and Degrees

Azusa Pacific University grants the Bachelor of Arts degree in the fields of art, athletic training, biblical studies, biochemistry, biology, business administration, chemistry, Christian ministries, cinema and broadcast arts, communication studies, English, global studies, graphic design, history, liberal studies, mathematics, mathematics/physics, music, natural science, philosophy, physical education, political science, psychology, social science, social work, sociology, Spanish, theater arts, theology, and youth ministry. The Bachelor of Science degree is awarded in the fields of accounting, applied health, biochemistry, biology, chemistry, computer information systems, computer science, finance, international business, marketing, mathematics, nursing, and physics.

Preprofessional programs are available in allied health and pharmacy, dentistry, law, and medicine. Pre-engineering degree programs (3-2 and 2-2) are also offered.

The Department of Religion and Philosophy offers a ministry credential program that combines academic study with practicum and leads to the Bachelor of Arts degree.

Academic Programs

Azusa Pacific University's undergraduate program operates on the semester system and offers two summer sessions. Many graduate programs are on the quarter system.

The minimum number of credits required for a bachelor's degree is 126. About half of these units must be completed in general studies requirements, as follows: skills and University requirements, 43 units; aesthetics and the creative arts, 3 units; heritage and institutions, 6 units; identity and relationships, 3 units; language and literature, 3 units; nature, 4 units; God's Word and the Christian response, 18 units; and integrative electives, 6 units. Areas of concentration vary in their requirements, and many offer several emphases within the major.

The University grants credit for certain scores on Advanced Placement tests and College-Level Examination Program tests, college courses taken while in high school, and the International Baccalaureate.

Academic Facilities

Azusa Pacific's libraries include the William V. Marshburn Memorial Library, the Hugh and Hazel Darling Library, the James L. Stamps Theological Library, and six regional-center libraries. The libraries offer enhanced traditional services as well as state-of-the-art features that facilitate research. Apolis2, the libraries' automated catalog system, is searchable on the World Wide Web, providing increased ease and convenience to aid users in the search process. A unified catalog identifies more than 215,000 books, media, and 1,800 serial titles. More than 630,000 microforms include the Library of American Civilization, Library of American Literature, *New York Times,* and Educational Resources Information Center collections. The University provides access to more than 100 electronic databases, including more than 12,000 full-text serial titles, in addition to an interlibrary loan system that offers access to more than 11 million books and resources to all students.

The holdings of the William V. Marshburn Memorial Library include collections supporting liberal arts and sciences, music, and business. Computer workstations and online services offer electronic access to materials from around the world. Special collections include many rare and valuable items. The Media Center has an extensive collection of scores, videocassettes, and compact discs as well as graphic art materials and equipment. Professional librarians are available for assistance.

The holdings of the Hugh and Hazel Darling Library include collections supporting computer science, education, nursing, and professional psychology and offer students a vast collection of printed books, reference materials, serials, and microfilm. Ninety-seven workstations offer access to more than 100 licensed databases and Web resources globally. There are also five classrooms that are equipped with video projectors, computers, and ISDN lines for distance learning; an auditorium with tiered seating; and a soundstage and TV control room. The design of the building is meant to meet the needs of the twenty-first-century learner.

The newest addition to the APU libraries is the James L. Stamps Theological Library, part of the $12.5-million Duke Academic Complex, which was completed in summer 2003. The library houses a three-story, 50,000-volume book stack dedicated to the APU theology collection; thirty-one workstations; and a number of periodicals. Denominational collections reflecting the rich traditions of the University's Christian heritage are available for research purposes. The rest of the 60,000-square-foot complex houses eighteen technologically advanced classrooms, a lecture hall, forty faculty and staff offices, and two conference rooms. The School of Theology and Department of Art currently reside in the complex.

APU offers a number of technology options on campus, with computer labs in every library and dorm and in the student union. These labs offer PC and Macintosh computers and laser printers.

All Access, the campuswide wireless network, provides Internet access anywhere on campus to all students and faculty and staff members with laptops and wireless connectivity. A wide variety of software is available to fulfill students' needs.

Outstanding features of the Carl E. Wynn Science Center include an electron microscope facility with both scanning and transmission instrumentation for use in cellular and molecular biology, physiology, and ecology courses and practical facilities, such as a greenhouse and a cadaver lab. The Departments of Biology, Chemistry, Mathematics, and Physics offer vigorous programs with the support of the science center.

APU enjoys the state-of-the-art School of Music and chapel complexes. The two-story School of Music contains three large rehearsal rooms, a recording studio, twenty-two instrumental and voice practice rooms, classrooms, and faculty offices. The Munson Chapel seats 300 and is used for intimate group gatherings, vocal and orchestra performances, and special chapel programs.

APU's attractive, landscaped, 103-acre campus houses many contemporary facilities, including Trinity Hall, a 350-bed, 103,000-square-foot residence hall that opened in fall 2003; the $5-million Wilden Hall of Business and Management; and a modern, lighted athletic complex. All facilities are barrier-free.

The 3,500-seat, $13.5-million Richard and Vivian Felix Event Center, which was designed to meet the University's and community's needs, opened in December 2000.

Costs

Expenses per year for 2006–07 were estimated as follows: tuition, $23,750; room, $3690; board, from $2350 (ten meals per week) to $3638 (300-block meal plan); and books and supplies, starting at $1224.

Financial Aid

Azusa Pacific University offers financial aid in the form of employment, loans, grants, and scholarships. Approximately 90 percent of the student body receives some form of aid. Each year, approximately $8 million in institutional aid is awarded. Students must reapply for aid yearly. Financial aid for international students may be more limited due to government restrictions and differences in educational systems.

Faculty

The student-faculty ratio is 14:1. There are 349 full-time faculty members, 28 part-time faculty members, and 549 adjunct professors. Seventy-three percent of the faculty members possess terminal degrees. The faculty is primarily a teaching staff. No graduate students serve as undergraduate instructors. Faculty members are highly supportive of and involved in many student activities; they also provide academic advising.

Student Government

The Associated Student Body (ASB) is responsible for representing the students' needs and desires to the administration. Through an annual survey, the ASB can pinpoint major issues that need to be targeted on the APU campus. Elections are held annually in the spring. The student government is made up of a senate and an executive council. ASB also assists student groups requesting funds and participates in student activities on campus.

Students are asked to use personal discretion in activities that may be spiritually or morally destructive. In particular, students are expected to refrain from smoking, drinking, and using or possessing illegal drugs while in residence at the University.

Admission Requirements

Azusa Pacific seeks students who are committed to their own personal, intellectual, and spiritual growth. Consequently, these areas are considered in the admission evaluation. Applicants are required to have earned a minimum GPA of 2.8 in high school or a minimum GPA of 2.2 in previous college work. Minimum SAT and ACT scores are 910 and 19, respectively. Both transfer students and international students who graduated from non-English-speaking schools also need a GPA of at least 2.8. Transfer, international, and older students are encouraged to apply.

Application and Information

Applicants must submit official transcripts of high school and/or previous college work, two references, a signed statement of agreement, and scores on either the ACT or SAT. A nonrefundable $45 application fee must be submitted with the application. International students do not need ACT or SAT scores, but a TOEFL score is required. A $65 application fee applies, and specific application deadlines are enforced. APU follows early action and rolling admission policies, depending on semester and class standing. Students should contact the Office of Undergraduate Admissions for enrollment application deadlines.

For further information, prospective students should contact:

Office of Undergraduate Admissions
Azusa Pacific University
901 East Alosta Avenue
P.O. Box 7000
Azusa, California 91702-7000
Phone: 626-812-3016
      800-TALK-APU (information requests, toll-free)
Fax: 626-812-3096
Web site: http://www.apu.edu/start/prospective/undergraduate

For further information, international students should contact:

Office of International Student Services
Azusa Pacific University
901 East Alosta Avenue
P.O. Box 7000
Azusa, California 91702-7000
Phone: 626-812-3055
Fax: 626-815-3801
Web site: http://www.apu.edu/international

The $8-million Hugh and Hazel Darling Library and $12.5-million Duke Academic Complex offer a spectacular array of resources in an environment that is conducive to learning.

CHAPMAN UNIVERSITY
ORANGE, CALIFORNIA

The University

During its 145-year history, Chapman has evolved from a small, traditional liberal arts college that was founded in 1861 by members of the First Christian Church (Disciples of Christ) into a midsized comprehensive liberal arts and sciences university that is distinguished for its nationally recognized programs in film and television production, business and economics, music, education, communication arts, and the natural and applied sciences. The mission of Chapman University is to provide personalized education of distinction that leads to inquiring, ethical, and productive lives as global citizens.

Chapman's parklike ivy-covered, tree-lined campus features a blending of fully refurbished historic structures with the newest in state-of-the-art Internet and satellite-connected learning environments. Five residence halls and six on-campus apartment buildings are conveniently located on the edge of the campus. Prominent in the center of the campus is Liberty Plaza, featuring a raised replica of a Lincoln chair that views a 10-ton section of the Berlin Wall.

Chapman University's academic structure includes the Wilkinson College of Letters and Sciences, the CILECT-accredited Dodge College of Film and Media Arts, the AACSB International–accredited Argyros School of Business and Economics, the School of Communication Arts, the CTC-approved School of Education, the ABA-accredited School of Law, and the NASM-accredited School of Music. Other nationally accredited programs include the IFT-accredited program in food sciences and the APTA-accredited program in physical therapy. Chapman has been further recognized by the Templeton Foundation as one of only 100 colleges nationally to be designated as a Templeton Foundation "Character-Building College" for its emphasis on global citizenry and for student involvement in community action and stewardship activities.

In addition to approximately 5,500 undergraduate, graduate, and professional school students enrolled on the campus in Orange, Chapman also enrolls another 8,000 undergraduate and graduate students annually through its Chapman University College and associated network of thirty University College corporate campus centers located in California and Washington.

The University environment is electric, involving, and outdoor-oriented. Along with the obvious benefits associated with the southern California climate, Chapman students enjoy a dynamic and involving student activities program. Although predominantly from California, Chapman students come from forty states; in addition, approximately 10 percent of its students come from thirty-four other countries. Over the past five years, Chapman students have been named Truman Scholars, Coro Fellows, *USA Today* All-USA College Academic Team members, NCAA All-Americans, and NCAA Academic All-Americans. Chapman's long and distinguished heritage in intercollegiate athletics includes five NCAA national championships in baseball, tennis, and softball. Chapman competes as an independent in the NCAA Division III level and fields teams in baseball, basketball (m/w), crew (m/w), cross-country (m/w), football, golf, lacrosse, soccer (m/w), softball, swimming (w), tennis (m/w), track and field (m/w), volleyball (w), and water polo (m/w). Approximately 20 percent of Chapman's student body participates in intercollegiate athletics. In 2005, 4 student-athletes were named NCAA All-Americans and 8 as NCAA Academic All-Americans.

More than seventy clubs and organizations are available, many with commitments to a wide range of community service efforts. Chapman's Greek system includes six nationally chartered fraternities for men and five nationally chartered sororities for women. A comprehensive intramural sports program involves myriad sports activities for all campus community members throughout the school year. On-campus intercollegiate athletic events and music, art, and theater productions provide students with extensive extracurricular activity options. Chapman's proximity to area recreational and cultural opportunities allows Chapman students to enjoy the essence of what makes Orange County's south coast area an enviable environment in which to live and learn.

Prominent Chapman alumni include the Honorable Loretta Sanchez '88, member of Congress; the Honorable David Bonior '72, member of Congress; Jose Gomez '75, member of the Panamanian National Assembly; television and film producers John Copeland '73, Jon Garcia '91, and John David Currey '98; cinematographer Gene Jackson '70; television sports analyst and former UCLA basketball coach Steve Lavin '88; major league baseball executive Gordon Blakely '76; former major league baseball stars Gary Lucas '80, Tim Flannery '80, Marty Castillo '80, and Randy Jones '72; Tony Award nominee and star of Broadway's *Showboat*, Michel Bell '68; and former U.S. Ambassador to Spain and philanthropist George L. Argyros '65.

Location

Orange County, California, was recently rated by *Places Rated Almanac* as "the #1 place to live in North America," citing superior climate, cultural, recreational, educational, and career-entree opportunities. Los Angeles is 35 miles to the north, and San Diego is 80 miles to the south. Nearby entertainment venues include Disneyland, Knott's Berry Farm, the Orange County Performing Arts Center, major-league baseball, and hockey. Pristine West Coast beaches are less than 10 miles from the campus, and seasonal snow skiing is 90 minutes away. The average year-round temperature on campus is 71°F, and the prevailing sea breeze coming off nearby southwest-facing beaches keeps the air clean and smog free.

Majors and Degrees

Chapman awards the Bachelor of Arts degree in the fields of art, biology, chemistry, communications, dance, economics, English and comparative literature, film and television, French, history, liberal studies (teaching), music, peace studies, philosophy, physical education, political science, psychology, religion, social science, sociology, Spanish, and theater. The Bachelor of Fine Arts degree is offered in creative writing, dance performance, film production, graphic design, studio art, television and broadcast journalism, and theater performance. The Bachelor of Science degree is offered in accounting, applied mathematics, biology, business administration, chemistry, computer information systems, computer science, and natural science. The Bachelor of Music degree is granted in composition, conducting, music education (vocal and instrumental), music performance (vocal and instrumental), and music therapy. Preprofessional or prevocational programs are offered in dentistry, law, medicine, physical therapy, social service, teaching, theology, and veterinary medicine.

Academic Programs

The requirements for graduation are commensurate with the liberal arts philosophy of education maintained by Chapman.

The program of studies is designed to ensure a breadth of subject matter selection in the liberal arts as well as depth of preparation in the student's major field. The minimum graduation requirements include successful completion (C average) of 124 semester credits, of which 36 must be earned in the upper division. Competence in reading, written communication, oral communication, computation, and library usage is required of all students. Chapman's general education sequence provides a broad introduction to the humanities, social sciences, and natural sciences. Students select general education classes with the guidance of their faculty adviser. A maximum of 32 semester credits may be gained through Advanced Placement (AP), College-Level Examination Program (CLEP), and departmental examinations.

Chapman's academic year operates on a 4-1-4 modified semester system. January is reserved for an optional Interterm. The University College corporate campus locations offer five 10-week terms annually.

Ample opportunities are available for alternative learning experiences. Internships and cooperative education programs are recommended. Students may also undertake in-depth individual study or research in their major field in conjunction with a faculty member.

Academic Facilities

Major facilities additions to the Chapman campus over the past year include the completion of the 100,000-square-foot Leatherby Libraries complex, housing eight discipline-specific individual libraries, a sculpture garden, a cyber courtyard, and a 24-hour study commons and coffee bar; the Oliphant Hall addition to the School of Music, which includes 24,000 square feet featuring fourteen teaching studios, a sixty-seat lecture hall, music therapy laboratory, and orchestra hall; and the new Interfaith Center, which features the 12,500-square-foot Wallace All-Faiths Chapel. The 90,000-square-foot Argyros Forum includes the primary campus dining area and conference and classroom facilities. The 1,000-seat Memorial Auditorium is listed on the National Register of Historic Places. Athletic facilities include the 4,000-seat Hutton Sports Center arena, a 5,000-seat outdoor stadium, four championship tennis courts, and training and fitness facilities for the campus and surrounding community. The recently completed Arnold Beckman Hall is the center for business and information technology, including the Argyros School of Business and Economics, the A. Gary Anderson Center for Economic Research, the Ralph Leatherby Center for Entrepreneurship and Business Ethics, and the Walter Schmid Center for International Business. The School of Communication Arts includes the Guggenheim Art Gallery and the 250-seat repertory-style Waltmar Theatre. The Hashinger Science Center features laboratories for nuclear science, radiation, crystallography, genetics, food science, and physical therapy.

Costs

For the 2006–07 academic year, full-time tuition and fees (including accident and sickness fee, health center fee, and associated student membership fee) were $30,598. Annual room and board costs averaged $10,110. The estimated cost for books was $700 per year.

Financial Aid

More than 85 percent of Chapman students benefit from some form of financial aid or scholarship assistance. Need-based financial awards include a combination of grants, scholarships, loans, and work-study jobs on campus. Awards are renewable, assuming that students complete the annual application process on time. By using a combination of Chapman's internal resources and federal and state funding, an individual financial aid package can be tailored to meet the student's financial need. Merit and talent scholarship awards, regardless of financial need, round out the types of financial assistance that Chapman offers. Chapman offers an Early Aid Estimator service that gives students an up-front picture of what their prospective aid/scholarship eligibility is, rather than waiting for the postadmission, official aid-awarding period. Students asking for information about Chapman automatically receive the Early Aid Estimator form, along with instructions for completion and submission for analysis.

Faculty

The University's faculty is composed of 256 full-time and 288 part-time members, more than 80 percent of whom hold doctoral or other terminal degrees. Their primary commitment is to undergraduate teaching, although most are also actively involved in scholarly research and publication. Many faculty members teach both undergraduate and graduate courses. Teaching assistants or graduate assistants are not used for the instruction of undergraduate classes. Chapman's favorable student-faculty ratio of 16:1 allows extensive interaction between the faculty members and students.

Student Government

Chapman has an associated student government that actively participates in the administration of the University.

Admission Requirements

Admission to Chapman is selective. In 2006, admission was granted to 51 percent of the applicant pool. The University is interested in admitting students whose prior records indicate that they will be successful in a competitive collegiate environment. Freshman applicants are considered for admission based primarily on the nature and sequence of their high school course work, the grade point average achieved, and their results on either the SAT or ACT examination. Transfer candidates are considered for admission on the basis of their course work and cumulative grade point average earned at other regionally accredited postsecondary institutions.

Application and Information

When applying, candidates are strongly encouraged to visit the campus and meet with a member of the admission staff. Arrangements for an interview or group information session and campus tour can be made through the Office of Admission. Freshman applicants can choose between a nonbinding November 30 early action application deadline or the January 31 regular application deadline. Transfer applicants must apply before the March 15 transfer deadline. Freshmen candidates who apply after January 31 and transfer candidates who apply after March 15 are considered on a space-available basis.

For further information, students should contact:

Michael O. Drummy
Assistant Vice President and Chief Admission Officer
Office of Admission
Chapman University
One University Drive
Orange, California 92866
Phone: 714-997-6711
       888-CUAPPLY (toll-free)
Fax: 714-997-6713
E-mail: admit@chapman.edu
Web site: http://www.chapman.edu

COLORADO STATE UNIVERSITY
FORT COLLINS, COLORADO

The University

In 1879, Colorado State University was designated Colorado's land-grant college. The land-grant concept of a balanced program of teaching, research, extension, and public service provides the foundation for the University's teaching and research programs. Today, Colorado State has a commitment to integrating first-rate academic programs with hands-on learning experiences inside and outside the classroom. Education at Colorado State encompasses the major areas of human knowledge—the sciences, the arts, the humanities, and the professions. The mission of the University is to graduate students who possess the knowledge and skills to compete in a global marketplace and live full, rewarding lives. The University historically has had a reputation for excellence in its programs from the baccalaureate to the postgraduate level and has achieved a worldwide reputation in a number of important fields. Colorado State offers graduate degrees in all eight colleges.

The 25,000 students enrolled at Colorado State represent all fifty states and eighty-five countries. The variety of students broadens the educational experience for all and enables students to share their backgrounds and heritages and learn about others in an atmosphere that encourages cultural exchange and an appreciation and respect for diversity.

The University provides a wide range of programs to meet the social, recreational, and academic needs of its diverse student population. There are more than 300 clubs and organizations, including student government, honor societies, sororities and fraternities, athletic clubs, cultural and religious organizations, advocacy offices, and major-oriented or professionally oriented clubs. The Lory Student Center provides a focal point for student life on campus. Many students participate in intramural and club sports. For the more serious-minded athlete, Colorado State offers men's and women's athletics in the Mountain West Conference (MWC) Division I of the National Collegiate Athletic Association (NCAA). All students have access to the sports facilities at the 100,000-square-foot Student Recreation Center, which is open daily for drop-in recreational use. This facility houses a gymnasium with multipurpose courts; an elevated running track; a ten-lane, 25-yard swimming pool and spa pool; and weight, cardio, exercise, and locker rooms; and more.

Colorado State has ten coed residence halls, each containing recreation and study areas, a laundry room, and vending machines. Residence hall dining centers provide many dining choices for students. The halls offer a wide variety of activities, including educational programs, social gatherings, and recreational events. Several floors within the residence halls are designated for either academic or leisure interests, providing the opportunity for students to live with others with similar interests. These living learning communities include honors, leadership, engineering, natural sciences, and pre–veterinary medicine. All residence halls are nonsmoking.

Location

Fort Collins, a city of 134,000, provides a unique blend of big-city amenities and small-college-town friendliness. It is scenically located at the western edge of the plains at the base of the Rocky Mountain foothills and conveniently located 65 miles north of Denver. The wide-open spaces and majestic Rockies make Fort Collins a very attractive place to live and learn. Areas for camping, hiking, skiing, swimming, boating, rafting, climbing, and fishing are within an easy driving distance of campus.

Majors and Degrees

Colorado State University offers bachelor's degrees through eight colleges. Bachelor of Science degrees are granted through the College of Agricultural Sciences in agricultural business, agricultural economics, agricultural education, animal science, equine science, horticulture, landscape architecture, landscape horticulture, and soil and crop sciences; through the College of Applied Human Sciences in apparel and merchandising, construction management, family and consumer sciences, health and exercise science, human development and family studies, interior design, nutrition and food science, and restaurant and resort management; through the College of Business in business administration, with concentrations in accounting, finance, information systems, management, marketing, and real estate; through the College of Engineering in chemical, civil, computer, electrical, environmental, and mechanical engineering and in engineering science; through the College of Natural Resources in fishery biology, forestry, geology, natural resources management, natural resource recreation and tourism, rangeland ecology, watershed science, and wildlife biology; through the College of Natural Sciences in applied computing technology, biochemistry, biological science, chemistry, computer science, mathematics, natural sciences, physics, psychology, and zoology; and through the College of Veterinary Medicine and Biomedical Sciences in biomedical sciences, environmental health, and microbiology.

Bachelor of Arts degrees are offered through the College of Applied Human Sciences in social work and through the College of Liberal Arts in anthropology; art; economics; English; history; languages, literatures, and cultures; liberal arts; music; performing arts; philosophy; political science; sociology; speech communication; and technical journalism. The Bachelor of Fine Arts and Bachelor of Music degrees are offered through the College of Liberal Arts in art and in music.

Teacher licensure is available in early childhood education; at the secondary level in English, French, German, mathematics, science (biology, chemistry, and geology), social studies, Spanish, and speech; and in grades K–12 in art and music. Vocational secondary education licensure is available in agricultural education, business education, consumer and family studies, marketing education, and trade and industrial education. Preprofessional advising programs are offered in chiropractic, dentistry, law, medicine, nursing, occupational therapy, optometry, pharmacy, physical therapy, physician assistant studies, podiatry, and veterinary medicine.

Academic Programs

More than 150 undergraduate programs of study are offered within the eight colleges, allowing students to shape a course of study that best meets their personal and professional goals. Depending on their degree program, students are required to complete a minimum of 120 credit hours for graduation.

Colorado State provides students with a well-rounded education through the All-University Core Curriculum (AUCC), the centerpiece of Colorado State's integrated learning experience. All students are required to complete the AUCC. Students usually meet the AUCC requirements in their freshman and sophomore years and devote their junior and senior years to specialization in their major field. A concentration—a sequence of at least 12 semester credits of selected courses designed to accommodate the specific interests of a student—may be designated within some majors. Students may also choose to pursue a double major, a minor, or an interdisciplinary studies program.

The Colorado State Honors Program provides academically motivated undergraduates in all majors with intellectual stimulation commensurate with their abilities. It offers small classes and fosters a close intellectual association of students and faculty members.

Off-Campus Programs

The Office of International Programs coordinates many study-abroad programs that allow students to study almost anywhere in the world. Study-abroad programs can range from two-week seminars to semester and yearlong periods of study in any major.

Academic Facilities

Colorado State comprises four campuses covering approximately 4,900 acres. The 579-acre main campus, with nearly 100 academic and administrative buildings, is virtually a city within itself. Classrooms and residence halls are in proximity. South of the main campus is the Veterinary Medical Center (103 acres), one of the nation's top facilities for teaching and research in the clinical sciences. A 1,433-acre agricultural campus supports instruction and research in agronomy and animal science, including the Equine Teaching and Research Center. The Foothills Campus, a 1,715-acre facility located 2 miles west of the main campus, is home to many of the University's renowned research projects. A 1,177-acre mountain campus, Pingree Park, located 55 miles west of the main campus at an elevation of 9,000 feet and bordering Rocky Mountain National Park, is used primarily for summer educational and research programs in forestry and natural resources.

The William E. Morgan Library houses collections totaling 2 million items and provides reading areas for more than 1,500 people. The library collections include books, periodicals, newspapers, journals, manuscripts, microfilms, records, and other reference items. The collection is enriched by a wide selection of electronic resources. The library also offers more than 300 public computers that allow access to specialized indexes and Web-based sources.

Costs

All stated costs are per semester. For 2006–07, tuition and fees for full-time (15 credits) undergraduates were $22,358 for Colorado residents and $8122 for nonresidents. The average cost of room and board for on-campus housing was $3163. Books are estimated at $450. Freshman students, unless they were living at home, married, or over 21 years of age, were required to live on campus and were therefore guaranteed a space in the residence halls. Upperclass students may choose to live in the Colorado State residence halls, in the University apartment housing (for student families, couples/partners, students 23 years and older, students under the age of 23 who were interested in an international experience, or graduate students), or in any of the numerous houses or apartments located nearby.

Financial Aid

Colorado State participates in and administers a wide variety of student financial aid programs, including loans, grants, scholarships, work-study, and student employment. Colorado State's Student Financial Services Web site (http://sfs.colostate.edu) describes in detail all scholarships and aid offered. Approximately 66 percent of the students at Colorado State received some type of financial assistance. Student Employment Services assists students with locating part-time positions both on and off campus.

Faculty

The Colorado State faculty teaches both graduate and undergraduate students. There are approximately 1,500 faculty members; 99 percent of the tenure-track faculty members hold doctorate, first professional, or other terminal degrees. The student-faculty ratio is 18:1. Faculty members are actively engaged in research, teach undergraduate classes, and serve as advisers.

Student Government

The Associated Students of Colorado State University (ASCSU) comprises all enrolled students. The ASCSU Senate acts as a liaison between the student body and the administration as well as the Board of Governors, the governing body of Colorado State. The ASCSU also offers free legal, consumer, and other services to Colorado State students.

Admission Requirements

Colorado State University selects for admission students who demonstrate the greatest academic potential for successfully attaining a degree and who appear to be the best qualified to benefit from and contribute to the academic and cultural environment of the University. Applications are carefully and individually reviewed. Colorado State is a selective university. In fall 2006, the middle 50 percent of entering freshmen had a GPA range of 3.2 to 3.8, an ACT composite score of 22 to 26, and an SAT (critical reading and math) combined score of 1010 to1210.

Students applying as freshmen must submit a completed application form, a $50 application processing fee, official high school transcripts that include high school class rank, college transcripts for any college course work, and scores from either the ACT or SAT. The personal essay and letters of recommendation from teachers, principals, or counselors are also recommended. Several factors are considered, including the applicant's grades, class rank, number of completed academic units, scores on either the ACT or SAT, rigor of high school curriculum, trend in quality of high school performances, leadership qualities, school or community service, and the ability to contribute to the campus community. Minimum freshman admission prerequisites include the completion of 18 units, 15 of which are academic units. These 15 academic units must include 5 units of a social science/natural science combination, with a minimum of 2 units from each area; 4 units of English; and 3 units of mathematics (algebra I, algebra II, and geometry). The completed application and all supporting documents must be received by July 1 for fall semester and December 1 for spring semester. Students are encouraged to apply early, as enrollment limits may be met prior to the deadline.

Undergraduate transfer students who wish to attend Colorado State must submit a completed application form, a $50 application processing fee, and official transcripts from all colleges and universities attended. The personal essay and letters of recommendation are also recommended. To be a strong candidate for admission, transfer applicants should have college-level academic course work and at least a 2.5 cumulative GPA with a minimum of more than 12 semester credits after high school graduation. These credits must be earned from a college or university accredited by one of the six regional associations of schools and colleges. Transfer applicants must also meet the admission requirement in mathematics. For details on meeting this requirement, students should visit http://admissions.colostate.edu/transfer. Other factors considered for admission include academic rigor and trend in grades. The completed application and all supporting documents must be received by July 1 for the fall semester, December 1 for the spring semester.

For current admission information and to apply online and pay the application processing fee, students should visit the Web site at http://admissions.colostate.edu.

Application and Information

The admissions office is open Monday through Friday, from 7:45 to 4:45 during the academic year and from 7:30 to 4:30 during the summer. Student-led campus tours and information sessions are given every weekday. Visit Day Programs are offered throughout the year. Students should visit the Office of Admissions Web site at http://admissions.colostate.edu/visit for more information regarding on-campus visits. Additional information and application forms are available by contacting:

Office of Admissions
Colorado State University
1062 Campus Delivery
Fort Collins, Colorado 80523-1062
Phone: 970-491-6909
Internet: http://admissions.colostate.edu

EASTERN WASHINGTON UNIVERSITY

CHENEY, WASHINGTON

The University

Established in 1882 as the Benjamin P. Cheney Academy, Eastern Washington University (EWU) has grown from a premier teachers' college into a comprehensive state university providing an excellent student-centered learning environment; professionally accomplished faculty members who are strongly committed to student learning; high-quality, integrated, interdependent academic programs; and exceptional student support services, resources, and facilities. The University retains the charm and personality of its founding on the parklike campus in Cheney. It also exhibits the distinctive marks of the modern comprehensive university in its newer facilities and the expansion of higher educational opportunities into downtown Spokane. Eastern is fully accredited by the Northwest Association of Schools and Colleges and by numerous professional accreditation agencies in specific disciplines. In addition to the undergraduate degrees that are listed, Eastern offers master's degrees in the arts and sciences, business administration, creative writing, education, nursing, public administration, social work, and urban and regional planning. Eastern also offers a doctorate in physical therapy.

Eastern's 10,000 students come from more than forty states and twenty-four countries. Nonwhite students make up 17 percent of the student body, and international students make up 4 percent. About 58 percent of Eastern's students are women. Educational and support services are available through the American Indian Studies, Chicano Education, African American Education, and Women's Studies Programs; the English Language Institute; and the Academic Support Center. Seven residence halls can accommodate 2,086 students on campus. Additional housing is available for married students and students with children. Fraternity and sorority housing, as well as off-campus housing within walking distance in Cheney, affords a variety of housing options. All residence halls are smoke free. Students and the University community enjoy one of the Northwest's premier sports and recreation centers. The PHASE complex includes a 5,500-seat pavilion, an indoor aquatics center, a field house with indoor track and tennis, and the main PHASE building, which houses indoor courts for basketball, volleyball, and racquetball; dance studios; a fitness center; and a large, multisurfaced rock for climbing practice. These facilities, totaling 100,000 square feet, and Woodward Field are the venues for the NCAA Division I Eagles, who compete in the Big Sky Conference.

Location

The University's main campus is located in Cheney, a comfortable and compact city of more than 10,000, where students may find a variety of services, facilities, and shopping while enjoying the pleasant, secure feel of a small town. Spokane, one of the state's largest cities and a regional hub for manufacturing, business, transportation, and health services for more than 450,000 residents, is just 17 miles away and offers a full range of social, cultural, recreational, and consumer opportunities. The Inland Northwest region offers virtually unlimited scenic and recreational attractions in a four-season climate. More than seventy-five lakes lie within 50 miles of the campus, and the mountains and many rivers are easily accessible. Other outdoor activities include excellent skiing within a short drive in nearly every direction. The University sits amid fascinating geological and geographic diversity, with the arid high country to the west, the rich Palouse farming area to the south, and the fir-covered mountains climbing from Spokane into Idaho and Montana. The Spokane International Airport, rail and bus service, and interstate access serve the region.

Majors and Degrees

EWU is responding to the needs of the state as defined by the Washington Council of the American Electronics Association by offering a new degree program in electrical engineering. As a comprehensive university, the following majors are available: anthropology; art; biology (including biochemistry/biotechnology, predental, premedicine, and pre–veterinarian); business administration (including accounting, economics, finance, general management, human resource management, international business, management information systems, marketing, operations management, and pre-M.B.A.); chemistry and biochemistry (including forensic science); communication disorders; communication studies (including interpersonal, organizational, public communication, and public relations); computer science (including computer information systems and multimedia programming and development); counseling, developmental, and educational psychology; criminal justice; dental hygiene; earth science; economics; education (including elementary and secondary options); electronic media and filmic arts; engineering and design (including computer engineering technology, construction design, electronics, visual communication design, manufacturing, and mechanical engineering technology); English (including creative writing, literary studies, and technical communication); environmental science; geography; geology (including environmental); government (including prelaw); health services administration; history; humanities; interdisciplinary studies; international affairs; journalism (including news editorial, public relations, and technology); mathematics (including computer science, economics, and statistics); military science; modern languages and literature (including French, German, and Spanish); music (including instrumental performance, liberal arts, music composition, piano performance, and vocal performance); natural science; nursing; occupational therapy; physical education, health, and recreation (including athletic training, coaching, community health education, exercise science, health, health and fitness/elementary or secondary education, health education, health promotion and wellness, outdoor recreation, recreation management, and therapeutic recreation); physics; psychology; social work; sociology; theater; and urban and regional planning.

Academic Programs

Eastern's mission is to prepare broadly educated, technologically proficient, and highly productive citizens to attain meaningful careers, to enjoy enriched lives, and to contribute to a culturally diverse society. Graduates must have well-developed skills in critical thinking and the ability to express themselves in oral, written, and quantitative forms of communication. The liberal arts core curriculum extends throughout the student's four-year program and includes both breadth and depth requirements as well as writing instruction and assessment in all areas of the curriculum. Small classes, a student-faculty ratio of 24:1, and facilities like the Writers' Center offer the student the resources to meet high expectations. Eastern's unique core curriculum and liberal arts goals were designed as a direct response to input from Eastern alumni, employers, and students. Minors are available in many areas of study, and teacher certification requirements and specific endorsements are available in conjunction with academic disciplines. The prestigious University Honors Program offers motivated students the opportunity to challenge their limits through special honors courses that are part of the core curriculum. University and departmental honor societies continue to provide these opportunities in the major fields. Career preparation is a focus during each student's entire program. Internships and career exploration opportunities for freshmen and sophomores assist in early career and major selection, enhanced employment skills, and locating professional internships as upper-division students.

Off-Campus Programs

Study-abroad opportunities are available for Eastern students as well as for students from other campuses. Programs are available in

more than twenty-five countries. In addition, internships are available for students in the Inland Northwest, across the United States, and internationally. These programs provide countless training and research opportunities for graduate and undergraduate students.

Academic Facilities

Eastern's campus includes more than 300 acres in Cheney. The University also maintains classroom, office, and laboratory/clinic facilities in downtown Spokane and shares facilities at the Riverpoint Higher Education Center, also in downtown Spokane. The University libraries include the Kennedy Library on the Cheney campus, with more than 800,000 items, online catalogs, and computer search capabilities covering Eastern as well as other Washington State libraries. Eastern and Washington State University jointly support a downtown library facility. Student computer labs, including a multimedia lab, are located throughout campus. The Pence Union Building houses the main computer lab, with Macintosh and IBM-compatible systems, on-site assistance, DEC mainframe access with faculty sponsorship, and Internet access. The residence halls are wired for both voice and data communications. Additional facilities for learning and teaching include the planetarium, the Robert Reid Laboratory School (an elementary school directly on campus that includes observation facilities), a speech and hearing clinic, and the Turnbull Laboratory for Ecological Studies.

Costs

Annual undergraduate tuition and fees for 2006–07 were $4695 for Washington State residents and $13,725 for nonresidents. Students participating in the Western Undergraduate Exchange Program paid $6609 for tuition and fees. Typical on-campus room and board cost about $6549.

Financial Aid

The Financial Aid and Scholarship Office assists students in identifying the most appropriate sources of funding for their college education. Students who are admitted to the University may apply for federal, state, and University funds by using the Free Application for Federal Student Aid and by applying before the priority deadline of February 15. Although most financial aid is based on need, a number of scholarships are available for students who meet competitive academic criteria. Academic scholarships also reward outstanding performance by continuing students at Eastern. The University scholarship application must be submitted for consideration by February 1. A reduction of the nonresident tuition is available to qualified students from Idaho, Montana, Nevada, New Mexico, North Dakota, Oregon, South Dakota, Utah, and Wyoming through the Western Undergraduate Exchange Program. Applicants interested in need-based financial aid and academic scholarships should contact the Financial Aid and Scholarship Office, 102 Sutton Hall, Eastern Washington University, Cheney, Washington, 99004.

Faculty

More than 600 faculty members provide highly personalized instruction to undergraduates at Eastern. Faculty members are committed to keeping class sizes small and to helping students graduate in a timely manner. Eastern's faculty members are teachers and take pride in innovative curricula, in maintaining close relationships with the community and with professionals outside of the University for the benefit of their students, and in their research, which brings new information and methods into the classroom.

Student Government

All students are members of the Associated Students of Eastern Washington University. A president, executive officers, and a 12-member council are elected annually. The 12 council members represent the students' interest in every facet of student life at Eastern. The student government is responsible for budgeting and managing student fees collected from all students. These funds are used for the operation of the student union, the Pence Union Building, athletic and intramural programs, and the more than seventy-five clubs and organizations that provide opportunities for involvement of students both on campus and in the community.

Admission Requirements

Freshman applicants are admitted based on their high school GPA and test scores on the SAT or the ACT with writing. Applicants also must meet the following core requirements in high school (having extra core classes is highly encouraged): English, 4; math, 3 (algebra I and II and geometry); social science, 3; science, 2 (including 1 lab science); foreign language, 2 (same language); and fine arts (or elective from above subject areas), 1. Transfer students with fewer than 40 transferable credits must meet the high school core and admissions index requirements and have a 2.0 cumulative GPA. Transfer students with more than 40 transferable credits must have a cumulative GPA of 2.0 and completed a minimum of precollege-level English and intermediate algebra with a 2.0 or better. Students who do not meet the academic criteria for admission may be considered on the basis of additional evidence of potential presented to the Office of Admissions. Many majors require considerably higher grade point averages for entry into the major field. Transfer students should consult the University catalog or contact the department for specific program requirements.

Application and Information

All freshman applicants should submit an application, complete high school (and any college) transcripts, and SAT or ACT with writing scores, and a personal statement to the Office of Admissions. Decisions for fall freshmen are made on December 1 and on a rolling basis thereafter. Transfer students should submit an application, an official high school transcript (if applicable), and official transcripts from all colleges and universities attended. A nonrefundable application fee of $50 is required of all applicants. A campus visit or participation in an overnight on-campus program is the best way to learn more about Eastern. Students should contact the Office of Admissions to find out more about these and other programs designed to provide an opportunity to explore Eastern Washington University. For additional information, students should contact:

Office of Admissions
101 Sutton Hall
Eastern Washington University
Cheney, Washington 99004

Phone: 509-359-2397
Fax: 509-359-6692
E-mail: admissions@mail.ewu.edu
Web site: http://www.ewu.edu

The state-of-the-art John F. Kennedy Library has 50 different databases available, 500 study carrels, wireless laptops that may be checked out, and more.

EMBRY-RIDDLE AERONAUTICAL UNIVERSITY

PRESCOTT, ARIZONA

The University

Embry-Riddle Aeronautical University's Prescott, Arizona, campus is recognized and respected worldwide as a center for cutting-edge instruction and training for tomorrow's leaders. The campus offers fourteen undergraduate degree programs and one master's-level program, all with a special emphasis on aviation and aerospace, security/intelligence, and related industries. Whether pursuing a career in the cockpit or engineering laboratories in computer science, space physics, or aviation business, Embry-Riddle–Arizona puts students far ahead in reaching their goals.

Embry-Riddle's reputation is based on its leadership role in aviation education as well as its commitment to a strong academic preparation and learning environment. Embry-Riddle is a private, independent, four-year university accredited by the Commission on Colleges of the Southern Association of Colleges and Schools.

The faculty and staff members take pride in providing Embry-Riddle–Arizona students with a unique combination of features not readily found on other campuses. A sense of belonging exists, with the total focus on students. Students share a love of aviation/aerospace, engineering, and a special motivation to succeed and become experts in their field. There is a close-knit residential atmosphere; nearly 850 students live in fourteen on-campus residence halls that offer both traditional rooms and apartment-style suites. Freshmen are required to live on campus. Most students take advantage of on-campus dining facilities and a variety of meal-plan options. The coed (18 percent women) student population of 1,650 undergraduates comes from fifty states and territories and thirty other countries. Three percent of the students are international.

There are more than seventy-five student clubs and organizations, including professional associations, fraternities and sororities, sports clubs, and intramural sports. The National Association of Intercollegiate Athletics (NAIA) men's soccer and wrestling teams, the NAIA women's soccer and volleyball teams, and the intercollegiate flight team compete both regionally and nationally. The Golden Eagles precision flight team has consistently ranked among the top in the country in the Safety and Flight Evaluation Conference (SAFECON) competitions and have captured the national championship title a record five times.

Guided by its worldwide network of alumni, Embry-Riddle's reputation has grown steadily in the aviation, aerospace, and business communities. Within one year of graduation, 95 percent of Embry-Riddle graduates from all campuses are either employed or have decided to continue their education.

Location

Just like its people, the University's location is warm and friendly. Prescott, a mile-high city on the Colorado Plateau, is home to the world's largest stand of ponderosa pine trees. The campus is about 100 miles northwest of Phoenix, 260 miles southeast of Las Vegas, and 375 miles east of Los Angeles. Prescott's climate reflects seasonable weather that is excellent for flying, with daytime averages of 80°F in the summer and 45°F in the winter. The local mountains exhibit the spirit of the rugged West, with students enjoying snow skiing, hiking, and tours of the Grand Canyon.

Known as a vacation getaway, Prescott offers shopping, entertainment, health, and recreational options and a friendly small-town atmosphere. For a flavor of city lights, Phoenix is a 1½-hour drive. The campus is situated on 539 acres, but campus life is centered in a 1-mile walking radius. The Flight Training Center is located nearby at the Prescott Municipal Airport.

Majors and Degrees

The Bachelor of Science in aeronautical science (professional pilot program) emphasizes multiengine training and prepares students for a career in the aviation industry with airlines, corporate and commercial aviation, or the military. Flight courses lead to certification as an instrument-rated commercial pilot. Certified Flight Instructor ratings are also available, although they are not required for the degree program. Students may also take professional-level courses in aircraft systems and flight methodology and many other flight-related topics.

The Bachelor of Science in aeronautics is designed for those students who work in aviation careers or wish to enter the field. The program provides an opportunity to acquire a broad-based education in aviation-specific courses and related instruction in business, computer science, economics, humanities, communication, social science, mathematics physical science, and other non-aviation-related fields.

The Bachelor of Science in aerospace engineering centers on the design of aircraft and spacecraft. The program focuses on the engineering of space-mission vehicles, aircraft, and other projects, with specializations of aeronautics and astronautics. Embry-Riddle is consistently rated as one of the country's best engineering schools by *U.S. News & World Report*'s "America's Best Colleges."

The Bachelor of Science in computer engineering degree gives a broad background in computer design, including embedded control systems, real-time systems, software engineering, and telecommunication systems. The program's emphasis on real-time embedded control systems and hardware/software interfaces provides program graduates with employment opportunities beyond those of graduates of traditional computer engineering programs.

The Bachelor of Science degree in electrical engineering is a systems-oriented program of study that includes analog and digital circuits, communication systems, computers, control systems, electromagnetic fields, energy sources and systems, and electronic devices. The student also gains specialization in avionics appropriate for entry-level engineering positions in the aerospace industry.

The Bachelor of Science in mechanical engineering is new for fall 2007. This degree program focuses on the design of propulsion systems or robotic systems, such as autonomous ground, air, or space vehicles. The curriculum combines a strong emphasis on the fundamentals of engineering with integrated analysis and design topics.

In the Bachelor of Science in computer science, studies consist of graphics, simulation, computer architecture, database management, operating systems, software engineering, artificial intelligence, and applications to the aviation industry.

The Bachelor of Science in global security and intelligence studies program focuses on global interrelationships in areas ranging from politics and economics to social change, public health, and other factors and the way these factors impact and influence the security of nations and the future of human society.

New in fall 2007, the Bachelor of Science in aviation environmental science program is the only undergraduate program in the country with aviation and aerospace industries as its focus. Graduates have the knowledge and technical skills needed to tackle the environmental and safety problems found in the aviation and aerospace industry.

The Bachelor of Science in applied meteorology provides a practical understanding of the physics and dynamics of the atmosphere and prepares the graduate for a range of meteorologist positions in government or industry. Students use a new state-of-the-art weather center and computer-equipped classrooms to understand and forecast complex atmospheric phenomena ranging from severe thunderstorms and tornadoes, cyclones, fronts, and jet streams to the global climate and how it is changing.

The Bachelor of Science degree in aviation business administration prepares the student for managerial and business-related positions in the constantly evolving aviation and aerospace industries. It is the only aviation business administration program approved by the Council on Aviation Accreditation (CAA).

The Bachelor of Science in space physics consists of four areas of concentration: astrophysics, particle physics and cosmology, advanced propulsion systems, and remote sensing. This program prepares students to excel in a wide range of careers and scientific pursuits, from solving problems associated with prolonged space missions to unraveling the mysteries of the universe.

The Bachelor of Science in aerospace studies is an interdisciplinary program that draws on a strong core of general education and advanced-level courses in a variety of areas to enhance communication, critical thinking, and technical skills; students also may choose three minor areas of study to create their own major.

Academic Programs

The undergraduate academic preparation provides a strong foundation for all students, whether or not they choose a career in aviation. Each major is a combination of general education, specialized focus, and applied technology. The general education component consists of courses in communication skills, social sciences/humanities, mathematics, computer science, and physical science.

Along with their major, students may opt to select a minor from many fields. Army and Air Force Reserve Officer Training Corps (ROTC) courses are also available to all Embry-Riddle students and may lead to a position as a commissioned officer.

Through participation in internships and cooperative education (co-op) arrangements, students in all fields of study gain valuable work experience with companies such as Continental Airlines, Delta Air Lines, the Federal Aviation Administration (FAA), Honeywell, Gulfstream Aerospace Corporation, Lockheed Martin, NASA, Northwest Airlines, the Naval Air Systems Command, the CIA, and Raytheon.

The academic year is divided into two semesters of fifteen weeks each. The average course load is 12–18 semester hours of credit. Two summer terms of approximately seven weeks each allow for additional enrollment. Many support programs exist to encourage students' development, such as academic advising and free tutoring, specialized career counselors in each college, and a writing center.

Academic Facilities

Tucked into the rolling hillsides, the campus blends nature with the layout of its eighty-four buildings, such as the Davis Learning Center auditorium and classrooms, the campus book store, and the Visitor Center. The center of campus focuses on student life and services such as the library, cafeteria, radio station and student government offices, student activities and financial aid offices, and the post office.

Embry-Riddle–Arizona's library is known for its outstanding aviation collections, which can be accessed by visiting the facility or the Web site. The library is home to the Aviation Safety and Security Archives as well as the Kalusa Collection, the world's largest to-scale collection of miniature airplane models. The new Hazy Library and Learning Center is under construction and scheduled to open in 2008.

Classroom buildings house specialized labs, including an airway science lab, the Robertson Aviation Safety Center, a physics lab, engineering graphics lab, aerospace engineering wind tunnel, optics lab, aerospace engineering structures, and aerospace engineering materials lab. The Aircraft Experimentation and Fabrication Building opened in fall 2006 with additional lab space for the hands-on portions of the engineering programs.

The 22,000-square-foot King Engineering and Technology Center houses a computer science classroom, the Computer-Aided Engineering Lab, and the UNIX Lab, which provide students with the latest in computer technologies. This center also houses the Linear Lab, Electrical Engineering Senior Design Lab, Electronics Power Lab, Honeywell Control, and System Integration Lab.

The Academic Complex has two computer design labs for engineering students, a weather center, faculty offices, and several classrooms.

Recreational and athletic facilities on campus include two gymnasiums; three athletic fields; a weight room; an aerobic, martial arts, and wrestling room; tennis courts; racquetball courts; a swimming pool; sand volleyball courts; a track; and several running trails.

Two miles from campus, the Embry-Riddle Flight Training Center occupies several buildings near the Prescott Municipal Airport. Embry-Riddle has more than thirty aircraft at Prescott. Currently, the Prescott fleet includes Cessna 152s (flight team), Cessna 172s, Piper Seminoles, American Champion Decathlons for extreme attitude recovery, and Cessna 182-RGs. Flight-training devices (FTDs) include three Cessna 172s and two Seminole Level 6 FTDs, all with 220-degree visual display, two Frasca 141 FTDs, one Frasca 142 FTD, and an Airbus A320 simulator.

Costs

The 2007–08 academic year tuition for all programs is $12,700 per semester. Flight fees are charged in addition to tuition. On-campus housing accommodations range from $1995 to $2960 per semester, depending on the accommodations; the required meal plan for freshmen is $1554 per semester. Students also need to account for the cost of books, transportation, and personal expenses.

Financial Aid

Students and their families find many sources of aid available to assist with paying the costs of a private university. Embry-Riddle participates in all national and state assistance programs. The completion of the Department of Education's Free Application for Federal Student Aid (FAFSA) form ensures students consideration for these funds. In addition, Embry-Riddle–Arizona provides assistance in the form of on-campus jobs, academic scholarships, veterans' educational benefits, and ROTC incentives.

Faculty

Easy access to faculty members is another strength of Embry-Riddle–Arizona. Faculty members, not graduate students, teach classes. The average class size is 21 students, with an overall student-faculty ratio of 14:1. Faculty members keep regular office hours and consider it their most important role to enhance the individual learning of each student. Faculty members bring both teaching and industry backgrounds to the classroom; most have extensive practical experience in their field, along with outstanding academic credentials.

Student Government

The Student Government Association (SGA) has an extremely important role. It provides many student activities, including service and community organizations, an Activities Planning Board, *Horizons* newspaper, and representation and funding for clubs and committees. The SGA is the key communication link to the University administration, and the council president serves as a member of the University Board of Trustees.

Admission Requirements

Each student receives individual consideration for admission, based on a variety of factors and circumstances. Completion of the Embry-Riddle–Arizona application for admission begins this process; official transcripts and score reports for either the SAT or ACT should also be submitted as well as two letters of recommendation. Notification takes place throughout the year.

Application and Information

A virtual tour of Embry-Riddle–Arizona is available online. For additional information, including information on campus visits, and application forms, students may contact:

Embry-Riddle Aeronautical University Admissions
3700 Willow Creek Road
Prescott, Arizona 86301
Phone: 928-777-6600
      800-888-3728 (toll-free)
E-mail: pradmit@erau.edu
Web site: http://www.embryriddle.edu/pr

FRESNO PACIFIC UNIVERSITY
FRESNO, CALIFORNIA

The University

Fresno Pacific University (FPU) is an independent university with a main campus in southeast Fresno and academic centers in Visalia, Bakersfield, and North Fresno. It serves about 1,200 undergraduates, 1,000 graduate students, plus thousands more in professional courses.

Academic programs prepare undergraduates for professional careers and graduate study in business, science and health, psychology, social work, teaching, communications, religious studies, and many other fields. Graduate students prepare for professional promotion and certification in business, several areas of education, and conflict resolution in organizations and communities.

The faculty is made up of experts dedicated to teaching. Most hold doctorates and publish regularly in their fields. As a Christian institution, all FPU programs emphasize the importance of values, ethics, and character development for professionals and leaders.

The University's success has been recognized nationally by such publications as *U.S. News & World Report,* which includes FPU in its top tier among Master's Universities—West.

Education at FPU is about equipping motivated students to become leaders; about developing knowledge skills and ethics that serve as tools to build successful futures. FPU does not see its job as filling students' minds with information, but helping them recognize the value of information, where to find it, and how to use it. FPU's reputation for academic excellence attracts both students and faculty members of the highest caliber.

Undergraduate enrollment has grown 60 percent in the last several years, attracting well-prepared students and reflecting the community's ethnic and cultural mosaic. The percentage of students of color in each new class is around 30 percent, while SAT scores and high school grade point averages are among the top quarter of each class rival those at several University of California campuses.

On-campus living arrangements include apartments and residence halls as well as University-sponsored houses. Apartment living is available near the University. Host family arrangements can be made for international students. Students are involved in many clubs, organizations and activities. Christian growth opportunities include various settings for worship, prayer, Bible study, and discipleship training. College Hour, a three-times-a-week gathering of the campus community, offers students and faculty members a look at a variety of issues from a Christian perspective as well as the sights and sounds of cultural and artistic presentations and various worship styles.

The Sunbird athletic teams of Fresno Pacific University are members of the National Association of Intercollegiate Athletics (NAIA) and compete at the intercollegiate level in men's basketball, cross-country, soccer, and track, and women's basketball, cross-country, soccer, track, and volleyball. Baseball and tennis programs were added in 2005. Intramural sports programs for both men and women are active throughout the school year. The music department has ensembles ranging from baroque to jazz, several of which tour. A highlight of the year is Unconcert, where students stage an evening of music of their choosing. The theater program produces two full-length productions each year as well as readings and one-act plays. The campus provides convenient access for handicapped people.

The Student Life Office provides personal, job, and career counseling and information on work and service opportunities as well as other support to students.

Location

Fresno Pacific University is the only accredited, private, residential four-year university in California's Central San Joaquin Valley offering bachelor's and master's degrees. The Fresno metropolitan area has an ethnically and culturally diverse population of 500,000. Yosemite, Kings Canyon, and Sequoia National Parks; ski areas; beaches; and cultural and entertainment attractions of San Francisco and Los Angeles are all accessible from Fresno.

Majors and Degrees

Fresno Pacific University offers bachelor's degrees in more than forty areas: applied mathematics, biblical and religious studies, biology, business accounting, business finance, business information systems, business marketing management, business nonprofit administration, chemistry, child development, church music, contemporary Christian ministries, English communication, English drama, English education, English literature, English writing, environmental science, environmental studies, history, intercultural studies, international business, mathematics education, music education, music performance/composition, philosophy, physical education exercise science, physical education health fitness, political science, psychology, social science education, social work, sociology, Spanish language and culture, and teaching/liberal studies. Preprofessional programs are available in law, medicine, and physical therapy.

Academic Programs

An FPU education begins with a broad foundation exposing the student to many areas of study. From this foundation, students learn the intellectual skills necessary to begin study in a major and a minor. Fresno Pacific University operates on a two-semester plus summer academic calendar. The academic year consists of an early fall semester, which ends before the Christmas holiday, and a spring semester, which concludes in May. The minimum number of units for a Bachelor of Arts degree is 124. The General Education Program includes four courses in biblical studies and religion. FPU grants credit for certain scores on Advanced Placement tests and College-Level Examination Program (CLEP) tests.

Off-Campus Programs

The University is part of several consortia that offer international and U.S. settings for off-campus education. Study-abroad programs are available in many countries of the world, including China, Ecuador, England, France, Germany, Greece, India, Japan, Mexico, Russia, and Spain. An American studies program is available in Washington, D.C., as is a film study program in Los Angeles, California. Short-term study-abroad programs led by FPU faculty members are also available to various countries in May of each year.

Academic Facilities

Hiebert Library is owned and operated jointly with the Mennonite Brethren Biblical Seminary. There are currently 150,000 volumes, 2,200 journal subscriptions, 250,000 microforms, and an audiovisual collection of 10,000 items. Three computer laboratories are available to all students, where they can access word processing, e-mail, Internet, spreadsheet, database, and other software for their use in class work, research, and writing, using either MS-DOS or Macintosh equipment, including Power Macs.

Recent facilities improvements also enhance learning. A revamped Alumni Hall, dedicated in April 2005, offers a fireplace lounge, coffee bar, and expanded campus bookstore. Steinert Campus Center opened in 2003 as a place to feed the spirit as well as the body. Students and faculty members eat together in the main dining room.

AIMS Hall of Mathematics and Science is more than a great place to learn about biology, physics, chemistry, and mathematics. Its design encourages faculty and students to gather, bringing together people as well as disciplines. The building also features a 41-foot Foucault Pendulum in the lobby—one of four in California and the only one in the Central Valley.

Athletic facilities are also being expanded. The track and soccer fields are among the best in the FPU's conference, and the Harold and Betty Haak Tennis Complex was dedicated in April 2005.

Fine arts facilities are part of the campus master plan, with designs being drawn up for a building for music and drama education and performance.

Costs

The tuition for academic year 2006–07 was $21,550 and room and board were $6600. Other fees were additional.

Financial Aid

Fresno Pacific University offers a variety of federal, state, and private financial aid programs to assist students who would benefit from an education but need financial aid. Such students are encouraged to apply for assistance. More than 97 percent of FPU undergraduate students receive financial assistance in the form of loans, grants, scholarships, and on-campus employment opportunities. Merit scholarships are awarded to students based on academic achievement. Other scholarships include service/leadership, music, drama, and athletics awards. Students wishing to apply for financial aid must be accepted for admission and complete the Free Application for Federal Student Aid (FAFSA) and the FPU Financial Aid Application. California students should complete the FAFSA before the March 2 California Grant deadline and submit the Cal Grant GPA Verification Form in order to be considered for the Cal Grant program. Financial aid for international students is also available on a limited basis. International students should complete the FPU Financial Aid Application only.

Faculty

The faculty members work with students to build relationships that encourage learning. In their first semester, freshmen are matched with a group of peers led by a faculty member to ease their integration into university life. All through their time at FPU, students find most classes have 20 or fewer students.

Two faculty members recently won Fulbright Scholarships. Many other faculty members share their talents in music, art, and drama or consult with businesses and nonprofit agencies. It has been said that the common thread among these dedicated teachers is that they set high goals for students, support their efforts, and celebrate their accomplishments.

Student Government

Fresno Pacific University is committed to helping students develop character and competence in order to become effective leaders who inspire, empower, and serve others. The Undergraduate Students of Fresno Pacific University offers a variety of services, provides student representation to the University, and gives many opportunities for personal, social, spiritual, and political growth for students. Members of the Student Executive Council also serve as members of standing staff and faculty committees within the University governance structure. The Student Executive Council is composed of the following positions: president, vice president, business manager, student ministries, social affairs, commuter representative, secretary, and class senators. Appointment to these leadership roles is conducted through student body elections and personal interviews.

Admission Requirements

Fresno Pacific University welcomes students who qualify academically, who demonstrate the physical and emotional capacity for university work, and who accept the purposes and standards of the University.

Acceptance for admission as a freshman student is based on an eligibility index score determined by a formula using the high school grade point average (excluding physical education, military science, and applied courses) and the total score from either the SAT or the ACT. Applicants must also have a high school diploma or a GED.

Transfer students may bring in a maximum of 70 units of credit from an accredited postsecondary institution. To be granted admission solely on college-level academic work, a minimum of 24 transferable units must have been completed with at least a 2.4 academic GPA.

International students are valuable to Fresno Pacific University. For those seeking improvement in their English language skills, the Intensive English Language Program (IELP) offers various levels of English language instruction. Students may receive university credits for language courses or may enroll in the Language and Culture Studies Program (LCS) to receive a certificate. International students need proficient English skills in order to succeed in undergraduate studies.

To study in regular undergraduate courses, students must reach a score of at least 500 (with 50 or higher on each section) on the TOEFL. SAT or ACT scores are useful in considering students for scholarships. An application file can be complete without TOEFL and SAT or ACT scores, although the University strongly recommends that they be submitted.

Application and Information

U.S. students entering directly from high school must submit an application for admission, a $40 nonrefundable application fee, official high school transcripts, SAT or ACT scores, and at least one letter of recommendation.

U.S. transfer students need to submit an application for admission, a $40 nonrefundable application fee, official transcripts from high school verifying graduation, official transcripts from each college attended, and at least one letter of recommendation. Test scores are not required, but they are recommended.

Requirements for international students include the international application form, a $40 nonrefundable application fee, certified and translated transcripts from all secondary schools and postsecondary institutions certifying academically acceptable marks/grades, a completed financial certification form, two letters of recommendation, and a TOEFL score.

For more information, students should contact:

Yammilette Rodriguez, Director of Undergraduate Admissions
Fresno Pacific University
1717 South Chestnut Avenue
Fresno, California 93702
Phone: 559-453-2039
      800-660-6089 (toll-free)
E-mail: ugadmis@fresno.edu
Web site: http://www.fresno.edu

For international student information, students should contact:

International Programs and Services Office
Fresno Pacific University
1717 South Chestnut Avenue
Fresno, California 93702
Phone: 559-453-2069
Fax: 559-453-5501
E-mail: ipso@fresno.edu
Web site: http://www.fresno.edu/dept/ipso

Since 1944, Fresno Pacific University has built a reputation for strong academics and character development.

GEORGE FOX UNIVERSITY
NEWBERG, OREGON

The University

George Fox University was founded in 1891 by the Society of Friends (Quakers) with the purpose of providing students a challenging academic atmosphere within a community of Christian faith. Today, George Fox maintains the same mission and has grown to an enrollment of more than 3,200 students.

Students find George Fox to be a place where spiritual growth and intellectual challenge take place in a friendly, caring environment. This tradition of integration of faith and learning has been recognized by the Templeton Foundation, which named George Fox University to its honor roll of character-building colleges.

The majority of George Fox students live in campus residence halls, suites, and apartments. Opportunities for extracurricular involvement are available in music, drama, journalism, student government, radio, clubs, and athletics. George Fox is a member of the NCAA Division III and competes in six men's sports (baseball, basketball, cross-country, soccer, tennis, and track) and eight women's sports (basketball, cross-country, golf, soccer, softball, tennis, track, and volleyball). Intramural sports are also played.

Regular chapel services bring the campus community together in worship. Students have the opportunity to put their faith into action on volunteer mission trips and during community outreach activities.

In addition to its undergraduate degrees, George Fox confers graduate degrees in business, counseling, education, organizational leadership, and psychology. George Fox Evangelical Seminary offers five seminary degrees; a sixth will be added in fall 2007.

Location

George Fox University is located in Newberg, a residential community of 20,000 people. The 85-acre tree-shaded campus is a 30-minute drive from the major metropolitan environment of Portland. The University is situated in the beautiful Pacific Northwest, with scenic Mt. Hood and the rugged Pacific coastline within short driving distances.

Tilikum Retreat Center, which is set on a 90-acre lake and just 10 minutes away, provides students a change of pace from the classroom. Students enjoy hiking, canoeing, and fishing at the camp. Tilikum has an extensive summer day camp program that employs many University students.

Majors and Degrees

George Fox confers the Bachelor of Arts and Bachelor of Science degrees. The following undergraduate majors are available: accounting, allied health, applied science, art, biblical studies, biology, business administration, chemistry, Christian ministries, cinema and media communications, cognitive science, communication arts, computer and information science, economics, elementary education, engineering, family and consumer sciences, health and human performance, history, interdisciplinary studies, international studies, mathematics, music, nursing, organizational communication, philosophy, political science, psychology, religion, social work, sociology, Spanish, theater, and writing/literature.

Academic Programs

The academic year at George Fox University is divided into two semesters of fifteen weeks. In addition to the two semesters, the University sponsors a three-week May Term. For graduation, students are required to earn 126 credit hours, including 54 general education and 42 upper-division credits.

Students may reduce the number of required courses and add flexibility to their undergraduate years with credit earned through Advanced Placement, International Baccalaureate (I.B.), the College-Level Examination Program, and credit by examination. All traditional undergraduates are given a personal computer to use and keep upon graduation.

George Fox demonstrates its commitment to freshmen by providing a Freshman Seminar program to assist students as they integrate themselves into the academic and social life of the University community.

Off-Campus Programs

The importance of international study is shown through a variety of programs. Each year during May Term, George Fox sponsors a number of three-week study tours, which are led by University faculty members. Transportation costs are subsidized by the University. These international learning experiences are designed for students completing their junior year. Through the Council for Christian Colleges and Universities, students are also given the opportunity to study for a semester in Africa, Australia, China, England, Latin America, the Middle East, Russia, and Washington, D.C.

Membership in the Christian College Consortium enables George Fox University students to attend for a semester one of twelve other colleges located throughout the United States.

Academic Facilities

The Edward F. Stevens Center provides 40,000 square feet of office and classroom space. All student service–oriented offices are now housed under one roof, providing greater efficiency and access for students. The building has been selected as part of the "Ten Shades of Green" by Portland General Electric for its use of recycled materials and minimal environmental impact.

The Murdock Learning Resource Center houses more than 140,000 books and periodicals. Its features include rare-book collections, study carrels, an audiovisual laboratory, and access to 19,000 journal titles in electronic format.

The Edwards/Holman Science Center is home to the University's science programs. The 36,000-square-foot building provides classrooms, offices, and laboratories for biology, chemistry, premedicine, mathematics, computer science, and engineering programs.

The William and Mary Bauman Auditorium seats 1,150 people in a facility that annually hosts the Oregon Symphony and other regional events. Rotating art exhibits appear in the adjoining Lindgren Gallery. All academic buildings and residence halls are equipped with wireless Web access.

Hoover Academic Building was named after former president Herbert Hoover and displays various photos and memorabilia from his life. Hoover was a student at Friends Pacific Academy, the forerunner of George Fox University. The newly remodeled facility houses the nursing program and the undergraduate psychology, religion, and sociology/social work departments.

Costs

Tuition for the 2006–07 year was $22,250. Room and board were $7210. Fees cost $320. Books are estimated to cost $700 per year.

Financial Aid

George Fox maintains that every qualified student should be able to attend the university of his or her choice without letting limited finances stand in the way. To this end, federal, state, and institutional need-based funds are available, as are merit awards. About 95 percent of all students receive financial aid.

Faculty

The faculty at George Fox University fosters an atmosphere of discussion and independent thinking in the classroom. Faculty members have found a healthy balance between teaching and research by devoting a majority of their time to educating students. The University employs 144 full-time and 116 part-time faculty members. Seventy percent of full-time faculty members hold doctoral degrees. Faculty members are personally committed Christians who are involved in the lives of their students. The student-faculty ratio is 13:1.

Student Government

The Associated Student Community of George Fox University serves as a unifying force and voice for the campus student community and plays a significant role in organizing cultural, social, and recreational activities.

Admission Requirements

Students admitted to George Fox University must show academic ability, high moral character, and social concern. These qualities are evaluated by consideration of each applicant's academic record, test scores, recommendations, interview reports, and participation in extracurricular activities. The priority application date is February 1. In order to provide a solid foundation for college-level work, it is recommended that the applicant present the equivalent of 16 academic units from an approved high school. The following units are suggested: English, 4; social studies, 3; science, 2; mathematics, 2; foreign language, 2; and health and physical education, 1.

Application and Information

For additional information, students should contact:

Office of Undergraduate Admissions
George Fox University
Newberg, Oregon 97132-2697

Phone: 800-765-4369 Ext. 2240 (toll-free)
E-mail: admissions@georgefox.edu
Web site: http://www.georgefox.edu

HAWAI'I PACIFIC UNIVERSITY

HONOLULU, HAWAI'I

The University

Hawai'i Pacific University (HPU) is an independent, coeducational, career-oriented comprehensive university with a foundation in the liberal arts. Undergraduate and graduate degrees are offered in more than fifty areas. Hawai'i Pacific prides itself on maintaining strong academic programs, small class sizes, individual attention to students, and a diverse faculty and student population. HPU is accredited by the Western Association of Schools and Colleges and the National League for Nursing Accrediting Commission.

HPU is the largest private university in Hawaii, with more than 8,000 students from every state in the union and more than 100 countries. The diversity of the student body stimulates learning about other cultures firsthand, both in and out of the classroom. There is no majority population at HPU. Students are encouraged to examine the values, customs, traditions, and principles of others to gain a clearer understanding of their own perspectives. HPU students develop friendships with students from throughout the United States and the world and important connections for success in the global economy of the twenty-first century.

In addition to the undergraduate programs, HPU offers eleven graduate programs: the M.B.A. (with eleven concentrations), the Master of Science in Information Systems (M.S.I.S.), the Master of Science in Nursing (M.S.N.), the Master of Education (M.Ed.) in secondary education, the Master of Social Work (M.S.W.), and the Master of Arts (M.A.) in communications, diplomacy and military studies, global leadership, human resource management, organizational change, and teaching English as a second language.

HPU has NCAA Division II intercollegiate sports. Men's athletic programs include baseball, basketball, cheerleading, cross-country, and tennis. Women's athletics include cheerleading, cross-country, softball, tennis, and volleyball.

The housing office at HPU offers many services and options for students. Residence halls with cafeteria service are available on the windward Hawai'i Loa campus, while off-campus apartments are available in the Honolulu and Waikiki areas for those seeking more independent living arrangements.

Location

With three campuses linked by shuttle, Hawai'i Pacific combines the excitement of an urban, downtown campus with the serenity of the windward Hawai'i Loa residential campus, which is set in the lush foothills of the Koolau Range. The main campus is located in downtown Honolulu, the business and financial center of the Pacific. Eight miles away, situated on 135 acres in Kaneohe, the windward Hawai'i Loa campus is the site of the School of Nursing, the marine science program, and a variety of other course offerings. The third campus, Oceanic Institute, is an applied aquaculture research facility located on a 56-acre site at Makapuu Point on the windward coast of Oahu, Hawaii, with facilities on the Big Island of Hawaii as well.

Six military campuses are located on Oahu: Pearl Harbor Naval Base, Hickam Air Force Base, Schofield Army Barracks, Tripler Army Medical Center, Marine Corps Base Hawaii–Kaneohe, and Marine Corps Base Hawaii–Camp H. M. Smith. These provide U.S. service members with educational opportunities. Students may take classes on whichever campus is most convenient.

The Hawai'i Loa campus is home to recreational facilities such as a soccer field, tennis courts, a softball field, a student center, and an exercise room. The beautiful weather, for which Hawaii is famous, allows for unlimited recreation opportunities year-round. The emphasis on a career-related curriculum keeps students focused on their academic goals. The economy in Hawaii makes cooperative education and internship opportunities hard to beat. Students desiring to expand their horizons in preparation for the changing global economy find Hawaii to be an exciting learning laboratory where East meets West. The many opportunities available at HPU provide for a healthy combination of school, work, and fun.

Majors and Degrees

Hawai'i Pacific University offers programs that lead to the degrees of Bachelor of Arts (B.A.), Bachelor of Science in Business Administration (B.S.B.A.), Bachelor of Science in Computer Science (B.S.C.S.), Bachelor of Science in environmental science, Bachelor of Science in marine science, Bachelor of Science in Nursing (B.S.N.), Bachelor of Science in premedical studies, and Bachelor of Social Work (B.S.W.).

Undergraduate majors include the B.A. in advertising, anthropology, applied sociology, communication (concentrations in speech and visual communication), East-West classical studies, economics, engineering (a 3-2 program), English, environmental studies, history, human resource development, human services, international relations, international studies (concentrations in American, Asian, comparative, European, and Pacific studies), justice administration, political science, psychology, social sciences, and teaching English as a second language. The College of Business programs include the B.S. in accounting, advertising, business economics, corporate communication, entrepreneurial studies, finance, human resource management, international business, management, marketing, public administration, and travel industry management. The B.S. is also available in applied mathematics, biology, computer information systems, computer science, diplomacy and military studies, environmental science, marine biology, nursing, oceanography, and premedical studies. Dual degrees, double majors, and minors are also offered.

Academic Programs

The baccalaureate student must complete at least 124 semester hours of credit. Forty-five of these credits provide the student with a strong foundation in the liberal arts, with the remaining credits composed of appropriate upper-division classes in the student's major and related areas. The academic year operates on a modified 4-1-4 semester system, featuring a five-week winter intersession. The University also offers extensive summer sessions. A student can earn up to 15 semester hours of credit during the summer. By attending these supplemental sessions, a student may complete the baccalaureate degree program in three years. A five-year B.S.B.A./M.B.A. program is also available.

Off-Campus Programs

Hawai'i Pacific's academic and cocurricular programs are intertwined with the world of work. The University offers a comprehensive cooperative education/internship program through the Career Services Center, in which a student may enroll throughout his or her course of study. This program enables students to gain significant experience in a career-related position as well as earn academic credit and a salary. HPU students have done co-ops and internships at some of the world's best-known companies and organizations, including American Express Financial Advisors; Deloitte & Touche, LLP; FBI; Hilton Hotels; Microsoft; Oceanic Institute; Polo Ralph Lauren; and Walt Disney World. The staff at the Career Services Center continues to work with students after graduation, from resume writing to job interview preparation.

Academic Facilities

The downtown campus comprises six buildings in the center of Honolulu's business district. HPU's newest facility is the Frear Center, which houses state-of-the-art classrooms, a communication lab, a robotics lab, and a graduate M.S.I.S. high-tech classroom. Hawai'i Pacific's Meader Library provides a large collection of circulating books, special reference resources, newspapers from around the world, and periodicals. A number of special collections are housed, with extensive business collections and a separate career development section. Meader Library has a tutoring center that provides free tutoring in all core subjects, a graduate reading room, and ample study space. A computerized search system allows students access to information from libraries throughout the nation. The Learning Assistance Center is the home of language labs and an audiotape and audiovisual library as well as the multimedia lab with the latest in interactive computer and CD-ROM technology. The recently expanded computer lab has more than 420 IBM-compatible PCs.

On the suburban and residential windward Hawai'i Loa campus, academic life revolves around the Amos N. Starr and Juliette Montague Cooke Academic Center (AC). The AC houses faculty and staff offices, classrooms, a theater, an art gallery, and the Atherton Learning Resources Center, which includes a library with extensive collections in the areas of Asian studies, marine science, and nursing. The Boyd MacNaughton Pacific Resource Room houses the Hawaiiana and Pacific special collections. The Academic Computer Center provides access to IBM computers.

Costs

For the 2007–08 academic year, tuition is $13,000 (for most majors), and books, supplies, and health insurance cost approximately $2300. For students who live in residence halls, room and board are $10,560. Tuition for marine science majors is $15,192, and tuition for junior- or senior-year nursing majors is $18,500.

Financial Aid

The University provides financial aid for qualified students through institutional, state, and federal aid programs. Approximately 40 percent of the University's undergraduate students receive financial aid. Among the forms of aid available are Federal Perkins Loans, Federal Stafford Student Loans, Guaranteed Parental Loans, Federal Pell Grants, and Federal Supplemental Educational Opportunity Grants. To apply for aid, students must submit the Free Application for Federal Student Aid (FAFSA). The FAFSA may be submitted at any time, but the priority deadline is March 1.

Faculty

HPU faculty members are renowned for the personal interest they take in each of their students. HPU is proud to offer more than 445 full-time and part-time faculty members with outstanding academic and business credentials from around the world, ensuring that HPU students can easily access a world's worth of knowledge and experiences. A vast majority of HPU faculty members hold the highest degrees in their fields. The student-faculty ratio is 18:1, and the average class size is less than 25.

Student Government

All registered students are members of the Associated Students of Hawai'i Pacific University (ASHPU), which is headed by elected officers and class representatives. ASHPU supervises more than eighty clubs, organizations, and activities, including a literary magazine; a national award–winning student newspaper; a pep band; an international vocal ensemble; preprofessional, cultural, and social organizations; service societies; dances; luaus; and cheerleading.

Admission Requirements

Hawai'i Pacific seeks students who are motivated and show academic promise. The admissions office requires that applicants complete and forward the admission application and their high school transcripts. Transfer students should also submit college transcripts. SAT and/or ACT scores should be submitted if these scores are not posted in the transcripts. First-time freshmen are expected to have a minimum GPA of 2.5 (on a 4.0 scale) in college-preparatory courses. Students with less than a 2.5 may be considered for admission but should also submit three letters of recommendation and a short essay on educational and personal objectives. HPU recommends that students complete 4 years of English, 2 years of math and social studies, and at least 1 year of history and science. Transfer students with 24 or more postsecondary credits are required to have a GPA of 2.0 or above. For students with less than 24 credits, a combination of college and high school GPA is used.

The marine science and environmental science programs require a high school GPA of 3.0 or above and 3 years of science, including biology, chemistry, and physics, as well as mathematics through precalculus (trigonometry). Transfer students must demonstrate ability in science and math at the college level. Students not meeting the above criteria are encouraged to enroll at HPU without declaring a major to demonstrate the ability to do college-level work in science and math.

Application and Information

Candidates are notified of admission decisions on a rolling basis, usually within two weeks of receipt of application materials. Early entrance and deferred entrance are available.

For further information and for application materials, students should contact:

Office of Admissions
Hawai'i Pacific University
1164 Bishop Street, Suite 200
Honolulu, Hawaii 96813
Phone: 808-544-0238
       866-CALL-HPU (toll-free in the U.S. and Canada)
Fax: 808-544-1136
E-mail: admissions@hpu.edu
Web site: http://www.hpu.edu

Students on the HPU windward campus.

LEWIS & CLARK COLLEGE
PORTLAND, OREGON

The College

Founded in 1867 in a small town south of Portland, Lewis & Clark College moved to its present location in Portland's southwest hills in 1942. The 137-acre campus is situated in a wooded residential area 6 miles from the center of the city and overlooks the lush Willamette Valley and Mount Hood in the distance.

The student body is known for its geographic diversity. In fall 2005, of the 1,964 undergraduates, 20 percent were from Oregon, and 80 percent came from forty-five states, plus the District of Columbia, and forty-two countries. Approximately 70 percent live in housing on campus, most of which is coed (91 percent). Residence halls allow for interaction among students, and the units are governed through student representation and hall councils. There are no fraternities or sororities.

The College offers numerous cocurricular activities, including seven music groups, nine media organizations, eight religious/spiritual life groups, and more than sixty student organizations. Cultural events such as lectures, symposia, art exhibits, theater productions, concerts, recitals, and dance performances occur on a regular basis. Currently, there are nineteen NCAA Division III varsity athletic teams, eight club teams, and eight to ten intramural sports. Athletic facilities include three basketball courts, a competition-size swimming pool, a weight-training room, a stadium, a baseball/softball complex, and six tennis courts, three of which are covered by an airdome. The renowned College Outdoors Program offers adventures such as backpacking, rafting, skiing, sea kayaking (and more!) in Oregon's and Washington's nearby wilderness areas.

Location

Portland has long been known for its livability and its excellent transportation service. Public buses and a free College shuttle run from the Lewis & Clark campus to the center of Portland. The metropolitan area (population 1.9 million) is bisected by the Willamette River. Mount Hood, offering skiing ten months per year, is 50 miles away, and Oregon's rugged coastline lies 90 miles to the west. The city has 10,447 acres of parks, thirty-three music associations, thirty-five theater and dance companies, more than ninety galleries and museums, and more than 1,000 restaurants. Professional sports teams compete in baseball, hockey, lacrosse, and NBA basketball.

Majors and Degrees

Lewis & Clark offers programs leading to the Bachelor of Arts degree. Academic majors include art, biochemistry and molecular biology, biology, chemistry, communications, computer science and mathematics, East Asian studies, economics, English, environmental studies, foreign languages, French studies, German studies, Hispanic studies, history, international affairs, mathematics, music, philosophy, physics, political science, psychology, religious studies, sociology/anthropology, and theater. Students may also design a major or pursue a double major and numerous minors. Preprofessional programs are available in dentistry, education, law, and medicine.

Dual-degree (3-2 and 4-2) programs in engineering are offered in cooperation with Columbia University, Washington University (St. Louis), the University of Southern California, and the Oregon Graduate Institute. A 4-2 B.A./M.B.A. program is offered in cooperation with the University of Rochester's Simon Graduate School of Business Administration. A 4-1 B.A./M.A.T. program is offered through Lewis & Clark's Graduate School of Education and Counseling.

Academic Programs

The liberal arts curriculum offers sufficient structure to ensure depth and breadth of study, but it also incorporates a high degree of freedom in order to promote creative and critical thinking. In the four-year plan of study, approximately one third of a student's time is devoted to general education, one third to a major program, and one third to elective courses. Students are also encouraged to participate in departmental honors programs, undergraduate research, independent study, and internships.

The academic calendar consists of two 15-week semesters. A normal load is four 4-semester-hour academic courses, plus one or more activity courses. By graduation a student is expected to have earned at least 128 semester hours—equivalent, roughly, to eight different classes a year. The fall semester begins early in September and ends before Christmas, and the spring semester begins in mid-January and ends in early May. There are also a limited number of courses offered during two summer sessions.

The community of scholars at Lewis & Clark College is dedicated to personal and academic excellence. Joining the Lewis & Clark community obligates each member to observe the principles of mutual respect, academic integrity, civil discourse, and responsible decision making.

Off-Campus Programs

Lewis & Clark offers nationally recognized international and off-campus study opportunities that have been in existence for more than forty years. Approximately twenty-five different overseas study programs and two domestic programs are available annually. Usually, 20 to 24 students, plus a faculty leader, participate in each program. Fifty-five percent of the College's graduates have taken advantage of these outstanding programs, often satisfying General Education or major requirements at the same time.

Overseas study may have either a general-culture focus or a specialized academic focus. On general-culture programs, students become immersed in the everyday life of the host country by living with local families, traveling, studying in classes and seminars, and working on independent projects. Programs with a more specific academic focus may include studying German language and literature in Munich; perfecting language skills in France, Ecuador, Russia, Japan, or China; or studying literature in England. Sites for overseas study programs from 2007 through 2010 are Australia, Chile, China, Cuba, Dominican Republic, Ecuador, England, France, Germany, Ghana, Greece, India, Italy, Japan, Kenya/Tanzania, Russia, Scotland, Senegal, Spain, and Vietnam. Domestic programs are available in New York, San Francisco, and Washington, D.C., for those interested in economics, political science, sociology, theater, or art. All programs, both overseas and domestic, are for credit and are similar in cost to full-time, on-campus study for the same period. Students with financial aid or scholarships can apply their assistance to the expenses of these programs.

Academic Facilities

The Aubrey R. Watzek Library (open 24 hours per day when school is in session) houses approximately 290,000 volumes and includes electronic access to thousands of periodical titles. Its mission is to provide a solid core of materials designed to support the curriculum and the research needs of the Lewis & Clark community. The library offers individualized reference assistance in the use of both print and electronic resources. The library's Web site provides access to its catalog as well as to a full range of electronic databases and links to useful Internet resources. The library is a member of Summit, a consortium of thirty-three academic libraries

that have a unified catalog that enables students to request and receive materials from member libraries within two days.

Music department facilities include Evans Auditorium, a 410-seat recital hall equipped with an orchestra pit and stage elevator; an extensive record, CD, and tape collection; twenty-two practice rooms; forty-three pianos, including several 6- and 7-foot concert grands and a 9-foot Steinway concert grand; two harpsichords; a Baroque organ; an electronic music studio with CD production capability; Zimbabwe marimbas; and an Indonesian gamelan orchestra. The 600-seat chapel houses an 85-rank Casavant organ.

The Fields Center for the Visual Arts is equipped with studio space for painting, drawing, ceramics, sculpture, design, and printmaking as well as a photography lab. The department also has a library of 50,000 slides and several thousand digital images representing artwork from a wide range of media, time periods, world regions, and cultures. The arts center contains gallery and classroom space as well. The humanities and social sciences also enjoy state-of-the-art classroom and lab facilities.

The natural sciences are housed in the Biology/Psychology, Bo-Dine, and Olin Buildings, which are well equipped with modern instrumentation to support the College's emphasis on collaborative student-faculty research. These buildings contain numerous research laboratories and equipment, used by students in classes or research projects, in addition to teaching labs and classrooms. Among the notable facilities are a laboratory for the study of human-computer interactions, a scanning electron microscope, a modern greenhouse, an astronomical observatory with several telescopes, a molecular modeling laboratory equipped with high-speed computers, a laboratory for the study of parallel computing, a laboratory for studying the biomechanics of animal locomotion, and an astrophysics laboratory that is equipped to remotely operate and acquire data from a specialized telescope at Kitts Peak, Arizona. All labs are computerized for acquiring and analyzing data and are networked to allow sharing and acquisition of data remotely. Ecological investigations and studies of the environmental impacts of human activity can be conducted both on the College's heavily wooded campus and at the nearby Tryon Creek State Park.

Computer facilities include several computer laboratories in academic buildings that are for student use. More than 130 Macintosh, IBM, and compatible computers are available for student use, along with peripherals such as color scanners, color printers, digital cameras, and digital video editing. All residence halls have direct Internet access. Parts of the campus also have wireless network capability.

Costs

Tuition and fees for 2006–07 were $29,772. The room and board charge was $7776 for fourteen meals per week; other meal plans were also available. The estimate for books and personal expenses was $1900.

Financial Aid

In 2005–06, 78 percent of the College's students received some form of financial assistance. Institutional, state, and federal resources, including Federal Pell Grants, Federal Supplemental Educational Opportunity Grants, Federal Perkins Loans, and Federal Work-Study awards, may be part of an aid award. Other options include low-interest Federal Stafford Student Loans and opportunities to work on and off campus. To receive priority consideration for financial aid, students must meet appropriate deadlines for admission and should submit the Free Application for Federal Student Aid (FAFSA) by March 1. Merit-based awards are offered to exceptional students who are selected as Neely Scholars (up to ten full-tuition scholarships), Trustee Scholars (up to fifteen half-tuition scholarships per year), and more than 100 Dean's Scholars ($4000–$10,000 scholarships per year). In addition, more than thirty $5000 Leadership and Service Awards are made annually. Students

designated as National Merit finalists with Lewis & Clark officially named as their first choice receive $1000.

Faculty

The 129 full-time members of the faculty are committed to undergraduate teaching and advising and are also active in research, writing, and publishing. Involving students in the research process is of high priority. Ninety-four percent of the full-time faculty members hold a Ph.D. or the highest advanced degree in their discipline. The student-faculty ratio is approximately 13:1. The average class size is 20, with an average size of 25 for first-year-level courses and 14 for upper-division courses.

Student Government

The Associated Students of Lewis & Clark (ASLC) has a decentralized structure that encourages cocurricular participation by students and places a high priority on participation with faculty and staff in the process of enriching the academic environment. ASLC consists of an Executive Council, governing boards, and appointed students who serve on faculty constitutional, standing, and special committees. The 25 members of the Student Academic Affairs Board (SAAB) are appointed on a departmental basis to solicit, evaluate, and support undergraduate and faculty research, instruction, curriculum, and program enhancement. One quarter of the total ASLC budget of more than $330,000 is used by SAAB in support of undergraduate research grants and speakers.

Admission Requirements

Lewis & Clark College seeks first-year and transfer applicants who are committed to academic excellence and personal growth. Admission is competitive. Applications are carefully reviewed and examined for degree of academic preparation, ability to express ideas in essay form, participation in activities, citizenship and community service, and support given by the school through recommendations. Campus visits are encouraged. Interviews are available but not required. Recommended high school preparation includes 4 years of English, 4 years of history or social science, 4 years of mathematics, 3 years of laboratory science, 2 to 3 years of foreign language, and 1 year of fine arts. The SAT or ACT is required, unless the student is applying via the Portfolio Path.

Application and Information

First-year applicants should submit the online Lewis & Clark or the Common Application (online or paper); a personal essay; an official academic transcript, including senior grades from the first marking period; one recommendation from a counselor; and at least one reference from an academic teacher. Lewis & Clark's online application can be found at the College's Web site. The application fee is waived if the applicant uses the College's online option or the online Common Application. Application deadlines are November 15 for Early Action (notification by January 15) and February 1 for Regular Decision (notification by April 1). The optional Portfolio Path admissions program provides an opportunity for applicants who have shown exceptional academic initiative to demonstrate the full extent of their pursuits by presenting a portfolio of their academic work. Under this plan, SAT or ACT scores are optional.

For more information about Lewis & Clark College or to arrange a visit, students should contact:

Office of Admissions
Lewis & Clark College
0615 Southwest Palatine Hill Road
Portland, Oregon 97219-7899
Phone: 503-768-7040
       800-444-4111 (toll-free)
Fax: 503-768-7055
E-mail: admissions@lclark.edu
Web site: http://www.lclark.edu

LINFIELD COLLEGE
MCMINNVILLE, OREGON

The College

Linfield College (1858) is an independent, coeducational, residential, comprehensive liberal arts and sciences college dedicated to providing an educational environment conducive to learning and participation. There are 1,750 full-time students on the McMinnville campus. These students come primarily from the thirteen Western states (twenty-six states overall) but also from nineteen other countries. Members of minority groups make up 11 percent of the student body, and 4 percent of students are international. Most students are between 18 and 22. Linfield is primarily residential, with one residence hall for men, three for women, and twelve that are coeducational, each accommodating between 10 and 100 residents. There are also four fraternity houses. Each hall establishes its own calendar of social, educational, and recreational events throughout the year. Students who reside on campus eat their meals in the College dining hall. Houses and apartments are available for upper-division students. Social clubs, professional organizations, sororities (one local: Sigma Kappa Phi, and three national: Alpha Phi, Phi Sigma Sigma, and Zeta Tau Alpha) and fraternities (one local: Delta Psi Delta, and three national: Kappa Sigma, Pi Kappa Alpha, and Theta Chi), service clubs, and almost forty other organizations play an important role in the daily life of a Linfield student. Linfield's winning athletics tradition fosters participation at all levels of competition. Women compete in intercollegiate basketball, cross-country, golf, lacrosse, soccer, softball, swimming, tennis, track and field, and volleyball. Men compete in intercollegiate baseball, basketball, cross-country, football, golf, soccer, swimming, tennis, and track and field. Water polo, Ultimate Frisbee, and men's lacrosse are club sports. Linfield also has an extensive and active year-round intramural program.

Linfield hosts the Oregon Nobel Laureate Symposium. (There are only five such symposiums worldwide.) At each symposium, several Nobel laureates come to share their backgrounds and expertise within the context of a basic theme.

The Linfield–Good Samaritan School of Nursing, an academic unit of the College at its Portland campus, prepares students for the B.S.N. or a degree in health science. This campus, at the Good Samaritan Hospital and Medical Center, has residence facilities, food service options, and a residence life program. The Portland campus median age is 24.

Location

Located in McMinnville, 40 miles southwest of Portland, Linfield College is a leader in the cultural, educational, and recreational events of the fast-growing community of 30,000. The seat of county government, McMinnville provides Linfield faculty and students with many opportunities to participate in community service activities. Cinemas, a community theater, bowling alleys, coffeehouses, and a wide variety of restaurants welcome Linfield students. Shopping is within walking distance. The central Oregon coast is an hour to the west, and the outdoor activity areas of the Oregon Cascade mountains, including year-round skiing at Mt. Hood, are 2 hours to the east. Salem, the state capital of Oregon, is 25 miles to the southeast, and Eugene is 80 miles south. Rainfall in western Oregon averages 42 inches annually, and the winter temperature averages 41°F.

Majors and Degrees

Linfield offers the Bachelor of Arts degree in art, communication, creative writing, English, European studies–German, French, German, history, Japanese, music, philosophy, political science, religious studies, sociology, Spanish, and theater arts. The Bachelor of Arts or Bachelor of Science degree is offered in accounting, anthropology, applied physics, athletic training, biology, business, chemistry, computing science, economics, elementary education, environmental studies, exercise science, finance, general science, health

education, health sciences, international business, mathematics, medical technology, nursing, physical education, physics, and psychology. The College has programs to prepare students for advanced study in dentistry, law, and medicine. The education department offers a strong program of teacher certification at the secondary and elementary levels. A 3-2 engineering program is available in cooperation with Oregon State University, Washington State University, and the University of Southern California.

Academic Programs

The academic year is divided into two 15-week semesters (fall and spring) and an optional four-week winter term in January. The January Term offers regular departmental courses and cultural-epochs study. Academic courses are assigned 1–5 semester credit hours each; 125 credits are required for a B.A. or a B.S. degree. Students divide their time equally among required general education courses, a major area of study, and elective subjects. The Linfield Curriculum courses, selected to provide a solid foundation in the liberal arts, require students to take 6 semester hours in at least two courses in each of the five areas of inquiry. These areas of inquiry are as follows: the Vital Past; Ultimate Questions; Individuals, Systems, and Societies; the Natural World; and Images and Arts. In addition, students are required to take a writing-intensive course, a course addressing global diversity, and a course dealing with American pluralism. Major requirements differ from department to department. Individually designed majors are available with faculty approval. Students majoring in a foreign language spend an academic year in a country in which the language being studied is the native tongue. Language majors have recently studied in such cities as Avignon, Guadalajara, Nantes, Munich, Quebec, and Valencia. The Advanced Placement (AP) Program of the College Board is recognized, and up to 5 semester hours of credit are granted for a score of 4 or 5 on an AP test. AP examinations do not satisfy general education requirements. The College recognizes the International Baccalaureate (IB) Diploma and awards up to 30 semester hours of credit for higher-level courses on a course-by-course basis. Total credit awarded by AP or IB may not exceed 30 semester hours.

The College offers courses in English with the English Language and Culture program. These courses are designed to help international students whose native language is not English to achieve competence in academic and social English skills, so that they may work effectively in their undergraduate classes at Linfield.

Off-Campus Programs

Off-campus educational experiences include the Semester Abroad Program, involving four months of study in San Ramon, Costa Rica; Aix, Angers, or Avignon, France; Vienna, Austria; Yokohama, Japan; Oaxaca, Mexico; Oslo, Norway; Hong Kong, China; Seoul, South Korea; Galway, Ireland; Nottingham, England; Quito and Galapagos, Ecuador; or various locations in Asia, as approved by the Director of International Programs. Sophomores, juniors, and seniors are encouraged to participate, and approximately 20 students are selected for each country each year. The program is designed to serve students who have successfully completed one year of study at Linfield in the appropriate language and who will return to the campus to share their international experiences with the College community. Transportation for the first round trip is included in the cost of tuition, and most of these study programs cost the same as a semester on campus. January Term study-abroad programs for four weeks are also offered. Recent offerings included the Emergence of Modern Ghana (West Africa); Mainland Southeast Asia History (Cambodia, Vietnam, and China); American Expatriate Writers in Europe: The Lost Generation Tour (nine European cities); and Australia: From Colony to Asian Power.

Academic Facilities

Murdock Hall houses the biology and chemistry departments and up-to-date laboratories and equipment. Laboratory and research space is provided for general and advanced chemistry and biology, organic chemistry, biochemistry, microbiology, bacteriology, immunology, ecology, botany, physiology, embryology, and gross and microscopic anatomy. There are approximately 200 IBM and Macintosh computers on campus available for student use. Services on the network that students can use include the two UNIX hosts (available for programming, e-mail, and other communication services), a connection to the Internet, file servers, and both laser and dot-matrix printers. Linfield students benefit from a communications and technology network, including phone service, voice mail, e-mail, and Internet connections in each residence hall room. In addition, there is wireless access in the library and other academic areas of the campus.

The Health and Physical Education/Recreation Complex houses three gymnasiums; weight rooms; fitness laboratories with a hydrostatic weighing tank, a metabolic and pulmonary measuring system, and an electrocardiovascular exercise ECG system; an eight-lane, 25-yard-long indoor pool; handball and racquetball courts; classrooms; offices; and a 28,000-square-foot field house.

Since 2000, there have been many exciting changes at Linfield. The College first opened six apartment buildings as well as the James F. Miller Fine Arts Center. In 2003, Linfield opened Nicholson library and the Marshall Theater and communication arts facility. The library covers 56,000 square feet and combines traditional collections of books and journals with the new and changing digital and electronic technology to provide access to the Web and Web-based designs. There is seating for up to 500 students, as well as thirty-five computer workstations and wireless access to the campus network, the Internet, and the World Wide Web for students who bring their own laptops or check out those available at the library. The studio theater has an audience seating capacity of up to 140, more than double the former facility. It includes space for set construction and design as well as faculty offices. In the fall of 2006, Linfield opened two new residence halls and the Vivian A. Bull Center for Music. Other facilities include art galleries and studios, a 250-watt FM radio station, an experimental psychology laboratory, dance and music studios, a preschool, and a 425-seat auditorium that houses a three-manual, 48-rank Casavant pipe organ.

Costs

For 2006–07, tuition and fees were $23,930 per two-semester year. Board was $3260, and a double room was $3760. There was a $131-per-credit fee for January Term classes.

Financial Aid

Eligibility for most of Linfield's assistance programs is based on need as determined by a federally approved needs analysis processor. The only form required for need-based programs is the Free Application for Federal Student Aid (FAFSA). Linfield participates in the Federal Perkins and Federal Stafford Student Loan programs, Federal Supplemental Educational Opportunity Grants, Federal Work-Study, and other forms of financial assistance on the basis of demonstrated need.

The College awards a number of scholarships to full-time students based on scholastic achievement, independent of financial need. These academic scholarships vary from 20 to 75 percent of tuition. To be considered, students must have a minimum GPA of 3.4. A number of other criteria are used when determining scholarships. Linfield sponsors special scholarships for National Merit finalists. The minimum award is 50 percent of tuition. Awards can range to full tuition, depending on financial need, provided the student has indicated that Linfield is his or her first-choice college. The College also sponsors the annual Academic Competitive Scholarship Program in early spring each year. Participation is limited to high school seniors who meet particular academic requirements. Each academic department offers prizes ranging from $10,000 to $16,000, divided over the student's four years at Linfield, provided the student maintains a grade point average of at least 3.0. Scholarships of varying amounts are awarded to entering students who are particularly talented in music performance. Amounts range from $1500 to $2500 annually. Interested students are required to audition either in person or by cassette tape by February 15. Financial assistance for non-U.S. citizens is limited to partial tuition scholarships and the opportunity to work part-time on campus. Other scholarships are available for students who demonstrate outstanding leadership and community service.

Faculty

There are 114 full-time and 64 part-time faculty members, each of whom is committed to undergraduate teaching and scholarship. Ninety-two percent have doctoral or other terminal degrees within their field. The faculty-student ratio is 1:12, and faculty members serve as academic advisers. There are no teaching assistants.

Student Government

Students have a significant voice in establishing and changing College policies and regulations. The Student Senate, chosen through campus elections, is the focus of student opinion and debate. Students are represented on most College governing councils and committees with faculty members and trustees, and they are encouraged to express and implement their ideas on academic or extracurricular matters.

Admission Requirements

Admission to Linfield College is selective. Admission is granted to students who are likely to grow and succeed in a personal and challenging liberal arts environment. Each applicant is judged on individual merit. A faculty admission committee evaluates candidates in a number of areas that commonly indicate academic potential. These include high school performance, a writing sample, recommendations from teachers and counselors, and precollege standardized test results (ACT or SAT). The committee also considers the depth and quality of an applicant's involvement in community and school activities. It reviews all applications as a group, selecting those students who show the greatest likelihood of benefiting from and contributing to the Linfield community. Linfield is a member of the Common Application Association.

International students whose education has been in a language other than English must submit certified English translations of their academic work. Proficiency in English is required, as demonstrated by an official TOEFL score report, including the Test of Written English (TWE; not available after September 2005, as the TOEFL will then include a test of speaking proficiency).

Application and Information

Early action applicants must apply by November 15, and notification is made by January 15. The priority application deadline for regular admission is February 15, with notification made on or before April 1. Admitted international students must show evidence of financial responsibility and submit a $2000 deposit.

Interviews are not required, but students are encouraged to visit. Appointments should be made in advance and can be requested online at http://www.linfield.edu/stopby. The Office of Admission is open Monday through Friday, 7:30 a.m. to 5:30 p.m., and on Saturdays during the school year from 9 a.m. to 2 p.m. The Linfield Web site provides students with information on student life, academic programs, and athletics. Students may also complete their application for admission online or ask for additional information. Interested students are encouraged to contact:

Director of Admission
Linfield College
McMinnville, Oregon 97128
Phone: 503-883-2213
      800-640-2287 (toll-free)
Fax: 503-883-2472
E-mail: admission@linfield.edu
Web site: http://www.linfield.edu

MULTNOMAH BIBLE COLLEGE AND BIBLICAL SEMINARY

PORTLAND, OREGON

The College

Multnomah Bible College and Biblical Seminary has been devoted to teaching the Bible to men and women since the 1930s. The mission of Multnomah Bible College is to produce, through collegiate education, biblically competent, culturally aware, maturing servants of Jesus Christ, whose love for God, His Word, and people shapes their lives into a transforming force in the church and world. Multnomah's education is more than time in the classroom—it's learning through hands-on ministry, late-night talks with friends in the coffee shop, and discovering the heart of God through prayer. At Multnomah, the Bible is central to everything students learn. Whether majoring in journalism or pastoral ministry, students are challenged at the end of the day to think and live biblically. Multnomah offers one of the most comprehensive Bible programs in the nation, requiring each student to complete 52 semester hours of Bible and theology. The College is accredited by the Northwest Commission on Colleges and Universities (NWCCU) and the Association of Biblical Higher Education (ABHE) and is recognized by the state of Oregon to award bachelor's degrees.

Effective education teaches the whole person. Community life presents challenges but provides tremendous opportunities to build lifelong friendships and to make service to others a lifelong habit. It allows faculty and staff members to give each student the individual attention befitting one created in God's image. But Multnomah does not leave its populace unprepared for the world's harsh realities. Rather, the College continually seeks ways to train students to have the greatest possible impact on the world today. Students are instructed in and saturated with a biblical, Christian worldview designed to prepare them for any situation encountered. Opportunities to make the world the classroom are offered through cross-cultural experiences and internships in the community. Students can work side-by-side with their instructors as they share the gospel in the community or minister in a home for abused women. The opportunities are endless.

Something is always happening on Multnomah's campus. Opportunities abound for students to get involved in a variety of activities, each designed to cultivate life skills that enhance their academic studies. Students can join the student government, intramural sports, the Ambassador Choir, or various chapel worship bands, among other activities.

Multnomah Biblical Seminary was launched to provide a complementary, nonrepetitive seminary option for the Bible college graduate. Programs include the graduate certificate, the Master of Divinity, the Master of Divinity in theological studies, and the Master of Arts in biblical studies or in pastoral studies (emphases in evangelism/church planting, family ministry, intercultural studies, ministry management, and women's ministry).

Location

The city of Portland offers an endless supply of adventure and excitement. The campus is only 15 minutes from downtown. On weekends, the Saturday Market offers a huge collection of handmade crafts, art, and ethnic food. Waterfront Park hosts the Rose Festival in late May, and many shops and restaurants overlook the Willamette River. The eclectic Hawthorne and northwest Portland districts have unique shopping and restaurants—including thirty-two Starbucks within 5 miles of campus. Portland is home to museums, concert venues, and the Trail Blazer basketball team. Less than 2 hours from Multnomah are Oregon's sandy beaches. An hour east of Portland lie the slopes of Mt. Hood, a favorite for skiers and snowboarders throughout the world. Portland International Airport (PDX) is less than 20 minutes from campus, and Portland has an excellent public transportation system.

Majors and Degrees

In addition to the Bible and theology major, students select a second major or minor in one of fifteen areas of study. Giving the Bible priority in their lives, most Multnomah students carry two majors (one of which is Bible) as they pursue their bachelor's degree. The Bachelor of Arts degree program provides students with more exposure to languages and humanities, while the Bachelor of Science degree program focuses more on social sciences. Areas of study include biblical Hebrew, educational ministries, elementary education, historical studies, intercultural studies, journalism, missionary aviation co-op, music ministry, New Testament Greek, pastoral ministry, speech communications, and youth ministry. Minors are now available in English, psychology, and Teaching English to Speakers of Other Languages (TESOL).

Academic Programs

Multnomah Bible College believes that there is no substitute for a thorough knowledge of the Word of God and that it is basic to all successful Christian service. For that reason, the College has made teaching the Bible its primary objective and enrolls all bachelor's students in the Bible major. As a result of the large proportion of Bible in the curriculum (52 semester hours of Bible and doctrine), students are able to obtain a sound and thorough training in the Word of God. A varied program of second majors and minors enables students to specialize in a particular area of interest for more effective Christian service and professional competency. General education provides learning experiences that enhance and complement the academic majors, giving the student an integrated Christian worldview. Students gain an understanding and awareness of broad areas of language, history, philosophy, communication, science, and human development.

A cooperative five-year program with Concordia University allows students in elementary education to receive two bachelor's degrees (one from Multnomah and one from Concordia) and a teaching certificate for public or private schools.

Off-Campus Programs

Multnomah offers a semester-abroad program, EduVenture, that integrates adventure (river journeying, trekking, and

mountain biking), short-term cultural immersion, and experiential learning with rigorous academics (field-based anthropology, cross-cultural communication, community development, missiological theory and practice, and spiritual formation). Currently, students can travel to Mexico or Indonesia. Although available in fall or spring, Multnomah recommends EduVenture for juniors in their spring semester.

Academic Facilities

The John and Mary Mitchell Library has a rich and developing collection of conventional and electronic resources to support the programs of study at Multnomah Bible College and Biblical Seminary. Multnomah is a member of a consortium of eight libraries with a union database of more than 500,000 library holdings. The library has more than 90,000 volumes and 1,000 full-text journals, a growing collection of videos and DVDs, and many online research tools. The library staff is pleased to assist patrons in locating materials and answer any questions about the library, its resources, and its use. The upper floor comprises stacks filled with a wide variety of books and a large study area for student and guest use. The lower floor has four classrooms, with seating capacities ranging from 38 to 55. A fifth classroom with auditorium-style seating accommodates 186 people. This classroom also has audiovisual computer capabilities. Two outside classrooms can seat 24 people. The Travis-Lovitt seminary building, the newest addition to campus, houses seven classrooms able to seat from 20 to 60 students. Each classroom is equipped with state-of-the-art audiovisual equipment.

Costs

In 2006–07, tuition and fees were $12,450 per year, and room and board averaged $5340, for a total of approximately $17,790.

Financial Aid

Multnomah provides a variety of aid through many sources, including federal and institutional aid. A variety of scholarships based on academics and experience are awarded. The President's Scholarship, Multnomah's most prestigious award, provides 50 percent of tuition. To qualify, the student must be an entering freshman and have at least a 3.5 GPA and a minimum SAT score of 1800 or ACT score of 27. The student must provide references from 3 people, including a person he or she has worked with in ministry, such as a pastor. The Multnomah Academic Dean's Scholarship is a second-tier scholarship providing 25 percent of tuition costs. Dean's Scholarship applicants must have a high school GPA of at least 3.25 or a minimum college-transfer GPA of 3.0 and an SAT score of at least 1650 or an ACT score of 24 or higher. Multnomah offers a variety of leadership opportunities on-campus that include financial assistance. Each student can apply for leadership opportunities after his or her first year at Multnomah.

Faculty

The faculty members are the foundation upon which programs of academic excellence are built. Though highly educated and respected as scholars, faculty members do not promote "ivory tower" scholarship in their classrooms. Faculty members are skilled communicators who make the ideas and principles they teach relevant to their students' lives. While the faculty members love to teach, they also consistently broaden their knowledge base—indicated by their publishing of books and journal articles and their involvement in various scholarly societies. They serve the church as pastors, church planters, counselors, and conference speakers. The content of their classroom instruction has been tested in the laboratory of experience, allowing them to teach with confidence.

Student Government

STUGO, the student government organization, organizes social events and ministries to help students become mature, Christ-like individuals. STUGO's Multnomah Community Outreach (MCO) provides opportunities for students to serve the surrounding community in after-school programs, workdays, and individual-care services. The Student World Outreach Team (SWOT) facilitates a world missionary vision through Monday chapels and missions-related events throughout the school year. All STUGO activities are designed to enrich the students' lives and contribute to their educational experience.

Admission Requirements

Because the academic load at Multnomah is rigorous, applicants should have a minimum 2.5 GPA. Students must complete the full application packet, which includes a personal statement and four reference forms (from one pastor, one employer or teacher, and two friends). Applicants must also submit official transcripts (from high school or community college), SAT or ACT scores, and the $40 application fee. The admissions committee also examines an applicant's character and his or her demonstrated commitment to Jesus Christ through service, leadership, and other factors.

Application and Information

Applicants should file admission forms well in advance of the enrollment date. Applications must arrive by July 15 for August admission (fall semester) or by November 15 for January admission (spring semester).

Admissions Office
Multnomah Bible College and Biblical Seminary
8435 Northeast Glisan Street
Portland, Oregon 97220
Phone: 503-251-6485
       800-275-4672 (toll-free)
E-mail: admiss@multnomah.edu
Web site: http://www.multnomah.edu/

NORTHERN ARIZONA UNIVERSITY
FLAGSTAFF, ARIZONA

The University

Northern Arizona University (NAU) is a fully accredited, state-supported, four-year institution with 11,945 full-time undergraduate students on its main campus. Since 1899, the University has made a major commitment to undergraduate education, and its goal is to preserve a friendly campus atmosphere and close student-faculty relationships through classroom teaching of the highest quality and faculty guidance for each student.

The University is composed of the Colleges of Arts and Letters, Business Administration, Education, Engineering and Natural Sciences, and Social and Behavioral Sciences and Professional Schools (Forestry, Health Sciences, Hotel and Restaurant Management, and Nursing). More than 150 undergraduate, master's, and doctoral degrees are offered in a number of interdisciplinary and preprofessional majors.

The University has a strong commitment to student advising, and regular office hours are maintained by faculty members. The Gateway Student Success Center offers academic advising services and career exploration assistance for all students who are undecided on a degree program. An average class size of 27 is another example of the institution's attention to high-quality education.

As a residential campus, Northern Arizona University provides an atmosphere of friendship and community. Fifty percent of the undergraduate students live in the seventeen residence halls and 297 family housing apartments located on the campus. Of the 11,945 full-time undergraduates enrolled in the 2006 fall semester, 4,853 are men (41 percent) and 7,092 are women (59 percent).

The campus includes three student unions, a student health center, an Olympic-size swimming and diving complex, a 16,230-seat multiuse wooden dome, and a multipurpose recreational facility.

Northern Arizona University is an Equal Opportunity/Affirmative Action institution.

Location

Northern Arizona University's 730-acre mountain campus is located in Flagstaff, which is a community with 61,000 residents. Flagstaff is located at an elevation of 7,000 feet, just south of the 12,600-foot-high San Francisco Peaks, a major winter-sports center. The University is at the junction of Interstate Highways 40 (U.S. 66) and 17, less than a 3-hour drive from Phoenix and about a 5-hour drive from Tucson, Arizona; Albuquerque, New Mexico; and Las Vegas, Nevada. The city is served by Amtrak, Greyhound buses, and a commercial airline. The campus is surrounded by scenic beauty and natural wonders such as the Grand Canyon and, a student favorite, Oak Creek Canyon. The varied landscape of mountains, gorges, forests, and lakes provides the University with natural classrooms and laboratories for research as well as recreation.

Majors and Degrees

Northern Arizona University offers baccalaureate degrees in approximately ninety-five major areas, embracing most of the recognized fields in the arts and sciences and a number of interdisciplinary majors. The University also offers a number of specialized programs, including criminal justice, dental hygiene, forestry, hotel and restaurant management, and parks and recreation management.

Academic Programs

A four-year baccalaureate degree program at Northern Arizona University requires the successful completion of 120 semester hours of course work, including 35 hours of liberal studies courses. The liberal studies program consists of foundation studies and studies in various disciplines designed to assist students in cultivating their abilities to recognize significant problems and to define, analyze, and defend solutions in a variety of contexts. Major-field requirements vary from 35 to 73 semester hours. Students may combine a major field with one or more 18-hour minors, take two majors or an extended major of 63 to 65 hours in a field of their interest, or select the merged major programs.

Northern Arizona University has a long-established honors program, which is designed to challenge the talented student. This leads to graduation with honors, and honor students may elect to take the special degree of Bachelor of Arts: Honors. The program provides special courses and seminars and offers superior students opportunities for independent study and research.

A three-year bachelor's degree program is available, offering intellectual and academic challenges for well-prepared and motivated students and allowing them to take the fast track to graduation and graduate programs.

Off-Campus Programs

The University actively cooperates in the work and research programs of several major scientific institutions that are located close to its campus. These include the Lowell Observatory; the U.S. Naval Observatory's Flagstaff station; various facilities of the U.S. Geological Survey, including its space-oriented Astrogeology Center; the U.S. Forest Service Rocky Mountain and Range Experiment station; and the Museum of Northern Arizona and its multidisciplinary Colton Research Center. The specialized libraries, laboratories, and other facilities of these institutions are available to qualified students at the University. Northern Arizona University also conducts scientific field work in many of the distinctive natural areas of northern Arizona, including the nearby Grand Canyon.

Northern Arizona University offers study-abroad opportunities at fifty-five universities in eighteen countries: Australia, Canada, China, Finland, France, Germany, Great Britain, Guatemala, Ireland, Italy, Japan, Mexico, Netherlands, New Zealand, South Korea, Spain, Sweden, and Switzerland. Opportunities to study abroad in conjunction with the University Studies Abroad Consortium offer another twenty-four locations. Students may study for a semester or a year. Through field trips and classroom study, students explore the history, literature, language, and culture of these regions. All students except freshmen may apply.

Through the National Student Exchange program, students have an opportunity to broaden their educational horizons by attending a college or university in another state for one semester or one year while paying tuition and fees at NAU. There are more than 180 participating institutions nationwide.

Academic Facilities

Northern Arizona University's facilities for education and research are extensive. The University's Cline Library provides both individual student and group research, study, and computing. Its collections include books, movies, audio recordings, and the Colorado Plateau Archives. The library's Web site provides access to electronic books, journals, services, and digital archives 24 hours a day, seven days a week. Within the library,

students have access to 150 computers, group study rooms, a coffee shop, and a multimedia production workstation.

State-of-the-art laboratories serve students in the sciences and health professions. Specially designed studios, workrooms, theaters, auditoriums, and an art gallery are available to students in the creative arts. Closed-circuit television hookups, student-paced audiovisual systems, language laboratories, an observatory, and a major computer center are used regularly by students for both learning and research.

The University makes extensive use of the spectacular Colorado Plateau country surrounding its campus as a natural laboratory for anthropology, biology, ecology, environmental sciences, geology, geophysics, paleontology, and other sciences. Prehistoric Indian ruins and the living cultures of the Navajo, Hopi, and many other Indian peoples of the Southwest provide rich resources for students of archaeology, anthropology, ethnology, and linguistics. Students have access to the 50,000-acre Centennial Forest for environmental and forestry research. The area's 7,000-foot elevation and unusually clear, dry air have made it a major center for astronomy and the atmospheric sciences.

Costs

For 2006–07, the charges for an academic year of two semesters for an in-state student were tuition and fees, $4546, and average board and room, $6260. Books and supplies averaged $828. The totaled estimated cost for Arizona residents was $11,634 per academic year. The out-of-state tuition and fees were $13,486, for an academic-year cost of $20,574. This does not included travel or personal expenses, which vary for each student. All costs are subject to change by the Arizona Board of Regents.

Financial Aid

Northern Arizona University maintains an extensive program of financial assistance to aid students in pursuing their educational goals. The amount of financial aid awarded to a student is based upon the student's need level, as computed from the Free Application for Federal Student Aid (FAFSA). However, some scholarships are awarded on the basis of a student's demonstration of academic excellence and/or participation in various University activities.

In the 2005–06 academic year, more than $110 million was available for loans, scholarships, grants, veterans' benefits, and work-study programs. About 66 percent of the students received some form of financial aid.

Along with grants, loans, and scholarships, on- and off-campus employment is available to help students meet financial obligations. More than 4,500 NAU students are currently employed in a wide variety of jobs on the campus.

Faculty

Northern Arizona University's faculty is made up of outstanding and dedicated professionals. More than 63 percent of the 755 full-time and 737 part-time faculty members hold doctoral degrees. Many are nationally distinguished scientists and scholars. The student-faculty ratio is 16:1, with more than 83 percent of the classes taught by faculty members rather than graduate assistants.

Student Government

Each student who enters the University is a member of the Associated Students of Northern Arizona University (ASNAU), which represents the students' interests in all matters that affect them.

Other student governing groups are the Associated Students for Women's Issues, Association of University Residence Halls, Pan-Hellenic Council, and Inter-Fraternity Council. About 40 percent of the students belong to one or more of the 120 student groups and organizations.

Admission Requirements

New freshmen are admitted if they have a cumulative GPA of 3.0 or better (on a 4.0 scale) or a minimum ACT composite score of 22 (24 for non-Arizona residents) or a minimum combined SAT score of 1040 (1100 for nonresidents) or a top 25 percent class rank and have no deficiencies in the high school course requirements. High school course requirements include 4 units of English, 4 units of math, 3 units of laboratory science, 2 units of social studies, 2 units of foreign language, and 1 unit of fine art. Students with both a math deficiency and a lab science deficiency are not admissible.

New freshmen are considered for admission if they have a cumulative GPA between 2.5 and 2.99 or a top 50 percent class rank and have no more than one deficiency in any two of the subject areas in the high school course requirements listed above. Transfer students who have earned fewer than 12 transferable academic semester credits must meet the same criteria as new freshmen.

Transfer students are offered admission if they have completed an associate degree, the Arizona General Education Curriculum (AGEC), or the California Inter-segmental General Education Transfer Curriculum (IGETC). Transfer students who have earned more than 12 college credits should visit NAU's Web site for complete admission requirements.

The priority deadlines are March 1 for the fall semester, December 1 for the spring semester, and May 1 for summer sessions. Applications and supporting documents received after these dates are processed on a space-available basis.

Application and Information

For more information, students should consult the University Web site or contact the Office of Admissions.

Office of Undergraduate Admissions
Northern Arizona University
Box 4084
Flagstaff, Arizona 86011-4084
Phone: 928-523-5511
    888-628-2968 (toll-free)
E-mail: undergraduate.admissions@nau.edu
Internet: http://home.nau.edu

A friendly residential campus and the four-season climate of Flagstaff, Arizona, attract about 11,900 undergraduate students each year to Northern Arizona University.

OREGON STATE UNIVERSITY
CORVALLIS, OREGON

The University

Exceptional students, an outstanding faculty, and a challenging curriculum combine to make Oregon State University (OSU) a nationally and internationally recognized comprehensive university.

OSU has earned the Carnegie Research Doctoral designation for commitment to education and research. Widely recognized research programs add to the quality of teaching by bringing new knowledge into the classroom and by encouraging undergraduate students to work with faculty members on research projects in many fields. As a member of the non-tiered Oregon University System, OSU is the premier research university in the state of Oregon.

The University's 19,000 students come from all fifty states and more than ninety-three countries around the world to pursue a wide choice of undergraduate programs that prepare them for careers and leadership positions in science, engineering and computer-related fields, natural resources, government, teaching and social service, pharmacy, and other professions. There were 162 valedictorians in the 2004 freshman class. Employers from across the nation recognize the value of an OSU degree, and more of them recruit at Oregon State University each year than at any other university in the state. Oregon State also ranks twenty-fifth nationally in Peace Corps volunteers.

OSU is committed to offering students the resources they need to be successful in their education. In 1997, Oregon State was named the leading institution in the U.S. and Canada for electronic services to students by the American Productivity and Quality Center. OSU continues to innovate by systematically adding wireless networks to classrooms, libraries, and common areas on campus. Students also have access to one of the largest open-source software labs in the world, where new shareware is developed, housed, and distributed.

Students also benefit from more than 300 cocurricular activities on campus. These include student government, student media, theater and music, intramural and club sports, and numerous social, academic, cultural, and professional clubs and organizations. In addition, Dixon Recreation Center offers opportunities for swimming and diving, weight training, aerobic exercise, and the largest collegiate rock-climbing center in the Northwest. A campus child-care facility offers educationally oriented day-care programs for children of students and faculty and staff members.

OSU offers a wide range of housing and dining options, including special-program residence halls, cooperative houses, student family housing, and fraternity and sorority housing. Many apartments and houses are available within biking or walking distance of OSU for students who choose to live off campus. There are more than fifteen restaurants on campus.

Graduate degrees are offered through the Colleges of Agricultural Sciences, Business, Engineering, Forestry, Health and Human Sciences, Liberal Arts, and Science. Graduate and professional degrees are also offered through the Colleges of Oceanic and Atmospheric Sciences, Pharmacy, and Veterinary Medicine, and through the School of Education.

Location

The OSU main campus is in Corvallis, which is consistently ranked as one of the safest university communities on the West Coast. With about 52,000 residents, Corvallis offers a friendly, university-oriented atmosphere. In fact, students rated OSU as

the fifth-friendliest campus in the U.S., according to Campus-Dirt.com. Miles of bike lanes and free city bus service make it easy for students to get around town. Within a couple hours of Corvallis are the Oregon Coast; the Cascade Mountains, with skiing, hiking, camping, and snowboarding; and Portland, Oregon's largest city. The OSU Cascades Campus in Bend, Oregon, represents a unique educational partnership involving four distinguished institutions, creating an innovative and collaborative university to serve the needs of central Oregon.

Majors and Degrees

Oregon State is a comprehensive university, with more than 200 academic programs. Undergraduate degrees are offered through the Colleges of Agricultural Sciences, Business, Education, Engineering, Forestry, Health and Human Sciences, Liberal Arts, and Science.

Students in any undergraduate major can strengthen their transcripts by earning an Honors Degree or an International Degree. Almost 600 top students are enrolled in the University Honors College, which offers a small-college atmosphere within the larger University. The University also offers twenty-eight preprofessional programs that prepare students for graduate programs and careers in fields such as health sciences, law, and education.

The OSU Cascades Campus offers a variety of undergraduate and graduate degree opportunities specific to the region. Geology, wildlife biology, botany, business, nursing, education, computer science, engineering, museum studies, outdoor recreation leadership, and tourism are among the many programs available.

Academic Programs

All undergraduate students at Oregon State complete the Baccalaureate Core, which helps develop skills and knowledge in writing, critical thinking, cultural diversity, the arts, science, literature, lifelong fitness, and global awareness, ensuring that as graduates they will be well prepared for life as well as a career.

Many students take advantage of OSU's first-year experience program, called Odyssey, which offers opportunities for new students to interact with faculty members and other students throughout the year, thus easing the transition to college life. The year begins with a five-day "Connect" orientation that features small-group meetings between faculty members and students, a barbecue, outdoor movies, open houses, and more.

Undergraduate research is an important component of many academic programs, and more than 2,000 OSU undergraduates participate with faculty members and graduate students on research projects each year. One example is the Howard Hughes Medical Institute Summer Research Program, which funds undergraduate researchers to the tune of $1.9 million.

OSU has more majors, minors, and special programs than any other college in Oregon and offers a University Exploratory Studies Program for students who want to try various options before choosing a major field. Oregon State uses the quarter system for its academic year. Most majors require between 180 and 192 credit hours for a bachelor's degree. There are no impacted majors at Oregon State University.

The Academic Success Center helps OSU students deal with problems and develop the skills they need in college and beyond. The Center for Writing and Learning, the Math Learning Center, and departmental resource centers assist students in preparing for

assignments in specific areas, while the African-American, Hispanic-American, Asian-American, and Native American education offices, along with the Educational Opportunities Program, help mentor students throughout their college careers. University Counseling and Psychological Services offers learning resource materials and professional assistance to help students deal with problems, both in and out of the classroom. Career Services assists students in locating internships and in finding jobs when they graduate.

Off-Campus Programs

Through the International Degree, study-abroad, and international internship programs, OSU students can study, work, or conduct research almost anywhere in the world. Programs, which range from a term to a full year, are offered in Australia, Canada, China, Denmark, Ecuador, England, France, Germany, Hungary, Italy, Japan, Korea, Mexico, New Zealand, Norway, Russia, Spain, Thailand, Tunisia, and Vietnam.

OSU also participates in the National Student Exchange Program, allowing students to spend up to a year at one of more than 160 colleges and universities in the U.S. and its possessions, while paying in-state tuition and fees.

Academic Facilities

OSU's Valley Library is a state-of-the-art facility that offers modern electronic services, including a wireless computer network, and unique special collections as well as traditional library services to students and the community. The OSU library is the first academic library to be named "Library of the Year" by *Library Journal* (1999). Library holdings include more than 2.5 million books, periodicals, and government documents on paper or microform. A reciprocal agreement makes more than 5 million additional volumes in the Oregon University System available to OSU students and faculty members. OSU's special collections include the papers and memorabilia of Linus Pauling, the only winner of two unshared Nobel Prizes, and the Atomic Energy Collection. The Valley Library is an official depository for U.S. government and state of Oregon publications.

Students at OSU have access to more than 2,200 computers at labs around the campus, including some that are available 24 hours per day. In addition, all rooms in campus residence facilities are wired for high-speed access to the Internet, and wireless networks are located throughout the campus. Special research facilities include OSU's Mark O. Hatfield Marine Science Center, Oregon Nanoscience and Microtechnologies Institute (ONAMI), Center for Gene Research and Biotechnology, Forest Research Laboratory, Radiation Center, and Hinsdale Wave Research Lab.

Costs

In-state undergraduate tuition and fees were approximately $5605 for the 2006–07 academic year, while nonresident charges were about $17,540. The average cost for a residence hall double room and meal plan was approximately $7345. Students who lived in a fraternity or sorority house paid about the same for housing and meals as those students who lived in residence halls.

Financial Aid

OSU offers the full range of scholarships, grants, work-study, and loans from federal, state, and University sources. Some form of financial assistance is received by 80 percent of the students at OSU. To qualify, students must have applied for admission and must submit the Free Application for Federal Student Aid (FAFSA), listing OSU as one of their top six choices (Title IV code: 003210). Some students help meet educational expenses with one of the many part-time jobs available on or near the campus. For financial aid information, interested students should contact the Office of Financial Aid and Scholarships, 218 Kerr Administration Building, Corvallis, Oregon 97331 (telephone: 541-737-2241, World Wide Web: http://oregonstate.edu/admin/finaid/).

Through the OSU Scholars Program, the University offers a variety of scholarships and additional scholarship search assis-

tance for new students who have strong academic records. University scholarships range from $500 to $6000 annually for up to four years. In addition, most OSU colleges offer scholarships to new students, and the OSU Foundation has a number of University-wide scholarships.

Faculty

Undergraduate education is a priority at OSU, and nationally prominent scholars and scientists regularly teach undergraduate courses at all levels. Students receive individual attention and the chance to know their professors both in and out of the classroom. Faculty members consistently receive awards for teaching and research, and many of them are nationally and internationally renowned. The more than $208 million in external research funds received annually by OSU faculty members exceeds that of all other Oregon public universities combined.

Student Government

The Associated Students of Oregon State University (ASOSU) plays a major role in making policy and regulating activities for students and in governing the University through student participation on more than fifty University-wide committees. In recent years, ASOSU has become more involved with local, state, and national issues that affect the welfare of students.

Admission Requirements

A minimum 3.0 high school GPA (on a 4.0 scale) qualifies students for freshman admission to OSU when all subject requirements are met. Applicants for undergraduate admission are required to complete an "Insight Resume," a written assessment designed to evaluate students' noncognitive attributes. These attributes include self-concept, realistic self-appraisal, handling the system, ability to set long-range goals, leadership, connections with a strong support person, community engagement, and nontraditional learning. High school subject requirements are 4 years of English, 3 years each of mathematics and social studies, and 2 years each of science and of the same foreign language. Students who do not meet the subject requirements may be considered for admission by earning a total score of at least 1410 on three SAT Subject Tests or by successfully completing course work to make up specific deficiencies. The alternatives must by completed by the time of high school graduation.

Transfer admission requires successful completion of at least 36 graded, transferable credits (24 semester credits) from accredited U.S. institutions, with a minimum GPA of 2.25. Grades of C- or better are required in college-level writing and mathematics. Students with less than 36 transferable credits are considered for admission on the basis of their high school records.

Application and Information

Applicants are encouraged to complete OSU's online application, which can be found at the Web site. An *OSU Viewbook*, with information on specific academic programs, housing, financial aid, scholarships, and activities, is sent to students upon request.

Prospective students are encouraged to visit OSU to determine in person whether the University meets their needs. A visit, including a campus tour and an opportunity to talk to faculty members in the student's area of interest, can be arranged by calling the Office of Admissions.

To request more information, students should contact:

Office of Admissions
104 Kerr Administration Building
Oregon State University
Corvallis, Oregon 97331-2106
Phone: 800-291-4192 (toll-free)
Fax: 541-737-2482
E-mail: osuadmit@oregonstate.edu
Web site: http://oregonstate.edu/admissions

PRESCOTT COLLEGE
Resident Degree Program
PRESCOTT, ARIZONA

The College

Prescott College is a small, private liberal arts college dedicated to environmental protection; social justice; service learning; experiential education; small, innovative classes; a large field-based curriculum; and the integration of the intellectual, emotional, spiritual, and social development of students. Prescott College, founded in 1966, is a small college trying to make a big difference in the world.

At Prescott College, a student's education is as individual as he or she is. The College believes that education should be personalized—a meaningful activity that goes beyond imparting facts. A Prescott College education instills values, critical-thinking skills, and the ability to adapt to the ever-changing internal landscape of ideas and knowledge as well as the ever-changing external landscape of today's social and physical ecology.

Prescott College offers bachelor's, master's, and Ph.D. degrees. A bachelor's degree can be earned via one of two routes: as a full-time resident student or as an adult student with limited residency. These routes are referred to, respectively, as the Resident Degree Program (RDP) and the Adult Degree Program (ADP). The 2005–06 resident degree enrollment was about 450 students. The information provided in this description pertains to the RDP. The Master of Arts degree is a limited-residency, independent, research-based degree program.

Location

Prescott is located in the mountains of central Arizona, surrounded by national forest at an elevation of more than 5,200 feet. The town is at the juncture of three ecosystems: interior chaparral, Ponderosa pines, and Pinon-Juniper. Desert or alpine ecosystems are within a short drive of Prescott.

With four mild seasons, more than a million acres of national forest, and almost 800 miles of trails, Prescott offers diverse outdoor activities, including rock climbing, hiking, mountain biking, horseback riding, and nearby canoeing, rafting, and snow skiing.

The Grand Canyon, the red rocks of Sedona, the old mining town of Jerome, and shopping and cultural events in Flagstaff, Phoenix, and Tucson are all within a few hours' drive. The Four Corners area, The Navajo Nation, Albuquerque, Las Vegas, San Diego, Mexico, Lake Powell, and Denver are all great destinations for weekend trips or extended visits during breaks.

Prescott is also the home of a lively and growing artistic community, with many art fairs and gallery openings. Many people are active in photography, music, weaving, and dance. The Mountain Artists Guild and the Prescott Fine Arts Association make a substantial cultural impact. The Phoenix Symphony, visiting ballet and opera companies, and numerous arts shows also provide regular programs.

Majors and Degrees

Prescott College offers the Bachelor of Arts (B.A.) degree in six general areas: adventure education, arts and letters, cultural and regional studies, education, environmental studies, and human development. Students create competence-based graduation plans in such topics as agroecology, conservation, counseling, ecological design, ecopsychology, education, environmental education, experiential education, field ecology, fine arts, holistic health, human ecology, literature, natural history, peace studies, philosophy, photography, psychology, religion, social and political studies, wilderness leadership, and writing.

Academic Programs

Prescott College is known for its innovative approach to higher education. It offers small classes (a student-faculty ratio of 10:1 in classrooms), extensive field work (a student-faculty ratio of 5:1 in the field), a close community atmosphere, and the opportunity for students to design their own educational paths. The philosophy of experiential education emphasizes the concept that learning is a lifelong process that helps students gain competence, creativity, and self-direction. In cooperation with an outstanding faculty, students are able to work in such special interdisciplinary fields as cultural and regional studies, ecopsychology, education and interpretation, human ecology, outdoor adventure education, social and political studies, and wilderness leadership.

Academic Facilities

Prescott College does not have a sprawling campus with ivy-covered towers. The campus, located near downtown Prescott, is an eclectic mix of buildings that once served other purposes. "Recycling" buildings is one tangible way in which the College demonstrates sustainability and minimizes its footprint upon the environment.

Prescott College's recently completed building, the Crossroads Center, incorporates various recycled or environmentally friendly elements in its design and construction. For example, the bathrooms feature original murals designed by Prescott students. The granite used in the murals was excess material donated to the project by a local enterprise that manufactures and installs countertops.

Many classes at the College are held in the field. Prescott uses the Southwest for ecological field studies, wilderness pursuits, social observations, artistic endeavors, and therapeutic facilitation. The fragile Southwestern desert can convey to students the vulnerability of the Equatorial rain forest and the destructibility of the Siberian tundra. The proximity to the Mexican border provides access to the crucial interactions between developing world politics, economics, and social and environmental issues. Thus, the Southwest provides a unique microcosm of the rapidly changing globe.

The Prescott College Information Commons (library) has a collection of more than 28,000 volumes, 125 microforms, 1,200 audiocassettes and videocassettes, and 408 periodical titles, all of which relate specifically to the College's program offerings. The Information Commons is computer-networked with all the regional libraries in the area, including two other college libraries and the public libraries. If students have difficulty locating information from any of these sources, the College librarian borrows books through the interlibrary loan system. Because the College places great emphasis on student services, faculty and staff members work diligently to assist each student in finding all information necessary for his or her pursuit of knowledge.

There are three fully equipped computer labs on campus. All labs are staffed full-time by a competent team of computer professionals and College work-study students. Laser printers are available, and students have access to the Internet for research and e-mail. The largest lab houses IBM-compatible computers. The Geographic Information Science Lab has its own computer lab for conducting research in land-use planning and management. The College also offers a Mac lab for fine arts students who are interested in graphic manipulation and digital imaging.

In addition, the College has a campus in Tucson and three off-campus research stations—Kino Bay, Walnut Creek Station, and Wolfberry Farm. The Tucson campus of Prescott College serves students who are enrolled in either the Adult Degree Program, through which working adults earn a bachelor's degree, or the Master of Arts degree program.

The Kino Bay Center for Cultural and Ecological Studies is Prescott's field station on the Sonoran shores of the Gulf of California, one of the most remote and unexplored seas remaining in the world today. The Kino Bay Center provides educational opportunities for hands-on field study in the areas of marine studies, environmental

sciences, resource conservation and management, cultural studies, Latin American studies, adventure education, writing, and Spanish language studies.

Wolfberry Farm is Prescott College's experimental farm dedicated to education, demonstration, and research in agroecology. The 30-acre farm is located 15 miles north of Prescott in Chino Valley, a town with a rich agricultural history. Students address the question: Can agriculture be more ecologically sustainable and economically viable? They experiment with water-saving irrigation technologies, regional and adapted crops, specialty crops, and fertility-generating rotations.

The Walnut Creek Station for Educational Research is run through a collaborative partnership between Prescott College, Yavapai College, Sharlot Hall Museum, Northern Arizona University, and the Prescott National Forest. During the high season, two or three classes per week use the station for courses, including Ecopsychology, Interpreting Nature Through Art and Photography, Geographical Information Systems, Drawing and Painting the Southwestern Landscape, Aboriginal Living Skills, Wildlife Management, Riparian Restoration, and many independent studies.

In addition, the station hosts research projects, such as the Hantavirus Longitudinal Study, which was funded by the Centers for Disease Control; the Arenavirus Distribution Study, funded by the National Institutes of Health; an Arizona Department of Water Resources inventory and monitoring study grant; and the Rattlesnake Radio Telemetry Project.

Costs

Tuition for 2006–07 was $18,576; tuition increases may occur in July of each year.

Financial Aid

The types of financial aid available are Federal Pell Grants, Prescott College grants, Arizona State Student Incentive Grants, Federal Supplemental Educational Opportunity Grants, student employment, Federal Stafford Student Loans, the Arizona Voucher Program, campus employment, and scholarships. More than 67 percent of the students at Prescott College receive financial aid.

Prescott College uses the Free Application for Federal Student Aid (FAFSA) to determine a student's financial need. Students wishing to apply for aid for the fall term should complete the financial aid form by April 15 for priority funding. Aid is awarded on a first-come, first-served basis until all available funds are used. FAFSA forms take four to six weeks to process, so students should submit them early, even if their plans are indefinite. Students who complete forms online may experience a quicker response than those who complete paper applications.

Faculty

Faculty members at Prescott College are devoted solely to the instruction of students. They are not burdened by the traditional "publish or perish" mandate faced by most educators; instead, they direct their energy toward being innovative instructors, positive role models, mentors, advisers, and friends. The College recognizes the importance of individualized attention and small classes. Faculty members are committed to the educational mission of Prescott College and thoroughly enjoy teaching, participating in College social activities, and working with individual students to help them comprehend challenging material. Approximately 60 percent of the 45 full-time RDP faculty members hold doctorates or terminal degrees.

Student Government

Students participate in all levels of governance at Prescott College. Currently, 1 student is a full voting member of the Board of Trustees. Students are also represented on hiring committees. The Student Union is composed of all full-time students, each of whom has a vote.

Admission Requirements

In evaluating an applicant, the Admissions Committee seeks evidence of preparation for college-level academic work, a strong sense of community, and a desire to become a self-directed learner. The Admissions Committee looks for the ability to plan and make decisions and commitments and carry them out effectively. The applicant's essays, letter of recommendation, and transcripts are the strongest determining factors in the admission decision. Visits to the College and personal interviews are strongly recommended, and, in some cases, they are required. Students who consider applying to Prescott College should first attempt to gain a thorough understanding of the College's educational philosophy and practices.

Prescott College has created a special learning environment that requires motivation, maturity, and a desire to be actively involved in learning.

Application and Information

The Admissions Office strongly encourages applicants to submit all required application materials by the priority filing date. Complete files are then reviewed by the Admissions Committee, and admissions decisions are communicated by the notification date. Files that are received or completed after the priority filing date are still considered on a rolling basis.

Once students are offered admission to an incoming class, they must submit a tuition deposit prior to the reply date to give evidence of intention to enroll and to reserve a space in that class. Tuition deposits are nonrefundable; applicants are advised to submit them only after determining that they are ready to commit to Prescott College. Tuition deposits received after the reply date are accepted on a first-come, first-served basis until the class has filled. Students whose deposits are received after the class is filled are placed on a wait list.

Applications for fall should be received by March 1; for spring, the priority filing date is November 1. The reply dates (deposit due dates) for fall and spring are, respectively, May 1 and December 1. Applications that are received or completed after the priority filing date are still considered. These applications are reviewed after those that were received and completed by the priority filing date.

For more information, students should contact:

Resident Degree Program–Admissions
Prescott College
220 Grove Avenue
Prescott, Arizona 86301
Phone: 928-350-2100
       877-350-2100 (toll-free)
E-mail: admissions@prescott.edu
Web site: http://www.prescott.edu

Prescott College students experience active education in a Southwestern classroom.

REGIS UNIVERSITY
DENVER, COLORADO

The University

In its 130th year, Regis University is the Rocky Mountain region's only Jesuit university and is well-known for innovation and educational leadership. Continuing a 450-year tradition of academic excellence, Regis is one of twenty-eight Jesuit colleges and universities located in the United States.

U.S. News & World Report named Regis University a "Top School" among colleges and universities in the western United States, marking the eleventh consecutive year Regis has been in the publication's top tier. The University was also recognized as one of the top 100 universities and colleges for leadership in the field of student character development in *The Templeton Guide: Colleges That Encourage Character Development*. Regis University is ranked by *U.S. News & World Report* as the fifth-best university in the western United States for the highest proportion of classes with 20 students or fewer.

The University has an American Rhodes Scholar, 2 *USA Today* College All-Academic Team selectees (in 1993 and 2000), the top female collegiate athlete in NCAA Division II for 1998–99, 5 Fulbright professors, 2 Fuld Fellows, and a wealth of other national recognition of outstanding academic excellence. More than 90 percent of Regis's full-time faculty members have a Ph.D. or terminal degree in their field.

However, Regis University was not always Regis. The school was started in 1877 in Las Vegas, New Mexico, by a group of exiled Italian Jesuits. It was known as Las Vegas College. In 1884, a second venture, known as Sacred Heart College, was started at Morrison, Colorado.

In 1887, Las Vegas College and Sacred Heart College moved to North Denver, where the joint operation became known as the College of the Sacred Heart. The college was renamed Regis in 1921, in honor of St. John Francis Regis, an eighteenth-century Jesuit missionary and saint who was revered for his exemplary work with poor people in the mountains of France.

On July 1, 1991, Regis College became Regis University, with three constituent schools: Regis College, the School for Professional Studies, and the Rueckert-Hartman School for Health Professions. Regis College is the traditional residential school, with 1,250 students, primarily in the 18- to 23-year-old range. The School for Professional Studies focuses on undergraduate and graduate adult higher education. The Rueckert-Hartman School for Health Professions educates men and women to be leaders who are committed to excellence within the health-care professions.

Regis College primarily serves traditional-aged, mostly residential undergraduate students. The college offers a full range of programs in the liberal arts, sciences, business, and education. Students may choose from twenty-four structured areas of study or design their own programs through the interdisciplinary and flexible major plans. A low student-faculty ratio permits small classes and learning formats that encourage critical thinking, thoughtful discussion, and well-developed communication skills. In the college, students receive highly personalized attention from 93 full-time skilled professors and dedicated scholars.

Four modern residence halls—O'Connell, DeSmet, West, and the townhouse complex—are fully staffed and offer computer labs, free cable TV, local phone service and voice mail, free laundry facilities, lounges, vending machines, and two phone and data lines in each room. More than 80 percent of freshmen live on campus.

Athletic opportunities are offered on all levels: recreational, intramural, and intercollegiate. Regis University is a member of NCAA Division II and the Rocky Mountain Athletic Conference and competes in twelve intercollegiate sports as well as a variety of intramural and club sport programs.

In addition to the undergraduate degree programs listed below, Regis offers a Master of Education (M.Ed.) degree in learning and teaching, a Master of Science (M.S.) degree in nursing, and a Doctor of Physical Therapy (D.P.T.) degree.

Location

Regis University is located near the base of the Rocky Mountains in a residential suburban neighborhood of northwest Denver, just north of I-70 and 25 minutes from Denver International Airport. Within 15 minutes of the campus is one of the most exciting international downtowns in the world. Thirty minutes west of the campus are the snowcapped peaks of the Rocky Mountains. Denver is one of America's fastest-growing metropolitan regions, with an abundance of cultural and recreational opportunities; it is one of only a few American cities with seven professional sports franchises. Denver has low humidity, and the sun shines about 300 days a year. The metropolitan area averages only 15 inches of precipitation a year, about the same as Los Angeles. Midwinter temperatures of 60 degrees are common. Colorado ski country is nearby; the campus is just 2 hours from Breckenridge, Vail, and Winter Park.

Majors and Degrees

Undergraduate degree offerings include the Bachelor of Arts (B.A.), Bachelor of Science (B.S.), Bachelor of Arts and Science, Classical Bachelor of Arts, and Bachelor of Science in Nursing (B.S.N.), as well as special majors.

Business programs include accounting (major and minor); accounting/M.B.A. (major); business administration, with concentrations in finance, international business, management, management information systems, and marketing (major and minor); economics (major and minor); flexible major; and political economy (major and minor).

Programs in humanities include art history (major), communication (major and minor), English (major and minor), fine arts: visual arts (major and minor), flexible major, French (major and minor), German (course work), Hispanic studies (minor), literature (minor), music (minor), Spanish (major and minor), women's studies (major and minor), and writing (minor).

The University offers natural sciences and mathematics programs in biochemistry (major and minor), biology (B.A. and B.S., major and minor), chemistry (major and minor), computer science (major and minor), environmental studies/human ecology (major and minor), exercise science (minor), mathematics (major and minor), neuroscience (major and minor), and physics (minor).

Programs in philosophy and religious studies include Catholic studies (minor), Christian leadership (minor), flexible major, philosophy (major and minor), and religious studies (major and minor).

Social sciences programs include anthropology (minor), criminology (minor), education (licensure), elementary education (licensure), flexible major, history (major and minor), leadership (minor), peace and justice studies (minor), physical education (minor), physical education: coaching/recreation (minor), politics (major and minor), psychology (major and minor), secondary education (licensure), sociology (major and minor), and special education (licensure).

Preprofessional programs are offered in dentistry, law, medicine, and physical therapy. A dual-degree engineering program is also offered.

Academic Programs

Regis is part of a 450-year-old Jesuit tradition that provides a values-centered liberal arts education and is known for service to others. The Core Curriculum, designed to prepare students for life as well as a career, requires students to reflect on the purpose of human existence, to understand the roots of modern culture, to embrace philosophical and religious perspectives, and to think critically. These courses enrich perceptions, challenge assumptions, and broaden visions.

A total of 128 semester hours is required for a bachelor's degree. Regis chooses a select group of students for its honors program each year and offers a schedule of undergraduate courses in the summer session. The University's Center for Service Learning actively involves students in community service projects. Internships and study abroad are offered as well. Other academic programs include the writing program, teacher licensure, the Commitment Program, Air Force Reserve Officer Training Corps, Air Force University Scholarship Program, and the Army Reserve Officer Training Corps (military science).

Academic Facilities

Regis is committed to providing state-of-the-art facilities. The University offers students 24-hour access to personal computers, online service, and research tools in common lab facilities. In addition, labs are located in the three coeducational residence halls, in the town houses, and in specific departments. All students are offered full access to an e-mail account on the Internet.

The University has two libraries, housing more than 280,000 volumes, 2,100 periodical subscriptions, 150,000 microforms, and a 90,000-slide art history collection. Its CARL online catalog is a comprehensive index to the collections and provides 10,000 databases, document delivery options, and full-text online journals. The main library, which includes media services, provides network ports at every place that a student studies for ease of access to the Internet and the Regis database.

The Coors Life Direction Center houses the Office of Career Services and Academic Internships, Personal Counseling, Disabilities Services, the Fitness Program, and the Health Center.

Costs

Undergraduate tuition and fees at Regis College for the 2006–07 academic year were $25,200. Room and board for the academic year cost $8470.

Financial Aid

In an effort to keep its high-quality Jesuit education affordable, Regis is committed to helping as many students as possible by continuing to increase scholarships and University grant funds. The student financial aid program invests more than $14 million in undergraduates. More than 90 percent of full-time Regis College students receive some financial assistance. Scholarships and grants are awarded on the basis of need, academic achievement, and leadership. The University participates in all federal and Colorado-supported programs. The Free Application for Federal Student Aid (FAFSA) or Renewal Application must be filed.

Faculty

Regis College has 93 full-time faculty members; 92 percent hold terminal degrees. Ten percent of the faculty members are Jesuit priests, and Regis has no graduate students/teaching assistants on its staff. The college has a 14:1 student-faculty ratio. Some professional staff members and Jesuit priests live and teach on Regis's campus. These committed adults are available for both academic and personal direction for Regis students. In addition, each undergraduate has an individual faculty adviser, who assists students in their academic choices.

Student Government

The Student Government at Regis is led by the Executive Board. The board is supported by the Senate, which comprises class representatives. The student leaders serve on University committees, plan entertainment, help determine student policy, and oversee more than thirty student organizations.

Admission Requirements

Regis College actively recruits students for equal opportunity and nondiscriminatory consideration of eligibility. The average ACT composite score for incoming freshmen is 23, and the average SAT combined score for Math and Critical Reading is 1108 (a new composite score that includes the Writing section has not been calculated yet). Admission is determined by a student's high school record, including grades, test scores, personal ability, and leadership qualities.

Requirements for freshman admission include high school graduation or its equivalent and evidence of college-level competency, as shown in high school courses, grades, ACT or SAT test scores, a personal essay, and recommendations. The new ACT writing component is not required. Freshmen should present a minimum of 15 academic units. Successful candidates must have a satisfactory high school or college record in order to be admitted.

Application and Information

Completed applications for admission should be submitted to the Director of Admissions. Applications may be submitted any time after the beginning of the year. The Office of Admissions usually notifies each applicant regarding the decision within four weeks after the completed application and supporting documents have been received by the Office of Admissions. All requests for information or application forms should be addressed to:

Director of Admissions
Regis College Office of Admissions, A-12
Regis University
3333 Regis Boulevard
Denver, Colorado 80221-1099
Phone: 303-458-4900
      800-388-2366 Ext. 4900 (toll-free)
Fax: 303-964-5534
E-mail: regisadm@regis.edu
Web site: http://www.regis.edu

The Regis University campus is located in a pleasant residential neighborhood with beautiful Rocky Mountain views, just a few minutes from downtown Denver.

ST. JOHN'S COLLEGE
SANTA FE, NEW MEXICO, AND ANNAPOLIS, MARYLAND

The College

Founded in Annapolis, Maryland, in 1696 as King William's School, St. John's College was chartered in 1784. A new campus opened in 1964 in Santa Fe, New Mexico. St. John's is accredited by the Maryland State Department of Education, the Middle States Association of Colleges and Secondary Schools, and by the Higher Learning Commission of the North Central Association of Colleges and Schools.

St. John's is a four-year, coeducational, liberal arts college with no religious affiliation and is known for its distinctive "great books" curriculum. The all-required course of study is based on the reading, study, and discussion of the most important books of the Western tradition. There are no majors and no departments; all students follow the same program. The classics of literature, philosophy, theology, psychology, political science, economics, history, mathematics, the laboratory sciences, and music are studied. No textbooks are used. The great books are read in roughly chronological order, beginning with authors from ancient Greece and continuing to modern times. All classes are discussion based. Instead of class lecture, the students meet together with faculty members (called tutors) to explore the books being read.

Both campuses offer extensive intramural sports programs, fencing, martial arts, and extracurricular fine and performing arts courses. Each campus has soundproof music practice rooms, an art gallery, and a music library. Major clubs and activities include student government, a newspaper, a yearbook, a film society, drama groups, a literary magazine, and opportunities for community service. The Annapolis campus has easy access to boating, sailing, and crew, while the Santa Fe campus offers skiing, hiking, and mountain rescue.

Each campus strives to keep the student population at 450 to 475 students. Freshman classes usually represent approximately thirty-five states and several other countries. Minority representation is about 10 percent on both campuses. The ratio of men to women is about 10 to 9. Annapolis students live in six centrally located dormitories, some dating back to the early nineteenth century. Dormitories on the Santa Fe campus are small modern units, clustered around central courtyards. About 60 percent of the students live on campus. Freshmen are guaranteed a room on campus. Dormitories are coed, usually by floor. There are no fraternities or sororities.

Location

The 36-acre eastern campus is located in the heart of historic Annapolis, which is the capital of Maryland. Annapolis is also a seaport town that is close to both Washington, D.C., and Baltimore.

The Santa Fe campus is a short walk from downtown museums, art galleries, Internet cafés, book stores, and coffee shops. Santa Fe is the state capital—historic yet sophisticated—and a cultural center of the Southwest.

Majors and Degrees

The Bachelor of Arts degree is awarded to all undergraduates upon the successful completion of the curriculum.

Academic Programs

The curriculum is an integrated arts and sciences program based on a chronological study of the seminal works of Western civilization. All students take Seminar, which comprises four years of interdisciplinary study (philosophy, theology, political science, literature, history, economics, and psychology); Language Tutorial, four years of language (ancient Greek, French, English composition, English poetry); Mathematics Tutorial, four years of mathematics (geometry, astronomy, algebra, calculus, relativity); Laboratory, three years of laboratory science (biology, physics, chemistry); and Music Tutorial, one year of music theory and composition. Students also participate in Preceptorials, which are two 8-week elective discussion sessions and a once-a-week lecture for the College as a whole.

Seminar readings include works of literature, philosophy, theology, political science, and history. The course of study is roughly chronological, beginning with the Greeks in freshman year and continuing to the twenty-first century in senior year. The chronological order in which the books are read is primarily a matter of convenience and intelligibility; it does not imply a historical approach to the subject matter. The St. John's curriculum seeks to convey to students an understanding of the fundamental problems that human beings have to face today and at all times, inviting students to reflect both on their continuities and their discontinuities.

In the Language Tutorial, students read foreign languages and translate them into English, compare them with each other and with English, and thus learn something of the nature of languages in general and of their own in particular. Throughout the four years, students explore language as the discourse of reason through the medium of foreign tongues—Greek in the first two years and French in the last two years.

The College believes that mathematics is an integral part of understanding the human intellect and the world. The Mathematics Tutorial gives students an insight into the fundamental nature and intention of mathematics and into the kind of reasoning that proceeds systematically from definitions and principles to necessary conclusions. Pure mathematics and the foundations of mathematical physics and astronomy are studied.

The sophomore Music Tutorial seeks to develop an understanding of music through attentive listening and through close study of musical theory and the analysis of works of music, including Bach, Beethoven, Mozart, Palestrina, Stravinsky, and Schoenberg, among others. Students undertake a thorough investigation of the diatonic system—a study of melody, counterpoint, and harmony—and of rhythm in words and notes.

The desire to follow more deeply the work of a particular author or to pursue a question of philosophy to another level is afforded by the Preceptorial, the closest offering the College has to an elective. For about seven or eight weeks in the middle of the year, seminars are suspended for juniors and seniors as they meet in smaller groups to study one book or explore a subject through the reading and discussion of several books. The tutors of junior and senior Seminar propose topics for the Preceptorials, and juniors and seniors submit their requests to the dean. Generally, not more than ten students meet with one tutor.

On Friday evening, the entire College assembles for a formal lecture by a tutor or a visitor. Afterward, the lecturer submits to lengthy questioning by students and faculty members. The evening serves two purposes—inculcating the habit of listening steadily and attentively to the exposition of a perhaps unfamiliar subject and granting the opportunity to exercise dialectical skills in a setting different from the classroom.

Academic Facilities

The libraries in Annapolis and Santa Fe contain more than 100,000 and 60,000 volumes, respectively. Each library houses a number of special collections, and each campus has a music library.

Costs

Tuition is $34,306, and room and board total $8270 a year. Students pay about $200 in required fees. A typical student budget includes about $275 for books and $800 for personal expenses and transportation.

Financial Aid

St. John's College is committed to making its unique program available to students of limited means. All financial aid awards are based on demonstrated need. In addition, educational loans, grants, and work-study positions are available through the federally funded programs administered by the College. The College receives support for financial aid from individuals, corporations, and foundations. The most generous of these is the Hodson Trust. Financial aid awards are made to approved applicants on a first-come, first-served basis. Sixty-five percent of St. John's students receive some form of financial aid. The typical financial aid package, which is combined with the family contribution and the student contribution, is usually made up of a St. John's College grant, loans, and jobs.

Faculty

At St. John's, the teaching members of the faculty are called tutors. The title professor is avoided to signify that it is not the chief role of the tutors to lecture in their fields of expertise but to guide the students through the program of study. Learning is cooperative rather than competitive, taking place in small discussion groups of mutually helpful members. Tutors, while specialists in various fields, are expected to participate in all parts of the curriculum; consequently, they exemplify and strengthen the program's integrated nature. The student-faculty ratio is 8:1.

Student Government

St. John's student government is not the standard collection of elected officials but a mix of elected officials and students who obtain voting privileges after attending three meetings. The Student Polity oversees some student organizations, promotes communication between students and faculty and staff members, and provides funding to some student activities. The government often holds town hall meetings where students can discuss their concerns openly and freely with faculty and staff members.

Admission Requirements

Although applications must be initiated and completed at one campus or the other, admission to either campus constitutes admission to the College as a whole. Applicants must submit the completed application, an official copy of all academic transcripts, letters of reference, and essays in which students discuss their previous education, their reasons for choosing St. John's, their reading habits, and an important experience. The submission of test scores is optional. Because the College welcomes all serious applicants, there is no application fee.

Application and Information

Due to the size of the freshman class on both campuses, as well as the limited financial aid and the intense competition for it, submitting applications early is extremely advantageous. Ideally, students should apply by January 1, allowing the admissions office to issue decisions within two weeks. Through March 1, admissions decisions are issued between two and three weeks. Students who are applying for financial aid should send in their applications by January 1 but no later than February 15.

Santa Fe Campus:
Director of Admissions
St. John's College
1160 Camino Cruz Blanca
Santa Fe, New Mexico 87505-4599

Phone: 505-984-6060
      800-331-5232 (toll-free)
E-mail: admissions@sjcsf.edu
Web site: http://www.stjohnscollege.edu

Annapolis Campus:
Director of Admissions
St. John's College
P.O. Box 2800
Annapolis, Maryland 21404-2800

Phone: 410-626-2522
      800-727-9238 (toll-free)
E-mail: admissions@sjca.edu
Web site: http://www.stjohnscollege.edu

Santa Fe campus.

SAN FRANCISCO ART INSTITUTE

SAN FRANCISCO, CALIFORNIA

sfai

san francisco. art. institute.
since 1871.

The Institute

Founded in 1871, San Francisco Art Institute (SFAI) has consistently offered one of the most open, innovative, and interdisciplinary environments in higher education. SFAI is committed to providing students with the best possible education by challenging them with a rigorous academic and studio program and by helping them meet the demands and expectations they will face as active community members and cultural contributors. SFAI is fully accredited by the Western Association of Schools and Colleges (WASC) and by the National Association of Schools of Art and Design (NASAD) and offers Bachelor of Arts, Bachelor of Fine Arts, Master of Arts, and Master of Fine Arts degrees and a post-baccalaureate certificate.

Students at SFAI build on a rich legacy of the kind of questioning that encourages the experimentation necessary for independent and collaborative invention. Students work closely with peers and faculty members from a wide variety of backgrounds and fields, and studio courses and seminars have a maximum of 15 students. Mixing the thinking of artists, sociologists, political scientists, philosophers, writers, historians, and others from around the world enables exciting ways for thoughtful, layered, and unexpected productions between these practitioners and students to take place.

Students in each of SFAI's programs participate in projects that allow them to move beyond the classroom and into the world. These programs combine SFAI's historic ways of teaching—through critique seminars, studio courses, and tutorials—with forms of research that emphasize the independent and collaborative nature of both teaching and learning. Internships, independent study, travel courses, and international exchange programs give students practical and professional experience.

To gain exposure to a wide range of historical and contemporary thinking and practices from a global context, all first-year undergraduate students enroll in Contemporary Practice, a core curriculum of research and writing, art history, critical thinking, and studio practice.

Location

SFAI's main campus was completed in 1926 in the residential neighborhood of Russian Hill. The architecture combines an historic Spanish-Italian colonial building with a distinctive modernist addition from 1970. Together, the two buildings offer traditional studios with natural light from windows and skylights; black-box performance, production, and editing studios; numerous galleries and exhibition spaces for student work; and seminar, screening, and lecture spaces. The campus features spectacular views of San Francisco Bay, including the Golden Gate Bridge, Bay Bridge, and Richmond Bridge as well as Alcatraz and Angel Island. Many of San Francisco's historic and diverse neighborhoods are also nearby, including North Beach, Chinatown, and SoMA—the South of Market area, which is home to many of the city's major museums, such as the San Francisco Museum of Modern Art and Yerba Buena Center for the Arts.

The San Francisco Bay area is the country's sixth-largest metropolitan area and is home to an exciting art scene that includes museums, galleries, and alternative spaces. The area also offers a wealth of cultural and educational resources—traditional and experimental theater, opera, dance, a wide range of music, cinemas, and libraries. Favored by a climate that is mild year-round, San Francisco is among the world's most livable cities.

Majors and Degrees

SFAI consists of two schools: the School of Studio Practice and the School of Interdisciplinary Studies. The School of Studio Practice offers the Bachelor of Fine Arts (B.F.A.) degree and a postbaccalaureate certificate in design+technology, film, new genres, painting, photography, printmaking, and sculpture. The School of Interdisciplinary Studies offers the Bachelor of Arts (B.A.) degree in history and theory of contemporary art and in urban studies. Students at SFAI receive a broad education that informs and enhances their primary area of study, choosing electives and fulfilling curriculum requirements from both schools.

Academic Programs

Education at SFAI is a process of dialogue and reflection. It is attuned to the challenges and responsibilities of the individual in a changing global world, and it engages a broad range of knowledge and technologies. This education is creative and generative, self-directed yet collaborative; it reflects the role artists play in shaping society's collective understanding. It encourages students to question the accepted definitions of art, build new tools for their practice, redefine the venues for the exhibition of art, and create new audiences for contemporary art. As alumni attest, SFAI educates students to be innovators and leaders in a wide range of professional endeavors.

In addition to working with SFAI's esteemed full- and part-time faculty members, students are introduced to a spectrum of visiting artists and scholars. SFAI provides students direct access to an exhibition program showcasing the work of regional and international artists as well as SFAI students; an extensive roster of lectures that brings more than 60 artists, designers, curators, and writers to the campus every year; and film screenings, symposia, and panel discussions that engage in contemporary issues and ideas.

Key elements of SFAI's approach to the intersection of academic and public inquiries are the new fellowships sponsored through the Centers of Interdisciplinary Study. Internationally recognized artists work in residence for a minimum of five weeks. Fellowships provide artists an environment to engage in the ongoing development of new ideas in their work, to test those ideas, and to teach and collaborate with SFAI students and faculty members. Recent Fellows include Raqs Media Collective from New Delhi; Alfredo Jaar, an artist, architect, and filmmaker known for his public interventions; and Hilton Als, a staff writer for *The New Yorker* and recent co-editor of *White Noise: An Eminem Reader.*

SFAI's focus on skills, experimentation, and constructive dialogue provides the perfect conditions for personal exploration. The Bachelor of Fine Arts and Bachelor of Arts degree programs are designed to help students develop their ability to think creatively and to give them the confidence to realize their visions. The programs provide equal parts skill development, guidance, challenging discussion, and the freedom to explore and experiment. SFAI's curriculum offers many opportunities, including studio practice, seminars, critiques, tutorials with individual faculty members, and internships, enabling students to design their own individualized learning program.

Academic Facilities

SFAI's main campus is located at 800 Chestnut Street in San Francisco's Russian Hill neighborhood. The campus houses large light-filled studios with 24-hour access for students; state-of-the-art digital media and imaging studios with large-format printers; black-and-white and color film processing facilities and darkrooms; facilities for processing 16mm film; film and sound editing studios, including HD video; lithography, etching, serigraphy, and letter-

press studios; a ceramics studio, woodshop, metal shop, and electronics lab; a lecture hall with 16mm and digital projection; numerous galleries; and a cafe.

SFAI's Anne Bremer Memorial Library is a valuable resource for books and primary-source material on artists. The library holds more than 29,000 volumes, including an outstanding collection of exhibition catalogues, artists' books, rare books, historic archives of original material documenting art in California since 1871, and subscriptions to over 200 periodicals as well as collections of slides, audiotapes, videotapes, films, and DVDs.

The Graduate Center is a large industrial loft building along the San Francisco Bay. The 62,000-square-foot facility provides individual and group studios (many with natural light), 24-hour access, and convenience to public transportation. The Graduate Center facilities include a digital lab, film and sound studios, darkrooms, a wood shop, seminar classrooms, a gallery, and installation critique rooms, where students can present finished works or works-in-progress. Graduate students also have access to all of the facilities on the main campus.

Costs

For the 2006–07 academic year, tuition for full-time undergraduate students was $27,200. The average cost for additional expenses included $2200 for supplies and books, $10,800 for housing and food, $3000 for personal expenses, and $400 for transportation. Most students live in private apartments or studios. Freshmen may live in college-leased housing. SFAI also maintains a roommate referral service and housing bulletin boards. SFAI requires all full-time students to purchase health insurance. This requirement may be waived upon presentation of proof of other coverage. The 2006–07 insurance premium was $1115.

Financial Aid

The San Francisco Art Institute administers four categories of aid: competitive scholarships, loans, grants, and work-study opportunities. In addition to making awards solely on the basis of demonstrated financial need, SFAI has established a prestigious scholarship competition, which awards merit-based scholarships each semester to students admitted for undergraduate study beginning in the subsequent semester.

Application for all types of need-based financial aid administered by SFAI requires a completed application for admission and the Free Application for Federal Student Aid (FAFSA). The FAFSA should be forwarded to the appropriate processing center. Students who apply by March 1 receive priority consideration for available financial aid funds. Approximately 80 percent of SFAI's students receive some form of financial aid.

Faculty

With a faculty of more than 130, SFAI enjoys an extraordinary student-faculty ratio of 5:1. Students work closely with faculty members and develop important and lasting relationships that continue beyond graduation.

SFAI's faculty includes artists, curators, writers, historians, theorists, activists, critics, urbanists, designers, performers, philosophers, musicians, and scientists. Okwui Enwezor, Dean of Academic Affairs, is a curator and writer and was the artistic director of the 2006 Bienal Internacional de Arte Contemporaneo in Seville, Spain. Renée Green is Dean of Graduate Studies at SFAI, and her work has been seen throughout the world in museums, galleries, biennials, and festivals. Hou Hanru, Chair of SFAI's Exhibitions and Museum Studies program, is the curator of the Chinese pavilion at the 2007 Venice Biennale and director of the 2007 Istanbul Biennial. Trisha Donnelly's work was included in the 2004 and 2006 Whitney Biennials. Martin Schmidt (of Matmos) has toured with Bjork and has a new CD, *The Rose Has Teeth In The Mouth Of The Beast.* Caitlin Mitchell-Dayton's paintings were used in the film *Art School Confidential.* Henry Wessel's photographs were recently published as a five-volume boxed set by Steidl. Jon Phillips is an open-source programmer for Creative Commons. Mark

Van Proyen is one of the editors of *AfterBurn: Reflections on Burning Man.* Amy Franceschini is the founder of FutureFarmers and has been involved in numerous projects aimed at raising public awareness to critical ecological issues. Thomas Humphrey is a nuclear physicist and director of exhibitions at the Exploratorium.

Student Government

The Student Union is the undergraduate forum for discussion and action concerning all matters of interest to students. Students are elected to SFAI's Board of Trustees and Faculty Senate and participate in other governing committees. Also under the jurisdiction of the Student Union are the exhibition program of the Diego Rivera Gallery, student publications, and various social functions. The Legion of Graduate Students (LOGS) includes all graduate students and encourages participation of graduate alumni. LOGS oversees the Swell Gallery, the Alternative Lecture Series, and serves as a forum for graduate students.

Admission Requirements

The admissions process is highly personalized and considers all of the information provided in each application. All applications are reviewed by faculty members and admissions staff members. Admission decisions are made on an individual basis, taking into account artistic and/or scholastic achievement, personal maturity, and dedication as well as the student's academic background.

B.A. and B.F.A. requirements include a written statement of purpose; a portfolio (B.F.A. applicants only); transcripts from high school, secondary school, and any colleges or universities previously attended; SAT or ACT scores; TOEFEL scores (international students); two letters of recommendation; and a $65 nonrefundable application fee ($75 for international applicants).

Application and Information

For B.A. and B.F.A. degree applicants, SFAI offers rolling admissions, with priority deadlines for scholarship consideration.

An online application and information are available at SFAI's Web site at http://www.sfai.edu.

Office of Admissions
San Francisco Art Institute
800 Chestnut Street
San Francisco, California 94133
Phone: 415-749-4500
         800-345-SFAI (toll-free)
E-mail: admissions@sfai.edu
Web site: http://www.sfai.edu

The Quad at SFAI, above San Francisco Bay.

SEATTLE UNIVERSITY
SEATTLE, WASHINGTON

The University

Seattle University (SU) provides an ideal environment for motivated students interested in self-reliance, awareness of different cultures, social justice, and the fulfillment that comes from making a difference. Its location in the center of one of the nation's most diverse and progressive cities attracts a varied student body, faculty, and staff. Its urban setting promotes the development of leadership skills and independence and provides a variety of opportunities for students to apply what they learn through internships, clinical experiences, and volunteer work.

As a Jesuit institution, Seattle University is part of a network of twenty-eight colleges and universities and forty-six high schools noted for academic strength across the United States. Academic offerings are designed to provide leadership opportunities, develop global awareness, and enable graduates to serve society through a demanding liberal arts and sciences foundation. In the Jesuit educational tradition, students are taught how to think, not what to think. Professional undergraduate offerings include highly respected Colleges of Business, Nursing, and Science and Engineering and career-oriented liberal arts programs such as communication, criminal justice, journalism, public affairs, and social work. The University's Colleges of Education, Law, and Theology and Ministry offer graduate-level opportunities.

Seattle University is noted for its focus on the individual through small, faculty-taught classes and excellent service. The result is mirrored by graduates who lead fulfilling and economically successful lives. SU is recognized as one of the leading institutions in the Pacific Northwest in producing Truman and Wilson scholars.

The fall quarter has a freshman class of 763, and 50 percent are from outside Washington State. The 4,135 undergraduate students represent forty-seven states and seventy-six nations. Approximately 7 percent are international students. The ethnic breakdown for the fall 2005 freshman class was 58 percent white, 23 percent Asian American, and 14 percent African American, Latino, and American Indian.

The residential campus has undergone $176 million in recent improvements. Although it is in the center of Seattle, the campus has been designated by Washington State as an Official Backyard Sanctuary for its distinctive landscaping and environmentally conscious practices.

There is a wide variety of on-campus housing that accommodates 1,600 students, including a new apartment complex, and 88 percent of freshmen live on campus. There is a two-year on-campus residence requirement.

Seattle University has more than eighty-five extracurricular clubs and organizations and has five varsity teams for men (basketball, cross-country, soccer, swimming, and track) and seven for women (basketball, cross-country, soccer, softball, swimming, track, and volleyball). SU is in NCAA Division II. The student life program includes sixty extracurricular clubs and organizations, including the Hawaiian Club, Associated Students of African Descent, Hiyu Coulee Hiking Club, Beta Alpha Psi (national accounting honorary), and other professional honoraries and clubs.

The Connolly Athletic Center serves as the major facility for varsity and intramural athletics and recreation. It features two swimming pools, two full-size gymnasiums, and locker room saunas. A 6-acre complex provides fields for outdoor sports.

Seattle University receives the highest professional accreditation from the Accreditation Board for Engineering and Technology, AACSB International–The Association to Advance Collegiate Schools of Business, American Bar Association, American Chemical Society, Association of Theological Schools, Commission on Accreditation of Allied Health Education Programs, National Association of Schools of Public Affairs and Administration, National Council for Accreditation of Teacher Education, Commission on Collegiate Nursing Education, Council on Social Work Education, and Northwest Commission on Colleges and Universities.

Location

Seattle University is located on First Hill in a port city of unsurpassed natural beauty. As the Pacific Northwest's largest city, Seattle is a scenic and cultural center in a setting that includes breathtaking mountain views of the Cascades to the east and the Olympics to the west; skiing is within 60 minutes of campus. In addition to being situated along Puget Sound, Seattle also contains Lakes Union and Washington; both provide a wide variety of recreational opportunities. Seattle's residents love the outdoors, and areas for hiking, backpacking, and climbing are minutes from campus. Biking is also popular and special trails for cycling and running are located throughout the city.

Seattle's sights and sounds, rich ethnic diversity, celebrated restaurants, first–run entertainment, major-league athletics, theater, opera, and ballet are within walking distance and enhance campus life.

Majors and Degrees

Seattle University offers the following undergraduate degrees: Bachelor of Arts, Bachelor of Science, Bachelor of Science in Nursing, Bachelor of Social Work, Bachelor of Criminal Justice, Bachelor of Public Affairs, and the Bachelor of Arts in Business Administration.

The University offers programs in six major academic units. The Albers School of Business and Economics awards degrees in accounting, business administration, business economics, e-commerce/information systems, finance, international business, management, and marketing. The College of Arts and Sciences grants degrees in art history, Asian studies, communication studies, criminal justice, cultural anthropology, drama, environmental studies, economics, English, fine arts, French, German, history, international studies, journalism, liberal studies, military science/ROTC, philosophy, political science, psychology, public affairs, social work, sociology, Spanish, theology/religious studies, and visual art. The College of Nursing offers a Bachelor of Science in Nursing degree. Matteo Ricci College awards degrees in humanities and humanities for teaching. The College of Science and Engineering offers degree programs in biochemistry, biology, chemistry, civil engineering, clinical laboratory science, computer engineering, computer science, diagnostic ultrasound, electrical engineering, environmental engineering, environmental science, general science, mechanical engineering, mathematics, and physics. Preprofessional programs include dentistry, law, medicine, optometry, and veterinary medicine.

Academic Programs

The Core Curriculum is known for its strength and has several distinguishing characteristics in keeping with the Jesuit tradition: it provides an integrated freshman year; it gives order and sequence to student learning; it provides experience in the meth-

ods and content of the range of liberal arts, sciences, philosophy, and theology; it calls for active learning in all classes for practice in writing and thinking, and for an awareness of values; and it fosters a global perspective and a sense of social and personal responsibility.

Seattle University offers two honors program options for students seeking the greatest possible challenge. The University Honors Program is a small, select two-year-long learning community. It is humanities focused, and its fully integrated curriculum examines the most significant texts and ideas of Western culture. The Core Honors Program involves seminar sections of nine required courses in English, history, philosophy, social science, and theology/religious studies. This option is particularly suited to students in profession-oriented majors where participation in University Honors is less feasible due to specific major requirements and scheduling conflicts.

SU operates on a quarter calendar. The fall quarter begins in mid-September; the winter quarter in early January; the spring quarter in late March; and the summer quarter in mid-June. Undergraduates typically take 15 credit hours each during the fall, winter, and spring quarters.

Off-Campus Programs

SU offers international study programs—one for French in France, one for Latin American studies in Mexico, one for Chinese in China, and two reciprocal exchange programs with the University of Graz in Austria and Sophia University in Japan. These are open to all students in all majors and emphasize appreciation of the language and culture. This is accomplished through the total immersion concept. Other programs include Campus Ministry missions in Nicaragua and Belize and Albers School of Business and Economics tours in Mexico, Italy, Hong Kong, and Vietnam. Seattle University maintains the only Calcutta Club in which students volunteer annually on behalf of Mother Teresa's ministry. Additional study-abroad programs in other nations, in conjunction with other colleges' overseas programs, are also offered. Arrangements are made through SU's Study Abroad Office.

Academic Facilities

The University is located on 45 acres in the First Hill neighborhood in the center of Seattle. There are twenty-eight buildings recently enhanced by $176 million in additions, renovations, and new construction.

Costs

In 2006–07, tuition was $24,615; room and meals were $7503. The estimate for books, fees, and personal expenses were an additional $4764. Travel costs vary among students. Costs were subject to change.

Financial Aid

Seattle University awarded $6.2 million in its own financial aid to fall 2005 freshmen, including 240 scholarships ranging from $6000 to $30,063. Sixty-eight percent of freshmen received University aid. Students are required to apply for financial aid by February 1 as awards are made early each spring for the following fall quarter. Applications that are received after this deadline will be evaluated in order received for any remaining aid. Students must submit the Free Application for Federal Student Aid (FAFSA) and be accepted for admission to be considered for financial assistance. There are also a number of scholarships for freshmen that are awarded on the basis of academic achievement, extracurricular involvement, and community service. Similar transfer scholarships are determined primarily on the basis of course selection and cumulative grade point average.

Faculty

There are 582 faculty members; 85 percent of full-time faculty members possess doctoral or terminal degrees. Like the University, the mission of faculty members who choose Seattle University is teaching. Most classes average 20; the faculty-student ratio is 1:13. All classes are taught by faculty members. The involvement of faculty members extends beyond the classroom. Faculty members are available to provide extra assistance, to help students with their research, and to assist in the arranging of internships. Faculty advisers provide guidance, direction, and encouragement throughout the year. New students are assigned faculty advisers according to major prior to registration.

Student Government

All undergraduates belong to the Associated Students of Seattle University (ASSU). This is the central student organization on campus. ASSU is organized around an elected president, an executive vice president, and an activities vice president. In addition, a 12-member representative council oversees every facet of the student body and is responsible for policymaking. Its primary responsibility is to provide a diverse activities program to meet the needs of SU's diverse student body. In addition, ASSU communicates student needs to the administration and faculty. ASSU oversees eighty-five clubs and organizations.

Admission Requirements

Freshman applicants are required to have a college-preparatory program, including 4 years of English, 3 years of social studies/history, 3 years of mathematics, 2 years of laboratory science, and 2 years of a foreign language. Applicants to the College of Science and Engineering must complete 4 units of college-preparatory mathematics for admission to any of its specific majors; applicants to the nursing major must complete laboratory biology and chemistry to be considered for admission. ACT or SAT scores, two recommendations, and an essay are also required. The middle 50 percent of freshman GPAs are between 3.3 and 3.8 on a 4.0 scale. The average score on the ACT is between 22 and 27, and the average SAT scores are between 510 and 630 (verbal) and 520 and 620 (math). Seattle University is an exclusive Common Application institution and requires its completion for admission consideration.

Essays or personal statements are required for admission and are carefully considered during application review.

College credit is awarded to those who have successfully completed Advanced Placement or International Baccalaureate examinations. Qualifying scores can be obtained by contacting the Office of the Registrar.

Application and Information

Applications can be obtained by contacting the Admissions Office. Secondary school students who have completed at least six semesters are encouraged to apply by January of their senior year. Transfer students must submit official transcripts from all postsecondary institutions attended, regardless of whether course work was completed. For fall admission, freshmen should complete the process by February 1 to receive consideration for scholarships and priority consideration for other Seattle University financial aid; the recommended admissions deadline for transfers is March 1. Please note that applications will be accepted after these dates on a space available basis, but funds for financial aid may no longer be available. Campus visits can be scheduled Monday through Friday and most Saturdays. Guests can attend a class, meet with a faculty adviser, participate in a campus tour, and speak individually with representatives from admissions and financial aid. For additional information students should contact:

Michael K. McKeon, Dean
Admissions Office
Seattle University
901 12th Avenue
Seattle, Washington 98122-1090
Phone: 206-296-2000
        800-426-7123 (toll-free)
E-mail: admissions@seattleu.edu
Web site: http://www.seattleu.edu

SOUTHERN OREGON UNIVERSITY

ASHLAND, OREGON

SOUTHERN
OREGON
UNIVERSITY

The University

Southern Oregon University (SOU) is a contemporary public liberal arts and sciences university with a growing national reputation for excellence in teaching. It places student learning, inside and outside the classroom, at the heart of all programs and services. SOU is proud of its strengths in the sciences and humanities; its continuing tradition of preparing outstanding teachers, business leaders, and other select professionals; and its designation as Oregon's Center of Excellence in the Fine and Performing Arts. SOU was recently elected to the prestigious Council of Public Liberal Arts Colleges, recognizing the campus as a leader in providing a high-quality liberal arts education.

The University offers undergraduate majors in thirty-five areas of study, minors in fifty-two areas, and eleven graduate programs that include management, applied psychology, and several areas of study in education. SOU also offers certificates in accounting, applied cultural anthropology, applied finance and economics, botany, business information systems, cultural resource management, interactive marketing and e-commerce, management of human resources, and Native American studies. Students may take preprofessional programs for entry into medicine, engineering, agriculture, law, and theology. The University offers nursing through its association with the nationally ranked nursing school at the Oregon Health Sciences University. SOU has an excellent Honors Program as well.

The combination of high-quality academics and a beautiful environment attracts approximately 5,000 students. SOU features small class sizes and a student-faculty ratio of 19:1. Students have special opportunities for research and internships with government agencies, such as the National Fish and Wildlife Forensics Lab on campus; businesses, such as the Bear Creek Corporation in Medford; media, including Jefferson Public Radio; outstanding public schools; and arts organizations, such as the internationally renowned Oregon Shakespeare Festival. Students gain multicultural perspectives in classes, extracurricular activities, the International Student Exchange, and from 150 currently enrolled international students from thirty-three countries. SOU study-abroad programs span more than twenty countries.

SOU offers an impressive variety of extracurricular activities, clubs, and organizations. The University's newspaper, literary publication, honor societies, social issue groups, social clubs, and religious, preprofessional, international, and academic organizations provide students with multiple opportunities for involvement. Extreme sports, including sky diving, bungee jumping, rock climbing, kayaking, and mountain bike racing, are very popular. More than 65 percent of the student body participates in intramural sports and many compete in intercollegiate club sports, including skiing (Northern California Intercollegiate Conference), aikido, baseball, climbing, karate, rugby, soccer, swimming, tennis, and wrestling.

The University is a member of NAIA Division II. Women's varsity sports include basketball, cross-country, soccer, softball, tennis, track and field, and volleyball. Men's varsity sports include basketball, cross-country, football, track and field, and wrestling. The campus is a culturally dynamic and stimulating environment. Annual concerts bring world-class musicians and performers to the campus. The theater department has two seasons and performs before capacity crowds. Music groups include the concert and chamber choirs, vocal jazz ensemble, symphonic band, woodwind quintet, gamelan ensemble, saxophone quartets, clarinet ensemble, Rogue Valley symphony, and opera workshop. Five art galleries feature the work of students, faculty members, and locally, nationally, and internationally acclaimed artists. The International Writer Series attracts recognized writers, poets, and novelists from around the world.

Approximately 25 percent of the student body lives in one of fourteen residence halls or in family housing units. Freshmen are required to live on campus. The majority of students living off campus live in the immediate surrounding area. The track; the football field; volleyball, basketball, and tennis courts; climbing walls; a large swimming pool; dance studios; and the student fitness center are all nearby. The Cas-

cade Food Court is open from 7 a.m. to 10 p.m. and offers a variety of healthy and delicious food choices for every range of tastes.

The University's Student ACCESS Center houses student support services, including counseling services, academic advising, career advising, disabled student services, a learning center, testing center, and tutorial programs—all in one location.

Location

The University's beautiful 175-acre campus is located in the idyllic community of Ashland. SOU was named by *Outside* magazine as one of the "coolest places to work, study, and live," recognizing Southern for its beautiful campus, incredible location, and abundant outdoor activities. Home of the Oregon Shakespeare Festival, the town of 20,000 draws 385,000 visitors each year to enjoy the lively downtown, exquisite Lithia Park, and abundant theater, music events, and other cultural happenings. The Ashland area has five fairs, thirteen festivals, twenty-five art galleries, and twenty-four museums. The town itself has sixty lodging facilities and eighty restaurants. Colorful flags and banners announcing events create a festive environment, and the many boutiques, cafés, coffee shops, movie theaters, and bookstores create an ideal environment for college students. Mt. Ashland and the Siskiyou Mountains serve as the town's backdrop and offer downhill skiing, cross-country skiing, snowboarding, hiking, and mountain biking. The Cascade Mountains, Rogue and Klamath Rivers, Crater Lake National Park, and numerous lakes offer world-class white water rafting, camping, hiking, sailing, kayaking, and rock climbing.

Majors and Degrees

The University is organized into five schools: Arts and Letters; Business; Education; Sciences; and Social Science, Health, and Physical Education. Bachelor of Arts (B.A.) and Bachelor of Science (B.S.) degrees are available in the following majors: anthropology, art, arts and letters, biology, business administration† (accounting; hotel, restaurant, and resort management; management; marketing; small business management), business-chemistry*, business-mathematics*, business-music*, business-physics*, chemistry†, communication† (human communication, journalism, media studies), computer science† (computer information science, computer programming and software, computer science and multimedia, computer security and information assurance), criminal justice†, early childhood development, economics†, English and writing†, environmental studies*, geography†, geology, health and physical education† (athletic training, health promotion and fitness management), history†, human services, interdisciplinary studies, international studies*, language and culture† (French, Spanish, German), mathematics†, mathematics-computer science*, music, nursing (with Oregon Health Sciences University), physics†, political science, psychology, science*, social science*, sociology, and theater arts. Bachelor of Fine Arts (B.F.A.) degrees are available in art and theater. (An * indicates interdisciplinary programs; majors with a † offer the accelerated-degree option.)

Preprofessional programs include agriculture, chiropractic medicine, dental hygiene, dentistry, engineering, law, medical technology, medicine, nursing, occupational therapy, optometry, pharmacy, physical therapy, physician's assistant studies, podiatry, resource management and conservation, theology, and veterinary medicine.

Minors include Africa-Middle East history; anthropology; applied multimedia; art history; biology; British literature; business administration; chemistry; communication; computer science; creative writing; criminology; economics; education; English education; European history; film studies; French; general studio art; geography; geology; German; hotel, restaurant, and resort management; human communication; interdisciplinary ethics; international peace studies; journalism; Latin American history; Latin American studies; media studies; mathematics; mathematics education; military science; music; Native American studies; philosophy; photography; physics; political science; psychology; public relations; Shakespeare studies; sociology; Spanish; theater arts; U.S. history; U.S. literature; video production; women's studies; and writing with professional applications.

Academic Programs

Students are required to complete general education requirements in addition to the major requirements. The general education requirements provide students with skills in effective communication, critical judgment, and research, and cultivate an awareness of the social, artistic, cultural, and scientific traditions of civilization. The required freshman Colloquium provides a solid foundation in reading, writing, communication, and critical thinking. Class size is limited to 28 students, and the Colloquium professor also serves as their first year adviser. Students in a four-year bachelor's program must have a minimum of 180 quarter credits to graduate. Students admitted to the Accelerated Baccalaureate Degree Program complete between 135 and 150 quarter credits to graduate.

Off-Campus Programs

Southern Oregon University offers a wide variety of study-abroad and overseas internship opportunities. The University also participates in National Student Exchange, which allows students to attend any of 140 colleges and universities nationwide and pay resident tuition.

Academic Facilities

The Hannon Library completed a significant expansion and renovation project in February 2005. The 120,000-square-foot library houses a coffee shop, group study and seminar rooms, classrooms, comfortable study areas, and an art exhibit area. Other recent developments on the SOU campus include the Center for Visual Arts, a 66,000-square-foot complex of modern glass and steel that serves as a showplace for art exhibition and education; a newly acquired biotechnology center featuring state of-the-art molecular biology instrumentation; and the acclaimed Institute for Environmental, Economic and Civic Studies.

SOU provides a strong information technology environment. Students have access to twenty-three computer labs on SOU's campus. The Main Computing Services Center lab is open more than 80 hours a week and houses more than 200 PCs and Macs, as well as printers and scanners. Other discipline-based and multimedia labs offer additional resources. Residence halls have labs, and student rooms are wired for computer access. Altogether, there are more than 600 workstations on the campus accessible to students. E-mail accounts, data storage, and access to the Internet are free of charge. The campus also offers extensive wireless Internet access.

Costs

For full-time undergraduate students taking 12 credits per term, 2005–06 tuition and fees were $4986 for residents and $14,691 for nonresidents. As a member of the Western Undergraduate Exchange, SOU offers most academic programs to residents of Alaska, Arizona, Colorado, Hawaii, Idaho, Montana, Nevada, New Mexico, North Dakota, South Dakota, Utah, Washington, and Wyoming for approximately $6834 (150 percent of the cost of in-state tuition and fees). Room and board costs, including a double room and the medium meal plan, were $6468. These prices are estimates at the time of printing and are subject to change.

Financial Aid

Financial aid is available in the form of grants, loans, and/or work-study. Approximately 65 percent of freshmen receive some form of financial aid. Students must file the Free Application for Federal Student Aid (FAFSA) to qualify. To be considered for financial aid at Southern Oregon University, students must have applied to the University for admission and have indicated the institution as one of their first six choices on the FAFSA. Students should mail the FAFSA by February 1 to receive maximum consideration for fall. The University offers merit and diversity scholarships to new freshmen and transfer students. Additional scholarships are available through departments and the Office of Financial Aid. For more information, students should contact the Financial Aid Office at 541-552-6161 or go online to http://www.sou.edu/finaid. For those seeking employment, the Student Employment Office lists the work-study and regular jobs available on and off campus.

Faculty

Ninety-three percent of the faculty members have Ph.D.s or the highest degree in their field. There are more than 200 full-time faculty members whose primary emphasis is on teaching and advising undergraduate students. Faculty members frequently include undergraduates in research projects, and many students have coauthored papers and made joint presentations at national conferences. Every student is assigned an adviser when they declare a major; freshmen have their Colloquium professor as their adviser.

Student Government

The Associated Students' governing body implements policies, makes budget recommendations, and participates in the allocation of more than $1.4 million each year to various clubs and organizations. They also work with the Oregon Student Association on issues important in higher education. Elected, appointed, and volunteer positions offer students valuable leadership experience.

Admission Requirements

Applicants for freshman admission must have achieved a minimum 2.75 cumulative high school GPA or a minimum combined math and critical reading score of 1010 on the SAT Reasoning Test or an ACT composite score of at least 21. In addition, applicants must have completed the following high school course requirements (with grades of C- or better, beginning with the high school graduating class of 2005): 4 years of English, 3 years of mathematics (including geometry, algebra I, and algebra II), 3 years of social science, 2 years of science (one of which must have a lab), and 2 years of one foreign language.

Students transferring from an accredited college or university must have earned at least 36 quarter credits of transfer-level credit with a minimum 2.25 GPA and, if a high school graduate of 1997 or later, meet the language requirement. Transfer applicants with less than 36 quarter credits must also meet the freshman admission requirements.

Home-schooled students and graduates of nonstandard or unaccredited high schools are eligible for admission if they meet the following requirements: a minimum combined math and critical reading score of 1010 on the SAT Reasoning Test and a score of at least 470 on the SAT Writing Test or a minimum score of 21 on the ACT. These students must also score an average 470 or above (940 total) on two SAT Subject Tests (Math Level I or IIC and another test of the student's choice). These students must also satisfy the second-language admission requirement if they graduated from a high school in 1997 or later.

Application and Information

Applicants must submit an application with a $50 nonrefundable application fee and official transcripts from each high school and/or university or college attended. Freshmen must submit official SAT or ACT scores. Students may apply after September 1 for the following academic year. Admission is rolling, but the priority deadline for the fall is June 1. Students may apply using either the paper application or online at http://www.sou.edu/admissions.

A campus visit is encouraged. Tours are offered at the Office of Admissions, Monday through Friday at 10 a.m. and 2 p.m. and on select Saturdays at 11 a.m. by appointment. For a tour or more information and summer tour hours, students should contact SOU at:

Southern Oregon University
Office of Admissions
1250 Siskiyou Boulevard
Ashland, Oregon 97520

Phone: 541-552-6411
        800-482-7672 (toll-free in Oregon and
            from area codes 916, 707, and 530)
E-mail: admissions@sou.edu
Web site: http://www.sou.edu

UNIVERSITY OF ADVANCING TECHNOLOGY
TEMPE, ARIZONA

The University

The University of Advancing Technology (UAT) is a unique, technology-infused private college founded by a techno-geek for techno-geeks. Its mission is to educate students in the fields of advancing technology to become innovators of the future. UAT's campus culture is devoted to continually nurturing a thriving geek community where everyone's personal lives and professional aspirations revolve around technology. UAT offers students a well-rounded education in a nontraditional setting. Students who are seeking a strictly career-oriented technical college experience will not find it here. Because of UAT's dedication to both scholastic excellence and technological innovation, it stands apart in academia as an ideal destination for the geeks of the world who feel disenfranchised by conventional institutions of higher learning. For the student who is looking at the future of technology and wishes to become a vital part of it, UAT beckons.

The beginning of the twenty-first century is an exciting time to be in the technology community, and UAT is serious about technology. As the twenty-first century unfolds, it is becoming more and more apparent how technology in all its manifestations profoundly alters how people work, live, play, and interact with each other. UAT students benefit from their fundamental understanding of both theoretical and applied aspects of technology. As technologists, UAT students see that there will always be newer and newer tools created to address mankind's emergent needs and desires. Changing the world through technology is inherent in UAT's mission. Current subjects of ongoing research and scholarship at UAT include robotics and embedded systems, artificial life programming, network security, game development, and other areas of advanced technology.

UAT has always devoted all of its resources to creating a vital academic environment where students are challenged to achieve, explore new and traditional concepts, and practice what they learn in real-world situations. This combination of research, scholarship, and application creates technically adept graduates who are equally at home in academia and the working world and valued by both. UAT graduates thrive in the digital age and meet and surpass every expectation of their high-technology employers and peers. They enter the professional world with accredited associate and bachelor's degrees, and many return to pursue a master's degree in the Graduate College of Applied Technology.

When the University of Advancing Technology was founded in 1983 (as the CAD Institute), it was conceived as a small school for training engineers and architects in the completely new field of computer-aided engineering. Its original students came to the CAD Institute seeking professional development training and certifications. From this beginning as a technical school, the institution became involved with advances in computer graphics and unique approaches to technology education. In 1998, the school moved to the new campus in Tempe, which was designed in accordance with Feng Shui principles. In 2002, the school changed its name to University of Advancing Technology to reflect its current broad technology focus.

UAT's 1,200 students (from all fifty states and many other countries) still find plenty of time to time to participate in clubs and other activities that enhance UAT's geek-friendly environment, such as ancient games, anime, technology philosophy, Yu-Gi-Oh, game developers, Web development, biking, C++, and photography. Special on-campus events include live-action games, Oktoberfest, LAN parties, Guitar Hero tournaments, and Thanksgiving dinner.

At any time, day or night, there are groups of students pounding coffee while working on course work and projects, looking to create the next big thing. It is not uncommon to see students burning the midnight oil, pulling all-nighters, exchanging ideas, and searching for solutions to perfect their creative innovations. There are students on their own laptops and PDAs, interacting and creating. There are also gatherings of students and instructors engaged in discussions of the latest technology developments and how they can make them better. UAT has an academic and social environment that integrates the contemporary and advancing principles of education and technology with its Year-Round Balanced Learning (YRBL) teaching model to create a unique collaborative educational environment.

Location

Located in sunny Tempe, Arizona, near the heart of downtown Phoenix, a booming urban center in the Sonoran desert, the University of Advancing Technology is 4 hours from Mexico and 2 hours from snowboarding. The campus is accessible from all parts of the Phoenix metropolitan region by public transportation, bicycle, or automobile. Students live on campus in Founder's Hall, the resident student complex, or off campus in nearby neighborhoods. The University is close to major freeways, bus lines, and Sky Harbor Airport, which is a major international airport that serves the entire Phoenix metropolitan area. Other local amenities include shopping, arts districts, and other attractions associated with a dynamic urban center.

Arizona is a land of incredible beauty, contrast, and opportunity. Tempe is located in the "Valley of the Sun", which is surrounded by beautiful mountain ranges. Within a short drive are attractions like the Grand Canyon (4½ hours), a variety of lakes and rivers (30–90 minutes), the red rocks of Sedona (2 hours), and the exquisite Sonoran Desert, just outside of town. UAT is close to every desert sport imaginable—golf, mountain biking, hiking, swimming, rollerblading, and skateboarding.

Majors and Degrees

UAT offers Bachelor of Arts, Bachelor of Science, Associate of Arts, and Associate of Science degrees in twenty advancing technology disciplines, including artificial life programming, computer forensics, digital animation, digital art and design, game art and animation, game design, game programming, network security, and robotics and embedded systems.

Academic Programs

The Bachelor of Arts and Bachelor of Science programs require a minimum of 120 semester credits, including 84 core credits, forty 300/400–level credits, and 36 general education credits. The Associate of Arts and Associate of Science programs require a minimum of 60 semester credits: 45 core credits, and 15 general education credits.

Academic Facilities

The University is open 24/7. In just about every corner of campus, there are hundreds of computers, including Macs and state-of-the-art video game consoles. Students at UAT are immersed in a world of technology. From the miles of cables and walls of servers in the open-viewed server rooms to the vast array of industry technology in the NT lab, students who love technology feel right at home.

As an institution, UAT is dedicated to planning, implementing, and sharing its research with others in technology and academia. The UAT research centers operate within the University to further knowledge creation, foster institutional and community awareness, and improve initiatives in their focal areas. In addition, each research center publishes works to the broader community through a variety of channels (technology journals, online journals, and conference papers. In 1992, the University founded its first research center, the Computer Reality Center. It performed research primarily for the computer graphics industry, with specific emphasis on the field of virtual reality. The center adopted the Hyperlearning model and developed UAT's current teaching model, Year-Round Balanced Learning. YRBL combines lecture, tutorial teaching, group recollection, student teachback, and discovery learning. Year-round classes are available both on the campus and online, and students produce projects for a graduation portfolio to demonstrate an understanding of what they are learning.

Through research of learning and teaching methodologies, the Center for Learning Excellence develops and supports educational models that enable the University to build innovative and balanced learning experiences. Its main goal is to apply its research toward developing the UAT Faculty Certification Program. This program ensures baseline effective teaching preparation within UAT's learning model for all faculty members before they are assigned to the classroom. The center routinely assesses instruction at UAT in relation to student learning outcomes.

The Center for Institutional Research is the center for ongoing institutional research that accumulates, generates, maintains, communicates, and disseminates institutional information to support assessment and general awareness of student learning. The center also evaluates and reviews the efficacy of institutional policies.

The Center for Technology Studies conducts original research and produces works published in the broader community and furthers community understanding of technology disciplines, their applications, and their relevance in the global society. Within the center is the Center for Information Assurance, which produces knowledge solely within the information assurance disciplines at UAT: computer forensics and network security at the undergraduate level and information security at the graduate level.

Whenever and wherever possible, the campus and technology resources are open to allow students and professionals alike to participate collaboratively in this endeavor, whether as team members on a student project, speaking at Technology Forum, or submitting work to the University's *Journal of Advancing Technology*.

Costs

Undergraduate tuition for 2007–08 is $7900 per semester. Tuition for UAT-Online students is $4700 per semester. Housing costs are about $6360 per year. Beginning fall 2007, a new dorm is scheduled to open, and all freshmen will be required to live on campus.

Financial Aid

Average aid per academic year for first-academic-year freshmen is $11,784. The percentage of freshmen who receive aid is 84 percent. The percentage of freshmen who receive UAT academic scholarships is 26 percent. The average amount of scholarships received per freshman student per academic year is $1200.

Faculty

UAT's faculty comprises members who are thinkers, teachers, technological gurus, industry experts, and student mentors. They garner their skills, knowledge, and expertise from a range of experiences—from the classrooms of academe to the boardrooms of industry, from community meeting halls to international conferences. They are a group governed by their passion for technology, their students, and their own academic and professional growth. Sixty-four faculty members, distinguished by their academic abilities and accomplishments within their respective fields, serve as both instructors and mentors.

Student Government

The University-sanctioned student government was formed to give the student body at UAT a collective voice and set traditions within the University. University Student Government (USG) performs important roles in encouraging self-directed Student Life organizations, coordinating student community service activities, and providing a venue for feedback between students and staff members. Students are encouraged to participate in the Student Government, which holds monthly open meetings.

Admission Requirements

The University of Advancing Technology strives to admit undergraduate students who embody its passion for technology, are a cultural match to the University, demonstrate adequate academic achievement, and have a dedication to lifelong learning. All undergraduate applicants are evaluated based on these criteria: academic history and achievements; personal expression; desire to attend UAT; how they might fit with UAT's geek-friendly culture, passion, and aptitude for technology; and the supportiveness of the applicant's network of family, friends, and peers to achieve their educational goals (for UAT-Online applicants, employer support is also evaluated). All applicants are encouraged to submit high school transcripts, ACT and/or SAT scores, Advanced Placement scores, and college transcripts, so UAT's Admissions Office may thoroughly review the applicant's academic history.

In addition to the standard admission requirements, non-U.S. citizens applying for admission to the University of Advancing Technology must provide proof of English proficiency in one of the following ways: Test of English as a Foreign Language (TOEFL) with a score of 550 or higher on the paper-based test, 79 or higher on the Internet-based test, or 213 or higher on the computer-based test; successful completion of Level 108 from an ELS Center; ASPECT English Language Proficiency Level 5; or attendance for one year at a regionally accredited U.S. college or university and completion of English 101 (or equivalent) with grade C or better. Proof of English proficiency is not required if English is the applicant's native language. Official transcripts must be submitted with an English translation and be evaluated as a U.S. high school equivalent by Educational Credential Evaluators, Inc., P.O. Box 17499, Milwaukee, Wisconsin 53217-0499, U.S.A. (http://www.ece.org).

Application and Information

UAT has an admissions application that helps both the student and the admissions staff determine if the applicant and UAT are a good match. Students should complete and submit the application to the UAT Admissions Office prior to consideration. Students may apply online at http://www.uat.edu/admissions. To request an application, students should either e-mail admissions@uat.edu or call 877-UAT-GEEK (toll-free).

UAT Admissions
University of Advancing Technology
2625 West Baseline Road
Tempe, Arizona 85283-1056
Phone: 602-383-8228
        800-658-5744 (toll-free)
E-mail: admission@uat.edu
Web site: http://www.uat.edu

UNIVERSITY OF ALASKA FAIRBANKS

FAIRBANKS, ALASKA

The University

Founded in 1917, the University provides education, research, and service in the "last frontier." The Fairbanks campus, one of three in the statewide system of higher education, is the primary administrative and research center, with branches in Bethel, Dillingham, Kotzebue, and Nome, along with rural centers throughout the state.

The total University of Alaska Fairbanks (UAF) enrollment is slightly over 10,000 students. Eighty-five percent of the students have Alaskan residency, although nearly half of the students graduated from high schools in forty-nine states and thirty-eight other countries. The nine residence halls on campus are renovated and are capable of lodging 1,322 students. The Student Apartment Complex has sixty furnished two-bedroom units reserved for sophomore and upperclass students. The Eileen Panigeo MacLean House, housing for rural students, holds 22 students. The University also manages 153 furnished apartments for students with families.

The large campus contains a core of academic buildings and residences, as well as miles of ski trails, two lakes, and an arboretum. Most of the University's research institutes, including the noted Geophysical Institute and the International Arctic Research Center, are clustered on the West Ridge. The University's Agricultural Experiment Station farm is on campus, as are a Cooperative Fish and Wildlife Research Unit and various state and federal agencies and laboratories. The University awards graduate degrees in many of the same areas as the undergraduate studies, often in conjunction with one of its research institutes. A natural science facility that houses chemistry, physics, geology, and earth sciences was completed relatively recently.

Intercollegiate athletics include men's and women's basketball, cross-country running and skiing, and riflery and women's volleyball and swim teams. The University sponsors an outstanding men's intercollegiate ice-hockey team, which plays at the 4,665-seat Carlson Center. The UAF hockey team is a member of the Central Collegiate Hockey Association (CCHA). The Student Recreation Complex houses a variety of sports and physical activities facilities, including multipurpose areas for basketball, volleyball, badminton, tennis, calisthenics, dance, gymnastics, judo, and karate; a rifle and pistol range; courts for handball, racquetball, and squash; an elevated 200-meter, three-lane jogging track; a swimming pool; weight-training and modern fitness equipment areas; an ice arena for recreational skating and hockey; a special aerobics area; and a three-story climbing wall. The cheery and roomy student union, the William Ransom Wood Center, is the focus of various out-of-class activities for students and faculty members. The center houses meeting and exhibit rooms, lounges and television areas, the student government offices, campus information, a pub, a bowling alley, a games room, a cafeteria, a snack bar, an espresso bar, and a photography darkroom.

Location

The campus of the University of Alaska Fairbanks is situated on a ridge overlooking the valley of the Tanana River and the city of Fairbanks. Serving a population of more than 85,000 within the 7,561-square-mile North Star Borough, Fairbanks is a major trade center for outlying villages in Interior Alaska. The city is connected with the rest of the state and the lower forty-eight states by air and highway. Municipal bus service is available between downtown Fairbanks, the surrounding area, and the campus. Shuttle bus service is available around the UAF campus.

Fairbanks offers the sophistication of larger cities through such luxuries as first-run movies and fine restaurants while maintaining the atmosphere of smaller, more personal towns. Denali National Park and other vast wilderness areas are close at hand, and Anchorage is 350 miles south via the Parks Highway. Members of the Fairbanks community and the University join together in the University-Fairbanks Symphony Orchestra and in many other musical and theatrical enterprises.

Majors and Degrees

The University of Alaska Fairbanks awards certificates, A.A. and A.A.S. degrees, and B.A., B.S., B.B.A., B.Ed., B.M., and B.F.A. degrees in accounting, airframe studies, Alaska Native studies, anthropology, applied accounting, applied business, applied physics, apprenticeship technology, art, arts and sciences, aviation maintenance technology, aviation technology, biochemistry, biological sciences, business administration, chemistry, civil engineering, communication, community health, computer science, culinary arts, dental assistant studies, drafting technology, early childhood, earth science, economics, electrical engineering, elementary education, emergency medical services, emergency services, English, Eskimo, fisheries, foreign languages, general science, geography (environmental studies), geological engineering, geology, ground vehicle maintenance technology, health-care reimbursement, health technology, history, human services, Japanese studies, journalism, justice, linguistics, maintenance technology, mathematics, mechanical engineering, medical assistant studies, microcomputer support specialist studies, mining engineering, molecular biology, music, Native language education, natural resources management (including forestry), Northern studies, office management and technology, paralegal studies, petroleum engineering, philosophy, phlebotomy, physics, political science, powerplant studies, process technology, psychology, renewable resources, rural development, rural human services, Russian studies, social work, sociology, statistics, technology, theater, tribal management, and wildlife biology. Preprofessional advising is available in dentistry, law, library science, medicine, physical therapy, and veterinary medicine.

Academic Programs

The academic year is divided into two semesters; registration is in early April for the fall semester and in November for the spring semester. Preregistration is available for returning students. In addition, there are three-week, six-week, and twelve-week summer sessions. UAF offers an early orientation for new students in the fall and spring semesters. The University is organized into four colleges and four professional schools: the College of Liberal Arts, the College of Natural Science and Mathematics, the College of Engineering and Mines, the College of Rural Alaska, and the Schools of Natural Resources and Agricultural Sciences, Education, Fisheries and Ocean Sciences, and Management. A minimum of 120 credits must be completed for the four-year baccalaureate degree programs.

Students who receive scores of 3 or higher on the College Board's Advanced Placement tests may be awarded credit by the University. Currently enrolled students may challenge courses for credit by successfully completing College-Level Examination Program (CLEP) examinations or by completing locally prepared examinations. Requests for advanced-placement credit and credit by examination are coordinated through the Office of Admissions.

The honors program is designed for highly motivated undergraduate students who wish to acquire a superior understanding of the natural and social sciences, the arts, and the humanities. Prospective honors students need a minimum ACT composite score of 29 or a minimum combined SAT score of approximately 1270, with a minimum 3.6 high school GPA.

Off-Campus Programs

The University maintains exchange programs with various universities in Canada; universities in Australia, Austria, Chile, Denmark, England, Finland, France, Germany, Japan, Mexico, Norway, Russia, Scotland, and Taiwan; and multiple other universities through the North 2 North Exchange program. The University also participates in the Northwest Interinstitutional Council for Study Abroad, providing students with an opportunity to enroll in liberal arts programs in Austria, England, France, Greece, Italy, and Spain. UAF is also a member of the National Student Exchange, participating with more than 180 colleges and universities throughout the United States, in U.S. territories, and at nine locations in Canada.

Academic Facilities

The Fine Arts Complex features a 480-seat theater, a 1,072-seat concert hall, FM public radio (KUAC) and educational-television (PBS) studios, an art gallery, and the Elmer E. Rasmuson Library. The library collection contains more than 1.75 million volumes, including the prestigious Alaska and Polar Regions Collection. Electronic catalogs provide access to collections in 11,000 libraries nationwide.

Students have free use of the University's academic computing facilities (Aurora), which are accessible from Windows and Macintosh computer labs and via remote access. Various schools and colleges have their own special-purpose computer labs.

The University Museum attracts more than 100,000 visitors each year to Interior Alaska and is located on the UAF campus. The museum collects, preserves, and exhibits materials from Alaska and the North.

Costs

In 2006–07, tuition and fees were $2135 per semester for full-time (15 credits) students. Nonresident students paid an additional $4185 for 15 credits of tuition each semester. Residents of Alaska, the Yukon Territory, British Columbia, and the Northwest Territories are exempt from the nonresident tuition fee. To qualify as a resident, a student must have been living in Alaska for two years. Students who initially register as nonresidents may apply for resident status after living in state for twelve months, under the University's "bona fide resident" provision. The approximate cost per semester for books and supplies was $500 and for personal items and recreation, $450. A double-occupancy residence hall room on campus costs $1495 per semester. Meals, which all residence hall occupants were required to purchase, cost approximately $1295 per semester. These costs are subject to change. Married student housing on campus was also available.

Financial Aid

A large portion of financial aid is derived from the Alaska Supplemental Education Loan Program, which is available to all students attending UAF, regardless of residency. Three kinds of aid are available: grants and scholarships (which need not be repaid), loans, and part-time employment. Students who seek financial assistance for the fall term should submit applications by February 15. Inquiries should be addressed to the Financial Aid Office, University of Alaska Fairbanks, P.O. Box 756560, Fairbanks, Alaska 99775-6560.

The Chancellor's Scholarship, a one-year tuition waiver, is available to entering freshmen with a minimum 3.0 GPA and 1150 SAT combined score or 25 ACT composite score. To apply, students should submit a scholarship application, an application for admission, a high school transcript, and test scores for review. The deadline for scholarships is February 15. National Merit finalists qualify for a four-year tuition waiver plus a $20,000 scholarship.

Faculty

Sixty-six percent of the 784 faculty members hold doctoral degrees, and many are actively engaged in research. In keeping with University policy, faculty members provide academic counseling for students. The combination of a student-faculty ratio of 15:1 and easy access to instructors for help outside of class produces a maximum educational benefit for students.

Student Government

The Associated Students of the University of Alaska Fairbanks (ASUAF) protects students' rights through its various governmental functions and also offers educational, social, recreational, and service activities. The school newspaper, *Sun Star*, is published weekly with the sponsorship of ASUAF, which also supports KSUA, the campus radio station; the international cinema and weekly movie series; and dances, concerts, and other entertainment. ASUAF publishes the results of its faculty evaluations and sends several student lobbyists to the Alaska state legislature in Juneau each spring. A student member sits on the Board of Regents of the University.

Admission Requirements

For admission to a baccalaureate program, applicants must be high school graduates with a cumulative grade point average of at least 2.0 and have earned a GPA of at least 2.5 in a high school core curriculum of 16 credits. Transfer students must also have a minimum grade point average of 2.0 in all previous college work. Applicants for a major in a scientific or technical field may be required to present a higher grade point average and to have completed specific background courses before being accepted into the major department. All entering freshmen are required to submit scores from the ACT or SAT examination prior to registration for placement in English and math courses.

Application and Information

The application deadlines are July 1 for the fall semester and November 1 for the spring semester. Applications are processed after the deadlines only as long as space is available. Applicants are notified of the admission decision as soon as all application material has been received. Only accepted students are allowed to apply for campus housing. Students who desire campus housing should apply for admission as early as possible.

For further information, applicants should contact:

Office of Admissions
University of Alaska Fairbanks
P.O. Box 757480
Fairbanks, Alaska 99775-7480
Phone: 907-474-7500
      800-478-1UAF (toll-free)
Web site: http://www.uaf.edu

The Plaza outside the classroom buildings at the University of Alaska Fairbanks. The flags represent the fifty states of the United States.

UNIVERSITY OF ALASKA SOUTHEAST
JUNEAU, KETCHIKAN, AND SITKA, ALASKA

The University

The University of Alaska Southeast (UAS) combines time-proven methods of learning with an innovative curriculum that relies heavily on the use of technology, fieldwork, and undergraduate research to create a new-century liberal arts approach. UAS graduates are excellent communicators, job-ready professionals, and well-prepared candidates for graduate school. The University does not mold its students to fit into a predictable box but guides individuals to explore and refine their unique talents and interests. UAS students discover their career paths through scientific and literary exploration, business internships, exposure to civic leaders, and artistic expression. The small class sizes and engaging faculty members allow the University to employ a more personal approach that ensures its students are being challenged academically and that the needs of each are being met. It is the mission of UAS to help students turn their passion into meaningful and fulfilling careers.

UAS has a total student population of approximately 4,100 students. The main campus in Juneau comprises 3,000 of those students; 65 percent of students are women and 35 percent are men. About 30 percent of the student body consists of people of Alaska Native, Asian, Pacific Island, African, and Hispanic ancestry.

Banfield Hall is reserved for freshman, but on-campus housing, including apartment-style housing, is available to all students. Meal plans are required for residents of Banfield Hall.

The new Student Recreation Center houses the basketball court, suspended running track, climbing wall, and weight-training and cardiovascular equipment. The new center also offers a student lounge with a wide-screen TV, pool tables, a dance floor, and a movie screen with a surround-sound system.

Location

Juneau's population is approximately 32,000. It is the third most populous city in the state and the largest city in Southeast Alaska. UAS is surrounded by the Tongass National Forest, which contains the world's last great expanse of ancient temperate rainforest. Juneau averages 56 inches of annual precipitation. The winters are surprisingly warm, with average temperatures in the high 20s, and average summer temperatures are in the high 60s.

Juneau has several daily flights to Anchorage and Seattle. It is accessible by plane and ferry but not by road. The state runs a year-round ferry service between Bellingham, Washington, and Southeast Alaska cities. Those who bring cars must use the barge service or the Alaska Marine Highway System. The ferries provide a spectacular cruise through the beautiful Inside Passage.

The main campus is located 11 miles from downtown Juneau between the shores of Auke Lake and Auke Bay. The campus is often referred to as the most beautiful place in Juneau. One glance across Auke Lake to the Mendenhall Towers, which cradle the Mendenhall Glacier, is all it takes for someone to know they've found the right place.

Majors and Degrees

UAS offers Bachelor of Arts degrees in elementary education, English (with emphases in creative writing, literature, and literature and the environment), and social science (with an emphases in anthropology, economics, government, history, psychology, and sociology). UAS also offers a Bachelor of Business Administration degree (with emphases in accounting, general business, management, and marketing); a Bachelor of Liberal Arts degree (with emphases in art, general studies, human communication, and language arts and communication); and Bachelor of Science degrees in biology, environmental science, information systems, marine biology, and mathematics.

UAS also offers associate degrees in apprenticeship technology, business administration, computer information and office systems, construction technology, early childhood education, environmental technology, fisheries technology, health information management, health sciences, nursing (through University of Alaska Anchorage), paralegal studies, and power technology (automotive, diesel, or USCG Marine Oiler).

In addition, certificate programs are available in accounting technician studies, automotive technology, child development, community wellness advocate, computer information and office systems, drafting technology, early childhood education, environmental technology, fisheries technology, health-care privacy, health information management coding specialist studies, law enforcement, outdoor skills and leadership, prenursing qualifications, preradiologic technology qualification, residential building science, small business management, and welding technology.

Academic Programs

UAS operates on a semester system, with the fall semester beginning in early September or late August, and the spring semester beginning in mid-January.

At minimum, 120 semester credits are required to complete a baccalaureate degree program, a minimum of 60 semester credits to complete an associate degree program, and a minimum of 30 semester credits to complete a certificate program. For all programs, students must maintain a minimum 2.0 GPA; in some core program areas, the minimum GPA requirement is higher.

Advanced placement credit is given to high school students who achieve scores of 3 or higher on the College Board's Advanced Placement tests. Students who are currently enrolled may challenge courses for credit through either the College-Level Examination Program (CLEP) or University challenge examinations. Requests by students for Advanced Placement credit and credit by examination are coordinated through the Office of Admissions and Records.

Academic Facilities

The Technical Education Center is located in downtown Juneau on the waterfront. It serves as the base for the vocational/technical programs, such as auto, construction, and power technology.

The Egan Library contains more than 420,000 volumes. This award-winning facility offers seating for more than 200 users, the most current computer technology for access to information, and extended hours for student study. The Learning Center, which offers tutoring programs and academic assistance, is housed in the Egan library.

The campus operates on a wireless network, which allows students access to the UAS network, the Internet, and e-mail from virtually anywhere on campus.

Costs

For purposes of tuition, a resident is any person who has been physically present in Alaska for two years and who declares their

intention to remain in Alaska indefinitely. Others exempt from nonresident fees are residents of British Columbia, Yukon, Northwest and Nunavut Territories, active military personnel stationed in Alaska and their dependents, and residents of several foreign sister cities. UAS also participates in the Western Undergraduate Exchange (WUE) program for all degree programs. Students from the fourteen-member states are eligible for WUE tuition rates.

For 2006–07, in-state full-time tuition cost $1530 a semester, or $128 per credit hour (average cost based on 12 credits). Full-time nonresident students paid $4788 a semester ($407 per credit hour, based on 12 credits). Tuition for Western Undergraduate Exchange students was $2250 a semester ($188 per credit hour, based on 12 credits).

Campus housing was available in Juneau. Freshman housing at Banfield Hall was $1750 per semester per person. Residents of Banfield Hall were required to have a roommate and purchase the meal plan, which cost an additional $985 per semester in 2006–07. Apartment-style housing with private rooms was available at a cost of $2000 per person per semester, and family housing was available at a cost of $4500 per semester. (Costs are estimated.)

Financial Aid

Prospective students should submit the Free Application for Federal Student Aid (FAFSA) at http://www.fafsa.ed.gov, using 001065 as the UAS federal school code, and visit the University's financial aid Web site at http://www.uas.alaska.edu/financial_aid.

UAS participates in the Federal Pell Grant, Federal Supplemental Educational Opportunity Grant, Federal Stafford Student Loan, and Federal Work-Study programs in addition to state student loan, family loan, and grant programs. Most aid is awarded on the basis of financial need. Some scholarships, however, are based on academic potential and performance. The deadline for merit-based UAS scholarships is February 15. To apply for need-based programs, students should request a packet from the financial aid office.

Faculty

UAS has an excellent student-faculty ratio of 12:1. The class size for lower-division courses averages between 15 and 20 students. Due to the small, intimate nature of the campus, faculty members play an integral role in their students' success and offer individual attention often unheard of at larger liberal arts institutions.

Student Government

The student government plays an important role in the development of UAS policies and activities. Students serve on a number of important committees and participate in lobbying the state legislature on behalf of students' interests.

Admission Requirements

UAS is an open-enrollment institution. Admission is on a rolling basis, and applications are processed in the order they are received. Applicants applying for the fall semester should aim to have their admissions packet complete by August 1 to allow adequate time for academic advising and financial aid planning.

Students are considered for admission when the University has the completed application, the application fee, and official transcripts (high school transcripts showing GPA and graduation date, and/or official postsecondary transcripts from all accredited institutions). Successful completion of the GED test is accepted as an equivalency of high school graduation. High school graduates from Alaska must also pass all sections of the High School Qualifying Exam to be admitted. Students wishing to pursue a bachelor's degree are required to submit SAT or ACT test scores as well. Applicants out of high school for longer than three years are not required to submit SAT or ACT test scores. Applicants generally receive an initial response within two weeks of receipt of the completed application packet.

It is the goal of UAS to help anyone who has a strong desire to pursue higher education. Students whose cumulative GPA is below 2.0 are admitted on probation and must maintain a minimum GPA of 2.0 during their first semester.

Application and Information

To apply, students must complete an application form and send it with the required $40 processing fee to the Office of Admissions and Records on the Juneau campus. Students can mail or fax applications or apply online.

For further information, application forms, or any other materials, prospective applicants can use the inquiry form on the UAS Web site or contact:

Office of Admissions and Records
University of Alaska Southeast
11120 Glacier Highway
Juneau, Alaska 99801
Phone: 907-796-6100
 877-465-4827 (toll-free)
Fax: 907-796-6365
E-mail: uas.info@uas.alaska.edu
Web site: http://www.uas.alaska.edu

Environmental science students at UAS have measured the face of the LeConte Glacier near Petersburg.

UNIVERSITY OF THE PACIFIC
STOCKTON, CALIFORNIA

The University

The University of the Pacific was established in 1851 as California's first chartered institution of higher education. The University's classic college environment combined with modern facilities provides students with the best of both worlds. An independent university known for the diversity of its academic programs and outstanding teaching faculty, Pacific has also acquired a reputation for educational innovation, as demonstrated by the development of its cooperative engineering program, numerous accelerated programs, and its three-year professional programs in pharmacy and dentistry. The University, which draws its 3,500 undergraduate students from more than forty states and fifty countries, is located in a residential area of the city of Stockton. The architecture and landscaping of the 175-acre main campus provide an Ivy League type of setting.

The University of the Pacific is a residential university, offering on-campus housing in fourteen residence halls, eight fraternity and sorority houses, and six apartment complexes (including a married student apartment complex). Approximately 70 percent of the undergraduate students live on campus. Excellent support services are available to Pacific students to enhance their academic and personal development; these are offered through the Career Resource Center, the Office of Services of Students with Disabilities, the Health and Wellness Center, and the Counseling Center. Extracurricular activities include plays, operas, concerts, speakers, and movies in one of four theater/auditoriums on campus; excellent athletic programs at the NCAA Division I intercollegiate, club, intramural, and physical education levels; broadcasting (on KUOP-FM, KPAC, and Tiger TV), journalism (the *Pacifican*), and forensics; professional organizations, a Greek Society, and honor societies; and more than 100 special interest clubs. The McCaffrey Center (student union) houses a grocery store, a bookstore, a movie theater, a games area, two additional dining areas, and the Associated Students of the University of the Pacific (ASUOP) offices. Recreation and athletic facilities include three gyms; playing fields; tennis, volleyball (indoor and outdoor), basketball (indoor and outdoor), and racquetball courts; a 28,000-seat stadium; the 6,000-seat Spanos Center; an Olympic-size swimming pool; an athletic training and fitness center; and a student fitness center.

The University's Arthur A. Dugoni School of Dentistry is located in San Francisco, and Pacific's McGeorge School of Law is in Sacramento. Professional and graduate programs on the Stockton campus include the Doctor of Pharmacy (Pharm.D.) degree; master's and doctoral programs in a variety of areas in education; Master of Arts programs in communication, music therapy, psychology, and sport sciences; Master of Business Administration; Master of Science programs in biological sciences, chemistry, pharmaceutical sciences, and speech-language pathology; and Doctor of Philosophy programs in chemistry and pharmaceutical sciences. Master of Science (M.S.), Doctor of Philosophy (Ph.D.), and Doctor of Physical Therapy (D.P.T.) programs are also available.

Location

Stockton (population 280,000) is California's largest inland port. Situated between San Francisco and the Sierra Nevada, the area provides unlimited cultural and recreational opportunities within a short drive, including entertainment in San Francisco; skiing, camping, and backpacking in the Sierra Nevada; and waterskiing and boating in the California Delta area. Stockton is served by Amtrak, bus lines, and three major freeways. Sacramento and Oakland International Airports are both within an hour drive from campus. The climate during the school year is pleasantly warm, with the rainy season generally restricted to the period between December and March. Summer temperatures are in the 80- and 90-degree ranges. Stockton has a diverse ethnic and economic background, offering opportunities for cultural enrichment and community service. For more information, prospective students should visit http://www.pacific.edu/stockton.

Majors and Degrees

The University of the Pacific offers the undergraduate degrees of Bachelor of Arts, Bachelor of Arts in Liberal Studies, Bachelor of Fine Arts, Bachelor of Music, Bachelor of Science, and Bachelor of Science in Engineering. Major areas are accounting, art, arts and entertainment management, Asian language and studies (emphasis in Japanese and Chinese), athletic training, biochemistry, biological sciences, business administration, business law, chemistry, chemistry-biology, communication, computer science, dental hygiene, economics, education (single and multiple subject teaching credentials), engineering (bio, civil, computer, electrical, management, and mechanical), engineering physics, English, entrepreneurship, finance, French, geology, geophysics, graphic design, history, human resources, international business, international relations and global studies, international studies, Japanese, liberal studies, management informational systems, marketing, mathematics, music (composition, education, history, jazz studies, management, performance, and therapy), philosophy, physical sciences, physics, political science, psychology, real estate management, religious and classic studies, social science, sociology, Spanish, speech-language pathology, sport management, sports medicine, studio art, and theater arts. For a complete listing of majors, prospective students should visit the University's Web site at http://www.pacific.edu/majors.

Special programs include a five-year bachelor's/M.B.A. option; a six-year bachelor's/J.D. option; several predental/D.D.S. accelerated programs; several prepharmacy/Doctor of Pharmacy accelerated programs; a five-year engineering program, which incorporates twelve months of mandatory and paid cooperative education work experience; a three-year accelerated Bachelor of Science degree in dental hygiene; an accelerated three-semester Master of Art program in international relations; an accelerated Bachelor of Science/Master of Science program in speech-language pathology; an accelerated Bachelor of Art/Master of Art or accelerated Bachelor of Art/Doctor of Physical Therapy (D.P.T.) or Doctor of Philosophy in physical therapy degree; an accelerated preliminary or secondary-teaching-credential program (that includes the year of student teaching); an optional cooperative education program in the liberal arts; and preprofessional studies in dentistry, law, medicine, pharmacy, physical therapy, and other fields.

Academic Programs

The University emphasizes a personal approach to education, featuring small classes and close working relationships between students and faculty members. The undergraduate academic programs are arranged through seven schools and colleges, each having its own distinctive features. Students enroll in one division but can take classes in the others and share common facilities. The College of the Pacific is a departmentally arranged liberal arts and sciences college, offering more than sixty different majors, minors, and preprofessional programs. Undergraduate professional divisions include the Conservatory of Music, the Eberhardt School of Business, the Benerd School of Education, the School of Engineering and Computer Science, and the School of International Studies. The Thomas J. Long School of Pharmacy and Health Sciences includes both undergraduate and first professional degree students. The Center for Professional and Continuing Education also offers special academic opportunities.

Each of the University's undergraduate divisions has its own academic requirements. However, the University emphasizes a commitment to the liberal arts and requires all students to have exposure to the humanities, behavioral sciences, natural sciences, and social sciences through a University-wide general education program. Many freshmen enter the University without having decided on a major area of study, and they work extensively with their academic advisers before selecting a major. The liberal arts college allows a considerable amount of flexibility in the academic programs, while the professional schools are more structured in their academic requirements. All divisions on the Stockton campus follow a semester calendar; however, the professional pharmacy, physical therapy, and dental hygiene programs have three terms per year.

Off-Campus Programs

The University of the Pacific currently participates in more than 100 programs in seventy countries in Africa, Asia, Central and South America, the Middle East, North America and the Caribbean, Oceania, and Western and Eastern Europe. Students may pursue interests in virtually any academic discipline and may be allowed independent study, travel, and homestay opportunities. Pacific has arrangements for participation in study abroad direct exchanges with individual universities as well as with the University Studies Abroad Consortium (USAC), the Council on International Education Exchange (CIEE), the Institute for the International Education of Students (IES), and the International Student Exchange Program (ISEP). For more information, students should visit http://www.pacific.edu/studentlife/ips.

Cooperative education and internships play important roles at the University. All engineering students spend two 6-month periods off campus working in full-time paid co-op positions. Students enrolled in all other University divisions have the option of participating in part-time or full-time internships, arranged through the Career Resource Center. For more information, prospective students should visit http://www.pacific.edu/exp.

Academic Facilities

Excellent equipment and facilities are available to assist students in their academic work outside the classroom. The Stockton campus of the University of the Pacific maintains a main library with 375,000 volumes, 1,400 print and more than 19,000 electronically accessible periodicals, 690,000 microform items, and 13,000 video and audio units. Approximately 105 computer workstations and 520 study spaces at tables, carrels, and group study rooms are available for student use. In addition, a science and technology library is maintained by the School of Pharmacy and Health Sciences. Students have access to extensive computer facilities. Also available for students are the Educational Resource Center, language laboratories, the drama studio, music practice rooms, the music laboratory, and the student advising center. For more information, prospective students should visit http://www.pacific.edu/onlinetour.

Costs

For 2006–07, tuition and fees were $26,920, and room and board were $8700.

Financial Aid

The University of the Pacific encourages students to apply for financial aid from all sources, including local clubs and organizations, state and federal programs, and the University. It is the intention of the University, within the limits of its resources, to provide assistance to promising students who would not otherwise be able to attend. To this end, the University has developed a financial aid program that includes scholarships, grants, loans, and job opportunities. Financial aid awards from Pacific are based on a combination of financial need and/or academic achievement. In recent years, Pacific has significantly increased its merit-based scholarship programs and, in 1997, became the first institution to provide matching scholarships to new students who receive a Cal Grant (California state gift aid). More than 75 percent of the student body receive some type of financial aid, and on-campus jobs are available through the Career Resource Center. The priority date to apply for financial aid is February 15 for the fall semester. For more information, prospective students should visit http://www.pacific.edu/financialaid.

Faculty

Of the 400 full-time faculty members on the Stockton campus, 93 percent have earned doctoral degrees or the highest degree in their field. The priority of Pacific's faculty is the education of individual students rather than research. The faculty members are actively engaged in classroom teaching and academic advising and also participate in numerous student social activities on campus. The faculty-student ratio is 1:14. For more information, prospective students should visit http://www.pacific.edu/faculty.

Student Government

The ASUOP, the student government organization, provides many services to the campus. The ASUOP president and Senate express the students' views as they work with the University administration. ASUOP operates a 200-seat movie theater, a grocery store, and a multicultural center. ASUOP Presents brings nationally known speakers and lecturers to the campus, and a very active social commission plans an extensive activities calendar that includes films, festivals, dances, and concerts on campus as well as off-campus events and trips. Each school and college also has its own student association, and all are concerned with both academic and social activities. Students are included on committees reviewing academic affairs and the curriculum structure, evaluating courses and faculty members, and planning future facilities and programs. For more information, prospective students should visit http://www.pacific.edu/asuop.

Admission Requirements

The University of the Pacific seeks freshman applicants who have had strong college-preparatory backgrounds of four academic subjects each semester. A challenging secondary school program of 4 years of English, 4 years of social studies, 3 years of mathematics, 2 years of laboratory sciences, and 2 or more years of foreign language is highly recommended. Science students should have an additional year of math and laboratory science that includes chemistry, physics, and higher mathematics. The University requires an official high school transcript, a counselor or teacher recommendation, SAT or ACT scores, and a personal essay. For more information, prospective students should visit http://www.pacific.edu/admission.

Application and Information

Out-of-state and international students are encouraged to apply, and approximately 240 transfer students and 825 freshmen enroll each year. Early action (nonbinding admission) is available for outstanding students (applying into most programs) who apply by November 15. All students applying for prepharmacy, predentistry, and dental hygiene also use the November 15 deadline. The regular fall application date (for all other programs) is January 15. All interested students are encouraged to arrange with the Office of Admissions to visit the campus. Further information may be obtained by contacting:

Office of Admissions
University of the Pacific
Stockton, California 95211

Phone: 209-946-2211
E-mail: admission@pacific.edu
Web site: http://www.pacific.edu/admission

These students are meeting outside the Holt Memorial Library with the Robert Burns Tower in the background.

UNIVERSITY OF WYOMING

LARAMIE, WYOMING

UNIVERSITY
OF WYOMING
New Thinking

The University

The University of Wyoming, a public land-grant institution founded in 1886, is a reflection of the global community it serves. The extensive range of academic programs offered at UW, as the school is affectionately known, inspires the development of new thinking and promotes fulfilling careers throughout the rapidly evolving world.

The research done by the professors and students of the University of Wyoming pushes the boundaries of modern science and technology, meriting UW's classification as a Carnegie Doctoral/Research University–Extensive.

It is this academic ambition that has allowed UW to provide high-quality undergraduate and graduate education, research, and service since its inception.

Wyoming, unique among the fifty states, has only one university. UW enjoys tremendous support from within its state as well as from an alumni network that spans the globe. More than 13,130 students from all parts of the U.S., and sixty-seven other countries attend UW classes in Laramie and at outreach sites around the state. The variety of students at UW enriches the educational experience for all by fostering a multicultural environment that encourages sharing and learning about those with different heritages and cultural backgrounds. It is this dialogue that continues to promote respect and appreciation for diversity.

UW offers bachelor's degree programs in six undergraduate colleges: the Colleges of Agriculture, Arts and Sciences, Business, Education, Engineering, and Health Sciences. Undergraduate education is a high priority at UW. More than 89 percent of the undergraduate courses are taught by professors, and the average class size is 29 students. UW also offers graduate and professional programs, including the Doctor of Pharmacy and the Juris Doctor.

There are more than 200 recognized campus clubs and organizations, including thirteen national fraternities and sororities, honor and professional societies, political and religious organizations, and special interest groups. Students have the opportunity to participate in more than sixty different intramural and club sports. UW is a Division I member of the NCAA and competes in the Mountain West Conference in seventeen men's and women's sports. Campus recreational facilities include the Wyoming Union, which recently underwent a $10-million renovation and includes the UW bookstore, eating establishments, student computers, study areas, and a variety of services and resources for students. Additional facilities on campus include Half Acre Gym, an indoor climbing wall, an eighteen-hole golf course, tennis and racquetball courts, weight rooms, two swimming pools, rifle and archery ranges, indoor and outdoor tracks, softball and baseball fields, and a hockey rink.

UW houses 2,400 students in six residence halls, and freshmen are required to live on campus during their first year. While primarily coed, the residence halls offer a number of unique living environments, including quiet/study floors, special interest floors, honors floors, single-sex floors, and other academic living environments. UW also offers fourteen different Freshman Interest Groups, which are learning communities that offer common living areas and clustered classes to students with similar academic areas of interest.

Location

UW's 785-acre campus is located at the foot of the Rocky Mountains in Laramie, a scenic town of 30,000 people in southeastern Wyoming. Many UW students enjoy the easy access to Alpine and Nordic skiing, snowboarding, snowmobiling, hiking, backpacking, camping, hunting, fishing, rock climbing, and mountain biking. Laramie—with its blue skies, clean air, and 320 days of sunshine a year—is a friendly and supportive university town, conveniently located 45 miles west of Wyoming's capital, Cheyenne, and only 130 miles northwest of Denver, Colorado.

Majors and Degrees

UW offers eighty undergraduate programs within its six colleges, leading to B.A., B.S., B.F.A., and B.S.N. degrees.

The College of Agriculture offers majors in agricultural business (with options in agribusiness management, farm and ranch management, and international agriculture), agricultural communications, agroecology, animal and veterinary sciences (with options in animal biology, business, communication, meat science and food technology, pre–veterinary science, production, and range livestock), family and consumer science (with options in child development, dietetics, family services, human nutrition and food, and textiles and merchandising), microbiology, molecular biology, and rangeland ecology and watershed management.

The College of Arts and Sciences offers majors in American studies, anthropology, art, astronomy/astrophysics, biology, botany, chemistry, communication, criminal justice, English, French, geography and recreation, geology (with options in earth science and environment/natural resources), German, history, humanities/fine arts, international studies, journalism, management, mathematical sciences, mathematics, music (with options in education, performance, and theory and composition), philosophy, physics, political science, psychology, Russian, social science, sociology, Spanish, statistics, theater and dance, wildlife/fisheries, women's studies, and zoology and physiology as well as the option of a self-designed major.

The College of Business offers majors in accounting, business administration, business economics, economics, finance, management, and marketing.

The College of Education offers majors in elementary and special education, elementary education, industrial technology education, secondary education (with options in agriculture, art, business, English, family and consumer sciences, industrial technology, mathematics, modern languages, sciences, and social studies), special education, and trades and industrial education.

The College of Engineering offers majors in architectural engineering, chemical engineering (with environmental and petroleum options), civil engineering, computer engineering, computer science, electrical engineering (with bioengineering and computer engineering options), management information systems (with accounting, business, and computer science options), and mechanical engineering.

The College of Health Sciences offers majors in dental hygiene, exercise and sports science, health education, health sciences, nursing, pharmacy, physical education teaching, social work, and speech-language and hearing sciences.

UW offers preprofessional programs in dentistry, forestry, law, medicine, nursing, occupational therapy, optometry, pharmacy, physical therapy, and veterinary medicine. The School of Environment and Natural Resources also offers interdisciplinary studies that can be combined with course work in seven other fields of study, including the humanities, physical sciences, and social sciences.

Academic Programs

The UW academic calendar consists of two semesters and a complete summer session. Depending on their degree program, students are required to complete 120 to 164 credit hours for graduation. Undergraduate programs for most majors can be completed in four years. Students may choose to double major within the same college, or they may pursue majors in two separate colleges for a cross-college major. Minors are also available in many areas. All students are required to complete the University Studies Program, which is a core curriculum that assists students in developing their knowledge of oral and written communication, mathematics, sci-

ence, diversity, global awareness, government, and culture. The University honors program provides academically ambitious undergraduates innovative and intellectual learning opportunities. Award-winning faculty members, unique and challenging course work, and senior research projects are the hallmarks of this program.

Off-Campus Programs

UW has approximately 350 international students and close to 100 international researchers/scholars during any given academic year. This diverse community represents some sixty-seven countries. International Students Services provides support to this population through an extensive orientation program, the Friendship Families program, the International Neighbors program, and the International Resource Center.

International Student Services coordinates the National Student Exchange (NSE), which is a domestic student exchange consortium of more than 180 colleges and universities throughout the U.S. In addition, NSE host sites are available in Canada, Puerto Rico, the Virgin Islands, and Guam. Membership in the NSE provides UW students with access to thousands of unique academic programs, classes, and faculty members on host campuses for either a semester or an academic year.

The UW Outreach School extends the university learning experience to Wyoming and the nation through credit and noncredit programs, University of Wyoming Television, Wyoming Public Radio, and the UW/Casper College Center. Credit programs are delivered via Internet/Web-based instruction, compressed video, audio teleconferencing, flexible enrollment (correspondence study), and on-site instruction. Select programs are offered, and degree availability may be limited.

Academic Facilities

The University libraries' collections number nearly 1.3 million volumes and offer links to a variety of library service collections. The William Robertson Coe Library houses materials in the social sciences, humanities, visual and performing arts, business, education, and health sciences as well as more than 2 million federal publications and the Audio Visual Library, a collection of 4,000 video and film titles. Other libraries include the Science Library, the Brinkerhoff Earth Resources Information Center (geology library), and the Rocky Mountain Herbarium Research Collection. Additional collections are housed in the American Heritage Center and the George W. Hooper Law Library. A branch library is located at the National Park Service Research Center in Jackson, Wyoming. UW libraries participate in the Colorado Alliance of Research Libraries and in Region Four of the National Network of Libraries of Medicine. In addition, FERRET provides high-speed access to UW's online library catalogs.

Costs

UW tuition and fees for full-time undergraduates in the 2007–08 academic year are $3366 for Wyoming residents and $9750 for non-residents (based on an average class load of 14 credit hours). Room and board (double occupancy, unlimited meal plan) costs are $7274. Estimated expenses include $1000 for books and $2000 for personal expenses.

Financial Aid

Nearly 80 percent of all UW students receive financial assistance. More than $67 million is available in the form of scholarships, loans, grants, and work-study opportunities. The Free Application for Federal Student Aid (FAFSA) is required for need-based assistance (loans, grants, work-study) and for many scholarships. Most scholarships at UW are based on academic merit. UW participates in the Western Undergraduate Exchange (WUE) program, which is awarded through the Peak Achievement Scholarship. The Peak Achievement Scholarship is also available to students from non-WUE states. The priority deadline for financial aid is March 1.

Faculty

More than 700 professors from the world's most respected colleges and universities have come to teach at UW. Recognized nationally and internationally as experts, 81 percent of the professors hold the highest degrees in their fields. UW professors are deeply committed to the success of their students. Only a small number of undergraduate courses are taught by graduate assistants, and many of the most distinguished and accomplished professors at UW teach first-year courses. UW maintains a low student-faculty ratio (15:1), which allows for individualized attention, instruction, and academic advising, as well as the inclusion of undergraduates in cutting-edge research projects.

Student Government

The Associated Students of the University of Wyoming (ASUW) is composed all students at UW. ASUW serves as the voice of the students, and its legislation impacts many aspects of student life. The ASUW Senate acts as a liaison between the student body and the administration as well as the UW Board of Trustees and local and state governments. The student body president also sits as an *ex officio* member of the UW Board of Trustees. UW encourages all students to actively participate in ASUW.

Admission Requirements

To ensure admission, high school graduates and new first-year students with fewer than 30 transferable college credit hours should have a cumulative high school GPA of 2.75 or above (Wyoming residents) or 3.0 or above (nonresidents). Students should have a composite ACT score of 20 or greater or an SAT verbal/math score of 960 or greater. In addition, all students have completed 4 units of English, 3 units of mathematics, 3 units of science (including a physical science), and 3 units of cultural context courses (behavioral or social sciences, visual arts, performing arts, humanities, or foreign languages). Admission with conditions can be granted to students who do not meet these standards but have a minimum 2.5 GPA or a 2.25 GPA with a composite ACT score of at least 20 or an SAT score of at least 960. Transfer students with 30 or more transferable semester credit hours must have a minimum cumulative college GPA of 2.0.

Application and Information

Students must submit a completed UW Application for Admission, official high school or college transcripts, ACT or SAT scores, and a $40 nonrefundable application fee. Students may apply and pay the application fee online at the Web address listed in this description. UW strongly encourages all prospective students and their parents to visit the campus.

Admissions Office
Department 3435
University of Wyoming
1000 East University Avenue
Laramie, Wyoming 82071-3435
Phone: 307-766-5160
        800-DIAL-WYO (342-5996; toll-free)
E-mail: why-wyo@uwyo.edu
Web site: http://www.uwyo.edu/

Historic Old Main at the University of Wyoming was built in 1886.

WARNER PACIFIC COLLEGE
PORTLAND, OREGON

The College

Warner Pacific College prepares the next generation of leaders by providing educational experiences in the liberal arts, purposefully taught with a Christian worldview. Its academic programs encourage students to explore life's most significant questions and learn to manage complex answers. The distinctive humanities core curriculum is designed to explore the paradoxes inherent in the human experience through a foundation of faith. Most importantly, Warner Pacific's liberal arts program equips students to lead and serve in a world challenged by a rapidly changing cultural landscape.

Since its founding in 1937, Warner Pacific has developed a diverse liberal arts curriculum. Today, more than twenty-three fields of undergraduate study are offered as well as a certificate in family life education, four preprofessional programs, an adult degree completion program, and four master's programs, opening the doors to more than a thousand possible futures.

Students are challenged in the classroom and encouraged to develop leadership skills by participating in on-campus activities and completing internships with organizations throughout the Portland metropolitan area. Applying theory to real life, students are able to maximize their learning experience. In addition, students are empowered to impact their world for Christ by serving in their community and beyond—consequently, Warner Pacific students tutor young children, visit the elderly, work with the homeless, and participate in many other worthwhile projects. Opportunities are also available for study-abroad programs through Warner Pacific's partnership with the Coalition for Christian Colleges and Universities.

Life on the Warner Pacific campus reverberates with activity, including residence life events aimed at building community, intramurals, drama, music, multicultural events, and ethics bowl competition. Warner Pacific is a member of the National Association of Intercollegiate Athletics (NAIA Division II) and the Cascade Collegiate Conference. Women's sports include basketball, cross-country, soccer, track and field, and volleyball. Men compete in basketball, cross-country, soccer, and track and field. In 2005, both the men's and women's basketball teams achieved national ranking, successfully competing in the NAIA Division II national tournament.

Total enrollment at Warner Pacific exceeds 650, with students representing twenty-one states, twelve countries, and twenty-seven denominations. Student housing includes traditional men's and women's residence halls, apartments, and houses. Residence rooms offer private phones and individual high-speed Internet connections. Wireless Internet connections are available for students throughout the campus.

Graduate programs are available that lead to a Master of Arts in biblical and theological studies, a Master of Religion, a Master of Education, and a Master of Science in management and organizational leadership (available through the Adult Degree Program).

Location

Warner Pacific is an urban campus adjacent to 195-acre Mt. Tabor Park, just 15 minutes from downtown Portland, Oregon. Situated in the beautiful Pacific Northwest, the city of Portland has been named by Next Generation Consulting as the sixth-hippest city in the nation. With reliable bus and light-rail transportation available, students are able to take advantage of diverse cultural, recreational, employment, and internship opportunities. Snow-capped mountains, rugged coastlines, and the Columbia gorge are all an hour away, where students enjoy skiing, hiking, kayaking, windsurfing, and exploring nature.

Majors and Degrees

Warner Pacific offers both Associate of Arts (A.A.) and Associate of Science (A.S.) degrees as well as Bachelor of Arts (B.A.) and Bachelor of Science (B.S.) degrees. A.A. degrees are offered in Christian education, general studies, organizational dynamics (through the Adult Degree Program), and youth ministries. A.S. degrees are offered in business administration, health sciences, and social sciences. Majors in American studies, English, history, liberal studies, music, music and youth ministries, and religion and Christian ministries lead to the B.A. degree. Majors in biological science, business administration, developmental psychology, early childhood/elementary education, health and human kinetics, human development, human development and family studies, middle/high school education, music business, music education, physical science, social science, and social work lead to the B.S. degree.

The Teacher Education Program is approved by the Oregon Teacher Standards and Practices Commission. The curriculum provides a Christian liberal arts education along with preparation in a teaching specialty. Extended field-based practicums and student-teaching experiences are an integral part of the program. Warner Pacific graduates have established an excellent reputation in the education community and are employed both nationally and internationally.

Academic Programs

In order to provide Christian excellence and an individualized education, students take courses in three categories: core studies, a major area of study, and elective credits. In general, each of these categories requires a third of a student's total program. A minor may be chosen as a part of the elective program. Unique at Warner Pacific is the humanities core curriculum, which is based on an interdisciplinary approach to learning designed to explore the ethical and pragmatic dilemmas of the human experience.

Course work to complete a bachelor's degree is available during the summer. In addition, the Adult Degree Program makes it possible for qualified adult learners to earn a Bachelor of Science in business administration or human development within a nontraditional course design and evening schedule.

The College operates on a semester calendar. The core studies include a minimum of 42 semester credits divided among specific requirements in communications, humanities, religion, mathematics, laboratory science, social science, fine arts, and physical education/health. The major area of study requires completion of certain courses as specified in the College course catalog. The remainder of the credits may be earned through elective course work and/or a minor concentration, for a total of 124 semester credit hours.

Off-Campus Programs

Through the Oregon Independent Colleges Association, Warner Pacific has cooperative relationships with all of the regionally accredited private colleges and universities in the state. In addition, Warner Pacific accepts the completed Associate of Arts transfer degree from Oregon community colleges and the Associate of Arts direct transfer agreement (DTA) degree from Clark

College in Vancouver, Washington, as having fulfilled the core requirements, with the exception of two religion and two upper-division humanities courses.

ROTC programs are available in cooperation with the University of Portland; study opportunities and laboratory access at the Oregon Health Sciences University in Portland are also available. The College participates in a consortium of colleges that maintains the Malheur (eastern Oregon) High Desert Study Center and is a member of the Council for Christian Colleges and Universities, which provides study opportunities in Oxford, England; Cairo, Egypt; Israel (Middle East Studies); Russia; Latin America; China; Sydney, Australia; Uganda; Los Angeles, California (Film Studies); Martha's Vineyard (Contemporary Music Studies); and Washington, D.C. (American Studies).

Academic Facilities

The Otto F. Linn Library provides study areas and housing for a collection of nearly 53,000 books and 450 periodicals. Access to more than 500,000 titles is available through the OPALL Consortium, a computer network that links the College with major public and university collections in Oregon and across the United States. Two biology, one physics, and two chemistry labs and an electron microscope are available. A performing arts auditorium and a small lecture/performance hall feature concerts and dramatic productions. There is a student computer lab as well as modem access in every student residence and wireless access in academic buildings.

Costs

Annual costs for the 2006–07 academic year were $20,480 for tuition (12 to 18 credits per semester) and $5740 for room and board.

Financial Aid

Warner Pacific believes that any student who demonstrates the ability and motivation to learn should have access to Christian higher education; therefore, the staff is committed to helping parents and students find the necessary financial resources through federal and state assistance, personal and federally insured loans, private scholarships and programs, institutional assistance, and parental and student contributions. More than 90 percent of Warner students receive some type of aid, whether institutional or otherwise. In order to determine the amount of assistance a student qualifies for, the Financial Aid Office should receive a completed Free Application for Federal Student Aid (FAFSA) by April 15.

The College manages nearly $3 million in institutional assistance each year in the form of competitive academic merit scholarships and fellowships, talent grants in music, international student awards, assistance designed to enhance ethnic diversity on campus, various types of church-related assistance (including a $2500 grant to members of the Church of God, which is headquartered in Anderson, Indiana), and awards for dependents of alumni. The scholarship priority application deadline is February 1. Students may be eligible to work on campus and are assisted in locating employment off campus.

Faculty

Warner Pacific faculty members are committed to excellence. With a 14:1 student-faculty ratio and small class sizes, students receive the individualized attention that meaningful scholarship requires. Each course is embedded with critical ethical issues

relevant to the subject matter. Students are challenged to think critically and reflect deeply to find their place in an increasingly complex world. Students thrive under the leadership of dedicated professors, many of whom serve as mentors, academic advisers, and advisers to student organizations and clubs.

Student Government

Democratic self-government is essential to the development of maturity, judgment, and leadership. Student life at Warner Pacific mirrors this process. Students, administration, and faculty members enter into this process by mutual consent. The Associated Students of Warner Pacific College (ASWPC) is the executive body, composed of duly elected and appointed officers and representatives. The ASWPC, operating under its own grant of powers, creates policy that contributes to the governance of student life and activities and organizes such activities. It develops and coordinates an active social and spiritual life program to meet the needs of all students.

Admission Requirements

Warner Pacific College selects candidates for admissions who value a Christian liberal arts education and provide evidence of academic achievement, aptitude, and the ability to benefit from and contribute to the opportunities at the College. Graduation from an accredited high school (or the test equivalent) is required for admission. A strong college-preparatory program is recommended. A minimum GPA of 2.5, along with a combined SAT score (critical reading and math) of at least 910 or an ACT composite score of at least 19, is required. The GPA of first-time freshmen averages 3.3. The average combined SAT score is 1010, and the average composite ACT score is 22. Official transcripts from each high school, college, or university attended should be sent directly from the institution to Warner Pacific College, Office of Admissions. An essay and signed community covenant is also required, along with a nonrefundable application fee of $50. A personal interview and references may be required. Students with a GPA of less than 2.5 may be considered for provisional acceptance. Transfer students with more than 20 semester credit hours are required to have a minimum 2.0 cumulative college GPA (4.0 scale).

Application and Information

Warner Pacific has a priority deadline of January 31 and a regular deadline of March 15. Applications are also accepted on a rolling basis throughout the calendar year. The following must be supplied in order for a student to be considered for admission: the application (including a signed community covenant and the nonrefundable $50 fee), the personal essay, an official transcript from high school and each college/university attended, as well as official SAT or ACT scores. Applicants can expect official notification of acceptance status within 24 hours of receipt of ALL required materials. Requests for further information and all forms should be addressed to:

Admissions Office
Warner Pacific College
2219 Southeast 68th Avenue
Portland, Oregon 97215
Phone: 503-517-1020
        800-804-1510 (toll-free)
Fax: 503-517-1352
E-mail: admissions@warnerpacific.edu
Web site: http://www.warnerpacific.edu

WESTMINSTER COLLEGE
SALT LAKE CITY, UTAH

The College

Westminster College is the only private, comprehensive liberal arts college in Utah. Impassioned teaching and active learning are the hallmarks of the Westminster experience. The College prepares its students for success through a strong foundation of liberal education combined with cutting-edge professional programs at both the undergraduate and graduate levels. The learning environment is interdisciplinary, experiential, and personal, led by faculty members who are here because they love to teach. Deeply committed to each student's success, Westminster College is a challenging and supportive community of learners where students take full advantage of the unique learning environment: the campus, the city, and the mountains.

Located where Salt Lake City meets the Rocky Mountains, Westminster is tucked into the quaint and eclectic Sugarhouse neighborhood of Salt Lake City and provides a welcome academic haven for learners. Distinguished by old-growth trees, a small creek, and a graceful blend of old and new architecture, the urban College campus still provides plenty of green space to enjoy in the midst of the city. The College's on-campus housing, which accommodates 500 students, includes new apartment-style suites featuring entertainment systems and cooking facilities. Off-campus rental housing is readily available in the neighborhood.

The current enrollment is approximately 2,500. Undergraduates make up 80 percent of the student body, with graduate students making up 20 percent. Students come to Westminster from twenty-six states and five countries. The average student age is 24, and the undergraduate ratio of men to women is 21:29.

Student life includes student government; the activities council, which plans social events; leadership development conferences; multiple lecture series; and more than sixty clubs and organizations that are focused on both academic and cocurricular activities.

Westminster College offers intercollegiate basketball, cross-country, golf, and soccer for men and basketball, cross-country, golf, soccer, and volleyball for women. Teams compete in the Frontier Conference (NAIA). Men's club lacrosse is also offered.

Student services include academic advising, career planning and placement, internships, personal counseling, tutoring, and testing.

Residential students are required to participate in a meal plan. Daily selections include a burger bar, a pizza station, a Mexican buffet, a fruit and salad bar, and daily specials.

Location

Salt Lake City, rated as one of the ten most fun places to live and home of the 2002 Winter Olympics and the Sundance Film Festival, is a metropolitan area of approximately 1.3 million people. Downtown Salt Lake is 10 minutes from the campus by bus, car, or bicycle. Attractions include professional sports events, ballet, theater, concerts, and shopping to suit all tastes. A new Campus Concierge program facilitates student access to cultural events, recreational and entertainment options, student discounts, and volunteer opportunities.

Salt Lake and the surrounding areas have four distinct seasons, with limited amounts of rain and snow in the valley and moderate temperatures. However, the Wasatch Mountains, a section of the Rockies that borders the Salt Lake Valley on the east, are famous for the "greatest snow on earth." With approximately 500 inches of annual snowfall, these mountains are ideal for winter sports enthusiasts as well as for those who enjoy summer hiking, biking, and camping. Ten world-class ski and snowboard resorts lie within an hour's drive of the campus, and sixteen national parks and recreational areas are within a day's drive or less. Golf, backpacking, mountain biking, kayaking, wakeboarding, mountain climbing, canyoneering, spelunking, and rafting are all within easy reach of the campus.

Majors and Degrees

Westminster College offers more than seventy academic programs, including Bachelor of Arts and Bachelor of Science degrees in the following areas: accounting, art, aviation, biology, business (accounting, finance, general business, human resource management, information resource management, management, and marketing), chemistry, communication, computer science, economics, education (early childhood, elementary, secondary, and special education), English, financial services, history, international business, justice studies, mathematics, nursing, philosophy, physics, political studies, preprofessional programs (dentistry, law, medicine, veterinary medicine, and 3-2 engineering), psychology, social science, and sociology.

In addition to the above-listed majors, the College offers minors in many of those program areas plus the following areas: anthropology, environmental studies, French, gender studies, music, political science, religion, Spanish, and theater arts.

Academic Programs

By integrating a liberal arts foundation with professional education, Westminster exhibits features of both a liberal arts college and a comprehensive university. Students are challenged to experiment with ideas, raise questions, critically examine alternatives, and make informed decisions. Students are also encouraged to accept responsibility for their own learning, to discover and pursue their passions, and to act with responsibility.

Each student must complete at least 124 semester hours to receive a bachelor's degree, of which approximately 40 hours consist of liberal arts education core requirements that are common to all students regardless of major. Semester-hour requirements vary among majors, but all students are exposed to liberal arts concepts as well as practical, career-oriented experiences. Credit is awarded for successful scores on Advanced Placement and CLEP examinations.

Students can participate in the U.S. Air Force Reserve Officer Training Corps program, the U.S. Army Reserve Officers' Training Corps program, and the U.S. Naval Reserve Officers' Training Corps program through cooperative programs at the University of Utah.

The College has a 4-4-1 calendar, consisting of two 15-week semesters followed by a one-month May term, as well as a summer session. Students who attend full-time during fall and spring semesters earn free May-term tuition.

Off-Campus Programs

Westminster students may participate in travel/study trips (for credit) during May term and the summer session. Students can also make individual arrangements for international study by advisement from the College's International Studies Chair and the Career Resource Center and through a cooperative agreement with the Foreign Study Office at the University of Utah.

Westminster is also a member of the Utah Asian Studies Consortium, which promotes connections between faculty members and students in Utah and businesses and schools in Asia, offering May-term trips, internships, semester study-abroad programs, and other opportunities in several Asian countries.

Academic Facilities

Classes are never more than a 5-minute walk away on the pristine, tree-filled 27 acres. The careful blend of architecture is illustrated by the newly completed Emma Eccles Jones Conservatory of Music and Theatre. The Gore School of Business, Aviation, and Entrepreneurship, one of the most technologically advanced business education facilities in the nation, integrates innovative, new laboratories and state-of-the-art classroom facilities with the Center for Financial Analysis, offering real-time access to world market data, a behavioral simulation lab, and a flight simulation and testing center.

The Flight Operations Center, which includes a state-of-the-art hangar, flight simulators, and fifteen new aircraft, is located at Salt Lake International Airport. Presently, the College is constructing a new health and wellness center that will include a lap pool, exercise facilities, and a climbing wall and will also house the School of Nursing and Health Sciences. Future plans include two additional facilities: a unique bilevel athletic field/parking garage structure and a new science center that promises to be one of the most innovative college science facilities in the West. Current facilities include major classroom buildings, multiple computer and presentation classrooms, a science building, an award-winning library, a ceramics studio, and a nursing laboratory.

All students have Internet access and e-mail accounts, using a high-speed gigabit network. A secure student Web portal consolidates online e-mail, course, and registration services. Network connections abound in all classrooms and every residence-hall room and library seat. Eighty percent of classrooms are set up for multimedia presentations. Technical support is available to students and faculty and staff members seven days a week.

Costs

Tuition and fees for 2006–07 were $21,030 for the academic year for a full-time student (12 to 16 semester hours). This figure includes costs for the fall semester, spring semester, and May term. Room and board costs were $6140 for the same period. Books and supplies were estimated at $1000 per year.

Financial Aid

Ninety-six percent of freshmen at Westminster receive some form of financial aid, averaging $16,743 each year per student. Aid programs include need-based institutional grants and need-based federal aid programs such as grants, loans, and employment (Federal Work-Study Program). The Free Application for Federal Student Aid (FAFSA) is the only form required for new students seeking financial aid. Students wishing to apply for federal aid programs should plan to submit applications by early April. Merit-based scholarships are available to incoming freshmen and transfer students as well as to continuing students through a generous endowment and institutional aid programs. Every full-time student is automatically considered for merit-based scholarships awarded by the College. The scholarships are based on their GPA from previous academic course work.

Faculty

Full-time faculty members number 123. The student-faculty ratio is 11:1. All faculty members teach; no full-time research faculty positions exist and no graduate students teach. Many full-time faculty members are actively involved as advisers and sponsors of campus-based student activities. Approximately 87 percent of the faculty members hold a Ph.D. or the highest degree available in their fields.

Student Government

The official student governing body is the Associated Students of Westminster College (ASWC), which sponsors all student activities and organizations and provides funding and authorization for them. The ASWC is made up of three branches: the executive cabinet, the legislative assembly, and the judiciary branch. The three branches function in a similar fashion to the federal government system. The president of the ASWC is considered the primary spokesperson for the student body and has access to all senior administrators of the College.

Admission Requirements

Individual applications are reviewed based on a student's potential for success at Westminster. Academic preparation, which includes both course work and grades, is most important. Also important to the review committee are items such as entrance exams (ACT or SAT), recommendations, and extracurricular activities. A campus visit to meet with an academic counselor is highly recommended, as it helps complete the picture for both the prospective student and the College.

Transfer students must have earned at least a 2.5 cumulative GPA in previous college work. In addition to all other admissions criteria, international students must have at least a 3.0 GPA in non-U.S. high school or college work and a Test of English as a Foreign Language (TOEFL) score of at least 550 (or equivalent).

Application and Information

To apply for admission, a student must submit an application for admission, an application fee, and official transcripts of previous high school and/or college class work. Freshman applicants must submit ACT or SAT scores. Applicants are notified of their admission status within two weeks of receipt of all required materials. All admission decisions are made on a rolling basis, and applications are processed until the date of class registration. New applicants are accepted for the start of all sessions. For application forms and additional information, students should contact:

Office of Admissions
Westminster College
1840 South 1300 East
Salt Lake City, Utah 84105
Phone: 801-832-2200
      800-748-4753 (toll-free)
Web site: http://www.westminstercollege.edu

Westminster College offers high-quality education in one of the most unique learning environments in the country.

WHITWORTH COLLEGE
SPOKANE, WASHINGTON

The College

Whitworth, founded in 1890, is among a select group of educational institutions known for both academic rigor and Christian commitment. The Whitworth faculty is committed to encouraging open intellectual inquiry as well as respect for diverse points of view. The College's community of scholars is also dedicated to the challenging task of integrating faith perspectives into all aspects of life and learning. This dual commitment distinguishes Whitworth among Christian colleges and universities.

The campus has thirty-eight buildings, mostly of red brick, which border the parklike Loop, including the Harriet Cheney Cowles Memorial Library, Cowles Memorial Auditorium, Hixson Union Building, Dixon Hall, and the Seeley Mudd Chapel. The Whitworth Fieldhouse is home to the Scotford Fitness and Aquatic Center, which has a 25-meter, six-lane pool with a movable bulkhead and a 15-foot diving pool. The Hixson Union Building houses the bookstore, post office, snack bar, and student media, student government offices, and a 450-seat dining hall.

The College's 2,100 full-time undergraduate students come from thirty-one states and twenty-five countries. Nearly 70 percent of the full-time undergraduate students live on campus in ten residential areas that range from suites and traditional dorms to cottage-size apartments and theme houses. Residence life is considered an essential part of a student's growth process, and living groups are encouraged, with the help of trained residence staff, to design their own living environments. Peer leaders in each residence hall include resident assistants, health coordinators, ministry coordinators, and cultural diversity advocates.

Also serving the personal development of each student are the Office of the Chaplain and Student Life Department. The Christian environment on campus is centered on midweek chapel and Hosanna, a late-evening student-led service. Small discussion groups and opportunities for service also originate in the Office of the Chaplain. The Student Life Program assists all students in adjusting to college life and defining individual goals by providing counseling, tutoring, services for international students and members of minority groups, job placement, career planning, and aptitude testing.

Whitworth College holds membership in the NCAA Division III and is a member of the Northwest Conference. Varsity teams for men compete in baseball, basketball, cross-country, football, golf, soccer, swimming, tennis, and track and field. Women's teams compete in basketball, cross-country, fast-pitch softball, golf, soccer, swimming, tennis, track and field, and volleyball. Twelve Whitworth teams have won conference championships in the past three years, and four teams have led the nation in team GPA for their sports in NCAA Division III. A broad intramural program, as well as club sports, offers athletic competition to everyone on campus, including faculty and staff members, and fitness evaluation services in the Scotford Fitness Center are available to all. Whitworth believes that physical development is an essential element in each student's pursuit of personal wholeness.

Location

Whitworth College is located just 10 minutes from downtown Spokane on a scenic, wooded 200-acre site, surrounded by quiet suburban residential areas. Spokane, a metropolitan area with a population of 414,500, is surrounded by an extraordinary outdoor recreation area, containing thousands of acres of state and national forests, four major ski resorts, and more than seventy-five lakes within an hour's drive. The city is the commercial and cultural center for more than a million people, and the size of this market area is reflected in the excellence of Spokane's many cultural and entertainment opportunities, restaurants, shopping centers, and transportation.

Majors and Degrees

Whitworth awards Bachelor of Arts and Bachelor of Science degrees. Programs and majors are available in accounting, American studies, art, arts administration, athletic training, biology, business management, chemistry, communication, computer science, cross-cultural studies, economics, education (elementary and secondary certification programs, with academic department emphases), English, environmental studies, French, German, history, international business, international studies, journalism and mass communications, kinesiology, leadership studies, liberal studies, marketing, mathematics, modern languages, music, organizational management, peace studies, philosophy, physical education, physics, political studies, pre-ministry, psychology, quantitative analysis, religion, sociology, Spanish, speech communication, theater, and women's studies.

Preprofessional programs are offered in dentistry, engineering (3-2), law, medical technology, medicine, occupational therapy, pharmacy, physical therapy, and veterinary medicine.

Academic Programs

The College is dedicated to academic excellence as expressed through its core of liberal arts and sciences and through rigorous disciplinary and interdisciplinary study. A Whitworth education is designed to broaden students' understanding of their cultural heritage, to promote critical thinking, to prepare students for productive work, and to stimulate creativity in responding to the challenges of life. As a Christian institution, Whitworth takes seriously its responsibility to help students understand and respond compassionately to the needs of the world. Recognizing that contemporary society is globally interdependent and increasingly multicultural, Whitworth seeks to foster in its students an attitude of curiosity and respect for diverse cultures.

The College's 4-1-4 calendar provides time for intensive study in a single subject during the month of January, often in an off-campus setting.

Off-Campus Programs

January terms and full semesters of off-campus study are available to encourage students to relate their education to real-life environments. Urban studies in San Francisco; international studies in Europe, Latin America, South Africa, Thailand, and the Middle East; music studies in Rome and Munich; and rural studies in various locales are offered to augment classroom learning. Students are not traveling as tourists; they are accompanied by faculty members who guide their research and studies and join them in experiencing the culture to the greatest degree possible.

Exchange-student arrangements are available through the International Student Exchange Program (ISEP). This program offers placements in any of the 150 member universities in Africa, Asia, Australia, Canada, Europe, or Latin America.

Cooperative education/internship opportunities are available for Whitworth students in Spokane or in almost any area of the country. For instance, political studies majors routinely intern in Washington, D.C. The co-op/internship program enables students to gain actual experience and build contacts in a chosen field prior to graduation. A January-term internship often leads to declaring a major, a modification of a career goal, or, just as often, a job opportunity.

Academic Facilities

With its state-of-the-art information retrieval technology and a capacity exceeding 250,000 volumes, the Harriet Cheney Cowles Memorial Library provides students and faculty members with a superb research facility. The library's computerized card catalogs and databases also provide access to the holdings of other libraries in the region and across the country. In addition, the library is home to three computer labs, six group study rooms, climate-controlled archives, a music library, a curriculum lab for teacher education, audiovisual services, and a Writing Center.

The Whitworth Music Building has the most advanced facilities available for music education. Laboratories for chemistry, physics, and biology are maintained in the Eric Johnston Science Center. A generous grant from the National Science Foundation provided funds to upgrade these laboratories. The Fine Arts Building contains studios for drawing, painting, and pottery and houses the John Koehler Gallery, which is used for student shows. The Dr. James P. Evans Sports Medicine Center includes a complete hydrotherapy center, ultrasound equipment, and a variety of ergometers and isokinetic machines.

Costs

For the 2007–08 academic year, tuition is $25,382 and room and board are $7284. Additional costs for books, fees, and personal expenses vary.

Financial Aid

More than 90 percent of Whitworth's students receive financial aid, with the average freshman scholarship and grant award exceeding $10,000. The Free Application for Federal Student Aid (FAFSA) is used to determine a student's financial need for awarding grants, scholarships, loans, and work-study. Academic scholarships and fine arts, pre-engineering, and science and journalism talent awards are available to exceptional students regardless of their demonstrated need. Student employment, under the Federal Work-Study Program, is available on campus for up to 20 hours per week through the Student Employment Office, which provides placement assistance for off-campus jobs as well. The following non-need-based federal loan programs are available to Whitworth students and their families: the Federal Unsubsidized Stafford Loan and the Federal PLUS loan for parents. Whitworth also recently joined The Tuition Plan program, offering tuition discounts and prepayment options to lock in tuition costs.

Faculty

The Whitworth faculty is made up of 120 full-time professors, most of whom have earned either a Ph.D. or the terminal degree in their field. These dedicated Christian scholars conduct important research, perform in demanding musical venues, write critically acclaimed books, and earn recognition in their fields. But their primary commitment is to teaching—sharing their knowledge, their faith journeys, and their friendship with students inside and outside the classroom.

Student Government

A full-time student activities coordinator works with the elected members of the Associated Students of Whitworth College (ASWC) and the appointed student managers to plan and carry out College activities, which range from Homecoming festivities to mountain climbs to political lobbying. Student government is responsible for the continuing involvement of students in the community, organizing outreach ministry opportunities on- and off-campus, and meeting the academic, social, and spiritual needs of the campus community. Individual students are full-fledged members, along with faculty members, of various councils that formulate major campus policies.

Admission Requirements

Whitworth selects its students from those applicants who, by reason of their academic achievement, measured aptitudes, and academic interests, demonstrate their ability to succeed at a rigorous Christian liberal arts college. Generally, 4 years of English; 3 years each of history, science (including lab science), and mathematics; and 2 years of a foreign language constitute a competitive college-preparatory program for a high school applicant. Transfer students are also welcome to apply; Whitworth grants junior standing and a waiver of most general graduation requirements to students who have earned an approved Associate of Arts degree at any Washington community college as well as North Idaho College.

Application and Information

High-achieving students who have decided that Whitworth College is their first or second choice are eligible to apply for early action. The early action application deadline is November 30. For regular admission, the deadline is March 1. Campus visits and admission interviews are welcome at any time throughout the calendar year but are recommended from the week after Labor Day in September through mid-May while classes are in session.

Application for admission may be made by submitting a completed Whitworth application form, a personal statement, an evaluation by the student's high school counselor or principal, a current transcript of high school work, and ACT or SAT scores.

For information and application forms, students should contact:

Office of Admissions
Whitworth College
West 300 Hawthorne Road
Spokane, Washington 99251-0106
Phone: 509-777-3212
       800-533-4668 (toll-free)
E-mail: admission@whitworth.edu
Web site: http://www.whitworth.edu

Whitworth students represent thirty-one states and twenty-five countries.

Profiles and Close-Ups of Other Colleges to Consider

Louisiana

UNIVERSITY OF NEW ORLEANS

New Orleans, Louisiana

University of New Orleans is a coed, public unit of Louisiana State University System, founded in 1958, offering degrees at the bachelor's, master's, and doctoral levels and postbachelor's certificates. It has a 345-acre campus in New Orleans.

Academic Information The faculty has 654 members (73% full-time), 56% with terminal degrees. The undergraduate student-faculty ratio is 17:1. The library holds 896,000 titles, 4,950 serial subscriptions, and 22,775 audiovisual materials. Special programs include academic remediation, services for learning-disabled students, an honors program, cooperative (work-study) education, study abroad, advanced placement credit, ESL programs, double majors, independent study, distance learning, self-designed majors, summer session for credit, part-time degree programs, adult/continuing education programs, internships, and arrangement for off-campus study with Southern University at New Orleans, Delgado Community College, Nunez Community College.

Student Body Statistics The student body totals 11,747, of whom 9,156 are undergraduates (1,021 freshmen). 54 percent are women and 46 percent are men. Students come from 46 states and territories and 74 other countries. 96 percent are from Louisiana. 2.8 percent are international students.

Expenses for 2007–08 *Application fee:* $40. *State resident tuition:* $3292 full-time, $521 per course part-time. *Nonresident tuition:* $10,336 full-time, $1859 per course part-time. *Mandatory fees:* $518 full-time, $53 per hour part-time. *College room and board:* $4734.

Financial Aid Forms of aid include need-based and non-need-based scholarships, athletic grants, and part-time jobs. The average aided 2006–07 undergraduate received an aid package worth an estimated $7119. The priority application deadline for financial aid is May 15.

Freshman Admission University of New Orleans requires a high school transcript, SAT or ACT scores, and TOEFL scores for international students. An essay, a minimum 2.0 high school GPA, 3 recommendations, an interview, and 2.0 high school GPA on high school core program are required for some. The application deadline for regular admission is rolling.

Transfer Admission The application deadline for admission is August 28.

Entrance Difficulty University of New Orleans assesses its entrance difficulty level as moderately difficult. For the fall 2006 freshman class, 77 percent of the applicants were accepted.

For Further Information Contact Mr. Robert Hensley, Director of Admissions, University of New Orleans, Lake Front, New Orleans, LA 70148. *Telephone:* 504-280-7013 or 800-256-5866 (toll-free out-of-state). *Fax:* 504-280-5522. *E-mail:* admissions@uno.edu. *Web site:* http://www.uno.edu/.

See page 224 for the College Close-Up.

New York

EUGENE LANG COLLEGE THE NEW SCHOOL FOR LIBERAL ARTS

New York, New York

SPONSOR
See Front Insert for Details!

Eugene Lang College The New School for Liberal Arts is a coed, private, four-year college of New School University, founded in 1978, offering degrees at the bachelor's level. It has a 5-acre campus in New York.

Academic Information The faculty has 122 members (40% full-time). The student-faculty ratio is 15:1. The library holds 4 million titles and 22,150 serial subscriptions. Special programs include study abroad, advanced placement credit, accelerated degree programs, ESL programs, independent study, distance learning, self-designed majors, summer session for credit, part-time degree programs, adult/continuing education programs, internships, and arrangement for off-campus study with Cooper Union for the Advancement of Science and Art, Bank Street College of Education, Sarah Lawrence College. The most frequently chosen baccalaureate field is liberal arts/general studies.

Student Body Statistics The student body is made up of 1,164 undergraduates (283 freshmen). 68 percent are women and 32 percent are men. Students come from 37 states and territories and 14 other countries. 29 percent are from New York. 3.2 percent are international students.

Expenses for 2006–07 *Application fee:* $50. *Comprehensive fee:* $40,960 includes full-time tuition ($28,600), mandatory fees ($610), and college room and board ($11,750). *College room only:* $8750. Full-time tuition and fees vary according to program. Room and board charges vary according to board plan and housing facility. *Part-time tuition:* $976 per credit. Part-time tuition varies according to course load, program, and reciprocity agreements.

Financial Aid Forms of aid include need-based and non-need-based scholarships and part-time jobs. The average aided 2006–07 undergraduate received an aid package worth an estimated $19,478. The application deadline for financial aid is continuous.

Freshman Admission Eugene Lang College The New School for Liberal Arts requires an essay, a high school transcript, a minimum 2.0 high school GPA, 2 recommendations, an interview, SAT or ACT scores, and TOEFL scores for international students. A minimum 3.0 high school GPA is recommended. The application deadline for regular admission is February 1 and for early decision it is November 15.

Transfer Admission The application deadline for admission is May 15.

Entrance Difficulty Eugene Lang College The New School for Liberal Arts assesses its entrance difficulty level as moderately difficult. For the fall 2006 freshman class, 66 percent of the applicants were accepted.

SPECIAL MESSAGE TO STUDENTS

Social Life Social life at the College is reflective of the cultural richness of New York City. The Theresa Lang Student Center provides a central location for student meetings and performances. A special program, Lang in the City, opens up the world of the arts at little or no additional cost to students. Undergraduates publish an award-winning literary magazine and a newspaper, produce several plays a year, and organize lectures and poetry readings. There are social and political groups, such as the Student Union, Latino and African American organizations, and a volunteer resource center.

Academic Highlights The academic structure at Eugene Lang College is interdisciplinary and emphasizes small seminar classes of no more than 20 students. Students develop a liberal arts program of study around twelve areas of concentration. Internships are also an integral component of the Eugene Lang College education and include placement at schools, media and publishing organizations, and nonprofit

Eugene Lang College The New School for Liberal Arts (continued)

organizations throughout the city. Students are encouraged to participate in the internship program as early as their sophomore year. Exchange programs with American and European universities are also options for students. One of eight distinct schools of The New School, Eugene Lang College has the full resources of a large urban university. Other schools that make up The New School: A University include Parsons The New School for Design, The New School for General Studies, The New School for Social Research, Milano The New School for Management and Urban Policy, Mannes College The New School for Music, The New School for Jazz and Contemporary Music, and The New School for Drama.

Interviews and Campus Visits The College's environment is distinctive and challenging, and, therefore, an interview for admission is highly recommended. Information about Eugene Lang College and the student is exchanged through informal conversation directed by the admissions officer. Students should come prepared to discuss their reasons for applying, their particular learning style, and their college expectations. Students are strongly encouraged to sit in on a seminar class and take a campus tour as part of their visit to the College. New York City provides a rich intellectual and cultural background for the College. Tours include the College and University facilities as well as historic and artistic sites. Points of interest include the Parsons School The New School for Design building, the Albert List Academic Center, the Orozco Murals (rendered in 1930), Loeb Student Residence Hall, the Theresa Lang Student Center, and the seminar classrooms. New York City architecture and parks are also highlights, especially the park at Union Square and the College's historic Greenwich Village neighborhood. For information about appointments and campus visits, students should call the Office of Admissions at 212-229-5665, Monday through Friday, 9 to 5, or e-mail the office. The fax number is 212-229-5355. The office is located at 65 West 11th Street, third floor, on the campus. The nearest commercial airport is John F. Kennedy International.

For Further Information Write to Nicole Curvin, Director of Admissions, Third Floor, Eugene Lang College The New School for Liberal Arts, 65 West 11th Street, New York, NY 10011. *E-mail:* lang@newschool.edu.

See page 218 for the College Close-Up.

North Carolina

NORTH CAROLINA AGRICULTURAL AND TECHNICAL STATE UNIVERSITY

Greensboro, North Carolina

North Carolina Agricultural and Technical State University is a coed, public unit of University of North Carolina System, founded in 1891, offering degrees at the bachelor's, master's, and doctoral levels. It has an 800-acre campus in Greensboro.

Academic Information The faculty has 495 members (74% full-time). The undergraduate student-faculty ratio is 24:1. The library holds 597,093 titles, 40,425 serial subscriptions, and 37,886 audiovisual materials. Special programs include academic remediation, services for learning-disabled students, an honors program, cooperative (work-study) education, study abroad, advanced placement credit, summer session for credit, part-time degree programs (daytime, evenings, summer), adult/continuing education programs, internships, and arrangement for off-campus study with University of North Carolina at Greensboro, Guilford College, Bennett College, High Point University, Greensboro College. The most frequently chosen baccalaureate fields are business/marketing, engineering, engineering technologies.

Student Body Statistics The student body totals 11,098, of whom 9,687 are undergraduates (2,094 freshmen). 53 percent are women and 47 percent are men. Students come from 43 states and territories. 75 percent are from North Carolina. 0.4 percent are international students.

Expenses for 2006–07 *Application fee:* $45. *One-time mandatory fee:* $10. *State resident tuition:* $1994 full-time. *Nonresident tuition:* $11,436 full-time. *Mandatory fees:* $1878 full-time. Full-time tuition and fees vary according to student level. *College room and board:* $6686. Room and board charges vary according to board plan and housing facility.

Financial Aid Forms of aid include need-based and non-need-based scholarships, athletic grants, and part-time jobs. The average aided 2005–06 undergraduate received an aid package worth $5898. The priority application deadline for financial aid is March 15.

Freshman Admission North Carolina Agricultural and Technical State University requires a high school transcript, a minimum 2.0 high school GPA, and TOEFL scores for international students. SAT or ACT scores are recommended. The application deadline for regular admission is rolling.

Transfer Admission The application deadline for admission is rolling.

Entrance Difficulty North Carolina Agricultural and Technical State University assesses its entrance difficulty level as moderately difficult. For the fall 2006 freshman class, 84 percent of the applicants were accepted.

For Further Information Contact Mr. Lee Young, Director of Admissions, North Carolina Agricultural and Technical State University, 1601 East Market Street, Webb Hall, Greensboro, NC 27411. *Telephone:* 336-334-7946 or 800-443-8964 (toll-free in-state). *Fax:* 336-334-7478. *E-mail:* uadmit@ncat.edu. *Web site:* http://www.ncat.edu/.

See page 220 for the College Close-Up.

Texas

UNIVERSITY OF DALLAS

Irving, Texas

University of Dallas is a coed, private, Roman Catholic university, founded in 1955, offering degrees at the bachelor's, master's, and doctoral levels and post-master's and postbachelor's certificates. It has a 750-acre campus in Irving near Dallas–Fort Worth.

Academic Information The faculty has 233 members (52% full-time), 64% with terminal degrees. The undergraduate student-faculty ratio is 11:1. The library holds 223,350 titles and 691 serial subscriptions. Special programs include services for learning-disabled students, study abroad, advanced placement credit, double majors, independent study, self-designed majors, summer session for credit, part-time degree programs (daytime, summer), internships, and arrangement for off-campus study. The most frequently chosen baccalaureate fields are English, biological/life sciences, social sciences.

Student Body Statistics The student body totals 2,941, of whom 1,188 are undergraduates (315 freshmen). 56 percent are women and 44 percent are men. Students come from 47 states and territories and 12 other countries. 56 percent are from Texas. 1.4 percent are international students. 40 percent of the 2006 graduating class went on to graduate and professional schools.

Expenses for 2007–08 *Application fee:* $40. *Comprehensive fee:* $30,882 includes full-time tuition ($21,819), mandatory fees ($1448), and college room and board ($7615). *College room only:* $4240. *Part-time tuition:* $975 per credit hour. *Part-time mandatory fees:* $1448 per year.

Financial Aid Forms of aid include need-based and non-need-based scholarships and part-time jobs. The average aided 2005–06 undergraduate received an aid package worth $17,668. The priority application deadline for financial aid is March 1.

Freshman Admission University of Dallas requires an essay, a high school transcript, 2 recommendations, SAT or ACT scores, and TOEFL scores for international students. An interview is recommended. An interview is required for some. The application deadline for regular admission is August 1 and for early action it is November 1.

Transfer Admission The application deadline for admission is July 1.

Entrance Difficulty University of Dallas assesses its entrance difficulty level as moderately difficult. For the fall 2006 freshman class, 85 percent of the applicants were accepted.

For Further Information Contact Sr. Mary Brian Bole, Assistant Dean of Enrollment Management, University of Dallas, 1845 East Northgate Drive, Irving, TX 75062-4799. *Telephone:* 972-721-5266 or 800-628-6999 (toll-free). *Fax:* 972-721-5017. *E-mail:* ugadmis@udallas.edu. *Web site:* http://www.udallas.edu/.

See page 222 for the College Close-Up.

EUGENE LANG COLLEGE
THE NEW SCHOOL FOR LIBERAL ARTS
NEW YORK, NEW YORK

The College

Eugene Lang College is the distinctive liberal arts division of The New School, formerly known as New School University. It is a major urban university with a tradition of innovative learning. Eugene Lang College offers all the benefits of a small and supportive college as well as the full range of opportunities found in a university setting.

Eugene Lang students are encouraged to participate in the creation and direction of their education. The desire to explore and the freedom to imagine shared by students and faculty members contribute to a distinctive academic community.

Eugene Lang College students currently come from forty-five states and thirteen countries. The ratio of men to women is approximately 2:3. About 45 percent of the College's 985 students come from outside the New York metropolitan area; 4 percent hold foreign citizenship and 23 percent are members of minority groups. The student body is composed of both residential and day students. The university operates residence halls within walking distance of classes; incoming freshmen and transfer students are given housing priority within these facilities, and housing is guaranteed for the first year for new students. Great diversity in interests and aspirations is found among the students. Through the Office of Student Services, students produce a student newspaper and an award-winning literary magazine. They organize and participate in dramatic, musical, and artistic events through the "Lang in the City Program," as well as numerous political, social, and cultural organizations at the university and throughout New York City.

The New School for Liberal Arts was founded in 1919 by such notable scholars and intellectuals as John Dewey, Alvin Johnson, and Thorstein Veblen. It has long been a home for leading artists, educators, and public figures. For example, the university was the first institution of higher learning to offer college-level courses in such "new" fields as black culture and race, taught by W. E. B. DuBois, and psychoanalysis, taught by Freud's disciple Sandor Ferenczi. Among the world-famous artists and performers who have taught at The New School for Liberal Arts are Martha Graham, Aaron Copland, and Thomas Hart Benton. Today, such noted scholars as Robert Heilbroner, Eric Hobsbawm, Jerome Bruner, and Rayna Rapp are among the hundreds of university faculty members accessible to Eugene Lang College students.

The other divisions of the university include The New School for General Studies, which offers nearly 1,000 credit and noncredit courses to students each semester and awards the B.A., B.S., M.A., M.S., and M.F.A. degrees; The New School for Social Research (founded in 1933 as the University in Exile), which grants M.A. and Ph.D. degrees; Milano The New School for Management and Urban Policy, which awards the M.S. and Ph.D. degrees; Parsons The New School for Design, one of the oldest and most influential art schools in the country; and Mannes College The New School for Music, a renowned classical conservatory. The total university enrollment in 2005–06 was approximately 8,700 degree-seeking students.

Location

The university is located in New York City's Greenwich Village, which historically has been a center for intellectual and artistic life. This slower-paced, more personal New York City neighborhood of town houses and tree-lined streets offers students a friendly and stimulating environment. Over and above the resources of Greenwich Village, New York City offers virtually unlimited cultural, artistic, recreational, and intellectual resources that make it one of the world's great cities.

Majors and Degrees

Eugene Lang College awards the Bachelor of Arts degree. Students are encouraged to design their own program of study in consultation with their faculty adviser. They must choose from twelve paths of study: the arts; cultural studies and media; education studies; history; literature; philosophy; psychology; religious studies; science, technology, and society; social and historical inquiry; urban studies; and writing. A student's concentration consists of eight to ten courses (32–40 credits) leading to relatively advanced and specialized knowledge of an area of study. In addition, students are encouraged to pursue an internship, where appropriate.

Students may also apply to a five-year B.A./B.F.A. program in conjunction with Parsons The New School for Design or The New School for Jazz and Contemporary Music, and advanced students may apply for the accelerated B.A./M.A. option offered in conjunction with the university's graduate divisions.

Academic Programs

When planning a program of study, Eugene Lang College students are encouraged to reflect on what their education means to them. Their program should parallel their own academic and personal development. By actively participating in the process of their education, students gain the knowledge to make informed choices about the direction of their studies with the help of their advisers and peers.

Small seminar classes serve as the focus of the academic program at the College. The maximum class size is 20 students. Classes are in-depth, interdisciplinary inquiries into topics or issues selected each semester by the College's outstanding faculty. Most important, the classes engage participants in the study of primary texts, rather than textbooks, and emphasize dialogue between teacher and student as a mode of learning. Here, not only is intellectual curiosity fostered by the small classes, but a genuine sense of community develops as well.

Although the College does not emphasize course requirements outside the path of study, freshmen are required to take one writing course and three other seminars of their choice in each of their first two semesters at the College. Upper-level students create their programs by selecting seminars from the College's curriculum, or they may combine offerings of the College with courses and workshops offered by The New School for General Study, The New School for Social Research, Milano The New School for Management and Urban Policy, and Parsons The New School for Design.

The College operates on a semester calendar; the first semester runs from September through mid-December, and the second runs from late January through mid-May. Students generally earn 16 credits per semester; a minimum of 120 credits is required for graduation.

Off-Campus Programs

Eugene Lang College recognizes the immense value of work undertaken beyond the classroom. The College arranges appropriate projects—internships with private and nonprofit organizations—which serve to strengthen the connection between theoretical work in the classroom and practical work on the job.

Sophomores and juniors have the option of spending a year on a sponsored exchange with Sarah Lawrence College and the University of Amsterdam. Other exchanges, both in the United States and abroad, are available.

Academic Facilities

Eugene Lang College is located on 11th Street between Fifth and Sixth Avenues in Greenwich Village. The university includes twelve academic buildings, including a student center, the University Computing Center with IBM and Macintosh stations, a 500-seat auditorium, art galleries, studios for the fine arts, classrooms, a writing center, and faculty offices. Eugene Lang College students have full and easy access to the Raymond Fogelman Library and the Adam and Sophie Gimbel Design Library. In addition, the university participates in the South Manhattan Library Consortium. Together, the libraries in the consortium house approximately 3 million volumes covering all the traditional liberal arts disciplines and the fine arts.

Costs

Tuition and fees for the 2005–06 academic year were $26,540. Room and board cost approximately $10,000, depending upon the student's choice of specific meal plan and dormitory accommodations. University fees were $100 per year.

Financial Aid

Students are encouraged to apply for aid by filing the Free Application for Federal Student Aid (FAFSA) and requesting that a copy of the need analysis report be sent to The New School (FAFSA code number 002780). Qualified College students are eligible for all federal and state financial aid programs in addition to university gift aid. University aid is awarded on the basis of need and merit and is part of a package consisting of both gift aid (grants and/or scholarships) and a self-help component (loans and Federal Work-Study Program awards). Aid is renewable each year as long as need continues and students maintain satisfactory academic standing at the College. Special attention is given to continuing students who have done exceptionally well.

Faculty

At Eugene Lang College, the faculty-student ratio is 1:10. Class size ranges from 10 to 20 students. Faculty members are graduates of outstanding colleges and universities and represent a wide variety of academic disciplines; 95 percent hold Ph.D.'s. College faculty members also serve as academic advisers, who are selected carefully in order to ensure thoughtful supervision of students' programs and academic progress.

Well-known faculty members from other divisions of the university teach at the College on a regular basis. In addition, every semester, the College hosts distinguished scholars and writers as visiting faculty and guest lecturers who further enrich the academic program of the College and the university.

Student Government

There is a student union at the College, which is an organized vehicle for student expression and action as well as a means of funding student projects and events. Students are encouraged to express their views and concerns about academic policies and community life through regular student-faculty member meetings.

Admission Requirements

Eugene Lang College welcomes admission applications from students of diverse racial, ethnic, religious, and political backgrounds whose past performance and academic and personal promise make them likely to gain from and give much to the College community. The College seeks students who combine inquisitiveness and seriousness of purpose with the ability to engage in a distinctive, rigorous liberal arts program. Each applicant to the College is judged individually; the Admissions Committee, which renders all admission decisions, considers both academic qualifications and the personal, creative, and intellectual qualities of each applicant. A strong academic background, including a college-preparatory program, is recommended. An applicant's transcript; teacher and counselor recommendations; SAT, ACT, or SAT Subject Test scores; and personal essays are all taken into consideration. In addition, an interview, a tour of university facilities, and a visit to Eugene Lang College seminars are optional but highly recommended.

High school students for whom the College is their first choice are strongly encouraged to apply as early decision candidates and are notified early of an admission decision. Early entrance is an option for qualified high school juniors who wish to enter college prior to high school graduation. Candidates for early entrance must submit two teacher recommendations.

Students who have successfully completed one full year or more at another accredited institution may apply as transfer candidates. If accepted, transfer students may enter upper-level seminars and pursue advanced work. International students may apply for admission as freshmen or transfers by submitting a regular application to the College. If English is spoken as a second language, TOEFL scores are required. The New York Connection Program invites students from other colleges to Eugene Lang College for a semester and incorporates an internship into their studies.

Students interested in applying for the combined B.A./B.F.A. degree program in fine arts or jazz studies are encouraged to apply for admission as freshmen to these special five-year programs. In addition to the admission requirements outlined above, a home exam and a portfolio are required for fine arts, and an audition is required for jazz studies.

Application and Information

Freshmen, transfers, and visiting students may apply for either the September (fall) or January (spring) semester. To apply for admission to the College, students must request an application packet and submit the required credentials and a $50 application fee by the appropriate deadline. The application fee may be waived in accordance with the College Board's Fee Waiver Service. For the semester beginning in January, the required credentials must be submitted by November 15, with notification by December 15. For the September semester, early decision candidates must submit the required credentials by November 15, with notification by December 15. For freshman candidates applying for general admission and freshman early entrants, the deadline is February 1, with notification by April 1. For transfers and visiting students, the deadline is rolling to May 15, with notification rolling until July 1.

For further information, students should contact:

Nicole Curvin
Director of Admissions
Eugene Lang College The New School for Liberal Arts
65 West 11th Street, Third Floor
New York, New York 10011

Phone: 212-229-5665
Fax: 212-229-5355
E-mail: lang@newschool.edu
Web site: http://www.lang.newschool.edu

NORTH CAROLINA AGRICULTURAL AND TECHNICAL STATE UNIVERSITY

GREENSBORO, NORTH CAROLINA

The University

North Carolina Agricultural and Technical State University (A&T) was founded in 1891 as one of two land-grant institutions in the state. Originally, it was established to provide postsecondary education and training for black students. Today, the University is a comprehensive institution of higher education with an integrated faculty and student body, and it has been designated a constituent institution of the University of North Carolina, offering degrees at the baccalaureate, master's, and doctoral levels. Located on a 191-acre campus, the University has 110 buildings, including single-sex and coeducational residence halls. Of a total of 10,475 undergraduates, 4,925 are men and 5,550 are women. The total population is 11,082.

North Carolina Agricultural and Technical State University provides outstanding academic programs through five undergraduate schools, two colleges, and a graduate school.

The mission of the University is to provide an intellectual setting in which students may find a sense of belonging, responsibility, and achievement that prepares them for roles of leadership and service in the communities where they will live and work. In this sense, the University serves as a laboratory for the development of excellence in teaching, research, and public service. As a result, A&T today stands as an example of well-directed higher education for all students.

Student life at the University is active and purposeful. The broad objective of the program provided by Student Development Services is to aid students in attaining the attitudes, understandings, insights, and skills that enable them to be socially competent. The program places special emphasis on campus relationships and experiences that complement formal instruction. Some of the services available are counseling, housing, health, and placement services. There is a University Student Union, and there are special services for international and minority students, veterans, and handicapped students. The University also provides a well-balanced program of activities to foster the moral, spiritual, cultural, and physical development of its students.

Location

Greensboro, North Carolina, is 300 miles south of Washington, D.C., and 349 miles north of Atlanta. It is readily accessible by air, bus, and automobile. The city offers a variety of cultural and recreational activities and facilities. These include sports events, concerts, bowling, boating, fishing, tennis, golf, and other popular forms of recreation. There are major shopping centers, churches, theaters, and medical facilities near the University. The heavy concentration of factories, service industries, government agencies, and shopping centers provides many job opportunities for students who desire part-time employment.

Majors and Degrees

North Carolina Agricultural and Technical State University grants the following degrees: Bachelor of Arts, Bachelor of Science, Bachelor of Fine Arts, Bachelor of Science in Nursing, and Bachelor of Social Work.

The School of Agriculture and Environmental Sciences offers programs in agricultural economics, agricultural economics (agricultural business), agricultural education, agricultural education (agricultural extension), agricultural science–earth and environmental science (earth and environmental science, landscape horticulture design, plant science, and soil science), agricultural science–natural resources (plant science), animal science, ani-

mal science (animal industry), child development, child development–early education and family studies B–K (teaching), family and consumer science (fashion merchandising and design), family and consumer science education, food and nutritional sciences, laboratory animal science, and landscape architecture.

In the College of Arts and Sciences, programs are available in applied mathematics, biology, biology–secondary education, broadcast production, chemistry, chemistry–secondary education, criminal justice, electronic/media journalism, English, English–secondary education, history, history–secondary education, journalism and mass communications, liberal studies–African-American studies, liberal studies–business, liberal studies–cultural change and social development, liberal studies-dance, liberal studies–interdisciplinary, liberal studies–international studies, liberal studies–prelaw, liberal studies–women's studies, mathematics, mathematics–secondary education, media management, music education, music-general, music-performance, physics, physics–secondary education, political science, print journalism, professional theater, psychology, public relations, sociology, social work, Romance languages and literatures–French, Romance languages and literatures–French secondary education, Romance languages and literatures–Spanish, Romance languages and literatures–Spanish secondary education, speech, speech (speech pathology/audiology), visual arts–art education, and visual arts–design.

The School of Business and Economics offers programs in accounting, business administration, business education, business education (administrative systems, vocational business education, and vocational business education–data processing), economics, finance, management, management (management information systems), marketing, and transportation.

In the School of Education, programs are available in elementary education, human performance and leisure studies (fitness/wellness management), human performance and leisure studies (teaching), human performance and leisure studies (sports science and fitness management), recreation administration, and special education.

In the College of Engineering, programs are offered in architectural engineering, bioenvironmental engineering, chemical engineering, civil engineering, computer engineering, computer science, electrical engineering, industrial engineering, and mechanical engineering.

The School of Nursing grants the Bachelor of Science in Nursing (B.S.N.) degree.

The School of Technology has programs in computer-aided drafting and design, construction management, electronics technology, electronics technology (computational technology), electronics technology (information technology), graphic communication systems, integrated Internet technologies, manufacturing systems, manufacturing systems (motor sports), occupational safety and health, printing and publishing, technology education (teaching), trade and industrial education (teaching), and training and development for industry.

Academic Programs

Students must complete a minimum of 124 semester hours to earn a bachelor's degree; the exact number varies with the program. Students are also required to demonstrate competence in English and mathematics.

As complements to the academic programs, the University's Army and Air Force ROTC programs and cooperative education program provide excellent opportunities for students to enrich their educational experiences. The ROTC programs are designed to prepare college graduates for military service careers. The cooperative education program provides an opportunity for qualified students to alternate periods of study on campus and meaningful employment off campus in private industrial or business firms or government agencies.

Academic Facilities

The University library has current holdings that include 507,036 book volumes and bound periodicals, as well as 5,446 current serials. As a select depository in North Carolina for U.S. government documents, the library contains a collection of more than 250,000 official publications. Among the library's other holdings are a collection of audiovisuals and 1,038,474 microforms, archives, and special collections in black studies and teacher-education materials. Special services are provided through formal and informal library instruction, interlibrary loans, and photocopying facilities.

The University's educational support centers are the Learning Assistance Center, the Audiovisual Center, the Closed Circuit Television Facility, a 1,000-watt student-operated educational radio station, the Computer Center, the Reading Center, the Language Laboratory, and the Center for Manpower Research and Training. The H. Clinton Taylor Art Gallery and the African Heritage Center are two exceptional art museums on campus. Throughout the year, these museums have on display a number of special exhibits of sculpture, paintings, graphics, and other media.

Costs

In 2006–07, tuition and fees for North Carolina residents were $3872 per year; for nonresidents of the state, they were $13,314. Board and lodging for the academic year were approximately $6650.

Financial Aid

Through the student financial aid program, the University makes every effort to ensure that no qualified student is denied the opportunity to attend because of a lack of funds. Students who demonstrate financial need and have the potential to achieve academic success at the University may obtain assistance to meet their expenses in accordance with the funds available. Financial aid is awarded without regard to race, religion, color, national origin, or sex. The University provides financial aid for students from four basic sources: grants, scholarships, loans, and employment. To apply for aid, students must submit the Free Application for Federal Student Aid (FAFSA). The priority filing deadline is March 15 for the fall semester. North Carolina residents may call 800-443-0835 (toll-free).

Faculty

The University's teaching faculty consists of more than 600 highly qualified members. Approximately 90 percent of them hold the doctoral degree or the first professional degree in their discipline. Faculty members are recruited from many areas and backgrounds, thereby bringing together a diverse cadre of academic professionals from many nations.

Student Government

The Student Government Association (SGA), which is composed of senators elected from the student body, is primarily a policy-recommending group and represents the views and concerns of the students. The president of the SGA reports directly to the vice-chancellor for student affairs. In addition, each student organization is represented by a senator, and these senators sit on the Faculty Senate.

Admission Requirements

Applicants for undergraduate admission are considered individually and in accordance with criteria applied flexibly to ensure that applicants with unusual qualifications are not denied admission. However, admission for out-of-state freshman students is competitive due to an 18 percent out-of-state enrollment cap. Students who are applying for admission as freshmen are expected to have completed a college-preparatory program in high school and to have taken the SAT or the ACT. General requirements include graduation from an accredited high school, including 4 units of English, 2 units of the same foreign language, 4 units of college-preparatory mathematics, 3 units of natural sciences, 2 units of social sciences, and American history; a satisfactory score on the SAT or ACT; and a respectable GPA and/or class rank. The General Educational Development (GED) test score results or a high school equivalency certificate from the state Department of Education may be submitted in lieu of the high school transcript for applicants receiving equivalency before January 1988.

North Carolina A&T State University welcomes applications from graduates of accredited community, technical, and junior colleges and from students who wish to transfer from other senior colleges.

Application and Information

The suggested application deadline for students who expect to live on campus is February 1; for commuting students, it is June 1. Applications are processed upon the receipt of the completed application form with the $45 application fee, official transcripts, and SAT or ACT scores. Out-of-state admission is limited; therefore, applications for admission should be filed by February 1.

To arrange an interview or a visit to the campus, students should contact:

Office of Admissions
B. C. Webb Hall
North Carolina Agricultural and Technical State University
Greensboro, North Carolina 27411
Phone: 336-334-7946 or 7947
      800-443-8964 (toll-free in North Carolina)
Web site: http://www.ncat.edu

A professor and students in the chemical engineering lab.

UNIVERSITY OF DALLAS
IRVING, TEXAS, AND ROME, ITALY

UNIVERSITY OF
DALLAS

The University

In 1955, the Roman Catholic Diocese of Dallas/Fort Worth purchased land for a university on a 1,000-acre tract of rolling hills northwest of Dallas, and in 1956, the University of Dallas (UD) opened. His Excellency Bishop Thomas K. Gorman, Chancellor of the new university, announced that it would be a coeducational institution, welcoming students of all faiths and ethnic backgrounds. Headed by a lay president and a lay academic dean, the faculty was composed of laymen, diocesan and Cistercian priests, and sisters of the Order of St. Mary of Namur.

Current undergraduate enrollment is about 1,200 men and women. Undergraduates come from all fifty states and thirty-three other countries. Although approximately 71 percent are Catholic, twenty faiths are represented on campus.

The University of Dallas was the first Catholic institution to have a board of trustees made up of both lay and religious members. Since its founding, many other universities and colleges have followed its example. The first class, a group of individuals who won significant honors, such as Fulbright and Woodrow Wilson fellowships, was graduated in 1960. There is a Phi Beta Kappa chapter on campus.

Through a $6-million endowment provided by the Blakley-Braniff Foundation, the Braniff Graduate School was established in 1966. Twelve graduate programs are now in existence, including doctoral programs in philosophy, politics, and literature and the M.F.A. program in art. The College of Business houses the Graduate School of Management, which is distinguished by its practice-oriented education, close ties with leading companies and professionals, and a global student body. In addition to its undergraduate programs, the College of Business offers Master of Business Administration (M.B.A.) and Master of Management degrees. The M.B.A. includes sixteen concentrations in the areas of finance, health care, information technology, management, marketing, and telecommunications.

The University of Dallas is a center of learning, and the experience on campus is intensive and highly directed. People choose to come to the University because they are serious students. While they engage in a full complement of extracurricular activities and independent study, it is the act of learning in association with their professors that shapes their college years. Because the undergraduate college is small and largely residential, it forms a close-knit community. The University sponsors a number of lectures, concerts, and art exhibits, ranging from the old masters to the UD international printmaking invitational. The Student Government sponsors weekly events and current and classic films. The *University News* has consistently won awards for excellence in writing and design. Collegium Cantorum, the a cappella liturgical choir, performs both nationally and internationally. Intercollegiate NCAA Division III sports include baseball, basketball, cross-country, golf, lacrosse, soccer, softball, tennis, track, and volleyball. Rugby is very popular at the club level. Eighty-five percent of the on-campus students are involved in intramurals: basketball, flag football, soccer, softball, paintball, and other sports. Traditional events include coffeehouses featuring student entertainment, Charity Week, Mallapalooza, Oktoberfest, Spring Olympics, and Groundhog.

For Catholic students, daily and weekly Mass, Reconciliation, and rosary are held in the 500-seat Church of the Incarnation. Transportation is arranged for students of other faiths to attend services nearby. Campus Ministry provides numerous volunteer opportunities, including annual service projects in Appalachia and Ecuador.

Location

Irving, Texas, a city of 195,000 on the northwest side of the city of Dallas, is about 15 minutes from downtown Dallas, 10 minutes from Love Field airport, and 15 minutes from DFW airport. The Dallas–Fort Worth Metroplex offers a diverse mix of cultural and entertainment attractions, including the Dallas Museum of Modern Art, the new Nasher Sculpture Center, and the Kimbell Museum in Fort Worth. The Dallas Theater Center and Stage One have built reputations as top-notch theaters and as proving grounds for Broadway-bound productions. Texas Stadium, home of the Dallas Cowboys, is just three blocks from the University. Dallas is home to professional sports teams in hockey, soccer, and basketball. Nearby Arlington is home to the Texas Rangers.

Majors and Degrees

The Constantin College of Liberal Arts offers programs leading to the Bachelor of Arts (B.A.) degree in art and art history, biology, business, chemistry, classics, computer science, drama, economics, economics and finance, education, English, history, mathematics, modern languages (French, German, and Spanish), philosophy, physics, politics, psychology, and theology. The Bachelor of Science degree is awarded in biochemistry, biology, chemistry, mathematics, and physics.

The College of Business offers Bachelor of Arts degrees in business leadership.

The University offers twenty-seven concentrations, or minors, including applied math, applied physics, art history, business, Christian contemplative studies, computer science, entrepreneurship, environmental science, international studies, journalism, math, medieval and Renaissance studies, modern language, music, and pure math.

Preprofessional programs in architecture, business, dentistry, engineering, law, medicine, and physical therapy are carefully integrated with the Core Curriculum of the Constantin College. The rate of acceptance and enrollment of the college's students by professional schools is exceptional. More than 60 percent go on to graduate school, and the rate of acceptance for medical and law school applicants is more than 90 percent.

A five-year, dual-degree program allows students to combine any undergraduate major with the graduate program in business management. Upon completion of the program, a student will have earned both the B.A. and M.B.A. degrees.

Academic Programs

The Core Curriculum is a shared series of specific courses that outline the development of Western thought and culture from classical to modern times. Every student becomes familiar with the same works of literature and the same great books and concepts, fostering a natural understanding and exchange of ideas. All students then go on to pursue their chosen major

discipline, reaching a level of maturity and competence in the discipline that they could not have attained in the absence of a broad general foundation. The student body has an active and personal involvement with the Core Curriculum.

The University observes a two-semester calendar, with the semester examinations occurring before the monthlong Christmas break. An interterm session and three summer sessions are also offered.

Off-Campus Programs

All undergraduates, regardless of major, are encouraged to spend one semester on the University's campus in Rome. While not compulsory, the Rome experience is an important part of the undergraduate education; to seek one's heritage in the liberal arts and to be a student of the Western world is, in a sense, to be a citizen of Rome. Courses offered in Rome are from the Core Curriculum and are taught by professors from the Texas campus. The Rome campus is located just outside of downtown Rome. Transfer students who need courses offered on the Rome campus may participate after one semester on the main campus. The cost for tuition, room, and board for all participants is roughly equivalent to that on the main campus. More than 80 percent of University of Dallas graduates have participated in the Rome program.

Academic Facilities

The Science Center, a $6-million, state-of-the-art facility, houses some of the most advanced tools for scientific research available, including a working observatory. The Haggerty Arts Village has established the University as a leading center for ceramics and fine arts in the Southwest. Drama productions are staged in the Margaret Jonsson Theater. Blakely Library holds more than 275,000 volumes, including the personal library of the late political philosopher Wilmoore Kendall.

Costs

Annual tuition and fees for 2007–08 are $23,222; room and board costs average $7615. Costs are the same for in-state and out-of-state students.

Financial Aid

Tuition, fees, room, and board are substantially lower at the University of Dallas than at many other nationally recognized universities. In addition, all high school seniors who apply for admission by the freshman scholarship priority deadline of January 15 receive priority consideration for all of the University's achievement-based awards. The University currently offers four types of achievement-based awards: academic achievements, community achievements, leadership achievements, and special talents. Talent areas that are currently recognized include art, business, chemistry, classics (Latin and Greek), German, French, math, physics, and Spanish. Students who apply for admission between January 16 and March 1 receive regular consideration for achievement-based awards. Those who apply for admission after March 1 are considered for achievement-based awards dependent on the availability of funding.

All students who submit a Free Application for Federal Student Aid (FAFSA) are considered for all forms of financial assistance based on their family's finances. These forms of assistance include scholarships, grants, loans, and work-study programs. Priority is given to applicants whose FAFSA is received by the University of Dallas on or before March 1. The school code for sending a FAFSA to the University of Dallas is 003651.

Faculty

The University prides itself on its teaching faculty. Ninety-two percent hold terminal degrees. There are no graduate assistants. With a faculty-student ratio of 1:12, extensive consultation and direction are possible. The average class size is 19. The faculty is characterized by authority in the various disciplines, and its members have published more than 1,000 books and articles and secured major research grants.

Student Government

The Student Government Association and various departmental and special clubs, such as the social, film, lecture, and fine arts committees, encourage an extracurricular life created by the students themselves.

Admission Requirements

Although no rigid cutoff point is adhered to in admission, 52 percent of the students who enter as freshmen rank in the top 10 percent of their high school class. General admission requirements include SAT or ACT scores, rank in the upper third of the high school class, and 16 college-preparatory units, including 4 in English, 3 in mathematics, 2 in the same foreign language, 2 in social science, and 2 in a laboratory science. Interviews are not required but are strongly recommended. Through the Office of Undergraduate Admission, counseling appointments, tours, and overnight accommodations on campus may be arranged. Transfer students are welcome.

Application and Information

A transcript, official rank in class, and SAT or ACT scores must be submitted along with a letter of recommendation and a completed application form, which is obtainable online or via mail or phone from the Office of Admission. Transfer students should submit all transcripts from colleges previously attended. A $40 application fee should accompany the application; the other material may follow as ready. The Early Action I deadline is November 1; the Early Action II deadline is December 1. The freshman priority scholarship deadline is January 15. The regular admission deadline is March 1. Rolling admission is March 2–August 1.

For applications or further information, students should contact:

Office of Undergraduate Admission and Financial Aid
University of Dallas
1845 East Northgate Drive
Irving, Texas 75062
Phone: 972-721-5266
        800-628-6999 (toll-free)
Web site: http://www.udallas.edu

University of Dallas students learning on-site at Sicily, Italy.

UNIVERSITY OF NEW ORLEANS
NEW ORLEANS, LOUISIANA

The University

The University of New Orleans (UNO) is part of the rich cultural tapestry of its hometown, which is one of the most extraordinary cities in the world. Established in 1956 to bring publicly supported higher education to the New Orleans area, UNO is fully accredited by the Commission on Colleges of the Southern Association of Colleges and Schools. With an enrollment of 11,800 (9,200 undergraduates and 2,600 graduate students) in fall 2006, UNO offers both undergraduate and graduate degrees through the doctoral level.

UNO derives its strength from its urban setting and strives to enhance the economic, social, and cultural amenities of New Orleans through its numerous research projects, outreach programs, and special cooperative agreements. The University of New Orleans attracts students from forty-eight states (approximately 10 percent) and 102 countries, with a majority of the students Louisiana residents (approximately 90 percent). The diverse student population (42 percent of students are members of ethnic minorities) provides an excellent opportunity for personal growth and understanding.

For students who are interested in on-campus housing, UNO offers three unique styles living. Privateer Place overlooks beautiful Lake Pontchartrain and includes a swimming pool and Jacuzzi. Privateer Place contains seventy-two 2-person unfurnished efficiency apartments, 216 furnished two-bedroom apartments, and sixty furnished four-bedroom apartments. Bienville Hall is a coeducational dormitory for single students and has 306 two-person rooms, including seventy-eight rooms that were recently remodeled. In fall 2007, UNO plans to open a new $38.5-million residence hall complex, composed of two 4-story buildings totaling about 220,000 square feet. The facility will include 236 suite-style units that can accommodate 749 students, as well as TV and recreation rooms, study lounges, laundry facilities, and a convenience store. All complexes have disability-accessible rooms available.

Campus dining facilities are conveniently located near all on-campus housing facilities and heavily populated student areas, with various hours of operation. Other student services include six on-campus computer labs that provide free Internet access, a learning resource center that offers additional tutoring services, student counseling services, an on-campus medical office and pharmacy, student legal counseling, and religious centers.

UNO has more than 100 active student organizations on campus, including academic, professional, Greek, social, political, and religious organizations. UNO's newest addition is the University pep band, the UNO Blue Zoo, which performs at all UNO home basketball games and other University-related events. *Bayou* is UNO's annual national literary magazine that collects submissions from writers worldwide. UNO's student newspaper, *Driftwood,* is published weekly, and *Ellipsis,* a literary magazine, is published annually.

As a Division I member of the National Collegiate Athletic Association (NCAA), UNO fields men's teams in basketball, baseball, and tennis and women's teams in basketball, volleyball, and tennis. UNO students can also participate in many recreational and intramural sports. Students have access to a new 85,000-square-foot Recreation and Fitness Center, which features a 12,000-square-foot cardiovascular, circuit, and free weight training room; an indoor track; a lap pool; racquetball courts; outdoor sundeck; juice bar; and social lounge.

Location

The University's 195-acre main campus is set in one of the most beautiful residential areas on the south shore of Lake Pontchartrain, only minutes from the fun and excitement of downtown New Orleans and the French Quarter. New Orleans is a cosmopolitan city, known for its great Southern hospitality and its unique tourist attractions. Renowned for Creole and Cajun cuisine, Mardi Gras,

and jazz music festivals, New Orleans culture offers a unique environment for students to grow, both socially and academically. Whether exploring the art galleries of the Warehouse District or strolling down stately St. Charles Avenue, New Orleans has something for everyone, and the University of New Orleans is a part of it all.

Many of UNO's hotel, restaurant, and tourism administration majors find internships in the city's best hotels and restaurants. Film students have the opportunity to work at the Nims Center film studio complex as New Orleans becomes the "Hollywood of the South." Naval architecture students have access to the nation's largest undergraduate program in naval architecture and marine engineering as well as to the UNO–Avondale Maritime Center. As New Orleans continues to attract computer technology–based businesses to what has been called "the Silicon Bayou," the UNO Research and Technology Park continues to expand, producing more than 8,000 new jobs. Computer science majors are able to network with potential employers in one of the fastest-growing computer technology markets in the country.

Majors and Degrees

Bachelor of Science degrees are offered in accounting; biological sciences; chemistry; civil and environmental engineering; computer science; earth and environmental science; electrical engineering; entrepreneurship; finance; general business administration; hotel, restaurant, and tourism administration; management; marketing; mathematics; mechanical engineering; naval architecture and marine engineering; physics; psychology; transportation studies; urban studies and planning; and preprofessional programs in dentistry; medicine (with biology, chemistry, and psychology tracks); nursing; pharmacy; physical therapy studies; and veterinary medicine.

Bachelor of Arts degrees are offered in anthropology; early childhood education; elementary education; English; English education; film, theater, and communication arts; fine arts–history; fine arts–studio (with options that include digital media, painting, photography, and sculpture); French; geography; history; international studies; mathematics education; music (with options including instrumental, jazz studies, theory and composition, and vocal); music education; philosophy; political science; secondary education; social science education; sociology; Spanish; and women's studies.

A four-year Bachelor of General Studies degree program is available for students who wish to design individual curricula. Credit programs in paralegal studies, medical coding, and medical transcripts are also offered. Additional interdisciplinary minors are offered in interdisciplinary studies in African studies, Asian studies, entrepreneurship, environmental studies, Latin American and Caribbean studies, medical coding, Native American studies, paralegal studies, and print journalism.

Academic Programs

All baccalaureate degree programs require a minimum of 128 semester hours with a minimum grade point average of 2.0 (C) in all work attempted in the college major. Also, all students must successfully complete an approved course demonstrating computer literacy. Other course requirements vary according to program. Programs leading to degrees with honors are offered in most academic majors. Credit for selected courses may be earned either through advanced-standing exams administered by the academic departments or through the College Board's Advanced Placement and College-Level Examination Program tests. College credit may also be gained for certain armed services and other nonacademic training. The academic year is composed of sixteen-week fall and spring semesters and three summer sessions.

Off-Campus Programs

The University of New Orleans Metropolitan College coordinates international study programs in Austria, Costa Rica, the Czech Republic, Ecuador, France, Greece, Honduras, and Italy. UNO's partnership with the University of Innsbruck, Austria, affords students an opportunity to participate in the largest international summer school of any American university in Europe. UNO offers college-credit exchange programs in Brazil and Canada. Students may also attend another school within the continental United States via the National Student Exchange (NSE) for one semester or one year.

UNO offers several off-campus facilities throughout the metropolitan New Orleans area, demonstrating UNO's commitment to community outreach. Off-campus locations offer both credit and non-credit courses, with hours varying from sunrise to evening and weekend classes.

Academic Facilities

The Earl K. Long Library's 1.5-million-volume collection includes approximately 12,000 journals, of which 3,800 are current subscriptions. Microform holdings include microfilm, microcard, and microfiche formats; microtext readers and reader-printers are also available. Other facilities include individual study carrels, a music listening room, computer terminals connected to the Computer Research Center, a Kurzweil reader for the visually impaired, and photocopy services. The Office of Educational Support Services includes a media resources center, which provides important media aids for the instructional staff in classroom presentations, and Television Resources, which coordinates a closed-circuit cable system and TV production studio. WWNO, the first public radio station in Louisiana, is located on the UNO campus.

All enrolled students and faculty and staff members receive a LAN and e-mail account. The University's computer network provides connections to approximately 5,000 locations campuswide as well as wireless connections in select buildings. High-speed ResNet service is available to students living in Privateer Place, and a free dial-up Internet modem pool provides access for all off-campus enrolled students and faculty and staff members.

The UNO Lee Circle Center for the Arts includes the Ogden Museum, which houses the largest collection of Southern art in the world. The center also houses the National D-Day Museum, which includes the world's largest collection of World War II color film. The 70,000-square-foot Nims Center, located 20 minutes from the main campus, houses a professional-quality sound stage, including a 10,000-square-foot studio for University film projects. The Nims Center is also available for professional film projects.

Costs

In 2006–07, combined undergraduate fees for full-time students for the fall and spring semesters were $3820 for Louisiana residents and $10,864 for nonresidents; summer session fees for full-time students were $1080 for Louisiana residents and $1630 for nonresidents. Residence hall and board fees totaled $3800 (double occupancy) for the fall and spring semesters. Costs of books and supplies totaled $800 per year. Additional charges included a $40 application fee, a $10 registration fee, field service and laboratory fees (usually $10 to $35) for some courses, an $80 car registration fee (includes parking pass), a $30 late application fee, a $30 late registration fee, a $5 per-credit-hour (maximum $75) technology fee, and a $10 per-credit-hour (maximum $120) academic enhancement fee. All fees are subject to change and can be confirmed by calling the Office of Admissions.

Financial Aid

The Office of Student Financial Aid develops financial aid packages to assist students with their educational expenses. This package is usually a combination of grants, loans, student employment, and/or scholarships, which, along with family contribution, help to finance the student's education. To be eligible for most federal financial aid programs, students must enroll for at least 6 credit hours (half-time) in an eligible program (one that leads to a degree or certificate). Approximately 90 percent of all freshmen in fall 2006 who showed financial need and took at least 6 credit hours were offered some form of financial aid. The priority date for the financial aid application is May 1. All applications postmarked on or before March 1 are considered for UNO's numerous academic scholarships, including those of international students. The University of New Orleans also offers scholarships in jazz studies; classical music; fine arts; film, theater, and communication arts; and creative writing. These scholarships require either an audition or the submission of a portfolio or manuscript along with the scholarship application.

Faculty

UNO has 525 full-time and 175 part-time faculty members, most of whom participate in both graduate and undergraduate instruction and research activity. Graduate students serve as teaching assistants in laboratory courses under the close supervision of the faculty. Approximately 80 percent of the faculty members hold doctorates. Most full-time faculty members devote themselves exclusively to University-related pursuits and are integrally involved in student affairs through counseling, teaching, research, and social activities. The student-faculty ratio is 17:1.

Student Government

Every student enrolled at UNO is a member of the Student Government (SG). SG offers students a way to create effective change, express opinions and concerns, and utilize resources to enhance their educational experiences. Some of the programs SG currently offers and/or sponsors are Student Legal Services, the Academic Travel Fund, 24-hour study hall during finals week, UNO pep band (The Blue Zoo), UNO Soccer Club, the Mechanical Engineering Mini Baja Competition, UNO Jazz Night at the University Center, musical excursions, UNO Ambassadors Fishing Rodeo, the UNO student literary magazine (Ellipsis), recreation and intramural sports, cheerleaders, and the Privateer dance team.

Admission Requirements

Students seeking admission to the University of New Orleans should submit their application as early as possible in their senior year. Admission requirements for Louisiana residents and nonresidents for fall 2007 include the completion of the Board of Regents core curriculum (in years): English (4), mathematics (3), science (3), social studies (3), foreign language (2), fine arts (1), and computer science (½). Residents must also have either a high school cumulative GPA of at least 2.5 or an ACT composite score of at least 23 (1060 SAT) or rank in the top 25 percent of their high school graduating class, and students must not require more than one developmental/remedial course. Out-of-state students who do not meet the GPA, test score, and rank requirements must have a minimum ACT composite score of 26 (SAT 1170) for automatic admission.

Transfer requirements include the completion of 18 semester hours of nondevelopmental work, a minimum 2.25 cumulative GPA, and completion of all developmental course work before transferring. Students with fewer than 18 semester hours must meet both freshman and transfer requirements.

Application and Information

The University of New Orleans has a rolling admissions policy. The application fee is $40. Priority deadlines for application are as follows: July 1 for the fall semester, November 15 for the spring semester, and May 1 for the summer semester. Deadlines for international students are June 1, October 1, and March 1, respectively.

Office of Admissions
103 Administration Building
University of New Orleans
2000 Lakeshore Drive
New Orleans, Louisiana 70148
Phone: 504-280-6595
        800-256-5-UNO (toll-free)
Fax: 504-280-5522
Web site: http://www.uno.edu

Indexes

Majors and Degrees

Accounting

Albertson Coll of Idaho, ID	B
Arizona State U, AZ	B
Arizona State U at the West campus, AZ	B
Azusa Pacific U, CA	B
Boise State U, ID	B
Brigham Young U, UT	B
Brigham Young U–Hawaii, HI	A,B
Brigham Young U–Idaho, ID	A
California Baptist U, CA	B
California Lutheran U, CA	B
California State Polytechnic U, Pomona, CA	B
California State U, Chico, CA	B
California State U, Dominguez Hills, CA	B
California State U, Fresno, CA	B
California State U, Fullerton, CA	B
California State U, Long Beach, CA	B
California State U, Northridge, CA	B
California State U, Sacramento, CA	B
California State U, San Bernardino, CA	B
California State U, San Marcos, CA	B
Central Washington U, WA	B
Chapman U, CA	B
Claremont McKenna Coll, CA	B
CollAmerica–Colorado Springs, CO	A
CollAmerica–Denver, CO	A
Coll of Santa Fe, NM	B
Coll of the Southwest, NM	B
Colorado Christian U, CO	B
Colorado State U, CO	B
Colorado State U–Pueblo, CO	B
Corban Coll, OR	B
Dixie State Coll of Utah, UT	B
Eastern New Mexico U, NM	B
Eastern Oregon U, OR	B
Eastern Washington U, WA	B
Everest Coll, Phoenix, AZ	A
Fort Lewis Coll, CO	B
Fresno Pacific U, CA	B
Gonzaga U, WA	B
Grand Canyon U, AZ	B
Hawai'i Pacific U, HI	A,B
Humboldt State U, CA	B
Idaho State U, ID	B
International Inst of the Americas, Mesa, AZ	A
International Inst of the Americas, Phoenix, AZ	A
International Inst of the Americas, Tucson, AZ	A
International Inst of the Americas, NM	A
Johnson & Wales U, CO	A,B
La Sierra U, CA	B
LDS Business Coll, UT	A
Lincoln U, CA	B
Linfield Coll, OR	B
Loyola Marymount U, CA	B

The Master's Coll and Seminary, CA	B
Mesa State Coll, CO	B
Montana State U–Billings, MT	B
Montana Tech of The U of Montana, MT	B
Morrison U, NV	A,B
Mount St. Mary's Coll, CA	B
National American U, Denver, CO	A,B
National U, CA	B
New Mexico Highlands U, NM	B
New Mexico State U, NM	B
North Carolina Ag and Tech State U, NC	B
Northern Arizona U, AZ	B
Northwest Nazarene U, ID	B
Northwest U, WA	B
Oregon Inst of Technology, OR	B
Pacific Lutheran U, WA	B
Pacific Union Coll, CA	B
Pacific U, OR	B
Pepperdine U, Malibu, CA	B
Pioneer Pacific Coll, Wilsonville, OR	A
Point Loma Nazarene U, CA	B
Portland State U, OR	B
Prescott Coll, AZ	B
Regis U, CO	B
Rocky Mountain Coll, MT	B
Saint Mary's Coll of California, CA	B
San Diego State U, CA	B
San Francisco State U, CA	B
San Jose State U, CA	B
Santa Clara U, CA	B
Seattle Pacific U, WA	B
Seattle U, WA	B
Southern Oregon U, OR	B
Southern Utah U, UT	B
U of Alaska Anchorage, AK	A,B
U of Alaska Fairbanks, AK	B
The U of Arizona, AZ	B
U of Colorado at Boulder, CO	B
U of Colorado at Colorado Springs, CO	B
U of Denver, CO	B
U of Great Falls, MT	B
U of Hawaii at Manoa, HI	B
U of Idaho, ID	B
U of La Verne, CA	B
The U of Montana, MT	B
U of Nevada, Las Vegas, NV	B
U of Nevada, Reno, NV	B
U of New Mexico–Gallup, NM	A
U of New Orleans, LA	B
U of Oregon, OR	B
U of Phoenix–Bay Area Campus, CA	B
U of Phoenix–Central Valley Campus, CA	B
U of Phoenix–Denver Campus, CO	B
U of Phoenix–Hawaii Campus, HI	B
U of Phoenix–Idaho Campus, ID	B

U of Phoenix–Las Vegas Campus, NV	A,B
U of Phoenix–New Mexico Campus, NM	B
U of Phoenix Online Campus, AZ	B
U of Phoenix–Oregon Campus, OR	B
U of Phoenix–Phoenix Campus, AZ	B
U of Phoenix–Sacramento Valley Campus, CA	B
U of Phoenix–San Diego Campus, CA	B
U of Phoenix–Southern Arizona Campus, AZ	B
U of Phoenix–Southern California Campus, CA	B
U of Phoenix–Southern Colorado Campus, CO	B
U of Phoenix–Utah Campus, UT	B
U of Phoenix–Washington Campus, WA	B
U of Portland, OR	B
U of Redlands, CA	B
U of San Diego, CA	B
U of San Francisco, CA	B
U of Southern California, CA	B
U of Utah, UT	B
U of Washington, WA	B
U of Wyoming, WY	B
Utah State U, UT	B
Utah Valley State Coll, UT	A,B
Vanguard U of Southern California, CA	B
Walla Walla Coll, WA	B
Washington State U, WA	B
Weber State U, UT	B
Western International U, AZ	B
Western State Coll of Colorado, CO	B
Western Washington U, WA	B
Westminster Coll, UT	B
Whitworth U, WA	B
Woodbury U, CA	B

Accounting and Business/Management

Alaska Pacific U, AK	B
LDS Business Coll, UT	A
U of Great Falls, MT	B

Accounting and Computer Science

California State U, Chico, CA	B
San Jose State U, CA	B
Western Washington U, WA	B

Accounting Related

Brigham Young U, UT	B
California State U, Sacramento, CA	B
Montana State U–Billings, MT	A
Rocky Mountain Coll, MT	B
Saint Mary's Coll of California, CA	B

Accounting Technology and Bookkeeping

DeVry U, Fremont, CA	A
DeVry U, Pomona, CA	A
DeVry U, Westminster, CO	A
DeVry U, Federal Way, WA	A
LDS Business Coll, UT	A
Lewis-Clark State Coll, ID	A,B
Montana State U–Billings, MT	A
U of Alaska Fairbanks, AK	A
The U of Montana, MT	A

Acting

Brigham Young U, UT	B
California Inst of the Arts, CA	B
California State U, Long Beach, CA	B
Coll of Santa Fe, NM	B
George Fox U, OR	B
U of Southern California, CA	B

Actuarial Science

Brigham Young U, UT	B
The Master's Coll and Seminary, CA	B
Oregon State U, OR	B

Administrative Assistant and Secretarial Science

Brigham Young U–Idaho, ID	A
Chief Dull Knife Coll, MT	A
Dixie State Coll of Utah, UT	A
Eastern Oregon U, OR	A
Idaho State U, ID	A
LDS Business Coll, UT	A
Lewis-Clark State Coll, ID	A,B
Mesa State Coll, CO	A,B
Montana State U–Billings, MT	A
Montana Tech of The U of Montana, MT	A
Morrison U, NV	A
North Carolina Ag and Tech State U, NC	B
Salish Kootenai Coll, MT	A
Stone Child Coll, MT	A
U of Alaska Fairbanks, AK	A
U of Alaska Southeast, AK	A
U of Idaho, ID	B
The U of Montana, MT	B
The U of Montana–Western, MT	A
U of New Mexico–Gallup, NM	A
Utah State U, UT	A,B
Weber State U, UT	A,B

Adult and Continuing Education

Biola U, CA	B
San Diego Christian Coll, CA	B
U of Nevada, Las Vegas, NV	B
U of San Francisco, CA	B

Adult Development and Aging

U of Northern Colorado, CO	B

Advertising

Academy of Art U, CA	A,B
Art Center Coll of Design, CA	B
The Art Inst of California–Los Angeles, CA	B

A—associate degree; B—bachelor's degree

The Art Inst of California–
  Orange County, CA   B
The Art Inst of California–San
  Diego, CA   A,B
The Art Inst of California–San
  Francisco, CA   B
The Art Inst of Colorado, CO   B
The Art Inst of Phoenix, AZ   B
The Art Inst of Portland, OR   B
Boise State U, ID   B
Brigham Young U, UT   B
Brigham Young U–Idaho, ID   A
California State U, Fullerton,
  CA   B
Chapman U, CA   B
Colorado State U–Pueblo, CO   B
Hawai'i Pacific U, HI   B
Johnson & Wales U, CO   A
Northern Arizona U, AZ   B
Notre Dame de Namur U, CA   B
Pepperdine U, Malibu, CA   B
Portland State U, OR   B
San Diego State U, CA   B
San Jose State U, CA   B
U of Colorado at Boulder, CO   B
U of Nevada, Reno, NV   B
U of Oregon, OR   B

Aeronautical/Aerospace Engineering Technology
Utah State U, UT   B

Aeronautics/Aviation/ Aerospace Science and Technology
Arizona State U at the
  Polytechnic Campus, AZ   B
Central Washington U, WA   B
Embry-Riddle Aeronautical U,
  AZ   B
San Jose State U, CA   B

Aerospace, Aeronautical and Astronautical Engineering
California Inst of Technology,
  CA   B
California Polytechnic State U,
  San Luis Obispo, CA   B
California State Polytechnic U,
  Pomona, CA   B
California State U, Long
  Beach, CA   B
Embry-Riddle Aeronautical U,
  AZ   B
New Mexico State U, NM   B
San Diego State U, CA   B
San Jose State U, CA   B
Stanford U, CA   B
United States Air Force
  Academy, CO   B
The U of Arizona, AZ   B
U of California, Davis, CA   B
U of California, Irvine, CA   B
U of California, Los Angeles,
  CA   B
U of California, San Diego, CA   B
U of Colorado at Boulder, CO   B
U of Southern California, CA   B
U of Washington, WA   B
Utah State U, UT   B
Weber State U, UT   B

Aerospace Science
Arizona State U, AZ   B

African-American/Black Studies
Arizona State U, AZ   B
California State U, Dominguez
  Hills, CA   B
California State U, Fresno, CA   B
California State U, Fullerton,
  CA   B
California State U, Long
  Beach, CA   B
California State U, Los
  Angeles, CA   B
California State U, Northridge,
  CA   B
Claremont McKenna Coll, CA   B
Loyola Marymount U, CA   B
Pitzer Coll, CA   B
Pomona Coll, CA   B
San Diego State U, CA   B
San Francisco State U, CA   B
San Jose State U, CA   B
Scripps Coll, CA   B
Sonoma State U, CA   B
U of California, Berkeley, CA   B
U of California, Davis, CA   B
U of California, Irvine, CA   B
U of California, Los Angeles,
  CA   B
U of California, Riverside, CA   B
U of California, Santa Barbara,
  CA   B
The U of Montana, MT   B
U of Nevada, Las Vegas, NV   B
U of New Mexico, NM   B
U of Northern Colorado, CO   B
U of Southern California, CA   B
U of Washington, WA   B

African Languages
U of California, Los Angeles,
  CA   B

African Studies
Portland State U, OR   B
Stanford U, CA   B
U of California, Los Angeles,
  CA   B

Agribusiness
Adams State Coll, CO   B
Brigham Young U, UT   B
Colorado State U, CO   B
New Mexico State U, NM   B
U of Wyoming, WY   B

Agricultural and Extension Education
Colorado State U, CO   B

Agricultural and Horticultural Plant Breeding
Colorado State U, CO   B

Agricultural Animal Breeding
U of Nevada, Reno, NV   B

Agricultural/Biological Engineering and Bioengineering
California Polytechnic State U,
  San Luis Obispo, CA   B
California State Polytechnic U,
  Pomona, CA   B
Oregon State U, OR   B
The U of Arizona, AZ   B
U of California, Los Angeles,
  CA   B

U of Idaho, ID   B
Utah State U, UT   B

Agricultural Business and Management
Arizona State U at the
  Polytechnic Campus, AZ   B
Brigham Young U, UT   B
Brigham Young U–Idaho, ID   A
California Polytechnic State U,
  San Luis Obispo, CA   B
California State Polytechnic U,
  Pomona, CA   B
California State U, Chico, CA   B
California State U, Fresno, CA   B
Eastern New Mexico U, NM   B
Eastern Oregon U, OR   B
Fort Lewis Coll, CO   B
Montana State U, MT   B
North Carolina Ag and Tech
  State U, NC   B
Oregon State U, OR   B
Rocky Mountain Coll, MT   B
San Diego State U, CA   B
U of Hawaii at Hilo, HI   B
U of Idaho, ID   B
Utah State U, UT   B

Agricultural Business and Management Related
U of California, Davis, CA   B
Utah State U, UT   B

Agricultural Communication/ Journalism
U of Wyoming, WY   B
Washington State U, WA   B

Agricultural Economics
Brigham Young U, UT   B
Brigham Young U–Idaho, ID   A
Colorado State U, CO   B
Eastern Oregon U, OR   B
New Mexico State U, NM   B
North Carolina Ag and Tech
  State U, NC   B
Oregon State U, OR   B
The U of Arizona, AZ   B
U of Hawaii at Manoa, HI   B
U of Idaho, ID   B
U of Nevada, Reno, NV   B
Utah State U, UT   B

Agricultural Mechanization
Montana State U, MT   B
North Carolina Ag and Tech
  State U, NC   B
U of Idaho, ID   B
Washington State U, WA   B

Agricultural Production
U of Hawaii at Manoa, HI   B

Agricultural Teacher Education
California State Polytechnic U,
  Pomona, CA   B
California State U, Chico, CA   B
California State U, Fresno, CA   B
Colorado State U, CO   B
Eastern New Mexico U, NM   B
Montana State U, MT   B
New Mexico State U, NM   B
North Carolina Ag and Tech
  State U, NC   B
The U of Arizona, AZ   B
U of Idaho, ID   B
U of Nevada, Reno, NV   B
U of Wyoming, WY   B

Utah State U, UT   B
Washington State U, WA   B

Agriculture
Brigham Young U–Idaho, ID   A
California Polytechnic State U,
  San Luis Obispo, CA   B
California State Polytechnic U,
  Pomona, CA   B
California State U, Stanislaus,
  CA   B
Chief Dull Knife Coll, MT   A
Colorado State U, CO   B
Dixie State Coll of Utah, UT   A
Fort Lewis Coll, CO   A
New Mexico State U, NM   B
North Carolina Ag and Tech
  State U, NC   B
Oregon State U, OR   B
Southern Utah U, UT   A
The U of Arizona, AZ   B
U of Hawaii at Hilo, HI   B
U of Idaho, ID   B
Utah State U, UT   B
Washington State U, WA   B

Agriculture and Agriculture Operations Related
U of California, Davis, CA   B
U of Wyoming, WY   B
Washington State U, WA   B

Agronomy and Crop Science
Brigham Young U–Idaho, ID   A
California Polytechnic State U,
  San Luis Obispo, CA   B
California State Polytechnic U,
  Pomona, CA   B
California State U, Chico, CA   B
California State U, Fresno, CA   B
Colorado State U, CO   B
Eastern Oregon U, OR   B
New Mexico State U, NM   B
Oregon State U, OR   B
Utah State U, UT   B
Washington State U, WA   B

Aircraft Powerplant Technology
Idaho State U, ID   A

Air Force ROTC/Air Science
U of Washington, WA   B
Weber State U, UT   B

Airframe Mechanics and Aircraft Maintenance Technology
U of Alaska Anchorage, AK   A
U of Alaska Fairbanks, AK   A
Utah State U, UT   A,B

Airline Pilot and Flight Crew
Dixie State Coll of Utah, UT   A
Embry-Riddle Aeronautical U,
  AZ   B
Rocky Mountain Coll, MT   B
U of Alaska Anchorage, AK   A
Utah Valley State Coll, UT   A,B
Westminster Coll, UT   B

Air Traffic Control
U of Alaska Anchorage, AK   A

American Government and Politics
Chapman U, CA   B
Claremont McKenna Coll, CA   B

A—associate degree; B—bachelor's degree

The Master's Coll and
  Seminary, CA   B
Northern Arizona U, AZ   B
The U of Montana, MT   B

American History
Chapman U, CA   B

American Indian/Native American Studies
Arizona State U, AZ   B
The Evergreen State Coll, WA   B
Fort Lewis Coll, CO   B
Humboldt State U, CA   B
Northern Arizona U, AZ   B
Portland State U, OR   B
Salish Kootenai Coll, MT   A
Sonoma State U, CA   B
Stanford U, CA   B
U of Alaska Fairbanks, AK   B
U of California, Berkeley, CA   B
U of California, Davis, CA   B
U of California, Los Angeles,
  CA   B
U of California, Riverside, CA   B
The U of Montana, MT   B
U of Washington, WA   B

American Literature
U of California, Los Angeles,
  CA   B
U of Great Falls, MT   B
U of Southern California, CA   B

American Native/Native American Languages
Idaho State U, ID   A

American Sign Language (ASL)
Idaho State U, ID   A

American Studies
Arizona State U at the West
  campus, AZ   B
Brigham Young U, UT   B
California State U, Chico, CA   B
California State U, Fullerton,
  CA   B
California State U, Long
  Beach, CA   B
California State U, San
  Bernardino, CA   B
Claremont McKenna Coll, CA   B
Colorado State U, CO   B
Idaho State U, ID   B
Mills Coll, CA   B
Mount St. Mary's Coll, CA   B
Occidental Coll, CA   B
Oregon State U, OR   B
Pitzer Coll, CA   B
Pomona Coll, CA   B
Reed Coll, OR   B
Saint Mary's Coll of California,
  CA   B
San Diego State U, CA   B
San Francisco State U, CA   B
San Jose State U, CA   B
Scripps Coll, CA   B
Sonoma State U, CA   B
Stanford U, CA   B
U of California, Berkeley, CA   B
U of California, Davis, CA   B
U of California, Los Angeles,
  CA   B
U of California, Santa Cruz,
  CA   B
U of Hawaii at Manoa, HI   B
U of Idaho, ID   B

U of New Mexico, NM   B
U of Southern California, CA   B
U of Wyoming, WY   B
Utah State U, UT   B
Warner Pacific Coll, OR   B
Washington State U, WA   B
Western State Coll of
  Colorado, CO   B
Western Washington U, WA   B
Whitworth U, WA   B
Willamette U, OR   B

Ancient/Classical Greek
Brigham Young U, UT   B
California State U, Long
  Beach, CA   B
Multnomah Bible Coll and
  Biblical Seminary, OR   B
St. John's Coll, NM   B
Santa Clara U, CA   B
Stanford U, CA   B
U of California, Berkeley, CA   B
U of California, Los Angeles,
  CA   B
U of California, Santa Cruz,
  CA   B
U of Washington, WA   B

Ancient Near Eastern and Biblical Languages
Bethany U, CA   B
Brigham Young U, UT   B
The Master's Coll and
  Seminary, CA   B
Northwest Nazarene U, ID   B
Walla Walla Coll, WA   B

Ancient Studies
Santa Clara U, CA   B
Stanford U, CA   B

Animal Physiology
California State U, Fresno, CA   B
San Francisco State U, CA   B
Sonoma State U, CA   B
U of California, San Diego, CA   B
U of California, Santa Barbara,
  CA   B
Utah State U, UT   B

Animal Sciences
Brigham Young U–Idaho, ID   A
California Polytechnic State U,
  San Luis Obispo, CA   B
California State Polytechnic U,
  Pomona, CA   B
California State U, Chico, CA   B
California State U, Fresno, CA   B
Colorado State U, CO   B
Montana State U, MT   B
New Mexico State U, NM   B
North Carolina Ag and Tech
  State U, NC   B
Oregon State U, OR   B
The U of Arizona, AZ   B
U of California, Davis, CA   B
U of Denver, CO   B
U of Hawaii at Hilo, HI   B
U of Hawaii at Manoa, HI   B
U of Idaho, ID   B
U of Nevada, Reno, NV   B
Utah State U, UT   B
Washington State U, WA   B

Animal Sciences Related
U of California, Davis, CA   B
U of Wyoming, WY   B

Animation, Interactive Technology, Video Graphics and Special Effects
Academy of Art U, CA   A,B
The Art Inst of California–
  Inland Empire, CA   B
The Art Inst of California–Los
  Angeles, CA   B
The Art Inst of California–
  Orange County, CA   B
The Art Inst of California–San
  Francisco, CA   B
The Art Inst of Phoenix, AZ   B
The Art Inst of Portland, OR   B
The Art Inst of Seattle, WA   A,B
Brigham Young U, UT   B
Cogswell Polytechnical Coll,
  CA   B
ITT Tech Inst, Tempe, AZ   B
ITT Tech Inst, Tucson, AZ   B
ITT Tech Inst, Anaheim, CA   B
ITT Tech Inst, Lathrop, CA   B
ITT Tech Inst, Oxnard, CA   B
ITT Tech Inst, Rancho
  Cordova, CA   B
ITT Tech Inst, San Bernardino,
  CA   B
ITT Tech Inst, San Diego, CA   B
ITT Tech Inst, San Dimas, CA   B
ITT Tech Inst, Sylmar, CA   B
ITT Tech Inst, Torrance, CA   B
ITT Tech Inst, CO   B
ITT Tech Inst, ID   B
ITT Tech Inst, NV   B
ITT Tech Inst, NM   B
ITT Tech Inst, OR   B
ITT Tech Inst, UT   B
ITT Tech Inst, Bothell, WA   B
ITT Tech Inst, Seattle, WA   B
ITT Tech Inst, Spokane, WA   B
National U, CA   A
Nevada State Coll at
  Henderson, NV   B
Platt Coll San Diego, CA   A,B

Anthropology
Albertson Coll of Idaho, ID   B
Arizona State U, AZ   B
Biola U, CA   B
Boise State U, ID   B
Brigham Young U, UT   B
Brigham Young U–Hawaii, HI   B
California State Polytechnic U,
  Pomona, CA   B
California State U, Chico, CA   B
California State U, Dominguez
  Hills, CA   B
California State U, Fresno, CA   B
California State U, Fullerton,
  CA   B
California State U, Long
  Beach, CA   B
California State U, Los
  Angeles, CA   B
California State U, Northridge,
  CA   B
California State U, Sacramento,
  CA   B
California State U, San
  Bernardino, CA   B
California State U, Stanislaus,
  CA   B
Central Washington U, WA   B
Claremont McKenna Coll, CA   B
The Colorado Coll, CO   B
Colorado State U, CO   B

Eastern New Mexico U, NM   B
Eastern Oregon U, OR   B
Eastern Washington U, WA   B
Eugene Lang Coll The New
  School for Liberal Arts, NY   B
Fort Lewis Coll, CO   A
Great Basin Coll, NV   A
Hawai'i Pacific U, HI   B
Humboldt State U, CA   B
Idaho State U, ID   B
Lewis & Clark Coll, OR   B
Linfield Coll, OR   B
Mesa State Coll, CO   B
Mills Coll, CA   B
Montana State U, MT   B
New Mexico Highlands U, NM   B
New Mexico State U, NM   B
Northern Arizona U, AZ   B
Occidental Coll, CA   B
Oregon State U, OR   B
Pacific Lutheran U, WA   B
Pitzer Coll, CA   B
Pomona Coll, CA   B
Portland State U, OR   B
Prescott Coll, AZ   B
Reed Coll, OR   B
Saint Mary's Coll of California,
  CA   B
San Diego State U, CA   B
San Francisco State U, CA   B
San Jose State U, CA   B
Santa Clara U, CA   B
Scripps Coll, CA   B
Sonoma State U, CA   B
Southern Oregon U, OR   B
Stanford U, CA   B
U of Alaska Anchorage, AK   B
U of Alaska Fairbanks, AK   B
The U of Arizona, AZ   B
U of California, Berkeley, CA   B
U of California, Davis, CA   B
U of California, Irvine, CA   B
U of California, Los Angeles,
  CA   B
U of California, Riverside, CA   B
U of California, San Diego, CA   B
U of California, Santa Barbara,
  CA   B
U of California, Santa Cruz,
  CA   B
U of Colorado at Boulder, CO   B
U of Colorado at Colorado
  Springs, CO   B
U of Colorado at Denver and
  Health Sciences Center, CO   B
U of Denver, CO   B
U of Hawaii at Hilo, HI   B
U of Hawaii at Manoa, HI   B
U of Hawaii–West Oahu, HI   B
U of Idaho, ID   B
U of La Verne, CA   B
The U of Montana, MT   B
U of Nevada, Las Vegas, NV   B
U of Nevada, Reno, NV   B
U of New Mexico, NM   B
U of New Orleans, LA   B
U of Oregon, OR   B
U of Redlands, CA   B
U of San Diego, CA   B
U of Southern California, CA   B
U of Utah, UT   B
U of Washington, WA   B
U of Wyoming, WY   B
Utah State U, UT   B
Vanguard U of Southern
  California, CA   B

Washington State U, WA	B
Western Oregon U, OR	B
Western State Coll of Colorado, CO	B
Western Washington U, WA	B
Westmont Coll, CA	B
Whitman Coll, WA	B
Willamette U, OR	B

Anthropology Related

U of Southern California, CA	B

Apparel and Accessories Marketing

California Design Coll, CA	A
FIDM/The Fashion Inst of Design & Merchandising, Los Angeles Campus, CA	A
The U of Montana, MT	A

Apparel and Textiles

Academy of Art U, CA	A,B
California State U, Long Beach, CA	B
Colorado State U, CO	B
FIDM/The Fashion Inst of Design & Merchandising, Los Angeles Campus, CA	A
New Mexico State U, NM	B
Seattle Pacific U, WA	B
U of California, Davis, CA	B
U of Idaho, ID	B
Washington State U, WA	B

Apparel and Textiles Related

California State U, Sacramento, CA	B

Applied Art

Academy of Art U, CA	A,B
Azusa Pacific U, CA	B
California Coll of the Arts, CA	B
California Polytechnic State U, San Luis Obispo, CA	B
California State U, Dominguez Hills, CA	B
Colorado State U-Pueblo, CO	B
Mesa State Coll, CO	B
Oregon State U, OR	B
Otis Coll of Art and Design, CA	B
Portland State U, OR	B
The U of Montana–Western, MT	A,B
U of Oregon, OR	B

Applied Economics

Brigham Young U, UT	B
U of San Francisco, CA	B

Applied History

Chapman U, CA	B

Applied Horticulture

Colorado State U, CO	B

Applied Mathematics

California Inst of Technology, CA	B
California State Polytechnic U, Pomona, CA	B
California State U, Chico, CA	B
California State U, Fullerton, CA	B
California State U, Long Beach, CA	B
Colorado State U, CO	B
Fresno Pacific U, CA	B
Hawai'i Pacific U, HI	A,B

Humboldt State U, CA	B
The Master's Coll and Seminary, CA	B
Mesa State Coll, CO	B
Montana Tech of The U of Montana, MT	B
North Carolina Ag and Tech State U, NC	B
Oregon State U, OR	B
Pacific Union Coll, CA	B
San Diego State U, CA	B
San Francisco State U, CA	B
San Jose State U, CA	B
Seattle U, WA	B
Sonoma State U, CA	B
U of Alaska Fairbanks, AK	B
U of California, Berkeley, CA	B
U of California, Davis, CA	B
U of California, Los Angeles, CA	B
U of California, San Diego, CA	B
U of California, Santa Cruz, CA	B
U of Colorado at Boulder, CO	B
U of Colorado at Colorado Springs, CO	B
U of Idaho, ID	B
The U of Montana, MT	B
U of Nevada, Las Vegas, NV	B
U of Washington, WA	B
Weber State U, UT	B

Applied Mathematics Related

Arizona State U, AZ	B
U of Wyoming, WY	B

Aquatic Biology/Limnology

U of California, Santa Barbara, CA	B

Arabic

Brigham Young U, UT	B
U of California, Los Angeles, CA	B
U of Utah, UT	B

Archeology

Claremont McKenna Coll, CA	B
Saint Mary's Coll of California, CA	B
Stanford U, CA	B
U of California, Los Angeles, CA	B
U of California, San Diego, CA	B
Weber State U, UT	A
Western Washington U, WA	B

Architectural Drafting and CAD/CADD

Dixie State Coll of Utah, UT	A
Montana Tech of The U of Montana, MT	A

Architectural Engineering

California Polytechnic State U, San Luis Obispo, CA	B
North Carolina Ag and Tech State U, NC	B
U of Colorado at Boulder, CO	B
U of Wyoming, WY	B

Architectural Engineering Technology

Brigham Young U–Idaho, ID	A
U of Alaska Anchorage, AK	A

Architecture

Arizona State U, AZ	B

California Coll of the Arts, CA	B
California Polytechnic State U, San Luis Obispo, CA	B
California State Polytechnic U, Pomona, CA	B
Portland State U, OR	B
Southern California Inst of Architecture, CA	B
The U of Arizona, AZ	B
U of California, Berkeley, CA	B
U of California, Los Angeles, CA	B
U of Hawaii at Manoa, HI	B
U of Idaho, ID	B
U of Nevada, Las Vegas, NV	B
U of New Mexico, NM	B
U of Oregon, OR	B
U of San Francisco, CA	B
U of Southern California, CA	B
U of Utah, UT	B
U of Washington, WA	B
Washington State U, WA	B
Western State Coll of Colorado, CO	B
Woodbury U, CA	B

Architecture Related

U of Utah, UT	B

Area, Ethnic, Cultural, and Gender Studies Related

Brigham Young U–Hawaii, HI	B
Claremont McKenna Coll, CA	B
The Evergreen State Coll, WA	B
Linfield Coll, OR	B
Northwest Christian Coll, OR	B
Saint Mary's Coll of California, CA	B
U of California, Irvine, CA	B

Area Studies

Hawai'i Pacific U, HI	B
United States Air Force Academy, CO	B
The U of Montana, MT	B

Area Studies Related

Claremont McKenna Coll, CA	B
Hawai'i Pacific U, HI	B
U of Alaska Fairbanks, AK	B
U of California, Los Angeles, CA	B
Utah State U, UT	B

Army ROTC/Military Science

Brigham Young U–Idaho, ID	A
U of Washington, WA	B

Art

Adams State Coll, CO	B
Albertson Coll of Idaho, ID	B
Arizona State U, AZ	B
Art Center Coll of Design, CA	B
The Art Inst of Colorado, CO	A,B
Boise State U, ID	B
Brigham Young U, UT	B
Brigham Young U–Hawaii, HI	B
Brigham Young U–Idaho, ID	A
California Coll of the Arts, CA	B
California Inst of the Arts, CA	B
California Lutheran U, CA	B
California State Polytechnic U, Pomona, CA	B
California State U Channel Islands, CA	B
California State U, Chico, CA	B
California State U, Dominguez Hills, CA	B

California State U, Fresno, CA	B
California State U, Fullerton, CA	B
California State U, Long Beach, CA	B
California State U, Los Angeles, CA	B
California State U, Monterey Bay, CA	B
California State U, Northridge, CA	B
California State U, Sacramento, CA	B
California State U, San Bernardino, CA	B
California State U, Stanislaus, CA	B
Central Washington U, WA	B
Chapman U, CA	B
Claremont McKenna Coll, CA	B
Colorado Christian U, CO	B
Colorado State U-Pueblo, CO	B
Concordia U, CA	B
Dixie State Coll of Utah, UT	A
Dominican U of California, CA	B
Eastern New Mexico U, NM	A,B
Eastern Oregon U, OR	B
The Evergreen State Coll, WA	B
Fort Lewis Coll, CO	B
George Fox U, OR	B
Gonzaga U, WA	B
Grand Canyon U, AZ	B
Great Basin Coll, NV	A
Humboldt State U, CA	B
Idaho State U, ID	A,B
La Sierra U, CA	B
Lewis & Clark Coll, OR	B
Linfield Coll, OR	B
Marylhurst U, OR	B
Mesa State Coll, CO	A,B
Mills Coll, CA	B
Montana State U, MT	B
Montana State U–Billings, MT	B
Mount St. Mary's Coll, CA	B
New Mexico Highlands U, NM	B
Northern Arizona U, AZ	B
Northwest Coll of Art, WA	B
Northwest Nazarene U, ID	B
Oregon State U, OR	B
Otis Coll of Art and Design, CA	B
Pacific Lutheran U, WA	B
Pacific Union Coll, CA	B
Pacific U, OR	B
Pepperdine U, Malibu, CA	B
Pitzer Coll, CA	B
Point Loma Nazarene U, CA	B
Pomona Coll, CA	B
Portland State U, OR	B
Prescott Coll, AZ	B
Reed Coll, OR	B
Rocky Mountain Coll, MT	B
Saint Mary's Coll of California, CA	B
San Francisco State U, CA	B
San Jose State U, CA	B
Scripps Coll, CA	B
Seattle Pacific U, WA	B
Seattle U, WA	B
Sierra Nevada Coll, NV	B
Sonoma State U, CA	B
Southern Oregon U, OR	B
Southern Utah U, UT	B
Stanford U, CA	B
U of Alaska Anchorage, AK	B

A—associate degree; B—bachelor's degree

U of Alaska Fairbanks, AK — B
U of California, Berkeley, CA — B
U of California, Irvine, CA — B
U of California, Los Angeles, CA — B
U of California, San Diego, CA — B
U of California, Santa Barbara, CA — B
U of California, Santa Cruz, CA — B
U of Colorado at Colorado Springs, CO — B
U of Dallas, TX — B
U of Denver, CO — B
U of Great Falls, MT — B
U of Hawaii at Hilo, HI — B
U of Hawaii at Manoa, HI — B
U of Idaho, ID — B
U of La Verne, CA — B
The U of Montana, MT — B
U of Nevada, Las Vegas, NV — B
U of Nevada, Reno, NV — B
U of New Mexico, NM — B
U of New Mexico–Gallup, NM — A
U of Oregon, OR — B
U of Puget Sound, WA — B
U of San Diego, CA — B
U of San Francisco, CA — B
U of Southern California, CA — B
U of the Pacific, CA — B
U of Utah, UT — B
U of Washington, WA — B
U of Wyoming, WY — B
Utah State U, UT — B
Walla Walla Coll, WA — B
Weber State U, UT — B
Western Oregon U, OR — B
Western State Coll of Colorado, CO — B
Westminster Coll, UT — B
Westmont Coll, CA — B
Whitman Coll, WA — B
Whitworth U, WA — B
Willamette U, OR — B

Art History, Criticism and Conservation

Boise State U, ID — B
Brigham Young U, UT — B
California State U, Chico, CA — B
California State U, Dominguez Hills, CA — B
California State U, Fullerton, CA — B
California State U, Long Beach, CA — B
California State U, San Bernardino, CA — B
Chapman U, CA — B
Claremont McKenna Coll, CA — B
Coll of Santa Fe, NM — B
The Colorado Coll, CO — B
Colorado State U, CO — B
Dixie State Coll of Utah, UT — A
Dominican U of California, CA — B
Eastern Washington U, WA — B
Humboldt State U, CA — B
Loyola Marymount U, CA — B
Mills Coll, CA — B
Northern Arizona U, AZ — B
Occidental Coll, CA — B
Oregon State U, OR — B
Pacific Lutheran U, WA — B
Pacific Union Coll, CA — B
Pitzer Coll, CA — B
Pomona Coll, CA — B
Portland State U, OR — B

Saint Mary's Coll of California, CA — B
San Diego State U, CA — B
San Jose State U, CA — B
Santa Clara U, CA — B
Scripps Coll, CA — B
Seattle U, WA — B
Sonoma State U, CA — B
Stanford U, CA — B
The U of Arizona, AZ — B
U of California, Berkeley, CA — B
U of California, Davis, CA — B
U of California, Irvine, CA — B
U of California, Los Angeles, CA — B
U of California, Riverside, CA — B
U of California, San Diego, CA — B
U of California, Santa Barbara, CA — B
U of California, Santa Cruz, CA — B
U of Dallas, TX — B
U of Denver, CO — B
U of La Verne, CA — B
The U of Montana, MT — B
U of Nevada, Las Vegas, NV — B
U of Nevada, Reno, NV — B
U of New Mexico, NM — B
U of New Orleans, LA — B
U of Oregon, OR — B
U of Redlands, CA — B
U of San Francisco, CA — B
U of Southern California, CA — B
U of the Pacific, CA — B
U of Utah, UT — B
U of Washington, WA — B
Washington State U, WA — B
Western State Coll of Colorado, CO — B
Western Washington U, WA — B
Willamette U, OR — B

Artificial Intelligence and Robotics

Montana Tech of The U of Montana, MT — B

Arts Management

Coll of Santa Fe, NM — B
Fort Lewis Coll, CO — B
Northern Arizona U, AZ — B
U of Portland, OR — B
U of San Francisco, CA — B
Whitworth U, WA — B

Art Teacher Education

Boise State U, ID — B
Brigham Young U, UT — B
Brigham Young U–Hawaii, HI — B
California Lutheran U, CA — B
California State U, Chico, CA — B
California State U, Fullerton, CA — B
California State U, Long Beach, CA — B
Central Washington U, WA — B
Colorado State U, CO — B
Colorado State U-Pueblo, CO — B
Eastern Washington U, WA — B
Grand Canyon U, AZ — B
Humboldt State U, CA — B
Montana State U–Billings, MT — B
Mount St. Mary's Coll, CA — B
New Mexico Highlands U, NM — B
North Carolina Ag and Tech State U, NC — B
Northern Arizona U, AZ — B
Northwest Nazarene U, ID — B

Pacific Lutheran U, WA — B
Pacific U, OR — B
Point Loma Nazarene U, CA — B
Rocky Mountain Coll, MT — B
Rocky Mountain Coll of Art & Design, CO — B
Seattle Pacific U, WA — B
Southern Utah U, UT — B
The U of Arizona, AZ — B
U of Dallas, TX — B
U of Denver, CO — B
U of Great Falls, MT — B
U of Idaho, ID — B
The U of Montana, MT — B
The U of Montana–Western, MT — B
U of Nevada, Reno, NV — B
U of New Mexico, NM — B
Walla Walla Coll, WA — B
Weber State U, UT — B
Western State Coll of Colorado, CO — B
Western Washington U, WA — B
Westmont Coll, CA — B
Whitworth U, WA — B

Art Therapy

Coll of Santa Fe, NM — B
Prescott Coll, AZ — B

Asian-American Studies

California State U, Fullerton, CA — B
California State U, Long Beach, CA — B
California State U, Los Angeles, CA — B
California State U, Northridge, CA — B
Claremont McKenna Coll, CA — B
Colorado State U, CO — B
Loyola Marymount U, CA — B
Pitzer Coll, CA — B
Scripps Coll, CA — B
U of California, Berkeley, CA — B
U of California, Davis, CA — B
U of California, Irvine, CA — B
U of California, Los Angeles, CA — B
U of California, Riverside, CA — B
U of California, Santa Barbara, CA — B
U of Denver, CO — B
U of Southern California, CA — B

Asian History

U of the West, CA — B

Asian Studies

Brigham Young U, UT — B
California State U, Chico, CA — B
California State U, Long Beach, CA — B
California State U, Los Angeles, CA — B
California State U, Sacramento, CA — B
Central Washington U, WA — B
Claremont McKenna Coll, CA — B
The Colorado Coll, CO — B
Colorado State U, CO — B
Fort Lewis Coll, CO — B
Gonzaga U, WA — B
Occidental Coll, CA — B
Pitzer Coll, CA — B
Pomona Coll, CA — B
San Diego State U, CA — B
Scripps Coll, CA — B

Stanford U, CA — B
U of California, Berkeley, CA — B
U of California, Los Angeles, CA — B
U of California, Riverside, CA — B
U of California, Santa Barbara, CA — B
U of California, Santa Cruz, CA — B
U of Colorado at Boulder, CO — B
U of Hawaii at Manoa, HI — B
The U of Montana, MT — B
U of New Mexico, NM — B
U of Oregon, OR — B
U of Puget Sound, WA — B
U of Redlands, CA — B
U of San Francisco, CA — B
U of Utah, UT — B
U of Washington, WA — B
Utah State U, UT — B
Washington State U, WA — B
Western Washington U, WA — B
Whitman Coll, WA — B
Willamette U, OR — B

Asian Studies (East)

Lewis & Clark Coll, OR — B
Pomona Coll, CA — B
Portland State U, OR — B
Scripps Coll, CA — B
Seattle U, WA — B
Stanford U, CA — B
The U of Arizona, AZ — B
U of California, Davis, CA — B
U of California, Irvine, CA — B
U of California, Los Angeles, CA — B
U of California, Santa Cruz, CA — B
The U of Montana, MT — B
U of Oregon, OR — B
U of Southern California, CA — B
U of Washington, WA — B
Western Washington U, WA — B

Asian Studies (South)

U of California, Santa Cruz, CA — B
U of Washington, WA — B

Asian Studies (Southeast)

U of California, Berkeley, CA — B
U of California, Los Angeles, CA — B
U of California, Santa Cruz, CA — B
U of Washington, WA — B

Astronomy

Brigham Young U, UT — B
Northern Arizona U, AZ — B
Pomona Coll, CA — B
San Diego State U, CA — B
San Francisco State U, CA — B
The U of Arizona, AZ — B
U of California, Los Angeles, CA — B
U of Colorado at Boulder, CO — B
The U of Montana, MT — B
U of Southern California, CA — B
U of Washington, WA — B
Whitman Coll, WA — B

Astronomy and Astrophysics Related

U of Wyoming, WY — B

Astrophysics
California Inst of Technology, CA — B
San Francisco State U, CA — B
U of California, Berkeley, CA — B
U of California, Los Angeles, CA — B
U of California, Santa Cruz, CA — B
U of New Mexico, NM — B

Athletic Training
Azusa Pacific U, CA — B
Boise State U, ID — B
Brigham Young U, UT — B
Brigham Young U–Idaho, ID — A
California Lutheran U, CA — B
California State U, Long Beach, CA — B
Chapman U, CA — B
Colorado State U, CO — B
Colorado State U-Pueblo, CO — B
Eastern Washington U, WA — B
Fort Lewis Coll, CO — B
Fresno Pacific U, CA — B
George Fox U, OR — B
Grand Canyon U, AZ — B
Hope International U, CA — B
Linfield Coll, OR — B
New Mexico State U, NM — B
Northwest Nazarene U, ID — B
Oregon State U, OR — B
Pacific U, OR — B
Pepperdine U, Malibu, CA — B
Point Loma Nazarene U, CA — B
Rocky Mountain Coll, MT — B
San Diego Christian Coll, CA — B
U of Idaho, ID — B
U of Nevada, Las Vegas, NV — B
Vanguard U of Southern California, CA — B
Washington State U, WA — B
Weber State U, UT — B
Western State Coll of Colorado, CO — B
Whitworth U, WA — B

Atmospheric Sciences and Meteorology
Embry-Riddle Aeronautical U, AZ — B
San Francisco State U, CA — B
San Jose State U, CA — B
United States Air Force Academy, CO — B
The U of Arizona, AZ — B
U of California, Berkeley, CA — B
U of California, Davis, CA — B
U of California, Los Angeles, CA — B
U of Utah, UT — B
U of Washington, WA — B

Atomic/Molecular Physics
San Diego State U, CA — B
U of California, San Diego, CA — B

Audio Engineering
The Art Inst of Seattle, WA — A
Cogswell Polytechnical Coll, CA — B

Audiology and Hearing Sciences
California State U, Long Beach, CA — B
U of Northern Colorado, CO — B

Audiology and Speech-Language Pathology
Brigham Young U, UT — B
California State U, Fresno, CA — B
California State U, Fullerton, CA — B
California State U, Long Beach, CA — B
California State U, Sacramento, CA — B
Eastern New Mexico U, NM — B
Eastern Washington U, WA — B
Idaho State U, ID — B
Loma Linda U, CA — B
San Francisco State U, CA — B
The U of Montana, MT — B
U of New Mexico, NM — B
U of Oregon, OR — B
U of Redlands, CA — B
U of the Pacific, CA — B
U of Utah, UT — B
U of Washington, WA — B
U of Wyoming, WY — B
Utah State U, UT — B
Western Washington U, WA — B

Audiovisual Communications Technologies Related
Nevada State Coll at Henderson, NV — B

Autobody/Collision and Repair Technology
Dixie State Coll of Utah, UT — A
Idaho State U, ID — A
Lewis-Clark State Coll, ID — A,B
Montana State U–Billings, MT — A
Montana Tech of The U of Montana, MT — A
Utah Valley State Coll, UT — A
Weber State U, UT — A

Automobile/Automotive Mechanics Technology
Boise State U, ID — A
Brigham Young U–Idaho, ID — A
Colorado State U-Pueblo, CO — B
Dixie State Coll of Utah, UT — A
Idaho State U, ID — A
Lewis-Clark State Coll, ID — A,B
Mesa State Coll, CO — A
Montana State U–Billings, MT — A
Montana Tech of The U of Montana, MT — A
Southern Utah U, UT — A
U of Alaska Anchorage, AK — A
U of New Mexico–Gallup, NM — A
Utah Valley State Coll, UT — A
Walla Walla Coll, WA — A,B
Weber State U, UT — A,B

Automotive Engineering Technology
Weber State U, UT — B

Aviation/Airway Management
California State U, Los Angeles, CA — B
Dixie State Coll of Utah, UT — A
Rocky Mountain Coll, MT — B
U of Alaska Anchorage, AK — A
U of Alaska Fairbanks, AK — A
Westminster Coll, UT — B

Avionics Maintenance Technology
U of Alaska Anchorage, AK — A
Walla Walla Coll, WA — A,B

Baking and Pastry Arts
The Art Inst of California–San Diego, CA — A,B
Johnson & Wales U, CO — A

Ballet
Brigham Young U, UT — B
U of Utah, UT — B

Banking and Financial Support Services
National U, CA — B
Utah Valley State Coll, UT — A

Behavioral Sciences
California Baptist U, CA — B
California State Polytechnic U, Pomona, CA — B
California State U, Dominguez Hills, CA — B
California State U, Monterey Bay, CA — B
Concordia U, CA — B
George Fox U, OR — B
Hawai'i Pacific U, HI — B
Lewis-Clark State Coll, ID — A
Mesa State Coll, CO — B
National U, CA — B
Notre Dame de Namur U, CA — B
Pacific Union Coll, CA — B
San Jose State U, CA — B
United States Air Force Academy, CO — B
U of La Verne, CA — B
U of Utah, UT — B
Utah Valley State Coll, UT — A,B
Western International U, AZ — B

Biblical Studies
Alaska Bible Coll, AK — A,B
Azusa Pacific U, CA — B
Bethany U, CA — B
Biola U, CA — B
Boise Bible Coll, ID — A,B
California Baptist U, CA — B
California Christian Coll, CA — A,B
Cascade Coll, OR — B
Colorado Christian U, CO — B
Corban Coll, OR — A,B
Eugene Bible Coll, OR — B
Fresno Pacific U, CA — A,B
George Fox U, OR — B
Grand Canyon U, AZ — B
Hope International U, CA — B
The Master's Coll and Seminary, CA — B
Multnomah Bible Coll and Biblical Seminary, OR — B
Nazarene Bible Coll, CO — A,B
Northwest Christian Coll, OR — B
Northwest U, WA — B
Pacific Union Coll, CA — A
Patten U, CA — A,B
Point Loma Nazarene U, CA — B
San Diego Christian Coll, CA — B
Shasta Bible Coll, CA — A,B
Simpson U, CA — A,B
Trinity Lutheran Coll, WA — A,B
Vanguard U of Southern California, CA — B
Warner Pacific Coll, OR — A,B

Bilingual and Multilingual Education
Biola U, CA — B
Boise State U, ID — B
California State Polytechnic U, Pomona, CA — B
California State U, Dominguez Hills, CA — B
Coll of the Southwest, NM — B
Fresno Pacific U, CA — B
Nevada State Coll at Henderson, NV — B
New Mexico Highlands U, NM — B
Prescott Coll, AZ — B
U of San Francisco, CA — B
U of Washington, WA — B
Washington State U, WA — B
Weber State U, UT — B

Biochemistry
Arizona State U, AZ — B
Azusa Pacific U, CA — B
Biola U, CA — B
Brigham Young U, UT — B
Brigham Young U–Hawaii, HI — B
California Lutheran U, CA — B
California Polytechnic State U, San Luis Obispo, CA — B
California State U, Chico, CA — B
California State U, Dominguez Hills, CA — B
California State U, Fullerton, CA — B
California State U, Long Beach, CA — B
California State U, Los Angeles, CA — B
California State U, Northridge, CA — B
California State U, San Bernardino, CA — B
California State U, San Marcos, CA — B
Chapman U, CA — B
Claremont McKenna Coll, CA — B
The Colorado Coll, CO — B
Colorado State U, CO — B
Eastern Washington U, WA — B
Fort Lewis Coll, CO — B
Gonzaga U, WA — B
Humboldt State U, CA — B
Idaho State U, ID — B
La Sierra U, CA — B
Lewis & Clark Coll, OR — B
Loyola Marymount U, CA — B
Mills Coll, CA — B
Mount St. Mary's Coll, CA — B
New Mexico State U, NM — B
Northwest Nazarene U, ID — B
Notre Dame de Namur U, CA — B
Occidental Coll, CA — B
Oregon State U, OR — B
Pacific Lutheran U, WA — B
Pacific Union Coll, CA — B
Pitzer Coll, CA — B
Point Loma Nazarene U, CA — B
Pomona Coll, CA — B
Portland State U, OR — B
Reed Coll, OR — B
Regis U, CO — B
Saint Mary's Coll of California, CA — B
San Francisco State U, CA — B
San Jose State U, CA — B
Scripps Coll, CA — B

A—associate degree; B—bachelor's degree

Seattle Pacific U, WA	B
Seattle U, WA	B
Southern Oregon U, OR	B
United States Air Force Academy, CO	B
The U of Arizona, AZ	B
U of California, Los Angeles, CA	B
U of California, Riverside, CA	B
U of California, San Diego, CA	B
U of California, Santa Barbara, CA	B
U of California, Santa Cruz, CA	B
U of Colorado at Boulder, CO	B
U of Dallas, TX	B
U of Denver, CO	B
The U of Montana, MT	B
U of Nevada, Las Vegas, NV	B
U of Nevada, Reno, NV	B
U of New Mexico, NM	B
U of Oregon, OR	B
U of Southern California, CA	B
U of the Pacific, CA	B
U of Washington, WA	B
Washington State U, WA	B
Western State Coll of Colorado, CO	B
Western Washington U, WA	B
Whitman Coll, WA	B

Biochemistry/Biophysics and Molecular Biology

California State U, Long Beach, CA	B

Biochemistry, Biophysics and Molecular Biology Related

Washington State U, WA	B

Bioinformatics

Brigham Young U, UT	B
U of Denver, CO	B

Biological and Biomedical Sciences Related

Arizona State U, AZ	B
Holy Names U, CA	B
Saint Mary's Coll of California, CA	B

Biological and Physical Sciences

Adams State Coll, CO	B
Brigham Young U, UT	B
California State U, Fresno, CA	B
Colorado Christian U, CO	B
Concordia U, OR	B
Eastern Oregon U, OR	B
Eastern Washington U, WA	B
The Evergreen State Coll, WA	B
Little Big Horn Coll, MT	A
Marylhurst, OR	B
The Master's Coll and Seminary, CA	B
Montana Tech of The U of Montana, MT	A,B
Oregon State U, OR	B
Portland State U, OR	B
San Francisco State U, CA	B
Santa Clara U, CA	B
Seattle U, WA	B
Sierra Nevada Coll, NV	B
United States Air Force Academy, CO	
U of Alaska Anchorage, AK	B
U of Alaska Fairbanks, AK	B
U of Denver, CO	B

U of Oregon, OR	B
Vanguard U of Southern California, CA	B
Warner Pacific Coll, OR	B
Western Washington U, WA	B

Biological Specializations Related

Arizona State U, AZ	B
San Jose State U, CA	B
Utah State U, UT	B

Biology/Biological Sciences

Adams State Coll, CO	B
Albertson Coll of Idaho, ID	B
Arizona State U, AZ	B
Arizona State U at the Polytechnic Campus, AZ	B
Arizona State U at the West campus, AZ	B
Azusa Pacific U, CA	B
Biola U, CA	B
Boise State U, ID	B
Brigham Young U, UT	B
Brigham Young U–Hawaii, HI	B
Brigham Young U–Idaho, ID	A
California Baptist U, CA	B
California Inst of Technology, CA	B
California Lutheran U, CA	B
California Polytechnic State U, San Luis Obispo, CA	B
California State Polytechnic U, Pomona, CA	B
California State U Channel Islands, CA	B
California State U, Chico, CA	B
California State U, Dominguez Hills, CA	B
California State U, Fresno, CA	B
California State U, Fullerton, CA	B
California State U, Long Beach, CA	B
California State U, Los Angeles, CA	B
California State U, Northridge, CA	B
California State U, Sacramento, CA	B
California State U, San Bernardino, CA	B
California State U, San Marcos, CA	B
California State U, Stanislaus, CA	B
Central Washington U, WA	B
Chapman U, CA	B
Claremont McKenna Coll, CA	B
Cleveland Chiropractic Coll-Los Angeles Campus, CA	A,B
Coll of the Southwest, NM	B
Colorado Christian U, CO	B
The Colorado Coll, CO	B
Colorado State U, CO	B
Colorado State U-Pueblo, CO	B
Concordia U, CA	B
Concordia U, OR	B
Dixie State Coll of Utah, UT	A
Dominican U of California, CA	B
Eastern New Mexico U, NM	B
Eastern Oregon U, OR	B
Eastern Washington U, WA	B
The Evergreen State Coll, WA	B
Fort Lewis Coll, CO	B
Fresno Pacific U, CA	A,B

George Fox U, OR	B
Gonzaga U, WA	B
Grand Canyon U, AZ	B
Harvey Mudd Coll, CA	B
Hawai'i Pacific U, HI	B
Holy Names U, CA	B
Humboldt State U, CA	B
Idaho State U, ID	A,B
Lewis & Clark Coll, OR	B
Lewis-Clark State Coll, ID	B
Linfield Coll, OR	B
Loyola Marymount U, CA	B
The Master's Coll and Seminary, CA	B
Mesa State Coll, CO	A,B
Mills Coll, CA	B
Montana State U, MT	B
Montana State U–Billings, MT	B
Montana Tech of The U of Montana, MT	A,B
Mount St. Mary's Coll, CA	B
National U, CA	B
Nevada State Coll at Henderson, NV	B
New Mexico Highlands U, NM	B
New Mexico Inst of Mining and Technology, NM	B
New Mexico State U, NM	B
North Carolina Ag and Tech State U, NC	B
Northern Arizona U, AZ	B
Northwest Nazarene U, ID	B
Notre Dame de Namur U, CA	B
Occidental Coll, CA	B
Oregon State U, OR	B
Pacific Lutheran U, WA	B
Pacific Union Coll, CA	B
Pacific U, OR	B
Pepperdine U, Malibu, CA	B
Pitzer Coll, CA	B
Point Loma Nazarene U, CA	B
Pomona Coll, CA	B
Portland State U, OR	B
Prescott Coll, AZ	B
Reed Coll, OR	B
Regis U, CO	B
Rocky Mountain Coll, MT	B
Saint Mary's Coll of California, CA	B
San Diego Christian Coll, CA	B
San Diego State U, CA	B
San Francisco State U, CA	B
San Jose State U, CA	B
Santa Clara U, CA	B
Scripps Coll, CA	B
Seattle Pacific U, WA	B
Seattle U, WA	B
Sonoma State U, CA	B
Southern Oregon U, OR	B
Southern Utah U, UT	B
Stanford U, CA	B
United States Air Force Academy, CO	B
U of Alaska Fairbanks, AK	B
U of Alaska Southeast, AK	B
The U of Arizona, AZ	B
U of California, Berkeley, CA	B
U of California, Davis, CA	B
U of California, Irvine, CA	B
U of California, Los Angeles, CA	B
U of California, Riverside, CA	B
U of California, San Diego, CA	B
U of California, Santa Barbara, CA	B

U of California, Santa Cruz, CA	B
U of Colorado at Colorado Springs, CO	B
U of Colorado at Denver and Health Sciences Center, CO	B
U of Dallas, TX	B
U of Denver, CO	B
U of Great Falls, MT	B
U of Hawaii at Hilo, HI	B
U of Hawaii at Manoa, HI	B
U of Idaho, ID	B
U of La Verne, CA	B
The U of Montana, MT	B
U of Nevada, Las Vegas, NV	B
U of Nevada, Reno, NV	B
U of New Mexico, NM	B
U of New Orleans, LA	B
U of Northern Colorado, CO	B
U of Oregon, OR	B
U of Portland, OR	B
U of Puget Sound, WA	B
U of Redlands, CA	B
U of San Diego, CA	B
U of San Francisco, CA	B
U of Southern California, CA	B
U of the Pacific, CA	B
U of Utah, UT	B
U of Washington, WA	B
U of Wyoming, WY	B
Utah State U, UT	B
Utah Valley State Coll, UT	A,B
Vanguard U of Southern California, CA	B
Walla Walla Coll, WA	B
Warner Pacific Coll, OR	B
Washington State U, WA	B
Western Oregon U, OR	B
Western State Coll of Colorado, CO	B
Western Washington U, WA	B
Westminster Coll, UT	B
Westmont Coll, CA	B
Whitman Coll, WA	B
Whitworth U, WA	B
Willamette U, OR	B

Biology/Biotechnology Laboratory Technician

California State Polytechnic U, Pomona, CA	B
California State U, Sacramento, CA	B
Weber State U, UT	A

Biology Teacher Education

Brigham Young U–Hawaii, HI	B
California State U, Chico, CA	B
California State U, Long Beach, CA	B
Central Washington U, WA	B
Colorado State U, CO	B
Corban Coll, OR	B
Fort Lewis Coll, CO	B
Montana State U–Billings, MT	B
Nevada State Coll at Henderson, NV	B
Northern Arizona U, AZ	B
Northwest Nazarene U, ID	B
Northwest U, WA	B
Rocky Mountain Coll, MT	B
Seattle Pacific U, WA	B
The U of Arizona, AZ	B
U of Great Falls, MT	B
The U of Montana–Western, MT	B
U of Utah, UT	B

U of Washington, WA — B
Utah State U, UT — B
Utah Valley State Coll, UT — B
Washington State U, WA — B
Weber State U, UT — B
Westminster Coll, UT — B

Biomathematics and Bioinformatics Related
U of California, Los Angeles, CA — B

Biomedical/Medical Engineering
Arizona State U, AZ — B
California Lutheran U, CA — B
California State U, Long Beach, CA — B
U of California, Berkeley, CA — B
U of California, Davis, CA — B
U of California, Irvine, CA — B
U of California, Los Angeles, CA — B
U of California, San Diego, CA — B
U of Idaho, ID — B
U of Southern California, CA — B
U of the Pacific, CA — B
U of Utah, UT — B
Walla Walla Coll, WA — B

Biomedical Sciences
Brigham Young U, UT — B
U of California, Riverside, CA — B
U of Colorado at Denver and Health Sciences Center, CO — B
U of Utah, UT — B

Biomedical Technology
Colorado State U-Pueblo, CO — B
DeVry U, Phoenix, AZ — B
DeVry U, Fremont, CA — B
DeVry U, Long Beach, CA — B
DeVry U, Pomona, CA — B
DeVry U, Westminster, CO — B
DeVry U, Federal Way, WA — B
Walla Walla Coll, WA — B

Biophysics
Brigham Young U, UT — B
Claremont McKenna Coll, CA — B
La Sierra U, CA — B
Oregon State U, OR — B
Pacific Union Coll, CA — B
U of California, Los Angeles, CA — B
U of California, San Diego, CA — B
U of Southern California, CA — B
Walla Walla Coll, WA — B
Washington State U, WA — B
Whitman Coll, WA — B

Biopsychology
Chapman U, CA — B
U of California, Santa Barbara, CA — B
U of Denver, CO — B
Western State Coll of Colorado, CO — B

Biostatistics
Brigham Young U, UT — B
U of California, Los Angeles, CA — B
U of Washington, WA — B

Biotechnology
Brigham Young U, UT — B
Dixie State Coll of Utah, UT — A

Eastern Washington U, WA — B
Montana State U, MT — B
Northern New Mexico Coll, NM — A
U of California, Davis, CA — B
U of California, Los Angeles, CA — B
U of California, San Diego, CA — B
U of Nevada, Reno, NV — B
Washington State U, WA — B

Botany/Plant Biology
Arizona State U, AZ — B
Brigham Young U, UT — B
Brigham Young U–Idaho, ID — A
California State Polytechnic U, Pomona, CA — B
California State U, Long Beach, CA — B
Colorado State U, CO — B
Dixie State Coll of Utah, UT — A
Humboldt State U, CA — B
Idaho State U, ID — B
Northern Arizona U, AZ — B
Oregon State U, OR — B
San Francisco State U, CA — B
Sonoma State U, CA — B
Southern Utah U, UT — B
U of California, Berkeley, CA — B
U of California, Davis, CA — B
U of California, Los Angeles, CA — B
U of California, Riverside, CA — B
U of California, Santa Cruz, CA — B
U of Great Falls, MT — B
U of Hawaii at Manoa, HI — B
U of Idaho, ID — B
The U of Montana, MT — B
U of Washington, WA — B
U of Wyoming, WY — B
Utah State U, UT — B
Weber State U, UT — B

Broadcast Journalism
Brigham Young U, UT — B
Brigham Young U–Idaho, ID — A
California State U, Long Beach, CA — B
Chapman U, CA — B
Colorado State U-Pueblo, CO — B
Columbia Coll Hollywood, CA — B
Dixie State Coll of Utah, UT — A
George Fox U, OR — B
Gonzaga U, WA — B
Humboldt State U, CA — B
Mesa State Coll, CO — B
Pacific Lutheran U, WA — B
Pacific U, OR — B
Point Loma Nazarene U, CA — B
U of Colorado at Boulder, CO — B
U of La Verne, CA — B
U of Nevada, Reno, NV — B
U of Oregon, OR — B
U of Southern California, CA — B
U of Utah, UT — B

Buddhist Studies
U of the West, CA — B

Building/Home/Construction Inspection
Utah Valley State Coll, UT — A

Business Administration and Management
Adams State Coll, CO — B

Alaska Pacific U, AK — A,B
Albertson Coll of Idaho, ID — B
Alliant International U, CA — B
Argosy U, Orange County, CA — A,B
Argosy U, San Francisco Bay Area, CA — B
Arizona State U, AZ — B
Arizona State U at the Polytechnic Campus, AZ — B
Azusa Pacific U, CA — B
Biola U, CA — B
Boise State U, ID — B
Brigham Young U, UT — B
Brigham Young U–Hawaii, HI — B
Brigham Young U–Idaho, ID — A
California Baptist U, CA — B
California Lutheran U, CA — B
California Maritime Academy, CA — B
California Polytechnic State U, San Luis Obispo, CA — B
California State Polytechnic U, Pomona, CA — B
California State U Channel Islands, CA — B
California State U, Chico, CA — B
California State U, Dominguez Hills, CA — B
California State U, Fresno, CA — B
California State U, Fullerton, CA — B
California State U, Long Beach, CA — B
California State U, Los Angeles, CA — B
California State U, Monterey Bay, CA — B
California State U, Northridge, CA — B
California State U, Sacramento, CA — B
California State U, San Bernardino, CA — B
California State U, San Marcos, CA — B
California State U, Stanislaus, CA — B
Cascade Coll, OR — B
Central Washington U, WA — B
Chapman U, CA — B
Chief Dull Knife Coll, MT — A
CollAmerica–Colorado Springs, CO — A
CollAmerica–Denver, CO — A
Coll of Santa Fe, NM — A,B
Coll of the Southwest, NM — B
Colorado Christian U, CO — B
Colorado State U, CO — B
Colorado State U-Pueblo, CO — B
Concordia U, CA — B
Concordia U, OR — A,B
Corban Coll, OR — A,B
DeVry U, Phoenix, AZ — B
DeVry U, Sherman Oaks, CA — B
DeVry U, Westminster, CO — B
DeVry U, NV — B
DeVry U, OR — B
DeVry U, Federal Way, WA — B
Dixie State Coll of Utah, UT — A,B
Dominican U of California, CA — B
Eastern New Mexico U, NM — B
Eastern Washington U, WA — B
The Evergreen State Coll, WA — B

FIDM/The Fashion Inst of Design & Merchandising, Los Angeles Campus, CA — B
Fort Lewis Coll, CO — B
Fresno Pacific U, CA — A,B
George Fox U, OR — B
Gonzaga U, WA — B
Grand Canyon U, AZ — B
Great Basin Coll, NV — A
Hawai'i Pacific U, HI — A,B
Holy Names U, CA — B
Hope International U, CA — B
Humboldt State U, CA — B
Idaho State U, ID — B
International Inst of the Americas, Mesa, AZ — A,B
International Inst of the Americas, Phoenix, AZ — A,B
International Inst of the Americas, Tucson, AZ — A,B
International Inst of the Americas, NM — A,B
ITT Tech Inst, Tempe, AZ — B
ITT Tech Inst, Tucson, AZ — B
ITT Tech Inst, Anaheim, CA — B
ITT Tech Inst, Clovis, CA — B
ITT Tech Inst, Lathrop, CA — B
ITT Tech Inst, Oxnard, CA — B
ITT Tech Inst, Rancho Cordova, CA — B
ITT Tech Inst, San Bernardino, CA — B
ITT Tech Inst, San Diego, CA — B
ITT Tech Inst, San Dimas, CA — B
ITT Tech Inst, Sylmar, CA — B
ITT Tech Inst, Torrance, CA — B
ITT Tech Inst, CO — B
ITT Tech Inst, ID — B
ITT Tech Inst, NV — B
ITT Tech Inst, NM — B
ITT Tech Inst, OR — B
ITT Tech Inst, Bothell, WA — B
ITT Tech Inst, Seattle, WA — B
Johnson & Wales U, CO — A
LA Coll International, CA — A,B
La Sierra U, CA — B
Lewis-Clark State Coll, ID — B
Lincoln U, CA — B
Little Big Horn Coll, MT — A
Loyola Marymount U, CA — B
Marylhurst U, CA — B
The Master's Coll and Seminary, CA — B
Menlo Coll, CA — B
Mesa State Coll, CO — A,B
Montana State U–Billings, MT — A,B
Montana Tech of The U of Montana, MT — B
Morrison U, NV — A,B
Mount St. Mary's Coll, CA — A,B
National American U, Denver, CO — A,B
National U, CA — B
Nevada State Coll at Henderson, NV — B
New Mexico Highlands U, NM — B
New Mexico Inst of Mining and Technology, NM — A,B
New Mexico State U, NM — B
North Carolina Ag and Tech State U, NC — B
Northern Arizona U, AZ — B
Northwestern Polytechnic U, CA — B
Northwest Nazarene U, ID — B

A—associate degree; B—bachelor's degree

Northwest U, WA	B
Notre Dame de Namur U, CA	B
Oregon Inst of Technology, OR	B
Oregon State U, OR	B
Pacific Lutheran U, WA	B
Pacific States U, CA	B
Pacific Union Coll, CA	B
Pacific U, OR	B
Patten U, CA	B
Pepperdine U, Malibu, CA	B
Pioneer Pacific Coll, Wilsonville, OR	A,B
Point Loma Nazarene U, CA	B
Portland State U, OR	B
Regis U, CO	B
Rocky Mountain Coll, MT	B
Saint Mary's Coll of California, CA	B
San Diego Christian Coll, CA	B
San Diego State U, CA	B
San Francisco State U, CA	B
San Jose State U, CA	B
Seattle Pacific U, WA	B
Seattle U, WA	B
Sierra Nevada Coll, NV	B
Simpson U, CA	B
Sonoma State U, CA	B
Southern Oregon U, OR	B
Southern Utah U, UT	B
Stone Child Coll, MT	A
Trinity Lutheran Coll, WA	B
United States Air Force Academy, CO	B
U of Alaska Anchorage, AK	A,B
U of Alaska Fairbanks, AK	A,B
U of Alaska Southeast, AK	A,B
U of California, Berkeley, CA	B
U of California, Los Angeles, CA	B
U of California, Riverside, CA	B
U of Colorado at Colorado Springs, CO	B
U of Denver, CO	B
U of Great Falls, MT	B
U of Hawaii at Hilo, HI	B
U of Hawaii–West Oahu, HI	B
U of La Verne, CA	B
The U of Montana–Western, MT	A
U of Nevada, Las Vegas, NV	B
U of New Mexico, NM	B
U of New Mexico–Gallup, NM	A
U of New Orleans, LA	B
U of Northern Colorado, CO	B
U of Oregon, OR	B
U of Phoenix–Bay Area Campus, CA	B
U of Phoenix–Central Valley Campus, CA	B
U of Phoenix–Denver Campus, CO	B
U of Phoenix–Eastern Washington Campus, Spokane Valley, WA	B
U of Phoenix–Hawaii Campus, HI	B
U of Phoenix–Idaho Campus, ID	B
U of Phoenix–Las Vegas Campus, NV	B
U of Phoenix–New Mexico Campus, NM	B
U of Phoenix Online Campus, AZ	B
U of Phoenix–Oregon Campus, OR	B

U of Phoenix–Phoenix Campus, AZ	B
U of Phoenix–Sacramento Valley Campus, CA	B
U of Phoenix–San Diego Campus, CA	B
U of Phoenix–Southern Arizona Campus, AZ	B
U of Phoenix–Southern California Campus, CA	B
U of Phoenix–Southern Colorado Campus, CO	B
U of Phoenix–Utah Campus, UT	B
U of Phoenix–Washington Campus, WA	B
U of Portland, OR	B
U of Redlands, CA	B
U of San Diego, CA	B
U of San Francisco, CA	B
U of Southern California, CA	B
U of the Pacific, CA	B
U of the West, CA	B
U of Utah, UT	B
U of Washington, WA	B
U of Washington, Bothell, WA	B
U of Washington, Tacoma, WA	B
U of Wyoming, WY	B
Utah State U, UT	B
Utah Valley State Coll, UT	A,B
Vanguard U of Southern California, CA	B
Walla Walla Coll, WA	A,B
Warner Pacific Coll, OR	B
Washington State U, WA	B
Weber State U, UT	B
Western International U, AZ	B
Western State Coll of Colorado, CO	B
Western Washington U, WA	B
Westminster Coll, UT	B
Whitworth U, WA	B
Woodbury U, CA	B

Business Administration, Management and Operations Related

California State U, Chico, CA	B
Embry-Riddle Aeronautical U, AZ	B
Northwest Christian Coll, OR	B
San Jose State U, CA	B
U of Phoenix–Idaho Campus, ID	B
U of Southern California, CA	B
William Jessup U, CA	B
Woodbury U, CA	B

Business Automation/ Technology/Data Entry

Montana State U–Billings, MT	A
Montana Tech of The U of Montana, MT	A
The U of Montana–Western, MT	A
Utah Valley State Coll, UT	A

Business/Commerce

Brigham Young U, UT	B
Everest Coll, Phoenix, AZ	A
Great Basin Coll, NV	A
Idaho State U, ID	A,B
Linfield Coll, OR	B
Montana State U, MT	B
Montana State U–Billings, MT	A,B
Montana Tech of The U of Montana, MT	B

New Mexico State U, NM	A,B
Northern Arizona U, AZ	B
Northern New Mexico Coll, NM	A
Saint Mary's Coll of California, CA	B
San Diego State U, CA	B
Touro U International, CA	B
The U of Arizona, AZ	B
U of Colorado at Denver and Health Sciences Center, CO	B
U of Denver, CO	B
U of Hawaii at Manoa, HI	B
The U of Montana, MT	B
The U of Montana–Western, MT	A,B
U of Nevada, Reno, NV	B
U of Phoenix–Las Vegas Campus, NV	A
U of Phoenix–San Diego Campus, CA	B
U of Puget Sound, WA	B
U of Redlands, CA	B
U of San Francisco, CA	B
U of Utah, UT	B
U of Washington, WA	B
Utah State U, UT	B
Utah Valley State Coll, UT	A,B
Washington State U, WA	B
Western Oregon U, OR	B
Westminster Coll, UT	B
Westmont Coll, CA	B

Business/Corporate Communications

Hawai'i Pacific U, HI	B
Holy Names U, CA	B
Point Loma Nazarene U, CA	B
The U of Montana–Western, MT	B
U of Phoenix–Bay Area Campus, CA	B
U of Phoenix–Denver Campus, CO	B
U of Phoenix–Hawaii Campus, HI	B
U of Phoenix–Idaho Campus, ID	B
U of Phoenix–Las Vegas Campus, NV	B
U of Phoenix–Oregon Campus, OR	B
U of Phoenix–Phoenix Campus, AZ	B
U of Phoenix–Sacramento Valley Campus, CA	B
U of Phoenix–San Diego Campus, CA	B
U of Phoenix–Southern Colorado Campus, CO	B
U of Phoenix–Utah Campus, UT	B
U of Phoenix–Washington Campus, WA	B

Business Family and Consumer Sciences/Human Sciences

Brigham Young U, UT	B

Business Machine Repair

Boise State U, ID	A
Idaho State U, ID	A
U of Alaska Anchorage, AK	A

Business, Management, and Marketing Related

The Art Inst of California–San Francisco, CA	A,B
California State U, Sacramento, CA	B
California State U, Stanislaus, CA	B
Corban Coll, OR	B
U of Denver, CO	B
U of Phoenix–Las Vegas Campus, NV	B
U of Southern California, CA	B
U of Utah, UT	B

Business/Managerial Economics

Boise State U, ID	B
California Inst of Technology, CA	B
California State U, Fullerton, CA	B
California State U, Long Beach, CA	B
California State U, San Bernardino, CA	B
Chapman U, CA	B
Eastern Oregon U, OR	B
Eastern Washington U, WA	B
Fort Lewis Coll, CO	B
Gonzaga U, WA	B
Grand Canyon U, AZ	B
Hawai'i Pacific U, HI	A,B
Mesa State Coll, CO	B
Mills Coll, CA	B
Montana State U–Billings, MT	B
Northern Arizona U, AZ	B
Notre Dame de Namur U, CA	B
Occidental Coll, CA	B
Seattle U, WA	B
Sonoma State U, CA	B
U of Alaska Anchorage, AK	B
The U of Arizona, AZ	B
U of California, Los Angeles, CA	B
U of California, Riverside, CA	B
U of California, Santa Barbara, CA	B
U of California, Santa Cruz, CA	B
U of Denver, CO	B
U of Hawaii at Manoa, HI	B
U of Judaism, CA	B
U of Nevada, Reno, NV	B
U of New Orleans, LA	B
U of San Diego, CA	B
U of Wyoming, WY	B
Washington State U, WA	B
Weber State U, UT	B
Westminster Coll, UT	B
Westmont Coll, CA	B

Business Statistics

Brigham Young U, UT	B
Southern Oregon U, OR	B

Business Teacher Education

Boise State U, ID	B
Brigham Young U–Hawaii, HI	B
Brigham Young U–Idaho, ID	A
Central Washington U, WA	B
Coll of Santa Fe, NM	B
Coll of the Southwest, NM	B
Colorado State U, CO	B
Corban Coll, OR	B
Eastern New Mexico U, NM	B
Eastern Washington U, WA	B

Grand Canyon U, AZ	B
Johnson & Wales U, CO	B
Mount St. Mary's Coll, CA	B
North Carolina Ag and Tech State U, NC	B
Pacific Union Coll, CA	B
Southern Utah U, UT	B
U of Idaho, ID	B
The U of Montana, MT	B
The U of Montana–Western, MT	B
U of Nevada, Reno, NV	B
Utah State U, UT	B
Utah Valley State Coll, UT	B
Walla Walla Coll, WA	B
Weber State U, UT	B

Cabinetmaking and Millwork
Utah Valley State Coll, UT	A

CAD/CADD Drafting/Design Technology
The Art Inst of Las Vegas, NV	A
ITT Tech Inst, Tempe, AZ	A
ITT Tech Inst, Tucson, AZ	A
ITT Tech Inst, Lathrop, CA	A
ITT Tech Inst, Oxnard, CA	A
ITT Tech Inst, Rancho Cordova, CA	A
ITT Tech Inst, San Bernardino, CA	A
ITT Tech Inst, San Diego, CA	A
ITT Tech Inst, San Dimas, CA	A
ITT Tech Inst, Sylmar, CA	A
ITT Tech Inst, Torrance, CA	A
ITT Tech Inst, CO	A
ITT Tech Inst, ID	A
ITT Tech Inst, NV	A
ITT Tech Inst, OR	A
ITT Tech Inst, UT	A
ITT Tech Inst, Bothell, WA	A
ITT Tech Inst, Seattle, WA	A
ITT Tech Inst, Spokane, WA	A

Canadian Studies
U of Washington, WA	B
Western Washington U, WA	B

Carpentry
Brigham Young U–Idaho, ID	A
Idaho State U, ID	A
Little Big Horn Coll, MT	A
Salish Kootenai Coll, MT	A
Southern Utah U, UT	A

Cartography
Brigham Young U, UT	B
Dixie State Coll of Utah, UT	A
U of Idaho, ID	B

Cell and Molecular Biology
California State U Channel Islands, CA	B
Fort Lewis Coll, CO	B
U of California, Berkeley, CA	B
U of California, Los Angeles, CA	B
U of Colorado at Boulder, CO	B
Western Washington U, WA	B

Cell Biology and Anatomical Sciences Related
Northern Arizona U, AZ	B

Cell Biology and Anatomy
Montana State U, MT	B

Cell Biology and Histology
California State U, Fresno, CA	B

California State U, Long Beach, CA	B
California State U, San Marcos, CA	B
Humboldt State U, CA	B
Oregon State U, OR	B
Pomona Coll, CA	B
San Francisco State U, CA	B
Sonoma State U, CA	B
The U of Arizona, AZ	B
U of California, Davis, CA	B
U of California, San Diego, CA	B
U of California, Santa Barbara, CA	B
U of California, Santa Cruz, CA	B
U of Utah, UT	B
U of Washington, WA	B
Western State Coll of Colorado, CO	B
Western Washington U, WA	B

Celtic Languages
U of California, Berkeley, CA	B

Ceramic Arts and Ceramics
Brigham Young U, UT	B
California Coll of the Arts, CA	B
California State U, Fullerton, CA	B
California State U, Long Beach, CA	B
Colorado State U, CO	B
Dixie State Coll of Utah, UT	A
Northwest Nazarene U, ID	B
U of Dallas, TX	B
U of Oregon, OR	B
U of Washington, WA	B
Western Washington U, WA	B

Ceramic Sciences and Engineering
U of Washington, WA	B

Chemical Engineering
Arizona State U, AZ	B
Brigham Young U, UT	B
Brigham Young U–Idaho, ID	A
California Inst of Technology, CA	B
California State Polytechnic U, Pomona, CA	B
California State U, Long Beach, CA	B
Colorado School of Mines, CO	B
Colorado State U, CO	B
Montana State U, MT	B
New Mexico Inst of Mining and Technology, NM	B
New Mexico State U, NM	B
North Carolina Ag and Tech State U, NC	B
Oregon State U, OR	B
San Jose State U, CA	B
Stanford U, CA	B
The U of Arizona, AZ	B
U of California, Berkeley, CA	B
U of California, Davis, CA	B
U of California, Irvine, CA	B
U of California, Los Angeles, CA	B
U of California, Riverside, CA	B
U of California, San Diego, CA	B
U of California, Santa Barbara, CA	B
U of Colorado at Boulder, CO	B
U of Idaho, ID	B

U of Nevada, Reno, NV	B
U of New Mexico, NM	B
U of Southern California, CA	B
U of Utah, UT	B
U of Washington, WA	B
U of Wyoming, WY	B
Washington State U, WA	B

Chemical Technology
Weber State U, UT	A

Chemistry
Adams State Coll, CO	B
Albertson Coll of Idaho, ID	B
Arizona State U, AZ	B
Azusa Pacific U, CA	B
Boise State U, ID	B
Brigham Young U, UT	B
Brigham Young U–Hawaii, HI	B
Brigham Young U–Idaho, ID	A
California Inst of Technology, CA	B
California Lutheran U, CA	B
California Polytechnic State U, San Luis Obispo, CA	B
California State Polytechnic U, Pomona, CA	B
California State U Channel Islands, CA	B
California State U, Chico, CA	B
California State U, Dominguez Hills, CA	B
California State U, Fresno, CA	B
California State U, Fullerton, CA	B
California State U, Long Beach, CA	B
California State U, Los Angeles, CA	B
California State U, Northridge, CA	B
California State U, Sacramento, CA	B
California State U, San Bernardino, CA	B
California State U, San Marcos, CA	B
California State U, Stanislaus, CA	B
Central Washington U, WA	B
Chapman U, CA	B
Claremont McKenna Coll, CA	B
The Colorado Coll, CO	B
Colorado School of Mines, CO	B
Colorado State U, CO	B
Colorado State U–Pueblo, CO	B
Concordia U, CA	B
Concordia U, OR	B
Dixie State Coll of Utah, UT	A
Eastern New Mexico U, NM	B
Eastern Oregon U, OR	B
Eastern Washington U, WA	B
Fort Lewis Coll, CO	B
Fresno Pacific U, CA	B
George Fox U, OR	B
Gonzaga U, WA	B
Grand Canyon U, AZ	B
Great Basin Coll, NV	A
Harvey Mudd Coll, CA	B
Humboldt State U, CA	B
Idaho State U, ID	A,B
La Sierra U, CA	B
Lewis & Clark Coll, OR	B
Lewis-Clark State Coll, ID	B
Linfield Coll, OR	B
Loyola Marymount U, CA	B

Mesa State Coll, CO	B
Mills Coll, CA	B
Montana State U, MT	B
Montana State U–Billings, MT	B
Montana Tech of The U of Montana, MT	B
Mount St. Mary's Coll, CA	B
New Mexico Highlands U, NM	B
New Mexico Inst of Mining and Technology, NM	B
New Mexico State U, NM	B
North Carolina Ag and Tech State U, NC	B
Northern Arizona U, AZ	B
Northwest Nazarene U, ID	B
Occidental Coll, CA	B
Oregon State U, OR	B
Pacific Lutheran U, WA	B
Pacific Union Coll, CA	B
Pacific U, OR	B
Pepperdine U, Malibu, CA	B
Pitzer Coll, CA	B
Point Loma Nazarene U, CA	B
Pomona Coll, CA	B
Portland State U, OR	B
Reed Coll, OR	B
Regis U, CO	B
Rocky Mountain Coll, MT	B
Saint Mary's Coll of California, CA	B
San Diego State U, CA	B
San Francisco State U, CA	B
San Jose State U, CA	B
Santa Clara U, CA	B
Scripps Coll, CA	B
Seattle Pacific U, WA	B
Seattle U, WA	B
Sonoma State U, CA	B
Southern Oregon U, OR	B
Southern Utah U, UT	B
Stanford U, CA	B
United States Air Force Academy, CO	B
U of Alaska Anchorage, AK	B
U of Alaska Fairbanks, AK	B
The U of Arizona, AZ	B
U of California, Berkeley, CA	B
U of California, Davis, CA	B
U of California, Irvine, CA	B
U of California, Los Angeles, CA	B
U of California, Riverside, CA	B
U of California, San Diego, CA	B
U of California, Santa Barbara, CA	B
U of California, Santa Cruz, CA	B
U of Colorado at Boulder, CO	B
U of Colorado at Colorado Springs, CO	B
U of Colorado at Denver and Health Sciences Center, CO	B
U of Dallas, TX	B
U of Denver, CO	B
U of Great Falls, MT	B
U of Hawaii at Hilo, HI	B
U of Hawaii at Manoa, HI	B
U of Idaho, ID	B
U of La Verne, CA	B
The U of Montana, MT	B
U of Nevada, Las Vegas, NV	B
U of Nevada, Reno, NV	B
U of New Mexico, NM	B
U of New Orleans, LA	B
U of Northern Colorado, CO	B

A—associate degree; B—bachelor's degree

U of Oregon, OR	B
U of Portland, OR	B
U of Puget Sound, WA	B
U of Redlands, CA	B
U of San Diego, CA	B
U of San Francisco, CA	B
U of Southern California, CA	B
U of the Pacific, CA	B
U of Utah, UT	B
U of Washington, WA	B
U of Wyoming, WY	B
Utah State U, UT	B
Utah Valley State Coll, UT	A,B
Vanguard U of Southern California, CA	B
Walla Walla Coll, WA	B
Washington State U, WA	B
Weber State U, UT	B
Western Oregon U, OR	B
Western State Coll of Colorado, CO	B
Western Washington U, WA	B
Westminster Coll, UT	B
Westmont Coll, CA	B
Whitman Coll, WA	B
Whitworth U, WA	B
Willamette U, OR	B

Chemistry Related

California State U, Chico, CA	B
California State U, Sacramento, CA	B
Northern Arizona U, AZ	B
Saint Mary's Coll of California, CA	B
San Diego State U, CA	B
U of California, Berkeley, CA	B
U of the Pacific, CA	B

Chemistry Teacher Education

Brigham Young U, UT	B
Brigham Young U–Hawaii, HI	B
California State U, Chico, CA	B
Central Washington U, WA	B
Colorado State U, CO	B
Eastern Washington U, WA	B
Fort Lewis Coll, CO	B
Montana State U–Billings, MT	B
Northwest Nazarene U, ID	B
Rocky Mountain Coll, MT	B
The U of Arizona, AZ	B
U of California, San Diego, CA	B
U of Great Falls, MT	B
Utah State U, UT	B
Utah Valley State Coll, UT	B
Washington State U, WA	B
Weber State U, UT	B
Western Washington U, WA	B
Westminster Coll, UT	B

Child-Care and Support Services Management

Brigham Young U, UT	B
Dixie State Coll of Utah, UT	A
Eastern New Mexico U, NM	A
Eastern Washington U, WA	B
Idaho State U, ID	A
Pacific Union Coll, CA	B
Weber State U, UT	A

Child-Care Provision

Brigham Young U, UT	B
Pacific Union Coll, CA	A
U of Alaska Fairbanks, AK	A

Child Development

Boise State U, ID	A
Brigham Young U, UT	B

Brigham Young U–Idaho, ID	A
California State U, Dominguez Hills, CA	B
California State U, Fresno, CA	B
California State U, Long Beach, CA	B
California State U, Los Angeles, CA	B
California State U, Northridge, CA	B
Eastern Washington U, WA	B
Hope International U, CA	B
Humboldt State U, CA	B
Lewis-Clark State Coll, ID	A,B
National U, CA	B
North Carolina Ag and Tech State U, NC	B
Pacific Oaks Coll, CA	B
Point Loma Nazarene U, CA	B
Portland State U, OR	B
Salish Kootenai Coll, MT	A
San Diego State U, CA	B
Southern Utah U, UT	A
U of Idaho, ID	B
U of La Verne, CA	B
U of Nevada, Reno, NV	B
U of Utah, UT	B
Weber State U, UT	A,B

Chinese

Brigham Young U, UT	B
Brigham Young U–Idaho, ID	A
California State U, Long Beach, CA	B
California State U, Los Angeles, CA	B
Claremont McKenna Coll, CA	B
Pacific Lutheran U, WA	B
Pacific U, OR	B
Pomona Coll, CA	B
Portland State U, OR	B
Reed Coll, OR	B
San Francisco State U, CA	B
San Jose State U, CA	B
Scripps Coll, CA	B
Stanford U, CA	B
U of California, Berkeley, CA	B
U of California, Davis, CA	B
U of California, Irvine, CA	B
U of California, Los Angeles, CA	B
U of California, Riverside, CA	B
U of California, San Diego, CA	B
U of California, Santa Barbara, CA	B
U of California, Santa Cruz, CA	B
U of Colorado at Boulder, CO	B
U of Hawaii at Manoa, HI	B
The U of Montana, MT	B
U of Oregon, OR	B
U of Utah, UT	B
U of Washington, WA	B

Chinese Studies

Claremont McKenna Coll, CA	B
U of the West, CA	B

Christian Studies

California Baptist U, CA	B

Cinematography and Film/Video Production

Academy of Art U, CA	A,B
Art Center Coll of Design, CA	B
The Art Inst of California–Los Angeles, CA	A,B
The Art Inst of Colorado, CO	A

The Art Inst of Seattle, WA	A
Brigham Young U, UT	B
California State U, Long Beach, CA	B
California State U, Northridge, CA	B
Chapman U, CA	B
Collins Coll: A School of Design and Technology, AZ	A
Colorado State U-Pueblo, CO	B
Columbia Coll Hollywood, CA	B
The Evergreen State Coll, WA	B
George Fox U, OR	B
Loyola Marymount U, CA	B
Montana State U, MT	B
San Francisco Art Inst, CA	B
U of Advancing Technology, AZ	B
U of California, Santa Cruz, CA	B
U of Southern California, CA	B
Vanguard U of Southern California, CA	B

City/Urban, Community and Regional Planning

Arizona State U, AZ	B
California Polytechnic State U, San Luis Obispo, CA	B
California State Polytechnic U, Pomona, CA	B
California State U, Chico, CA	B
Eastern Oregon U, OR	B
Eastern Washington U, WA	B
New Mexico State U, NM	B
Portland State U, OR	B
The U of Arizona, AZ	B
U of California, Davis, CA	B
U of California, Los Angeles, CA	B
The U of Montana, MT	B
U of Nevada, Las Vegas, NV	B
U of Oregon, OR	B
U of San Francisco, CA	B
U of Southern California, CA	B
U of Washington, WA	B

Civil Drafting and CAD/CADD

Montana Tech of The U of Montana, MT	A

Civil Engineering

Arizona State U, AZ	B
Boise State U, ID	B
Brigham Young U, UT	B
California Polytechnic State U, San Luis Obispo, CA	B
California State Polytechnic U, Pomona, CA	B
California State U, Chico, CA	B
California State U, Fresno, CA	B
California State U, Fullerton, CA	B
California State U, Long Beach, CA	B
California State U, Los Angeles, CA	B
Colorado School of Mines, CO	B
Colorado State U, CO	B
Gonzaga U, WA	B
Idaho State U, ID	B
Loyola Marymount U, CA	B
Montana State U, MT	B
Montana Tech of The U of Montana, MT	B
New Mexico Inst of Mining and Technology, NM	B
New Mexico State U, NM	B

North Carolina Ag and Tech State U, NC	B
Northern Arizona U, AZ	B
Oregon Inst of Technology, OR	B
Oregon State U, OR	B
Portland State U, OR	B
San Diego State U, CA	B
San Francisco State U, CA	B
San Jose State U, CA	B
Santa Clara U, CA	B
Seattle U, WA	B
Stanford U, CA	B
United States Air Force Academy, CO	B
U of Alaska Anchorage, AK	B
U of Alaska Fairbanks, AK	B
The U of Arizona, AZ	B
U of California, Berkeley, CA	B
U of California, Davis, CA	B
U of California, Irvine, CA	B
U of California, Los Angeles, CA	B
U of Colorado at Boulder, CO	B
U of Colorado at Denver and Health Sciences Center, CO	B
U of Hawaii at Manoa, HI	B
U of Idaho, ID	B
U of Nevada, Las Vegas, NV	B
U of Nevada, Reno, NV	B
U of New Mexico, NM	B
U of New Orleans, LA	B
U of Portland, OR	B
U of Southern California, CA	B
U of the Pacific, CA	B
U of Utah, UT	B
U of Washington, WA	B
U of Wyoming, WY	B
Utah State U, UT	B
Walla Walla Coll, WA	B
Washington State U, WA	B

Civil Engineering Related

California State U, Sacramento, CA	B
U of Southern California, CA	B

Civil Engineering Technology

Brigham Young U–Idaho, ID	A
Colorado State U-Pueblo, CO	B
Idaho State U, ID	A

Classical, Ancient Mediterranean and Near Eastern Studies and Archaeology

Brigham Young U, UT	B
U of California, Berkeley, CA	B
U of California, Davis, CA	B
U of California, Irvine, CA	B
U of California, Los Angeles, CA	B

Classics

Pitzer Coll, CA	B
The U of Arizona, AZ	B
U of Hawaii at Manoa, HI	B

Classics and Classical Languages Related

California State U, Long Beach, CA	B
U of California, Los Angeles, CA	B

Classics and Languages, Literatures and Linguistics

Brigham Young U, UT	B
Claremont McKenna Coll, CA	B
The Colorado Coll, CO	B

Classics and Languages, Literatures and Linguistics

The Evergreen State Coll, WA — B
Loyola Marymount U, CA — B
Pacific Lutheran U, WA — B
Pitzer Coll, CA — B
Pomona Coll, CA — B
Reed Coll, OR — B
St. John's Coll, NM — B
San Diego State U, CA — B
San Francisco State U, CA — B
Santa Clara U, CA — B
Scripps Coll, CA — B
Seattle Pacific U, WA — B
Stanford U, CA — B
U of California, Berkeley, CA — B
U of California, Irvine, CA — B
U of California, Los Angeles, CA — B
U of California, Riverside, CA — B
U of California, San Diego, CA — B
U of California, Santa Barbara, CA — B
U of California, Santa Cruz, CA — B
U of Colorado at Boulder, CO — B
U of Dallas, TX — B
U of Idaho, ID — B
The U of Montana, MT — B
U of New Mexico, NM — B
U of Oregon, OR — B
U of Puget Sound, WA — B
U of Southern California, CA — B
U of the Pacific, CA — B
U of Utah, UT — B
U of Washington, WA — B
Western Washington U, WA — B
Whitman Coll, WA — B
Willamette U, OR — B

Clinical Laboratory Science/ Medical Technology
Arizona State U, AZ — B
Boise State U, ID — B
Brigham Young U, UT — B
California State U, Chico, CA — B
California State U, Dominguez Hills, CA — B
Eastern New Mexico U, NM — B
Humboldt State U, CA — B
Idaho State U, ID — B
Loma Linda U, CA — B
Oregon State U, OR — B
Pacific Union Coll, CA — B
Seattle U, WA — B
The U of Arizona, AZ — B
U of Idaho, ID — B
The U of Montana, MT — B
U of Nevada, Las Vegas, NV — B
U of New Orleans, LA — B
U of Utah, UT — B
Utah State U, UT — B
Walla Walla Coll, WA — B
Weber State U, UT — A,B

Clinical/Medical Laboratory Technology
Brigham Young U–Idaho, ID — A
California State U, Dominguez Hills, CA — B
Sonoma State U, CA — B
U of Alaska Anchorage, AK — A
The U of Montana, MT — B
U of New Mexico, NM — B
U of New Mexico–Gallup, NM — A
U of Utah, UT — B
Weber State U, UT — A,B

Clinical Psychology
Biola U, CA — B
California State U, Fullerton, CA — B
Colorado State U-Pueblo, CO — B
George Fox U, OR — B
Western State Coll of Colorado, CO — B

Clothing/Textiles
Brigham Young U–Idaho, ID — A
North Carolina Ag and Tech State U, NC — B
Oregon State U, OR — B
San Francisco State U, CA — B

Cognitive Psychology and Psycholinguistics
California State U, Stanislaus, CA — B
George Fox U, OR — B
Occidental Coll, CA — B
U of California, San Diego, CA — B
U of California, Santa Cruz, CA — B

Cognitive Science
George Fox U, OR — B
U of California, Berkeley, CA — B
U of California, Los Angeles, CA — B

Commercial and Advertising Art
Academy of Art U, CA — A,B
Art Center Coll of Design, CA — B
The Art Inst of California–San Diego, CA — A,B
The Art Inst of California–San Francisco, CA — A,B
The Art Inst of Colorado, CO — A,B
Biola U, CA — B
Boise State U, ID — B
Brigham Young U–Idaho, ID — A
California Coll of the Arts, CA — B
California Inst of the Arts, CA — B
California Polytechnic State U, San Luis Obispo, CA — B
California State Polytechnic U, Pomona, CA — B
California State U, Dominguez Hills, CA — B
California State U, Fresno, CA — B
California State U, Fullerton, CA — B
California State U, Long Beach, CA — B
Collins Coll: A School of Design and Technology, AZ — A
Colorado State U, CO — B
Dixie State Coll of Utah, UT — A
FIDM/The Fashion Inst of Design & Merchandising, Los Angeles Campus, CA — A
Grand Canyon U, AZ — B
Mesa State Coll, CO — B
New Mexico Highlands U, NM — B
Northwest Coll of Art, WA — B
Northwest Nazarene U, ID — B
Notre Dame de Namur U, CA — B
Otis Coll of Art and Design, CA — B
Platt Coll San Diego, CA — A
Portland State U, OR — B
U of Advancing Technology, AZ — B

U of Denver, CO — B
U of Oregon, OR — B
U of the Pacific, CA — B
U of Washington, WA — B
Utah Valley State Coll, UT — A
Walla Walla Coll, WA — A,B
Weber State U, UT — B
Western State Coll of Colorado, CO — B
Woodbury U, CA — B

Commercial Photography
Art Center Coll of Design, CA — B

Communication and Journalism Related
Arizona State U at the Polytechnic Campus, AZ — B
The Art Inst of California–San Diego, CA — B
Brigham Young U, UT — B
Brigham Young U–Hawaii, HI — B
California Baptist U, CA — B
Eastern Washington U, WA — B
Hawai'i Pacific U, HI — B
Northern Arizona U, AZ — B
Notre Dame de Namur U, CA — B
Saint Mary's Coll of California, CA — B
San Diego State U, CA — B

Communication and Media Related
Cascade Coll, OR — B

Communication Disorders
Arizona State U, AZ — B
Biola U, CA — B
California State U, Chico, CA — B
California State U, Fresno, CA — B
California State U, Fullerton, CA — B
California State U, Long Beach, CA — B
California State U, Los Angeles, CA — B
California State U, Northridge, CA — B
Eastern Washington U, WA — B
San Diego State U, CA — B
San Jose State U, CA — B
The U of Arizona, AZ — B
U of Oregon, OR — B

Communication/Speech Communication and Rhetoric
Adams State Coll, CO — B
Arizona State U, AZ — B
Arizona State U at the West campus, AZ — B
Azusa Pacific U, CA — B
Brigham Young U–Hawaii, HI — A
California Baptist U, CA — B
California State U, Fresno, CA — B
California State U, Fullerton, CA — B
California State U, Los Angeles, CA — B
California State U, Monterey Bay, CA — B
California State U, Sacramento, CA — B
California State U, San Marcos, CA — B
California State U, Stanislaus, CA — B
Chapman U, CA — B

Colorado Christian U, CO — B
Colorado State U, CO — B
Concordia U, CA — B
Corban Coll, OR — B
Dixie State Coll of Utah, UT — A
Dominican U of California, CA — B
Eastern New Mexico U, NM — B
Eastern Washington U, WA — B
George Fox U, OR — B
Hawai'i Pacific U, HI — B
Humboldt State U, CA — B
Idaho State U, ID — A,B
La Sierra U, CA — B
Lewis & Clark Coll, OR — B
Lewis-Clark State Coll, ID — B
Linfield Coll, OR — B
Montana Tech of The U of Montana, MT — B
Multnomah Bible Coll and Biblical Seminary, OR — B
Northern Arizona U, AZ — B
Northwest Christian Coll, OR — B
Northwest Nazarene U, ID — B
Notre Dame de Namur U, CA — B
Oregon Inst of Technology, OR — B
Pepperdine U, Malibu, CA — B
Point Loma Nazarene U, CA — B
Prescott Coll, AZ — B
Regis U, CO — B
Rocky Mountain Coll, MT — B
Saint Mary's Coll of California, CA — B
San Diego Christian Coll, CA — B
Santa Clara U, CA — B
Seattle Pacific U, WA — B
Simpson U, CA — B
Sonoma State U, CA — B
Southern Oregon U, OR — B
Stanford U, CA — B
Trinity Lutheran Coll, WA — B
U of Alaska Fairbanks, AK — B
The U of Arizona, AZ — B
U of California, Davis, CA — B
U of California, Los Angeles, CA — B
U of California, Santa Barbara, CA — B
U of Colorado at Boulder, CO — B
U of Colorado at Colorado Springs, CO — B
U of Colorado at Denver and Health Sciences Center, CO — B
U of Denver, CO — B
U of Hawaii at Manoa, HI — B
U of Idaho, ID — B
U of La Verne, CA — B
The U of Montana, MT — B
U of Nevada, Las Vegas, NV — B
U of Nevada, Reno, NV — B
U of New Mexico–Gallup, NM — A
U of New Orleans, LA — B
U of Northern Colorado, CO — B
U of Puget Sound, WA — B
U of San Francisco, CA — B
U of Southern California, CA — B
U of the Pacific, CA — B
U of Utah, UT — B
U of Washington, WA — B
U of Wyoming, WY — B
Utah Valley State Coll, UT — A
Vanguard U of Southern California, CA — B
Washington State U, WA — B
Western Washington U, WA — B
Westminster Coll, UT — B

A—associate degree; B—bachelor's degree

Westmont Coll, CA	B
Woodbury U, CA	B

Communications Systems Installation and Repair Technology

Idaho State U, ID	A

Communications Technology

ITT Tech Inst, Tempe, AZ	B
ITT Tech Inst, Tucson, AZ	A
ITT Tech Inst, Anaheim, CA	B
ITT Tech Inst, Lathrop, CA	B
ITT Tech Inst, Rancho Cordova, CA	B
ITT Tech Inst, Sylmar, CA	B
ITT Tech Inst, Torrance, CA	B
ITT Tech Inst, ID	B
ITT Tech Inst, OR	A
ITT Tech Inst, Bothell, WA	B

Community Health and Preventive Medicine

U of California, Los Angeles, CA	B
Utah Valley State Coll, UT	A

Community Health Services Counseling

California State U, Sacramento, CA	B
Central Washington U, WA	B
Western Washington U, WA	B

Community Organization and Advocacy

Corban Coll, OR	B
New Mexico State U, NM	B
U of Alaska Fairbanks, AK	B
U of New Mexico, NM	A
U of New Mexico–Gallup, NM	A
U of Oregon, OR	B

Community Psychology

Montana State U–Billings, MT	B

Comparative Literature

Brigham Young U, UT	B
California State U, Fullerton, CA	B
California State U, Long Beach, CA	B
The Colorado Coll, CO	B
Mills Coll, CA	B
Occidental Coll, CA	B
Oregon State U, OR	B
San Diego State U, CA	B
San Francisco State U, CA	B
Stanford U, CA	B
U of California, Berkeley, CA	B
U of California, Davis, CA	B
U of California, Irvine, CA	B
U of California, Los Angeles, CA	B
U of California, Riverside, CA	B
U of California, Santa Barbara, CA	B
U of California, Santa Cruz, CA	B
U of La Verne, CA	B
U of Nevada, Las Vegas, NV	B
U of New Mexico, NM	B
U of Oregon, OR	B
U of Southern California, CA	B
U of Washington, WA	B
Willamette U, OR	B

Computational Mathematics

California Inst of Technology, CA	B
U of California, Davis, CA	B
U of California, Los Angeles, CA	B

Computer and Information Sciences

Arizona State U at the West campus, AZ	B
Biola U, CA	B
Boise State U, ID	B
California Lutheran U, CA	B
California State Polytechnic U, Pomona, CA	B
California State U, Los Angeles, CA	B
California State U, Sacramento, CA	B
California State U, San Bernardino, CA	B
California State U, Stanislaus, CA	B
Central Washington U, WA	B
Chapman U, CA	B
Claremont McKenna Coll, CA	B
Colorado Christian U, CO	B
Colorado State U, CO	B
Colorado State U-Pueblo, CO	B
DeVry U, Phoenix, AZ	B
DeVry U, Fremont, CA	B
DeVry U, Pomona, CA	B
DeVry U, Sherman Oaks, CA	B
DeVry U, Westminster, CO	B
DeVry U, OR	B
DeVry U, Federal Way, WA	B
Eastern New Mexico U, NM	B
Eastern Washington U, WA	B
The Evergreen State Coll, WA	B
Fresno Pacific U, CA	B
George Fox U, OR	B
Hawai'i Pacific U, HI	B
Idaho State U, ID	B
Lewis-Clark State Coll, ID	A,B
The Master's Coll and Seminary, CA	B
Montana State U–Billings, MT	A
Montana Tech of The U of Montana, MT	B
National American U, Denver, CO	A,B
Neumont U, UT	B
New Mexico State U, NM	B
Northern Arizona U, AZ	B
Northern New Mexico Coll, NM	A
Northwest Christian Coll, OR	B
Oregon Inst of Technology, OR	B
Pacific Union Coll, CA	B
Portland State U, OR	B
Prescott Coll, AZ	B
Sierra Nevada Coll, NV	B
U of Alaska Anchorage, AK	A
U of Alaska Fairbanks, AK	B
The U of Arizona, AZ	B
U of California, Irvine, CA	B
U of Colorado at Colorado Springs, CO	B
U of Colorado at Denver and Health Sciences Center, CO	B
U of Denver, CO	B
U of Great Falls, MT	B
U of Hawaii at Manoa, HI	B
The U of Montana, MT	B
The U of Montana–Western, MT	A
U of Nevada, Reno, NV	B
U of New Mexico, NM	B
U of Oregon, OR	B

Computer and Information Sciences and Support Services Related

California State U, Chico, CA	B
California State U, Los Angeles, CA	B
LDS Business Coll, UT	A
Montana State U–Billings, MT	A
U of California, Irvine, CA	B
U of Great Falls, MT	B
Utah State U, UT	B

Computer and Information Sciences Related

National American U, Denver, CO	A,B
Neumont U, UT	B
U of Great Falls, MT	B

Computer and Information Systems Security

ITT Tech Inst, Tempe, AZ	A
ITT Tech Inst, Tucson, AZ	B
ITT Tech Inst, Anaheim, CA	B
ITT Tech Inst, Lathrop, CA	B
ITT Tech Inst, Oxnard, CA	B
ITT Tech Inst, Rancho Cordova, CA	B
ITT Tech Inst, San Bernardino, CA	B
ITT Tech Inst, San Diego, CA	B
ITT Tech Inst, San Dimas, CA	B
ITT Tech Inst, Sylmar, CA	B
ITT Tech Inst, Torrance, CA	B
ITT Tech Inst, CO	B
ITT Tech Inst, ID	B
ITT Tech Inst, NV	B
ITT Tech Inst, NM	B
ITT Tech Inst, OR	B
ITT Tech Inst, UT	B
ITT Tech Inst, Bothell, WA	B
ITT Tech Inst, Seattle, WA	B
ITT Tech Inst, Spokane, WA	B
U of Great Falls, MT	B
U of Phoenix–Bay Area Campus, CA	B
U of Phoenix–Denver Campus, CO	B
U of Phoenix–Hawaii Campus, HI	B
U of Phoenix–Idaho Campus, ID	B
U of Phoenix–Las Vegas Campus, NV	B
U of Phoenix–Phoenix Campus, AZ	B
U of Phoenix–Sacramento Valley Campus, CA	B
U of Phoenix–Southern California Campus, CA	B
U of Phoenix–Washington Campus, WA	B

Computer Engineering

Arizona State U, AZ	B

Computer Engineering (continued)

Brigham Young U, UT	B
California Inst of Technology, CA	B
California Polytechnic State U, San Luis Obispo, CA	B
California State Polytechnic U, Pomona, CA	B
California State U, Chico, CA	B
California State U, Fresno, CA	B
California State U, Long Beach, CA	B
California State U, Sacramento, CA	B
Colorado State U, CO	B
Embry-Riddle Aeronautical U, AZ	B
Gonzaga U, WA	B
Loyola Marymount U, CA	B
Montana State U, MT	B
Montana Tech of The U of Montana, MT	B
Northwestern Polytechnic U, CA	B
Oregon State U, OR	B
Pacific Lutheran U, WA	B
Portland State U, OR	B
San Diego State U, CA	B
San Jose State U, CA	B
Santa Clara U, CA	B
Stanford U, CA	B
The U of Arizona, AZ	B
U of California, Irvine, CA	B
U of California, Los Angeles, CA	B
U of California, San Diego, CA	B
U of California, Santa Barbara, CA	B
U of California, Santa Cruz, CA	B
U of Colorado at Boulder, CO	B
U of Colorado at Colorado Springs, CO	B
U of Denver, CO	B
U of Idaho, ID	B
U of La Verne, CA	B
U of Nevada, Las Vegas, NV	B
U of Nevada, Reno, NV	B
U of New Mexico, NM	B
U of Portland, OR	B
U of Southern California, CA	B
U of the Pacific, CA	B
U of Utah, UT	B
U of Washington, WA	B
U of Wyoming, WY	B
Utah State U, UT	B
Washington State U, WA	B

Computer Engineering Related

DigiPen Inst of Technology, WA	B
U of Southern California, CA	B

Computer Engineering Technology

Arizona State U at the Polytechnic Campus, AZ	B
California State U, Long Beach, CA	B
Colorado State U-Pueblo, CO	B
DeVry U, Phoenix, AZ	B
DeVry U, Fremont, CA	B
DeVry U, Long Beach, CA	B
DeVry U, Pomona, CA	B
DeVry U, Westminster, CO	B
DeVry U, Federal Way, WA	B
Eastern Washington U, WA	B
ITT Tech Inst, Tempe, AZ	B

ITT Tech Inst, Tucson, AZ — A
ITT Tech Inst, Anaheim, CA — A
ITT Tech Inst, Clovis, CA — A
ITT Tech Inst, Lathrop, CA — A
ITT Tech Inst, Oxnard, CA — A
ITT Tech Inst, Rancho Cordova, CA — A
ITT Tech Inst, San Bernardino, CA — A
ITT Tech Inst, San Diego, CA — A
ITT Tech Inst, San Dimas, CA — A
ITT Tech Inst, Sylmar, CA — A
ITT Tech Inst, Torrance, CA — A
ITT Tech Inst, CO — A
ITT Tech Inst, ID — A
ITT Tech Inst, NV — A
ITT Tech Inst, NM — A
ITT Tech Inst, OR — A
ITT Tech Inst, UT — A
ITT Tech Inst, Bothell, WA — A
ITT Tech Inst, Seattle, WA — A
Oregon Inst of Technology, OR — A,B
Utah State U, UT — B
Weber State U, UT — A

Computer Graphics
Academy of Art U, CA — A,B
The Art Inst of California–Orange County, CA — A,B
The Art Inst of California–San Francisco, CA — A,B
The Art Inst of Colorado, CO — A,B
California Inst of the Arts, CA — B
California State U, Chico, CA — B
Cogswell Polytechnical Coll, CA — B
Dominican U of California, CA — B
Platt Coll San Diego, CA — A
U of Advancing Technology, AZ — A,B
U of Great Falls, MT — B

Computer/Information Technology Services Administration Related
Holy Names U, CA — B
National American U, Denver, CO — A,B
Seattle Pacific U, WA — B
U of Great Falls, MT — B

Computer Management
Pacific Union Coll, CA — B
U of Great Falls, MT — B
Western International U, AZ — B

Computer Programming
Brigham Young U–Hawaii, HI — B
Brigham Young U–Idaho, ID — A
CollAmerica–Colorado Springs, CO — A
CollAmerica–Denver, CO — A
ITT Tech Inst, CO — A
Montana Tech of The U of Montana, MT — B
National American U, Denver, CO — A,B
Neumont U, UT — B
Nevada State Coll at Henderson, NV — B
New Mexico Highlands U, NM — B
Oregon Inst of Technology, OR — A,B
Pacific Union Coll, CA — B
U of Advancing Technology, AZ — A,B
U of Great Falls, MT — B

U of Phoenix Online Campus, AZ — B
Walla Walla Coll, WA — A

Computer Programming Related
National American U, Denver, CO — A,B
Neumont U, UT — B

Computer Programming (Specific Applications)
The Art Inst of California–San Francisco, CA — B
DeVry U, Phoenix, AZ — B
DeVry U, Fremont, CA — B
DeVry U, Long Beach, CA — B
DeVry U, Pomona, CA — B
DeVry U, Westminster, CO — B
DeVry U, Federal Way, WA — B
Idaho State U, ID — A
National American U, Denver, CO — A,B
Neumont U, UT — B
U of Puget Sound, WA — B

Computer Programming (Vendor/Product Certification)
Neumont U, UT — B

Computer Science
Arizona State U, AZ — B
Azusa Pacific U, CA — B
Boise State U, ID — B
Brigham Young U, UT — B
Brigham Young U–Hawaii, HI — B
Brigham Young U–Idaho, ID — A
California Inst of Technology, CA — B
California Lutheran U, CA — B
California Polytechnic State U, San Luis Obispo, CA — B
California State Polytechnic U, Pomona, CA — B
California State U Channel Islands, CA — B
California State U, Chico, CA — B
California State U, Dominguez Hills, CA — B
California State U, Fresno, CA — B
California State U, Fullerton, CA — B
California State U, Long Beach, CA — B
California State U, Los Angeles, CA — B
California State U, Northridge, CA — B
California State U, San Bernardino, CA — B
California State U, San Marcos, CA — B
Chapman U, CA — B
Claremont McKenna Coll, CA — B
CollAmerica–Colorado Springs, CO — A
CollAmerica–Denver, CO — A
Coll of Santa Fe, NM — B
Coll of the Southwest, NM — B
Colorado School of Mines, CO — B
Colorado State U, CO — B
Corban Coll, OR — B
Dixie State Coll of Utah, UT — A,B
Eastern Oregon U, OR — B
Fort Lewis Coll, CO — B
Gonzaga U, WA — B

Harvey Mudd Coll, CA — B
Hawai'i Pacific U, HI — B
Humboldt State U, CA — B
LA Coll International, CA — A,B
La Sierra U, CA — B
Lewis & Clark Coll, OR — B
Lewis-Clark State Coll, ID — B
Lincoln U, CA — B
Linfield Coll, OR — B
Little Big Horn Coll, MT — A
Loyola Marymount U, CA — B
Mesa State Coll, CO — A,B
Mills Coll, CA — B
Montana State U, MT — B
Montana Tech of The U of Montana, MT — A,B
Morrison U, NV — A
National U, CA — B
Neumont U, UT — B
New Mexico Highlands U, NM — B
New Mexico Inst of Mining and Technology, NM — B
North Carolina Ag and Tech State U, NC — B
Northwestern Polytechnic U, CA — B
Northwest Nazarene U, ID — B
Notre Dame de Namur U, CA — B
Oregon State U, OR — B
Pacific Lutheran U, WA — B
Pacific States U, CA — B
Pacific Union Coll, CA — B
Pacific U, OR — B
Pepperdine U, Malibu, CA — B
Point Loma Nazarene U, CA — B
Pomona Coll, CA — B
Portland State U, OR — B
Regis U, CO — B
Rocky Mountain Coll, MT — B
Salish Kootenai Coll, MT — A
San Diego State U, CA — B
San Francisco State U, CA — B
San Jose State U, CA — B
Santa Clara U, CA — B
Scripps Coll, CA — B
Seattle Pacific U, WA — B
Seattle U, WA — B
Sonoma State U, CA — B
Southern Oregon U, OR — B
Southern Utah U, UT — B
Stanford U, CA — B
Stone Child Coll, MT — A
United States Air Force Academy, CO — B
U of Alaska Anchorage, AK — B
U of Alaska Fairbanks, AK — B
U of California, Berkeley, CA — B
U of California, Irvine, CA — B
U of California, Los Angeles, CA — B
U of California, Riverside, CA — B
U of California, San Diego, CA — B
U of California, Santa Barbara, CA — B
U of California, Santa Cruz, CA — B
U of Colorado at Boulder, CO — B
U of Colorado at Colorado Springs, CO — B
U of Great Falls, MT — B
U of Hawaii at Hilo, HI — B
U of Hawaii at Manoa, HI — B
U of Idaho, ID — B
U of La Verne, CA — B
The U of Montana, MT — B

U of Nevada, Las Vegas, NV — B
U of Nevada, Reno, NV — B
U of New Orleans, LA — B
U of Oregon, OR — B
U of Portland, OR — B
U of Puget Sound, WA — B
U of Redlands, CA — B
U of San Diego, CA — B
U of San Francisco, CA — B
U of Southern California, CA — B
U of the Pacific, CA — B
U of Utah, UT — B
U of Washington, WA — B
U of Wyoming, WY — B
Utah Valley State Coll, UT — A,B
Walla Walla Coll, WA — B
Washington State U, WA — B
Weber State U, UT — A,B
Western Oregon U, OR — B
Western State Coll of Colorado, CO — B
Western Washington U, WA — B
Westminster Coll, UT — B
Westmont Coll, CA — B
Whitworth U, WA — B
Willamette U, OR — B

Computer Software and Media Applications Related
Eastern Washington U, WA — B
Holy Names U, CA — B
Neumont U, UT — B
Platt Coll San Diego, CA — A
U of Great Falls, MT — B
U of Phoenix–Denver Campus, CO — B

Computer Software Engineering
Embry-Riddle Aeronautical U, AZ — B
ITT Tech Inst, Tempe, AZ — B
ITT Tech Inst, Tucson, AZ — B
ITT Tech Inst, Lathrop, CA — B
ITT Tech Inst, Torrance, CA — B
ITT Tech Inst, CO — A
ITT Tech Inst, ID — B
ITT Tech Inst, Seattle, WA — B
ITT Tech Inst, Spokane, WA — A
National U, CA — B
Notre Dame de Namur U, CA — B
U of Phoenix–Bay Area Campus, CA — B
U of Phoenix–Denver Campus, CO — B
U of Phoenix–Idaho Campus, ID — B
U of Phoenix–Las Vegas Campus, NV — B
U of Phoenix–Phoenix Campus, AZ — B
U of Phoenix–Sacramento Valley Campus, CA — B
U of Phoenix–Southern Colorado Campus, CO — B
U of Phoenix–Washington Campus, WA — B

Computer Software Technology
ITT Tech Inst, Tempe, AZ — B
ITT Tech Inst, Tucson, AZ — B
ITT Tech Inst, Lathrop, CA — A
ITT Tech Inst, Oxnard, CA — B
ITT Tech Inst, Torrance, CA — B
ITT Tech Inst, NV — A

A—associate degree; B—bachelor's degree

ITT Tech Inst, UT   B
ITT Tech Inst, Bothell, WA   A

Computer Systems Analysis
Arizona State U at the
  Polytechnic Campus, AZ   B
Montana Tech of The U of
  Montana, MT   B
Seattle Pacific U, WA   B
U of Advancing Technology,
  AZ   B
U of Denver, CO   B
U of Great Falls, MT   B

Computer Systems Networking and Telecommunications
Boise State U, ID   B
CollAmerica–Colorado Springs,
  CO   A
CollAmerica–Denver, CO   A
DeVry U, Phoenix, AZ   B
DeVry U, Fremont, CA   A,B
DeVry U, Long Beach, CA   A,B
DeVry U, Pomona, CA   A,B
DeVry U, Sherman Oaks, CA   A,B
DeVry U, Westminster, CO   B
DeVry U, Federal Way, WA   A,B
ITT Tech Inst, Tempe, AZ   B
ITT Tech Inst, Tucson, AZ   B
ITT Tech Inst, Anaheim, CA   A
ITT Tech Inst, Clovis, CA   A
ITT Tech Inst, Lathrop, CA   B
ITT Tech Inst, Oxnard, CA   A
ITT Tech Inst, Rancho
  Cordova, CA   A
ITT Tech Inst, San Bernardino,
  CA   A
ITT Tech Inst, San Diego, CA   A
ITT Tech Inst, Sylmar, CA   A
ITT Tech Inst, Torrance, CA   A
ITT Tech Inst, CO   A
ITT Tech Inst, ID   A
ITT Tech Inst, NV   A
ITT Tech Inst, NM   A
ITT Tech Inst, OR   A
ITT Tech Inst, UT   A
ITT Tech Inst, Bothell, WA   B
ITT Tech Inst, Seattle, WA   A
ITT Tech Inst, Spokane, WA   A
National American U, Denver,
  CO   A,B
Remington Coll–Colorado
  Springs Campus, CO   A
U of Great Falls, MT   B
Weber State U, UT   B

Computer Teacher Education
Eastern Washington U, WA   B

Computer Technology/ Computer Systems Technology
Collins Coll: A School of
  Design and Technology, AZ   A
DeVry U, Phoenix, AZ   B
DeVry U, Pomona, CA   A
DeVry U, Sherman Oaks, CA   B
DeVry U, Westminster, CO   A,B

Conducting
Loyola Marymount U, CA   B

Conservation Biology
Arizona State U, AZ   B
Brigham Young U, UT   B
California State U, Sacramento,
  CA   B

Construction Engineering
Arizona State U, AZ   B
California State U, Long
  Beach, CA   B
National U, CA   B
Oregon State U, OR   B
U of Nevada, Las Vegas, NV   B
U of Southern California, CA   B

Construction Engineering Technology
Brigham Young U–Idaho, ID   A
California State Polytechnic U,
  Pomona, CA   B
California State U, Chico, CA   B
California State U, Fresno, CA   B
California State U, Long
  Beach, CA   B
California State U, Sacramento,
  CA   B
Colorado State U–Pueblo, CO   B
Eastern Washington U, WA   B
Montana State U, MT   B
Northern Arizona U, AZ   B
Southern Utah U, UT   B
U of Nevada, Reno, NV   B
U of New Mexico–Gallup, NM   A

Construction Management
Boise State U, ID   B
California State U, Fresno, CA   B
California State U, Long
  Beach, CA   B
ITT Tech Inst, Tempe, AZ   B
ITT Tech Inst, Anaheim, CA   B
ITT Tech Inst, Clovis, CA   B
ITT Tech Inst, Lathrop, CA   B
ITT Tech Inst, Oxnard, CA   B
ITT Tech Inst, Rancho
  Cordova, CA   B
ITT Tech Inst, San Bernardino,
  CA   B
ITT Tech Inst, San Diego, CA   B
ITT Tech Inst, San Dimas, CA   B
ITT Tech Inst, Sylmar, CA   B
ITT Tech Inst, Torrance, CA   B
ITT Tech Inst, ID   B
ITT Tech Inst, NV   B
ITT Tech Inst, NM   B
ITT Tech Inst, OR   B
ITT Tech Inst, UT   B
ITT Tech Inst, Bothell, WA   B
ITT Tech Inst, Seattle, WA   B
ITT Tech Inst, Spokane, WA   B
North Carolina Ag and Tech
  State U, NC   B
Oregon State U, OR   B
U of Denver, CO   B
U of Washington, WA   B

Construction Trades
U of Alaska Southeast, AK   A
Utah Valley State Coll, UT   A

Consumer Economics
U of Alaska Southeast, AK   A
The U of Arizona, AZ   B

Consumer Merchandising/ Retailing Management
FIDM/The Fashion Inst of
  Design & Merchandising, Los
  Angeles Campus, CA   A
San Francisco State U, CA   B

Cooking and Related Culinary Arts
The Art Inst of California–Los
  Angeles, CA   A,B

The Art Inst of California–
  Orange County, CA   A
The Art Inst of California–San
  Diego, CA   A,B

Corrections
Colorado State U–Pueblo, CO   B
Eastern Washington U, WA   B
Lewis-Clark State Coll, ID   B
U of Great Falls, MT   B
U of New Mexico, NM   B
U of New Mexico–Gallup, NM   A
Weber State U, UT   A,B
Western Oregon U, OR   B

Corrections Administration
U of Great Falls, MT   B

Corrections and Criminal Justice Related
U of Alaska Fairbanks, AK   B
U of Great Falls, MT   B
U of Phoenix–Bay Area
  Campus, CA   B
U of Phoenix–Central Valley
  Campus, CA   B
U of Phoenix Online Campus,
  AZ   B
U of Phoenix–Sacramento
  Valley Campus, CA   B
U of Phoenix–Southern
  Arizona Campus, AZ   B
U of Phoenix–Southern
  Colorado Campus, CO   B

Cosmetology
U of New Mexico–Gallup, NM   A

Counseling Psychology
Coll of Santa Fe, NM   B
Oregon Inst of Technology, OR   B
San Diego Christian Coll, CA   B
U of Great Falls, MT   B
Western State Coll of
  Colorado, CO   B

Counselor Education/School Counseling and Guidance
California State Polytechnic U,
  Pomona, CA   B
Mesa State Coll, CO   B
Northern Arizona U, AZ   B
U of Hawaii at Manoa, HI   B
Western Washington U, WA   B

Crafts, Folk Art and Artisanry
Brigham Young U, UT   B
Oregon Coll of Art & Craft,
  OR   B

Creative Writing
Albertson Coll of Idaho, ID   B
California State U, Long
  Beach, CA   B
California State U, San
  Bernardino, CA   B
Chapman U, CA   B
Coll of Santa Fe, NM   B
The Colorado Coll, CO   B
Colorado State U, CO   B
Dominican U of California, CA   B
Eastern Washington U, WA   B
Eugene Lang Coll The New
  School for Liberal Arts, NY   B
Lewis-Clark State Coll, ID   B
Linfield Coll, OR   B
Marylhurst U, OR   B
Mills Coll, CA   B
New Coll of California, CA   B
Pacific U, OR   B

Pitzer Coll, CA   B
San Diego State U, CA   B
San Francisco State U, CA   B
Seattle U, WA   B
The U of Arizona, AZ   B
U of California, Riverside, CA   B
U of California, San Diego, CA   B
U of California, Santa Cruz,
  CA   B
U of Denver, CO   B
U of Great Falls, MT   B
The U of Montana, MT   B
U of Puget Sound, WA   B
U of Redlands, CA   B
U of Southern California, CA   B
U of Washington, WA   B
Western State Coll of
  Colorado, CO   B
Western Washington U, WA   B

Credit Management
U of Phoenix–Las Vegas
  Campus, NV   B

Criminal Justice/Law Enforcement Administration
Argosy U, Orange County, CA   A
Arizona State U at the West
  campus, AZ   B
Boise State U, ID   A,B
Brigham Young U–Idaho, ID   A
California Baptist U, CA   B
California Lutheran U, CA   B
California State U, Dominguez
  Hills, CA   B
California State U, Fullerton,
  CA   B
California State U, Long
  Beach, CA   B
California State U, Sacramento,
  CA   B
California State U, San
  Bernardino, CA   B
California State U, Stanislaus,
  CA   B
Central Washington U, WA   B
Coll of Santa Fe, NM   B
Eastern Washington U, WA   B
Gonzaga U, WA   B
Grand Canyon U, AZ   B
Hawai'i Pacific U, HI   B
International Inst of the
  Americas, Mesa, AZ   A
International Inst of the
  Americas, Tucson, AZ   A
International Inst of the
  Americas, NM   A
ITT Tech Inst, Tempe, AZ   B
ITT Tech Inst, Tucson, AZ   B
ITT Tech Inst, Anaheim, CA   B
ITT Tech Inst, Clovis, CA   B
ITT Tech Inst, Lathrop, CA   B
ITT Tech Inst, Oxnard, CA   B
ITT Tech Inst, Rancho
  Cordova, CA   B
ITT Tech Inst, San Bernardino,
  CA   B
ITT Tech Inst, San Diego, CA   B
ITT Tech Inst, San Dimas, CA   B
ITT Tech Inst, Sylmar, CA   B
ITT Tech Inst, Torrance, CA   B
ITT Tech Inst, CO   B
ITT Tech Inst, ID   B
ITT Tech Inst, NV   B
ITT Tech Inst, NM   B
ITT Tech Inst, OR   B
ITT Tech Inst, UT   B

ITT Tech Inst, Bothell, WA — B
ITT Tech Inst, Seattle, WA — B
ITT Tech Inst, Spokane, WA — B
Johnson & Wales U, CO — A
Mesa State Coll, CO — A
National U, CA — B
Nevada State Coll at Henderson, NV — B
Northern Arizona U, AZ — B
Portland State U, OR — B
Regis U, CO — B
Remington Coll–Colorado Springs Campus, CO — A,B
San Diego State U, CA — B
San Francisco State U, CA — B
Seattle U, WA — B
Sonoma State U, CA — B
Southern Utah U, UT — A
U of Alaska Anchorage, AK — B
The U of Arizona, AZ — B
U of Great Falls, MT — B
U of Hawaii–West Oahu, HI — B
U of Nevada, Las Vegas, NV — B
U of New Mexico–Gallup, NM — A
U of Phoenix–Bay Area Campus, CA — B
U of Phoenix–Denver Campus, CO — B
U of Phoenix–Eastern Washington Campus, Spokane Valley, WA — B
U of Phoenix–Hawaii Campus, HI — B
U of Phoenix–Idaho Campus, ID — B
U of Phoenix–Las Vegas Campus, NV — B
U of Phoenix–New Mexico Campus, NM — B
U of Phoenix–Oregon Campus, OR — B
U of Phoenix–Phoenix Campus, AZ — B
U of Phoenix–Sacramento Valley Campus, CA — B
U of Phoenix–San Diego Campus, CA — B
U of Phoenix–Southern California Campus, CA — B
U of Phoenix–Utah Campus, UT — B
U of Phoenix–Washington Campus, WA — B
U of Washington, WA — B
Utah Valley State Coll, UT — A,B
Washington State U, WA — B
Western International U, AZ — B
Western Oregon U, OR — B
Western State Coll of Colorado, CO — B

Criminal Justice/Police Science
Brigham Young U–Idaho, ID — A
Everest Coll, Phoenix, AZ — A,B
Idaho State U, ID — A
Pioneer Pacific Coll, Wilsonville, OR — A,B
U of Great Falls, MT — B
Weber State U, UT — A,B
Western Oregon U, OR — B

Criminal Justice/Safety
Arizona State U, AZ — B
California State U, Chico, CA — B

California State U, Los Angeles, CA — B
Cambridge Coll, CO — A
Coll of the Southwest, NM — B
Colorado State U, CO — B
Dixie State Coll of Utah, UT — A
Eastern New Mexico U, NM — B
Great Basin Coll, NV — A
Idaho State U, ID — A
New Mexico Highlands U, NM — B
New Mexico State U, NM — A,B
Northern New Mexico Coll, NM — A
Prescott Coll, AZ — B
San Jose State U, CA — B
U of Great Falls, MT — B
U of Idaho, ID — B
U of Northern Colorado, CO — B
U of Portland, OR — B
U of Wyoming, WY — B
Weber State U, UT — A,B

Criminology
California State U, Fresno, CA — B
Colorado State U–Pueblo, CO — B
Mesa State Coll, CO — B
New Mexico Highlands U, NM — B
Southern Oregon U, OR — B
U of California, Irvine, CA — B
U of Denver, CO — B
U of La Verne, CA — B
U of Nevada, Reno, NV — B

Crop Production
Colorado State U, CO — B
Washington State U, WA — B

Culinary Arts
The Art Inst of California–San Diego, CA — A
The Art Inst of Colorado, CO — A,B
The Art Inst of Phoenix, AZ — A,B
The Art Inst of Seattle, WA — A
Boise State U, ID — A
Idaho State U, ID — A
Johnson & Wales U, CO — A,B
Mesa State Coll, CO — A
U of Alaska Anchorage, AK — A
U of Alaska Fairbanks, AK — A
The U of Montana, MT — A
U of Nevada, Las Vegas, NV — B
Utah Valley State Coll, UT — A

Cultural Studies
Azusa Pacific U, CA — B
Boise State U, ID — B
Brigham Young U–Hawaii, HI — B
California State Polytechnic U, Pomona, CA — B
California State U, Fullerton, CA — B
California State U, Sacramento, CA — B
Fort Lewis Coll, CO — B
Mills Coll, CA — B
New Coll of California, CA — B
Oregon State U, OR — B
Sonoma State U, CA — B
U of California, Irvine, CA — B
U of California, Riverside, CA — B
U of California, San Diego, CA — B
U of Colorado at Boulder, CO — B
U of Nevada, Las Vegas, NV — B
U of Oregon, OR — B
U of Southern California, CA — B
U of Washington, WA — B
Western Washington U, WA — B

Curriculum and Instruction
The U of Montana, MT — B
Utah State U, UT — B

Cytotechnology
California State U, Dominguez Hills, CA — B
Loma Linda U, CA — B

Dairy Science
Brigham Young U–Idaho, ID — A
California Polytechnic State U, San Luis Obispo, CA — B
Utah State U, UT — B

Dance
Arizona State U, AZ — B
Brigham Young U, UT — B
Brigham Young U–Idaho, ID — A
California Inst of the Arts, CA — B
California State U, Fresno, CA — B
California State U, Fullerton, CA — B
California State U, Long Beach, CA — B
California State U, Los Angeles, CA — B
California State U, Sacramento, CA — B
Chapman U, CA — B
Claremont McKenna Coll, CA — B
The Colorado Coll, CO — B
Colorado State U, CO — B
Dixie State Coll of Utah, UT — A
Loyola Marymount U, CA — B
Mills Coll, CA — B
New Mexico State U, NM — B
Pitzer Coll, CA — B
Pomona Coll, CA — B
Prescott Coll, AZ — B
Reed Coll, OR — B
Saint Mary's Coll of California, CA — B
San Diego State U, CA — B
San Francisco State U, CA — B
San Jose State U, CA — B
Scripps Coll, CA — B
Southern Utah U, UT — B
The U of Arizona, AZ — B
U of California, Berkeley, CA — B
U of California, Irvine, CA — B
U of California, Los Angeles, CA — B
U of California, Riverside, CA — B
U of California, San Diego, CA — B
U of California, Santa Barbara, CA — B
U of California, Santa Cruz, CA — B
U of Colorado at Boulder, CO — B
U of Hawaii at Manoa, HI — B
U of Idaho, ID — B
The U of Montana, MT — B
U of Nevada, Las Vegas, NV — B
U of New Mexico, NM — B
U of Oregon, OR — B
U of Utah, UT — B
U of Washington, WA — B
Utah State U, UT — B
Utah Valley State Coll, UT — A
Weber State U, UT — B
Western Oregon U, OR — B
Westmont Coll, CA — B

Dance Related
Brigham Young U, UT — B

California State U, Long Beach, CA — B
Chapman U, CA — B

Data Entry/Microcomputer Applications
National American U, Denver, CO — A,B

Data Modeling/Warehousing and Database Administration
National U, CA — B
Neumont U, UT — B

Data Processing and Data Processing Technology
Brigham Young U–Idaho, ID — A
Dixie State Coll of Utah, UT — A
Great Basin Coll, NV — A
Hawai'i Pacific U, HI — A
Montana State U–Billings, MT — A
Montana Tech of The U of Montana, MT — A
Pacific Union Coll, CA — B
U of Advancing Technology, AZ — B
The U of Montana–Western, MT — A
U of Washington, WA — B
Utah Valley State Coll, UT — A,B

Dental Assisting
U of Alaska Anchorage, AK — A

Dental Hygiene
Brigham Young U–Idaho, ID — A
Dixie State Coll of Utah, UT — A
Eastern Washington U, WA — B
Idaho State U, ID — B
Loma Linda U, CA — B
Montana State U–Billings, MT — A
Northern Arizona U, AZ — B
Oregon Inst of Technology, OR — B
Salish Kootenai Coll, MT — A
U of Alaska Anchorage, AK — A
U of Colorado at Denver and Health Sciences Center, CO — B
U of Hawaii at Manoa, HI — B
U of New Mexico, NM — A,B
U of Southern California, CA — B
U of Washington, WA — B
U of Wyoming, WY — B
Utah Valley State Coll, UT — B
Weber State U, UT — A,B

Dental Laboratory Technology
Idaho State U, ID — A

Design and Applied Arts Related
Art Center Coll of Design, CA — B
The Art Inst of California–San Diego, CA — B
U of California, Los Angeles, CA — B

Design and Visual Communications
Brigham Young U, UT — B
California State U, Chico, CA — B
Collins Coll: A School of Design and Technology, AZ — A,B
FIDM/The Fashion Inst of Design & Merchandising, Los Angeles Campus, CA — A
Montana State U, MT — B
San Diego State U, CA — B
San Francisco Art Inst, CA — B

A—associate degree; B—bachelor's degree

U of Advancing Technology,
AZ — B
Weber State U, UT — B
Western Washington U, WA — B

Developmental and Child Psychology
California Polytechnic State U,
San Luis Obispo, CA — B
California State U, San
Bernardino, CA — B
Colorado State U-Pueblo, CO — B
Eastern Washington U, WA — B
Fresno Pacific U, CA — A,B
Humboldt State U, CA — B
Mills Coll, CA — B
Mount St. Mary's Coll, CA — B
Sonoma State U, CA — B
U of California, Santa Cruz,
CA — B
U of Utah, UT — B
Western Washington U, WA — B

Developmental Biology and Embryology
U of Colorado at Boulder, CO — B

Development Economics and International Development
Point Loma Nazarene U, CA — B
U of California, Los Angeles,
CA — B

Diagnostic Medical Sonography and Ultrasound Technology
Seattle U, WA — B
Weber State U, UT — B

Diesel Mechanics Technology
Dixie State Coll of Utah, UT — A
Great Basin Coll, NV — A
Idaho State U, ID — A
Lewis-Clark State Coll, ID — A,B
Montana State U–Billings, MT — A
U of Alaska Anchorage, AK — A
Utah Valley State Coll, UT — A
Weber State U, UT — A

Dietetics
Bastyr U, WA — B
Brigham Young U, UT — B
Brigham Young U–Idaho, ID — A
California State Polytechnic U,
Pomona, CA — B
California State U, Chico, CA — B
California State U, Fresno, CA — B
California State U, Long
Beach, CA — B
California State U, Los
Angeles, CA — B
California State U, San
Bernardino, CA — B
Colorado State U, CO — B
Idaho State U, ID — B
Loma Linda U, CA — A,B
North Carolina Ag and Tech
State U, NC — B
Point Loma Nazarene U, CA — B
San Francisco State U, CA — B
San Jose State U, CA — B
U of Hawaii at Manoa, HI — B
U of Northern Colorado, CO — B

Digital Communication and Media/Multimedia
Academy of Art U, CA — A,B
The Art Inst of California–San
Diego, CA — B

California Lutheran U, CA — B
California State U, Sacramento,
CA — B
Cogswell Polytechnical Coll,
CA — B
Eastern Washington U, WA — B
Platt Coll San Diego, CA — A
U of Phoenix–Bay Area
Campus, CA — B
U of Phoenix–Denver Campus,
CO — B
U of Phoenix–Hawaii Campus,
HI — B
U of Phoenix–Phoenix Campus,
AZ — B
U of Phoenix–Sacramento
Valley Campus, CA — B
U of Phoenix–Southern
California Campus, CA — B
U of Phoenix–Utah Campus,
UT — B
U of Phoenix–Washington
Campus, WA — B
Utah Valley State Coll, UT — A,B
Washington State U, WA — B

Directing and Theatrical Production
Brigham Young U, UT — B
California State U, Long
Beach, CA — B
George Fox U, OR — B
U of Southern California, CA — B

Divinity/Ministry
Azusa Pacific U, CA — B
Bethany U, CA — B
Biola U, CA — B
Boise Bible Coll, ID — A,B
Concordia U, CA — B
Corban Coll, OR — B
Eugene Bible Coll, OR — B
Fresno Pacific U, CA — B
Grand Canyon U, AZ — B
Marylhurst U, OR — B
The Master's Coll and
Seminary, CA — B
Northwest Nazarene U, ID — B
Northwest U, WA — B
Patten U, CA — B
San Diego Christian Coll, CA — B
Warner Pacific Coll, OR — A,B

Drafting and Design Technology
Boise State U, ID — A
Brigham Young U–Idaho, ID — A
Idaho State U, ID — A
Lewis-Clark State Coll, ID — A,B
Montana State U–Billings, MT — A
Montana Tech of The U of
Montana, MT — A
Pacific Union Coll, CA — B
Southern Utah U, UT — A
U of Alaska Anchorage, AK — A
Utah State U, UT — A
Utah Valley State Coll, UT — A
Weber State U, UT — A

Drafting/Design Engineering Technologies Related
Eastern Washington U, WA — B
Idaho State U, ID — B
National U, CA — B

Drafting/Design Technology
ITT Tech Inst, Clovis, CA — A

Drama and Dance Teacher Education
Brigham Young U, UT — B
Central Washington U, WA — B
Eastern Washington U, WA — B
Northern Arizona U, AZ — B
The U of Arizona, AZ — B
U of Utah, UT — B
Utah Valley State Coll, UT — B
Weber State U, UT — B

Dramatic/Theater Arts
Adams State Coll, CO — B
Albertson Coll of Idaho, ID — B
Arizona State U, AZ — B
Bethany U, CA — B
Boise State U, ID — B
Brigham Young U, UT — B
Brigham Young U–Hawaii, HI — A
Brigham Young U–Idaho, ID — A
California Baptist U, CA — B
California Inst of the Arts, CA — B
California Lutheran U, CA — B
California State Polytechnic U,
Pomona, CA — B
California State U, Chico, CA — B
California State U, Dominguez
Hills, CA — B
California State U, Fresno, CA — B
California State U, Fullerton,
CA — B
California State U, Long
Beach, CA — B
California State U, Los
Angeles, CA — B
California State U, Monterey
Bay, CA — B
California State U, Northridge,
CA — B
California State U, Sacramento,
CA — B
California State U, San
Bernardino, CA — B
California State U, Stanislaus,
CA — B
Central Washington U, WA — B
Chapman U, CA — B
Claremont McKenna Coll, CA — B
Coll of Santa Fe, NM — B
Coll of the Southwest, NM — B
Colorado Christian U, CO — B
The Colorado Coll, CO — B
Colorado State U, CO — B
Concordia U, CA — B
Concordia U, OR — B
Dixie State Coll of Utah, UT — A
Eastern New Mexico U, NM — B
Eastern Oregon U, OR — B
Eastern Washington U, WA — B
Eugene Lang Coll The New
School for Liberal Arts, NY — B
The Evergreen State Coll, WA — B
Fort Lewis Coll, CO — B
George Fox U, OR — B
Gonzaga U, WA — B
Grand Canyon U, AZ — B
Humboldt State U, CA — B
Idaho State U, ID — B
Lewis & Clark Coll, OR — B
Linfield Coll, OR — B
Loyola Marymount U, CA — B
Mesa State Coll, CO — A,B
Montana State U, MT — B
Montana State U–Billings, MT — B
Naropa U, CO — B
New Mexico State U, NM — B

North Carolina Ag and Tech
State U, NC — B
Northern Arizona U, AZ — B
Northwest U, WA — B
Notre Dame de Namur U, CA — B
Occidental Coll, CA — B
Pacific Lutheran U, WA — B
Pacific U, OR — B
Pepperdine U, Malibu, CA — B
Pitzer Coll, CA — B
Point Loma Nazarene U, CA — B
Pomona Coll, CA — B
Portland State U, OR — B
Prescott Coll, AZ — B
Reed Coll, OR — B
Rocky Mountain Coll, MT — B
Saint Mary's Coll of California,
CA — B
San Diego State U, CA — B
San Francisco State U, CA — B
San Jose State U, CA — B
Santa Clara U, CA — B
Scripps Coll, CA — B
Seattle Pacific U, WA — B
Seattle U, WA — B
Sonoma State U, CA — B
Southern Oregon U, OR — B
Southern Utah U, UT — B
Stanford U, CA — B
U of Alaska Anchorage, AK — B
U of Alaska Fairbanks, AK — B
The U of Arizona, AZ — B
U of California, Berkeley, CA — B
U of California, Irvine, CA — B
U of California, Los Angeles,
CA — B
U of California, Riverside, CA — B
U of California, San Diego, CA — B
U of California, Santa Barbara,
CA — B
U of California, Santa Cruz,
CA — B
U of Colorado at Boulder, CO — B
U of Colorado at Denver and
Health Sciences Center, CO — B
U of Dallas, TX — B
U of Denver, CO — B
U of Hawaii at Manoa, HI — B
U of Idaho, ID — B
U of La Verne, CA — B
The U of Montana, MT — B
The U of Montana–Western,
MT — B
U of Nevada, Las Vegas, NV — B
U of Nevada, Reno, NV — B
U of New Mexico, NM — B
U of Northern Colorado, CO — B
U of Oregon, OR — B
U of Portland, OR — B
U of Puget Sound, WA — B
U of San Diego, CA — B
U of Southern California, CA — B
U of the Pacific, CA — B
U of Utah, UT — B
U of Washington, WA — B
U of Wyoming, WY — B
Utah State U, UT — B
Utah Valley State Coll, UT — A
Vanguard U of Southern
California, CA — B
Washington State U, WA — B
Weber State U, UT — B
Western Oregon U, OR — B
Western State Coll of
Colorado, CO — B
Western Washington U, WA — B

Westmont Coll, CA — B
Whitman Coll, WA — B
Whitworth U, WA — B
Willamette U, OR — B

Dramatic/Theater Arts and Stagecraft Related
Brigham Young U, UT — B
California Inst of the Arts, CA — B
California State U, Chico, CA — B
Coll of Santa Fe, NM — B
U of Nevada, Las Vegas, NV — B
U of Northern Colorado, CO — B

Drawing
Academy of Art U, CA — A,B
Biola U, CA — B
Boise State U, ID — B
Brigham Young U, UT — B
California Coll of the Arts, CA — B
California State U, Fullerton, CA — B
California State U, Long Beach, CA — B
Colorado State U, CO — B
Dixie State Coll of Utah, UT — A
Otis Coll of Art and Design, CA — B
Portland State U, OR — B
Sonoma State U, CA — B
U of California, Santa Cruz, CA — B
The U of Montana, MT — B
U of Oregon, OR — B
U of San Francisco, CA — B
Western Washington U, WA — B

Dutch/Flemish
U of California, Berkeley, CA — B

Early Childhood Education
Brigham Young U, UT — B
California State U, Chico, CA — B
California State U, Fullerton, CA — B
California State U, Los Angeles, CA — B
Cascade Coll, OR — B
Central Washington U, WA — B
Coll of Santa Fe, NM — B
Eastern Washington U, WA — B
Fort Lewis Coll, CO — B
Naropa U, CO — B
New Mexico State U, NM — B
San Diego State U, CA — B
San Jose State U, CA — B
Trinity Lutheran Coll, WA — B
The U of Arizona, AZ — B
U of Great Falls, MT — A
U of New Mexico, NM — B
U of New Orleans, LA — B
Utah Valley State Coll, UT — A,B
Washington State U, WA — B

East Asian Languages
U of California, Los Angeles, CA — B
U of Oregon, OR — B
U of Southern California, CA — B

East Asian Languages Related
Arizona State U, AZ — B
Claremont McKenna Coll, CA — B

Ecology
Brigham Young U–Idaho, ID — A
California State U, Chico, CA — B
California State U, Fresno, CA — B

California State U, Long Beach, CA — B
California State U, San Marcos, CA — B
Dixie State Coll of Utah, UT — A
Idaho State U, ID — B
New Coll of California, CA — B
Northern Arizona U, AZ — B
Pitzer Coll, CA — B
Pomona Coll, CA — B
Prescott Coll, AZ — B
San Francisco State U, CA — B
Sierra Nevada Coll, NV — B
Sonoma State U, CA — B
U of California, Irvine, CA — B
U of California, Los Angeles, CA — B
U of California, San Diego, CA — B
U of California, Santa Barbara, CA — B
U of California, Santa Cruz, CA — B
U of Colorado at Colorado Springs, CO — B
Utah State U, UT — B
Washington State U, WA — B
Western State Coll of Colorado, CO — B

Ecology, Evolution, Systematics and Population Biology Related
Brigham Young U, UT — B
U of California, Davis, CA — B
U of Colorado at Boulder, CO — B

E-Commerce
Dominican U of California, CA — B
ITT Tech Inst, San Dimas, CA — B
National U, CA — B
U of La Verne, CA — B
U of Phoenix–Bay Area Campus, CA — B
U of Phoenix–Denver Campus, CO — B
U of Phoenix–Hawaii Campus, HI — B
U of Phoenix–Idaho Campus, ID — B
U of Phoenix–Las Vegas Campus, NV — B
U of Phoenix–Oregon Campus, OR — B
U of Phoenix–Phoenix Campus, AZ — B
U of Phoenix–Sacramento Valley Campus, CA — B
U of Phoenix–Washington Campus, WA — B
Washington State U, WA — B

Econometrics and Quantitative Economics
The Colorado Coll, CO — B
U of California, San Diego, CA — B

Economics
Albertson Coll of Idaho, ID — B
Arizona State U, AZ — B
Boise State U, ID — B
Brigham Young U, UT — B
Brigham Young U–Idaho, ID — A
California Inst of Technology, CA — B
California Lutheran U, CA — B

California Polytechnic State U, San Luis Obispo, CA — B
California State Polytechnic U, Pomona, CA — B
California State U Channel Islands, CA — B
California State U, Chico, CA — B
California State U, Dominguez Hills, CA — B
California State U, Fresno, CA — B
California State U, Fullerton, CA — B
California State U, Long Beach, CA — B
California State U, Los Angeles, CA — B
California State U, Northridge, CA — B
California State U, Sacramento, CA — B
California State U, San Bernardino, CA — B
California State U, San Marcos, CA — B
California State U, Stanislaus, CA — B
Central Washington U, WA — B
Claremont McKenna Coll, CA — B
The Colorado Coll, CO — B
Colorado School of Mines, CO — B
Dixie State Coll of Utah, UT — A
Eastern Oregon U, OR — B
Eastern Washington U, WA — B
Eugene Lang Coll The New School for Liberal Arts, NY — B
Fort Lewis Coll, CO — B
George Fox U, OR — B
Gonzaga U, WA — B
Grand Canyon U, AZ — B
Hawai'i Pacific U, HI — B
Humboldt State U, CA — B
Idaho State U, ID — B
Lewis & Clark Coll, OR — B
Lincoln U, CA — B
Linfield Coll, OR — B
Loyola Marymount U, CA — B
Mills Coll, CA — B
Montana State U, MT — B
National U, CA — B
New Mexico State U, NM — B
North Carolina Ag and Tech State U, NC — B
Northern Arizona U, AZ — B
Occidental Coll, CA — B
Oregon State U, OR — B
Pacific Lutheran U, WA — B
Pacific U, OR — B
Pepperdine U, Malibu, CA — B
Pitzer Coll, CA — B
Pomona Coll, CA — B
Portland State U, OR — B
Reed Coll, OR — B
Regis U, CO — B
Rocky Mountain Coll, MT — B
Saint Mary's Coll of California, CA — B
San Diego State U, CA — B
San Francisco State U, CA — B
San Jose State U, CA — B
Santa Clara U, CA — B
Scripps Coll, CA — B
Seattle Pacific U, WA — B
Seattle U, WA — B
Sonoma State U, CA — B
Southern Oregon U, OR — B

Southern Utah U, UT — B
Stanford U, CA — B
United States Air Force Academy, CO — B
U of Alaska Anchorage, AK — B
U of Alaska Fairbanks, AK — B
The U of Arizona, AZ — B
U of California, Berkeley, CA — B
U of California, Davis, CA — B
U of California, Irvine, CA — B
U of California, Los Angeles, CA — B
U of California, Riverside, CA — B
U of California, San Diego, CA — B
U of California, Santa Barbara, CA — B
U of California, Santa Cruz, CA — B
U of Colorado at Boulder, CO — B
U of Colorado at Colorado Springs, CO — B
U of Colorado at Denver and Health Sciences Center, CO — B
U of Dallas, TX — B
U of Denver, CO — B
U of Hawaii at Hilo, HI — B
U of Hawaii at Manoa, HI — B
U of Hawaii–West Oahu, HI — B
U of Idaho, ID — B
U of La Verne, CA — B
The U of Montana, MT — B
U of Nevada, Las Vegas, NV — B
U of New Mexico, NM — B
U of New Orleans, LA — B
U of Northern Colorado, CO — B
U of Oregon, OR — B
U of Puget Sound, WA — B
U of Redlands, CA — B
U of San Diego, CA — B
U of San Francisco, CA — B
U of Southern California, CA — B
U of the Pacific, CA — B
U of Utah, UT — B
U of Washington, WA — B
Utah State U, UT — B
Walla Walla Coll, WA — B
Washington State U, WA — B
Weber State U, UT — B
Western Oregon U, OR — B
Western State Coll of Colorado, CO — B
Western Washington U, WA — B
Westmont Coll, CA — B
Whitman Coll, WA — B
Whitworth U, WA — B
Willamette U, OR — B

Economics Related
California State U, Chico, CA — B
Claremont McKenna Coll, CA — B
The Colorado Coll, CO — B
Nevada State Coll at Henderson, NV — B
U of Dallas, TX — B

Education
Bethany U, CA — B
Biola U, CA — B
Boise State U, ID — B
Brigham Young U–Hawaii, HI — B
Brigham Young U–Idaho, ID — A
California State U Channel Islands, CA — B
Coll of the Southwest, NM — B
Colorado State U-Pueblo, CO — B
Concordia U, OR — B

A—associate degree; B—bachelor's degree

Corban Coll, OR — B
Eastern Oregon U, OR — B
Eugene Lang Coll The New School for Liberal Arts, NY — B
Fresno Pacific U, CA — B
Humboldt State U, CA — B
The Master's Coll and Seminary, CA — B
Mesa State Coll, CO — B
Montana State U–Billings, MT — A,B
Mount St. Mary's Coll, CA — B
National U, CA — A
Nevada State Coll at Henderson, NV — B
New Coll of California, CA — B
New Mexico Highlands U, NM — B
North Carolina Ag and Tech State U, NC — B
Northern Arizona U, AZ — B
Northwest U, WA — B
Notre Dame de Namur U, CA — B
Pacific Lutheran U, WA — B
Pacific Union Coll, CA — B
Pacific U, OR — B
Pepperdine U, Malibu, CA — B
Prescott Coll, AZ — B
Regis U, CO — B
Rocky Mountain Coll, MT — B
San Diego Christian Coll, CA — B
Shasta Bible Coll, CA — B
Southern Utah U, UT — B
U of Alaska Anchorage, AK — B
U of Alaska Fairbanks, AK — B
U of Alaska Southeast, AK — B
U of California, Los Angeles, CA — B
U of Dallas, TX — B
U of Hawaii at Manoa, HI — B
U of La Verne, CA — B
The U of Montana, MT — B
The U of Montana–Western, MT — B
U of Nevada, Las Vegas, NV — B
U of New Mexico–Gallup, NM — A
U of Oregon, OR — B
U of Portland, OR — B
U of Redlands, CA — B
U of San Francisco, CA — B
U of Southern California, CA — B
U of the Pacific, CA — B
U of Utah, UT — B
U of Washington, WA — B
U of Washington, Tacoma, WA — B
Vanguard U of Southern California, CA — B
Warner Pacific Coll, OR — B
Washington State U, WA — B
Western State Coll of Colorado, CO — B
Western Washington U, WA — B
Westmont Coll, CA — B
William Jessup U, CA — B

Educational/Instructional Media Design
California State U, Chico, CA — B
Western Oregon U, OR — B

Educational Leadership and Administration
Northern Arizona U, AZ — B
Shasta Bible Coll, CA — B
U of California, Los Angeles, CA — B
U of Oregon, OR — B
U of San Francisco, CA — B
Western Washington U, WA — B

Education (K–12)
Biola U, CA — B
Pacific Union Coll, CA — B
San Diego Christian Coll, CA — B
The U of Montana–Western, MT — B
Walla Walla Coll, WA — B

Education (Multiple Levels)
Northwest Christian Coll, OR — B
U of Great Falls, MT — B
U of Washington, WA — B
Utah State U, UT — B
Western Washington U, WA — B

Education Related
Alliant International U, CA — B
Brigham Young U, UT — B
Dominican U of California, CA — B
Eastern Washington U, WA — B
Marylhurst U, OR — B

Education (Specific Levels and Methods) Related
Brigham Young U, UT — B

Education (Specific Subject Areas) Related
Brigham Young U, UT — B
Eastern Washington U, WA — B
Northern Arizona U, AZ — B
The U of Arizona, AZ — B
U of Nevada, Reno, NV — B
Utah State U, UT — B

Electrical and Electronic Engineering Technologies Related
Boise State U, ID — A

Electrical, Electronic and Communications Engineering Technology
Boise State U, ID — A
Brigham Young U–Idaho, ID — A
California State Polytechnic U, Pomona, CA — B
California State U, Long Beach, CA — B
Central Washington U, WA — B
Cogswell Polytechnical Coll, CA — B
DeVry U, Phoenix, AZ — A,B
DeVry U, Fremont, CA — A,B
DeVry U, Long Beach, CA — A,B
DeVry U, Pomona, CA — A,B
DeVry U, Sherman Oaks, CA — A,B
DeVry U, Westminster, CO — A,B
DeVry U, NV — A
DeVry U, OR — A
DeVry U, Federal Way, WA — A,B
Eastern Washington U, WA — B
Great Basin Coll, NV — A
Idaho State U, ID — A
ITT Tech Inst, Tempe, AZ — B
ITT Tech Inst, Tucson, AZ — A,B
ITT Tech Inst, Anaheim, CA — B
ITT Tech Inst, Lathrop, CA — A,B
ITT Tech Inst, Oxnard, CA — A,B
ITT Tech Inst, Rancho Cordova, CA — B
ITT Tech Inst, San Bernardino, CA — B
ITT Tech Inst, San Diego, CA — B
ITT Tech Inst, San Dimas, CA — A,B
ITT Tech Inst, Sylmar, CA — B
ITT Tech Inst, Torrance, CA — B
ITT Tech Inst, CO — A,B
ITT Tech Inst, ID — B

ITT Tech Inst, NV — B
ITT Tech Inst, NM — B
ITT Tech Inst, OR — B
ITT Tech Inst, UT — B
ITT Tech Inst, Bothell, WA — B
ITT Tech Inst, Seattle, WA — B
ITT Tech Inst, Spokane, WA — A,B
Mesa State Coll, CO — A
Northern New Mexico Coll, NM — A
Oregon Inst of Technology, OR — A,B
Pacific Union Coll, CA — B
Southern Utah U, UT — A,B
U of Alaska Anchorage, AK — A
U of California, Santa Barbara, CA — B
The U of Montana, MT — A
Utah Valley State Coll, UT — A
Weber State U, UT — A,B
Western Washington U, WA — B

Electrical, Electronics and Communications Engineering
Arizona State U, AZ — B
Boise State U, ID — B
Brigham Young U, UT — B
California Inst of Technology, CA — B
California Polytechnic State U, San Luis Obispo, CA — B
California State Polytechnic U, Pomona, CA — B
California State U, Chico, CA — B
California State U, Fresno, CA — B
California State U, Fullerton, CA — B
California State U, Long Beach, CA — B
California State U, Los Angeles, CA — B
California State U, Sacramento, CA — B
Cogswell Polytechnical Coll, CA — B
Colorado School of Mines, CO — B
Colorado State U, CO — B
Embry-Riddle Aeronautical U, AZ — B
George Fox U, OR — B
Gonzaga U, WA — B
Idaho State U, ID — B
Loyola Marymount U, CA — B
Montana State U, MT — B
New Mexico Inst of Mining and Technology, NM — B
New Mexico State U, NM — B
North Carolina Ag and Tech State U, NC — B
Northern Arizona U, AZ — B
Northwestern Polytechnic U, CA — B
Oregon State U, OR — B
Pacific Lutheran U, WA — B
Pacific States U, CA — B
Portland State U, OR — B
San Diego State U, CA — B
San Francisco State U, CA — B
San Jose State U, CA — B
Santa Clara U, CA — B
Seattle Pacific U, WA — B
Seattle U, WA — B
Stanford U, CA — B
United States Air Force Academy, CO — B
U of Alaska Fairbanks, AK — B
The U of Arizona, AZ — B
U of California, Berkeley, CA — B

U of California, Davis, CA — B
U of California, Irvine, CA — B
U of California, Los Angeles, CA — B
U of California, Riverside, CA — B
U of California, San Diego, CA — B
U of California, Santa Barbara, CA — B
U of California, Santa Cruz, CA — B
U of Colorado at Boulder, CO — B
U of Colorado at Colorado Springs, CO — B
U of Colorado at Denver and Health Sciences Center, CO — B
U of Denver, CO — B
U of Hawaii at Manoa, HI — B
U of Idaho, ID — B
U of Nevada, Las Vegas, NV — B
U of Nevada, Reno, NV — B
U of New Mexico, NM — B
U of New Orleans, LA — B
U of Portland, OR — B
U of San Diego, CA — B
U of Southern California, CA — B
U of the Pacific, CA — B
U of Utah, UT — B
U of Washington, WA — B
U of Wyoming, WY — B
Utah State U, UT — B
Walla Walla Coll, WA — B
Washington State U, WA — B

Electrical/Electronics Equipment Installation and Repair
Arizona State U at the Polytechnic Campus, AZ — B
Idaho State U, ID — A
Lewis-Clark State Coll, ID — A,B

Electromechanical Technology
Idaho State U, ID — A
Utah Valley State Coll, UT — A
Walla Walla Coll, WA — A

Elementary Education
Adams State Coll, CO — B
Alaska Pacific U, AK — A,B
Arizona State U, AZ — B
Arizona State U at the Polytechnic Campus, AZ — B
Arizona State U at the West campus, AZ — B
Bethany U, CA — B
Biola U, CA — B
Boise State U, ID — B
Brigham Young U, UT — B
Brigham Young U–Hawaii, HI — B
Brigham Young U–Idaho, ID — A
Cascade Coll, OR — B
Central Washington U, WA — B
Coll of Santa Fe, NM — B
Coll of the Southwest, NM — B
Colorado State U-Pueblo, CO — B
Concordia U, OR — B
Corban Coll, OR — B
Dixie State Coll of Utah, UT — A,B
Eastern New Mexico U, NM — B
Eastern Washington U, WA — B
Fort Lewis Coll, CO — B
Fresno Pacific U, CA — B
George Fox U, OR — B
Gonzaga U, WA — B
Grand Canyon U, AZ — B
Great Basin Coll, NV — A,B
Hope International U, CA — B

Elementary Education

Humboldt State U, CA	B
Idaho State U, ID	B
La Sierra U, CA	B
Lewis-Clark State Coll, ID	B
Linfield Coll, OR	B
Little Big Horn Coll, MT	A
The Master's Coll and Seminary, CA	B
Mesa State Coll, CO	B
Montana State U, MT	B
Montana State U–Billings, MT	B
Mount St. Mary's Coll, CA	B
New Mexico Highlands U, NM	A,B
New Mexico State U, NM	B
North Carolina Ag and Tech State U, NC	B
Northern Arizona U, AZ	B
Northern New Mexico Coll, NM	A
Northwest Nazarene U, ID	B
Northwest U, WA	B
Notre Dame de Namur U, CA	B
Pacific Lutheran U, WA	B
Pacific Oaks Coll, CA	B
Pacific Union Coll, CA	B
Pacific U, OR	B
Pepperdine U, Malibu, CA	B
Prescott Coll, AZ	B
Regis U, CO	B
Rocky Mountain Coll, MT	B
San Diego Christian Coll, CA	B
Simpson U, CA	B
Southern Utah U, UT	B
Trinity Lutheran Coll, WA	B
U of Alaska Anchorage, AK	B
U of Alaska Fairbanks, AK	B
The U of Arizona, AZ	B
U of Dallas, TX	B
U of Great Falls, MT	B
U of Hawaii at Hilo, HI	B
U of Hawaii at Manoa, HI	B
U of Idaho, ID	B
U of La Verne, CA	B
The U of Montana, MT	B
The U of Montana–Western, MT	B
U of Nevada, Las Vegas, NV	B
U of Nevada, Reno, NV	B
U of New Mexico, NM	B
U of New Mexico–Gallup, NM	A,B
U of New Orleans, LA	B
U of Phoenix–Las Vegas Campus, NV	B
U of Phoenix–Utah Campus, UT	B
U of Portland, OR	B
U of Redlands, CA	B
U of San Francisco, CA	B
U of Utah, UT	B
U of Washington, WA	B
U of Wyoming, WY	B
Utah State U, UT	B
Walla Walla Coll, WA	B
Warner Pacific Coll, OR	B
Washington State U, WA	B
Weber State U, UT	B
Western State Coll of Colorado, CO	B
Western Washington U, WA	B
Westminster Coll, UT	B
Westmont Coll, CA	B
Whitworth U, WA	B

Emergency Medical Technology (EMT Paramedic)

Brigham Young U–Idaho, ID	A
Central Washington U, WA	B
Dixie State Coll of Utah, UT	A
Idaho State U, ID	A
Loma Linda U, CA	B
Montana State U–Billings, MT	A
U of Alaska Anchorage, AK	A
Weber State U, UT	A

Engineering

Arizona State U at the Polytechnic Campus, AZ	B
Brigham Young U–Idaho, ID	A
California State U, Fullerton, CA	B
California State U, Long Beach, CA	B
California State U, Los Angeles, CA	B
California State U, Northridge, CA	B
Claremont McKenna Coll, CA	B
Colorado School of Mines, CO	B
Dixie State Coll of Utah, UT	A
George Fox U, OR	B
Gonzaga U, WA	B
Harvey Mudd Coll, CA	B
Idaho State U, ID	B
Mesa State Coll, CO	A
Mills Coll, CA	B
Montana Tech of The U of Montana, MT	A,B
New Mexico Highlands U, NM	B
Northern Arizona U, AZ	B
Oregon State U, OR	B
Pacific Union Coll, CA	B
Pitzer Coll, CA	B
Saint Mary's Coll of California, CA	B
San Diego State U, CA	B
San Jose State U, CA	B
Santa Clara U, CA	B
Stanford U, CA	B
United States Air Force Academy, CO	B
The U of Arizona, AZ	B
U of California, Los Angeles, CA	B
U of California, San Diego, CA	B
U of Denver, CO	B
U of Idaho, ID	B
U of Portland, OR	B
U of Southern California, CA	B
U of Utah, UT	B
U of Washington, WA	B
Walla Walla Coll, WA	B

Engineering/Industrial Management

California State U, Long Beach, CA	B
Claremont McKenna Coll, CA	B
Fort Lewis Coll, CO	B
The U of Arizona, AZ	B
U of Portland, OR	B
U of the Pacific, CA	B

Engineering Mechanics

New Mexico Inst of Mining and Technology, NM	B
United States Air Force Academy, CO	B

Engineering Physics

Colorado School of Mines, CO	B
Colorado State U, CO	B
Fort Lewis Coll, CO	B
Loyola Marymount U, CA	B
New Mexico State U, NM	B
North Carolina Ag and Tech State U, NC	B
Northern Arizona U, AZ	B
Northwest Nazarene U, ID	B
Oregon State U, OR	B
Pacific Lutheran U, WA	B
Point Loma Nazarene U, CA	B
Santa Clara U, CA	B
The U of Arizona, AZ	B
U of California, Berkeley, CA	B
U of California, San Diego, CA	B
U of Colorado at Boulder, CO	B
U of Nevada, Reno, NV	B
U of the Pacific, CA	B
Westmont Coll, CA	B

Engineering Related

Brigham Young U–Idaho, ID	A
California State U, Chico, CA	B
California State U, Long Beach, CA	B
Claremont McKenna Coll, CA	B
Hawai'i Pacific U, HI	B
Idaho State U, ID	B
Montana State U–Billings, MT	A
Pacific Union Coll, CA	B
The U of Arizona, AZ	B
U of California, Davis, CA	B
Western Washington U, WA	B

Engineering-Related Technologies

U of Alaska Southeast, AK	A

Engineering Science

California Polytechnic State U, San Luis Obispo, CA	B
California State U, Fullerton, CA	B
Claremont McKenna Coll, CA	B
Colorado School of Mines, CO	B
Colorado State U, CO	B
Montana Tech of The U of Montana, MT	B
Pacific Lutheran U, WA	B
Seattle Pacific U, WA	B
Sonoma State U, CA	B
United States Air Force Academy, CO	B
U of California, Berkeley, CA	B
U of California, San Diego, CA	B
U of New Mexico, NM	B
U of New Orleans, LA	B
U of Portland, OR	B

Engineering Technologies Related

California Maritime Academy, CA	B
California State Polytechnic U, Pomona, CA	B

Engineering Technology

Brigham Young U, UT	B
Brigham Young U–Idaho, ID	A
California State Polytechnic U, Pomona, CA	B
California State U, Long Beach, CA	B
Colorado State U–Pueblo, CO	B
Eastern New Mexico U, NM	B

Eastern Washington U, WA	B
Montana Tech of The U of Montana, MT	A
New Mexico State U, NM	A,B
Pacific Union Coll, CA	A,B
U of Alaska Anchorage, AK	A
Walla Walla Coll, WA	B
Western Washington U, WA	B

English

Adams State Coll, CO	B
Albertson Coll of Idaho, ID	B
Arizona State U, AZ	B
Arizona State U at the West campus, AZ	B
Azusa Pacific U, CA	B
Bethany U, CA	B
Biola U, CA	B
Boise State U, ID	B
Brigham Young U, UT	B
Brigham Young U–Hawaii, HI	B
Brigham Young U–Idaho, ID	A
California Baptist U, CA	B
California Inst of Technology, CA	B
California Lutheran U, CA	B
California Polytechnic State U, San Luis Obispo, CA	B
California State Polytechnic U, Pomona, CA	B
California State U Channel Islands, CA	B
California State U, Chico, CA	B
California State U, Dominguez Hills, CA	B
California State U, Fresno, CA	B
California State U, Fullerton, CA	B
California State U, Long Beach, CA	B
California State U, Los Angeles, CA	B
California State U, Northridge, CA	B
California State U, Sacramento, CA	B
California State U, San Bernardino, CA	B
California State U, San Marcos, CA	B
California State U, Stanislaus, CA	B
Cascade Coll, OR	B
Central Washington U, WA	B
Chapman U, CA	B
Claremont McKenna Coll, CA	B
Coll of Santa Fe, NM	A,B
Coll of the Southwest, NM	B
Colorado Christian U, CO	B
The Colorado Coll, CO	B
Colorado State U, CO	B
Colorado State U–Pueblo, CO	B
Concordia U, CA	B
Concordia U, OR	B
Corban Coll, OR	B
Dixie State Coll of Utah, UT	A
Dominican U of California, CA	B
Eastern New Mexico U, NM	B
Eastern Oregon U, OR	B
Eastern Washington U, WA	B
Eugene Lang Coll The New School for Liberal Arts, NY	B
Fort Lewis Coll, CO	B
Fresno Pacific U, CA	A,B
George Fox U, OR	B

A—associate degree; B—bachelor's degree

Gonzaga U, WA — B
Grand Canyon U, AZ — B
Great Basin Coll, NV — A
Hawai'i Pacific U, HI — B
Holy Names U, CA — B
Humboldt State U, CA — B
Idaho State U, ID — A,B
La Sierra U, CA — B
Lewis & Clark Coll, OR — B
Lewis-Clark State Coll, ID — B
Linfield Coll, OR — B
Loyola Marymount U, CA — B
The Master's Coll and
 Seminary, CA — B
Mesa State Coll, CO — A,B
Mills Coll, CA — B
Montana State U, MT — B
Montana State U–Billings, MT — B
Mount St. Mary's Coll, CA — B
Naropa U, CO — B
National U, CA — B
Nevada State Coll at
 Henderson, NV — B
New Mexico Highlands U, NM — B
New Mexico State U, NM — B
North Carolina Ag and Tech
 State U, NC — B
Northern Arizona U, AZ — B
Northwest Nazarene U, ID — B
Northwest U, WA — B
Notre Dame de Namur U, CA — B
Oregon State U, OR — B
Pacific Lutheran U, WA — B
Pacific Union Coll, CA — B
Pacific U, OR — B
Pepperdine U, Malibu, CA — B
Pitzer Coll, CA — B
Pomona Coll, CA — B
Portland State U, OR — B
Reed Coll, OR — B
Regis U, CO — B
Rocky Mountain Coll, MT — B
St. John's Coll, NM — B
Saint Mary's Coll of California,
 CA — B
San Diego Christian Coll, CA — B
San Diego State U, CA — B
San Francisco State U, CA — B
San Jose State U, CA — B
Santa Clara U, CA — B
Scripps Coll, CA — B
Seattle Pacific U, WA — B
Seattle U, WA — B
Simpson U, CA — B
Sonoma State U, CA — B
Southern Oregon U, OR — B
Southern Utah U, UT — B
Stanford U, CA — B
United States Air Force
 Academy, CO — B
U of Alaska Anchorage, AK — B
U of Alaska Fairbanks, AK — B
The U of Arizona, AZ — B
U of California, Berkeley, CA — B
U of California, Davis, CA — B
U of California, Irvine, CA — B
U of California, Los Angeles,
 CA — B
U of California, Riverside, CA — B
U of California, San Diego, CA — B
U of California, Santa Barbara,
 CA — B
U of Colorado at Boulder, CO — B
U of Colorado at Colorado
 Springs, CO — B

U of Colorado at Denver and
 Health Sciences Center, CO — B
U of Dallas, TX — B
U of Denver, CO — B
U of Great Falls, MT — B
U of Hawaii at Hilo, HI — B
U of Hawaii at Manoa, HI — B
U of Hawaii–West Oahu, HI — B
U of Idaho, ID — B
U of La Verne, CA — B
The U of Montana, MT — B
The U of Montana–Western,
 MT — B
U of Nevada, Las Vegas, NV — B
U of Nevada, Reno, NV — B
U of New Mexico, NM — B
U of New Orleans, LA — B
U of Northern Colorado, CO — B
U of Oregon, OR — B
U of Portland, OR — B
U of Puget Sound, WA — B
U of Redlands, CA — B
U of San Diego, CA — B
U of San Francisco, CA — B
U of Southern California, CA — B
U of the Pacific, CA — B
U of the West, CA — B
U of Utah, UT — B
U of Washington, WA — B
U of Wyoming, WY — B
Utah State U, UT — B
Utah Valley State Coll, UT — A,B
Vanguard U of Southern
 California, CA — B
Walla Walla Coll, WA — B
Warner Pacific Coll, OR — B
Washington State U, WA — B
Weber State U, UT — B
Western Oregon U, OR — B
Western State Coll of
 Colorado, CO — B
Western Washington U, WA — B
Westminster Coll, UT — B
Westmont Coll, CA — B
Whitman Coll, WA — B
Whitworth U, WA — B
Willamette U, OR — B

English as a Second/Foreign Language (Teaching)

Brigham Young U, UT — B
Brigham Young U–Hawaii, HI — B
Eastern Washington U, WA — B
Hawai'i Pacific U, HI — B
Northern Arizona U, AZ — B
Northwest U, WA — B
The U of Arizona, AZ — B
U of California, Los Angeles,
 CA — B
U of Hawaii at Manoa, HI — B
The U of Montana, MT — B
U of Washington, WA — B
Washington State U, WA — B

English Composition

Brigham Young U, UT — B
Northwest U, WA — B
U of Colorado at Denver and
 Health Sciences Center, CO — B
U of Great Falls, MT — B
U of Nevada, Reno, NV — B

English Language and Literature Related

Fort Lewis Coll, CO — B
Point Loma Nazarene U, CA — B

Saint Mary's Coll of California,
 CA — B
U of Alaska Southeast, AK — B
U of California, Los Angeles,
 CA — B
U of California, Santa Cruz,
 CA — B
U of Great Falls, MT — B
U of Nevada, Reno, NV — B

English/Language Arts Teacher Education

Brigham Young U, UT — B
Brigham Young U–Hawaii, HI — B
California State U, Chico, CA — B
California State U, Long
 Beach, CA — B
Central Washington U, WA — B
Coll of Santa Fe, NM — B
Colorado State U, CO — B
Concordia U, OR — B
Corban Coll, OR — B
Eastern Washington U, WA — B
Fort Lewis Coll, CO — B
Hope International U, CA — B
Lewis-Clark State Coll, ID — B
Montana State U–Billings, MT — B
Nevada State Coll at
 Henderson, NV — B
Northern Arizona U, AZ — B
Northwest Nazarene U, ID — B
Northwest U, WA — B
Prescott Coll, AZ — B
Rocky Mountain Coll, MT — B
Seattle Pacific U, WA — B
Simpson U, CA — B
The U of Arizona, AZ — B
U of Great Falls, MT — B
The U of Montana–Western,
 MT — B
U of Nevada, Reno, NV — B
U of New Orleans, LA — B
Utah Valley State Coll, UT — B
Washington State U, WA — B
Weber State U, UT — B
Westmont Coll, CA — B

English Literature (British and Commonwealth)

Marylhurst U, OR — B
U of Southern California, CA — B

Entomology

Colorado State U, CO — B
Oregon State U, OR — B
U of California, Davis, CA — B
U of California, Riverside, CA — B
U of Hawaii at Manoa, HI — B
U of Idaho, ID — B
Utah State U, UT — B
Washington State U, WA — B

Entrepreneurship

Brigham Young U, UT — B
California State U, Fullerton,
 CA — B
Hawai'i Pacific U, HI — B
Johnson & Wales U, CO — A,B
LDS Business Coll, UT — A
National U, CA — B
The U of Arizona, AZ — B
U of Nevada, Reno, NV — B
U of New Mexico–Gallup, NM — A
Washington State U, WA — B
Western State Coll of
 Colorado, CO — B

Environmental Biology

California Polytechnic State U,
 San Luis Obispo, CA — B
California State U, Monterey
 Bay, CA — B
Colorado State U-Pueblo, CO — B
Eastern Washington U, WA — B
Fort Lewis Coll, CO — B
Grand Canyon U, AZ — B
Humboldt State U, CA — B
The Master's Coll and
 Seminary, CA — B
Oregon State U, OR — B
U of La Verne, CA — B
Western Washington U, WA — B

Environmental Design/ Architecture

Art Center Coll of Design, CA — B
Montana State U, MT — B
Otis Coll of Art and Design,
 CA — B
Prescott Coll, AZ — B
U of California, Irvine, CA — B
U of Colorado at Boulder, CO — B
U of New Mexico, NM — B

Environmental Education

Prescott Coll, AZ — B
Sonoma State U, CA — B
The U of Montana, MT — B
Western Washington U, WA — B

Environmental Engineering Technology

California State U, Long
 Beach, CA — B
Mesa State Coll, CO — A
Utah Valley State Coll, UT — A

Environmental/Environmental Health Engineering

Arizona State U at the
 Polytechnic Campus, AZ — B
California Inst of Technology,
 CA — B
California Polytechnic State U,
 San Luis Obispo, CA — B
Colorado School of Mines, CO — B
Colorado State U, CO — B
Humboldt State U, CA — B
Montana Tech of The U of
 Montana, MT — B
New Mexico Inst of Mining
 and Technology, NM — B
Northern Arizona U, AZ — B
Oregon State U, OR — B
Seattle U, WA — B
Stanford U, CA — B
United States Air Force
 Academy, CO — B
U of California, Berkeley, CA — B
U of California, Irvine, CA — B
U of California, Riverside, CA — B
U of Colorado at Boulder, CO — B
U of Nevada, Reno, NV — B
U of Southern California, CA — B
U of Utah, UT — B
Utah State U, UT — B

Environmental Health

Boise State U, ID — B
California State U, Northridge,
 CA — B
Colorado State U, CO — B
Colorado State U-Pueblo, CO — B
New Mexico State U, NM — B
Oregon State U, OR — B

U of California, Los Angeles, CA — B
U of Utah, UT — B
U of Washington, WA — B

Environmental Science
Alaska Pacific U, AK — B
Brigham Young U, UT — B
California State U Channel Islands, CA — B
California State U, Fresno, CA — B
California State U, Long Beach, CA — B
Coll of Santa Fe, NM — B
The Colorado Coll, CO — B
Eastern Washington U, WA — B
Hawai'i Pacific U, HI — B
Mills Coll, CA — B
Montana State U, MT — B
National U, CA — B
Nevada State Coll at Henderson, NV — B
Northwest U, WA — B
Pitzer Coll, CA — B
Rocky Mountain Coll, MT — B
San Diego State U, CA — B
Santa Clara U, CA — B
Scripps Coll, CA — B
The U of Arizona, AZ — B
U of California, Berkeley, CA — B
U of California, Los Angeles, CA — B
U of Hawaii at Manoa, HI — B
U of New Mexico, NM — B
U of Oregon, OR — B
U of San Francisco, CA — B
U of Washington, Bothell, WA — B
U of Washington, Tacoma, WA — B
Washington State U, WA — B
Western State Coll of Colorado, CO — B
Western Washington U, WA — B
Willamette U, OR — B

Environmental Studies
Boise State U, ID — B
California State U, Monterey Bay, CA — B
California State U, Sacramento, CA — B
California State U, San Bernardino, CA — B
Claremont McKenna Coll, CA — B
Coll of the Southwest, NM — B
Concordia U, OR — B
Dixie State Coll of Utah, UT — A
Dominican U of California, CA — B
The Evergreen State Coll, WA — B
Great Basin Coll, NV — A
Hawai'i Pacific U, HI — B
Humboldt State U, CA — B
Lewis & Clark Coll, OR — B
Linfield Coll, OR — B
Marylhurst U, OR — B
Mills Coll, CA — B
Montana State U, MT — B
Montana State U–Billings, MT — B
Naropa U, CO — B
New Mexico Highlands U, NM — B
New Mexico Inst of Mining and Technology, NM — B
New Mexico State U, NM — B
Northern Arizona U, AZ — B
Northern New Mexico Coll, NM — A
Oregon Inst of Technology, OR — B

Oregon State U, OR — B
Pacific Lutheran U, WA — B
Pacific U, OR — B
Pitzer Coll, CA — B
Pomona Coll, CA — B
Portland State U, OR — B
Prescott Coll, AZ — B
Regis U, CO — B
Rocky Mountain Coll, MT — B
Salish Kootenai Coll, MT — A,B
San Diego State U, CA — B
San Jose State U, CA — B
Scripps Coll, CA — B
Seattle U, WA — B
Sierra Nevada Coll, NV — B
Sonoma State U, CA — B
Southern Oregon U, OR — B
Stanford U, CA — B
The U of Arizona, AZ — B
U of California, Berkeley, CA — B
U of California, Davis, CA — B
U of California, Riverside, CA — B
U of California, San Diego, CA — B
U of California, Santa Barbara, CA — B
U of California, Santa Cruz, CA — B
U of Colorado at Boulder, CO — B
U of Denver, CO — B
U of Hawaii at Manoa, HI — B
U of Idaho, ID — B
The U of Montana, MT — B
The U of Montana–Western, MT — B
U of Nevada, Las Vegas, NV — B
U of New Orleans, LA — B
U of Oregon, OR — B
U of Portland, OR — B
U of Redlands, CA — B
U of San Diego, CA — B
U of San Francisco, CA — B
U of Southern California, CA — B
U of the Pacific, CA — B
U of Utah, UT — B
U of Washington, WA — B
U of Wyoming, WY — B
Walla Walla Coll, WA — B
Western State Coll of Colorado, CO — B
Western Washington U, WA — B
Westminster Coll, UT — B

Environmental Toxicology
U of California, Davis, CA — B

Epidemiology
U of California, Los Angeles, CA — B

Equestrian Studies
Colorado State U, CO — B
Rocky Mountain Coll, MT — B
The U of Montana–Western, MT — A

Ethics
St. John's Coll, NM — B

Ethnic, Cultural Minority, and Gender Studies Related
California State Polytechnic U, Pomona, CA — B
California State U, Chico, CA — B
California State U, Sacramento, CA — B
Claremont McKenna Coll, CA — B
The Colorado Coll, CO — B

Dominican U of California, CA — B
Marylhurst U, OR — B
U of California, Berkeley, CA — B
U of Hawaii at Manoa, HI — B
U of Oregon, OR — B
Washington State U, WA — B

European History
Chapman U, CA — B
U of California, Santa Cruz, CA — B

European Studies
Claremont McKenna Coll, CA — B
Fort Lewis Coll, CO — B
Loyola Marymount U, CA — B
Pitzer Coll, CA — B
Saint Mary's Coll of California, CA — B
San Diego State U, CA — B
Scripps Coll, CA — B
Seattle Pacific U, WA — B
U of California, Irvine, CA — B
U of California, Los Angeles, CA — B
U of New Mexico, NM — B
U of Washington, WA — B

European Studies (Central and Eastern)
Brigham Young U, UT — B
Portland State U, OR — B
San Diego State U, CA — B
U of Oregon, OR — B

European Studies (Western)
Claremont McKenna Coll, CA — B
Seattle U, WA — B

Evolutionary Biology
Oregon State U, OR — B
U of Colorado at Boulder, CO — B

Executive Assistant/Executive Secretary
LDS Business Coll, UT — A
Montana Tech of The U of Montana, MT — A
The U of Montana, MT — A
Utah Valley State Coll, UT — A

Exercise Physiology
Chapman U, CA — B
U of California, Davis, CA — B

Experimental Psychology
Colorado State U-Pueblo, CO — B
La Sierra U, CA — B

Family and Community Services
Brigham Young U–Idaho, ID — A
Oregon State U, OR — B
Point Loma Nazarene U, CA — B
Southern Utah U, UT — B
U of California, Santa Cruz, CA — B
U of Utah, UT — B

Family and Consumer Economics Related
Brigham Young U, UT — B
California State U, Fresno, CA — B
California State U, Sacramento, CA — B
Oregon State U, OR — B
Seattle Pacific U, WA — B
U of Utah, UT — B
Utah State U, UT — B

Family and Consumer Sciences/Home Economics Teacher Education
Brigham Young U, UT — B
Brigham Young U–Idaho, ID — A
Colorado State U, CO — B
Johnson & Wales U, CO — B
New Mexico State U, NM — B
North Carolina Ag and Tech State U, NC — B
Seattle Pacific U, WA — B
Southern Utah U, UT — B
The U of Arizona, AZ — B
U of Idaho, ID — B
U of Nevada, Reno, NV — B
U of Utah, UT — B
Utah State U, UT — B
Washington State U, WA — B

Family and Consumer Sciences/Human Sciences
Brigham Young U, UT — B
Brigham Young U–Idaho, ID — A
California State Polytechnic U, Pomona, CA — B
California State U, Long Beach, CA — B
California State U, Northridge, CA — B
Central Washington U, WA — B
Colorado State U, CO — B
Eastern New Mexico U, NM — B
George Fox U, OR — B
Idaho State U, ID — B
The Master's Coll and Seminary, CA — B
Montana State U, MT — B
North Carolina Ag and Tech State U, NC — B
Oregon State U, OR — B
Point Loma Nazarene U, CA — B
San Francisco State U, CA — B
Southern Utah U, UT — B
U of Alaska Anchorage, AK — A
U of Hawaii at Manoa, HI — B
U of New Mexico, NM — B
U of Oregon, OR — B
U of Utah, UT — B
U of Wyoming, WY — B

Family and Consumer Sciences/Human Sciences Business Services Related
Brigham Young U, UT — B

Family and Consumer Sciences/Human Sciences Related
California State U, Long Beach, CA — B
Washington State U, WA — B

Family Psychology
Corban Coll, OR — B

Family Resource Management
Arizona State U, AZ — B
Brigham Young U, UT — B
U of Utah, UT — B

Family Systems
Brigham Young U, UT — B
Weber State U, UT — B

Farm and Ranch Management
Brigham Young U–Idaho, ID — A
California Polytechnic State U, San Luis Obispo, CA — B

A—associate degree; B—bachelor's degree

California State Polytechnic U, Pomona, CA — B
Colorado State U, CO — B
Idaho State U, ID — A,B

Fashion/Apparel Design
Academy of Art U, CA — A,B
The Art Inst of California–San Francisco, CA — A,B
The Art Inst of Portland, OR — A,B
The Art Inst of Seattle, WA — A
Brigham Young U–Idaho, ID — A
California Coll of the Arts, CA — B
California Design Coll, CA — A
FIDM/The Fashion Inst of Design & Merchandising, Los Angeles Campus, CA — A
Oregon State U, OR — B
Otis Coll of Art and Design, CA — B
U of Hawaii at Manoa, HI — B
Woodbury U, CA — B

Fashion Merchandising
Academy of Art U, CA — A,B
The Art Inst of Phoenix, AZ — B
The Art Inst of Seattle, WA — A
Brigham Young U–Idaho, ID — A
California Design Coll, CA — A
California State U, Long Beach, CA — B
Central Washington U, WA — B
FIDM/The Fashion Inst of Design & Merchandising, Los Angeles Campus, CA — A
George Fox U, OR — B
Johnson & Wales U, CO — A
Oregon State U, OR — B
The U of Montana, MT — B
Utah State U, UT — B
Weber State U, UT — A
Woodbury U, CA — B

Fiber, Textile and Weaving Arts
Academy of Art U, CA — A,B
California Coll of the Arts, CA — B
California State U, Long Beach, CA — B
Colorado State U, CO — B
U of Oregon, OR — B
U of Washington, WA — B
Western Washington U, WA — B

Filipino/Tagalog
U of Hawaii at Manoa, HI — B

Film/Cinema Studies
Academy of Art U, CA — A,B
Arizona State U, AZ — B
Art Center Coll of Design, CA — B
Brigham Young U, UT — B
California Coll of the Arts, CA — B
California Inst of the Arts, CA — B
California State U, Long Beach, CA — B
California State U, Northridge, CA — B
Chapman U, CA — B
Claremont McKenna Coll, CA — B
Coll of Santa Fe, NM — B
The Colorado Coll, CO — B
Columbia Coll Hollywood, CA — B
George Fox U, OR — B
Pitzer Coll, CA — B
Pomona Coll, CA — B
Prescott Coll, AZ — B
San Francisco State U, CA — B

Stanford U, CA — B
U of California, Berkeley, CA — B
U of California, Davis, CA — B
U of California, Irvine, CA — B
U of California, Los Angeles, CA — B
U of California, San Diego, CA — B
U of California, Santa Barbara, CA — B
U of California, Santa Cruz, CA — B
U of Colorado at Boulder, CO — B
U of Nevada, Las Vegas, NV — B
U of New Mexico, NM — B
U of Southern California, CA — B
U of Utah, UT — B
Whitman Coll, WA — B

Film/Video and Photographic Arts Related
Art Center Coll of Design, CA — B
Brigham Young U, UT — B
California Inst of the Arts, CA — B
Rocky Mountain Coll of Art & Design, CO — B
Scripps Coll, CA — B
Woodbury U, CA — B

Finance
Arizona State U, AZ — B
Boise State U, ID — B
Brigham Young U–Idaho, ID — A
California State Polytechnic U, Pomona, CA — B
California State U, Chico, CA — B
California State U, Dominguez Hills, CA — B
California State U, Fresno, CA — B
California State U, Fullerton, CA — B
California State U, Long Beach, CA — B
California State U, Sacramento, CA — B
California State U, San Bernardino, CA — B
Colorado State U, CO — B
Colorado State U-Pueblo, CO — B
Corban Coll, OR — B
Eastern New Mexico U, NM — B
Eastern Washington U, WA — B
Fort Lewis Coll, CO — B
Fresno Pacific U, CA — B
George Fox U, OR — B
Gonzaga U, WA — B
Grand Canyon U, AZ — B
Hawai'i Pacific U, HI — A,B
Idaho State U, ID — B
Linfield Coll, OR — B
The Master's Coll and Seminary, CA — B
Mesa State Coll, CO — B
Montana State U–Billings, MT — B
Montana Tech of The U of Montana, MT — B
National U, CA — B
New Mexico State U, NM — B
Northern Arizona U, AZ — B
Northwest Nazarene U, ID — B
Notre Dame de Namur U, CA — B
Oregon State U, OR — B
Pacific Lutheran U, WA — B
Pacific Union Coll, CA — B
Pacific U, OR — B
Portland State U, OR — B
San Diego State U, CA — B
San Francisco State U, CA — B

San Jose State U, CA — B
Santa Clara U, CA — B
Seattle U, WA — B
U of Alaska Anchorage, AK — B
The U of Arizona, AZ — B
U of Colorado at Boulder, CO — B
U of Colorado at Colorado Springs, CO — B
U of Denver, CO — B
U of Hawaii at Manoa, HI — B
U of Idaho, ID — B
The U of Montana, MT — B
U of Nevada, Las Vegas, NV — B
U of Nevada, Reno, NV — B
U of New Orleans, LA — B
U of Oregon, OR — B
U of Phoenix–Denver Campus, CO — B
U of Phoenix–Hawaii Campus, HI — B
U of Phoenix–Idaho Campus, ID — B
U of Phoenix Online Campus, AZ — B
U of Phoenix–Oregon Campus, OR — B
U of Phoenix–Phoenix Campus, AZ — B
U of Phoenix–Sacramento Valley Campus, CA — B
U of Phoenix–Southern Arizona Campus, AZ — B
U of Phoenix–Southern Colorado Campus, CO — B
U of Phoenix–Utah Campus, UT — B
U of Phoenix–Washington Campus, WA — B
U of Portland, OR — B
U of San Francisco, CA — B
U of Utah, UT — B
U of Wyoming, WY — B
Utah State U, UT — B
Vanguard U of Southern California, CA — B
Washington State U, WA — B
Weber State U, UT — B
Western International U, AZ — B
Western State Coll of Colorado, CO — B
Western Washington U, WA — B
Westminster Coll, UT — B

Finance and Financial Management Services Related
Johnson & Wales U, CO — B
Saint Mary's Coll of California, CA — B
San Diego State U, CA — B
San Jose State U, CA — B

Financial Planning and Services
Brigham Young U, UT — B

Fine Arts Related
Art Center Coll of Design, CA — B
California State U, Long Beach, CA — B
Oregon Coll of Art & Craft, OR — B
Point Loma Nazarene U, CA — B
U of California, Los Angeles, CA — B

Fine/Studio Arts
Academy of Art U, CA — A,B
Art Center Coll of Design, CA — B

Biola U, CA — B
Brigham Young U, UT — B
California Coll of the Arts, CA — B
California Inst of the Arts, CA — B
California State U, Chico, CA — B
California State U, Dominguez Hills, CA — B
California State U, Fullerton, CA — B
California State U, Long Beach, CA — B
California State U, Stanislaus, CA — B
Chapman U, CA — B
Claremont McKenna Coll, CA — B
Coll of Santa Fe, NM — B
Colorado Christian U, CO — B
The Colorado Coll, CO — B
Colorado State U, CO — B
Eastern Washington U, WA — B
The Evergreen State Coll, WA — B
George Fox U, OR — B
Grand Canyon U, AZ — B
Humboldt State U, CA — B
La Sierra U, CA — B
Loyola Marymount U, CA — B
Mills Coll, CA — B
Montana State U, MT — B
Naropa U, CO — B
New Mexico State U, NM — B
Northern New Mexico Coll, NM — A
Notre Dame de Namur U, CA — B
Occidental Coll, CA — B
Otis Coll of Art and Design, CA — B
Pacific Lutheran U, WA — B
Pacific Union Coll, CA — B
Pitzer Coll, CA — B
Pomona Coll, CA — B
Reed Coll, OR — B
San Diego State U, CA — B
San Jose State U, CA — B
Scripps Coll, CA — B
Seattle U, WA — B
Sierra Nevada Coll, NV — B
Sonoma State U, CA — B
Stanford U, CA — B
The U of Arizona, AZ — B
U of California, Davis, CA — B
U of California, Irvine, CA — B
U of California, Riverside, CA — B
U of California, San Diego, CA — B
U of California, Santa Barbara, CA — B
U of Colorado at Boulder, CO — B
U of Colorado at Colorado Springs, CO — B
U of Colorado at Denver and Health Sciences Center, CO — B
U of Dallas, TX — B
U of Denver, CO — B
U of Great Falls, MT — B
U of Idaho, ID — B
U of New Orleans, LA — B
U of Northern Colorado, CO — B
U of Oregon, OR — B
U of Redlands, CA — B
U of San Francisco, CA — B
U of Southern California, CA — B
U of the Pacific, CA — B
Washington State U, WA — B
Western State Coll of Colorado, CO — B
Western Washington U, WA — B

Whitworth U, WA — B
Willamette U, OR — B

Fire Protection and Safety Technology
Montana State U–Billings, MT — A

Fire Science
Cogswell Polytechnical Coll, CA — B
Eastern Oregon U, OR — B
Idaho State U, ID — A
Lewis-Clark State Coll, ID — A,B
U of Alaska Anchorage, AK — A
U of Alaska Fairbanks, AK — A
Utah Valley State Coll, UT — A

Fire Services Administration
California State U, Los Angeles, CA — B
Utah Valley State Coll, UT — B
Western Oregon U, OR — B

Fish/Game Management
Humboldt State U, CA — B
Oregon State U, OR — B
U of Idaho, ID — B

Fishing and Fisheries Sciences and Management
Colorado State U, CO — B
Humboldt State U, CA — B
Oregon State U, OR — B
U of Alaska Fairbanks, AK — B
U of Washington, WA — B

Folklore
U of Oregon, OR — B

Foods and Nutrition Related
California State U, Long Beach, CA — B
Utah State U, UT — B

Food Science
Brigham Young U, UT — B
California Polytechnic State U, San Luis Obispo, CA — B
North Carolina Ag and Tech State U, NC —
Oregon State U, OR — B
San Jose State U, CA — B
U of California, Davis, CA — B
U of Idaho, ID — B
U of Utah, UT — B
Washington State U, WA — B

Food Service and Dining Room Management
Johnson & Wales U, CO — B

Foods, Nutrition, and Wellness
Arizona State U at the Polytechnic Campus, AZ — B
Bastyr U, WA — B
Brigham Young U–Idaho, ID — A
California Polytechnic State U, San Luis Obispo, CA —
California State Polytechnic U, Pomona, CA — B
California State U, Fresno, CA — B
California State U, Los Angeles, CA —
California State U, San Bernardino, CA — B
Central Washington U, WA — B
Colorado State U, CO — B
George Fox U, OR — B
Idaho State U, ID —

The Master's Coll and Seminary, CA — B
New Mexico State U, NM — B
North Carolina Ag and Tech State U, NC — B
Oregon State U, OR — B
Pepperdine U, Malibu, CA — B
Point Loma Nazarene U, CA — B
Seattle Pacific U, WA — B
U of Idaho, ID — B
U of Nevada, Reno, NV — B
U of New Mexico, NM — B
Washington State U, WA — B

Food Technology and Processing
Brigham Young U, UT — B

Foreign Languages and Literatures
California State U, Monterey Bay, CA — B
Central Washington U, WA — B
Colorado State U, CO — B
Dixie State Coll of Utah, UT — A
Dominican U of California, CA — B
Lewis & Clark Coll, OR — B
Montana State U, MT — B
New Mexico State U, NM — B
Pitzer Coll, CA — B
St. John's Coll, NM — B
Scripps Coll, CA — B
U of Alaska Anchorage, AK — B
U of Alaska Fairbanks, AK — B
U of California, San Diego, CA — B
U of California, Santa Cruz, CA — B
U of Idaho, ID — B
The U of Montana, MT — B
U of New Mexico, NM — B
U of Northern Colorado, CO — B
U of Utah, UT — B
Washington State U, WA — B

Foreign Languages Related
Saint Mary's Coll of California, CA — B
U of Alaska Fairbanks, AK — A
U of California, Berkeley, CA — B
U of California, Los Angeles, CA — B

Foreign Language Teacher Education
Brigham Young U, UT — B
The U of Arizona, AZ — B
U of Nevada, Reno, NV — B
U of New Orleans, LA — B
Washington State U, WA — B

Forensic Science and Technology
Northwest Nazarene U, ID — B
Seattle U, WA — B
U of Great Falls, MT — B

Forest Engineering
Oregon State U, OR — B
U of Washington, WA — B

Forest/Forest Resources Management
Oregon State U, OR — B
U of California, Berkeley, CA — B
The U of Montana, MT — B
U of Washington, WA — B

Forest Resources Production and Management
Oregon State U, OR — B

Forestry
Brigham Young U–Idaho, ID — A
California Polytechnic State U, San Luis Obispo, CA — B
Dixie State Coll of Utah, UT — A
Humboldt State U, CA — B
Oregon State U, OR — B
Salish Kootenai Coll, MT — A
U of California, Berkeley, CA — B
U of Idaho, ID — B
The U of Montana, MT — B
U of Nevada, Reno, NV — B
U of Washington, WA — B
Utah State U, UT — B
Washington State U, WA — B

Forestry Related
Utah State U, UT — B

Forestry Technology
Salish Kootenai Coll, MT — A

Forest Sciences and Biology
Colorado State U, CO — B
Northern Arizona U, AZ — B
U of Washington, WA — B

French
Arizona State U, AZ — B
Boise State U, ID — B
Brigham Young U, UT — B
Brigham Young U–Idaho, ID — A
California Lutheran U, CA — B
California State U, Chico, CA — B
California State U, Dominguez Hills, CA — B
California State U, Fresno, CA — B
California State U, Fullerton, CA — B
California State U, Long Beach, CA — B
California State U, Los Angeles, CA — B
California State U, Northridge, CA — B
California State U, Sacramento, CA — B
California State U, San Bernardino, CA — B
California State U, Stanislaus, CA — B
Chapman U, CA — B
Claremont McKenna Coll, CA — B
The Colorado Coll, CO — B
Colorado State U, CO — B
Eastern Washington U, WA — B
Gonzaga U, WA — B
Humboldt State U, CA — B
Idaho State U, ID — A,B
Lewis & Clark Coll, OR — B
Linfield Coll, OR — B
Loyola Marymount U, CA — B
Mills Coll, CA — B
Mount St. Mary's Coll, CA — B
North Carolina Ag and Tech State U, NC — B
Northern Arizona U, AZ — B
Occidental Coll, CA — B
Oregon State U, OR — B
Pacific Lutheran U, WA — B
Pacific U, OR — B
Pepperdine U, Malibu, CA — B
Pitzer Coll, CA — B

Pomona Coll, CA — B
Portland State U, OR — B
Reed Coll, OR — B
Regis U, CO — B
St. John's Coll, NM — B
Saint Mary's Coll of California, CA — B
San Diego State U, CA — B
San Francisco State U, CA — B
San Jose State U, CA — B
Santa Clara U, CA — B
Scripps Coll, CA — B
Seattle Pacific U, WA — B
Seattle U, WA — B
Sonoma State U, CA — B
Southern Oregon U, OR — B
Southern Utah U, UT — B
Stanford U, CA — B
The U of Arizona, AZ — B
U of California, Berkeley, CA — B
U of California, Davis, CA — B
U of California, Irvine, CA — B
U of California, Los Angeles, CA — B
U of California, Riverside, CA — B
U of California, San Diego, CA — B
U of California, Santa Barbara, CA — B
U of California, Santa Cruz, CA — B
U of Colorado at Boulder, CO — B
U of Colorado at Denver and Health Sciences Center, CO — B
U of Dallas, TX — B
U of Denver, CO — B
U of Hawaii at Manoa, HI — B
U of Idaho, ID — B
U of La Verne, CA — B
The U of Montana, MT — B
U of Nevada, Las Vegas, NV — B
U of Nevada, Reno, NV — B
U of New Mexico, NM — B
U of New Orleans, LA — B
U of Northern Colorado, CO — B
U of Oregon, OR — B
U of Puget Sound, WA — B
U of Redlands, CA — B
U of San Diego, CA — B
U of San Francisco, CA — B
U of Southern California, CA — B
U of the Pacific, CA — B
U of Utah, UT — B
U of Washington, WA — B
U of Wyoming, WY — B
Utah State U, UT — B
Walla Walla Coll, WA — B
Washington State U, WA — B
Weber State U, UT — B
Western State Coll of Colorado, CO — B
Western Washington U, WA — B
Westmont Coll, CA — B
Whitman Coll, WA — B
Whitworth U, WA — B
Willamette U, OR — B

French Language Teacher Education
Brigham Young U, UT — B
California Lutheran U, CA — B
California State U, Chico, CA — B
Central Washington U, WA — B
Colorado State U, CO — B
Eastern Washington U, WA — B
The U of Arizona, AZ — B

A—associate degree; B—bachelor's degree

U of Utah, UT	B
Washington State U, WA	B
Weber State U, UT	B

French Studies

Claremont McKenna Coll, CA	B
The Colorado Coll, CO	B
Mills Coll, CA	B
Santa Clara U, CA	B

General Retailing/Wholesaling

Dixie State Coll of Utah, UT	A

General Studies

Antioch U Santa Barbara, CA	B
Arizona State U at the Polytechnic Campus, AZ	B
Eastern New Mexico U, NM	A
Hope International U, CA	A
Idaho State U, ID	A,B
Montana State U–Billings, MT	A
National U, CA	B
New Mexico Inst of Mining and Technology, NM	A
New Mexico State U, NM	B
Northern Arizona U, AZ	B
Northwest U, WA	B
St. John's Coll, NM	B
Seattle Pacific U, WA	B
Simpson U, CA	A
U of Alaska Southeast, AK	A,B
U of Idaho, ID	B
U of Nevada, Reno, NV	B
U of New Mexico, NM	B
U of New Mexico–Gallup, NM	A,B
U of New Orleans, LA	B
U of Phoenix Online Campus, AZ	B
U of Southern California, CA	B
U of Washington, WA	B
Utah State U, UT	A
Utah Valley State Coll, UT	A
Western Washington U, WA	B

Genetics

U of California, Davis, CA	B
Washington State U, WA	B

Geochemistry

California Inst of Technology, CA	B
Northern Arizona U, AZ	B
Pomona Coll, CA	B
U of California, Los Angeles, CA	B

Geography

Arizona State U, AZ	B
Brigham Young U, UT	B
Brigham Young U–Idaho, ID	A
California State Polytechnic U, Pomona, CA	B
California State U, Chico, CA	B
California State U, Dominguez Hills, CA	B
California State U, Fresno, CA	B
California State U, Fullerton, CA	B
California State U, Long Beach, CA	B
California State U, Los Angeles, CA	B
California State U, Northridge, CA	B
California State U, Sacramento, CA	B
California State U, San Bernardino, CA	B

California State U, Stanislaus, CA	B
Central Washington U, WA	B
Eastern Washington U, WA	B
Humboldt State U, CA	B
New Mexico State U, NM	B
Northern Arizona U, AZ	B
Oregon State U, OR	B
Portland State U, OR	B
San Diego State U, CA	B
San Francisco State U, CA	B
San Jose State U, CA	B
Sonoma State U, CA	B
Southern Oregon U, OR	B
United States Air Force Academy, CO	B
U of Alaska Fairbanks, AK	B
The U of Arizona, AZ	B
U of California, Berkeley, CA	B
U of California, Los Angeles, CA	B
U of California, Santa Barbara, CA	B
U of Colorado at Boulder, CO	B
U of Colorado at Colorado Springs, CO	B
U of Colorado at Denver and Health Sciences Center, CO	B
U of Denver, CO	B
U of Hawaii at Hilo, HI	B
U of Hawaii at Manoa, HI	B
U of Idaho, ID	B
The U of Montana, MT	B
U of Nevada, Reno, NV	B
U of New Mexico, NM	B
U of New Orleans, LA	B
U of Northern Colorado, CO	B
U of Oregon, OR	B
U of Southern California, CA	B
U of Utah, UT	B
U of Washington, WA	B
U of Wyoming, WY	B
Utah State U, UT	B
Weber State U, UT	B
Western Oregon U, OR	B
Western Washington U, WA	B

Geography Related

Brigham Young U, UT	B
U of California, Los Angeles, CA	B

Geological and Earth Sciences/Geosciences Related

Brigham Young U, UT	B
California State U, Chico, CA	B
San Jose State U, CA	B
U of California, Los Angeles, CA	B
U of Nevada, Las Vegas, NV	B
U of Utah, UT	B
U of Wyoming, WY	B

Geological Engineering

The U of Arizona, AZ	B

Geological/Geophysical Engineering

Colorado School of Mines, CO	B
Montana Tech of The U of Montana, MT	B
Oregon State U, OR	B
U of Alaska Fairbanks, AK	B
U of California, Berkeley, CA	B
U of California, Los Angeles, CA	B
U of Idaho, ID	B

U of Nevada, Reno, NV	B
U of Utah, UT	B

Geology/Earth Science

Adams State Coll, CO	B
Arizona State U, AZ	B
Boise State U, ID	B
Brigham Young U, UT	B
Brigham Young U–Idaho, ID	A
California Inst of Technology, CA	B
California Lutheran U, CA	B
California State Polytechnic U, Pomona, CA	B
California State U, Chico, CA	B
California State U, Dominguez Hills, CA	B
California State U, Fresno, CA	B
California State U, Fullerton, CA	B
California State U, Long Beach, CA	B
California State U, Los Angeles, CA	B
California State U, Monterey Bay, CA	B
California State U, Northridge, CA	B
California State U, Sacramento, CA	B
California State U, San Bernardino, CA	B
California State U, Stanislaus, CA	B
Central Washington U, WA	B
The Colorado Coll, CO	B
Colorado State U, CO	B
Dixie State Coll of Utah, UT	A
Eastern New Mexico U, NM	B
Eastern Washington U, WA	B
Fort Lewis Coll, CO	B
Great Basin Coll, NV	A
Humboldt State U, CA	B
Idaho State U, ID	A,B
Mesa State Coll, CO	A,B
Montana State U, MT	B
National U, CA	B
New Mexico Inst of Mining and Technology, NM	B
New Mexico State U, NM	B
Northern Arizona U, AZ	B
Occidental Coll, CA	B
Oregon State U, OR	B
Pacific Lutheran U, WA	B
Pomona Coll, CA	B
Portland State U, OR	B
Rocky Mountain Coll, MT	B
San Diego State U, CA	B
San Francisco State U, CA	B
San Jose State U, CA	B
Scripps Coll, CA	B
Sonoma State U, CA	B
Southern Oregon U, OR	B
Southern Utah U, UT	B
Stanford U, CA	B
U of Alaska Fairbanks, AK	B
The U of Arizona, AZ	B
U of California, Berkeley, CA	B
U of California, Davis, CA	B
U of California, Irvine, CA	B
U of California, Los Angeles, CA	B
U of California, Riverside, CA	B
U of California, San Diego, CA	B
U of California, Santa Barbara, CA	B

U of California, Santa Cruz, CA	B
U of Colorado at Boulder, CO	B
U of Hawaii at Hilo, HI	B
U of Hawaii at Manoa, HI	B
U of Idaho, ID	B
The U of Montana, MT	B
U of Nevada, Las Vegas, NV	B
U of Nevada, Reno, NV	B
U of New Mexico, NM	B
U of New Orleans, LA	B
U of Northern Colorado, CO	B
U of Oregon, OR	B
U of Puget Sound, WA	B
U of Southern California, CA	B
U of the Pacific, CA	B
U of Utah, UT	B
U of Washington, WA	B
U of Wyoming, WY	B
Utah State U, UT	B
Utah Valley State Coll, UT	A,B
Washington State U, WA	B
Weber State U, UT	B
Western State Coll of Colorado, CO	B
Western Washington U, WA	B
Whitman Coll, WA	B

Geophysics and Seismology

Boise State U, ID	B
California Inst of Technology, CA	B
New Mexico Inst of Mining and Technology, NM	B
Occidental Coll, CA	B
Oregon State U, OR	B
Stanford U, CA	B
U of California, Los Angeles, CA	B
U of California, Riverside, CA	B
U of California, Santa Barbara, CA	B
U of California, Santa Cruz, CA	B
U of Nevada, Reno, NV	B
U of New Orleans, LA	B
U of Utah, UT	B
U of Washington, WA	B
Western Washington U, WA	B

Geotechnical Engineering

Montana Tech of The U of Montana, MT	B

German

Arizona State U, AZ	B
Boise State U, ID	B
Brigham Young U, UT	B
Brigham Young U–Idaho, ID	A
California Lutheran U, CA	B
California State U, Chico, CA	B
California State U, Fullerton, CA	B
California State U, Long Beach, CA	B
California State U, Northridge, CA	B
Claremont McKenna Coll, CA	B
The Colorado Coll, CO	B
Colorado State U, CO	B
Gonzaga U, WA	B
Humboldt State U, CA	B
Idaho State U, ID	A,B
Lewis & Clark Coll, OR	B
Linfield Coll, OR	B
Northern Arizona U, AZ	B
Oregon State U, OR	B
Pacific Lutheran U, WA	B

Pacific U, OR — B
Pepperdine U, Malibu, CA — B
Pitzer Coll, CA — B
Pomona Coll, CA — B
Portland State U, OR — B
Reed Coll, OR — B
Saint Mary's Coll of California, CA — B
San Diego State U, CA — B
San Francisco State U, CA — B
San Jose State U, CA — B
Scripps Coll, CA — B
Seattle Pacific U, WA — B
Seattle U, WA — B
Southern Oregon U, OR — B
Southern Utah U, UT — B
Stanford U, CA — B
The U of Arizona, AZ — B
U of California, Berkeley, CA — B
U of California, Davis, CA — B
U of California, Irvine, CA — B
U of California, Los Angeles, CA — B
U of California, Riverside, CA — B
U of California, San Diego, CA — B
U of California, Santa Barbara, CA — B
U of California, Santa Cruz, CA — B
U of Dallas, TX — B
U of Denver, CO — B
U of Hawaii at Manoa, HI — B
U of Idaho, ID — B
U of La Verne, CA — B
The U of Montana, MT — B
U of Nevada, Las Vegas, NV — B
U of Nevada, Reno, NV — B
U of New Mexico, NM — B
U of Northern Colorado, CO — B
U of Oregon, OR — B
U of Puget Sound, WA — B
U of Redlands, CA — B
U of Southern California, CA — B
U of the Pacific, CA — B
U of Utah, UT — B
U of Washington, WA — B
U of Wyoming, WY — B
Utah State U, UT — B
Walla Walla Coll, WA — B
Washington State U, WA — B
Weber State U, UT — B
Western Oregon U, OR — B
Western Washington U, WA — B
Whitman Coll, WA — B
Willamette U, OR — B

Germanic Languages
Claremont McKenna Coll, CA — B
U of Colorado at Boulder, CO — B

Germanic Languages Related
U of California, Los Angeles, CA — B

German Language Teacher Education
Brigham Young U, UT — B
California Lutheran U, CA — B
California State U, Chico, CA — B
Central Washington U, WA — B
Colorado State U, CO — B
Eastern Washington U, WA — B
The U of Arizona, AZ — B
U of Utah, UT — B
Washington State U, WA — B
Weber State U, UT — B

German Studies
Claremont McKenna Coll, CA — B
Santa Clara U, CA — B
Stanford U, CA — B
U of California, Irvine, CA — B

Gerontology
California State U, Chico, CA — B
California State U, Dominguez Hills, CA — B
California State U, Sacramento, CA — B
Central Washington U, WA — B
Mount St. Mary's Coll, CA — B
San Diego State U, CA — B
U of Nevada, Las Vegas, NV — B
U of Southern California, CA — B
Weber State U, UT — B

Graphic and Printing Equipment Operation/Production
California Polytechnic State U, San Luis Obispo, CA — B
Idaho State U, ID — A
Lewis-Clark State Coll, ID — A,B
U of New Mexico–Gallup, NM — A

Graphic Communications
Academy of Art U, CA — A,B
Arizona State U at the Polytechnic Campus, AZ — B
Point Loma Nazarene U, CA — B

Graphic Design
Academy of Art U, CA — A,B
Arizona State U, AZ — B
Art Center Coll of Design, CA — B
The Art Inst of California–Inland Empire, CA — A,B
The Art Inst of California–Los Angeles, CA — A,B
The Art Inst of California–Orange County, CA — A,B
The Art Inst of California–San Diego, CA — A,B
The Art Inst of California–San Francisco, CA — B
The Art Inst of Phoenix, AZ — A,B
The Art Inst of Portland, OR — A,B
The Art Inst of Seattle, WA — A,B
Brigham Young U, UT — B
California Inst of the Arts, CA — B
California State U, Chico, CA — B
California State U, Fullerton, CA — B
California State U, Long Beach, CA — B
California State U, Sacramento, CA — B
Chapman U, CA — B
CollAmerica–Colorado Springs, CO — A
CollAmerica–Denver, CO — A
Collins Coll: A School of Design and Technology, AZ — B
George Fox U, OR — B
ITT Tech Inst, UT — B
Northwest Nazarene U, ID — B
Platt Coll San Diego, CA — A
Point Loma Nazarene U, CA — B
Rocky Mountain Coll of Art & Design, CO — B
San Diego State U, CA — B
San Jose State U, CA — B
U of San Francisco, CA — B

Health and Physical Education
Western State Coll of Colorado, CO — B
Western Washington U, WA — B

Health and Physical Education
Brigham Young U, UT — B
Brigham Young U–Hawaii, HI — B
California State U, Chico, CA — B
California State U, Fullerton, CA — B
California State U, Sacramento, CA — B
Colorado Christian U, CO — B
Eastern Washington U, WA — B
George Fox U, OR — B
La Sierra U, CA — B
Linfield Coll, OR — B
The Master's Coll and Seminary, CA — B
Montana State U, MT — B
Montana State U–Billings, MT — B
Northwest Nazarene U, ID — B
Point Loma Nazarene U, CA — B
Saint Mary's Coll of California, CA — B
San Diego State U, CA — B
San Jose State U, CA — B
U of Great Falls, MT — B
U of Hawaii at Manoa, HI — B
U of San Francisco, CA — B
U of Utah, UT — B
Utah Valley State Coll, UT — A
Vanguard U of Southern California, CA — B
Walla Walla Coll, WA — B
Washington State U, WA — B
Weber State U, UT — B

Health and Physical Education Related
Arizona State U at the Polytechnic Campus, AZ — B
Brigham Young U, UT — B
California Baptist U, CA — B
California State U, Long Beach, CA — B
California State U, Sacramento, CA — B
Naropa U, CO — B
Rocky Mountain Coll, MT — B
Saint Mary's Coll of California, CA — B
Utah Valley State Coll, UT — A,B

Health/Health Care Administration
Alaska Pacific U, AK — B
California State U, Dominguez Hills, CA — B
California State U, Long Beach, CA — B
California State U, Sacramento, CA — B
California State U, San Bernardino, CA — B
CollAmerica–Colorado Springs, CO — A
CollAmerica–Denver, CO — A
Concordia U, OR — B
Eastern Washington U, WA — B
Idaho State U, ID — B
International Inst of the Americas, Mesa, AZ — A
International Inst of the Americas, Phoenix, AZ — A

International Inst of the Americas, Tucson, AZ — A
International Inst of the Americas, NM — A
Montana State U, MT — B
Montana State U–Billings, MT — B
Mount St. Mary's Coll, CA — B
National American U, Denver, CO — A,B
New Mexico Highlands U, NM — B
Oregon State U, OR — B
Pioneer Pacific Coll, Wilsonville, OR — A,B
San Jose State U, CA — B
Touro U International, CA — B
The U of Arizona, AZ — B
U of Great Falls, MT — B
U of La Verne, CA — B
U of Nevada, Las Vegas, NV — B
U of Phoenix–Bay Area Campus, CA — B
U of Phoenix–Central Valley Campus, CA — B
U of Phoenix–Denver Campus, CO — B
U of Phoenix–Eastern Washington Campus, Spokane Valley, WA — B
U of Phoenix–Hawaii Campus, HI — B
U of Phoenix–Idaho Campus, ID — B
U of Phoenix–New Mexico Campus, NM — B
U of Phoenix Online Campus, AZ — B
U of Phoenix–Phoenix Campus, AZ — B
U of Phoenix–Sacramento Valley Campus, CA — B
U of Phoenix–San Diego Campus, CA — B
U of Phoenix–Southern Arizona Campus, AZ — B
U of Phoenix–Utah Campus, UT — B
U of Phoenix–Washington Campus, WA — B
Weber State U, UT — B
Western International U, AZ — B

Health Information/Medical Records Administration
Boise State U, ID — A
LDS Business Coll, UT — A
Loma Linda U, CA — B
Montana State U–Billings, MT — A
Regis U, CO — B

Health Information/Medical Records Technology
DeVry U, Fremont, CA — A
DeVry U, Long Beach, CA — A
DeVry U, Pomona, CA — A
DeVry U, Sherman Oaks, CA — A
DeVry U, Westminster, CO — A
Idaho State U, ID — A
ITT Tech Inst, Rancho Cordova, CA — A
ITT Tech Inst, San Bernardino, CA — A
ITT Tech Inst, San Diego, CA — A
ITT Tech Inst, San Dimas, CA — A
ITT Tech Inst, Sylmar, CA — A
ITT Tech Inst, Torrance, CA — A
ITT Tech Inst, ID — A

A—associate degree; B—bachelor's degree

ITT Tech Inst, OR	A
ITT Tech Inst, UT	A
ITT Tech Inst, Seattle, WA	A
U of Phoenix–Hawaii Campus, HI	B
Weber State U, UT	A

Health/Medical Physics
California State U, Northridge, CA	B
U of Nevada, Las Vegas, NV	B

Health/Medical Preparatory Programs Related
U of Nevada, Reno, NV	B

Health Professions Related
Arizona State U at the Polytechnic Campus, AZ	
California State U, Fullerton, CA	B
California State U, Los Angeles, CA	B
California State U, Sacramento, CA	B
Dixie State Coll of Utah, UT	A
Saint Mary's Coll of California, CA	B
San Diego State U, CA	B
U of Alaska Southeast, AK	A
U of Nevada, Reno, NV	B
U of Utah, UT	B

Health Science
Azusa Pacific U, CA	B
Bastyr U, WA	B
Boise State U, ID	B
Brigham Young U–Idaho, ID	A
California State U, Dominguez Hills, CA	B
California State U, Fresno, CA	B
California State U, Long Beach, CA	B
California State U, Los Angeles, CA	B
California State U, Northridge, CA	B
California State U, San Bernardino, CA	B
Chief Dull Knife Coll, MT	A
Corban Coll, OR	B
Montana Tech of The U of Montana, MT	B
National U, CA	B
Northwest U, WA	A
Oregon State U, OR	B
Pacific U, OR	B
San Francisco State U, CA	B
Sonoma State U, CA	B
U of Alaska Anchorage, AK	B
U of Colorado at Colorado Springs, CO	B
U of Nevada, Las Vegas, NV	B
U of Southern California, CA	B
Walla Walla Coll, WA	B
Warner Pacific Coll, OR	B

Health Services Administration
Northwest Christian Coll, OR	B
U of California, Los Angeles, CA	B
U of Phoenix–Bay Area Campus, CA	B
U of Phoenix–Hawaii Campus, HI	B
U of Phoenix–Idaho Campus, ID	B

U of Phoenix–Las Vegas Campus, NV	B
U of Phoenix–Oregon Campus, OR	B
U of Phoenix–Phoenix Campus, AZ	B
U of Phoenix–Sacramento Valley Campus, CA	B
U of Phoenix–San Diego Campus, CA	B
U of Phoenix–Southern California Campus, CA	B
U of Phoenix–Southern Colorado Campus, CO	B
U of Phoenix–Utah Campus, UT	B
U of Phoenix–Washington Campus, WA	B
Utah Valley State Coll, UT	B

Health Services/Allied Health/Health Sciences
California State U, Chico, CA	B
California State U, Sacramento, CA	B
Corban Coll, OR	B
Idaho State U, ID	B
National American U, Denver, CO	A
National U, CA	B
San Diego State U, CA	B
San Jose State U, CA	B
U of Utah, UT	B
U of Wyoming, WY	B

Health Teacher Education
California State U, Chico, CA	B
California State U, San Bernardino, CA	B
Central Washington U, WA	B
Eastern Washington U, WA	B
George Fox U, OR	B
Idaho State U, ID	B
Montana State U–Billings, MT	B
New Mexico Highlands U, NM	B
North Carolina Ag and Tech State U, NC	B
Northern Arizona U, AZ	B
Portland State U, OR	B
Rocky Mountain Coll, MT	B
San Francisco State U, CA	B
Southern Oregon U, OR	B
Touro U International, CA	B
The U of Arizona, AZ	B
U of Great Falls, MT	B
The U of Montana, MT	B
The U of Montana–Western, MT	B
U of Nevada, Las Vegas, NV	B
U of Nevada, Reno, NV	B
U of New Mexico, NM	B
U of New Mexico–Gallup, NM	A
U of Utah, UT	B
U of Wyoming, WY	B
Utah State U, UT	B
Utah Valley State Coll, UT	B
Washington State U, WA	B
Western Washington U, WA	B

Heating, Air Conditioning, Ventilation and Refrigeration Maintenance Technology
Boise State U, ID	A
Lewis-Clark State Coll, ID	A,B
Montana State U–Billings, MT	A
U of Alaska Anchorage, AK	A
Utah Valley State Coll, UT	A

Heavy Equipment Maintenance Technology
Mesa State Coll, CO	A
U of Alaska Anchorage, AK	A
The U of Montana, MT	A

Hebrew
Brigham Young U, UT	B
Multnomah Bible Coll and Biblical Seminary, OR	B
U of California, Los Angeles, CA	B
U of Oregon, OR	B

Herbalism
Bastyr U, WA	B

Hispanic-American, Puerto Rican, and Mexican-American/Chicano Studies
Arizona State U, AZ	B
California State U, Dominguez Hills, CA	B
California State U, Fresno, CA	B
California State U, Fullerton, CA	B
California State U, Long Beach, CA	B
California State U, Los Angeles, CA	B
California State U, Northridge, CA	B
Claremont McKenna Coll, CA	B
The Colorado Coll, CO	B
Lewis & Clark Coll, OR	B
Loyola Marymount U, CA	B
Mills Coll, CA	B
Pitzer Coll, CA	B
Pomona Coll, CA	B
San Diego State U, CA	B
San Francisco State U, CA	B
Scripps Coll, CA	B
Sonoma State U, CA	B
Stanford U, CA	B
The U of Arizona, AZ	B
U of California, Berkeley, CA	B
U of California, Davis, CA	B
U of California, Irvine, CA	B
U of California, Los Angeles, CA	B
U of California, Riverside, CA	B
U of California, Santa Barbara, CA	B
U of California, Santa Cruz, CA	B
U of Northern Colorado, CO	B
U of San Diego, CA	B
U of Southern California, CA	B
U of Washington, WA	B

Historic Preservation and Conservation
Saint Mary's Coll of California, CA	B

History
Adams State Coll, CO	B
Albertson Coll of Idaho, ID	B
Arizona State U, AZ	B
Arizona State U at the West campus, AZ	B
Azusa Pacific U, CA	B
Biola U, CA	B
Boise State U, ID	B
Brigham Young U, UT	B
Brigham Young U–Hawaii, HI	B
Brigham Young U–Idaho, ID	A
California Baptist U, CA	B

California Inst of Technology, CA	B
California Lutheran U, CA	B
California Polytechnic State U, San Luis Obispo, CA	B
California State Polytechnic U, Pomona, CA	B
California State U Channel Islands, CA	B
California State U, Chico, CA	B
California State U, Dominguez Hills, CA	B
California State U, Fresno, CA	B
California State U, Fullerton, CA	B
California State U, Long Beach, CA	B
California State U, Los Angeles, CA	B
California State U, Northridge, CA	B
California State U, Sacramento, CA	B
California State U, San Bernardino, CA	B
California State U, San Marcos, CA	B
California State U, Stanislaus, CA	B
Central Washington U, WA	B
Claremont McKenna Coll, CA	B
Coll of the Southwest, NM	B
Colorado Christian U, CO	B
The Colorado Coll, CO	B
Colorado State U, CO	B
Colorado State U-Pueblo, CO	B
Concordia U, CA	B
Dixie State Coll of Utah, UT	A
Dominican U of California, CA	B
Eastern New Mexico U, NM	B
Eastern Oregon U, OR	B
Eastern Washington U, WA	B
Eugene Lang Coll The New School for Liberal Arts, NY	B
Fort Lewis Coll, CO	B
Fresno Pacific U, CA	A,B
George Fox U, OR	B
Gonzaga U, WA	B
Grand Canyon U, AZ	B
Great Basin Coll, NV	A
Hawai'i Pacific U, HI	B
Holy Names U, CA	B
Humboldt State U, CA	B
Idaho State U, ID	A,B
La Sierra U, CA	B
Lewis & Clark Coll, OR	B
Linfield Coll, OR	B
Loyola Marymount U, CA	B
The Master's Coll and Seminary, CA	B
Mesa State Coll, CO	B
Mills Coll, CA	B
Montana State U, MT	B
Montana State U–Billings, MT	B
Mount St. Mary's Coll, CA	B
Multnomah Bible Coll and Biblical Seminary, OR	B
National U, CA	B
Nevada State Coll at Henderson, NV	B
New Mexico Highlands U, NM	B
New Mexico State U, NM	B
North Carolina Ag and Tech State U, NC	B
Northern Arizona U, AZ	B
Northwest Nazarene U, ID	B

Northwest U, WA	B	U of the Pacific, CA	B	Utah State U, UT	B	Hawai'i Pacific U, HI	B

Northwest U, WA — B
Notre Dame de Namur U, CA — B
Occidental Coll, CA — B
Oregon State U, OR — B
Pacific Lutheran U, WA — B
Pacific Union Coll, CA — B
Pacific U, OR — B
Pepperdine U, Malibu, CA — B
Pitzer Coll, CA — B
Point Loma Nazarene U, CA — B
Pomona Coll, CA — B
Portland State U, OR — B
Prescott Coll, AZ — B
Reed Coll, OR — B
Regis U, CO — B
Rocky Mountain Coll, MT — B
St. John's Coll, NM — B
Saint Mary's Coll of California, CA — B
San Diego Christian Coll, CA — B
San Diego State U, CA — B
San Francisco State U, CA — B
San Jose State U, CA — B
Santa Clara U, CA — B
Scripps Coll, CA — B
Seattle Pacific U, WA — B
Seattle U, WA — B
Simpson U, CA — B
Sonoma State U, CA — B
Southern Oregon U, OR — B
Southern Utah U, UT — B
Stanford U, CA — B
United States Air Force Academy, CO — B
U of Alaska Anchorage, AK — B
U of Alaska Fairbanks, AK — B
U of Alaska Southeast, AK — B
The U of Arizona, AZ — B
U of California, Berkeley, CA — B
U of California, Davis, CA — B
U of California, Irvine, CA — B
U of California, Los Angeles, CA — B
U of California, Riverside, CA — B
U of California, San Diego, CA — B
U of California, Santa Barbara, CA — B
U of California, Santa Cruz, CA — B
U of Colorado at Boulder, CO — B
U of Colorado at Colorado Springs, CO — B
U of Colorado at Denver and Health Sciences Center, CO — B
U of Dallas, TX — B
U of Denver, CO — B
U of Great Falls, MT — B
U of Hawaii at Hilo, HI — B
U of Hawaii at Manoa, HI — B
U of Hawaii–West Oahu, HI — B
U of Idaho, ID — B
U of La Verne, CA — B
The U of Montana, MT — B
U of Nevada, Las Vegas, NV — B
U of Nevada, Reno, NV — B
U of New Mexico, NM — B
U of New Orleans, LA — B
U of Northern Colorado, CO — B
U of Oregon, OR — B
U of Portland, OR — B
U of Puget Sound, WA — B
U of Redlands, CA — B
U of San Diego, CA — B
U of San Francisco, CA — B
U of Southern California, CA — B

U of the Pacific, CA — B
U of the West, CA — B
U of Utah, UT — B
U of Washington, WA — B
U of Wyoming, WY — B
Utah State U, UT — B
Utah Valley State Coll, UT — B
Vanguard U of Southern California, CA — B
Walla Walla Coll, WA — B
Warner Pacific Coll, OR — B
Washington State U, WA — B
Weber State U, UT — B
Western Oregon U, OR — B
Western State Coll of Colorado, CO — B
Western Washington U, WA — B
Westminster Coll, UT — B
Westmont Coll, CA — B
Whitman Coll, WA — B
Whitworth U, WA — B
Willamette U, OR — B
Woodbury U, CA — B

History and Philosophy of Science and Technology
Oregon State U, OR — B
U of Washington, WA — B

History of Philosophy
St. John's Coll, NM — B

History of Science and Technology
California Inst of Technology, CA — B

History Related
Brigham Young U, UT — B
The Colorado Coll, CO — B
Hawai'i Pacific U, HI — B
Marylhurst U, OR — B

History Teacher Education
Brigham Young U, UT — B
Central Washington U, WA — B
Montana State U–Billings, MT — B
Nevada State Coll at Henderson, NV — B
Northern Arizona U, AZ — B
Northwest Nazarene U, ID — B
Rocky Mountain Coll, MT — B
The U of Arizona, AZ — B
U of Great Falls, MT — B
The U of Montana–Western, MT — B
U of Utah, UT — B
Washington State U, WA — B
Weber State U, UT — B

Home Furnishings and Equipment Installation
Brigham Young U, UT — B

Horticultural Science
Boise State U, ID — A
Brigham Young U–Idaho, ID — A
California Polytechnic State U, San Luis Obispo, CA — B
California State Polytechnic U, Pomona, CA — B
Colorado State U, CO — B
Montana State U, MT — B
New Mexico State U, NM — B
Oregon State U, OR — B
U of Hawaii at Hilo, HI — B
U of Idaho, ID — B

Utah State U, UT — B
Washington State U, WA — B

Hospital and Health Care Facilities Administration
U of Phoenix–Hawaii Campus, HI — B

Hospitality Administration
Lewis-Clark State Coll, ID — A,B
National U, CA — B
San Diego State U, CA — B
San Francisco State U, CA — B
San Jose State U, CA — B
Touro U International, CA — B
U of Denver, CO — B
U of Nevada, Las Vegas, NV — B
U of Nevada, Reno, NV — B
U of New Orleans, LA — B
U of Phoenix–Bay Area Campus, CA — B
U of Phoenix–Denver Campus, CO — B
U of Phoenix–Hawaii Campus, HI — B
U of Phoenix–Idaho Campus, ID — B
U of Phoenix–Las Vegas Campus, NV — B
U of Phoenix–Phoenix Campus, AZ — B
U of Phoenix–Sacramento Valley Campus, CA — B
U of Phoenix–Washington Campus, WA — B
Utah Valley State Coll, UT — A,B
Washington State U, WA — B

Hospitality Administration Related
San Diego State U, CA — B

Hotel and Restaurant Management
Johnson & Wales U, CO — B

Hotel/Motel Administration
Alliant International U, CA — B
Brigham Young U–Hawaii, HI — B
California State Polytechnic U, Pomona, CA — B
California State U, Long Beach, CA — B
Colorado State U, CO — B
Mesa State Coll, CO — A
Northern Arizona U, AZ — B
San Diego State U, CA — B
Sierra Nevada Coll, NV — B
Southern Oregon U, OR — B
U of Denver, CO — B
U of San Francisco, CA — B

Housing and Human Environments
Utah State U, UT — B

Housing and Human Environments Related
U of Nevada, Reno, NV — B

Human Development and Family Studies
Brigham Young U, UT — B
California State U, Long Beach, CA — B
California State U, San Bernardino, CA — B
Colorado State U, CO — B

Hawai'i Pacific U, HI — B
Hope International U, CA — B
Montana State U, MT — B
New Mexico State U, NM — B
Oregon State U, OR — B
Pacific Oaks Coll, CA — B
Prescott Coll, AZ — B
San Diego Christian Coll, CA — B
The U of Arizona, AZ — B
U of California, Davis, CA — B
U of California, Riverside, CA — B
U of Hawaii at Manoa, HI — B
U of Nevada, Reno, NV — B
U of New Mexico, NM — B
U of Utah, UT — B
Utah State U, UT — B
Warner Pacific Coll, OR — B
Washington State U, WA — B

Human Development and Family Studies Related
Utah State U, UT — A

Human Ecology
Prescott Coll, AZ — B
Regis U, CO — B
U of California, Irvine, CA — B
U of California, San Diego, CA — B

Humanities
Biola U, CA — B
Brigham Young U, UT — B
Brigham Young U–Hawaii, HI — B
Brigham Young U–Idaho, ID — A
California State Polytechnic U, Pomona, CA — B
California State U, Chico, CA — B
California State U, Dominguez Hills, CA — B
California State U, Monterey Bay, CA — B
California State U, Northridge, CA — B
California State U, Sacramento, CA — B
California State U, San Bernardino, CA — B
Coll of Santa Fe, NM — B
Colorado State U, CO — B
Concordia U, CA — B
Concordia U, OR — B
Corban Coll, OR — B
Dixie State Coll of Utah, UT — A
Dominican U of California, CA — B
Eastern Washington U, WA — B
Eugene Lang Coll The New School for Liberal Arts, NY — B
The Evergreen State Coll, WA — B
Fort Lewis Coll, CO — B
Fresno Pacific U, CA — B
Hawai'i Pacific U, HI — B
Holy Names U, CA — B
Loyola Marymount U, CA — B
Mesa State Coll, CO — A,B
New Coll of California, CA — B
Northern Arizona U, AZ — B
Pacific U, OR — B
Pepperdine U, Malibu, CA — B
Pomona Coll, CA — B
Portland State U, OR — B
Prescott Coll, AZ — B
Regis U, CO — B
St. John's Coll, NM — B
San Diego State U, CA — B
San Francisco State U, CA — B
San Jose State U, CA — B

A—associate degree; B—bachelor's degree

Seattle U, WA	B
Sierra Nevada Coll, NV	B
Stanford U, CA	B
United States Air Force Academy, CO	B
U of Alaska Southeast, AK	A,B
U of California, Irvine, CA	B
U of California, Riverside, CA	B
U of Colorado at Boulder, CO	B
U of Hawaii–West Oahu, HI	B
U of New Mexico, NM	B
U of Oregon, OR	B
U of San Diego, CA	B
U of Utah, UT	B
U of Washington, WA	B
U of Wyoming, WY	B
Utah Valley State Coll, UT	A
Walla Walla Coll, WA	B
Washington State U, WA	B
Western Oregon U, OR	B
Western Washington U, WA	B
Willamette U, OR	B

Human/Medical Genetics
U of California, Los Angeles, CA	B

Human Nutrition
Washington State U, WA	B

Human Resources Development
Brigham Young U, UT	B

Human Resources Management
Boise State U, ID	B
Brigham Young U, UT	B
California Polytechnic State U, San Luis Obispo, CA	B
California State Polytechnic U, Pomona, CA	B
California State U, Chico, CA	B
California State U, Dominguez Hills, CA	B
California State U, Fresno, CA	B
California State U, Long Beach, CA	B
California State U, Sacramento, CA	B
Dominican U of California, CA	B
Eastern New Mexico U, NM	B
Eastern Washington U, WA	B
Grand Canyon U, AZ	B
Hawai'i Pacific U, HI	B
Holy Names U, CA	B
Idaho State U, ID	B
Mesa State Coll, CO	B
Montana State U–Billings, MT	A
Montana Tech of The U of Montana, MT	A
National U, CA	B
Portland State U, OR	B
San Jose State U, CA	B
Simpson U, CA	B
U of Alaska Fairbanks, AK	B
The U of Arizona, AZ	B
U of Hawaii at Manoa, HI	B
U of Idaho, ID	B
The U of Montana–Western, MT	A
U of Nevada, Las Vegas, NV	B
U of Nevada, Reno, NV	B
Utah State U, UT	B
Washington State U, WA	B
Weber State U, UT	B
Western State Coll of Colorado, CO	B

Western Washington U, WA	B
Westminster Coll, UT	B

Human Services
Alaska Pacific U, AK	B
California State U, Dominguez Hills, CA	B
California State U, Monterey Bay, CA	B
California State U, San Bernardino, CA	B
Hawai'i Pacific U, HI	B
Holy Names U, CA	B
Mesa State Coll, CO	B
Northern New Mexico Coll, NM	A
Northwest Christian Coll, OR	B
Notre Dame de Namur U, CA	B
Pacific Oaks Coll, CA	B
Salish Kootenai Coll, MT	A,B
Stone Child Coll, MT	A
U of Alaska Anchorage, AK	A
U of Great Falls, MT	A,B
U of Nevada, Las Vegas, NV	B
U of Northern Colorado, CO	B
U of Oregon, OR	B
U of Phoenix–Bay Area Campus, CA	B
U of Phoenix–Denver Campus, CO	B
U of Phoenix–Hawaii Campus, HI	B
U of Phoenix–Idaho Campus, ID	B
U of Phoenix–Las Vegas Campus, NV	B
U of Phoenix–New Mexico Campus, NM	B
U of Phoenix–Oregon Campus, OR	B
U of Phoenix–Phoenix Campus, AZ	B
U of Phoenix–Sacramento Valley Campus, CA	B
U of Phoenix–San Diego Campus, CA	B
U of Phoenix–Southern California Campus, CA	B
U of Phoenix–Southern Colorado Campus, CO	B
U of Phoenix–Utah Campus, UT	B
U of Phoenix–Washington Campus, WA	B
Western Washington U, WA	B

Hydrology and Water Resources Science
California State U, Chico, CA	B
Humboldt State U, CA	B
U of California, Davis, CA	B
U of California, Santa Barbara, CA	B

Illustration
Academy of Art U, CA	A,B
Art Center Coll of Design, CA	B
Brigham Young U, UT	B
California State U, Fullerton, CA	B
California State U, Long Beach, CA	B
Rocky Mountain Coll of Art & Design, CO	B
U of San Francisco, CA	B

Industrial and Organizational Psychology
California State U, Sacramento, CA	B
Coll of Santa Fe, NM	B
Corban Coll, OR	B
Point Loma Nazarene U, CA	B
Saint Mary's Coll of California, CA	B

Industrial Arts
Brigham Young U–Idaho, ID	A
California State U, Fresno, CA	B
Colorado State U-Pueblo, CO	B
Humboldt State U, CA	B
New Mexico Highlands U, NM	B
North Carolina Ag and Tech State U, NC	B
San Francisco State U, CA	B
Southern Utah U, UT	B
The U of Montana, MT	A
The U of Montana–Western, MT	B
Walla Walla Coll, WA	B
Weber State U, UT	A
Western State Coll of Colorado, CO	B

Industrial Design
Academy of Art U, CA	A,B
Arizona State U, AZ	B
Art Center Coll of Design, CA	B
The Art Inst of California–Orange County, CA	B
The Art Inst of Colorado, CO	B
The Art Inst of Seattle, WA	A
Brigham Young U, UT	B
Brigham Young U–Idaho, ID	A
California Coll of the Arts, CA	B
California State U, Long Beach, CA	B
George Fox U, OR	B
San Francisco State U, CA	B
San Jose State U, CA	B
U of Washington, WA	B
Western Washington U, WA	B

Industrial Electronics Technology
Lewis-Clark State Coll, ID	A,B

Industrial Engineering
Arizona State U, AZ	B
California Polytechnic State U, San Luis Obispo, CA	B
California State Polytechnic U, Pomona, CA	B
California State U, Long Beach, CA	B
Colorado State U-Pueblo, CO	B
Montana State U, MT	B
New Mexico State U, NM	B
North Carolina Ag and Tech State U, NC	B
Northern New Mexico Coll, NM	A
Oregon State U, OR	B
San Jose State U, CA	B
Seattle U, WA	B
Stanford U, CA	B
U of Alaska Fairbanks, AK	B
U of Idaho, ID	B
U of San Diego, CA	B
U of Washington, WA	B

Industrial/Manufacturing Engineering
The U of Arizona, AZ	B

Industrial Production Technologies Related
Utah State U, UT	B

Industrial Radiologic Technology
Boise State U, ID	A,B
Mesa State Coll, CO	A
Northern New Mexico Coll, NM	A
Oregon Inst of Technology, OR	B

Industrial Technology
Arizona State U at the Polytechnic Campus, AZ	B
Boise State U, ID	B
Brigham Young U–Idaho, ID	A
California Polytechnic State U, San Luis Obispo, CA	B
California State U, Fresno, CA	B
California State U, Long Beach, CA	B
California State U, Los Angeles, CA	B
Central Washington U, WA	B
Great Basin Coll, NV	A
ITT Tech Inst, OR	B
Mesa State Coll, CO	A
North Carolina Ag and Tech State U, NC	B
U of Alaska Fairbanks, AK	A
U of Idaho, ID	B
Weber State U, UT	A,B
Western Washington U, WA	B

Information Science/Studies
Boise State U, ID	B
Brigham Young U–Hawaii, HI	B
Brigham Young U–Idaho, ID	A
California Baptist U, CA	B
California Lutheran U, CA	B
California State Polytechnic U, Pomona, CA	B
California State U, Dominguez Hills, CA	B
California State U, Fullerton, CA	B
California State U, Northridge, CA	B
California State U, Stanislaus, CA	A
Cambridge Coll, CO	A
Colorado State U, CO	B
Fort Lewis Coll, CO	B
George Fox U, OR	B
Gonzaga U, WA	B
Hawai'i Pacific U, HI	B
Humboldt State U, CA	B
Idaho State U, ID	B
La Sierra U, CA	B
Mesa State Coll, CO	B
Montana Tech of The U of Montana, MT	B
Morrison U, NV	A
National American U, Denver, CO	A,B
National U, CA	B
New Mexico Highlands U, NM	B
New Mexico State U, NM	B
Oregon State U, OR	B
Pacific Union Coll, CA	A,B
Pioneer Pacific Coll, Wilsonville, OR	A
San Diego State U, CA	B
San Francisco State U, CA	B
Southern Utah U, UT	A
U of Alaska Anchorage, AK	A

U of California, Los Angeles, CA — B
U of California, Santa Cruz, CA — B
U of Great Falls, MT — B
The U of Montana, MT — B
The U of Montana–Western, MT — A
U of San Francisco, CA — B
U of the Pacific, CA — B
U of Washington, WA — B
Utah State U, UT — B
Weber State U, UT — A,B
Western International U, AZ — B
Woodbury U, CA — B

Information Technology
Brigham Young U, UT — B
California State U Channel Islands, CA — B
California State U, Chico, CA — B
California State U, Los Angeles, CA — B
Concordia U, CA — B
DeVry U, Phoenix, AZ — B
DeVry U, Long Beach, CA — B
DeVry U, Pomona, CA — B
DeVry U, Westminster, CO — B
DeVry U, Federal Way, WA — B
LDS Business Coll, UT — A
National American U, Denver, CO — A,B
National U, CA — B
Neumont U, UT — B
New Mexico Inst of Mining and Technology, NM — B
New Mexico State U, NM — B
Pioneer Pacific Coll, Wilsonville, OR — B
Rocky Mountain Coll, MT — B
San Diego State U, CA — B
San Jose State U, CA — B
U of Great Falls, MT — B
The U of Montana, MT — B
U of Phoenix–Bay Area Campus, CA — B
U of Phoenix–Denver Campus, CO — B
U of Phoenix–Eastern Washington Campus, Spokane Valley, WA — B
U of Phoenix–Hawaii Campus, HI — B
U of Phoenix–Idaho Campus, ID — B
U of Phoenix–Las Vegas Campus, NV — B
U of Phoenix–New Mexico Campus, NM — B
U of Phoenix–Oregon Campus, OR — B
U of Phoenix–Phoenix Campus, AZ — B
U of Phoenix–Sacramento Valley Campus, CA — B
U of Phoenix–San Diego Campus, CA — B
U of Phoenix–Southern Arizona Campus, AZ — B
U of Phoenix–Southern California Campus, CA — B
U of Phoenix–Southern Colorado Campus, CO — B
U of Phoenix–Utah Campus, UT — B

U of Phoenix–Washington Campus, WA — B
Utah Valley State Coll, UT — A,B

Instrumentation Technology
Colorado State U-Pueblo, CO — B
Idaho State U, ID — A

Insurance
California State Polytechnic U, Pomona, CA — B
California State U, Sacramento, CA — B
Seattle U, WA — B
Washington State U, WA — B

Intercultural/Multicultural and Diversity Studies
The Evergreen State Coll, WA — B
Northwest U, WA — B
Trinity Lutheran Coll, WA — B
Western Oregon U, OR — B
William Jessup U, CA — B

Interdisciplinary Studies
Arizona State U, AZ — B
Arizona State U at the Polytechnic Campus, AZ — B
Arizona State U at the West campus, AZ — B
Bethany U, CA — B
Boise State U, ID — B
Brigham Young U–Hawaii, HI — B
California Baptist U, CA — B
California Lutheran U, CA — B
California State U, Dominguez Hills, CA — B
California State U, Long Beach, CA — B
California State U, Los Angeles, CA — B
California State U, Monterey Bay, CA — B
California State U, San Bernardino, CA — B
Concordia U, OR — B
Corban Coll, OR — B
Eastern Washington U, WA — B
Eugene Lang Coll The New School for Liberal Arts, NY — B
George Fox U, OR — B
Great Basin Coll, NV — A
Hawai'i Pacific U, HI — B
Hope International U, CA — B
Lewis-Clark State Coll, ID — B
Marylhurst U, OR — B
Mills Coll, CA — B
National U, CA — B
New Coll of California, CA — B
New Mexico State U, NM — B
Northwest U, WA — B
Oregon State U, OR — B
Pacific Union Coll, CA — B
Pepperdine U, Malibu, CA — B
Pitzer Coll, CA — B
Pomona Coll, CA — B
Prescott Coll, AZ — B
Rocky Mountain Coll, MT — B
Saint Mary's Coll of California, CA — B
San Diego Christian Coll, CA — B
Santa Clara U, CA — B
Sonoma State U, CA — B
Southern Oregon U, OR — B
Stanford U, CA — B
Thomas Aquinas Coll, CA — B

United States Air Force Academy, CO — B
U of Alaska Anchorage, AK — B
U of California, San Diego, CA — B
U of California, Santa Barbara, CA — B
U of Hawaii at Hilo, HI — B
U of Hawaii at Manoa, HI — B
U of Judaism, CA — B
The U of Montana, MT — B
U of Nevada, Las Vegas, NV — B
U of Northern Colorado, CO — B
U of Portland, OR — B
U of Puget Sound, WA — B
U of Redlands, CA — B
U of San Francisco, CA — B
U of Southern California, CA — B
U of the Pacific, CA — B
U of Washington, WA — B
Vanguard U of Southern California, CA — B
Western Oregon U, OR — B
Western State Coll of Colorado, CO — B
Western Washington U, WA — B
Woodbury U, CA — B

Interior Architecture
Arizona State U, AZ — B
The Art Inst of California–San Diego, CA — B
California Coll of the Arts, CA — B
U of Idaho, ID — B
U of Nevada, Las Vegas, NV — B
U of Oregon, OR — B
U of Washington, WA — B
Woodbury U, CA — B

Interior Design
Academy of Art U, CA — A,B
Art Center Coll of Design, CA — B
The Art Inst of California–Inland Empire, CA — B
The Art Inst of California–Los Angeles, CA — B
The Art Inst of California–Orange County, CA — B
The Art Inst of California–San Diego, CA — B
The Art Inst of California–San Francisco, CA — B
The Art Inst of Colorado, CO — B
The Art Inst of Las Vegas, NV — A,B
The Art Inst of Phoenix, AZ — B
The Art Inst of Portland, OR — A,B
The Art Inst of Seattle, WA — A,B
Brigham Young U, UT — B
Brigham Young U–Idaho, ID — A
California State U, Chico, CA — B
California State U, Fresno, CA — B
California State U, Long Beach, CA — B
California State U, Sacramento, CA — B
Collins Coll: A School of Design and Technology, AZ — B
Colorado State U, CO — B
Dixie State Coll of Utah, UT — A
FIDM/The Fashion Inst of Design & Merchandising, Los Angeles Campus, CA — A
LDS Business Coll, UT — A
Marylhurst U, OR — B
Northern Arizona U, AZ — B
Oregon State U, OR — B

Otis Coll of Art and Design, CA — B
Rocky Mountain Coll of Art & Design, CO — B
San Diego State U, CA — B
San Francisco State U, CA — B
San Jose State U, CA — B
Southern Utah U, UT — A
U of Idaho, ID — B
Utah State U, UT — B
Washington State U, WA — B
Weber State U, UT — A

Intermedia/Multimedia
Art Center Coll of Design, CA — B
The Art Inst of California–San Diego, CA — B
The Art Inst of Colorado, CO — A
The Art Inst of Portland, OR — A,B
The Art Inst of Seattle, WA — A,B
Coll of Santa Fe, NM — B
DigiPen Inst of Technology, WA — A,B
The Evergreen State Coll, WA — B
George Fox U, OR — B
Mills Coll, CA — B
National U, CA — B
Platt Coll San Diego, CA — A
U of California, San Diego, CA — B
U of Oregon, OR — B
Western Washington U, WA — B

International Agriculture
U of California, Davis, CA — B
Utah State U, UT — B

International Business/Trade/Commerce
Albertson Coll of Idaho, ID — B
Alliant International U, CA — B
Arizona State U at the West campus, AZ — B
Boise State U, ID — B
Brigham Young U–Hawaii, HI — B
California State Polytechnic U, Pomona, CA — B
California State U, Dominguez Hills, CA — B
California State U, Fresno, CA — B
California State U, Long Beach, CA — B
California State U, Monterey Bay, CA — B
California State U, Sacramento, CA — B
Chapman U, CA — B
Claremont McKenna Coll, CA — B
Coll of Santa Fe, NM — B
Concordia U, CA — B
Dominican U of California, CA — B
Fort Lewis Coll, CO — B
Fresno Pacific U, CA — B
George Fox U, OR — B
Gonzaga U, WA — B
Grand Canyon U, AZ — B
Hawai'i Pacific U, HI — B
Johnson & Wales U, CO — B
Lincoln U, CA — B
Linfield Coll, OR — B
Mount St. Mary's Coll, CA — B
New Mexico State U, NM — B
Northwest Nazarene U, ID — B
Notre Dame de Namur U, CA — B
Oregon State U, OR — B
Pacific Lutheran U, WA — B
Pacific Union Coll, CA — B

A—associate degree; B—bachelor's degree

Pepperdine U, Malibu, CA — B
Saint Mary's Coll of California, CA — B
San Diego State U, CA — B
San Francisco State U, CA — B
San Jose State U, CA — B
Seattle U, WA — B
U of Denver, CO — B
U of Hawaii at Manoa, HI — B
U of La Verne, CA — B
The U of Montana, MT — B
U of Nevada, Las Vegas, NV — B
U of Nevada, Reno, NV — B
U of Oregon, OR — B
U of Phoenix–Bay Area Campus, CA — B
U of Phoenix–Hawaii Campus, HI — B
U of Phoenix–Idaho Campus, ID — B
U of Phoenix–Las Vegas Campus, NV — B
U of Phoenix–Oregon Campus, OR — B
U of Phoenix–Phoenix Campus, AZ — B
U of Phoenix–Sacramento Valley Campus, CA — B
U of Phoenix–Washington Campus, WA — B
U of Portland, OR — B
U of Puget Sound, WA — B
U of San Francisco, CA — B
U of Southern California, CA — B
U of Washington, WA — B
Utah Valley State Coll, UT — B
Vanguard U of Southern California, CA — B
Washington State U, WA — B
Western International U, AZ — B
Western State Coll of Colorado, CO — B
Western Washington U, WA — B
Westminster Coll, UT — B
Whitworth U, WA — B

International Economics
Albertson Coll of Idaho, ID — B
California State U, Chico, CA — B
Claremont McKenna Coll, CA — B
The Colorado Coll, CO — B
Loyola Marymount U, CA — B
Seattle U, WA — B
U of California, Los Angeles, CA — B
U of California, Santa Cruz, CA — B
U of Puget Sound, WA — B

International Finance
Brigham Young U, UT — B

International/Global Studies
Arizona State U, AZ — B
Colorado Christian U, CO — B
Concordia U, CA — B
Dominican U of California, CA — B
The Evergreen State Coll, WA — B
George Fox U, OR — B
National U, CA — B
Oregon State U, OR — B
Pitzer Coll, CA — B
Point Loma Nazarene U, CA — B
U of California, Irvine, CA — B
U of Colorado at Boulder, CO — B
U of Colorado at Denver and Health Sciences Center, CO — B
U of New Orleans, LA — B

U of Utah, UT — B
Willamette U, OR — B

International Marketing
Brigham Young U, UT — B

International Relations and Affairs
Alliant International U, CA — B
Azusa Pacific U, CA — B
Bethany U, CA — B
Brigham Young U, UT — B
California Lutheran U, CA — B
California State U, Chico, CA — B
California State U, Long Beach, CA — B
California State U, Monterey Bay, CA — B
Chapman U, CA — B
Claremont McKenna Coll, CA — B
Eastern Washington U, WA — B
Embry-Riddle Aeronautical U, AZ — B
Eugene Lang Coll The New School for Liberal Arts, NY — B
Gonzaga U, WA — B
Grand Canyon U, AZ — B
Hawai'i Pacific U, HI — B
Holy Names U, CA — B
Lewis & Clark Coll, OR — B
Mills Coll, CA — B
Northern Arizona U, AZ — B
Northwest Nazarene U, ID — B
Occidental Coll, CA — B
Oregon State U, OR — B
Pacific Lutheran U, WA — B
Pacific U, OR — B
Pepperdine U, Malibu, CA — B
Pitzer Coll, CA — B
Pomona Coll, CA — B
Portland State U, OR — B
Reed Coll, OR — B
Saint Mary's Coll of California, CA — B
San Diego State U, CA — B
San Francisco State U, CA — B
Scripps Coll, CA — B
Seattle U, WA — B
Sonoma State U, CA — B
Southern Oregon U, OR — B
Stanford U, CA — B
U of California, Davis, CA — B
U of Denver, CO — B
U of Idaho, ID — B
U of La Verne, CA — B
U of Nevada, Reno, NV — B
U of Oregon, OR — B
U of Puget Sound, WA — B
U of Redlands, CA — B
U of San Diego, CA — B
U of Southern California, CA — B
U of the Pacific, CA — B
U of Washington, WA — B
U of Wyoming, WY — B
Western International U, AZ — B
Western Oregon U, OR — B
Whitworth U, WA — B

Islamic Studies
U of California, Los Angeles, CA — B
U of California, Santa Barbara, CA — B

Italian
Arizona State U, AZ — B
Brigham Young U, UT — B

California State U, Long Beach, CA — B
Claremont McKenna Coll, CA — B
The Colorado Coll, CO — B
Gonzaga U, WA — B
Saint Mary's Coll of California, CA — B
San Francisco State U, CA — B
Santa Clara U, CA — B
Scripps Coll, CA — B
Stanford U, CA — B
The U of Arizona, AZ — B
U of California, Berkeley, CA — B
U of California, Davis, CA — B
U of California, Los Angeles, CA — B
U of California, San Diego, CA — B
U of California, Santa Barbara, CA — B
U of California, Santa Cruz, CA — B
U of Colorado at Boulder, CO — B
U of Denver, CO — B
U of Oregon, OR — B
U of Southern California, CA — B
U of Washington, WA — B

Italian Studies
Santa Clara U, CA — B
U of California, Santa Cruz, CA — B

Japanese
Brigham Young U, UT — B
California State U, Fullerton, CA — B
California State U, Long Beach, CA — B
California State U, Los Angeles, CA — B
Claremont McKenna Coll, CA — B
Linfield Coll, OR — B
Pacific U, OR — B
Pomona Coll, CA — B
Portland State U, OR — B
San Diego State U, CA — B
San Francisco State U, CA — B
San Jose State U, CA — B
Scripps Coll, CA — B
Stanford U, CA — B
U of Alaska Fairbanks, AK — B
U of California, Berkeley, CA — B
U of California, Davis, CA — B
U of California, Irvine, CA — B
U of California, Los Angeles, CA — B
U of California, San Diego, CA — B
U of California, Santa Barbara, CA — B
U of California, Santa Cruz, CA — B
U of Colorado at Boulder, CO — B
U of Hawaii at Hilo, HI — B
U of Hawaii at Manoa, HI — B
The U of Montana, MT — B
U of Oregon, OR — B
U of the Pacific, CA — B
U of Utah, UT — B
U of Washington, WA — B

Japanese Studies
Claremont McKenna Coll, CA — B
U of San Francisco, CA — B
Willamette U, OR — B

Jazz/Jazz Studies
Brigham Young U, UT — B
California Inst of the Arts, CA — B

U of Nevada, Las Vegas, NV — B
U of Oregon, OR — B
U of Southern California, CA — B
Western Washington U, WA — B

Jewish/Judaic Studies
California State U, Chico, CA — B
San Diego State U, CA — B
Scripps Coll, CA — B
The U of Arizona, AZ — B
U of California, Los Angeles, CA — B
U of California, San Diego, CA — B
U of Judaism, CA — B
U of Oregon, OR — B
U of Southern California, CA — B
U of Washington, WA — B

Journalism
Alliant International U, CA — B
Arizona State U, AZ — B
Brigham Young U, UT — B
Brigham Young U–Idaho, ID — A
California Baptist U, CA — B
California Lutheran U, CA — B
California Polytechnic State U, San Luis Obispo, CA — B
California State Polytechnic U, Pomona, CA — B
California State U, Chico, CA — B
California State U, Fresno, CA — B
California State U, Fullerton, CA — B
California State U, Long Beach, CA — B
California State U, Northridge, CA — B
California State U, Sacramento, CA — B
Central Washington U, WA — B
Colorado State U, CO — B
Colorado State U–Pueblo, CO — B
Corban Coll, OR — B
Dixie State Coll of Utah, UT — A
Eastern Washington U, WA — B
Gonzaga U, WA — B
Hawai'i Pacific U, HI — B
Humboldt State U, CA — B
Multnomah Bible Coll and Biblical Seminary, OR — B
New Mexico Highlands U, NM — B
New Mexico State U, NM — B
Northern Arizona U, AZ — B
Pacific Lutheran U, WA — B
Pacific Union Coll, CA — B
Pacific U, OR — B
Pepperdine U, Malibu, CA — B
Point Loma Nazarene U, CA — B
San Diego State U, CA — B
San Francisco State U, CA — B
San Jose State U, CA — B
Seattle U, WA — B
U of Alaska Anchorage, AK — B
U of Alaska Fairbanks, AK — B
The U of Arizona, AZ — B
U of California, Irvine, CA — B
U of Colorado at Boulder, CO — B
U of Denver, CO — B
U of Hawaii at Manoa, HI — B
U of Idaho, ID — B
U of La Verne, CA — B
The U of Montana, MT — B
U of Nevada, Reno, NV — B
U of New Mexico, NM — B
U of Northern Colorado, CO — B
U of Oregon, OR — B
U of Portland, OR — B

U of Southern California, CA	B
U of Utah, UT	B
U of Wyoming, WY	B
Utah State U, UT	B
Walla Walla Coll, WA	B
Weber State U, UT	B
Western State Coll of Colorado, CO	B
Western Washington U, WA	B
Whitworth U, WA	B

Journalism Related

California State U, Long Beach, CA	B
Eastern Washington U, WA	B

Judaic Studies

San Diego State U, CA	B
The U of Arizona, AZ	B

Kindergarten/Preschool Education

Arizona State U, AZ	B
Bethany U, CA	A,B
Boise State U, ID	B
Brigham Young U–Idaho, ID	A
California Polytechnic State U, San Luis Obispo, CA	B
Central Washington U, WA	B
Concordia U, OR	B
Dixie State Coll of Utah, UT	A
Eastern New Mexico U, NM	B
Great Basin Coll, NV	A
Hope International U, CA	A
Humboldt State U, CA	B
Mesa State Coll, CO	A
Mount St. Mary's Coll, CA	B
New Mexico Highlands U, NM	B
New Mexico State U, NM	B
North Carolina Ag and Tech State U, NC	B
Oregon State U, OR	B
Pacific Lutheran U, WA	B
Pacific Oaks Coll, CA	B
Pacific Union Coll, CA	A,B
Pacific U, OR	B
Patten U, CA	B
Prescott Coll, AZ	B
Salish Kootenai Coll, MT	A
U of Alaska Anchorage, AK	B
U of Alaska Fairbanks, AK	A
The U of Arizona, AZ	B
U of Great Falls, MT	A,B
The U of Montana–Western, MT	A
U of Nevada, Las Vegas, NV	B
U of New Mexico–Gallup, NM	B
U of Utah, UT	B
Utah State U, UT	B
Warner Pacific Coll, OR	B
Washington State U, WA	B
Weber State U, UT	B
Western Washington U, WA	B
Westminster Coll, UT	B

Kinesiology and Exercise Science

Adams State Coll, CO	B
Albertson Coll of Idaho, ID	B
Arizona State U, AZ	B
Bastyr U, WA	B
Biola U, CA	B
Boise State U, ID	B
Brigham Young U, UT	B
Brigham Young U–Hawaii, HI	B
California Baptist U, CA	B
California Lutheran U, CA	B

California State U, Chico, CA	B
California State U, Long Beach, CA	B
California State U, Los Angeles, CA	B
California State U, Northridge, CA	B
California State U, Sacramento, CA	B
Central Washington U, WA	B
Colorado State U, CO	B
Colorado State U-Pueblo, CO	B
Concordia U, CA	B
Eastern Washington U, WA	B
Fort Lewis Coll, CO	B
Gonzaga U, WA	B
Grand Canyon U, AZ	B
Humboldt State U, CA	B
La Sierra U, CA	B
Lewis-Clark State Coll, ID	B
Linfield Coll, OR	B
The Master's Coll and Seminary, CA	B
Mesa State Coll, CO	B
Northern Arizona U, AZ	B
Northwest Nazarene U, ID	B
Occidental Coll, CA	B
Oregon State U, OR	B
Pacific Union Coll, CA	B
Pacific U, OR	B
Point Loma Nazarene U, CA	B
Rocky Mountain Coll, MT	B
Saint Mary's Coll of California, CA	B
San Diego Christian Coll, CA	B
Seattle Pacific U, WA	B
Sonoma State U, CA	B
U of California, Los Angeles, CA	B
U of Hawaii at Manoa, HI	B
U of La Verne, CA	B
U of Nevada, Las Vegas, NV	B
U of Northern Colorado, CO	B
U of Puget Sound, WA	B
U of Southern California, CA	B
U of the Pacific, CA	B
U of Utah, UT	B
U of Wyoming, WY	B
Vanguard U of Southern California, CA	B
Walla Walla Coll, WA	B
Warner Pacific Coll, OR	B
Washington State U, WA	B
Weber State U, UT	B
Western State Coll of Colorado, CO	B
Western Washington U, WA	B
Westmont Coll, CA	B
Willamette U, OR	B

Kinesiotherapy

California State U, Long Beach, CA	B

Korean

Brigham Young U, UT	B
U of California, Los Angeles, CA	B
U of Hawaii at Manoa, HI	B

Korean Studies

Claremont McKenna Coll, CA	B

Labor and Industrial Relations

California State U, Dominguez Hills, CA	B
San Francisco State U, CA	B

Landscape Architecture

Arizona State U, AZ	B
Brigham Young U–Idaho, ID	A
California Polytechnic State U, San Luis Obispo, CA	B
California State Polytechnic U, Pomona, CA	B
Colorado State U, CO	B
North Carolina Ag and Tech State U, NC	B
The U of Arizona, AZ	B
U of California, Berkeley, CA	B
U of California, Davis, CA	B
U of Hawaii at Manoa, HI	B
U of Idaho, ID	B
U of Nevada, Las Vegas, NV	B
U of Oregon, OR	B
U of Southern California, CA	B
U of Washington, WA	B
Utah State U, UT	B
Washington State U, WA	B

Landscaping and Groundskeeping

Colorado State U, CO	B

Language Interpretation and Translation

Brigham Young U, UT	B

Laser and Optical Technology

Idaho State U, ID	A
Oregon Inst of Technology, OR	B

Latin

Brigham Young U, UT	B
Claremont McKenna Coll, CA	B
Idaho State U, ID	A
Loyola Marymount U, CA	B
Saint Mary's Coll of California, CA	B
Santa Clara U, CA	B
Scripps Coll, CA	B
Seattle Pacific U, WA	B
Stanford U, CA	B
U of California, Berkeley, CA	B
U of California, Los Angeles, CA	B
U of California, Santa Cruz, CA	B
U of Idaho, ID	B
The U of Montana, MT	B
U of Oregon, OR	B
U of Washington, WA	B

Latin American Studies

Alliant International U, CA	B
Brigham Young U, UT	B
California State U, Chico, CA	B
California State U, Fullerton, CA	B
California State U, Los Angeles, CA	B
Claremont McKenna Coll, CA	B
Colorado State U, CO	B
Fort Lewis Coll, CO	B
Pitzer Coll, CA	B
Portland State U, OR	B
Prescott Coll, AZ	B
Saint Mary's Coll of California, CA	B
San Diego State U, CA	B
Scripps Coll, CA	B
Seattle Pacific U, WA	B
The U of Arizona, AZ	B
U of California, Berkeley, CA	B

Landscape Architecture *(continued)*

U of California, Los Angeles, CA	B
U of California, Riverside, CA	B
U of California, San Diego, CA	B
U of California, Santa Barbara, CA	B
U of California, Santa Cruz, CA	B
U of Denver, CO	B
U of Idaho, ID	B
U of New Mexico, NM	B
U of San Francisco, CA	B
U of Washington, WA	B
Western Washington U, WA	B
Willamette U, OR	B

Latin Teacher Education

Brigham Young U, UT	B

Legal Administrative Assistant/Secretary

LDS Business Coll, UT	A
Lewis-Clark State Coll, ID	A,B
Mesa State Coll, CO	A
Montana State U–Billings, MT	A
Montana Tech of The U of Montana, MT	A
Morrison U, NV	A
Pacific Union Coll, CA	A
The U of Montana, MT	A

Legal Assistant/Paralegal

Boise State U, ID	A
California State U, Chico, CA	B
Everest Coll, Phoenix, AZ	A
International Inst of the Americas, Mesa, AZ	A
International Inst of the Americas, Phoenix, AZ	A
International Inst of the Americas, Tucson, AZ	A
Lewis-Clark State Coll, ID	A,B
Morrison U, NV	A
Pioneer Pacific Coll, Wilsonville, OR	A
U of Alaska Anchorage, AK	A
U of Alaska Fairbanks, AK	A
U of Great Falls, MT	A,B
U of La Verne, CA	B
The U of Montana, MT	A
U of New Mexico–Gallup, NM	A
Utah Valley State Coll, UT	A,B

Legal Studies

California State U, Chico, CA	B
Chapman U, CA	B
Claremont McKenna Coll, CA	B
National U, CA	B
Scripps Coll, CA	B
United States Air Force Academy, CO	B
U of Alaska Southeast, AK	A
U of California, Berkeley, CA	B
U of California, Santa Cruz, CA	B
The U of Montana, MT	A,B

Liberal Arts and Sciences and Humanities Related

Brigham Young U, UT	B
The Colorado Coll, CO	B
Northern Arizona U, AZ	B
Northwest Christian Coll, OR	B
St. John's Coll, NM	B
Saint Mary's Coll of California, CA	B

A—associate degree; B—bachelor's degree

U of California, Los Angeles, CA — B
U of Utah, UT — B

Liberal Arts and Sciences/ Liberal Studies

Adams State Coll, CO — A,B
Alaska Pacific U, AK — B
Antioch U Los Angeles, CA — B
Arizona State U, AZ — B
Azusa Pacific U, CA — B
Bethany U, CA — A,B
Boise State U, ID — B
Brigham Young U, UT — B
Brigham Young U–Idaho, ID — A
California Baptist U, CA — B
California Lutheran U, CA — B
California Polytechnic State U, San Luis Obispo, CA — B
California State Polytechnic U, Pomona, CA — B
California State U Channel Islands, CA — B
California State U, Chico, CA — B
California State U, Dominguez Hills, CA — B
California State U, Fresno, CA — B
California State U, Fullerton, CA — B
California State U, Long Beach, CA — B
California State U, Los Angeles, CA — B
California State U, Monterey Bay, CA — B
California State U, Northridge, CA — B
California State U, Sacramento, CA — B
California State U, San Bernardino, CA — B
California State U, San Marcos, CA — B
California State U, Stanislaus, CA — B
Cascade Coll, OR — B
Chapman U, CA — B
Chief Dull Knife Coll, MT — A
Colorado Christian U, CO — A,B
Colorado State U, CO — B
Concordia U, CA — B
Concordia U, OR — A,B
Corban Coll, OR — B
Dixie State Coll of Utah, UT — A
Dominican U of California, CA — B
Eastern New Mexico U, NM — B
Eastern Oregon U, OR — B
Eastern Washington U, WA — B
Eugene Lang Coll The New School for Liberal Arts, NY — B
The Evergreen State Coll, WA — B
Fort Lewis Coll, CO — B
Fresno Pacific U, CA — A,B
Gonzaga U, WA — B
Grand Canyon U, AZ — B
Hawai'i Pacific U, HI — B
Holy Names U, CA — B
Humboldt State U, CA — B
La Sierra U, CA — B
LDS Business Coll, UT — A
Lewis-Clark State Coll, ID — A
Little Big Horn Coll, MT — A
Loyola Marymount U, CA — B
Marymount Coll, Palos Verdes, California, CA — A
The Master's Coll and Seminary, CA — B

Menlo Coll, CA — B
Mesa State Coll, CO — A,B
Mills Coll, CA — B
Montana State U–Billings, MT — A,B
Montana Tech of The U of Montana, MT — A,B
Mount St. Mary's Coll, CA — A
Nevada State Coll at Henderson, NV — B
Northern Arizona U, AZ — B
Northwest Nazarene U, ID — B
Notre Dame de Namur U, CA — B
Oregon Inst of Technology, OR — A
Oregon State U, OR — B
Pacific U, OR — B
Patten U, CA — A,B
Pepperdine U, Malibu, CA — B
Point Loma Nazarene U, CA — B
Pomona Coll, CA — B
Portland State U, OR — B
Prescott Coll, AZ — B
Regis U, CO — B
Rocky Mountain Coll, MT — A
St. John's Coll, NM — B
Saint Mary's Coll of California, CA — B
Salish Kootenai Coll, MT — A
San Diego Christian Coll, CA — B
San Diego State U, CA — B
San Francisco State U, CA — B
San Jose State U, CA — B
Santa Clara U, CA — B
Seattle Pacific U, WA — B
Seattle U, WA — B
Simpson U, CA — B
Soka U of America, CA — B
Sonoma State U, CA — B
Southern Oregon U, OR — B
Stone Child Coll, MT — A
Thomas Aquinas Coll, CA — B
U of Alaska Fairbanks, AK — A
U of Alaska Southeast, AK — A,B
The U of Arizona, AZ — B
U of California, Los Angeles, CA — B
U of California, Riverside, CA — B
U of Idaho, ID — B
U of Judaism, CA — B
U of La Verne, CA — A,B
The U of Montana, MT — B
The U of Montana–Western, MT — B
U of New Mexico, NM — B
U of New Mexico–Gallup, NM — A
U of Oregon, OR — B
U of Redlands, CA — B
U of San Diego, CA — B
U of San Francisco, CA — B
U of Utah, UT — B
U of Washington, WA — B
Utah State U, UT — B
Warner Pacific Coll, OR — B
Weber State U, UT — B
Western International U, AZ — A,B
Western Oregon U, OR — A
Western State Coll of Colorado, CO — B
Western Washington U, WA — B
Westmont Coll, CA — B

Library Assistant

Northern New Mexico Coll, NM — A

Library Science Related

U of California, Los Angeles, CA — B
U of Great Falls, MT — B

Lineworker

Utah Valley State Coll, UT — A

Linguistic and Comparative Language Studies Related

Brigham Young U, UT — B
U of California, Los Angeles, CA — B

Linguistics

Brigham Young U, UT — B
California State U, Chico, CA — B
California State U, Dominguez Hills, CA — B
California State U, Fresno, CA — B
California State U, Fullerton, CA — B
California State U, Northridge, CA — B
Pitzer Coll, CA — B
Pomona Coll, CA — B
Portland State U, OR — B
Reed Coll, OR — B
San Diego State U, CA — B
San Jose State U, CA — B
Scripps Coll, CA — B
Stanford U, CA — B
U of Alaska Fairbanks, AK — B
The U of Arizona, AZ — B
U of California, Berkeley, CA — B
U of California, Davis, CA — B
U of California, Irvine, CA — B
U of California, Los Angeles, CA — B
U of California, Riverside, CA — B
U of California, San Diego, CA — B
U of California, Santa Barbara, CA — B
U of California, Santa Cruz, CA — B
U of Colorado at Boulder, CO — B
U of Hawaii at Hilo, HI — B
U of Hawaii at Manoa, HI — B
The U of Montana, MT — B
U of New Mexico, NM — B
U of Oregon, OR — B
U of Southern California, CA — B
U of Utah, UT — B
U of Washington, WA — B
Washington State U, WA — B
Western Washington U, WA — B

Literature

Boise State U, ID — B
California State U, Dominguez Hills, CA — B
California State U, Long Beach, CA — B
Chapman U, CA — B
Claremont McKenna Coll, CA — B
Eastern Washington U, WA — B
Eugene Lang Coll The New School for Liberal Arts, NY — B
Fresno Pacific U, CA — B
Gonzaga U, WA — B
Grand Canyon U, AZ — B
Hawai'i Pacific U, HI — B
New Coll of California, CA — B
Northwest U, WA — B
Oregon State U, OR — B
Pacific Lutheran U, WA — B
Pacific U, OR — B
Pitzer Coll, CA — B
Prescott Coll, AZ — B
Reed Coll, OR — B
St. John's Coll, NM — B

Saint Mary's Coll of California, CA — B
San Francisco State U, CA — B
Sonoma State U, CA — B
U of California, Irvine, CA — B
U of California, San Diego, CA — B
U of California, Santa Cruz, CA — B
U of Judaism, CA — B
The U of Montana–Western, MT — B
U of Redlands, CA — B
Western Washington U, WA — B

Logistics and Materials Management

Brigham Young U, UT — B
Portland State U, OR — B
U of Nevada, Reno, NV — B
Weber State U, UT — B

Machine Tool Technology

Boise State U, ID — A
Brigham Young U–Idaho, ID — A
Idaho State U, ID — A
Mesa State Coll, CO — A
Utah Valley State Coll, UT — A
Weber State U, UT — A

Management Information Systems

Alliant International U, CA — B
Arizona State U, AZ — B
Azusa Pacific U, CA — B
Brigham Young U, UT — B
California Polytechnic State U, San Luis Obispo, CA — B
California State U, Chico, CA — B
California State U, Dominguez Hills, CA — B
California State U, Fresno, CA — B
California State U, Long Beach, CA — B
California State U, Sacramento, CA — B
California State U, San Bernardino, CA — B
Coll of Santa Fe, NM — B
Colorado Christian U, CO — A,B
Corban Coll, OR — B
Eastern New Mexico U, NM — B
Eastern Washington U, WA — B
Fort Lewis Coll, CO — B
George Fox U, OR — B
Hawai'i Pacific U, HI — B
Lincoln U, CA — B
The Master's Coll and Seminary, CA — B
National American U, Denver, CO — B
National U, CA — B
New Mexico Highlands U, NM — B
Northern Arizona U, AZ — B
Northwest Christian Coll, OR — B
Oregon Inst of Technology, OR — B
Oregon State U, OR — B
Pacific Lutheran U, WA — B
Pacific Union Coll, CA — B
Point Loma Nazarene U, CA — B
Rocky Mountain Coll, MT — B
Santa Clara U, CA — B
Seattle U, WA — B
Simpson U, CA — B
Touro U International, CA — B

Majors and Degrees

Management Information Systems

U of Alaska Anchorage, AK — B
The U of Arizona, AZ — B
U of Denver, CO — B
U of Hawaii at Manoa, HI — B
U of Idaho, ID — B
U of Nevada, Las Vegas, NV — B
U of New Orleans, LA — B
U of Phoenix–Bay Area
Campus, CA — B
U of Phoenix–Central Valley
Campus, CA — B
U of Phoenix–Denver Campus,
CO — B
U of Phoenix–Hawaii Campus,
HI — B
U of Phoenix–Idaho Campus,
ID — B
U of Phoenix–Las Vegas
Campus, NV — B
U of Phoenix–New Mexico
Campus, NM — B
U of Phoenix–Oregon Campus,
OR — B
U of Phoenix–Phoenix Campus,
AZ — B
U of Phoenix–Sacramento
Valley Campus, CA — B
U of Phoenix–San Diego
Campus, CA — B
U of Phoenix–Southern
Arizona Campus, AZ — B
U of Phoenix–Southern
Colorado Campus, CO — B
U of Phoenix–Utah Campus,
UT — B
U of Phoenix–Washington
Campus, WA — B
U of Redlands, CA — B
U of San Francisco, CA — B
U of Utah, UT — B
U of Washington, WA — B
U of Wyoming, WY — B
Utah Valley State Coll, UT — B
Walla Walla Coll, WA — B
Washington State U, WA — B
Weber State U, UT — A,B
Western State Coll of
Colorado, CO — B
Western Washington U, WA — B

Management Information Systems and Services Related
California State U, Chico, CA — B
Westminster Coll, UT — B

Management Science
Colorado Christian U, CO — B
New Mexico State U, NM — B
Prescott Coll, AZ — B
Rocky Mountain Coll, MT — B
U of California, San Diego, CA — B
U of Great Falls, MT — B
U of Phoenix–Bay Area
Campus, CA — B
U of Phoenix–Denver Campus,
CO — B
U of Phoenix–Hawaii Campus,
HI — B
U of Phoenix–Idaho Campus,
ID — B
U of Phoenix–Las Vegas
Campus, NV — B
U of Phoenix–New Mexico
Campus, NM — B
U of Phoenix Online Campus,
AZ

U of Phoenix–Oregon Campus,
OR — B
U of Phoenix–Phoenix Campus,
AZ — B
U of Phoenix–Sacramento
Valley Campus, CA — B
U of Phoenix–Southern
Arizona Campus, AZ — B
U of Phoenix–Southern
Colorado Campus, CO — B
U of Phoenix–Utah Campus,
UT — B
U of Phoenix–Washington
Campus, WA — B
U of Washington, WA — B
U of Wyoming, WY — B
Washington State U, WA — B

Manufacturing Engineering
Brigham Young U, UT — B
U of California, Berkeley, CA — B
U of California, Los Angeles,
CA — B

Manufacturing Technology
Arizona State U at the
Polytechnic Campus, AZ — B
California State U, Long
Beach, CA — B
Eastern Washington U, WA — B
Lewis-Clark State Coll, ID — A,B
Utah Valley State Coll, UT — A
Western Washington U, WA — B

Marine Biology
U of Hawaii at Manoa, HI — B

Marine Biology and Biological Oceanography
Alaska Pacific U, AK — B
Brigham Young U–Idaho, ID — A
California State U, Long
Beach, CA — B
Dixie State Coll of Utah, UT — A
Hawai'i Pacific U, HI — B
Humboldt State U, CA — B
Northern Arizona U, AZ — B
San Francisco State U, CA — B
San Jose State U, CA — B
Sonoma State U, CA — B
U of California, Los Angeles,
CA — B
U of California, Santa Barbara,
CA — B
U of California, Santa Cruz,
CA — B
Western Washington U, WA — B

Marine Science/Merchant Marine Officer
Prescott Coll, AZ — B
U of San Diego, CA — B

Marine Technology
California Maritime Academy,
CA — B

Marketing/Marketing Management
Arizona State U, AZ — B
Azusa Pacific U, CA — B
Boise State U, ID — A,B
Brigham Young U, UT — B
Brigham Young U–Idaho, ID — A
California Lutheran U, CA — B
California State Polytechnic U,
Pomona, CA — B
California State U, Chico, CA — B

California State U, Dominguez
Hills, CA — B
California State U, Fresno, CA — B
California State U, Fullerton,
CA — B
California State U, Long
Beach, CA — B
California State U, Sacramento,
CA — B
California State U, San
Bernardino, CA — B
Cascade Coll, OR — B
Coll of the Southwest, NM — B
Colorado State U, CO — B
Colorado State U–Pueblo, CO — B
Eastern New Mexico U, NM — B
Eastern Washington U, WA — B
Fort Lewis Coll, CO — B
Fresno Pacific U, CA — B
George Fox U, OR — B
Gonzaga U, WA — B
Grand Canyon U, AZ — B
Hawai'i Pacific U, HI — A,B
Holy Names U, CA — B
Humboldt State U, CA — B
Idaho State U, ID — A,B
Johnson & Wales U, CO — A,B
Mesa State Coll, CO — B
Montana State U–Billings, MT — B
Mount St. Mary's Coll, CA — B
National U, CA — B
New Mexico Highlands U, NM — B
New Mexico State U, NM — B
Northern Arizona U, AZ — B
Northwest Nazarene U, ID — B
Northwest U, WA — B
Notre Dame de Namur U, CA — B
Oregon State U, OR — B
Pacific Lutheran U, WA — B
Pacific Union Coll, CA — B
Pacific U, OR — B
Portland State U, OR — B
San Diego State U, CA — B
San Francisco State U, CA — B
San Jose State U, CA — B
Santa Clara U, CA — B
Seattle U, WA — B
Southern Oregon U, OR — B
U of Alaska Anchorage, AK — B
The U of Arizona, AZ — B
U of Colorado at Boulder, CO — B
U of Colorado at Colorado
Springs, CO — B
U of Denver, CO — B
U of Great Falls, MT — B
U of Hawaii at Manoa, HI — B
U of Idaho, ID — B
U of La Verne, CA — B
The U of Montana, MT — B
U of Nevada, Las Vegas, NV — B
U of Nevada, Reno, NV — B
U of New Mexico–Gallup, NM — A
U of New Orleans, LA — B
U of Oregon, OR — B
U of Phoenix–Bay Area
Campus, CA — B
U of Phoenix–Central Valley
Campus, CA — B
U of Phoenix–Denver Campus,
CO — B
U of Phoenix–Hawaii Campus,
HI — B
U of Phoenix–Idaho Campus,
ID — B

U of Phoenix–Las Vegas
Campus, NV — B
U of Phoenix–New Mexico
Campus, NM — B
U of Phoenix–Oregon Campus,
OR — B
U of Phoenix–Phoenix Campus,
AZ — B
U of Phoenix–Sacramento
Valley Campus, CA — B
U of Phoenix–San Diego
Campus, CA — B
U of Phoenix–Southern
Arizona Campus, AZ — B
U of Phoenix–Southern
Colorado Campus, CO — B
U of Phoenix–Utah Campus,
UT — B
U of Phoenix–Washington
Campus, WA — B
U of Portland, OR — B
U of San Francisco, CA — B
U of Utah, UT — B
U of Wyoming, WY — B
Utah State U, UT — B
Utah Valley State Coll, UT — B
Vanguard U of Southern
California, CA — B
Walla Walla Coll, WA — B
Washington State U, WA — B
Weber State U, UT — A,B
Western International U, AZ — B
Western State Coll of
Colorado, CO — B
Western Washington U, WA — B
Westminster Coll, UT — B
Woodbury U, CA — B

Marketing Related
U of Utah, UT — B

Marriage and Family Therapy/Counseling
U of Nevada, Las Vegas, NV — B

Massage Therapy
Cambridge Coll, CO — A

Mass Communication/Media
Boise State U, ID — B
Brigham Young U, UT — B
Brigham Young U–Idaho, ID — A
California Lutheran U, CA — B
California State Polytechnic U,
Pomona, CA — B
California State U, Dominguez
Hills, CA — B
California State U, Fresno, CA — B
California State U, Long
Beach, CA — B
California State U, Sacramento,
CA — B
Central Washington U, WA — B
Colorado State U–Pueblo, CO — B
Fresno Pacific U, CA — A,B
Gonzaga U, WA — B
Grand Canyon U, AZ — B
Hawai'i Pacific U, HI — B
Idaho State U, ID — B
Loyola Marymount U, CA — B
Marylhurst U, OR — B
The Master's Coll and
Seminary, CA — B
Menlo Coll, CA — B
Mesa State Coll, CO — B
Montana State U–Billings, MT — B
New Mexico Highlands U, NM — B

A—associate degree; B—bachelor's degree

North Carolina Ag and Tech State U, NC — B
Northwest Nazarene U, ID — B
Pacific Lutheran U, WA — B
Pacific Union Coll, CA — B
Pacific U, OR — B
Point Loma Nazarene U, CA — B
San Diego State U, CA — B
Seattle U, WA — B
Sonoma State U, CA — B
Southern Utah U, UT — B
U of Alaska Anchorage, AK — B
U of California, Berkeley, CA — B
U of California, San Diego, CA — B
U of Oregon, OR — B
U of Portland, OR — B
U of San Diego, CA — B
U of San Francisco, CA — B
U of Southern California, CA — B
U of Utah, UT — B
Walla Walla Coll, WA — B
Western State Coll of Colorado, CO — B
Whitworth U, WA — B

Mass Communications
Arizona State U, AZ — B
Brigham Young U, UT — B

Materials Engineering
Arizona State U, AZ — B
California Polytechnic State U, San Luis Obispo, CA — B
California State Polytechnic U, Pomona, CA — B
California State U, Long Beach, CA
Montana Tech of The U of Montana, MT — B
New Mexico Inst of Mining and Technology, NM
San Jose State U, CA — B
Stanford U, CA — B
U of California, Davis, CA — B
U of California, Irvine, CA — B
U of California, Los Angeles, CA
U of Utah, UT — B
U of Washington, WA — B
Washington State U, WA — B

Materials Science
California Inst of Technology, CA — B
Montana Tech of The U of Montana, MT — B
Stanford U, CA — B
United States Air Force Academy, CO — B
The U of Arizona, AZ — B
U of California, Berkeley, CA — B
U of California, Los Angeles, CA — B
U of Utah, UT — B
Washington State U, WA — B

Maternal/Child Health and Neonatal Nursing
U of Washington, WA — B

Mathematics
Adams State Coll, CO — B
Albertson Coll of Idaho, ID — B
Arizona State U, AZ — B
Azusa Pacific U, CA — B
Biola U, CA — B
Boise State U, ID — B
Brigham Young U, UT — B

Brigham Young U–Hawaii, HI — B
Brigham Young U–Idaho, ID — A
California Baptist U, CA — B
California Inst of Technology, CA — B
California Lutheran U, CA — B
California Polytechnic State U, San Luis Obispo, CA
California State Polytechnic U, Pomona, CA — B
California State U Channel Islands, CA — B
California State U, Chico, CA — B
California State U, Dominguez Hills, CA — B
California State U, Fresno, CA — B
California State U, Fullerton, CA — B
California State U, Long Beach, CA — B
California State U, Los Angeles, CA — B
California State U, Northridge, CA — B
California State U, Sacramento, CA — B
California State U, San Bernardino, CA — B
California State U, San Marcos, CA — B
California State U, Stanislaus, CA — B
Central Washington U, WA — B
Chapman U, CA — B
Claremont McKenna Coll, CA — B
Coll of the Southwest, NM — B
Colorado Christian U, CO — B
The Colorado Coll, CO — B
Colorado School of Mines, CO — B
Colorado State U, CO — B
Colorado State U-Pueblo, CO — B
Concordia U, CA — B
Corban Coll, OR — B
Dixie State Coll of Utah, UT — A
Eastern Oregon U, OR — B
Eastern Washington U, WA — B
Fort Lewis Coll, CO — B
Fresno Pacific U, CA — A,B
George Fox U, OR — B
Gonzaga U, WA — B
Grand Canyon U, AZ — B
Great Basin Coll, NV — A
Harvey Mudd Coll, CA — B
Humboldt State U, CA — B
Idaho State U, ID — A,B
La Sierra U, CA — B
Lewis & Clark Coll, OR — B
Lewis-Clark State Coll, ID — B
Linfield Coll, OR — B
Little Big Horn Coll, MT — A
Loyola Marymount U, CA — B
The Master's Coll and Seminary, CA — B
Mesa State Coll, CO — A,B
Mills Coll, CA — B
Montana State U, MT — B
Montana State U–Billings, MT — B
Montana Tech of The U of Montana, MT — B
Mount St. Mary's Coll, CA — B
National U, CA — B
New Mexico Highlands U, NM — B
New Mexico Inst of Mining and Technology, NM — B
New Mexico State U, NM — B

North Carolina Ag and Tech State U, NC — B
Northern Arizona U, AZ — B
Northwest Nazarene U, ID — B
Occidental Coll, CA — B
Oregon State U, OR — B
Pacific Lutheran U, WA — B
Pacific Union Coll, CA — B
Pacific U, OR — B
Pepperdine U, Malibu, CA — B
Pitzer Coll, CA — B
Point Loma Nazarene U, CA — B
Pomona Coll, CA — B
Portland State U, OR — B
Reed Coll, OR — B
Regis U, CO — B
Rocky Mountain Coll, MT — B
St. John's Coll, NM — B
Saint Mary's Coll of California, CA — B
San Diego Christian Coll, CA — B
San Diego State U, CA — B
San Francisco State U, CA — B
San Jose State U, CA — B
Santa Clara U, CA — B
Scripps Coll, CA — B
Seattle Pacific U, WA — B
Seattle U, WA — B
Simpson U, CA — B
Sonoma State U, CA — B
Southern Oregon U, OR — B
Southern Utah U, UT — B
Stanford U, CA — B
United States Air Force Academy, CO — B
U of Alaska Anchorage, AK — B
U of Alaska Fairbanks, AK — B
U of Alaska Southeast, AK — B
The U of Arizona, AZ — B
U of California, Berkeley, CA — B
U of California, Davis, CA — B
U of California, Irvine, CA — B
U of California, Los Angeles, CA — B
U of California, Riverside, CA — B
U of California, San Diego, CA — B
U of California, Santa Barbara, CA — B
U of California, Santa Cruz, CA — B
U of Colorado at Boulder, CO — B
U of Colorado at Colorado Springs, CO — B
U of Colorado at Denver and Health Sciences Center, CO — B
U of Dallas, TX — B
U of Denver, CO — B
U of Great Falls, MT — A,B
U of Hawaii at Hilo, HI — B
U of Hawaii at Manoa, HI — B
U of Idaho, ID — B
U of La Verne, CA — B
The U of Montana, MT — B
U of Nevada, Las Vegas, NV — B
U of Nevada, Reno, NV — B
U of New Mexico, NM — B
U of New Orleans, LA — B
U of Northern Colorado, CO — B
U of Oregon, OR — B
U of Portland, OR — B
U of Puget Sound, WA — B
U of Redlands, CA — B
U of San Diego, CA — B
U of San Francisco, CA — B
U of Southern California, CA — B
U of the Pacific, CA — B

U of Utah, UT — B
U of Washington, WA — B
U of Wyoming, WY — B
Utah State U, UT — B
Utah Valley State Coll, UT — A,B
Vanguard U of Southern California, CA — B
Walla Walla Coll, WA — B
Washington State U, WA — B
Weber State U, UT — B
Western Oregon U, OR — B
Western State Coll of Colorado, CO — B
Western Washington U, WA — B
Westminster Coll, UT — B
Westmont Coll, CA — B
Whitman Coll, WA — B
Whitworth U, WA — B
Willamette U, OR — B

Mathematics and Computer Science
The Colorado Coll, CO — B
Saint Mary's Coll of California, CA — B
Southern Oregon U, OR — B
Stanford U, CA — B
U of Oregon, OR — B

Mathematics and Statistics Related
Saint Mary's Coll of California, CA — B
Seattle Pacific U, WA — B

Mathematics Related
Eastern Washington U, WA — B
U of California, Los Angeles, CA — B

Mathematics Teacher Education
Brigham Young U, UT — B
Brigham Young U–Hawaii, HI — B
California Lutheran U, CA — B
California State U, Chico, CA — B
California State U, Long Beach, CA — B
Central Washington U, WA — B
Colorado State U, CO — B
Colorado State U-Pueblo, CO — B
Concordia U, OR — B
Corban Coll, OR — B
Eastern Washington U, WA — B
Lewis-Clark State Coll, ID — B
Montana State U–Billings, MT — B
Nevada State Coll at Henderson, NV — B
Northern Arizona U, AZ — B
Northwest Nazarene U, ID — B
Prescott Coll, AZ — B
Rocky Mountain Coll, MT — B
San Diego State U, CA — B
Seattle Pacific U, WA — B
The U of Arizona, AZ — B
U of California, San Diego, CA — B
U of California, Santa Cruz, CA — B
U of Great Falls, MT — B
The U of Montana, MT — B
The U of Montana–Western, MT — B
U of Nevada, Reno, NV — B
U of New Orleans, LA — B
U of Utah, UT — B
Utah State U, UT — B
Utah Valley State Coll, UT — B

Washington State U, WA	B
Westmont Coll, CA	B

Mechanical Design Technology

Brigham Young U–Idaho, ID	A

Mechanical Drafting and CAD/CADD

Dixie State Coll of Utah, UT	A
Montana Tech of The U of Montana, MT	A

Mechanical Engineering

Arizona State U, AZ	B
Brigham Young U, UT	B
California Inst of Technology, CA	B
California Maritime Academy, CA	B
California Polytechnic State U, San Luis Obispo, CA	B
California State Polytechnic U, Pomona, CA	B
California State U, Chico, CA	B
California State U, Fresno, CA	B
California State U, Fullerton, CA	B
California State U, Long Beach, CA	B
California State U, Los Angeles, CA	B
California State U, Sacramento, CA	B
Colorado School of Mines, CO	B
Colorado State U, CO	B
George Fox U, OR	B
Gonzaga U, WA	B
Idaho State U, ID	B
Loyola Marymount U, CA	B
Montana State U, MT	B
Montana Tech of The U of Montana, MT	B
New Mexico Inst of Mining and Technology, NM	B
New Mexico State U, NM	B
North Carolina Ag and Tech State U, NC	B
Northern Arizona U, AZ	B
Oregon State U, OR	B
Portland State U, OR	B
San Diego State U, CA	B
San Francisco State U, CA	B
San Jose State U, CA	B
Santa Clara U, CA	B
Seattle U, WA	B
Stanford U, CA	B
United States Air Force Academy, CO	B
U of Alaska Fairbanks, AK	B
The U of Arizona, AZ	B
U of California, Berkeley, CA	B
U of California, Davis, CA	B
U of California, Irvine, CA	B
U of California, Los Angeles, CA	B
U of California, Riverside, CA	B
U of California, San Diego, CA	B
U of California, Santa Barbara, CA	B
U of Colorado at Boulder, CO	B
U of Colorado at Colorado Springs, CO	B
U of Colorado at Denver and Health Sciences Center, CO	B
U of Denver, CO	

U of Hawaii at Manoa, HI	B
U of Idaho, ID	B
U of Nevada, Las Vegas, NV	B
U of Nevada, Reno, NV	B
U of New Mexico, NM	B
U of New Orleans, LA	B
U of Portland, OR	B
U of San Diego, CA	B
U of Southern California, CA	B
U of the Pacific, CA	B
U of Utah, UT	B
U of Washington, WA	B
U of Wyoming, WY	B
Utah State U, UT	B
Walla Walla Coll, WA	B
Washington State U, WA	B

Mechanical Engineering/ Mechanical Technology

Arizona State U at the Polytechnic Campus, AZ	B
Boise State U, ID	B
Brigham Young U–Idaho, ID	A
California Polytechnic State U, San Luis Obispo, CA	B
California State Polytechnic U, Pomona, CA	B
California State U, Long Beach, CA	B
California State U, Sacramento, CA	B
Central Washington U, WA	B
Colorado State U-Pueblo, CO	B
Eastern Washington U, WA	B
Montana State U, MT	B
Oregon Inst of Technology, OR	B
Weber State U, UT	A,B

Mechanics and Repair

Idaho State U, ID	A
Lewis-Clark State Coll, ID	A,B

Medical Administrative Assistant and Medical Secretary

Boise State U, ID	A
LDS Business Coll, UT	A
Mesa State Coll, CO	A
Montana State U–Billings, MT	A
Montana Tech of The U of Montana, MT	A
Morrison U, NV	A
Pacific Union Coll, CA	A
The U of Montana, MT	A

Medical/Clinical Assistant

Argosy U, Orange County, CA	A
California State U, Dominguez Hills, CA	B
Cambridge Coll, CO	A
Everest Coll, Phoenix, AZ	A
Idaho State U, ID	A
LDS Business Coll, UT	A
Montana State U–Billings, MT	A
National American U, Denver, CO	A
Pioneer Pacific Coll, Wilsonville, OR	A
U of Alaska Anchorage, AK	A
U of Alaska Fairbanks, AK	A

Medical/Health Management and Clinical Assistant

Lewis-Clark State Coll, ID	A,B
National American U, Denver, CO	A

Medical Informatics

DeVry U, Phoenix, AZ	B
DeVry U, Fremont, CA	B
DeVry U, Long Beach, CA	B
DeVry U, Westminster, CO	B
DeVry U, Federal Way, WA	B

Medical Insurance Coding

Cambridge Coll, CO	A
LDS Business Coll, UT	A

Medical Laboratory Technology

ITT Tech Inst, Tempe, AZ	A
ITT Tech Inst, Tucson, AZ	A
ITT Tech Inst, Anaheim, CA	A
ITT Tech Inst, Lathrop, CA	A
ITT Tech Inst, Oxnard, CA	A
ITT Tech Inst, CO	A
ITT Tech Inst, NV	A
ITT Tech Inst, NM	A
ITT Tech Inst, Bothell, WA	A
ITT Tech Inst, Spokane, WA	A
U of Nevada, Las Vegas, NV	B

Medical Microbiology and Bacteriology

Arizona State U, AZ	B
California Polytechnic State U, San Luis Obispo, CA	B
California State Polytechnic U, Pomona, CA	B
California State U, Dominguez Hills, CA	B
Colorado State U, CO	B
Humboldt State U, CA	B
Idaho State U, ID	B
Montana State U, MT	B
New Mexico State U, NM	B
Northern Arizona U, AZ	B
Oregon State U, OR	B
Pomona Coll, CA	B
San Francisco State U, CA	B
Sonoma State U, CA	B
U of California, Los Angeles, CA	B
U of California, San Diego, CA	B
U of California, Santa Barbara, CA	B
U of Idaho, ID	B
The U of Montana, MT	B
U of Washington, WA	B
Utah State U, UT	B
Weber State U, UT	B

Medical Office Assistant

LDS Business Coll, UT	A
Lewis-Clark State Coll, ID	A,B

Medical Pharmacology and Pharmaceutical Sciences

The U of Montana, MT	B

Medical Radiologic Technology

California State U, Long Beach, CA	B
Cambridge Coll, CO	A
Idaho State U, ID	A,B
Loma Linda U, CA	A,B
Northern New Mexico Coll, NM	A
Oregon Health & Science U, OR	B
U of Nevada, Las Vegas, NV	B
U of New Mexico, NM	A,B
Weber State U, UT	A,B

Medical Transcription

LDS Business Coll, UT	A

Medicinal and Pharmaceutical Chemistry

U of California, San Diego, CA	B

Medieval and Renaissance Studies

U of California, Santa Barbara, CA	B

Mental and Social Health Services and Allied Professions Related

U of Alaska Fairbanks, AK	A

Mental Health/Rehabilitation

Chief Dull Knife Coll, MT	A
Prescott Coll, AZ	B

Merchandising, Sales, and Marketing Operations Related (General)

Brigham Young U, UT	B
Oregon State U, OR	B

Metal and Jewelry Arts

Academy of Art U, CA	A,B
California Coll of the Arts, CA	B
California State U, Long Beach, CA	B
Colorado State U, CO	B
U of Oregon, OR	B
U of Washington, WA	B

Metallurgical Engineering

Colorado School of Mines, CO	B
Montana Tech of The U of Montana, MT	B
Oregon State U, OR	B
U of Idaho, ID	B
U of Nevada, Reno, NV	B
U of Utah, UT	B
U of Washington, WA	B

Metallurgical Technology

Brigham Young U–Idaho, ID	A

Meteorology

U of Hawaii at Manoa, HI	B
U of Utah, UT	B

Microbiological Sciences and Immunology Related

U of California, Los Angeles, CA	B

Microbiology

Brigham Young U, UT	B
California State U, Chico, CA	B
California State U, Long Beach, CA	B
California State U, Los Angeles, CA	B
Idaho State U, ID	B
New Mexico State U, NM	B
Oregon State U, OR	B
San Diego State U, CA	B
U of California, Berkeley, CA	B
U of California, Davis, CA	B
U of California, Irvine, CA	B
U of California, Santa Barbara, CA	B
U of Hawaii at Manoa, HI	B
U of Wyoming, WY	B
Washington State U, WA	B

A—associate degree; B—bachelor's degree

Middle/Near Eastern and Semitic Languages Related
U of California, Los Angeles, CA — B

Middle School Education
Alaska Pacific U, AK — B
Coll of the Southwest, NM — B
Colorado State U-Pueblo, CO — B
The Master's Coll and Seminary, CA — B
Mesa State Coll, CO — B
Prescott Coll, AZ — B
U of Great Falls, MT — B
U of New Orleans, LA — B
Warner Pacific Coll, OR — B

Military Studies
Hawai'i Pacific U, HI — A,B
United States Air Force Academy, CO — B

Military Technologies
U of Idaho, ID — B

Mining and Mineral Engineering
Colorado School of Mines, CO — B
Montana Tech of The U of Montana, MT — B
New Mexico Inst of Mining and Technology, NM — B
Oregon State U, OR — B
The U of Arizona, AZ — B
U of Idaho, ID — B
U of Nevada, Reno, NV — B
U of Utah, UT — B

Mining and Petroleum Technologies Related
U of Alaska Fairbanks, AK — B

Missionary Studies and Missiology
Biola U, CA — B
Corban Coll, OR — B
Eugene Bible Coll, OR — B
George Fox U, OR — B
Hope International U, CA — A,B
Multnomah Bible Coll and Biblical Seminary, OR — B
Northwest Nazarene U, ID — B
Northwest U, WA — B
Simpson U, CA — B
Vanguard U of Southern California, CA — B

Modern Greek
Boise Bible Coll, ID — B
Claremont McKenna Coll, CA — B
Loyola Marymount U, CA — B
Saint Mary's Coll of California, CA — B
U of California, Los Angeles, CA — B
U of Oregon, OR — B
U of Utah, UT — B

Modern Languages
Claremont McKenna Coll, CA — B
Lewis & Clark Coll, OR — B
Pacific Lutheran U, WA — B
Pacific U, OR — B
Pomona Coll, CA — B
Saint Mary's Coll of California, CA — B
Scripps Coll, CA — B
Walla Walla Coll, WA — B
Westmont Coll, CA — B

Molecular Biochemistry
U of California, Davis, CA — B
U of California, Irvine, CA — B
U of California, Los Angeles, CA — B

Molecular Biology
Arizona State U, AZ — B
Brigham Young U, UT — B
California Lutheran U, CA — B
California State U, Fresno, CA — B
California State U, Sacramento, CA — B
California State U, San Marcos, CA — B
Chapman U, CA — B
Humboldt State U, CA — B
Pitzer Coll, CA — B
Pomona Coll, CA — B
San Francisco State U, CA — B
San Jose State U, CA — B
Scripps Coll, CA — B
U of California, Los Angeles, CA — B
U of California, San Diego, CA — B
U of California, Santa Barbara, CA — B
U of California, Santa Cruz, CA — B
U of Denver, CO — B
U of Idaho, ID — B
U of Washington, WA — B
U of Wyoming, WY — B
Western State Coll of Colorado, CO — B
Whitman Coll, WA — B

Molecular Pharmacology
U of California, Los Angeles, CA — B

Molecular Physiology
U of California, Los Angeles, CA — B

Molecular Toxicology
U of California, Los Angeles, CA — B

Multi-/Interdisciplinary Studies Related
Arizona State U, AZ — B
Arizona State U at the Polytechnic Campus, AZ — B
Arizona State U at the West campus, AZ — B
Brigham Young U–Hawaii, HI — B
California Lutheran U, CA — B
California State U, Chico, CA — B
California State U, Long Beach, CA — B
California State U, Los Angeles, CA — B
California State U, Stanislaus, CA — B
Coll of Santa Fe, NM — B
The Colorado Coll, CO — B
Eastern New Mexico U, NM — B
The Evergreen State Coll, WA — B
Hawai'i Pacific U, HI — B
Idaho State U, ID — B
Lewis-Clark State Coll, ID — B
Montana State U–Billings, MT — B
Naropa U, CO — B
Nevada State Coll at Henderson, NV — B
Rocky Mountain Coll, MT — B

(Music continued)
Saint Mary's Coll of California, CA — B
San Diego Christian Coll, CA — B
San Diego State U, CA — B
San Francisco Art Inst, CA — B
San Jose State U, CA — B
Scripps Coll, CA — B
Sonoma State U, CA — B
Thomas Aquinas Coll, CA — B
U of Alaska Fairbanks, AK — A,B
The U of Arizona, AZ — B
U of California, Berkeley, CA — B
U of California, Davis, CA — B
U of California, Irvine, CA — B
U of California, Los Angeles, CA — B
U of California, Santa Barbara, CA — B
U of Colorado at Denver and Health Sciences Center, CO — B
U of Denver, CO — B
U of Idaho, ID — B
U of Northern Colorado, CO — B
U of Washington, Bothell, WA — B
U of Washington, Tacoma, WA — B
U of Wyoming, WY — B
Utah State U, UT — B

Music
Adams State Coll, CO — B
Albertson Coll of Idaho, ID — B
Arizona State U, AZ — B
Azusa Pacific U, CA — B
Biola U, CA — B
Boise State U, ID — B
Brigham Young U, UT — B
Brigham Young U–Hawaii, HI — A,B
Brigham Young U–Idaho, ID — A
California Baptist U, CA — B
California Inst of the Arts, CA — B
California Lutheran U, CA — B
California Polytechnic State U, San Luis Obispo, CA — B
California State Polytechnic U, Pomona, CA — B
California State U, Chico, CA — B
California State U, Dominguez Hills, CA — B
California State U, Fresno, CA — B
California State U, Fullerton, CA — B
California State U, Long Beach, CA — B
California State U, Los Angeles, CA — B
California State U, Northridge, CA — B
California State U, Sacramento, CA — B
California State U, San Bernardino, CA — B
California State U, Stanislaus, CA — B
Central Washington U, WA — B
Chapman U, CA — B
Claremont McKenna Coll, CA — B
Colorado Christian U, CO — B
The Colorado Coll, CO — B
Colorado State U, CO — B
Colorado State U-Pueblo, CO — B
Concordia U, CA — B
Corban Coll, OR — B
Dixie State Coll of Utah, UT — A
Dominican U of California, CA — B
Eastern New Mexico U, NM — B
Eastern Oregon U, OR — B
Eastern Washington U, WA — B

(Music continued)
Fort Lewis Coll, CO — B
Fresno Pacific U, CA — A,B
George Fox U, OR — B
Gonzaga U, WA — B
Grand Canyon U, AZ — B
Holy Names U, CA — B
Humboldt State U, CA — B
Idaho State U, ID — B
La Sierra U, CA — B
Lewis & Clark Coll, OR — B
Linfield Coll, OR — B
Loyola Marymount U, CA — B
Marylhurst U, OR — B
The Master's Coll and Seminary, CA — B
Mesa State Coll, CO — A,B
Mills Coll, CA — B
Montana State U, MT — B
Montana State U–Billings, MT — B
Mount St. Mary's Coll, CA — B
New Mexico Highlands U, NM — B
Northern Arizona U, AZ — B
Northwest Nazarene U, ID — B
Northwest U, WA — B
Notre Dame de Namur U, CA — B
Occidental Coll, CA — B
Oregon State U, OR — B
Pacific Union Coll, CA — B
Pacific U, OR — B
Pepperdine U, Malibu, CA — B
Pitzer Coll, CA — B
Point Loma Nazarene U, CA — B
Pomona Coll, CA — B
Portland State U, OR — B
Reed Coll, OR — B
Saint Mary's Coll of California, CA — B
San Diego Christian Coll, CA — B
San Francisco Conservatory of Music, CA — B
San Francisco State U, CA — B
San Jose State U, CA — B
Santa Clara U, CA — B
Scripps Coll, CA — B
Seattle Pacific U, WA — B
Sierra Nevada Coll, NV — B
Simpson U, CA — B
Sonoma State U, CA — B
Southern Oregon U, OR — B
Southern Utah U, UT — B
Stanford U, CA — B
U of Alaska Anchorage, AK — B
U of Alaska Fairbanks, AK — B
The U of Arizona, AZ — B
U of California, Berkeley, CA — B
U of California, Davis, CA — B
U of California, Irvine, CA — B
U of California, Los Angeles, CA — B
U of California, Riverside, CA — B
U of California, San Diego, CA — B
U of California, Santa Barbara, CA — B
U of California, Santa Cruz, CA — B
U of Colorado at Boulder, CO — B
U of Colorado at Denver and Health Sciences Center, CO — B
U of Denver, CO — B
U of Hawaii at Hilo, HI — B
U of Hawaii at Manoa, HI — B
U of La Verne, CA — B
The U of Montana, MT — B
U of Nevada, Las Vegas, NV — B
U of Nevada, Reno, NV — B
U of New Orleans, LA — B

U of Northern Colorado, CO	B	U of Denver, CO	B	Marylhurst U, OR	B	U of Puget Sound, WA	B

U of Northern Colorado, CO B
U of Oregon, OR B
U of Portland, OR B
U of Puget Sound, WA B
U of Redlands, CA B
U of San Diego, CA B
U of Southern California, CA B
U of the Pacific, CA B
U of Utah, UT B
U of Washington, WA B
U of Wyoming, WY B
Utah State U, UT B
Utah Valley State Coll, UT A
Vanguard U of Southern
California, CA B
Walla Walla Coll, WA B
Warner Pacific Coll, OR B
Washington State U, WA B
Weber State U, UT B
Western Oregon U, OR B
Western State Coll of
Colorado, CO B
Western Washington U, WA B
Westmont Coll, CA B
Whitman Coll, WA B
Whitworth U, WA B
Willamette U, OR B

Musical Instrument Fabrication and Repair
U of Washington, WA B

Music History, Literature, and Theory
Brigham Young U, UT B
California State U, Fresno, CA B
California State U, Fullerton,
CA B
California State U, Long
Beach, CA B
Eugene Lang Coll The New
School for Liberal Arts, NY B
Loyola Marymount U, CA B
U of California, Los Angeles,
CA B
U of California, San Diego, CA B
U of Idaho, ID B
U of Redlands, CA B
U of the Pacific, CA B
U of Washington, WA B
Western Washington U, WA B

Music Management and Merchandising
Boise State U, ID B
California State U, Sacramento,
CA B
Central Washington U, WA B
Grand Canyon U, AZ B
The Master's Coll and
Seminary, CA B
Northwest Christian Coll, OR B
Southern Oregon U, OR B
U of Idaho, ID B
U of Puget Sound, WA B
U of Southern California, CA B
U of the Pacific, CA B
Warner Pacific Coll, OR B
Western State Coll of
Colorado, CO B

Musicology and Ethnomusicology
Loyola Marymount U, CA B
U of California, Los Angeles,
CA B

U of Denver, CO B
U of Washington, WA B

Music Pedagogy
Brigham Young U, UT B
California State U, Sacramento,
CA B
Holy Names U, CA B

Music Performance
Adams State Coll, CO B
Arizona State U, AZ B
Brigham Young U, UT B
Brigham Young U–Hawaii, HI B
California Baptist U, CA B
California Inst of the Arts, CA B
California State U, Chico, CA B
California State U, Fullerton,
CA B
California State U, Long
Beach, CA B
California State U, Los
Angeles, CA B
California State U, Stanislaus,
CA B
Chapman U, CA B
The Colburn School
Conservatory of Music, CA B
Colorado Christian U, CO B
Colorado State U, CO B
Corban Coll, OR B
Dominican U of California, CA B
Eastern Washington U, WA B
Fort Lewis Coll, CO B
George Fox U, OR B
Holy Names U, CA B
Idaho State U, ID B
Naropa U, CO B
New Mexico State U, NM B
Northern Arizona U, AZ B
Northwest Nazarene U, ID B
Northwest U, WA B
Notre Dame de Namur U, CA B
Pacific U, OR B
Point Loma Nazarene U, CA B
Rocky Mountain Coll, MT B
San Francisco Conservatory of
Music, CA B
San Jose State U, CA B
U of Alaska Anchorage, AK B
The U of Arizona, AZ B
U of California, Irvine, CA B
U of Denver, CO B
U of Idaho, ID B
The U of Montana, MT B
U of Nevada, Reno, NV B
U of New Mexico, NM B
U of Oregon, OR B
U of Puget Sound, WA B
U of Redlands, CA B
U of Southern California, CA B
U of Washington, WA B
U of Wyoming, WY B
Washington State U, WA B
Weber State U, UT B
Willamette U, OR B

Music Related
Brigham Young U, UT B
California Inst of the Arts, CA B
California State U, Chico, CA B
California State U, Sacramento,
CA B
Claremont McKenna Coll, CA B
Coll of Santa Fe, NM B
Colorado Christian U, CO B

Marylhurst U, OR B
San Diego State U, CA B
The U of Arizona, AZ B
U of Southern California, CA B

Music Teacher Education
Arizona State U, AZ B
Bethany U, CA B
Boise State U, ID B
Brigham Young U, UT B
Brigham Young U–Hawaii, HI B
Brigham Young U–Idaho, ID A
California Lutheran U, CA B
California State U, Chico, CA B
California State U, Dominguez
Hills, CA B
California State U, Fresno, CA B
California State U, Fullerton,
CA B
Central Washington U, WA B
Chapman U, CA B
Colorado Christian U, CO B
Colorado State U, CO B
Colorado State U–Pueblo, CO B
Corban Coll, OR B
Eastern New Mexico U, NM B
Eastern Washington U, WA B
Fort Lewis Coll, CO B
Fresno Pacific U, CA B
George Fox U, OR B
Gonzaga U, WA B
Grand Canyon U, AZ B
Hope International U, CA B
Humboldt State U, CA B
Idaho State U, ID B
La Sierra U, CA B
The Master's Coll and
Seminary, CA B
Mesa State Coll, CO B
Montana State U, MT B
Montana State U–Billings, MT B
Mount St. Mary's Coll, CA B
New Mexico Highlands U, NM B
New Mexico State U, NM B
North Carolina Ag and Tech
State U, NC B
Northern Arizona U, AZ B
Northwest Nazarene U, ID B
Northwest U, WA B
Pacific Lutheran U, WA B
Pacific Union Coll, CA B
Pacific U, OR B
Pepperdine U, Malibu, CA B
Point Loma Nazarene U, CA B
Prescott Coll, AZ B
Rocky Mountain Coll, MT B
San Diego Christian Coll, CA B
San Diego State U, CA B
Seattle Pacific U, WA B
Simpson U, CA B
Sonoma State U, CA B
Southern Utah U, UT B
U of Alaska Anchorage, AK B
The U of Arizona, AZ B
U of Colorado at Boulder, CO B
U of Idaho, ID B
The U of Montana, MT B
The U of Montana–Western,
MT B
U of Nevada, Reno, NV B
U of New Mexico, NM B
U of New Orleans, LA B
U of Northern Colorado, CO B
U of Oregon, OR B
U of Portland, OR B

U of Puget Sound, WA B
U of Redlands, CA B
U of Southern California, CA B
U of the Pacific, CA B
U of Utah, UT B
U of Washington, WA B
U of Wyoming, WY B
Utah State U, UT B
Walla Walla Coll, WA B
Warner Pacific Coll, OR B
Washington State U, WA B
Weber State U, UT B
Western State Coll of
Colorado, CO B
Western Washington U, WA B
Whitworth U, WA B

Music Theory and Composition
Arizona State U, AZ B
Brigham Young U, UT B
California Baptist U, CA B
California Inst of the Arts, CA B
California State U, Chico, CA B
California State U, Long
Beach, CA B
California State U, Sacramento,
CA B
Central Washington U, WA B
Chapman U, CA B
Eastern Washington U, WA B
George Fox U, OR B
Loyola Marymount U, CA B
Northwest Nazarene U, ID B
Point Loma Nazarene U, CA B
San Francisco Conservatory of
Music, CA B
U of Idaho, ID B
U of Nevada, Las Vegas, NV B
U of Redlands, CA B
U of Southern California, CA B
U of the Pacific, CA B
U of Washington, WA B
U of Wyoming, WY B
Washington State U, WA B
Willamette U, OR B

Music Therapy
Arizona State U, AZ B
Chapman U, CA B
Colorado State U, CO B
U of the Pacific, CA B
Utah State U, UT B

Natural Resources and Conservation Related
U of Alaska Fairbanks, AK B
U of California, Davis, CA B
Utah State U, UT B

Natural Resources/ Conservation
California State U, Sacramento,
CA B
Coll of Santa Fe, NM B
Dixie State Coll of Utah, UT A
Humboldt State U, CA B
Montana State U, MT B
Prescott Coll, AZ B
U of Alaska Southeast, AK A,B
U of California, Berkeley, CA B
U of California, Davis, CA B
The U of Montana, MT B
U of Nevada, Reno, NV B
U of Wyoming, WY B
Washington State U, WA B

A—associate degree; B—bachelor's degree

Natural Resources Management
Central Washington U, WA — B
U of Hawaii at Manoa, HI — B

Natural Resources Management and Policy
Alaska Pacific U, AK — B
California State U, Chico, CA — B
Chief Dull Knife Coll, MT — A
Coll of Santa Fe, NM — B
Colorado State U, CO — B
Dixie State Coll of Utah, UT — A
Eastern Oregon U, OR — B
Humboldt State U, CA — B
New Mexico Highlands U, NM — B
Oregon State U, OR — B
Prescott Coll, AZ — B
Salish Kootenai Coll, MT — A
U of Alaska Fairbanks, AK — A
U of California, Berkeley, CA — B
U of California, San Diego, CA — B
U of Idaho, ID — B
U of La Verne, CA — B
The U of Montana, MT — B
U of Nevada, Reno, NV — B
U of Washington, WA — B

Natural Sciences
Azusa Pacific U, CA — B
California State U, Fresno, CA — B
California State U, Los Angeles, CA — B
California State U, San Bernardino, CA — B
Concordia U, OR — B
Eastern Washington U, WA — B
The Evergreen State Coll, WA — B
Fresno Pacific U, CA — A,B
Humboldt State U, CA — B
Lewis-Clark State Coll, ID — B
Loyola Marymount U, CA — B
The Master's Coll and Seminary, CA — B
Pepperdine U, Malibu, CA — B
Salish Kootenai Coll, MT — A
San Jose State U, CA — B
U of Alaska Anchorage, AK — B
U of Hawaii at Hilo, HI — B
U of La Verne, CA — B
U of Puget Sound, WA — B
Utah Valley State Coll, UT — A
Western Oregon U, OR — B

Naval Architecture and Marine Engineering
U of New Orleans, LA — B

Navy/Marine Corps ROTC/ Naval Science
U of Washington, WA — B

Near and Middle Eastern Studies
Claremont McKenna Coll, CA — B
Portland State U, OR — B
The U of Arizona, AZ — B
U of California, Berkeley, CA — B
U of California, Los Angeles, CA — B
U of California, Santa Barbara, CA — B
U of Utah, UT — B
U of Washington, WA — B

Neurobiology and Neurophysiology
U of California, Davis, CA — B
U of California, Los Angeles, CA — B

Neuroscience
Brigham Young U, UT — B
The Colorado Coll, CO — B
Montana State U, MT — B
Pitzer Coll, CA — B
Pomona Coll, CA — B
Regis U, CO — B
Scripps Coll, CA — B
U of California, Irvine, CA — B
U of California, Los Angeles, CA — B
U of California, Riverside, CA — B
U of Southern California, CA — B
Washington State U, WA — B
Westmont Coll, CA — B

Nonprofit Management
Fresno Pacific U, CA — B

Norwegian
Brigham Young U, UT — B

Nuclear Engineering
Oregon State U, OR — B
The U of Arizona, AZ — B
U of California, Berkeley, CA — B
U of New Mexico, NM — B

Nuclear Medical Technology
California State U, Dominguez Hills, CA — B
U of Nevada, Las Vegas, NV — B
Weber State U, UT — B

Nursing Administration
U of Phoenix–Denver Campus, CO — B
U of San Francisco, CA — B

Nursing Assistant/Aide and Patient Care Assistant
Montana Tech of The U of Montana, MT — A

Nursing (Licensed Practical/ Vocational Nurse Training)
Lewis-Clark State Coll, ID — A
Montana State U–Billings, MT — A
The U of Montana, MT — A
U of Phoenix–Hawaii Campus, HI — B
U of Phoenix–Phoenix Campus, AZ — B
U of Phoenix–Sacramento Valley Campus, CA — B

Nursing (Registered Nurse Training)
Arizona State U, AZ — B
Azusa Pacific U, CA — B
Biola U, CA — B
Boise State U, ID — A,B
Brigham Young U, UT — B
Brigham Young U–Idaho, ID — A
California State U, Chico, CA — B
California State U, Dominguez Hills, CA — B
California State U, Fresno, CA — B
California State U, Fullerton, CA — B
California State U, Long Beach, CA — B
California State U, Los Angeles, CA — B
California State U, Northridge, CA — B
California State U, Sacramento, CA — B
California State U, San Bernardino, CA — B
California State U, Stanislaus, CA — B
Colorado State U-Pueblo, CO — B
Concordia U, OR — B
Dixie State Coll of Utah, UT — A,B
Dominican U of California, CA — B
Eastern New Mexico U, NM — B
Eastern Washington U, WA — B
George Fox U, OR — B
Gonzaga U, WA — B
Grand Canyon U, AZ — B
Great Basin Coll, NV — A,B
Hawai'i Pacific U, HI — B
Holy Names U, CA — B
Humboldt State U, CA — B
Idaho State U, ID — B
International Inst of the Americas, Phoenix, AZ — A
Lewis-Clark State Coll, ID — B
Loma Linda U, CA — A,B
Mesa State Coll, CO — A,B
Montana State U, MT — B
Montana Tech of The U of Montana, MT — A
Mount St. Mary's Coll, CA — A,B
Nevada State Coll at Henderson, NV — B
New Mexico State U, NM — B
North Carolina Ag and Tech State U, NC — B
Northern Arizona U, AZ — B
Northwest Nazarene U, ID — B
Northwest U, WA — B
Oregon Health & Science U, OR — B
Pacific Lutheran U, WA — B
Pacific Union Coll, CA — A,B
Point Loma Nazarene U, CA — B
Regis U, CO — B
Saint Mary's Coll of California, CA — B
Salish Kootenai Coll, MT — A
Samuel Merritt Coll, CA — B
San Diego State U, CA — B
San Francisco State U, CA — B
San Jose State U, CA — B
Seattle Pacific U, WA — B
Seattle U, WA — B
Sonoma State U, CA — B
Southern Oregon U, OR — B
U of Alaska Anchorage, AK — A,B
The U of Arizona, AZ — B
U of California, Los Angeles, CA — B
U of Colorado at Colorado Springs, CO — B
U of Colorado at Denver and Health Sciences Center, CO — B
U of Hawaii at Hilo, HI — B
U of Hawaii at Manoa, HI — B
U of Nevada, Las Vegas, NV — B
U of Nevada, Reno, NV — B
U of New Mexico, NM — B
U of New Mexico–Gallup, NM — A,B
U of Northern Colorado, CO — B
U of Phoenix–Denver Campus, CO — B
U of Phoenix–Hawaii Campus, HI — B

U of Phoenix–New Mexico Campus, NM — B
U of Phoenix–Oregon Campus, OR — B
U of Phoenix–Phoenix Campus, AZ — B
U of Phoenix–San Diego Campus, CA — B
U of Phoenix–Southern Arizona Campus, AZ — B
U of Phoenix–Southern California Campus, CA — B
U of Phoenix–Southern Colorado Campus, CO — B
U of Phoenix–Utah Campus, UT — B
U of Portland, OR — B
U of San Francisco, CA — B
U of Utah, UT — B
U of Washington, WA — B
U of Washington, Bothell, WA — B
U of Washington, Tacoma, WA — B
U of Wyoming, WY — B
Utah Valley State Coll, UT — A,B
Walla Walla Coll, WA — B
Warner Pacific Coll, OR — A
Washington State U, WA — B
Weber State U, UT — A,B
Westminster Coll, UT — B
Whitworth U, WA — B

Nursing Related
California State U, Fullerton, CA — B
San Diego State U, CA — B
U of California, Los Angeles, CA — B

Nursing Science
Holy Names U, CA — B
National U, CA — A,B
U of Phoenix–Bay Area Campus, CA — B
U of Phoenix–Central Valley Campus, CA — B
U of Phoenix–Denver Campus, CO — B
U of Phoenix–Hawaii Campus, HI — B
U of Phoenix–New Mexico Campus, NM — B
U of Phoenix–Sacramento Valley Campus, CA — B
U of Phoenix–Southern Arizona Campus, AZ — B

Nutritional Sciences
California State U, Los Angeles, CA — B

Nutrition Science
Washington State U, WA — B

Nutrition Sciences
Brigham Young U, UT — B
Chapman U, CA — B
The U of Arizona, AZ — B
U of California, Berkeley, CA — B
U of California, Davis, CA — B
U of Nevada, Las Vegas, NV — B

Occupational Health and Industrial Hygiene
California State U, Fresno, CA — B
Montana Tech of The U of Montana, MT — B

Occupational Safety and Health Technology

California State U, Fresno, CA	B
Central Washington U, WA	B
Montana Tech of The U of Montana, MT	A,B
National U, CA	B
North Carolina Ag and Tech State U, NC	B
Oregon State U, OR	B
Utah State U, UT	B

Occupational Therapist Assistant

Idaho State U, ID	A
Loma Linda U, CA	A
Mount St. Mary's Coll, CA	A

Occupational Therapy

Brigham Young U–Idaho, ID	A
Dominican U of California, CA	B
Loma Linda U, CA	B
San Jose State U, CA	B
U of Southern California, CA	B
U of Utah, UT	B
U of Washington, WA	B

Ocean Engineering

California State U, Long Beach, CA	B

Oceanography (Chemical and Physical)

Hawai'i Pacific U, HI	B
Humboldt State U, CA	B
U of Washington, WA	B

Office Management

Central Washington U, WA	B
Chief Dull Knife Coll, MT	A
Great Basin Coll, NV	A
Weber State U, UT	B

Office Occupations and Clerical Services

U of Alaska Fairbanks, AK	A

Operations Management

Boise State U, ID	B
California State U, Chico, CA	B
California State U, Long Beach, CA	B
California State U, Sacramento, CA	B
Central Washington U, WA	B
Great Basin Coll, NV	A
National U, CA	B
Remington Coll–Colorado Springs Campus, CO	B
San Diego State U, CA	B
Seattle U, WA	B
The U of Arizona, AZ	B
U of Idaho, ID	B
U of Phoenix–Bay Area Campus, CA	B
U of Phoenix–Denver Campus, CO	
U of Phoenix–Hawaii Campus, HI	B
U of Phoenix–Las Vegas Campus, NV	B
U of Phoenix–Phoenix Campus, AZ	B
U of Phoenix–Sacramento Valley Campus, CA	B
U of Phoenix–Southern Colorado Campus, CO	

U of Phoenix–Washington Campus, WA	B
Utah State U, UT	B
Utah Valley State Coll, UT	B
Washington State U, WA	B
Western Washington U, WA	B

Operations Research

California State U, Fullerton, CA	B
United States Air Force Academy, CO	B
U of California, Berkeley, CA	B
U of Denver, CO	B

Optical Sciences

The U of Arizona, AZ	B

Organizational Behavior

Chapman U, CA	B
National U, CA	B
Pitzer Coll, CA	B
Scripps Coll, CA	B
Simpson U, CA	B
U of Phoenix–Bay Area Campus, CA	B
U of Phoenix–Hawaii Campus, HI	B
U of Phoenix–Las Vegas Campus, NV	B
U of Phoenix–Phoenix Campus, AZ	B
U of Phoenix–Sacramento Valley Campus, CA	B
U of Phoenix–Washington Campus, WA	B
U of San Francisco, CA	B
Woodbury U, CA	B

Organizational Communication

Brigham Young U, UT	B
California State U, Chico, CA	B
California State U, Sacramento, CA	B
Eastern Washington U, WA	B
Northwest U, WA	B
Western State Coll of Colorado, CO	B

Ornamental Horticulture

Brigham Young U–Idaho, ID	A
California Polytechnic State U, San Luis Obispo, CA	B
California State Polytechnic U, Pomona, CA	B
California State U, Fresno, CA	B
Utah State U, UT	A,B

Orthotics/Prosthetics

U of Washington, WA	B

Pacific Area/Pacific Rim Studies

Brigham Young U–Hawaii, HI	B
Claremont McKenna Coll, CA	B
U of Hawaii at Manoa, HI	B

Painting

Academy of Art U, CA	A,B
Art Center Coll of Design, CA	B
Brigham Young U, UT	B
California Coll of the Arts, CA	B
California State U, Fullerton, CA	B
California State U, Long Beach, CA	B
Coll of Santa Fe, NM	B
Colorado State U, CO	B

Dixie State Coll of Utah, UT	A
Northwest Nazarene U, ID	B
Rocky Mountain Coll of Art & Design, CO	B
San Francisco Art Inst, CA	B
U of Dallas, TX	B
U of Oregon, OR	B
U of San Francisco, CA	B
U of Washington, WA	B
Western Washington U, WA	B

Paralegal/Legal Assistant

Argosy U, Orange County, CA	A
Utah Valley State Coll, UT	A,B

Parks, Recreation and Leisure

Alaska Pacific U, AK	B
Arizona State U, AZ	B
Arizona State U at the West campus, AZ	B
Brigham Young U, UT	B
Brigham Young U–Idaho, ID	A
California Polytechnic State U, San Luis Obispo, CA	B
California State U, Chico, CA	B
California State U, Dominguez Hills, CA	B
California State U, Fresno, CA	B
California State U, Long Beach, CA	B
California State U, Northridge, CA	B
California State U, Sacramento, CA	B
Central Washington U, WA	B
Colorado State U–Pueblo, CO	B
Eastern Washington U, WA	B
Humboldt State U, CA	B
North Carolina Ag and Tech State U, NC	B
Northern Arizona U, AZ	B
Northwest Nazarene U, ID	B
Oregon State U, OR	B
Pacific Union Coll, CA	B
Prescott Coll, AZ	B
San Diego State U, CA	B
San Francisco State U, CA	B
San Jose State U, CA	B
U of Hawaii at Manoa, HI	B
U of Idaho, ID	B
The U of Montana, MT	B
U of Nevada, Las Vegas, NV	B
U of Nevada, Reno, NV	B
U of New Mexico, NM	B
U of Utah, UT	B
Utah State U, UT	B
Utah Valley State Coll, UT	A,B
Western State Coll of Colorado, CO	B
Western Washington U, WA	B

Parks, Recreation and Leisure Facilities Management

California State U, Chico, CA	B
California State U, Fresno, CA	B
California State U, Sacramento, CA	B
Colorado State U, CO	B
Eastern Washington U, WA	B
Humboldt State U, CA	B
Johnson & Wales U, CO	B
New Mexico State U, NM	B
Oregon State U, OR	B
U of Northern Colorado, CO	B
U of Utah, UT	B

U of Wyoming, WY	B
Western State Coll of Colorado, CO	B

Parks, Recreation, and Leisure Related

Brigham Young U, UT	B
Utah State U, UT	B
Washington State U, WA	B

Pastoral Counseling and Specialized Ministries Related

Multnomah Bible Coll and Biblical Seminary, OR	B

Pastoral Studies/Counseling

Bethany U, CA	B
Biola U, CA	B
Boise Bible Coll, ID	A,B
Coll of Santa Fe, NM	B
Corban Coll, OR	B
Eugene Bible Coll, OR	B
Fresno Pacific U, CA	B
George Fox U, OR	B
Marylhurst U, OR	B
The Master's Coll and Seminary, CA	B
Multnomah Bible Coll and Biblical Seminary, OR	B
Nazarene Bible Coll, CO	B
Northwest Nazarene U, ID	B
Northwest U, WA	B
Pacific Union Coll, CA	B
Patten U, CA	B
San Diego Christian Coll, CA	B
Vanguard U of Southern California, CA	B
Warner Pacific Coll, OR	B

Pathology/Experimental Pathology

U of California, Los Angeles, CA	B

Peace Studies and Conflict Resolution

Chapman U, CA	B
U of California, Berkeley, CA	B
U of California, Santa Cruz, CA	B
U of Hawaii at Manoa, HI	B
Whitworth U, WA	B

Perfusion Technology

Boise State U, ID	A

Petroleum Engineering

California State Polytechnic U, Pomona, CA	B
Colorado School of Mines, CO	B
Montana Tech of The U of Montana, MT	B
New Mexico Inst of Mining and Technology, NM	B
Stanford U, CA	B
U of Alaska Fairbanks, AK	B
U of Southern California, CA	B

Petroleum Technology

Montana State U–Billings, MT	A
Montana Tech of The U of Montana, MT	A
U of Alaska Anchorage, AK	A

Pharmacology

U of California, Santa Barbara, CA	B

A—associate degree; B—bachelor's degree

Pharmacology and Toxicology

Washington State U, WA	B

Pharmacy

The U of Montana, MT	B
U of New Mexico, NM	B
U of the Pacific, CA	B
U of Utah, UT	B
U of Washington, WA	B

Pharmacy, Pharmaceutical Sciences, and Administration Related

U of Utah, UT	B

Pharmacy Technician

Idaho State U, ID	A
The U of Montana, MT	B

Philosophy

Albertson Coll of Idaho, ID	B
Arizona State U, AZ	B
Azusa Pacific U, CA	B
Biola U, CA	B
Boise State U, ID	B
Brigham Young U, UT	B
California Baptist U, CA	B
California Inst of Technology, CA	B
California Lutheran U, CA	B
California Polytechnic State U, San Luis Obispo, CA	
California State Polytechnic U, Pomona, CA	B
California State U, Chico, CA	B
California State U, Dominguez Hills, CA	B
California State U, Fresno, CA	B
California State U, Fullerton, CA	B
California State U, Long Beach, CA	B
California State U, Los Angeles, CA	B
California State U, Northridge, CA	B
California State U, Sacramento, CA	B
California State U, San Bernardino, CA	B
California State U, Stanislaus, CA	B
Central Washington U, WA	B
Chapman U, CA	B
Claremont McKenna Coll, CA	B
The Colorado Coll, CO	B
Colorado State U, CO	B
Dixie State Coll of Utah, UT	A
Dominican School of Philosophy and Theology, CA	B
Eastern Washington U, WA	B
Eugene Lang Coll The New School for Liberal Arts, NY	B
Fort Lewis Coll, CO	B
George Fox U, OR	B
Gonzaga U, WA	B
Holy Names U, CA	B
Humboldt State U, CA	B
Idaho State U, ID	B
Lewis & Clark Coll, OR	B
Linfield Coll, OR	B
Loyola Marymount U, CA	B
Mills Coll, CA	B
Montana State U, MT	B
Mount St. Mary's Coll, CA	B
New Mexico State U, NM	B
Northern Arizona U, AZ	B
Northwest Nazarene U, ID	B
Northwest U, WA	B
Notre Dame de Namur U, CA	B
Occidental Coll, CA	B
Oregon State U, OR	B
Pacific Lutheran U, WA	B
Pacific U, OR	B
Pepperdine U, Malibu, CA	B
Pitzer Coll, CA	B
Point Loma Nazarene U, CA	B
Pomona Coll, CA	B
Portland State U, OR	B
Prescott Coll, AZ	B
Reed Coll, OR	B
Regis U, CO	B
Rocky Mountain Coll, MT	B
St. John's Coll, NM	B
Saint Mary's Coll of California, CA	B
San Diego State U, CA	B
San Francisco State U, CA	B
San Jose State U, CA	B
Santa Clara U, CA	B
Scripps Coll, CA	B
Seattle Pacific U, WA	B
Seattle U, WA	B
Sonoma State U, CA	B
Stanford U, CA	B
U of Alaska Fairbanks, AK	B
The U of Arizona, AZ	B
U of California, Berkeley, CA	B
U of California, Davis, CA	B
U of California, Irvine, CA	B
U of California, Los Angeles, CA	B
U of California, Riverside, CA	B
U of California, San Diego, CA	B
U of California, Santa Barbara, CA	B
U of California, Santa Cruz, CA	B
U of Colorado at Boulder, CO	B
U of Colorado at Colorado Springs, CO	B
U of Colorado at Denver and Health Sciences Center, CO	B
U of Dallas, TX	B
U of Denver, CO	B
U of Hawaii at Hilo, HI	B
U of Hawaii at Manoa, HI	B
U of Hawaii–West Oahu, HI	B
U of Idaho, ID	B
U of La Verne, CA	B
The U of Montana, MT	B
U of Nevada, Las Vegas, NV	B
U of Nevada, Reno, NV	B
U of New Mexico, NM	B
U of New Orleans, LA	B
U of Northern Colorado, CO	B
U of Oregon, OR	B
U of Portland, OR	B
U of Puget Sound, WA	B
U of Redlands, CA	B
U of San Diego, CA	B
U of San Francisco, CA	B
U of Southern California, CA	B
U of the Pacific, CA	B
U of the West, CA	B
U of Utah, UT	B
U of Washington, WA	B
U of Wyoming, WY	B
Utah State U, UT	B
Utah Valley State Coll, UT	A,B
Walla Walla Coll, WA	B
Washington State U, WA	B
Western Oregon U, OR	B
Western Washington U, WA	B
Westminster Coll, UT	B
Westmont Coll, CA	B
Whitman Coll, WA	B
Whitworth U, WA	B
Willamette U, OR	B

Philosophy and Religious Studies Related

California State U, Sacramento, CA	B
Claremont McKenna Coll, CA	B
Holy Names U, CA	B
Point Loma Nazarene U, CA	B
St. John's Coll, NM	B

Philosophy Related

Claremont McKenna Coll, CA	B
St. John's Coll, NM	B
U of Southern California, CA	B

Photographic and Film/Video Technology

Dixie State Coll of Utah, UT	A

Photography

Academy of Art U, CA	A,B
Art Center Coll of Design, CA	B
The Art Inst of Colorado, CO	B
The Art Inst of Seattle, WA	A
Brigham Young U, UT	B
Brigham Young U–Idaho, ID	A
California Coll of the Arts, CA	B
California Inst of the Arts, CA	B
California State U, Fullerton, CA	B
California State U, Long Beach, CA	B
California State U, Sacramento, CA	B
Coll of Santa Fe, NM	B
Colorado State U, CO	B
Dixie State Coll of Utah, UT	A
Northern Arizona U, AZ	B
Otis Coll of Art and Design, CA	B
Pacific Union Coll, CA	A
Prescott Coll, AZ	B
San Francisco Art Inst, CA	B
Seattle U, WA	B
U of California, Santa Cruz, CA	B
U of Idaho, ID	B
U of Oregon, OR	B
U of Washington, WA	B
Weber State U, UT	B

Physical Education Teaching and Coaching

Albertson Coll of Idaho, ID	B
Azusa Pacific U, CA	B
Biola U, CA	B
Boise State U, ID	B
Brigham Young U, UT	B
Brigham Young U–Hawaii, HI	B
Brigham Young U–Idaho, ID	A
California Lutheran U, CA	B
California Polytechnic State U, San Luis Obispo, CA	
California State Polytechnic U, Pomona, CA	B
California State U, Chico, CA	B
California State U, Dominguez Hills, CA	B
California State U, Fresno, CA	B
California State U, Fullerton, CA	B
California State U, Long Beach, CA	B
California State U, San Bernardino, CA	B
California State U, Stanislaus, CA	B
Central Washington U, WA	B
Coll of the Southwest, NM	B
Colorado State U-Pueblo, CO	B
Concordia U, OR	B
Corban Coll, OR	B
Dixie State Coll of Utah, UT	A
Eastern New Mexico U, NM	B
Eastern Oregon U, OR	B
Eastern Washington U, WA	B
Fort Lewis Coll, CO	B
Fresno Pacific U, CA	A,B
George Fox U, OR	B
Gonzaga U, WA	B
Grand Canyon U, AZ	B
Humboldt State U, CA	B
Idaho State U, ID	B
Lewis-Clark State Coll, ID	B
The Master's Coll and Seminary, CA	B
Mesa State Coll, CO	B
Montana State U–Billings, MT	B
New Mexico Highlands U, NM	B
New Mexico State U, NM	B
North Carolina Ag and Tech State U, NC	B
Northern Arizona U, AZ	B
Northwest Nazarene U, ID	B
Northwest U, WA	B
Oregon State U, OR	B
Pacific Lutheran U, WA	B
Pacific Union Coll, CA	B
Pepperdine U, Malibu, CA	B
Prescott Coll, AZ	B
Rocky Mountain Coll, MT	B
San Diego Christian Coll, CA	B
San Francisco State U, CA	B
Seattle Pacific U, WA	B
Sonoma State U, CA	B
Southern Oregon U, OR	B
Southern Utah U, UT	B
U of Alaska Anchorage, AK	B
The U of Arizona, AZ	B
U of Great Falls, MT	B
U of Hawaii at Manoa, HI	B
U of Idaho, ID	B
U of La Verne, CA	B
The U of Montana, MT	B
The U of Montana–Western, MT	B
U of Nevada, Las Vegas, NV	B
U of Nevada, Reno, NV	B
U of New Mexico, NM	B
U of New Mexico–Gallup, NM	A
U of New Orleans, LA	B
U of San Francisco, CA	B
U of Utah, UT	B
U of Wyoming, WY	B
Utah State U, UT	B
Utah Valley State Coll, UT	B
Vanguard U of Southern California, CA	B
Walla Walla Coll, WA	B
Warner Pacific Coll, OR	B
Washington State U, WA	B
Weber State U, UT	B
Western State Coll of Colorado, CO	B
Western Washington U, WA	B
Westmont Coll, CA	B
Whitworth U, WA	B

Physical Sciences

Biola U, CA	B

Brigham Young U–Hawaii, HI — B
Brigham Young U–Idaho, ID — A
California Polytechnic State U, San Luis Obispo, CA — B
California State U, Sacramento, CA — B
California State U, Stanislaus, CA — B
Colorado State U, CO — B
Concordia U, OR — B
Eastern Washington U, WA — B
The Evergreen State Coll, WA — B
Grand Canyon U, AZ — B
Humboldt State U, CA — B
La Sierra U, CA — B
Linfield Coll, OR — B
The Master's Coll and Seminary, CA — B
Mesa State Coll, CO — B
New Mexico Inst of Mining and Technology, NM — B
Northern Arizona U, AZ — B
Oregon State U, OR — B
Pacific Union Coll, CA — B
St. John's Coll, NM — B
San Diego State U, CA — B
San Francisco State U, CA — B
Southern Utah U, UT — B
U of California, Berkeley, CA — B
U of New Mexico–Gallup, NM — A
U of Southern California, CA — B
U of the Pacific, CA — B
U of Utah, UT — B
Utah Valley State Coll, UT — A
Warner Pacific Coll, OR — B
Washington State U, WA — B

Physical Sciences Related
New Mexico Inst of Mining and Technology, NM — B
U of California, Davis, CA — B
U of Utah, UT — B

Physical Therapist Assistant
Idaho State U, ID — A
Loma Linda U, CA — A
Mount St. Mary's Coll, CA — A

Physical Therapy
Brigham Young U–Idaho, ID — A
California State U, Fresno, CA — B
Eastern Washington U, WA — B
Hope International U, CA — B
Northwest Nazarene U, ID — B
The U of Montana, MT — B
U of Utah, UT — B
U of Washington, WA — B
Vanguard U of Southern California, CA — B

Physician Assistant
Boise State U, ID — B
California State U, Dominguez Hills, CA — B
Rocky Mountain Coll, MT — B
U of New Mexico, NM — B
U of Washington, WA — B

Physics
Albertson Coll of Idaho, ID — B
Arizona State U, AZ — B
Azusa Pacific U, CA — B
Boise State U, ID — B
Brigham Young U, UT — B
Brigham Young U–Idaho, ID — A
California Inst of Technology, CA — B

California Lutheran U, CA — B
California Polytechnic State U, San Luis Obispo, CA — B
California State Polytechnic U, Pomona, CA — B
California State U, Chico, CA — B
California State U, Dominguez Hills, CA — B
California State U, Fresno, CA — B
California State U, Fullerton, CA — B
California State U, Long Beach, CA — B
California State U, Los Angeles, CA — B
California State U, Northridge, CA — B
California State U, Sacramento, CA — B
California State U, San Bernardino, CA — B
California State U, Stanislaus, CA — B
Central Washington U, WA — B
Claremont McKenna Coll, CA — B
The Colorado Coll, CO — B
Colorado State U, CO — B
Colorado State U-Pueblo, CO — B
Dixie State Coll of Utah, UT — A
Eastern New Mexico U, NM — B
Eastern Oregon U, OR — B
Eastern Washington U, WA — B
Fort Lewis Coll, CO — B
Gonzaga U, WA — B
Great Basin Coll, NV — A
Harvey Mudd Coll, CA — B
Humboldt State U, CA — B
Idaho State U, ID — A,B
Lewis & Clark Coll, OR — B
Linfield Coll, OR — B
Loyola Marymount U, CA — B
Mesa State Coll, CO — A,B
Montana State U, MT — B
New Mexico Inst of Mining and Technology, NM — B
New Mexico State U, NM — B
North Carolina Ag and Tech State U, NC — B
Northern Arizona U, AZ — B
Northwest Nazarene U, ID — B
Occidental Coll, CA — B
Oregon State U, OR — B
Pacific Union Coll, CA — B
Pacific U, OR — B
Pitzer Coll, CA — B
Point Loma Nazarene U, CA — B
Pomona Coll, CA — B
Portland State U, OR — B
Reed Coll, OR — B
St. John's Coll, NM — B
Saint Mary's Coll of California, CA — B
San Diego State U, CA — B
San Francisco State U, CA — B
San Jose State U, CA — B
Santa Clara U, CA — B
Scripps Coll, CA — B
Seattle Pacific U, WA — B
Seattle U, WA — B
Sonoma State U, CA — B
Southern Oregon U, OR — B
Stanford U, CA — B
United States Air Force Academy, CO — B
U of Alaska Fairbanks, AK — B

The U of Arizona, AZ — B
U of California, Berkeley, CA — B
U of California, Davis, CA — B
U of California, Irvine, CA — B
U of California, Los Angeles, CA — B
U of California, Riverside, CA — B
U of California, San Diego, CA — B
U of California, Santa Barbara, CA — B
U of California, Santa Cruz, CA — B
U of Colorado at Boulder, CO — B
U of Colorado at Colorado Springs, CO — B
U of Colorado at Denver and Health Sciences Center, CO — B
U of Dallas, TX — B
U of Denver, CO — B
U of Hawaii at Hilo, HI — B
U of Hawaii at Manoa, HI — B
U of Idaho, ID — B
U of La Verne, CA — B
The U of Montana, MT — B
U of Nevada, Las Vegas, NV — B
U of Nevada, Reno, NV — B
U of New Mexico, NM — B
U of New Orleans, LA — B
U of Northern Colorado, CO — B
U of Oregon, OR — B
U of Portland, OR — B
U of Puget Sound, WA — B
U of Redlands, CA — B
U of San Diego, CA — B
U of San Francisco, CA — B
U of Southern California, CA — B
U of the Pacific, CA — B
U of Utah, UT — B
U of Washington, WA — B
U of Wyoming, WY — B
Utah State U, UT — B
Utah Valley State Coll, UT — A,B
Walla Walla Coll, WA — B
Washington State U, WA — B
Weber State U, UT — B
Western State Coll of Colorado, CO — B
Western Washington U, WA — B
Westminster Coll, UT — B
Westmont Coll, CA — B
Whitman Coll, WA — B
Whitworth U, WA — B
Willamette U, OR — B

Physics Related
Brigham Young U, UT — B
California State U, Chico, CA — B
Embry-Riddle Aeronautical U, AZ — B
Northern Arizona U, AZ — B
U of California, Davis, CA — B
U of Nevada, Las Vegas, NV — B

Physics Teacher Education
Brigham Young U, UT — B
Brigham Young U–Hawaii, HI — B
Colorado State U, CO — B
Eastern Washington U, WA — B
Northern Arizona U, AZ — B
The U of Arizona, AZ — B
U of California, San Diego, CA — B
U of Utah, UT — B
Utah State U, UT — B
Weber State U, UT — B

Physiological Psychology/Psychobiology
Claremont McKenna Coll, CA — B
Holy Names U, CA — B
Hope International U, CA — B
La Sierra U, CA — B
Mills Coll, CA — B
Occidental Coll, CA — B
Saint Mary's Coll of California, CA — B
Scripps Coll, CA — B
U of California, Los Angeles, CA — B
U of California, Riverside, CA — B
U of California, Santa Cruz, CA — B
U of Southern California, CA — B

Physiology
Brigham Young U, UT — B
California State U, Long Beach, CA — B
San Jose State U, CA — B
The U of Arizona, AZ — B
U of California, Los Angeles, CA — B
U of California, Santa Barbara, CA — B
U of Oregon, OR — B

Piano and Organ
Brigham Young U, UT — B
Brigham Young U–Hawaii, HI — B
Brigham Young U–Idaho, ID — A
California Inst of the Arts, CA — B
California State U, Chico, CA — B
California State U, Fullerton, CA — B
California State U, Sacramento, CA — B
Central Washington U, WA — B
The Colburn School Conservatory of Music, CA — B
Eastern Washington U, WA — B
Grand Canyon U, AZ — B
The Master's Coll and Seminary, CA — B
Notre Dame de Namur U, CA — B
Pacific Lutheran U, WA — B
Pacific Union Coll, CA — B
San Francisco Conservatory of Music, CA — B
U of Redlands, CA — B
U of the Pacific, CA — B
U of Washington, WA — B
Walla Walla Coll, WA — B
Weber State U, UT — B
Whitworth U, WA — B
Willamette U, OR — B

Planetary Astronomy and Science
California Inst of Technology, CA — B

Plant Genetics
Brigham Young U, UT — B

Plant Pathology/Phytopathology
Dixie State Coll of Utah, UT — A
New Mexico State U, NM — B

Plant Protection
U of Hawaii at Manoa, HI — B

A—associate degree; B—bachelor's degree

Plant Protection and Integrated Pest Management

California State Polytechnic U, Pomona, CA	B
Dixie State Coll of Utah, UT	A
Washington State U, WA	B

Plant Sciences

California State U, Fresno, CA	B
Colorado State U, CO	B
Montana State U, MT	B
The U of Arizona, AZ	B
U of California, Los Angeles, CA	B
U of California, Santa Cruz, CA	B
U of Idaho, ID	B
Utah State U, UT	B
Washington State U, WA	B

Plant Sciences Related

Utah State U, UT	B

Plastics Engineering Technology

Brigham Young U–Idaho, ID	A
Western Washington U, WA	B

Playwriting and Screenwriting

Brigham Young U, UT	B
Loyola Marymount U, CA	B
U of Southern California, CA	B

Political Science and Government

Adams State Coll, CO	B
Albertson Coll of Idaho, ID	B
Arizona State U, AZ	B
Arizona State U at the West campus, AZ	B
Azusa Pacific U, CA	B
Boise State U, ID	B
Brigham Young U, UT	B
Brigham Young U–Hawaii, HI	B
Brigham Young U–Idaho, ID	A
California Baptist U, CA	B
California Inst of Technology, CA	B
California Lutheran U, CA	B
California Polytechnic State U, San Luis Obispo, CA	B
California State Polytechnic U, Pomona, CA	B
California State U Channel Islands, CA	B
California State U, Chico, CA	B
California State U, Dominguez Hills, CA	B
California State U, Fresno, CA	B
California State U, Fullerton, CA	B
California State U, Long Beach, CA	B
California State U, Los Angeles, CA	B
California State U, Northridge, CA	B
California State U, Sacramento, CA	B
California State U, San Bernardino, CA	B
California State U, San Marcos, CA	B
California State U, Stanislaus, CA	B
Central Washington U, WA	B
Chapman U, CA	B
Claremont McKenna Coll, CA	B

Coll of Santa Fe, NM	B
Colorado Christian U, CO	B
The Colorado Coll, CO	B
Colorado State U, CO	B
Colorado State U-Pueblo, CO	B
Concordia U, CA	B
Dixie State Coll of Utah, UT	A
Dominican U of California, CA	B
Eastern New Mexico U, NM	B
Eastern Washington U, WA	B
Eugene Lang Coll The New School for Liberal Arts, NY	B
The Evergreen State Coll, WA	B
Fort Lewis Coll, CO	B
Fresno Pacific U, CA	A,B
Gonzaga U, WA	B
Grand Canyon U, AZ	B
Hawai'i Pacific U, HI	B
Humboldt State U, CA	B
Idaho State U, ID	A,B
La Sierra U, CA	B
Lewis & Clark Coll, OR	B
Linfield Coll, OR	B
Loyola Marymount U, CA	B
The Master's Coll and Seminary, CA	B
Mesa State Coll, CO	B
Mills Coll, CA	B
Montana State U, MT	B
Mount St. Mary's Coll, CA	B
New Mexico Highlands U, NM	B
New Mexico State U, NM	B
North Carolina Ag and Tech State U, NC	B
Northern Arizona U, AZ	B
Northwest Nazarene U, ID	B
Northwest U, WA	B
Notre Dame de Namur U, CA	B
Occidental Coll, CA	B
Oregon State U, OR	B
Pacific Lutheran U, WA	B
Pacific Union Coll, CA	B
Pacific U, OR	B
Pepperdine U, Malibu, CA	B
Pitzer Coll, CA	B
Point Loma Nazarene U, CA	B
Pomona Coll, CA	B
Portland State U, OR	B
Prescott Coll, AZ	B
Reed Coll, OR	B
Regis U, CO	B
Rocky Mountain Coll, MT	B
Saint Mary's Coll of California, CA	B
San Diego State U, CA	B
San Francisco State U, CA	B
San Jose State U, CA	B
Santa Clara U, CA	B
Scripps Coll, CA	B
Seattle Pacific U, WA	B
Seattle U, WA	B
Sonoma State U, CA	B
Southern Oregon U, OR	B
Southern Utah U, UT	B
Stanford U, CA	B
United States Air Force Academy, CO	B
U of Alaska Anchorage, AK	B
U of Alaska Fairbanks, AK	B
The U of Arizona, AZ	B
U of California, Berkeley, CA	B
U of California, Davis, CA	B
U of California, Irvine, CA	B
U of California, Los Angeles, CA	B
U of California, Riverside, CA	B

U of California, San Diego, CA	B
U of California, Santa Barbara, CA	B
U of California, Santa Cruz, CA	B
U of Colorado at Boulder, CO	B
U of Colorado at Colorado Springs, CO	B
U of Colorado at Denver and Health Sciences Center, CO	B
U of Denver, CO	B
U of Great Falls, MT	B
U of Hawaii at Hilo, HI	B
U of Hawaii at Manoa, HI	B
U of Hawaii–West Oahu, HI	B
U of Idaho, ID	B
U of Judaism, CA	B
U of La Verne, CA	B
U of Nevada, Las Vegas, NV	B
U of Nevada, Reno, NV	B
U of New Mexico, NM	B
U of New Orleans, LA	B
U of Northern Colorado, CO	B
U of Oregon, OR	B
U of Portland, OR	B
U of Puget Sound, WA	B
U of Redlands, CA	B
U of San Diego, CA	B
U of San Francisco, CA	B
U of Southern California, CA	B
U of the Pacific, CA	B
U of Utah, UT	B
U of Washington, WA	B
U of Wyoming, WY	B
Utah State U, UT	B
Utah Valley State Coll, UT	B
Vanguard U of Southern California, CA	B
Washington State U, WA	B
Weber State U, UT	B
Western Oregon U, OR	B
Western State Coll of Colorado, CO	B
Western Washington U, WA	B
Westminster Coll, UT	B
Westmont Coll, CA	B
Whitman Coll, WA	B
Whitworth U, WA	B
Willamette U, OR	B
Woodbury U, CA	B

Political Science and Government Related

Claremont McKenna Coll, CA	B
Saint Mary's Coll of California, CA	B
U of California, Davis, CA	B

Polymer/Plastics Engineering

U of Southern California, CA	B

Portuguese

Brigham Young U, UT	B
Stanford U, CA	B
U of California, Los Angeles, CA	B
U of California, Santa Barbara, CA	B
U of New Mexico, NM	B
U of Southern California, CA	B

Pre-Dentistry Studies

Adams State Coll, CO	B
Boise State U, ID	B
California State U, Chico, CA	B
California State U, Dominguez Hills, CA	B
Claremont McKenna Coll, CA	B

Colorado State U-Pueblo, CO	B
Eastern Oregon U, OR	B
Eastern Washington U, WA	B
Grand Canyon U, AZ	B
Humboldt State U, CA	B
La Sierra U, CA	B
Mount St. Mary's Coll, CA	B
Notre Dame de Namur U, CA	B
Pacific Union Coll, CA	B
Pacific U, OR	B
Pepperdine U, Malibu, CA	B
Regis U, CO	B
Seattle Pacific U, WA	B
Sonoma State U, CA	B
U of Colorado at Colorado Springs, CO	B
U of Dallas, TX	B
The U of Montana–Western, MT	B
U of Oregon, OR	B
U of Portland, OR	B
U of Puget Sound, WA	B
U of San Francisco, CA	B
Utah State U, UT	B
Walla Walla Coll, WA	B
Western State Coll of Colorado, CO	B
Westmont Coll, CA	B
Whitworth U, WA	B

Pre-Engineering

Adams State Coll, CO	B
Azusa Pacific U, CA	B
Boise State U, ID	A
Brigham Young U–Idaho, ID	A
Lewis & Clark Coll, OR	B
Mesa State Coll, CO	A
Montana State U–Billings, MT	A
Southern Utah U, UT	A
The U of Montana, MT	B
Utah Valley State Coll, UT	A

Pre-Law Studies

Adams State Coll, CO	B
Azusa Pacific U, CA	B
Biola U, CA	B
California State Polytechnic U, Pomona, CA	B
California State U, Dominguez Hills, CA	B
California State U, Fresno, CA	B
Claremont McKenna Coll, CA	B
Colorado State U-Pueblo, CO	B
Corban Coll, OR	B
Dixie State Coll of Utah, UT	A
Eastern Oregon U, OR	B
Eastern Washington U, WA	B
Fresno Pacific U, CA	B
Grand Canyon U, AZ	B
Humboldt State U, CA	B
La Sierra U, CA	B
The Master's Coll and Seminary, CA	B
Montana State U–Billings, MT	B
Mount St. Mary's Coll, CA	B
National U, CA	B
New Mexico Highlands U, NM	B
Northern Arizona U, AZ	B
Northwest Nazarene U, ID	B
Notre Dame de Namur U, CA	B
Pacific Union Coll, CA	B
Pepperdine U, Malibu, CA	B
Regis U, CO	B
Seattle Pacific U, WA	B
Sonoma State U, CA	B
Southern Oregon U, OR	B
U of California, Riverside, CA	B

U of California, Santa Barbara, CA — B
U of Colorado at Colorado Springs, CO — B
U of Dallas, TX — B
U of La Verne, CA — B
The U of Montana, MT — B
The U of Montana–Western, MT — B
U of Portland, OR — B
U of Puget Sound, WA — B
Utah State U, UT — B
Vanguard U of Southern California, CA — B
Walla Walla Coll, WA — B
Warner Pacific Coll, OR — B
Washington State U, WA — B
Western State Coll of Colorado, CO — B
Westmont Coll, CA — B
Whitworth U, WA — B

Pre-Medical Studies

Adams State Coll, CO — B
Albertson Coll of Idaho, ID — B
Boise State U, ID — B
California Polytechnic State U, San Luis Obispo, CA —
California State Polytechnic U, Pomona, CA — B
California State U, Chico, CA — B
California State U, Dominguez Hills, CA — B
Claremont McKenna Coll, CA — B
Colorado State U-Pueblo, CO — B
Concordia U, OR — B
Eastern Oregon U, OR — B
Eastern Washington U, WA — B
Fresno Pacific U, CA — B
Grand Canyon U, AZ — B
Hawai'i Pacific U, HI — B
Humboldt State U, CA — B
La Sierra U, CA — B
The Master's Coll and Seminary, CA — B
Montana State U–Billings, MT — B
Mount St. Mary's Coll, CA — B
New Mexico Highlands U, NM — B
Northern Arizona U, AZ — B
Northwest Nazarene U, ID — B
Notre Dame de Namur U, CA — B
Oregon Inst of Technology, OR — B
Pacific Union Coll, CA — B
Pacific U, OR — B
Pepperdine U, Malibu, CA — B
Pitzer Coll, CA — B
Pomona Coll, CA — B
Regis U, CO — B
St. John's Coll, NM — B
Scripps Coll, CA — B
Seattle Pacific U, WA — B
Sonoma State U, CA — B
Southern Oregon U, OR — B
U of Colorado at Colorado Springs, CO — B
U of Dallas, TX — B
U of Idaho, ID — B
U of Judaism, CA — B
The U of Montana, MT — B
The U of Montana–Western, MT — B
U of Nevada, Reno, NV — B
U of Oregon, OR — B
U of Portland, OR — B
U of Puget Sound, WA — B

U of San Diego, CA — B
U of San Francisco, CA — B
Utah State U, UT — B
Walla Walla Coll, WA — B
Warner Pacific Coll, OR — B
Washington State U, WA — B
Western State Coll of Colorado, CO —
Westmont Coll, CA — B
Whitworth U, WA — B

Pre-Nursing Studies

Adams State Coll, CO — B
Brigham Young U, UT — B
Montana State U–Billings, MT — B
Nevada State Coll at Henderson, NV — B

Pre-Pharmacy Studies

Adams State Coll, CO — B
Colorado State U-Pueblo, CO — B
Montana State U–Billings, MT — B
Oregon State U, OR — B
The U of Montana, MT — B
U of Utah, UT — B
Westmont Coll, CA — B

Pre-Theology/Pre-Ministerial Studies

California Baptist U, CA — B
California Christian Coll, CA — B
Concordia U, OR — B
Corban Coll, OR — B
Nazarene Bible Coll, CO — A
Point Loma Nazarene U, CA — B
U of Dallas, TX — B
Westmont Coll, CA — B

Pre-Veterinary Studies

Adams State Coll, CO — B
Boise State U, ID — B
California State Polytechnic U, Pomona, CA — B
California State U, Chico, CA — B
California State U, Dominguez Hills, CA — B
Colorado State U, CO — B
Colorado State U-Pueblo, CO — B
Eastern Oregon U, OR — B
Eastern Washington U, WA — B
Grand Canyon U, AZ — B
Humboldt State U, CA — B
Mesa State Coll, CO — B
Northern Arizona U, AZ — B
Pacific Union Coll, CA — B
Regis U, CO — B
Sonoma State U, CA — B
The U of Arizona, AZ — B
U of Colorado at Colorado Springs, CO — B
The U of Montana–Western, MT — B
U of Nevada, Reno, NV — B
U of Puget Sound, WA — B
U of San Francisco, CA — B
Utah State U, UT — B
Walla Walla Coll, WA — B
Warner Pacific Coll, OR — B
Western State Coll of Colorado, CO — B
Westmont Coll, CA — B
Whitworth U, WA — B

Printmaking

Academy of Art U, CA — A,B
Brigham Young U, UT — B
California Coll of the Arts, CA — B

California State U, Fullerton, CA — B
California State U, Long Beach, CA — B
Coll of Santa Fe, NM — B
Colorado State U, CO — B
Dixie State Coll of Utah, UT — A
San Francisco Art Inst, CA — B
Sonoma State U, CA — B
U of California, Santa Cruz, CA — B
U of Dallas, TX — B
U of Oregon, OR — B
U of San Francisco, CA — B
U of Washington, WA — B
Western Washington U, WA — B

Psychology

Adams State Coll, CO — B
Alaska Pacific U, AK — B
Albertson Coll of Idaho, ID — B
Alliant International U, CA — B
Argosy U, Orange County, CA — B
Argosy U, San Francisco Bay Area, CA — B
Arizona State U, AZ — B
Arizona State U at the West campus, AZ — B
Azusa Pacific U, CA — B
Bastyr U, WA — B
Bethany U, CA — B
Biola U, CA — B
Boise State U, ID — B
Brigham Young U, UT — B
Brigham Young U–Hawaii, HI — B
Brigham Young U–Idaho, ID — A
California Baptist U, CA — B
California Lutheran U, CA — B
California Polytechnic State U, San Luis Obispo, CA — B
California State Polytechnic U, Pomona, CA — B
California State U Channel Islands, CA — B
California State U, Chico, CA — B
California State U, Dominguez Hills, CA — B
California State U, Fresno, CA — B
California State U, Fullerton, CA — B
California State U, Long Beach, CA — B
California State U, Los Angeles, CA — B
California State U, Northridge, CA — B
California State U, Sacramento, CA — B
California State U, San Bernardino, CA — B
California State U, San Marcos, CA — B
California State U, Stanislaus, CA — B
Cascade Coll, OR — B
Central Washington U, WA — B
Chapman U, CA — B
Claremont McKenna Coll, CA — B
Coll of Santa Fe, NM — B
Coll of the Southwest, NM — B
Colorado Christian U, CO — B
The Colorado Coll, CO — B
Colorado State U, CO — B
Colorado State U-Pueblo, CO — B
Concordia U, CA — B

Concordia U, OR — B
Corban Coll, OR — B
Dixie State Coll of Utah, UT — A
Dominican U of California, CA — B
Eastern New Mexico U, NM — A,B
Eastern Oregon U, OR — B
Eastern Washington U, WA — B
Eugene Lang Coll The New School for Liberal Arts, NY —
Fort Lewis Coll, CO — B
Fresno Pacific U, CA — A,B
George Fox U, OR — B
Gonzaga U, WA — B
Grand Canyon U, AZ — B
Great Basin Coll, NV — A
Hawai'i Pacific U, HI — B
Holy Names U, CA — B
Hope International U, CA — B
Humboldt State U, CA — B
Idaho State U, ID — B
La Sierra U, CA — B
Lewis & Clark Coll, OR — B
Lewis-Clark State Coll, ID — B
Linfield Coll, OR — B
Loyola Marymount U, CA — B
Marylhurst U, OR — B
Mesa State Coll, CO — B
Mills Coll, CA — B
Montana State U, MT — B
Montana State U–Billings, MT — A,B
Mount St. Mary's Coll, CA — B
Naropa U, CO — B
National U, CA — B
Nevada State Coll at Henderson, NV — B
New Coll of California, CA — B
New Mexico Highlands U, NM — B
New Mexico Inst of Mining and Technology, NM — B
New Mexico State U, NM — B
North Carolina Ag and Tech State U, NC — B
Northern Arizona U, AZ — B
Northwest Nazarene U, ID — B
Northwest U, WA — B
Notre Dame de Namur U, CA — B
Occidental Coll, CA — B
Oregon State U, OR — B
Pacific Lutheran U, WA — B
Pacific Union Coll, CA — B
Pacific U, OR — B
Pepperdine U, Malibu, CA — B
Pitzer Coll, CA — B
Point Loma Nazarene U, CA — B
Pomona Coll, CA — B
Portland State U, OR — B
Prescott Coll, AZ — B
Reed Coll, OR — B
Regis U, CO — B
Rocky Mountain Coll, MT — B
Saint Mary's Coll of California, CA — B
San Diego Christian Coll, CA — B
San Diego State U, CA — B
San Francisco State U, CA — B
San Jose State U, CA — B
Santa Clara U, CA — B
Scripps Coll, CA — B
Seattle Pacific U, WA — B
Seattle U, WA — B
Simpson U, CA — B
Sonoma State U, CA — B
Southern Oregon U, OR — B
Southern Utah U, UT — B
Stanford U, CA — B

A—associate degree; B—bachelor's degree

Trinity Lutheran Coll, WA	B
U of Alaska Anchorage, AK	B
U of Alaska Fairbanks, AK	B
The U of Arizona, AZ	B
U of California, Berkeley, CA	B
U of California, Davis, CA	B
U of California, Irvine, CA	B
U of California, Los Angeles, CA	B
U of California, Riverside, CA	B
U of California, San Diego, CA	B
U of California, Santa Barbara, CA	B
U of California, Santa Cruz, CA	B
U of Colorado at Boulder, CO	B
U of Colorado at Colorado Springs, CO	B
U of Colorado at Denver and Health Sciences Center, CO	B
U of Dallas, TX	B
U of Denver, CO	B
U of Great Falls, MT	B
U of Hawaii at Hilo, HI	B
U of Hawaii at Manoa, HI	B
U of Hawaii–West Oahu, HI	B
U of Idaho, ID	B
U of Judaism, CA	B
U of La Verne, CA	B
The U of Montana, MT	B
U of Nevada, Las Vegas, NV	B
U of Nevada, Reno, NV	B
U of New Mexico, NM	B
U of New Orleans, LA	B
U of Northern Colorado, CO	B
U of Oregon, OR	B
U of Phoenix–Bay Area Campus, CA	B
U of Phoenix–Denver Campus, CO	B
U of Phoenix–Hawaii Campus, HI	
U of Phoenix–Idaho Campus, ID	B
U of Phoenix–Las Vegas Campus, NV	B
U of Phoenix–Oregon Campus, OR	B
U of Phoenix–Phoenix Campus, AZ	B
U of Phoenix–Sacramento Valley Campus, CA	B
U of Phoenix–Southern Colorado Campus, CO	B
U of Phoenix–Utah Campus, UT	B
U of Phoenix–Washington Campus, WA	B
U of Portland, OR	B
U of Puget Sound, WA	B
U of Redlands, CA	B
U of San Diego, CA	B
U of San Francisco, CA	B
U of Southern California, CA	B
U of the Pacific, CA	B
U of the West, CA	B
U of Utah, UT	B
U of Washington, WA	B
U of Wyoming, WY	B
Utah State U, UT	B
Vanguard U of Southern California, CA	B
Walla Walla Coll, WA	B
Warner Pacific Coll, OR	B
Washington State U, WA	B
Weber State U, UT	B

Western Oregon U, OR	B
Western State Coll of Colorado, CO	B
Western Washington U, WA	B
Westminster Coll, UT	B
Westmont Coll, CA	B
Whitman Coll, WA	B
Whitworth U, WA	B
Willamette U, OR	B
William Jessup U, CA	B
Woodbury U, CA	B

Psychology Related

Arizona State U at the Polytechnic Campus, AZ	B
Northwest Christian Coll, OR	B
Saint Mary's Coll of California, CA	B

Psychology Teacher Education

Brigham Young U, UT	B
California Lutheran U, CA	B

Public Administration

Boise State U, ID	B
California State Polytechnic U, Pomona, CA	B
California State U, Chico, CA	B
California State U, Dominguez Hills, CA	B
California State U, Fresno, CA	B
California State U, Fullerton, CA	B
California State U, San Bernardino, CA	B
Coll of Santa Fe, NM	B
Eastern Washington U, WA	B
Hawai'i Pacific U, HI	B
Nevada State Coll at Henderson, NV	B
San Diego State U, CA	B
Seattle U, WA	B
The U of Arizona, AZ	B
U of California, Los Angeles, CA	B
U of California, Riverside, CA	B
U of Denver, CO	B
U of Hawaii–West Oahu, HI	B
U of La Verne, CA	B
U of Oregon, OR	B
U of Phoenix–Bay Area Campus, CA	B
U of Phoenix–Hawaii Campus, HI	
U of Phoenix–Idaho Campus, ID	B
U of Phoenix–Las Vegas Campus, NV	B
U of Phoenix–Oregon Campus, OR	B
U of Phoenix–Phoenix Campus, AZ	B
U of Phoenix–Sacramento Valley Campus, CA	B
U of Phoenix–Southern California Campus, CA	B
U of Phoenix–Southern Colorado Campus, CO	B
U of Phoenix–Washington Campus, WA	B
U of San Francisco, CA	B
U of Southern California, CA	B
U of Washington, WA	B
Western Oregon U, OR	B

Public Administration and Social Service Professions Related

U of Phoenix–Central Valley Campus, CA	B
U of Phoenix–Denver Campus, CO	B
U of Phoenix–Hawaii Campus, HI	B
U of Phoenix–Las Vegas Campus, NV	B
U of Phoenix–New Mexico Campus, NM	B
U of Phoenix–Sacramento Valley Campus, CA	B
U of Phoenix–Southern Arizona Campus, AZ	B
U of Phoenix–Utah Campus, UT	B

Public/Applied History and Archival Administration

U of California, Santa Barbara, CA	B

Public Health

Boise State U, ID	B
California State U, Dominguez Hills, CA	B
California State U, Long Beach, CA	B
New Mexico State U, NM	B
Oregon State U, OR	B
Touro U International, CA	B
U of Alaska Fairbanks, AK	A
U of Washington, WA	B

Public Health/Community Nursing

U of Washington, WA	B

Public Health Education and Promotion

California State U, Long Beach, CA	B
New Mexico State U, NM	B
U of Northern Colorado, CO	B
U of Southern California, CA	B
Walla Walla Coll, WA	B

Public Health Related

U of California, Berkeley, CA	B
U of California, Los Angeles, CA	B
Utah State U, UT	B

Public Policy Analysis

Brigham Young U, UT	B
Central Washington U, WA	B
Mills Coll, CA	B
Northern Arizona U, AZ	B
Occidental Coll, CA	B
Pomona Coll, CA	B
Stanford U, CA	B
U of California, Los Angeles, CA	B
U of Oregon, OR	B
Western State Coll of Colorado, CO	B

Public Relations

Marylhurst U, OR	B
San Diego State U, CA	B

Public Relations, Advertising, and Applied Communication Related

Brigham Young U, UT	B
California Lutheran U, CA	B

Public Relations/Image Management

California Lutheran U, CA	B
California State Polytechnic U, Pomona, CA	B
California State U, Chico, CA	B
California State U, Dominguez Hills, CA	B
California State U, Fresno, CA	B
California State U, Fullerton, CA	B
California State U, Long Beach, CA	B
Central Washington U, WA	B
Colorado State U, CO	B
Colorado State U-Pueblo, CO	B
George Fox U, OR	B
Gonzaga U, WA	B
Hawai'i Pacific U, HI	B
Johnson & Wales U, CO	B
Marylhurst U, OR	B
The Master's Coll and Seminary, CA	B
Mesa State Coll, CO	B
Montana State U–Billings, MT	B
Northern Arizona U, AZ	B
Northwest Nazarene U, ID	B
Pacific Union Coll, CA	B
Pepperdine U, Malibu, CA	B
San Diego State U, CA	B
San Jose State U, CA	B
Seattle U, WA	B
U of Idaho, ID	B
U of Oregon, OR	B
U of Southern California, CA	B
U of Utah, UT	B
Walla Walla Coll, WA	B
Weber State U, UT	B

Purchasing, Procurement/Acquisitions and Contracts Management

Arizona State U, AZ	B

Quality Control Technology

California State U, Long Beach, CA	B
San Jose State U, CA	B

Radiation Protection/Health Physics Technology

Oregon State U, OR	B

Radio and Television

Academy of Art U, CA	A,B
Biola U, CA	B
Brigham Young U–Idaho, ID	A
California State U, Chico, CA	B
California State U, Fresno, CA	B
California State U, Fullerton, CA	B
California State U, Long Beach, CA	B
California State U, Los Angeles, CA	B
Central Washington U, WA	B
Colorado State U, CO	B
Colorado State U-Pueblo, CO	B
Columbia Coll Hollywood, CA	B
Dixie State Coll of Utah, UT	A
George Fox U, OR	B
The Master's Coll and Seminary, CA	B
Mesa State Coll, CO	B
Northern Arizona U, AZ	B
Pacific Lutheran U, WA	B
Pacific U, OR	B
San Diego State U, CA	B

San Francisco State U, CA — B
San Jose State U, CA — B
The U of Arizona, AZ — B
U of Idaho, ID — B
The U of Montana, MT — B
U of Oregon, OR — B
U of Southern California, CA — B
U of Utah, UT — B
Vanguard U of Southern California, CA — B
Walla Walla Coll, WA — B
Weber State U, UT — B
Western State Coll of Colorado, CO — B

Radio and Television Broadcasting Technology
Northwest Nazarene U, ID — B

Radiologic Technology/ Science
Boise State U, ID — A,B
Brigham Young U–Idaho, ID — A
Lewis-Clark State Coll, ID — A
Mesa State Coll, CO — A
Oregon Inst of Technology, OR — B
The U of Montana, MT — A

Radio, Television, and Digital Communication Related
Brigham Young U, UT — B
California State Polytechnic U, Pomona, CA — B
Dixie State Coll of Utah, UT — B

Range Science and Management
Brigham Young U, UT — B
Brigham Young U–Idaho, ID — A
California State U, Chico, CA — B
Colorado State U, CO — B
Dixie State Coll of Utah, UT — A
Humboldt State U, CA — B
Montana State U, MT — B
New Mexico State U, NM — B
Oregon State U, OR — B
U of Idaho, ID — B
U of Wyoming, WY — B
Utah State U, UT — B

Reading Teacher Education
Boise State U, ID — B
Eastern Washington U, WA — B
Pacific Lutheran U, WA — B
U of Great Falls, MT — B
The U of Montana, MT — B
Washington State U, WA — B

Real Estate
Arizona State U, AZ — B
Arizona State U at the Polytechnic Campus, AZ — B
California State Polytechnic U, Pomona, CA — B
California State U, Dominguez Hills, CA — B
California State U, Fresno, CA — B
California State U, Sacramento, CA — B
Colorado State U, CO — B
Marylhurst U, OR — B
San Diego State U, CA — B
San Francisco State U, CA — B
U of Denver, CO — B
U of Nevada, Las Vegas, NV — B
Washington State U, WA — B

Receptionist
The U of Montana, MT — A

Regional Studies
Coll of Santa Fe, NM — B
Pitzer Coll, CA — B

Rehabilitation and Therapeutic Professions Related
Montana State U–Billings, MT — B

Rehabilitation Therapy
California State U, Los Angeles, CA — B
Montana State U–Billings, MT — B

Religious Education
Biola U, CA — B
Boise Bible Coll, ID — A,B
Concordia U, CA — B
Concordia U, OR — B
Corban Coll, OR — B
Eugene Bible Coll, OR — B
George Fox U, OR — B
The Master's Coll and Seminary, CA — B
Multnomah Bible Coll and Biblical Seminary, OR — B
Nazarene Bible Coll, CO — A,B
Northwest Nazarene U, ID — B
Northwest U, WA — B
Pepperdine U, Malibu, CA — B
Seattle Pacific U, WA — B
Simpson U, CA — B
Vanguard U of Southern California, CA — B
Warner Pacific Coll, OR — A,B

Religious/Sacred Music
Bethany U, CA — B
Boise Bible Coll, ID — A,B
Corban Coll, OR — B
Eugene Bible Coll, OR — B
Fresno Pacific U, CA — B
Grand Canyon U, AZ — B
Hope International U, CA — B
The Master's Coll and Seminary, CA — B
Multnomah Bible Coll and Biblical Seminary, OR — B
Nazarene Bible Coll, CO — A,B
Northwest Nazarene U, ID — B
Northwest U, WA — B
Pacific Lutheran U, WA — B
Patten U, CA — B
Point Loma Nazarene U, CA — B
San Diego Christian Coll, CA — B
Trinity Lutheran Coll, WA — B

Religious Studies
Albertson Coll of Idaho, ID — B
Arizona State U, AZ — B
Azusa Pacific U, CA — B
Biola U, CA — B
Boise Bible Coll, ID — A,B
California Lutheran U, CA — B
California State U, Chico, CA — B
California State U, Dominguez Hills, CA — B
California State U, Fresno, CA — B
California State U, Fullerton, CA — B
California State U, Long Beach, CA — B
California State U, Northridge, CA — B
Central Washington U, WA — B

Chapman U, CA — B
Claremont McKenna Coll, CA — B
Coll of Santa Fe, NM — B
The Colorado Coll, CO — B
Concordia U, OR — B
Corban Coll, OR — B
Dominican U of California, CA — B
Eastern New Mexico U, NM — B
Eugene Lang Coll The New School for Liberal Arts, NY — B
Fresno Pacific U, CA — B
George Fox U, OR — B
Gonzaga U, WA — B
Grand Canyon U, AZ — B
Holy Names U, CA — B
Humboldt State U, CA — B
La Sierra U, CA — B
Lewis & Clark Coll, OR — B
Linfield Coll, OR — B
Marylhurst U, OR — B
The Master's Coll and Seminary, CA — B
Mount St. Mary's Coll, CA — B
Naropa U, CO — B
Northern Arizona U, AZ — B
Northwest Nazarene U, ID — B
Northwest U, WA — B
Notre Dame de Namur U, CA — B
Occidental Coll, CA — B
Pacific Lutheran U, WA — B
Pacific Union Coll, CA — B
Pepperdine U, Malibu, CA — B
Pitzer Coll, CA — B
Pomona Coll, CA — B
Queen of the Holy Rosary Coll, CA — A
Reed Coll, OR — B
Regis U, CO — B
Rocky Mountain Coll, MT — B
St. John's Coll, NM — B
Saint Mary's Coll of California, CA — B
San Diego State U, CA — B
San Francisco State U, CA — B
San Jose State U, CA — B
Santa Clara U, CA — B
Scripps Coll, CA — B
Seattle U, WA — B
Stanford U, CA — B
The U of Arizona, AZ — B
U of California, Berkeley, CA — B
U of California, Davis, CA — B
U of California, Los Angeles, CA — B
U of California, Riverside, CA — B
U of California, San Diego, CA — B
U of California, Santa Barbara, CA — B
U of California, Santa Cruz, CA — B
U of Colorado at Boulder, CO — B
U of Denver, CO — B
U of Great Falls, MT — B
U of Hawaii at Manoa, HI — B
U of La Verne, CA — B
U of New Mexico, NM — B
U of Oregon, OR — B
U of Puget Sound, WA — B
U of Redlands, CA — B
U of San Diego, CA — B
U of San Francisco, CA — B
U of Southern California, CA — B
U of the Pacific, CA — B
U of Washington, WA — B

Vanguard U of Southern California, CA — B
Walla Walla Coll, WA — B
Warner Pacific Coll, OR — B
Washington State U, WA — B
Westmont Coll, CA — B
Whitman Coll, WA — B
Whitworth U, WA — B
Willamette U, OR — B

Religious Studies Related
Claremont McKenna Coll, CA — B
Point Loma Nazarene U, CA — B
U of the West, CA — B

Resort Management
Western State Coll of Colorado, CO — B

Respiratory Care Therapy
Boise State U, ID — B
Loma Linda U, CA — A,B
The U of Montana, MT — A
Weber State U, UT — A,B

Restaurant, Culinary, and Catering Management
The Art Inst of California– Orange County, CA — B
The Art Inst of California–San Diego, CA — B
The Art Inst of Las Vegas, NV — B

Restaurant/Food Services Management
The Art Inst of California–San Diego, CA — B
Johnson & Wales U, CO — A,B
U of San Francisco, CA — B

Retailing
Brigham Young U, UT — B

Retail Management
U of Phoenix–Bay Area Campus, CA — B
U of Phoenix–Hawaii Campus, HI — B
U of Phoenix–Idaho Campus, ID — B
U of Phoenix–Las Vegas Campus, NV — B
U of Phoenix–Oregon Campus, OR — B
U of Phoenix–Phoenix Campus, AZ — B
U of Phoenix–Sacramento Valley Campus, CA — B
U of Phoenix–Southern Colorado Campus, CO — B
U of Phoenix–Washington Campus, WA — B

Robotics Technology
ITT Tech Inst, San Dimas, CA — B

Romance Languages
Pitzer Coll, CA — B
Point Loma Nazarene U, CA — B
Pomona Coll, CA — B
U of Nevada, Las Vegas, NV — B
U of Oregon, OR — B
U of Washington, WA — B

Romance Languages Related
The Colorado Coll, CO — B

Russian
Arizona State U, AZ — B
Brigham Young U, UT — B

A—associate degree; B—bachelor's degree

Brigham Young U–Idaho, ID · A
Claremont McKenna Coll, CA · B
The Colorado Coll, CO · B
Pitzer Coll, CA · B
Pomona Coll, CA · B
Portland State U, OR · B
Reed Coll, OR · B
San Diego State U, CA · B
San Francisco State U, CA · B
Scripps Coll, CA · B
Seattle Pacific U, WA · B
The U of Arizona, AZ · B
U of California, Davis, CA · B
U of California, Irvine, CA · B
U of California, Los Angeles, CA · B
U of California, Riverside, CA · B
U of California, San Diego, CA · B
U of Denver, CO · B
U of Hawaii at Manoa, HI · B
The U of Montana, MT · B
U of New Mexico, NM · B
U of Oregon, OR · B
U of Southern California, CA · B
U of Utah, UT · B
U of Washington, WA · B
U of Wyoming, WY · B
Washington State U, WA · B

Russian Studies
California State U, Fullerton, CA · B
Claremont McKenna Coll, CA · B
The Colorado Coll, CO · B
San Diego State U, CA · B
U of Alaska Fairbanks, AK · B
U of California, Los Angeles, CA · B
U of California, Riverside, CA · B
U of California, San Diego, CA · B
U of California, Santa Cruz, CA · B
U of Colorado at Boulder, CO · B
The U of Montana, MT · B
U of New Mexico, NM · B
U of Washington, WA · B

Sales and Marketing/Marketing and Distribution Teacher Education
Colorado State U, CO · B
Eastern New Mexico U, NM · B
Utah State U, UT · B

Sales, Distribution and Marketing
LDS Business Coll, UT · A
Pioneer Pacific Coll, Wilsonville, OR · A
Sierra Nevada Coll, NV · B

Sanskrit and Classical Indian Languages
U of Hawaii at Manoa, HI · B

Scandinavian Languages
Pacific Lutheran U, WA · B
U of California, Berkeley, CA · B
U of California, Los Angeles, CA · B
U of Washington, WA · B

Scandinavian Studies
U of Washington, WA · B

School Librarian/School Library Media
Eastern Washington U, WA · B
U of Great Falls, MT · B

School Psychology
Western State Coll of Colorado, CO · B

Science Teacher Education
Boise State U, ID · B
Brigham Young U, UT · B
Brigham Young U–Hawaii, HI · B
California Lutheran U, CA · B
California State U, Chico, CA · B
California State U, San Marcos, CA · B
Central Washington U, WA · B
Coll of the Southwest, NM · B
Colorado State U, CO · B
Colorado State U-Pueblo, CO · B
Concordia U, OR · B
Eastern Washington U, WA · B
Fresno Pacific U, CA · B
Grand Canyon U, AZ · B
Lewis-Clark State Coll, ID · B
The Master's Coll and Seminary, CA · B
Mesa State Coll, CO · B
Montana State U–Billings, MT · B
Nevada State Coll at Henderson, NV · B
New Mexico Highlands U, NM · B
Northern Arizona U, AZ · B
Pacific Lutheran U, WA · B
Prescott Coll, AZ · B
Seattle Pacific U, WA · B
The U of Arizona, AZ · B
U of Great Falls, MT · B
The U of Montana, MT · B
The U of Montana–Western, MT · B
U of Nevada, Reno, NV · B
U of New Orleans, LA · B
U of Utah, UT · B
U of Washington, WA · B
Utah State U, UT · B
Utah Valley State Coll, UT · B
Warner Pacific Coll, OR · B
Washington State U, WA · B
Weber State U, UT · B
Western State Coll of Colorado, CO · B
Western Washington U, WA · B

Science Technologies Related
Arizona State U at the Polytechnic Campus, AZ · B
Northern Arizona U, AZ · B
The U of Arizona, AZ · B
Willamette U, OR · B

Science, Technology and Society
Embry-Riddle Aeronautical U, AZ · B
Pitzer Coll, CA · B
Scripps Coll, CA · B
Stanford U, CA · B
U of Alaska Anchorage, AK · B
U of Nevada, Reno, NV · B
U of Puget Sound, WA · B

Sculpture
Academy of Art U, CA · A,B
Brigham Young U, UT · B
California Coll of the Arts, CA · B
California Inst of the Arts, CA · B
California State U, Fullerton, CA · B
California State U, Long Beach, CA · B
Coll of Santa Fe, NM · B

Colorado State U, CO · B
Dixie State Coll of Utah, UT · A
Northwest Nazarene U, ID · B
Otis Coll of Art and Design, CA · B
Portland State U, OR · B
Rocky Mountain Coll of Art & Design, CO · B
San Francisco Art Inst, CA · B
Sonoma State U, CA · B
U of California, Santa Cruz, CA · B
U of Dallas, TX · B
U of Oregon, OR · B
U of Washington, WA · B
Western Washington U, WA · B

Secondary Education
Adams State Coll, CO · B
Arizona State U, AZ · B
Arizona State U at the Polytechnic Campus, AZ · B
Arizona State U at the West campus, AZ · B
Biola U, CA · B
Boise State U, ID · B
Brigham Young U–Hawaii, HI · B
Coll of Santa Fe, NM · B
Coll of the Southwest, NM · B
Colorado State U-Pueblo, CO · B
Concordia U, OR · B
Corban Coll, OR · B
Dixie State Coll of Utah, UT · A
Fort Lewis Coll, CO · B
Fresno Pacific U, CA · B
Gonzaga U, WA · B
Grand Canyon U, AZ · B
Great Basin Coll, NV · B
Humboldt State U, CA · B
Idaho State U, ID · B
La Sierra U, CA · B
The Master's Coll and Seminary, CA · B
Mesa State Coll, CO · B
Montana State U, MT · B
Montana State U–Billings, MT · B
Mount St. Mary's Coll, CA · B
New Mexico Highlands U, NM · B
New Mexico State U, NM · B
Northwest Nazarene U, ID · B
Northwest U, WA · B
Notre Dame de Namur U, CA · B
Pacific Lutheran U, WA · B
Pacific U, OR · B
Pepperdine U, Malibu, CA · B
Prescott Coll, AZ · B
Rocky Mountain Coll, MT · B
San Diego Christian Coll, CA · B
Southern Utah U, UT · B
U of Alaska Anchorage, AK · B
The U of Arizona, AZ · B
U of Dallas, TX · B
U of Great Falls, MT · B
U of Hawaii at Hilo, HI · B
U of Hawaii at Manoa, HI · B
U of Idaho, ID · B
The U of Montana, MT · B
The U of Montana–Western, MT · B
U of Nevada, Las Vegas, NV · B
U of New Mexico, NM · B
U of Portland, OR · B
U of Redlands, CA · B
U of San Francisco, CA · B
U of Utah, UT · B
U of Washington, WA · B
U of Wyoming, WY · B

Utah State U, UT · B
Vanguard U of Southern California, CA · B
Warner Pacific Coll, OR · B
Washington State U, WA · B
Weber State U, UT · B
Western Oregon U, OR · B
Western State Coll of Colorado, CO · B
Western Washington U, WA · B
Westmont Coll, CA · B
Whitworth U, WA · B

Security and Protective Services Related
U of Phoenix–Hawaii Campus, HI · B
U of Phoenix–Idaho Campus, ID · B
U of Phoenix–Las Vegas Campus, NV · B
U of Phoenix–Oregon Campus, OR · B
U of Phoenix–Southern California Campus, CA · B
U of Phoenix–Southern Colorado Campus, CO · B
U of Phoenix–Washington Campus, WA · B

Sheet Metal Technology
Montana State U–Billings, MT · A

Sign Language Interpretation and Translation
Idaho State U, ID · B
U of New Mexico, NM · B
Western Oregon U, OR · B

Slavic Languages
Stanford U, CA · B
U of California, Berkeley, CA · B
U of California, Los Angeles, CA · B
U of California, Santa Barbara, CA · B
U of Southern California, CA · B
U of Washington, WA · B

Small Business Administration
Lewis-Clark State Coll, ID · A,B

Small Engine Mechanics and Repair Technology
The U of Montana, MT · A

Social Psychology
Brigham Young U, UT · B
U of California, Irvine, CA · B
U of California, Santa Cruz, CA · B
U of Nevada, Reno, NV · B

Social Sciences
Adams State Coll, CO · B
Arizona State U at the West campus, AZ · B
Azusa Pacific U, CA · B
Bethany U, CA · B
Biola U, CA · B
Boise State U, ID · B
California Baptist U, CA · B
California Lutheran U, CA · B
California Polytechnic State U, San Luis Obispo, CA · B
California State Polytechnic U, Pomona, CA · B
California State U, Chico, CA · B
California State U, Los Angeles, CA · B

California State U, Sacramento, CA   B
California State U, San Bernardino, CA   B
California State U, San Marcos, CA   B
California State U, Stanislaus, CA   B
Coll of the Southwest, NM   B
Colorado Christian U, CO   B
Colorado State U, CO   B
Colorado State U-Pueblo, CO   B
Concordia U, OR   B
Corban Coll, OR   B
Eastern New Mexico U, NM   B
Eugene Lang Coll The New School for Liberal Arts, NY   B
The Evergreen State Coll, WA   B
Fresno Pacific U, CA   B
Grand Canyon U, AZ   B
Hawai'i Pacific U, HI   B
Hope International U, CA   B
Humboldt State U, CA   B
Lewis-Clark State Coll, ID   B
Marylhurst U, OR   B
Mesa State Coll, CO   A,B
Mount St. Mary's Coll, CA   B
New Coll of California, CA   B
North Carolina Ag and Tech State U, NC   B
Northern Arizona U, AZ   B
Northwest Nazarene U, ID   B
Notre Dame de Namur U, CA   B
Pacific Union Coll, CA   B
Point Loma Nazarene U, CA   B
Portland State U, OR   B
Saint Mary's Coll of California, CA   B
San Diego Christian Coll, CA   B
San Diego State U, CA   B
San Francisco State U, CA   B
San Jose State U, CA   B
Southern Oregon U, OR   B
Southern Utah U, UT   B
United States Air Force Academy, CO   B
U of Alaska Southeast, AK   B
U of California, Irvine, CA   B
U of California, Riverside, CA   B
U of Denver, CO   B
U of Great Falls, MT   B
U of Hawaii–West Oahu, HI   B
U of La Verne, CA   B
The U of Montana, MT   B
The U of Montana–Western, MT   B
U of Nevada, Las Vegas, NV   B
U of Northern Colorado, CO   B
U of Southern California, CA   B
U of the Pacific, CA   B
U of Utah, UT   B
U of Washington, WA   B
U of Wyoming, WY   B
Warner Pacific Coll, OR   A,B
Washington State U, WA   B
Western Oregon U, OR   B
Western State Coll of Colorado, CO   B
Westminster Coll, UT   B
Westmont Coll, CA   B

Social Sciences Related

The Colorado Coll, CO   B
Concordia U, CA   B
Northwest Christian Coll, OR   B

Saint Mary's Coll of California, CA   B
U of California, Berkeley, CA   B
U of Denver, CO   B

Social Science Teacher Education

Brigham Young U, UT   B
Brigham Young U–Hawaii, HI   B
California Lutheran U, CA   B
California State U, Chico, CA   B
Central Washington U, WA   B
Corban Coll, OR   B
Hope International U, CA   B
Lewis-Clark State Coll, ID   B
Montana State U–Billings, MT   B
Nevada State Coll at Henderson, NV   B
Northern Arizona U, AZ   B
Northwest Nazarene U, ID   B
Prescott Coll, AZ   B
Seattle Pacific U, WA   B
Simpson U, CA   B
The U of Arizona, AZ   B
U of Great Falls, MT   B
The U of Montana, MT   B
The U of Montana–Western, MT   B
U of Nevada, Reno, NV   B
U of Utah, UT   B
Weber State U, UT   B
Western State Coll of Colorado, CO   B
Westminster Coll, UT   B
Westmont Coll, CA   B

Social Studies Teacher Education

Colorado State U, CO   B
Colorado State U-Pueblo, CO   B
Concordia U, OR   B
Corban Coll, OR   B
Eastern Washington U, WA   B
Rocky Mountain Coll, MT   B
The U of Arizona, AZ   B
U of Great Falls, MT   B
U of Nevada, Reno, NV   B
U of New Orleans, LA   B
U of Utah, UT   B
Utah State U, UT   B
Washington State U, WA   B
Weber State U, UT   B

Social Work

Arizona State U, AZ   B
Arizona State U at the West campus, AZ   B
Azusa Pacific U, CA   B
Boise State U, ID   B
Brigham Young U, UT   B
Brigham Young U–Hawaii, HI   B
Brigham Young U–Idaho, ID   A
California State U, Chico, CA   B
California State U, Fresno, CA   B
California State U, Long Beach, CA   B
California State U, Los Angeles, CA   B
California State U, Sacramento, CA   B
California State U, San Bernardino, CA   B
Chapman U, CA   B
Colorado State U, CO   B
Colorado State U-Pueblo, CO   B
Concordia U, OR   B

Dixie State Coll of Utah, UT   A
Eastern Washington U, WA   B
Fresno Pacific U, CA   B
George Fox U, OR   B
Great Basin Coll, NV   B
Hawai'i Pacific U, HI   B
Hope International U, CA   B
Humboldt State U, CA   B
Idaho State U, ID   B
La Sierra U, CA   B
Lewis-Clark State Coll, ID   B
New Mexico Highlands U, NM   B
New Mexico State U, NM   B
North Carolina Ag and Tech State U, NC   B
Northern Arizona U, AZ   B
Northwest Nazarene U, ID   B
Pacific Lutheran U, WA   B
Pacific Union Coll, CA   B
Pacific U, OR   B
Point Loma Nazarene U, CA   B
San Diego State U, CA   B
San Francisco State U, CA   B
San Jose State U, CA   B
Seattle U, WA   B
Trinity Lutheran Coll, WA   B
U of Alaska Anchorage, AK   B
U of Alaska Fairbanks, AK   B
U of California, Berkeley, CA   B
U of California, Los Angeles, CA   B
U of Hawaii at Manoa, HI   B
The U of Montana, MT   B
U of Nevada, Las Vegas, NV   B
U of Nevada, Reno, NV   B
U of Portland, OR   B
U of Utah, UT   B
U of Washington, WA   B
U of Washington, Tacoma, WA   B
U of Wyoming, WY   B
Utah State U, UT   B
Walla Walla Coll, WA   B
Warner Pacific Coll, OR   B
Weber State U, UT   B

Sociology

Adams State Coll, CO   B
Albertson Coll of Idaho, ID   B
Arizona State U, AZ   B
Arizona State U at the West campus, AZ   B
Azusa Pacific U, CA   B
Biola U, CA   B
Boise State U, ID   B
Brigham Young U, UT   B
Brigham Young U–Idaho, ID   A
California Baptist U, CA   B
California Lutheran U, CA   B
California State Polytechnic U, Pomona, CA   B
California State U Channel Islands, CA   B
California State U, Chico, CA   B
California State U, Dominguez Hills, CA   B
California State U, Fresno, CA   B
California State U, Fullerton, CA   B
California State U, Long Beach, CA   B
California State U, Los Angeles, CA   B
California State U, Northridge, CA   B

California State U, Sacramento, CA   B
California State U, San Bernardino, CA   B
California State U, San Marcos, CA   B
California State U, Stanislaus, CA   B
Central Washington U, WA   B
Chapman U, CA   B
Claremont McKenna Coll, CA   B
The Colorado Coll, CO   B
Colorado State U, CO   B
Colorado State U-Pueblo, CO   B
Dixie State Coll of Utah, UT   A
Eastern New Mexico U, NM   B
Eastern Oregon U, OR   B
Eastern Washington U, WA   B
Eugene Lang Coll The New School for Liberal Arts, NY   B
Fort Lewis Coll, CO   B
Fresno Pacific U, CA   A
George Fox U, OR   B
Gonzaga U, WA   B
Grand Canyon U, AZ   B
Great Basin Coll, NV   A
Hawai'i Pacific U, HI   B
Holy Names U, CA   B
Humboldt State U, CA   B
Idaho State U, ID   B
La Sierra U, CA   B
Lewis & Clark Coll, OR   B
Linfield Coll, OR   B
Loyola Marymount U, CA   B
Mesa State Coll, CO   B
Mills Coll, CA   B
Montana State U, MT   B
Montana State U–Billings, MT   A,B
Mount St. Mary's Coll, CA   B
National U, CA   B
New Mexico Highlands U, NM   B
New Mexico State U, NM   B
North Carolina Ag and Tech State U, NC   B
Northern Arizona U, AZ   B
Notre Dame de Namur U, CA   B
Occidental Coll, CA   B
Oregon State U, OR   B
Pacific Lutheran U, WA   B
Pacific Union Coll, CA   B
Pacific U, OR   B
Pepperdine U, Malibu, CA   B
Pitzer Coll, CA   B
Point Loma Nazarene U, CA   B
Pomona Coll, CA   B
Portland State U, OR   B
Prescott Coll, AZ   B
Reed Coll, OR   B
Regis U, CO   B
Rocky Mountain Coll, MT   B
Saint Mary's Coll of California, CA   B
San Diego State U, CA   B
San Francisco State U, CA   B
San Jose State U, CA   B
Santa Clara U, CA   B
Scripps Coll, CA   B
Seattle Pacific U, WA   B
Seattle U, WA   B
Sonoma State U, CA   B
Southern Oregon U, OR   B
Southern Utah U, UT   B
Stanford U, CA   B
U of Alaska Anchorage, AK   B
U of Alaska Fairbanks, AK   B

A—associate degree; B—bachelor's degree

The U of Arizona, AZ — B
U of California, Berkeley, CA — B
U of California, Davis, CA — B
U of California, Irvine, CA — B
U of California, Los Angeles, CA — B
U of California, Riverside, CA — B
U of California, San Diego, CA — B
U of California, Santa Barbara, CA — B
U of California, Santa Cruz, CA — B
U of Colorado at Boulder, CO — B
U of Colorado at Colorado Springs, CO — B
U of Colorado at Denver and Health Sciences Center, CO — B
U of Denver, CO — B
U of Great Falls, MT — B
U of Hawaii at Hilo, HI — B
U of Hawaii at Manoa, HI — B
U of Hawaii–West Oahu, HI — B
U of Idaho, ID — B
U of La Verne, CA — B
The U of Montana, MT — B
U of Nevada, Las Vegas, NV — B
U of Nevada, Reno, NV — B
U of New Mexico, NM — B
U of New Orleans, LA — B
U of Northern Colorado, CO — B
U of Oregon, OR — B
U of Portland, OR — B
U of Puget Sound, WA — B
U of Redlands, CA — B
U of San Diego, CA — B
U of San Francisco, CA — B
U of Southern California, CA — B
U of the Pacific, CA — B
U of Utah, UT — B
U of Washington, WA — B
U of Wyoming, WY — B
Utah State U, UT — B
Vanguard U of Southern California, CA — B
Walla Walla Coll, WA — B
Washington State U, WA — B
Weber State U, UT — B
Western Oregon U, OR — B
Western State Coll of Colorado, CO — B
Western Washington U, WA — B
Westminster Coll, UT — B
Westmont Coll, CA — B
Whitman Coll, WA — B
Whitworth U, WA — B
Willamette U, OR — B

Soil Conservation
California State Polytechnic U, Pomona, CA — B

Soil Science and Agronomy
Dixie State Coll of Utah, UT — A
New Mexico State U, NM — B
U of California, Davis, CA — B
U of Idaho, ID — B
Utah State U, UT — B
Washington State U, WA — B

Soil Sciences
Oregon State U, OR — B
The U of Arizona, AZ — B

Soil Sciences Related
Brigham Young U, UT — B

South Asian Languages
Claremont McKenna Coll, CA — B
U of Hawaii at Manoa, HI — B

Spanish
Adams State Coll, CO — B
Albertson Coll of Idaho, ID — B
Arizona State U, AZ — B
Arizona State U at the West campus, AZ — B
Azusa Pacific U, CA — B
Biola U, CA — B
Boise State U, ID — B
Brigham Young U, UT — B
Brigham Young U–Idaho, ID — A
California Lutheran U, CA — B
California State Polytechnic U, Pomona, CA — B
California State U Channel Islands, CA — B
California State U, Chico, CA — B
California State U, Dominguez Hills, CA — B
California State U, Fresno, CA — B
California State U, Fullerton, CA — B
California State U, Long Beach, CA — B
California State U, Los Angeles, CA — B
California State U, Northridge, CA — B
California State U, Sacramento, CA — B
California State U, San Bernardino, CA — B
California State U, San Marcos, CA — B
California State U, Stanislaus, CA — B
Chapman U, CA — B
Claremont McKenna Coll, CA — B
The Colorado Coll, CO — B
Colorado State U, CO — B
Colorado State U-Pueblo, CO — B
Eastern New Mexico U, NM — B
Eastern Washington U, WA — B
Fort Lewis Coll, CO — B
Fresno Pacific U, CA — A,B
George Fox U, OR — B
Gonzaga U, WA — B
Holy Names U, CA — B
Humboldt State U, CA — B
Idaho State U, ID — A,B
La Sierra U, CA — B
Lewis & Clark Coll, OR — B
Linfield Coll, OR — B
Loyola Marymount U, CA — B
Mills Coll, CA — B
Montana State U–Billings, MT — B
Mount St. Mary's Coll, CA — B
New Mexico Highlands U, NM — B
Northern Arizona U, AZ — B
Northwest Nazarene U, ID — B
Occidental Coll, CA — B
Oregon State U, OR — B
Pacific Lutheran U, WA — B
Pacific Union Coll, CA — B
Pacific U, OR — B
Pepperdine U, Malibu, CA — B
Pitzer Coll, CA — B
Point Loma Nazarene U, CA — B
Pomona Coll, CA — B
Portland State U, OR — B
Prescott Coll, AZ — B
Reed Coll, OR — B
Regis U, CO — B
Saint Mary's Coll of California, CA — B
San Diego State U, CA — B

San Francisco State U, CA — B
San Jose State U, CA — B
Santa Clara U, CA — B
Scripps Coll, CA — B
Seattle Pacific U, WA — B
Seattle U, WA — B
Sonoma State U, CA — B
Southern Oregon U, OR — B
Southern Utah U, UT — B
Stanford U, CA — B
The U of Arizona, AZ — B
U of California, Berkeley, CA — B
U of California, Davis, CA — B
U of California, Irvine, CA — B
U of California, Los Angeles, CA — B
U of California, Riverside, CA — B
U of California, San Diego, CA — B
U of California, Santa Barbara, CA — B
U of California, Santa Cruz, CA — B
U of Colorado at Boulder, CO — B
U of Colorado at Colorado Springs, CO — B
U of Colorado at Denver and Health Sciences Center, CO — B
U of Dallas, TX — B
U of Denver, CO — B
U of Hawaii at Manoa, HI — B
U of Idaho, ID — B
U of La Verne, CA — B
The U of Montana, MT — B
U of Nevada, Las Vegas, NV — B
U of Nevada, Reno, NV — B
U of New Mexico, NM — B
U of New Orleans, LA — B
U of Northern Colorado, CO — B
U of Oregon, OR — B
U of Portland, OR — B
U of Puget Sound, WA — B
U of Redlands, CA — B
U of San Diego, CA — B
U of San Francisco, CA — B
U of Southern California, CA — B
U of the Pacific, CA — B
U of Utah, UT — B
U of Washington, WA — B
U of Wyoming, WY — B
Utah State U, UT — B
Utah Valley State Coll, UT — B
Vanguard U of Southern California, CA — B
Walla Walla Coll, WA — B
Washington State U, WA — B
Weber State U, UT — B
Western Oregon U, OR — B
Western State Coll of Colorado, CO — B
Western Washington U, WA — B
Westmont Coll, CA — B
Whitman Coll, WA — B
Whitworth U, WA — B
Willamette U, OR — B

Spanish and Iberian Studies
Santa Clara U, CA — B

Spanish Language Teacher Education
Brigham Young U, UT — B
California Lutheran U, CA — B
California State U, Chico, CA — B
Central Washington U, WA — B
Colorado State U, CO — B
Colorado State U-Pueblo, CO — B
Eastern Washington U, WA — B

Montana State U–Billings, MT — B
Northern Arizona U, AZ — B
Northwest Nazarene U, ID — B
The U of Arizona, AZ — B
U of Utah, UT — B
Utah Valley State Coll, UT — B
Washington State U, WA — B
Weber State U, UT — B

Special Education
Arizona State U, AZ — B
Arizona State U at the West campus, AZ — B
Boise State U, ID — B
Brigham Young U, UT — B
Brigham Young U–Hawaii, HI — B
Central Washington U, WA — B
Coll of the Southwest, NM — B
Eastern New Mexico U, NM — B
Eastern Oregon U, OR — B
Eastern Washington U, WA — B
Gonzaga U, WA — B
Grand Canyon U, AZ — B
Idaho State U, ID — B
La Sierra U, CA — B
Montana State U–Billings, MT — A,B
New Mexico Highlands U, NM — B
New Mexico State U, NM — B
North Carolina Ag and Tech State U, NC — B
Northern Arizona U, AZ — B
Pacific Lutheran U, WA — B
Pacific Oaks Coll, CA — B
Prescott Coll, AZ — B
Seattle Pacific U, WA — B
Southern Utah U, UT — B
The U of Arizona, AZ — B
U of California, Los Angeles, CA — B
U of Great Falls, MT — B
U of Hawaii at Manoa, HI — B
U of Idaho, ID — B
U of Nevada, Las Vegas, NV — B
U of Nevada, Reno, NV — B
U of New Mexico, NM — B
U of Northern Colorado, CO — B
U of the Pacific, CA — B
U of Utah, UT — B
U of Wyoming, WY — B
Utah State U, UT — B
Washington State U, WA — B
Western State Coll of Colorado, CO — B
Western Washington U, WA — B
Westminster Coll, UT — B
Whitworth U, WA — B

Special Education (Early Childhood)
Eastern Washington U, WA — B

Special Education (Gifted and Talented)
U of Great Falls, MT — B

Special Education Related
Nevada State Coll at Henderson, NV — B
U of Wyoming, WY — B

Special Education (Speech or Language Impaired)
New Mexico State U, NM — B
Northern Arizona U, AZ — B

Special Products Marketing
Brigham Young U–Idaho, ID — A
Oregon State U, OR — B
San Francisco State U, CA — B

Speech and Rhetoric

Adams State Coll, CO	B
Brigham Young U, UT	B
California Polytechnic State U, San Luis Obispo, CA	B
California State U, Chico, CA	B
California State U, Fresno, CA	B
California State U, Fullerton, CA	B
California State U, Long Beach, CA	B
California State U, Los Angeles, CA	B
Gonzaga U, WA	B
Grand Canyon U, AZ	B
Humboldt State U, CA	B
The Master's Coll and Seminary, CA	B
North Carolina Ag and Tech State U, NC	B
Northern Arizona U, AZ	B
Oregon State U, OR	B
Pepperdine U, Malibu, CA	B
Portland State U, OR	B
San Diego State U, CA	B
San Francisco State U, CA	B
San Jose State U, CA	B
Southern Utah U, UT	B
U of Alaska Fairbanks, AK	B
U of California, Berkeley, CA	B
U of Hawaii at Manoa, HI	B
The U of Montana, MT	B
U of New Mexico, NM	B
U of Utah, UT	B
U of Washington, WA	B
Utah State U, UT	B
Vanguard U of Southern California, CA	B
Walla Walla Coll, WA	B
Whitworth U, WA	B
Willamette U, OR	B

Speech-Language Pathology

Nevada State Coll at Henderson, NV	B
U of Nevada, Reno, NV	B
U of Northern Colorado, CO	B

Speech Teacher Education

Brigham Young U, UT	B
The U of Arizona, AZ	B

Speech Therapy

Brigham Young U–Idaho, ID	A
U of Redlands, CA	B

Sport and Fitness Administration/Management

Albertson Coll of Idaho, ID	B
Central Washington U, WA	B
Concordia U, OR	B
Corban Coll, OR	B
Fort Lewis Coll, CO	B
Fresno Pacific U, CA	B
George Fox U, OR	B
Gonzaga U, WA	B
Montana State U, MT	B
Montana State U–Billings, MT	B
National U, CA	B
Saint Mary's Coll of California, CA	B
U of Nevada, Las Vegas, NV	B
Washington State U, WA	B
Western State Coll of Colorado, CO	B

Statistics

Brigham Young U, UT	B
California Polytechnic State U, San Luis Obispo, CA	B
California State Polytechnic U, Pomona, CA	B
California State U, Chico, CA	B
California State U, Fullerton, CA	B
California State U, Long Beach, CA	B
Eastern New Mexico U, NM	B
Mesa State Coll, CO	B
San Diego State U, CA	B
San Francisco State U, CA	B
Sonoma State U, CA	B
Stanford U, CA	B
U of California, Berkeley, CA	B
U of California, Davis, CA	B
U of California, Los Angeles, CA	B
U of California, Riverside, CA	B
U of California, Santa Barbara, CA	B
U of Denver, CO	B
The U of Montana, MT	B
U of Nevada, Las Vegas, NV	B
U of New Mexico, NM	B
U of Washington, WA	B
U of Wyoming, WY	B
Utah State U, UT	B

Statistics Related

Brigham Young U, UT	B

Structural Engineering

U of California, San Diego, CA	B
U of Southern California, CA	B

Substance Abuse/Addiction Counseling

Bethany U, CA	B
U of Great Falls, MT	A,B

Surgical Technology

Boise State U, ID	A
Cambridge Coll, CO	A
Loma Linda U, CA	A
Montana State U–Billings, MT	A
The U of Montana, MT	A

Survey Technology

California State Polytechnic U, Pomona, CA	B
California State U, Fresno, CA	B
Idaho State U, ID	B
New Mexico State U, NM	B
Oregon Inst of Technology, OR	B
U of Alaska Anchorage, AK	A,B

Swedish

Brigham Young U, UT	B

System Administration

National American U, Denver, CO	A,B
U of Great Falls, MT	B

System, Networking, and LAN/WAN Management

DeVry U, Phoenix, AZ	A
DeVry U, Fremont, CA	A
DeVry U, Long Beach, CA	A
DeVry U, Pomona, CA	A
DeVry U, Sherman Oaks, CA	A
DeVry U, Westminster, CO	A
DeVry U, Federal Way, WA	A
ITT Tech Inst, Tucson, AZ	A

ITT Tech Inst, San Dimas, CA	A
ITT Tech Inst, CO	A
ITT Tech Inst, NM	A
LDS Business Coll, UT	A
National American U, Denver, CO	A,B
U of Great Falls, MT	B

Systems Engineering

Montana Tech of The U of Montana, MT	B
The U of Arizona, AZ	B
U of California, San Diego, CA	B
U of Southern California, CA	B

Systems Science and Theory

Stanford U, CA	B

Taxation

California State U, Fullerton, CA	B

Teacher Assistant/Aide

Boise State U, ID	A
New Mexico Highlands U, NM	A
New Mexico State U, NM	A
U of New Mexico, NM	A

Technical and Business Writing

Boise State U, ID	B
Coll of Santa Fe, NM	B
Montana Tech of The U of Montana, MT	B
New Mexico Inst of Mining and Technology, NM	B
San Francisco State U, CA	B
The U of Montana, MT	B
U of Washington, WA	B
Weber State U, UT	B

Technical Teacher Education

U of Idaho, ID	B
Utah State U, UT	B

Technology/Industrial Arts Teacher Education

Brigham Young U, UT	B
Central Washington U, WA	B
Montana State U, MT	B
Northern Arizona U, AZ	B
U of Idaho, ID	B
The U of Montana–Western, MT	B
U of Nevada, Reno, NV	B
U of New Mexico, NM	B
U of Wyoming, WY	B
Utah State U, UT	B

Telecommunications

California State Polytechnic U, Pomona, CA	B
California State U, Monterey Bay, CA	B
Colorado State U-Pueblo, CO	B
Columbia Coll Hollywood, CA	A,B
National U, CA	B
Pacific U, OR	B
Pepperdine U, Malibu, CA	B

Theater Design and Technology

Brigham Young U, UT	B
California Inst of the Arts, CA	B
Coll of Santa Fe, NM	B
George Fox U, OR	B
Rocky Mountain Coll, MT	B
U of Alaska Fairbanks, AK	B
The U of Arizona, AZ	B

U of California, Santa Cruz, CA	B
U of New Mexico, NM	B
U of Southern California, CA	B

Theater Literature, History and Criticism

Saint Mary's Coll of California, CA	B

Theater/Theater Arts Management

California Inst of the Arts, CA	B
Coll of Santa Fe, NM	B
U of Southern California, CA	B

Theological and Ministerial Studies Related

California Baptist U, CA	B
Northwest Christian Coll, OR	B
Point Loma Nazarene U, CA	B

Theology

Azusa Pacific U, CA	B
Bethany U, CA	B
Biola U, CA	B
California Baptist U, CA	B
Concordia U, CA	B
Concordia U, OR	B
Corban Coll, OR	B
Grand Canyon U, AZ	B
Loyola Marymount U, CA	B
The Master's Coll and Seminary, CA	B
Multnomah Bible Coll and Biblical Seminary, OR	B
Northwest Nazarene U, ID	B
Pacific Union Coll, CA	B
Saint Mary's Coll of California, CA	B
San Diego Christian Coll, CA	B
Seattle Pacific U, WA	B
U of Dallas, TX	B
U of Great Falls, MT	B
U of Portland, OR	B
U of San Francisco, CA	B
Walla Walla Coll, WA	B
Warner Pacific Coll, OR	B
William Jessup U, CA	A,B

Theology and Religious Vocations Related

Simpson U, CA	B

Theoretical and Mathematical Physics

San Diego State U, CA	B

Therapeutic Recreation

Brigham Young U, UT	B
California State U, Chico, CA	B
Eastern Washington U, WA	B
Pacific Lutheran U, WA	B

Tool and Die Technology

Utah State U, UT	B

Tourism and Travel Services Management

Alliant International U, CA	B
Brigham Young U–Hawaii, HI	A,B
Fort Lewis Coll, CO	B
Hawai'i Pacific U, HI	B
Mesa State Coll, CO	A
Morrison U, NV	B
New Mexico Highlands U, NM	B
San Diego State U, CA	B
U of Hawaii at Manoa, HI	B

A—associate degree; B—bachelor's degree

The U of Montana–Western, MT — A
U of Nevada, Las Vegas, NV — B

Tourism and Travel Services Marketing
Dixie State Coll of Utah, UT — A
The U of Montana–Western, MT — A,B

Tourism Promotion
New Mexico State U, NM — B

Tourism/Travel Marketing
Western State Coll of Colorado, CO — B

Toxicology
Humboldt State U, CA — B
U of California, Berkeley, CA — B

Trade and Industrial Teacher Education
Brigham Young U–Idaho, ID — A
California Polytechnic State U, San Luis Obispo, CA — B
California State U, Fresno, CA — B
California State U, Long Beach, CA — B
California State U, San Bernardino, CA — B
Central Washington U, WA — B
North Carolina Ag and Tech State U, NC — B
San Diego State U, CA — B
San Francisco State U, CA — B
U of Idaho, ID — B
U of Nevada, Reno, NV — B
U of Wyoming, WY — B

Transportation Technology
North Carolina Ag and Tech State U, NC — B
San Francisco State U, CA — B

Turf and Turfgrass Management
Colorado State U, CO — B

Urban Forestry
U of California, Davis, CA — B

Urban Studies/Affairs
Arizona State U, AZ — B
California State Polytechnic U, Pomona, CA — B
California State U, Northridge, CA — B
Eugene Lang Coll The New School for Liberal Arts, NY — B
Loyola Marymount U, CA — B
Mount St. Mary's Coll, CA — A
Portland State U, OR — B
San Diego State U, CA — B
San Francisco State U, CA — B
Stanford U, CA — B
U of California, Berkeley, CA — B
U of California, San Diego, CA — B
U of New Orleans, LA — B
U of San Diego, CA — B
U of Southern California, CA — B
U of Utah, UT — B
U of Washington, Tacoma, WA — B

Vehicle/Equipment Operation
The U of Montana, MT — A

Vehicle Maintenance and Repair Technologies Related
U of Alaska Fairbanks, AK — A

Veterinary/Animal Health Technology
Brigham Young U, UT — B

Veterinary Sciences
Washington State U, WA — B

Violin, Viola, Guitar and Other Stringed Instruments
Brigham Young U, UT — B
California Inst of the Arts, CA — B
California State U, Fullerton, CA — B
The Colburn School Conservatory of Music, CA — B
Notre Dame de Namur U, CA — B
San Francisco Conservatory of Music, CA — B
U of Southern California, CA — B
U of Washington, WA — B
Willamette U, OR — B

Visual and Performing Arts
Arizona State U at the West campus, AZ — B
Art Center Coll of Design, CA — B
California Baptist U, CA — B
California State U Channel Islands, CA — B
California State U, San Marcos, CA — B
Claremont McKenna Coll, CA — B
The Evergreen State Coll, WA — B
Naropa U, CO — B
New Mexico State U, NM — B
Regis U, CO — B
San Jose State U, CA — B
The U of Arizona, AZ — B
U of San Diego, CA — B
U of San Francisco, CA — B
U of Utah, UT — B
Western Washington U, WA — B
William Jessup U, CA — B

Visual and Performing Arts Related
Brigham Young U, UT — B
Claremont McKenna Coll, CA — B
Dominican U of California, CA — B
Saint Mary's Coll of California, CA — B
San Francisco Art Inst, CA — B
Scripps Coll, CA — B
U of California, Davis, CA — B
U of California, Los Angeles, CA — B

Vocational Rehabilitation Counseling
U of Northern Colorado, CO — B

Voice and Opera
Brigham Young U, UT — B
Brigham Young U–Hawaii, HI — B
California Inst of the Arts, CA — B
California State U, Fullerton, CA — B
California State U, Long Beach, CA — B
Central Washington U, WA — B
Chapman U, CA — B
Corban Coll, OR — B
Eastern Washington U, WA — B
Grand Canyon U, AZ — B
Loyola Marymount U, CA — B
The Master's Coll and Seminary, CA — B
Mount St. Mary's Coll, CA — B
Notre Dame de Namur U, CA — B

Pacific Lutheran U, WA — B
San Diego Christian Coll, CA — B
San Francisco Conservatory of Music, CA — B
U of Idaho, ID — B
U of Redlands, CA — B
U of the Pacific, CA — B
U of Washington, WA — B
Walla Walla Coll, WA — B
Whitworth U, WA — B
Willamette U, OR — B

Water Resources Engineering
Dixie State Coll of Utah, UT — A
The U of Arizona, AZ — B
U of Nevada, Reno, NV — B
U of Southern California, CA — B

Web/Multimedia Management and Webmaster
Academy of Art U, CA — A,B
ITT Tech Inst, Tempe, AZ — A
ITT Tech Inst, Tucson, AZ — A
ITT Tech Inst, Rancho Cordova, CA — A
ITT Tech Inst, CO — A
ITT Tech Inst, ID — A
ITT Tech Inst, NV — A
ITT Tech Inst, NM — A
ITT Tech Inst, OR — A
ITT Tech Inst, UT — A
ITT Tech Inst, Bothell, WA — A
ITT Tech Inst, Seattle, WA — A
ITT Tech Inst, Spokane, WA — A
Lewis-Clark State Coll, ID — A,B
Pioneer Pacific Coll, Wilsonville, OR — A
Platt Coll San Diego, CA — A
U of Great Falls, MT — A

Web Page, Digital/Multimedia and Information Resources Design
The Art Inst of California–Inland Empire, CA — B
The Art Inst of California–Los Angeles, CA — A,B
The Art Inst of California–San Francisco, CA — B
The Art Inst of Phoenix, AZ — B
The Art Inst of Portland, OR — A,B
Azusa Pacific U, CA — B
Dixie State Coll of Utah, UT — A
ITT Tech Inst, Tempe, AZ — A
ITT Tech Inst, Tucson, AZ — A
ITT Tech Inst, Anaheim, CA — A
ITT Tech Inst, Lathrop, CA — A
ITT Tech Inst, Oxnard, CA — A
ITT Tech Inst, Rancho Cordova, CA — A
ITT Tech Inst, San Bernardino, CA — A
ITT Tech Inst, San Diego, CA — A
ITT Tech Inst, San Dimas, CA — A
ITT Tech Inst, Sylmar, CA — A
ITT Tech Inst, Torrance, CA — A
ITT Tech Inst, CO — A
ITT Tech Inst, ID — A
ITT Tech Inst, NV — A
ITT Tech Inst, NM — A
ITT Tech Inst, OR — A
ITT Tech Inst, UT — A
ITT Tech Inst, Bothell, WA — A
ITT Tech Inst, Seattle, WA — A
ITT Tech Inst, Spokane, WA — A
LDS Business Coll, UT — A

National American U, Denver, CO — A,B
Neumont U, UT —
Platt Coll San Diego, CA — A,B
U of Great Falls, MT — B

Welding Technology
Boise State U, ID — A
Brigham Young U–Idaho, ID — A
Great Basin Coll, NV — A
Idaho State U, ID — A
Lewis-Clark State Coll, ID — A,B
Mesa State Coll, CO — A
Montana Tech of The U of Montana, MT — B
U of Alaska Anchorage, AK — A
The U of Montana, MT — A
U of New Mexico–Gallup, NM — A
Utah Valley State Coll, UT — A

Western Civilization
St. John's Coll, NM — B
Thomas Aquinas Coll, CA — B

Wildlife and Wildlands Science and Management
Brigham Young U, UT — B
Brigham Young U–Idaho, ID — A
Colorado State U, CO — B
Dixie State Coll of Utah, UT — A
Eastern New Mexico U, NM — B
Humboldt State U, CA — B
New Mexico State U, NM — B
Northern Arizona U, AZ — B
Oregon State U, OR — B
Prescott Coll, AZ — B
U of Alaska Fairbanks, AK — B
The U of Arizona, AZ — B
U of Idaho, ID — B
The U of Montana, MT — B
U of Nevada, Reno, NV — B
U of Washington, WA — B
Utah State U, UT — B
Washington State U, WA — B

Wildlife Biology
Grand Canyon U, AZ — B
New Mexico State U, NM — B
Western State Coll of Colorado, CO — B

Wind/Percussion Instruments
California State U, Fullerton, CA — B
Chapman U, CA — B
Grand Canyon U, AZ — B
San Francisco Conservatory of Music, CA — B
U of Southern California, CA — B

Women's Studies
Arizona State U, AZ — B
Arizona State U at the West campus, AZ — B
California State U, Chico, CA — B
California State U, Fresno, CA — B
California State U, Fullerton, CA — B
California State U, Long Beach, CA — B
California State U, Northridge, CA — B
California State U, Sacramento, CA — B
California State U, San Marcos, CA — B
Claremont McKenna Coll, CA — B
The Colorado Coll, CO — B
Dominican U of California, CA — B

Eugene Lang Coll The New
  School for Liberal Arts, NY   B
Fort Lewis Coll, CO   B
Mills Coll, CA   B
Nazarene Bible Coll, CO   A
Northern Arizona U, AZ   B
Occidental Coll, CA   B
Pacific Lutheran U, WA   B
Pitzer Coll, CA   B
Pomona Coll, CA   B
Portland State U, OR   B
Saint Mary's Coll of California,
  CA   B
San Diego State U, CA   B
San Francisco State U, CA   B
Scripps Coll, CA   B
Sonoma State U, CA   B
Stanford U, CA   B
The U of Arizona, AZ   B
U of California, Berkeley, CA   B
U of California, Davis, CA   B
U of California, Irvine, CA   B
U of California, Los Angeles,
  CA   B

U of California, Riverside, CA   B
U of California, San Diego, CA   B
U of California, Santa Barbara,
  CA   B
U of California, Santa Cruz,
  CA   B
U of Colorado at Boulder, CO   B
U of Denver, CO   B
U of Hawaii at Manoa, HI   B
The U of Montana, MT   B
U of Nevada, Las Vegas, NV   B
U of Nevada, Reno, NV   B
U of New Mexico, NM   B
U of New Orleans, LA   B
U of Oregon, OR   B
U of Utah, UT   B
U of Washington, WA   B
U of Wyoming, WY   B
Washington State U, WA   B
Western Washington U, WA   B
Willamette U, OR   B

Wood Science and Wood Products/Pulp and Paper Technology
Oregon State U, OR   B

U of Idaho, ID   B
U of Washington, WA   B

Work and Family Studies
Brigham Young U, UT   B

Youth Ministry
California Baptist U, CA   B
Colorado Christian U, CO   B
Corban Coll, OR   B
Eugene Bible Coll, OR   B
George Fox U, OR   B
Multnomah Bible Coll and
  Biblical Seminary, OR   B
Northwest U, WA   B
Point Loma Nazarene U, CA   B
Vanguard U of Southern
  California, CA   B

Zoology/Animal Biology
Brigham Young U, UT   B
Brigham Young U–Idaho, ID   A
California State Polytechnic U,
  Pomona, CA   B
California State U, Fresno, CA   B

California State U, Long
  Beach, CA   B
Colorado State U, CO   B
Dixie State Coll of Utah, UT   A
Humboldt State U, CA   B
Idaho State U, ID   B
Northern Arizona U, AZ   B
Oregon State U, OR   B
San Francisco State U, CA   B
Sonoma State U, CA   B
Southern Utah U, UT   B
U of California, Davis, CA   B
U of California, Santa Barbara,
  CA   B
U of Hawaii at Manoa, HI   B
U of Idaho, ID   B
The U of Montana, MT   B
U of Washington, WA   B
U of Wyoming, WY   B
Utah State U, UT   B
Washington State U, WA   B
Weber State U, UT   B

A—associate degree; B—bachelor's degree

Athletic Programs and Scholarships

Archery

California State U, Long Beach, CA	M, W
Seattle U, WA	M, W

Badminton

California State U, Chico, CA	M, W
California State U, Dominguez Hills, CA	M, W
California State U, Long Beach, CA	M, W
Claremont McKenna Coll, CA	M, W
Eastern Washington U, WA	M
San Jose State U, CA	M, W
U of California, Irvine, CA	M, W
U of Oregon, OR	M, W
U of Wyoming, WY	M, W

Baseball

Albertson Coll of Idaho, ID	M(s)
Arizona State U, AZ	M(s)
Azusa Pacific U, CA	M(s)
Bethany U, CA	M
Biola U, CA	M(s)
Brigham Young U, UT	M(s)
California Baptist U, CA	M(s)
California Inst of Technology, CA	M
California Lutheran U, CA	M
California Polytechnic State U, San Luis Obispo, CA	M(s)
California State Polytechnic U, Pomona, CA	M(s)
California State U, Chico, CA	M(s)
California State U, Fresno, CA	M(s)
California State U, Fullerton, CA	M(s)
California State U, Los Angeles, CA	M(s)
California State U, Northridge, CA	M(s)
California State U, Sacramento, CA	M(s)
California State U, San Bernardino, CA	M(s)
California State U, Stanislaus, CA	M
Central Washington U, WA	M(s)
Chapman U, CA	M
Claremont McKenna Coll, CA	M
Coll of the Southwest, NM	M(s)
Colorado School of Mines, CO	M(s)
Colorado State U-Pueblo, CO	M
Concordia U, CA	M(s)
Concordia U, OR	M(s)
Corban Coll, OR	M(s)
Dixie State Coll of Utah, UT	M(s)
Eastern New Mexico U, NM	M(s)
Eastern Oregon U, OR	M
Eastern Washington U, WA	M
Fort Lewis Coll, CO	M
Fresno Pacific U, CA	M
George Fox U, OR	M
Gonzaga U, WA	M(s)
Grand Canyon U, AZ	M(s)
Harvey Mudd Coll, CA	M
Hawai'i Pacific U, HI	M(s)
Johnson & Wales U, CO	M
Lewis & Clark Coll, OR	M
Lewis-Clark State Coll, ID	M(s)
Linfield Coll, OR	M

Loyola Marymount U, CA	M(s)
The Master's Coll and Seminary, CA	M(s)
Menlo Coll, CA	M
Mesa State Coll, CO	M(s)
Montana State U–Billings, MT	M
New Mexico Highlands U, NM	M(s)
New Mexico State U, NM	M(s)
North Carolina Ag and Tech State U, NC	M(s)
Northwest Nazarene U, ID	M(s)
Occidental Coll, CA	M
Oregon Inst of Technology, OR	M
Oregon State U, OR	M(s)
Pacific Lutheran U, WA	M
Pacific U, OR	M
Pepperdine U, Malibu, CA	M(s)
Pitzer Coll, CA	M
Point Loma Nazarene U, CA	M(s)
Pomona Coll, CA	M
Portland State U, OR	M(s)
Regis U, CO	M(s)
Saint Mary's Coll of California, CA	M(s)
San Diego State U, CA	M(s)
San Francisco State U, CA	M(s), W(s)
San Jose State U, CA	M(s)
Santa Clara U, CA	M(s)
Seattle U, WA	M, W
Simpson U, CA	M
Sonoma State U, CA	M(s)
Southern Utah U, UT	M(s)
Stanford U, CA	M(s)
United States Air Force Academy, CO	M
The U of Arizona, AZ	M(s)
U of California, Berkeley, CA	M(s)
U of California, Davis, CA	M
U of California, Irvine, CA	M(s)
U of California, Los Angeles, CA	M(s)
U of California, Riverside, CA	M(s)
U of California, San Diego, CA	M
U of California, Santa Barbara, CA	M(s)
U of Colorado at Boulder, CO	M
U of Colorado at Colorado Springs, CO	M
U of Dallas, TX	M
U of Hawaii at Hilo, HI	M(s)
U of Hawaii at Manoa, HI	M(s)
U of Idaho, ID	M
U of La Verne, CA	M
The U of Montana, MT	M
U of Nevada, Las Vegas, NV	M(s)
U of Nevada, Reno, NV	M(s)
U of New Mexico, NM	M
U of New Orleans, LA	M(s)
U of Northern Colorado, CO	M(s)
U of Oregon, OR	M
U of Portland, OR	M(s)
U of Puget Sound, WA	M
U of Redlands, CA	M
U of San Diego, CA	M(s)
U of San Francisco, CA	M(s)
U of Southern California, CA	M(s)
U of the Pacific, CA	M(s)

U of Utah, UT	M(s)
U of Washington, WA	M(s)
U of Wyoming, WY	M
Utah State U, UT	M
Utah Valley State Coll, UT	M(s)
Vanguard U of Southern California, CA	M(s)
Washington State U, WA	M(s)
Weber State U, UT	M
Western Oregon U, OR	M
Western State Coll of Colorado, CO	M
Westmont Coll, CA	M(s)
Whitman Coll, WA	M
Whitworth U, WA	M
Willamette U, OR	M

Basketball

Adams State Coll, CO	M(s), W(s)
Albertson Coll of Idaho, ID	M(s), W(s)
Arizona State U, AZ	M(s), W(s)
Azusa Pacific U, CA	M(s), W(s)
Bethany U, CA	M(s), W(s)
Biola U, CA	M(s), W(s)
Boise State U, ID	M(s), W(s)
Brigham Young U, UT	M(s), W(s)
Brigham Young U–Hawaii, HI	M(s)
California Baptist U, CA	M(s), W(s)
California Christian Coll, CA	M
California Inst of Technology, CA	M, W
California Lutheran U, CA	M, W
California Maritime Academy, CA	M(s), W(s)
California Polytechnic State U, San Luis Obispo, CA	M(s), W(s)
California State Polytechnic U, Pomona, CA	M(s), W(s)
California State U, Chico, CA	M(s), W(s)
California State U, Dominguez Hills, CA	M(s), W(s)
California State U, Fresno, CA	M(s), W(s)
California State U, Fullerton, CA	M(s), W(s)
California State U, Long Beach, CA	M(s), W(s)
California State U, Los Angeles, CA	M(s), W(s)
California State U, Monterey Bay, CA	M, W
California State U, Northridge, CA	M(s), W(s)
California State U, Sacramento, CA	M(s), W(s)
California State U, San Bernardino, CA	M(s), W(s)
California State U, Stanislaus, CA	M, W
Cascade Coll, OR	M(s), W(s)
Central Washington U, WA	M(s), W(s)
Chapman U, CA	M, W
Claremont McKenna Coll, CA	M, W
Colorado Christian U, CO	M(s), W(s)
The Colorado Coll, CO	M, W
Colorado School of Mines, CO	M(s), W(s)
Colorado State U, CO	M(s), W(s)
Colorado State U-Pueblo, CO	M(s), W(s)
Concordia U, CA	M(s), W(s)
Concordia U, OR	M(s), W(s)
Corban Coll, OR	M(s), W(s)
Dixie State Coll of Utah, UT	M(s), W(s)
Dominican U of California, CA	M(s), W(s)
Eastern New Mexico U, NM	M(s), W(s)

M—for men; W—for women; (s)—scholarship offered

Basketball

Eastern Oregon U, OR	M, W
Eastern Washington U, WA	M(s), W(s)
Eugene Bible Coll, OR	M
The Evergreen State Coll, WA	M(s), W(s)
Fort Lewis Coll, CO	M(s), W(s)
Fresno Pacific U, CA	M(s), W(s)
George Fox U, OR	M, W
Gonzaga U, WA	M(s), W(s)
Grand Canyon U, AZ	M(s), W(s)
Harvey Mudd Coll, CA	M, W
Hawai'i Pacific U, HI	M(s)
Holy Names U, CA	M(s), W(s)
Hope International U, CA	M(s), W(s)
Humboldt State U, CA	M(s), W(s)
Idaho State U, ID	M(s), W(s)
Johnson & Wales U, CO	M, W
La Sierra U, CA	M, W
Lewis & Clark Coll, OR	M, W
Lewis-Clark State Coll, ID	M(s), W(s)
Linfield Coll, OR	M, W
Little Big Horn Coll, MT	M, W
Loyola Marymount U, CA	M(s), W(s)
The Master's Coll and Seminary, CA	M(s), W(s)
Menlo Coll, CA	M, W
Mesa State Coll, CO	M(s), W(s)
Montana State U, MT	M(s), W(s)
Montana State U–Billings, MT	M(s), W(s)
Montana Tech of The U of Montana, MT	M(s), W(s)
Multnomah Bible Coll and Biblical Seminary, OR	M
New Mexico Highlands U, NM	M(s), W(s)
New Mexico State U, NM	M(s), W(s)
North Carolina Ag and Tech State U, NC	M(s), W(s)
Northern Arizona U, AZ	M(s), W(s)
Northwest Christian Coll, OR	M(s), W(s)
Northwest Nazarene U, ID	M(s), W(s)
Northwest U, WA	M(s), W(s)
Notre Dame de Namur U, CA	M, W
Occidental Coll, CA	M, W
Oregon Inst of Technology, OR	M(s), W
Oregon State U, OR	M(s), W(s)
Pacific Lutheran U, WA	M, W
Pacific Union Coll, CA	M, W
Pacific U, OR	M, W
Patten U, CA	M(s), W(s)
Pepperdine U, Malibu, CA	M(s), W(s)
Pitzer Coll, CA	M, W
Point Loma Nazarene U, CA	M(s), W(s)
Pomona Coll, CA	M, W
Portland State U, OR	M(s), W(s)
Reed Coll, OR	M
Regis U, CO	M(s), W(s)
Saint Mary's Coll of California, CA	M(s), W(s)
San Diego Christian Coll, CA	M(s), W(s)
San Diego State U, CA	M(s), W(s)
San Francisco State U, CA	M(s), W(s)
San Jose State U, CA	M(s), W(s)
Santa Clara U, CA	M(s), W(s)
Scripps Coll, CA	W
Seattle Pacific U, WA	M(s), W(s)
Seattle U, WA	M(s), W(s)
Simpson U, CA	M, W
Sonoma State U, CA	M(s), W(s)
Southern Oregon U, OR	M(s), W(s)
Southern Utah U, UT	M(s), W(s)
Stanford U, CA	M(s), W(s)
United States Air Force Academy, CO	M, W
U of Alaska Anchorage, AK	M(s), W(s)
U of Alaska Fairbanks, AK	M(s), W(s)
The U of Arizona, AZ	M(s), W(s)
U of California, Berkeley, CA	M(s), W(s)
U of California, Davis, CA	M, W
U of California, Irvine, CA	M(s), W(s)

U of California, Los Angeles, CA	M(s), W(s)
U of California, Riverside, CA	M(s), W(s)
U of California, San Diego, CA	M, W
U of California, Santa Barbara, CA	M(s), W(s)
U of California, Santa Cruz, CA	M, W
U of Colorado at Boulder, CO	M(s), W(s)
U of Colorado at Colorado Springs, CO	M(s), W(s)
U of Dallas, TX	M, W
U of Denver, CO	M(s), W(s)
U of Great Falls, MT	M(s), W(s)
U of Hawaii at Hilo, HI	M(s)
U of Hawaii at Manoa, HI	M(s), W(s)
U of Idaho, ID	M(s), W(s)
U of La Verne, CA	M, W
The U of Montana, MT	M(s), W(s)
The U of Montana–Western, MT	M(s), W(s)
U of Nevada, Las Vegas, NV	M(s), W(s)
U of Nevada, Reno, NV	M(s), W(s)
U of New Mexico, NM	M(s), W(s)
U of New Orleans, LA	M(s), W(s)
U of Northern Colorado, CO	M(s), W(s)
U of Oregon, OR	M(s), W(s)
U of Portland, OR	M(s), W(s)
U of Puget Sound, WA	M, W
U of Redlands, CA	M, W
U of San Diego, CA	M(s), W(s)
U of San Francisco, CA	M(s), W(s)
U of Southern California, CA	M(s), W(s)
U of the Pacific, CA	M(s), W(s)
U of Utah, UT	M(s), W(s)
U of Washington, WA	M(s), W(s)
U of Wyoming, WY	M(s), W(s)
Utah State U, UT	M(s), W(s)
Utah Valley State Coll, UT	M(s), W(s)
Vanguard U of Southern California, CA	M(s), W(s)
Walla Walla Coll, WA	M, W
Warner Pacific Coll, OR	M(s), W(s)
Washington State U, WA	M(s), W(s)
Weber State U, UT	M(s), W(s)
Western Oregon U, OR	M, W
Western State Coll of Colorado, CO	M(s), W(s)
Western Washington U, WA	M(s), W(s)
Westminster Coll, UT	M, W
Westmont Coll, CA	M(s), W(s)
Whitman Coll, WA	M, W
Whitworth U, WA	M, W
Willamette U, OR	M, W
William Jessup U, CA	M, W

Bowling

California State U, Chico, CA	M, W
California State U, Fullerton, CA	M, W
California State U, Long Beach, CA	M, W
California State U, Sacramento, CA	M, W
Central Washington U, WA	M, W
San Jose State U, CA	M, W
U of California, Santa Barbara, CA	M, W
U of Colorado at Boulder, CO	M, W
U of Oregon, OR	M, W
U of Utah, UT	M, W
Washington State U, WA	M, W
Weber State U, UT	M, W

Cheerleading

Brigham Young U, UT	M(s), W(s)
California Lutheran U, CA	M, W
California State U, Chico, CA	M, W
California State U, Sacramento, CA	M, W
Central Washington U, WA	M, W
Claremont McKenna Coll, CA	M, W
Dominican U of California, CA	W
Fort Lewis Coll, CO	M, W
Hawai'i Pacific U, HI	M(s), W(s)
Hope International U, CA	M, W

Johnson & Wales U, CO	M, W
Montana State U, MT	M(s), W(s)
Occidental Coll, CA	W
Pacific Lutheran U, WA	M, W
Pacific U, OR	M, W
Pepperdine U, Malibu, CA	M, W
San Jose State U, CA	M, W
Seattle U, WA	M, W
Simpson U, CA	W
United States Air Force Academy, CO	M, W
U of California, San Diego, CA	M, W
U of Great Falls, MT	M, W
U of Nevada, Las Vegas, NV	M(s), W(s)
U of Nevada, Reno, NV	M, W
U of Oregon, OR	M(s), W(s)
U of Puget Sound, WA	M, W
U of Utah, UT	M(s), W(s)
U of Wyoming, WY	M(s), W(s)
Weber State U, UT	M(s), W(s)
Western State Coll of Colorado, CO	W
Western Washington U, WA	M, W

Crew

California Maritime Academy, CA	M, W
California State U, Long Beach, CA	M, W
California State U, Sacramento, CA	M(s), W(s)
Chapman U, CA	W
Gonzaga U, WA	M, W
Humboldt State U, CA	M, W
Lewis & Clark Coll, OR	M, W
Loyola Marymount U, CA	M, W(s)
Mills Coll, CA	W
Occidental Coll, CA	W
Oregon State U, OR	M, W
Pacific Lutheran U, WA	M, W
Pepperdine U, Malibu, CA	M, W
Reed Coll, OR	M, W
Saint Mary's Coll of California, CA	M, W
Santa Clara U, CA	M, W
Seattle Pacific U, WA	M, W
Seattle U, WA	M, W
Stanford U, CA	M, W(s)
U of California, Berkeley, CA	M(s), W(s)
U of California, Irvine, CA	M(s), W(s)
U of California, Los Angeles, CA	W
U of California, San Diego, CA	M, W
U of California, Santa Barbara, CA	M, W
U of Colorado at Boulder, CO	M, W
The U of Montana, MT	M, W
U of Oregon, OR	M, W
U of Puget Sound, WA	M, W
U of San Diego, CA	M, W
U of Southern California, CA	W(s)
U of Washington, WA	M(s), W(s)
Washington State U, WA	M, W
Western Washington U, WA	M(s), W(s)
Willamette U, OR	M, W

Cross-Country Running

Adams State Coll, CO	M(s), W(s)
Alliant International U, CA	M(s), W(s)
Arizona State U, AZ	M(s), W(s)
Azusa Pacific U, CA	M(s), W(s)
Biola U, CA	M(s), W(s)
Boise State U, ID	M(s), W(s)
Brigham Young U, UT	M(s), W(s)
Brigham Young U–Hawaii, HI	M(s), W(s)
California Inst of Technology, CA	M, W
California Lutheran U, CA	M, W
California Polytechnic State U, San Luis Obispo, CA	
California State Polytechnic U, Pomona, CA	M(s), W(s)
California State U, Chico, CA	M(s), W(s)
California State U, Fresno, CA	M(s), W(s)
California State U, Fullerton, CA	M(s), W(s)

M—for men; W—for women; (s)—scholarship offered

California State U, Long Beach, CA M(s), W(s)
California State U, Los Angeles, CA W(s)
California State U, Monterey Bay, CA M, W
California State U, Northridge, CA M(s), W(s)
California State U, Sacramento, CA M(s), W(s)
California State U, San Marcos, CA M, W
California State U, Stanislaus, CA M, W
Cascade Coll, OR M(s), W(s)
Central Washington U, WA M(s), W(s)
Chapman U, CA M, W
Claremont McKenna Coll, CA M, W
Coll of the Southwest, NM M(s), W(s)
Colorado Christian U, CO M, W
The Colorado Coll, CO M, W
Colorado School of Mines, CO M(s), W(s)
Colorado State U, CO M(s), W(s)
Colorado State U-Pueblo, CO W(s)
Concordia U, CA M(s), W(s)
Corban Coll, OR M(s), W(s)
Eastern New Mexico U, NM M(s), W(s)
Eastern Oregon U, OR M, W
Eastern Washington U, WA M(s), W(s)
The Evergreen State Coll, WA M(s), W(s)
Fort Lewis Coll, CO M(s), W(s)
Fresno Pacific U, CA M(s), W(s)
George Fox U, OR M, W
Gonzaga U, WA M, W
Harvey Mudd Coll, CA M, W
Hawai'i Pacific U, HI M(s), W(s)
Holy Names U, CA M(s), W(s)
Humboldt State U, CA M(s), W(s)
Idaho State U, ID M(s), W(s)
Lewis & Clark Coll, OR M, W
Lewis-Clark State Coll, ID M(s), W(s)
Linfield Coll, OR M, W
Loyola Marymount U, CA M(s), W(s)
The Master's Coll and Seminary, CA M(s), W(s)
Menlo Coll, CA M, W
Mesa State Coll, CO W(s)
Mills Coll, CA W
Montana State U, MT M(s), W(s)
Montana State U–Billings, MT M(s), W(s)
Montana Tech of The U of Montana, MT M, W
New Mexico Highlands U, NM M(s), W(s)
New Mexico State U, NM M(s), W(s)
North Carolina Ag and Tech State U, NC M(s), W(s)
Northern Arizona U, AZ M(s), W(s)
Northwest Nazarene U, ID M(s), W(s)
Northwest U, WA M(s), W(s)
Notre Dame de Namur U, CA M, W
Occidental Coll, CA M, W
Oregon Inst of Technology, OR M(s), W(s)
Pacific Lutheran U, WA M, W
Pacific Union Coll, CA M, W
Pacific U, OR M, W
Patten U, CA M(s), W(s)
Pepperdine U, Malibu, CA M(s), W(s)
Pitzer Coll, CA M, W
Point Loma Nazarene U, CA M(s), W(s)
Pomona Coll, CA M, W
Portland State U, OR M(s), W(s)
Saint Mary's Coll of California, CA M(s), W(s)
San Diego Christian Coll, CA M(s), W(s)
San Diego State U, CA W(s)
San Francisco State U, CA M(s), W(s)
San Jose State U, CA M(s), W(s)
Santa Clara U, CA M(s), W(s)
Scripps Coll, CA W
Seattle Pacific U, WA M(s), W(s)
Seattle U, WA M(s), W(s)
Simpson U, CA M, W
Soka U of America, CA M, W
Sonoma State U, CA W(s)
Southern Oregon U, OR M(s), W(s)

Southern Utah U, UT M, W
Stanford U, CA M(s), W(s)
United States Air Force Academy, CO M, W
U of Alaska Anchorage, AK M(s)
U of Alaska Fairbanks, AK M(s), W(s)
The U of Arizona, AZ M(s), W(s)
U of California, Berkeley, CA M(s), W(s)
U of California, Davis, CA M, W
U of California, Irvine, CA M(s), W(s)
U of California, Los Angeles, CA M(s), W(s)
U of California, Riverside, CA M(s), W(s)
U of California, San Diego, CA M, W
U of California, Santa Barbara, CA M(s), W(s)
U of California, Santa Cruz, CA M, W
U of Colorado at Boulder, CO M(s), W(s)
U of Colorado at Colorado Springs, CO M(s), W(s)
U of Dallas, TX M, W
U of Great Falls, MT M, W
U of Hawaii at Hilo, HI M(s), W(s)
U of Hawaii at Manoa, HI W(s)
U of Idaho, ID M(s), W(s)
U of La Verne, CA M, W
The U of Montana, MT M(s), W(s)
U of Nevada, Las Vegas, NV W(s)
U of Nevada, Reno, NV W(s)
U of New Mexico, NM M(s), W(s)
U of New Orleans, LA M(s), W(s)
U of Northern Colorado, CO W(s)
U of Oregon, OR M(s), W(s)
U of Portland, OR M(s), W(s)
U of Puget Sound, WA M, W
U of Redlands, CA M, W
U of San Diego, CA M(s), W(s)
U of San Francisco, CA M(s), W(s)
U of Southern California, CA M(s), W(s)
U of the Pacific, CA W(s)
U of Utah, UT W(s)
U of Washington, WA M(s), W(s)
U of Wyoming, WY M(s), W(s)
Utah State U, UT M(s), W(s)
Utah Valley State Coll, UT M(s), W(s)
Vanguard U of Southern California, CA M(s), W(s)
Warner Pacific Coll, OR M(s), W(s)
Washington State U, WA M(s), W(s)
Weber State U, UT M(s), W(s)
Western Oregon U, OR M, W
Western State Coll of Colorado, CO M(s), W(s)
Western Washington U, WA M(s), W(s)
Westmont Coll, CA M(s), W(s)
Whitman Coll, WA M, W
Whitworth U, WA M, W
Willamette U, OR M, W

Equestrian Sports
California Polytechnic State U, San Luis Obispo, CA M, W
California State U, Fresno, CA W(s)
The Colorado Coll, CO M, W
New Mexico State U, NM M, W
Sierra Nevada Coll, NV M, W
Stanford U, CA M, W
U of California, Santa Barbara, CA M, W
U of California, Santa Cruz, CA M, W
U of Colorado at Boulder, CO M, W
The U of Montana, MT M, W
U of Nevada, Las Vegas, NV W
U of Oregon, OR M, W
U of San Diego, CA W
U of Wyoming, WY M, W
Utah State U, UT M, W
Washington State U, WA M, W

Fencing
California Inst of Technology, CA M, W
California State U, Fullerton, CA M(s), W(s)

California State U, Long Beach, CA M, W
Central Washington U, WA M, W
Fort Lewis Coll, CO M, W
Reed Coll, OR M, W
St. John's Coll, NM M, W
Scripps Coll, CA W
Stanford U, CA M(s), W(s)
United States Air Force Academy, CO M, W
U of California, Irvine, CA M, W
U of California, San Diego, CA M, W
U of California, Santa Barbara, CA M, W
U of California, Santa Cruz, CA M, W
U of Colorado at Boulder, CO M, W
The U of Montana, MT M, W
U of Oregon, OR M, W
U of Wyoming, WY M, W
Weber State U, UT M, W

Field Hockey
California State U, Chico, CA M, W
The Colorado Coll, CO M, W
Pepperdine U, Malibu, CA W
Stanford U, CA M, W(s)
U of California, Berkeley, CA W(s)
U of California, Santa Barbara, CA W
U of Colorado at Boulder, CO M, W
The U of Montana, MT W
U of the Pacific, CA W(s)

Football
Adams State Coll, CO M(s)
Arizona State U, AZ M(s)
Azusa Pacific U, CA M(s)
Boise State U, ID M(s)
Brigham Young U, UT M(s)
California Lutheran U, CA M
California Polytechnic State U, San Luis Obispo, CA M(s)
California State U, Fresno, CA M(s)
California State U, Northridge, CA M(s)
California State U, Sacramento, CA M(s)
Central Washington U, WA M(s)
Chapman U, CA M
Claremont McKenna Coll, CA M
The Colorado Coll, CO M
Colorado School of Mines, CO M(s)
Colorado State U, CO M(s)
Dixie State Coll of Utah, UT M(s)
Eastern New Mexico U, NM M(s)
Eastern Oregon U, OR M
Eastern Washington U, WA M(s)
Fort Lewis Coll, CO M(s)
Harvey Mudd Coll, CA M
Humboldt State U, CA M(s)
Idaho State U, ID M(s)
Lewis & Clark Coll, OR M
Linfield Coll, OR M
Menlo Coll, CA M
Mesa State Coll, CO M(s)
Montana State U, MT M(s)
Montana Tech of The U of Montana, MT M(s)
New Mexico Highlands U, NM M(s)
New Mexico State U, NM M(s)
North Carolina Ag and Tech State U, NC M(s)
Northern Arizona U, AZ M(s)
Occidental Coll, CA M
Oregon State U, OR M(s)
Pacific Lutheran U, WA M
Pitzer Coll, CA M
Pomona Coll, CA M
Portland State U, OR M(s)
San Diego State U, CA M(s)
San Jose State U, CA M(s)
Southern Oregon U, OR M(s)
Southern Utah U, UT M(s)

Football

Stanford U, CA	M(s)
United States Air Force Academy, CO	M
The U of Arizona, AZ	M(s)
U of California, Berkeley, CA	M(s)
U of California, Davis, CA	M
U of California, Los Angeles, CA	M(s)
U of Colorado at Boulder, CO	M(s)
U of Hawaii at Manoa, HI	M(s)
U of Idaho, ID	M(s)
U of La Verne, CA	M
The U of Montana, MT	M(s)
The U of Montana–Western, MT	M(s)
U of Nevada, Las Vegas, NV	M(s)
U of Nevada, Reno, NV	M(s)
U of New Mexico, NM	M(s)
U of Northern Colorado, CO	M(s)
U of Oregon, OR	M(s)
U of Puget Sound, WA	M
U of Redlands, CA	M
U of San Diego, CA	M
U of Southern California, CA	M(s)
U of Utah, UT	M(s)
U of Washington, WA	M(s)
U of Wyoming, WY	M(s)
Utah State U, UT	M(s)
Washington State U, WA	M(s)
Weber State U, UT	M(s)
Western Oregon U, OR	M
Western State Coll of Colorado, CO	M(s)
Western Washington U, WA	M(s)
Whitworth U, WA	M
Willamette U, OR	M

Golf

Adams State Coll, CO	M(s)
Albertson Coll of Idaho, ID	M(s), W(s)
Arizona State U, AZ	M(s), W(s)
Azusa Pacific U, CA	M(s)
Bethany U, CA	M, W
Boise State U, ID	M(s), W(s)
Brigham Young U, UT	M(s), W(s)
California Baptist U, CA	W
California Inst of Technology, CA	M
California Lutheran U, CA	M
California Maritime Academy, CA	M(s), W
California Polytechnic State U, San Luis Obispo, CA	M(s)
California State U, Chico, CA	M(s), W(s)
California State U, Fresno, CA	M(s)
California State U, Long Beach, CA	M, W
California State U, Monterey Bay, CA	M, W
California State U, Northridge, CA	M(s)
California State U, Sacramento, CA	M(s), W
California State U, San Bernardino, CA	M(s)
California State U, San Marcos, CA	M(s), W
California State U, Stanislaus, CA	M
Central Washington U, WA	M, W
Chapman U, CA	M, W
Claremont McKenna Coll, CA	M
Coll of the Southwest, NM	M(s), W(s)
Colorado Christian U, CO	M
Colorado School of Mines, CO	M(s)
Colorado State U, CO	M(s), W(s)
Colorado State U–Pueblo, CO	M(s), W(s)
Concordia U, OR	M(s), W(s)
Corban Coll, OR	M
Dixie State Coll of Utah, UT	M(s)
Eastern Washington U, WA	M, W(s)
Fort Lewis Coll, CO	M(s)
Gonzaga U, WA	M, W
Grand Canyon U, AZ	M(s)
Harvey Mudd Coll, CA	M
Hawai'i Pacific U, HI	M(s), W(s)
Holy Names U, CA	M(s)

Idaho State U, ID	M(s), W(s)
Johnson & Wales U, CO	M
Lewis & Clark Coll, OR	M, W
Lewis-Clark State Coll, ID	M(s), W(s)
Linfield Coll, OR	M, W
Loyola Marymount U, CA	M(s)
Marymount Coll, Palos Verdes, California, CA	M, W
The Master's Coll and Seminary, CA	M(s)
Menlo Coll, CA	M, W
Mesa State Coll, CO	W(s)
Montana State U, MT	W(s)
Montana State U–Billings, MT	M, W
Montana Tech of The U of Montana, MT	M(s), W(s)
New Mexico Inst of Mining and Technology, NM	M, W
New Mexico State U, NM	M(s), W(s)
Northern Arizona U, AZ	W(s)
Northwest Nazarene U, ID	M(s)
Notre Dame de Namur U, CA	M, W
Occidental Coll, CA	M, W
Oregon State U, OR	M(s), W(s)
Pacific Lutheran U, WA	M, W
Pacific U, OR	M, W
Patten U, CA	M(s)
Pepperdine U, Malibu, CA	M(s), W(s)
Pitzer Coll, CA	M
Point Loma Nazarene U, CA	M(s)
Pomona Coll, CA	M, W
Portland State U, OR	M(s), W(s)
Regis U, CO	M(s), W(s)
Saint Mary's Coll of California, CA	M(s)
San Diego State U, CA	M(s), W(s)
San Jose State U, CA	M(s), W(s)
Santa Clara U, CA	M(s), W(s)
Scripps Coll, CA	W
Seattle U, WA	M, W
Sonoma State U, CA	M
Southern Utah U, UT	M(s)
Stanford U, CA	M(s), W(s)
United States Air Force Academy, CO	M
The U of Arizona, AZ	M(s), W(s)
U of California, Berkeley, CA	M(s), W(s)
U of California, Davis, CA	M, W
U of California, Irvine, CA	M, W
U of California, Los Angeles, CA	M(s), W(s)
U of California, San Diego, CA	M
U of California, Santa Barbara, CA	M(s), W
U of California, Santa Cruz, CA	W
U of Colorado at Boulder, CO	M(s), W(s)
U of Colorado at Colorado Springs, CO	M(s)
U of Dallas, TX	M
U of Denver, CO	M(s), W(s)
U of Great Falls, MT	M, W
U of Hawaii at Hilo, HI	M(s)
U of Hawaii at Manoa, HI	M(s), W(s)
U of Idaho, ID	M(s), W(s)
U of La Verne, CA	M
The U of Montana, MT	W
The U of Montana–Western, MT	M(s), W(s)
U of Nevada, Las Vegas, NV	M(s)
U of Nevada, Reno, NV	M(s), W(s)
U of New Mexico, NM	M(s), W(s)
U of New Orleans, LA	M(s), W(s)
U of Northern Colorado, CO	M(s), W(s)
U of Oregon, OR	M(s), W(s)
U of Portland, OR	M(s), W(s)
U of Puget Sound, WA	M, W
U of Redlands, CA	M, W
U of San Diego, CA	M(s)
U of San Francisco, CA	M(s), W(s)
U of Southern California, CA	M(s), W(s)
U of the Pacific, CA	M(s)

U of Utah, UT	M(s)
U of Washington, WA	M(s), W(s)
U of Wyoming, WY	M(s), W(s)
Utah State U, UT	M(s)
Utah Valley State Coll, UT	M(s)
Walla Walla Coll, WA	M
Washington State U, WA	M(s), W(s)
Weber State U, UT	M(s), W(s)
Western Washington U, WA	M(s), W(s)
Westminster Coll, UT	M, W
Whitman Coll, WA	M, W
Whitworth U, WA	M, W
Willamette U, OR	M, W

Gymnastics

Arizona State U, AZ	W(s)
Boise State U, ID	W(s)
Brigham Young U, UT	W(s)
California Polytechnic State U, San Luis Obispo, CA	W(s)
California State U, Fullerton, CA	W(s)
California State U, Sacramento, CA	W(s)
Oregon State U, OR	W(s)
San Jose State U, CA	W(s)
Seattle Pacific U, WA	W(s)
Southern Utah U, UT	W(s)
Stanford U, CA	M(s), W(s)
United States Air Force Academy, CO	M, W
U of Alaska Anchorage, AK	W(s)
The U of Arizona, AZ	W(s)
U of California, Berkeley, CA	M(s), W(s)
U of California, Davis, CA	W
U of California, Los Angeles, CA	W(s)
U of California, Santa Barbara, CA	M, W(s)
U of Denver, CO	W(s)
U of Utah, UT	W(s)
U of Washington, WA	W(s)
Utah State U, UT	W(s)

Ice Hockey

California Inst of Technology, CA	M
California State U, Sacramento, CA	M
Central Washington U, WA	M, W
The Colorado Coll, CO	M(s), W
Eastern Washington U, WA	M
Fort Lewis Coll, CO	M, W
San Jose State U, CA	M, W
Stanford U, CA	M
United States Air Force Academy, CO	M
U of Alaska Anchorage, AK	M(s)
U of Alaska Fairbanks, AK	M(s)
The U of Arizona, AZ	M
U of Colorado at Boulder, CO	M, W
U of Denver, CO	M(s)
U of Idaho, ID	M
The U of Montana, MT	M, W
U of Oregon, OR	M
U of San Diego, CA	M
U of Utah, UT	M
U of Wyoming, WY	M, W
Utah State U, UT	M
Walla Walla Coll, WA	M
Washington State U, WA	M, W
Weber State U, UT	M
Western State Coll of Colorado, CO	M
Whitman Coll, WA	M

Lacrosse

Brigham Young U, UT	M
California State U, Chico, CA	M, W
California State U, Sacramento, CA	M, W
Claremont McKenna Coll, CA	M, W
The Colorado Coll, CO	M, W
The Evergreen State Coll, WA	M, W
Fort Lewis Coll, CO	M
Harvey Mudd Coll, CA	W

M—for men; W—for women; (s)—scholarship offered

Humboldt State U, CA	M, W
Lewis & Clark Coll, OR	M, W
Linfield Coll, OR	W
Loyola Marymount U, CA	M, W
Notre Dame de Namur U, CA	M
Occidental Coll, CA	M, W
Pacific Lutheran U, WA	M, W
Pacific U, OR	W
Pepperdine U, Malibu, CA	M
Pitzer Coll, CA	W
Regis U, CO	W(s)
Saint Mary's Coll of California, CA	M, W
Santa Clara U, CA	M, W
Scripps Coll, CA	W
Stanford U, CA	M, W
United States Air Force Academy, CO	M
The U of Arizona, AZ	M, W
U of California, Berkeley, CA	W(s)
U of California, Davis, CA	M, W
U of California, Irvine, CA	M, W
U of California, Santa Barbara, CA	M, W
U of California, Santa Cruz, CA	M, W
U of Colorado at Boulder, CO	M, W
U of Dallas, TX	W
U of Denver, CO	M(s), W(s)
The U of Montana, MT	M, W
U of Northern Colorado, CO	M
U of Oregon, OR	M, W(s)
U of Puget Sound, WA	W
U of Redlands, CA	W
U of San Diego, CA	M, W
Washington State U, WA	M, W
Weber State U, UT	M, W
Western State Coll of Colorado, CO	M, W
Westmont Coll, CA	W
Whitman Coll, WA	M, W
Willamette U, OR	M

Racquetball

Brigham Young U, UT	M, W
California State U, Sacramento, CA	M, W
Stanford U, CA	M, W
U of California, Irvine, CA	M, W
U of Colorado at Boulder, CO	M, W
U of Oregon, OR	M, W
U of Utah, UT	M, W
Weber State U, UT	M, W

Riflery

Seattle U, WA	M, W
United States Air Force Academy, CO	M, W
U of Alaska Fairbanks, AK	M(s), W(s)
U of Alaska Southeast, AK	M, W
U of Idaho, ID	M, W
U of Nevada, Reno, NV	M(s), W(s)
U of San Francisco, CA	M(s), W(s)
U of Wyoming, WY	M, W

Rock Climbing

California State U, Chico, CA	M, W
Fort Lewis Coll, CO	M, W

Rugby

Brigham Young U, UT	M
California Inst of Technology, CA	M
California Maritime Academy, CA	M
California State U, Chico, CA	M, W
California State U, Fullerton, CA	M
California State U, Long Beach, CA	M
California State U, Sacramento, CA	M, W
Central Washington U, WA	M, W
Claremont McKenna Coll, CA	M, W
The Colorado Coll, CO	M, W
The Evergreen State Coll, WA	W
Humboldt State U, CA	M, W
Loyola Marymount U, CA	M
Montana Tech of The U of Montana, MT	M, W

New Mexico Inst of Mining and Technology, NM	M, W
Occidental Coll, CA	M, W
Pacific Lutheran U, WA	M
Pepperdine U, Malibu, CA	M
Saint Mary's Coll of California, CA	M, W
San Jose State U, CA	M
Santa Clara U, CA	M, W
Scripps Coll, CA	W
Stanford U, CA	M, W
United States Air Force Academy, CO	W
The U of Arizona, AZ	M, W
U of California, Berkeley, CA	M(s)
U of California, Irvine, CA	M
U of California, Santa Barbara, CA	M
U of California, Santa Cruz, CA	M, W
U of Colorado at Boulder, CO	M, W
U of Hawaii at Manoa, HI	M
U of Idaho, ID	M, W
The U of Montana, MT	M, W
U of Northern Colorado, CO	M, W
U of Oregon, OR	M, W
U of Portland, OR	M
U of Puget Sound, WA	M, W
U of San Diego, CA	M
U of Utah, UT	M
U of Wyoming, WY	M, W
Utah State U, UT	M, W
Washington State U, WA	M, W
Weber State U, UT	M, W
Western Oregon U, OR	M, W
Western State Coll of Colorado, CO	M, W
Westmont Coll, CA	M
Whitman Coll, WA	M, W

Sailing

California Maritime Academy, CA	M, W
California State U, Long Beach, CA	M, W
Pepperdine U, Malibu, CA	M, W
Reed Coll, OR	M, W
San Jose State U, CA	M, W
Stanford U, CA	M, W
U of California, Irvine, CA	M, W
U of California, Santa Barbara, CA	M, W
U of California, Santa Cruz, CA	M, W
U of Hawaii at Manoa, HI	M, W
U of Oregon, OR	M, W

Skiing (Cross-Country)

Albertson Coll of Idaho, ID	M, W
Eastern Oregon U, OR	M, W
Fort Lewis Coll, CO	M, W
Gonzaga U, WA	M, W
Montana State U, MT	M(s), W(s)
Stanford U, CA	M, W
United States Air Force Academy, CO	M, W
U of Alaska Anchorage, AK	M(s), W(s)
U of Alaska Fairbanks, AK	M(s), W(s)
U of Colorado at Boulder, CO	M(s), W(s)
U of Denver, CO	M(s), W(s)
U of Idaho, ID	M, W
U of Nevada, Reno, NV	M(s), W(s)
U of New Mexico, NM	M(s), W(s)
U of Utah, UT	M(s), W(s)
Washington State U, WA	M, W
Western State Coll of Colorado, CO	M(s), W(s)
Whitman Coll, WA	M, W

Skiing (Downhill)

Albertson Coll of Idaho, ID	M(s), W(s)
Boise State U, ID	W
California State U, Long Beach, CA	M, W
California State U, Sacramento, CA	M, W
Claremont McKenna Coll, CA	M, W
The Colorado Coll, CO	M, W
Colorado School of Mines, CO	M
Eastern Oregon U, OR	M, W
Fort Lewis Coll, CO	M, W

Gonzaga U, WA	M, W
Idaho State U, ID	M, W
Montana State U, MT	M(s), W(s)
Reed Coll, OR	W
Scripps Coll, CA	W
Seattle U, WA	M, W
Sierra Nevada Coll, NV	M(s), W(s)
Southern Oregon U, OR	M, W
Stanford U, CA	M, W
United States Air Force Academy, CO	M, W
U of Alaska Anchorage, AK	M(s), W(s)
U of California, Santa Barbara, CA	M, W
U of Colorado at Boulder, CO	M(s), W(s)
U of Denver, CO	M(s), W(s)
U of Idaho, ID	M, W
The U of Montana, MT	M, W
U of Nevada, Reno, NV	M(s), W(s)
U of New Mexico, NM	M(s), W(s)
U of Oregon, OR	M, W
U of Puget Sound, WA	M, W
U of Utah, UT	M(s), W(s)
U of Wyoming, WY	M, W
Washington State U, WA	M, W
Weber State U, UT	M, W
Western State Coll of Colorado, CO	M(s), W(s)
Whitman Coll, WA	M, W

Soccer

Albertson Coll of Idaho, ID	M(s), W(s)
Alliant International U, CA	M(s), W(s)
Arizona State U, AZ	W(s)
Azusa Pacific U, CA	M(s), W(s)
Bethany U, CA	M, W
Biola U, CA	M(s), W(s)
Boise State U, ID	W
Brigham Young U, UT	M, W(s)
California Baptist U, CA	M(s), W(s)
California Inst of Technology, CA	M, W
California Lutheran U, CA	M, W
California Maritime Academy, CA	M(s)
California Polytechnic State U, San Luis Obispo, CA	M, W
California State Polytechnic U, Pomona, CA	M(s), W(s)
California State U, Chico, CA	M(s), W(s)
California State U, Dominguez Hills, CA	M(s), W(s)
California State U, Fresno, CA	M(s), W(s)
California State U, Fullerton, CA	M(s), W(s)
California State U, Long Beach, CA	M, W(s)
California State U, Los Angeles, CA	M(s), W(s)
California State U, Monterey Bay, CA	M, W
California State U, Northridge, CA	M(s)
California State U, Sacramento, CA	M(s), W(s)
California State U, San Bernardino, CA	M(s), W(s)
California State U, Stanislaus, CA	M, W
Cascade Coll, OR	M(s), W(s)
Central Washington U, WA	M, W(s)
Chapman U, CA	M, W
Claremont McKenna Coll, CA	M, W
Coll of the Southwest, NM	M(s), W(s)
Colorado Christian U, CO	M(s), W(s)
The Colorado Coll, CO	M, W(s)
Colorado School of Mines, CO	M
Colorado State U-Pueblo, CO	M, W
Concordia U, CA	M(s), W(s)
Concordia U, OR	M(s), W(s)
Corban Coll, OR	M(s), W(s)
Dixie State Coll of Utah, UT	W(s)
Dominican U of California, CA	M(s), W(s)
Eastern New Mexico U, NM	W(s)
Eastern Oregon U, OR	W
Eastern Washington U, WA	W(s)
Eugene Bible Coll, OR	M, W
The Evergreen State Coll, WA	M(s), W(s)
Fort Lewis Coll, CO	M(s), W(s)

Fresno Pacific U, CA	M(s), W(s)
George Fox U, OR	M, W
Gonzaga U, WA	M(s), W(s)
Grand Canyon U, AZ	M(s), W(s)
Harvey Mudd Coll, CA	M, W
Hawai'i Pacific U, HI	M(s), W(s)
Holy Names U, CA	M(s), W(s)
Hope International U, CA	M(s), W(s)
Humboldt State U, CA	M(s), W(s)
Johnson & Wales U, CO	M
La Sierra U, CA	M
Lewis & Clark Coll, OR	M, W
Linfield Coll, OR	M, W
Loyola Marymount U, CA	M(s), W(s)
The Master's Coll and Seminary, CA	M(s), W(s)
Menlo Coll, CA	M, W
Mesa State Coll, CO	W(s)
Mills Coll, CA	W
Montana State U–Billings, MT	M(s), W(s)
Montana Tech of The U of Montana, MT	M, W
New Mexico Highlands U, NM	W(s)
New Mexico Inst of Mining and Technology, NM	M, W
Northern Arizona U, AZ	W(s)
Northwest Nazarene U, ID	W(s)
Northwest U, WA	M(s)
Notre Dame de Namur U, CA	M, W
Occidental Coll, CA	M, W
Oregon Inst of Technology, OR	W
Oregon State U, OR	M(s), W(s)
Pacific Lutheran U, WA	M, W
Pacific U, OR	M, W
Patten U, CA	M(s), W(s)
Pepperdine U, Malibu, CA	M, W(s)
Pitzer Coll, CA	M, W
Point Loma Nazarene U, CA	M(s), W(s)
Pomona Coll, CA	M, W
Portland State U, OR	W(s)
Reed Coll, OR	M, W
Regis U, CO	M(s), W(s)
St. John's Coll, NM	M, W
Saint Mary's Coll of California, CA	M(s), W(s)
San Diego Christian Coll, CA	M(s), W(s)
San Diego State U, CA	M(s), W(s)
San Francisco State U, CA	M(s), W(s)
San Jose State U, CA	M(s), W(s)
Santa Clara U, CA	M(s), W(s)
Scripps Coll, CA	W
Seattle Pacific U, WA	M(s), W(s)
Seattle U, WA	M(s), W(s)
Simpson U, CA	M, W
Sonoma State U, CA	M(s), W(s)
Southern Oregon U, OR	W(s)
Stanford U, CA	M(s), W(s)
United States Air Force Academy, CO	M, W
The U of Arizona, AZ	M, W(s)
U of California, Berkeley, CA	M(s), W(s)
U of California, Davis, CA	M, W
U of California, Irvine, CA	M(s), W(s)
U of California, Los Angeles, CA	M(s), W(s)
U of California, San Diego, CA	M, W
U of California, Santa Barbara, CA	M(s), W(s)
U of California, Santa Cruz, CA	M, W
U of Colorado at Boulder, CO	M, W(s)
U of Colorado at Colorado Springs, CO	M(s), W
U of Dallas, TX	M, W
U of Denver, CO	M(s), W(s)
U of Great Falls, MT	W(s)
U of Hawaii at Manoa, HI	W(s)
U of Idaho, ID	M, W(s)
U of La Verne, CA	M, W
The U of Montana, MT	W
U of Nevada, Las Vegas, NV	M(s), W(s)

U of Nevada, Reno, NV	W(s)
U of New Mexico, NM	M(s), W(s)
U of Northern Colorado, CO	M, W(s)
U of Oregon, OR	M, W
U of Portland, OR	M(s), W(s)
U of Puget Sound, WA	M, W
U of Redlands, CA	M, W
U of San Diego, CA	M(s), W(s)
U of San Francisco, CA	M(s), W(s)
U of Southern California, CA	W(s)
U of the Pacific, CA	W(s)
U of Utah, UT	M, W(s)
U of Washington, WA	M(s), W
U of Wyoming, WY	M, W(s)
Utah State U, UT	M, W(s)
Utah Valley State Coll, UT	W(s)
Vanguard U of Southern California, CA	M(s), W(s)
Walla Walla Coll, WA	M
Warner Pacific Coll, OR	M, W
Washington State U, WA	M, W(s)
Weber State U, UT	M, W(s)
Western Oregon U, OR	W
Western State Coll of Colorado, CO	M, W
Western Washington U, WA	M(s), W(s)
Westminster Coll, UT	M
Westmont Coll, CA	M(s), W(s)
Whitman Coll, WA	M(s), W(s)
Whitworth U, WA	M, W
Willamette U, OR	M, W
William Jessup U, CA	M, W

Softball

Adams State Coll, CO	W(s)
Albertson Coll of Idaho, ID	W(s)
Arizona State U, AZ	W(s)
Azusa Pacific U, CA	W(s)
Bethany U, CA	W(s)
Biola U, CA	W(s)
Brigham Young U, UT	W(s)
Brigham Young U–Hawaii, HI	W(s)
California Baptist U, CA	W(s)
California Lutheran U, CA	W
California Polytechnic State U, San Luis Obispo, CA	W(s)
California State U, Chico, CA	W(s)
California State U, Fresno, CA	W(s)
California State U, Fullerton, CA	W(s)
California State U, Long Beach, CA	W(s)
California State U, Northridge, CA	W(s)
California State U, Sacramento, CA	W(s)
California State U, San Bernardino, CA	W(s)
California State U, Stanislaus, CA	W
Central Washington U, WA	W(s)
Chapman U, CA	W
Claremont McKenna Coll, CA	W
Coll of the Southwest, NM	W(s)
The Colorado Coll, CO	W
Colorado School of Mines, CO	W(s)
Colorado State U, CO	W(s)
Colorado State U-Pueblo, CO	W(s)
Concordia U, CA	W(s)
Concordia U, OR	W(s)
Corban Coll, OR	W(s)
Dixie State Coll of Utah, UT	W(s)
Dominican U of California, CA	W(s)
Eastern New Mexico U, NM	W(s)
Eastern Oregon U, OR	W
Fort Lewis Coll, CO	W(s)
George Fox U, OR	W
Harvey Mudd Coll, CA	W
Hawai'i Pacific U, HI	W(s)
Hope International U, CA	W(s)
Humboldt State U, CA	W(s)

Lewis & Clark Coll, OR	W
Linfield Coll, OR	W
The Master's Coll and Seminary, CA	W(s)
Menlo Coll, CA	W
Mesa State Coll, CO	W(s)
Montana State U–Billings, MT	W
New Mexico Highlands U, NM	W(s)
New Mexico State U, NM	W(s)
North Carolina Ag and Tech State U, NC	W
Northwest Christian Coll, OR	W(s)
Northwest Nazarene U, ID	W(s)
Notre Dame de Namur U, CA	W
Occidental Coll, CA	W
Oregon Inst of Technology, OR	W(s)
Oregon State U, OR	W(s)
Pacific Lutheran U, WA	W
Pacific U, OR	W
Patten U, CA	W(s)
Pitzer Coll, CA	W
Point Loma Nazarene U, CA	W(s)
Pomona Coll, CA	W
Portland State U, OR	W(s)
Regis U, CO	W(s)
Saint Mary's Coll of California, CA	W(s)
San Diego State U, CA	W(s)
San Francisco State U, CA	W(s)
San Jose State U, CA	W
Santa Clara U, CA	W(s)
Scripps Coll, CA	W
Seattle U, WA	W(s)
Sonoma State U, CA	W(s)
Southern Oregon U, OR	W(s)
Southern Utah U, UT	W(s)
Stanford U, CA	W(s)
United States Air Force Academy, CO	W
The U of Arizona, AZ	W(s)
U of California, Berkeley, CA	W(s)
U of California, Davis, CA	W
U of California, Irvine, CA	M, W
U of California, Los Angeles, CA	W(s)
U of California, Riverside, CA	W(s)
U of California, San Diego, CA	W
U of California, Santa Barbara, CA	W(s)
U of California, Santa Cruz, CA	W
U of Colorado at Boulder, CO	W
U of Colorado at Colorado Springs, CO	W(s)
U of Dallas, TX	W
U of Great Falls, MT	W
U of Hawaii at Hilo, HI	W(s)
U of Hawaii at Manoa, HI	W(s)
U of La Verne, CA	W
U of Nevada, Las Vegas, NV	W(s)
U of Nevada, Reno, NV	W(s)
U of New Mexico, NM	W(s)
U of Northern Colorado, CO	W(s)
U of Oregon, OR	W(s)
U of Puget Sound, WA	W
U of Redlands, CA	W
U of San Diego, CA	W
U of San Francisco, CA	M, W
U of the Pacific, CA	W(s)
U of Utah, UT	W
U of Washington, WA	W(s)
Utah State U, UT	W(s)
Utah Valley State Coll, UT	W(s)
Vanguard U of Southern California, CA	W(s)
Walla Walla Coll, WA	W
Washington State U, WA	W
Weber State U, UT	W
Western Oregon U, OR	W
Western Washington U, WA	W(s)
Whitman Coll, WA	M, W

M—for men; W—for women; (s)—scholarship offered

Whitworth U, WA	W
Willamette U, OR	W

Squash
Reed Coll, OR	M, W
Stanford U, CA	M, W
U of Colorado at Boulder, CO	M, W

Swimming and Diving
Arizona State U, AZ	M(s), W(s)
Biola U, CA	M(s), W(s)
Brigham Young U, UT	M(s), W(s)
California Baptist U, CA	M(s), W(s)
California Inst of Technology, CA	M, W
California Lutheran U, CA	M, W
California Polytechnic State U, San Luis Obispo, CA	M, W
California State U, Fresno, CA	W(s)
California State U, Northridge, CA	M(s), W(s)
California State U, San Bernardino, CA	M(s), W(s)
Chapman U, CA	M, W
Claremont McKenna Coll, CA	M, W
The Colorado Coll, CO	M, W
Colorado School of Mines, CO	M(s), W(s)
Colorado State U, CO	W(s)
Harvey Mudd Coll, CA	M, W
Lewis & Clark Coll, OR	M, W
Linfield Coll, OR	M, W
Loyola Marymount U, CA	W(s)
Mills Coll, CA	W
Montana Tech of The U of Montana, MT	M, W
New Mexico State U, NM	W(s)
North Carolina Ag and Tech State U, NC	W(s)
Northern Arizona U, AZ	W(s)
Occidental Coll, CA	M, W
Oregon State U, OR	W(s)
Pacific Lutheran U, WA	M, W
Pacific U, OR	M, W
Pepperdine U, Malibu, CA	W(s)
Pitzer Coll, CA	M, W
Pomona Coll, CA	M, W
San Diego State U, CA	W(s)
San Francisco State U, CA	M(s), W(s)
San Jose State U, CA	W(s)
Scripps Coll, CA	W
Seattle U, WA	M(s), W(s)
Soka U of America, CA	M, W
Stanford U, CA	M(s), W(s)
United States Air Force Academy, CO	M, W
U of Alaska Anchorage, AK	M(s)
U of Alaska Fairbanks, AK	W(s)
The U of Arizona, AZ	M(s), W(s)
U of California, Berkeley, CA	M(s), W(s)
U of California, Davis, CA	M, W
U of California, Irvine, CA	M(s), W(s)
U of California, Los Angeles, CA	W(s)
U of California, San Diego, CA	M, W
U of California, Santa Barbara, CA	M(s), W(s)
U of California, Santa Cruz, CA	M, W
U of Colorado at Boulder, CO	M, W
U of Denver, CO	M(s), W(s)
U of Hawaii at Manoa, HI	M(s), W(s)
U of La Verne, CA	M, W
U of Nevada, Las Vegas, NV	M(s), W(s)
U of Nevada, Reno, NV	W(s)
U of New Mexico, NM	W(s)
U of Northern Colorado, CO	W(s)
U of Oregon, OR	M, W
U of Puget Sound, WA	M, W
U of Redlands, CA	M, W
U of San Diego, CA	W(s)
U of Southern California, CA	M(s), W(s)
U of the Pacific, CA	M(s), W(s)
U of Utah, UT	M(s), W(s)

U of Washington, WA	M(s), W(s)
U of Wyoming, WY	M(s), W(s)
Washington State U, WA	W(s)
Weber State U, UT	M, W
Whitman Coll, WA	M, W
Whitworth U, WA	M, W
Willamette U, OR	M, W

Table Tennis
California State U, Long Beach, CA	M
Northwestern Polytechnic U, CA	M
U of California, Irvine, CA	M, W
U of California, Santa Cruz, CA	M, W
U of Oregon, OR	M, W
U of Utah, UT	M, W

Tennis
Albertson Coll of Idaho, ID	M(s), W(s)
Alliant International U, CA	M(s), W(s)
Arizona State U, AZ	M(s), W(s)
Azusa Pacific U, CA	M(s)
Biola U, CA	W(s)
Boise State U, ID	M(s), W(s)
Brigham Young U, UT	M(s), W(s)
Brigham Young U–Hawaii, HI	M(s), W(s)
California Baptist U, CA	W
California Inst of Technology, CA	M, W
California Lutheran U, CA	M, W
California Polytechnic State U, San Luis Obispo, CA	M, W
California State Polytechnic U, Pomona, CA	M(s), W(s)
California State U, Fresno, CA	M(s), W(s)
California State U, Fullerton, CA	W(s)
California State U, Long Beach, CA	W(s)
California State U, Los Angeles, CA	W(s)
California State U, Northridge, CA	W(s)
California State U, Sacramento, CA	M(s), W(s)
Chapman U, CA	M, W
Claremont McKenna Coll, CA	M, W
Coll of Santa Fe, NM	M(s), W(s)
Colorado Christian U, CO	M, W
The Colorado Coll, CO	M, W
Colorado School of Mines, CO	M(s), W(s)
Colorado State U, CO	W(s)
Colorado State U–Pueblo, CO	M(s), W(s)
Dominican U of California, CA	M(s), W(s)
Eastern New Mexico U, NM	W(s)
Eastern Washington U, WA	M(s), W(s)
Fresno Pacific U, CA	M, W
George Fox U, OR	M, W
Gonzaga U, WA	M(s), W(s)
Grand Canyon U, AZ	W(s)
Harvey Mudd Coll, CA	M, W
Hawai'i Pacific U, HI	M(s), W(s)
Hope International U, CA	M(s), W(s)
Idaho State U, ID	M(s), W(s)
Johnson & Wales U, CO	M, W
Lewis & Clark Coll, OR	M, W
Lewis-Clark State Coll, ID	M(s), W(s)
Linfield Coll, OR	M, W
Loyola Marymount U, CA	M(s), W(s)
Marymount Coll, Palos Verdes, California, CA	M(s), W(s)
Mesa State Coll, CO	M(s), W(s)
Mills Coll, CA	W
Montana State U, MT	M(s), W(s)
Montana State U–Billings, MT	M(s), W(s)
New Mexico State U, NM	M(s), W(s)
North Carolina Ag and Tech State U, NC	M(s), W(s)
Northern Arizona U, AZ	M(s), W(s)
Occidental Coll, CA	M, W
Pacific Lutheran U, WA	M, W
Pacific U, OR	M, W
Pepperdine U, Malibu, CA	M(s), W(s)
Pitzer Coll, CA	M, W

Point Loma Nazarene U, CA	M(s), W(s)
Pomona Coll, CA	M, W
Portland State U, OR	M(s), W(s)
Saint Mary's Coll of California, CA	M(s), W(s)
San Diego State U, CA	M(s), W(s)
San Jose State U, CA	W(s)
Santa Clara U, CA	M(s), W(s)
Scripps Coll, CA	W
Sonoma State U, CA	M(s), W(s)
Southern Oregon U, OR	W(s)
Southern Utah U, UT	W(s)
Stanford U, CA	M(s), W(s)
United States Air Force Academy, CO	M, W
The U of Arizona, AZ	M(s), W(s)
U of California, Berkeley, CA	M(s), W(s)
U of California, Davis, CA	M, W
U of California, Irvine, CA	M(s), W(s)
U of California, Los Angeles, CA	M(s), W(s)
U of California, Riverside, CA	M(s), W(s)
U of California, San Diego, CA	M, W
U of California, Santa Barbara, CA	M(s), W(s)
U of California, Santa Cruz, CA	M, W
U of Colorado at Boulder, CO	M(s), W(s)
U of Colorado at Colorado Springs, CO	M(s), W(s)
U of Dallas, TX	M, W
U of Denver, CO	M(s), W(s)
U of Hawaii at Hilo, HI	M(s), W(s)
U of Hawaii at Manoa, HI	M(s), W(s)
U of Idaho, ID	M(s), W(s)
U of La Verne, CA	M, W
The U of Montana, MT	M(s), W(s)
U of Nevada, Las Vegas, NV	M(s), W(s)
U of Nevada, Reno, NV	M(s), W(s)
U of New Mexico, NM	M(s), W(s)
U of New Orleans, LA	M(s), W(s)
U of Northern Colorado, CO	M(s), W(s)
U of Oregon, OR	M(s), W(s)
U of Portland, OR	M(s), W(s)
U of Puget Sound, WA	M, W
U of Redlands, CA	M, W
U of San Diego, CA	M(s), W(s)
U of San Francisco, CA	M(s), W(s)
U of Southern California, CA	M(s), W(s)
U of the Pacific, CA	M(s), W(s)
U of Utah, UT	M(s), W(s)
U of Washington, WA	M(s), W(s)
U of Wyoming, WY	W(s)
Utah State U, UT	M(s), W(s)
Vanguard U of Southern California, CA	M(s), W(s)
Washington State U, WA	W(s)
Weber State U, UT	M(s), W(s)
Westmont Coll, CA	M(s), W(s)
Whitman Coll, WA	M, W
Whitworth U, WA	M, W
Willamette U, OR	M, W

Track and Field
Adams State Coll, CO	M(s), W(s)
Alliant International U, CA	M(s), W(s)
Arizona State U, AZ	M(s), W(s)
Azusa Pacific U, CA	M(s), W(s)
Biola U, CA	M(s), W(s)
Boise State U, ID	M(s), W(s)
Brigham Young U, UT	M(s), W(s)
California Inst of Technology, CA	M, W
California Lutheran U, CA	M, W
California Polytechnic State U, San Luis Obispo, CA	M(s), W(s)
California State Polytechnic U, Pomona, CA	M(s), W(s)
California State U, Chico, CA	M(s), W(s)
California State U, Fresno, CA	M(s), W(s)
California State U, Fullerton, CA	M(s), W(s)
California State U, Long Beach, CA	M(s), W(s)
California State U, Los Angeles, CA	M(s), W(s)

California State U, Northridge, CA	M(s), W(s)
California State U, Sacramento, CA	M(s), W(s)
California State U, San Marcos, CA	M, W
California State U, Stanislaus, CA	M, W
Cascade Coll, OR	M(s), W(s)
Central Washington U, WA	M(s), W(s)
Chapman U, CA	W
Claremont McKenna Coll, CA	M, W
Coll of the Southwest, NM	M(s), W(s)
The Colorado Coll, CO	M, W
Colorado School of Mines, CO	M(s), W(s)
Colorado State U, CO	M(s), W(s)
Concordia U, CA	M, W
Concordia U, OR	M(s), W(s)
Eastern New Mexico U, NM	M(s), W(s)
Eastern Oregon U, OR	M, W
Eastern Washington U, WA	M(s), W(s)
The Evergreen State Coll, WA	M, W
Fort Lewis Coll, CO	M, W
Fresno Pacific U, CA	M(s), W(s)
George Fox U, OR	M, W
Gonzaga U, WA	M, W
Harvey Mudd Coll, CA	M, W
Humboldt State U, CA	M(s), W(s)
Idaho State U, ID	M(s), W(s)
Lewis & Clark Coll, OR	M, W
Linfield Coll, OR	M, W
Montana State U, MT	M(s), W(s)
New Mexico Highlands U, NM	M, W
New Mexico State U, NM	W(s)
North Carolina Ag and Tech State U, NC	M(s), W(s)
Northern Arizona U, AZ	M(s), W(s)
Northwest Nazarene U, ID	M(s), W(s)
Northwest U, WA	M(s), W(s)
Occidental Coll, CA	M, W
Oregon Inst of Technology, OR	M(s), W(s)
Pacific Lutheran U, WA	M, W
Pacific U, OR	M, W
Pitzer Coll, CA	M, W
Point Loma Nazarene U, CA	M(s), W(s)
Pomona Coll, CA	M, W
Portland State U, OR	M(s), W(s)
San Diego State U, CA	W(s)
San Francisco State U, CA	M(s), W(s)
Santa Clara U, CA	M, W
Scripps Coll, CA	W
Seattle Pacific U, WA	M(s), W(s)
Seattle U, WA	M(s), W(s)
Soka U of America, CA	M, W
Sonoma State U, CA	W(s)
Southern Oregon U, OR	M(s), W(s)
Southern Utah U, UT	M(s), W(s)
Stanford U, CA	M(s), W(s)
United States Air Force Academy, CO	M, W
The U of Arizona, AZ	M(s), W(s)
U of California, Berkeley, CA	M(s)
U of California, Davis, CA	M, W
U of California, Irvine, CA	M(s), W(s)
U of California, Los Angeles, CA	M(s), W(s)
U of California, Riverside, CA	M(s), W(s)
U of California, San Diego, CA	M, W
U of California, Santa Barbara, CA	M, W
U of California, Santa Cruz, CA	M, W
U of Colorado at Boulder, CO	M(s), W(s)
U of Colorado at Colorado Springs, CO	M, W
U of Dallas, TX	M, W
U of Hawaii at Manoa, HI	W(s)
U of Idaho, ID	M(s), W(s)
U of La Verne, CA	M, W
The U of Montana, MT	M(s), W(s)
U of Nevada, Las Vegas, NV	W(s)
U of Nevada, Reno, NV	W(s)
U of New Mexico, NM	M(s), W(s)

U of New Orleans, LA	M(s), W(s)
U of Northern Colorado, CO	M(s), W(s)
U of Oregon, OR	M(s), W(s)
U of Portland, OR	M(s), W(s)
U of Puget Sound, WA	M, W
U of Redlands, CA	M, W
U of San Francisco, CA	W(s)
U of Southern California, CA	M(s), W(s)
U of Utah, UT	W(s)
U of Washington, WA	M(s), W(s)
U of Wyoming, WY	M(s), W(s)
Utah State U, UT	M(s), W(s)
Utah Valley State Coll, UT	M(s), W(s)
Vanguard U of Southern California, CA	M(s), W(s)
Warner Pacific Coll, OR	M, W
Washington State U, WA	M(s), W(s)
Weber State U, UT	M(s), W(s)
Western Oregon U, OR	M, W
Western State Coll of Colorado, CO	M(s), W(s)
Western Washington U, WA	M(s), W(s)
Westmont Coll, CA	M(s), W(s)
Whitman Coll, WA	M, W
Whitworth U, WA	M, W
Willamette U, OR	M, W

Ultimate Frisbee

California State U, Chico, CA	M, W
The Colorado Coll, CO	M, W
Fort Lewis Coll, CO	M, W
Occidental Coll, CA	M, W
Pacific Lutheran U, WA	M, W
Pomona Coll, CA	M, W
Stanford U, CA	M, W
U of California, Santa Barbara, CA	M, W
U of California, Santa Cruz, CA	M, W
U of Colorado at Boulder, CO	M, W
The U of Montana, MT	M, W
U of Oregon, OR	M, W
U of Wyoming, WY	M, W
Whitman Coll, WA	M, W

Volleyball

Adams State Coll, CO	W(s)
Albertson Coll of Idaho, ID	W(s)
Alliant International U, CA	W(s)
Arizona State U, AZ	W(s)
Azusa Pacific U, CA	M, W(s)
Bethany U, CA	M(s), W(s)
Biola U, CA	W(s)
Boise State U, ID	W(s)
Brigham Young U, UT	M(s), W(s)
Brigham Young U–Hawaii, HI	W(s)
California Baptist U, CA	M(s), W(s)
California Christian Coll, CA	W
California Inst of Technology, CA	M, W
California Lutheran U, CA	W
California Maritime Academy, CA	W(s)
California Polytechnic State U, San Luis Obispo, CA	W(s)
California State Polytechnic U, Pomona, CA	W(s)
California State U, Chico, CA	M, W
California State U, Dominguez Hills, CA	W(s)
California State U, Fresno, CA	W(s)
California State U, Fullerton, CA	W(s)
California State U, Long Beach, CA	M(s), W(s)
California State U, Los Angeles, CA	W(s)
California State U, Monterey Bay, CA	W
California State U, Northridge, CA	M(s), W(s)
California State U, Sacramento, CA	M, W(s)
California State U, San Bernardino, CA	W(s)
California State U, Stanislaus, CA	W
Cascade Coll, OR	W(s)

Central Washington U, WA	W(s)
Chapman U, CA	W
Claremont McKenna Coll, CA	M, W
Coll of the Southwest, NM	W(s)
Colorado Christian U, CO	W(s)
The Colorado Coll, CO	M, W
Colorado School of Mines, CO	W(s)
Colorado State U, CO	W(s)
Colorado State U-Pueblo, CO	W(s)
Concordia U, CA	W(s)
Concordia U, OR	W(s)
Corban Coll, OR	W(s)
Dixie State Coll of Utah, UT	W(s)
Dominican U of California, CA	W(s)
Eastern New Mexico U, NM	W(s)
Eastern Oregon U, OR	M, W
Eastern Washington U, WA	W(s)
Embry-Riddle Aeronautical U, AZ	W(s)
Eugene Bible Coll, OR	W
The Evergreen State Coll, WA	W(s)
Fort Lewis Coll, CO	W(s)
Fresno Pacific U, CA	M, W(s)
George Fox U, OR	W
Gonzaga U, WA	W(s)
Grand Canyon U, AZ	W(s)
Harvey Mudd Coll, CA	W
Hawai'i Pacific U, HI	W(s)
Holy Names U, CA	M(s), W(s)
Hope International U, CA	M(s), W(s)
Humboldt State U, CA	M, W(s)
Idaho State U, ID	W(s)
La Sierra U, CA	M, W
Lewis & Clark Coll, OR	W
Lewis-Clark State Coll, ID	W(s)
Linfield Coll, OR	W
Loyola Marymount U, CA	M, W(s)
The Master's Coll and Seminary, CA	W(s)
Menlo Coll, CA	W
Mesa State Coll, CO	W(s)
Mills Coll, CA	W
Montana State U, MT	W(s)
Montana State U–Billings, MT	W(s)
Montana Tech of The U of Montana, MT	W(s)
Multnomah Bible Coll and Biblical Seminary, OR	W
New Mexico Highlands U, NM	W(s)
New Mexico State U, NM	W(s)
North Carolina Ag and Tech State U, NC	W(s)
Northern Arizona U, AZ	W(s)
Northwest Nazarene U, ID	M, W(s)
Northwest U, WA	W(s)
Notre Dame de Namur U, CA	W
Occidental Coll, CA	M, W
Oregon Inst of Technology, OR	W(s)
Oregon State U, OR	W(s)
Pacific Lutheran U, WA	M, W
Pacific Union Coll, CA	M, W
Pacific U, OR	M, W
Pepperdine U, Malibu, CA	M(s), W(s)
Pitzer Coll, CA	W
Point Loma Nazarene U, CA	W(s)
Pomona Coll, CA	W
Portland State U, OR	W(s)
Regis U, CO	W(s)
Saint Mary's Coll of California, CA	M, W(s)
San Diego Christian Coll, CA	W(s)
San Diego State U, CA	M, W(s)
San Francisco State U, CA	W(s)
San Jose State U, CA	M, W(s)
Santa Clara U, CA	M, W(s)
Scripps Coll, CA	W
Seattle Pacific U, WA	W(s)
Seattle U, WA	M, W

M—for men; W—for women; (s)—scholarship offered

Simpson U, CA	W
Sonoma State U, CA	W(s)
Southern Oregon U, OR	W(s)
Stanford U, CA	M(s), W(s)
United States Air Force Academy, CO	W
U of Alaska Anchorage, AK	W(s)
U of Alaska Fairbanks, AK	W(s)
The U of Arizona, AZ	M, W(s)
U of California, Berkeley, CA	W(s)
U of California, Davis, CA	M, W
U of California, Irvine, CA	M(s), W(s)
U of California, Los Angeles, CA	M(s), W(s)
U of California, Riverside, CA	W(s)
U of California, San Diego, CA	M, W
U of California, Santa Barbara, CA	M(s), W(s)
U of California, Santa Cruz, CA	M, W
U of Colorado at Boulder, CO	M, W(s)
U of Colorado at Colorado Springs, CO	M, W(s)
U of Dallas, TX	W
U of Denver, CO	M, W(s)
U of Great Falls, MT	W(s)
U of Hawaii at Hilo, HI	W(s)
U of Hawaii at Manoa, HI	M(s), W(s)
U of Idaho, ID	W(s)
U of La Verne, CA	W
The U of Montana, MT	M, W(s)
The U of Montana–Western, MT	W(s)
U of Nevada, Las Vegas, NV	W(s)
U of Nevada, Reno, NV	W(s)
U of New Mexico, NM	W(s)
U of New Orleans, LA	W(s)
U of Northern Colorado, CO	W(s)
U of Oregon, OR	M, W(s)
U of Portland, OR	W(s)
U of Puget Sound, WA	W
U of Redlands, CA	W
U of San Diego, CA	M, W(s)
U of San Francisco, CA	M, W(s)
U of Southern California, CA	M(s), W(s)
U of the Pacific, CA	M(s), W(s)
U of Utah, UT	W(s)
U of Washington, WA	W(s)
U of Wyoming, WY	W(s)
Utah State U, UT	M, W(s)
Utah Valley State Coll, UT	W(s)

Vanguard U of Southern California, CA	W(s)
Walla Walla Coll, WA	M, W
Warner Pacific Coll, OR	W(s)
Washington State U, WA	M, W(s)
Weber State U, UT	W(s)
Western Oregon U, OR	W
Western State Coll of Colorado, CO	M, W(s)
Western Washington U, WA	W(s)
Westminster Coll, UT	W
Westmont Coll, CA	M, W(s)
Whitman Coll, WA	M(s), W(s)
Whitworth U, WA	W
Willamette U, OR	W
William Jessup U, CA	W

Water Polo

Arizona State U, AZ	W
Brigham Young U–Hawaii, HI	M(s)
California Baptist U, CA	M(s), W(s)
California Inst of Technology, CA	M, W
California Lutheran U, CA	M, W
California Maritime Academy, CA	M, W
California State U, Chico, CA	M, W
California State U, Long Beach, CA	M(s), W(s)
Central Washington U, WA	M, W
Chapman U, CA	M, W
Claremont McKenna Coll, CA	M, W
The Colorado Coll, CO	M, W
Colorado State U, CO	W(s)
Harvey Mudd Coll, CA	M, W
Loyola Marymount U, CA	M(s), W(s)
Occidental Coll, CA	M, W
Pepperdine U, Malibu, CA	M(s), W
Pitzer Coll, CA	M, W
Pomona Coll, CA	M, W
Saint Mary's Coll of California, CA	M, W
San Diego State U, CA	W(s)
San Jose State U, CA	W(s)
Santa Clara U, CA	M(s), W
Scripps Coll, CA	W
Seattle U, WA	M, W
Soka U of America, CA	M, W
Sonoma State U, CA	W
Stanford U, CA	M(s), W(s)
United States Air Force Academy, CO	M
U of California, Davis, CA	M, W
U of California, Irvine, CA	M(s), W

U of California, Los Angeles, CA	M(s), W(s)
U of California, San Diego, CA	M, W
U of California, Santa Barbara, CA	M(s), W(s)
U of California, Santa Cruz, CA	M, W
U of Colorado at Boulder, CO	M, W
U of Hawaii at Manoa, HI	W(s)
U of La Verne, CA	M, W
U of Oregon, OR	M, W
U of Redlands, CA	M, W
U of Southern California, CA	M(s), W(s)
U of the Pacific, CA	M(s), W(s)
Washington State U, WA	M
Weber State U, UT	M, W

Weight Lifting

Reed Coll, OR	M, W
United States Air Force Academy, CO	M, W
U of California, Irvine, CA	M, W

Wrestling

Adams State Coll, CO	M(s)
Arizona State U, AZ	M(s)
Boise State U, ID	M(s)
California Polytechnic State U, San Luis Obispo, CA	M(s)
California State U, Fresno, CA	M(s)
California State U, Fullerton, CA	M(s)
Colorado School of Mines, CO	M(s)
Embry-Riddle Aeronautical U, AZ	M(s)
Fort Lewis Coll, CO	M, W
Menlo Coll, CA	M, W
Oregon State U, OR	M(s)
Pacific U, OR	M, W
Portland State U, OR	M(s)
San Francisco State U, CA	M(s)
San Jose State U, CA	M, W
Southern Oregon U, OR	M(s)
Stanford U, CA	M(s)
United States Air Force Academy, CO	M
The U of Arizona, AZ	M
U of California, Davis, CA	M
U of Colorado at Boulder, CO	M
U of Great Falls, MT	M(s)
U of Northern Colorado, CO	M(s)
U of Oregon, OR	M(s)
U of Washington, WA	M
U of Wyoming, WY	M(s)
Utah Valley State Coll, UT	M(s)
Western State Coll of Colorado, CO	M(s), W

ROTC Programs

Alaska Pacific U, AK	AF(c)
Albertson Coll of Idaho, ID	A(c)
Alliant International U, CA	A(c)
Arizona State U, AZ	A, AF
Arizona State U at the Polytechnic Campus, AZ	A(c), AF(c)
Azusa Pacific U, CA	A(c)
Biola U, CA	A(c), AF(c)
Boise State U, ID	A
Brigham Young U, UT	A, AF
Brigham Young U–Hawaii, HI	A(c), N(c), AF(c)
Brigham Young U–Idaho, ID	A
California Baptist U, CA	A(c), AF(c)
California Inst of Technology, CA	A(c), AF(c)
California Lutheran U, CA	A(c), AF(c)
California Polytechnic State U, San Luis Obispo, CA	A
California State Polytechnic U, Pomona, CA	A, AF(c)
California State U, Dominguez Hills, CA	A(c), AF(c)
California State U, Fresno, CA	A, AF
California State U, Fullerton, CA	A
California State U, Long Beach, CA	A
California State U, Los Angeles, CA	A(c), AF(c)
California State U, Northridge, CA	A(c), AF(c)
California State U, Sacramento, CA	A(c), AF
California State U, San Bernardino, CA	A, AF
California State U, San Marcos, CA	A(c), N(c), AF(c)
Cascade Coll, OR	A(c), AF(c)
Central Washington U, WA	A, AF
Chapman U, CA	A(c), AF(c)
Claremont McKenna Coll, CA	A, AF(c)
Coll of Santa Fe, NM	AF(c)
Colorado Christian U, CO	A(c)
The Colorado Coll, CO	A(c)
Colorado School of Mines, CO	A
Colorado State U, CO	A, AF
Colorado State U–Pueblo, CO	A
Concordia U, OR	AF(c)
Corban Coll, OR	A(c), AF(c)
DeVry U, Phoenix, AZ	AF
Eastern Oregon U, OR	A
Eastern Washington U, WA	A
Embry-Riddle Aeronautical U, AZ	A, AF
George Fox U, OR	AF(c)

Gonzaga U, WA	A
Grand Canyon U, AZ	A, AF(c)
Harvey Mudd Coll, CA	A(c), AF
Hawai'i Pacific U, HI	A(c), AF(c)
Holy Names U, CA	A(c), AF(c)
Idaho State U, ID	A(c)
LDS Business Coll, UT	AF(c)
Lewis-Clark State Coll, ID	A, AF(c)
Linfield Coll, OR	AF(c)
Loyola Marymount U, CA	A(c), AF
Menlo Coll, CA	A(c)
Montana State U, MT	A, AF
Montana Tech of The U of Montana, MT	A
National U, CA	A(c), AF(c)
Nevada State Coll at Henderson, NV	A(c)
New Mexico State U, NM	A, AF
North Carolina Ag and Tech State U, NC	A, AF
Northern Arizona U, AZ	A, AF
Northwest Christian Coll, OR	A(c)
Northwest Nazarene U, ID	A
Northwest U, WA	A(c)
Occidental Coll, CA	A(c), AF(c)
Oregon Health & Science U, OR	A(c)
Oregon Inst of Technology, OR	A(c)
Oregon State U, OR	A, N, AF
Pacific Lutheran U, WA	A
Pacific U, OR	A(c), AF(c)
Pepperdine U, Malibu, CA	A(c), AF(c)
Pitzer Coll, CA	A(c), AF(c)
Point Loma Nazarene U, CA	A(c), N(c), AF(c)
Pomona Coll, CA	A(c), AF(c)
Portland State U, OR	A, AF(c)
Regis U, CO	A(c), AF(c)
Saint Mary's Coll of California, CA	A(c), AF(c)
Samuel Merritt Coll, CA	A(c), AF(c)
San Diego Christian Coll, CA	A(c), AF(c)
San Diego State U, CA	A, N, AF
San Francisco State U, CA	A(c), N(c), AF(c)
San Jose State U, CA	A, AF
Santa Clara U, CA	A, AF(c)
Scripps Coll, CA	A(c), AF(c)
Seattle Pacific U, WA	A(c), N(c), AF(c)
Seattle U, WA	A, AF(c)
Sierra Nevada Coll, NV	A(c)
Sonoma State U, CA	A(c), AF(c)
Southern Utah U, UT	A
Stanford U, CA	A(c), N(c), AF(c)
U of Alaska Anchorage, AK	AF
U of Alaska Fairbanks, AK	A
The U of Arizona, AZ	A, N, AF

U of California, Berkeley, CA	A, N, AF
U of California, Davis, CA	A, N(c), AF(c)
U of California, Irvine, CA	A(c), AF(c)
U of California, Los Angeles, CA	A, N, AF
U of California, Riverside, CA	A(c), AF(c)
U of California, San Diego, CA	A(c)
U of California, Santa Barbara, CA	A
U of California, Santa Cruz, CA	A(c), N(c), AF(c)
U of Colorado at Boulder, CO	A, N, AF
U of Colorado at Colorado Springs, CO	A
U of Colorado at Denver and Health Sciences Center, CO	A, AF(c)
U of Dallas, TX	A(c), AF(c)
U of Denver, CO	A(c), AF(c)
U of Hawaii at Manoa, HI	A, AF
U of Hawaii–West Oahu, HI	A(c), AF(c)
U of Idaho, ID	A, N, AF(c)
U of La Verne, CA	A(c)
The U of Montana, MT	A
U of Nevada, Reno, NV	A
U of New Mexico, NM	A, N, AF
U of New Orleans, LA	A(c), N(c), AF(c)
U of Northern Colorado, CO	A, AF
U of Oregon, OR	A, AF(c)
U of Portland, OR	A, AF
U of Puget Sound, WA	A(c)
U of Redlands, CA	A(c), AF(c)
U of San Diego, CA	A(c), N, AF(c)
U of San Francisco, CA	A, AF(c)
U of Southern California, CA	A, N, AF
U of the Pacific, CA	AF(c)
U of Utah, UT	A, N, AF
U of Washington, WA	A, N, AF
U of Washington, Bothell, WA	A(c), AF(c)
U of Washington, Tacoma, WA	A(c), N(c), AF(c)
U of Wyoming, WY	A, AF
Utah State U, UT	A, AF
Utah Valley State Coll, UT	A, AF(c)
Vanguard U of Southern California, CA	AF(c)
Warner Pacific Coll, OR	A(c), AF(c)
Washington State U, WA	A, N(c), AF
Weber State U, UT	A, N, AF
Western Oregon U, OR	A, AF(c)
Westminster Coll, UT	A(c), N(c), AF(c)
Westmont Coll, CA	A(c), AF(c)
Whitworth U, WA	A(c)
Willamette U, OR	AF(c)

A—Army; N—Navy; AF—Air Force; (c)—available through a cooperating host institution

290

Alphabetical Listing of Colleges and Universities

In this index, the page locations of the **Profiles** are printed in regular type, **Profiles** with **Special Messages** in *italics*, and **Close-Ups** in **bold type**.

Alphabetical Listing of Colleges and Universities

Notes

Notes

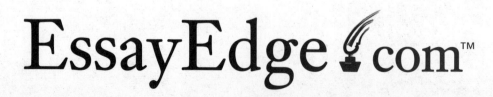

Peterson's
Book Satisfaction Survey

Give Us Your Feedback

Thank you for choosing Peterson's as your source for personalized solutions for your education and career achievement. Please take a few minutes to answer the following questions. Your answers will go a long way in helping us to produce the most user-friendly and comprehensive resources to meet your individual needs.

When completed, please tear out this page and mail it to us at:

> Publishing Department
> Peterson's, a Nelnet company
> 2000 Lenox Drive
> Lawrenceville, NJ 08648

You can also complete this survey online at **www.petersons.com/booksurvey.**

1. **What is the ISBN of the book you have purchased? (The ISBN can be found on the book's back cover in the lower right-hand corner.)** _____

2. **Where did you purchase this book?**
   - ❏ Retailer, such as Barnes & Noble
   - ❏ Online reseller, such as Amazon.com
   - ❏ Petersons.com
   - ❏ Other (please specify) _____

3. **If you purchased this book on Petersons.com, please rate the following aspects of your online purchasing experience on a scale of 4 to 1 (4 = Excellent and 1 = Poor).**

	4	3	2	1
Comprehensiveness of Peterson's Online Bookstore page	❏	❏	❏	❏
Overall online customer experience	❏	❏	❏	❏

4. **Which category best describes you?**
   - ❏ High school student
   - ❏ Parent of high school student
   - ❏ College student
   - ❏ Graduate/professional student
   - ❏ Returning adult student
   - ❏ Teacher
   - ❏ Counselor
   - ❏ Working professional/military
   - ❏ Other (please specify) _____

5. **Rate your overall satisfaction with this book.**

Extremely Satisfied	Satisfied	Not Satisfied
❏	❏	❏

6. Rate each of the following aspects of this book on a scale of 4 to 1 (4 = Excellent and 1 = Poor).

	4	3	2	1
Comprehensiveness of the information	❑	❑	❑	❑
Accuracy of the information	❑	❑	❑	❑
Usability	❑	❑	❑	❑
Cover design	❑	❑	❑	❑
Book layout	❑	❑	❑	❑
Special features (e.g., CD, flashcards, charts, etc.)	❑	❑	❑	❑
Value for the money	❑	❑	❑	❑

7. This book was recommended by:
- ❑ Guidance counselor
- ❑ Parent/guardian
- ❑ Family member/relative
- ❑ Friend
- ❑ Teacher
- ❑ Not recommended by anyone—I found the book on my own
- ❑ Other (please specify) _____

8. Would you recommend this book to others?

Yes	Not Sure	No
❑	❑	❑

9. Please provide any additional comments.

_____

_____

_____

_____

_____

Remember, you can tear out this page and mail it to us at:

Publishing Department
Peterson's, a Nelnet company
2000 Lenox Drive
Lawrenceville, NJ 08648

or you can complete the survey online at **www.petersons.com/booksurvey.**

Your feedback is important to us at Peterson's, and we thank you for your time!

If you would like us to keep in touch with you about new products and services, please include your e-mail address here: _____